Special Edition

USING
Windows® 95

Special Edition

USING
Windows® 95

Written by

Ron Person

R. Michael O'Mara

Gerald Paul Honeycutt Jr.

Roger Jennings

Rob Tidrow

Ian Stokell

Dick Cravens

William S. Holderby

Michael Marchuk

Gordon Meltzer

Glenn Fincher

Francis Moss

Paul E. Robichaux

Doug Kilarski

Jim Boyce

Sue Plumley

Alex Leavens

Lisa A. Bucki

Dave Plotkin

Peter Kent

QUe®

Special Edition Using Windows 95

Copyright© 1995 by Que® Corporation.

Library of Congress Catalog No.: 95-70648

ISBN: 1-56529-921-3

97 96 95   6 5 4 3 2

Interpretation of the printing code: the rightmost double-digit number is the year of the book's printing; the rightmost single-digit number, the number of the book's printing. For example, a printing code of 95-1 shows that the first printing of the book occurred in 1995.

Screen reproductions in this book were created using Collage Plus from Inner Media, Inc., Hollis, NH.

Composed in *Stone Serif* and *MCPdigital* by Que Corporation.

Credits

About the Authors

Ron Person has written more than 12 books for Que Corporation, including *Using Excel 5 for Windows*, Special Edition, and *Using Word 6 for Windows*, Special Edition. Ron is the principal consultant for Ron Person & Co. He has an M.S. in physics from Ohio State University and an M.B.A. from Hardin-Simmons University.

Ron Person & Co., based in San Francisco, has attained Microsoft's highest rating for Microsoft Excel and Word for Windows consultants—Microsoft Solutions Partner. Ron was one of Microsoft's 12 original Consulting Partners. The firm trains Excel and Visual Basic for Applications developers and support staff for corporations nationally and internationally. If your company plans to develop applications using Microsoft Excel or integrating multiple Microsoft applications, you will gain significantly from the courses taught by Ron Person & Co. For information on course content, on-site corporate classes, or consulting, contact Ron Person & Co. at the following address:

> Ron Person & Co.
> P.O. Box 5647
> Santa Rosa, CA 95402

R. Michael O'Mara is a freelance author and technical writer. Previously, he was a staff author with The Cobb Group where he wrote innumerable articles about leading computer software programs and served as Editor-in-Chief of several monthly software journals. He coauthored a best-selling book about Microsoft Windows and has recently contributed to other Que books, including *Using DOS*, *Using Windows 3.11*, and *Special Edition Using CompuServe*. He's been a member of the online community for about 10 years, participating on CompuServe, local BBSs, and the Internet. Mr. O'Mara can be reached on CompuServe at **76376,3441**.

Gerald "Jerry" Paul Honeycutt Jr. is a business-oriented technical manager, with experience developing large-scale applications for Windows using C, C++, and Visual Basic. He is experienced with all aspects of software development, including conception, specification, coding, testing, and delivery. Jerry has provided leadership and technical skills to The Travelers, IBM, Nielsen North America, and, most recently, Information Retrieval Methods, Inc.

When he is not busily delivering products, he is an author and frequent speaker at Comdex and Windows World. You can reach Jerry on the Internet at **jerry@dfw.net**, on CompuServe at **76477,2751**, or on The Microsoft Network at **Honeycutt**.

Roger Jennings is a principal of OakLeaf Systems, a northern California consulting firm specializing in Windows multimedia and database applications. He has more than 25 years of computer-related experience, was a radio-TV broadcast engineer, and is an amateur musician, arranger, and composer. Roger is the author of Que's *Unveiling Windows 95; Using Windows Desktop Video,* Special Edition; *Using Access 2 for Windows,* Special Edition; *Access Hot Tips;* and *Discover Windows 3.1 Multimedia.* He's also a contributing editor for Fawcette Technical Publication, Inc.'s *Visual Basic Programmer's Journal.* Roger's CompuServe address is **70233,2161**, and you can reach him as **Roger_Jennings** on The Microsoft Network.

Rob Tidrow has been using computers for the past six years and has used Windows for the past four years. Mr. Tidrow is a technical writer and recently was the Manager of Product Development for New Riders Publishing, a division of Macmillan Computer Publishing. Rob is coauthor of the best-selling *Windows for Non-Nerds* and has coauthored several other books, including *Inside the World Wide Web; New Riders' Official CompuServe Yellow Pages; Inside Microsoft Office Professional; Inside WordPerfect 6 for Windows; Riding the Internet Highway, Deluxe Edition;* and the *AutoCAD Student Workbook.* In the past, Mr. Tidrow created technical documentation and instructional programs for use in a variety of industrial settings. He has a degree in English from Indiana University. He resides in Indianapolis with his wife, Tammy, and two boys, Adam and Wesley. You can reach him on the Internet at **rtidrow@iquest.net**.

Ian Stokell is a freelance writer and editor living in the Sierra Foothills of northern California with his wife and three young children. He is also Managing Editor of Newsbytes News Network, an international daily newswire covering the computer and telecommunications industries. His writing career began with a 1981 article published in the UK's *New Statesman* and has since encompassed over 1,500 articles in a variety of computing and noncomputing publications. He wrote the "Networking" chapter of Que's *Using the Macintosh,* Special Edition, and has also written on assignment for such magazines as *PC World* and *MacWeek.* He is currently seeking representation for two completed novels and a screenplay.

Dick Cravens lives and works in Columbia, MO, where he is a product manager at Datastorm Technologies, Inc., a publisher of PC communications software. Dick and his 10-year-old son, Jesse, are both members of the University of Missouri Internet User's Group, and are active on America Online, CIS, many local BBS systems, the World Wide Web, and the Columbia Online Information System (the local gateway to the Internet).

William S. Holderby is a computer engineering graduate from the University of Central Florida. He has 20 years of experience in systems design and applications development for the federal government and commercial markets. Mr. Holderby frequently contributes magazine articles covering computer systems technology. He is a network systems developer and integrator and is currently working with the Naval Computer Telecommunications Station based in New Orleans, LA.

Michael Marchuk has been working in the computer industry since 1979 when he started as a part-time BASIC programming instructor. Along with his bachelor's degree in finance from the University of Illinois, he has received certification as a NetWare CNE and a Compaq Advanced Systems Engineer. He has designed and built an international, multi-protocol, wide area network for a Fortune 500 company and now serves as an Integration Engineer and the Network Security Chairman for a Forbes 400 corporation.

Gordon Meltzer has been teaching himself about computers since they were made with vacuum tubes. Recently, Gordon had designed and built workgroup networks for a music marketing division of Time-Warner and several New York City law firms. He is a consultant on computing issues to NBC Post Production, also in Manhattan. Gordon has produced a number of jazz records for people like Miles Davis, Michel LeGrand, Al Di Meola, and Wallace Roney, and has a special interest in using computers in the business side of the music industry.

Glenn Fincher has worked in the computer industry for the last 12 years. Working in the fast-moving electronic manufacturing industry, he spent the early years in Test Engineering at SCI Systems, Inc., the world's largest computer contract manufacturer. Spending the bulk of the SCI years in component, board, and unit testing, he became intimately familiar with the building blocks of today's computer technology. He joined Intergraph Corporation in 1991 as a Customer Support Analyst and has applied his wealth of computer knowledge to providing Intergraph's customers with quality, timely, and accurate support for the MicroStation CAD product. Leading the software certification efforts for the successful release of MicroStation 5.0,

Glenn continues to be involved in the day-to-day world of Intergraph's partner Bentley Systems' MicroStation product. Sharing the knowledge gained in the experience of these years in the industry has always been a priority, so it is no surprise that he is in demand as a speaker, writer, and presenter throughout Intergraph. With his present involvement in Intergraph's WWW effort as Webmaster for Intergraphs Software Solutions, Glenn remains at the leading edge of this industry. Continually seeking to stay on this edge has required both the support and understanding of wife Jan and their three children—Ashley, Will, and Aimee—without whom this and all his other endeavors would have been a lonely journey indeed. Glenn can be reached by electronic mail at **gtfinche@ingr.com**.

Francis Moss has been involved with computers for 12 years, a Microsoft beta tester for 5 years, and a writer—primarily in television but more recently books—for 15 years. With his writing partner, he is coauthor of *Internet for Kids*. He likes computers because he enjoys cursing at unarmed inanimate objects. With his wife and two children, he lives in North Hollywood, CA. He can be reached at **fcmoss@directnet.com**.

Paul Robichaux is a software developer and author with a wide range of experience developing, and writing about, desktop operating systems, applications software, and the Internet. He lives in Huntsville, AL with his family.

Doug Kilarski is a freelance writer and an accomplished computer industry analyst. Doug is a former technical editor for *Computer Shopper* magazine and former Editor-in-Chief for *Computer Monthly* and *Reseller World* magazines. He is currently developing global marketing and distribution strategies for the internetworking and telephony industries. Doug can be reached on the Internet at **dkilarski@mcimail.com**.

Jim Boyce is a contributing editor and columnist for *Windows Magazine*, a columnist for *Cadence* magazine, and the author and contributing author of over two dozen books on computers and software. You can reach Jim at **76516.3403@compuserve.com.**

Sue Plumley owns and operates Humble Opinions, a consulting firm that offers training in popular software programs and network installation and maintenance. Sue's husband, Carlos, joined her company two years ago as a CNE. Sue is the author of 12 Que books, including *Crystal Clear DOS*, *Crystal Clear Word 6*, and *Microsoft Office Quick Reference*, and coauthor of 16 additional books, including *Using WordPerfect 6 for DOS*, Special Edition; *Using*

OS/2 2.1, Special Edition, and *Special Edition Using Microsoft Office* for Que and its sister imprints.

Alex Leavens is a software developer with more than 15 years experience. He has developed products that have sold more than a million copies and is one of the few software designers whose work can be found in the permanent collection of the National Museum of American History at the Smithsonian. He develops Windows products and books and can be reached on CompuServe at **70444,43.** In Addition to writing Appendix E, Alex acquired and assembled the materials on the CD-ROM.

Lisa Bucki has been involved in the computer book business for more than five years. She has written Que's *Guide to WordPerfect Presentations 3.0 for Windows*, *10 Minute Guide to Harvard Graphics*, *10 Minute Guide to Harvard Graphics for Windows*, *One Minute Reference to Windows 3.1*, and other titles. She has contributed chapters dealing with presentation graphics and multimedia for other books, as well as assisting with the product development for such titles as *Upgrading Your PC to Multimedia*, also from Que. Bucki resides in Fishers, Indiana.

Dave Plotkin is a Business Area Analyst with Integral Systems in Walnut Creek, California. He has extensive experience in designing and implementing databases, both at the desktop and on client-server systems. He writes extensively for various computer periodicals, and his favorite editor is his wife, Marisa.

Peter Kent lives in Lakewood, Colorado. He's spent the last 14 years training users, documenting software, and designing user interfaces. Working as an independent consultant for the last 9 years, Peter has worked for companies such as MasterCard, Amgen, Data General, and Dvorak Development and Publishing. Much of his consulting work has been in the telecommunications business.

Peter is the author of the best-selling Internet book *The Complete Idiot's Guide to the Internet* (QUE). He's also written another six Internet-related books—including *The Complete Idiot's Guide to the World Wide Web*—and a variety of other works, such as *The Technical Writer's Freelancing Guide* and books on Windows NT and Windows 3.1. His articles have appeared in many periodicals, including *Internet World*, *Windows Magazine*, *Windows User*, the *Dallas Times Herald*, and *Computerworld*. Peter can be reached electronically at **PeterKent** (Microsoft Network), **71601,1266** (CompuServe), or **pkent@lab-press.com** (Internet).

We'd Like to Hear from You!

As part of our continuing effort to produce books of the highest possible quality, Que would like to hear your comments. To stay competitive, we *really* want you, as a computer book reader and user, to let us know what you like or dislike most about this book or other Que products.

You can mail comments, ideas, or suggestions for improving future editions to the address below, or send us a fax at (317) 581-4663. For the online inclined, Macmillan Computer Publishing has a forum on CompuServe (type **GO QUEBOOKS** at any prompt) through which our staff and authors are available for questions and comments. The address of our Internet site is **http://www.mcp.com** (World Wide Web).

In addition to exploring our forum, please feel free to contact me personally to discuss your opinions of this book: I'm **lwagner@que.mcp.com** on the Internet.

Thanks in advance—your comments will help us to continue publishing the best books available on computer topics in today's market.

Lisa D. Wagner
Product Development Specialist
Que Corporation
201 W. 103rd Street
Indianapolis, Indiana 46290
USA

Contents at a Glance

Introducing Windows 95

Working with Windows 95

Working with Applications

Disks and Files

Networking

Online Communications

Windows 95 Multimedia

Appendixes

Indexes

Contents

6 Controlling Printers   167

11 Working with DOS Applications in Windows 95

18 Backing Up and Protecting Your Data   555

24 Using Microsoft Exchange   723

25 Working with Network Printers   771

26 Network Management and Security   795

VII Windows 95 Multimedia 947

31 Understanding Windows 95 Multimedia 949

32 Installing and Using a CD-ROM Drive 969

VIII Appendixes   1075

A Installing and Uninstalling Windows 95   1077

Preface

Windows 95 will significantly change the way computers are used at home and in offices around the world. And *Special Edition Using Windows 95* is your reference guide to learning and understanding what Microsoft's newest operating system is all about.

Years of research went into creating this new operating system known as Windows 95 and here at Que we have spent over a year studying and researching what Windows 95 is all about and how it will affect computer users of every level. We gathered the best authoring team in the business and put our top-notch developers and editors in place to produce the most comprehensive book about Windows 95. *Special Edition Using Windows 95* is the result of all this hard work.

Que has established itself over the course of the past decade as the premier publisher of high-quality computer books. While we are proud of our reputation for excellence, we are not content to rest on our laurels. A tradition of excellence is only useful as long as a continuing commitment to quality exists.

When we started planning this book, we knew from the start how important it would be to you. As you make the switch from Windows 3.1 to Windows 95 (or use Windows for the first time), nothing is more important to your computing needs than understanding how to use your new operating system. Without a grasp of how to use Windows 95, you will never get the most out of your computing time.

With this in mind, Que looked at what you would need from a book about Windows 95. It was clear to us that any attempt to rewrite or augment an existing Windows 3.1 book would not do proper service to our readers. Consequently, this book is built new from the ground up and designed especially to fit the way you will use Windows 95.

The other essential ingredient in our plan was an extensive commitment to technical accuracy. Windows 95 has been in beta testing for over a year and we have been there every step of the way. There have been many beta test versions but every technical detail, task, and procedure in each chapter of this book has been carefully checked against the final version of Windows 95. This is the only way to ensure that what you see in this book matches what you find when you start using Windows 95.

With these efforts, we hope you find this book to be valuable as you learn and use Windows 95. I believe it to be the best available book of its type. I sincerely hope it meets or exceeds your expectations.

Roland Elgey
President
Que Corporation

Introduction

With Windows 3.0 and 3.1, Microsoft altered forever the face of PC computing. Microsoft brought an easy-to-use graphical interface to tens of millions of personal computers. At one time regarded as a plaything and not for serious users, Windows became the standard for hardware and software compatibility. Now with Windows 95, Microsoft has added a new look to computers and the look and feel of graphical PC computing has taken another major turn.

Microsoft has devoted years of extensive research to making Windows 95 easier to learn and use than its predecessors. New users will be able to start programs, create documents, and become productive much more quickly with Windows 95.

However, despite its ease of use and graphical interface, Windows 95 is not entirely intuitive. In fact, many experienced users will find that the number and scope of changes to the interface will take them some time to get accustomed to. But, after a short period of transition and learning, you should become more productive and efficient with Windows 95 than you were with Windows 3.1.

And that's where *Special Edition Using Windows 95* steps in to help. This book is the single source you need to get quickly up to speed and greatly enhance your productivity with Windows 95.

How to Use This Book

This book was designed and written from the ground up with two important purposes in mind:

- First, *Special Edition Using Windows 95* makes it easy for you to find any task you need to accomplish and see how to do it most effectively.

■ Second, this book covers Windows 95 in a breadth and depth that you won't find anywhere else. So not only does the book show you how to do things quickly and efficiently, you also find out how to accomplish tasks that simply aren't covered by online help, documentation, or other books.

With those goals in mind, how do you use this book?

If you have used Windows 3.1, you may just want to skim through the first few chapters of this book to see what changes there are in Windows 95. After all, you may have read magazine articles and heard from colleagues about all of the new features. The first two chapters help you get a grip on what changes to expect. After that, keep *Special Edition Using Windows 95* handy by your computer as a reference. When you have a question or need to see how to accomplish something, look it up in the table of contents or index and read how to do it. We don't waste your time with anecdotes, witty banter, or cartoons. We do give you the most comprehensive and detailed coverage of Windows 95 of any book on the market and clearly focus that coverage to satisfy the needs of all types of Windows users.

If you are using Windows for the first time, you should find that *Special Edition Using Windows 95* is a clear presentation of the fundamentals of Windows computing. This is a book that can help you understand Windows and use it well. And, if you need to learn more about Windows than just the basics, *Special Edition Using Windows 95* will be there when you need it. To get started with Windows 95, read the first two chapters to get a feel for what Windows does, and then go through Chapters 3 and 4 while sitting at your computer. Once you're comfortable with Windows, move on to the chapters that cover the additional topics you want to learn about.

How this Book is Organized

Special Edition Using Windows 95 is a comprehensive book on Windows 95. The book is divided into nine parts, 35 chapters, and six appendixes to help you quickly find the coverage you need. The parts begin with the most common and basic topics and move forward into more specialized or advanced subjects. This rest of this section describes the content more specifically, chapter by chapter.

Part I: Introducing Windows 95

Chapter 1, "What's New in Windows 95?," shows you an overview of the new features in Windows 95. After reading this chapter, you should be aware of why you moved or need to begin the move from Windows 3.1 to Windows 95.

Chapter 2, "Understanding Windows 95," presents the big picture to understanding Windows 95. If you're a new user, you'll want to get a feel for the important concepts and see where you are going. If you're an experienced user, you'll want to know what's different from previous versions of Windows and what's remained the same.

Part II: Working with Windows 95

Chapter 3, "Getting Started with Windows 95," gives you an explanation of the parts of the Windows screen, how to use the keyboard and mouse, and how to start Windows and applications.

Chapter 4, "Starting and Working with Applications," teaches you information that carries over to all Windows applications. The skills gained from this chapter help you operate control features, such as menus and dialog boxes, and control parts of the display, such as the size and position of the windows in which different documents or applications display. This chapter also covers IRQs, hardware profiles, and I/Os.

Chapter 5, "Customizing Windows 95," shows you how to customize Windows 95 to fit the way you work. You learn to customize the taskbar, the Start menu, the Program menu, the desktop pattern or graphic, as well as all the colors used by Windows elements.

Chapter 6, "Controlling Printers," explains how to use Windows 95 printing. It also introduces each of the new printing features, describes the options, and explains how to create a quality print job.

Chapter 7, "Working with Fonts," explains fonts and how Windows 95 uses them. It also shows you how to install and manage fonts in Windows 95.

Chapter 8, "Plug and Play and Legacy Device Installation." The objective of Plug and Play is to make new device installation a "hands-off" process. Thus, much of this chapter is devoted to explaining what happens "behind-the-scenes" to make Plug and Play work. This chapter also describes how to install the many devices that do not take advantage of Plug and Play.

Chapter 9, "Special Features for Notebook Users," describes how to take advantage of Windows 95 support for PC Cards (formerly called PMCIA adapter cards), advanced power management, docking stations, file synchronization with My Briefcase, and all of the other new features that are of particular use to laptop users.

Part III: Working with Applications

Chapter 10, "Installing, Running, and Uninstalling Windows Applications." With all its power, most users will find Windows to be of little value without installing application software. After all, Windows 95 is just the operating system—to do something, you need applications. This chapter shows you how to install Windows applications (both Windows 95 and older applications are covered), how to run applications, and how to remove applications, including coverage of uninstalling software with Windows 95's new Remove feature.

Chapter 11, "Working with DOS Applications in Windows 95," shows you how to use DOS programs in Windows. This version of Windows makes more memory available to DOS applications and runs DOS games faster and better than previous versions.

Chapter 12, "Using WordPad to Create Documents," shows how to use WordPad, a simple but powerful word processor for Windows. This simple accessory is ideal for many day-to-day word processing tasks. You learn to create and edit a document in WordPad, format and print documents, and save and open documents.

Chapter 13, "Using Paint, Calculator, and other Accessories," shows you how to use Paint to create and edit pictures that you can insert in documents created with other applications, use Calculator to perform calculations, set the clock that displays on the taskbar, and insert special characters into any Windows document with Character Map.

Chapter 14, "Simple Ways of Sharing Data between Applications." Generally, all Windows applications provide some means for sharing data with another application. This chapter shows how to use the most basic and commonly used of these means, including cutting, copying, and pasting within and between documents in Windows and DOS applications, as well as how to link data from one document to another.

Chapter 15, "Building Compound Documents with OLE," shows how to create and modify documents based on the concept of *compound documents*—documents you create by using multiple types of data. You see how to build documents that incorporate different types of data, such as text from a word processor, a spreadsheet, and graphics. You also learn how to use this data within a single application without having to switch between applications to edit the different data types.

Part IV: Working with Disks and Files

Chapter 16, "Working with Disks and Disk Drives," shows you how to work with and maintain your floppy and hard disks. Before you put data on a disk, you usually have to format it to get it ready to receive data. Floppy and hard disks are susceptible to damage, which is very trying when you're dealing with irreplaceable data. Windows 95 comes with a tool to help you check for and repair some kinds of damage. You can monitor the performance of your system using the System Monitor. You can improve the performance of your hard disks by using Disk Defragmenter and enable your system to act as if has more memory (RAM) than is actually installed by using *virtual memory*. This chapter covers all these topics and more.

Chapter 17, "Managing Your Files with Explorer." The first part of this chapter explains how Windows 95 organizes files. The remainder of the chapter is devoted to showing you how to use Windows Explorer to work with and manage the files on your computer. You also learn how to carry out many file management tasks using My Computer.

Chapter 18, "Backing Up and Protecting Your Data," explains how to copy one or more files from your hard disk to another location (usually a floppy disk, a tape drive, or another computer on your network), restore your backed up files to any location you choose (including their original locations), and compare files on your backup disks with the original files to ensure their validity.

Part V: Networking with Windows 95

Chapter 19, "Understanding Networks," introduces one of the most improved features in Windows 95—networking capabilities. This chapter covers the basic concepts of networking and Windows 95. You see what types of networks are supported in Windows 95, how to install hardware and Windows 95 drivers for them, and how to use tools such as Windows Explorer and Network Neighborhood to make use of network resources.

Chapter 20, "Setting Up a Windows 95 Peer-to-Peer Network," presents Windows 95 built-in peer-to-peer networking. Windows 95 peer-to-peer networking brings all the resources of the network to your desktop. You can share any of your PC's resources with other PCs on the network. You can easily make use of the printer down the hall or the CD on your associate's new high-speed desktop. This chapter presents the basics of setting up the network software and hardware to work with Windows 95 and your computer.

Chapter 21, "Sharing Windows 95 Peer-to-Peer Resources," shows how to make resources on your computer available to others on the Windows 95 peer-to-peer network. You see how to share hard drives, CD-ROMs, printers, and fax-modems, and how to manage these shared resources.

Chapter 22, "Connecting Windows 95 to a Novell Network," shows you how to take advantage of Windows 95 and Novell NetWare compatibility. It presents the basics of setting up the network software and hardware to work with Windows 95 and your computer. If your primary network is currently Novell NetWare, Windows 95 seamlessly integrates with your current network.

Chapter 23, "Using Novell Network Resources in Windows 95," shows how to take advantage of some of the advanced networking features available with NetWare and Windows 95. You see how to use network monitoring and maintenance tools, as well as make backups on network tape drives.

Chapter 24, "Using Microsoft Exchange," shows how to use Microsoft Exchange, a central communications client that organizes "received" electronic mail and faxes in one convenient location. You learn how to use Exchange as your universal in-box and how to compose, store, organize, and send messages via e-mail and fax.

Chapter 25, "Working with Network Printers," takes printing a step farther and discusses printing issues from a network perspective. Specifically, you learn to print using network printers, optimize print resources, manage print files, solve common network printing problems, and use custom print managers and utilities.

Chapter 26, "Network Management and Security," presents valuable information for anyone tasked with setting up and maintaining a network in conjunction with Windows 95. You learn how to control the installation and configuration of your network. This chapter exposes weaknesses in network design and tells you how to work around them. It provides tips for keeping your network up and running and for simplifying it without losing functionality. This chapter also provides a guide to help you understand the philosophy behind the Windows 95 network and shows you how to make it work in your individual situation.

Part VI: Online Communications with Windows 95

Chapter 27, "Installing and Configuring Your Modem," explains how Windows' communications system works for you, how to install your Plug and Play modem or legacy modem, how to configure your modem after it's installed, and what TAPI means and does.

Chapter 28, "Communicating with HyperTerminal," discusses using HyperTerminal, the Windows accessory which allows you to connect your computer to another PC or online service. HyperTerminal is a full-featured communications tool that greatly simplifies getting online. With HyperTerminal, you can connect to a friend's computer, a university network, an Internet service provider, or even CompuServe. In this chapter, you learn how to use HyperTerminal by using it for some common tasks, such as creating a connection or downloading a file, and how to configure HyperTerminal and customize your connections.

Chapter 29, "Getting Connected to the Internet," introduces you to the Internet and World Wide Web, two of the fastest growing and most talked about topics in computing. You learn what TCP/IP is, how to choose an Internet service provider, how to connect to the Internet with Windows 95 built-in connectivity tools, and how to use other Internet apps with Windows 95.

Chapter 30, "Using FTP, the World Wide Web, and other Internet Services," covers what to do once you get connected to the Internet. You see how to use Microsoft's FTP program to connect to large archives of shareware and freeware to find and download software, how to log in to remote computers on the Internet with Telnet, how to cruise the Web with Microsoft's Internet Explorer (part of Microsoft Plus!), and how to create Web pages with Microsoft's Internet Assistant.

Part VII: Windows 95 Multimedia

Chapter 31, "Understanding Windows 95 Multimedia," introduces the basic concepts of multimedia and Windows 95. Windows' multimedia features are greatly improved in Windows 95. In this chapter, you see what improvements have been made for multimedia hardware and software and how to install hardware and configure Windows 95 drivers for multimedia.

Chapter 32, "Installing and Using a CD-ROM Drive," shows how to install drivers for Plug and Play and legacy CD-ROM drives, how to use CD-ROM applications, and how to optimize your CD-ROM.

Chapter 33, "Working with Windows 95 Sound Capabilities," shows how to install drivers for Plug and Play and legacy sound cards. You see how to use Windows accessories for recording, playing, and editing sound files and how to play audio CDs on your computer.

Chapter 34, "Using Windows 95 Full-Motion Video Options," describes video enhancements in Windows 95 and shows how the video enhancements have also improved graphics-intensive DOS games. You see the procedure for installing video drivers, adding to your video capabilities with QuickTime for Windows, and how to play videos with Media Player.

Chapter 35, "Desktop Video Production under Windows 95," highlights the improvements to Windows video by showing how to use several applications for video capture and production.

Part VIII: Appendixes

Appendix A, "Installing and Uninstalling Windows 95," presents the steps for preparing your computer for Windows 95 and then for installing Windows 95. Standard and custom installation options are discussed, including a multiple-boot configuration. The appendix also explains how to remove Windows 95 from your system.

Appendix B, "Using Microsoft Network," describes how to get started using Microsoft Network (MSN). MSN is fully integrated into Windows and offers you online access to the world by giving you access to a variety of people and resources. With MSN, you can exchange electronic mail (e-mail) with other people, exchange ideas on bulletin boards, participate in live discussions in chat rooms, access the resources of the Internet, and more. This appendix also describes some of the interesting forum areas and services currently available.

Appendix C, "Exploring the Windows 95 Resource Kit," describes the components of this set of additional documentation and utilities designed primarily for system administrators and other power users.

Appendix D, "Using Microsoft Plus!," shows you how to install and use DriveSpace 3, Internet Explorer, Desktop Themes, and the other special utilities and tools in this add-in from Microsoft.

Appendix E, "What's on the CD," describes the software and utilities you find on the CD that accompanies this book.

Appendix F, "Glossary," provides a great reference for Windows 95 terms and computer terminology in general.

Part IX: Indexes

"Index of Common Problems." This feature goes hand in hand with the Troubleshooting elements. If you are having a problem with Windows 95 and don't know where to look in the book for an answer, look to the Index of Common Problems, located near the back of the book, immediately preceding the index. Use the Index of Common Problems to find all the Troubleshooting sections in the book and other discussions of common problems and fixes.

The Indexes part also contains a stardard topic index that lets you quickly find information you need throughout the book.

Other Books of Interest

You may wonder how you could ever need to know anything else about Windows than what we've presented in this book. But with the enormous potential of Windows 95, you'll soon see that depending on your area of special interest, there is much more you can do with Windows. So, here is a short list of other Que books that may be of interest, depending on your computing needs:

- *Killer Windows 95*. If you consider yourself a "power-user," you'll find the advanced techniques and tools presented in this book to be invaluable additions to your Windows 95 tools.

- *Surviving the Move to Windows 95*. This is a good book for users that need a short reference detailing the features that have changed in this version of Windows.

- *Windows 95 Connectivity*. Network and online connectivity are key improved features in Windows 95. This book examines these features in detail.

- *Special Edition Using Microsoft Office*. This book covers everything you need to know about Microsoft's new Windows 95 release of the popular Microsoft Office suite. It includes detailed coverage of Word, Excel, and PowerPoint and how to use those applications together. Other books of interest if you need more detailed coverage of one of the individual Office applications include *Special Edition Using Word for Windows 95, Special Edition Using Excel for Windows 95,* and *Special Edition Using PowerPoint for Windows 95.*

■ *Special Edition Using the Internet*, 2nd Edition. Windows 95 is the first version of Windows that makes connecting to the Internet a snap. If you want detailed coverage of the many aspects of the Internet such as the World Wide Web, FTP, HTML, e-mail and more, this book is for you.

Special Features in the Book

Que has over a decade of experience writing and developing the most successful computer books available. With that experience, we've learned what special features help readers the most. Look for these special features throughout the book to enhance your learning experience.

Chapter Roadmaps

Near the beginning of each chapter is a list of topics to be covered in the chapter. This list serves as a roadmap to the chapter so you can tell at a glance what is covered. It also provides a useful outline of the key topics you'll be reading about.

Notes

Notes present interesting or useful information that isn't necessarily essential to the discussion. This secondary track of information enhances your understanding of Windows, but you can safely skip notes and not be in danger of missing crucial information. Notes look like this:

> **Note**
>
> If you have many applications open, you may not be able to read the application and document name on the taskbar button. If the application and document name are truncated, pause the pointer over the button. A button tip appears showing the full names.

Tip
Any open application appears as a button on the taskbar. Click the button to activate the application.

Tips

Tips present short advice on quick or often overlooked procedures. These include shortcuts that save you time. A tip is shown in the margin as an example.

Cautions

Cautions serve to warn you about potential problems that a procedure may cause, unexpected results, and mistakes to avoid. Cautions look like this:

Caution

If you have a wallpaper selected with the Display Tile option selected, you will not be able to see your pattern. A full-screen wallpaper shows over the top of the pattern. To see the pattern, select (None) from the Wallpaper list.

Troubleshooting

No matter how carefully you follow the steps in the book, you eventually come across something that just doesn't work the way you think it should. Troubleshooting sections anticipate these common errors or hidden pitfalls and present solutions. A troubleshooting section looks like this:

Troubleshooting

When I double-click a linked or embedded object, a `cannot edit` *error message occurs.*

This means that the source file cannot be opened. Make sure the application you need to edit the file is on your machine. Also make sure that you have enough system memory to run both the container and source applications. Keep in mind that compound documents demand more memory than simple documents.

Cross References

Throughout the book in the margins, you see references to other sections and pages in the book, like the one next to this paragraph. These cross references point you to related topics and discussions in other parts of the book.

▶ See "Using Drag-and-Drop to Copy Information between Documents," p. 421

In addition to these special features, there are several conventions used in this book to make it easier to read and understand. These conventions include the following.

Underlined Hot Keys, or Mnemonics

Hot keys in this book appear underlined, like they appear on-screen. For example, the F in File is a hot key, or shortcut for opening the File menu. In Windows, many menus, commands, buttons, and other options have these hot keys. To use a hot-key shortcut, press Alt and the key for the underlined character. For instance, to choose the Properties button, press Alt and then R.

Shortcut Key Combinations

In this book, shortcut key combinations are joined with plus signs (+). For example, Ctrl+V means hold down the Ctrl key, press the V key, and then release both keys (Ctrl+V is a shortcut for the Paste command).

Menu Commands

Instructions for choosing menu commands have this form:

Choose File, New.

This example means open the File menu and select New, which in this case opens a new file.

Instructions involving the new Windows 95 Start menu are an exception. When you are to choose something through this menu, the form is

Open the Start menu and choose Programs, Accessories, WordPad.

In this case, you open the WordPad word processing accessory. Notice that in the Start menu you simply drag the mouse pointer and point at the option or command you want to choose (even through a whole series of submenus); you don't need to click anything.

This book also has the following typeface enhancements to indicate special text, as indicated in the following table.

Typeface	Description
Italic	Italics are used to indicate new terms and variables in commands or addresses.
Boldface	Bold is used to indicate text you type, and Internet addresses and other locators in the online world.
`Computer type`	This command is used for on-screen messages and commands (such as DOS copy or UNIX commands).
MYFILE.DOC	File names and directories are set in all caps to distinguish them from regular text, as in MYFILE.DOC.

What's on the CD

The CD-ROM included with this book provides you with a variety of software to use with Windows 95. This software includes programs and data files for everyone, no matter what your interests and level of computer use.

Among the programs on the CD-ROM are Windows utilities, communications programs, editors, graphics programs, and games. There are even video utilities included. The disc also provides popular online service and Internet software that will help get you up and running online.

For those interested in multimedia, the disc offers many great files to use with Windows 95 enhanced multimedia capabilities. In fact, you'll find more than 150M of graphics files, wallpaper, bitmap patterns for your desktop, sound files, and digital video files.

Appendix E, "What's on the CD," discusses the contents of the disc in detail.

Part I

Introducing
Windows 95

Chapter 1

What's New in Windows 95?

by Ron Person

Windows 95 will change the way you work with computers. Microsoft's new operating system is more than just a better interface or an easier way of working with the computer. It incorporates more features, better performance, and greater compatibility than any previous operating system. This chapter will give you an overview of the new features in Windows 95. After reading this chapter, you should be aware of why you need to begin the move from Windows to Windows 95.

Windows 95 is an improvement over Windows 3.11 and Windows for Workgroups 3.11. Both of these programs, although significantly easier to use than DOS, needed enhancements to accommodate both first-time users and experienced "power" users.

Some of the problems faced by computer novices when using Windows were:

- Overlapping windows caused confusion due to visual clutter. Windows that filled the screen hid other programs that were open

- Windows seemed to disappear when minimized

- The hierarchical display of directory structures in the File Manager was intimidating and not intuitive to non-technical users

- The File Manager and Program Manager shared some functionality, such as starting applications, but they used different metaphors and appearance

- Switching between running applications and knowing which applications were running was not obvious. Many users started multiple instances of the same application, thereby using up system resources and increasing the potential for an application failure

■ Double-clicking and many keystrokes, such as Alt+Tab, while very important, were hidden in manuals and were inaccessible

■ File names were limited to eight characters with a three-letter extension

Windows 95 was created to make work easier for novice and beginning computer users. Yet at the same time it contains many extensions and features that add value for advanced or power users. Some of the areas where power users faced problems with previous versions of Windows were:

■ Resources and utilities needed for customizing and fine-tuning were scattered all over the Windows system in different groups, such as Control Panel, Print Manager, Setup, File Manager, and Program Manager

■ Information such as IRQ and I/O address settings were difficult to find

■ Many graphical elements could not be customized

■ Networking with non-Microsoft networks required a lot of study, work, and workarounds

■ Power users always want faster performance

■ Hardware was difficult to install and could easily cause conflicts with existing hardware. The conflicts were difficult to resolve

This chapter introduces

■ Windows 95 compatibility with DOS and previous Windows programs and data

■ The ease with which Windows 95 is installed

■ Windows 95's improved performance in many areas including file handling, memory management, and application speed

■ A graphical interface using the Start menu, taskbar, and desktop that make Windows much easier for first-time users

■ Property sheets about items in Windows 95 that show you information about the item and enable you to customize the item

■ Program startup and file management, both of which can be handled from within the same My Computer windows

- Shortcut icons that start programs and documents and give you quick access to frequently used folders

- Long names for files and folders that make file management easier than previously

- Networking and communication that is much easier to install. The networking works with adapters and protocols from more vendors than before

- Easier hardware installation where Windows 95 recognizes the hardware and installs the appropriate drivers and settings automatically

- Features for road warriors who travel with a portable computer, but must occasionally work with a desktop computer

Note

Windows 95 addresses all of these issues. Look through this chapter to get a quick overview of how Windows 95 has improved. From here, you will want to go to Chapter 2, "Understanding Windows 95," for a quick understanding of the basic concepts in Windows 95 and then go on to chapters about specific topics in which you are interested.

Compatibility with Windows 3.1 and DOS Programs

With more than 60 million people using Windows 3.1, Microsoft had to include a high degree of compatibility in Windows 95 so that data and applications from previous versions of Windows would still work. Windows 95 also handles DOS programs better. DOS programs can now run in a window that includes a toolbar for commonly used features.

File Manager and Program Manager Are Available

A company with thousands or tens of thousands of Windows users may not want to think about having to train them on how to use Windows 95. One way to make this transition and upgrade smoother is to continue to use the File Manager and Program Manager that are familiar to users of previous versions of Windows. This allows your users to keep what they are familiar with and lets you gain the customizability, performance, and enhancements of Windows 95. You can then help your users migrate over time to the File

▶ See "Using Windows 3.1 File Manager or Program Manager," p. 77

Manager and Program Manager replacement—either My Desktop or Windows Explorer.

Windows 3.1 and DOS Data Files Are Compatible

The effective use of data seems to be what differentiates winners from losers in the information age. With that in mind, files created in Windows 95 are compatible with files from earlier versions of DOS and Windows.

▶ See "Using Long File Names," p. 334

Windows 95 is capable of handling file names up to 255 characters long. The long file names can include spaces. For example, what used to be BUDGET96.DOC can now be RON'S VACATION BUDGET FOR 1996.DOC. When you move a file with a long name to a system that uses the older eight-character name with a three-letter extension, the older system sees only an abbreviated version of the long name.

Caution

Don't use file utility software designed for DOS and older versions of Windows in Windows 95 or on files from Windows 95. Windows 95 stores name and file tracking information in different locations. Although this makes no difference to applications, some file-manipulation utilities can scramble this data. The types of utilities to beware of do such things as recover lost files.

Tip
To see the device drivers you have and information about them, open the Start menu and choose Settings, Control Panel. Double-click the System icon and select the Device Manager tab. Double-click any device to see its Properties sheet.

▶ See "Getting Help," p. 79

Compatible Drivers

Device drivers act as translators between hardware and software. They make sure the two work together efficiently. Windows 95 comes with 32-bit device drivers for major hardware such as disk drives, display adapters, and CD-ROM drives. This means that when you install Windows 95, it will install new device drivers that give you the hardware's advanced features as well as any speed that comes from a 32-bit driver. Unfortunately, there are thousands of different hardware devices. This makes it almost impossible for Microsoft to ensure that every device driver has been included in the set that initially installs with Windows. Because of that, if Windows 95 cannot find a new device driver during installation, it continues to use any 16-bit device driver that you have already installed from a previous version of Windows or from MS-DOS.

If you want to ensure you have the latest device driver, contact the manufacturer of your hardware device. Microsoft has made device drivers much easier to create for Windows 95, and your hardware manufacturer should have a new version available.

Installing Windows 95 Is Easy

You don't have to be a hardware guru to install Windows 95. In previous versions of Windows you were often forced into making choices about hardware configurations. It was up to you to select the appropriate options and settings so that hardware and software were compatible. Windows 95 takes care of many of those decisions and options for you. If you have newer Plug and Play hardware, Windows 95 can detect exactly what is installed and how Windows 95 should be configured to work. If you have hardware, such as modems that aren't Plug and Play, Windows 95 will prompt you for the information necessary for setup.

▶ See "Installing Plug and Play Hardware," p. 246

▶ See "Installing a Plug and Play Modem," p. 833

▶ See "Using Windows 95 Setup," p. 1084

Improved Performance

One of the design goals for Windows 95 is that its speed should be the same or better than Windows 3.11. As memory is added, the performance should improve. At the low end, Windows 95 should be able to run with the same or better speed as Windows 3.11 running on low-end 386DX computers with only 4M of RAM.

Everyone expects new software to run faster, and Windows 95 does. As you add more memory, you find that Windows' performance improves proportionally. You should see a significant performance improvement for new 32-bit applications designed for Windows 95, too. Microsoft Excel for Windows 95 and Microsoft Word for Windows 95 are up to 50 percent faster in many of their operations.

Even 16-bit applications will have improved performance in Windows 95 in areas that involve the 32-bit system, such as printing and file handling. That Windows terror, the out of memory error, is less likely to occur. Although Windows 95 still uses a 64K heap to store systems information for 16-bit applications, a lot of the information that was stored in this area by older versions of Windows is now stored elsewhere. As a result, there is less chance of your application failing.

Windows 95 uses a new 32-bit VCACHE, which replaces the older SmartDrive that ran under DOS and previous versions of Windows. VCACHE uses more intelligent caching algorithms to improve the apparent speed of your hard drive as well as your CD-ROM and 32-bit network redirectors. Unlike SmartDrive, VCACHE dynamically allocates itself. Based on the amount of free system memory, VCACHE allocates or reallocates memory used by the cache.

▶ See "Improving Performance with Disk Defragmenter," p. 486

An Easier but More Powerful Interface

To most personal computer users, the interface they see on-screen *is* the computer. Because of that, the world of DOS computers was too difficult for many people. There was a lot of learning involved just to get started with simple tasks. And there was no way to learn as you worked. You had to devote part of your time to learning DOS and the applications, and use the remaining time trying to get productive work done. The advent of Windows improved this quite a bit. With a few hours of instruction on Windows, you could learn on your own by exploring. The work-to-learning ratio improved significantly.

Research by Microsoft found that Windows was still difficult to learn for many people and some people were still too timid to explore and learn on their own. For that reason they had two primary design goals for Windows 95:

- To make Windows more accessible to novice users so that they can quickly get what they need.

- To make Windows more customizable and productive for advanced users by including accessible shortcuts and power techniques.

Windows 95 does a good job on both of these goals. Tests in Microsoft's usability laboratory show that inexperienced computer users are able to find and start applications significantly faster with Windows 95 than with previous versions of Windows. For example, the Start menu enables anyone familiar with a mouse to open a menu and search for the application he or she wants. In earlier versions of Windows, users had to learn about the Program Manager, group windows, and program item icons before they could start their first application.

Tip

Without an overview of Windows 95, your previous experience with Windows may get in the way of how easy it is to use Windows 95.

Experienced and novice computer users will want to review the basics of Windows 95 in order to get a good idea as to how much easier Windows 95 is to operate than previous operating systems. The Windows 95 desktop interface is shown in figure 1.1.

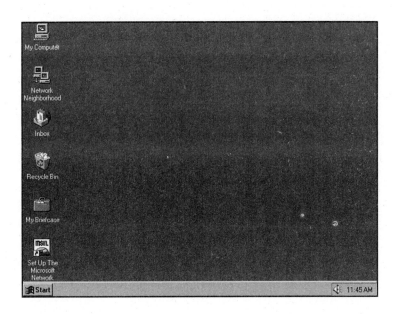

Fig. 1.1
When Windows 95 first loads, your desktop will look similar to this. Depending on the type of setup you used, you may have additional icons or some of these icons may not be present.

The Start Button Makes Starting Applications Easier

The Start button is one of the most important changes to Windows 95. It makes Windows 95 more accessible. Research from Microsoft's usability labs shows that people start applications three to nine times faster when using the Start button than they do when using the old Program Manager. By clicking the Start button, you open the Start menu, which is your avenue to Windows 95.

The Start button not only makes Windows easier to use for beginners, it's an excellent improvement for power users. When you click the Start button, or press Ctrl+Esc, you see a menu that includes not only applications, but also lists of frequently used documents, customizable settings, and frequently used features such as Find, Help, and Run (see fig. 1.2).

Note

Ctrl+Esc is a shortcut key combination used to access the Start menu. Throughout this book, when you see a key+key combination, that signifies a shortcut to accessing an application or opening a menu.

Fig. 1.2
Tests show that
Windows 95 is
easier to use for
beginners and
more customizable
for experts.

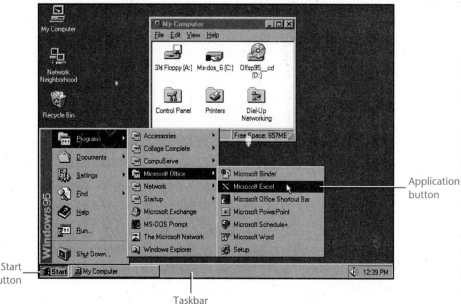

Start
button

Application
button

Taskbar

The Taskbar Makes It Easy to Switch between Applications

▶ See "Customiz-
ing the Task-
bar," p. 122

One of the problems both novice and advanced users face is keeping track of
which applications are currently running, and then switching to an already
running application. In previous versions of Windows, switching between
applications was difficult to figure out. Microsoft estimates that nearly 70
percent of users didn't know they could press Alt+Tab to switch between
applications (the Alt+Tab combination still works in Windows 95). With the
new taskbar, all the applications that are running appear as buttons on the
taskbar (refer to fig. 1.2). Clicking a button opens that running application
into its own window.

Tip
Nearly every item
in Windows 95
contains a prop-
erty sheet you can
customize. Right-
click on an item
and choose Prop-
erties to see its
properties.

Right Mouse Button Information

Windows 95 has many customizable features and the key to unlocking them
is clicking the right mouse button. Nearly every item you see on the Windows 95 screen contains a shortcut menu. To see that shortcut menu, right-
click on the item. For example, if you want to customize the taskbar, put the
tip of the mouse pointer on a gray area of the taskbar and click the right
mouse button, then choose Properties. The Taskbar Properties sheet displays
(see fig. 1.3). In it, you can change how the taskbar appears and what it
contains.

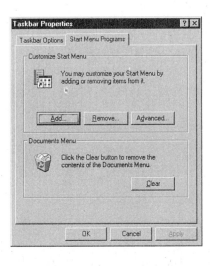

Fig. 1.3
Clicking the right mouse button on the taskbar brings up the Taskbar Properties sheet.

> **Note**
>
> Properties dialogs in Windows 95 are referred to as sheets. When you click a tab within the sheets, the open dialogs are referred to as pages. Figure 1.3 displays the Start Menu Programs page of the Taskbar Properties sheet.

My Computer for Easy Understanding of What's in Your Computer

Hierarchical displays of directories and files confused many new computer users. Microsoft developed My Computer and Network Neighborhood to resolve that problem. Double-click the My Computer icon to see a window that displays the resources available on your computer (see fig. 1.4). Doing the same on the Network Neighborhood icon displays all the resources available on any network to which you are connected. The Network Neighborhood icon does not display unless Windows has been installed for a network.

Notice in the My Computer Window that the drives and resources available within your computer are displayed. In the example in figure 1.4, the computer has an A, C, and D drive. My Computer will always display a Control Panel icon and in this case a Printers and Dial-Up Networking icon.

Tip
If you find it confusing to have too many windows open, you can specify that all the views of My Computer or Network Neighborhood appear in the same window.

> **Note**
>
> The name of the C drive in this example depends on the hard drive having a volume name prior to Windows 95 installation. Most My Computer windows will just show a (C:) drive.

Fig. 1.4
Use the My Computer window to access the drives on your computer. Double-clicking a drive will display the folders and files within that drive.

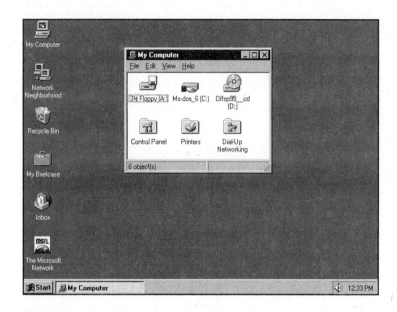

Folders Make File Management More Intuitive

Directories and files are not a familiar concept to people who are new to computers. But everyone who has worked in an office is familiar with folders and documents. The metaphor of folders and documents in Windows 95 makes file management easier to understand. Double-clicking the My Computer icon on the desktop displays the My Computer window shown in figure 1.4. This window shows the drives on your computer and other peripherals. You can get to files and directories by double-clicking any of the drives.

Double-clicking on the Ms-dos 6 (C:) icon that represents a hard drive in the computer opens the window C:\. Within this window, double-clicking on the My Documents folder opens the window titled C:\My Documents. This window contains document icons. Notice that each icon represents a type of file.

▶ See "Using My Computer to Manage Files," p. 551

You can perform work on documents by dragging their icon into other folders, onto the desktop (the background), or dropping them onto other icons that represent resources such as printers or applications. Use a right mouse click on a document icon to see frequently used tasks that control documents or to see the properties of the document.

In figure 1.5, the My Computer icon has been opened to show selected contents of the computer. The first window open is the My Computer window. This was opened by double-clicking on the My Computer icon at the top left of the desktop. The name My Computer shows in the title bar. The next window, with the title bar Ms-dos_6 (C:), was opened by double-clicking on the C: drive icon in the My Computer window. Notice that the Ms-dos_6 (C:) window overlaps the My Computer window. Finally, the My Documents window was opened by double-clicking on the My Documents folder visible in the Ms-dos_6 (C:) window. Notice that as each window opens it overlaps the window from which it came.

Each of these windows shows a different view of the computer resources available to you. As the windows open, they layer over the previous window.

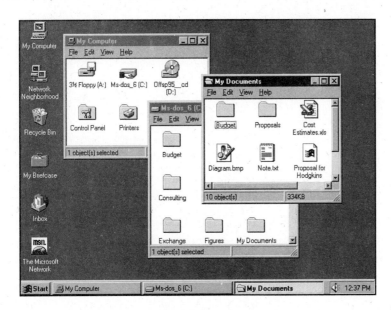

Fig. 1.5
Double-clicking on items in My Computer windows either opens the item to show its contents or opens the document or program.

Windows Explorer for Powerful File Management

Expert users may find My Computer and Network Neighborhood limiting when they need to do a lot of file management and examine different types of computer resources. Windows provides the Windows Explorer (see fig. 1.6) for more advanced users. It uses a single window composed of two panes. The left side shows a hierarchical structure of all the computer resources from hard drives and CD-ROMs to Control Panels and printers. Once you understand how to use the Windows Explorer, you will be able to do more than you could with the old File Manager. For example, you can drag files and folders from the right panel in the Explorer to a subfolder at any level in the right panel. You also can right-click on files to display a shortcut menu that enables you to view the file, print, create a shortcut, and see the file's properties.

▶ See "Using the Windows Explorer to View Files and Folders," p. 499

I

Introducing Windows 95

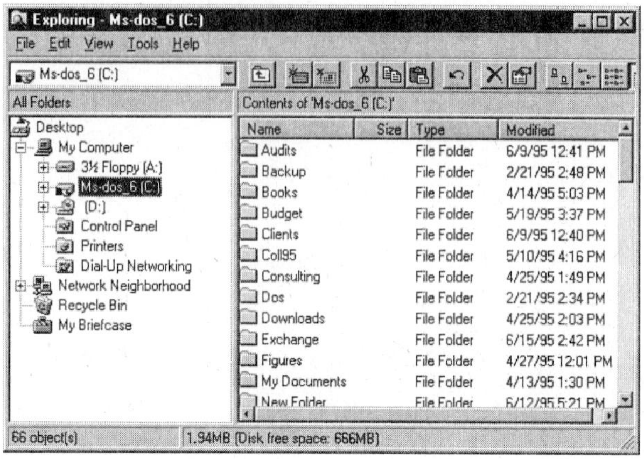

Fig. 1.6
Windows Explorer
is a powerful file
management tool.

Displaying Properties of Programs, Documents, and Resources

▶ See "Changing
Settings and
Properties with
the Right
Mouse Button,"
p. 107

Almost everything in Windows can be customized. If you can't customize it, you can at least see what its current settings or properties are. To change or view properties of an object such as the desktop background, the taskbar, the Recycle Bin, a file, a folder, and so on, click the right mouse button on the item. When a shortcut menu displays, choose Properties. A properties sheet displays. Figure 1.7 shows the property sheet for the desktop. It appears when you right-click the desktop, choose Properties, and then select one of the tabs. You can use it to change the colors, background, and screen savers in Windows.

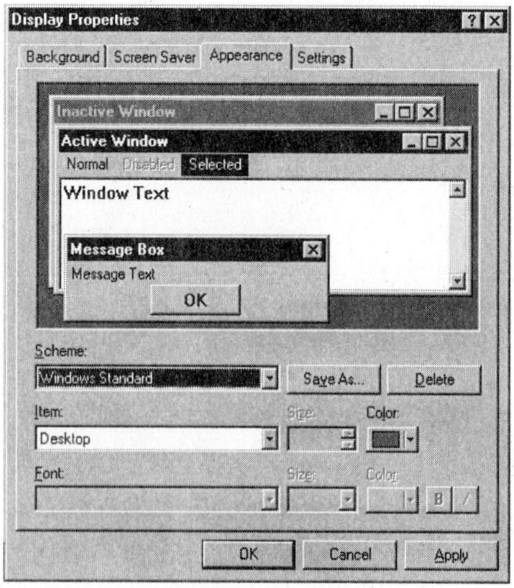

Fig. 1.7
Right-click almost
any item and
choose Properties
to display a
property sheet
like this Display
Properties sheet.

Shortcuts Add Power

Shortcuts are a powerful way of customizing your desktop. You can use a shortcut to start applications, load a document, act as a drop-box into a folder located elsewhere, and so on. You can even put a printer shortcut on your desktop. Dragging a file onto a printer shortcut will then print the file. You can put shortcuts anywhere on the desktop or in any folder.

▶ See "Creating Shortcut Icons on the Desktop to Start Programs," p. 68

Quick View Displays File Previews

Quick View enables you to see a preview of a file without starting the application that created the file and opening the file. It's a handy browser that can save you time. Quick View works with the files from most major applications. Figure 1.8 shows a Quick View of an Excel sheet.

▶ See "Previewing a Document with Quick View," p. 527

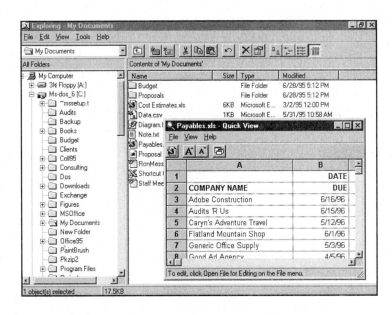

Fig. 1.8
Use Quick View to preview a file without opening it.

Long File Names Make File Names Easier to Read

One of the most aggravating things faced by everyone who used DOS or previous versions of Windows was the 8.3 file-naming restriction. File names were a maximum of eight characters and file extensions were a maximum of three characters. This limit lead to very inventive, but pretty undecipherable, file names. In Windows 95, you can use file names that are up to 255 characters long—they can even include space characters. When a file with a long name is brought back to an 8.3 file system, the long file name is truncated, so that files are still compatible.

Introducing Windows 95

Help Is Easy to Use

Help has been simplified, while at the same time it contains more information. Help now enables you to type in phrases and get back a list of related items. Help also includes graphical displays that are designed to help you understand the big picture of how a function or feature works.

More Useful Accessories

Windows includes accessories that are helpful in routine work and doing work such as file and disk management. The simple word processor, WordPad, is more than adequate for most school work or personal letter writing. And it uses a file format that is compatible with Word for Windows, the powerful and most widely sold word processor. Windows also includes accessories such as a new paint program, a calculator, and a clock.

A valuable set of disk management accessories comes with Windows. These accessories improve the performance, integrity, and safety of data on your hard drives. DriveSpace compresses data on your disk so that you can fit almost twice as much data on a drive. The ScanDisk utility checks your hard disk for errors. Disk Defragmenter collects file segments that are stored all over the disk and relocates them so that files are stored in contiguous segments. As a result, your disk runs faster and wastes less storage space. Finally, Windows includes Backup. You can use the Backup utility to make magnetic tape or disk backups of all or parts of your hard disk.

Windows 9 has been improved for use with multimedia equipment. As such, it includes the CD Player that enables you to play music CDs on computers equipped with a CD-ROM and sound board.

Improved Printing

Windows has had a number of improvements in the area of printing. Printing speed is something that everyone will appreciate. Windows now uses a 32-bit print subsystem that enables you to print in the background without causing the application you are using to show significant delays. The apparent print time has been improved because it takes less time for Windows to return to your control after you give a print command.

If you need high-quality print output, you will be able to take advantage of Windows' support for PostScript Level II printers as well as better color matching between the display and output devices.

Mobile computer users will be able to take advantage of *deferred printing*. This enables people with laptop computers to print even though their laptop is not in a docking station. Once it is connected in a docking station, it will automatically print.

Windows also supports more than 800 different models. With newer models that support the Plug and Play standard, installation is very simple. Network administrators will enjoy the automatic printer driver installation from Windows 95, Windows NT, or Novell NetWare servers.

Networking and Communication in Windows 95

Windows 95 is designed to meet the requirements of a corporate networking environment. At the same time, it is easier to use for people on the network and for mobile computer users who connect to the network. Windows 95 includes HyperTerminal, an improved 32-bit version of the basic communications program Terminal that came with previous versions of Windows.

Windows uses a high-performance 32-bit network architecture that includes 32-bit versions of network client software, file and print sharing software, network protocols, and network card drivers. It supports multiple redirectors, protocols, and network card device drivers. It also supports the industry standards TCP/IP, IPX, SNMP, and DMI.

You can build your own network using the integrated networking capability of Windows. Windows 95 is capable of supporting up to ten 32-bit, Protected-mode network clients. With today's heterogeneous networking environments, it's important that Windows be able to run as a client for many different networks. Windows runs client support for Windows NT Server, NetWare, Banyan, DEC PathWorks, and Sun NFS.

▶ See "Windows 95 Peer to Peer Networking Features," p. 617

▶ See "Automatic Installation of Windows 95 NetWare Support," p. 678

In addition to supporting corporate networking, Windows 95 has access to Microsoft Network and the Internet. Windows includes TCP/IP support, Windows Socket services, and widely used protocols such as Point to Point Protocol (PPP) and SLIP, so you can connect to the Internet through your corporate network or directly via your own modem or ISDN connection.

Microsoft Network promises to be a collection of resources that will greatly expand the services and information available online. In addition, you will be able to get online help for your Windows software from Microsoft and other companies. If you have a modem in your system, you will be able to subscribe to Microsoft Network during installation. You can install at a later time by double-clicking the MSN icon.

Windows 95 also includes a feature for organizing all your e-mail in one place. This is called the *Inbox*. With this properly set up and configured, you can read all your incoming mail from the Microsoft Network, your LAN's Microsoft mail, CompuServe mail, and even Internet mail in the same place rather than having to use all of these different applications to read mail.

Better Features for the Road Warrior

More and more people are taking advantage of the benefits of mobile computing: being able to work where you want, taking your computer home, taking it to clients, or taking it into the field. However, mobile computing comes with a plethora of difficulties. Windows now addresses many of those difficulties.

Moving your mobile computer usually requires some changes in your hardware configuration. If you are using a desktop monitor, the desktop monitor and your laptop screen may use different colors and resolutions. Some laptops come with pointer devices integrated into the keyboard, yet at your desk you might prefer to use a mouse. And then there is the problem of connecting and disconnecting from a network. When you return from a trip, there is the problem of synchronizing files—integrating the most up-to-date files between laptop and network. Prior to Windows 95, these changes required separate configuration files.

With Windows 95, mobile computer users can easily switch between different named setup configurations. If the mobile computer uses a docking station, the software transition can be completely automatic. Putting the laptop in the docking station causes the laptop to reboot in the correct configuration and connect to the appropriate network, printers, and so on.

The use of PCMCIA cards also has been improved (in Windows 95, however, PCMCIA cards are now referred to as PC Cards). You can install newer PC Cards while the computer is on. Windows will recognize the new card through Plug and Play, and immediately will make its features available.

▶ See "Synchronizing Files," p. 533

One of the advances that Windows 95 includes is the Briefcase to store files shared between desktop and mobile computers. The Briefcase will automatically update files between the systems and ask you to judge files that may be in conflict.

Any mobile computer user will tell you how important power management is. You can't have a battery go dead at the wrong time. In laptop computers that support the new Power Management APIs, Windows can monitor system power, reduce power wastage, and warn you when power gets low.

▶ See "Special Features for Notebook Users," p. 265

Easier Plug and Play Hardware Installation

One of the most aggravating situations you can face with a computer is installing a sound board, disk drive, or network adapter card with which you are unfamiliar. In fact, many hardware devices used with computers require some arcane knowledge and a few tricks that aren't in the book before they finally work. Plug and Play is designed to do away with the trickery and make the hardware side of computers as easy as installing refrigerators and toasters.

The Plug and Play specification is an industry-wide specification designed to make adding hardware easy. Plug and Play enables you to install or connect Plug-and-Play-compatible devices and let Windows figure out the technical details such as IRQs, I/O addresses, DMA channels, and memory addresses. Where there is conflict, Windows resolves the problem rather than you having to spend hours trying different settings. The information about all installed hardware and software is stored in the Registry, a database of system information. Plug and Play even makes it easier to install hardware that does not meet Plug and Play specifications, so-called "legacy hardware." Windows detects that the legacy hardware may cause a conflict with current system settings and then gives you information from the Registry that makes it easier for you to decide how to install the hardware. You don't have to keep notecards containing all the settings from previous hardware you installed. Nor do you have to pull out hardware manuals that you have probably misplaced.

Plug and Play's ease of use is apparent with, for example, the use of Plug and Play printers or PC cards. With a Plug and Play printer, as soon as you connect the printer, your computer recognizes the new printer, installs a new device driver for it, and sets up your printer configuration to print with that printer. With PC cards used in portable computers, you can slide in a modem card and immediately send a message. Plug and Play configures the modem card for you.

▶ See "Installing Plug and Play Hardware," p. 246

Improved Multimedia and Games

Windows 95 not only has improved multimedia capability. Windows includes Video for Windows so that you don't have to install video drivers. It also includes drivers for the most commonly used CD-ROM drives and sound cards. And to make it easy for anyone at home to use games or edutainment software, Windows automatically installs and runs newer CD-ROMs when you put them in the computer. Its improvements aren't limited to multimedia, however; Windows now includes Win-G, a programming interface used by game programmers, so they can write faster games that run on Windows. ❖

Chapter 2

Understanding Windows 95

by Ron Person

This chapter gives you "the big picture" to help you understand Windows 95. If you're a new user, you'll want to get a feel for the important concepts and see where you are going. If you're an experienced Windows user, you'll want to know what is different and what is the same in this new version of Windows compared to previous versions. And if you are a power user or consultant, you'll want a quick introduction to ways you can customize and troubleshoot Windows 95.

After reading this chapter, you should have a good idea what sections to read to get started learning about Windows 95. Throughout this chapter, you'll find recommendations for three different approaches to learning more. These three approaches are based on whether you are an inexperienced Windows user, an experienced Windows user, or a power user.

This chapter gives you an overview of the most important concepts for controlling Windows 95. It also tells you which book sections are probably appropriate to your experience level. In this chapter, you get an overview of the following concepts:

- The important screen elements in Windows

- The most frequently used ways of starting programs and documents

- How to customize by changing property sheets

- Whether you should use My Computer or the Windows Explorer for file management

Tip

People who have used previous versions of Windows should read this chapter so that they can quickly grasp what has changed.

Tip

Throughout this chapter, important concepts are broken up by experience level. Rather than repeating basic concepts for each experience level, you should read the concepts from the inexperienced user level up to your level.

- How to learn more about Windows through online Help

- Important differences from previous versions of Windows

- Which control methods are best suited for your work style and experience level

Understanding the Most Important Screen Elements in Windows 95

The appearance of the Windows 95 screen, shown in figure 2.1, is completely different from MS-DOS or previous versions of Windows. The backdrop of the screen is called the *desktop*. On the desktop, you'll find icons that represent programs or documents, a taskbar containing a Start button and minimized application buttons, and windows that contain programs. If your Windows 95 has been used previously and customized, it may appear slightly different from the figure.

Fig. 2.1
The Windows 95 screen is designed to be easier to use for first-time users, yet more powerful and customizable for power users.

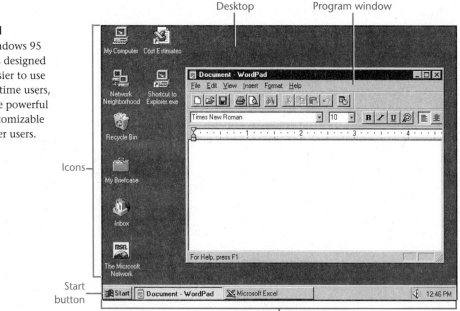

Beginning Users of Windows 95

If you are unfamiliar with previous versions of Windows, the important things to notice are:

- Each graphical item on the screen responds in a particular way when you put the tip of the mouse pointer on the item and click or double-click the left or right mouse button.

- Icons represent programs, documents, or shortcuts. *Shortcuts* are pointers to a program or document.

- You use the taskbar and Start button shown at the bottom of figure 2.1 to start and switch between programs.

- Running programs appear in three ways: as a button on the taskbar, in a window on the screen, or filling the entire screen.

Experienced and Power Users of Previous Windows Versions

If you are familiar with previous versions of Windows or even consider yourself a power user, the important things to notice are:

- Much more of Windows can be customized. Customize by clicking an item with the right mouse button, clicking Properties, and then changing options on the Properties sheet for the item.

- The Program Manager is gone. In its place are icons that appear on the desktop and a taskbar with Start button shown at the bottom of figure 2.1.

- You can drag icons on the desktop to any location and they will stay there. You can even place folders on the desktop. (*Folders* are the new name for directories.)

- *Shortcut* icons on the desktop act as pointers to programs or documents that you don't want to put directly on the desktop. Shortcuts display a small curved arrow at their lower-left corner. Double-clicking a shortcut icon opens the document or program. Deleting a shortcut icon does not delete the file to which it points.

▶ See "Learning the Parts of the Windows Display," p. 58

▶ See "Starting Applications from the Start Menu and Taskbar," p. 62

▶ See "Customizing the Mouse," p. 147

▶ See "Making Windows Accessible for the Hearing, Sight, and Movement Impaired," p. 150

▶ See "Creating Shortcut Icons on the Desktop to Start Programs," p. 68

Introducing Windows 95

The main purpose for the shortcut is to have access to a program or document from multiple places without having to have it physically stored in both places. If it's a shortcut to a document, you don't have to worry about which icon (the original or the shortcut) was used to open it because, either way, there is only one file that is being modified.

How to Start Programs and Documents

Microsoft has found that starting programs with Windows 95 is much easier than it was in previous versions of Windows. Depending on your experience level and the task, you can start programs or documents in different ways.

Starting from the Start Button

The Start button is a significant enhancement to Windows. Clicking the Start button displays a menu like the one directly above the Start button in figure 2.2. As you move the pointer over an item on the menu, a submenu appears. When you see the program or document you want to open, click it.

Fig. 2.2
Click the Start button to display the Start menu and your computer's programs and documents.

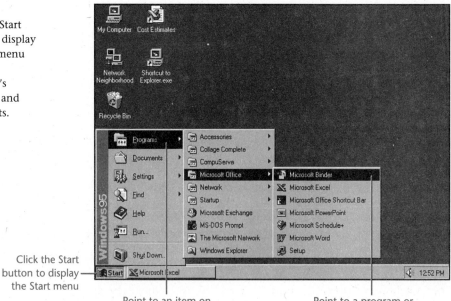

Click the Start button to display the Start menu

Point to an item on the Start menu to open a submenu

Point to a program or document to open it

Beginning Users of Windows 95

If you are unfamiliar with previous versions of Windows, the important things to notice are:

- Starting a program or document is easy. Move the mouse pointer over the Start button and click the left mouse button.

- Windows 95 lists your programs on the Start menu.

- Start a recently used document by pointing to the Documents menu item and then clicking the document. The program opens automatically.

- Find documents or programs by pointing to the Find button and clicking Files or Folders. Enter information about the document or program file you want to find.

- Get Help or demonstrations by pointing to the Help button and clicking.

- Shut down Windows by opening the Start menu and choosing Shut Down.

▶ See "Starting a Program from the Start Menu," p. 65

▶ See "Quitting Windows Applications," p. 77

Experienced Users of Previous Windows Versions

If you are familiar with previous versions of Windows, the important things to notice are:

- You no longer need to open and close Group windows in the Program Manager to find program or document icons.

- Your existing Group windows from the Program Manager in previous versions of Windows now appear as submenus off the Programs item of the Start menu.

- Click the Start button to see your programs and most frequently used documents. Click the item you want to open.

- Go directly to the Control Panel or printer settings from the Settings item on the Start menu.

- Make frequently used programs more accessible on the Start menu by dragging their file icon from the Explorer or My Computer and dropping it on the Start button.

▶ See "Running Programs on Startup," p. 52

▶ See "Specifying Documents to Open at Startup," p. 54

▶ See "Customizing the Start Menu," p. 128

Introducing Windows 95

Power Users Very Experienced with Windows

▶ See "Controlling How Startup Programs Appear," p. 54

If you consider yourself a power user and are very experienced with Windows, the important things to notice are:

■ At first the Start menu may seem to slow you down compared to quickly clicking your way through the Program Manager. It will be faster, however, if you customize by adding your own submenus and repositioning programs and documents on the menu.

▶ See "Customizing the Taskbar," p. 122

■ Customize the Start menu to include your own submenus by adding a folder to the Start menu.

▶ See "Managing Windows after an Application Failure," p. 78

■ Change the properties of programs so that they open as a button on the taskbar, as a window, or maximized to fill the screen.

Starting from Shortcuts

Shortcuts are icons that point to files. When you double-click a shortcut, it starts the program or opens the document. You can put folder shortcuts on your desktop so that when you drag a file onto the folder shortcut, the file is stored in the folder.

Fig. 2.3
Double-click a shortcut icon to open the program or document.

Shortcut icons have a small curved arrow at their lower-left corner

Beginning Users of Windows 95

If you are unfamiliar with previous versions of Windows, the important things to notice are:

▶ See "Starting Programs from a Shortcut Icon on the Desktop," p. 68

■ Shortcuts represent documents, programs, or folders.

■ Double-clicking a shortcut opens the document or program.

■ You can delete a shortcut icon without deleting the file or folder it represents.

Experienced Users of Previous Windows Versions

If you are familiar with previous versions of Windows, the important thing to notice is:

▶ See "Creating Shortcut Icons on the Desktop to Start Programs," p. 68

■ You can create a shortcut for any program, document, or folder by dragging the file or folder from the Explorer or My Computer with the right mouse button and dropping it on the desktop.

Power Users Very Experienced with Windows

If you consider yourself a power user and are very experienced with Windows, the important things to notice are:

■ You can create shortcuts that automatically run procedures or programs. For example, in Word or Excel you can create a shortcut to a document or spreadsheet that contains a macro that runs when opened. Another example is the Windows 95 Backup program. It enables you to create shortcuts that automatically backup selected files.

■ Customize shortcuts by right-clicking the Shortcut icon, clicking Properties and then clicking the Shortcut tab in the shortcut's Properties sheet. You can add shortcut keys, change the file to which the shortcut points, specify how a program runs, and change the icon.

▶ See "Modifying and Deleting Shortcuts," p. 72

Starting from My Computer or the Explorer

My Computer and the Explorer are windows used to manage the program and document files on your computer. Figures 2.4 and 2.5 show My Computer and the Explorer windows.

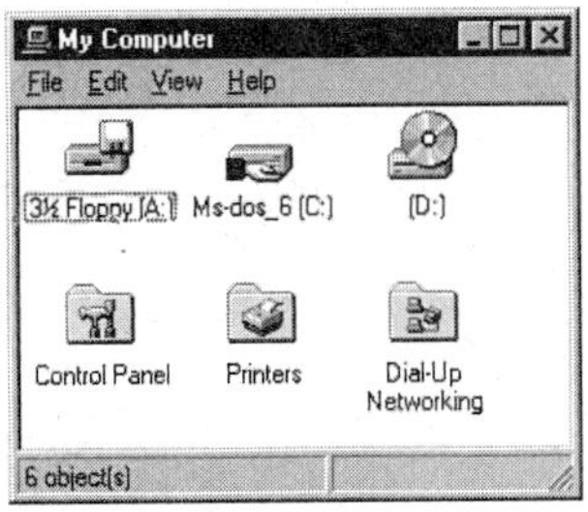

Fig. 2.4
The My Computer window.

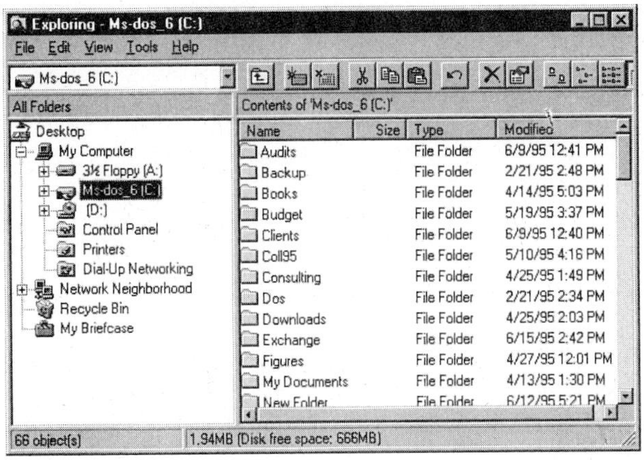

Fig. 2.5
The Explorer window.

Introducing Windows 95

Beginning Users of Windows 95

If you are unfamiliar with previous versions of Windows, the important things to notice are:

- You should use the Start menu to open programs whenever possible. Open documents from within the program. If it is a frequently used document, you may find it on the <u>D</u>ocuments submenu off of the Start menu.

▶ See "Using My Computer to Open Documents," p. 76

▶ See "Opening a Document or Application from the Explorer," p. 73

▶ See "Using the Windows Explorer to View Files and Folders," p. 499

▶ See "Managing Your Files and Folders," p. 513

- If there is a program that you can't find on the Start menu, use a window from My Computer to display program files. When you find the program you want, double-click the program's icon.

Experienced Users of Previous Windows Versions

If you are familiar with previous versions of Windows, the important things to notice are:

- If you are familiar with opening program or document files in the File Manager, you'll know how to open programs or documents from within My Computer or the Explorer. Find the file and double-click it.

- You can register a file type with an application so that double-clicking on a file of that type opens a specific application and loads the file. Most file types are automatically registered, but you can manually register a file or change a file type's registration by choosing <u>V</u>iew, <u>O</u>ptions, and then selecting the File Types tab and either adding a new type or editing an existing type.

Power Users Very Experienced with Windows

If you consider yourself a power user and are very experienced with Windows, the important thing to notice is:

▶ See "Registering Files to Automatically Open an Application," p. 539

- Open multiple files at the same time from My Computer or Explorer by selecting the files with Shift+Click or Ctrl+Click, and then right-click one of the selected files. From the shortcut menu, click <u>O</u>pen.

How to Customize and See Property Sheets

Property sheets are an important part of Windows 95. Nearly all items you see on-screen have a property sheet that describes the item. To display a properties sheet, click an item with the right mouse button and then click P<u>r</u>operties from the shortcut menu. Figure 2.6 shows the Taskbar Properties sheet.

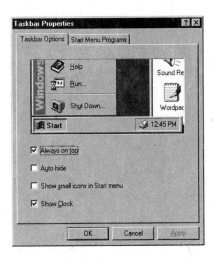

Fig. 2.6
Use properties
sheets to get
information about
an item and
change how the
item behaves.

Beginning Users of Windows 95

If you are unfamiliar with previous versions of Windows, the important
things to notice are:

- You can get a description and change the behavior of many items by
  displaying the Properties sheets.

- Even within some applications, you can see the properties of a document by displaying the file's Properties sheet from within the Open
  dialog box.

Experienced Users of Previous Windows Versions

If you are familiar with previous versions of Windows, the important things
to notice are:

- You don't have to go through the Control Panel to customize items
  anymore. Start clicking with the right mouse button and notice what
  items have a properties sheet.

- You can customize Windows by right-clicking items you want to
  change, such as the desktop, and then clicking Properties.

Power Users Very Experienced with Windows

If you consider yourself a power user and are very experienced with Windows, the important things to notice are:

- You can create logon profiles that change Windows hardware configuration depending on a selection at startup. This is useful for laptops that
  also serve as desktop computers.

▶ See "Changing
Settings and
Properties with
the Right
Mouse Button,"
p. 107

▶ See "Customiz-
ing the Desk-
top Colors and
Background,"
p. 131

▶ See "Changing
the Screen
Resolution,
Font Size, and
Color Palette,"
p. 142

▶ See "Changing
Custom Set-
tings for Each
User," p. 156

■ You can use log on IDs to identify different users on a network or isolated computer. Windows will start up with the customized settings which that user has created.

How to Manage Files

Windows 95 has two different approaches to managing files. If you're a new or inexperienced user, you may want to use My Computer. It uses a folder metaphor where files appear as program or document icons (see fig. 2.7). These icons can be moved or copied between folder icons. If you're on a network, examine Network Neighborhood. It shows network files in the same way.

The second way of managing files in Windows 95 is through the Explorer (see fig. 2.8). The Explorer displays folders and files using two panes in a window. The left pane shows the hierarchical relationship between folders—which folder is inside another. The right pane displays the contents of the folder that has been selected in the left pane.

Fig. 2.7
My Computer displays the contents of your computer in windows that contain folders and program/document icons.

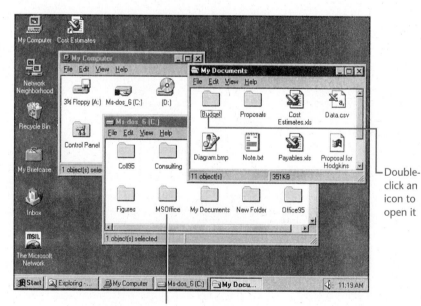

Double-click an icon to open it

Double-click a folder to open it

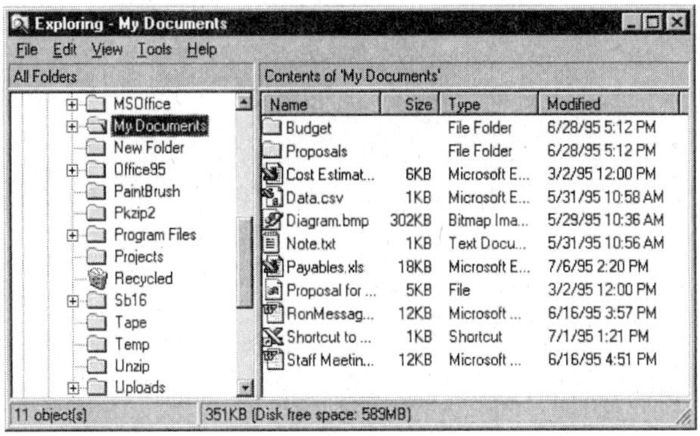

Fig. 2.8
The hierarchical relationship of folders shows in the left pane of the Explorer window.

Beginning Users of Windows 95

If you are unfamiliar with previous versions of Windows, the important things to notice are:

■ You should use My Computer to see the contents of your computer. Open disk drives and folders by double-clicking the icon.

■ Use My Computer to copy and delete files.

■ Create your own folders in a window by clicking File, New, Folder.

▶ See "Using My Computer to Manage Files," p. 551

Experienced Users of Previous Windows Versions

If you are familiar with previous versions of Windows, the important things to notice are:

■ Use either the folder metaphor in My Computer or the hierarchical panes in Explorer to manage your computer's files.

■ If you need to see the relationships of folders—how folders are grouped inside other folders—use the Explorer.

■ Right-click files in My Computer or Explorer to see the numerous short-cut commands for copying, deleting, printing, and so on.

■ At first, you may get frustrated using the Explorer because it doesn't allow multiple windows. You can actually do more in the Explorer than you did in File Manager, but it may take time to figure out how.

■ You can change the displays in either My Computer or Explorer to show lists of names with details, and small or large icons.

▶ See "Managing Your Files and Folders," p. 513

▶ See "Working with Long File Names," p. 509

▶ See "Improving Performance with Disk Defragmenter," p. 486

I

Introducing Windows 95

■ My Computer and Explorer also give you access to features such as the Control Panel and Printers. Double-click these folders to change computer and printer settings.

Power Users Very Experienced with Windows

► See "Synchronizing Files," p. 533

► See "Using Explorer with Shared Resources on a Network," p. 544

► See "Monitoring Your System," p. 483

If you consider yourself a power user and are very experienced with Windows, the important things to notice are:

■ You'll probably prefer to use the Explorer because you can see more file and folder information at a glance.

■ If you are used to side-by-side windows from the File Manager, you can recreate them in the Explorer. Open two instances of the Explorer, right-click in a gray area of the taskbar, and then click Tile Vertically.

■ All system resources are visible and most are changeable by opening the Control Panel and then System. Click the Device Manager tab. To see properties of any hardware device, click the device and then click Properties. (Select the Computer item to see IRQ and I/O settings for all devices.) ❖

Part II

Working with Windows 95

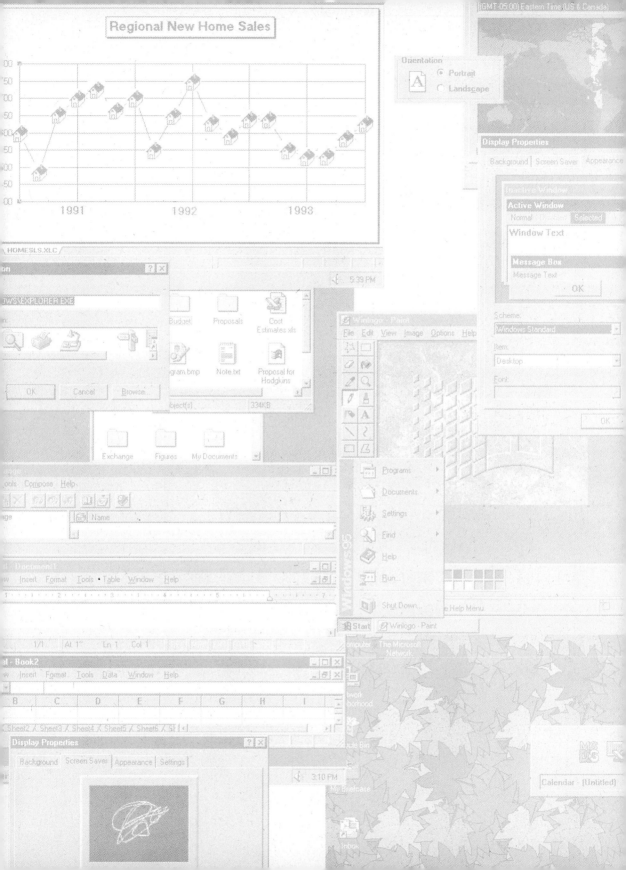

Chapter 3

Getting Started with Windows 95

by Ron Person

What you learn in this and the next chapter will help you operate Windows and any Windows application. This chapter describes the parts of the Windows screen and explains how to use the keyboard and mouse and how to start Windows and applications. You learn that there are many different ways to start an application. This chapter not only describes these different methods, it also tells you which ways you might prefer to use, depending on your experience and the type of task that you are doing.

This chapter also briefly introduces the Windows Explorer and My Computer (which Chapter 17, "Managing Your Files with Explorer," covers in more detail) and teaches you some tricks for getting out of trouble when Windows or one of your programs misbehaves.

In this chapter, you learn

- How to start and quit Windows

- How to start Windows after computer problems occur

- The terms for and parts of Windows and Windows applications

- How to use the mouse or keyboard to operate Windows

- How to run programs automatically at startup

- How to start applications from the Start menu

- How to add programs to the Start menu

- How to create shortcuts for starting programs

■ How to use the Explorer and My Computer to start applications

■ How to manage Windows when a program fails

Starting and Quitting Windows

If you have not yet installed Windows, turn to Appendix A, "Installing and Uninstalling Windows 95," to learn how. After you install Windows, you can start and display Windows simply by turning on your computer. If you are familiar with previous versions of Windows, you might expect Windows 95 to go directly into DOS as it starts, but in most cases Windows 95 starts as soon as you turn on your computer. If your computer requires DOS drivers, you may see a DOS-like text screen as the drivers load. Also, if your Windows has multiple configurations installed—as a laptop or desktop version, for example—a text screen will display asking you to choose between the configurations. Once you make your choice, Windows starts.

Tip

The first time you start Windows, you will see a Welcome to Windows 95 dialog box. You can turn this dialog box off by clicking the Show this Welcome Screen check box.

When Windows appears, you will see a login sheet in which you should type your password. Windows uses the password from the login sheet for two purposes. If the computer is connected to a network, it logs you into the network using your network password. Windows can also use the password from the login sheet to detect which person is using the computer. Because different people may have customized Windows in different ways, the login sheet enables Windows to customize itself to the way you prefer to work with Windows.

Once login sheets are completed, Windows starts and displays the desktop with My Computer, Recycle Bin, and Network Neighborhood icons. You might also see a My Briefcase icon and shortcut icons created by prior users. The *taskbar* usually appears at the bottom of the screen, although it might appear in another location or not at all.

> **Caution**
>
> Incorrectly exiting Windows can result in the loss of data. Be sure you see a display message saying it is safe to turn off your computer before you turn it off.

When you finish running Windows applications and Windows, you must not turn off the computer until you correctly exit Windows. Windows stores some data in memory and does not write it to your hard disk until you choose the Shut Down command. If you turn off the computer without correctly exiting, you might lose this data. To exit Windows correctly, follow these steps:

1. Save the data in the applications in which you are working. If you forget to do so, most applications ask whether you want to save open documents when you exit the application.

2. Exit any DOS applications that you are running.

3. Open the Start menu and choose Shut Down. The dialog box shown in figure 3.1 displays. (Your options may vary depending on your configuration.)

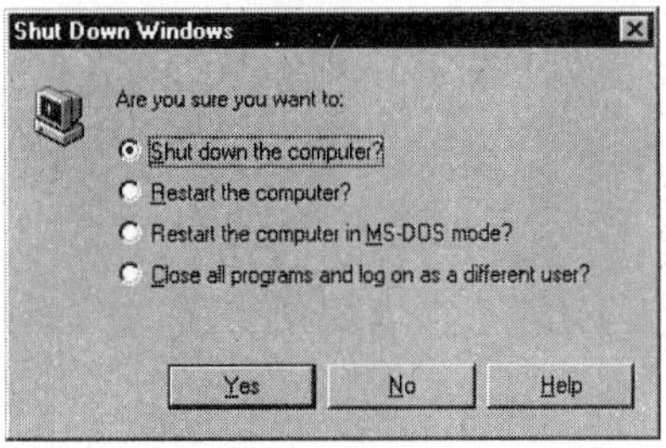

Fig. 3.1
Windows enables you to shut down the computer, restart Windows, restart the computer in DOS mode, or close all applications and log on with another user ID.

4. Choose the Shut Down the Computer? option.

5. Click Yes.

6. Turn off your computer when you see the message that says that it is safe to do so.

If your computer and Windows are set up to work on a network, you see the Close All Programs and Log On as a Different User? option when you choose the Shut Down command from the Start menu.

Do not turn off the computer hardware until you see a message saying that you can safely do so. This message might take as long as two or three minutes to appear. Turning off the computer before you see this message might result in your losing the data for applications you were working in or not updating the Registry if you made changes to applications.

Tip
If you share a computer with others, you must restart to use your customized features. Shut down with the Close All Programs and Log On as a Different User? option.

Starting Applications at Startup

If you work with certain programs each time that you use your computer, you can tell Windows to start these programs automatically when you turn on your computer. You can even tell Windows how you want the program to appear at startup—either in a window, maximized, or minimized—so that it appears as a button in the taskbar.

You can also specify that Windows open certain documents at startup. In this case, Windows starts the program associated with the document in addition to opening the document.

Running Programs on Startup

▶ See "Customizing the Start Menu," p. 128

To specify the programs that you want to run at startup, you add them to the Startup folder. The easiest way to do this is with the Taskbar Properties sheet, which has a Wizard that guides you through the process step by step. Any programs that you add to the Startup folder appear in the Startup menu, which is a submenu of the Programs menu (see fig. 3.2).

Fig. 3.2
Programs that you add to the Startup folder appear in the Startup menu and run automatically when you start Windows.

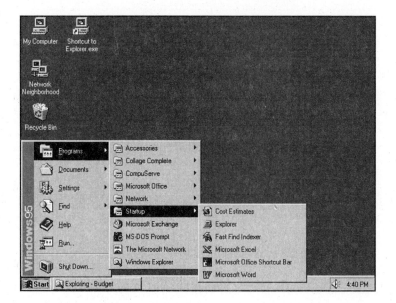

To specify programs that you want Windows to run at startup, follow these steps:

1. Open the Start menu and choose Settings, Taskbar.

2. Select the Start Menu Programs tab, as shown in figure 3.3.

3. Choose Add and then Browse.

4. Select the program that you want to add to the Startup folder by double-clicking the folder in which the program is located and then double-clicking the program.

5. Click Next.

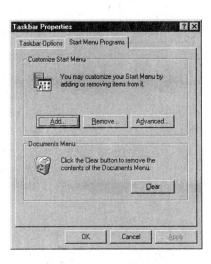

Fig. 3.3
Use the Start Menu
Programs page to
specify programs
to run at startup.

II

Working with Windows 95

6. Double-click the Startup folder.

7. Accept the default title for the program or type a new title in the Select a Name for the Shortcut text box. The name that you enter appears in the Startup menu.

8. Click Finish.

9. Repeat steps 3 through 8 to add more programs to the Startup folder, or choose OK if you are finished adding programs.

> **Note**
>
> If you frequently change the programs or documents that you want to run on startup, make the Startup folder accessible on the desktop so you can drag program or document files in and out of it. First, create a shortcut icon on the desktop for the Startup folder. Use a right mouse drag-and-drop to drag program or document files from Windows Explorer or My Computer into the Startup folder. Creating shortcuts is described in the section "Creating Shortcut Icons on the Desktop to Start Programs" later in this chapter.

To remove a program from the Startup folder, follow these steps:

1. Choose Remove on the Start Menu Programs page.

2. Double-click the Startup folder.

3. Select the program that you want to remove and choose <u>R</u>emove.

4. Choose Close.

Specifying Documents to Open at Startup

▶ See "Register-
ing Files to
Automatically
Open an Appli-
cation," p. 539

If you regularly work with particular documents each time that you use your computer—for example, if you have a budget worksheet that you work on every day—you can tell Windows to open such documents automatically at startup. For Windows to open a document automatically, the document must be associated with a program. For many programs, Windows automatically associates the documents it creates with the program. This association enables you to open a document and the program that created it simultaneously.

To specify a document to open at startup, you follow the same procedure outlined in the preceding section, "Running Programs on Startup," except that in step 4, you select a document rather than a program. After you do so, the program associated with the document automatically runs at startup and the specified document opens.

Controlling How Startup Programs Appear

Tip

Alternatively, you can double-click the shortcut icon you just created.

After specifying that a program run at startup, you can tell Windows how you want the program to display when it starts. By default, Windows runs the program in a normal window. However, you can also choose to have the program run *maximized*, so that it fills the screen, or *minimized*, so that it appears as a button on the taskbar.

To control how a program appears on startup, follow these steps:

1. Add the program to the Startup folder, as described earlier in the section "Running Programs on Startup."

▶ See "Using the
Windows
Explorer to
View Files and
Folders," p. 499

2. Open the Startup folder in either My Computer or Explorer. The Startup folder is located as a subfolder in WINDOWS\START MENU\PROGRAMS\STARTUP.

3. On the program that you want to appear on startup, click the right mouse button; then choose P<u>r</u>operties.

4. Select the Shortcut tab.

5. Select one of the three options from the <u>R</u>un drop-down list, as shown in figure 3.4.

6. Choose OK.

Fig. 3.4
The Properties
sheet is being used
to configure how
the application
Calendar will run
on startup.

Starting Windows after Technical Problems Occur

If you have any trouble starting Windows after you install it, it's good to
know some of the avenues that you can take to get out of trouble. In this
section, you learn how to create a startup disk, which enables you to start
Windows if it doesn't start normally. You also learn how to start Windows in
safe mode, which can be helpful if you are having certain kinds of problems.

Creating a Startup Disk

If you have trouble starting Windows, you might need to use a startup disk
to start your computer. For example, if you inadvertently delete a file that
Windows needs for startup, you must start Windows with the startup disk in
your disk drive and then remedy the problem so that you can start Windows
normally.

When you install Windows, you have an opportunity to create a startup disk,
which you should label and always keep on hand. If you didn't create the
startup disk during installation or have misplaced the disk, you can create
one after Windows is installed. Be sure to do so now, before you need the
disk. Otherwise, if you have problems starting Windows, you won't be able to
get into Windows to create the startup disk. (You might, however, be able to
use another computer to create a startup disk.)

To create a startup disk, follow these steps:

1. Open the Start menu and choose Settings, Control Panel.

2. Double-click the Add/Remove Programs button.

3. Click the Startup Disk tab, as shown in figure 3.5.

Fig. 3.5
To create a startup disk, click the Startup Disk tab in the Add/Remove Programs Properties sheet.

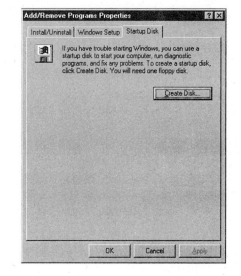

4. Insert a disk in your disk drive. The contents of this disk will be deleted.

If you have both a 5 1/4-inch and 3 1/2-inch drive, use the A drive (usually the 3 1/2-inch drive on newer computers). This is the drive from which your computer attempts to boot if a disk is in the drive.

5. Choose Create Disk and follow the instructions as they appear on-screen.

To create the startup disk, you must have your original Windows program disks (or CD-ROM) handy.

6. Click OK.

Store your startup disk somewhere safe and easy to remember. If you have a laptop, you should store your startup disk in your laptop case.

To use the startup disk, insert it in the disk drive and reboot the computer. You can now diagnose and correct the problem so that you can start

Windows normally. If you are having problems getting Windows started, or it starts but the video or some other piece of hardware does not operate correctly, read the next section for instructions on diagnosing and correcting problems.

Starting Windows in Safe Mode

Sometimes when you have trouble starting Windows, starting Windows in *safe mode* is helpful. When you do so, Windows uses basic default settings that at least get you back into the Windows environment, where you can fix the problem. For example, if you install the wrong driver for a new monitor, you might not be able to see the Windows display when you restart Windows. In this case, restarting Windows with the default settings helps because you can see the screen, enter the Control Panel, and set up a different display.

The default settings use a generic VGA monitor driver, no network settings, the standard Microsoft mouse driver, and the minimum device drivers necessary to start Windows. (*Device drivers* are software that enables hardware to work with Windows.) When you start Windows with the default settings, you cannot access any CD-ROM drives, printers, or other extra hardware devices. But you can at least access Windows and then diagnose and correct the problem.

▶ See "Getting Help," p. 79

To start Windows in a different mode, follow these steps:

1. Turn on the computer. Make sure that you also turn on the display monitor so that you can see the screen as Windows attempts to start. Be ready to press the F8 key.

2. When the message Starting Windows appears on-screen, press F8 to display the Windows 95 Startup Menu. This displays a menu of choices for starting Windows in different modes. Safe Mode is choice 3; Safe Mode with Network Support is choice 4. Or select one of the other startup modes.

3. Type the selection number for the Safe Mode or Safe Mode with Network Support. Press Enter.

To skip the Startup Menu and start directly in a mode, start your computer and press one of the key combinations in the following table when the message Starting Windows appears.

II

Working with Windows 95

Key Combination	Operating Mode
F5	Loads HIMEM.SYS and IFSHLP.SYS, loads DoubleSpace or DriveSpace if present, then runs Windows 95 WIN.COM. Starts in safe mode.
Shift+F5	Loads COMMAND.COM and loads DoubleSpace or DriveSpace if present.
Ctrl+F5	Loads COMMAND.COM.
F6	Loads HIMEM.SYS and IFSHLP.SYS. Processes the Registry, loads COMMAND.COM, loads DoubleSpace or DriveSpace if present, runs Windows 95 WIN.COM, loads network drivers, and runs NETSTART.BAT.

▶ See "Checking Performance Settings," p. 164

A message informs you that Windows is running in safe mode and that some of your devices might not be available. The words Safe mode appear at each corner of the screen.

Learning the Parts of the Windows Display

Windows screens display many graphical elements. Learning the names of these graphic elements or icons is important because you'll see these terms throughout this book. Likewise, you need to be familiar with these elements and icons because you can invoke a command for Windows or a Windows program by clicking the mouse pointer on many of them.

Figure 3.6 shows a Windows desktop that contains multiple applications, each in its own window. The figure also identifies the parts of a typical Windows screen.

In the desktop shown in figure 3.6, the Start button appears in the lower-left corner. This button provides one of the easiest ways to start programs or to open documents that you have recently used. (The Start button and taskbar may appear along different edges of the screen if a previous user has moved them.) With the mouse, you can click the Start button to open the Start menu. With the keyboard, you press Ctrl+Esc.

▶ See "Customizing the Taskbar," p. 122

Across the bottom of the screen is the taskbar. The taskbar displays all programs currently open and running. You can switch between different programs by clicking the mouse pointer on the program that you want in the taskbar. To use the keyboard, press Alt+Tab to select the program and then release the keys.

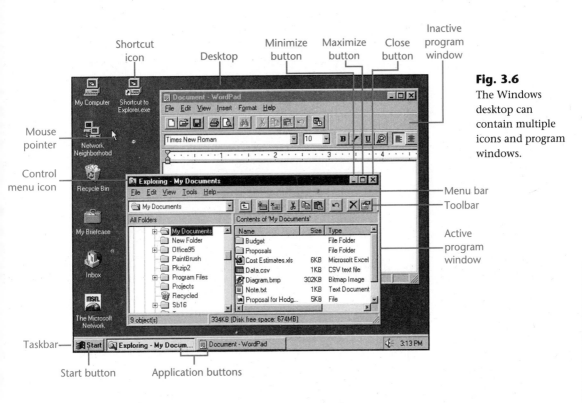

Shortcut icon — Desktop — Minimize button — Maximize button — Close button — Inactive program window

Mouse pointer — Control menu icon

Fig. 3.6
The Windows desktop can contain multiple icons and program windows.

Menu bar — Toolbar — Active program window

Taskbar — Start button — Application buttons

▶ See "Moving the Taskbar," p. 124

The taskbar might appear in a different location on your screen. You can move the taskbar by dragging it to another location. You can also remove the taskbar from the screen by customizing your screen as described in Chapter 5, "Customizing Windows 95."

With the mouse pointer, you can control Windows applications quickly and intuitively. The mouse pointer enables you to choose commands, select options, and move on-screen items. When you move the mouse, the mouse pointer moves synchronously. At different locations on the screen, the mouse pointer changes shape to indicate that it has capabilities specific to its current location. To select an item on the screen, you position the pointer on the item and then press or hold down the mouse button. You use four actions to affect on-screen items that are under the tip of the pointer: clicking, double-clicking, right-clicking, and dragging.

Windows enables you to run more than one program at the same time. Each program appears in its own window or as an item on the taskbar at the bottom of the screen. When programs are in windows, the program in the top-most window is the *active* program in the *active* window. Usually, the color of the active windows title bar differs from that of inactive windows. The active

II

Working with Windows 95

window receives your keyboard commands. One of the advantages of Windows is that even while you are working with the active program in the active window, other programs can be working.

The title bar at the top of each window displays the name of the application in the window. After you save a file, the title bar also shows the file name. (The active window is the one on top; it contains the currently running application.)

The menu bar, which is directly under the title bar, displays the menu names. Windows applications use the same menu headings for common functions (such as File, Edit, Window, and Help), which makes it easier for you to learn new applications. To open a menu, click on its name with the left mouse button, or press Alt and then the underlined letter in the menu name.

Icons are small, graphic representations. To reduce the clutter of a filled desktop, you can minimize windows so that they appear as icons on the taskbar. Even if not currently displayed in a window, an application is still running if the taskbar displays its icon. The taskbar appears at the bottom of figure 3.6.

Troubleshooting

Pressing Alt+Tab just seems to alternate between two applications.

Hold down the Alt key as you press Tab and you will see a bar displaying icons of all the running applications. As you continue to hold down the Alt key, each press of the Tab key selects the next application icon on the bar. When the application you want is selected, release both the Alt and the Tab keys.

Using the Mouse and Keyboard on the Desktop

With the dominance of the *graphical user interface* (GUI) on today's personal computers, using a mouse has become second nature to most computer users. In Windows 95, you use the mouse even more than in earlier versions of Windows. Although you can still perform most tasks in the Windows environment with the keyboard, you can accomplish them much more quickly with the mouse. Also, many shortcuts are accessible only with the mouse. For example, in Windows 95 you use the right mouse button extensively to access shortcut menus that can significantly reduce the number of steps that it takes to invoke a command. Even if you are a diehard keyboard addict, you should explore the Windows environment with your mouse. You might be surprised by the things that you can now do with the mouse.

This section explains the basic steps that you need to know to perform tasks with the mouse. If you already know how to use the mouse, you might want to skip this section.

▶ See "Customiz-
ing the Mouse,"
p. 147

▶ See "Customiz-
ing the Key-
board," p. 148

Windows users routinely use the mouse to select text, objects, menus and their commands, toolbar buttons, and dialog box options, and to scroll through documents. To perform such tasks, you need to know how to point and click with the mouse.

To click items using the mouse, follow these steps:

1. Move the mouse so that the tip of the mouse pointer, usually an arrow, is on the menu, command, dialog box item, graphics object, or a position within the text. (When moved over editable text, the pointer changes to the shape of the letter I, also called the *I-beam*.)

2. With a single, quick motion, press and release the left mouse button.

Throughout this book, this two-step process is called *clicking*. Clicking the mouse button twice in rapid succession while pointing is called *double-clicking*. Double-clicking produces an action different than clicking. In a word processing application, for example, you often click to position the insertion point but double-click to select a word.

You also can use the mouse for *dragging*. Dragging selects multiple text characters or moves graphic objects such as windows.

To drag with the mouse, follow these steps:

1. Move the mouse so that the tip of the pointer is on the object or at the beginning of the text that you want to select. (When over text, the pointer appears as an I-beam.)

2. Press and hold down the left mouse button.

3. Move the mouse while holding down the mouse button. If you are dragging a graphical object, the object moves when you move the mouse. If you are selecting text, the highlighted text area expands as you move the mouse.

4. Release the mouse button.

II

Working with Windows 95

An important enhancement to Windows 95 is the extensive use of the right mouse button. Putting the tip of the pointer on many objects on-screen and clicking the right mouse button displays a shortcut menu with commands specific to that object. For example, right-clicking a file name produces a shortcut menu containing commands such as Copy, Delete, and Rename. In some situations, such as dragging a file name onto the desktop, you will want to drag using the right mouse button. In this case, you would drag as you would using the left mouse button, but hold down the right mouse key. When you release the item, a shortcut menu will appear, from which you can quickly choose your next action.

The mouse is a useful tool, but you can use the keyboard to do nearly everything that you can do with the mouse. The mouse and the keyboard work as a team for controlling Windows applications. You can perform some tasks more easily with the mouse and some more easily with the keyboard. With most Windows applications, you can perform all functions with either. Experiment with the mouse and the keyboard, and use each where it works best for you. The next section gives you detailed information on how to use the mouse and keyboard to accomplish various tasks in the Windows environment.

Starting Applications from the Start Menu and Taskbar

Most of the work that you do on your computer consists of opening a program, using the program to create or modify a document, saving the document as a file, and then closing the program. Windows is designed to make these routine tasks as simple as possible.

One of the most important tasks that you must know how to do is to open or start programs in Windows. This task is very simple to do in Windows. You can open a program in several ways, so you can choose which works best for you. This section describes the different methods for starting programs and for using the Start menu, shortcuts, the Windows Explorer, and My Computer. You also learn what to do if a program fails or locks up when you are using it.

Using the Start Menu

The simplest way for a new Windows user to open a program is to use the Start menu. When you install Windows, the installation program usually places each of your programs on a submenu that appears off the Start menu. You can open the program simply by selecting it from a menu (see fig. 3.7).

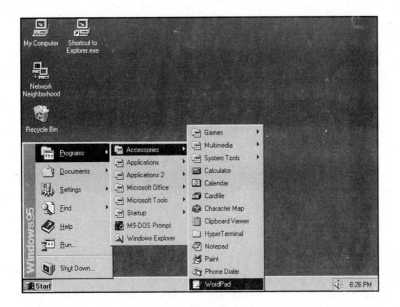

Fig. 3.7
You can select the program that you want to start from one of the menus that cascades from the Start menu. Here, the user is choosing to start WordPad.

II

Working with Windows 95

Note

If you are upgrading from an older version of Windows to Windows 95, the Group windows that appeared within the Program Manager will become submenus that appear off Programs in the Start menu.

If you are familiar with Windows and want to make your programs more accessible, you can add the programs that you use most frequently to the Start menu. Then you don't have to move through a series of menus to start these programs. In this chapter, you also learn how to create a shortcut icon on the desktop that starts an application. These powerful features of Windows give you immediate access to your programs. You learn these techniques later in this section.

When to Work from the Start Menu

If you are just getting started with Windows 95, you will probably want to use the Start menu to start your programs. Then all you have to learn is how to open the Start menu and select the programs that you want.

After you become more comfortable or familiar with Windows, you might still want to use the Start menu. However, you first will want to add your frequently used programs to the first level of the Start menu. This gives you immediate access to your programs and saves you from having to work your way through a series of submenus.

▶ See "Customizing the Start Menu," p. 128

Understanding the Start Menu

The Start menu is the starting place for many of the tasks you want to accomplish in Windows. You can open the Start menu at any time, from within any program, with one mouse click. From the Start menu, you can open your programs, customize the look and feel of Windows, find files and folders, get help, and shut down your computer (see fig. 3.8). While providing all the power of immediate access, the Start menu also is integral to the clean look of the Windows desktop, enabling you to minimize the clutter on your desktop.

Fig. 3.8
The Start menu is just a mouse click away and gives you instant access to all your programs and many other Windows features.

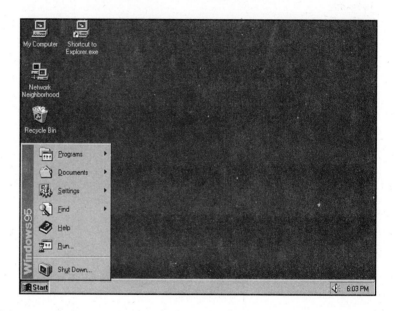

Tip
If you are an experienced Windows user, do not be put off by the Start menu. Windows 95 can be customized to be much faster to use than previous versions of Windows.

Use the Start menu whenever you need to open a program or access other features of Windows. You can open the Start menu at any time, even when you are working in another application such as Paint, as shown in figure 3.9. This is much simpler than in earlier versions of Windows, where you had to switch back to Program Manager to open other programs.

Troubleshooting

The windows of some programs written for older versions of Windows cover the taskbar, so it is difficult to switch between applications or click the Start button.

Even when you can't see the taskbar, you can switch between applications by holding down the Alt key and pressing Tab. A bar appears with icons for each application. Press Tab until the application you want is selected, then release both keys.

To simultaneously display the taskbar and open the Start menu, press Ctrl+Esc.

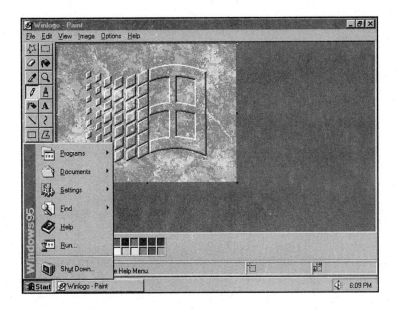

Fig. 3.9
You can open
the Start menu
without having to
leave the program
in which you are
working. Here, the
Start menu appears
at the bottom of
the Paint program.

Starting a Program from the Start Menu

To start a program from the Start menu, use the mouse to select the program
from a menu and then click. It's that easy. You can also use the keyboard,
although Windows is definitely designed to work most efficiently with a
mouse.

To start a program using the Start menu, follow these steps:

1. Click the Start button in the taskbar to open the Start menu.

   If you have customized your computer, you might not see the taskbar
   and Start button at the bottom of your screen. If you see a gray line at
   one edge of the screen, move the pointer to that edge to display the
   taskbar. With the keyboard you can press Ctrl+Esc to display the taskbar
   and open the Start menu.

2. Point to Programs on the Start menu. The Program menu then appears
   to the right. Then point to the program that you want to start and click.

   If the Programs menu doesn't list the program you want to start, click
   the folder that contains the program. In figure 3.10, the user has selected WordPad from the Accessories submenu; when the user clicks the
   mouse, Windows opens that program. To find the program that you
   want, you might have to move through a series of submenus.

Fig. 3.10

Open the menu that contains the program you want to start and then click the program.

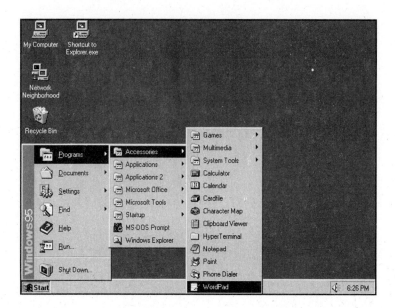

If you are using a keyboard and do not have a mouse available, open the Start menu by pressing Ctrl+Esc, and then use arrow keys to move up and down the menu. Press Enter to select the currently highlighted menu or program.

▶ See "Switching between Applications," p. 118

When you open a program, a button for the program appears in the taskbar. These buttons tell you which programs are open and enable you to move quickly from one open program to another.

▶ See "Customizing the Start Menu," p. 128

Note

Usually you should find the program that you want to open in one of the Start menu's submenus. When you install Windows, the installation program looks for all your applications and puts each in one of the menus. If, however, you can't find your program in the Start menus, you can add a program or folder to the Start menu by following the procedures described in Chapter 5.

Starting a Document from the Start Menu

After you click the Start button, notice a Documents command in the Start menu. When you choose this command, the Documents submenu appears with a listing of the files that you have worked on recently (see fig. 3.11). To open a document in this list, simply click on it. Windows then automatically starts the associated application, if it is not already running, and opens the document.

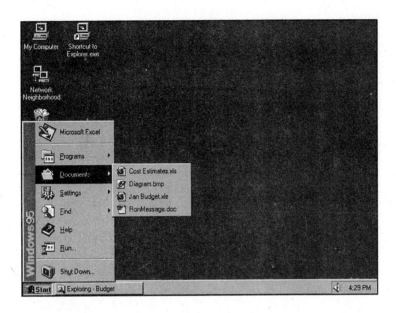

Fig. 3.11
The Start menu maintains a list of the documents that you have worked with most recently. Click on one to load it into its application.

After a while, the listing in the Documents menu can become quite long and contain documents that you no longer are working with. To clear the list, click the Start button, choose Settings, and then choose Taskbar. Select the Start Menu Programs tab on the Taskbar Properties sheet and choose the Clear button (see fig. 3.12). Click OK to close the Properties sheet.

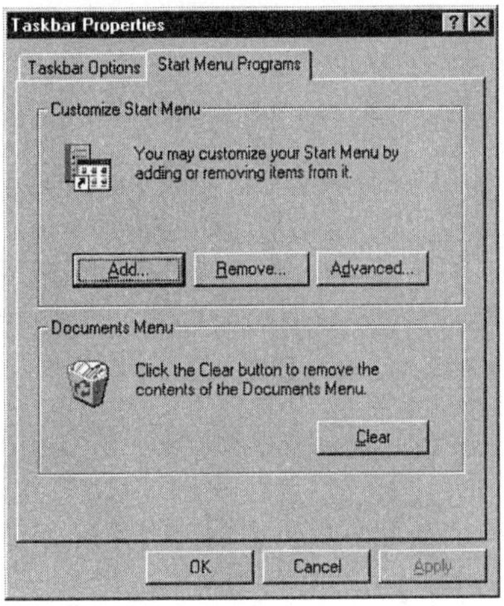

Fig. 3.12
You can clear the Documents list from the Start Menu Programs page.

II

Working with Windows 95

Starting Programs from a Shortcut Icon on the Desktop

Another method for starting programs is to create shortcuts for the programs that you use most frequently. These shortcuts can appear as icons on your desktop. To start a program, you simply double-click its icon. If you don't like using menus to start your programs, you might prefer using shortcuts. A drawback to this method, however, is that to access the shortcut icons, your desktop must be visible. If a program is maximized, you cannot see the shortcuts.

You can always tell whether an icon represents a shortcut, because a little arrow appears beneath the icon (see fig. 3.13).

Fig. 3.13
This desktop has three shortcuts, as indicated by the arrows. To start an application, you double-click its icon.

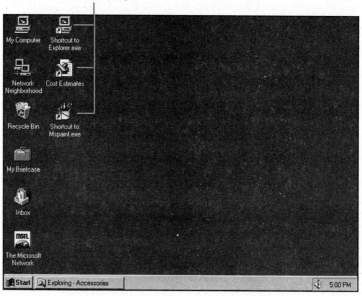

Double-click a shortcut icon
to start the program

Creating Shortcut Icons on the Desktop to Start Programs

To create a shortcut for a program on your desktop, follow these steps:

1. Using the Explorer or My Computer, locate the program for which you want to create a shortcut.

See Chapter 17, "Managing Your Files with Explorer," to learn how to use the Explorer and My Computer for browsing files and folders.

2. Select the program in the Explorer or My Computer window.

3. Click the program with the right mouse button and choose Copy.

4. Click the desktop with the right mouse button and choose Paste Shortcut.

The icon now appears on your desktop. You can drag the icon to any location. Refer to figure 3.13 earlier, which shows the desktop with three shortcuts.

You also can create a shortcut for a document. Find the document in the Explorer or My Computer, and create a shortcut for the document as described in the preceding steps. If the document is associated (or registered) with a program, you can start the program and open the document by double-clicking its shortcut.

Tip

Drag a file from My Computer or Explorer onto the desktop with the right mouse button. Drop the file and select Create Shortcut(s) Here to create a shortcut icon on the desktop.

Troubleshooting

Double-clicking a shortcut icon no longer opens the document or program.

What may have happened is that the file to which the shortcut pointed was moved or deleted. To correct this problem, you can either delete and then re-create the shortcut, or you can correct its Properties sheet. To delete the shortcut icon, right-click the icon, and then choose Delete. Choose Yes when asked to confirm the deletion. Re-create the shortcut with the methods described in this section. To fix a shortcut to a file that has moved, right-click on the icon, and then choose Properties. Click on the Shortcut tab. Check the file and path name in the Target box. They may be wrong. To find the file, click on the Find Target button. This opens a window in My Computer to the file if it is found. If it cannot be found, you can search in My Computer for the correct file and path name.

Setting the Properties for a Shortcut Icon

You can change how a shortcut icon acts and how it appears by opening its Properties sheet and changing its properties. On the Properties sheet, you can find information such as when a shortcut was created. You also can make a variety of changes, such as the following:

- Change the file that the shortcut opens.

- Make an application start in a folder you specify.

- Add a shortcut key that activates the shortcut.

- Indicate whether you want the document or application to run minimized, maximized, or in a window.

- Change the icon used for a shortcut.

To display the Properties sheet and set the properties for a shortcut icon, follow these steps:

1. Right-click on the shortcut icon.

2. Click the Properties command to display the General page of the Shortcut Properties sheet, shown in figure 3.14.

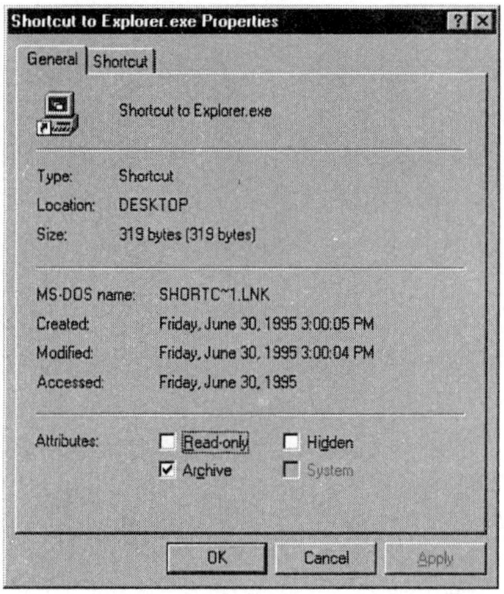

Fig. 3.14
The General page shows you file information about the shortcut icon.

On the General page, you can read where the LNK file for the shortcut is stored, as well as when it was created, modified, and last used. You also can change its file attributes.

3. Click the Shortcut tab to see the Shortcut page, shown in figure 3.15.

At the top of the page, you can read the type of shortcut it is and the folder in which it is located. In the figure, the shortcut is to the Explorer application in the WINDOWS folder.

4. If you want a different file to start from the shortcut, click in the Target edit box and type the folder and file name.

Tip
If your data files for a program are not in the same directory as the program, use the Start In edit box to enter the path to your data files.

If you are unsure of the location, click Find Target to open a My Computer window in which you can look for the file and folder you want. Once you find the folder and file, close the My Computer window and type the name in the Target text box.

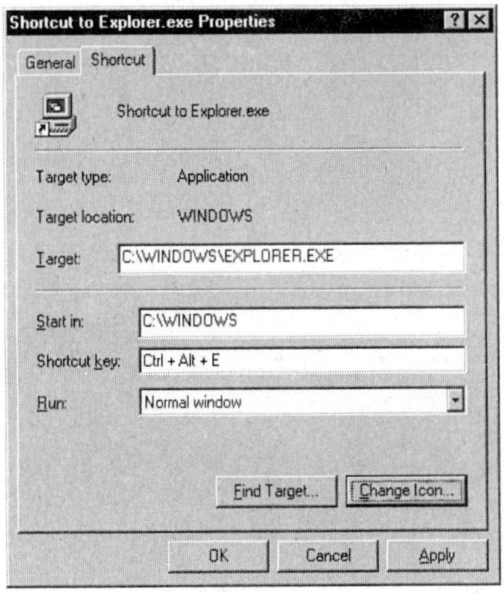

Fig. 3.15
The Shortcut page enables you to specify the file, startup folder, shortcut key, and icon used by a shortcut.

II

Working with Windows 95

5. To specify a folder that contains the file or files necessary for operation, click in the Start In text box and enter the drive and folders.

6. To specify a shortcut key that will activate this shortcut icon, click in the Shortcut Key text box and then press the key you want as the shortcut key. The key must be a letter or a number. You cannot use Esc, Enter, Tab, the space bar, Print Screen, or Backspace. To clear the Shortcut Key text box, select the box and press the space bar.

   To use this shortcut key, you press Ctrl+Alt and the key you indicated. Shortcut keys you enter take precedence over other access keys in Windows.

Tip
You can press a shortcut's key combination to run the shortcuts program or document even when another program is active.

7. To specify the type of window in which the application or document will run, click on the Run drop-down list. Select from Normal Window, Minimized, or Maximized.

8. To change the icon displayed for the shortcut, click Change Icon to display the Change Icon dialog box, shown in figure 3.16.

   The Change Icon dialog box displays a scrolling horizontal list of icons stored in files with the extensions EXE, DLL, and ICO.

Fig. 3.16
You can select the
icon you want for
your shortcut.

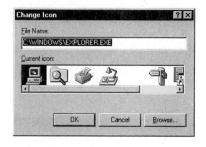

9. Select the icon you want and then choose OK.

10. Click the OK button to make your changes and close the Shortcut Properties sheet. Click Apply to make your changes and keep the Shortcut Properties sheet open for more changes.

> **Note**
>
> When selecting icons for a shortcut, you don't have to restrict yourself to the icons in the file the shortcut points to. You can select an icon from any other DLL, EXE, or ICO file. To see other icon files from the Change Icon dialog box, click the Browse button.

Tip
Online computer services and computer clubs maintain large collections of icon files that are available for free.

Modifying and Deleting Shortcuts

If you want to modify the name that appears under the icon, click once on the icon to select it. Then click once on the name to select the text in the name. At this point, the pointer changes to an I-beam. You can press Delete to delete the name or click the pointer where you want the insertion point. After you edit the name, press Enter.

To delete a shortcut, click on it with the right mouse button and choose Delete. Choose Yes when the confirmation dialog box appears.

Tip
You can arrange icons on the desktop by right-clicking on the desktop, and then choosing the Arrange Icons command. You are given alternative ways of arranging them.

> **Caution**
>
> Be careful when deleting shortcuts from the desktop. When you delete a shortcut for a file, you delete only the shortcut, not the file. However, when you delete an icon that represents a file, you delete the file. You can always tell whether an icon represents a shortcut because an arrow appears beneath the icon.
>
> If, for example, you drag a document from My Computer to the desktop with the left mouse button, the icon actually represents the file; if you then delete the icon, you also delete the file. Make sure that you know what you are doing before you delete an icon on your desktop.

Starting Programs and Documents from the Explorer or My Computer

The Windows Explorer is an application that comes with Windows 95. The Explorer is similar to the earlier Windows version's File Manager but is much more powerful. You can use the Explorer to view the files and folders on your computer; move, copy, rename, and delete files and folders; and perform other file-management tasks. You can also start programs and open documents from the Explorer. The time that you spend learning how to work with this very useful and powerful tool is well invested.

My Computer is similar to the Explorer. The main difference between them is that, unlike the Explorer window, the My Computer window does not enable you to view the overall structure of or relationships among all your computer's resources. Typically, when you use My Computer, you view the contents of one folder at a time. For some users, this window is less confusing than the Explorer window, which presents a lot of information at once.

This section focuses on starting programs and opening documents. For detailed instructions on using the Explorer and My Computer to manage your files, see Chapter 17, "Managing Your Files with Explorer."

Opening a Document or Application from the Explorer

You can use the Explorer to find any file on your computer. After you find the file, you can also use the Explorer to start the program or document. If the file is a program file, you can start the program by double-clicking on its file in the Explorer. If the file is a document, you can start its associated application and open the document simultaneously. If the application is already running, Windows opens the document in that application.

To open an application or document in the Explorer, follow these steps:

1. Open the Start menu and choose Programs, Windows Explorer. The Explorer window appears, as shown in figure 3.17.

2. In the Explorer's left pane, locate and select the folder that contains the program or document that you want to start or open. Click on the + sign to open a folder or the – sign to close a folder.

   In figure 3.18, the user has selected a folder called Sales Department, and the Explorer's right pane displays the files in that folder.

II

Working with Windows 95

Tip
Access the Explorer quickly by right-clicking the Start button and then choosing Explore.

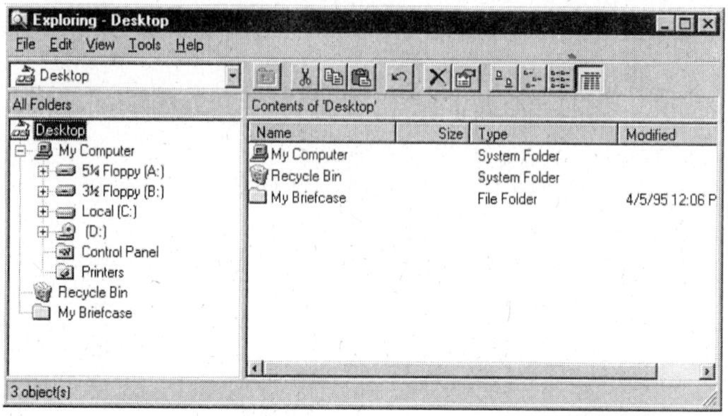

Fig. 3.17
The Explorer window displays all your computer's resources, including folders and files.

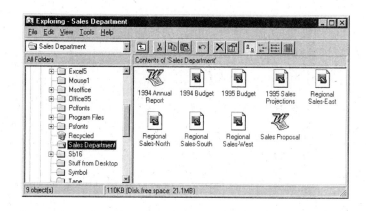

Fig. 3.18
The user has selected the Sales Department folder in the Explorer's left pane, so the right pane displays that folder's contents.

Each document in the folder is represented by an icon that indicates the application that was used to create the document. The name of the document appears beneath the icon. For more detailed information on each file, choose View, Details. The Explorer's right pane then lists the files along with information on the size, type, and the date and time that each file was last modified, as shown in figure 3.19.

3. Double-click the document that you want to open.

If a document is associated with an application such as a word processor or spreadsheet program, Windows starts the application and opens the document. If the associated application is already running, Windows simply opens the document.

4. To open another document in the same folder, click the Exploring button in the taskbar to redisplay the Explorer, and double-click the document you want to open.

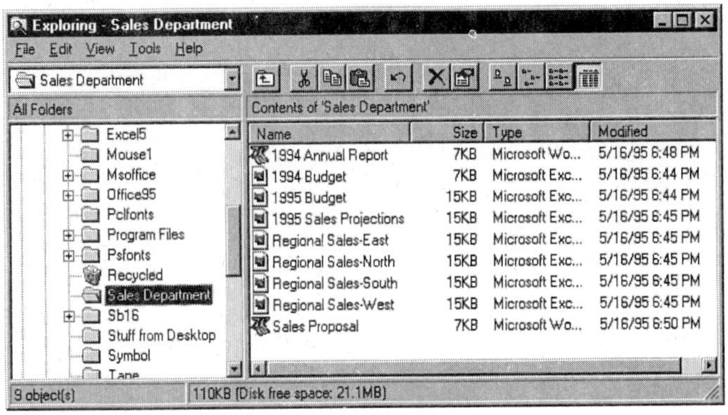

Fig. 3.19

Choose View, Details to display more information for each file in a folder.

5. To open a document in another folder, click the Exploring button in the taskbar to redisplay the Explorer, locate and select the folder containing the document in the left pane, and double-click the document in the right pane.

Troubleshooting

Double-clicking a file in the Explorer doesn't open the file. An Open With dialog box displays, asking which program should be used to open the file.

Windows does not recognize the application to use when opening the document you double-clicked. Windows displays the Open With dialog box so you can select the application to open. Windows records this application so that it can open the same application the next time you double-click on this type of document.

▶ See "Registering Files to Automatically Open an Application," p. 539

If you decide to use the Explorer routinely to open your documents, you can leave it open on your desktop. When you exit and restart Windows, it automatically opens the Explorer window in the same position as you left it.

Figure 3.20 shows how the Explorer window might look if a financial consultant organized her documents by client, creating one folder for each client. Within each folder she would keep all the documents associated with that client and could easily move from client to client, opening documents simply by double-clicking on them. With this approach to document management, the Explorer, rather than the Start menu, becomes the starting point for your work. You can still use the Start menu to access other Windows applications that you use less frequently or that are not associated with documents. Such applications include the Control Panel, which you use to customize Windows.

II

Working with Windows 95

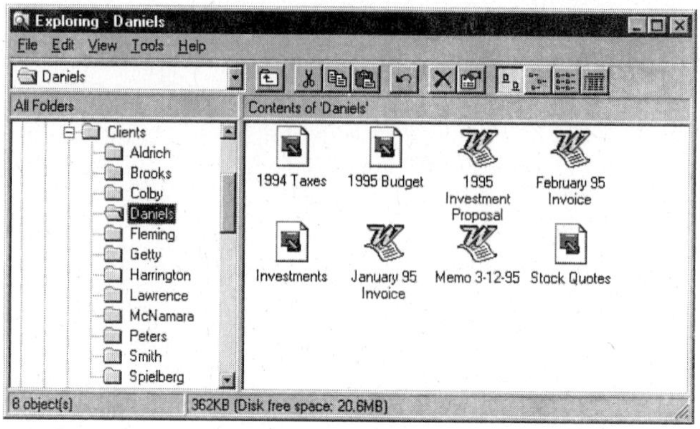

Fig. 3.20

In this desktop, the user has created a folder for each client, and each folder contains all the documents for that client.

Using My Computer to Open Documents

The first time that you start Windows, you will notice an icon called My Computer on your desktop. If you double-click on this icon, the My Computer window appears, as shown in figure 3.21. You can use My Computer to view your computer's resources, including folders and files. Figure 3.22 shows a window of folders that displays after double-clicking on the C: drive icon. My Computer is a different way of viewing folders, files and computer resources than that used by the Explorer.

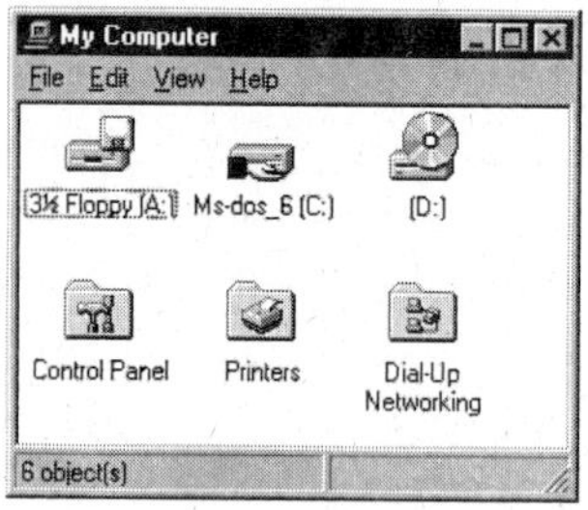

Fig. 3.21

Use the My Computer window to view your computer's resources.

After you open a window for a folder so that you can view its contents, you can open a document (or application) by double-clicking its icon, just as you did in the Explorer earlier in this chapter. Figure 3.22 shows the folders within a C: drive. Some users find this window simpler and less confusing than the Explorer window shown in figure 3.20.

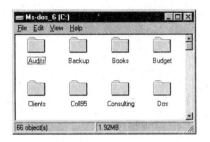

Fig. 3.22
Double-click on a
folder to display its
contents.

Using Windows 3.1 File Manager or Program Manager

If you upgraded your Windows 3.1 or Windows 3.11 to Windows 95, you still have copies of File Manager and Program Manager available. Although My Computer and Explorer are more flexible, you may prefer to make the transition slowly and take your time learning the new features of Windows 95.

If you prefer to use File Manager and Program Manager, you can easily do so. Their files, WINFILE.EXE and PROGMAN.EXE, are located in the WINDOWS folder. You can use the procedures described in this chapter to add these programs to your Start menu, create shortcut icons for the desktop, or run them when Windows starts.

Quitting Windows Applications

Most Windows applications operate the same way. To quit a Windows application, follow these steps:

1. Activate the application by clicking on the application's window or by pressing Alt+Tab until you have selected the application.

2. Click the Close button, or choose File, Exit.

Note

Throughout this book, instuctions such as "Choose File, Exit" mean that you click the File menu (or press Alt+F) and then click the Exit command (or press Alt+X).

II

Working with Windows 95

If the application contains documents that you have modified since the last time that you saved them, the application prompts you to save your changes before the application quits.

Managing Windows after an Application Failure

Under Windows 3.0, if an application quit working, the user had two options: prayer and prayer. A hung program meant lost data. Windows 3.1 improved on this by allowing *local reboot*, the ability to trap errant application behavior, thus protecting other applications and data. Under Windows 3.1's local reboot, pressing Ctrl+Alt+Del didn't restart your computer; it closed the misbehaving application and was supposed to leave Windows and other applications running correctly.

Local reboot had two main problems, however:

- People didn't always know which application was misbehaving, so pressing Ctrl+Alt+Del often closed the wrong appplication.

- Windows 3.1 didn't always respond quickly to the Ctrl+Alt+Del command. Users would continue to press Ctrl+Alt+Del until the computer restarted. (A single Ctrl+Alt+Del would bring up a blue screen warning that a second Ctrl+Alt+Del would reset the system.)

Windows 95 significantly improves on how failed or misbehaving applications are handled. Windows 95 continuously polls the applications to see if they are running and responding. When an application fails to respond, Windows 95 displays the Not Responding dialog box, like the one shown in figure 3.23. In this dialog box, you can click the End Task button to close down the application. You lose all changes to data in the application since the last time you saved. Click Cancel to return to the application.

If the application misuses memory or has a fatal error that causes the application to crash, other applications in Windows will not usually be involved. When an application fails to respond—for example, clicks or keystrokes get no response—press Ctrl+Alt+Del to display the Close Program dialog box shown in figure 3.24.

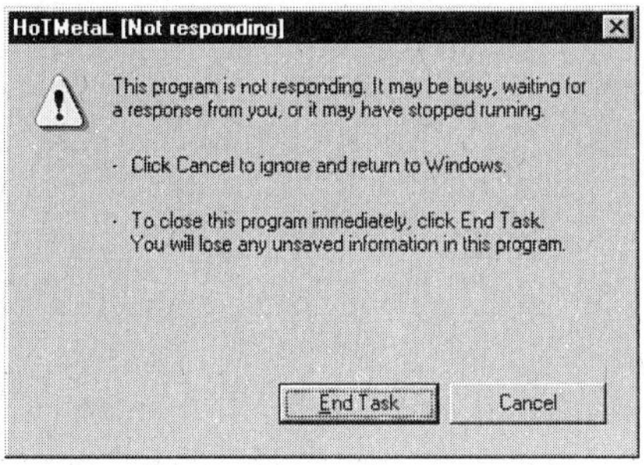

Fig. 3.23
Windows displays
the Not Respond-
ing dialog box
when an applica-
tion fails to
respond.

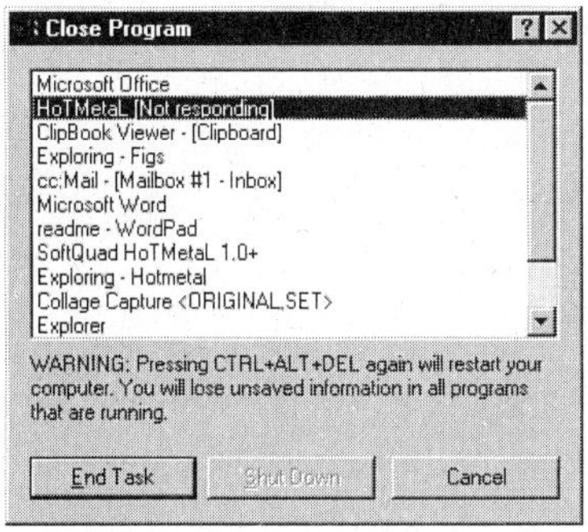

Fig. 3.24
You can check
which programs
may have failed
and shut them
down by pressing
Ctrl+Alt+Del to
display the Close
Program dialog
box.

The application that has trouble will show the phrase [Not responding]. To
continue working in Windows on your other applications, you must shut
down this application. Select the application and click End Task. If you click
Shut Down or press Ctrl+Alt+Delete again, all applications and Windows 95
will shut down. You may be able to click Cancel and return to the application
with no problems. However, you should probably be safe and save any work
in that application to a new file and close it then restart.

Getting Help

Windows applications and accessories have extensive Help screens to help
you find information on procedures, commands, techniques, and terms.
Many applications even include numbered lists of steps in Help to guide you
through complex procedures. The tools in Windows Help enable you to
search for topics, print Help information, annotate the Help screens with
your own notes, and copy to the Clipboard information from the Help
screens for use in other applications.

II

Working with Windows 95

Many Windows accessories and applications use similar kinds of commands and procedures. Each application's Help screens differs, however. You can learn how to use the application's Help system by opening the Help menu (from the application's menu bar) and choosing a command such as How to Use Help.

Understanding Windows Help

You start Windows Help by opening the Start menu and choosing Help. Figure 3.25 shows the Contents tab of the Help dialog box. This is the Help dialog box for Windows 95; other Windows applications provide Help dialog boxes that look different, perhaps offering more or fewer Help topics.

Fig. 3.25

The Windows Help screens offer help regarding all aspects of Windows.

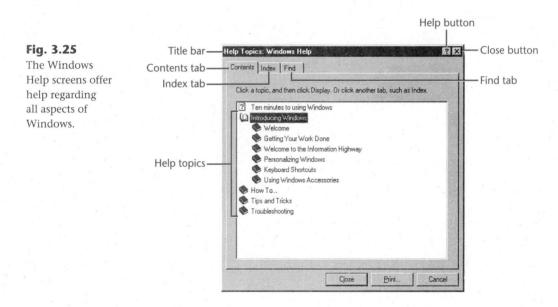

The following table describes the parts of the Help Topics dialog box:

Part	Description
Title bar	Includes the Help button (use it to display pop-up help, discussed later in the chapter), and the Close button.
Contents tab	Displays the available Help topics.
Index tab	Enables you to search through the available Help topics.

Part	Description
Close	Closes the selected book icon on the Contents page.
Open button	Opens the selected book icon on the Contents page.
Display button	Displays the selected Help item from the Index or Contents page.
Cancel button	Closes Help.
Print button	Displays the Print dialog box, from which you can print the selected topic.

The Help Topics dialog box uses the standard Windows controls: scroll bars (as needed), and the Close button.

> **Note**
>
> To start Help from within a Windows application, you can press the F1 key. Help then appears for the active application or window.

Using Pop-Up Help

In most Windows applications, a question mark button (?) appears at the top-right corner of many dialog boxes and windows. You can use this button to find out information about items on the screen. This information can help you learn how to use the dialog box or window. If you see a data-entry box and are unfamiliar with how it works or what it does, click on the Help (?) button and then click on the data-entry box. A pop-up window then displays Help information about the item you clicked.

For example, you might be interested in learning how to check your hardware devices. To get to the Device Manager, you must open the System application from the Control Panel, and then click on the Device Manager tab. Once on the Device Manager page, you can learn how the list of hardware devices works by clicking on the Help (?) button and then clicking on the list. Figure 3.26 shows the pop-up window that tells you about the list in the Device Manager.

II

Working with Windows 95

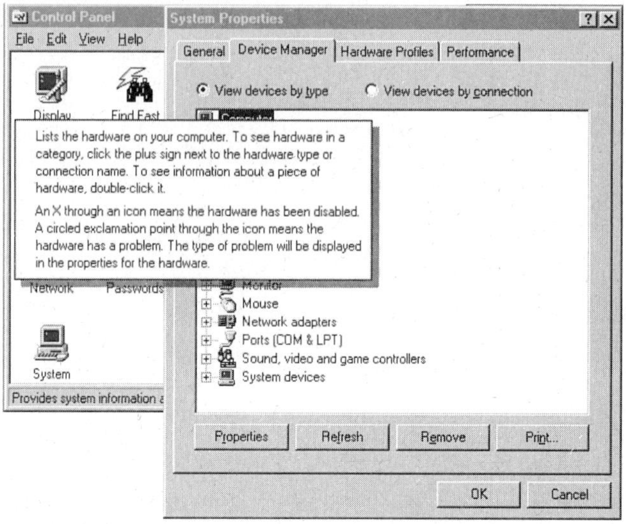

Fig. 3.26

To view a pop-up Help window describing a control on a Properties sheet or dialog box, click on the Help (?) button and then on any control.

The Help (?) button on the title bar of many Properties sheets and dialog boxes enables you to get help on how to use the sheet or dialog box. To use the Help (?) button, follow these steps:

1. Click the Help (?) button. A large question mark attaches to the pointer.

2. Click the control that you have a question about—for example, a list or check box. A description box displays adjacent to the control.

3. Click the left mouse button to close the description box.

Using the Contents Page

The Contents page of the Help Topics window lists Help topics that are available in the Windows application in which you chose Help (refer to fig. 3.25). Topics are categorized into books. Each Help topic icon first appears as a closed book. When you open a book, you see page icons. Displaying a page icon reveals the Help contents for that topic.

Figure 3.27 shows a Help window's contents. In addition to a list of steps, the window also contains a shortcut button. Clicking on that button immediately displays the Password Properties sheet that the Help screen discusses. You can keep the Help window open as you work in the Password Properties sheet. Many of the topics include tips and tricks that offer shortcuts and other timesaving techniques.

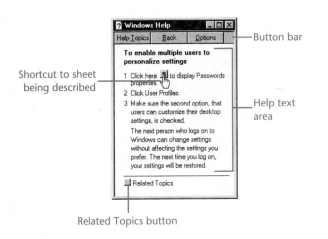

Button bar

Shortcut to sheet being described

Help text area

Related Topics button

Fig. 3.27
The Windows Help windows display procedural steps and buttons to open dialog boxes described in the procedure.

To display a Help window about one of the topics on the Contents page, follow these steps:

1. Open the Start menu and choose <u>H</u>elp.

2. Click the Contents tab.

3. Scroll through the list of topics to locate the topic that you want.

4. Double-click a book to display its contents. The contents of the topic display as page icons.

5. Double-click a page icon to display its contents, or select the topic and choose <u>D</u>isplay. The Help topic displays in a window sized to fit its contents. You can resize the window to make it easier to work in your application.

Using the Help Window

After you select a Help topic from either the Contents or Index tab, the Windows Help window appears (refer to fig. 3.27). The following table describes the toolbar in the Windows Help window:

Button	Description
Help <u>T</u>opics	Displays the Help Topics window.
<u>B</u>ack	Moves the Help window back to the previous topic.
<u>O</u>ptions	Displays a menu of commands that enables you to use the contents of the Help window in different ways. Following sections in this chapter describe these commands. Options include: Annotate, Copy, Print Topic, Font, Keep Help on Top.

II

Working with Windows 95

Button	Description
Related Topics button	Displays a list of related Help topics.

Using the Index Page

The Index Help page provides a search feature that finds the topic you want (see fig. 3.28). For example, if you want to learn about adding shortcuts to the desktop, you can type **sho**. The selection bar then moves through the list of index entries to *shortcuts (links), putting on the desktop*. The more letters you type, the closer you get to the topic name.

Fig. 3.28
Find a Help topic with the Windows Help Index.

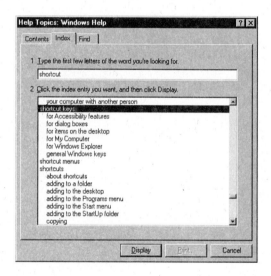

To use the Help Index, follow these steps:

1. Open the Start menu and choose <u>H</u>elp.

2. Click the Index tab.

3. Click in the text box and type the name of the subject that you want help on. As you type, the selection bar moves through the list of topics.

4. When you have selected your topic, double-click it, or click it and choose <u>D</u>isplay. The Help screen displays.

Jumping between Topics

You can easily jump between Help topics by returning to either the Contents or Index page. Simply click the Contents or Index tab in the Help window. For example, if you finish reading a Help window and want to read about another topic, click the Contents tab and the Contents page redisplays. Then select a new topic from the Contents page. The Index tab redisplays the Index page.

When more information related to the topic that you're viewing is available, the Help window includes a Related Topics button. Click the Related Topics button to see a list of related topics. The Topics Found window displays and lists the additional related topics. Click the topic that you want and then click Display to view the topics Help.

Printing a Help Topic

Often, having a printed copy of the Help topic in which you are interested can help you understand the topic more clearly. When the topic for which you want information is in the Help window, choose the Options button and then Print Topic to display the Print dialog box. Click OK to print.

> **Note**
>
> Some of the handiest information that you can print or copy from Help is an application's shortcut keys. If you didn't get a shortcut keystroke template for your application, look in the application's Help contents for a topic similar to Keyboard Shortcuts. Copy these topics (by pressing Ctrl+C) to a word processor, reorganize them, and print them. Alternatively, you can print the topics directly from Help. You can then copy the contents at a reduced size and paste them onto 3-by-5 cards.

Customizing Help

Help is more than just a list of procedures or word definitions. You can print Help screens, copy screens into word processors, and even add notes to help windows so that Help becomes customized to the kind of work that you do.

Adding Custom Notes to Help Topics

You can customize Help information in a Windows application to make Help information more useful to you or to coworkers. You might want to include information about your company's default settings, for example, in a Help window on document formatting, or attach a note that names the templates for mailing labels to a built-in Help window that describes how to create mailing labels. To add such information, you use *annotations*.

To create an annotation, follow these steps:

1. Display the topic that you want to annotate.

2. Click the Options button and then choose Annotate. The Annotate dialog box, a small notepad, appears.

3. Type the notes that you want to save regarding this Help topic.

4. Choose the Save button.

A paper clip icon appears to the left of the topic title in the Help window. Whenever you want to read an annotation, just click the paper clip icon.

To remove an annotation, click on the paper clip icon. When the Annotate dialog box appears, choose the Delete button.

Copying Help Information to Another Application

▶ See "Using the Windows Clipboard," p. 411

You can create a collection of Help topics by copying Help information and pasting this data into a word processor document file. You can copy and paste into another application any information that you see in a Help window. The information transfers as editable text.

To copy the contents of a Help window, choose the Options button and then the Copy command. To paste this information into another Windows application, such as a word processor, open the other application, position the insertion point wherever you want to paste the information, and choose Edit, Paste, or press Ctrl+V.

Finding Help, Support, and Resources

Windows is one of the most popular software applications ever written. Therefore, much support is available for Windows. The following sections describe resources that can help you get the most from Windows.

Getting Telephone Support

Use the following telephone numbers to get technical support or product sales information about Windows or Windows applications.

For questions specific to Windows installation, Explorer, or Windows accessories, call Microsoft Corporation's Windows support line at (206) 637-7098. For customer service and product upgrade information, call (800) 426-9400.

If Windows or applications came preinstalled on your computer, your technical support for the preinstalled software will probably be through the hardware vendor who supplied your equipment.

Getting Online Help

You can also find support online, through the Microsoft Network and various computer bulletin board forums.

The Microsoft Network. Microsoft Network is available to users of Windows 95 who have a modem correctly installed. Once you sign on to Microsoft Network, you have access to forums, libraries of software, and technical support forums.

▶ See "Connecting to the Microsoft Network," p. 1110

To start Microsoft Network, double-click on The Microsoft Network icon on the desktop. Once you are connected, the Welcome to MSN Central window appears. MSN Central contains the main menu to various parts of MSN. The Member Assistance icon is the one you want to access for help.

After you click Member Assistance, several items appear. For online support, double-click the MSN Center folder. Here you will find the MSN Support Bulletin Board. The Bulletin Board contains support folders for Internet access, e-mail, file transfer, and billing, to name just a few.

Computer Bulletin Board Forums. Computer bulletin boards are computer services that enable you to retrieve information over the telephone line. Some bulletin boards contain a wealth of information about Windows and Windows applications. One of the largest public bulletin boards is CompuServe.

CompuServe contains *forums* where Windows and Windows applications are discussed. You can submit questions electronically to Microsoft operators, who will answer questions usually within a day. CompuServe also contains libraries of sample files and new printer and device drivers. The Knowledgebase available in Microsoft's region of CompuServe has much of the same troubleshooting information that Microsoft's telephone support representatives use. You can search through the Knowledgebase by using key words. The Microsoft region of CompuServe is divided into many different areas, such as Windows users, Windows software developers, Microsoft, Excel, and Microsoft languages, and sections for each of the major Microsoft and non-Microsoft applications that run under Windows.

After you become a CompuServe member, you can access the Microsoft user forums, library files, and Knowledgebase. (You must join CompuServe and get a passcode before you can use the bulletin board.) When you join

II

Working with Windows 95

CompuServe, make sure that you get a copy of WinCIM, the Windows CompuServe Information Manager. It enables you to avoid typing so many commands, and thus makes using CompuServe significantly easier.

For more information, contact CompuServe at the following address:

CompuServe
5000 Arlington Centre Blvd.
P.O. Box 20212
Columbus, OH 43220
(800) 848-8990

▶ See "Using FTP," p. 912

▶ See "Surfing the Web with Internet Explorer," p. 920

Internet Support. Microsoft provides two Internet sites that provide access to free software, updates, technical papers, and device drivers. From within your Internet browser, you can access the Microsoft FTP site with this URL:

FTP:\\ftp.microsoft.com

You can access the same information by using your browser on the World Wide Web with this URL:

HTTP:\\http.microsoft.com

Consultants and Training

Microsoft Solution Providers develop and support applications written for the Windows environment with Microsoft products. They are independent consultants who have met the strict qualifying requirements imposed by Microsoft.

Microsoft also certifies training centers. A certified training center has instructors who have passed a competency exam and use Microsoft-produced training material.

You can find the Microsoft Solution Providers and training centers in your area by calling the following number:

(800) SOL-PROV

Chapter 4

Starting and Working with Applications

by Ron Person

The information that you learn in this chapter carries over to all Windows applications. This "learning carry-over" is important: after you learn how to use one Windows application, you understand most of the concepts necessary to operate other applications. The skills that you acquire in this chapter will help you operate such control features as menus and dialog boxes and learn how to control such display aspects as the size and position of the windows in which different documents or applications display.

In this chapter, you learn how to do the following:

■ Open menus and choose commands

■ Change the location and size of windows

■ Display the properties of the desktop, file, or taskbar

■ Work in applications

■ Drag-and-drop objects as a shortcut for such actions as opening files or printing documents

Working in the Windows Environment

Windows uses concepts that, for many people, make computers easier to use. The basic organizational concept is that all applications run on a desktop and that each application runs in its own window. Windows can run multiple

▶ See "Making Windows Accessible for the Hearing, Sight, and Movement Impaired," p. 150

applications, just as you might have stacks of papers on your desk from more than one project. You can move the windows and change their size just as you can move and rearrange the stacks of papers on your desk.

► See "Using the Windows Clipboard," p. 411

Just as you can cut, copy, and paste parts between papers on your real desktop, Windows enables you to cut or copy information from one application and paste the information into another. Some Windows applications even share live information; when you change data in one application, Windows automatically updates linked data in other applications.

► See "Using Embedding to Link Informa-tion," p. 440

The process for making entries, edits, and changes to text, numbers, or graphics is similar in all Windows applications. The basic procedure is as follows:

1. Activate the window that contains the desired application.

2. Select the text, number, or graphics object that you want to change. You can select items with the mouse or the keyboard.

3. Choose a command from the menu bar at the top of the application.

4. If a dialog box appears, select options to modify how the command works. Then execute the command by choosing the OK button.

An *application window* is the window that contains an application. *Document windows* appear inside application windows and contain documents. In many (but not all) applications, you can have several document windows open at a time; you switch between them by pressing Ctrl+F6 or by selecting from the Window menu the document that you want.

Tip
To minimize all windows with one command, click on a clear area in the taskbar with the right mouse button and choose Minimize All Windows.

The Control menu contains commands to control a window's location, size, and status (open or closed). Each application and each document window within the application window has its own Control menu. The application Control menu appears at the left edge of the application's title bar. The document Control menu appears at the left edge of the document's title bar (if the document window is smaller than a full screen) or at the left edge of the menu bar (if the document window is a full screen). To open an application Control menu, click once on the application Control Menu icon (the icon at the top-left corner of the program window), or press Alt+space bar. To open a document Control menu, click once on the document Control Menu icon (the icon at the top-left corner of a document window), or press Alt+hyphen (-).

To maximize a window so it fills the screen, click on the Maximize button, a square window icon in the window's top-right corner (see fig. 4.1) or double-click the title bar. You can also minimize a window and place it on the taskbar. To do so, you click on another icon in the window's top-right corner, the Minimize button, which looks like an underline representing the taskbar (see fig. 4.1).

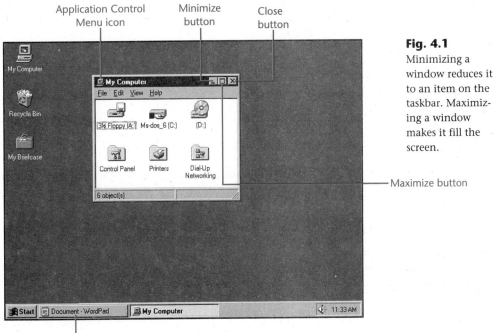

Application Control
Menu icon

Minimize
button

Close
button

Maximize button

Minimized application
on taskbar

Fig. 4.1
Minimizing a window reduces it to an item on the taskbar. Maximizing a window makes it fill the screen.

II

Working with Windows 95

When you minimize a program, its window shrinks to become an icon and name on the taskbar. The program still runs even though it is not in a window. To make a program on the taskbar appear in a window, click on the program in the taskbar. (To use the keyboard to activate a program, press Alt+Tab repeatedly until you have selected the appropriate program, and then release the keys.)

You can resize a window by dragging its window border with the mouse, or by choosing the Size command from the Control menu. You can move a window without resizing it by dragging its title bar with the mouse, or by choosing the Move command from the Control menu.

Tip
To restore all minimized windows with one command, right-click a clear area in the taskbar and choose Undo Minimize All.

▶ See "Customizing the Mouse," p. 147

▶ See "Customizing the Keyboard," p. 148

Table 4.1 introduces keystrokes that perform certain actions. You may want to refer back to this table as you read through the book or begin working with Windows 95.

Table 4.1 Keystrokes to Control Windows	
Keystroke	**Action**
Alt+Esc	Activates the next application window.
Alt+Tab	Displays a program bar showing open programs as icons. Each press of Alt+Tab selects the next icon. Releasing Alt+Tab activates the program selected in the program bar.
Alt+Shift+Tab	Moves the selection through the program bar in the opposite direction of Alt+Tab. Releasing Alt+Shift+Tab activates the selected program.
Ctrl+F6	Activates the next document window (if an application has multiple document windows open).
Ctrl+Esc	Displays the Start menu. Press the up- or down-arrow keys to select from the menu.
Alt+space bar	Displays the Control menu for the active program icon or window. Use the Control menu to change the location, size, and status of the program window.
Alt+hyphen (-)	Displays the Control menu for the active document window within the program. Use this Control menu to change the location, size, and status of the document window.

Using Menus and Dialog Boxes

▶ See "Making Windows Accessible for the Hearing, Sight, and Movement Impaired," p. 150

Every properly designed Windows application operates in a similar way. As you will learn, you can move and resize all windows the same way in every Windows application. You also execute commands the same way in all Windows applications.

You can choose a command from a menu by using the mouse or the keyboard (also, many time-saving shortcuts exist for choosing commands). If a command requires information from you before executing, a dialog box appears when you choose the command. In the dialog box, you use the mouse or the keyboard to choose options or enter values that control the command.

Choosing Menus and Commands

When you click on a menu, a list of commands drops down under the menu, as shown in figures 4.2 and 4.3. If you're not sure where to find a command, try browsing through the menus by clicking on them until you find the command that you want. Many applications use similar commands for similar actions—a practice that makes learning multiple Windows applications easier.

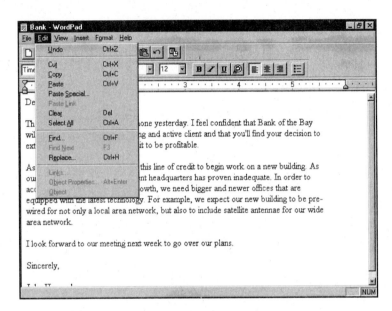

Fig. 4.2
WordPad's Edit menu displays shortcut keys.

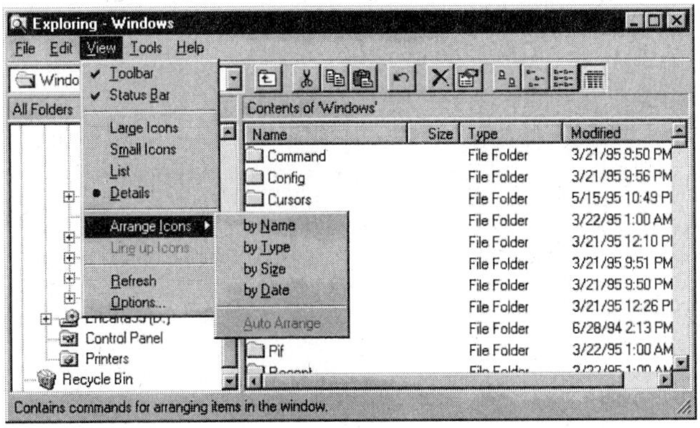

Fig. 4.3
In the Explorer, when you choose View, Arrange Icons, you see a submenu that displays additional commands.

II

Working with Windows 95

Tip
To change the colors of the text in menu commands, see "Creating Custom Color and Text Schemes" in Chapter 5.

To choose a menu or command with the mouse, move the tip of the pointer over the menu or command name and click the left mouse button. To choose a menu or command with the keyboard, press Alt+*letter* where *letter* is the underlined letter in the menu. When the menu displays, press the key for the underlined letter in the command. For example, to choose the File menu's Open command, you press Alt, then F, and then O.

You can choose commands that appear in a menu in solid black (bold) type. You *cannot* choose commands that appear in gray in a menu, even though you can see them. Gray commands or options are *disabled*. Commands or options appear in bold only when they are available, or *enabled*. For example, the Edit menu's Copy command appears in bold type only when you have selected something to copy.

Command names followed by an ellipsis (...) display an additional dialog box or window from which you can choose options or enter data. If you choose Edit, Find... from a Windows application, for example, a dialog box appears in which you type the word that you want to find.

Commands with a check mark to the left are commands that toggle on and off. A check mark indicates that the command is on; no check mark indicates that the command is off.

Commands with key combinations listed to the right have shortcuts. In Windows Explorer, for example, the Edit menu lists a shortcut for the Copy command, Ctrl+C. Therefore, to copy text, you can choose Edit, Copy, or press Ctrl+C.

Commands with an arrowhead next to them, as in figure 4.3, have submenus that list additional commands. In the Explorer, the Arrange Icons command in the View menu has an arrowhead to its right, indicating that a submenu will show the ways in which you can arrange icons.

If you don't want to make a choice after displaying a menu, click the pointer a second time on the menu name or click outside the menu. If you are using the keyboard, press Esc to exit a menu without making a choice. Continue to press Esc until no commands or menus are selected.

> **Note**
>
> If a dialog box appears on-screen and you aren't sure what to do, you can escape without making any changes. Click the Cancel button or press the Esc key to cancel the current dialog box and ignore any changes to options.
>
> Most Windows applications have an Undo command. If you complete a command and then decide that you want to undo it, check whether the Edit menu includes an Undo command.

Selecting Options from Dialog Boxes

Commands that require more information before they work display a *dialog box*—a window similar to those shown in figures 4.4 and 4.5. Dialog boxes like the one in figure 4.4 have areas in which you enter text (such as the File Name text box) or select from a scrolling list of choices (see the Name list box of file names). Many applications also include drop-down list boxes with lists that appear only when you select the box and press the down-arrow key, or click on the down arrow on the right side of the text box.

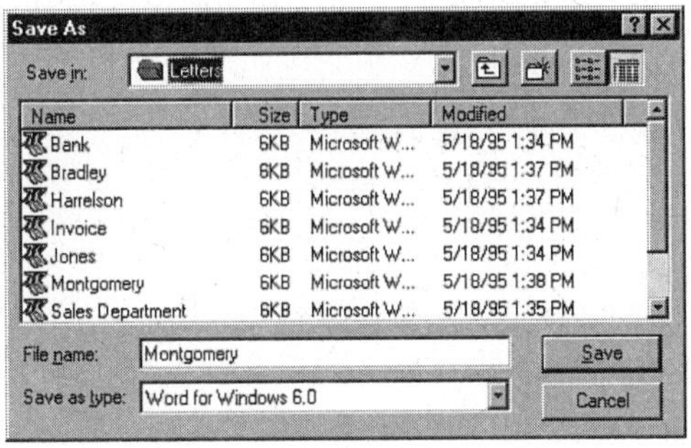

Fig. 4.4
The Save As dialog box is similar among Windows programs.

Figure 4.5 shows that dialog boxes can have round *option* buttons and square *check boxes*. The option buttons are clustered in a group labeled Hidden Files. When options are in such groups, you can choose only one of them. Check boxes act independently of other check boxes so you can select as many of them as you want. After you select options or make text entries, you accept the contents of the dialog box by choosing the OK button or cancel them by choosing the Cancel button.

II

Working with Windows 95

Fig. 4.5

Option buttons, check boxes, and scrolling lists appear in the View tab of the Explorer's Options dialog box.

Option buttons ⎯

Scrolling list ⎯

Check boxes ⎯

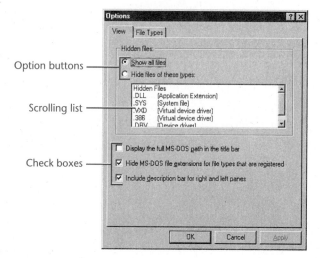

If a dialog box hides something that you want to see on-screen, you can move the dialog box with the mouse by dragging the dialog box by its title bar to a new position. With the keyboard, press Alt+space bar to open the dialog Control menu and then choose Move. A four-headed arrow appears. Press any arrow key to move an outline of the dialog box. Press Enter when the outline of the dialog box is where you want to place the dialog box. (Before you press Enter, you can cancel the move by pressing Esc instead.)

Figure 4.6 shows the five types of controls used in dialog boxes, and table 4.2 summarizes them.

Fig. 4.6

Some of the types of controls presented in dialog boxes.

Option buttons

Check boxes

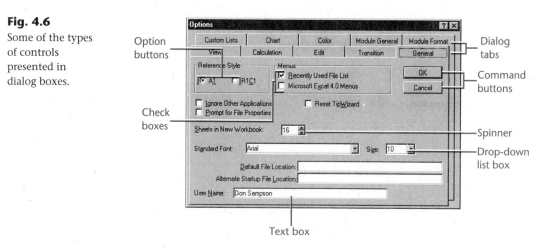

Dialog tabs

Command buttons

Spinner

Drop-down list box

Text box

Table 4.2   Types of Dialog Box Controls

Control	Use
Text box	Move the pointer over the text box until it changes to an I-beam shape, then click. Type text entries manually. If you make a mistake, press the Backspace or Delete key to erase characters.
List box	You will see two types of lists. *Scrolling lists* show a columnar list of choices (refer to fig. 4.5). Click on the up or down arrow on the right side of the list to scroll through the list, and then click on the item that you want. The selected item appears in highlighted text (and might also appear in the text box above the list). The second type of list, a *drop-down list*, like the one shown in figure 4.6, displays its scrolling list after you click the down arrow.
Option button	Click on one option from within a group of option buttons. (You can select only one option button in each group.) The selected option button has a darkened center. To remove a selection, select a different option in the same group.
Check box	Click on a check box to turn it on or off. Check boxes are square and contain an X when selected. You can select more than one check box at a time.
Spinner	Click the up or down arrow on the right side of a spinner to make the number change in increments of one.
Command button	Click on a command button to complete the command, cancel the command, or open an additional dialog box for more alternatives.
Dialog tab	Click on a dialog tab to see another grouping of options.

▶ See "Editing Text in Text Boxes," p. 102

II

Working with Windows 95

Using the Mouse in Dialog Boxes

To select an option button or check box, click on it. Clicking on a blank check box selects it by putting an X in it. Clicking on a check box that already has an X removes the X. To turn off an option button, click on one of the other option buttons in the group.

To choose command buttons such as OK, Cancel, Yes, or No, click on them.

To select from a scrolling list box, click in the list box and then scroll through the list by clicking on the up or down arrow in the scroll bar at the right side of the list box. To jump through large sections of the list, click in the scroll bar's shaded area. For long moves, drag the scroll bar's square to the new location. When the desired selection appears in the list box, click once on that selection.

Some Windows applications use drop-down list boxes. When closed, these list boxes look like the Printer list box shown in figure 4.7; when open, they look like the same list box as shown in figure 4.8. To select from a drop-down list box, click on the down arrow on the text box's right side. When the scrolling list appears, select from it the same way that you select from any scrolling list box: click on the item that you want.

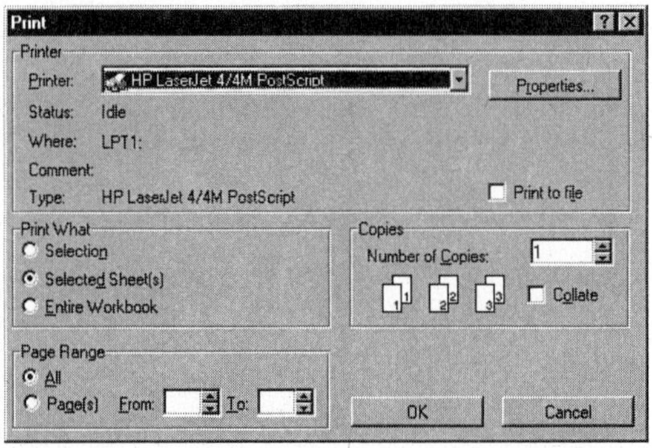

Fig. 4.7
The Printer pull-down list box when closed.

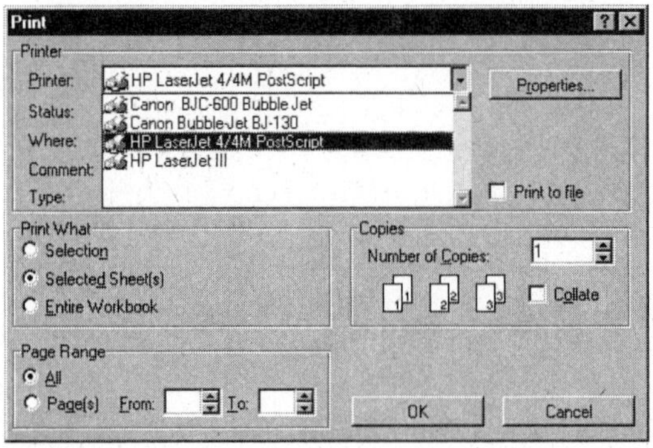

Fig. 4.8
The Printer pull-down list box when open.

Note

In some dialog boxes, double-clicking on an option button or an item in a list selects that option and simultaneously chooses the OK command button. In the Open dialog box, for example, you can double-click on a file name to select and open the file. Experiment with the dialog boxes in your applications to determine whether double-clicking is a viable shortcut.

Using the Keyboard in Dialog Boxes

Some drawing or graphics applications require that you use the mouse. In most Windows applications, however, you have the same functionality available from either the keyboard or the mouse. You might find that in some situations using the keyboard to control Windows is faster or more convenient.

To access a group of option buttons with the keyboard, you press Alt+*letter*, where *letter* is the underlined character that appears in an option's label. If the individual options do not have an underlined letter, press Alt+*letter*, where the underlined *letter* is in the title of the option group; then use the arrow keys to select an option.

To select a check box, press Alt+*letter*, where *letter* is the underlined character in the check box's label. Each time that you press Alt+*letter*, you toggle the check box between selected and deselected. An X appears in the check box when the box is selected. You also can toggle the active check box between selected and deselected by pressing the space bar.

To make an entry in a text box, select the text box by pressing Alt+*letter*, where *letter* is the underlined character in the name of the text box. Press Alt+N, for example, to select the File Name text box in the Save As dialog box shown in figure 4.9. Type a text entry or edit the existing entry by using the editing techniques described in the upcoming section "Editing Text in Text Boxes."

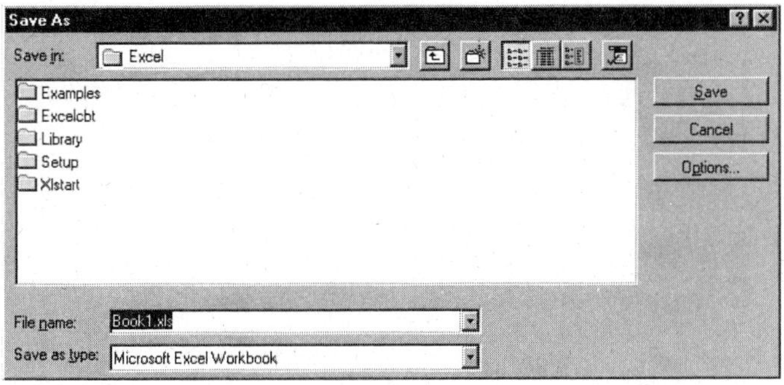

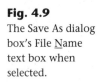

Fig. 4.9

The Save As dialog box's File Name text box when selected.

To select from a list of alternatives in a scrolling list box, select the list box by pressing Alt+*letter*, where *letter* is the underlined character in the name of the list box. When the list box is active, use the up- or down-arrow key or Page Up or Page Down to move through the list. The text is selected and displayed in reversed type. (To use the keyboard to display a drop-down scrolling list, press Alt+*letter* to activate the list and then press Alt+down-arrow to drop the list. Then select items by pressing the up- or down-arrow keys.)

To select a command button, press Alt+*letter*, or if no letter is underlined, press Tab or Shift+Tab until a dashed line encloses the name of the button that you want. Press the space bar to select the active button indicated by the dashed enclosure. At any time, you can select the command button that appears in bold type, usually the OK button, by pressing Enter. Press Esc to choose the Cancel button and escape from a dialog box without making any changes.

Changing Folders in Save As and Open Dialog Boxes

When you save a file on your hard disk, Windows places the file in a folder in your hard disk. Folders are analogous to the file drawers and file folders that you use in your office to help you organize and locate your papers. You can locate files more easily if you store related files together in a folder. For example, you can store all the business letters that you create with your word processor in a folder named LETTERS and all your proposals in a folder named PROPOSALS.

▶ See "Using the Windows Explorer to View Files and Folders," p. 499

Don't store the files that you create in the folders that store your program files. If you ever have to reinstall or upgrade a program, you might lose files that you store in the program folders. Also, these folders are already full of files, and it will be difficult to find yours. Create your own folders, and folders within folders, to store your files.

▶ See "Working with Long File Names," p. 509

The first time that you use the File, Open or File, Save As command in a program session, the application usually assumes that you want to open or save a document in that program's default folder. Usually, however, you want to open or save a file in one of your own folders. You must tell the program where the file that you want to open is located or where you want to save a file—whether that location is a different folder or a different drive on your hard disk. To switch folders or drives, use the appropriate list boxes in the Open and Save As dialog boxes, as discussed in the following paragraphs.

Note

Most applications have a place where you can set the default folder for data files. If any of yours don't, you can get the same result with these steps:

1. Create a shortcut to the application.

2. Right-click on the new icon.

3. Click the Shortcut tab.

4. In the Start In box, type the path for the folder where you want to store data files.

The selected folder appears in the Look In drop-down list (see fig. 4.10). You can display this list to select another drive.

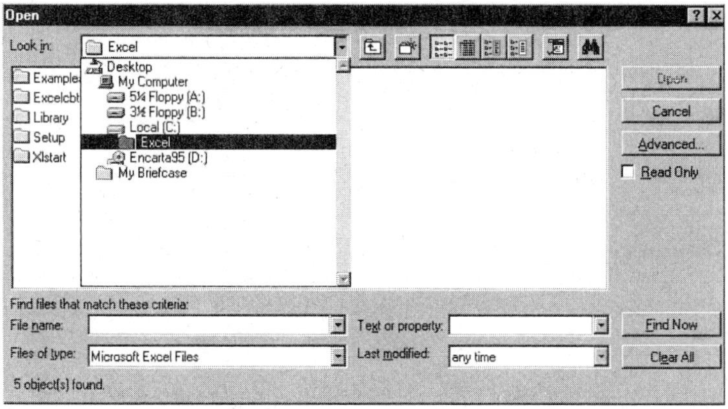

Fig. 4.10
Open the Look In drop-down list to select a different drive in the Open and Save As dialog boxes.

The list box includes all the folders in the current folder. An icon that resembles a file folder represents each folder. If you want to open a file in a folder contained within another folder, you first must open that folder. You can do so by double-clicking on the folder icon.

To change disk drives or folders in the Open or Save As dialog boxes, follow these steps:

1. Display the Look In drop-down list and select the drive that you want.

2. To select a folder, double-click on the folder icon. You can also click the Up One Level button to move up one level in the folder structure.

3. Select the file from the list, or type the file name in the File Name text box.

4. Choose Open or Save.

Editing Text in Text Boxes

You can use the text-editing techniques that you learn in this section in all Windows applications. Although the editing techniques described are specifically for the text boxes that appear in dialog boxes, they also apply to editing text in other locations in Windows applications.

To use a mouse when editing text in a text box, you position the pointer over the text where you want to place the insertion point, and then click. When moving over editable text, the pointer changes from an arrowhead to an I-beam shape. To select multiple characters, drag across the characters.

While positioned in a text box, you can press left- or right-arrow keys to move left or right. End to move to the end of the text, and Home to move to the beginning of the text.

To delete a character to the right of the flashing insertion point, press Delete. Press Backspace to delete a character to the left of the insertion point.

Replace existing text with new text by selecting the text that you want to replace and then typing the new text. Select text with the mouse by dragging the I-beam across the text as you hold down the mouse button. To select text with the keyboard, move the insertion point to the left of the first character that you want to select, press and hold down Shift, and press the right-arrow key.

> **Note**
>
> When editing text in an application, you usually can use Edit menu commands such as Undo, Copy, and Paste. Although these commands often do not work in dialog boxes, the keystroke equivalents Ctrl+C (to copy), Ctrl+X (to cut), and Ctrl+V (to paste) frequently do work.

Controlling the Size and Position of Windows

Just as you move papers on your desktop, you can move and reorder windows on-screen. In fact, you can resize windows, expand them to full size, shrink them to a small icon to save space, and restore them to their original size.

The easiest way to resize and reposition application or document windows is with the mouse. As you will see, you can simply drag title bars or edges to move windows or change their size.

As you move the mouse pointer over edges of application or document windows, the pointer changes shape. Each shape, shown in table 4.3, indicates the type of window change that you can make by dragging that edge or corner. Before you can move a window, it must be active—that is, the window must be on top. To activate a window, you can click on it or press Alt+Tab until you select the application.

Table 4.3 Pointer Shapes When Moving or Resizing Windows		
Shape	**Pointer**	**Mouse Action**
↔	Left/right	Drag the edge left or right
↕	Up/down	Drag the edge up or down
↘	Corner	Drag the corner in any direction

Using Taskbar Shortcuts to Arrange Windows

There are times when you want to quickly arrange a few applications on your desktop so that you can compare documents, drag-and-drop between documents, and so forth. Manually moving and resizing each Window is a tedious job, so Windows 95 has a few shortcuts that can make this type of work easier.

First, you can make your desktop easier to work on by minimizing all applications so they appear as buttons on the taskbar. To do this quickly, right-click on a gray area of the taskbar. When the shortcut menu appears, click on Minimize All Windows.

If you want to compare documents in two or three applications, minimize all applications except the two or three you want to work with and then right-click on a gray area of the taskbar. When the shortcut menu appears, click on either Tile Horizontally or Tile Vertically. Your applications will appear in adjacent windows that fill the screen as shown in figure 4.11.

If you want to be able to quickly see all the application title bars so that you can click title bars to switch between many application windows, right-click in the gray area of the taskbar. When the shortcut menu appears, click on Cascade. The windows will arrange as shown in figure 4.12.

Tip

When the taskbar has a lot of application buttons, the titles may be too truncated to read. Pause the pointer over a button to see a pop-up title.

II

Working with Windows 95

Fig. 4.11
Tiling application windows horizontally or vertically makes it easy to compare documents or to drag-and-drop contents.

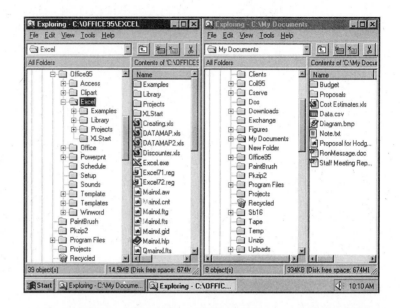

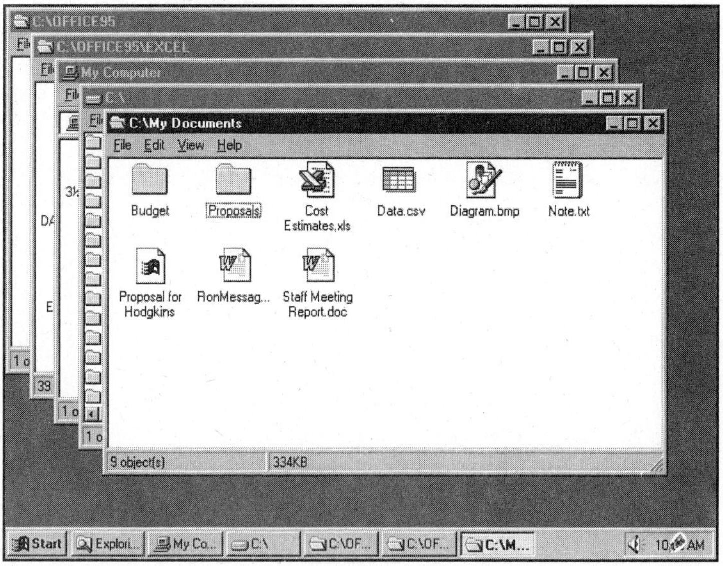

Fig. 4.12
Cascading application windows overlays them so that you can see each title bar. It is then easy to move among windows by clicking the title bars.

Tip
You cannot size a maximized window—a window that fills the screen—because you cannot make it any larger.

Moving a Window or a Desktop Icon

If an application window is not maximized (does not fill the screen), you can move the application's window. Move the pointer over the application's title at the top of its window, hold down the left mouse button, and drag the window to its new location. Windows displays an outline that indicates the application's position. When you release the mouse button, the window moves.

To drag document windows within the application, you use the same technique. As long as the document is within a window, you can drag its title bar. You can more easily arrange some documents within the application by choosing Window, Arrange All. This command puts document windows in predefined layouts.

Changing the Size of a Window

To change the size of a window with the mouse, you first activate the window by clicking on it. Move the pointer to one edge or corner of the window until the pointer changes to a two-headed arrow (refer to table 4.3). Press and hold down the mouse button, and then drag the double-headed arrow to move the edge or corner of the window to resize it. The moving edge appears as an outline until you release the mouse button.

To move two edges at once with the mouse, move the pointer to the corner of a window so that the pointer becomes a two-headed arrow tilted at a 45-degree angle. Drag the corner to its new location and release the mouse button.

Learning about Drag-and-Drop

After becoming proficient at operating Windows and its programs with commands, you will want to learn some of the faster but less obvious methods of controlling Windows and its programs. One of the most powerful methods is *drag-and-drop*.

The term *drag-and-drop* specifies exactly the action that the method uses. You click on an object, such as a folder, and then hold down the mouse button as you drag the object to a new location. You drop the object by releasing the mouse button.

For drag-and-drop methods to work, each Windows object has to know how to behave when dropped on other Windows objects. For example, if in the Explorer you drag the icon of a file and drop it on the icon for a program, the program starts and loads that file.

Figure 4.13 illustrates how you can use drag-and-drop to make frequently used folders more accessible. Instead of tediously having to find the folder each time in the Explorer, you can put on the desktop a shortcut icon that enables you to open the folder directly. To create a shortcut icon with drag-and-drop, follow these steps:

1. Double-click the My Computer icon to open its window. Make sure that the window does not fill the screen.

▶ See "Drag-and-Drop Printing from the Desktop," p. 178

▶ See "Embedding an Excel Object by Dragging and Dropping," p. 448

▶ See "Backing Up with a Simple Drag-and-Drop," p. 572

II

Working with Windows 95

2. Double-click the local drive icon for your computer.

3. Click on a folder that you frequently use, then hold down the right mouse button and drag the folder out of the window and over the desktop.

In figure 4.13, the user has dragged the Budgets folder to the desktop.

Fig. 4.13

The user has dragged the reverse-colored Budgets folder (by holding down the right mouse button) and dropped the folder to the desktop. When you release the mouse button, a shortcut menu appears.

4. Release the right mouse button. A menu appears over the folder on the desktop as shown in figure 4.13.

5. Choose the Create Shortcut(s) Here command.

Tip

You can tell at a glance that an icon is a shortcut by the small arrow at the lower left corner.

The Shortcut to Budgets icon, shown in figure 4.14, remains on the desktop even after you close the My Computer windows. You can open the folder at any time by double-clicking on the shortcut icon.

Caution

When dragging and dropping a file or folder, make sure that you use the right mouse button and choose Create Shortcut(s) Here from the shortcut menu. This creates a shortcut icon while leaving the original file or folder in its original location. If you delete the shortcut icon, the original file or folder remains intact. If you delete an original icon (which you create by dragging with the left mouse button) from your desktop, Windows deletes the original file or folder along with the icon. If the file is important, this causes a disaster and a lot of intra-office panic.

Fig. 4.14
Choosing the Create Shortcut(s) Here command produces on the desktop a shortcut icon that you can click to start the application.

Note

Drag-and-drop features are available only with Windows applications that are compatible with Object Linking and Embedding (OLE).

There are many ways that you can use the drag-and-drop method to save time. You can move and copy files and folders, which makes reorganizing the contents on your computer easy. You can drag a shortcut for your printer onto your desktop, drag documents from My Computer or the Explorer, and then drop them onto the printer icon, which prints the documents. With applications compatible with the OLE 2 specifications, you can even drag and drop objects from one application to another. For example, you can drag a table from a spreadsheet into a word processing document.

▶ See "Using Embedding to Link Information," p. 440

▶ See "Creating an Example Compound Document," p. 446

Throughout this book, you accomplish your computer tasks by using drag-and-drop methods. Always look for ways to use these methods for saving time and trouble.

Changing Settings and Properties with the Right Mouse Button

One important Windows concept is that most objects that you see on-screen have *properties* related to them. Properties can include such characteristics as an object's appearance and behavior.

You can change some properties, but others are *read-only*—you can view them, but cannot change them. For example, changeable properties of the Windows desktop include the types of patterns and wallpapers used as backgrounds and the color of different screen elements. Read-only properties that you can see but not change include a file's size or a program's version number.

You can experiment to find properties in Windows, the Explorer, and most Windows 95 applications. To see an object's properties, point to the object and click the right mouse button (that is, you *right-click* the object). A Properties sheet displays, or a menu displays a Properties command. For example, you can place the pointer's tip on most objects, such as the desktop or a file, and then click the right mouse button. From the menu that appears, select the Properties command.

Note

Don't be afraid to experiment when you look for properties. To discover how you can customize Windows, right-click on files, taskbars, and so on. If you do not want to change the object's properties, press the Esc key or click the Cancel button in the Properties sheet that appears.

To see the properties that you can change on the desktop, right-click on the desktop and then choose the Properties command. The Display Properties sheet shown in figure 4.15 appears. In this dialog box, you can change the display's background, color, and screen saver, and display adapter settings. To learn how to change these settings, see Chapter 5, "Customizing Windows 95." Click the Cancel button to remove the dialog box without making changes.

If you want to change how the taskbar operates, right-click on a blank area of the taskbar and then choose the Properties command. The Taskbar Properties sheet displays. On this sheet, you can add or remove applications from the Start menu, or change when and how the taskbar displays. Chapter 5, "Customizing Windows 95," describes this Properties sheet and how to customize the taskbar. Click the Cancel button to remove the dialog box without making changes.

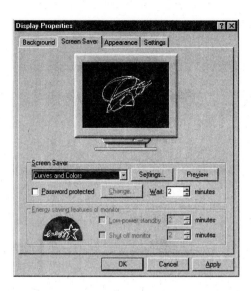

Fig. 4.15
Right-click on the
desktop and then
choose Properties
to see the desktop
properties. The
Screen Saver page,
shown here,
enables you to
choose a screen
saver.

Working with Applications

Many operations are similar among Windows applications. Nearly all Windows applications, for example, start with the File and Edit menus. The File menu includes commands for opening, closing, saving, and printing files. The Edit menu includes commands for cutting, copying, pasting, and other editing actions specific to the application. The procedures you use to control menus and select items in dialog boxes is the same in nearly all Windows applications.

Opening, Saving, and Closing Documents

When you create or edit a document and then save the document, you create a *file* that Windows stores in a magnetic recording on disk. The file contains all the information necessary to recreate the document in your program. When this book uses the term *file*, it usually refers to the information stored on the computer's hard disk or on a removable disk.

When first started, many applications present a new, empty document—a blank page if the application is a word processing, graphics, or desktop publishing application, an empty worksheet if the application is a spreadsheet application. If you finish working on one file, you can start a new file by choosing File, New. Your application might ask you for information about the type of new file to start.

Tip
Double-click on a
file name in the
Open dialog box
to open that file.

To open an existing file, choose File, Open. An Open dialog box similar to
the one shown in figure 4.16 appears. In the Look In drop-down list, select
the drive that contains your file. The Look In drop-down list displays your
computer's drives as icons. Click on the drive you want to look in. In the
Look In box, select the folder that contains your file and then choose OK to
display the list of files in that folder. From the files presented, select the one
that you want to open and then choose OK or press Enter.

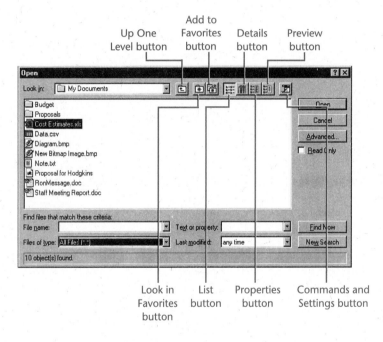

Fig. 4.16
The Open dialog
box is common to
many Windows
applications.

You can do far more in a Windows 95 Open dialog box than meets the eye.
Click on a button at the top of the dialog box to get the result you want.
Table 4.4 lists the buttons and their results.

Table 4.4   Open Dialog Box Buttons

Button	Result
Up One Level button	Move up to the next higher folder
Look in Favorites button	Look at a list of favorite or frequently used files
Add to Favorites button	Add the selected file to the Favorites list
List button	Display files in a list view

Button	Result
Details button	Display files with all file details shown
Properties button	Display a file or folder properties
Preview button	Display the contents of a file using QuickView
Commands and Settings button	Select from a shortcut menu to print, sort, or search for files and map to a network drive

Explore with your right mouse button by clicking on files or folders to see some of the things you can do to files and folders. When you right-click on a file or folder, a shortcut menu appears with various commands you can choose from. The specific commands on the menu can vary, depending on the file type. Table 4.5 lists the basic options that are available for most file types.

Table 4.5   Shortcut Commands for Files and Folders

Command	Result
Open	Opens the file.
Open Read Only	Open as a read-only document that must be saved to a different file name.
Print	Print the file.
Quick View	Display a preview of the file.
Send To	Copy the file to a shortcut folder, floppy disk, mail or Fax address.
Cut	Remove the file or folder from its location in preparation to paste elsewhere.
Copy	Copy the file or folder in preparation to copy the file elsewhere.
Paste	Paste a file or folder that has been cut or copied. This command appears only when it is appropriate.
Create Shortcut	Create a shortcut to the file or folder.
Delete	Delete the selection(s).
Properties	Display the file or folder properties.

Tip
In some applications, you can open multiple documents by selecting the files with Ctrl+click and then clicking the Open button.

II

Working with Windows 95

The File menu contains two commands for saving files: Save As and Save. Choose one of these commands the first time that you save a file. They tell Windows where to save the file and enable you to name your file. If you choose File, Save As, you can create a new version of an existing file by specifying a new name for the file. The Save As dialog box is often similar to the Open dialog box shown in figure 4.16. In the Save As dialog box, you must specify the drive and folder to which you want to save your file and name the file.

After you type the file name in the File name text box, choose Save or press Enter to save the file. After you name your file, you can choose File, Save to save the file without changing its name or location. The File, Save command replaces the original file.

To close a document, you often can choose File, Close. If you choose File, Exit, you exit the application. When you close or exit a Windows application, most prompt you to save any changes that you made since you last saved your document.

Scrolling in a Document

Most applications include scroll bars at the right and bottom edges of the screen, as shown in figure 4.17. You can use the vertical scroll bar at the right to scroll up and down in your document. You can use the horizontal scroll bar to scroll left and right. To scroll a short distance, click on the arrow at either end of a scroll bar; you scroll in the direction that the arrow points. To scroll a longer distance, click in the gray area next to the arrow or drag the scroll bar box to a new location. In many applications, the scroll bars are optional; if you want more working space, you can turn them off.

To scroll with the keyboard, you can press the arrow keys to move a character or line at a time, or press the Page Up or Page Down keys to move a screen at a time. The Home key usually scrolls you to the left margin, and the End key takes you to the end of the line or the right side. Holding down the Ctrl key while pressing any other scrolling key extends the scroll: Ctrl+Home, for example, takes you to the beginning of your file; Ctrl+End takes you to the end of the file; Ctrl+left-arrow or Ctrl+right-arrow moves you a word at a time rather than a character at a time. Most applications have many shortcuts for scrolling.

If you use the scroll bars to scroll, the insertion point does not move; it remains where it was before you scrolled. If you use the keyboard to scroll, the insertion point moves as you scroll.

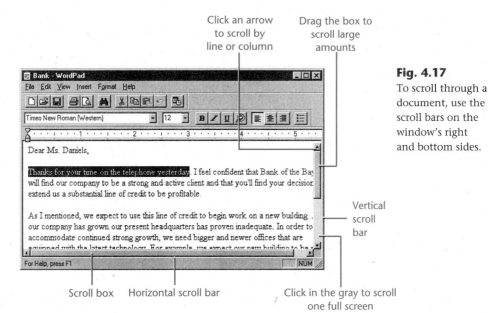

Click an arrow
to scroll by
line or column

Drag the box to
scroll large
amounts

Fig. 4.17
To scroll through a
document, use the
scroll bars on the
window's right
and bottom sides.

Vertical
scroll
bar

Scroll box   Horizontal scroll bar   Click in the gray to scroll
one full screen

Using Simple Editing Techniques

Editing text and objects is similar in all Windows applications. When you
work with text, in your document or in a dialog box, the mouse pointer turns
into an I-beam when you move it over editable text. You can use the I-beam
to move the insertion point and select text. The flashing vertical insertion
point is where the text that you type appears. (The insertion point is equivalent to the cursor in DOS applications.)

You can use the mouse or the keyboard to move the insertion point. To use
the mouse, position the I-beam where you want the insertion point in the
text and click the left mouse button. (If you cannot see the insertion point, it
might be under the I-beam. Move the mouse a little to move the I-beam.) To
use the keyboard to move the insertion point, press the arrow keys.

To insert text at the insertion point, you simply type. Most applications push
existing text to the right to make room for the new text (although some applications enable you to select an overtype mode, which replaces existing text
as you type). To delete text to the left of the insertion point, press the Backspace key. To delete text to the right of the insertion point, press the Delete
key.

Tip
Although the
pointer changes to
an I-beam over
editable text, you
cannot edit at the
location until you
click the mouse
button.

II

Working with Windows 95

> **Caution**
>
> If you accidentally press the Insert key, you turn on Overtype mode, which types new text over existing text. If this happens, press the Insert key again. Some applications display OVR or a similar indicator in the status bar to show when they are in Overtype mode.

Selecting Text and Objects

Tip

Most applications contain an "oops" function: the Edit, Undo command. This command undoes your most recent edit (or more, depending on the program). Use this command when you make an edit that you instantly regret.

You can sum up one of the most important editing rules in all Windows applications with three simple words: select, then do. You must select text or an object before you can do anything to it (if you don't select first, the application doesn't know where to apply your command).

To select text and objects, you can use the mouse or the keyboard. To select text with the mouse, position the I-beam at the beginning of the text that you want to select, click and hold down the left mouse button, drag to the end of the text that you want to select, and release the mouse button. To select text with the keyboard, position the insertion point at the beginning of the text that you want to select, press and hold down the Shift key, use arrow keys to move to the end of the text that you want to select, and then release the Shift and arrow keys. The selected text appears in reverse type, as shown in figure 4.17.

Many shortcuts exist for selecting. Some of the following shortcuts apply to text in many Windows documents and dialog boxes:

- To select a word with the mouse, double-click on the word.

- To select a word using the keyboard, hold down Ctrl+Shift while pressing the left- or right-arrow key.

- To select a length of text with the mouse, you can drag until you touch the end of the screen, which causes the screen to scroll.

- To select a length of text with the keyboard, position the I-beam where you want to start the selection, hold down the Shift key, and scroll to the end of the selection by using any keyboard scrolling technique.

After you select a word, you can change its appearance. For example, you might make the word bold or change its font. In most applications, typing replaces the selection, which enables you to replace text by selecting it and typing the new text. If you select a graphic, you can resize it or apply formatting.

To use the mouse to select an object such as a picture, click on the object. (To select multiple objects, hold down Shift while you click on each one in turn.) To select objects with the keyboard, position the insertion point beside the object, hold down Shift, and press an arrow key to move the object in the direction indicated by the arrow key. Selected objects, such as graphics, usually appear with *selection handles* (small black boxes) on each side and corner.

Copying and Moving

After selecting text or an object, you can use the Edit menu to copy or move the selection. The Edit menu commands that all Windows applications use to copy and move are Cut, Copy, and Paste. The Edit, Cut command removes the selection from your document, and Edit, Copy duplicates it. Both commands transfer the selection to the Clipboard, a temporary holding area. The Edit, Paste command copies the selection from the Clipboard and into your document at the insertion point's location. Your selection remains in the Clipboard until you replace it with another selection.

To copy a selection, choose Edit, Copy; then move the insertion point to where you want to duplicate the selection, and choose Edit, Paste. To move a selection, choose Edit, Cut; then move the insertion point to where you want to move it, and choose Edit, Paste. Many shortcuts exist for copying and moving. Ctrl+X usually cuts a selection, Ctrl+C copies a selection, and Ctrl+V usually pastes the Clipboard's contents. Many Windows applications also take advantage of the Windows drag-and-drop feature, which enables you to use the mouse to drag a selection to its new location and drop it into place.

Because all applications running under Windows share the Clipboard, you can move or copy a selection between documents and between applications as easily as you can move and copy within a file. The next two sections explain how to switch between documents and applications.

Switching between Document Windows

In many (but not all) Windows applications, you can easily open more than one document and switch between the documents in the same application. Use these techniques when you want to copy or move information from one document to another. To open multiple documents, choose File, Open multiple times, each time opening a different document. If your application doesn't support multiple documents, it closes the current file, asking whether you want to save any changes that you made since you last saved.

If your application supports multiple documents, each document opens in its own document window as shown in figure 4.18. Multiple document windows

Tip

To copy and paste between documents and dialog boxes, try using the shortcut keys described in this section.

▶ See "Using the Windows Clipboard," p. 411

▶ See "Using Drag-and-Drop to Copy Information between Documents," p. 421

II

Working with Windows 95

have a document Control menu to control the active document window's size and position.

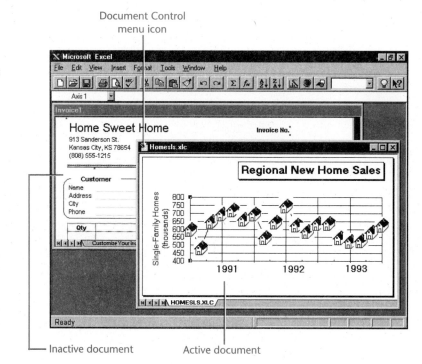

Fig. 4.18
Control document
windows with
these buttons.

Document Control menu icon

Inactive document   Active document

The document Control menu appears to the left of the document title bar, or if the document is displayed as a full screen, to the left of the menu bar. You can click on the document Control menu icon to display the Control menu. This menu enables you to change the window's size or close the document. If you are using the keyboard, press Alt+hyphen (-). There is, however, an easier way to control document windows than through the document Control menu.

A faster way to control documents in Windows is to use the buttons that appear at the top-right corner of each document, as shown in figures 4.19 and 4.20. If the document fills the application window, the Restore Document button appears to the right of the menu bar as shown in figure 4.19.

If a document is in its own window, three buttons appear at the top-right corner of the document's title bar, as shown in figure 4.20. Click on one of these buttons to reduce the document to an icon, enlarge the document to fill the application window, or close the document.

Minimize Document
button

Close Document
button

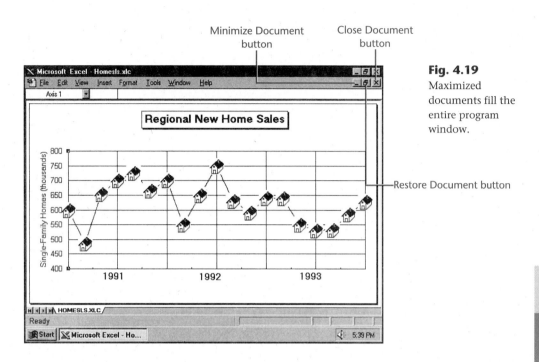

Fig. 4.19
Maximized
documents fill the
entire program
window.

Restore Document button

Maximize
Document button

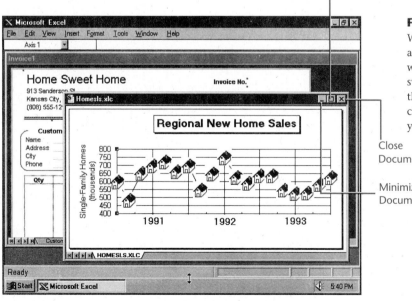

Fig. 4.20
When documents
are in their own
windows, you can
switch between
them quickly by
clicking the one
you want active.

Close
Document button

Minimize
Document button

II

Working with Windows 95

Reducing a document window creates an icon in the application window
such as that shown in figure 4.21. Notice that this icon has three buttons that

you can click to restore the document to a window, enlarge it to full screen, or close it.

Fig. 4.21
Documents reduced to icons require less space in the program's window.

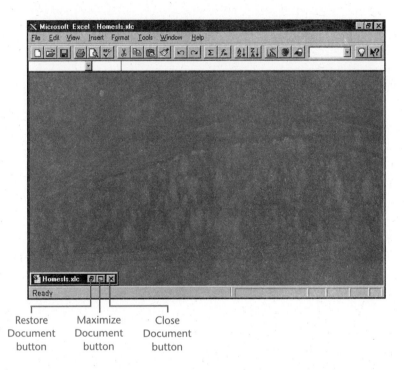

Restore   Maximize   Close
Document   Document   Document
button   button   button

Switching between Applications

◄ See "Using Taskbar Short-cuts to Arrange Windows," p. 103

When you run several applications, you need an easy way to switch between them. If the taskbar is visible, you can switch to another application by clicking on the application's button in the taskbar. If you cannot see the taskbar, press Ctrl+Esc to display it and open the Start menu.

Another way to switch between applications is to hold down the Alt key and press Tab. When you first press Alt+Tab, a bar with open applications appears as shown in figure 4.22. Continue holding the Alt key to keep the bar on-screen. Each time you press Alt+Tab the next application on the bar is selected. A box encloses the icon of the active application. Press Shift+Alt+Tab to move the selection to the application to the left. Release Alt+Tab when you have selected the application that you want to activate.

Fig. 4.22
Press Alt+Tab to
switch to another
open application.

To switch between document windows with the mouse, click on the window
that you want to activate. If the window that you want to activate is not
visible, you might have to move or size the active window on top. (To move a
window, drag its title bar; to size a window, drag its border.) To use the keyboard to switch between document windows, open the <u>W</u>indow menu and
select from the list of open windows the document that you want.❖

Chapter 5

Customizing Windows 95

by Ron Person

The more you use Windows, the more you'll appreciate its customization options. You can save time by setting features so that they normally appear or act in the way you prefer. You can change date and time formats, languages, keyboards, mouse settings, and more. And you can set colors, fonts, and desktop backgrounds so that they are personal to you.

Many Windows users feel more comfortable with their computers after they customize the Windows screen. Applying a personally selected color, pattern, and background makes their computer seem more like a personal belonging. Another way you can customize the screen, and even add protection from prying eyes, is to enable the screen saver that comes with Windows.

There are a number of simple things you can do to make working in Windows easier. For example, you can customize your taskbar to appear only when you want it to. That gives your applications more room on-screen. You can also position the taskbar in locations other than at the bottom of the screen. If you frequently use the same applications, you can add them to the Start menu so they are easy to find.

If you work with different types of Windows software and have a more up-to-date video adapter and monitor, you will want to take advantage of Windows' capability to switch between different display resolutions. This can be useful when you're running different types of applications or when switching a mobile computer between mobile and desktop operation.

In this chapter, you learn to:

■ Customize the taskbar and add programs to the Start menu and Program menu

■ Customize the desktop pattern or graphic as well as all the colors used by elements in Windows

■ Control how your mouse works

■ Control how your keyboard works

■ Change your computer's date and time

■ Change international settings

■ Add a password to protect the settings you customize

Customizing the Taskbar

The taskbar is one of the most important and innovative features in Windows 95. It accounts for a lot of the reasons why Windows 95 is easier to use than previous versions of Windows. While the basic taskbar makes Windows easier to use for novices, once you have some experience you can customize the taskbar to fit the way you work. That makes it both easier and more efficient.

When you begin working in Windows 95, the taskbar appears as a simple gray bar at the bottom of the screen, displaying only the Start menu and the clock. As you begin working with applications, you notice that each open application adds a button to the taskbar. These buttons show you what applications are running. Clicking these buttons switches you from application to application.

Tip

Any open application appears as a button on the taskbar. Click the button to activate the application.

If you work with a lot of open applications, your screen can become cluttered with many open windows. Rather than clutter the screen with several open windows, you can reduce the applications you're not using currently to buttons on the taskbar. As more buttons appear on the taskbar, the other buttons shrink to make room. To activate an application, you simply click its button on the taskbar. Figure 5.1 shows a taskbar with several buttons.

Fig. 5.1

Use the taskbar to temporarily store applications while you're not using them.

Note

If you have many applications open, you may not be able to read the application and document name on the taskbar button. If the application and document name are truncated, pause the pointer over the button. A button tip will appear showing the full names.

To reduce an application to a button on the taskbar, click the Minimize button. To reactivate an application, click its button in the taskbar.

Troubleshooting

Right-clicking on the taskbar displays a shortcut menu that appears to control the applications that are minimized as buttons. The taskbar shortcut menu doesn't appear.

Right-click in the gray area between buttons to see the taskbar shortcut menu.

After clicking on Auto Hide in the Taskbar Properties sheet, the taskbar "hides" when an application opens, but when a window is maximized the taskbar won't come back, even dragging the mouse pointer to the bottom of the screen doesn't display it.

Usually you should set two properties when you want the taskbar to automatically hide. But first you must get the taskbar displayed again. When you get stuck without a taskbar, press Ctrl+Esc to display the taskbar and Start menu. Press Esc once to remove the menu so just the taskbar shows. Click with the right mouse in a gray area of the taskbar, then click Properties. Select both the Auto Hide and the Always on Top check boxes. Without the Always on Top option the mouse pointer can't touch the thin gray line at the screen edge that reactivates the taskbar.

Resizing the Taskbar

You can change the size of the taskbar to accommodate a large number of buttons or to make it easier to read the full description written on a button. To resize the taskbar, follow these steps:

1. Point to the edge of the taskbar. The pointer becomes a double-pointing arrow.

2. Hold down the left mouse button, drag to the size you want, and then release the button.

The taskbar resizes in full button widths. If the taskbar is horizontal against the top or bottom of the screen, you can change its height. If the taskbar is positioned vertically against a side, you can change its width.

Moving the Taskbar

The taskbar can be positioned horizontally (the default) along the top or bottom of the desktop or vertically along the side of the desktop (see fig. 5.2). To reposition the taskbar, follow these steps:

1. Point to a position on the taskbar where no button appears, either below or between buttons.

2. Hold down the left mouse button and drag to the edge of the screen where you want to position the taskbar. A shaded line indicates the new position of the taskbar.

3. Release the mouse button.

When the taskbar is positioned at the side of the desktop, it may be so wide that you don't have enough space to work. If so, you can drag the edge of the taskbar to give it a new width. When the taskbar is against a side, you can change its width in pixel increments, not just in full button widths.

Using the Taskbar Menu

As in other Windows screen areas, you can click the right mouse button in a gray area of the taskbar to display a menu (see fig. 5.3). Use the taskbar menu to rearrange windows on the desktop, to reduce applications to buttons, and to change the properties of the taskbar.

Fig. 5.2
Reposition the taskbar for your convenience.

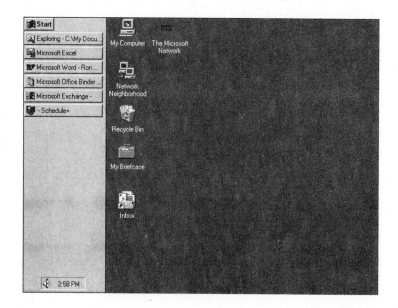

The following table describes each of the commands on the taskbar menu.

Command	Description
Cascade	Display windows one over the other from left to right, top to bottom (see fig. 5.4).
Undo Cascade	(Available only after using Cascade.) Returns windows to their previous sizes and positions after using Cascade.
Tile Horizontally	Display windows top to bottom without overlapping (see fig. 5.5).
Tile Vertically	Display windows left to right without overlapping (see fig. 5.6).
Undo Tile	(Available only after using Tile Horizontally or Tile Vertically.) Returns windows to their previous sizes and positions after using one of the Tile commands.
Minimize All Windows	Reduces all open windows to buttons on the taskbar.
Properties	Displays the Taskbar Properties sheet where you can change the Start menu or taskbar options.

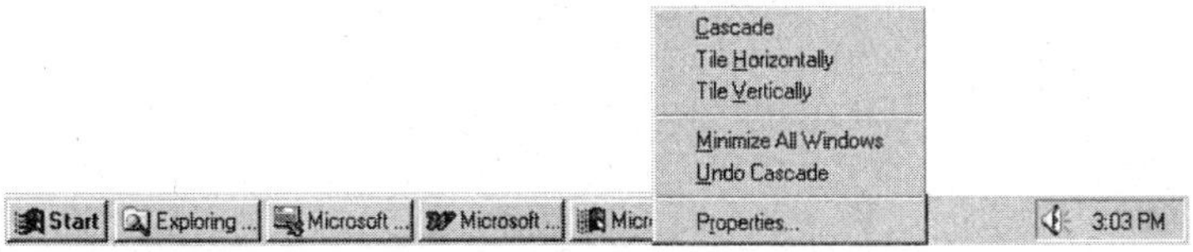

Fig. 5.3
Right-click in the gray area of the taskbar to display the shortcut menu.

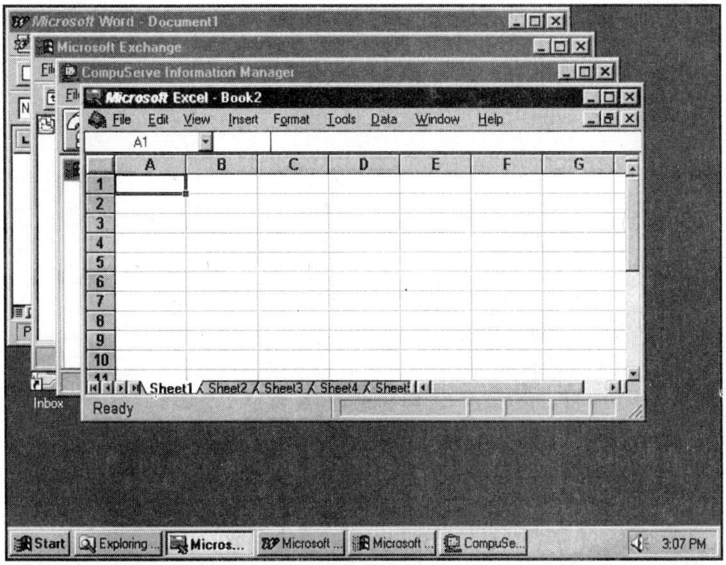

Fig. 5.4
Cascading windows.

II

Working with Windows 95

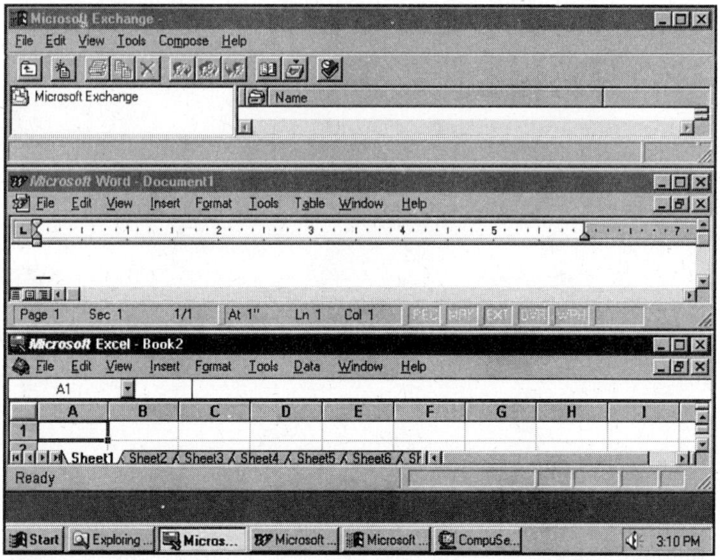

Fig. 5.5
Windows tiled
horizontally.

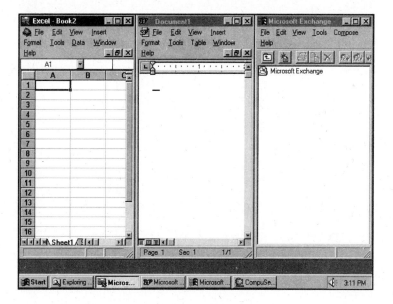

Fig. 5.6
Windows tiled
vertically.

Changing the Taskbar Options

You can hide or display the taskbar using the Taskbar Properties sheet. Figure 5.7 shows the commands available from the Taskbar Options tab. You also can turn the clock area of the taskbar on and off.

To change taskbar properties, follow these steps:

1. Point to a position on the taskbar where no button appears, either below or between buttons, and right-click. Choose Properties.

   or

   Open the Start menu and choose Settings, Taskbar.

2. Click the Taskbar Options tab.

3. Click a check box to turn an item on or off. The options are explained in the following table.

4. Click OK.

Option	Description
Always On Top	The taskbar displays over all open windows.
Auto Hide	Hides the taskbar to make more space available on your desktop and in application windows. To see the taskbar, move your mouse pointer to the bottom of the screen (or wherever the taskbar is if you have moved it) and the taskbar reappears. When you move the pointer away, the taskbar disappears again.
Show Small Icons In Start Menu	Displays the Start menu with small icons and without the Windows banner. This enables you to see more of what's on-screen while in the Start menu.
Show Clock	Hides or displays the clock in one corner of the taskbar.

▶ See "Using the Taskbar Clock," p. 406

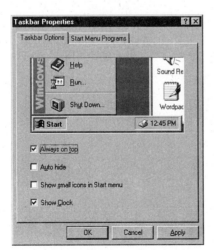

Fig. 5.7
Right-click in the gray area of the taskbar and then choose Properties when you want to change how your taskbar operates.

II

Working with Windows 95

Customizing the Start Menu

Tip

To quickly add a program to the highest level of the Start menu, drag the program's file from the Explorer or My Computer window and drop it on the Start button.

The contents of the Start menu can be customized. You can add a list of applications you use frequently, and then start those applications directly from the menu. By adding programs to the Start menu, you avoid having to display additional menus.

To add a program to the Start menu, follow these steps:

1. Right-click on a gray area between buttons on the taskbar. Choose Properties.

   or

   Open the Start menu and choose Settings, Taskbar.

2. Click the Start Menu Programs tab.

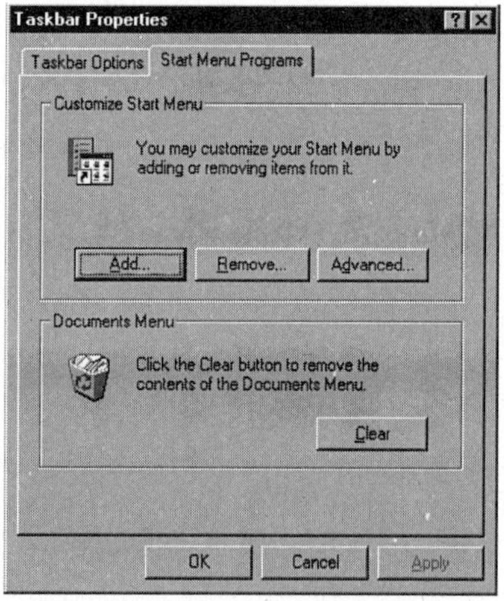

Fig. 5.8

The Start Menu Programs page enables you to add programs to the Start menu.

3. Click Add to display the Create Shortcut dialog box shown in figure 5.9.

◀ See "Opening, Saving, and Closing Documents," p. 109

4. Click Browse to display the Browse dialog box. This dialog box looks very similar to an Open File dialog box.

5. Find and click the file that starts the program or document file you want to add to the Start menu. Choose the Open button once you have selected the file.

   You can limit the displayed files to program files by selecting Programs from the Files of Type list at the bottom of the dialog box. For example, if you wanted to start Excel, you would open the Office95 folder, open the Excel folder, and then click on EXCEL.EXE. Most program files use an EXE extension.

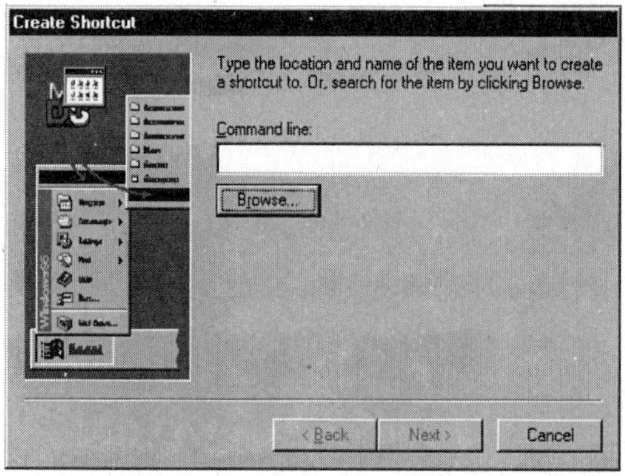

Fig. 5.9
In the Create Shortcut dialog box, you want to type or select the file of the program you want to add to the Start menu.

6. Click Next> to display the Select Program Folder dialog box shown in figure 5.10.

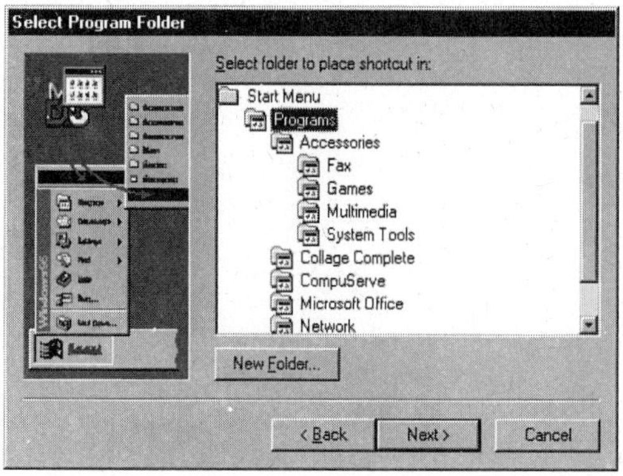

Fig. 5.10
You can position your document or application anywhere on the Start menu.

7. Select the folder that corresponds to the location on the Start menu where you want the program to appear. Choose Next>.

For example, if you wanted the program you selected to appear at the top of the Start menu, you would select the Start Menu folder. If you wanted the program to appear as an item on the Programs menu, then you would select the Programs folder.

8. Type the name or words you want to appear on the Start menu in the edit box. Choose Finish.

Tip
Adding a document's file to the Start menu enables you to open the document in its related application.

◀ See "Starting
Programs from
a Shortcut Icon
on the Desk-
top," p. 68

Note

If you frequently copy files to the same folders, put Shortcuts to those folders in the WINDOWS\SENDTO folder. The shortcuts to the folders will then show up on the Send To menu that appears when you right-click on a file.

To remove a program from the Start menu, you follow a similar process:

1. Display the Taskbar Properties sheet as described earlier in this chapter.

2. Click the Start Menu Programs tab.

3. Click the Remove button to display the Remove Shortcuts/Folders dialog box shown in figure 5.11.

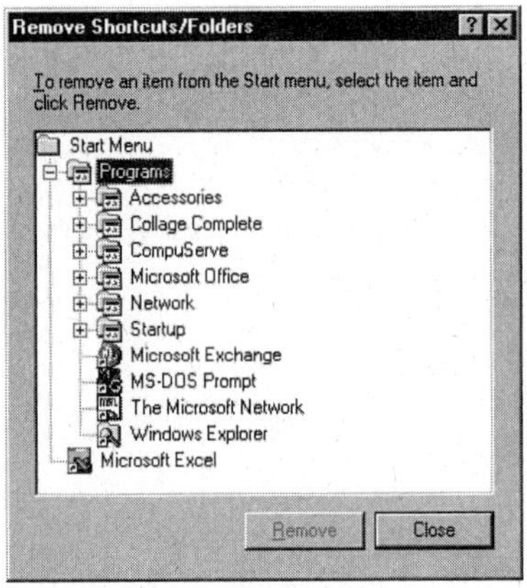

Fig. 5.11
In the Remove
Shortcuts/Folders
dialog box, select
the file or folder
you want to
remove from the
Start menu.

4. Select the shortcut or folder you want to remove from the Start menu.

5. Click the Remove button to remove the file or folder.

6. Remove additional items or choose Close. Choose OK when you return to the Taskbar Properties sheet.

The Start menu contains a Documents item that shows a list of recently used documents. At times this list may become too long, or you may want to clear the list so that documents are easier to find. To clear the documents from the Documents menu, follow these steps:

1. Display the Taskbar Properties sheet.

2. Click the Start Menu Programs tab.

3. Click Clear in the Documents Menu portion of the page.

4. Choose OK.

Customizing the Desktop Colors and Background

Changing colors is just one way you can customize the windows you see on-screen. You also can change the pattern used in the desktop background, add a graphical wallpaper as a background, change the border width of windows, and more.

Wallpaper options you select for the desktop background can include graphics that come with Windows—including some wild and colorful ones—and designs you create or modify with Windows Paint. The graphic images you use as wallpaper are nothing more than computer drawings saved in a bitmap (BMP) format. You also can use the Windows Paint program to create your own bitmap drawings to use as screen backgrounds.

▶ See "Saving Paint Files," p. 395

▶ See "Changing the Windows Desktop with Paint," p. 393

You can put wallpaper over just the center portion of the desktop, or you can tile the desktop with wallpaper. When tiling, the wallpaper reproduces itself to fill the screen.

Changing Windows Colors

After working in the drab and dreary DOS or mainframe computer world, one of the first changes many people want to make is to add color to their Windows screens. You can pick colors for window titles, backgrounds, bars—in fact, all parts of the window. Predesigned color schemes range from the brilliant to the cool and dark. You also can design and save your own color schemes and blend your own colors.

Using Existing Color Schemes

Windows comes with a list of predefined color schemes. Each color scheme maps a different color and text to a different part of the screen.

You can select from existing schemes, or you can devise your own (described in the next section). Figure 5.12 shows the Appearance page. To select one of the predefined schemes, follow these steps:

1. Right-click the desktop, choose Properties, and then select the Appearance tab.

Tip

Large, complex bitmap drawings consume a lot of memory. If Windows' performance slows when a large wallpaper is used, you may want to return to a small bitmap that is tiled over the screen, or use no bitmap at all.

II

Working with Windows 95

You can also open the Start menu and choose $\underline{S}$ettings, $\underline{C}$ontrol Panel; then double-click the Display icon and select the Appearance tab.

The Appearance page of the Display Properties sheet displays, as shown in figure 5.12.

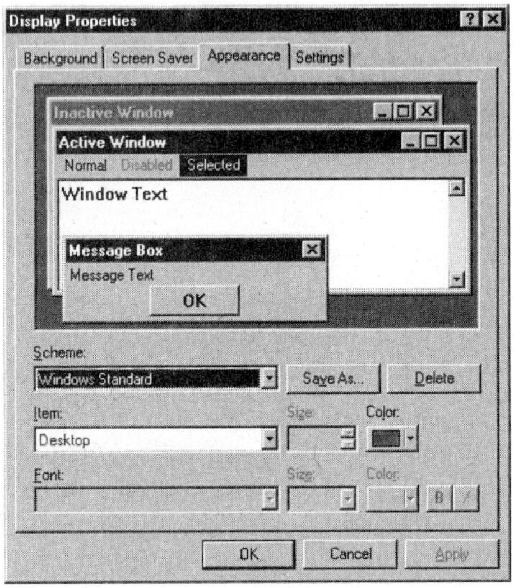

Fig. 5.12

Select from existing color and text schemes on the Appearance page to customize Windows' appearance.

Tip

If you have trouble reading the menus and seeing icons, choose Windows Standard (Large) or Windows Standard (Extra Large) from the $\underline{S}$cheme list.

2. Select the $\underline{S}$cheme list and select a predefined color and text scheme from the list. The sample screen at the top of the sheet illustrates what this color scheme looks like.

3. Choose OK to use the displayed color scheme or return to step 2 for other predefined schemes.

Creating Custom Color and Text Schemes

If you don't like the predesigned color and text schemes, you can create your own or modify one of the existing schemes. You can change all or some of the colors in a scheme, the text, and even the color and width of borders. To create new color schemes while the Appearance page is open, follow these steps:

1. If you want to use an existing scheme as a base (as opposed to using Windows Standard as a base), select the scheme from the $\underline{S}$cheme list.

2. Select from the Item list the screen element you want to modify. Or click on a screen element in the sample window at the top of the sheet. You can select elements such as the Menu Bar, Button, Active Border, and so on.

3. Select from the Size, Font, and Color lists how you want to change the selected element. Some options are only available for certain elements.

4. Choose one of these alternatives for the colors you have selected:

   ■ If you want to color another window element, return to step 2.

   ■ If you want to use these colors now but not save them for the next time you run Windows, choose OK or press Enter.

   ■ If you want to save these colors so that you can use them now or return to them at any time, choose the Save As button. Then type a name in the Save Scheme dialog box and choose OK.

   ■ If you want to cancel these colors and return to the original scheme, select that scheme from the Scheme list if it was saved, or choose Cancel.

To remove a scheme from the list, select the scheme you want to remove from the Scheme list and click Delete.

Wallpapering Your Desktop with a Graphic

Using a graphic or picture as the Windows desktop is a nice personal touch. For special business situations or for custom applications, you may want to use a color company logo or pictorial theme as the wallpaper.

Windows comes with a collection of graphics for the desktop. You can modify these images or draw new images for the desktop with the Windows Paint accessory. For high-quality pictorials, use a scanner to create a digitized black-and-white or color image.

▶ See "Changing the Windows Desktop with Paint," p. 393

Figure 5.13 shows one of the many wallpaper patterns that come with Windows. Figure 5.14 shows a logo used as a backdrop. Many companies scan and then enhance their corporate logo as a BMP file, then use it as the desktop background. Most of the patterns must be tiled to fill the entire screen, which you learn how to do in the following steps.

II

Working with Windows 95

Fig. 5.13
One of the many
Windows images
you can use to
wallpaper your
desktop.

Fig. 5.14
Edit existing
wallpaper files or
create your own
with Paint.

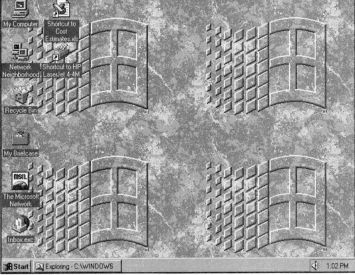

Tip
Using a complex
or detailed back-
ground or pattern
on your desktop
may make icons
on the desktop
difficult to read.

To select wallpaper, follow these steps:

1. Right-click the desktop, choose P<u>r</u>operties, and then select the Background tab.

   or

Open the Start menu and choose Settings, Control Panel; then double-click the Display icon, and select the Background tab.

The Background page of the Display Properties sheet will display as shown in figure 5.15.

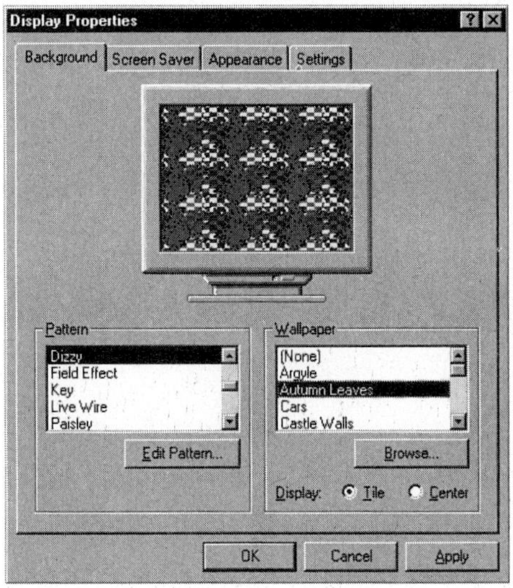

Fig. 5.15
Use the Background tab in Display Properties to select new wallpapers and patterns.

2. Choose a wallpaper in the Wallpaper list box. If the graphic file (with a BMP extension) is located in a folder other than Windows, select the Browse button to find and select the graphic file.

3. If the graphic is large enough to fill the screen, select Display, Center to center the wallpaper in the desktop. If the graphic is small and must be repeated to fill the screen, select Display, Tile.

4. Choose OK if you are finished or make other display property changes.

When you choose a wallpaper from the Wallpaper list, you see a miniature rendition of it in the display shown in the upper portion of the Display Properties sheet. This allows you to preview wallpapers before settling on the one to use.

Wallpaper is created from files stored in a bitmap format. They are located in the Windows folder. These files end with the BMP extension and must be stored in the Windows folder. You can edit BMP formats with the Windows Paint accessory. You also can read and edit files with PCX format in Paint and then save them in BMP format to use as a desktop wallpaper.

Tip
Bitmap images displayed as the desktop wallpaper use more memory than a colored or patterned desktop. If you run low on memory, remove the wallpaper.

II

Working with Windows 95

You can create your own desktop wallpapers in one of three ways:

- Buy clip art from a software vendor. If the clip art is not in PCX or BMP format, use a graphics-conversion application to convert the image to one of these formats. Use Windows Paint to read PCX format and resave the figure in BMP format. Computer bulletin boards, online services, and the Internet have thousands of BMP graphics files.

- Scan a black-and-white or color picture using a digital scanner. Save the scanned file as BMP format or convert it to BMP format.

- Modify an existing desktop wallpaper, or create a new one with Windows Paint or a higher-end graphics program. Save the files with the BMP format.

Store your new BMP (bitmap) graphics files in the Windows folder so that they appear in the Wallpaper Files drop-down list of the Display Properties sheet.

To remove a wallpaper file from the Wallpaper list, delete or remove its BMP file from the Windows folder. To remove the wallpaper from the desktop, repeat the previous steps but select None as the type of wallpaper.

Troubleshooting

After adding a beautiful and very intricate Chinese dragon to my wallpaper, my computer seems to run slower. I'm running with minimally acceptable memory so Windows is already slow.

Wallpapers consume memory. If you have a very complex wallpaper it's large size could consume enough memory to make Windows slower. You need to install more memory or use less ambitious artwork.

Changing the Background Pattern

Wallpapers, while pretty and often amusing, can consume a lot of memory. If you want a simpler background or want to conserve memory, you can use a background pattern. The pattern is a small grid of dots that repeats to fill the screen. The Sample area of figure 5.16 shows how one background pattern appears. Windows comes with predefined patterns you can select; you also can create your own. The color of the pattern is the same as the color selected for Window Text in the Color dialog box.

> **Caution**
>
> If you have a wallpaper selected with the Display, Tile option selected, then you will not be able to see your pattern. A full-screen wallpaper shows over the top of the pattern. To see the pattern, select None from the Wallpaper list.

To select a pattern, follow these steps:

1. Right-click the desktop, choose Properties, and then select the Background tab.

   or

   Open the Start menu and choose Settings, Control Panel; then double-click the Display icon and select the Background tab. The Background page of the Display Properties sheet displays as shown in figure 5.16.

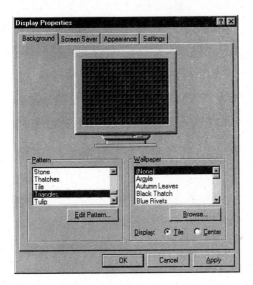

Fig. 5.16
Background patterns are simpler and conserve memory.

2. Select a pattern from the Pattern list. Some of the built-in repetitive patterns you can select are 50% Gray, Boxes, Diamonds, Weave, and Scottie.

3. Choose OK to add the pattern to the desktop. Alternatively, use the following procedure to edit the pattern just selected.

You can edit or create new patterns only if you have a mouse. To edit an existing pattern or create a new pattern while the Background page is displayed, follow these steps:

1. Select a pattern from the Pattern list.

2. Click the Edit Pattern button to display the Pattern Editor dialog box shown in figure 5.17.

3. Click in the editing grid in the location where you want to reverse a dot in the pattern. Watch the Sample area to see the overall effect.

4. Continue to click in the grid until the pattern is what you want.

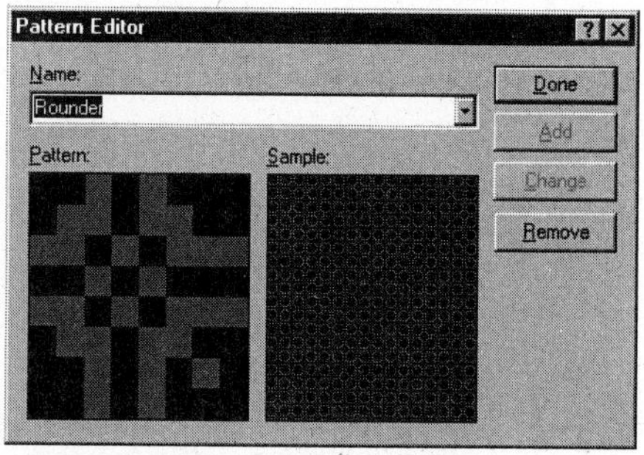

Fig. 5.17
Editing your pattern using an existing pattern as a base may be easier than working from the None pattern.

5. When you are finished creating or editing, continue with one of the following options:

   - If you want to change an existing pattern, click Change.

   - If you want to add a new pattern, type a new name in the Name list box and choose the Add button.

6. When you are finished editing, click Done. Choose OK in the Display Properties sheet.

To remove an unwanted pattern from the list, select the pattern and click Remove. Confirm the deletion by choosing Yes. The Remove button is available only after you select a new pattern name.

Having Fun with the Screen Saver

Screen savers display a changing pattern on-screen when you haven't typed or moved the mouse for a predetermined amount of time. Screen savers were designed to prevent an image from burning onto your screen if the document on-screen did not change frequently. With new display screens this is rarely a problem, but screen savers remain. They are fun and afford a degree of protection against others seeing your work. You can specify the delay before the screen saver activates, and you can set up various attributes—including a password—for most of the screen savers.

To select and set up a screen saver, follow these steps:

1. Right-click the desktop and choose Properties; then select the Screen Saver tab.

   or

   Open the Start menu and choose Settings, Control Panel; then double-click the Display icon and select the Screen Saver tab.

   The Screen Saver page of the Display Properties sheet displays (see fig. 5.18).

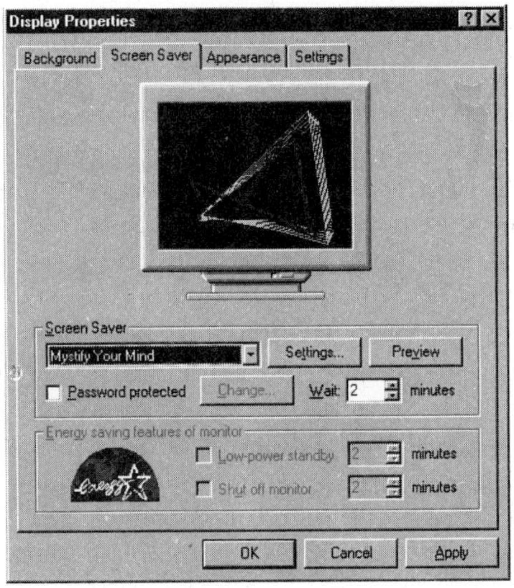

Fig. 5.18
Screen savers display when your computer sits idle for a predetermined amount of time.

II

Working with Windows 95

2. Select a screen saver from the Screen Saver list.

3. The miniature display shows you a preview of the screen saver. To see a full-screen view, click Preview. Click anywhere on-screen to return to the sheet from the preview.

4. To test other screen savers, return to step 2.

5. To customize the appearance and properties of your screen saver, click Settings. The options and settings for each screen saver are different. Figure 5.19 shows the options to customize the Flying Through Space screen saver. Click OK when you're finished.

6. In the Wait box, type or select the number of minutes you want the screen to be idle before the screen saver displays. A range from 5 to 15 minutes is usually a good time.

7. Choose Apply to apply the Display Property changes you have selected so far. You will see the changes take effect, but the Display Properties sheet stays open. Choose OK to accept the changes and close the sheet.

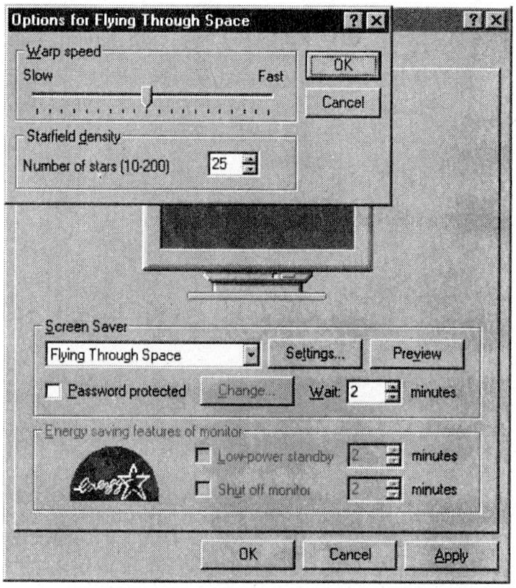

Fig. 5.19
You can customize screen savers so that they act differently.

Tip
When your screen saver is on, you need to be careful about pressing keys that might affect the active program. Either move the mouse or press Shift to go back to the normal display.

Protecting Your Computer with a Screen Saver Password

◄ See "Starting and Quitting Windows," p. 50

Although each screen saver has unique settings, all except Blank Screen have an area where you can specify password protection. If you don't want uninvited users to use your computer, you can specify a password that is associated with a screen saver, so that only those who know the password can clear the screen saver and use your computer.

To protect your computer using a password, follow these steps:

1. Click with the right mouse button anywhere on the desktop then choose Properties to open the Display Properties sheet.

2. Click the Screen Saver tab.

3. Select a screen saver from the Screen Saver drop-down list and set its options.

4. Select the Password Protected option and then choose Change.

5. Type your password in the New Password text box, and then confirm your password by typing it again in the Confirm New Password text box.

   Asterisks will appear in the text boxes as you type your password to prevent others from seeing it (see fig. 5.20).

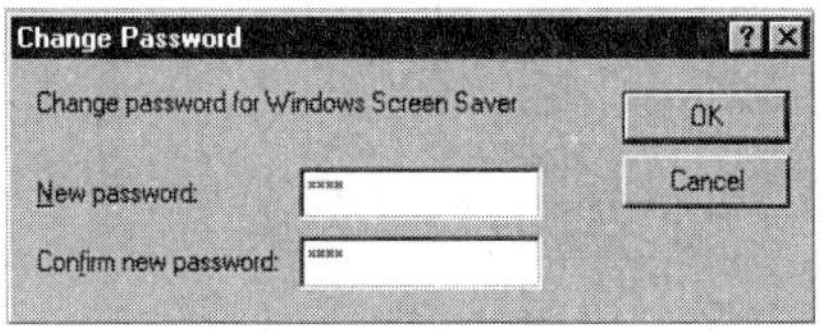

Fig. 5.20
Enter a password for the screen saver in the Change Password dialog box.

6. Choose OK, and when the confirmation message appears, choose OK again.

Now when the screen saver appears and you press a key on the keyboard or move the mouse, a dialog box appears in which you have to type your password to clear the screen saver.

Using Your Display's Energy-Saving Feature

If you leave your computer on continuously, or if you leave your desk for long periods of time while your computer continues to run, you will want to conserve energy by using the energy-saving features that are built in to many newer monitors. Although the energy used by one monitor may seem small, when multiplied by the millions of computers in use across the nation, it is easy to see that selecting this option one time can save a lot of energy and reduce pollution. When you multiply the cost of running the tens of thousands of monitors in a single large corporation, the dollar savings can be significant.

Monitors that satisfy EPA requirements usually display an "Energy Star" sticker on the monitor or in the manual. Older monitors do not have the energy-saving feature.

► See "Understanding Plug and Play Architecture," p. 230

If you have a monitor that is an Energy Star but the Energy Saving Features of Monitor options are not available in the Screen Saver page, you should install the correct display drivers for your monitor. To check which display driver is installed, open the Display Properties sheet, choose the Settings tab, and then

► See "Creating and Modifying Hardware Profiles," p. 273

II

Working with Windows 95

choose the Change Display Type button. From the dialog box that appears, you can install the display driver for your manufacturer and model. Once you have the correct driver, select the Monitor Is Energy Star Compliant checkbox. Selecting this checkbox does no good if the monitor is not compliant.

To set Windows so that it takes advantage of the energy-saving features of Energy Star compliant monitors, follow these steps:

1. Click the right mouse button on the desktop and choose Properties.

2. Choose the Settings tab (refer to fig. 5.18).

3. Choose the Low-Power Standby check box, and then select the number of minutes the computer should be idle before the monitor goes into low-power standby. This mode reduces power requirements but keeps the monitor ready to be instantly used.

4. Choose the Shut Off Monitor check box, and then select the number of minutes the computer should be idle before the monitor shuts down. This mode completely turns off your monitor.

5. Choose OK.

When you return to your workstation, you can press any key or move the mouse to return to normal monitor use from low-power standby. The Shut Off Monitor mode shuts off the monitor rather than putting it in standby mode. This saves the most energy. The manual for your monitor will describe the best way to turn the monitor on again.

Changing the Screen Resolution, Font Size, and Color Palette

With Windows, you have the ability to change how your application displays even while you work. This can help you if you run applications that operate with different screen resolutions, or use programs that look better in different font sizes. Some applications, such as graphics programs or multimedia, work better when they use 256 colors and higher resolution.

The resolution is the number of dots shown on-screen. The more dots on-screen, the more detail you can work with. However, with a high-resolution screen, icons or fonts that appeared an adequate size on a VGA screen may now appear small.

Changing the resolution while Windows is running enables you to switch between VGA mode (640 × 480 pixels on-screen) to the more detailed and wider view of SVGA mode (1024 × 768 pixels). This can come in handy when you work on different types of tasks. You may, for example, have a laptop computer that displays on its LCD screen in VGA mode. When you work at your desk and have a high-resolution monitor connected to the laptop, you want to work in SVGA mode.

Changing the Screen Resolution

You can change the screen resolution—the number of dots on the screen—if your display is capable of running Super VGA 800 × 600 resolution or better and Super VGA or better is currently set as the monitor type.

You can change or examine your monitor type by following these steps:

1. Open the Display Properties sheet and click on the Settings tab.

2. Choose the Change Display Type button to display the Change Display Type dialog box.

3. Choose the Change button next to the Monitor Type box.

4. Select the resolution you want to use for your monitor from the Select Device dialog box. Choose the Show All Devices option if you do not see your monitor. If you are unsure, choose the (Standard Monitor Types) option from the Manufacturers list.

5. Choose OK, then choose Close.

6. When you return to the Display Properties sheet, you can change other display properties. Choose OK.

When you exit the Display Properties sheet, you may need to restart Windows in order to implement the new monitor type. You will be asked whether you want to restart at that time.

Caution

Changing to an incorrect monitor type that cannot be implemented may cause your screen to be unreadable. If that happens, shut off your computer. Restart the computer and watch the screen carefully. When the phrase, Starting Windows 95 appears, press F8. This displays a text menu that enables you to start Windows in *safe mode.* Safe mode displays Windows on any screen, but many resources will not be available such as networking and CD-ROMs. While in safe mode, repeat the steps described in the section, "Changing the Screen Resolution," and select either a monitor type you are sure of or a resolution that will work from the (Standard Monitor Types) list.

Once your monitor is in Super VGA mode or better, you can change between different screen resolutions by dragging the slider in the Desktop area portion of the Settings tab.

Changing the Number of Colors Available to Your Monitor

Depending on your display adapter and the monitor, you can have the same resolution screen, but with a different palette of colors available. For example, you may have some business applications that use only 16 colors, while most games and multimedia use 256 or more colors. Depending on the amount of video memory your video card has, not all color choices will be available at all monitor resolutions.

To change the size of your color palette, click on the down arrow next to Color Palette in the Settings page, then click on the number of colors you need.

Changing Font Sizes

Need glasses to read the screen? You can enlarge (or reduce) the size of the font Windows uses on-screen. All text on-screen will change size. You have to restart Windows, however, to see the change.

You can select from any of the following font size options:

- Small Fonts scales fonts to 100 percent of normal size.

- Large Fonts scales fonts to 125 percent of normal size.

- Custom displays the Custom Font Size dialog box where you can specify your own size.

To change the size of screen fonts, follow these steps:

1. Click the right mouse button on the Desktop and choose Properties.

2. Click the Settings tab to display the page shown in figure 5.21.

3. Click the down arrow next to the Font size box and choose Large Fonts or Small Fonts.

   or

   Click Custom to display the Custom Font Size dialog box (see fig. 5.22). Type or select a percentage of normal size in the Scale box, or drag across the ruler then release the mouse button to resize. Notice the sample font and its size below the ruler. Choose OK.

4. Click OK to accept the change and close the Display Properties sheet.

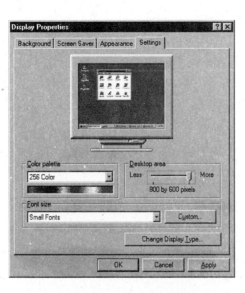

Fig. 5.21
Change your display's appearance in the Settings page.

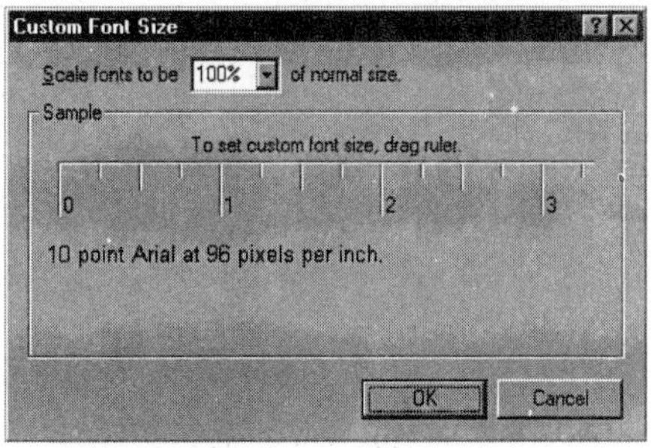

Fig. 5.22
You can create your own custom font size.

Changing the Sounds Related to Windows Events

Windows has sounds related to different events such as errors, closing programs, exiting windows, emptying the Recycle Bin, and so on. You can change the sounds used for each of these events. You can even use your own sound files. (Of course, you need a sound card to hear these sounds.)

To change the sounds related to an event, follow these steps:

1. Open the Start menu and choose Settings, Control Panel.

2. Double-click on Sounds to display the Sounds Properties sheet shown in figure 5.23.

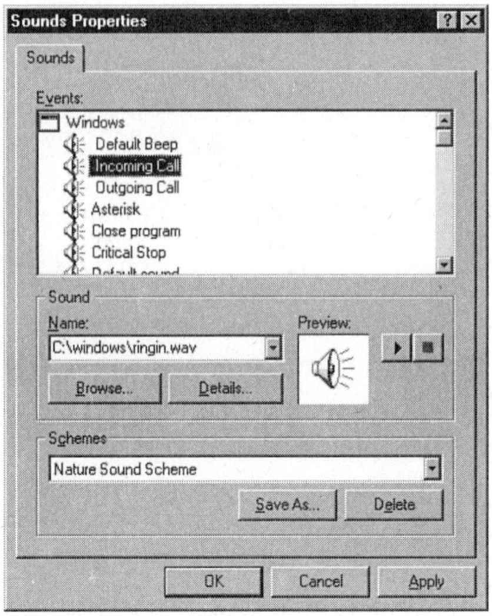

Fig. 5.23
You can assign
your own sound
files to different
Windows or
application events.

3. Scroll through the E̲vents list until you see the event whose sound you want to change, then click on that event.

4. Select the WAV file that contains the sound for that event by clicking on the B̲rowse button and selecting a WAV file. Click OK.

   The Browse dialog box opens in the WINDOWS\MEDIA folder, but you can change to any folder.

5. Preview the sound by clicking on the Go button to the right of the Preview icon.

6. Click OK.

> **Note**
>
> You can create your own collection of WAV files by following the procedures de-scribed in Chapter 33, "Working with Windows Sound Capabilities." You also may want to look on public bulletin boards, online services, and the Internet. They con-tain thousands of free WAV files.

Entire collections of sounds have been grouped already for you as sound schemes. To change all the sounds involved in a sound scheme, select the scheme you want by choosing it from the S̲chemes list.

If you create your own scheme of sounds/events, you can save it with a name so you can return to it by clicking the Save As button, entering a name, and clicking OK.

Customizing the Mouse

If you are left-handed, or if you like a fast or slow mouse, you need to know how to modify your mouse's behavior. Mouse options can be changed at the Mouse Properties sheet, shown in figure 5.24.

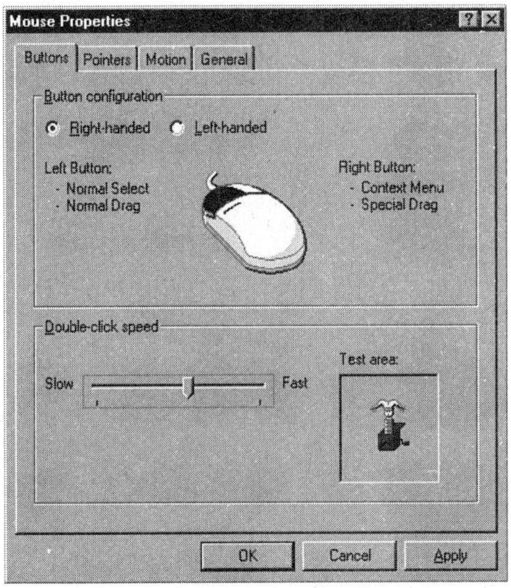

Fig. 5.24
You can change the speed of your mouse and more in the Mouse Properties sheet.

To change how your mouse behaves and appears, follow these steps:

1. Open the Start menu and choose Settings, Control Panel; then double-click Mouse. The Mouse Properties sheet appears.

2. Click a tab and make the changes you want.

3. Click Apply to accept the changes and to continue making changes, or click OK to accept the changes and close the Mouse Properties sheet.

Mouse options are grouped on three tabs—Buttons, Pointers, Motion, and General. Each tab is described in the following table. (Depending on the brand of your mouse, you may have different, though similar, options.)

Tip
Double-click on a pointer shape while in the Pointers page to replace one shape within a scheme.

II

Working with Windows 95

Tab	Description
Buttons	Select either a Right-Handed mouse or Left-Handed mouse. Set the Double-Click Speed, and then double-click in the Test Area to determine whether you have set a speed you're comfortable with. When you double-click at the right speed in the Test Area, you'll be surprised by what appears.
Pointers	Change the size and shape of the pointer. You can select schemes of pointer shapes so that all pointer shapes for different activities take on a new appearance.
Motion	You can set the Pointer Speed to make the mouse move more slowly or quickly across the screen. You can add a Pointer Trail to the mouse to leave a trail of mouse pointers on-screen. This feature is especially useful if you have a LCD screen where the mouse pointer can sometimes get lost. This option cannot be shown for video display drivers that don't support it.
General	To add a new mouse to your system, click Change and the Select Device dialog box displays. Make your selection from there. You also can add a new mouse with the Add New Hardware wizard, available from the Control Panel.

▶ See "Installing Legacy Cards after Setting Up Drivers," p. 255

▶ See "LCD Screen Mouse Trails," p. 298

Customizing the Keyboard

Although changing the keyboard speed doesn't result in a miracle that makes you type faster, it does speed up the rate at which characters are repeated. You also can change the delay before the character repeats.

To change keyboard properties, follow these steps.

1. Open the Start menu and choose Settings, Control Panel; then double-click Keyboard. The Keyboard Properties sheet appears (see fig. 5.25).

2. Click a tab and make the changes you want.

3. Click Apply to accept the changes and to continue making changes, or click OK to accept the changes and close the Keyboard Properties sheet.

Keyboard options are grouped on three tabs—Speed, Language, and General. They are described in the following table. (These tabs will vary for other keyboard and language drivers.)

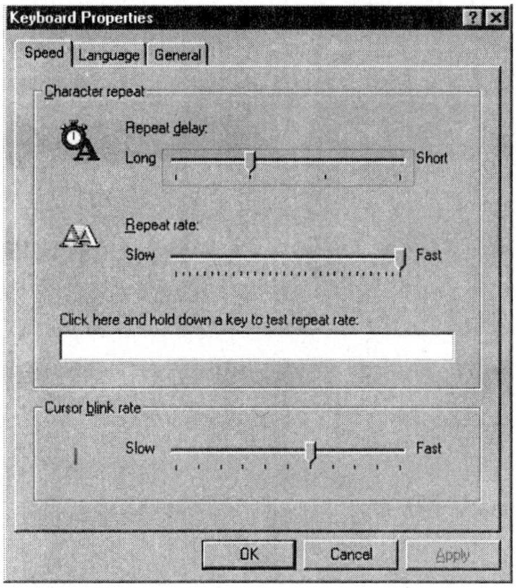

Fig. 5.25
You can change the keyboard repeat and more in the Keyboard Properties sheet.

Tab	Description
Speed	Change the keyboard repeat speed. Drag the Long/Short pointer to change the Repeat Delay speed (how long before the first repeat) or drag the Slow/Fast pointer to change the Repeat Rate. Click in the Click Here box to test the results. Drag the Slow/Fast pointer for Cursor Blink Rate to change the speed the cursor blinks.
Language	Use the Language page to select the language you use. Click Add to display the Add Language dialog box and select a language from the drop-down list. Click Properties to select an appropriate keyboard layout. Click Remove to remove a language from the list. Click the up and down arrows to change the order of the languages you have selected. Changing this option enables your applications to accurately sort words that may contain non-English characters, such as accent marks. However, changing the language setting does not change the language used by Windows. You need to purchase a different language version of Windows to accomplish this.
General	To change keyboards, click the Change button and the Select Device dialog box displays. Make your selection from there. You can also add a new keyboard with the Add New Hardware wizard, available from the Control Panel.

Making Windows Accessible for the Hearing, Sight, and Movement Impaired

In an effort to make computers more available to the more than 30 million people with some form of disability, Microsoft has added accessibility properties that you can use to adjust the computer's sound, display, and physical interface.

To make accessibility adjustments, follow these steps:

1. Click the Start button and choose Settings, Control Panel.

2. Double-click the Accessibility Options icon. The Accessibility Properties sheet appears (see fig. 5.26).

3. Make your selections and click OK.

Troubleshooting

The Accessibility Options icon does not appear in my Control Panel.

Reinstall Windows using a custom installation and select Accessibility Options. Appendix A describes how to reinstall options in Windows.

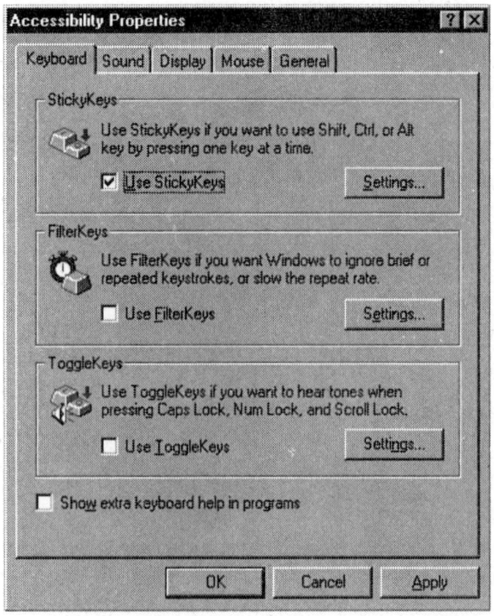

Fig. 5.26

Use the Accessibility Properties sheet to make Windows easier to use for a person with a disability.

The accessibility properties include the following tabs:

Tab	Description
Keyboard	Make the keyboard more tolerant and patient. Select Use StickyKeys if you need to press multiple keys simultaneously but are able to press keys only one at a time. Select Use FilterKeys to ignore short or repeated keystrokes. Select Use ToggleKeys to make a sound when you press Caps Lock, Num Lock, and Scroll Lock.
Sound	Provide visual warnings and captions for speech and sounds. Select Use SoundSentry to make Windows use a visual warning when a sound alert occurs. Select Use ShowSounds to display captions instead of speech or sounds.
Display	Select colors and fonts for easy reading. Select Use High Contrast to use color and font combinations that produce greater screen contrast.
Mouse	Control the pointer with the numeric keypad. Select Use MouseKeys to use the numeric keypad and other keys in place of the mouse. The relationship of keys to mouse controls appears in the table that follows.
General	Turn off accessibility features, give notification, and add an alternative input device. Use Automatic Reset to set Windows so accessibility features remain on at all times, are turned off when Windows restarts, or are turned off after a period of inactivity. Notification tells users when a feature is turned on or off. The SerialKey device enables Windows to receive keyboard or mouse input from alternative input devices through a serial port.

Some of these accessibility features could be difficult for a person with disabilities to turn on or off through normal Windows procedures. To alleviate this problem, Windows includes special *hotkeys*. Pressing the keys or key combinations for the designated hotkey turns an accessibility feature on or off, or changes its settings. The following table gives the hotkeys for different features.

Feature	Hotkey	Result
High-contrast mode	Left-Alt+left-Shift+ Print Screen pressed simultaneously	Alternates the screen through different text/ background combinations
StickyKeys	Press the Shift key five consecutive times	Turned on or off

(continues)

Feature	Hotkey	Result
FilterKeys	Hold down right Shift key for eight seconds	Turned on or off
ToggleKeys	Hold down NumLock key for five seconds	Turned on or off
MouseKeys	Press left-Alt+ left-Shift+NumLock simultaneously	Turned on or off

MouseKeys can be very useful for portable or laptop computer users and graphic artists as well as for people unable to use a mouse. Graphic artists will find MouseKeys useful because it enables them to produce finer movements than those done with a mouse. Once MouseKeys is turned on, you can produce the same effects as a mouse by using these keys:

Action	Press This Key(s)
Movement	Any number key except 5
Large moves	Hold down Ctrl as you press number keys
Single pixel moves	Hold down Shift as you press number keys
Single-click	5
Double-click	+
Begin drag	Insert (Ins)
Drop after drag	Delete (Del)
Select left mouse button	/
Select right mouse button	-
Select both mouse buttons	*

> **Caution**
>
> Use the numeric keypad with MouseKeys, not the numbered keys across the top of the keypad. Make sure the NumLock key is set so that the keypad is in numeric mode rather than cursor mode.

Setting the Date and Time

Use the Date/Time Properties sheet to change the date or time in your system (see fig. 5.27). You also can change the format of the date and time to match another country's standard.

▶ See "Using the Taskbar Clock," p. 406

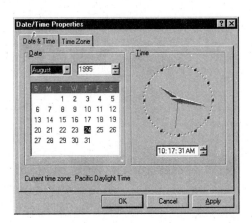

Fig. 5.27

You can change the system date and time at the Date/Time Properties sheet.

To change date and time properties, follow these steps.

1. Double-click the clock on the taskbar.

   or

   Open the Start menu and choose Settings, Control Panel; then double-click Date/Time.

   The Date/Time Properties sheet appears.

2. Click a tab and make the changes you want. See the following table for a description of things you can change.

3. Click Apply to accept the change and to continue making changes, or click OK to accept the change and close the Properties for Date/Time sheet.

Date and time options are grouped on two tabs—Date & Time and Time Zone. They are described in the following table.

Tip

To display the current date, point to the clock on the taskbar and the date will pop up.

Working with Windows 95

Tab	Description
Date & Time	To change the <u>D</u>ate, click the down arrow and select a month, or the up and down arrows to select a year. Click on the day of the month in the calendar to change the date.
	To change the time, click on the element you want to change in the digital time display. For example, to change hours, click on the first two numbers. Click the up and down arrows next to the time display.
Time Zone	Click the down arrow to select a new time zone (see fig. 5.28). Click the Automatically Adjust Clock for <u>D</u>aylight Savings Changes box to have the time automatically adjust for daylight savings time (a check indicates that it is on).

Fig. 5.28
You can change the time zone to reflect the time in any area of the world.

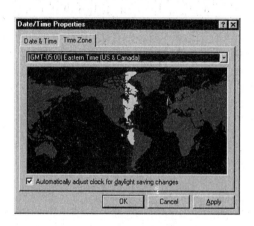

Customizing for Your Country and Language

Windows has the capacity to switch between different international character sets, time and date displays, and numeric formats. The international settings you choose in Control Panel affect applications, such as Microsoft Excel, that take advantage of these Windows features.

> **Note**
>
> Although you can change the language and country formats, doing so does not change the language used in menus or Help information. To obtain versions of Windows and Microsoft applications for countries other than the United States, check with your local Microsoft representative. Check with the corporate offices of other software vendors for international versions of their applications.

The Regional Settings Properties sheet (see fig. 5.29) provides five tabs. The region you select on the Regional Settings page will automatically affect the settings in the other pages.

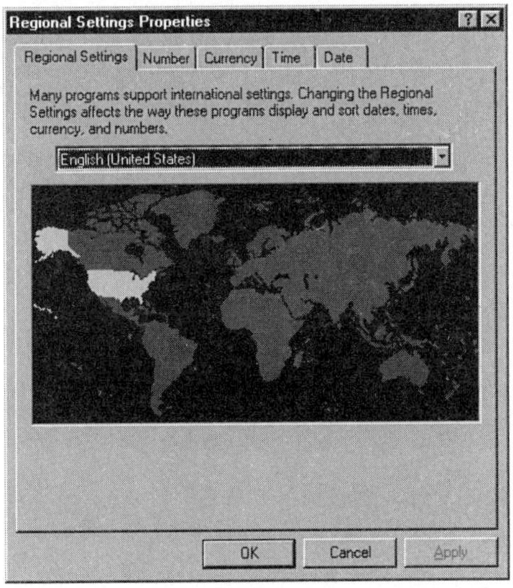

Fig. 5.29

You can change settings, such as number formats on the Number tab, to reflect any region of the world.

To change Regional Settings properties, follow these steps:

1. Open the Start menu and choose Settings, Control Panel; then double-click on Regional Settings. The Regional Settings Properties sheet appears (refer to fig. 5.29).

2. Click a tab and make the changes you want.

3. Click Apply to accept the changes and to continue making changes, or click OK to accept the change and close the Regional Settings Properties sheet.

Each Regional Setting page is described in the following table.

Tab	Description
Regional Settings	Click the down arrow and select your geographic region, or click your region on the global map. This selection automatically changes other settings in the sheet.
Number	To make a change to the format, click the down arrow next to the box you want to change and choose what you want, or click in the box and type what you want.

(continues)

Tab	Description
Currency	To make a change to the format, click the down arrow next to the box you want to change and choose what you want, or click in the box and type what you want. To select some currency symbols, you may have to select a different keyboard first. The No. of Digits After Decimal setting can be overridden by some applications, such as spreadsheets.
Time	Change the symbols, separator, and style of the time display. To make a change to the format, click the down arrow next to the box you want to change and choose what you want, or click in the box and type what you want.
Date	To make a change to the format, click the down arrow next to the box you want to change and choose what you want, or click in the box and type what you want.

Changing Custom Settings for Each User

Windows accomodates situations where people share a computer or move between computers. Windows enables you to store your custom settings for colors, accessibility features, and so on with your logon name. When you log on to the computer, Windows resets the computer with your settings.

User profiles are stored with your user logon ID. But you must tell Windows that you want to store user profiles for each different logon ID.

To create or remove a custom user profile for each logon ID, follow these steps:

1. Open the Start menu and choose Settings, Control Panel; then double-click Passwords.

2. Click the User Profiles tab to display the page shown in figure 5.30.

3. Select one of the following:

   ■ Select All Users of This PC if you want all users to use the same settings. Go to step 5.

   ■ Select Users Can Customize Their Preferences if you want Windows to use the customization setup during the last use of that logon ID.

4. If you make the second selection in step 3, you can choose from the following:

- Select Include Desktop Icons and Network Neighborhood Contents in User Settings if the user profile should remember changes to these items.

- Select Include Start Menu and Program Groups in User Settings if the user profile should remember changes to these items.

5. Click OK.

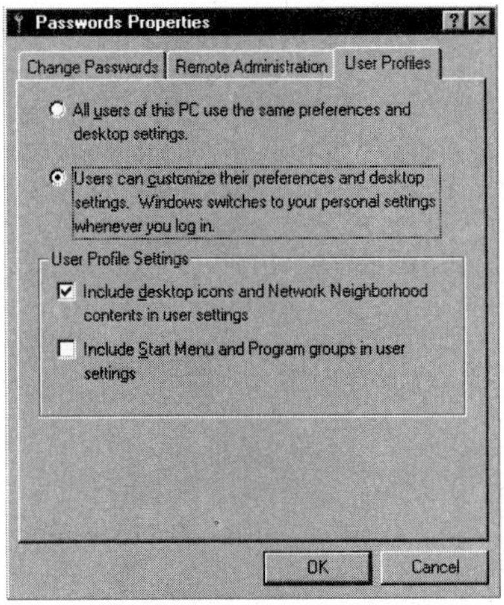

Fig. 5.30
You can customize the size of screen fonts.

When you are done with a Windows computer shared by multiple users, log off the computer so that others can log on and use their custom user profiles. To log off, click the Start button, click Shut Down, then click the option Close All Programs and Log On as a Different User. Choose OK.

If you made the selection Users Can Customize Their Preferences, then whenever a person logs on to Windows and customizes settings, those settings are saved with that logon ID. The next time someone logs on with that logon ID, Windows changes to the settings for that ID.

Preventing Others from Using Windows

You may work in an area where you need to keep your computer secure. For example, your work may involve financial, market, or personnel data that is confidential. One way you can help to protect this information is to require a password before Windows will start.

▶ See "Securing Your Network Resources," p. 640

To change or create your Windows password, follow these steps:

1. Open the Passwords Properties sheet as described in the previous section.

2. Click the Change Passwords tab, then click the Change Windows Password button to display the Change Windows Password dialog box.

   If you have network passwords, they will be listed so that you can change them to match your Windows password.

3. Type your old password in the Old Password box.

4. Type your new password in the New Password and Confirm Password boxes.

5. Choose OK, then OK again.

Windows provides security for the network environment from the other pages on the Password Properties.

Reviewing Your Computer's System Information

One of the more gruesome aspects of using DOS or earlier versions of Windows was working with configuration files whenever you wanted to customize or optimize your computer. People who wanted to install sound cards or network adapters, change memory usage, or specify I/O (Input/Output) or IRQ (interrupt request) settings faced immersion in the arcane world of configuration files. Configuration files gave you no help; yet if you made an error, part of your hardware might not be recognized, your system might run slower, or it might not run at all.

Windows 95 makes specifying configurations easier. Now you can select only allowable options from straightforward dialog boxes, and you can see settings from other hardware devices that might cause conflicts.

Reading Your Registration and Version Number

You can see your registration number, the version number of Windows, and the type of processor on which Windows is running on the General page of the System Properties sheet. To see this page, follow these steps:

1. Open the Start menu; then choose Settings, Control Panel to display the Control Panel window.

2. Double-click on the System icon.

3. Click the General tab of the System Properties sheet as shown in figure 5.31.

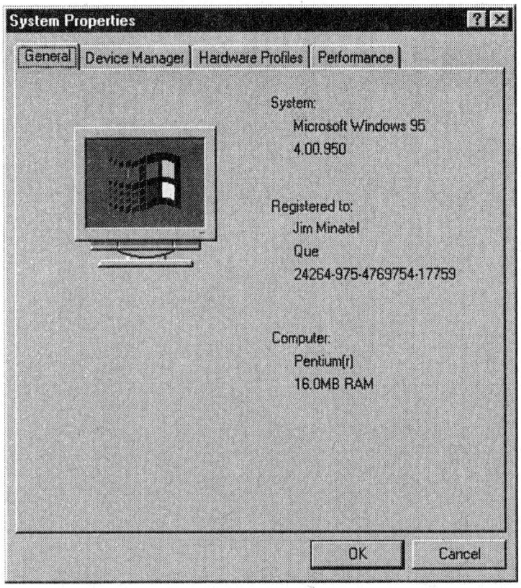

Fig. 5.31

View your registration number and Windows' version number on the System Properties General page.

Examine the Hardware on Your Computer

You may need to examine the configuration settings and drivers for hardware connected to your computer. You also can use the System Properties sheet to help you troubleshoot hardware. If you need to see a list of IRQ and I/O settings, you need to use the Device Manager.

To display the Device Manager page, follow these steps:

1. Open the Start menu; then choose Settings, Control Panel to display the Control Panel window.

2. Double-click on the System icon.

3. Click the Device Manager tab of the System Properties sheet (see fig. 5.32).

4. To see the drivers installed for a device, click on the + sign to the left of the device. To see information about a device or to remove the device, select one of the following buttons:

▶ See "Installing Plug and Play Hardware," p. 246

▶ See "Installing Legacy Cards after Setting Up Drivers," p. 255

▶ See "Installing Plug and Play CD-ROM Drives," p. 975

▶ See "Installation of Full-Motion Video Device Drivers," p. 1012

II

Working with Windows 95

Button	Action
Properties	Displays a listing of properties appropriate to the device. Select the Computer item to see IRQ and I/O settings.
Refresh	Windows reexamines the installed hardware and attempts to update the list.
Remove	Removes the selected device or driver.
Print	Prints a report of configuration settings.

    5. Choose OK.

Fig. 5.32

View the hardware devices and their drivers on the System Properties Device Manager page.

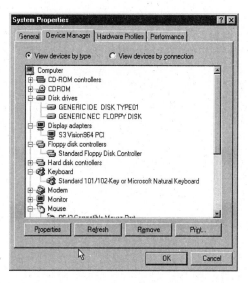

Checking IRQ, I/O, DMA, and Memory Settings

▶ See "Installing a Plug and Play Modem," p. 833

▶ See "Configuring Your Modem," p. 843

Hardware devices each require a unique section of memory (I/O address). Some hardware devices also require an interrupt request (IRQ) or direct memory access (DMA) to operate. If any of these settings conflicts with the settings for another device, either or both of the devices may not work.

You can see a list of these settings in your computer by selecting the Computer icon on the Device Manager page of the System Properties sheet and then clicking Properties. Select from the option buttons to display the list of settings you want to see. Figure 5.33 shows the list of IRQ settings.

In MS-DOS and in prior versions of Windows, it was difficult to tell the cause of conflicts between hardware devices. In many cases, all that you knew was that something didn't work. The exact cause was often a mystery to the novice. Even for an experienced hardware specialist, resolving such problems often took considerable trial and error and required a lot of time reading manuals. Now the Device Manager shows you lists of IRQ and I/O settings. You can scan through the lists and see where you have accidentally installed two device drivers for the same device or you have set two different devices to the same or overlapping IRQ or I/O settings.

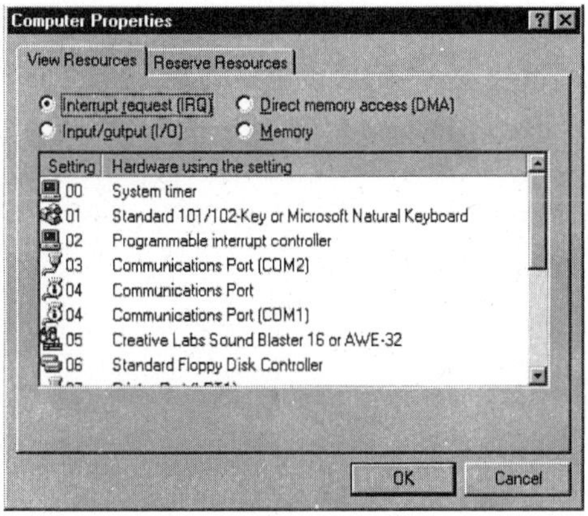

Fig. 5.33
Use the View Resources page to track down conflicts in IRQ and I/O settings.

If you find you have installed two drivers for the same device, you can delete one of them. If you find a conflict because two hardware devices are using the same memory or IRQ settings, you can resolve the conflict easily through the Device Manager. The approach you might take to resolve a conflict is to look through the lists in the Device Manager to find an open IRQ or I/O setting, check the two manuals for the particular devices to determine what other IRQ or I/O settings they will work with, and then change the settings for one of the devices so that it doesn't conflict.

Troubleshooting

One of the hardware devices on a computer is not working.

Click the Device Manager tab on the System Properties sheet and check for an X through a device. This means the hardware has been disabled. Double-click on that device to check its settings. If a device icon has a circled exclamation point, the hardware has problem. Double-click the icon to inspect the type of problem.

It took a couple different attempts with different driver selections before some of the hardware would work. Now some of the devices on the system work slowly, intermittently, or incorrectly.

(continues)

II

Working with Windows 95

(continued)

Check the Device Manager page of the System Properties sheet to see if you have multiple drivers installed for the same hardware device. Delete all the drivers except the driver for your specific manufacturer and model. If there are multiple drivers, but not one specific to your hardware device, keep the generic driver.

The computer works with either a sound card or a network adapter card, but not both.

The usual cause of this problem is a conflict between IRQ ports and I/O addresses. Each hardware device must have its own IRQ port and its own I/O address. Sound cards and network adapters are notorious for conflicting with each other over these. To see the IRQ port and I/O address used by each device, display the Device Manager page, select the Computer icon, and choose Properties. On the View Resources page that appears, you can select the Interrupt Request (IRQ) or Input/Output (I/O) option to view a list of settings for each device on your computer. Write down the current settings and watch for conflicts. Then change the settings for devices that conflict with others.

Creating, Naming, and Copying Hardware Profiles

▶ See "Using Your Laptop with a Docking System," p. 273

Hardware profiles are collections of hardware settings. Hardware profiles are useful if you use different collections of hardware on your computer. For example, you might have a laptop computer that uses a VGA LCD monitor on the road, but uses an SVGA large-screen monitor on the desktop. If you have an older laptop that cannot detect when PC Cards are inserted or removed or cards that cannot be "hot-swapped" (inserted or removed while the machine is on), you also may find a need to set up hardware profiles.

By saving a collection of hardware settings as a profile, you only need to choose the profile you want rather than manually change hardware settings whenever you want to run a different combination of hardware.

When you start a Windows 95 computer that has multiple hardware configurations, you have the option of choosing the named hardware profile you want to use. From a text screen in Startup, you see something similar to this:

```
Windows cannot determine what configuration your computer is in.
Select one of the following:

1. Original Configuration
2. Multimedia
3. Desktop
4. None of the above

Enter your choice:
```

Type the number of the profile you want to use and press Enter. Windows 95 then starts with that configuration of hardware, only loading the hardware drivers required.

In order to make use of the distinct hardware profiles, you must first copy the existing default profile. The default profile is named Original Configuration. After you have copied a profile, you can then edit the devices included in it and rename it to help you recognize it. To copy or rename a hardware profile, follow these steps:

1. Open the Start menu; then choose Settings, Control Panel to display the Control Panel window.

2. Double-click on the System icon.

3. Click the Hardware Profile tab of the System Properties sheet (see fig. 5.34).

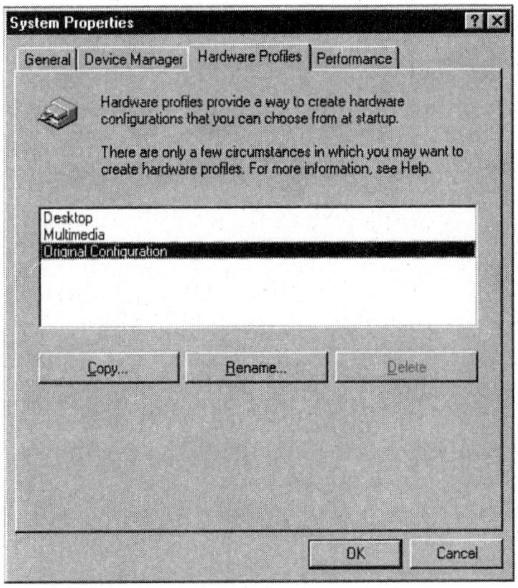

II

Fig. 5.34
Keep different combinations of hardware devices stored as a named hardware profile.

Working with Windows 95

4. Select the hardware profile you want to work with and then click one of the following buttons:

Button	Action
Copy	Displays a Copy Profile dialog box in which you can enter a new name. Copies the hardware configuration from the selected profile to this new profile.
Rename	Changes the name of a profile.
Delete	Deletes a profile.

5. Choose OK.

To create a new profile or change an existing profile, follow these steps:

1. If you want to create a new profile, copy an existing profile as described in the preceding series of steps. Use a unique, descriptive name for the profile.

2. Click the Device Manager tab on the System Properties sheet.

3. Click the plus sign next to the hardware type you want to change for the configuration; then double-click the specific hardware you want to change. This displays the device's Properties sheet.

4. In the Device Usage area of the Properties sheet, deselect any hardware profile that you don't want to use this device with. By default, all of your devices will be used with all of your profiles until you make changes.

5. Choose OK.

6. Repeat steps 3–5 until you have configured all the hardware for this profile.

7. Choose OK.

Depending on the changes you made, you may be prompted to restart your computer.

Checking Performance Settings

▶ See "Improving Performance with Disk Defragmenter," p. 486

You can check the performance parameters of your computer on the Performance page of the System Properties. To see this page, follow these steps:

1. Open the Start menu; then choose Settings, Control Panel to display the Control Panel window.

2. Double-click on the System icon.

3. Click the Performance tab of the System Properties sheet as shown in figure 5.35.

4. View the performance status parameters on the Performance page, or choose File System, Graphics, or Virtual Memory for advanced performance tuning options.

5. Choose OK.

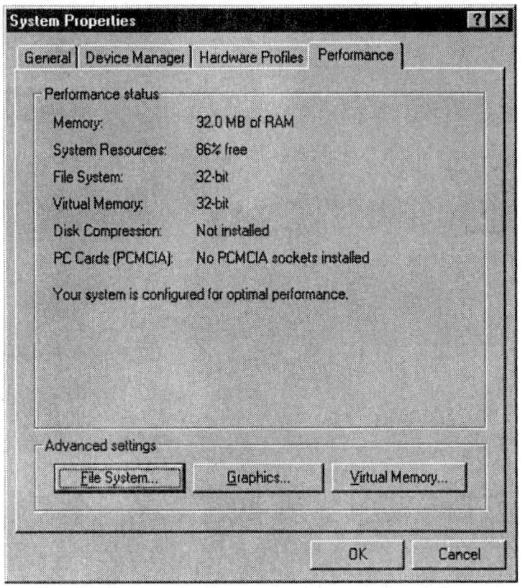

Fig. 5.35
The System
Properties Perfor-
mance page
provides informa-
tion on your
computer's
performance
parameters.

Caution

In general, do not change the settings available on the Performance page. Windows 95 usually sets these parameters optimally.

Chapter 6

Controlling Printers

by William S. Holderby

Microsoft has packed a great deal of its past experience into the features of the Windows 95 printing system.

To appreciate Windows 95 printing, you should take a brief look at the new feature changes Microsoft has made to create faster printing while producing a higher quality output. Although some changes, at first glance, appear to be ho-hum, don't be fooled. Windows 95's new print model is both faster than its predecessors and designed with the user in mind.

In this chapter, we discuss each of the new printing features and how they work in concert to produce a quality print job.

Windows 95 new printing features:

- *Rapid return from printing* is enabled by the 32-bit printer drivers, preemptive spooler, and enhanced meta file spooling.

- *Deferred Printing* enables you to configure your PC to conveniently print to a file when you are on the road or away from your printer. Once the printer has been reattached, simply release the print files to the appropriate printer.

- *Bi-directional printer communications* sends print files to your printer and listens for a response. Windows can quickly identify a printer that cannot accept a print file.

- *Plug and Play* supports the addition of new printers by quickly identifying the brand and model of a printer and assisting you in configuring the appropriate drivers for that printer.

- *Extended capability port support* enables Windows 95 to use the latest in high-speed parallel-port technology to connect your printer.

You learn, in this chapter, how to use Windows 95 printing. This chapter introduces you to each of the new printing features, describes the options, and explains how to create a quality print job. Specifically, you learn how to

- Print from Windows applications

- Print a document from the desktop

- Install, delete, and configure printers

- Understand special printing issues related to printing from MS-DOS applications

- Work with special printing features for laptop and docking station users

- Solve common printing problems

Printing from Applications

When you print from an application under Windows 95, you use the same commands and techniques available under previous versions of Windows; however, there have been changes. You find that application printing now takes less time, the operating system releases your resources quicker, and the color/gray scale found in the printer output is substantially more consistent and accurate. However, many details of the printing architecture are transparent to application users.

Basic Windows 95 Printing Procedure

▶ See "Printing a Document," p. 371

▶ See "Printing a Painting," p. 400

Depending on the application from which you are printing, you may have some slightly different printing options. In this section, we look at the printing options available to all applications written for the Windows 95 operating system. The two most common Windows 95 applications are WordPad and Paint, included with Windows 95. The options you see in these applications are the same as the options in many Windows 95 applications.

To print from an application, perform the following steps:

1. Load the file to be printed.

2. Initiate the printing command. In most Windows applications, do this by choosing File, Print. Figure 6.1 shows a typical Print dialog box. The controls in this dialog box let you specify the portion of the file to be printed and the printer designated to complete the job.

Note

Most Windows applications that have toolbars also have a button for printing (similar to the one shown here). In some applications (such as Word, Excel, and other MS Office applications), clicking the Print button immediately prints the document using the current print settings—there are no dialog boxes to go through. Other applications open the Print dialog box shown in figure 6.1 after you click the Print button.

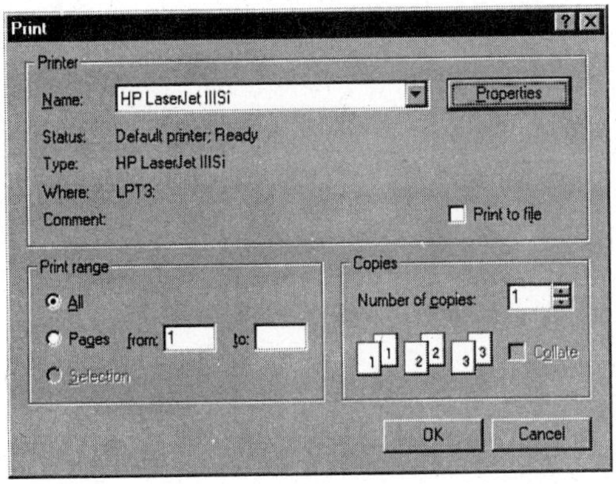

Fig. 6.1
A typical application's Print dialog box lets you send a print job to a specific printer.

3. Determine whether the printer shown in the Name box is the printer you want to use for this document. If it is not the desired printer, click the drop-down arrow for this box and select the desired printer.

4. Specify the number of copies you want to print by clicking the up and down arrows on the Number of Copies control. You may also select the default setting and type a number to replace the default number 1.

5. By default, most applications choose All as the print range. If you want to print something other than the entire document, you must define the print range. To do this, choose one of the three radio buttons in the Print Range box:

   ■ *All*. Prints all pages contained within the document.

   ■ *Selection*. Prints only those portions of the document you have selected using the selection features of the application.

▶ See "Selecting and Editing Text," p. 363

II

Working with Windows 95

Tip
Some applications allow more complicated ranges to be specified. See "Applications with Special Print Options," later in this chapter.

Tip
The sheets-of-paper icon next to the collate option show whether or not the print job will be collated.

▶ See "The Print Manager," p. 173

> **Note**
>
> The Selection option is not available in all applications. In applications that do have this option, it is available only when part of the document has been selected.

■ *Pages.* Prints the page range you specify in the boxes located to the right of the radio button. Specify a beginning page in the From box and an ending page in the To box.

6. If you are printing more than one copy of the document, you can have the copies collated (each copy of the multipage document is printed completely before the next copy of the document). To collate copies, select the Collate check box. If you don't select this option, all the copies of each page are printed together (for example, four copies of page 1 are printed and then four copies of page 2). The Collate option is not available in all applications.

7. To output the printer information to a print file, select the Print to File check box. Windows 95 prompts you for a file name and directs the print output to the specified file, rather than to a printer. Print files also are used for transferring data between applications with dissimilar file formats.

8. To initiate the links between your application and the Windows print drivers, click OK. Your application should now begin printing the specified document.

If you change your mind and don't want to print, click Cancel to return to the document without making any changes or starting the print job.

> **Note**
>
> If you plan to print to a file frequently, set up a bogus printer. Use the Add Printer Wizard in the Printers folder to install a new printer; accept the current driver if you already have a printer installed or add the driver if you don't have one installed. Follow the preceding procedures to direct this printer's output to a file. When you're ready to print from the application, choose File, Print Setup (Windows 3.x applications) or use Name drop-down list in the Print dialog box (Windows 95 applications) to select the bogus printer and print.

This basic printing procedure applies to most applications, even if their Print dialog boxes are slightly different than the one shown in figure 6.1. Some applications have additional options, as discussed in the next two sections.

Applications with Special Print Options

Some applications take the basic printing features in Windows 95 and add a few features of their own. This section looks at some of the additional features you may find in other programs, with Word 95 as an example. Although these features vary from application to application, this section should give you an idea of what to look for.

Figure 6.2 shows the Word 95 Print dialog box.

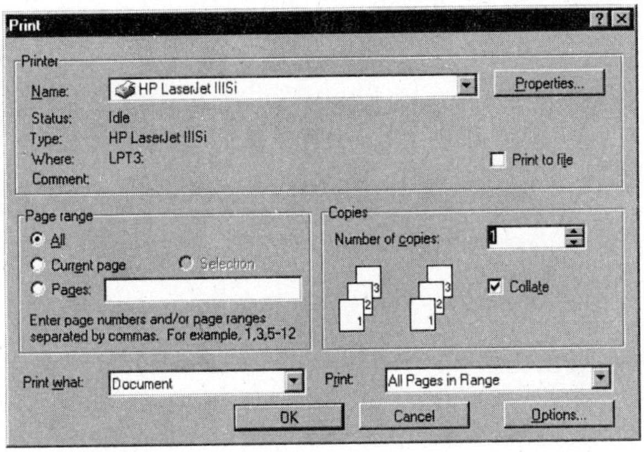

Fig. 6.2
The Print dialog box in Word 95 includes several enhancements not found in the standard Windows 95 Print dialog box.

Here is a quick summary of some of the additional (and different) options provided by this application compared to the standard Windows 95 printing options:

- The Current Page option in the Page Range section. When this option is selected, Word prints the page in which the insertion point is currently located.

- An enhanced Pages option. This enhanced option allows you to specify a page range in the variable box located to the right of the Pages label. The range can be individual pages separated by a comma, a page range separated by a hyphen, or both: for example, 1,2,4-8,10. In this example, pages 1, 2, 4, 5, 6, 7, 8, and 10 are printed.

II

Working with Windows 95

- The Print <u>W</u>hat drop-down list. In Word, you can select to print the document itself or other information such as summary information, annotations, and styles.

- The P<u>r</u>int option. From this drop-down list, you select to print odd, even, or all pages in the range.

- The <u>O</u>ptions button. When you click this button, Word displays the Options dialog box, opened to the Print tab. Use this dialog box to set printing options specific to Word.

> **Note**
>
> For a more complete discussion of Word's printing features, see Que's *Special Edition Using Word for Windows 95.*

Keep in mind that the options described here are not the same in all applications.

Windows 3.1 Applications with Special Print Options

The other common type of Print dialog box you may encounter is from a Windows 3.1 application that has a customized dialog box, such as the one for Word 6 shown in figure 6.3.

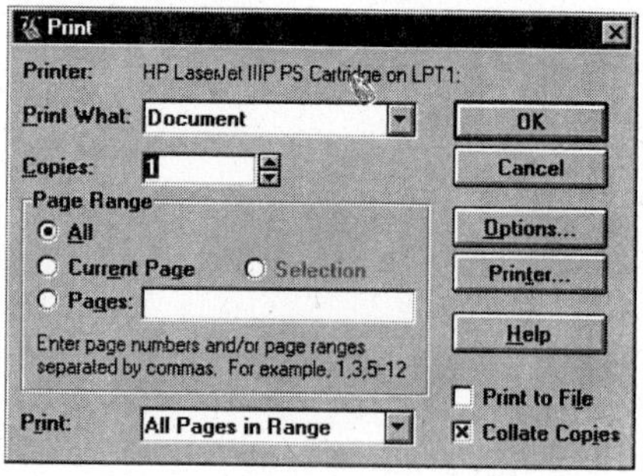

Fig. 6.3

The Word 6 dialog box is still styled like a Windows 3.1 dialog box.

Most options in this dialog box are the same as those shown in figures 6.1 and 6.2. However, there are some differences:

■ There is no status entry or comment field that describes the printer's current activity.

■ You select a different printer by clicking the Printer button and selecting from a dialog box instead of choosing a printer from a drop-down list.

▶ See "Options for Your Printer," p. 187

■ There is no Properties button.

As with the other printing options discussed in this chapter, the options displayed in the Print dialog box vary from application to application.

Managing Print Jobs

Like Windows 3.1, Windows 95 offers the option of printing directly to the configured port or using its 32-bit Print Manager. For most applications, the Print Manager provides facilities to better manage the printing of documents.

Tip
If you have a shortcut to your printer on your desktop, you can open its window by double-clicking the shortcut icon. To create a short-cut for your printer, see " Create a Desktop Printer Icon," later in this chapter.

The Print Manager

To start the Print Manager, open the Start menu and choose Settings, Printers; then double-click the icon for the printer you want to manage in the Printers window (see fig. 6.4). Depending on the printers you have installed, your window will differ from the one shown in the figure.

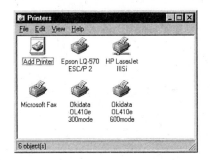

Fig. 6.4
The Printer control panel has icons for each of your installed printers as well as the icon to add a new printer.

Unlike Windows 3.1, Windows 95 uses a separate Print Manager for each printer. Therefore, make certain that you choose the correct Print Manager to view the status of your print jobs.

The Print Manager shown in figure 6.5 displays the current printer status for each print job.

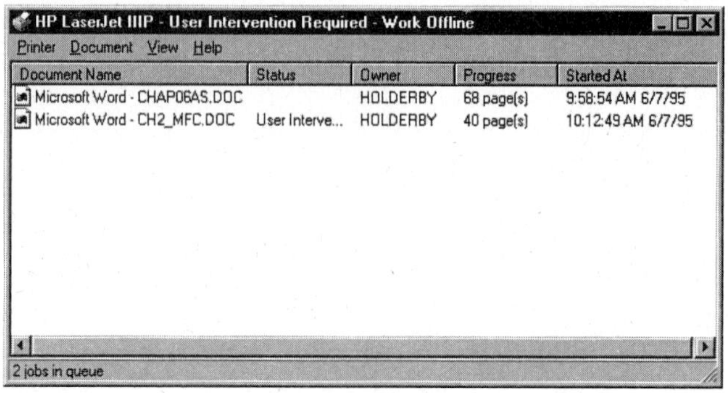

Fig. 6.5
Each printer has
its own Print
Manager; make
sure that you
select from the
Printer control
panel the correct
printer for the
print jobs you
want to check.

The printer status includes the following information:

- The Document Name section shows the name of each application that has submitted a print job as well as the name of each document job in the print queue.

▶ See "Managing Print Files and Sharing," p. 784

- The Status column describes the current condition of each print job, such as paused or spooling.

- The user's name associated with each document. A print job on your printer may belong to someone else when you share your printer.

Tip

By default, print jobs are listed in the order they entered the queue. You can sort them according to name, status, owner, progress, or start time by clicking the appropriate column heading.

- The relative progress of each job in the print queue. The progress of each job monitors the printing of each document and provides information concerning the number of pages printed and the number of pages left to print.

- The time and date when each print job was submitted to the print queue. This is important for those users with deferred print jobs.

Controlling Printing

The Print Manager coordinates and schedules the printing of files received from your applications. These applications may be Windows based or MS-DOS based.

The Print Manager pull-down menus provide you with the following capabilities, all of which are described in the next several sections:

- Pause Printing

- Purge Printing

- Work Off-Line

- Set Printer as Default

- Change a Printer's Properties

- Pause a Selected Document's Printing

- Cancel a Selected Document's Printing

- View the Status Bar

- Access Windows Help

Note

If you are using a network printer, you can cancel only your own print jobs. You cannot pause printing, even of your own documents. Canceling someone else's print jobs or pausing printing requires network supervisor rights.

▶ See "Managing Print Files and Sharing," p. 784

Pausing Printing

Pausing a printer temporarily stops print jobs from being sent to that printer. Once a paused printer is restarted all pending print jobs are started and sequentially sent to the printer. This feature is useful when changing toner or performing printer maintenance.

To pause printing, choose Printer, Pause Printing. The Print jobs are paused and the Print Manager's title bar displays `Paused`.

To restart printing, choose Printer, Pause Printing again, which is now prefaced by a check mark. The Pause Printing check mark disappears and printing resumes.

Purging Print Jobs

The Purge Print Jobs command permanently removes all queued print jobs. Choose Printer, Purge Print Jobs. The documents listed by the Print Manager disappear.

Troubleshooting

The printer has started my print job and the Purge Print Jobs command won't stop it.

Purging print jobs stops Windows 95 from sending print jobs to the printer. However, it does not purge the print jobs currently being processed by the printer. You may have to reset the printer to terminate unwanted printing.

▶ See "Using
Your Laptop
with a Docking
System," p. 273

▶ See "Under-
standing Net-
work Printing,"
p. 772

▶ See "Configura-
tion of the EMF
Print Spooler,"
p. 194

Working Off-Line

Windows 95 enables you to initiate a print job without being physically attached to a printer. This feature is known as Deferred Printing, or Working
Offline. Deferred Printing is available for network printers and laptop users
with docking stations. Deferred Printing tracks deferred print jobs and releases them under configuration control when the computer is connected to
the printer locally, networked or attached through a docking station.

> **Note**
>
> The spooler must be turned on for you to use Deferred Printing.

To configure a printer to work offline, choose Printer, Work Off-Line. A check
mark appears in front of the Work Off-Line command. The Printer is now
configured to work offline and defer printouts. The Print Manager changes its
title to read *<printer name>* User Intervention Required. This information is
then placed in the status line of each print job being sent to this printer.
The Print manager defers printouts until you change the status of the Work
Off-Line flag.

To change the status of the Work Off-Line flag, choose Work Off-Line a second time. The check mark disappears and the deferred printouts are sent to
the printer.

The taskbar normally displays a clock at the lower right of the screen. This
box also displays a printer when a document is being printed. If deferred
documents are pending, the icon changes to include a question mark circled
in red as shown in figure 6.6.

Fig. 6.6
When deferred
printouts are
stored, the taskbar
displays the
Printer icon with a
question mark to
remind you to
release the jobs
to the printer.

To print documents that have been deferred, follow these steps:

1. Physically connect the target printer to the system by putting the
   laptop in the docking station or connecting to the network printer.

2. From the Print Manager window, choose Printer. Then choose the
   Work Off-Line option to remove its check mark.

3. Verify that printing begins immediately to the target printer and that
   the deferred print jobs are no longer displayed by the Print Manager.

Setting a Default Printer

If you have more than one printer available (either locally or on a network), you should choose which printer you want to use as the default. The default printer is used by all applications unless you choose another printer from within the application.

To set a printer as the default, start that printer's Print Manager and then choose Printer, Set as Default. A check mark appears next to the Set as Default command on the pull-down menu, signifying that this printer is now the Windows default printer.

To remove the printer as the system default, select the Printer, Set as Default command from the Print Manager of another printer. Windows allows only one default printer.

Pausing a Document

You can pause a document if the Print Manager has not started sending it to the printer, or if the printer is local. You cannot pause a document that Print Manager has already started sending to a network printer. Pausing a document that has already been sent to a local printer prevents any other documents from being printed. If Print Manager has not yet started sending a document, pausing that document places it "on hold," while other documents continue to print.

To pause a document, choose one or more documents from the list of documents in the print queue. (Choosing a document highlights the document's entry in the Print Manager.) Choose Document, Pause. The selected documents now display a Paused status.

To release a paused document, choose the paused documents from the list of documents in the print queue. Choose Document, Pause. The selected documents no longer display a Paused status.

Canceling a Document from Printing

You also can permanently remove selected documents from the list of documents being printed. To cancel documents, choose one or more documents from the documents in the print queue; then choose Document, Cancel.

> **Caution**
>
> Once you cancel a document, Windows immediately removes that document from the print queue. You do not receive a confirmation prompt. You might try Pause first and make certain that you want this document's printout terminated.

Turning the Status Bar Off and On

The status bar lists the status of the print queue and contains the number of print jobs remaining to be printed. To turn off the display of the status bar, choose View, Status Bar. Repeat this action to turn the status bar display back on. The Status Bar option is a standard Windows toggle control: if the option is not preceded by a check mark, the status bar is not visible.

Closing Print Manager

To close the Print Manager, choose Printer, Close; or click the Close button.

> **Note**
>
> Closing the Print Manager in Windows 95 does not purge the associated print jobs (unlike Windows 3.1). Printing continues based on the print Manager's settings.

To rearrange the print queue, select a document, drag it to the correct queue position, and drop it. Dragging-and-dropping a document in the print queue works only with documents that are not currently being printed.

Drag-and-Drop Printing from the Desktop

Tip
Make sure that the document is associated with an application that is available to Windows, or your printing will terminate.

A new feature of the Windows 95 operating system is the ability to print a document without first initiating the associated application or the File Manager. Using desktop icons, you can quickly launch print jobs from the desktop.

In earlier versions of Windows, printing used a four-step operation: open an application, load a file, initiate printing, and finally shut down the application after printing. Windows 95 uses a two-step printing procedure that is quick and convenient. However, before you can print from the desktop, you must take certain steps to set up your system.

Create a Desktop Printer Icon

◀ See "Starting Programs from a Shortcut Icon on the Desktop," p. 68

Before you can drag-and-drop documents to desktop icons, you must first create the icons. Although some icons are automatically created during Windows setup, printer icons are not.

To create a shortcut icon for a printer, follow these steps:

1. Open the Start menu, choose Settings, and then choose Printers. You also can open the Printers folder by double-clicking the Printers icon in the Control Panel window. The Printer's folder is now open.

2. Select the desired printer, drag it onto the desktop, and release it.

3. Windows displays a question window that asks permission to create a shortcut (see fig. 6.7). Answer Y̲es; the shortcut icon is created.

After you have created the shortcut to the printer, you can modify it by creating a shortcut key or changing the icon. Modifying shortcuts is discussed in Chapter 3, "Getting Started with Windows 95."

◀ See "Modifying and Deleting Shortcuts," p. 72

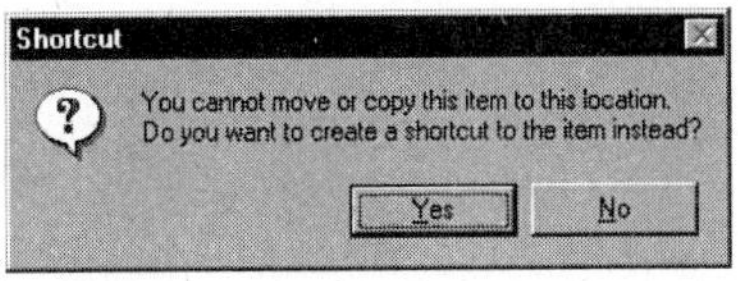

Fig. 6.7
A Windows question window asks your permission to create a shortcut.

Print from the Desktop

Once you have created a shortcut icon on the desktop for your printer, you can print any document from the desktop. To print from the desktop, follow these steps:

1. Open any folder (either in My Computer or Windows Explorer) that contains a printable document.

2. Select that document using the left mouse button.

3. While holding down the left mouse button, drag the document's icon from its folder to a printer desktop icon. Don't worry: this action makes no changes to the file.

4. When the document icon is on top of the printer desktop icon, release the mouse button.

▶ See "Selecting Files and Folders," p. 513

▶ See "Using My Computer to Manage Files," p. 551

Windows starts the associated application configured to handle that file type. Windows executes that application's print command. Once the printing has been committed to the background print spooler, Windows releases the associated application, closes it, and background prints the spooled files.

Why all the fuss about such a simple control function? Consider the time it saves you: If you have to print documents quickly, simply point, click, and drag the document to the printer; then you can go back to your other applications. Windows delivers hard copy with minimum effort.

Desktop Printing of Multiple Documents

Using Windows, you can print several files at once by dragging them to the shortcut icon on the desktop. Follow these steps to print several files at once:

II

Working with Windows 95

Tip
You can select
and print mul-
tiple docu-
ments created
using different
applications.

1. Select several documents to print by dragging around them or by hold-ing down the Ctrl key and clicking the documents.

2. Drag the selected documents to the desktop printer icon.

3. Drop the documents on the icon.

4. The message window shown in figure 6.8 appears. Select Yes to print. Select No only if you want to stop all documents from printing.

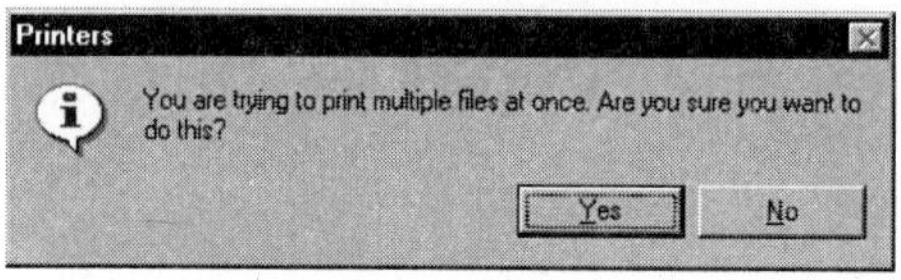

Fig. 6.8
A message window
asks permission to
print the multiple
documents.

Windows starts each of the applications associated with the selected docu-ments and begins printing.

Installing and Deleting Printers

Before you can take advantage of Windows' newest printing features, you must first install a printer. The printer installation process depends largely on the make and model of the printer you have. The next sections describe how to fully install a printer—with an emphasis on the specific areas in which you can expect to find printer differences. The following sections use as an ex-ample printer the HP LaserJet 4.

Installing a New Printer

Before you install a printer, you should know the following information:

- Review your printer to find the make and model (for example, Hewlett-Packard IIIP).

- Refer to the printer manual or print a test page using the printer's test feature to find the amount of RAM contained in your printer (for ex-ample, 2M).

- Identify the type of communications interface required to connect your printer to the computer (for example, serial, parallel, or a special interface).

- Identify any special features or functions supported by your printer, such as PostScript compatibility. Some printers are multimode and may require installation as two separate printers (for example, the HP LaserJet IV with PostScript option).

■ Find the location of a suitable port on your PC to connect your printer. The selected port must correspond to the same port type as required by your printer (that is, serial to serial, parallel to parallel).

This information is required by the Windows printer installation wizard later in the installation process.

Installing a Printer with the Printer Wizard

Microsoft Office's suite of desktop applications pioneered the use of wizards to step a user through an often complex series of operations. The Windows 95 print architecture incorporates a printer installation wizard to step you through the labor-intensive chore of installing a printer.

A quick explanation of the use of the Wizard buttons is in order. The Back button steps you back one Wizard screen every time you click it. The Next button steps you forward one Wizard screen. The Cancel button halts the entire Wizard process and discards all inputs made during this Wizard session. Use these buttons to back up and make changes if later configurations prove to be incorrect.

1. Open the Windows 95 Start menu and choose Settings, Printers. If the control panel is open, double-click the Printer folder. The Printers window appears (see fig. 6.9), showing each installed printer as an icon. Don't worry if you have no installed printers yet: the window also includes the Add New Printer icon. The program associated with the Add New Printer icon is the Add Printer Wizard. You use the Printers window often because it is useful in managing your printers.

Fig. 6.9
Starting a printer installation by opening the Printers window.

2. Double-click the Add New Printer icon to start the Add Printer Wizard. Windows displays the initial Wizard screen.

3. Choose Next. Windows displays the Add Printer Wizard screen shown in figure 6.10.

II

Working with Windows 95

Fig. 6.10
The Add Printer Wizard steps you through the printer installation procedure by first asking whether you are installing a local or network printer.

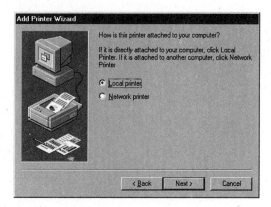

▶ See "Installing a Network Printer," p. 774

4. Choose the <u>L</u>ocal Printer option to install a printer attached directly to your PC. Choose Next. The screen shown in figure 6.11 appears.

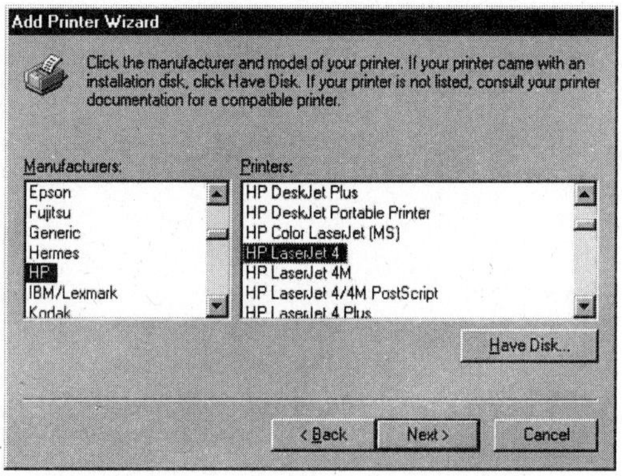

Fig. 6.11
Select the make and model of the printer you are installing from the lists provided.

5. Locate the make and model of your printer by scrolling through the Wizard's screen lists. Windows 95 has drivers that support over 300 printers. When you have selected the appropriate options, choose Next to display the screen shown in figure 6.12.

If you're adding a printer after initial installation, you need the Windows 95 installation disks or CD available. Windows will ask for these if it does not have an existing driver available. You may also use a manufacturer's disk to install custom printer drivers.

Scroll the screen on the far left to identify your printer's manufacturer. Then select the appropriate printer model. If your printer is not on the list, you can install your printer by choosing either the generic printer or the Have <u>D</u>isk button. If your printer came with its own software driver, insert the floppy disk from your printer manufacturer into either

Tip
Many laser printers are Hewlett-Packard compatible and dot-matrix printers are Epson compatible. If you can't get a driver or the generic driver doesn't work well, try one of the commonly emulated printers.

drive A or B and choose the Have Disk button to complete the requirements of this screen.

Note

If your printer is not listed, you should contact your printer manufacturer for an updated driver. Choose a generic printer until you can obtain an updated driver version.

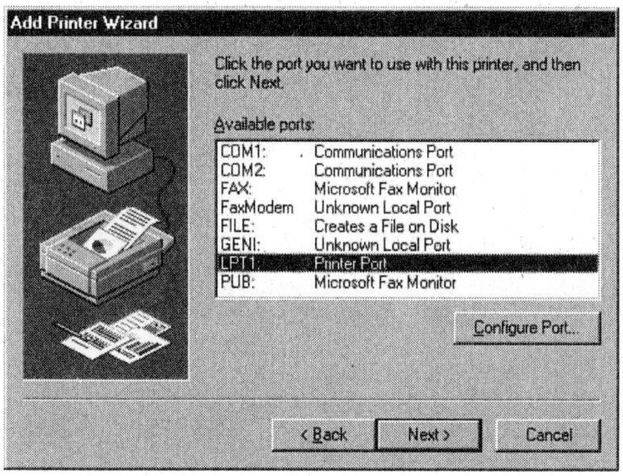

Fig. 6.12
Selecting the printer port to which you want to attach the printer.

6. Provide the printer port information. The Wizard screen shown in figure 6.12 displays ports based on the survey Windows did of your PC hardware. You may have several COM and LPT ports. Refer to the list of information you compiled before you started the installation and choose the port to which you want to attach the printer. The port selected in figure 6.12 is LPT1, a very typical selection.

7. Choose the Configure Port button. The Wizard displays the Configure Port window (see fig. 6.13). The window contains a check box that enables Windows 95 to spool your MS-DOS print jobs. This box should always be checked to enable MS-DOS printing, unless your MS-DOS applications prove to be incompatible with Windows 95 printing. Enable the Check Port State before Printing check box if you want Windows 95 to determine if the printer port is available prior to starting the print job.

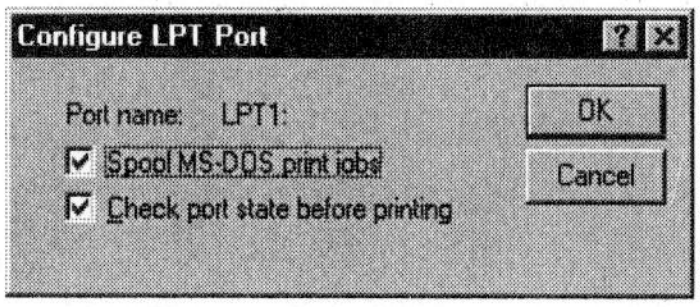

Fig. 6.13
Configuring your parallel printer port enables MS-DOS applications to use the same driver.

8. After you configure the port, choose OK and then Next to display the dialog box shown in figure 6.14. Use this dialog box to name the new printer and define it as your default printer if desired. In the Printer Name field, type the name of the printer. The name can be up to 128 characters long and can contain spaces and nonalphanumeric symbols. The printer's name should include location or ownership.

Fig. 6.14

The printer name and default status are specified using this Wizard screen.

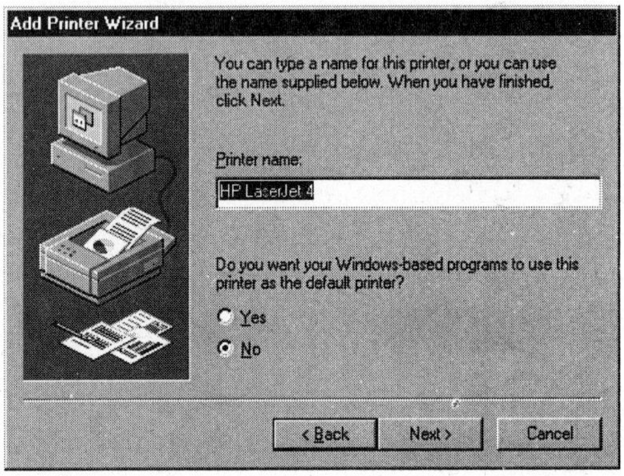

Note

If you have access to two printers of the same type, appropriate names would be to name the first one "HP LaserJet Series II Room 5, Building 10" and the second one "HP LaserJet Series II Room 25, Building 15."

9. Choose Yes to set this printer as the system default. By setting this printer as your default, you instruct all applications to use this printer, unless you tell the application to use a different printer. (You can set the default to any other installed printer at any time.) Click Next to continue. The final Wizard screen, shown in figure 6.15, appears.

10. Specify whether you want to print a test page. Printing a test page tests the overall operation of the printer based on the settings you've just entered. Choose Yes and click Finish to print the test page. The Wizard then copies the necessary driver files to your system, prompting you to insert one of the Windows 95 source disks if necessary.

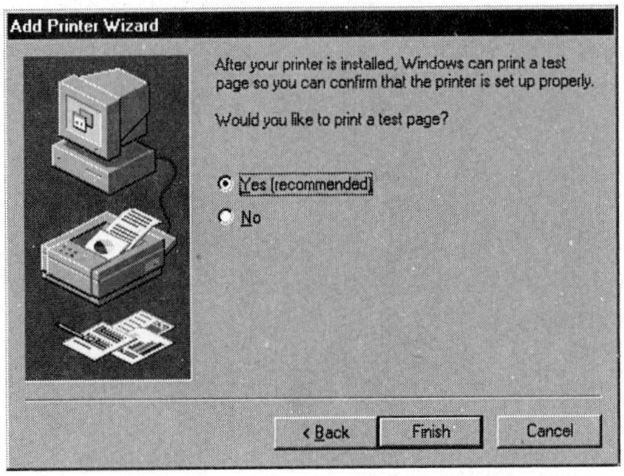

Fig. 6.15
Printing a test page is the final step in configuring and testing your printer installation.

> **Note**
>
> The test page contains information specific to your printer, its configuration, and the drivers Windows uses to interface with it. Once this page is printed, save it for future reference. If your PC is used by others, you may some day have to return to a known installation configuration.

Installing a Plug-and-Play Printer

In addition to the Add Printer Wizard, Windows 95 supports the Plug and Play standards that assist the user in configuring the printer software. Plug and Play technology automatically provides answers to configuration questions you've scratched your head over in the past. Remember the list of information you compiled before you began installing your printer? Plug and Play printers interact with Windows to automatically configure printers by using a dialog transparent to the user. Many printer manufacturers have cooperated with Microsoft to not only make configuration easier, but to automatically update the software when you make changes to the printer hardware configuration.

If your printer is Plug and Play compatible, see Chapter 8, "Plug and Play and Legacy Device Installation," for an explanation of how Plug and Play devices are installed.

Renaming an Existing Printer

Printers named during installation can be quickly renamed using the Printers folder. The Printers folder displays all installed printers, with their individual names located immediately below the printer's icon (refer to fig. 6.9).

To rename a printer after it is installed, follow these steps:

1. Open the Printers folder by opening the Start menu, choosing Settings, and then choosing Printers. If Control Panel is open, double-click the Printers folder.

◄ See "Changing Settings and Properties with the Right Mouse Button," p. 107

2. Select the desired printer and choose File, Rename. Alternatively, right-click the printer icon to open the shortcut menu and choose Rename.

   Windows creates a text box around the printer name and highlights that name.

3. Change the name by typing a new name or deleting portions of the existing name.

4. When finished, press the Enter key. The new printer name is used throughout the Windows operating system.

Deleting an Existing Printer

You can delete an installed printer from the Printers window, which displays all installed printers as icons. To delete a printer from the Printers window, follow these steps:

1. Select the printer you want to delete. Choose File, Delete; alternatively, right-click the printer icon to open the shortcut menu and choose Delete.

   Windows opens a dialog box and asks whether you're sure that you want to delete the printer. The dialog box provides two control buttons: OK and Cancel.

2. Choose OK; the printer is now deleted. Windows then asks whether it can remove the associated software from your hard disk and presents the same OK and Cancel buttons.

> **Caution**
>
> If you have a similar printer that could use the same drivers, do not remove the software. Deleting the associated software may remove that driver from use by other printers.

3. Choose OK to remove the deleted printer's software driver.

The printer and its driver are now removed. Windows signifies this event by removing that printer icon from the Printers window.

> **Note**
>
> If you plan to reattach this printer in the future, do not remove the software drivers. This can save you time when reattaching the printer. If you do not plan to reattach this printer or are upgrading the software drivers, remove the software to free up disk space and avoid confusion.

Configuring Your Printer

By now, you have installed one or more printers for use by Windows 95 applications. Both Windows and MS-DOS applications can use these resources without further effort. The initial installation of the printer created a default configuration. You may want to make changes to that configuration. Because few default configurations satisfy all printing requirements, you may want to change the printer's configuration frequently.

> **Note**
>
> Windows 3.1 provided a setting to change the priority of background printing. This feature does not appear in Windows 95.

Tip

If you change printer settings frequently, you can install duplicate printers and configure each printer with its own set of properties. This eliminates repeated property changes.

II

Working with Windows 95

Options for Your Printer

Printer properties are preset during installation of the printer. The preset values for the many variables may not meet your current printing needs. You may also have to make changes to meet special printing needs or to solve any performance problems that arise.

Like many other printing issues discussed in this chapter, the exact options available depend on the capabilities of your printer. The following discussion focuses on the basic procedures; you must adapt these to fit your specific printer.

To change printer options, open the printer's Properties sheet using one of these two methods:

- If the Print Manager for the printer whose options you want to change is open, choose Printer, Properties.

- Open the Printer window and select the printer whose options you want to change. Choose File, Properties or right-click the printer icon and choose Properties from the shortcut menu.

Both methods open the printer's Properties sheet (see fig. 6.16). This dialog box has several tabs. The settings on each page depend on the manufacturer, printer model, and printer options.

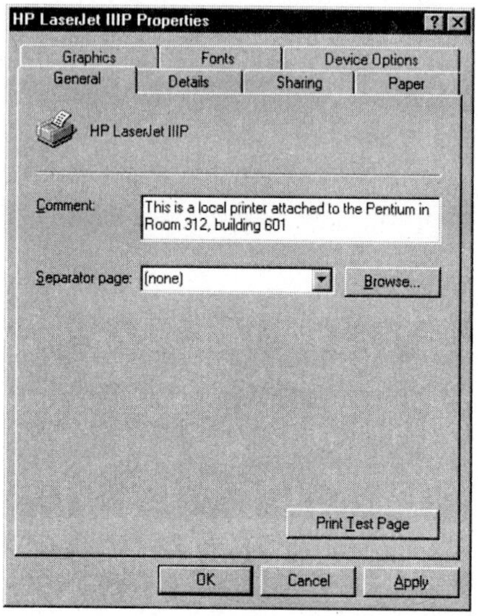

Fig. 6.16

Use the General page of the printer's Properties sheet to get and specify basic information about the printer.

The Properties sheet typically contains the following information. (The details of these pages will change with different printers.)

- *The General page.* Enables you to identify your printer, print a test page, and choose a separator page. A separator page is used to separate print jobs from different users. Each page includes a user name and job specific information such as date, time, and file name. The General page enables you to perform the following actions:

  - Fill in a comment field to identify a printer whose properties are being changed.

  - Specify that Windows will print a separator page between each print job.

  - Print a test page using the Print Test Page control.

- *The Details page.* Contains controls to attach or change ports, add or delete ports, change timeout periods, and specify how Windows will process print files. Use the Details page to configure enhanced meta file printing and the spooler. Typical controls include

- Print to the Following Port specifies the printer port that Windows 95 will use to access the printer.

- Add Port permits the user to add another port.

- Delete Port deletes a port.

- Print Using the Following Driver displays which driver the operating system will use to print to this printer.

- New Driver adds another printer driver for possible use with this printer.

- Capture Printer Port captures a network printer port.

- Release Printer Port releases a network printer port.

- Time-Out Settings enables you to set the time out and not selected periods for printing.

- Spool Settings enables you to configure the print spooler.

- Port Settings enables MS-DOS printing.

■ *The Sharing page.* Enables a printer to be shared or not be shared with other workstations attached to your PC over a network.

■ *The Paper page.* Provides several controls that set the printer's default paper handling, orientation, and the number of pages to be printed. Commonly included controls are

- Paper Size specifies paper or envelope size.

- The Layout block specifies from one to four reduced pages per printed page.

- The Orientation block specifies Portrait or Landscape printing.

- Paper Source specifies which paper tray is the default.

- Copies specifies single or multiple copies.

■ *The Graphics page.* Sets the resolution and other options that define how the printer treats graphic files. Typical settings include

- Default printing resolution.

- The way Windows employs halftoning to create grayscale images from color graphics.

- For PostScript printers, controls that allow you to create negative images and print mirror images.

- Scaling that reduces the size occupied by a printout on the printed page.

■ *The Fonts page*. Enables you to adjust how fonts are treated by Windows for this printer. Configurable fonts include printer, cartridge, and software fonts. Typical controls include

- Sending TrueType fonts to a printer according to the Font Substitution Table.

- Always Use Built-In Printer Fonts instead of TrueType fonts.

- Always Use TrueType Fonts instead of any other fonts.

■ *The Device Options page*. Configures the options associated with the printer's hardware. The number and type of controls are specific to the printer's make, model, and hardware. Typical controls include

- Set printer memory capacity to change the amount of memory in your printer.

- Specify device-specific options such as Page Protection.

Tip
Be certain to accurately configure the available printer memory. An incorrect value in this variable can change the speed of your printouts or cause your printer to time out or fail during printing sessions.

Printing with Color

Microsoft uses licensed Image Color Matching (ICM) technology from Kodak to create an image environment that treats color consistently from the screen to the printed page. The Windows ICM goal is to be able to repeatedly and consistently reproduce color-matched images from source to destination.

In earlier versions of Windows, printout and display quality were application- and vendor-dependent. Using ICM technology, Windows 95 provides a higher quality color rendering. ICM provides more consistent, repeatable quality among various brands of printers and scanners. The term *color* includes grayscale rendering.

The most important feature is consistency between the video screen and the printed page. Now both software applications and hardware devices adapt to improve output quality. The phrase "What You See Is What You Get" (WYSIWYG) takes on much deeper meaning. Not only are black-and-white printouts consistent from screen to printer, but the color, texture, and tone are no longer solely dependent on price.

Many newer printers are capable of printing color in addition to grayscale. Choose a printer that is color aware and compliant with Kodak's ICM specification. For color printers, printouts more closely match the colors and shades seen on your display. Grayscale printers also reproduce outputs with much higher correspondence to the screen using grayscale and shading.

Setting Color Printing Properties

The Graphics page in the printer's Properties sheet for a color printer is shown in figure 6.17. It provides several controls for setting color consistency in the printed output. The controls in this page allow you to configure your printer to produce the best color possible.

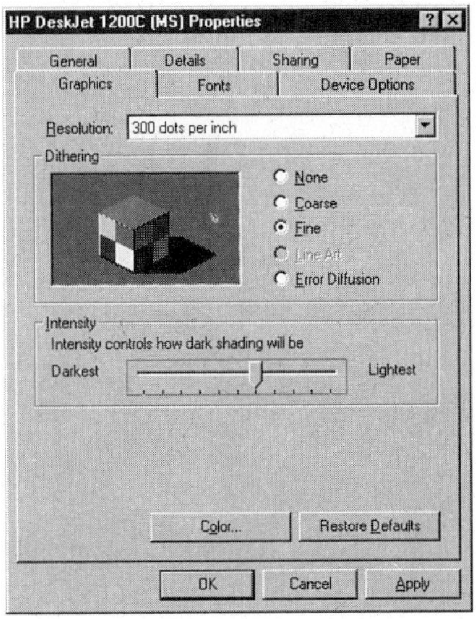

Fig. 6.17
The Graphics page of the printer's Properties sheet for a color printer lets you adjust color and output quality.

- *Resolution*. This drop-down list box specifies the number of dots per inch (dpi) that the printer can produce. The higher the dpi, the clearer the graphics.

- *Dithering*. Dithering is an error-correcting tool used by Windows 95 to more accurately represent an object's color and grayscale.

- *Intensity*. Intensity is a brightness control to lighten or darken a printout to more accurately reflect its screen appearance and to compensate for deficiencies in toner or paper quality.

To access the color settings for a color printer, click the Color button. This dialog box shown in figure 6.18 appears; use this dialog box to set ICM compliance alternatives.

The color settings are used to adjust the level of compliance of your printer with the ICM standards. The dialog box is also useful for trial-and-error adjustment of color printer output quality. Following is a list of the settings:

■ *Color Control.* A macro command that enables you to direct the printer to print only black and white or to specify whether or not you want ICM technology.

■ *Color Rendering Intent.* Provides the best ICM settings for three of the major uses of color printing: presentations, photographs, and true color screen display printing. Select the choice that works best for your purpose.

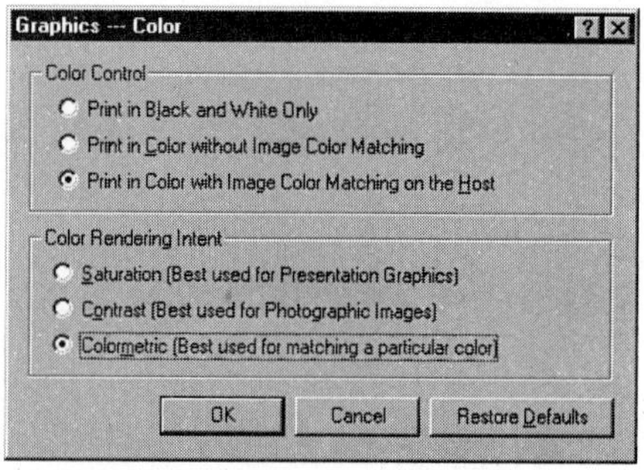

Fig. 6.18
Display the Graphics—Color dialog box by selecting the Color button on the Graphics page of the printer's Properties sheet.

Using the 32-Bit Subsystem

◄ See "Improved Performance," p. 21

Naturally, a 32-bit application is faster than its 16-bit equivalent. However, in Windows 95, 32-bit performance means more than speed. It also means safety. 32-bit applications run in their own address space so that a failure in one application doesn't propagate to others. Because printing is a resource-dependent function, 32-bit performance results in better use of your resources. It permits Windows 95 designers to provide a more robust, feature-rich user interface.

When using the 32-bit printing subsystem, you will find the following differences in Windows 95 versus Windows 3.1 performance.

■ *Return from Printing.* When an application prints, it shares memory and resources with the print system. In the Windows 32-bit architecture, 32-bit applications do not share the same memory—each has its own virtual memory resources. Virtual memory, combined with the faster performance of 32-bit drivers, results in the printing subsystem quickly releasing resources. Thirty-two-bit printer drivers share existing resources more equitably, resulting in smoother background printing.

■ *System Stalls.* Because the printing subsystem runs in its own 32-bit virtual processor, a printing failure no longer locks out other applications. Another benefit from this design is that Windows can clean up resources after a print failure.

■ *Printing Independence.* 32-bit virtual drivers enables Windows to support each printer with an individual, dedicated Print Manager. Multiple Print Managers result in the independent configuration of each printer and maximize the use of all printers without the need for frequent reconfiguration.

To verify that all Windows 95 printing components are 32-bit, perform the following checks:

■ Using the Port Configuration dialog box, verify that all port drivers are VxD files. The VxD extension designates a virtual device driver.

■ Using the Print Manager Properties sheet, print a test page from the General page. The test page displays the name and version of the current printer driver. Verify that the version of the driver is the latest available for Windows 95. As a general rule, this driver should also have a VxD (virtual device driver) extension. If your drivers are not VxD, check with your printer manufacturer to obtain the latest releases of these drivers. Then perform the Add a Printer installation procedure using the new drivers.

Using Enhanced Meta File Spooling (EMF)

The new Enhanced Meta File (EMF) feature appears to fall in the "so-what" category—or does it? Historically, PostScript printing has employed meta files to produce excellent hardcopy results. A printer meta file contains specific printer instructions to produce a hardcopy printout. Many printer manufacturers use proprietary meta file formats, such as PostScript, to produce their best results. Now meta files can be created within the operating system and be standardized for most printers.

The EMF Process

An application submits a print stream to Windows. If the printer is configured to support Enhanced Meta Files, the print stream is converted into a series of high level printer instructions.

The process of changing a print stream to a meta file converts each page into a series of printer-recognizable macro instructions. Printing EMF files transfers much of the processing overhead from the PC to the printer. Windows uses its 32-bit Graphics Device Interface (GDI) and its Device Independent Bitmap (DIB) engine to create the image to print.

Print Spooling

Print spooling creates a temporary disk file that stores print files. It is temporary because Windows only stores these files until it has finished printing. The spooler is an integral part of the Windows 32-bit print architecture. The spooler itself is a 32-bit virtual device driver.

An application sends a print stream to Windows for printing. The printer driver reviews the printer configuration and verifies that the spooler is required.

The spooler creates a memory-mapped file on the system's hard disk to store the application's print stream. Although this process takes time, it uses fewer system resources for a shorter period of time than does sending the print stream directly to the printer.

Using the spooler enables Windows to smooth out background printing and more quickly return resources to the application.

Configuration of the EMF Print Spooler

The Enhanced Meta File (EMF) Print Spooler is responsible for converting your documents into a printable format prior to sending them to the printer. The spooler is important because it affects both printing speed and how quickly Windows returns control to you after printing.

> **Note**
>
> You cannot configure PostScript printers using the EMF Print Spooler. PostScript is itself a substitute for EMF, and Windows will only configure RAW for PostScript printers.

To use the spooler, follow these steps:

1. Open the Start menu and choose <u>S</u>ettings, <u>P</u>rinters.

2. Right-click on a non-PostScript printer to open its context menu, and then choose Properties to open the printer's Properties sheet.

3. Click the Details tab to display the Details page.

4. Select Spo<u>o</u>l Settings. Windows displays the Spool Settings dialog box, shown in figure 6.19. The Spool Settings dialog box has four basic controls: spooler printing, bypassing the spooler, spooler formats, and printer communications.

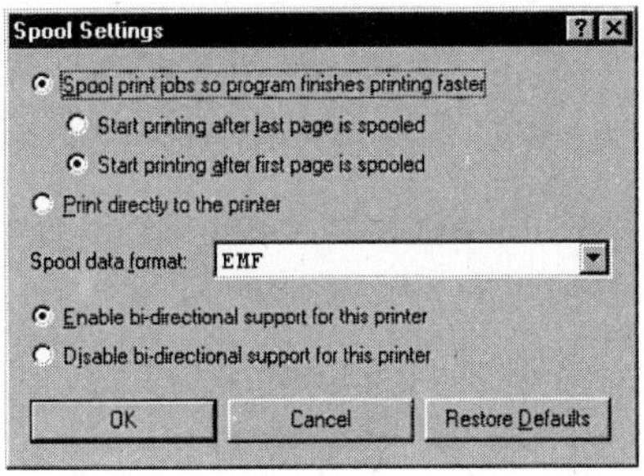

Fig. 6.19
The Spool Settings
dialog box
provides controls
to modify the
operation of the
Windows printer
spooler.

5. Select the Spool Print Jobs So Program Finishes Printing Faster radio
   button. Selecting this option enables the spooler.

   Alternatively, select Print Directly to the Printer; this option disables
   the spooler.

6. If you selected the Select the Spool Print Jobs So Program Finishes Printing Faster radio button, you can then choose when you want Windows
   to start printing during the spooling process. Because this is a radio
   button list, you can only select one of the following two options:

   ■ *Start Printing after First Page Is Spooled.* This option tells the Print
     Manager to print after the first page is spooled.

   ■ *Start Printing after Last Page Is Spooled.* Printing after the last page
     is spooled provides the smoothest background printing, even
     though you wait longer for the printout.

7. Specify EMF in the Spool Data Format drop-down list box. The list has
   two options: RAW or EMF. RAW saves the print stream to a spooler, but
   does not convert the print stream to Enhanced Meta File format. Select
   RAW when printing to a PostScript printer or to a printer with a proprietary meta file print driver. The EMF setting should produce superior
   results on most printers. However, if your printing slows down or
   produces poor-quality graphics, try the RAW setting for possible
   improvement.

8. Select the Enable Bi-Directional Support or Disable Bi-Directional Support radio button to specify whether or not Windows can communicate
   in both directions with the attached printer. If a printer cannot support
   any level of bi-directional communications or is not attached, the correct choice is Disable Bi-Directional Support. In all other cases, the appropriate choice is Enable Bi-Directional Support, which allows the
   Print Manager to monitor the printer status during the printing process.

II

Working with Windows 95

> **Note**
>
> If your printer or port does not support these options, the options will be dimmed in the dialog box.

Configuring the Printer Port

In addition to configuring settings that affect the printer itself, you can make a few configuration changes to the port to which the printer is attached. These options vary depending on which port you use to print. The most common printing port is an LPT port, usually LPT1 (or LPT2 if you have a second LPT port). Changing the printer port may be required if you attach a printer to a serial port or add a printer switch.

Follow these steps to change the configuration options for port LPT1:

1. Open the Start menu and choose Settings, Control Panel.

2. Double-click the System icon.

3. Windows displays the System Properties sheet; choose the Device Manager tab to configure printer ports (see fig. 6.20).

Fig. 6.20
The Device Manager tab of the System Properties sheet identifies the port, its present state of operation, and the hardware configuration being used.

4. Double-click the Ports icon to show the attached ports. Choose the printer port whose configuration you want to change, such as LPT1 or COM1. For this example, choose LPT1. If your printer is attached to another parallel port or a COM (serial) port, choose that port instead.

5. Click Properties. The Printer Port Properties sheet shown in figure 6.21 appears. Note that Printer Port Properties are divided among three pages: General, Driver, and Resources.

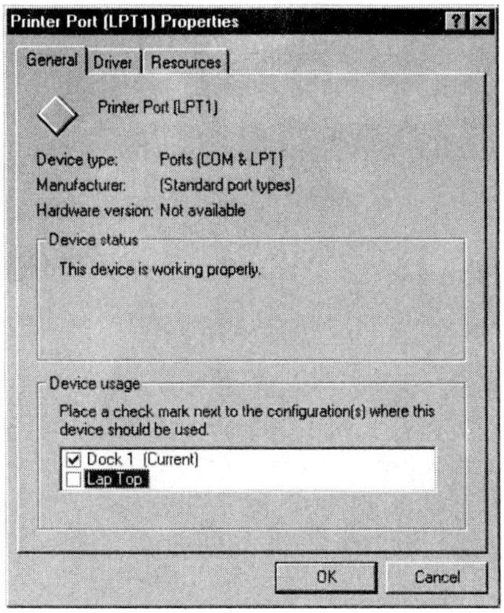

Fig. 6.21

The General page of the Printer Port Properties sheet provides current status and information about the port's hardware.

6. Choose the Driver tab.

7. Verify that the driver file selected on the Driver page is the most current printer driver available (see fig. 6.22). Note that the VxD extension signifies a 32-bit virtual driver that can be expected to provide the best performance. If you have a driver with a .DRV extension, you are not using a 32-bit driver. Check with your printer manufacturer for the latest version.

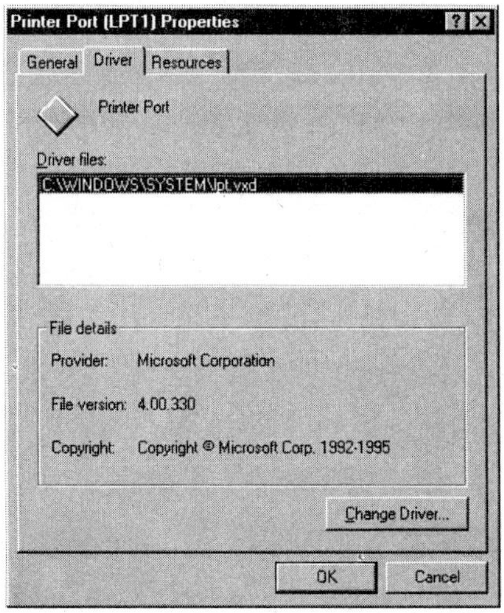

Fig. 6.22

The Driver page of the Printer Port Properties sheet provides the name and version of the currently installed port driver.

8. To install a different driver, click Change Driver. Windows displays the Select Device dialog box shown in figure 6.23. Use this dialog box to load a new driver from either a vendor-supplied disk or choose a previously installed driver. If you have a vendor-supplied disk that contains the new port driver, choose Have Disk.

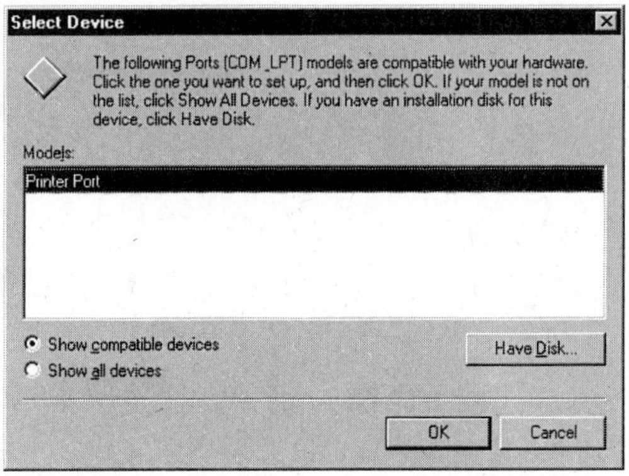

Fig. 6.23

Select a new or existing printer port driver.

9. Windows displays an instruction window that directs you to insert the manufacturer's disk in drive A. Change the drive by typing the appropriate drive letter over the letter *A*. The window also allows you to browse and select a driver from another location. Windows requests a vendor disk. Insert the appropriate disk and select the OK control button. Otherwise, select the Cancel control button to stop the installation process. Windows installs the vendor software and links it to the selected printer port.

The Resources page contains detailed information about the printer port's addresses and any configuration conflicts. Reviewing this information is a convenient way to verify that Windows has properly installed the driver. In the background, Windows cross-checked the ports configuration with the system startup settings. Windows can and does spot configuration problems but doesn't necessarily notify the user that there's a problem. The resources contain the Input/Output Range of addresses. The addresses of the LPT1 port are shown under the Setting column. If a device uses an interrupt, that interrupt is also shown. If Windows spots a problem, it will designate that a conflict exists and list the information in this window. You can then choose alternative configurations to test other configurations.

To configure the printer port, click the Resources tab. The critical information is the Conflicting Device List (see fig. 6.24). This list contains all items that conflict with your printer port. When installing new hardware, always verify that its address and interrupts do not conflict with existing hardware properties.

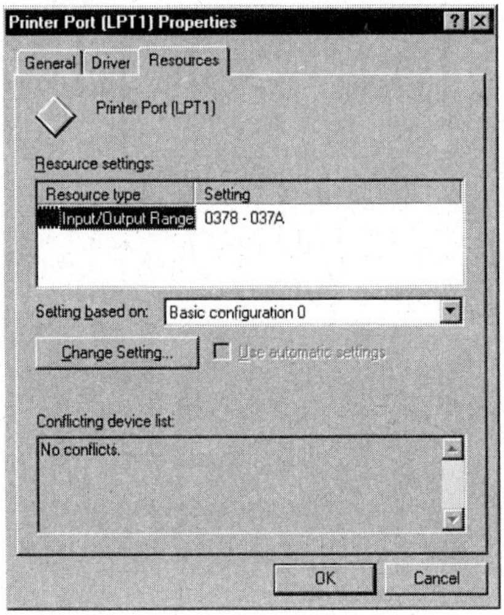

Fig. 6.24
The Resources page of the Printer Port Properties sheet displays detailed hardware information vital to port operation and the diagnosis of communications problems.

You should normally choose Use Automatic Settings. If you have any conflict problems, the Settings Based On list box shown in figure 6.24 provides several optional configurations that Windows can use to configure the printer port.

To use this control, first uncheck the Use Automatic Settings box. You then can use the Settings Based On control to select from a list of Windows configurations. Each configuration shows the port configured to different devices and interrupts. As each configuration is considered, problems associated with the new configuration are shown in the Conflicting Device List information box at the bottom of the tab.

> **Note**
>
> Carefully review the hardware properties for all devices to identify potential conflicts. Windows cannot discover and display all problems in normal operation. Use the Device Manager to check for conflicting devices; doing so may prevent problems later.

Most printer installations do not require changes to the printer port settings. However, unusual address conflicts from older equipment or Enhanced

II

Working with Windows 95

Capability Ports (ECP) technology provide more configuration options. The number of possible decisions and potential conflicts between pieces of hardware increase as the number of options increase. Select OK to complete the port configuration.

Printing from MS-DOS Applications

Windows provides support for printing from MS-DOS applications in much the same way it does for printing from Windows applications. Although EMF support for MS-DOS applications is not supported, the print stream is spooled using the RAW setting for the print spooler. The result is faster return to MS-DOS applications and the ability to mix Windows and MS-DOS print streams (avoiding contention problems that occurred under Windows 3.1).

Under Windows 3.1, MS-DOS applications could not access the Windows printing facilities. In the past, printing from a DOS application was neither robust nor fail-safe. When printing simultaneously from both Windows and MS-DOS applications, you often received notice of a printer conflict. In most cases, this caused either the MS-DOS application or the Windows application to stall, and you had to reboot.

The major change Windows 95 brings to MS-DOS applications is direct access to the Windows print spooler. MS-DOS applications no longer compete for a share of the printer; you can actually use the Print Manager to queue your MS-DOS printouts with those of Windows applications.

When you print from an MS-DOS application in the Windows environment, the DOS application spools print jobs to the 32-bit print spooler, which takes the output destined for the printer port and spools it before printing. Windows automatically installs the print spooler for MS-DOS applications; the spooler is transparent to users. Although your MS-DOS printouts automatically use the 32-bit spooler, they cannot be processed into Enhanced Meta Files.

Printing from a Docking Station

▶ See "Using Your Laptop with a Docking System," p. 273

Every time you start Windows, it performs an inventory check of all attached hardware. Windows also provides a choice of configurations during startup (that is, it lists the configurations it recognizes). You must choose one of the selections from this list.

You can configure Windows to work offline when the PC is undocked and online when the PC is docked. You can set the system configurations for the printer port to be configured only when the laptop is attached to the docking station. You also can configure the port to be automatically unavailable when the system is being used as a laptop.

Configuring a Hardware Profile

A hardware profile specifies whether Windows will use or not use a specific peripheral. Hardware profiles provide a tool that you can use to specify the hardware configurations to operate your system. Hardware configurations are created and changed through the Control Panel's System icon.

Because the printer is not a system resource, it is not part of the hardware configuration. However, the printer is attached to the system through the LPT1 port. This port *is* a system resource and can be configured to be available when the computer is in a docking station. The port can also be configured as unavailable when the system is used as a laptop.

Use the following steps to create the hardware profile:

1. Open the Start menu and choose Settings, Control Panel.

2. Double-click the System icon. The System Properties sheet appears.

3. Choose the Hardware Profiles tab. The page contains a text window with a single item: Dock 1. When Windows is first installed at a docking station, it creates the Dock 1 setting in the text window.

4. Select the Dock 1 setting and click Copy.

> **Note**
>
> Windows will automatically detect most docking stations and create a Dock 1 profile. Even if you initially install Windows on a laptop, Windows checks the system components each time it starts and will create profiles automatically when it finds changes.

5. Change the name of the newly created configuration from Dock 1 to Lap Top or some other name that indicates that the laptop is not in its docking station. Click OK.

6. Choose the Device Manager tab from the System Properties sheet.

7. Select the port (COM or LPT) from the Device Manager page.

8. Choose the printer's port (LPT1).

The Printer Port (LPT1) Properties sheet that appears contains a Device Usage block with a hardware configuration window (see fig. 6.25). The Device Usage block now contains two hardware configurations: the initial Dock 1 and the new Lap Top. The two items are check box controls. A check in the Dock 1 box directs Windows to include port LPT1 in its hardware configuration whenever a docking station has been detected.

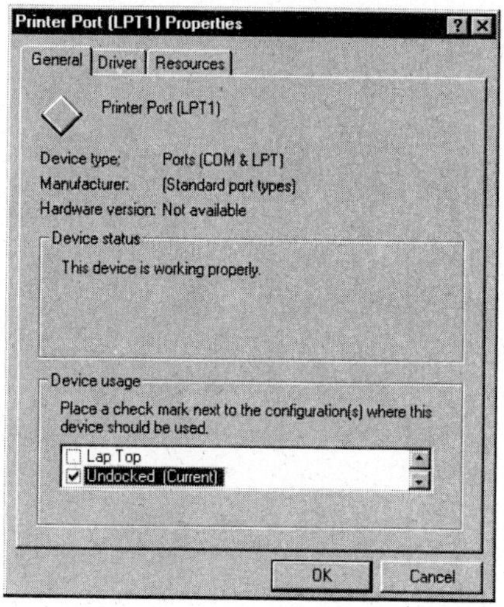

Fig. 6.25

The Printer Port Properties sheet showing which hardware profile is currently configured.

9. Check the Dock 1 box. Leave the Lap Top box unchecked.

10. Reboot your Windows system. During initial boot-up, Windows asks for a configuration. Choose Lap Top.

To verify that you have configured the hardware profile correctly, do not change the hardware and follow these steps:

1. After Windows has started, open the Start menu and choose Settings, Control Panel.

2. Double-click Device Manager.

3. Select the port (COM or LPT) from the Device Manager page.

4. Note that the printer port is now offline, signified by a red X through the port's icon. Printing now results in a diagnostic message that the printer is not attached. The Print Manager deletes all print files.

Therefore, you must set the printer to <u>W</u>ork Off-Line so that the system will save all print files.

Repeat the process first by rebooting Windows, this time selecting the Dock 1 configuration setting. The printer port returns. The saved print files can then be released for printing.

Common Printer Problems

You install a printer only on occasion. But you troubleshoot printer problems frequently. The most useful tool in identifying and correcting printer problems is a thorough knowledge of your printer's installation and properties. During installation, test your printer and the wide range of properties available to better identify a starting point for dissecting most problems.

Windows provides fundamental troubleshooting aid with Bi-Directional Printer Communication. If a printer can talk to its drivers, many potential causes for problems can be routinely identified.

Advance preparation is always an excellent safeguard against any PC problem. The following checklists can be useful when you are diagnosing a local printer problem.

Before the Problem: Initial Preparation

Following initial installation of the printer, perform these steps:

1. Make a test-page printout and save the resulting printout for future use. The test page can contain important configuration information including the current printer driver, memory size, and port information. On PostScript printers, it will contain version level and settings.

◄ See "Options for Your Printer," p. 187

2. If your printer can perform a self test, make a printer self-test printout. For most printers, this test page contains the printer's internal configuration. This information may contain the number of pages printed, memory size, a list of configured options, and internal software revision level. Save the printout for future use. This information may be useful in describing your printer to its manufacturer at a later date for upgrading or troubleshooting.

3. Note the proper configuration of your printer's indicators: the Ready or Online light and the display status.

4. Make a record of your printer's internal menu settings for paper size, orientation, interface, and so on.

5. Record the installation results and the information from the Printer Properties screens.

Diagnosing the Problem: Basic Troubleshooting

For a local printer, perform the following steps to start diagnosing a problem:

1. Verify that all cabling is free of nicks, tears, or separations.

2. Verify that all cabling is fully inserted and locked at both the PC and the printer ends.

3. Verify that the printer is online and that all proper indicators are lit (for example, that the Online or Ready indicators are lit).

4. Verify that the printer is properly loaded with paper and that there are no paper jams.

5. Verify that the printer has toner (laser), ink (inkjet), or a good ribbon (dot-matrix).

6. Verify that cabinet doors and interlocks are closed and locked.

7. Verify that the printer's display, if available, shows a normal status.

8. Verify that the Windows printer driver can communicate with the printer using the Printer Properties screens. You should be able to print a test page to verify communication. If you cannot print a test page, Windows generates a diagnostic message providing you with a starting point to diagnose the problem.

9. Verify that the Windows Printer Properties screens display the same information that was contained in the Properties screens when you installed the printer.

10. Attempt to print to the errant printer using another application and a different type of print file (for example, print a text file or a graphics file).

Troubleshooting Tools

If the basic troubleshooting steps listed in the preceding section fail, Windows comes with three important tools you can use to further investigate printer problems. The first tool is Windows 95's new Help file. Initiate the Help file from the Print Manager's Help menu. Then select the Troubleshooting icon.

The Troubleshooter steps you through several of the most probable causes of printing problems (see fig. 6.26). Primarily, this tool verifies that the printer can communicate with the PC. If basic communication is lost, none of the software tools can provide any real assistance. You must resort to hardware exchange until you resolve which component or components are defective. However, with the exception of toner and paper problems, most printing problems are not hardware failures; the problems are primarily software settings or corrupted printer drivers.

Fig. 6.26
The Windows Print Trouble-shooter assists you in isolating problems using logical fault-isolation techniques.

The Windows 95 Print Manager provides a diagnostic tool that can aid you during the process of equipment interchange. The diagnostic screen shown in figure 6.27 is usually the first indication you receive that a printer fault has occurred. The information on this screen varies (Windows provides as much detail as possible about the problem). The increased amount of information is a result of the Bi-Directional Communications between the PC and the printer. For those printers without bi-directional capability, you will receive a standard "Unable to print" diagnostic.

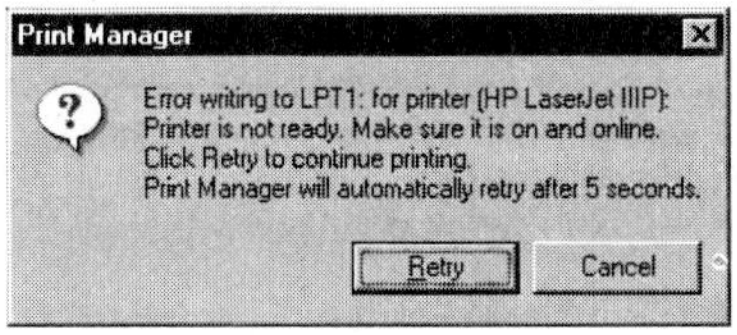

Fig. 6.27
The Print Manager diagnostic reports problems as they are found and continues until either the problem is fixed or the print job is canceled.

If you click the diagnostic's Retry button, Windows continues to monitor the printer's status at approximately five-second intervals. If you click the Cancel button, the diagnostic discontinues and the Print Manager pauses the print file.

The third troubleshooting tool is the Enhanced Print Troubleshooter, shown in figure 6.28. This software application steps you through your problem by asking you questions concerning the problem. As you answer each question, you are provided with a range of possible alternatives to help you narrow in on the potential source of the problem. Clicking the hot buttons next to the most accurate answer brings up another screen with additional insight and questions. This tool is a Windows 95 executable file named EPTS.EXE.

Fig. 6.28

The Enhanced Print Trouble-shooter steps you through a printer problem using plain English-language questions.

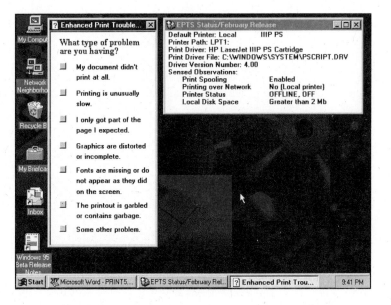

Most Common Printer Problems

The most common printing problems are printing supplies running out or a change that has recently taken place in either the printer or the operating system. In any event, a check list is an excellent place to start because it lets you consider each possible problem. The most common problems, in order of probability, are listed here:

■ **The printer is either not selected or is not the default.**

Make the printer the system default using the Print Manager's Printer menu.

■ **The printer doesn't appear to be turned on.**

Verify that the printer has been plugged in and that the power is in the on position.

■ **The printer does not begin printing even though my PC says that I am printing a document.**

If your system is attached to more than one printer, make sure the appropriate printer is being printed to by checking the Print Manager of each attached printer to find the current print job.

■ **The printer is offline.**

Set the printer online.

■ **The printer is out of paper.**

Reload the printer's paper supply.

■ **The printer is out of toner.**

Reload the printer's supply of toner.

■ **The printer is out of ink.**

Reload the printer's ink cartridge.

■ **The printer's ribbon is no longer functional.**

Remove and replace the printer's ribbon with a new one.

■ **The printer's door is open or has a failed interlock.**

Check for open doors or covers.

■ **The printer cable is not properly connected to either the printer or PC.**

Replace or reseat the cable.

■ **The Printer is not connected to the correct port.**

Remove the cable and connect it to the appropriate port.

■ **The printer's software configuration has changed or the drivers have been corrupted.**

Delete and reinstall the printer.

■ **New hardware has been added to either the printer or the PC and a conflict has resulted in addressing or interrupts.**

Review the installation records of the printer and reconfigure it if required.

■ **Additional software has been added to Windows that changed the printer's configuration files.**

Check the printer's configuration for driver files that have changed using the printed test page created during installation.

■ **An application has indicated that it can no longer print to a corrupted print driver and to the selected printer.**

Delete and reinstall the printer.

■ **The operating system has been stalled during a print operation.**

Reboot Windows 95 and verify printer operation, by printing a test document.

■ **A printout stops halfway through printing a large detailed graphic.**

Using your application, set the print quality to draft. If the graphic printout completes, check your printer's documentation to possibly increase the amount of memory in your printer. If it doesn't complete, run a printer self-test to print a test page.

■ **A printer with a cartridge option does not report that the cartridge is installed.**

Turn the printer off and then check to verify that the cartridge is properly seated. Turn the printer on and retest.

■ **A hardware problem may have occurred in either the PC or printer that stops during the printing of a document.**

Reinitiate printing the document. If it fails again, review the installation records of the printer and note any changes.

Chapter 7

Working with Fonts

by William S. Holderby

Fonts are specifications that tell Windows how to display and print text. Font technology has evolved so much over the last few years that the number of font types now available has grown tremendously. Font types exist for the basic text characters of many of the world's languages, and some special font types display pictures rather than text. These fonts are useful for lines, universal sign language, and many other specialized applications. Fonts are more than just specifications, you must be able to change them to meet your needs. Changing fonts may mean resizing them, changing character spacing, or rotating them to better fit your document. Fonts have names like Courier, Times Roman, Arial; each font creates its own impression on the printed page.

This chapter deals with the standard font offerings that Windows uses to print text. Although Windows comes equipped with several font technologies, the Windows preference is the TrueType font technology. TrueType technology was developed by Microsoft to provide standard fonts, capable of being both displayed and printed with minimal changes in appearance. TrueType fonts were included with previous versions of Windows. Microsoft has included new architectural features that improve their display speed for both the operating system and applications, such as the 32-bit Rasterizer.

▶ See "TrueType Fonts," p. 216

This chapter discusses the following issues:

- How Windows uses fonts

- How to install and delete TrueType fonts

- How to manage fonts in Windows 95

- How to work with other font types

Understanding Fonts

Individual fonts belong to a family of similar fonts that share various characteristics such as style, size, and special effects. For example, a Times Roman font is really more than a single entity because a character set is associated with the font. To review fonts, you should first understand a few terms:

- *Font size* is the definition of how large, or small, a font character is displayed or printed. Sizes are normally described in points. Each point is approximately 1/72 of an inch.

- *Font style* consists of bold, normal, italic, or bold italic. The style determines how the characters belonging to a font are displayed.

- *Font effects* defines color, special instructions (such as an underline or strikethrough), and in some cases, gradient grayscale fill for outlined fonts.

- *Serif fonts* have projections (serifs) that extend the upper and lower strokes of the set's characters beyond their normal boundaries. The Courier font is an example of a serif font. San-Serif fonts, such as Arial, do not have these projections.

- *Font spacing* refers to the space between characters on the screen or printed page. Fixed-spaced fonts have the same space between each character. Courier is a fixed-spaced font. Proportional-spaced fonts, such as Arial, adjust the inter-character space based on the shape of the individual characters.

- *Font width* describes the width of individual characters. These widths can be fixed, normal, condensed, or expanded. In Windows, certain fonts are fixed, such as the OEM font. Other fonts use variable width to display characters that are out of proportion.

Font technology can seem complex and confusing because of the large number of fonts in use, the somewhat obscure constraints, and the advantages touted by various vendors. Windows and your applications provide standard font choices that eliminate much of the confusion, while allowing you to customize their selection. Windows 95 supports numerous font technologies from many vendors. New fonts are available from Adobe, Bitstream, and other software suppliers.

32-Bit TrueType Font Rasterizer

Microsoft has included a new *rasterizer* that improves the time it takes to create TrueType fonts. A rasterizer prepares a TrueType font for either display, or printing, from a file that contains a mathematical model of the fonts characters. The Microsoft 32-bit TrueType Font Rasterizer was developed as part of Windows new 32-bit printing architecture. A scalable font such as TrueType can be made larger or smaller without losing its distinctive shape and appearance; for example, the appearance of a character shown in size 6 is identical to the same font character at size 18. The Rasterizer creates new sizes and parameters to use in displaying font characters of different sizes, orientations, and effects (such as Arial 12 Bold, Italic).

▶ See "Reviewing Types of Fonts," p. 213

In Windows 95, a single file—the TTF file—replaces the FOT and TTF TrueType font families. The TTF file contains all the information needed to create fonts of different sizes and complexity.

The FOT file was called a display hint file, because it provided hints to the Windows 3.1 Rasterizer as to where it should begin to create a displayable font. In other words, the FOT file speeded up the Rasterizer by providing initial conditions. Windows 95's new rasterizer eliminates the need for hint files by using an entirely new algorithm to create fonts from the TTF file in less time.

Registry-Based Font Support

In Windows 3.1, fonts were identified and loaded using INI files. Windows 3.1 dutifully loaded each font during startup. The time Windows 3.1 took to start increased as more and more fonts were loaded into the system. In addition, the number of fonts available was restricted under Windows 3.1.

Windows 95 attaches fonts through the Registry. Because Windows has immediate access to these fonts, as needed, it no longer has to load all of them, thereby reducing time and overhead. The Registry also provides better management and enables access to many more fonts. Windows uses the Registry instead of the INI files to configure software options for Windows access. The Registry provides a systematic structure and interface that is available to all software regardless of manufacturer.

Changing to Registry-based fonts provides the following benefits:

- The number of fonts that Windows can configure is limited only by available disk space. The number of fonts you can simultaneously use and print in the same document is approximately 1,000.

II

Working with Windows 95

- Registry-based fonts create an environment where more than one person can use your PC hardware. Each user can individually configure a unique environment, which can include individual font selection.

- Improved font handling through the universal Registry enables an efficient standard access for both Windows and applications.

Windows 3.1 used initialization files to identify which font files were available for use. Some 16-bit Windows applications use the WIN.INI file to identify which fonts are installed. Under Windows 95, 32-bit applications use the system Registry to access installed fonts. Windows still maintains the WIN.INI file to stay compatible with some 16-bit applications.

Required Fonts for Windows

The number of fonts that Windows 95 requires is defined by the applications that you plan to run under the operating system. If you are primarily interested in word processing, then 10 to 12 scalable fonts is more than adequate. A page of text may require only one or two fonts for emphasis. If you plan to use CAD (computer-aided design), desktop publishing, or imaging applications, consult these packages for their special requirements. Because fonts provide an additional dimension you can use to create special effects or to distinguish a particular area of a document, CAD or desktop publishing documents may require a large number of fonts.

Standard Windows fonts or fonts shipped with the product include:

- *System fonts,* which are used by Windows to draw menus and controls, and to create specialized control text. System fonts are proportional fonts that Windows can size and manipulate quickly. Therefore, Windows uses these fonts to save time when it creates your screen environment.

- *Fixed-width fonts,* which are included with Windows 95 to maintain compatibility with earlier versions of Windows 2.0 and 3.0.

- *OEM fonts,* which are provided to support older installed products. The term *OEM* refers to Original Equipment Manufacturers. This font family includes a character set designed to be compatible with older equipment and software applications.

Fonts You Should Keep

Unlike Windows 3.1, Windows 95 does not slow down when loaded with additional fonts. However, these extra fonts do take up valuable disk real estate. You should carefully weigh the value of these fonts before you load them on your system. Microsoft has optimized the font-handling drivers for the TrueType font family, but you still may use other fonts. The decision about which fonts to keep depends on which applications you use.

The only way to make this determination is to experiment by adding, changing, displaying, printing, and eventually deleting unneeded fonts. Experiment with all the fonts on both the display and printed page before you make this decision.

> **Note**
>
> Experimenting with other font families from various manufacturers provides you with a wide range of optional selections. Other font families can be added to Windows, such as fonts from Adobe. However, Adobe fonts require more Windows resources because they require the Adobe Type Manager to be running. You may want to look for TrueType fonts that will serve your needs if your applications don't specifically require ATM.

Reviewing Types of Fonts

Some fonts are designed to be compatible with special printing devices. These fonts use mathematical outline descriptions to create their character set. The resulting characters can be scaled and rotated. However, fonts designed for special printers are often difficult to display. To solve this problem, Adobe has created the Adobe Type Manager (ATM), a Windows application that converts Adobe PostScript printer fonts into displayable characters for use by Windows 95 applications.

> **Note**
>
> Many printer vendors have designed custom software drivers to support their printers. Your printer manufacturer may have special Windows 95 handler software.

These output devices involve different font handling technology and drivers:

- PostScript printers use PostScript meta file printing which is similar to, but not compatible with Windows Enhanced Meta Files (EMF).

◀ See "Using Enhanced Meta File Spooling (EMF)," p. 193

- Dot-matrix printers range from older, very simple models to newer Near Letter Quality (NLQ) printers. Many of the older dot matrix printers did not support downloading of soft fonts and some of the newer printers may provide better results using proprietary drivers.

II

Working with Windows 95

- Hewlett-Packard PCL printers use various levels of HP's Printer Control Language (PCL)—for example, the Laserjet II supported level 4 and Laserjet III supports level 5 PCL. Both Windows and HP provide up-to-date drivers that provide the best font settings.

- Plotters primarily use vector fonts as plotter software converts plotter outputs into a series of straight lines.

- Specialized OEM printers may use proprietary fonts to create unique symbols or increase the speed of graphic character creation. Most of the specialized printers provide optimum performance when they are inter-faced with their manufacturer's proprietary drivers.

> **Note**
>
> If your printer came with special drivers, check with the manufacturer for the latest updated Windows 95 driver.

We speak of fonts as belonging to *technologies,* or families, that include many styles and variations. A technology determines how a font is created, stored, and what device limitations it has. We use the term *technologies* and *families* interchangeably to refer to a group of fonts with similar attributes.

Standard Windows provides support for three font technologies:

- *Raster fonts.* Fonts that are bit-mapped for fast display. These fonts are created in specific sizes and rotation angles.

- *Vector fonts.* Fonts that are created from mathematical line models, each character consisting of a series of lines (vectors). Vector fonts are an outgrowth of plotter technology. Pen Plotters are used extensively in computer-aided design (CAD) to create line drawings.

- *TrueType fonts.* Scalable, rotatable fonts created from mathematical models. These fonts are a compromise between displayable and print-able fonts.

The following sections discuss these and some other font technologies.

Raster Fonts

The name *raster fonts* describes a font set that was designed primarily for the raster display. You cannot scale raster fonts in odd multiples or rotate them effectively. Raster fonts consist of arrays of dots and are stored in bit-map files with the extension FON. Raster fonts need separate files for each point size, resolution, and display device. Therefore, each raster font file has a letter designating its targeted device:

- D = printer

- E = VGA display

- F = 8514 display

The Courier raster font has three files associated with it: COURD.FON for the printer font, COURE.FON for the VGA font, and COURF.FON for the fonts optimized for the 8514 display. Each raster file is optimized for its intended display device and contains attribute-specific information:

- Font type

- Font character set

- Font sizes

- Font optimized resolution

You can scale raster fonts in even multiples up to the point where they no longer appear smooth. By their nature, bit maps that are expanded too far lose their orderly appearance and smoothness. However, these fonts are quickly displayed and reduce the Windows screen refresh time.

Raster fonts are printable only if the chosen font set is compatible with your printer's horizontal and vertical resolution.

Note

Not all printers can print raster fonts acceptably. Before you combine any font type with your printer, you should first test the compatibility. You can test the appearance of printed fonts by creating a page of text using that font type and then printing that page. Another way to test printed fonts is to print the font family from the Control Panel's font folder, shown later in this chapter.

Five raster fonts are supplied with Windows 95, and several other vendors supply additional font sizes. The supplied raster fonts are MS Serif, MS Sans Serif, Courier, System, and Terminal.

II

Working with Windows 95

Vector Fonts

Vector fonts are derived from lines or vectors that describe each character's shape. You can scale vector fonts to any size or aspect ratio. The characters are stored as a set of points and interconnecting lines that Windows 95 can use to scale the font to any required size. These fonts are very applicable for plotting and CAD. As with the raster fonts, vector fonts are stored in FON files. The way Windows 95 treats this font type is to rasterize the various characters by using function calls to the Graphics Device Interface (GDI). The number of calls required for each font increases the display time required to create the characters and to refresh the display. The fonts are useful for CAD and desktop publishing because they are readily extensible. Large vector font sizes maintain the same aspect ratio as smaller sizes. Windows 95 supplies three vector fonts: ROMAN, SCRIPT, and MODERN. Additional fonts are available from several sources including CAD and desktop publishing software vendors.

TrueType Fonts

In Windows 95, TrueType fonts are each stored in a single TTF file. This file contains both the outline information and the ratios necessary to scale the font. FOT files were used in previous versions of Windows to provide the operating system with a hint to use in creating a displayable font character. Using hints increased creation speed and enabled Windows to display new fonts more quickly. With the new Windows Rasterizer, hints are no longer needed because the speed of creating fonts has increased significantly. Removing the FOT file frees disk real estate.

The Windows 95 print architecture includes a new 32-bit TrueType font Rasterizer for rendering and displaying these fonts faster and with greater accuracy. The Rasterizer uses a technique that Microsoft calls *anti-aliasing* to smooth display mode curves and reduce the jagged effects of the font enlargement. Windows 95 supplies many TrueType fonts including ARIAL.TTF, COUR.TTF (New Courier), and TIMES.TTF (Times New Roman).

Other Fonts

In addition to raster, vector, and TrueType fonts, other fonts exist that perform specialized services. Your printer may have an entire set of fonts or may be capable of being configured with font sets through the use of font cartridges or additional cards. The following list describes additional Windows fonts:

- *System fonts*. The system font files included with Windows 95 are 8514SYS.FON and VGASYS.FON.

- *OEM fonts*. The OEM font files included with Windows 95 are 8514OEM.FON and VGAOEM.FON.

- *Fixed fonts*. The fixed font files included with Windows 95 are 8514FIX.FON and VGASYS.FON.

- *MS-DOS legacy fonts*. Windows 95 includes several MS-DOS compatible font files for DOS applications to use while running in the Windows 95 environment. These files provide backward compatibility to the real-mode DOS environment. Files included are CGA40WOA.FON, CGA80WOA.FON, DOSAPP.FON, EGA40WOA.FON, and EGA80WOA.FON. Although these fonts are primarily used for application display, the DOSAPP.FON is a good choice for printing.

- *Printer soft fonts*. Depending on your printing hardware, you may download soft fonts to your printer. Downloading fonts reduces the time taken by the printer to process printouts. You download soft fonts once to speed up subsequent print jobs.

Installing and Deleting Fonts

During the Windows installation process, Windows loads its standard suite of font files onto the system disk. Windows and your applications use these files as default fonts. You have the option of installing and deleting fonts from your system to change the look of your desktop environment, word-processing, spreadsheet applications, or for use by special application needs, such as CAD.

> **Caution**
>
> Be careful when deleting seemingly useless font sets. Deleting certain sets like fixed, OEM, or system fonts may drastically alter the look and proportion of your Windows desktop and applications. When fonts are deleted, you may see applications and even Windows dialog boxes change appearance. Even though Windows substitutes existing fonts to replace deleted ones, you may not like the substitution. Make sure you have a backup copy of all fonts you delete, as you may want to replace them for aesthetic reasons.

II

Working with Windows 95

Installing New Fonts

Windows enables you to quickly install new fonts using the Control Panel. Fonts may be installed from the Windows disks or from vendor-supplied disks. This procedure installs new fonts into the Windows Registry for use by both Windows and applications.

1. Open the Start menu and choose Settings; then choose Control Panel. Double-click the Fonts folder in the Control Panel.

2. Windows displays the Fonts window that contains a list of all the fonts currently registered by the system (see fig. 7.1).

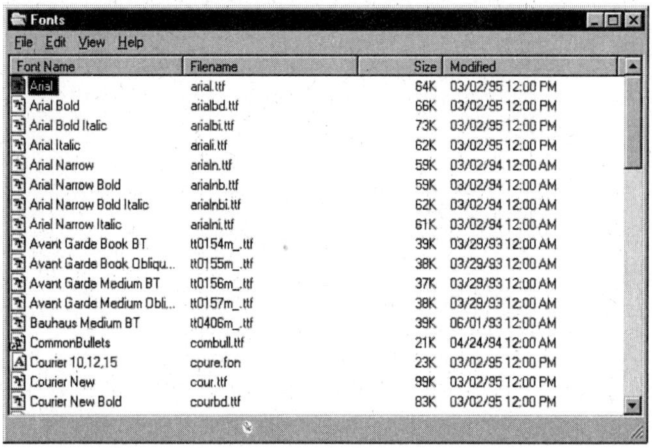

Fig. 7.1

The Fonts window shows which fonts are loaded along with their file name, size, and configuration date.

You can display the list as individual icons with the name of each font below the icons. Or you can display a detailed list that contains the name of the font, the name and extension of the font file, the size of the file, and the date of its creation.

3. To change the look of this list, choose View and then choose Large Icons, List, or Details. Refer to figure 7.1 for an example of Details view.

> **Note**
>
> On occasion, you may want to look at the list of font types displayed without their many variations (such as Bold). You may choose this option in conjunction with other View menu selections by choosing View, Hide Variations (Bold, Italic, and so on).

4. Choose Files, Install. Windows displays the Add Fonts dialog box, shown in figure 7.2.

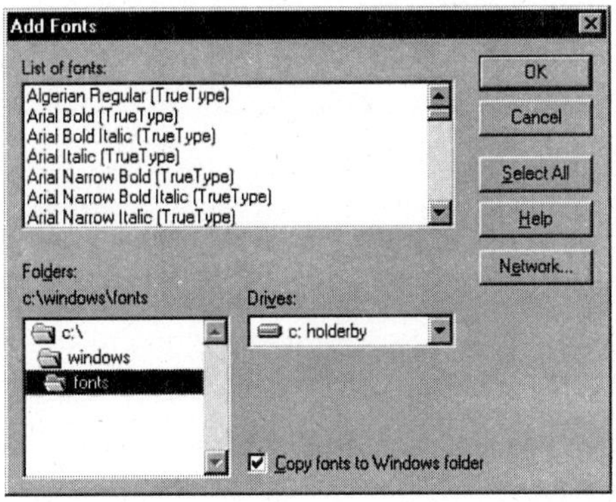

Fig. 7.2
The Add Fonts dialog box provides the controls needed to add a new font to Windows 95.

5. Using the Drives and Folders controls, choose the location of the font you want to install. This location may be a directory on the hard drive or a manufacturer's floppy disk.

6. Windows displays a roster in the List of Fonts window. Select the font or fonts to add.

   If these fonts are located in a location other than the Windows font directory, you may have the files automatically copied to this directory by checking the Copy Fonts to Windows Folder box at the bottom of the Add Fonts dialog box.

7. Choose OK to add the selected font(s). Windows installs the new fonts and enters them in its Registry.

> **Note**
>
> You can also install fonts by dragging and dropping them from a disk into the Fonts Folder, using the Windows Explorer. However, this procedure doesn't always register the font correctly. After you install a font this way, print a test copy to verify installation.

Deleting Fonts from the Hard Disk

Windows also enables you to quickly delete installed fonts from the Control Panel. The following procedure deletes unwanted fonts and removes them from the Windows Registry.

1. Open the Start menu and choose Settings; then choose Control Panel. Double-click the Fonts folder in the Control Panel. In the Fonts window, Windows displays the fonts currently registered by the system (refer to fig. 7.1).

II

Working with Windows 95

2. Highlight the font or fonts to delete.

3. Choose <u>F</u>ile, <u>D</u>elete.

Tip
If you mistakenly delete fonts, you may recover them from the Recycle Bin.

▶ See "Restoring Deleted Files," p. 520

4. Windows displays a warning asking you if you really want to delete these fonts. Choose Yes. Windows shows the font being sent to the Recycle bin as it removes the deleted fonts from the Registry.

> **Note**
>
> For faster deletion, you can also delete fonts by dragging and dropping them from the Fonts Folder into the Recycle bin, using the Windows Explorer.

Using TrueType Fonts

TrueType fonts are created by Microsoft and are integrated as part of the operating system. While all font technologies are optimized for specific applications or hardware, TrueType font design is a compromise between printed text and displayed text. The TrueType text, either displayed or printed, shows virtually no variation, which enables you to create documents that most closely resemble the on-screen representation of your work.

Understanding the Pros and Cons of TrueType

Because TrueType fonts are an integral part of Windows 95, many font styles come bundled with the operating system. The new Windows Rasterizer provides greater speed and accuracy for displaying and printing TrueType fonts.

Windows uses an anti-aliasing, character-generation algorithm that increases font smoothness. However, this technology needs a 256-color mode or higher, requiring more complex and higher priced hardware. For specific printing applications and CAD applications, PostScript fonts repeatedly provide better printing results. In addition, not every printer is compatible with TrueType fonts, causing some printers to treat TrueType fonts as graphics and thus reducing printer efficiency.

Determining Which Fonts Are TrueType

Through the use of icons in the Fonts folder, Windows makes it easy to identify your TrueType fonts. If you work with many MS-DOS applications, you should note that TrueType and other fonts are also distinguishable by their file extensions:

1. Open the Start menu and choose Settings; then choose Control Panel. Double-click the Fonts folder in the Control Panel. Windows displays the Fonts window containing the list of registered fonts.

2. Display the fonts as individual icons with the name of the font below the icon by choosing View, Large Icon. TrueType fonts are shown by an icon containing the letters T_T.

   In the List and Details view, TrueType fonts are shown prefaced by a smaller icon showing T_T. In the Details view, TrueType fonts also are denoted by their file type TTF. Other font types are shown as file type FON.

Adding or Removing TrueType Fonts

You add or delete TrueType fonts the same way you add or delete other font types. To add or remove TrueType fonts, use the previously described Add a Font or Delete a Font procedures, selecting only fonts with TTF file extensions.

Using Windows 3.1 TrueType Fonts

In Windows 3.1, each TrueType font was maintained by two files, TTF and FOT. Windows 95 eliminates the need for an FOT by implementing faster font creation. You can add your existing TrueType fonts to Windows 95 by specifying the TTF file when adding a font. Windows will not ask for a separate FOT file and accepts Windows 3.1 TrueType fonts as well as fonts created from most existing applications.

Using Only TrueType Fonts

To select only TrueType fonts in your applications, you can set the appropriate font option. Microsoft has integrated TrueType fonts into the Windows operating system. If you want to only use TrueType fonts in your applications follow this procedure:

1. Choose the Fonts folder from the Control Panel. Windows displays the Fonts folder containing a list of the registered fonts.

2. Choose View, Options.

3. Choose the TrueType tab in the Options dialog box (see fig. 7.3).

4. Check the box that reads Show Only TrueType Fonts in the Programs on my Computer. Now, only TrueType fonts are shown as available to applications.

II

Working with Windows 95

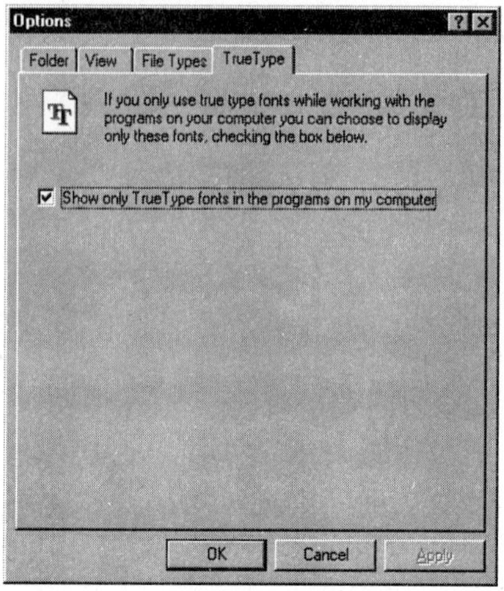

Fig. 7.3

To configure only TrueType fonts for applications, check the box in the Options dialog box that reads Show Only TrueType Fonts in the Programs on My Computer.

Other Font Configurations

◄ See "Displaying Properties of Programs, Documents, and Resources," p. 28

Each printer is configurable through its Printer Properties sheets. The printer property options vary from printer to printer. Many of the printers support downloaded soft fonts. Many printers support TrueType fonts as downloaded soft fonts or printing them as graphics. These options can be readily set on the appropriate Printer Properties Fonts page.

Printing TrueType fonts as graphics increases your printing time, but on some printers it substantially improves the look and quality of the printed font. Downloading TrueType fonts as soft fonts stores the fonts in your printer. If your printer has adequate memory to store fonts, downloading speeds up the printing operation. If the printer is unable to store these fonts, you'll usually receive a "memory overflow" error on the printer following the download.

> **Note**
>
> Assuming that your printer has adequate memory, the look and quality of using graphics mode versus download mode is identical. But if your printer is short on memory and your document is heavy on graphics, using graphics mode may help because the entire font may not have to be downloaded into memory.

PostScript printers provide an option to substitute PostScript fonts for TrueType fonts by use of a Font Substitution Table. The Printer Properties Fonts page for those printers enables you to change which fonts are substituted by changing the table.

Managing Fonts in Windows 95

In Windows 95, fonts are a managed resource. Applications can quickly access fonts through standardized registration, making your fonts quickly available for viewing, printing, comparing, sorting, adding, and deleting.

Previewing and Printing Font Samples

Before you use a font, you may want to preview it or print a sample before committing it to a document. Windows provides quick access to this information by performing the following steps:

1. Open the Start menu and choose Settings; then choose Control Panel. Double-click the Fonts folder in the Control Panel. Windows displays the Fonts window containing the list of registered fonts.

    You have the option to display the font list as either a <u>D</u>etails list or as Large icons through the <u>V</u>iew menu.

2. Select the font you want to view and choose <u>F</u>ile, <u>O</u>pen; or double-click the font to view it. Windows displays the font in various sizes (see fig. 7.4).

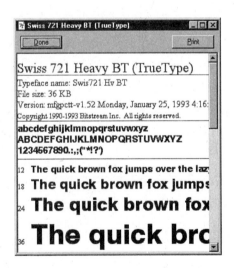

Fig. 7.4

A sample of a font type showing sizes and font detail information.

3. To print the sample page, choose <u>P</u>rint.

4. When you are done previewing and printing the font, choose <u>D</u>one.

Showing Font Properties

Fonts, like most other Windows objects, have properties. The properties include version information that may contain important information for

Tip

You also can print a sample from the Fonts folder by selecting the font and choosing <u>F</u>ile, <u>P</u>rint.

II

Working with Windows 95

purposes of upgrading your fonts. Although at present there is no way to change these font properties, you can view the information contained in these screens through the following procedure.

1. Open the Start menu and choose Settings; then choose Control Panel. Double-click the Fonts folder in the Control Panel. Windows displays the Fonts window containing the list of registered fonts.

2. Select the font you want to view.

3. Choose File, Properties. Windows displays a Properties sheet like the one shown in figure 7.5. The Properties sheet contains version and management information for each font type registered by Windows.

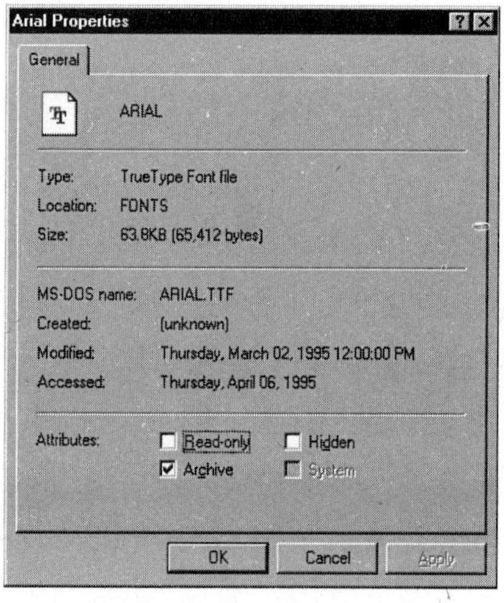

Fig. 7.5
A Properties sheet for the Arial TrueType font provides file and configuration information.

Viewing Fonts by Similarity

Fonts are distinguished by their differences, but they also can be grouped by similar features. Grouping fonts by similarity may be important to you when showing subtly different text in a document or when your printed document doesn't match the display. Substituting a similar font may correct this problem. You will find fonts listed by similarity, except where Windows has insufficient Panose information to make a comparison. *Panose* refers to a Windows internal description that assigns each font a PANOSE ID number. Windows uses several internal descriptions to categorize fonts. The PANOSE information is used to register a font class and is a means to compare similar font features. You can group similar fonts by following this procedure.

1. Open the Start menu and choose Settings; then choose Control Panel. Double-click the Fonts folder in the Control Panel. Windows displays the Fonts window containing the list of registered fonts.

2. Open the <u>V</u>iew menu and choose <u>D</u>etails, <u>L</u>ist, or Large icons.

3. Select the font to use as a master against which you want to test other fonts for similarity.

4. Choose <u>V</u>iew, List files by <u>S</u>imilarity. Windows redisplays the Font list as shown in figure 7.6. The list now shows all fonts with an assessment of their similarity to the master font. In the case shown in figure 7.6, the Arial font is the master font. The Swiss 721, shown, is listed as being fairly similar to Arial. Compare the similarity between the Swiss 721 and the Arial font.

Fonts are shown as being very similar, fairly similar, not similar, or insufficient Panose information available.

Tip
You can test the similarity of other fonts by selecting the <u>L</u>ist Fonts by Similarity To control and choosing another font type.

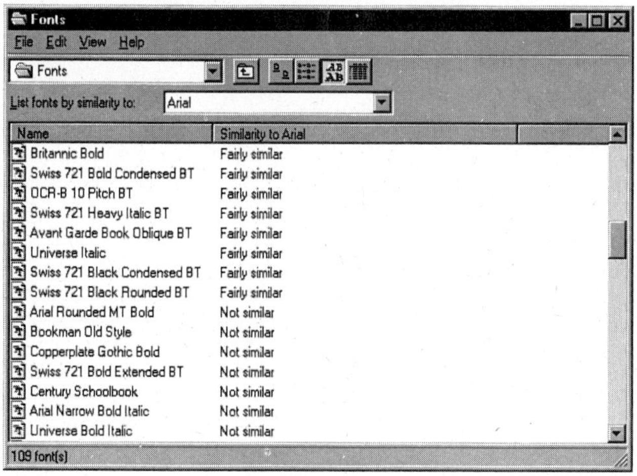

Fig. 7.6
This list shows how closely other font types match the Arial font.

II

Working with Windows 95

Installing Printer Fonts

Printer fonts reside in the printer as a cartridge or within the printer's memory. You can install printer fonts through Windows or through installation applications that usually accompany your printer. Follow these steps to install printer fonts using Windows:

1. Open the Print Manager for the selected printer.

2. Choose <u>P</u>rinter, P<u>r</u>operties.

3. Choose the Fonts tab on the Properties sheet. See the Printer Properties Fonts page shown in figure 7.7. Note that each printer type is supported by a different set of Properties pages, which depend on the make, model, and hardware configuration of the printer.

◄ See "The Print Manager," p. 173

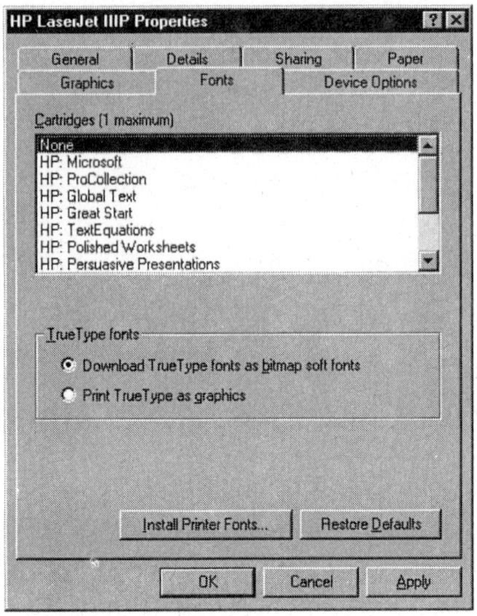

Fig. 7.7

A typical Printer Properties Fonts page.

4. Choose Install Printer Fonts. A dialog box similar to the one in figure 7.8 appears. The printer fonts installer for your printer may look different from the one shown in the figure, but all installers perform similar functions.

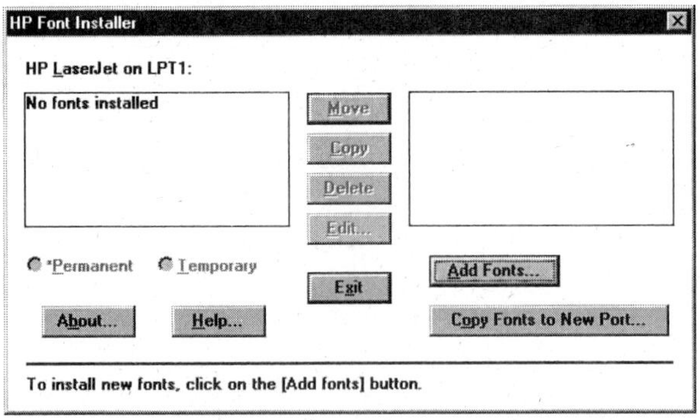

Fig. 7.8

The HP Font Installer dialog box.

> **Note**
>
> The HP Fonts Installer shown in figure 7.8 cannot be used to download TrueType fonts to HP printers. PCL printers can download only PCL-compatible fonts. Be certain that your printer and the fonts being specified for download are compatible. Refer to the installer's help file for more information on compatible fonts.

5. Select the fonts to be installed in the list on the right side of the Font Installer dialog box.

6. Choose Copy to move the selected fonts to the left window.

7. Choose Add Fonts to register the printer's fonts. A dialog box is then displayed asking for the location of the fonts. This box provides a Browse button to enable you to find the disk location of the fonts to be installed.

8. Identify where the font files are located and select OK to enable Windows to install the selected fonts.

Downloading Fonts as Permanent or Temporary

Most Printer Properties Fonts pages include a set of radio button controls that enable you to select whether a font is to be temporarily or permanently downloaded.

Download frequently used fonts as permanent. This allows you to print faster. However, permanent downloaded fonts limit the amount of printer memory available for printing. Therefore, to stay within normal printer memory limits, keep the number of fonts you specify as permanent to three of four.

Downloading fonts as temporary does not store the font in the printer's memory until it is needed. The font is loaded only temporarily in the printer before a document is printer and removed after the document is complete. This increases printing time, but it increases the amount of available printer memory and reduces print overrun errors. Downloading fonts as temporary is the default setting and works well with most applications.❖

II

Working with Windows 95

Chapter 8

Plug and Play and Legacy Device Installation

by Roger Jennings

Adding a new hardware device, such as a multimedia upgrade kit, to a pre-Windows 95 PC is best described as a daunting experience. The new device—and possibly even your PC—may not work the first time you test the installation, especially if you have a few other special-purpose adapter cards installed in your PC. So you pull out the card, change some miniature jumpers on the upgrade kit's sound card or one of the other adapter cards in your PC (assuming that you didn't lose the jumper under your desk), and then test the device again. The most common refrain during this cut-and-try process is "Let's see—what IRQ and DMA and device addresses did I try last time?"

Windows 95's new Plug and Play (PnP) features, combined with a PnP-compliant PC, take the mystery and the frustration out of installing new hardware devices. Plug and Play abolishes jumpers and software configuration programs; plug in a PnP adapter card, and your PnP-compatible computer makes the card play the first time around. Plug and Play is the most important distinguishing feature of the Windows 95 operating system; no other operating system for Intel-architecture PCs currently offers Plug and Play support.

The hitch in the PnP scenario is that relatively few PnP-compliant adapter cards were available when Windows 95 hit the retail shelves, and most users of Windows 95 don't have new PCs with PnP system BIOS on the motherboard. Microsoft calls hardware that's not PnP-compliant a *legacy* device—a rather derisive term for the vast majority of the PC motherboards and adapter cards in use today. Fortunately, Windows 95 includes new features that help you install legacy devices, too.

Most of the chapters in this book are devoted to hands-on advice for getting the most out of Windows 95. The objective of Plug and Play is to make new-device installation a "hands-off" process. Therefore, much of this chapter is devoted to explaining what happens behind the scenes to make Plug and Play work. This chapter covers the following topics:

- The PnP architecture

- What PC hardware you need to take advantage of new PnP devices

- How Windows 95 handles installation of legacy devices

- Troubleshooting device installation

Understanding Plug and Play Architecture

▶ See "Using PC Card Devices," p. 266

Plug and Play is a computer-industry standard that automates the process of adding new capabilities to your PC or changing PCMCIA adapters in your notebook PC. (*PCMCIA* stands for Personal Computer Memory Card Interface Association.) The PnP standard is a joint development of Intel Corporation and Microsoft Corporation. Other industry leaders—such as Phoenix Technologies Ltd., Compaq Computer Corporation, NEC Technologies Inc., and Toshiba Computer Systems Division—contributed their expertise to the development of the set of eight specifications that make up the PnP standard.

Microsoft defines a Plug and Play computer system, qualifying for the "Designed for Windows 95" logo, as having the following components:

- *Plug and Play BIOS version 1.0a.* The PnP BIOS (basic input/output system) provides the basic instructions for identifying the devices necessary to boot the computer during the POST (power-on self-test) process. The standard minimum set of devices is a display, keyboard, and disk drive to load the operating system—in this case, a fixed-disk drive to load Windows 95. Computers that sport the "Designed for Windows 95" logo are required to have PnP BIOS version 1.0a or later.

- *Plug and Play operating system.* Windows 95 is the first PnP operating system, but limited support for Plug and Play features is available in MS-DOS 5, Windows 3.1, and later versions of both programs. Microsoft is likely to add Plug and Play features to a future version of Windows NT.

- *Plug and Play hardware.* Plug and Play hardware is a set of PC devices that are autoconfigurable by the PnP operating system. PnP hardware primarily consists of adapter cards (or their equivalent circuitry) on the PC's motherboard; but printers, external modems, and other devices connected to the PC's COM (serial) and LPT (parallel) ports also may support PnP. PCI adapters qualify as Plug and Play hardware. ISA and most EISA adapter cards require modification for PnP autoconfiguration. Microsoft requires PnP compliance for hardware devices to carry the "Designed for Windows 95" logo.

■ *Plug and Play device drivers.* Microsoft includes 32-bit device drivers (*VxDs*, which are virtual *anything* drivers) for basic PnP devices, such as IDE and SCSI-2 fixed-disk and CD-ROM drives. Hardware manufacturers are responsible for providing VxDs to support specialty adapters, such as sound and video capture cards. When you install a PnP-compliant device that requires a driver that's not included in the retail version of Windows 95, you're asked to insert the setup disk for the PnP device that has the required device driver.

Virtually every PC manufacturer and assembler offers products claiming PnP compliance and displaying the "Designed for Windows 95" logo. Simply replacing the motherboard's BIOS chip with one that meets the Plug and Play BIOS Specification 1.0a (described in the following section) doesn't make an assembled computer PnP-compliant. The adapter cards, fixed-disk and CD-ROM drives, and other components of the system also must comply with the appropriate PnP specification.

Following are the eight specifications that comprised the Plug and Play standard when Windows 95 was released:

■ *Plug and Play BIOS Specification 1.0a*, developed by Compaq, Phoenix Technologies, and Intel. This basic document defines the way that PnP works. (The PnP BIOS specification is described in additional detail in the following section.)

■ *Plug and Play ISA Specification 1.0a*, developed by Microsoft and Intel. The purpose of the PnP ISA specification is to define how non-PnP and PnP-compliant cards can coexist on the ISA bus without getting in each other's way.

■ *Plug and Play SCSI Specification 1.0*, developed by Adaptec, AT&T Global Information Solutions, Digital Equipment Corporation, Future Domain, Maxtor, and Microsoft. The SCSI 1.0 spec defines the SCSI host adapter card. An additional specification—SCAM (SCSI Configured AutoMagically)—defines the means by which individual SCSI devices (such as fixed-disk drives) support autoconfiguration features similar to

II

PnP. The SCSI standard is maintained by Committee X3T9.2 of the American National Standards Institute (ANSI).

■ *Plug and Play IDE Specification*, developed by Microsoft in conjunction with the ANSI X3T10 Committee and Phoenix Technologies, Ltd. The IDE (Integrated Device Electronics) specification defines the requirements for PnP-compliant adapters on PC motherboards and plug-in ISA and PCI cards for IDE fixed-disk and CD-ROM drives.

■ *Plug and Play LPT Specification 1.0*, developed by Microsoft, defines the method by which devices connected to the parallel port identify themselves to the PnP BIOS. Printers, modems, network adapters, and parallel-port SCSI adapters are among the devices defined by the PnP LPT specification. If you plug a Hewlett-Packard LaserJet 4M into your computer's parallel port, Windows 95 finds the driver for the printer and loads the driver automatically.

■ *Plug and Play COM Specification 0.94*, developed by Microsoft and Hayes Microcomputer Products, defines the way that serial devices (such as mice, modems, printers, and uninterruptible power supplies) identify themselves. Windows 95 usually is quite capable of identifying the type of mouse and modem installed, even without PnP identification. The PnP COM spec was a draft version when this book was written.

■ *Plug and Play APM Specification 1.1*, developed by Microsoft and Intel, handles advanced power management for laptop and energy-efficient desktop PCs.

■ *Plug and Play Device Driver Interface Specification for Microsoft Windows and MS-DOS 1.0c*, developed by Microsoft, provides limited support for PnP assignment of I/O, IRQs, DMA, and memory ranges under MS-DOS and Windows 3.1 and later.

Note

In addition to the specifications in the preceding list, the ATAPI specification defines the identification process for PnP-compatible CD-ROM drives that attach to the enhanced, PnP-compliant IDE interface. The Extended System Configuration Data specification (ESCD 1.0) is designed to provide additional information about ISA and EISA adapter cards to the PnP BIOS.

The primary reason for boring you with the preceding list of specifications is this: you may need to inquire whether a computer, motherboard, or device that you are planning to purchase truly is PnP-compatible. The ability to name the applicable specification precisely is more likely to elicit a forthright response than "Is *whatever* Plug and Play?"

A second reason for the list is that it enables you to download current copies of each of the preceding specifications from the libraries of the Plug and Play Forum (GO PLUGPLAY) on CompuServe. Copies of these specifications are not readily available elsewhere. A white paper titled *Microsoft Windows and the Plug and Play Framework Architecture* is available in WINPNP.ZIP (which contains WINPNP.DOC) from Library 1 of the PLUGPLAY forum and (as PNP.ZIP) from the WINNEWS forum. (PNP.ZIP includes Word 6.0, ASCII text, and PostScript versions of the backgrounder.) Library 1 of the Plug and Play Forum also includes the *Plug and Play Catalog*, a Microsoft Word document that contains the latest list of PnP devices and the names, addresses, and telephone numbers of the device manufacturers.

Plug and Play BIOS Specification 1.0a

Clearly, the most important element of a PnP computer system is the PnP system BIOS. *Plug and Play BIOS Specification 1.0a* adds the following major components to the conventional PC's system BIOS:

- *Resource management* handles the basic system resources: direct memory access (DMA), interrupt requests (IRQs), input/output (I/O), and shared memory address ranges. A variety of devices need these system resources, and this situation often leads to the conflicts discussed at the beginning of this chapter. The Plug and Play BIOS resource manager is responsible for configuring boot devices on the motherboard, as well as any PnP devices.

- *Runtime management* of configuration is new to PCs. PnP BIOS includes the capability to reconfigure devices after the operating system loads. This feature is particularly important for notebook PCs that have PCMCIA devices that you can change at will. Previously, the operating system considered all devices detected by the BIOS to be static; static detection requires that you restart the notebook after swapping a PCMCIA device.

- *Event management* detects when devices have been removed or added to the system while the computer is running. PnP BIOS 1.0a provides event management, such as detecting when your laptop or notebook PC is connected to a docking adapter (only for portable PCs, because hot swapping adapter devices of desktop PCs is not a safe practice). Event management relies on runtime management to reconfigure the system.

▶ See "Using Your Laptop with a Docking System," p. 273

If your PC doesn't have a BIOS ROM chip that meets the requirements of PnP BIOS Specification 1.0a, you're likely to be out of luck in the PnP department. The only exceptions are the following situations:

- Your computer has flash BIOS that you can upgrade with a floppy disk from the computer or motherboard supplier. Flash BIOS is a nonvolatile memory chip (NVRAM) that retains the BIOS instructions when the power is turned off.

- The supplier of your computer or motherboard offers a PnP BIOS 1.0a upgrade kit. In this case, you simply remove the existing BIOS chip(s) and plug in the replacement(s).

If the manufacturer or assembler of your computer doesn't offer one of the two preceding options, you need to replace the motherboard to gain the benefits of PnP. Of course, you need PnP-compliant PC adapter cards, such as PCI-bus components, or PCMCIA devices to gain the *full* benefit of Plug and Play.

Determining Whether Your Computer Supports Plug and Play

Some computers' BIOS display a line indicating Plug and Play compliance during the boot process. If you have a PC with an 80486DX2/66 or faster motherboard manufactured in 1995 or later, and you don't know whether the PC supports Plug and Play, follow these steps to check its capabilities:

1. Double-click Control Panel's System icon to open the System Properties sheet.

2. Click the Device Manager tab to display Devices by Type. (Click the Devices by Type option button, if necessary.)

3. Double-click the System Devices icon in the device list to expand the System Devices list.

4. If your PC supports Plug and Play, you see a Plug and Play BIOS entry (see fig. 8.1). The I/O Read Data Port for ISA Plug and Play Enumerator item appears regardless of whether your PC supports Plug and Play.

5. Double-click the Plug and Play BIOS icon to open the Properties sheet for the Plug and Play BIOS.

6. Click the Driver tab to display the device driver (BIOS.VXD) that Windows 95 uses to connect to the PnP feature of your system BIOS (see fig. 8.2).

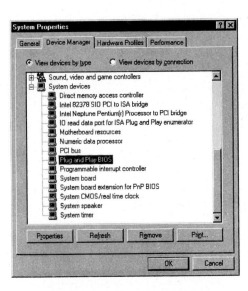

Fig. 8.1
Check the System
Devices list to
determine whether
your PC has Plug
and Play BIOS.

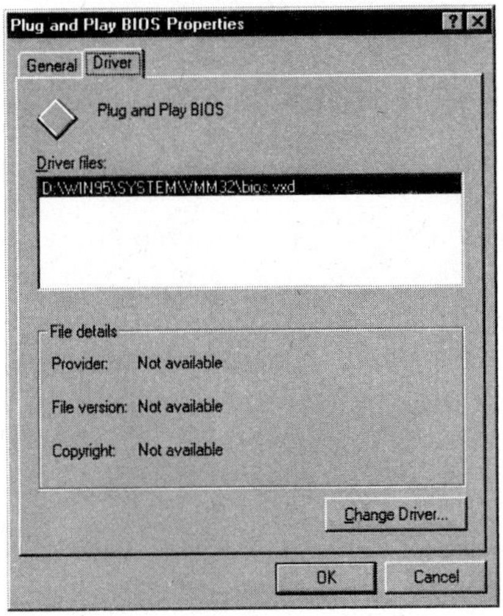

Fig. 8.2
Click the Driver
tab to check the
properties of
Windows 95's Plug
and Play BIOS
device driver.

PC hardware suppliers have used the term "plug and play" for several years
as a generic description of devices that are purported to be easy to install. If
you're purchasing a new PC or upgrading your PC's motherboard, make sure
that you use the preceding method to verify that the system BIOS supports
Plug and Play before you take delivery of your new or upgraded PC.

> **Caution**
>
> Some brands of computers whose motherboards were produced in 1994 display messages during the boot process, indicating that the motherboard supports Plug and Play. Many of these motherboards, however, have early versions of the PnP BIOS, which does not conform to the 1.0a specification. Even if your computer displays a PnP message during the boot process, check Device Manager for the Plug and Play BIOS entry to verify that you have PnP BIOS 1.0a.

Plug and Play Support for Fixed-Disk Drives

▶ See "Understanding What Your Disk Drive Does," p. 460

Windows 95 supports virtually every type of fixed-disk drive, even including ancient MFM (modified frequency modulation) and RLL (run-length limited MFM) drives. Windows 95 provides Plug and Play support only for IDE and SCSI-2 fixed-disk and CD-ROM drives. The following sections describe how Plug and Play simplifies the installation and configuration of your PC's fixed-disk and CD-ROMs.

Integrated Device Electronics (IDE) Drives

Fixed-disk drives in early IBM PC-ATs and clones required an adapter card that held most of the electronics that the drive needed to communicate with the ISA bus. Subsequently, PC and fixed-disk drive manufacturers determined that there were technical and economic advantages to moving the circuitry from the adapter card to the drive itself. The result was the Integrated Device Electronics (IDE) interface standard for fixed-disk drives. The IDE interface is very simple to implement with a few chips on an adapter card or the PC motherboard.

In mid-1994, the IDE specification was upgraded to provide a higher data rate (11M per second), accommodate up to four fixed-disk drives, support larger disk drives, and provide for PnP support. Today, the majority of drives that have 512M or lesser capacity use IDE. Newer PCs support 1G and larger IDE drives through Logical Block Addressing (LBA) or compatible Cylinder/Head/Sector (CHS) addressing for IDE drives up to 8.4G (1,024 cylinders, 255 heads, and 63 sectors maximum). Windows 95 supports both the LBA and CHS drive geometries.

> **Note**
>
> Limitations in the size of the DOS file allocation table (FAT) require that the fixed-disk cluster size increase as the capacity of the drive increases. 512M drives use 16K clusters, and 1G drives require 32K clusters. Each directory and every file, no matter how small, occupies a single cluster. The empty space in the cluster is called *slack*. A common practice is to partition, with FDISK.EXE, large disks into two or more logical volumes to reduce the cluster size and slack. An alternative is to use Windows 95's DriveSpace disk data compression utility on large drives. DriveSpace creates its own file allocation system, which minimizes slack.

▶ See "Compressing a Disk," p. 469

Standard IDE adapter cards connect two floppy-disk drives and two fixed-disk drives. Most of these cards now include the functions of the I/O card, providing two serial ports and one or two parallel ports. Most PC manufacturers now incorporate the floppy-disk and one or two IDE drive connectors, plus two serial ports and one parallel port on the motherboard. You can attach one or two IDE devices to each IDE connector (primary and secondary), for a maximum four devices supported by today's system BIOS. (New modem/audio adapter cards with on-board IDE connectors, such as Creative Lab's ViBRA product line, let you add additional IDE devices that the system BIOS doesn't recognize during the boot process.) The primary master IDE device is your boot drive (C); the second primary drive (D) is a slave. The secondary IDE connector, if you have one, also accommodates a master (E) and slave (F) drive.

Detection of the drive and drive geometry, as well as the assignment of drive letters, ordinarily is the responsibility of the PC's system BIOS. Windows 95 has its own automatic drive-geometry-detection system in its Installable File System (IFS) VxD for IDE drives. If Windows 95 can't resolve the drive geometry from BIOS data, IDE fixed-disk access falls back to the system BIOS.

Most manufacturers of CD-ROM drives now offer IDE versions, and IDE (ATAPI) CD-ROM drives that support PnP are likely to be the standard for moderately priced, multimedia-ready PCs. This situation means that manufacturers of audio adapter cards can eliminate the CD-ROM drive interface or substitute a simple IDE interface. (Creative Labs took the latter route for the firm's new Sound Blaster 32.)

Windows 95's built-in drivers support IDE devices that comply with the new ATA-2 (AT Attachment, version 2) standard and ATAPI devices that comply with the SFF8020 2.0 specification. Almost all IDE drives manufactured after

II

Working with Windows 95

mid-1994 are ATA-2 compliant, and every IDE CD-ROM drive conforms to ATAPI requirements. Fortunately, you don't need Plug and Play BIOS to take advantage of Windows 95's automatic configuration features for IDE drives.

Troubleshooting

I just installed an additional IDE drive, but it doesn't appear in My Computer or Explorer.

Most PCs with recent system BIOS automatically detect an additional drive connected to the primary IDE controller as a primary slave drive. If you have an older BIOS, you need to use the PC's BIOS setup application to specify the type of drive installed (number of cylinders, number of heads, landing zone, and other drive parameters). If you connect a third drive to a PC with a recent BIOS, you need to enable the secondary IDE controller in the BIOS setup program so BIOS can recognize the drive. IDE CD-ROM drives connected to sound cards usually can be installed as secondary, tertiary, or quaternary IDE drives. Use the default (secondary) setting for an IDE CD-ROM if you don't have a secondary IDE controller in your PC; if your PC has a secondary IDE controller, use the tertiary I/O base address and interrupt for the CD-ROM.

Small Computer Systems Interface (SCSI-2) and SCAM Drives

The Small Computer Systems Interface (SCSI, pronounced "scuzzy") bus is not a PC architecture, but a means of connecting multiple peripheral devices—such as fixed-disk drives, CD-ROM drives, tape backup drives, and graphic scanners—to the PC. You can connect up to seven internal or external SCSI devices to a single SCSI-2 adapter card or a SCSI-2 port on your PC's motherboard, if it has one.

Figure 8.3 is a block diagram of a typical SCSI-2 setup, with an internal SCSI fixed-disk drive, external CD-ROM and tape backup drives, and a page scanner.

Apple Computer was the first major manufacturer to support the SCSI bus; SCSI has been the primary means of attaching most external devices to the Macintosh. The majority of CD-ROM drives use SCSI-2, which is the second iteration of the SCSI bus, and many sound cards include a simple SCSI-2 adapter to connect CD-ROM drives. The advantage of the SCSI-2 bus is that the devices connected to the bus have built-in "intelligence": circuitry that takes some of the processing load off the PC. SCSI devices can "talk" to one another as well as to the PC. The extra circuitry for this intelligence causes SCSI-2 devices, such as disk and CD-ROM drives, to be somewhat more expensive than devices that have IDE or proprietary interfaces.

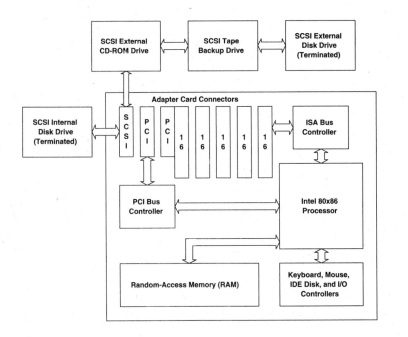

Fig. 8.3
A typical SCSI installation uses a PCI SCSI-2 host adapter to connect up to seven internal and external SCSI devices.

The original SCSI specification was a rather loosely worded document, and the SCSI devices sold by one manufacturer often didn't work with another manufacturer's products. The SCSI-2 specification tightened the requirements and provided a substantial increase in bus operating speed. Today, almost all SCSI-2 devices are fully compatible with one another. SCSI-2 has become the standard architecture for the high-capacity disk drives that are used in network file servers and client–server computing.

> **Note**
>
> SCSI-2 adapter cards have a 50-pin internal SCSI connector that connects to SCSI devices, such as fixed-disk and CD-ROM drives, mounted in your PC's housing. The SCSI-2 connector for external devices is much smaller than the original SCSI-1 connector. You need a special SCSI-2-to-SCSI-1 cable to mate the external connector of the new SCSI-2 adapter cards with conventional 50-pin "Micro Blue Ribbon" connectors used by the majority of today's external SCSI devices, such as scanners.

A recent improvement to the SCSI-2 bus, called fast-SCSI, increases bus speed from about 5M per second to 10M per second. Wide-SCSI uses a 16-bit or 32-bit bus structure to provide a theoretical 40M-per-second (40-M/s) data rate. Wide-SCSI is the basis for the new SCSI-3 specification. PCI multichannel wide-SCSI adapter cards, such as the Adaptec AHA-3940, provide up to a 133-M/s burst rate and 20-M/s synchronous data transfer across two channels.

▶ See "Video," p. 964

II

Working with Windows 95

The performance of the basic SCSI-2 bus is adequate for all but the most demanding network file server, client–server, and nonlinear digital-video-editing duties.

> **Note**
>
> SCSI-2 currently is the preferred bus for new 3.5-inch removable media disk drives, such as Iomega's external 100M Zip and forthcoming 1G Jaz drives. The Jaz drive is expected to have a data rate of 6 M/s or faster, making it suitable for recording digital-video data. Iomega plans an internal IDE version of the Zip drive, but Windows 95's support for removable-media IDE read-write devices is "rudimentary," according to a Microsoft white paper.

Even if your computer doesn't have Plug and Play BIOS, Windows 95 automatically detects all popular SCSI-2 host adapters, including SCSI-2 ports on sound cards, and installs the required SCSI *mini-port* driver (MPD file) for the device. Mini-port drivers adapt Windows 95's built-in SCSI-2 device driver for specific SCSI-2 host adapters or SCSI-2 interface chipsets.

Figure 8.4 shows the Device Manager item for the Adaptec AIC-6X60 ISA Single-Chip SCSI Controller used to connect SCSI-2 CD-ROM drives to Creative Labs' Sound Blaster 16 SCSI adapter card. Double-clicking the Adaptec AID-6X60 item displays the Properties sheet for the SCSI controller.

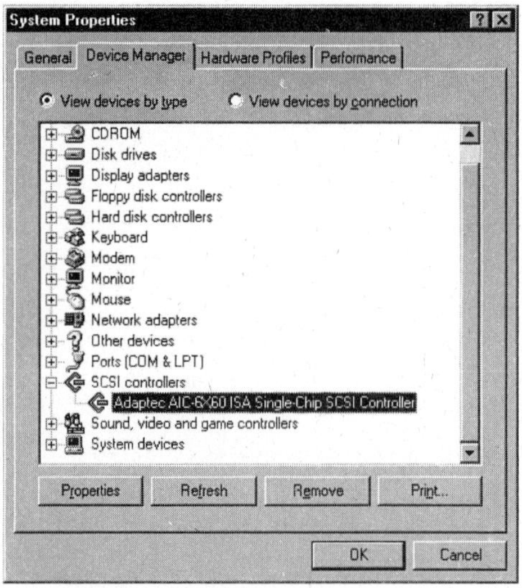

Fig. 8.4

The SCSI-2 controller of the Sound Blaster 16 SCSI adapter card appears in the Device Manager's list of SCSI controllers.

The Resources page of the controller's Properties sheet, shown in figure 8.5, enumerates the Input/Output Range, Interrupt Request, and Direct Memory Address (DMA) channel used by the controller. Device resources are one of the subjects covered in "Dealing with Legacy Hardware" later in this chapter.

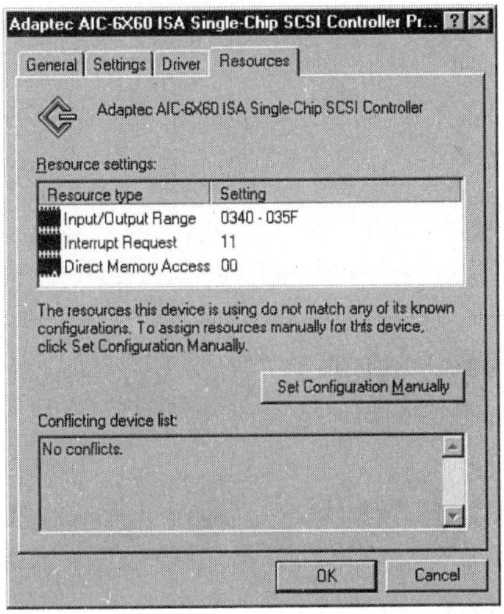

Fig. 8.5
Clicking the Resources tab of the Properties sheet displays the Input/Output Range and Interrupt Request settings for the Adaptec AIC-6X60 ISA Single-Chip SCSI Controller.

SCSI Configured AutoMagically (SCAM) is Plug and Play for the SCSI-2 bus, not just for PCs running Windows 95. The conventional SCSI bus has two basic problems: SCSI buses must be terminated by a set of resistors to prevent reflected signals, and each SCSI device on the bus must have a unique ID number (1 to 7 for SCSI-2; 0 is reserved for the SCSI adapter card). You set the "hard" ID number of SCSI devices with a small rotary switch or jumpers. SCAM-compliant SCSI-2 devices negotiate their own "soft" ID numbers, eliminating the need to set hard ID numbers.

SCSI-2 devices must comply with SCAM Level 1 (one SCSI master with a hard ID) or Level 2 (all soft ID devices) to carry the "Designed for Windows 95" logo. In addition, the internal SCSI-2 cabling, rather than the last SCSI device in the chain, must provide the termination resistors. (External SCSI-2 devices use a plug-in terminator.) Quantum's Lightning series drives were the first commercial SCAM-compliant fixed-disk drives. Make sure that any new SCSI-2 device you buy carries the "Designed for Windows 95" or SCAM logo.

> **Note**
>
> New SCSI-2 devices are quite reliable, but a variety of mishaps can kill the SCSI-2 bus. Therefore, many users of SCSI-2 devices install an IDE drive as the boot device (C) that stores Windows 95 and connect their SCSI-2 drives (D and higher) to a high-speed SCSI host adapter card. Booting from the IDE primary master device allows you to start Windows 95 even if a problem exists with your SCSI controller, device(s), or cabling.

IDE, SCSI, and the PCI Bus

Intel Corporation designed the Peripheral Control Interconnect (PCI) bus in conjunction with the development of the Pentium processor. The PCI bus, like the EISA and MCA (IBM Microchannel Architecture) buses, incorporates the hardware necessary to implement Plug and Play. Most PC motherboards that implement the PCI bus have seven active slots. Four slots are 16-bit ISA; two slots are 32-bit PCI; and one slot has a shared set of ISA/PCI connectors, into one of which you can plug either type of adapter card. You need a mouse that has an IBM PS/2 round (DIN) connector or a PS/2 mouse adapter for most PCI motherboards, because the system also provides mouse support. (If you elect to use a standard serial mouse, you lose one of the two serial COM ports.)

Although the PCI bus got off to a slow start in 1994, the fact that Intel designed the PCI bus carries a great deal of weight in the PC industry. Based on the number of references to PCI in Microsoft's PnP-related documents, PCI is the preferred bus structure for Windows 95. By mid-1995, the PCI bus had displaced the VESA (Video Electronic Standards Association) Local Bus (VLB) as the most popular high-speed bus for Windows graphics accelerator cards and fixed-disk controllers. PCI adapter cards are sure to dominate the digital-video capture and playback market in 1996 and beyond.

The PCI bus and the system BIOS's PCI features comprise a subset of the Plug and Play specification. Windows 95 supports the PCI bus with the following system devices:

■ *PCI Bus,* to specify the Windows 95 device driver for the bus (PCI.VXD).

■ *Processor to PCI Bridge,* to make the high-speed connection between an 80486DX or Pentium processor and the PCI bus.

■ *PCI to ISA Bridge,* to allow legacy ISA adapter cards for IDE drives to use PCI features.

- *PCI-to-PCI Bridge,* to provide the capability for a single PCI adapter card (such as the Adaptec AHA-3940, described earlier in this chapter) to use two PCI data channels. If the system BIOS doesn't include PCI-to-PCI-Bridge support, which usually is implemented only in high-end Pentium motherboards, you can't use multichannel PCI devices.

Even if your PCI-bus PC doesn't have Plug and Play BIOS, Windows 95 takes advantage of the PCI bus and the system BIOS's PCI features to provide basic Plug and Play installation and operation of PCI devices.

How the Windows 95 Operating System Orchestrates Plug and Play

When you boot a PnP computer, the following five steps occur:

1. The system BIOS identifies the devices on the motherboard (including the type of bus), as well as external devices such as disk drives, keyboard, video display, and other adapter cards that are required for the boot process.

2. The system BIOS determines the resource (IRQ, DMA, I/O, and memory address) requirements of each device. Some devices don't require all four of these resources. At this step, the system BIOS determines which devices are legacy devices that have fixed resource requirements and which are PnP devices for which resource requirements can be reconfigured.

3. The operating system (Windows 95) allocates the resources remaining after allowing for legacy resource assignments to each PnP device. If many legacy and PnP devices are in use, Windows 95 may require many iterations of the allocation process to eliminate all resource conflicts by changing the resource assignments of the PnP devices.

4. Windows 95 creates a final system configuration and stores the resource allocation data for this configuration in the registration database (Registry).

5. Windows 95 searches the \WINDOWS 95\SYSTEM directory to find the required driver for the device. If the device driver is missing, a dialog box appears, asking you to insert into drive A the manufacturer's floppy disk that contains the driver software. Windows 95 loads the driver in memory and then completes its startup operations.

II

Working with Windows 95

Figure 8.6 illustrates the preceding steps in the form of a simple flow diagram. Although the process appears simple on the surface, a substantial amount of low-level BIOS and high-level programming code is required to implement the PnP feature set. Compaq, Intel, Microsoft, and Phoenix Technologies deserve congratulations for making the Plug and Play magic work.

Fig. 8.6

A flow diagram best describes the PnP system configuration process.

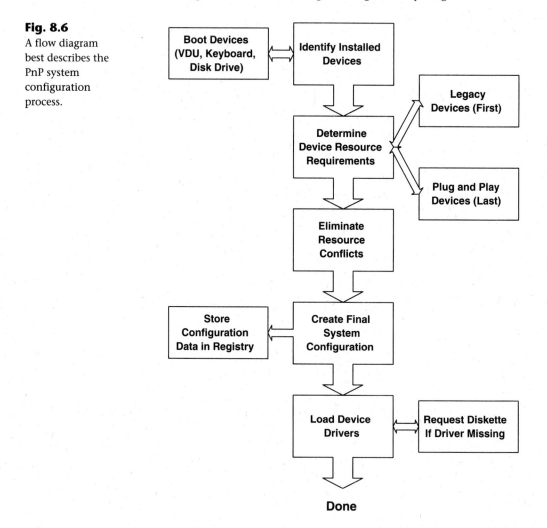

Done

Buying a Windows 95-Ready Plug and Play PC

At this point, you may have learned more than you ever wanted to know about PC architecture. Familiarity with acronyms such as PCI, VLB, IDE, and SCSI is necessary to distinguish between the offerings of suppliers that sell PCs carrying the "Designed for Windows 95" logo. However, your local clone dealer isn't likely to have taken all the necessary steps to be able to apply the Microsoft logo. If you plan to purchase a new PC or upgrade your current PC for Windows 95, the guidelines in the following list ensure that you'll get a "Designed for Windows 95" PC (even if the PC doesn't bear the logo):

- Pentium will be the standard processor for running Windows 95, especially if you're interested in multimedia applications. Pentium PCs now dominate the home-computer market. If you're on a budget, you can save some money by purchasing an 80486-architecture PC. You don't need a clock-tripled, 100-MHz 80486DX4, however, because Windows 95 runs like a champ on the standard 66-MHz 80486DX2 processor used to write this chapter and even on plain-vanilla 80486DX33s. For almost all users of Windows 95, 256K of cache RAM is adequate; discerning the performance improvement offered by a 512K cache is difficult.

- Don't even think about buying a PC or a new motherboard that doesn't have PnP BIOS 1.0a or later and a PCI bus. Plain-vanilla ISA PCs are obsolete, and the VLB is obsolescent; Plug and Play with PCI is where today's action is. Even if you don't plan to experiment with digital video or with playing and recording hi-fi sound today, you likely will be tempted to upgrade to PCI when you discover the 32-bit multimedia features of Windows 95. The cost differential between plain ISA or ISA/VLB and ISA/PCI bus motherboards is inconsequential.

- Buy as much RAM as you can afford. Like money, you never can have too much RAM (or fixed-disk space). The practical minimum for running today's Windows 3.1 and later applications is 8M, and Windows 95 requires about the same amount of RAM as Windows 3.1 and later. The good news is that Windows 95 makes better use of added RAM than Windows 3.1 and later does. For most users who don't run more than one Microsoft Office application at a time, 12M is optimum, but 16M gives a noticeable performance boost to the programs of Microsoft Office 95, especially Access 7.

II

Working with Windows 95

▶ See "Codec
Implementa-
tion in Win-
dows 95,"
p. 1009

■ If you're interested in graphics and/or multimedia, make sure that you include a DCI-compliant PCI graphics accelerator card with digital video acceleration in your purchase specification. If you're seriously interested in digital video, buy at least a 90-MHz Pentium so that you can play MPEG-encoded CD-ROMs (video CDs), using the software MPEG codec that Microsoft licensed in mid-1995 from Mediamatics, Inc. The $200 that you save because you don't need a hardware-assisted MPEG-1 playback card more than covers the extra charge for a fast Pentium.

■ Make sure that you purchase a fixed-disk drive with 600M or larger capacity. Remember that each full installation of a productivity application (such as Microsoft Excel, Word, PowerPoint, or Access) occupies about the same amount of disk space as Windows 95 itself—or even more. IDE drives with 1G capacity have a street price of less than $400.

■ Verify that the adapter cards or the equivalent circuitry on the motherboard is PnP-compliant and that the fixed-disk and CD-ROM drives support PnP. This guideline is especially important for SCSI-2 controllers and fixed-disk drives. Also make sure that the internal modem and sound card (if your purchase includes them) support PnP.

▶ See "Using
Your Laptop
with a Docking
System,"
p. 273

■ If you're buying a laptop or notebook PC, make sure that the PCMCIA cards and the docking station that you purchase are PnP-compliant and come with PnP drivers for Windows 95. Otherwise, you won't gain the advantages of hot swapping and hot docking.

Installing Plug and Play Hardware

Installing a PnP adapter card in your desktop PnP-compliant PC is a simple and straightforward process, at least in most instances. You follow these steps to install both the card and the 32-bit driver (VxD) required for use with Windows 95:

1. Turn off the power to your PC.

2. Open the case and install the adapter card.

3. Close the case and repower your PC.

4. Insert the driver floppy disk in your A or B drive, if requested.

5. Restart Windows 95, if requested.

If the driver for your adapter card is included with Windows 95, you might not need the card's driver floppy disk; Windows 95 automatically sets up the driver for your device. Compare the dates of the driver files, and use whichever is most recent. If Windows applications come with the adapter card, you install the applications by running SETUP.EXE or INSTALL.EXE from the floppy disk after installing the card.

Installing in PCs that have PnP-compliant serial and parallel ports PnP-compliant peripheral devices, such as printers, scanners, and external modems, follows a procedure similar to the one in the preceding list. When you add or change a peripheral device, you don't need to open the PC and, in some cases (modems, for example), a new driver isn't required. If you plug in a Hewlett-Packard LaserJet 4 Plus to your PC's parallel port, as an example, Windows 95 identifies the printer and automatically loads the required printer driver that's included with Windows 95. (You may be instructed to insert the CD-ROM or a specified distribution floppy disk that holds the printer driver.)

Troubleshooting

When I try to install a Plug and Play adapter card, I get a "resource conflict" message and the installation fails.

Most PC adapter cards require at least one I/O base address and one or more interrupts. (The "Setting Resource Values for Legacy Adapter Cards" section that follows shortly describes I/O base addresses and interrupts.) Most adapter cards support only a few of the available I/O base addresses and interrupts. If you already have several legacy adapter cards in your PC, you may have a situation where the I/O base addresses or, more likely, the interrupts supported by the new card are occupied by existing legacy cards. In this case, you need to change the settings of one or more of your legacy cards to free the required resource(s) for use by your new card. The worst-case condition occurs in PCI-bus PCs where all of the available interrupts are assigned before you install the new card. (In many PCI-bus PCs, PCI slots consume one interrupt each, whether or not the slot is in use.) The only solution in the worst case is to free an interrupt by reconfiguring your PC's system BIOS to reassign an interrupt from an unused PCI slot. If your system BIOS doesn't permit reconfiguration, you must remove an existing adapter card to free an interrupt.

Dealing with Legacy Hardware

Almost all PC adapter cards require at least one interrupt request (IRQ) level and a set of I/O base memory addresses for communication with your PC's processor. Some cards require one or more DMA (Direct Memory Access) channels for high-speed communication with your PC's RAM. IRQs, I/O memory, and DMA channels collectively are called *device resources*. Legacy adapter cards use the following two methods for setting their device resource values:

- *Mechanical jumpers* that create a short circuit between two pins of a multipin header. Jumpers commonly are used to designate resource values for sound cards.

- *Nonvolatile memory* (NVM) for storing resource assignments. Nonvolatile memory—such as electrically erasable, programmable read-only memory (EEPROM)—retains data when you turn off your PC's power. Network adapter cards (Intel's EtherExpress products) and sound cards (the Media Vision product line) commonly use NVM.

> **Note**
>
> PCI adapter cards don't have jumpers or nonvolatile memory to designate resource values. Instead, the system BIOS and Windows 95 automatically allocate resources needed by PCI adapter cards during the boot process.

▶ See "Under-
standing the
Unimodem
Driver,"
p. 841

▶ See "Using
Your CD-ROM
Drive," p. 970

▶ See "Adding a
Sound Board,"
p. 984

The following sections describe how Windows 95 deals with a variety of legacy adapter cards. Later chapters of this book describe in detail the installation process for specific device types, such as modems, CD-ROM drives, and sound cards.

Legacy-Device Detection during Windows 95 Setup

When you run Windows 95's Setup program, Windows 95 attempts to detect all the hardware devices in your PC, including legacy devices such as ISA sound cards and network adapters. If you install Windows 95 over an existing installation of DOS and Windows 3.1 or later, Windows uses the real-mode (16-bit) device drivers that it finds in your current CONFIG.SYS file. In addition, Windows 95 follows any instructions in your AUTOEXEC.BAT file to set up the device to use the drivers and to specify the IRQs, I/O base addresses, and DMA channels used by the device. To use the 32-bit protected-mode device drivers provided with Windows 95, you must disable these instructions manually from CONFIG.SYS and/or AUTOEXEC.BAT (by typing **REM** before entries).

When you install Windows 95 on a new computer or elect to use dual-boot mode, Setup performs a device-detection process similar to the one described in the preceding paragraph. In this case, however, Windows 95 installs its own protected-mode drivers for popular legacy adapter cards, such as sound cards, modems, and network cards. Using Windows 95's drivers eliminates the need to use the real-mode drivers supplied on floppy disk with the legacy card. If Windows 95 detects the device but doesn't have the appropriate built-in driver, a message box asks you to insert the driver disk for the device. If Windows can't identify the legacy device, you need to install the device manually. "Installing Legacy Cards after Setting Up Drivers," later in this chapter, explains the manual installation method.

Setting Resource Values for Legacy Adapter Cards

You must set the IRQ, I/O base address, and DMA channel of a new adapter card to values that do not conflict with the resource values that already are assigned to system devices, PCI slots, or other legacy adapter cards. One of the problems with the basic design of IBM-compatible PCs is that only 16 interrupts are available, and the majority of these interrupts are likely to be in use. Therefore, your choice of IRQs is limited.

> **Note**
>
> The word *base* in *I/O base address* refers to the location at which the block of I/O addresses for the adapter card begins. The actual number of address bytes occupied by the I/O system of the adapter card varies with the type of card. I/O addresses are separated by 16 bytes, and most adapter cards require fewer than 16 bytes of I/O address space.

Table 8.1 lists the PCs' IRQs and the most common use of each interrupt level.

Table 8.1   Interrupt Assignments and Options for ISA Cards Installed in 80x86-Based PCs

IRQ	Function	Comment
0	Internal timer	Dedicated; not accessible
1	Keyboard	Dedicated; not accessible
2	Tied to IRQ9	Dedicated; see IRQ9
3	Second serial port	COM2 and COM4; usually assigned to a modem
4	First serial port	COM1 and COM3; usually for a serial mouse

(continues)

II

Working with Windows 95

IRQ	Function	Comment
	Table 8.1 Continued	
5	Second parallel printer	Often used for bus mouse, network, and scanner cards
6	Floppy disk drives	Dedicated; do not use
7	First parallel printer	Used by some scanner cards; otherwise available
8	Time-of-day clock	Dedicated; not accessible
9	IRQ2 on 80x86 computers	IRQ2 is rerouted to IRQ9; often shown as IRQ2/9
10	Unassigned	Good choice for a sound card, if offered
11	Unassigned	Not a common option; use if 12 is assigned
12	Usually unassigned	Sometimes dedicated to an IBM-style mouse port
13	80x87 coprocessor	Dedicated; do not use even if an 80x87 is not installed
14	Fixed-disk drive	Dedicated; do not use
15	Usually unassigned	Used for secondary IDE controller, if installed

Virtually all PCs come with two serial port devices (COM1 and COM2) and one parallel port (LPT1) device. Unless your PC has a separate IBM PS/2-compatible mouse port, which requires an assignable interrupt, COM1 ordinarily is occupied by the serial mouse. The default interrupt for the Sound Blaster and most MPC-compatible audio adapter cards is IRQ5. Although IRQ7 is assigned to the second parallel printer (LPT2), few users have two printers, and printers seldom require an interrupt; therefore, IRQ7 usually is free. Network cards often use IRQ5.

The upshot of the preceding paragraph is this: use the highest IRQ that your legacy adapter card supports, leaving the lower IRQs for cards that don't support interrupts above IRQ9 or IRQ10. The Sound Blaster 16 audio adapter card, for example, supports only IRQ2/9, IRQ5 (the default), IRQ7, and IRQ10. The Intel Smart Video Recorder Pro video capture card allows you to choose IRQ9, IRQ10, IRQ11, or IRQ15; the best choice for the video capture card is IRQ15 (if you aren't using the secondary IDE connector) or IRQ11.

> **Note**
>
> If your computer has a PCI bus, the BIOS autoconfiguration feature usually assigns one interrupt to each PCI adapter-card slot. You may need to use the BIOS setup feature to assign a specific set of interrupts to the ISA adapter-card slots. In addition, some video overlay and capture cards require sharing upper-memory blocks with the ISA bus, which usually is accomplished by making an entry in one of the pages that appear during the BIOS setup process. See your PC's instruction manual for details on assigning interrupts and shared-memory locations to the ISA bus. Make a note of the IRQs that already are used by adapter cards in your PC.

Many more options exist for I/O base addresses than for IRQ levels, so you seldom encounter an I/O address conflict between adapter cards. The default I/O base address for the Sound Blaster 16 card and most other sound cards is 220H for the digital audio functions and 330H for the MIDI IN and OUT signals (MPU-401 UART). The H or h suffix indicates that the hexadecimal system is used to specify the I/O address. You occasionally see hexadecimal addresses specified in the syntax of the C language (0x220 or 0x240).

> **Note**
>
> Most legacy PC adapter cards use jumpers to set resource values. Cards that store resource settings in nonvolatile RAM require that you run their setup application to set IRQ, I/O base address, and (if applicable, DMA channel). If the setup program unavoidably installs real-mode drivers for the device, don't forget to disable the real-mode drivers by adding temporary REM prefixes before restarting Windows 95.

Installing Adapter Cards with Automatic Detection

The easiest way to install a new legacy card in a Windows 95 PC is to use the Add New Hardware Wizard's automatic-detection feature to identify your added card. The Wizard also is capable of determining whether you have removed a card. Auto-detection is best suited for PCs that have few or no specialty adapter cards, such as sound and video capture cards, already installed. (If you have many specialty adapter cards installed, the manual process described in the next section is a more foolproof approach.) The following steps describe the automatic-detection process in replacing a Sound Blaster 16 SCSI card with a Media Vision Premium 3D sound card:

1. Set nonconflicting resource values for your new adapter card, using jumpers or the card's setup program.

II

Working with Windows 95

2. Shut down Windows 95, and turn off the power to your PC.

3. Install the new adapter card in an empty ISA slot (remove the existing adapter card, if applicable), and make any required external connections, such as audio inputs and speaker outputs for sound cards.

4. Turn the PC power on, and restart Windows 95.

5. Launch Control Panel, and double-click the Add New Hardware icon to start the Add New Hardware Wizard (see fig. 8.7).

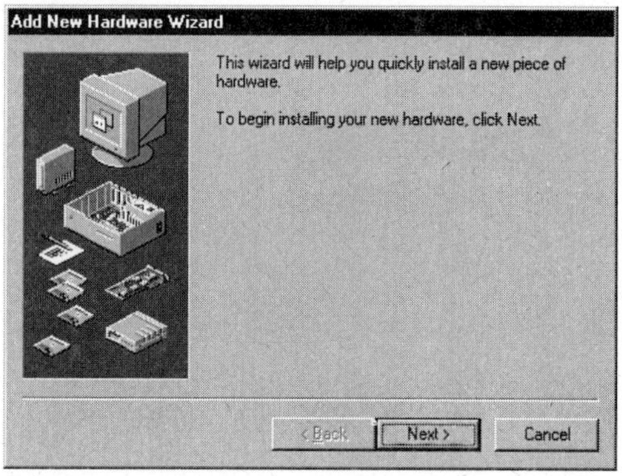

Fig. 8.7

This figure shows the opening dialog box of the Add New Hardware Wizard.

6. Click the Next button. You go to the Wizard dialog box that allows you to choose between manual and automatic hardware detection and installation. Accept the default Yes (Recommended) option (see fig. 8.8).

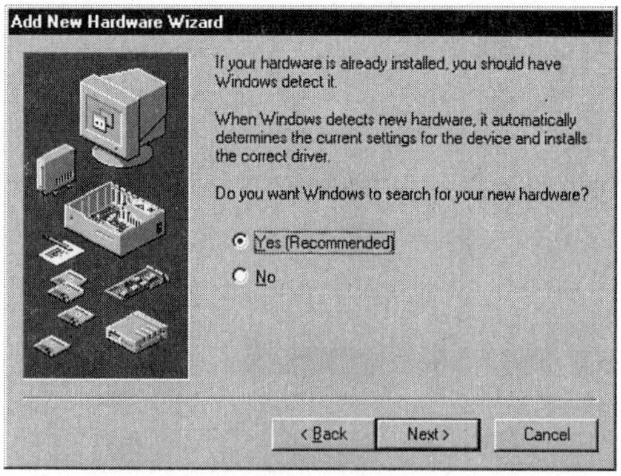

Fig. 8.8

You choose automatic or manual hardware detection in the Wizard's second dialog box.

7. Click the Next button to display the Wizard's boilerplate (see fig. 8.9).

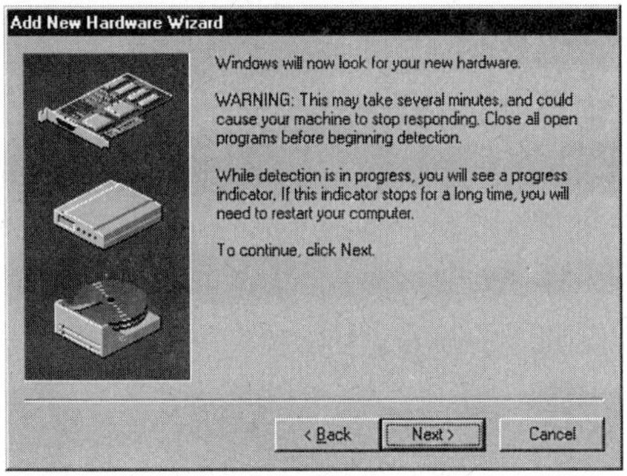

Fig. 8.9
The Wizard warns
that detection may
take a long time
or may lock up
Windows.

8. Click the Next button to start the detection process (see fig. 8.10).

After a few minutes of intense disk activity, often interspersed with periods of seeming inactivity, the wizard advises that detection is complete (see fig. 8.11).

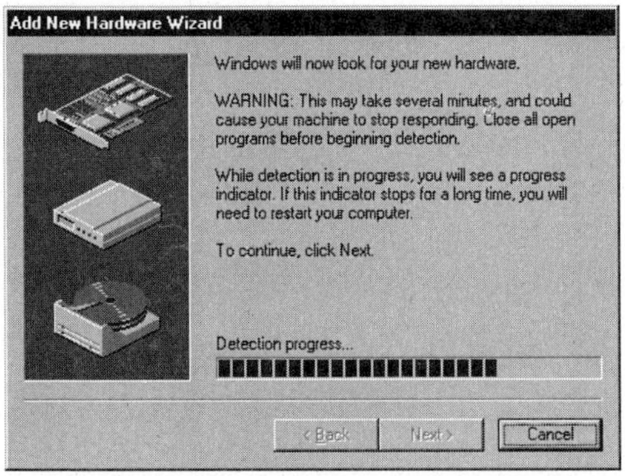

Fig. 8.10
The Wizard
detection-progress
dialog box tells
you when
detection is
complete.

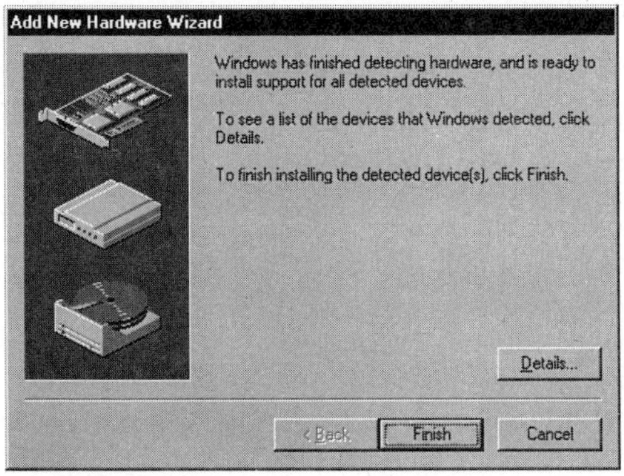

Fig. 8.11
Good news: the
Wizard has finally
finished the
detection process.

II

Working with Windows 95

9. Click the Details button to display what the Wizard detected. Figure 8.12 indicates that drivers for the Sound Blaster 16 SCSI card are to be removed and drivers for the Media Vision Pro/Premium 3D card are to be installed.

   If the Wizard doesn't detect your newly installed card, you must install the card manually; click Cancel to terminate the automatic-detection process.

Fig. 8.12
Success: the Wizard detected that the Sound Blaster 16 SCSI card has been replaced by a Media Vision Pro/ Premium 3D card.

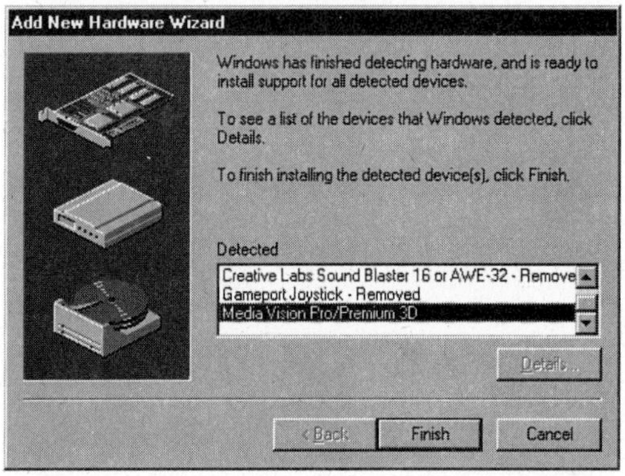

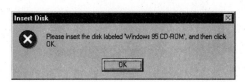

10. Click the Finish button to install the required drivers from the Windows 95 CD-ROM or floppy disks. The message box shown in figure 8.13 indicates the expected medium—in this case, the Windows 95 CD-ROM.

Fig. 8.13
The message box tells you the medium on which Windows 95 expects to find the required drivers.

11. Insert the Windows 95 CD-ROM into the drive, and click OK to install the drivers.

12. If Windows 95 can't find the required device-driver file in the expected location, you see the series of dialog boxes shown in figure 8.14.

   In this example, if your CD-ROM drive previously was connected to the Sound Blaster 16 SCSI card and now is connected to the Media Vision card, Windows 95 cannot read the CD-ROM. You must use the Windows 95 distribution floppy disks to install the drivers. The required setup cabinet file, WIN95_08.CAB, is located on disk 8. Insert the proper disk, click OK to close the Open dialog box, and then click OK again to close the Copying Files dialog box and continue the installation process.

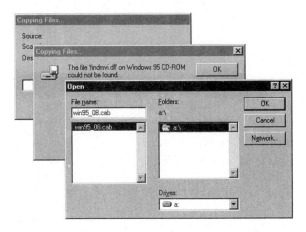

Fig. 8.14
This cascade of dialog boxes is required to change the location or type of the distribution medium for Windows 95.

13. When driver installation is complete, a message box advises you that system settings have changed and asks whether you want to restart Windows 95. Click Restart Now so that your driver changes take effect.

Tests with a variety of modems, sound cards, Windows graphics accelerator cards, and digital video capture cards indicate that the Wizard detects all but very specialized (and, therefore, uncommon) devices.

Installing Legacy Cards after Setting Up Drivers

The alternative to automatic device detection, described in the preceding section, is installing the new adapter card manually after you install its drivers. The advantage to this method is that you can determine in advance resource settings that don't conflict with existing devices. (You also eliminate the CD-ROM driver dilemma described in the preceding section if you install the driver for the new CD-ROM drive before installing the adapter card for the drive.) The following steps describe the process of reinstalling the drivers for the Sound Blaster 16 SCSI card:

1. Launch the Add New Hardware Wizard from Control Panel, and click the Next button in the opening dialog box to display the Wizard dialog box that allows you to choose between manual and automatic hardware detection and installation (refer to fig. 8.8).

2. Choose the No option to select manual installation; then click the Next button to display the Wizard's Hardware Types dialog box (see fig. 8.15).

Fig. 8.15

The Add New Hardware Wizard's Hardware Types dialog box lists a variety of adapter card categories.

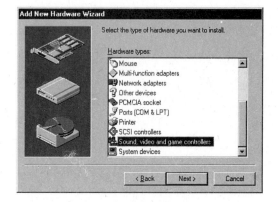

3. Select the card type in the Hardware Types list; then click the Next button to display the Manufacturers and Models dialog box (see fig. 8.16).

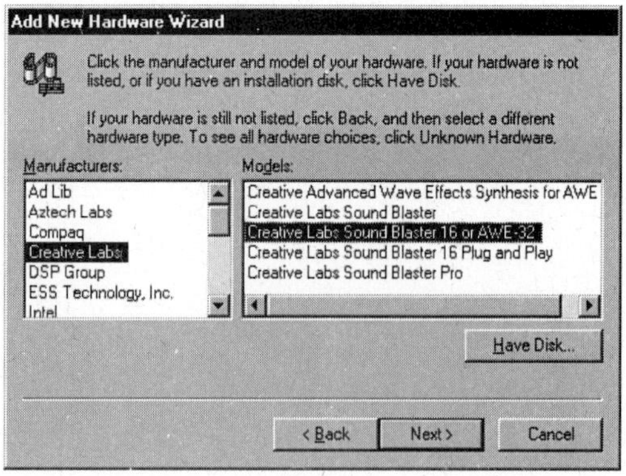

Fig. 8.16

The Wizard dialog box lists manufacturers and models of devices for which drivers are included on the Windows 95 distribution media.

4. Make the appropriate selections in the Manufacturers and Models list boxes; then click the Next button to display the default settings for the new device.

If you don't see the manufacturer or model in the list boxes, you need a floppy disk or CD-ROM that contains Windows 95 drivers for your device (Windows 3.1 or later drivers won't work). If you have the required Windows 95 drivers, click the Have Disk button to install the drivers from floppy disk or CD-ROM. If you don't have Windows 95 drivers, click the Cancel button to terminate the installation.

5. Windows 95 can't tell what resource value settings you made for your new or replacement adapter card, so the manufacturer's default settings for the device appear in the Wizard's Resource Settings dialog box (see fig. 8.17). Write down or print these default settings.

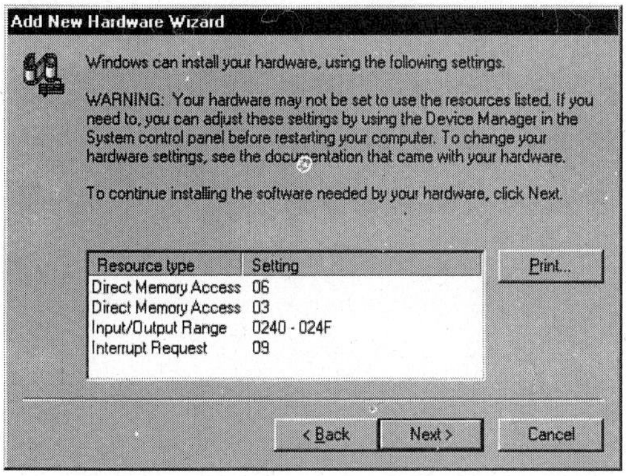

Fig. 8.17
Default values for the Sound Blaster 16 SCSI card appear when opening the Resource Setting dialog box.

6. Click the Next button to display the System Settings Change message box (see fig. 8.18).

   If the default settings in the preceding step correspond to the resource settings of your card, click the Yes button to shut down Windows 95. If you haven't installed the card (which is the normal situation for manual device detection), turn off the power to your PC, install the card, turn the power back on, and restart Windows 95 with the new card activated.

   If any of the resource values in the preceding step are incorrect or you receive a "resource conflict" message, click the No button in the System Settings Change message box so that you can alter the resource values as necessary.

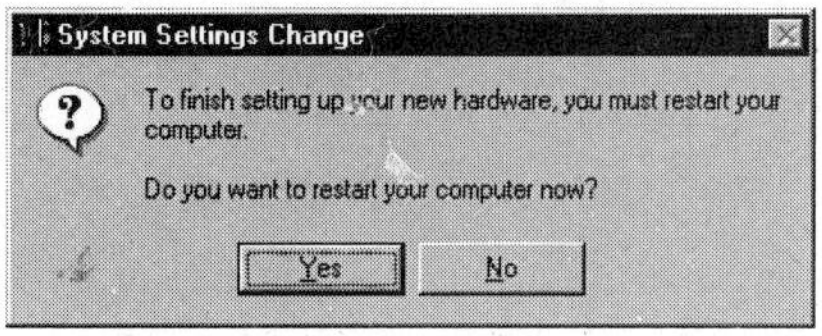

Fig. 8.18
The System Settings Change message box gives you the option to restart Windows 95.

7. Open Control Panel's System Properties sheet, click the Device Manager tab, and expand the entries for the type of device that you're installing.

Exclamation points superimposed on the device's icon(s) indicate that the device is not yet fully installed or has been removed from your PC.

8. If you're replacing a card, entries for both cards appear in the Device Manager list. To remove the old entry, select the entry and click the Remove button. A message box requests that you confirm the removal process (see fig. 8.19).

Fig. 8.19
You're asked to confirm removal of an unneeded device with the Device Manager.

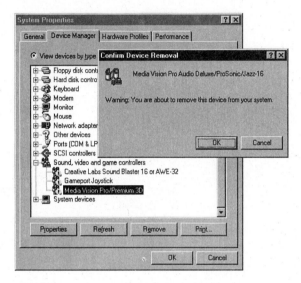

9. Double-click the entry for the new adapter card to display the Properties sheet for the device.

10. In the Resource Settings list box, select the resource whose value you want to change; then click the Change Setting button to display the Edit Interrupt Request dialog box for the resource.

11. Use the spin buttons of the Value text box to select the value that corresponds to the preset value for your adapter card. If a conflict with an existing card occurs, the card that has the conflicting value is identified in the Conflict Information text box (see fig. 8.20).

12. Change the Value setting to a value that displays No devices are conflicting in the Conflict Information box; then make the corresponding change in the card, using the jumpers or nonvolatile RAM. (Turn off power to your PC before making jumper changes.) Figure 8.21 shows an I/O base address setting changed to remove a conflict at Input/Output Range 0260 - 026F.

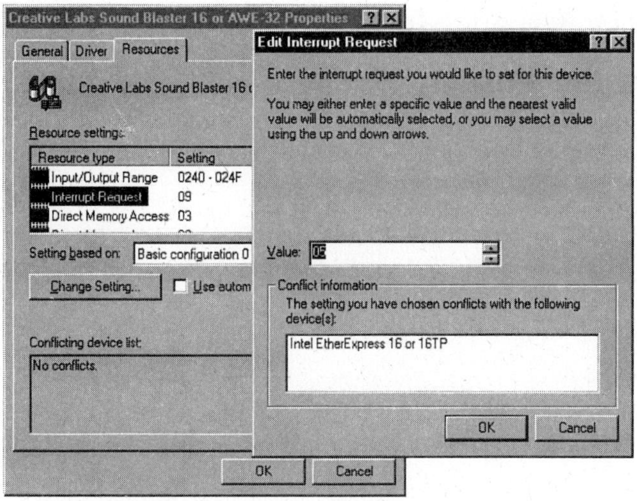

Fig. 8.20
Change the IRQ
setting for the new
adapter card to
avoid a conflict;
IRQ5 conflicts
with the network
card's IRQ in this
example.

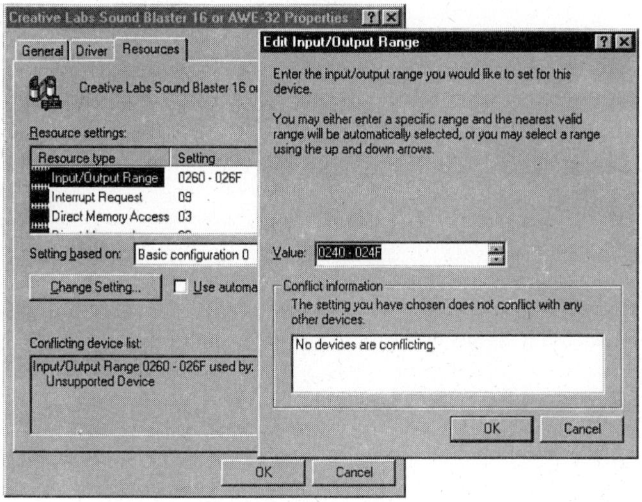

Fig. 8.21
Change the I/O
base address
(Input/Output
Range) to a
nonconflicting
value.

II

Working with Windows 95

13. After making all the changes necessary to remove resource conflicts, click OK to close the resource's Edit Input/Output Range dialog box, and then click OK to close the Properties sheet for the device.

14. Click OK to close the System Properties sheet.

15. Shut down and restart Windows 95 so that your new settings take effect.

The process of manually installing a legacy device, described in the preceding steps appears to be complex, but it's a more foolproof process than the one used by Windows 3.1 and later. In particular, the capability to detect resource conflicts with proposed resource value settings for legacy adapter cards eliminates many of the problems associated with installing new devices under Windows 3.1 and later.

> **Note**
>
> Windows 95 includes drivers for an extraordinary number of popular devices but not for low-volume products, such as digital video capture and MPEG-1 playback cards. Reputable manufacturers of specialty legacy devices likely will provide 32-bit protected-mode drivers for Windows 95 in late 1995 and early 1996. You can expect updated Windows 95 drivers to be posted in manufacturers' technical-support forums on CompuServe, in BBSs on the Microsoft Network, and at vendors' World Wide Web sites.

Removing Unneeded Drivers for Legacy Devices

If you remove a legacy device from your PC and don't intend to reinstall it, it's good Windows 95 housekeeping to remove the driver for the device from Device Manager's list. Follow these steps to remove the Device Manager entry for permanently removed adapter cards:

1. Double-click Control Panel's System icon to open the System Properties sheet.

2. Click the Device Manager tab and double-click the icon for the hardware type of the device removed to display the list of installed devices. An exclamation point superimposed on a device icon indicates a removed or inoperable device.

3. Click the list item to select the device you want to remove and then click the Remove button.

4. Confirm that you want to remove the device by clicking OK in the Confirm Device Removal message box (refer to fig. 8.19).

   If you have more than one hardware configuration, a modified version of the Confirm Device Removal message box appears. Make sure the default Remove from All Configurations option button is selected; then click OK to remove the device and close the message box.

Using Windows 95's Registry Editor to Troubleshoot Hardware-Compatibility Problems

In most cases, you can solve hardware-resource-conflict problems by changing jumper positions or using the card's setup program to alter nonvolatile RAM values and then making corresponding changes in resource values in the device's Properties sheet. If you have a problem that changing resource settings doesn't solve, the card supplier's product-support staff probably will need additional information about your system. The primary source of system information is Windows 95's Registry; all device information that appears in Device Manager is obtained from entries in the Registry.

To examine the Registry, you need to set up and use the Registry Editor (RegEdit) application, REGEDIT.EXE. Windows 95 doesn't add a Start menu choice for RegEdit automatically, because Windows 95 neophytes and the faint of heart should not attempt to change Registry values.

If you need to check the Registry values for an adapter card, follow these steps:

1. Open the Start menu, and choose <u>R</u>un.

2. Type **regedit** to open the Registry Editor.

3. Choose <u>F</u>ind, <u>E</u>dit to open the Find dialog box.

4. In the Fi<u>n</u>d What text box, type the key word for the card in question; then click the <u>F</u>ind Next button to locate the first instance of the key word.

   The support person usually gives you the key word on which to search. The phrase *sound blaster*, for example, finds all references to Sound Blaster hardware in the Registry.

5. The first or second instance of the key word is likely to display the Plug and Play device assignment data for the card. Press F3 to find the successive instances of the key word.

   Figure 8.22 shows the PnP device data for the Sound Blaster 16 card.

6. Pressing F3 might continue finding additional instances of Registry entries for the device in question. Figure 8.23 shows the Registry entry that defines the driver for the Line Input device of the Sound Blaster 16, SB16SND.DRV.

II

Working with Windows 95

Tip

If you use RegEdit often, create a shortcut for it. The REGEDIT.EXE file is in the \WINDOWS directory.

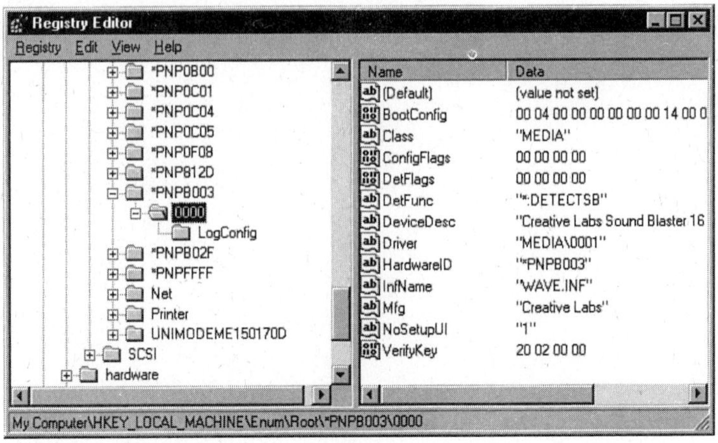

Fig. 8.22

The Windows 95 Registry Editor displays Plug and Play device assignment values for a Sound Blaster 16 card.

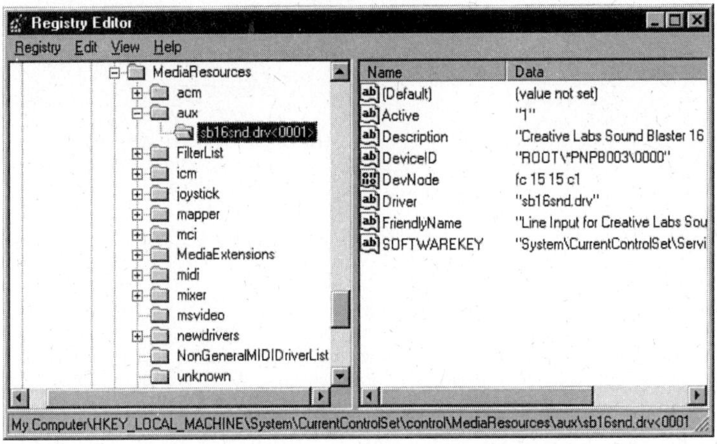

Fig. 8.23

Continued searching in RegEdit displays the settings of the driver for the Line Input device of the Sound Blaster 16 card.

Caution

Do not make any changes in Registry data unless you are instructed to do so by a competent technician who is fully conversant with Windows 95. Improper values of Registry entries can prevent proper operation of Windows 95 and may prevent you from booting Windows 95.

Using Multiple Hardware Configurations

Windows 95 allows you to create multiple hardware configurations for your PC. (Multiple hardware configurations aren't necessary, however, if you have a PC that has PnP BIOS and if all your devices also are PnP-compliant.) The most common use of a multiple hardware configuration is to reflect the docking or undocking of a laptop or notebook PC in a non-PnP docking station. You also can use multiple hardware configurations if you repeatedly change legacy adapter cards in your PC.

To set up one or more alternative hardware profiles, follow these steps:

1. Open the System Properties sheet (by double-clicking Control Panel's System icon), and click the Hardware Profiles tab.

2. In the Hardware Profiles list box, select the Original Configuration profile; then click the Copy button to open the Copy Profile dialog box.

3. In the To text box, type the name of the new profile (see fig. 8.24); then click the OK button to create the new hardware profile.

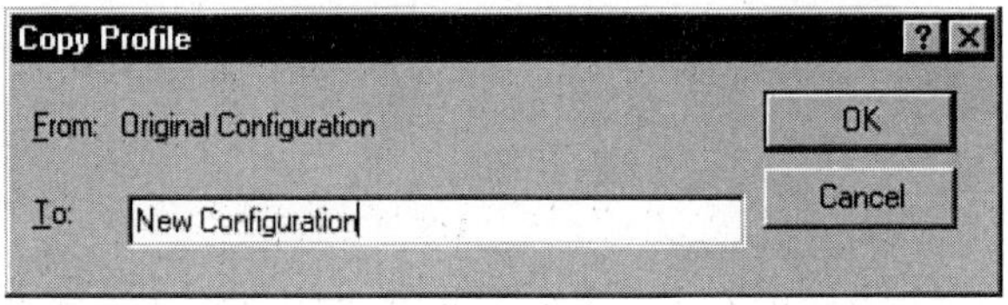

Fig. 8.24
Create a copy of the Original Profile to serve as an alternative hardware profile.

4. Click the Device Manager tab, and select a device that you don't want to use in the new alternative profile.

   By default, all devices in the Original Profile are enabled in the new alternative profile, as indicated by a check in the check box to the left of the hardware-profile name (see fig. 8.25).

5. To prevent a device from being used in the alternative profile, clear the check box for the device.

II

Working with Windows 95

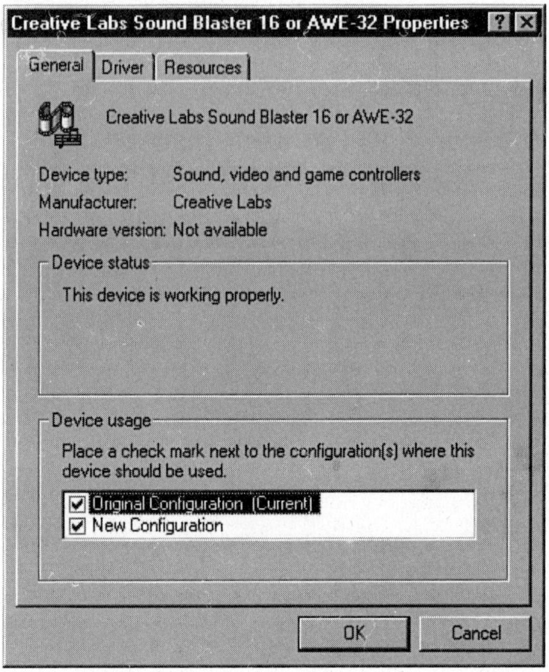

Fig. 8.25
Device Manager
shows a device
enabled in both
the Original
Profile and the
new profile.

6. To set the default hardware profile for startup, select the profile on the Hardware Profiles page; then click OK to close the System Properties sheet.

7. Shut down and restart Windows to activate the selected hardware profile.

The use of alternative hardware profiles in Windows 95 is uncommon, but it is an example of Microsoft developers' attention to detail, which enables Windows 95 to accommodate almost any set of hardware-related changes.❖

Chapter 9

Special Features for Notebook Users

by Jim Boyce with Doug Kilarski

As computing moved beyond the desktop, Microsoft recognized the need for system services and end-user functionality to improve the mobile-computing experience. With portable PCs forecasted to comprise 33 percent or more of the entire computer system production in 1995, mobile computer support couldn't be an afterthought. Portable support had to be foremost in the minds of Windows 95 developers.

Many business professionals want to be able to take their office with them. Portable technology and Windows 95 make a hard-to-beat combination. Portable PCs enable you to work nearly anywhere, and Windows 95's features for portable computing—which include 32-bit support for PC Card (PCMCIA) devices, file synchronization, Dial-Up Networking, remote mail, and more—make Windows 95 a perfect operating system for your portable PC. Not only does Windows 95 make it easy for you to take your work with you, but features such as Dial-Up Networking and remote mail enable you to keep in touch with coworkers and access disk and printer resources in your main office from anywhere in the world.

> **Note**
>
> What were formerly called "PCMCIA" devices are now referred to as "PC Card" devices.

Simply put, Windows 95 enables users to better utilize their portable PCs. Mobile users have universally asked for three areas of portable-specific features:

- Get the most out of their portable PC hardware

- Maintain access to office LAN resources

- Keep organized

Windows 95 delivers on all three points. PC Card, Plug and Play, disk compression, power management, and support for port replicators and docking stations all complement portable PC hardware. Windows 95 architectural enhancements conserve battery power and manage configuration changes, which helps extend the life of older portables. Dial-Up Networking enables you to access your office file server(s) using your modem and send and receive e-mail to coworkers. Windows 95 keeps users organized as well. Using an advanced file synchronization system called Briefcase and a deferred printing option, roaming users remain "in sync" with their desktop environments (and vice versa).

To help you understand how to get the most from Windows 95's features for portable computing, this chapter explores the following:

- Using PC Card (PCMCIA) devices

- Using a docking system

- Using a direct cable connection to share resources

- Using power management

- Using Dial-Up Networking

- Synchronizing files with Briefcase

- Using mouse trails

Using PC Card Devices

Many notebook PCs contain one or two special bus slots called *PC Card slots* (formerly PCMCIA slots) that accommodate credit card-sized adapters for various functions. Although initially only flash memory cards were available in PCMCIA format, today many types of devices—including modems, hard disks, network cards, sound cards, and other devices—are available in PC Card/PCMCIA format. In addition, PC Card docking stations enable you to use PC Card devices in desktop PCs, making it possible, for example, to use the same PC Card modem in a notebook PC and a desktop PC.

> **Note**
>
> There are three official types of PC Card slots, referred to as Type I, Type II, and Type III. The specification for a fourth type of slot—Type IV—is being finalized by the PCMCIA organization (Personal Computer Memory Card International Association). One of the primary differences between the types of PC Card slots is that each higher-numbered slot accommodates a thicker PC Card than the previous slot. PC Card hard disks, for example, generally require a Type III slot, but modems can be installed in a Type I or Type II slot. Most of today's newer notebook PCs can accommodate one Type III device, or two Type II devices (or any combination of two Type I and Type II devices).

◀ See "Installing Plug and Play Hardware," p. 246

The primary advantage of PC Card devices for portable PC users is that these devices make it possible to expand the capabilities of portable PCs in the same way you can expand desktop systems, enabling you to add optional hardware to the portable PC. Windows 95 improves on the PCMCIA support in DOS and Windows 3.x by providing 32-bit device drivers to support the PC Card controllers in most PCs. This makes it possible for Windows 95 to support a wide variety of PC Card devices without requiring 16-bit, real mode drivers that slow down the system and use conventional memory.

Another improvement for PC Card devices in Windows 95 is expanded support for *hot swapping*, which is the ability to remove and insert PC Card devices in the PC without powering down the computer. If you need to temporarily remove your network card to use a modem, for example, you first use the PC Card object in the Control Panel to turn off the network card (see fig. 9.1). Then, you simply remove the network card from its slot and insert the modem. Windows 95 disables the network driver(s) temporarily and enables the modem drivers.

II

Working with Windows 95

Fig. 9.1

Use the PC Card (PCMCIA) Properties sheet to enable and disable PC Card devices.

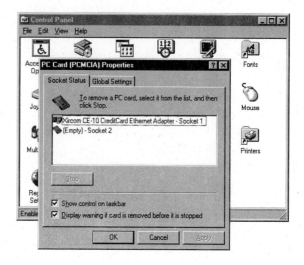

Installing PC Card Support

Each computer with PC Card slots or a PC Card docking station includes a PC Card controller that enables the CPU to communicate with the PC Card bus. This controller requires a set of drivers that enable the operating system (in this case, Windows 95) to communicate using the PC Card bus. In addition, each PC Card device requires a device-specific driver that enables the device to function and communicate with the operating system. If you are using a PC Card network card, for example, Windows 95 requires a set of drivers for the PC Card slot itself and a separate driver for the network card.

When you install Windows 95, Setup automatically detects your PC's PC Card controller and installs support for it. Setup does not, however, enable the 32-bit PC Card controller drivers. Setup takes this approach because some portable PCs require that you continue to use 16-bit drivers (which come with the portable PC) to control the PC Card slots.

Note

Windows 95 supports 32-bit drivers for systems based on either an Intel PCIC-compatible PC Card controller or Databook PC Card controller.

In addition to enabling 32-bit PC Card support (if your PC supports it), you must install the drivers for the PC Card devices you'll be using. In many cases, Windows 95 can install these devices automatically using Plug and

Play, even on systems without a Plug and Play BIOS. To install a PC Card modem, for example, simply insert the modem in its slot. Windows 95 detects the new device and starts the Add New Modem Wizard to install the modem driver.

Enabling 32-Bit PC Card Support

After you install Windows 95, you must use the PC Card object in the Control Panel to enable 32-bit support for your PC Card controller. Enabling 32-bit support provides better overall system performance and more effective memory use. In addition, enabling 32-bit PC Card support is required to support Plug and Play installation of PC Card devices and hot-swapping.

> **Note**
>
> When Windows 95 enables 32-bit PC Card support, your existing 16-bit real mode PC Card drivers are disabled. If you are installing Windows 95 from a network server, you must have local access to the Windows 95 source files. Therefore, you must have a set of Windows 95 floppy disks or have a CD-ROM connected to your portable PC to enable Windows 95 to read the 32-bit driver files for the PC Card controller. Optionally, you can copy the Windows 95 cabinet files from the network server to your portable PC's hard disk prior to enabling 32-bit support.

To enable 32-bit PC Card support for your PC, use the following steps:

1. Verify that you have local access to the Windows 95 cabinet files as explained in the previous note.

2. Open the Start menu and choose Settings, Control Panel.

3. Choose the PC Card (PCMCIA) object. The first time you open this object, the PC Card (PCMCIA) Wizard appears (see fig. 9.2).

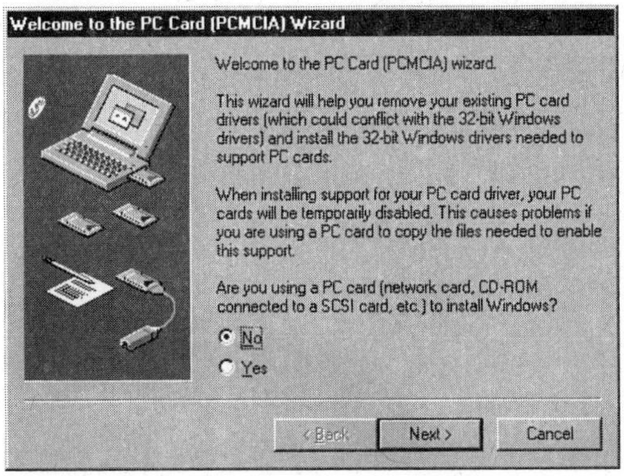

Fig. 9.2
The opening dialog box of the PC Card (PCMCIA) Wizard.

II

Working with Windows 95

4. Choose No and then Next to inform the Wizard that you are not setting up Windows 95 from a network server. (If your Windows 95 setup disk is on a network server or another device such as a CD-ROM drive connected through a PC Card adapter, choose Yes.)

5. If the PC Card Wizard detects existing real-mode PC Card drivers, it displays the dialog box shown in figure 9.3, enabling you to view the drivers and control the way the Wizard handles the existing drivers. If you want the Wizard to automatically remove the drivers, choose No and then choose Next. If you want to view and verify the deletion of the existing real-mode PC Card drivers, choose Yes and then choose Next.

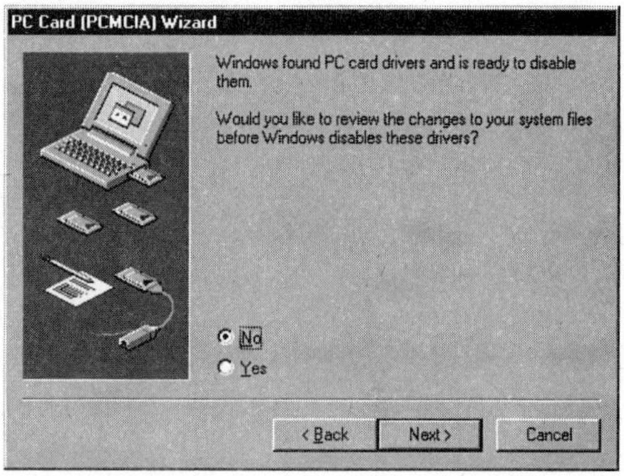

Fig. 9.3

To verify your drivers, choose Yes.

6. If you select Yes, the Wizard displays a set of dialog boxes that show the device entries in CONFIG.SYS, AUTOEXEC.BAT, and SYSTEM.INI that it will delete (see fig. 9.4). If you do not want the wizard to delete a specific driver from one of these files, deselect the line in the appropriate dialog box, and then choose Next.

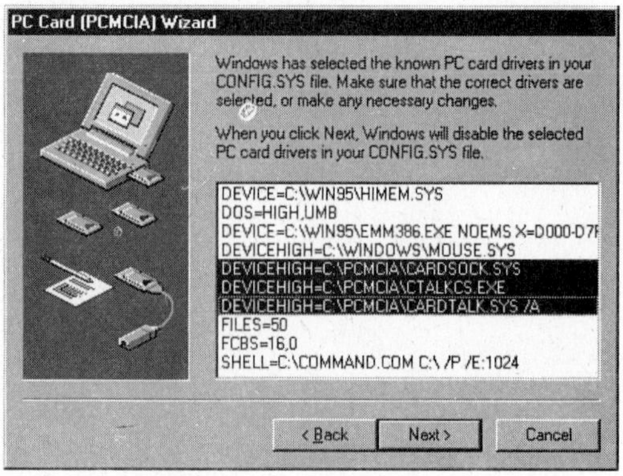

Fig. 9.4

The PC Card (PCMCIA) Wizard enables you to verify real-mode driver deletion.

7. After the PC Card Wizard removes the real-mode drivers (if any) as directed by you, it displays a final dialog box that prompts you to choose Finish to complete the PC Card setup process and enable 32-bit PC Card support. Choose the Finish button to complete the process. Windows 95 shuts down so the change takes effect.

Installing PC Card Devices

After you enable 32-bit PC Card support, Windows 95 can typically install PC Card devices automatically. If you insert a network card in the PC, for example, Windows 95 detects the new card and automatically installs the necessary drivers for the card. If, for some reason, Windows 95 does not automatically recognize your PC Card device, you must manually install support for it.

To manually install a PC Card device other than a modem or network adapter, use the following procedure:

1. Insert the new PC Card device in the appropriate slot. (Check the PC Card device's manual to determine if the device must be installed in a specific slot.)

2. Open the Control Panel and choose the Add New Hardware object to start the Add New Hardware Wizard. Then choose Next.

3. Choose <u>Y</u>es and then Next to enable the Wizard to automatically detect your new PC Card device.

4. If the Wizard is unable to detect the new device, the Wizard displays a hardware selection dialog box similar to the one shown in figure 9.5. Choose the type of device you are installing and then choose Next.

▶ See "Installing and Configuring the Network Adapter Cards," p. 624

▶ See "Installing and Configuring Your Modem," p. 831

II

Working with Windows 95

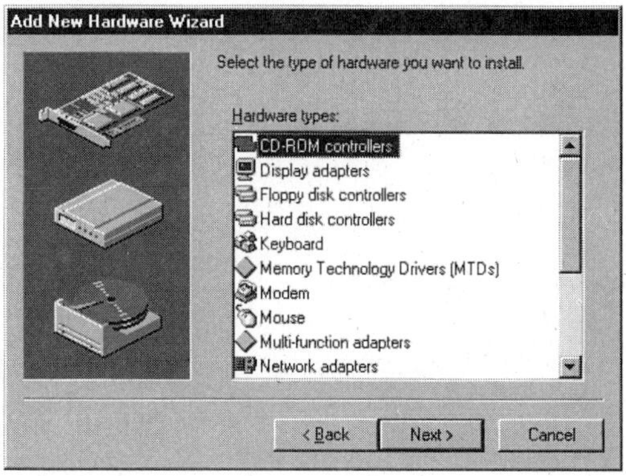

Fig. 9.5
Choose the type of device you are installing and then choose Next.

Tip

If you are install-
ing a PC Card
network adapter,
use the Network
object in the Con-
trol Panel to install
it. If you are in-
stalling a PC Card
modem, use the
Modems object in
the Control Panel.

5. From the <u>M</u>anufacturers list, choose the manufacturer of the device you
   are installing. Then from the Mo<u>d</u>els list, choose the device model. If
   your manufacturer or model is not listed and you have a driver disk for
   the device, choose <u>H</u>ave Disk and then follow the prompts to direct the
   Wizard to the directory on the floppy disk where the necessary files are
   located.

6. After you have selected the correct manufacturer and model, choose OK
   to complete the setup process.

Hot-Swapping PC Cards

Windows 95 enables you to remove a PC Card device and replace it with
another without powering down the system. This capability enables you to
quickly swap PC Card devices. Before you remove a device, however, you
should first shut down the device. To do so, choose the PC Card object in the
Control Panel. Windows 95 displays a PC Card (PCMCIA) Properties sheet
similar to the one shown in figure 9.6, which displays information about the
PC's PC Card slots and any currently inserted devices.

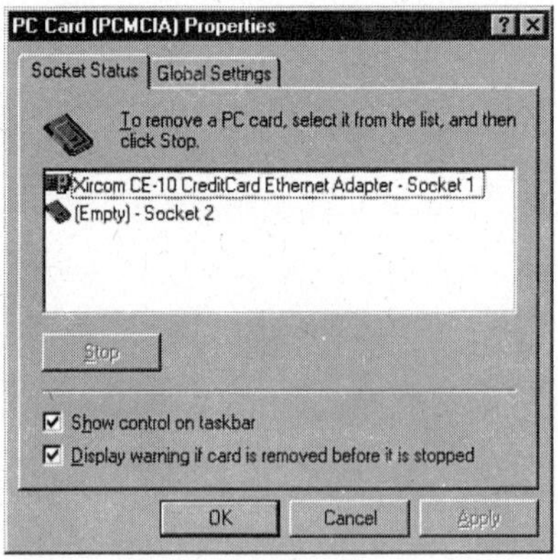

Fig. 9.6

You can view
information about
slots and installed
devices.

To remove a PC Card device from the system, first select the device from the
list on the Socket Status page and then choose <u>S</u>top. Windows 95 shuts down
the device and temporarily disables its drivers. After Windows 95 disables the
device, the socket is listed as empty. You then can remove the PC Card
device.

To insert a new device, simply insert the device in the proper slot. If you have
previously installed support for the device, Windows 95 detects the device
and automatically enables its drivers. If you have not used the device in the

PC previously, Windows 95 detects the new hardware and automatically installs support for the device.

Using Your Laptop with a Docking System

Before docking stations (see fig. 9.7) and port replicators, portable PC users were often trading mobility for compromises in storage, video quality, and display size. Beyond the lack of accessible resources, the general incompatibility and undynamic docking posed even greater problems. Much time was spent reconfiguring and rebooting systems during docking and undocking.

Fig. 9.7
A docked notebook.

With Windows 95, *hot-docking support* integrates hardware and software for quick and easy docking. Docking and undocking can occur when the power is on or off. Windows 95 automatically detects any configuration changes and manages any conflicts or file disruptions. It also loads and unloads hardware drivers as required. To undock your PC when Windows 95 is running, open the Start menu and choose Eject PC. Windows 95 reconfigures the system automatically for the undocked configuration and then prompts you to remove the PC from the docking station.

Creating and Modifying Hardware Profiles

Windows 95 enables you to create multiple hardware profiles to accommodate different hardware configurations, such as when your PC is docked and when it is undocked. Windows 95 automatically creates two hardware profiles for you—one for the docked configuration and a second profile for the undocked configuration. Windows 95 detects which profile is required at startup and automatically uses the correct one.

Note

If your portable PC contains a Plug and Play BIOS, Windows 95 does not have to use multiple hardware profiles to accommodate hot docking. Instead, the Plug and Play BIOS can detect which devices are available and Windows 95 can configure the system accordingly.

If you want to change an existing profile or create a new one, you can do so through the Control Panel. Use the following procedure to create a new hardware profile:

1. Open the Start menu and choose Settings, Control Panel.

2. Double-click the System icon to display the System Properties sheet.

3. Click the Hardware Profiles tab to display the Hardware Profiles page (see fig. 9.8).

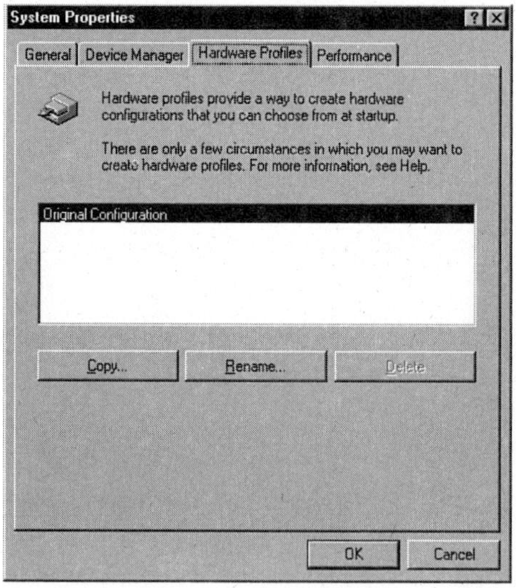

Fig. 9.8
The Hardware Profiles page enables you to modify and create hardware profiles.

4. Select the hardware profile you want to use as a basis for the new profile, and then choose Copy. Windows 95 displays a Copy Profile dialog box in which you specify the name for the new hardware profile (see fig. 9.9).

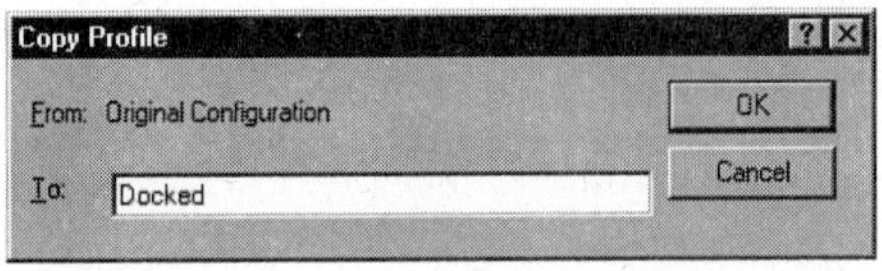

Fig. 9.9
Specify a name for
the hardware
profile.

5. Enter a name for the new profile and choose OK. The new hardware profile appears in the Hardware Profiles list.

In some cases, you might want to modify a hardware profile. If Windows 95 is unable to properly detect the hardware in a particular configuration, for example, you can modify the profile to add and remove hardware from the profile.

To modify a hardware profile, use the following procedure:

1. Open the Control Panel and double-click the System icon; then click the Device Manager tab to display the Device Manager property page (see fig. 9.10).

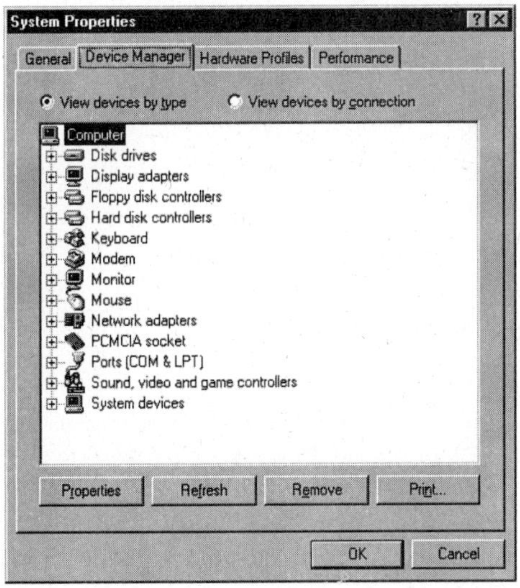

Fig. 9.10
Use the Device
Manager page to
modify a hardware
profile.

2. Select the hardware device that you want to add or remove from a particular profile, and then choose Properties to display the General page of its Properties sheet (see fig. 9.11).

Working with Windows 95

II

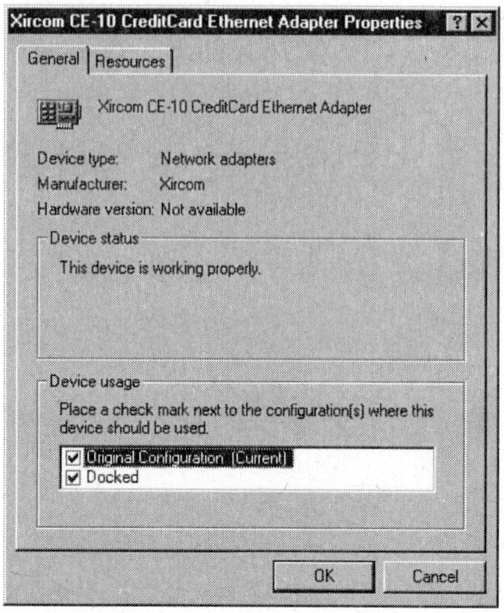

Fig. 9.11

Use the Device
Usage list to add
and remove
hardware from
a profile.

3. At the bottom of the device's General page is a Device Usage list that defines which profiles use the device. Place a check in the check box beside a hardware profile to enable the device for that profile. Clear the check box to disable the device for that profile.

4. Choose OK to apply the changes.

When you start the system, Windows 95 detects the hardware configuration you are using and automatically applies the appropriate hardware profile. If the hardware profiles are so similar that Windows 95 cannot determine which profile should be used, Windows 95 displays a menu containing a list of the available profiles and prompts you to select the profile to be used.

Working with Different Configurations

Most hardware settings in Windows 95 are stored relative to the current hardware profile. Changes that you make to a device's settings are applied to the current profile, but not to other hardware profiles. It therefore is possible to maintain different settings for the same device in two or more different hardware profiles. For example, you might use a display resolution of 640 X 480 in one profile, but use 800 X 600 in a different profile. Such is probably the case when you are using an external monitor with your PC. You probably use 640 X 480 with the portable's LCD display and a higher resolution with the external monitor.

To configure unique settings for a device, first start Windows 95 using the hardware profile in which you want the changes to be made. If you want to use a high-resolution mode with an external monitor, for example, select the hardware profile you normally use with the external monitor (or create a profile for use with the external monitor as explained in the previous section). After you've started Windows 95 with the appropriate hardware profile, change the settings for the device. The changes are applied to the current hardware profile and do not affect other profiles you have created.

Troubleshooting

Windows 95 did not automatically select the LCD monitor for my laptop's LCD when I ran setup.

Check the monitor type in the hardware profile that is used when you are working with the internal display. To set the monitor type, right-click on the desktop and choose Properties. Click the Settings tab to display the Settings page. Choose Change Display Type to display the Change Display Type dialog box. Choose the Change button to display the Select Device dialog box. Choose the Show All Devices option button, choose Standard Monitor Types from the Manufacturers list, and then choose the appropriate Laptop Display Panel selection from the Models list.

Using Deferred Printing

When your portable PC is docked, you probably have access to a printer connected to the docking station or that is available across the network. When your PC is not docked, however, it is unlikely that you'll have access to a printer. Even though you might not have access to a printer, however, Windows 95 still makes it possible for you to print documents through *deferred printing*. When you print a document, Windows 95 places the document in the printer's queue, even if the printer is not available. The document remains in the printers's queue even when you turn off your computer.

◀ See "Controlling Printing," p. 174

When you dock your computer and the printer once again becomes available, Windows 95 senses that the printer is available and begins spooling the document to the printer. Deferred printing is handled automatically by Windows 95. You simply print the document, and when the printer becomes available, Windows 95 begins sending the document to the printer.

Sharing Local Resources via Parallel or Serial Connection

A growing number of portable users also have a desktop system. They regularly transfer files between systems by using either a floppy disk and/or a direct parallel or serial cable, and a third-party application to handle the transfer. Windows 95 includes a feature called Direct Cable Connection that integrates the same capability within Windows 95—essentially, you can use a serial or parallel cable to network together your portable and desktop PCs, creating a small peer-to-peer network. The two computers then can access each other's files and other resources (such as a fax modem) as if they were joined by a traditional network interface.

In a direct cable connection, one computer acts as the host (server) and the other computer acts as a guest (client). The host PC also can act as a gateway, enabling the client to access the network to which the host is connected. The host can serve as a gateway for NetBEUI and/or IPX/SPX protocols, but cannot serve as a gateway for TCP/IP.

Setting Up Direct Cable Connection

If you select the Portable option when you install Windows 95, Setup installs Direct Cable Connection on your PC. If you use a different option or deselected the Direct Cable Connection option during Setup, you must install it. To add Direct Cable Connection, use the following procedure:

1. Open the Start menu and choose Settings, Control Panel.

2. Double-click the Add/Remove Programs icon.

3. Click the Windows Setup tab to display the Windows Setup page.

4. Select Communications from the Components list, and then choose Details.

5. Place a check beside Direct Cable Connection, and then choose OK.

6. Choose OK again to cause Windows 95 to add Direct Cable Connection to your PC.

> **Note**
>
> If Direct Cable Connection is already checked in the Components list, the software is already installed on your PC.

After installing the Direct Cable Connection software, you must connect the two computers with an appropriate cable. You can use either a parallel or null-modem serial cable to connect your two PCs. The types of cables you can use for the connection are described in the following list:

- Standard 4-bit null-modem cable, and LapLink and InterLink cables made prior to 1992.

- Extended Capabilities Port (ECP) cable. To use this type of cable, your parallel port must be configured as an ECP port in your system BIOS.

- Universal Cable Module (UCM) cable, which supports connecting together different types of parallel ports. You can use a UCM cable to connect together two ECP ports for fastest performance.

As indicated above, configuring your parallel ports as ECP ports provides the best performance. To use ECP, however, your PC's ports must be ECP-capable, and the ports must be configured as ECP ports in the system BIOS. Older PCs do not contain ECP-capable parallel ports.

▶ See "Client/ Server Net- works," p. 582

The final step in setting up the Direct Cable Connection is to ensure that both the guest and host computers are using the same network protocol. You can use the NetBEUI, IPX/SPX, or TCP/IP protocols. In addition, you must use an appropriate network client, such as Client for NetWare Networks or Client for Microsoft Networks. The host computer must be running either the File and Printer Sharing for Microsoft Networks service or the File and Printer Sharing for NetWare Networks service.

Setting Up the Host

In a Direct Cable Connection between two PCs, one PC acts as the host and the other PC acts as the guest. The first step in enabling the connection is to configure the host. To do so, use the following procedure:

1. Open the Start menu and choose Programs, Accessories, Direct Cable Connection. Windows 95 displays the dialog box shown in figure 9.12.

2. Select Host option and then choose Next. Windows 95 displays the dialog box shown in figure 9.13.

II

Working with Windows 95

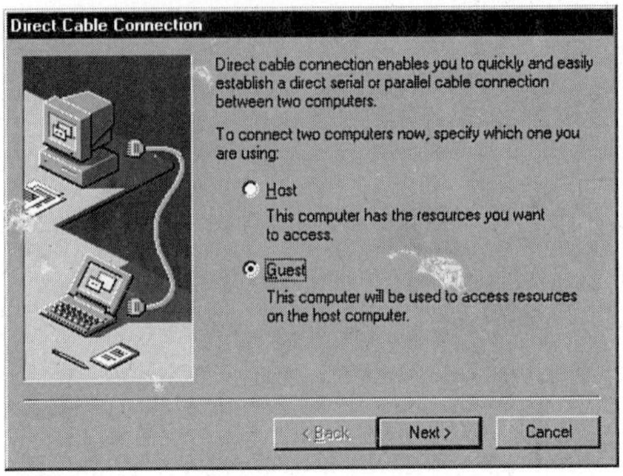

Fig. 9.12
Choose whether
the PC will act as
host or guest.

3. Choose the port you want to use on the host for the connection. You can choose one of the host's parallel or serial ports. After selecting the port, choose Next.

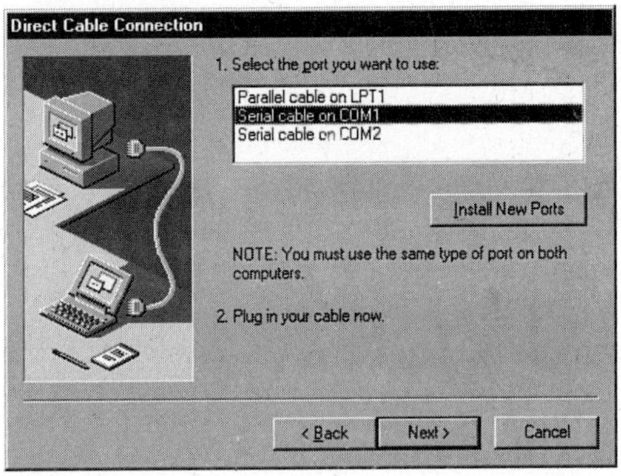

Fig. 9.13
Select the port to
be used by the
connection.

4. Specify whether you want to use password protection to prevent unauthorized access to the host. To use password protection, enable the Use Password Protection check box. Then choose Set Password, which displays a simple dialog box in which you enter the password that must be provided by the guest computer to access the host. When you've specified the desired password settings, choose Finish to complete host setup.

Setting Up the Guest

After configuring the host, you're ready to configure the guest computer. To do so, use the following procedure:

1. On the guest computer, open the Start menu and choose Programs, Accessories, Direct Computer Connection.

2. From the Direct Cable Connection dialog box, choose Guest and then Next.

3. Choose the port on the guest PC through which the connection will be made and then choose Next.

4. Choose Finish to complete the setup.

Before you begin sharing files using the Direct Cable Connection, you must share a directory in which the files will be transferred. To set up sharing, see Chapter 21, "Sharing Windows 95 Peer-to-Peer Resources."

Using the Direct Cable Connection

When you want to begin using your mini-network connection, you need to start the Direct Cable Connection software on both the host and the guest computers. On the host, open the Start menu and choose Programs, Accessories, Direct Cable Connection. Windows 95 displays a dialog box similar to the one shown in figure 9.14.

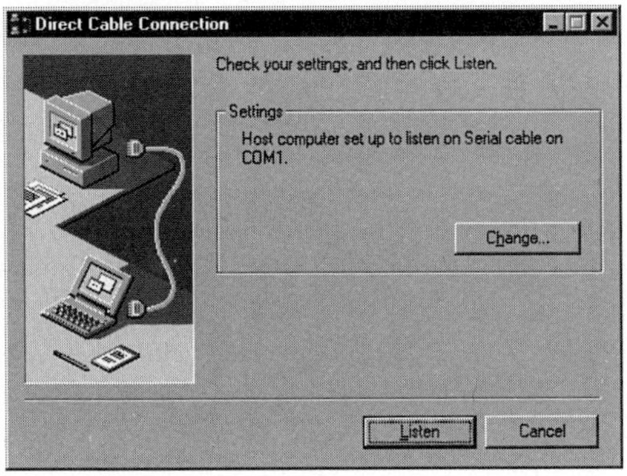

Fig. 9.14

Choose Listen to set up the host for the connection.

▶ See "Windows 95 Peer-to-Peer Networking Features," p. 618

▶ See "Understanding File Sharing," p. 643

If the settings you specified previously are correct, choose Listen to place the host computer in listen mode to listen for a connection by the guest. If you need to change the password or port settings, choose Change.

After placing the host computer in listen mode, start the Direct Cable Connection software on the guest computer. Open the Start menu and choose Programs, Accessories, Direct Cable Connection. Windows 95 displays a dialog box similar to the one shown figure 9.14, except the Listen button is replaced by a Connect button. Choose Connect to connect to the host and begin using the connection.

Using Power Management

Tip
In order for your PC to use power management, the PC's BIOS must include support for power management, and power management must be enabled in the PC's BIOS.

Most portable PCs (and an increasing number of desktop PCs) support some form of power management that allows the PC's devices to be shut down to conserve power while the computer remains on. Power management, for example, can power down the hard disk when the disk is not being used, conserving battery power. When the system is idle, power management can shut down the display and even the CPU to further conserve power. Windows 95 integrates power management into the operating system and adds features to the interface that enable you to easily take advantage of power management.

If your portable PC supports power management, and power management software (such as MS-DOS's POWER.EXE) is enabled when you install Windows 95, Setup adds support for power management automatically. If power management software was not enabled during Setup, you must enable power management yourself through the Control Panel. The following steps explain how to enable power management:

1. Open the Start menu and choose Settings, Control Panel.

2. Double-click the System icon.

3. Click the Device Manager tab and then double-click the System devices item to expand the System devices tree.

4. Select the Advanced Power Management support item and then choose Properties.

5. Click the Settings tab to display the Settings page shown in figure 9.15.

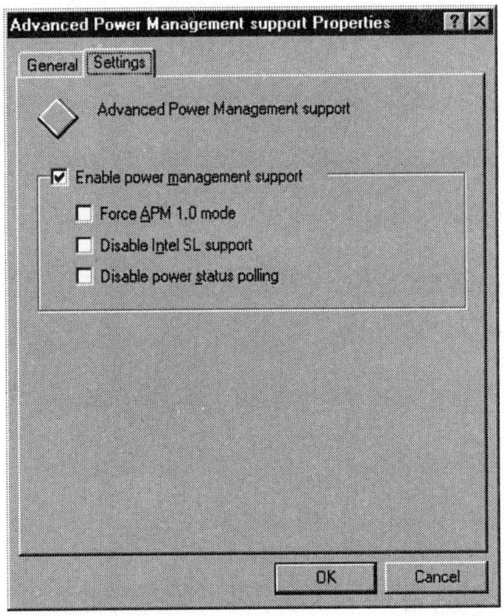

Fig. 9.15
Use the Settings page to control power management.

6. Place a check in the Enable Power Management Support check box and then choose OK.

7. Choose OK to close the System Properties sheet. Windows 95 prompts you to restart the computer for the change to take effect.

The other options on the Settings page control the way power management works. These options are explained in the following list:

■ *Force APM 1.0 Mode*. Enable this option if your PC's power management features do not work properly. This option causes Windows 95 to use an APM 1.1 BIOS in 1.0 mode, which overcomes problems with some portable PCs.

■ *Disable Intel SL Support*. If your computer uses the SL chipset and stops responding at startup, enable this option.

■ *Disable Power Status Polling*. Enable this option if your PC shuts down unexpectedly while you are using it. This option prevents Windows 95 from calling the APM BIOS to check battery status, consequently also disabling the battery meter in the tray.

II

Working with Windows 95

Setting Power Management Options

▶ See "Setting SL Options," p. 285

The Power object in the Control Panel enables you to specify options that control power management features. Selecting the Power object in the Control Panel displays the Power Properties sheet shown in figure 9.16. The large SL button appears on the Power page only if your PC uses an SL processor.

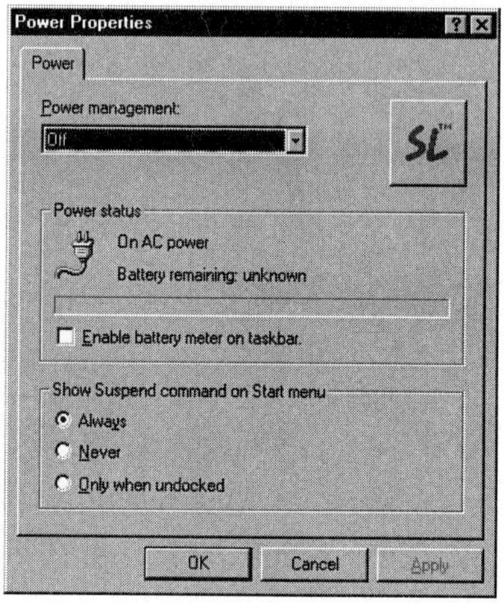

Fig. 9.16

Use the Power page to set power management options.

Tip

When you want to place the PC in suspend mode, open the Start menu and choose Suspend. Windows 95 will immediately place the PC in suspend mode. If you have files open across the network, you should first save or close the files before placing the PC in suspend mode to avoid losing data.

The Power Management list enables you to specify the level of power management your system uses. The options you can select are explained in the following list:

- *Standard.* Choose this setting to use only the power management features supported by your PC's BIOS. Additional features, such as battery status monitoring, are not enabled when you choose this feature.

- *Advanced.* Choose this setting to use full power management support, including features provided by Windows 95 in addition to those provided by your PC's BIOS. These include battery status monitoring and power status display on the tray.

- *Off.* Choose this setting to turn off power management.

Additional options on the Power property page control whether or not the Suspend command is displayed in the Start menu. Choose Always if you want the Suspend command always displayed on the Start menu. Choose Never if you do not want it to appear on the Start menu, even when the system is undocked. Choose Only when Undocked if you want the Suspend command to appear on the Start menu only when the PC is not connected to a docking station.

The Power property page also displays information about battery status and enables you to turn on or off the power status indicator on the taskbar. To view the amount of power remaining in your battery, rest the cursor on the power indicator on the taskbar for a second and Windows 95 will display a Tool Tip listing battery power remaining. Or, double-click the power indicator to display a Battery Meter dialog box similar to the one shown in figure 9.17.

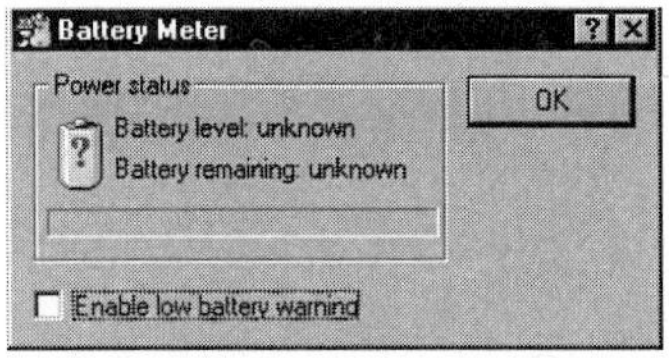

Fig. 9.17
The Battery Meter dialog box shows power remaining.

> **Note**
>
> As you can see in figure 9.17, Windows 95 cannot always detect the amount of power remaining in the battery. This is often due to the way in which the batteries used in portable PCs drain their charges. The voltage remains fairly steady through the battery's cycle, then begins to drop rapidly as the battery nears the end of its useful charge.

Setting SL Options

If your PC uses an Intel SL processor such as the 486SL, you can use SL-specific options to control additional power management features. As previously explained, an SL button appears on the Power property page on systems containing an SL processor. Choosing the SL button displays the SL Enhanced Options dialog box shown in figure 9.18.

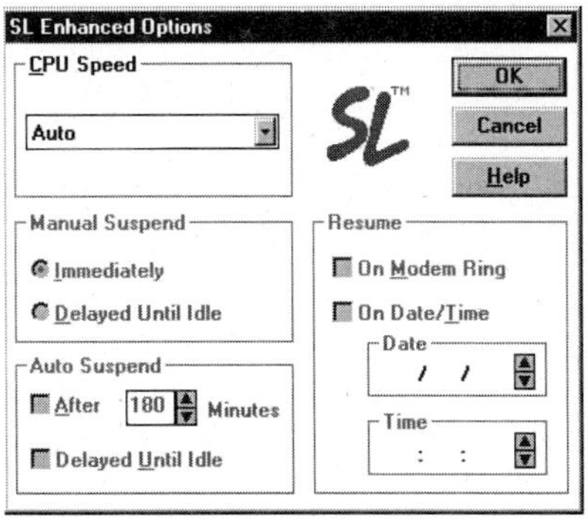

Fig. 9.18
The SL Enhanced Options dialog box controls SL-specific power options.

II

Working with Windows 95

The following list explains the groups in the SL Enhanced Options dialog box:

- *CPU Speed.* This drop-down list enables you to control how the CPU is managed. Choose Auto to cause the CPU to run at full speed but power down whenever possible to conserve power. Choose 10 percent, 25 percent, or 50 percent to run the CPU at a specific reduced speed. Choose 100 percent to run the CPU at full speed and prevent the CPU from powering down.

- *Manual Suspend.* The two settings in this group control the way the system powers down when you press the Suspend button, close the display (on a notebook PC), or choose Suspend in the Start menu. Choose Immediately in the Manual Suspend group to cause the PC to suspend immediately when you press the PC's Suspend button or close the display. Windows will suspend all applications even if they are currently processing. Choose the Delayed Until Idle option to cause Windows to wait for all applications to finish processing before it powers down the PC. Some applications appear to Windows to be processing when they actually are just waiting for input, so the system might not enter suspend mode if such an application is running and the Delayed Until Idle option is selected.

- *Auto Suspend.* This option controls how the system powers down automatically after a specified period of time with no keyboard or mouse activity. The After option lets you specify an amount of time after which the system powers down automatically. The Delayed Until Idle option causes the system to power down automatically only if there are no active applications. These settings don't affect the screen, hard disk, or other devices individually. Instead, they control shutdown of the entire system, including the CPU.

- *Resume.* These settings control how the system resumes after it has been suspended. The On Modem Ring option, if enabled, causes the system to resume if a call comes in to a line that is connected to the PC's modem. The On Date/Time option enables you to specify a specific date and time at which the system will resume.

Using Dial-Up Networking

Windows for Workgroups includes a remote access client that enables you to dial into remote servers to access files and other network resources such as printers and e-mail. Windows 95 expands and improves on the remote access client in Windows for Workgroups, integrating remote access almost seamlessly within the Windows 95 interface. With the remote access features in Windows 95—collectively called *Dial-Up Networking*—you can connect to a remote computer to access its files and printer(s). If the remote computer is connected to a network and you have the necessary access rights on the remote LAN, dialing into the server is just like connecting locally to the network. You can use the shared resources of any computer on the network, send and receive e-mail, print, and perform essentially any task remotely that you can perform with a workstation connected directly to the network.

▶ See "Creating a Connection," p. 290

> **Note**
>
> A Windows NT server can act as a TCP/IP gateway, routing TCP/IP traffic for your dial-in PC. If your office network is connected to the Internet, for example, you can dial into a server to gain access to the Internet from home. To use this capability, you must install the TCP/IP network protocol and bind it to the dial-up adapter. The Windows NT server's Remote Access Server service must also be configured to allow TCP/IP dial-in and route TCP/IP traffic.

If you did not install Dial-Up Networking when you installed Windows 95, you must do so with the following procedure:

1. Open the Start menu and choose Settings, Control Panel, and then double-click the Add/Remove Programs icon; then choose the Windows Setup tab to display the Windows Setup dialog box.

2. Double-click the Communications item to display the Communications dialog box.

3. Place a check in the Dial-Up Networking check box, then choose OK. Choose OK again and Windows 95 installs Dial-Up Networking on your PC.

Before you can begin using Dial-Up Networking, you must install the dial-up adapter and network protocol required by the remote server. The next section explains how to set up Dial-Up Networking.

II

Working with Windows 95

Setting Up Dial-Up Networking

Setting up Dial-Up Networking requires four steps: installing the dial-up adapter, installing the network protocol(s) used by the remote server, installing a network client, and installing an appropriate file and printer sharing service.

The dial-up adapter is a special driver supplied with Windows 95 that acts as a virtual network adapter, performing much the same function that a typical hardware network adapter performs. Instead of handling network traffic across a network cable, the dial-up adapter handles network traffic through your PC's modem.

To install the dial-up adapter, follow these steps:

1. Open the Control Panel and double-click the Network icon.

2. In the Configuration page of the Network property sheet, choose Add.

3. Choose Adapter from the Select Network Component Type dialog box, and then choose Add. Windows 95 displays the Select Network Adapters dialog box shown in figure 9.19.

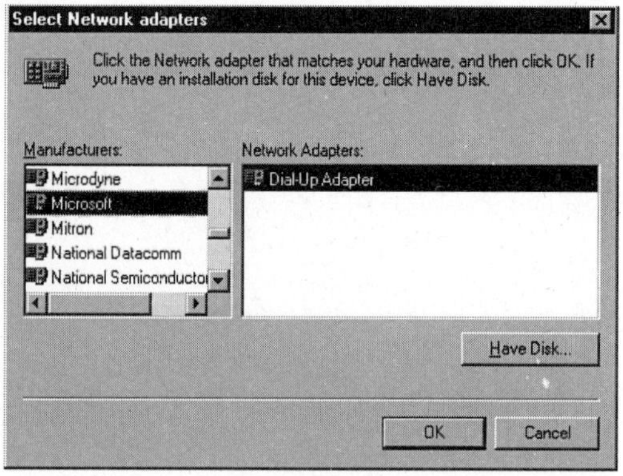

Fig. 9.19
You must install the dial-up adapter before you can use Dial-Up Networking.

4. From the Manufacturers list, choose Microsoft.

5. From the Network Adapters list, choose Dial-Up Adapter, then choose OK. Windows 95 will add the dial-up adapter to your system.

After you install the dial-up adapter, you must install at least one network protocol to be used for the dial-up connection. The protocol you select depends on the protocol used by the remote server. On Microsoft-based networks, the protocol used typically is NetBEUI. On NetWare-based networks, the protocol typically used is IPX/SPX. If you are connecting to a remote network that uses TCP/IP, you should install the TCP/IP protocol.

To install a protocol and bind it to the dial-up adapter, use the following procedure:

1. Open the Control Panel and double-click the Network icon.

2. From the Configuration page, choose the Add button.

3. Choose Protocol from the Select Network Component Type dialog box, then choose Add.

4. From the Manufacturers list, choose Microsoft.

5. From the Network Protocols list, choose the appropriate network protocol, then choose OK.

In addition to a network protocol, you also might need to install a network client. The network client enables your PC to access files and printers on the remote server and network. If you are connecting to a Microsoft network-based computer or network, you should install the Client for Microsoft Networks client. If you are connecting to a NetWare system, you should install the Client for NetWare Networks client.

To install a network client and bind it to the dial-up adapter, use the following procedure:

1. Open the Control Panel, double-click the Network icon, and then choose Add from the Configuration page.

2. From the Select Network Component Type dialog box, choose Client, then choose Add.

3. From the Manufacturer's list, choose Microsoft, choose the appropriate client from the Network Clients list, then choose OK.

4. In the Configuration property page, select Dial-Up Adapter from the list of installed network components, and then choose Properties. This displays the Dial-Up Adapter Properties sheet.

5. Choose the Bindings tab to display the Bindings property page shown in figure 9.20.

Tip

If you are using TCP/IP to gain access to the Internet through a dial-up server, and do not want to have access to the remote server's files or shared resources on the LAN to which the server is connected, you do not need to install a network client.

II

Working with Windows 95

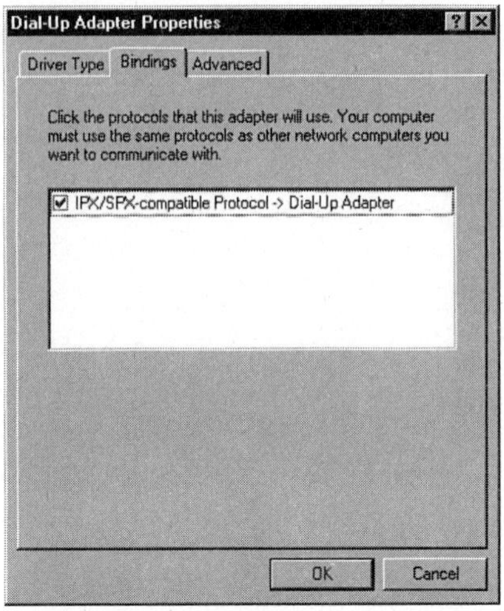

Fig. 9.20
Use the Bindings
page to bind a
network protocol
to the dial-up
adapter.

6. Place a check beside the network protocols you want to use with the dial-up adapter, then choose OK. Choose OK again to close the Network dialog box.

▶ See "Installing and Configuring Your Modem," p. 831

Your PC is now configured to act as a Dial-Up Networking client. Making a connection is explained in the next section.

Note

If you have not already installed your modem, do so before continuing. Your modem must be installed in order to use Dial-Up Networking.

Creating a Connection

To create a new Dial-Up Networking connection, first open My Computer, then choose the Dial-Up Networking folder. The Dial-Up Networking folder contains an object named Make New Connection that starts a wizard to help you create Dial-Up Networking connections. The following steps help you start the wizard and create a Dial-Up Networking connection:

1. Open the Dial-Up Networking folder and double-click the Make New Connection object. Windows 95 displays the Make New Connection wizard box shown in figure 9.21.

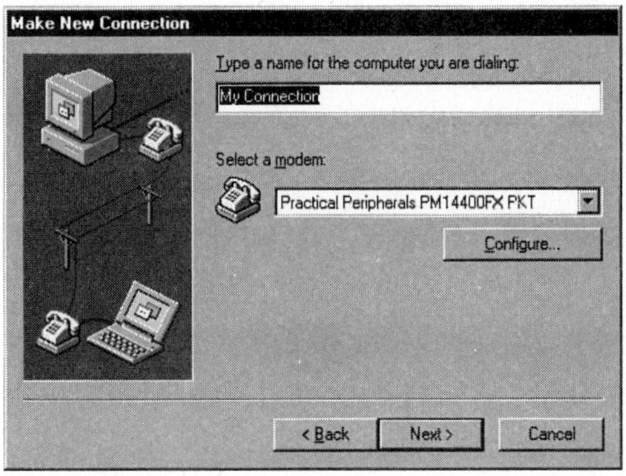

Fig. 9.21
The Make New Connection wizard helps you create Dial-Up Networking connections.

2. By default, the wizard names the connection "My Connection." Highlight the name and enter a name that describes the remote system to which you are connecting. This is the name that will appear under the connection's icon in the Dial-Up Networking folder.

3. Use the Select a Modem drop-down list to choose the modem you want to use for the Dial-Up Networking connection, and then choose Next. The dialog box changes as shown in figure 9.22.

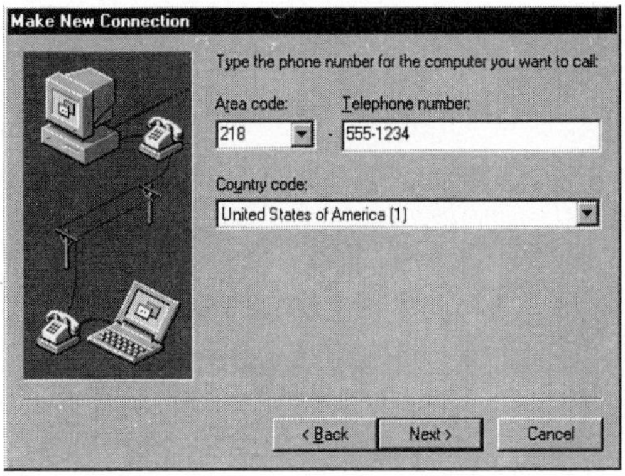

Fig. 9.22
Specify the phone number for the remote connection.

4. Enter the area code and telephone number in the appropriate text boxes.

5. Use the Country Code drop-down list to choose the country in which the remote system is located, and then choose Next.

6. Choose Finish to create the connection and add its icon to the Dial-Up Networking folder.

II

Working with Windows 95

Connecting to a Remote System

Connecting to a remote system through a Dial-Up Networking connection is simple. Open the Dial-Up Networking folder, and then double-click the icon of the server to which you want to connect. Windows 95 displays a dialog box for the Dial-Up Networking connection similar to the one shown in figure 9.23.

Fig. 9.23
You can verify and change settings prior to making the connection.

▶ See "Using Network Neighborhood to View Network Resources," p. 550

In the User Name and Password text boxes, enter the account name and password required by the remote server. If you want Windows 95 to save the password so you don't have to enter it each time you use the Dial-Up Networking connection, enable the Save password check box.

Next, verify that the phone number and dialing location specified in the connection are correct; then choose Connect. Dial-Up Networking dials the remote server and attempts to connect and log on using the name and password you have provided. After the connection is established, you can begin using the shared resources of the remote server and the shared resources of other computers on the remote network as if your PC were connected locally to the network.

Maintaining Laptop and Desktop Files with Briefcase

Many users of portable PCs also use a desktop system and often need to juggle files between the two systems. You might, for example, have a set of reports you are preparing with your desktop system and you need to move those files to your portable to work on them while you are out of town.

Windows 95 includes a feature called Briefcase that simplifies the task of synchronizing the files on your desktop and portable PCs, helping you keep track of which copy of the file(s) is most current.

The following is a simplified example of how you might use the Briefcase:

- You create a Briefcase (which appears as a typical folder) on your portable PC.

- You copy one or more files to the Briefcase using a direct cable connection to your desktop PC or through your docking station's network connection.

- You work on the documents contained in the Briefcase while you are away from the office, modifying and updating the files.

- While you are away from the office, a co-worker modifies one of the files on your desktop system that you copied to your Briefcase.

- When you return to the office, you reconnect your portable to your desktop PC, and then open the Briefcase on your portable.

- You use the Briefcase to update the files. The Briefcase informs you which files have been modified and enables you to easily copy the files from the Briefcase to their original locations on the desktop PC. The Briefcase also informs you that a file on your desktop PC (the file modified by your coworker), has changed, and gives you the option of updating your copy in the Briefcase.

The Briefcase also can detect when the original and Briefcase copies of a file have been changed. The Briefcase then prompts you to specify which copy of the file should be retained. The Briefcase also supports *reconciliation* of the two copies of the file. This means that if the document's source application supports reconciliation, the Briefcase uses OLE to communicate with the source application and merge the two files together, retaining the changes made in each copy of the file.

Note

Because the Briefcase is a new feature, few applications currently support reconciliation, but the number of applications that support it should grow as developers take advantage of this new feature.

II

Working with Windows 95

▶ See "Synchro-
nizing Files
with a Floppy
Disk," p. 296

You are not limited to creating a Briefcase on your portable PC. In fact, you can create a Briefcase on a floppy disk or your desktop PC. You might find a Briefcase useful for synchronizing files on which multiple users on the network collaborate. And, you are not limited to creating a single Briefcase—you can create as many as you like. For example, you might create a separate Briefcase for each project on which you are currently working.

> **Note**
>
> Placing a Briefcase on a floppy disk is useful if you do not have the necessary cable to connect your desktop and portable PCs using Direct Cable Connection, or your docking station is not connected to the network. Simply create the Briefcase, then move it to a floppy disk. Drag files from your desktop PC to the Briefcase, then move the Briefcase disk to your portable and begin working on the files.

Creating a Briefcase

If your PC does not already include a Briefcase on your desktop, you can easily create a new Briefcase. To create a Briefcase, follow these steps:

1. Decide where you want the Briefcase to be created (on the desktop, in a floppy disk folder, in a folder on the hard disk, etc.).

2. Right-click in the location in which you want the Briefcase created. If you want the Briefcase created on the desktop, for example, right-click the desktop.

3. From the pop-up menu, choose New, Briefcase. Windows 95 will create a Briefcase and add an icon for it in the location you have selected.

4. If you want to rename the Briefcase, click the Briefcase icon to select it, then click the Briefcase's description. Type a new description and press Enter.

As previously explained, you can create as many Briefcases as you like. By default, Windows 95 creates a Briefcase called My Briefcase on your desktop. You can rename the default Briefcase to suit your preferences.

Placing Files in the Briefcase

Although the Briefcase is a special type of folder, it behaves almost identically to a standard directory folder. You can move or copy files to a Briefcase in the same way you move or copy files to any folder. Simply open the folder in which the files are located, then drag them to the Briefcase. Hold down the Ctrl key while dragging to copy the files, or hold down the Shift key to move the files. If you prefer, you can open Explorer (open the Start menu and choose Programs, Windows Explorer) and drag the files from Explorer into the Briefcase.

In addition to using standard file copying and moving techniques to place files in the Briefcase, you also can use Send To. Locate the file(s) you want to place in the Briefcase, then right-click one of the files. From the pop-up menu, choose Send To, and then choose the Briefcase to which you want to send the selected file(s). Windows 95 will copy the file(s) in the Briefcase.

Tip

If you right-drag a document to the Briefcase, the pop-up menu includes an item labeled Make Sync Copy. Choose this option to create a copy of the object in the Briefcase.

Synchronizing Files

If you travel or work at home on your portable with files copied to your Briefcase from your desktop PC, Briefcase can keep your files updated. When your PC is undocked or you are working remotely, use your files as you normally would, opening and saving them in the Briefcase. When you return to the office desktop or remote network, first reconnect your portable to your desktop system or network, or insert the Briefcase floppy disk in your desktop PC. Then, simply open the Briefcase and choose Briefcase, Update All. Briefcase displays a dialog box similar to the one shown in figure 9.24.

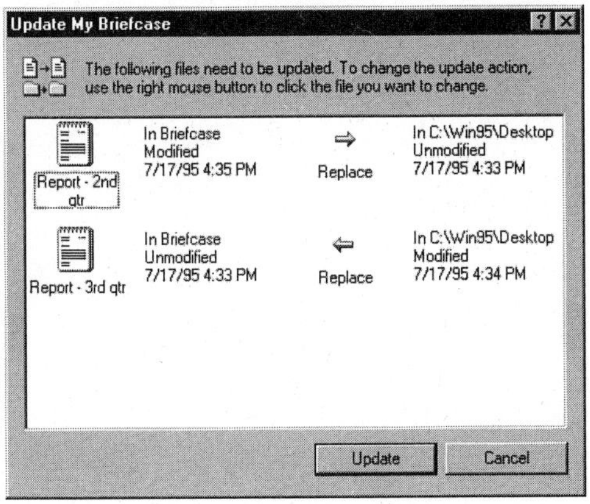

Fig. 9.24
Briefcase prompts you to specify how modified files should be handled.

The left column lists the name of the file, and the second column lists the status of the file in the Briefcase. The third column specifies the update action that occurs if you do not choose a different action. The fourth column indicates the status of the original copy of the file.

If the update actions listed for each file are appropriate, click Update to update the files. To change the update action for a file, right-click the file. Briefcase opens a dialog box as shown in figure 9.24. Choose the appropriate update action, and Briefcase changes the action for the file. When all of the files are set the way you want them, click Update.

Tip

To select a group of files in the Briefcase, hold down the Ctrl key and click on each file you want to update.

> **Note**
>
> If you update a file on a network server, you have no guarantee that another user won't modify the file after you have updated it, placing it once again out of sync with your Briefcase copy. If you again update the files in the Briefcase, however, the Briefcase will indicate that the original copy of the file located on the network server has changed.

If you prefer to only update a few of the files in the Briefcase, simply select the files you want to update, then choose Briefcase, Update Selection. Briefcase lists in the Update My Briefcase dialog box only those files you have selected.

After your selection of files is complete, choose Briefcase, Update Selection to update the selected files. You also can right-click a file in the Briefcase to open a dialog box, and then choose Update from the shortcut menu to update the selected file(s).

Synchronizing Files with a Floppy Disk

You can move a Briefcase to a floppy disk to simplify transferring files between your portable and desktop PCs. To move your Briefcase to a floppy disk, follow these steps:

1. If you do not yet have a Briefcase on the desktop PC, create one; right-click the Windows 95 desktop, and then choose New, Briefcase.

2. Open the My Computer folder and position the folder so you can see the Briefcase icon.

3. Open the folder containing the files you want to place in the Briefcase, then right-drag the files from their folder to the Briefcase icon. From the shortcut menu, choose Make Sync Copy.

4. Place a formatted disk in the desktop PC's floppy disk drive.

5. Right-drag the Briefcase from the desktop to the floppy drive icon in My Computer, and then choose <u>M</u>ove Here.

6. Remove the floppy disk containing the Briefcase and insert it in the portable's floppy disk drive.

7. On the portable, work on the files in the Briefcase, opening and saving them in the Briefcase.

8. When you're ready to synchronize the files, place the floppy disk containing the Briefcase in the desktop PC's floppy disk drive. Open My Computer; then open the floppy disk folder. Right-drag the Briefcase from the disk folder to the desktop, then choose <u>M</u>ove Here.

9. Open the Briefcase, and then synchronize the files as explained in the previous section.

Synchronizing Files with a Network

You can use a Briefcase to help you synchronize files on a network server on which you collaborate with other users. The process for working with the Briefcase and synchronizing files is the same as for a desktop PC/portable PC scenario. Create the Briefcase on your desktop, and then copy the files from the network server to the Briefcase. Edit the files in the Briefcase. When you're ready to synchronize them again with the original files on the server, open the Briefcase, and synchronize the files as previously explained.

Checking the Status of Briefcase Files

The update status of each file is listed in the Briefcase folder if you use <u>D</u>etails to display the contents of the Briefcase as a detailed list. To configure the Briefcase to display a detailed list, choose <u>V</u>iew, <u>D</u>etails.

You also can view the status of files in the Briefcase by selecting the files, then choosing <u>B</u>riefcase, <u>U</u>pdate Selection. You also can view the status of individual files in the same way. In addition, you can use a file's pop-up menu to view its status. With the Briefcase open, right-click the file or folder that you want to check. Choose <u>P</u>roperties to display the file's property sheet, then choose the Update Status tab to display the Update Status page shown in figure 9.25.

Tip

If you want to check the status of all your Briefcase files, choose <u>B</u>riefcase, Update <u>A</u>ll. A status window pops up, enabling you to view the status of all files in the Briefcase. Choose Update to update the files, or Cancel to close the dialog box without making any changes.

II

Working with Windows 95

Fig. 9.25
A file's property
sheet shows its
update status.

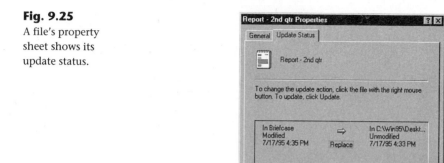

Splitting the Briefcase File from the Original Files

Occasionally, you might want to disassociate (called *splitting*) a file in the
Briefcase from its original. Splitting a file removes the link between the two
files. To split a file, first open the Briefcase and select the file you want to
split. After selecting the file, choose Briefcase, Split From Original. After a
file is split from an original, it is labeled an orphan and can no longer be
updated.

LCD Screen Mouse Trails

Pointing device features are also enhanced with the mobile user in mind.
Switching between integrated pointing devices—track ball or clip-on mouse—
to a desktop mouse (Plug and Play-compatible) is now automatically detected
and enabled by Windows 95. Installing a serial, Plug and Play mouse
amounts to plugging it in, and the system enables its use.

Like Windows for Workgroups, Windows 95 also adds a few special features
that make it easier to see the cursor on a passive-matrix LCD panel, which
many portable PCs use for their displays (active-matrix panels have much
better image quality, and consequently it is much easier to see the cursor on
an active matrix LCD). The following sections explain these features.

Using Mouse Trails

When you move the cursor on a passive LCD display, the display typically cannot update fast enough to adequately display the pointer as it moves across the display. This makes it difficult to see the cursor. To alleviate the problem, you can turn on *mouse trails*. When mouse trails is enabled, a set of "ghost" pointers trail the pointer as it moves across the display. This makes it much easier to locate the cursor.

To enable mouse trails, open the Start menu and choose S̲ettings, C̲ontrol Panel. From the Control Panel, double-click the Mouse icon, and then click the Motion tab to display the Motion property page shown in figure 9.26.

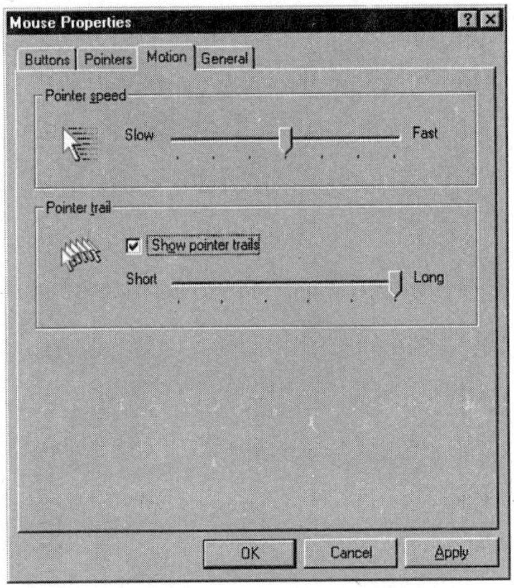

Fig. 9.26
Use the Show Pointer Trails check box to turn on mouse trails.

Place a check in the Sh̲ow Pointer Trails check box to enable mouse trails. Use the accompanying slider control to specify the length of the mouse trail; then choose OK to apply the changes.

Using Large Pointers

In addition to using mouse trails, you also might want to increase the size of pointer you use on your portable to make it easier to see the pointer. Windows 95 enables you to create pointer schemes much like you create desktop color schemes, saving the pointer schemes by name. Windows 95 includes a small selection of predefined schemes, two of which use large pointers that are much easier to see on a passive LCD panel than the standard Windows 95 mouse pointers.

> **Note**
>
> If you did not install the optional pointers when you installed Windows 95, you must install them before you can use the large pointer schemes. To do so, open the Control Panel, then choose the Add/Remove Programs icon. Double-click Accessories, then scroll through the Accessories list to find the Mouse Pointers item. Place a check beside Mouse Pointers, then choose OK, and OK a second time to add the pointers to your system.

To use a large-pointer scheme, open the Control Panel and choose the Mouse icon, then choose the Pointers tab to display the Pointers property page (see fig. 9.27). From the Schemes drop-down list, choose either the Windows Standard (Large) or Windows Standard (Extra Large) scheme, then choose OK. Windows 95 immediately begins using the new pointers.

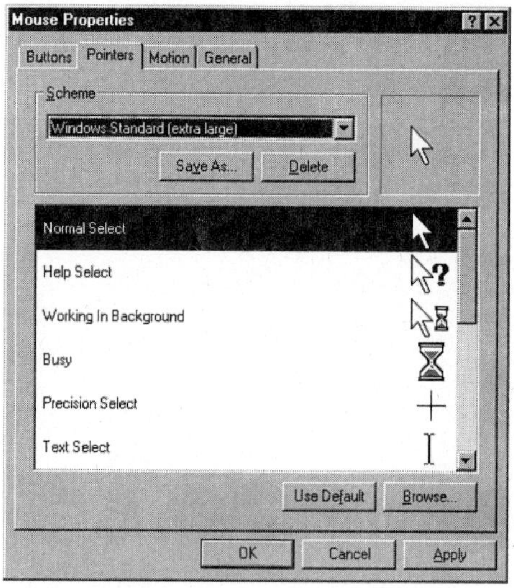

Fig. 9.27

Use the Pointers page to specify a pointer scheme.

Tip

To add a new scheme, customize as many pointers as you want; then click Save As on the Pointers property page to identify the new scheme.

In addition to using a predefined scheme, you also can create your own custom schemes. Display the Pointers property page as described earlier, then select the pointer you wish to change. Choose Browse, and Windows 95 displays a dialog box from which you can select a pointer file. When you select a pointer file, a sample of the pointer appears in the Preview box. When you have selected the pointer you want to use, choose Open to select the pointer and return to the Pointers page. Choose Save As to specify a name for your new pointer scheme.❖

Part III

Working with Applications

Chapter 10

Installing, Running, and Uninstalling Windows Applications

by Michael O'Mara

An operating system provides the foundation for applications such as word processors, spreadsheets, and graphics programs. The applications don't come with the operating system; you must purchase and install your applications separately.

In the old days of DOS-based applications, installing a new program was fairly simple. Usually you just copied files into a directory on your hard disk. Efforts to integrate the application into your system seldom went beyond adding a couple of lines to your AUTOEXEC.BAT or CONFIG.SYS file. Each application stood alone with minimal interaction with the operating system and no interaction with other applications.

Now things have changed. Applications are bigger, more powerful, and much more complex. They've become so intertwined with the operating system that it's hard to tell where the dividing line is between Windows and an application. And nearly every Windows application has the potential to interact with any other Windows application on your system.

Not surprisingly, the process of installing and removing applications has grown more complex as well. Fortunately, as application installation grew more complicated, application developers turned to automated setup programs to handle most installation chores. And Windows 95 adds new features to further automate adding and removing applications.

In this chapter, you learn how to

- Install older 16-bit applications in Windows 95
- Install Windows 95 applications
- Add and remove Windows' component applications
- Uninstall applications

Not long ago, the typical PC user worked with only a couple of applications, and never used more than one program at a time. Now, multitasking is a way of life. The average Windows user probably works with a dozen applications regularly, several of which are likely to be open and running simultaneously. To juggle all those concurrent tasks effectively, you need to understand how Windows manages tasks behind the scenes.

Installing Applications in Windows 95

▶ See "Installing MS-DOS Applications," p. 345

To install any Windows application, you usually use a setup program or install utility. Installing DOS-based applications is a different matter (and the subject of Chapter 11, "Working with DOS Applications in Windows 95"). These setup programs for Windows applications take care of all the details of installing the application. You don't have to concern yourself with creating directories, copying files, and integrating the application into Windows. That's good, because installing sophisticated applications can be complex. A manual installation of a major software suite is beyond the capabilities of the average user, and a dreaded chore for even the most advanced user.

What Does Setup Do?

A typical setup or installation program begins by prompting you for some information and then installs the application automatically. The better setup programs provide feedback during installation to keep you informed of what it's doing to your system and the progress of the installation. Depending on the complexity of the application you are installing, the setup program might give you an opportunity to select various options and customize the installation. The program might limit your input to accepting or changing the path where you install the application, selecting whether to install various optional components, or specifying configuration settings for the new application.

After receiving your input, the setup program proceeds to perform some or all of the following steps automatically:

- Search for an existing copy of the application it's about to install and switch to upgrade mode if appropriate.

- Scan your system to determine whether your hard disk has enough room for the necessary files and perhaps check for the existence of special hardware or other system requirements.

- Create directories and copy files. Often, the setup program must expand files that are stored in a compressed form on the distribution disks.

- Create a shortcut that you can use to launch the application.

- Add a folder and/or shortcuts to your Start menu.

- Update Windows' configuration files.

- Update the Windows Registry.

- Register the application as an OLE server.

- Register the application's file types so Windows can recognize the file name extensions for the application's document and data files.

- Install fonts, support utilities, and so on.

- Configure or personalize the application.

What If There's No Setup Program?

A few Windows programs don't include a setup utility to install the application—the developer just didn't supply one. Such an application is probably a small utility program for which installation consists of copying a couple of files to your hard disk and perhaps adding a shortcut to your Start menu to launch the application. You'll probably find instructions for installing the application in an accompanying manual or README file.

The installation instructions may assume that you're installing the program in Windows 3.1, not Windows 95. (At least that's likely to be the case for a while after Microsoft releases Windows 95.) Fortunately, this isn't a serious problem. Most of the procedures for installing an application in Windows 3.1 work equally well in Windows 95. For instance, although Windows 95 supplies new tools for managing files, the underlying process of creating directories (folders) and copying files is the same in both versions of Windows. Also, for backward compatibility, Windows 95 includes full support for WIN.INI

III

Working with Applications

and SYSTEM.INI files, so any additions that you're instructed to make to those files should work as expected.

◀ See "Cus-
tomizing the
Start Menu,"
p. 128

▶ See "Register-
ing Files to
Automatically
Open an Appli-
cation," p. 539

There are two common manual installation procedures that you must adapt for Windows 95. First, if the Windows 3.1 installation instructions require that you create a file association in File Manager, you must substitute the Windows 95 equivalent of registering a file type. Second, instead of creating a program item in Program Manager, you add a program to the Start menu.

Using Windows 3.1 Applications in Windows 95

According to Microsoft, Windows 95 features full backward compatibility with 16-bit Windows 3.1 applications, and thus you can install and use your Windows 3.1 applications in Windows 95 without modification. And in fact, with only rare exceptions, Windows 3.1 applications do indeed run success-fully in Windows 95.

Tip

After the release of Windows 95, technical support facilities will undoubtedly be swamped—especially for applications with compatibility problems. Avoid the logjam by checking online services such as CompuServe and America Online for program patches and infor-mation on workarounds.

If you encounter a compatibility problem with a *legacy application*—an older application designed for a previous version of DOS or Windows—running in Windows 95, check with the application's developer for a patch or work-around for the problem. In some cases, perhaps the only solution is an up-grade to a new, Windows 95 version of the application.

Installing Windows 3.1 Applications

You install Windows 3.1 applications in Windows 95 the same way that you do in Windows 3.1. You simply insert the first disk of the program's installa-tion disks in your floppy disk or CD-ROM drives, run the Setup program, and follow the prompts and instructions.

The installation instructions for most Windows 3.1 applications direct you to use the Run command to start the setup program and begin installing the application. The instructions might mention that you can find the Run com-mand on the File menu in either Program Manager or File Manager. However, in Windows 95, you find the Run command on the Start menu.

Note

You might prefer a different technique for launching the Setup program. Open the My Computer window and double-click the drive icon for the drive that contains the installation disk. Then locate the Setup program's icon and launch the program by double-clicking it.

When you use this technique, you need not type the command in the Run dialog box to start the Setup program. The technique also lets you scan the disk for README files before installing the application.

Of course, the Setup program for a legacy application will be tailored to Windows 3.1 instead of Windows 95. For example, the installation program will probably offer to create Program Manager groups (see fig. 10.1) and update INI files. Fortunately, you can just accept those options when the program offers them. Windows 95 will intercept Program Manager updates and automatically convert them to Start menu shortcuts. Windows 95 also transfers WIN.INI and SYSTEM.INI entries into the Registry.

Tip

For a current list of programs with known incompatibility problems with Windows 95 and suggested fixes or workarounds, read the file PROGRAMS.TXT in the Windows folder.

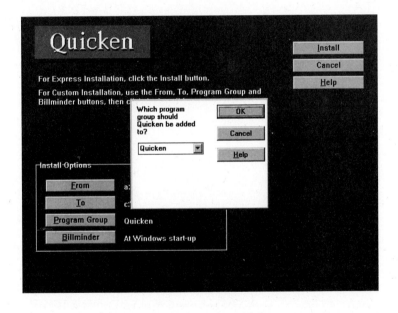

Fig. 10.1
Windows 95 translates some actions of a Windows 3.1 application's Setup program into their Windows 95 equivalent.

If you install Windows 95 as an upgrade to Windows 3.1, the Setup program should take care of such issues. The Windows 95 Setup program automatically transfers information about your existing applications to the Registry when you install Windows 95 onto your existing Windows 3.1 directory. As a result, you shouldn't have to reinstall applications.

Setting Up Existing Applications in a Dual Boot Configuration

If, however, you choose to create a dual-boot system by installing Windows 95 in a directory separate from Windows 3.1, Windows 95 won't know about

III

Working with Applications

▶ See "Setting Up a Dual Boot System," p. 1105

any Windows 3.1 applications already on your disk. Just adding those applications to your Start menu isn't enough to let you run them successfully in Windows 95.

Caution

Before reinstalling a Windows 3.1 application in Windows 95, be sure to note the directory in which the application is currently installed. You must specify *exactly* the same directory when you reinstall the application. Otherwise, you might waste valuable disk space by having two copies of the same application on your system.

It isn't necessary to have a separate copy of an application on your hard disk in order to use it in Windows 95 as well as Windows 3.1. You can use the same application in both versions of Windows. However, most applications expect to find certain initialization and support files in the Windows directory. If you attempt to run the application from Windows 95, it expects to find those files in the Windows 95 directory. But if you installed the program under Windows 3.1, those files are in the Windows 3.1 directory, not in the Windows 95 directory. In some cases, if you copy the Windows 3.1 applications' initialization and support files to the Windows 95 directory, you can run the applications. But usually, you have to reinstall your Windows 3.1 applications in Windows 95 before you can use them. You'll certainly need to reinstall an application if it uses features such as OLE.

Troubleshooting

When I try to use the same application under both Windows 3.1 and Windows 95 on a dual-boot system, why does the application keep "forgetting" changes I make in the application's user preference settings?

If you change user settings in an application when running it under Windows 3.1, they may not be there when you run the application under Windows 95—and vice versa. Even though there's only one copy of the application on your hard disk, you may have two sets of the initialization files where user preference settings are stored; one each in the Windows 3.1 and Windows 95 directories. The application uses the settings from (and stores revised settings in) the initialization files it finds in the default Windows directory for the version of Windows you're running at the time. Unfortunately, there's no way to keep two sets of initialization files in sync automatically.

Running Windows 3.1 Applications

After installing a Windows 3.1 application in Windows 95, you can launch and run the application just like any other Windows application. Windows 95 changes the application's appearance automatically, giving it the new Windows look (see fig. 10.2). The application window's title bar will have the new format, complete with new style of Minimize, Maximize, and Close buttons, and most buttons and other window elements will take on the new three-dimensional look.

◀ See "Starting and Quitting Windows," p. 50

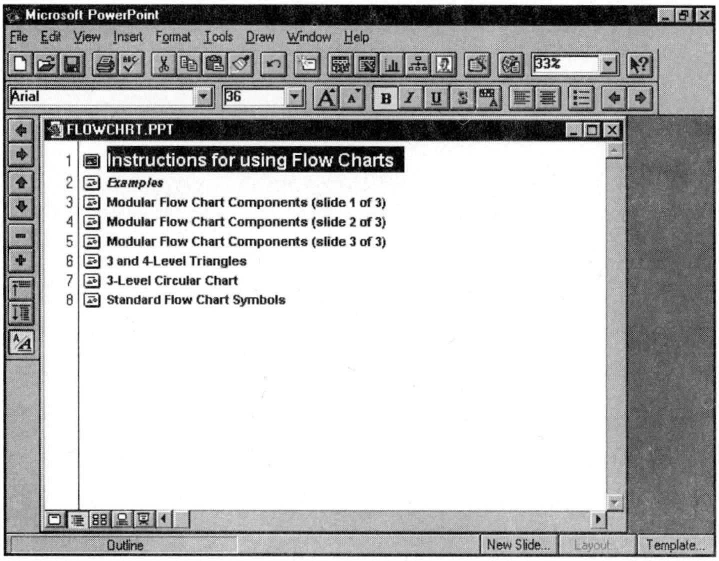

Fig. 10.2
Running a Windows 3.1 application in Windows 95 gives the program an automatic facelift. However, despite the change of appearance, the application performs the same as in Windows 3.1.

Beneath the superficial appearance changes, the application works the same as it did under Windows 3.1. The application might benefit from some Windows 95 performance improvements such as more efficient printing. However, to take maximum advantage of the features and capabilities of Windows 95's 32-bit operating system, you must upgrade to a new version of the application. In the meantime, you should be able to continue using your 16-bit Windows 3.1 applications effectively and efficiently.

Installing Windows 95 Applications in Windows 95

The basic technique for installing Windows 95 applications is essentially the same as installing other Windows applications. You just run Setup (or Install) and follow the prompts. The Setup program takes care of all the details of installing the application. However, the Run feature is located in the Start menu in Windows 95.

One new feature of Windows 95 is an optional way to start an application's Setup program: a new Install Programs Wizard accessible via the Add/Remove Programs icon in the Control Panel. The Add/Remove Programs dialog box provides a common starting point for adding and removing Windows applications and Windows system components and accessories.

When you're ready to run the Install Programs Wizard and use it to install a Windows application, follow these steps:

1. Open the Start menu and choose Settings, Control Panel. This opens the Control Panel window shown in figure 10.3.

> **Note**
>
> Depending on the applications you already have installed, your Control Panel folder may contain different icons.

Fig. 10.3
The Windows 95 Control Panel contains a new Wizard to make installing applications easier.

2. In the Control Panel window, double-click Add/Remove Programs to open the Add/Remove Programs Properties sheet shown in figure 10.4. By default, the Install/Uninstall tab should be active.

3. To start the Install Program Wizard, choose Install.

4. When the Install Program from Floppy Disk or CD-ROM dialog box appears (see fig. 10.5), insert the application's distribution disk (the first floppy disk or compact disk) in the appropriate drive and click Next.

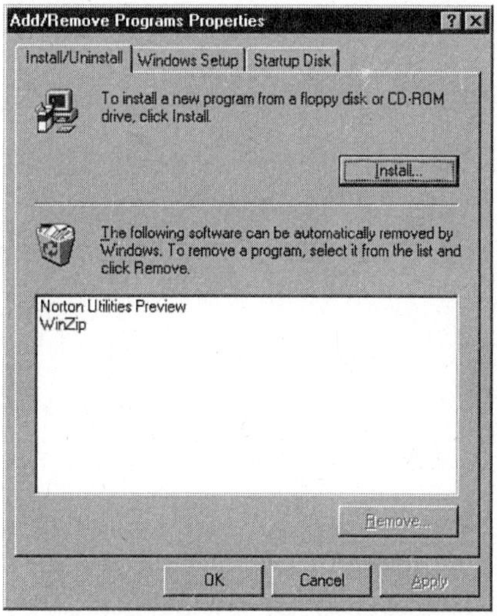

Fig. 10.4
The Add/Remove Programs Properties sheet is master control for adding and removing applications.

Fig. 10.5
The Install Program Wizard takes you through each installation step.

5. The Wizard searches the disk's root directory for an installation program (usually named SETUP.EXE or INSTALL.EXE) and displays the command line in the Run Installation Program dialog box (see fig. 10.6).

6. If the Wizard fails to find the setup program (perhaps because it is in a subdirectory or has a non-standard file name) or you want to run a different setup program (perhaps from a network drive), you can use Browse and select a different file in the Browse dialog box (see fig. 10.7). Choose Open to insert the selected file name in the Wizard.

III

Working with Applications

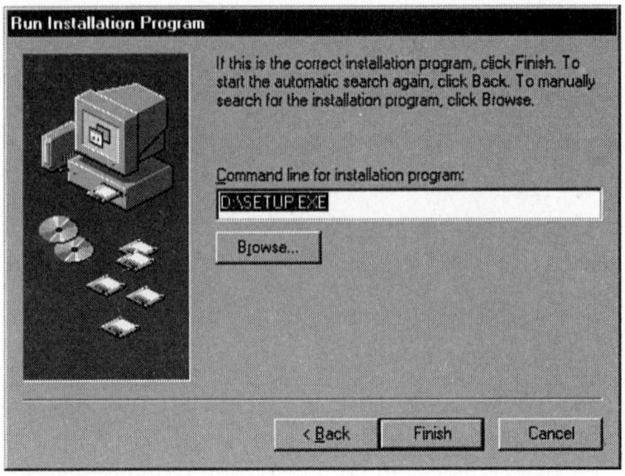

Fig. 10.6
Usually the
Wizard finds the
application's setup
program on the
disk.

7. After the correct command line for the Setup program appears in the Run Installation Program dialog box, click Finish to start the Setup program and begin the application installation.

The application's Setup program then proceeds to install the application. You'll probably need to respond to several prompts during the installation process. If the Setup program includes a Windows 95-compatible uninstall feature, the Wizard notes this and adds the new application to a list of programs that you can remove automatically. (The section "Removing Windows Applications," later in this chapter, discusses this new feature in more detail.)

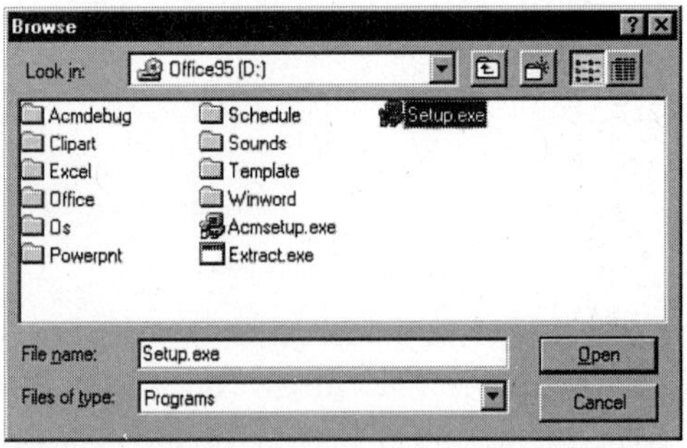

Fig. 10.7
If the Wizard
needs help
locating the Setup
program, you can
browse for the
correct file.

Note

You also can use the Install Programs Wizard to install Windows 3.1 applications. However, using the Wizard for this purpose yields no significant advantage. Windows 3.1 Setup programs lack the special features that let you use the Add/Remove Programs control panel to remove the applications later.

Adding Windows Component Applications

The Add/Remove Programs icon in Control Panel lets you install and remove Windows components and accessories as well as applications. Therefore, you can reconfigure your copy of Windows 95 without reinstalling it. The feature is a more powerful version of the Windows 3.1 Setup utility.

Adding and Removing Windows Components

To use the Windows Setup feature to add or remove a Windows component, follow these steps:

1. Open the Start menu and choose Settings, Control Panel.

2. Open the Add/Remove Programs Properties sheet by double-clicking the Add/Remove Programs icon.

3. Click the Windows Setup tab to display a list of Windows components as shown in figure 10.8.

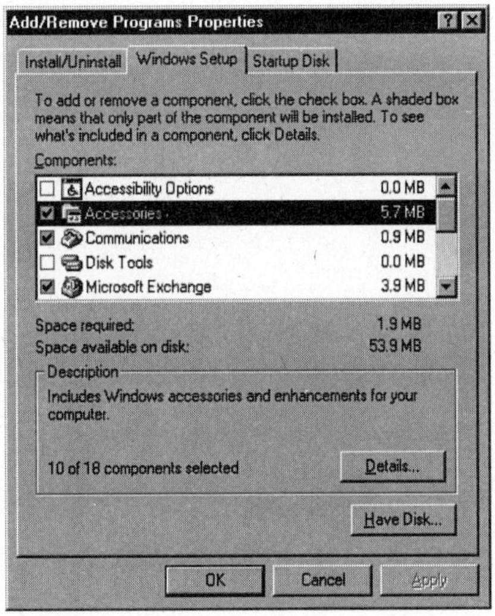

Fig. 10.8
The Windows Setup page of the Add/Remove Program Properties sheet lets you add and remove parts of Windows.

In the Components list box, a check mark next to an item indicates that the component is already installed on your system. If the check box is gray, the Windows component is composed of more than one sub-component and some (but not all) sub-components are currently installed. For instance, in figure 10.8, only some of the sub-components (accessories such as Calculator, Paint, and WordPad) of the Accessories component are installed. To see what's included in a component, choose <u>D</u>etails.

4. Select a component in the <u>C</u>omponents list box. When you do, the Description box in the lower portion of the dialog box displays a description of that component.

5. If the component you selected consists of more than one sub-component, choose <u>D</u>etails to open a dialog box listing the sub-components. (For example, figure 10.9 shows the Accessories dialog box listing the sub-components of the main Accessories component.) Sometimes in this dialog box, you can choose <u>D</u>etails to narrow your selection further.

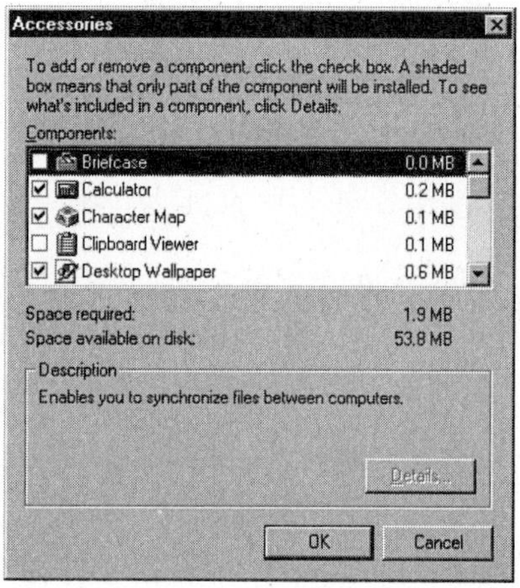

Fig. 10.9

The Accessories dialog box lists a component's parts. By choosing <u>D</u>etails, you can narrow your selections.

6. Mark components for installation or removal by clicking the check box beside that item in the <u>C</u>omponents list. Adding a check mark to a previously blank check box marks that item for installation. Conversely, clearing a previously checked box instructs Windows to uninstall that component.

7. If you're selecting sub-components in a dialog box you opened by choosing <u>D</u>etails, click OK to close that dialog box and return to the Add/Remove Programs Properties sheet.

8. When the check marks in the <u>C</u>omponents list specifies the components that you want composing your Windows system, choose <u>A</u>pply in the Add/Remove Programs Properties sheet. You'll need to supply the Windows Setup disks or CD when prompted.

Troubleshooting

When I use the Windows Setup feature to add new components, it adds those components, but it also removes other components. Why?

Windows Setup adds or removes components as necessary to make the list of components installed on your system match the list of components you checked in the Add/Remove Programs Properties sheet.

Contrary to what you might think, when you mark components in the list, you're not telling Windows Setup what items you want to *add* to your system. You're telling it you want to make sure the item is included in your Windows installation. Windows Setup will check your hard disk and add the component if it isn't already there. Similarly, clearing a checkbox doesn't mean you want to leave the item alone, it means you don't want that component installed on your system. If you clear a previously checked checkbox, Windows Setup will dutifully remove the component from your Windows system.

Installing Unlisted Components

Eventually, you might want to install a Windows component that doesn't appear on the Components list in the Windows Setup tab of the Add/Remove Program Properties sheet. For example, you might want to install one of the system-management utilities from the Windows 95 Resource Kit.

To install a Windows component not listed in the Components list box, open the Add/Remove Program Properties sheet, click the Windows Setup tab, and choose the Have Disk button at bottom of the dialog box. This opens the Install From Disk dialog box (see fig. 10.10).

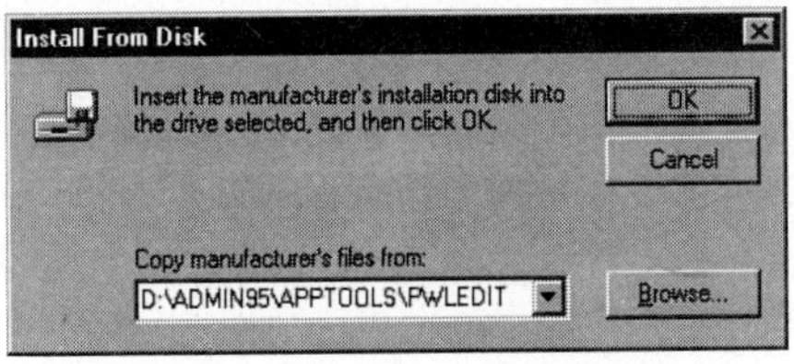

Tip

Alternatively, you can right-click the INF file in a folder window and choose Install from the shortcut menu.

Fig. 10.10
When adding Windows components from a supplemental disk, you must supply the full path to the correct INF file.

In the Copy Manufacturer's Files From field, specify the path to the setup information file (INF) for the Windows component that you want to install. (The setup information file tells Windows Setup what is available to install and how to do it.) You can either type the path and file name or choose Browse and select the file in the Browse dialog box. After specifying the correct path, click OK. Windows opens the Have Disk dialog box (see fig. 10.11), which lists the components available for installation. Check the ones that

III

Working with Applications

you want to install, then choose Install. You might have to supply disks and browse for needed files when prompted.

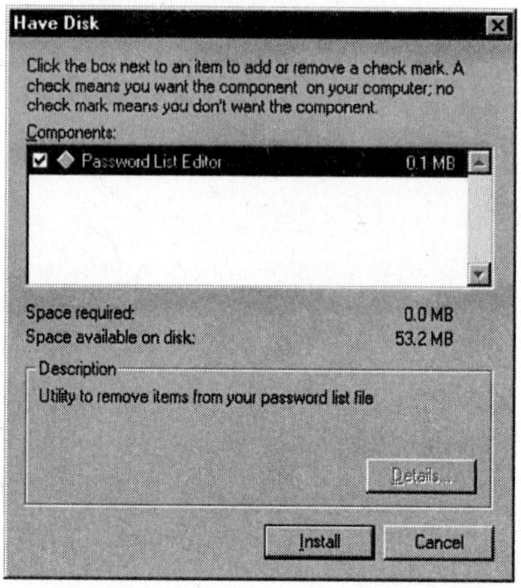

Fig. 10.11
The Have Disk dialog box lists the Windows components available on the supplemental disk, or at least the components described in the INF file that you selected.

Windows not only installs the component, but also adds the component to the Components list in the Windows Setup tab. Later, you can remove the component just like any other in the list.

▶ See "Installing MS-DOS Applications," p. 345

Installing components for DOS applications is different than the procedure used with Windows. In most cases, installing many of the major DOS applications requires suspending Windows 95 and switching to the "exclusive" DOS mode. This procedure is described in detail in Chapter 11, "Working with DOS Applications in Windows 95."

Running Applications

◀ See "Starting Applications from the Start Menu and Taskbar," p. 62

After you install your application's and Windows' accessories, Windows 95 gives you many options for launching them. You can use any of the methods to run any application. The technique that you choose depends on your personal preferences, working style, and what you're doing at the time.

◀ See "Starting Programs from a Shortcut Icon on the Desktop," p. 68

The various methods for launching applications are discussed in more detail in Chapter 3, "Getting Started with Windows 95," and Chapter 17, "Managing Your Files with Explorer." The following is a summary of the techniques:

■ Choose the application's shortcut from the Start menu.

■ Create and use a shortcut on the desktop.

■ Right-click the application's icon in Windows Explorer or the My Computer window, then click <u>O</u>pen in the context menu.

◀ See "Compatibility with Windows 3.1 and DOS Programs," p. 19

■ Double-click the application's icon in the My Computer window or Windows Explorer.

■ Choose the <u>R</u>un command from the Start menu and then type the path and file name of the application's executable file.

■ Choose the <u>R</u>un command from the Start menu, then drag an EXE file from My Computer or Network Neighborhood and drop the file into the Run dialog box.

■ Use the Windows 3.1 Program Manager and run the application by double-clicking its program item.

> **Note**
>
> Windows 95 includes updated versions of both Program Manager and File Manager. The optional 3.1 interface will add applications to the Program Manager during installation. If you opt for the Windows 3.1 interface, you also can add program items to the Program Manager manually.

■ Open a document or data file associated with the application. When you open a file, Windows launches the application automatically and then opens the file in that application. There are as many ways to open files as there are ways to launch applications. For instance, you can open files in Explorer, by choosing a recently used file from the <u>D</u>ocuments submenu on the Start menu, or by double-clicking a shortcut on your desktop.

■ Finally, for a bizarre twist, try this method of launching a Windows application: you can open a MS-DOS window and type the command to start the application at the DOS prompt (or type **start** followed by the command). You would expect to get an error message saying the program requires Windows to run. But, instead, Windows 95 launches the Windows application for you.

Understanding How Windows Runs Applications

Windows 95 can run applications designed specifically for Windows 95. It also can run most older Windows 3.1 applications, DOS-based applications, and applications designed for Windows NT. Windows 95 no longer requires the traditional CONFIG.SYS, AUTOEXEC.BAT, and INI files for configuration information. However, for backward compatibility, Windows 95 can use settings from INI files and can maintain its own versions of CONFIG.SYS and AUTOEXEC.BAT in order to support loading real-mode device drivers.

Although Windows 95 can run various kinds of applications successfully, it provides different kinds of support for each category of application. Windows applications fall into one of two general categories: 32-bit applications (designed for Windows NT and Windows 95) and 16-bit applications (designed for Windows 3.1 and lower versions). This section describes how Windows 95 runs these programs. Chapter 11, "Working with DOS Applications in Windows 95," discusses DOS-based applications.

Support for Win32 applications

Windows 95 offers several significant advantages over Windows 3.1. Some advantages, such as preemptive multitasking and multithreading support, are available only to 32-bit applications.

▶ See "Working with Long File Names," p. 509

Support for long file names is one feature of Windows 95's 32-bit operating system that is available to any application designed to make use of it. Of course, all Windows 95 applications will let you create file names containing up to 255 characters, allowing you to assign files names such as "First Quarter Sales Results" instead of "1QSALES." Theoretically, program developers can adapt 16-bit applications to use long file names as well. However, don't expect many older Windows applications to add long file name support; the programmers are likely to concentrate on converting the application to full-fledged 32-bit status instead of spending time on minor upgrades.

◀ See "Managing Windows after an Application Failure," p. 78

Most applications benefit from Windows 95's 32-bit architecture, which makes memory addressing more efficient. In addition, Windows 95 runs each 32-bit application in its own memory space. Ordinarily, such details are of interest only to programmers. However, these advantages have a side-effect that all users will appreciate. If a 32-bit application hangs or crashes, the problem is isolated, confined to the application's own address space, and thus unlikely to affect other running applications. You can simply exit the problem application and, without even rebooting, have Windows 95 clean up the affected memory.

Advantages of Preemptive Multitasking and Multithreading

Despite appearances, our computers can't really perform multiple tasks from several different applications all at the same instant. Generally, computers perform only one or two tasks at a time, but they can do so very fast. There-fore, if the applications are designed to break operations into small tasks, the operating system can switch between tasks from several applications so quickly that it seems that all the applications and their processes are running simultaneously.

Programmers had to design Windows 3.1 applications to surrender control of the CPU voluntarily at various points of execution, enabling Windows to switch to another task. This scheme is called *cooperative multitasking*. How-ever, some applications were more cooperative than others. If an application was reluctant to share CPU capacity with other applications, Windows 3.1 couldn't do much about it.

Preemptive multitasking, on the other hand, enables the Windows 95 operating system to take control away from one running task and pass it to another task, depending on the system's needs. The system doesn't have to wait for an application or process to surrender control of the CPU before another application can take its turn.

With preemptive multitasking, Windows 95 doesn't depend on the fore-sight of application programmers to ensure that an application performs multitasking successfully. Windows 95 has more power to arbitrate the de-mands of various running applications.

Multithreading enables an application to create and run separate concurrent *threads* or processes and thus handle different internal operations. Each pro-cess gets its own share of Windows 95's multitasking resources. For example, a word processing application might use one thread to handle keyboard input and display it on-screen. At the same time, a separate thread can run in the background to check spelling while another thread prints a document.

Some Windows 3.1 applications implement their own internal multithreading, with varying degrees of success. Now, Windows 95 makes multithreading an integral feature of the operating system, available to all 32-bit applications.

Increased System Resources

One of the most troubling limitations of Windows 3.1 is the restricted size of a special chunk of memory called System Resources. System Resources is where Windows stores things such as menus and other vital parts of the user interface for Windows and Windows applications.

Running a couple of elaborate applications in Windows 3.1 can nearly exhaust the available System Resources memory. You can't run another application if the System Resources doesn't have enough room for the application to load its user interface and other components. Consequently, the size of the System Resources became the principal factor limiting the number of applications that you can run simultaneously in Windows 3.1. Under Windows 3.1, you often run out of System Resources long before you begin to tax the limits of RAM or CPU power.

> **Note**
>
> In Windows 3.1, attempting to launch an application when there was insufficient system resources often resulted in Not Enough Memory errors even though there was ample RAM and disk memory available. In Windows 3.1, things like having lots of installed fonts, running in high resolution, and high color display modes would tax system resources. With 32-bit applications, you won't have this problem in Windows 95.

Windows 95 doesn't remove the limitation on System Resources completely, but the improvement is dramatic. The system limits on some kinds of programming information that Windows 3.1 severely restricted are now unlimited. Windows 95 still limits other kinds of programming information, but those limits are significantly higher than in Windows 3.1. As a result, you can run more applications, create more windows, use more fonts, and so on—all without running out of system resources. For instance, as I write this I have two very large, resource-hungry applications running, plus a communications program, a personal organizer, the Explorer, and CD Player. That's more than enough to exhaust system resources in Windows 3.1 and precipitate a flurry of error messages. But in Windows 95, I still have more than 80 percent of the available system resources free.

Support for Windows 3.1 Applications

Most Windows 3.1 applications run in Windows 95 without modification or special settings. Microsoft claims that 16-bit Windows applications run at least as well in Windows 95 as in Windows 3.1.

Windows 3.1 applications continue to use cooperative multitasking; they cannot use Windows 95's preemptive multitasking and multithreading. However, 16-bit applications can benefit from the advantages Windows 95 derives from 32-bit device drivers and improved printing throughput due to multitasking at the operating system level.

Windows 3.1 applications running in Windows 95 all run in the same virtual machine and share the same address space—just as they do when running in

Windows 3.1. As a result, they don't share the same crash protection as Windows 95 applications. If one 16-bit application hangs or crashes, it's likely to affect other 16-bit applications that are running at the same time. In other words, any application failure that would have required rebooting or restarting Windows 3.1 will require you to shut down all the 16-bit applications you're running. However, a failure of a 16-bit application should not affect 32-bit applications, and Windows 95 probably can clean up after an errant 16-bit application without requiring a reboot to recover System Resources and clear memory.

◀ See "Managing Windows after an Application Failure," p. 78

> **Note**
>
> Many times, you can avoid losing data in other open 16-bit applications by pressing the familiar Ctrl+Alt+Del and choosing the offending application from the Close Program dialog box. Quite often, Windows shuts down the errant program and leaves your other 16-bit applications running as normal.

Removing Windows Applications

Installing a Windows application can be a complicated venture. Windows applications are often tightly integrated with the operating system. Installing such applications not only requires copying the application's files into the application's own directory, but also adds numerous support files to your Windows directory and changes Windows' settings. Fortunately, nearly all applications provide Setup programs to automate the installation process.

Removing an application can be similarly complicated. Finding all the support files and settings added or changed during the application's installation can be nearly impossible. Fortunately, many application Setup programs now offer an uninstall option to automate the process when you need to remove the application from your system.

Windows 95 takes this welcome trend a step further by adding a facility to remove applications. That facility is in the same Control Panel dialog box that you use to install applications and Windows components.

Removing Applications Automatically

Windows 95's Add/Remove Programs Wizard adds to the capability of individual setup programs by tracking an application's components in the Registry. This lets Windows delete an application's files and settings but still identify and retain any files that another application might share and use.

III

Working with Applications

> **Note**
>
> Only applications that provide uninstall programs specifically designed to work with Windows 95 appear in the list of applications that Windows 95 can remove automatically.

To uninstall an application automatically, start by opening the Control Panel and double-clicking the Add/Remove Programs icon. This opens the Add/Remove Programs Properties sheet—the same sheet you used to install the application (see fig. 10.12).

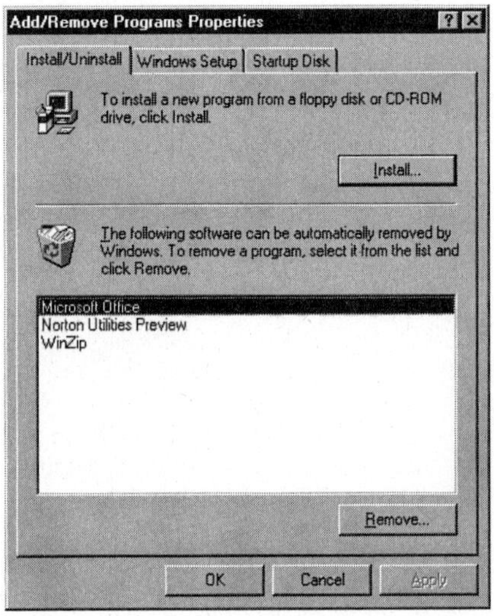

Fig. 10.12
In the Add/Remove Programs Properties sheet, you can remove applications as well as install them.

The lower portion of the sheet lists applications that you can remove. To remove an application, select it from the list and choose Remove. After you confirm that you want to remove the program, Windows runs the selected application's uninstall program.

Removing Applications Manually

If you want to remove an application from your system, just hope that it's one that Windows can remove automatically. Removing an application manually can be difficult, and possibly dangerous.

Remove Files from the Application Directory

Getting rid of the files in an application's own directory is fairly straightforward. In fact, that should probably be the first step in removing an application manually.

Tip
If you find support files in your Windows directory that you think are unnecessary, copy them to a separate folder before you remove them. If you don't encounter any problems after a few months, you can delete that folder.

Many applications install support files in the Windows directories. It's nearly impossible to tell what application added which files, and to make matters worse, several applications can share the same files. If you ignore the files in the Windows directories when you remove an application, you can leave numerous orphaned files on your system needlessly consuming hard disk space. However, if you make a mistake and delete the wrong file or one that another application also uses, you might render the other application unusable.

Remove Shortcuts and Folders from the Start Menu

After you remove an application's files from your hard disk, you want to get rid of any shortcuts that pointed to the application. To delete a shortcut icon from your desktop, simply drag and drop the shortcut onto the Recycle Bin icon on your desktop. The Recycle Bin is like a trash can that stores deleted files until the Bin reaches a certain capacity.

◀ See "Understanding the Most Important Screen Elements in Windows 95," p. 36

To remove the application from the Start menu, open the Start menu and choose Settings, Taskbar. Then, in the Taskbar Properties sheet, click the Start Menu Programs page. Next, choose Remove to open the Remove Shortcuts/ Folders dialog box (see fig. 10.13). You also can right-click the Start button and choose Explore from the shortcut menu.

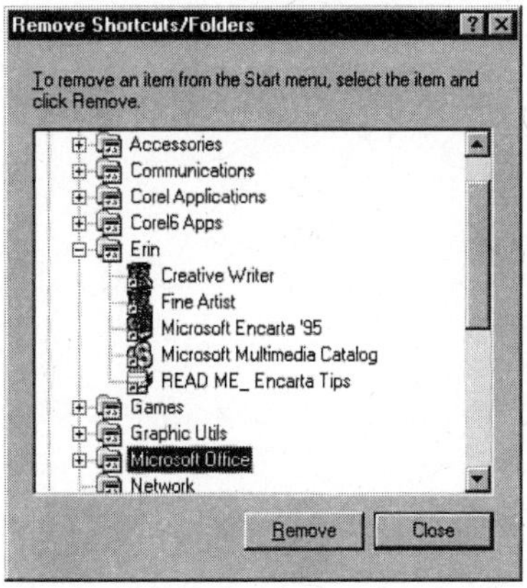

Fig. 10.13

After removing an application, you open the Remove Shortcuts/Folders dialog box to remove the application's folder and shortcuts from your Start menu.

III

The Remove Shortcuts/Folders dialog box, like the Explorer, displays a hierarchical list of folders and files. To expand the display and show a folder's contents, you can click the plus sign beside the folder. Select the folder or shortcut that you want to delete, then choose Remove. To remove other items, repeat the process as necessary. When you finish removing items, click Close.

▶ See "Managing Your Files and Folders," p. 513

Working with Applications

Remove File Associations

After you remove an application, you can remove any associations that might have existed between file extensions and the defunct application. After all, you don't want Windows to try to launch the nonexistent application when you double-click a document file.

To remove the link between a file extension and an application, start by opening the My Computer window. Next, choose View, Options to open the Options dialog box, then click the File Types tab. You then see the screen shown in figure 10.14. Scroll down the Registered File Types list and select the file type that you want to delete, then choose Remove. Windows asks you to confirm your choice. If you answer Yes, Windows abolishes the registration of that file type.

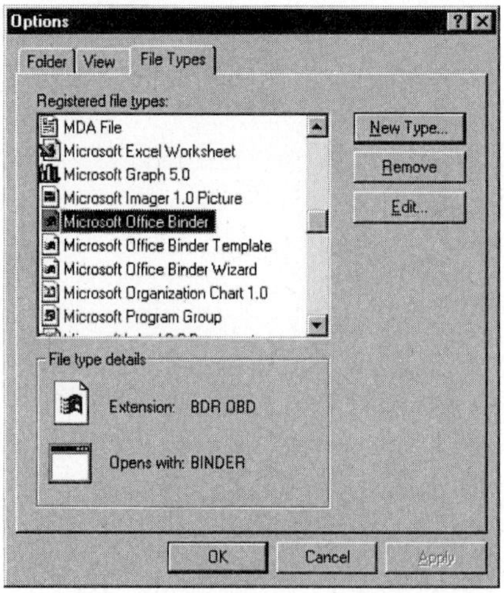

Fig. 10.14
Using the Options dialog box to remove a file type registration is easier and safer than editing the Registry directly.

Caution

Third-party utility programs designed to remove applications from Windows 3.1 probably won't work in Windows 95 because they won't be able to cope with the Registry and other changes. You should check with the company's support staff before using third-party utility programs to see if they work in Windows 95.

Chapter 11

Working with DOS Applications in Windows 95

by Dick Cravens

Although Windows 95 is designed from the ground up to shield the user from the often-confusing world of the command line, AUTOEXEC.BAT, CONFIG.SYS, and the arcane voodoo of memory-management practices, it offers surprisingly rich support for those users who still desire or need to work in the MS-DOS environment. If you have a favorite MS-DOS application, utility, or game, there's absolutely no need to give it up or suffer performance loss. In fact, Windows 95 offers greatly enhanced MS-DOS support compared to earlier versions.

None of this comes without a small price: you must learn a few new concepts and controls to master Windows 95 MS-DOS operations. If you're used to adjusting PIF files, you'll be applying some of that knowledge to Windows 95 Properties management, and learning some new tricks as well. The reward is far greater control over MS-DOS application environments under Windows 95 than under previous versions.

If you're currently using another brand of DOS other than Microsoft MS-DOS, have no fear—Windows 95 MS-DOS support is so compatible and configurable, you can easily adjust for any minor variations between DOS versions from other vendors such as IBM's PC-DOS, or Novell/Digital Research DR-DOS.

In this chapter, you learn:

- What's new in MS-DOS for Windows 95

- How Windows 95 works with MS-DOS applications

- Optimizing Windows 95 MS-DOS Graphics mode support

- Installing, configuring, and uninstalling MS-DOS applications

- Starting and running MS-DOS programs

Understanding How Windows 95 Works with MS-DOS Applications

Just as Windows 3.1 improved drastically on version 3.0 support for MS-DOS applications, Windows 95 improves on its predecessor. Applications that simply would not run under earlier versions of the Windows MS-DOS prompt now perform admirably. For applications that still won't run under the new Windows, a special mode helps you run them quickly and easily from within Windows, and then automatically return to your Windows session when you're finished.

The following are some of the improvements in MS-DOS support Windows now offers to users:

- Better local reboot support

- Zero conventional memory usage for Protected-mode components

- Consolidated setup for MS-DOS-based applications

- Toolbar support for windowed MS-DOS applications

- Graceful shutdown for windowed MS-DOS sessions

- Long file name support, with full backwards compatibility for "8.3" format file names

- Execution of Windows programs from the MS-DOS session

- The capability to open documents from the command line

- Better control over MS-DOS window fonts

- User-scalable MS-DOS session windows

- Improved Cut/Paste/Copy commands for integrating MS-DOS and Windows application information

- Universal Naming Convention (UNC) path name support

- Spooling of MS-DOS-based print jobs

Windows 95 makes dealing with MS-DOS/Windows integration quicker and easier than ever, and makes working with MS-DOS applications very close to working on a machine running only MS-DOS. In addition, MS-DOS emulation under Windows 95 gives the user many of the other benefits of Windows 95: the graphical user interface, multitasking, and networking support.

Gone are the confusing variations and limitations of Real, Standard, and Enhanced-mode MS-DOS. Chances are, you'll never have to make an adjustment to Windows MS-DOS support; but if you do, you'll find the controls vastly simplified, well consolidated, and more reliable than ever.

Note

An added bonus of the overall design of Windows 95 is the greater conservation of conventional memory (that below the 640K mark). By loading eligible device drivers and TSR (terminate-and-stay-resident) programs in Protected mode, above the first-megabyte mark in memory, Windows frees more working memory for MS-DOS applications than any previous version.

Some MS-DOS applications simply couldn't run under Windows 3.1. By the time mouse, network, SCSI, and other necessary drivers were loaded, there simply wasn't enough RAM below 640K. Windows 95 alleviates this situation by checking each driver specified in your installation against a "safe list" of known drivers, and loading approved ones in extended memory, or substituting equivalent drivers.

For example, if your PC is on a NetWare network, uses a SCSI CD-ROM drive, the SMARTDrive disk cache, DriveSpace disk compression, and an MS-DOS mouse driver, you can save more than 250K in conventional memory using the MS-DOS system in Windows 95.

III

Working with Applications

Caution

Just as with earlier versions of Windows, don't run anything in a Windows MS-DOS session that alters the File Allocation Table, or other system-critical files. Examples of this type of software are MS-DOS disk defragmentors and unerase or undelete utilities. Windows now comes with many of these utilities, so use the Windows versions instead (don't just boot to MS-DOS to use your older utilities; some of them will corrupt the Windows 95 long file name system).

Starting the MS-DOS Prompt Session

Getting started with MS-DOS under Windows is as simple as selecting a menu item. To begin a session, follow these steps:

1. Open the Start menu and choose Programs. Windows displays a continuation menu, as shown in figure 11.1.

Fig. 11.1
It's simply a matter of two mouse clicks to start MS-DOS.

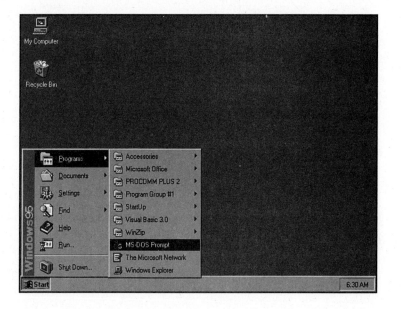

2. Choose the MS-DOS Prompt menu item. Windows opens the MS-DOS Prompt window, as shown in figure 11.2.

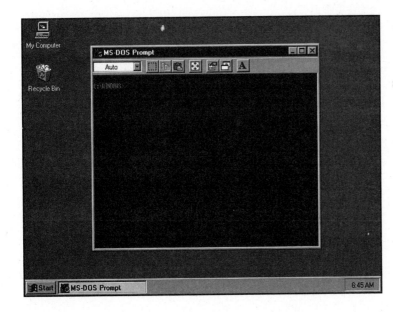

Fig. 11.2
The MS-DOS
Prompt window
awaits your every
command.

Ending MS-DOS Prompt Sessions

Now that you've started an MS-DOS Prompt session, practice closing it before
you move on to the finer points of operation. To close the MS-DOS Prompt
window, follow these steps:

1. Click in the MS-DOS Prompt window to bring it to the foreground.

2. Find the flashing cursor near the MS-DOS command prompt. At the
   flashing cursor near the MS-DOS command prompt, type **exit**.

3. Press Enter, and Windows closes the MS-DOS Prompt session window.

Tip

Don't leave MS-
DOS Prompt ses-
sions open any
longer than you
need to. Every
session takes a big
chunk out of avail-
able CPU time,
slowing down your
entire Windows
performance in all
applications.

III

Working with Applications

Note

As with most other procedures under Windows, several other ways to close an MS-
DOS Prompt session are available. As alternatives, try each of the following:

- Double-click the MS-DOS icon in the upper-left corner of the MS-DOS Prompt
  session window.

- Click the MS-DOS icon; then choose Close from the menu.

- Click the Close icon in the upper-right corner of the MS-DOS
  Prompt window.

- Right-click anywhere in the MS-DOS Prompt window title bar.
  Windows displays a menu, from which you can choose Close.

Ending Sessions with Running Applications

Windows also allows you to close sessions that have applications open; but by default, it warns you if the application is running or has open files.

Besides giving you options for more gracefully ending a session, Windows 95 improves on previous versions by performing better session "cleanup," releasing memory and deallocating system resources much more consistently.

To close an active session, simply follow the same procedures that you tried earlier to close a session with just an MS-DOS prompt. This time, however, Windows displays the warning dialog box shown in figure 11.3.

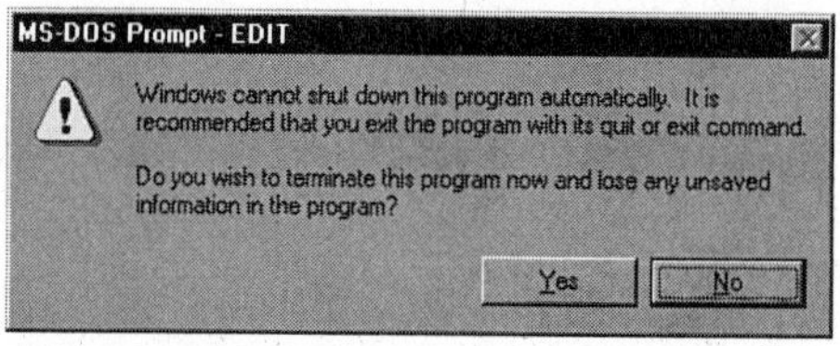

Fig. 11.3
Windows warns you if you try to exit an MS-DOS session while an application is active.

```
MS-DOS Prompt - EDIT                                    ☒

    ⚠    Windows cannot shut down this program automatically.  It is
          recommended that you exit the program with its quit or exit command.

          Do you wish to terminate this program now and lose any unsaved
          information in the program?

                                   Yes          No
```

If you choose No, Windows returns you to the MS-DOS Prompt session, and you can exit the program before you close the MS-DOS session.

Otherwise, choose Yes and Windows shuts down the MS-DOS session and terminates the running application. It's not recommended that you close sessions this way, but you can do it in an emergency (for example, if the application is hung and simply won't *let* you exit gracefully).

Troubleshooting

My MS-DOS application simply won't respond, and none of the close procedures you list are working. What can I do to shut down this bad apple and get back to work? Will I lose all my data in other applications?

One great addition to Windows 3.1 was the capability to *local reboot,* or close crashed applications without closing all of Windows. Windows 95 extends this capability with even greater control over shutting down errant applications.

The method used is the same as under Windows 3.1: use the classic "three-fingered salute," Ctrl+Alt+Del, after which Windows 95 displays the Close Program dialog box, instead of the classic Windows 3.1 "Blue Screen of Impending Doom." Windows 95, however, does a much better job of recovering from application failure, because it gives you a choice of which task to shut down, instead of assuming the one in the foreground is the culprit. After you select the application task to deal with, you have the choice of ending the errant task, shutting down the entire computer, rebooting using Ctrl+Alt+Del again, or canceling.

You learn a way to override the Windows warnings about closing an active MS-DOS Prompt session later in this chapter—see the section "Miscellaneous Properties."

▶ See "Miscellaneous Properties," p. 353

Controlling the MS-DOS Prompt Session

Now that you know how to get in and out of the car, start the engine, and shut it down, you're ready to get behind the wheel and take her for a spin! Windows 95 offers many great options to dress up the classic MS-DOS session.

Using the MS-DOS Prompt Toolbar

Windows MS-DOS sessions now have a variety of interface controls. The toolbar will be familiar to you if you've been using the Windows Explorer.

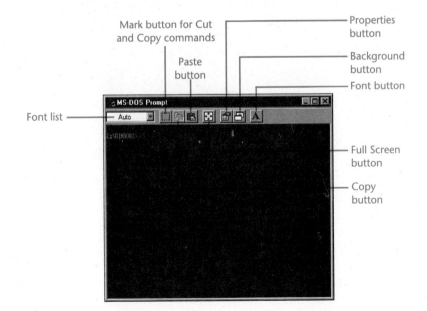

Fig. 11.4
The MS-DOS Prompt toolbar offers tools for quickly controlling the session interface.

Figure 11.4 shows the MS-DOS Prompt toolbar and its controls.

Controlling the MS-DOS Prompt Interface

Although Windows 3.1 offered a choice of fonts for windowed MS-DOS sessions, that choice was limited to bitmapped fonts that restricted the sizing options for the window. It was workable, but it offered nothing like the flexibility available in Windows 95 MS-DOS support.

Windows now offers TrueType scalable fonts in addition to the familiar system fonts, allowing on-the-fly resizing of the entire session window. To try the new font features, open an MS-DOS session and perform the following steps:

1. Click on the toolbar's Font list; then choose TT7 X 14 (the TrueType font for TT7 X 14 resolution). The window should now appear as shown in figure 11.5 (assuming that you're using 640 X 480 standard VGA display resolution).

Fig. 11.5
You can use the toolbar to control TrueType fonts in your MS-DOS Prompt session.

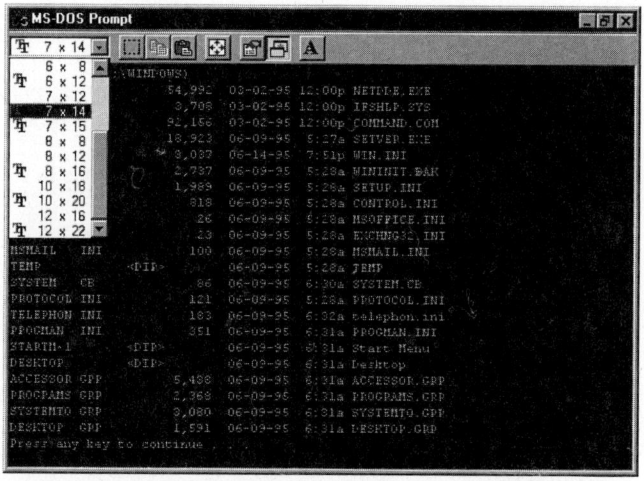

Tip
Windows 3.*x* veterans know one of the most basic and useful control tools for MS-DOS sessions: the Alt+Enter key sequence. This great shortcut changes the MS-DOS session from full-screen to windowed and back again, in a flash.

2. Grab the window borders in the bottom-right corner and resize the window. Note that the vertical and horizontal window scroll bar controls appear on the window, but the text in the window remains the same, as shown in figure 11.6.

3. Repeat the procedure in the preceding step 1 to select the 4 X 6 font mode. Notice that the text in the window is much smaller, and the window has shrunk to match (see fig. 11.7). Grab the window borders again and try to enlarge the window; note how it is limited to a maximum size.

4. Repeat the procedure in the preceding step 1 to select Auto mode. The window does not change.

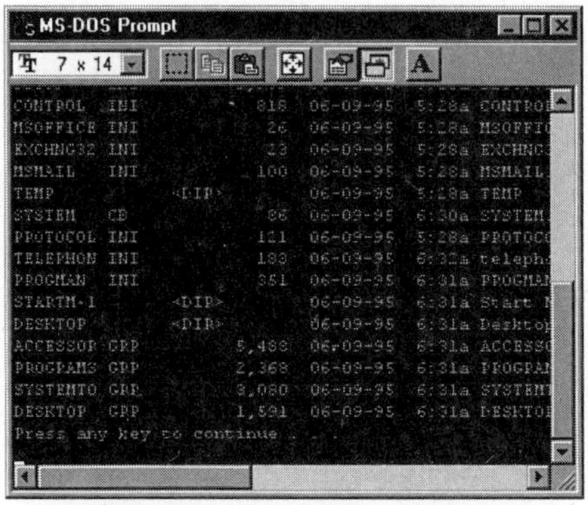

Fig. 11.6
Windows now supports dynamic resizing of the MS-DOS Prompt window. You can access any hidden areas of the session using standard scroll bar controls.

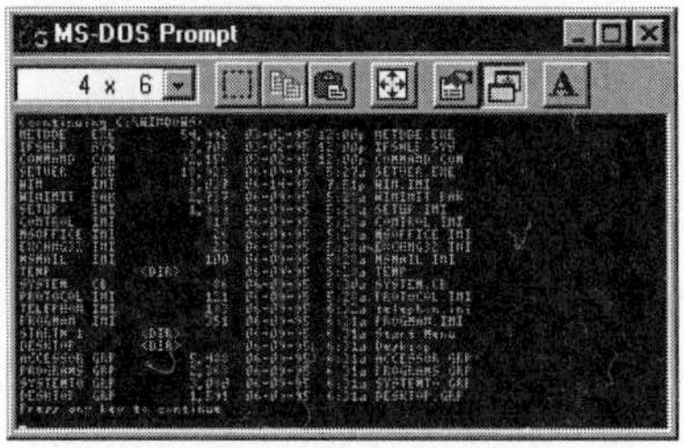

Fig. 11.7
If you choose a font that allows full viewing of the MS-DOS Prompt session, Windows won't let you resize the window larger than the session.

5. Grab the window borders and pull the window to a larger size. Note how Windows alters the font on the fly. When you change the window size again (try a square, or a vertical rectangle), the font adjusts automatically to the nearest available size.

Using the Windows Clipboard with the MS-DOS Prompt

Windows now offers even easier access to the data in your MS-DOS session, via the toolbar. Copying information from your session into a Windows application is quick and easy. Follow these steps to try it out:

1. Using the mouse, click on the Mark tool and highlight text in your MS-DOS application.

2. Click the Copy tool on the MS-DOS Prompt toolbar. Windows places a copy of the text in the Clipboard.

3. Using the mouse, click on your Windows application (for example, NotePad) to make it active. Position the cursor where you want to insert the text; then choose Edit, Paste from the NotePad menu. NotePad displays the text copied from your MS-DOS session window.

III

Working with Applications

Troubleshooting

*I used to be able to use the mouse to highlight text in an MS-DOS session, and then press
Enter to copy the text to the Clipboard, but now it doesn't work.*

This still works under Windows 95; it simply isn't enabled by default. You can use the
mouse to highlight and copy text if the application you're running supports it (for
example, EDIT); but the MS-DOS prompt itself won't (for example, you can't mark
and copy the results of the `dir` command that MS-DOS writes to your window). If
you use the toolbar on your MS-DOS sessions, just click on the Mark tool on the
toolbar before you select the text. If you've set up your MS-DOS sessions so the
toolbar doesn't show, then you can tell Windows 95 to enable the QuickEdit feature.

To enable this feature, simply click the window system icon (the MS-DOS icon in the
upper-left corner) and choose Properties; then choose the Misc tab when the Properties sheet appears. Check the QuickEdit box under the Mouse section; then click OK,
and you're ready to go.

Using Long File Names

One of the most bothersome limitations of the MS-DOS environment has
been the 8.3 file name format. Windows now supports longer file names, and
the MS-DOS Prompt offers support for them, too. To see how this works,
follow these steps:

1. Using the Windows Desktop, create a new folder called Incredibly Long
   Folder Name on the root of drive C:, as shown in figure 11.8.

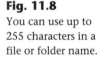

Fig. 11.8

You can use up to
255 characters in a
file or folder name.

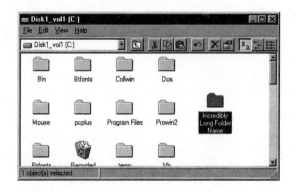

2. Using the Start menu, open an MS-DOS Prompt. At the prompt, type
   dir c:*. The MS-DOS window displays the directory listing for the root
   of drive C: (an example is shown in fig. 11.9).

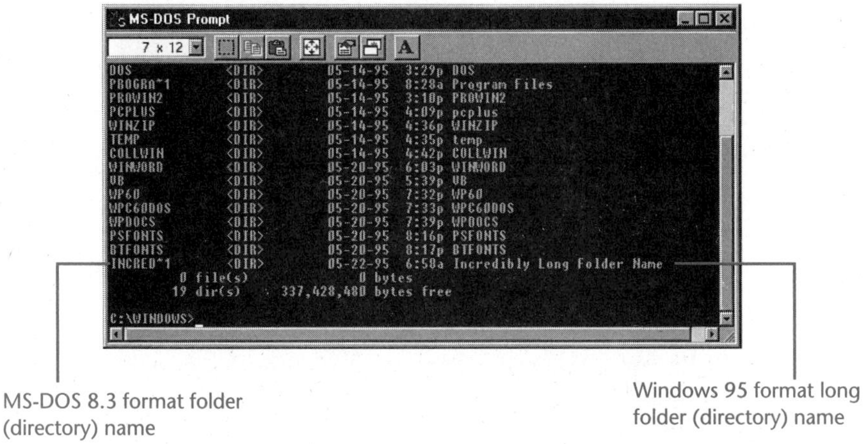

Fig. 11.9
The MS-DOS Prompt session supports and displays both long and short file and folder (directory) names.

MS-DOS 8.3 format folder (directory) name

Windows 95 format long folder (directory) name

Note the dual display of both the 8.3-format and long-format folder names. Windows and MS-DOS coordinate both naming systems, but not without a price; the 8.3 format name uses the tilde character (~) to show the inevitable truncation. Even under Windows, some long names may be shortened using the ellipsis characters (...) when space is at a premium.

▶ See "Registering Files to Automatically Open an Application," p. 539

To ensure complete backwards compatibility, file extensions are still used, even though they are not displayed in the Windows Explorer or on the Desktop. If you rename a file from the Windows environment, it does not change the hidden file name extension. Windows still uses the extension for file associations with applications and viewers.

Note

Not all applications support long file names just because Windows does. It's doubtful that any MS-DOS applications will support long file names because most were written prior to this version of Windows. Most 16-bit Windows applications won't support longer file names until their first release after Windows 95, if then (some software companies will probably wait for the first release of their application as a true 32-bit program to include this feature).

Many of the native MS-DOS commands in Windows 95 have been enhanced to provide support for long file names. For example, the dir and copy commands both support long file names.

III

Working with Applications

Using Universal Naming Convention Path Names

More and more PCs are on *local area networks* (*LANs*). Most shared resources on a LAN are stored on *servers*, or PCs dedicated for a particular network task, such as printing, file storage, or database storage.

Gaining access to other PCs on the network, whether server or workstation, can be a tiresome process of mapping the other machine to a virtual drive letter on your system. The Windows 95 MS-DOS Prompt offers a way around this with *Universal Naming Convention (UNC)* support. This is a fancy way of saying that you can view, copy, or run files on another machine without having to assign it a drive letter on your computer. It also means that if you are running short of logical drive letters, you can get to servers that you use only intermittently with a simple command from the MS-DOS Prompt.

For example, if you want to run an application called SHARED.EXE in the directory STUFF on server FRED1, you can enter the following at the command prompt:

\\fred1\stuff\shared.exe

You also can use this feature with any legal MS-DOS command. For example, to see the contents of the directory STUFF, use the familiar dir command as follows:

dir \\fred1\stuff

This yields a standard directory listing of the contents of that area of the server.

Printing from the MS-DOS Prompt

The biggest change in printing support for MS-DOS applications comes in the form of better conflict resolution and print job queuing. Windows now handles printer port contention between MS-DOS and Windows applications by shuttling all MS-DOS print tasks to the same printer management utility used by Windows applications.

Understanding MS-DOS Mode

◀ See "Printing
from MS-DOS
Applications,"
p. 200

Even the most perfect host can't entertain someone who really doesn't want to be at the party. Windows has the same problem with some poorly designed MS-DOS applications—some MS-DOS applications demand total control over system resources and access hardware in the most direct way, bypassing "standard" Windows methods.

Windows 95 accommodates a poorly behaved guest to the best of its ability, via *MS-DOS mode*. This mode is the equivalent to the Real mode present in older versions of Windows, with some "real" improvements.

MS-DOS mode works by giving the errant MS-DOS application the entire system for the duration of the session. Windows removes itself from memory, leaving only a small "stub" loader in preparation for its return to power.

To use this mode, the user sets a property in the Advanced Program Settings dialog box. When the MS-DOS application runs, Windows literally shuts down, loads the application, and then returns automatically when the application is finished. This process can be slow and cumbersome, but it is faster and more convenient than exiting Windows manually, using the dual boot option, and reloading Windows.

Knowing When to Use MS-DOS Mode

Before you decide to enable MS-DOS mode for an application, try these other options:

- Confirm that you've optimized the MS-DOS session settings for that application. Check the program's documentation for special memory requirements or other unusual needs. You may be able to adjust Windows' MS-DOS support to make the application work in a standard MS-DOS session.

  ▶ See "Configuring Your MS-DOS Application," p. 347

- Try running the application in full-screen mode, using the Alt+Enter key sequence.

If either of the preceding methods works, you will have a faster, more convenient alternative, allowing you the full benefit of Windows' multitasking and other features, all of which disappear during the MS-DOS mode session.

Customizing MS-DOS Mode

Just as you can customize the MS-DOS Prompt session properties, you can alter MS-DOS mode properties as well. If your problem application has special needs beyond those addressed by the default MS-DOS session settings, you can override the Windows defaults via the settings in the Advanced Program Settings dialog box, as shown in figure 11.10.

III

Working with Applications

Fig. 11.10
Windows allows
you to override
the default
settings for MS-
DOS mode
support. You can
even run a special
CONFIG.SYS and
AUTOEXEC.BAT
file for each
application.

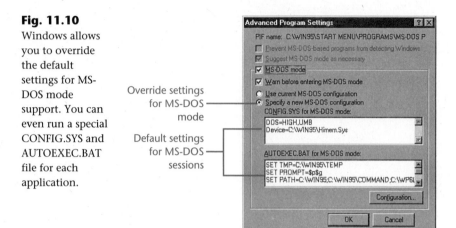

Override settings
for MS-DOS
mode

Default settings
for MS-DOS
sessions

Troubleshooting

I set my main MS-DOS Prompt to run in MS-DOS mode, and now whenever I start it, Windows shuts down completely! How can I set it back if I can't get to the properties? Will I have to reinstall Windows? I just want my windowed MS-DOS back.

Have no fear! You can access the properties of any program or file from the Windows Desktop without running the program or opening the file. When Windows restarts after the MS-DOS Mode session, locate the icon for the MS-DOS prompt program (in the WINDOWS\START MENU\PROGRAMS directory) with the Windows Explorer and right-click the icon to get the menu that offers the Properties function.

When the Properties sheet opens, go to the Program page and choose the Advanced button, which opens the Advanced Program Settings dialog box, as shown earlier in figure 11.10. Simply uncheck the MS-DOS Mode box, and choose OK twice to close the Properties sheet and return to the desktop. See "Configuring Your MS-DOS Application" later in this chapter.

Using PIF Files

Windows 3.1 offered a straightforward, if awkward, means of controlling the session settings for an MS-DOS application through the use of *Program Infor-mation Files* (commonly referred to by their extension, *PIF*). Although PIFs offered a high degree of control over the virtualized MS-DOS environment, the user had to understand the relationship between Windows, MS-DOS, the

PIF, the Program Manager icon assigned to the PIF, and the application itself. Advanced training in MS-DOS memory management didn't hurt either. If you add an MS-DOS batch file to the equation, it could be really confusing.

Windows 95 solves this whole mess by using the same mechanism for MS-DOS applications and data that's now used for Windows files: the Properties sheet. With a simple right-click of the mouse, you can directly view and alter the entire gamut of controls for your MS-DOS application. No separate editor, no hunting for the PIF and confirming that it's the correct one. Although Windows 95 still uses PIF files, there's a unified means of viewing the PIF properties for a given application, via the Properties sheet.

One of the more confusing issues under Windows 3.1 was the need to create a PIF file for each MS-DOS application that required custom settings. Windows 95 takes care of that chore automatically—all you need to do is view the properties for your MS-DOS application.

To view an example Properties sheet for an MS-DOS application, follow these steps:

1. Using the Windows Explorer, find the Windows folder. Then open the Command folder.

2. Right-click to open the shortcut menu, and choose Properties. Windows displays the Edit Properties sheet, as shown in figure 11.11.

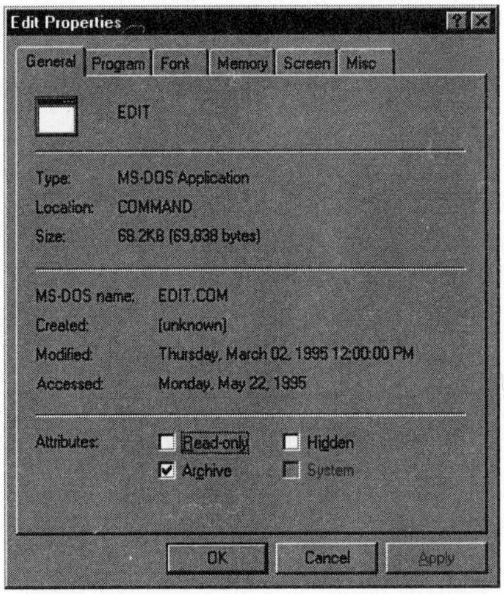

Fig. 11.11
The Windows Properties sheet for MS-DOS applications has several tabs unique to the needs of the MS-DOS environment.

If you're mystified by some of the terms and control types you see here, don't worry. The "Configuring Your MS-DOS Application" section, later in this chapter, shows examples of how these controls can help you maximize Windows' performance when you run MS-DOS applications.

Graphic-Intensive Applications

One great example of the enhanced MS-DOS support available under Windows 95 is the capability to run some applications in graphics mode, in a window. Although this doesn't sound like a big trick, remember that earlier versions of Windows don't support this at all; you are forced to run MS-DOS Graphics-mode applications full screen.

Why would you want to take advantage of running MS-DOS applications in a window? For some of the same reasons you like Windows applications: the capability to quickly and easily move back and forth between applications and the capability to easily cut and paste information between programs.

Also, in earlier versions of Windows, moving from a full-screen MS-DOS application in Graphics mode back to Windows involves a time lag during which the display has to reset for a completely different video mode and resolution; some monitors handle this gracefully, but most don't. Running your MS-DOS program in a window avoids this altogether.

> **Note**
>
> Windows 95 contains the capability to self-configure for many popular MS-DOS programs. These configurations are derived from research with the most-used applications and are stored in a file called APPS.INF. When you install an MS-DOS application, Windows checks to see if it's registered in the APPS.INF database; if the application is listed in the APPS.INF file but no PIF file exists, Windows uses the information to create a PIF for future use.

Although this new capability is wonderful, be aware that not all MS-DOS applications are supported. Not all applications follow the "official" guidelines for MS-DOS hardware access (some programmers break or bend the rules to gain faster performance—for example, writing directly to the video hardware versus using the MS-DOS service calls for video); hence, Windows 95 can't support them in a windowed, virtualized MS-DOS environment. The same application may run perfectly full-screen, because there are fewer layers of virtualization for Windows to provide. A great example of this scenario is a game program, which constantly attempts to use the system timer, video, and sound resources as directly as possible.

How do you know if your application will run in Graphics mode in a Windows 95 window? The best test is to try it. Follow these steps to test your program:

1. Locate the icon for the MS-DOS graphics program you want to test and double-click it to start the program. Windows starts the program in full-screen mode, unless you've configured it otherwise or the program was installed with a windowed default. If the program opens in a window, press Alt+Enter to return to full-screen mode.

2. If the program supports both Character and Graphics modes, activate the program feature that requires Graphics mode (such as Page or Print Preview).

3. When the screen has reformatted for graphics display, press Alt+Enter to return to windowed display mode. Windows displays the application as shown in the example in figure 11.12.

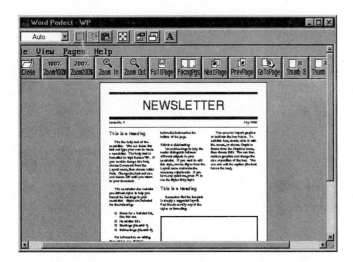

Fig. 11.12
Windows can display MS-DOS graphics mode for many applications, such as the WordPerfect Print Preview feature.

4. If Windows can't support the application in this mode, you see the warning box displayed in figure 11.13.

III

Working with Applications

Fig. 11.13
Although
Windows now
offers improved
support for MS-
DOS graphics
mode, some
applications still
don't work in a
window.

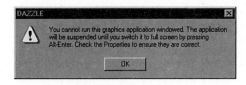

Improved Memory Protection

A bitter lesson learned from running MS-DOS applications under Windows
3.1 was that those applications often inadvertently corrupted the operating
system memory areas. MS-DOS programs, not written for a multitasking environment, believe that they have the right to alter the memory for the entire
system. This can have catastrophic results in a multitasking environment
such as Windows and has been the cause of many a lockup.

Windows 95 offers a much higher level of memory protection for the entire
system and specifically for MS-DOS applications. You can specify special
protection for conventional system memory by checking the Protected check
box on the Memory property page, as shown in figure 11.14.

Fig. 11.14
Windows 95
allows you to
protect conven-
tional memory
from errant
applications via
the Protected
setting on the
Memory property
page.

Select to enable
MS-DOS session
memory
protection

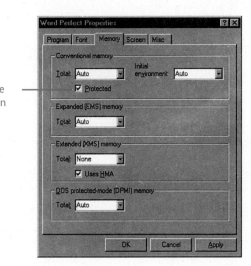

Although it might seem logical to enable this option by default for all MS-
DOS applications, enough overhead is involved in tracking this for each session that it's really best to turn it on only for those applications that have
proven they require it.

Enhanced Virtual Machine Support

MS-DOS application support requires the presence of a virtual MS-DOS environment, or *virtual machine.* This concept and technique, originally from the mainframe environment, is the primary reason for the success and popularity of the Microsoft Windows product. A virtual machine is basically an effective "clone" of the same operating system that MS-DOS applications are written for. Windows provides this environment within Windows so that you can run multiple MS-DOS sessions simultaneously with both Windows and MS-DOS applications.

◀ See "Managing Windows after an Application Failure," p. 78

One problem with Windows 3.1 virtual machine support was that version's particular technique of implementing multiple virtual machines. Because it ran on top of MS-DOS, Windows 3.1 took a "snapshot" of the first megabyte of MS-DOS memory and stored it for later use. When the user asked for an MS-DOS session, Windows re-created this virtual one-megabyte environment, complete with all the original running programs, device drivers, terminate-and-stay-resident programs, and so on, regardless of whether the MS-DOS application running in the virtual environment needed them.

This approach, although workable, had two major problems: it wasted system memory and restricted the customization of individual virtual MS-DOS sessions. Program Information Files (PIFs) allowed the user to alter some parameters of the memory model for each successive virtual machine session, but the overall settings could not be altered once Windows 3.1 was started.

Windows 95 offers many improvements over this model. Because Windows 95 doesn't require a complete, preexisting Real-mode MS-DOS environment before it runs, you can control almost every aspect of the virtual MS-DOS environment because it is more "truly" virtual. You can even run batch files within the session to customize the environment for your application's needs.

Windows 95 also offers better management of MS-DOS session closings. Under Windows 3.1, not all system memory and resources were released when a virtual machine session ended. This resulted in a slow erosion of performance with the eventual inability to open additional applications, requiring the user to restart Windows.

III

Working with Applications

Enhanced Local Reboot Support

Under Windows 3.0, if an application quit working, the user had two options: prayer and prayer. A hung program meant lost data. Windows 3.1 improved on this scenario by allowing *local reboot*, the capability to trap errant application behavior, thus protecting other applications and data. Under Windows 3.1's local reboot, the Ctrl+Alt+Del key sequence didn't restart the machine; it closed the misbehaving application and theoretically left Windows and all other applications fat and happy.

Local reboot had two main problems:

- Users didn't always know which application was hung, so when they used Ctrl+Alt+Del, Windows often closed the wrong one (sometimes offering to shut itself down!).

- Windows 3.1 didn't always respond quickly to the Ctrl+Alt+Del command, and the user "sat" on the keys, resulting in a complete machine reset. (A single Ctrl+Alt+Del would bring up a blue screen warning that a second Ctrl+Alt+Del would reset the system; often this screen was a blue blip as the world came crashing down, and the annual report went to the Great Bit Bucket Beyond.)

Windows 95 improves on this bad scenario by putting a menu between you and data loss. A single Ctrl+Alt+Del displays the Close Program dialog box.

If an application creates a problem or freezes, Windows now indicates that it is "not responding," and you have the choice of ending that task or completing an orderly shutdown of the entire system. Although this doesn't totally insulate your computer from errant applications, it does drastically improve your ability to control otherwise disastrous circumstances.

Troubleshooting

I'm really pleased with how my new computer works with Windows 95 and Windows applications, but it's really slow when I use MS-DOS programs. It also keeps losing my MS-DOS programs, and I have to restart them!

You're probably running too many MS-DOS sessions at once. If you switch back to the Windows Desktop or a Windows application, the MS-DOS application "disappears" (actually it's still open, just hidden by Windows, because it can't display a full-screen MS-DOS session and Windows at the same time). In full-screen MS-DOS mode, Windows can't display the taskbar to show all running applications. If you're running MS-DOS in a window, it's even easier to "lose" it behind another running program's window.

If you restart your MS-DOS application from the same icon, you're really creating a second instance of the program, not moving back to the first one. This only serves to slow down the entire system because every MS-DOS session divides your computing resources by the same amount as all running Windows applications together.

If you can't see your running MS-DOS application, use the old Alt+Tab key trick. Hold down the Alt key and press the Tab key once; this brings up a small window in center screen with icons for all running programs. Another press of the Tab key moves the icon cursor to the next running program, allowing you to move through all open applications "carousel" style. Windows 3.1 didn't show all of the running programs at once in the Alt+Tab window, so many users don't realize they have more than one MS-DOS session open (the icons all look the same, you just have more of them!). Windows 95 Alt+Tab lets you see all running programs' icons at once.

Use the Windows taskbar to help you view and return to running applications. It's really one of the most useful additions to the new Windows, especially for MS-DOS users.

Installing MS-DOS Applications

Now that you have explored the basic concepts, tools, and techniques behind MS-DOS Prompt session support under Windows 95, look at the steps required to install and configure an MS-DOS application.

◀ See "Installing, Running, and Uninstalling Windows Applications," p. 303

You can install any application in the following two basic ways:

- Locate and run the installation program for the application.

- Create a directory for the application and copy the files to that directory.

Note

Although Windows can handle complete installations of true Windows applications, it relies on structures and capabilities that are simply not present in most MS-DOS applications. Thus, you need to set up application shortcuts and Start button menu items manually.

III

Working with Applications

Using MS-DOS Application Installation Programs

Most professionally written MS-DOS applications have an installation or setup program that handles the details of installation for you. Besides simply creating a storage area for the application and moving the files to it, these installation programs perform the additional operating system configuration chores that may be necessary for successful operation.

> **Note**
>
> MS-DOS installation programs that are Windows-aware may handle some of the preceding tasks for you, but most won't—you'll have to handle some of the tasks yourself. How do you know what alterations to make? Look for the documentation for the manual program installation instructions in the program directory. Often this is a simple text file, labeled README.TXT or INSTALL.TXT.

Installing MS-DOS Applications from the MS-DOS Prompt

While it's just as easy to find and run your MS-DOS application installation program from the Windows Explorer or the Start button Run command, you may want to go directly to the MS-DOS Prompt session and install your application directly, or your application may not have a structured installation program. In either case, Windows certainly allows you this level of control.

Using an Installation Program from the MS-DOS Prompt

Running the installation program from an MS-DOS prompt is just like doing it on a machine that's running only MS-DOS. Follow these steps to begin:

1. Open a new MS-DOS session from the Start menu.

2. At the MS-DOS prompt, enter the command to start the installation program (for example, **a:\install.exe**) and press Enter.

◄ See "Ending MS-DOS Prompt Sessions," p. 329

3. When the installation program is finished, close the MS-DOS session manually or run the application if you want.

Installing MS-DOS Programs Manually from the MS-DOS Prompt

Some MS-DOS applications don't have installation programs at all. This is most common with shareware applications or small utility programs.

To install your application manually, follow these simple steps:

1. Open a new MS-DOS session from the Start menu.

2. At the MS-DOS prompt, enter the command to create a directory for your program (for example, **md c:\myprog**) and press Enter.

3. Enter the command to copy the program to the new directory, such as **xcopy a:*.* c:\myprog**. MS-DOS copies the files to the new directory.

> **Note**
>
> You may need to alter the preceding routine slightly if your application comes as a compressed archive (such as a ZIP or an ARJ file). Usually all this means is an additional step for decompression once the files are copied.

Configuring Your MS-DOS Application

Before you explore the myriad options for customizing the MS-DOS environment for your application, there's one point that needs to be stressed: the odds are very good that your program will run perfectly without any reconfiguration at all. Microsoft has done a truly admirable job in observing the reality of how people use MS-DOS applications under Windows, and the design of Windows 95 MS-DOS defaults reflects that. Preset configurations for the most popular MS-DOS applications are stored in Windows, awaiting your installation of the program. So before you begin messing around with all the options, be smart and run the program a few times. The old adage truly applies: if it isn't broke, don't fix it.

Understanding and Configuring MS-DOS Application Properties

You've already been introduced to the Windows Properties sheet and seen how Windows now uses it in place of the PIF Editor. Now you take a closer look at specific property options and how they relate to your application.

◀ See "Displaying Properties of Programs, Documents, and Resources," p. 28

III

Working with Applications

General Properties

The General properties page is primarily informational, with minimal controls other than file attributes (see fig. 11.15).

Fig. 11.15
The General properties page gives you most of the basic information about the file and easy access to control of the file attributes. Context-sensitive help is available at any time by using the "?" tool.

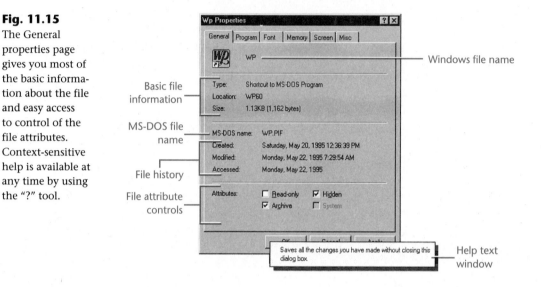

Windows file name

Basic file information

MS-DOS file name

File history

File attribute controls

Help text window

The only real controls exposed in the General properties page are the file attribute settings. These are used mainly to protect documents (by setting the read-only attribute), and you shouldn't alter them unless you have a specific reason.

> **Note**
>
> A running MS-DOS application displays only five Properties tabs. (The General tab is not shown when the program is in use.)

Program Properties

The Program properties page gives you control over the basic environment your application starts with (see fig. 11.16).

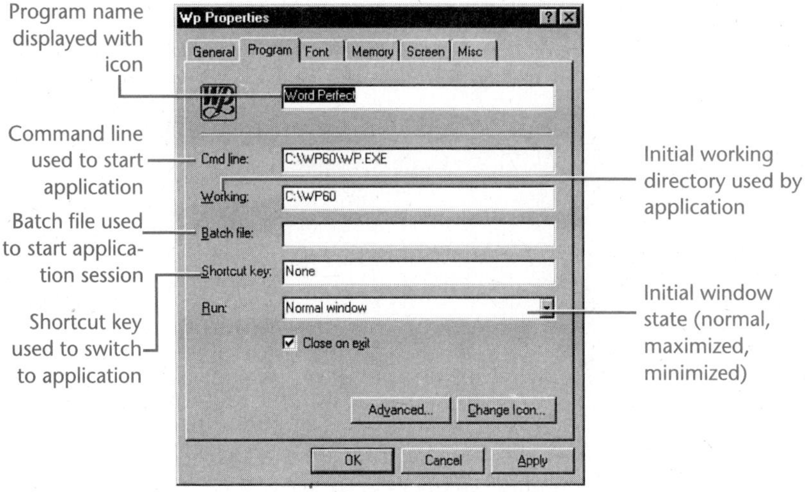
Program name displayed with icon
Command line used to start application
Batch file used to start application session
Shortcut key used to switch to application
Initial working directory used by application
Initial window state (normal, maximized, minimized)
Wp Properties
General
Program
Font
Memory
Screen
Misc
Word Perfect
Cmd line:
C:\WP60\WP.EXE
Working:
C:\WP60
Batch file:
Shortcut key:
None
Run:
Normal window
Close on exit
Advanced...
Change Icon...
OK
Cancel
Apply

Fig. 11.16
The Program properties page allows you to alter the variables used to name and start the application.

Advanced Program Settings. Clicking the Advanced button in the Program properties page produces the Advanced Program Settings dialog box, shown in figure 11.17.

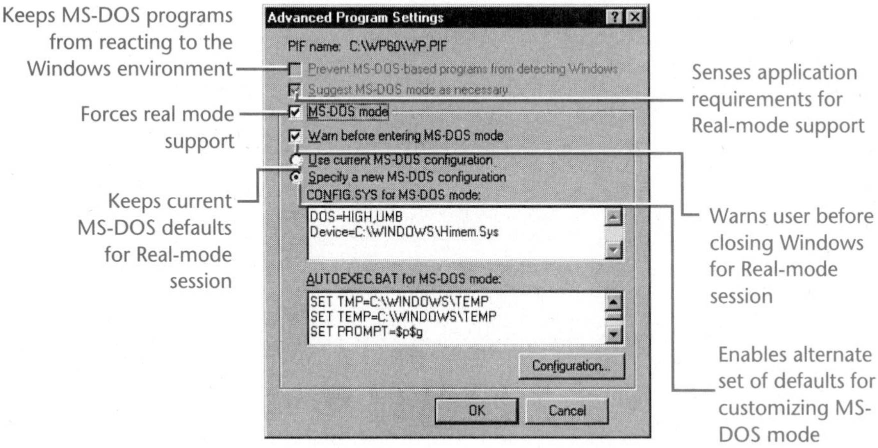
Keeps MS-DOS programs from reacting to the Windows environment
Forces real mode support
Keeps current MS-DOS defaults for Real-mode session
Senses application requirements for Real-mode support
Warns user before closing Windows for Real-mode session
Enables alternate set of defaults for customizing MS-DOS mode
Advanced Program Settings
PIF name: C:\WP60\WP.PIF
Prevent MS-DOS-based programs from detecting Windows
Suggest MS-DOS mode as necessary
MS-DOS mode
Warn before entering MS-DOS mode
Use current MS-DOS configuration
Specify a new MS-DOS configuration
CONFIG.SYS for MS-DOS mode:
DOS=HIGH,UMB
Device=C:\WINDOWS\Himem.Sys
AUTOEXEC.BAT for MS-DOS mode:
SET TMP=C:\WINDOWS\TEMP
SET TEMP=C:\WINDOWS\TEMP
SET PROMPT=pg
Configuration...
OK
Cancel

Fig. 11.17
The Advanced Program Settings dialog box enables you to define the precise mode and environment for your MS-DOS session.

If you need to run your application in MS-DOS mode, here's where you can enable it. You can even set up custom CONFIG.SYS and AUTOEXEC.BAT values for your session. If you click the Specify a New MS-DOS Configuration radio button, you can edit the special CONFIG.SYS and AUTOEXEC.BAT values right in this dialog box.

If you click the Configuration button, you see the dialog box displayed in figure 11.18.

Fig. 11.18
The Select MS-DOS Mode Configuration Options dialog box lets you control expanded memory, disk caching, disk access, and command-line editing.

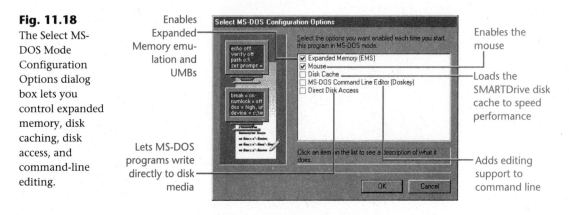

All the settings under the Advanced dialog box should be altered only if your MS-DOS application simply won't run in a standard session with the default settings. For that matter, don't even enable MS-DOS mode unless your application demands it.

◀ See "Knowing When to Use MS-DOS Mode," p. 337

Changing MS-DOS Application Icons. If you click the Change Icon button shown in figure 11.16, the Change Icon dialog box displays (see fig. 11.19).

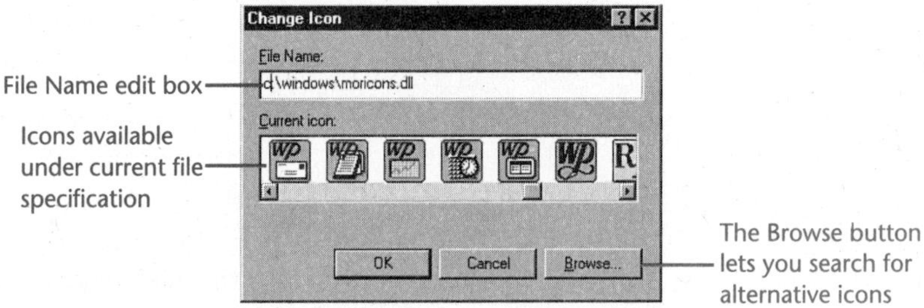

Fig. 11.19
The Change Icon dialog box lets you customize the icon for your MS-DOS application.

File Name edit box

Icons available under current file specification

The Browse button lets you search for alternative icons

It's likely that your MS-DOS application won't come with any icons. Windows 95 will show you the icons in the file PIFMGR.DLL when you choose Change Icon. You can choose icons from other applications simply by specifying them in this dialog box. Or you may want to look in an icon archive that comes with Windows 3.1, MORICONS.DLL. Microsoft threw in icons for a few of the most popular programs so that you can have a choice. If you didn't upgrade from Windows 3.1, MORICONS.DLL probably won't be on your system.

Font Properties

The Font properties page is primarily informational, with minimal controls other than file attributes (see fig. 11.20). It works just like the Font list control on the MS-DOS session toolbar.

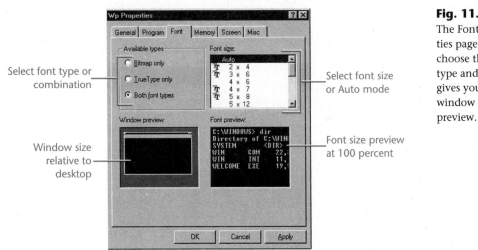

Select font type or combination

Window size relative to desktop

Select font size or Auto mode

Font size preview at 100 percent

Fig. 11.20

The Font properties page lets you choose the font type and size, and gives you both a window and font preview.

Memory Properties

The Memory properties page makes simple work of the traditional maze of MS-DOS memory management (see fig. 11.21). With a few mouse clicks, you can configure your application memory precisely as needed.

Several dozen entire books have been written on the subject of MS-DOS memory management. Let's keep it simple: if your application works without altering these values, *do not change them*. If your application doesn't work with the default settings, *consult the documentation* to determine what the appropriate settings are. *Then* you can alter the values in this dialog box. Proceeding in any other way, unless you have considerable experience with the techniques involved, can severely inhibit the performance of your system.

◀ See "Controlling the MS-DOS Prompt Interface," p. 331

◀ See "Improved Memory Protection," p. 342

III

Working with Applications

Fig. 11.21
The Memory properties page vastly simplifies this formerly arcane management issue.

Sets conventional memory to specific value
Enables protection for session memory range
Enables High Memory Area
Sets DPMI memory value
Sets MS-DOS environment memory value
Sets EMS emulation value
Sets XMS emulation value
Wp Properties
General
Program
Font
Memory
Screen
Misc
Conventional memory
Total:
Auto
Initial environment:
Auto
Protected
Expanded (EMS) memory
Total:
Auto
Extended (XMS) memory
Total:
None
Uses HMA
DOS protected-mode (DPMI) memory
Total:
Auto
OK
Cancel
Apply

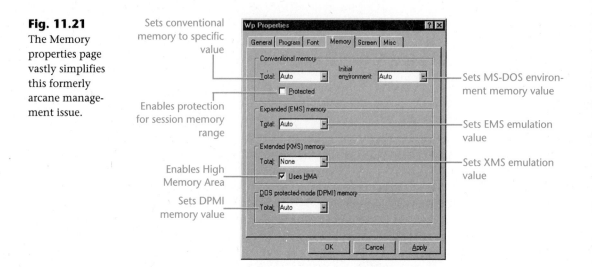

Screen Properties

The Screen properties page lets you control the appearance of the MS-DOS session (see fig. 11.22).

Fig. 11.22
The Screen properties page gives you control of the size, type, and performance of the MS-DOS interface.

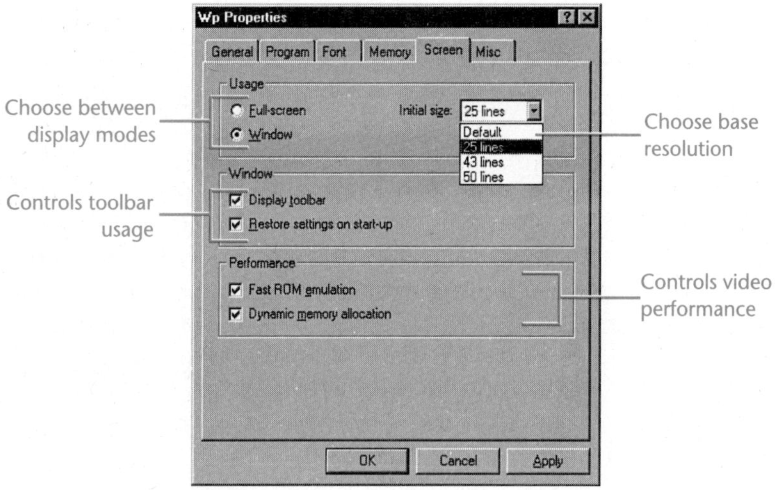

Choose between display modes
Controls toolbar usage
Choose base resolution
Controls video performance
Wp Properties
General
Program
Font
Memory
Screen
Misc
Usage
Full-screen
Window
Initial size:
25 lines
Default
25 lines
43 lines
50 lines
Window
Display toolbar
Restore settings on start-up
Performance
Fast ROM emulation
Dynamic memory allocation
OK
Cancel
Apply

You may find that certain MS-DOS programs (especially those running in Graphics mode) respond poorly to the video emulation used in windowed mode. If so, try defeating the performance defaults by unchecking the Fast ROM Emulation and Dynamic Memory Allocation items. Fast ROM Emulation tells the Windows 95 display driver to mimic the video hardware to help display MS-DOS programs faster. Dynamic Memory Allocation releases display memory to other programs when the MS-DOS session isn't using it. If you experience strange display problems with your MS-DOS programs, try changing these settings.

Miscellaneous Properties

The Misc properties page covers the remaining configuration items that don't fit under the other categories (see fig. 11.23).

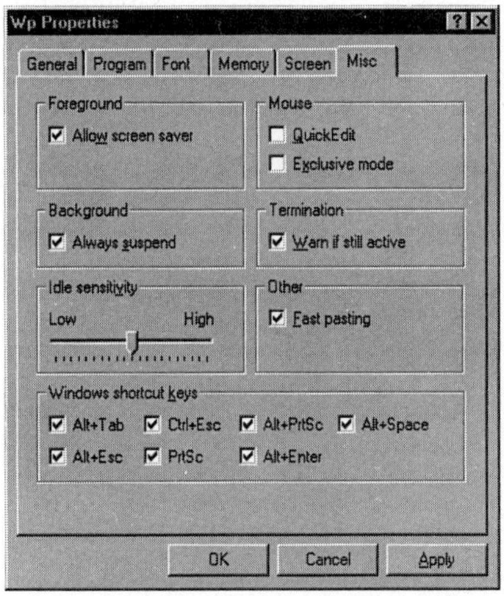

Fig. 11.23

The Misc properties page controls screen saver, mouse, background operation, program termination, shortcut key, and editing options.

- The Allow Screen Saver control lets your default Windows screen saver operate even if your MS-DOS session has the foreground.

- Always Suspend freezes your MS-DOS application when you bring another application (either MS-DOS or Windows) to the foreground. If you have an application that must perform time-sensitive operations (such as a communications program), make sure to disable this option.

III

Working with Applications

- Idle Sensitivity tells your MS-DOS program to yield the system to other applications if it really isn't doing anything important. A word processor, for example, won't have a problem letting go of the system clock when you're not using it. A communications program, however, may need to respond quickly, so you want to set its idle sensitivity to Low.

- The Mouse controls enable QuickEdit mode (letting you mark text using just the mouse) and Exclusive Mode (the MS-DOS application has control of the mouse cursor when the application is in the foreground, even if you try to move the mouse out of the MS-DOS window).

- The Warn If Still Active Item in the Termination box tells Windows to notify you before the MS-DOS session is closed. It's really best to leave this enabled, unless you are absolutely certain that the MS-DOS program will never, ever have open data files when you close it.

- The Fast Pasting setting simply tells Windows that your MS-DOS program can handle a raw data stream dump from the Windows Clipboard. Some MS-DOS programs clog at full speed, so if you paste to your MS-DOS application and you consistently lose characters, turn this one off.

- Windows Shortcut Keys allows you to override the standard quick navigation aids built into the Windows environment, just for your MS-DOS session (some MS-DOS programs think they can get away with using the same keys, and something has to give—Windows!). By default, Windows "owns" these shortcuts, but you can lend them to your MS-DOS application by unchecking them here.

Running Installed MS-DOS Applications

Windows comes set up with a default MS-DOS Prompt configuration designed to run the vast majority of applications. Although your application may have special needs, odds are it will work fine if you start it from within a running MS-DOS Prompt session.

To start your application from an MS-DOS Prompt session, follow these steps:

1. Open a new MS-DOS Prompt session from the Start menu.

2. At the MS-DOS prompt, enter the command to move to the directory of the program you want to start (for example, **cd \wp60**) and press Enter. The MS-DOS prompt now shows the current directory, as shown in figure 11.24.

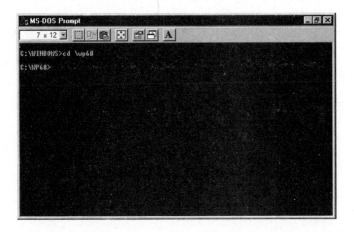

Fig. 11.24
Once you're in the MS-DOS Prompt session, all the basic MS-DOS commands can be used to start your application

3. At the MS-DOS prompt, enter the command to start your application (for example, **wp**) and press Enter. The MS-DOS Prompt window now displays the application you've started, as shown in figure 11.25.

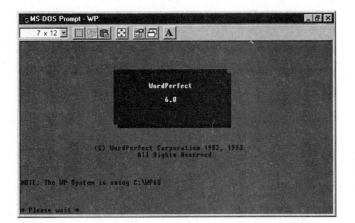

Fig. 11.25
Once your application starts, Windows displays it in the MS-DOS Prompt window space. Note that the window title reflects the command name of the program running.

III

Working with Applications

◀ See "How to
Start Programs
and Docu-
ments," p. 38

Although running an application from within the MS-DOS Prompt window works well and seems familiar to the veteran command-line user, it's not really the most convenient method under Windows.

In addition to the default Windows MS-DOS Prompt, Windows 95 offers four other ways to start an application:

- The Windows Explorer

- The Start button <u>R</u>un option

- The Start button <u>P</u>rograms menu

- The Application shortcut

These startup methods work just like they do for their Windows counterparts.

Removing MS-DOS Applications

If you decide to remove your MS-DOS application from your computer, there are two easy ways to do it:

- Use the MS-DOS Prompt `dir` and `deltree` commands

- Use the Windows Explorer and Recycle Bin

Caution

Regardless of which technique you use, make sure that you don't have any data stored with the application you're removing. Some applications allow you to store your documents or data files in the same directory as the application code itself. Although this is inherently poor design, it still happens; and if you don't tell the application to save your files to another folder or directory, you may be very sorry after you've deleted the program itself.

Using MS-DOS Commands to Remove an MS-DOS Application

Perhaps the most straightforward way to remove an MS-DOS application is to use the MS-DOS tools themselves. To do this, follow these steps:

1. Open MS-DOS Prompt session from the Start menu.

2. At the MS-DOS prompt, type the command **dir c:\appdir /p** (where *appdir* is the directory in which your doomed application awaits its final moments). In this example, you'll use **c:\wp60 /p**. The MS-DOS Prompt session displays a directory listing similar to that shown in figure 11.26.

▶ See "Moving and Copying Files and Folders," p. 515

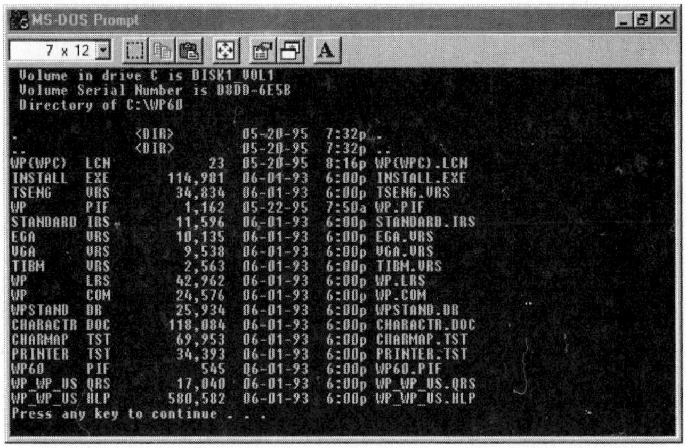

Fig. 11.26
The dir command shows the contents of the directory you want to delete. The /p switch displays the listing in a page at a time. Simply press any key to continue through the listing.

3. Look for any files that contain your personal data (be sure to check in any subdirectories). If necessary, copy or move these files to another location.

4. After you've saved any personal data, proceed to delete the application. At the MS-DOS prompt, type **deltree c:\appdir** (where *appdir* is the directory containing the application to be deleted) and press Enter. MS-DOS displays a message asking you to confirm the deletion. If you're absolutely sure, type **y** and press Enter. MS-DOS deletes the application directory and all subdirectories.

Tip
If you need help with an MS-DOS command, try the built-in MS-DOS help system. Simply add **/?** after the MS-DOS command at the prompt (that is, **move /?**) and you'll get help text for that command.

Using the Explorer to Remove an MS-DOS Application

An even simpler way to remove an MS-DOS application is to use the Explorer and the Recycle Bin. It's really as simple as locating the application folder, checking it for your personal data, and then dragging it to the "trash."

For complete instructions on using the Explorer to remove an application, see Chapter 17, "Managing Your Files with Explorer."

III

Working with Applications

► See "Deleting Files and Folders," p. 518

Cleaning Up Shortcuts and the Start Menu

Be sure to remove shortcuts to applications after you've removed the application itself. If you don't, Windows will still try to load the application, and ask you to help find it when it can't—a real hassle. If you've placed the shortcut on your Desktop, simply drag it to the Recycle Bin.

◄ See "Removing Windows Applications," p. 321

If you used the Control Panel Add/Remove Programs feature discussed in Chapter 10 to add the shortcut to the Start menu, just follow the removal steps outlined in that chapter.❖

Chapter 12

Using WordPad to Create Documents

by Ron Person

WordPad is a simple but powerful word processor that comes with Windows 95. This accessory is ideal for many day-to-day word processing needs. WordPad offers many of the editing and formatting capabilities commonly found in more advanced applications, along with the ability to share information with other applications and files. You can cut, copy, and paste text and graphics between WordPad documents and between WordPad and other applications. WordPad uses the same structure of menus, commands, icons, and dialog boxes that all Windows 95 applications use. What you learn about managing text in WordPad applies to most of the Windows 95 applications involving text.

In this chapter, you learn to

- Create and edit a document
- Format text or an entire document
- Print a document
- Open and save a document
- Customize WordPad's Settings

Creating Documents in WordPad

WordPad is easy to use. The features you've learned in other word processors—like how to select commands, enter text, and format text—also work here. Creating a WordPad document is as simple as starting the application and typing the text. Because the margins, a font, and tabs are already set, you can actually begin a new WordPad document as soon as you start the application.

Starting WordPad

Tip
If you want quick access to WordPad, add a shortcut icon to the desktop. Then just double-click the icon to start WordPad.

To start WordPad from the desktop, follow these steps:

1. Open the Start menu and choose Programs; then choose Accessories.

2. Choose WordPad. WordPad starts up and displays the WordPad window (see fig. 12.1).

> **Note**
>
> If your WordPad screen doesn't include the same elements as the one shown in figure 12.1, see the "Changing the Screen Display" section later in this chapter for information on how to add and remove screen elements from the display.

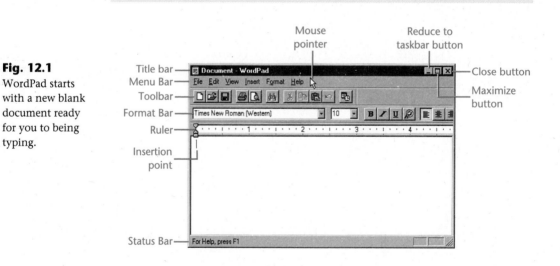

Fig. 12.1
WordPad starts with a new blank document ready for you to being typing.

Creating a New WordPad Document

◀ See "Starting Programs from a Shortcut Icon on the Desktop," p. 68

Unlike more robust Windows applications, WordPad can contain only one document at a time. When you open a new blank document you will be asked if you want to save the current document.

To create a new document once you have started WordPad, follow these steps:

1. Choose <u>F</u>ile, <u>N</u>ew, or click the New button in the toolbar. The New
   dialog box appears (see fig. 12.2).

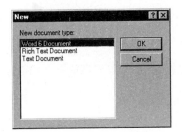

Fig. 12.2
You can create
new documents in
any one of three
formats.

2. Select one of the following document types:

   ■ *Word 6 Document.* This format can be opened and edited in
   Microsoft Word 6.0 or Word 95.

   ■ *Rich Text Document.* This format is compatible with several word
   processors and includes fonts, tabs, and character formatting.

   ■ *Text Document.* This format includes no text formatting and can
   be used in any word processor.

3. Click OK.

Opening WordPad Documents

To open a file that has already been created and saved, follow these steps:

1. Choose <u>F</u>ile, <u>O</u>pen, or click the Open button in the toolbar. The Open
   dialog box appears (see fig. 12.3).

   ◄ See "Changing
   Folders in Save
   As and Open
   Dialog Boxes,"
   p. 100

   > **Caution**
   >
   > If you open a file that was created in another word processor such as Word for
   > Windows, same of the formatting can be lost or converted incorrectly.

2. If the file is on a different disk, click the down arrow to the right of the
   Look <u>I</u>n box and select the drive that contains the file you want.

3. Double-click the folder that contains the file you want to open.

4. Click the down arrow to the right of the Files of <u>T</u>ype box and select the
   type of files you want to list.

III

Working with Applications

5. Double-click the file you want open.

or

Type in the File Name box the name of the file you want to open and click Open.

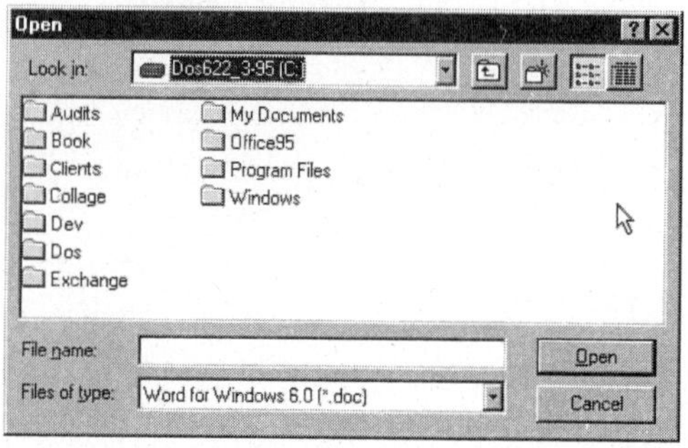

Fig. 12.3

You can open documents from the Open dialog box.

Tip

Try using WordPad on older, less powerful laptop computers. It is a small application using less memory and hard disk space, yet it gives you basic word processing features.

Tip

To work with multiple WordPad documents, open the WordPad application multiple times.

◄ See "Changing Folders in Save As and Open Dialog Boxes," p. 100

► See "Working with Long File Names," p. 509

Note

If a Word for Windows file will not open, try opening it in WordPad. If it opens you may see symbols and characters you do not recognize. Start a new instance of Word for Windows and open a blank document in it. Base this new document on the same template as the document that would not open. Now return to WordPad and copy the entire document. Switch to the blank document in Word for Windows and paste. Reapply paragraph styles as necessary. WordPad seems to be able to open documents that contain file errors that make Word balk.

In WordPad, you can work on only one document at a time. You can start a new document (or open a different document), but the existing document closes. If you haven't saved changes to the existing document, the program asks whether you want to save the changes.

Typing, Saving, and Naming the Document

In the WordPad text area is a flashing insertion point (also known as the cursor). This is where your typing or edits will appear. You can begin typing as soon as you open a file. Use the same word processing techniques you would use in any Windows word processor. As you type, notice that *word-wrap* makes lines of text break and wrap to the next lower line. As you fill the page, the screen scrolls down (or left and right), keeping the insertion point in view.

As you work on your WordPad document, you should save it periodically to avoid losing your work in case of a power failure or equipment malfunction. To save and name a file, follow these steps:

1. Choose File, Save As, or click the Save button in the toolbar. The Save As dialog box appears (see fig. 12.4).

Save As dialog box:

```
Save As                                          ? X
Save in:  [ Dos622_3-95 (C:) ]  [v] [↑] [📁] [::] [▦]

📁 Audits          📁 My Documents
📁 Book            📁 Office95
📁 Clients         📁 Program Files
📁 Collage         📁 Windows
📁 Dev
📁 Dos
📁 Exchange

File name:     [Document              ]        [ Save  ]
Save as type:  [ Word for Windows 6.0 ] [v]    [ Cancel ]
```

Fig. 12.4
Give a file a name and also indicate where you want it saved in the Save As dialog box.

2. Select the drive where you want to save the file in the Save In box.

3. Double-click the folder in which you want to save the file.

4. Type the file name in the File Name text box.

5. If you want to save the file in a format other than WordPad, select a format from the Save as Type list.

6. Click Save or press Enter.

To resave a file with its current name, choose File, Save; or click the Save button.

Selecting and Editing Text

You can make simple edits in your WordPad documents by moving the insertion point and deleting or inserting text. To make simple insertions, place the insertion point where you want to add text and type. To erase one character at a time, position the insertion point next to the character and press Backspace (to delete characters to the left), or Delete (to delete characters to the right).

However, many edits you need to make are more complex than simply entering or deleting one character at a time. You may want to change a word, delete a sentence, or move a whole paragraph. To do these things, you must identify the text you want to edit or format by selecting it. Selected text appears highlighted (or in reverse video) on-screen, as shown in figure 12.5.

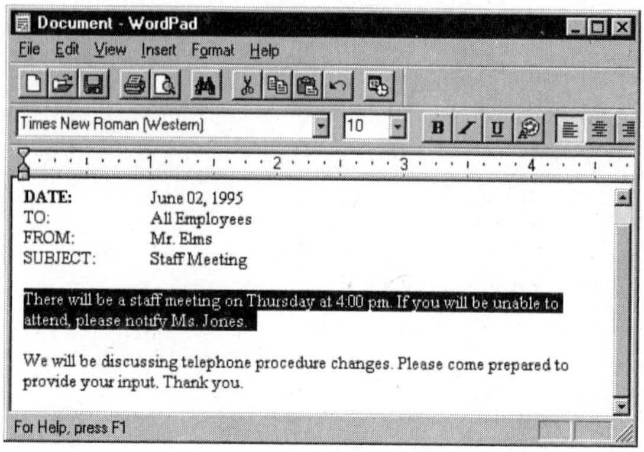

Fig. 12.5
Two sentences
selected for
editing.

Note

WordPad lets you change your mind about an edit you just made or a sentence you just typed. To undo, choose Edit, Undo; press Alt+Backspace or Ctrl+Z; or click the Undo button in the toolbar. You can restore text you just deleted, delete text you just added, or remove formatting. You can even undo the undo. If you find that Edit Undo removes too much typing, choose Edit, Undo a second time to undo the undo.

Tip
Many of the selection shortcuts you learn in WordPad work in Microsoft Word for Windows.

To select text with the mouse, position the I-beam at the beginning of the text, hold down the mouse button, drag to the end of the text, and release the mouse button. WordPad also offers time-saving selection shortcuts, such as double-clicking to select a word. Techniques for selecting with the mouse are shown in table 12.1.

Table 12.1   Mouse Techniques for Selecting Text

Selection	Action
One word	Double-click the word
Several words	Double-click the first word and drag to the end of the last word
Any amount of text	Press the mouse button and drag from the beginning to the end of the text
Between two points	Move the insertion point to the beginning, click, move to the second point, press and hold down Shift, and click at the second point
One line	Click the selection bar (white space) to the left of the line

Selection	Action
Several lines	Press the mouse button and drag up or down in the selection bar
Paragraph	Double-click in the selection bar (blank area) to the left of the paragraph
Entire document	Press Ctrl and click in the selection bar

To select text with the keyboard, press and hold down the Shift key while moving the insertion point with the arrow keys. You can extend the selection by pressing Shift+Ctrl+an arrow key to select a word at a time. Or, press Shift+End to select text to the end of the line.

◀ See "Selecting Text and Objects," p. 114

To deselect text with the mouse, click once anywhere in the text portion of the window. To deselect text with the keyboard, press any arrow key. Deselected text returns to its normal appearance.

To delete a block of text, select it and press Delete or Backspace or choose Edit, Cut. You also can replace text by selecting it and then typing; WordPad deletes the selected block and inserts the new words.

Moving and Copying Text

Any amount of text—a letter, a word, part of a sentence, or several pages—can be moved from one place in a document to another. You also can copy text from one place in a document to another or to many other places.

To move or copy text, follow these steps:

1. Select the text you want to move or copy.

2. Choose Edit, Cut, or press Shift+Del or Ctrl+X, or click the Cut button (to move text).

   Or choose Edit, Copy, or press F2, Ctrl+Ins, or Ctrl+C, or click the Copy button (to copy text).

3. Move the insertion point to where you want to move or copy the text.

◀ See "Copying and Moving," p. 115

4. Choose Edit, Paste, press Shift+Ins or Ctrl+V, or click the Paste button.

◀ See "Learning About Drag-and-Drop," p. 105

To quickly move selected text, you can use the drag-and-drop technique. Select the text, point to it with the mouse, hold down the left mouse button, and drag to a new location. Release the mouse and the text is dropped. Hold down the Control key while you perform the process to copy the selection.

III

Working with Applications

> **Note**
>
> To make it easier to copy text between applications, minimize applications that are not involved so they are on the taskbar. Right-click in a gray area of the taskbar and choose Tile Horizontal or Tile Vertical. This will put the two application windows side-by-side and make it easy to work.

Finding and Replacing Text

You can use WordPad to search a document and find or change text—for example, to change a misspelled name or correct an old date. The Edit menu includes three commands that help you find text and make changes quickly: Find (you also can click the Find button), Find Next (repeats the previous search), and Replace.

The Find and Replace commands operate through dialog boxes (see fig. 12.6). After you enter the text you want to find or change, WordPad starts at the insertion point and searches forward through the document, locating and selecting the first occurrence of the text.

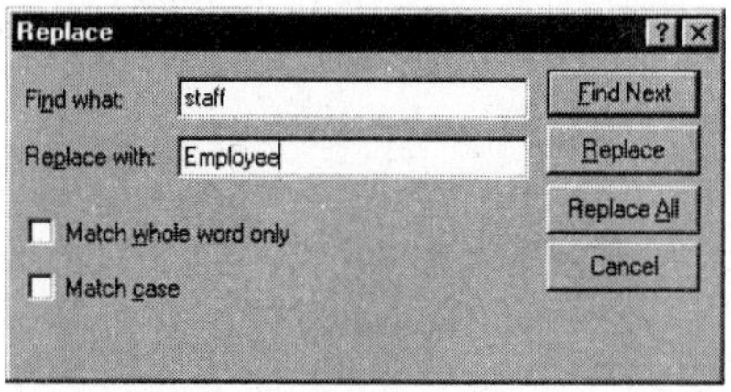

Fig. 12.6
Use the Edit, Replace command to quickly change text.

Formatting the Document

WordPad offers a number of ways to customize the look of your documents. You can add emphasis to individual characters or words with bold or italic, specify the font and point size of the text, and so on. These formats are called *character formatting* and apply to individual characters within words.

You can format paragraphs individually or as a group. For example, you can set up tables with special column alignment, center headings and quotations, and so on. This type of formatting is called *paragraph formatting*.

When the text of your document is finished, it's time to think about the *document formatting*. Do you plan to print the document on letterhead or other special paper that requires certain margins to fit correctly? Document formatting controls the look of the document as a whole.

The following sections describe the three types of WordPad formatting in detail.

Character Formatting

You can control, or enhance, the appearance of characters with the Format, Font command or from the Format bar. You can select, for example, a new font or font size, or select bold to emphasize an important point. If you already have typed the characters, you can change their appearance by selecting the text and choosing options from the Format bar or by choosing Format, Font. If you have not yet typed the text, position the insertion point where you want the enhanced text to begin, choose the enhancement, and type the text.

Many of the character enhancement options, shown in the Font dialog box in figure 12.7, "toggle" on and off like a light switch. You turn them on the same way you turn them off, by simply choosing the command. To make plain text bold, for example, select the text and click the Bold button. To make bold text plain, do the same thing.

To change character formatting, select the text you want to change and select character formatting options from the Format bar or with the Format, Font command.

Tip
To add bold from the keyboard, select the text you want bold and press Ctrl+B. Press Ctrl+I for italic, and Ctrl+U for underline.

> **Note**
>
> You can quickly make up a font chart for reference purposes by using the right click feature in the Font dialog box or the Format bar. When you display the Font dialog box, you can right-click in the Font, Font style, or Size boxes and select Cut, Copy, Paste, or Delete from the menu that displays. (Right-click in the Font or Size boxes in the Format bar for the same menu.) If you select a font, for example, right-click, and choose Copy, you can return to your document, right-click and choose Paste to insert the font name (style or size) into the document. Do that with the entire list of fonts and you will have a sample of each font displayed with its name.

> **Note**
>
> Add special symbols from the ANSI code (check your printer manual for the codes) by pressing and holding Alt as you type the sequence of four digits that describe the letter. The numbers must be typed on the numeric pad. There must be four digits so fill in unused digits with zeros. For example, press Alt+0169, then release Alt to insert the copyright symbol.

III

Working with Applications

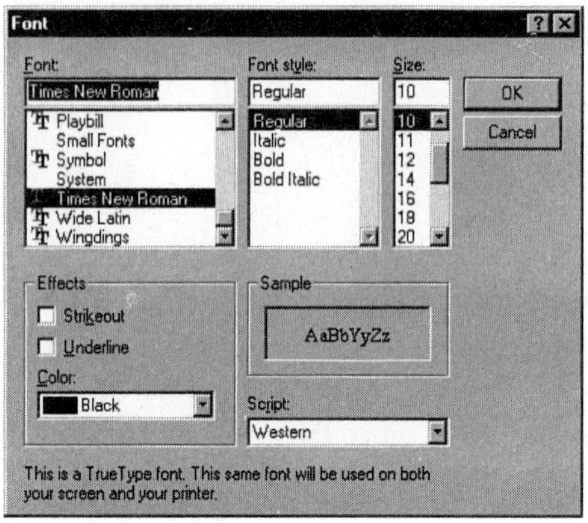

Fig. 12.7
Change the
character format-
ting at the Font
dialog box.

Paragraph Formatting

Paragraph formatting describes the appearance of a paragraph (or of a single line that stands by itself as a paragraph). This level of formatting includes text alignment and indentation. Some formatting choices were made for you already: by default, text is left-aligned, and no paragraphs are indented, as you can see in the Paragraph dialog box in figure 12.8.

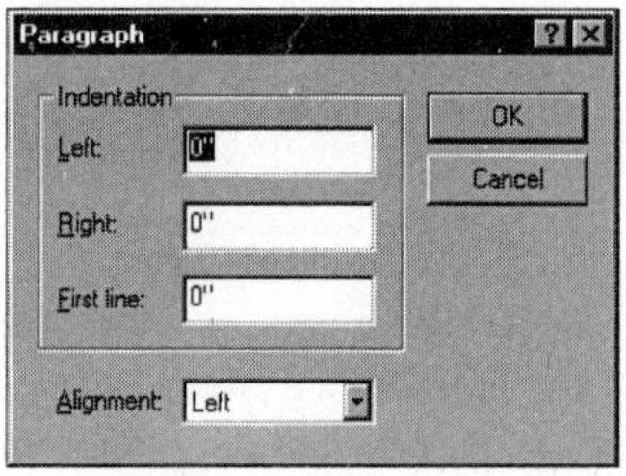

Fig. 12.8
Change the
paragraph
formatting at the
Format Paragraph
dialog box.

In WordPad, paragraphs can be aligned with the left or right margin, or in the center between the margins. You can set alignment with either the For-mat, Paragraph command or with the alignment buttons in the Format bar.

Paragraphs can be indented to set them off from the main body of text— for example, for long quotations. Also, the first lines of paragraphs can be indented so that you do not have to press Tab at the beginning of each paragraph.

Indentations, like all measurements in WordPad, are measured in inches rather than characters, because WordPad supports different font sizes and proportional spacing. (Measurement units can be changed. See the "Chang-ing WordPad Settings" section later in this chapter for more information.)

The indentation options are available in the Paragraph dialog box (refer to fig. 12.8), and also on the Ruler.

▶ See "Changing the Screen Display," p. 373

> **Note**
>
> In *proportional* spacing, the widths of letters are proportional; for example, the letter *i* is narrower than the letter *m*. If margins and indentations were measured in characters, WordPad would not know how large to make an indentation: an inch might contain 16 *i*'s but only 12 *m*'s. Similarly, varying font sizes means that WordPad cannot measure the length of a page by lines.

To indent a paragraph with the ruler, follow these steps:

1. Choose <u>V</u>iew, <u>R</u>uler to display the ruler, if it is not currently displayed.

2. Position the insertion point inside the paragraph or select those paragraphs you want to change.

3. Drag the indent markers to the left or right (see fig. 12.9).

First-line
indent marker

Left
indent
marker

First-line and left
indent marker

Right indent
marker

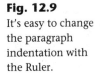

Fig. 12.9
It's easy to change the paragraph indentation with the Ruler.

Document Formatting

Document formatting affects an entire document and its appearance. In a new WordPad document, many document formatting choices are made for you already. Margins, for example, are set to 1.25 inches on the left and right, and 1 inch on the top and bottom. Default tab settings are set every .5 inch. The paper is portrait-oriented.

You can change tabs with the F<u>o</u>rmat, <u>T</u>abs command or on the ruler. All tabs are left-aligned. Set tabs in inches from the left margin (as shown in figure 12.10), not from another tab setting. The ruler may be the easiest way to set tabs. Click on the ruler where you want a tab set. Move tab settings by dragging the tab arrows left or right. Remove tabs by dragging them down off the ruler.

III

Working with Applications

Fig. 12.10
Set tabs on the Tab ruler by clicking the position where you want the new tab set.

Tab settings

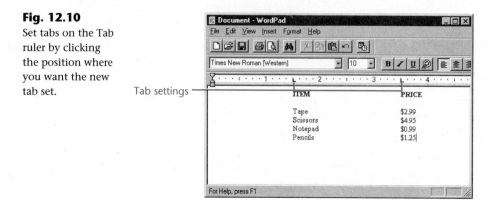

Margins and paper instructions, as well as printer selection, are set at the Page Setup dialog box (see fig. 12.11). Follow these steps:

1. Choose File, Page Setup. The Page Setup dialog box displays.

2. Select the Top, Bottom, Left, and Right boxes in turn and type a decimal measurement for each margin.

3. Select a paper Size, Source, or Orientation.

4. Click Printer to select a printer.

5. Click OK or press Enter.

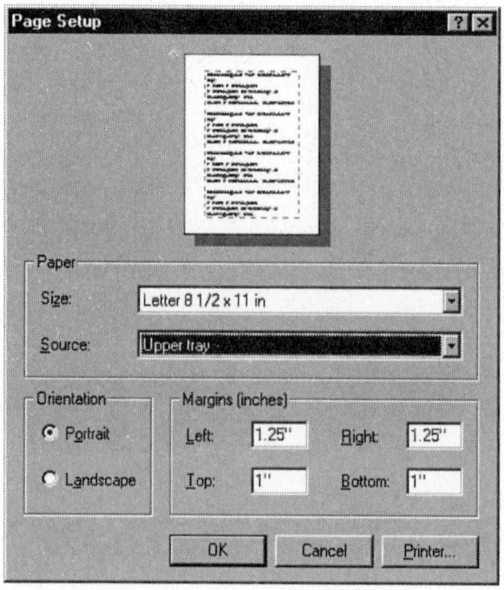

Fig. 12.11
Change the margins in the Page Setup dialog box.

Printing a Document

Printing with WordPad involves two steps—selecting the printer, and specifying what you want to print.

◀ See "Printing from Applications," p. 168

The Print Preview screen displays your document as it will appear in print (see fig. 12.12). Use it to ensure that what you're about to print is what you expect. You'll save printing time and paper.

The pointer at the Print Preview screen becomes a magnifying glass and works like the Zoom In and Zoom Out buttons. To preview your document, choose File, Print Preview, or click the Print Preview button.

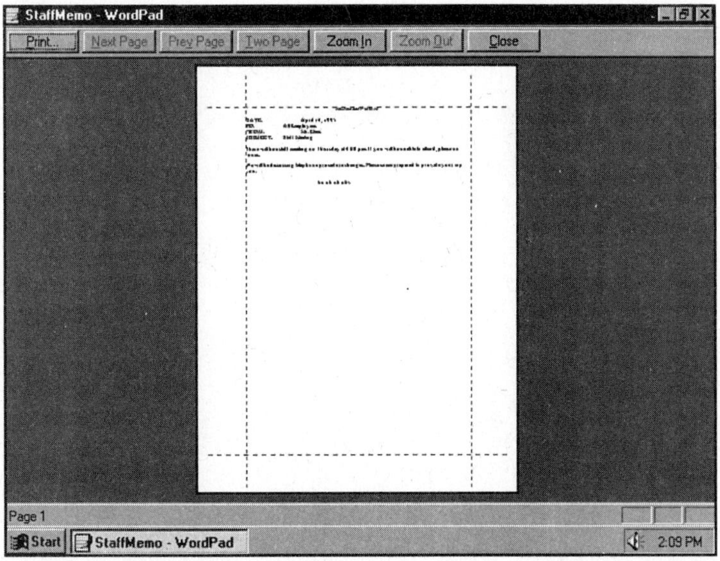

Fig. 12.12
WordPad provides a preview screen where you can examine your document before you print.

Selecting a Printer

Before you can print, you must select a printer. Once a printer is selected, it remains selected for all documents—you won't have to select a printer again unless you want to change to a different printer. To identify and set up the default printer, follow these steps:

1. Choose File, Page Setup (the Page Setup dialog box appears) and click Printer; or choose File, Print (the Print dialog box appears).

2. Select a printer from the Name box.

3. Click OK.

III

Working with Applications

Tip
You can add a
shortcut printer
icon to the desk-
top and then drag
a saved file onto it.
The file will print.

◀ See "Print from
the Desktop,"
p. 179

The printer list includes all the printers installed on the computer for Windows. Click the P̲roperties button to select additional information, such as paper size and graphics resolution.

Printing a File

To print a document, follow these steps:

1. Choose F̲ile, P̲rint. The Print dialog box appears (see fig. 12.13).

2. Select Print range A̲ll to print all the pages; select S̲election to print only the selected text; or type a range of pages to print in the Pages f̲rom and Pages t̲o text boxes.

3. Mark the Print to Fil̲e check box to print to a file rather than to the printer. You are prompted to provide a filename and a location.

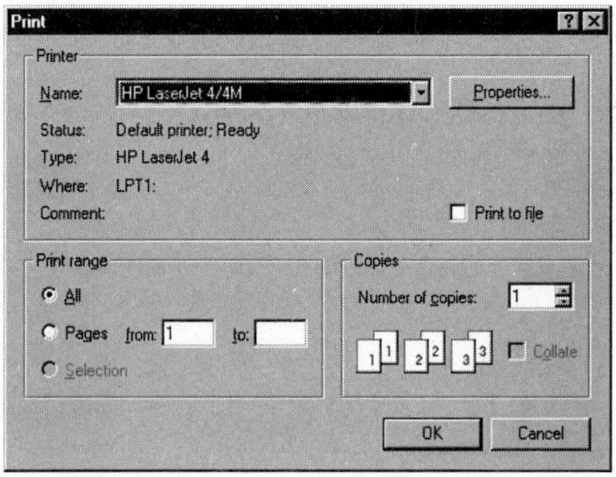

Fig. 12.13
In the Print dialog
box you can vary
the number of
copies you print
and select exactly
which pages you
print.

Tip
To print the whole
document without
selecting any
special options,
simply click the
Print button.

<table>
<tr><td colspan="2">**Print**   ? X</td></tr>
<tr><td colspan="2">Printer</td></tr>
<tr><td>N̲ame:</td><td>HP LaserJet 4/4M ▾   P̲roperties...</td></tr>
<tr><td>Status:</td><td>Default printer; Ready</td></tr>
<tr><td>Type:</td><td>HP LaserJet 4</td></tr>
<tr><td>Where:</td><td>LPT1:</td></tr>
<tr><td>Comment:</td><td>☐ Print to fil̲e</td></tr>
</table>

Print range — ⦿ A̲ll ○ Pages f̲rom:1 t̲o: ○ S̲election

Copies — Number of c̲opies: 1 — ☐ C̲ollate

OK   Cancel

4. Type the number of copies you want to print in the Number of c̲opies box.

5. Select Collate to collate multiple copies of the document (available if your printer supports collating).

6. Click OK or press Enter.

Changing the Screen Display

WordPad provides options from the View menu that let you add or remove elements from the screen display. Each of these elements, including Toolbar, Format Bar, Ruler, and Status Bar, can be toggled on and off. A check mark in the menu indicates that an item is turned on. To toggle screen elements on or off, click the View menu and choose the command you want. The View menu also includes the Options command for customizing some of the WordPad settings.

Changing WordPad Settings

You can change several of the WordPad default settings in the Options dialog box (see fig. 12.14). Your choices, available on each of the six tabs, include setting the measurement units, determining how word wrap operates, and presetting the toolbars that will display. Choose View, Options, click the tab you want, make your selections, and click OK.

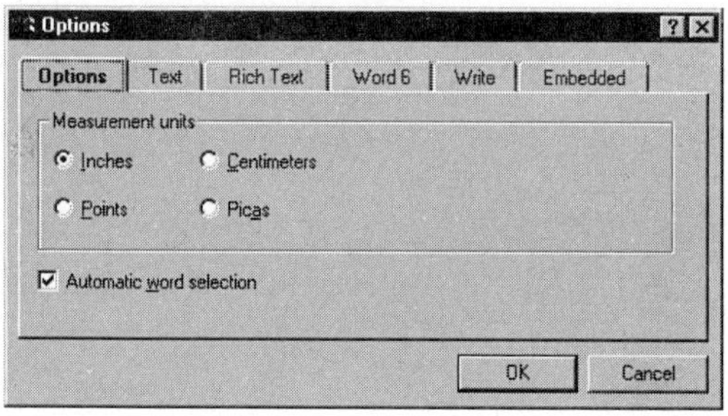

Fig. 12.14
You can customize some of the WordPad defaults in the Options dialog box.

III

Working with Applications

Exiting WordPad

After you finish writing or are ready to stop for the day, exit WordPad and return to the Windows desktop by choosing File, Exit or by clicking the Close button in the upper-right corner of the application window.

Using Notepad

Notepad is a miniature text editor. Just as you use a notepad on the desk, you can use Notepad to take notes on-screen while working in other Windows applications. Notepad uses little memory and is useful for editing text that you want to copy in a Windows or DOS application that lacks editing capability.

Notepad retrieves and saves files in text format. This feature makes Notepad a convenient editor for creating and altering text-based files. Because Notepad stores files in text format, almost all word processors can retrieve Notepad's files.

Use Notepad to hold text you want to move to another application. Clipboard can hold only one selection at a time, but the Notepad can serve as a text scrapbook when you are moving several items as a group.

Starting Notepad

To start Notepad, follow these steps:

1. Open the Start menu and choose Programs; then choose Accessories.

2. Choose Notepad. Notepad starts up and displays a blank document in the Notepad window (see fig. 12.15). You can begin typing.

Fig. 12.15

The initial blank Notepad file is ready for text.

Caution

Be careful when you edit with Notepad. Because Notepad creates text files, you can open and edit important system, application, and data files. To avoid loss of data or applications, make sure that you open only files with which you are familiar.

Working with Documents in Notepad

Unlike most word processing applications, Notepad doesn't by default wrap text to the following line. You must either choose Edit, Word Wrap, or press Enter at the end of each line.

You can move the insertion point by using either the mouse or the keyboard. You select and edit text in Notepad the same way you select and edit text in WordPad.

◀ See "Selecting and Editing Text," p. 363

Limited formatting is available from the File, Page Setup command. You can change margins and add a header or footer. You cannot format characters or paragraphs in any way, although you can use Tab, the space bar, and Backspace to align text. Tab stops are preset at every eight characters.

◀ See "Copying and Moving," p. 115

With Notepad's Edit commands, you can cut, copy, and move text from one place in a file to another. Text you cut or copy is stored in the Clipboard. When you paste text, this text is copied from the Clipboard to the document at the insertion point.

Creating a Time-Log File with Notepad

By typing a simple command at the top of a Notepad document, **.LOG**, you can have Notepad enter the current time and date at the end of a document each time you open the file. This feature is convenient for taking phone messages or for calculating the time spent on a project. As an alternative, you can choose Edit, Time/Date or press F5 to insert the current time and date at the insertion point.❖

III

Working with Applications

Chapter 13

Using Paint, Calculator, and other Accessories

by Ron Person

The desktop accessories that come with Windows can help you perform special tasks related to a current project without leaving the application. You may be working in Word for Windows, for example, and need to make a quick calculation; the Windows Calculator can do the job. You can create computer "paintings" in Paint to illustrate a story, to emphasize an important point in a report, or to clarify instructions.

The desktop accessories take advantage of one of Windows' most powerful features: the capability of running several applications simultaneously. As you work in the main application, you can keep the Windows desktop applications running at the same time. Because so little of the computer's memory is used, the desktop accessories don't slow you down.

In this chapter, you learn to

- Use Paint to create and edit pictures that can be inserted into other applications

- Use Calculator to perform calculations

- Set the clock that displays on the taskbar

- Insert special characters into any Windows document with Character Map

III

Working with Applications

Using Windows Paint

Even though Paint is a simple, easy-to-use graphics application, it may be as powerful a graphics application as you will ever need. Paint is fun, but it also is a serious business tool. With Paint, you can create everything from free-flowing drawings to precise mathematical charts, and you can use your creations in other Windows applications, such as WordPad or Word for Windows.

The following are some of the graphic effects you can create with Paint:

- Lines in many widths, shades, and colors

- Brush strokes in a variety of styles, widths, shades, and colors

- Unfilled or filled shapes with shades or colors

- Text in many sizes, styles, and colors

- Special effects such as rotating, tilting, and inverting

Because Paint is a bitmap graphics application, the shapes you create are painted on-screen in one layer. You cannot reshape a box or move an object behind another object, but you can cut out a box and move it somewhere else, cut out a picture of a house and tilt it, cut out a pattern and flip it, or change the colors of your painting. You can also erase your painting (or part of it) and paint something new.

Starting Windows Paint

To start Paint, follow these steps:

1. Open the Start menu; then choose Programs, Accessories.

2. Choose Paint.

Paint starts up and opens a new, empty Paint file (see fig. 13.1).

To open a previously saved Paint file, choose File, Open. Select the file from the Open dialog box.

Selecting Tools and Colors

To paint, draw, fill, color or shade, write, and edit in Paint, you first must select the appropriate tool and shade or color. Figure 13.2 shows the individual tools in the toolbox on the left side of the screen.

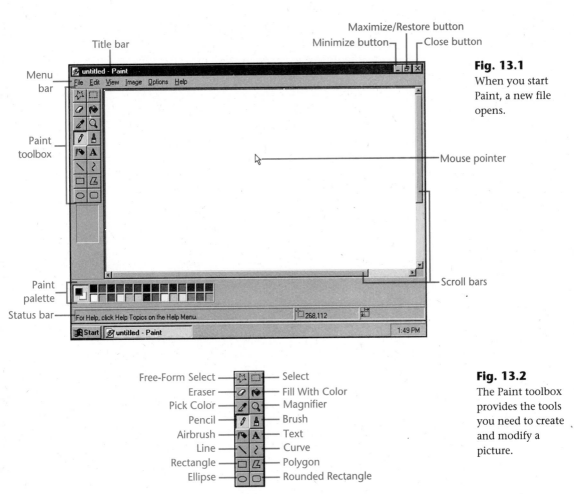

Fig. 13.1
When you start
Paint, a new file
opens.

Free-Form Select — Select
Eraser — Fill With Color
Pick Color — Magnifier
Pencil — Brush
Airbrush — Text
Line — Curve
Rectangle — Polygon
Ellipse — Rounded Rectangle

Fig. 13.2
The Paint toolbox
provides the tools
you need to create
and modify a
picture.

The palette offers two choices: foreground and background shade or color.
At the left end of the palette is a box overlaying a box (see fig. 13.3). The top
box is the foreground color; the bottom box is the background color. The
color you use depends on which mouse button you use to draw lines, brush
strokes, and shapes. The left mouse button selects the foreground color; the
right mouse button selects the background color. For example, when you
draw a shaded box with the left mouse button, the foreground color borders
the box and the background color fills the box. The opposite is true when
you draw the box with the right mouse button. (Drawing is discussed in the
next section, "Using the Paint Toolbox.")

Tip
If you draw
with the right
mouse button,
the foreground
and back-
ground colors
will be reversed.

III

Working with Applications

Fig. 13.3

Choose foreground and background colors from the Paint palette.

Foreground color — (left mouse button)

Background color (right mouse button)

To select a tool or color, position the pointer on the tool or foreground color that you want and click the left mouse button. To select a background color, point to the color you want and click the right mouse button.

Using the Paint Toolbox

The Paint toolbox includes tools for selecting areas, airbrushing, typing text, erasing, filling, brushing, drawing curves or straight lines, and drawing filled or unfilled shapes. Most of the tools operate using a similar process.

To draw with the tools in the Paint toolbox, follow these steps:

1. Click to select the tool you want to use.

2. Move the pointer to where you want to begin drawing.

3. Press and hold down the mouse button as you drag the mouse.

4. Release the mouse button to stop drawing.

Three exceptions to this process are

■ The Text tool, which works by clicking and typing.

■ The Paint Fill tool, which works by pointing and clicking.

■ The Curve tool, which works by clicking, dragging, and clicking.

Aligning Drawn Objects

When you want lines or shapes to line up accurately on-screen, refer to the cursor position indicators in the status bar at the bottom of Paint's window. The two numbers that display tell you the position of the insertion point or drawing tool on-screen. The position is given in X, Y coordinates, measured in pixels, from the top left corner of the painting. The left number is the X-coordinate (the position relative to the left edge of the painting); the right number is the Y-coordinate (the position relative to the top of the painting). If the numbers in the Cursor Position window read *42, 100*, for example, the cursor is 42 pixels from the left edge of the painting and 100 pixels down from the top of the painting.

Whichever tool you use, <u>E</u>dit, <u>U</u>ndo is a useful ally. Use it to undo your most recent action. <u>U</u>ndo will undo up to the last three actions. Just continue to select <u>U</u>ndo to undo the number of actions you desire.

> **Note**
>
> Several tools, including the Selection and Shape tools, use the right mouse button to undo. To cancel the shape you're currently drawing, click the right mouse button *before* you release the left mouse button.

Troubleshooting

What if I choose the wrong option or change my mind?

You can choose <u>E</u>dit, <u>U</u>ndo to undo your last choice. If you undo something by mistake, you can choose <u>E</u>dit, <u>R</u>epeat to redo it. Because Undo can only undo the last three changes you've made it is a good idea to save your work with a different file name every ten or fifteen minutes. When you finish working delete the unneeded files.

The following sections describe how to use each of the toolbox tools.

Selecting a Free-Form Area

The Free-Form Select tool selects areas inside the line you draw. Click the Free-Form Select tool and select either Transparent (doesn't include the background) or Opaque (does include the background) at the bottom of the toolbox. Draw in any shape to enclose an area of the drawing. If you make a mistake while using the Free-Form Select tool, click the left mouse button outside the cutout area to cancel the cutout and try again. Once enclosed, an area can be moved, cut or copied (and then pasted), resized, tilted, flipped, or inverted with the <u>E</u>dit menu commands. If you cut an area, the selected background color shows the color the cleared area will be. With an area selected, press Delete to delete it from the picture.

Selecting a Rectangular Area

The Select tool selects areas inside the rectangle you drag. Click the Select tool and select either Transparent or Opaque at the bottom of the toolbox. Drag to size a rectangular area. If you make a mistake while using the Select tool, click the left mouse button outside the cutout area to cancel the cutout and try again. Once enclosed, the area can be moved, cut or copied (and then pasted), resized, tilted, flipped, or inverted with the Edit menu commands. If you cut an area, the selected background color shows the color the cleared area will be. With an area selected, press Delete to delete it from the picture.

Erasing Parts of Your Picture

The Eraser tool erases as you drag it over your picture, just like an eraser on a blackboard. Click the Eraser tool and then select the eraser size from the bottom of the toolbox. Drag across the picture with the left mouse button pressed to erase. The selected background color shows the color the erased area will be. Choose Edit, Undo if you want to restore what you have erased.

Filling an Area with Color

The Fill With Color tool fills inside a shape. Click the Fill With Color tool and select foreground and background colors from the palette. Position the pointed tip of the Fill With Color tool inside the shape that you want to fill. Click the left mouse button to fill with the foreground color, or the right mouse button to fill with the background color.

Picking Up a Color from the Drawing

The Pick Color tool picks up the color on which you click for use in the current tool. To pick up the color of the spot where you click, click the Pick Color tool and then click anywhere in the painting. You can resume using the previous tool or select another tool and paint with the new color.

Magnifying the View of the Drawing

The Magnifier tool magnifies the view of the drawing. Click the Magnifier tool and then select a magnification at the bottom of the toolbox (1x, 2x, 6x, or 8x). Position the rectangle over the area you want to enlarge and click the left mouse button. You can work with the individual pixels that make up the painting. You can use any of the tools in the magnified view. To reset the drawing size with the Magnifier tool, choose 1x.

Figure 13.4 shows the original 1x magnification (top) and the area magnified 6x (bottom).

Drawing a Free-Form Line

The Pencil tool draws a one-pixel-wide free-form line in the currently selected color. Draw with the left mouse button pressed to use the foreground color; draw with the right mouse button pressed to draw with the background color.

Fig. 13.4
Use the Magnifier tool to enlarge a portion of the picture so you can easily modify it. In this example, the picture has been magnified six times to enable pixel-by-pixel modifications.

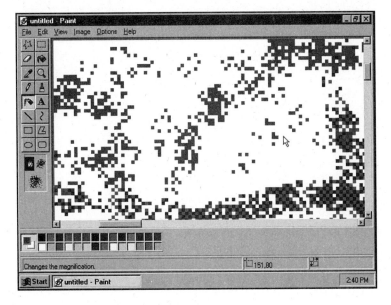

Painting with a Brush

The Brush tool paints with a brush. Click the brush and select from the brush shapes that display at the bottom of the toolbox. Paint with the left mouse button pressed to use the foreground color; paint with the right mouse button pressed to use the background color.

Painting with an Airbrush

The Airbrush tool paints with an airbrush effect. Click the Airbrush tool and select from the sprayer sizes that display at the bottom of the toolbox. Select a color from the Color palette: the left mouse button sprays with the foreground color; the right mouse button sprays with the background color. The Airbrush sprays a transparent mist of color; the more densely you spray, the heavier your coverage.

Adding Text to a Picture

Use the Text tool to add text to your painting. Click the Text tool and select Opaque (the background color fills the text box behind the text) or Transparent (the picture appears behind the text) in the area below the toolbox. Next, in the picture area, drag to determine the size of the text box. Choose View, Text Toolbar to display the Paint Fonts toolbar. Select a font, point size, and bold, italic, or underline options. Click in the text box and type. Use the limited set of editing tools, including word-wrap and Backspace. Text appears in the foreground color. Figure 13.5 shows text added to a painting and the Paint Fonts toolbar.

Tip

If your painting will include a lot of text, type the text in Word or WordPad, select and copy it, and then paste it into Paint.

Tip

If your document will have more text than graphics, create the graphic in Paint and copy it; then paste it into your Word or WordPad document.

Troubleshooting

Text Toolbar is not available from the View menu.

You must click the Text tool and drag a text area before Text Toolbar is available from the View menu.

An error message appears saying that I need to resize the text box.

The text box isn't large enough to hold the text you are pasting into it. Enlarge the box and try again.

Drawing a Straight Line

The Line tool draws a straight line. Click the Line tool and select a line width from the display at the bottom of the toolbox. Drag the mouse to draw a straight line. The left mouse button draws with the foreground color; the right mouse button draws with the background color. To undo the line that you're drawing, click the right mouse button before you release the left mouse button. To draw a line that is perfectly vertical, horizontal, or at a 45-degree angle, press and hold down the Shift key as you draw.

Fig. 13.5
Add text to your
picture with the
Text tool.

Drawing Curves

The Curve tool draws a curve. To draw a curve, follow these steps:

1. Click the Curve tool.

2. Select a line width from the display at the bottom of the toolbox.

3. Draw a straight line and release the mouse button.

4. Click the left mouse button and drag away from the line to pull the line into a curve.

5. When you've achieved the shape you want, release the mouse button to complete the line. Repeat the process on the other side of the line to create an *s*-shaped curve (see fig. 13.6).

Tip
The left mouse
button draws
with the fore-
ground color; the
right mouse
button draws
with the back-
ground color.

Drawing Rectangles and Squares

The Rectangle tool draws a rectangle or square with different borders or fill color. Click the Rectangle tool and select Border Only, Border and Fill, or Fill Only from the bottom of the toolbox. To create the size box you want, press and hold down the mouse button and drag to that size. Release the mouse button when you have the size you want. Use the left mouse button to border with the foreground color and fill with the background color; use the right mouse button to border with the background color and fill with the foreground color. The size of the border is determined by the last line size you selected.

Tip
To draw a square,
select the rectangle
tool, and then
press and hold
down the Shift key
as you draw.

III

Working with Applications

Fig. 13.6
Draw curves with
the Curve tool.

S-curves

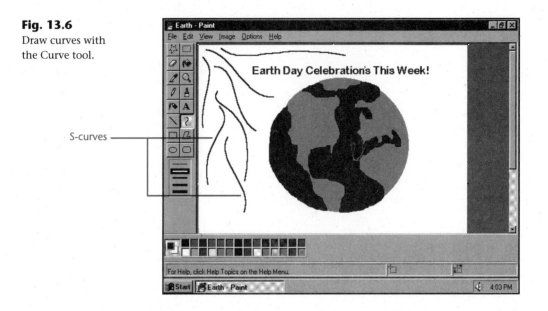

Drawing Objects with Many Sides (Polygons)

The Polygon tool draws a multisided shape. Each side on the shape is a
straight line. To draw a polygon, follow these steps:

1. Click the Polygon tool and select Border Only, Border and Fill, or Fill
   Only from the bottom of the toolbox.

2. Click and drag to draw the first side of the polygon.

3. Release the mouse button and click to draw each of the other sides.

4. Double-click to finish.

Use the left mouse button to border with the foreground color and fill with
the background color; use the right mouse button to border with the background color and fill with the foreground color. The size of the border is
determined by the last line size you selected.

Drawing Ellipses and Circles

The Ellipse tool draws an *ellipse* (an oval) or circle. Click the Ellipse tool and
select Border Only, Border and Fill, or Fill Only from the bottom of the
toolbox. To draw a circle, press and hold down the Shift key as you draw.

Use the left mouse button to border with the foreground color and fill with the background color; use the right mouse button to border with the background color and fill with the foreground color. The size of the border is determined by the last line size you selected.

Drawing Rectangles with Rounded Corners

Use the Rounded Rectangle tool to draw a rectangle with rounded edges. Click the Rounded Rectangle tool and select Border Only, Border and Fill, or Fill Only from the bottom of the toolbox. Press and hold down the mouse button and drag to create the size box you want. Release the mouse button when you have the size you want.

Tip
To draw a square with rounded corners, press and hold down the Shift key as you draw.

Use the left mouse button to border with the foreground color and fill with the background color; use the right mouse button to border with the background color and fill with the foreground color. The size of the border is determined by the last line size you selected.

Editing a Painting

With Paint, you can edit a painting. As you edit, however, be aware that completed objects cannot be edited, only erased or painted over and replaced. The method that you use to complete an object depends on the object. To complete a straight line, for example, you *release* the mouse button; to complete text, you *click* the mouse button. Any object that has not been completed is subject to edits. You can cancel a line or curve before you complete it, for example, by clicking the right mouse button; you can change the appearance of text *before* you complete it by making a selection from the Text toolbar.

The following sections describe how to use each of the Edit menu commands.

Undoing Changes

To undo changes, choose Edit, Undo (or press Ctrl+Z). Choose Edit, Undo again to continue undoing up to three previous changes.

Repeating a Change

Choose Edit, Repeat (or press F4) to redo the last change you made with the Edit, Undo command.

Cutting to the Clipboard

Use Edit, Cut to remove a part of your painting and place it into the Clipboard. Select the area you want to cut or copy, and then choose Edit, Cut (Ctrl+X).

▶ See "Using the Clipboard to Exchange Data," p. 424

III

Working with Applications

Copying to the Clipboard

Use Edit, Copy to copy a part of your painting and place it into the Clipboard. Select the area you want to cut or copy, and then choose Edit, Copy (Ctrl+C).

Pasting from the Clipboard

Use Edit, Paste to place a copy of the contents of the Clipboard into your painting. Display the area of the painting where you want to paste the contents of the Clipboard and choose Edit, Paste (Ctrl+V). The pasted object appears at the top left of the screen and is enclosed by a dotted line to show that the object still is selected. Drag the selection to the location you want and click outside it.

Removing a Selected Object or Area

Select the area you want to remove. Choose Edit, Clear Selection, or press the Delete key; it is deleted from the painting. This option does not place the selected object into the Clipboard.

Copying Part of Your Painting to a File

Use Edit, Copy To to save a portion of your painting in a file. Select the portion of the painting you want to save to a file. Open the Edit menu and choose Copy To. Give the file a name (use the file extension that is appropriate for the type of graphic file you want to create, such as PCX), select a directory or another drive, and click OK.

Pasting a File into Your Painting

Use the Edit, Paste From command to insert a file into your painting. Use the Rectangular Select tool to select the area of the painting into which you want to paste the file. Choose the Edit, Paste From command. Type the file name, select a directory or another drive, and click OK. The file is pasted in the top left corner of the screen. Drag it to a new location.

Many of the commands described in the preceding sections are also available from a shortcut menu. When you select a portion of your painting with either of the Pick tools and click the right mouse button, a menu appears (see fig. 13.7). Additional commands in the shortcut menu are described in the later section, "Creating Special Effects."

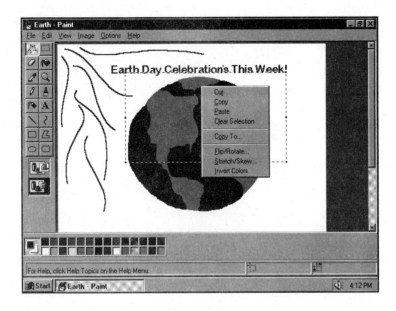

Fig. 13.7
A shortcut menu
appears when you
click the right
mouse button over
a selected area of
your painting.

Moving a Selection

You can move an object or area on-screen after you select it. (The object
is still selected if you just pasted it.) To move a selection, follow these steps:

1. Use one of the Select tools to select an object or area of the drawing.
   Select either Transparent (to leave the background showing) or Opaque
   (to hide the background). A dashed line encloses the selection.

2. Move the crosshair over the selection. The crosshair becomes an arrow.

3. Press and hold down the left mouse button to drag the selection to
   its new location. To copy the selection to a new location rather than
   moving it, hold down the Ctrl key as you drag the object to its new
   location.

4. Release the mouse button, and click outside the selection to fix it in its
   new location.

Getting Different Views of the Painting

You can zoom in to get a closer look at your painting or zoom out to see the
whole page. Use either the View, Zoom command or the Magnifier tool.

◄ See "Magnifying
the View of the
Drawing," p. 382

The larger magnifications of the picture display the *pixels*, or tiny squares
of color, that make up your painting. You can paint pixels in the selected

III

Working with Applications

foreground color by clicking the dots with the left mouse button, and in the background color by clicking the right mouse button.

To zoom in for a close-up view of your painting, follow these steps:

1. Choose View, Zoom.

2. Select Normal Size (Ctrl+Page Up), Large Size (Ctrl+Page Down), or Custom. If you select Custom, the View Zoom dialog box appears. Select 100%, 200%, 400%, 600%, or 800%.

3. Use the scroll bars to display the part of the painting you want.

To zoom back out to regular editing view, choose View, Zoom again and select Normal Size. Or, click the Magnifier tool and then click in the picture.

You can choose View, View Bitmap (Ctrl+F) when you are in the regular view to display a reduced picture of the entire page. When you choose View, View Bitmap, all toolboxes, menus, and scroll bars disappear, and your picture expands to fill the window. You can only view in this mode; you cannot edit your painting in Picture mode. Click anywhere in the display to return to normal size.

With an enlarged view of your picture, you can choose to add a grid for more exact drawing. Choose View, Zoom, Show Grid (Ctrl+G). You can also add a thumbnail, a small display of the portion of the drawing that has been enlarged. Choose View, Zoom, Show Thumbnail (see fig. 13.8).

Fig. 13.8
Turn on the Grid and the Thumbnail displays to give you more information about your painting as you work.

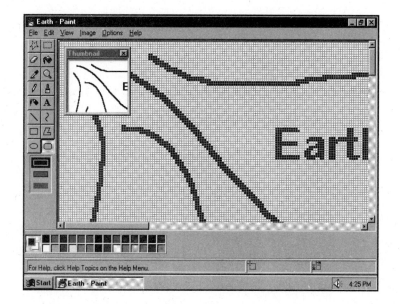

You also can switch the Tool Box, Color Box, and Status Bar on or off at the View menu.

Creating Special Effects

Using the Image menu, you can flip, stretch, invert, shrink, enlarge, or tilt objects you select. These special effects can help you refine your painting by altering selected objects in subtle or not-so-subtle ways. The following sections describe each of the Image menu commands.

Flipping or Rotating a Selection

With the Flip/Rotate command, you can flip a selection in two ways: horizontally (left to right) or vertically (top to bottom). Flipping horizontally reverses an image from left to right; you can use this technique to create mirror images by copying the selection and then flipping the pasted copy. Flipping vertically flips an image from top to bottom, making it upside-down.

Alternatively, you can rotate the selection by 90 degrees, 180 degrees, or 270 degrees.

Tip

Select the area you want to flip, rotate, stretch, or skew. Place the pointer over it, and click the right mouse button to display a shortcut menu.

Stretching or Skewing a Selection

With the Stretch/Skew command, you can stretch or skew a selection horizontally or vertically the number of degrees you enter. Figure 13.9 shows a selection that has been skewed horizontally 45 degrees. Use this command to tilt objects precisely.

Fig. 13.9
Stretch or skew selections with the Image Stretch/ Skew command.

Inverting the Colors in a Selection

Use the Invert Colors command to invert the colors in your painting, changing them to their opposites on the red/green/blue color wheel. In an inverted black-and-white painting, for example, black becomes white, and white becomes black; in an inverted green-and-yellow painting, green becomes purple, and yellow becomes blue (any white border area turns black). Use this technique to *reverse* a selected object.

III

Working with Applications

Inverting the Colors in a Selection

With the Attributes command, you can override the *default* image area by resizing the image area to make it smaller or larger. Change the following attributes of the picture: Width, Height, the Units of measurement (Inches, Cm, Pels), and Colors (Black and White or Colors). If your picture was originally in black and white, for example, you can switch to Colors and add color to the painting. To return to the default image area size, click Default. Figure 13.10 shows colors converted to black and white.

Fig. 13.10
Colors have been switched to black and white with Image, Attributes.

Clearing the Painting

The Clear Image command is used to clear the screen of all painting you've done without saving or exiting.

Troubleshooting

There's one drawn object in the picture, a circle, that needs to be resized. But there doesn't seem to be a way to change that circle once other objects are drawn.

Paint is a bitmap drawing program. When you draw, you change the dots of color on the screen. Once you complete the object you are drawing, it becomes part of the screen's pattern—you can't resize or recolor it. Drawing programs that are object-based enable you to select the individual items that have been drawn and edit them. Items can also be grouped together to act as a single object. There are many stand-alone object-based drawing programs. Some applications, such as Microsoft Excel and Microsoft Word, include object-based drawing tools so you can draw within their documents.

Changing the Windows Desktop with Paint

You can change the appearance of the desktop directly from Paint with File, Set as Wallpaper (Tiled) or Set as Wallpaper (Centered). Select Tiled to repeat the painting over the entire desktop, or Centered to display it once in the center of the desktop.

◀ See "Wallpapering Your Desktop with a Graphic," p. 133

To use your painting or part of your painting as wallpaper, follow these steps:

1. Display the painting you want to use as wallpaper.

2. If you want to use only part of the painting on the Desktop, select that part.

3. Choose File, Set as Wallpaper (Tiled) to repeat the painting as a pattern over the desktop, or Set as Wallpaper (Centered) to display the painting in the center of the desktop.

Working with Color

Color is a tremendously important component in daily life; it gives meaning to what you see. If you have a color monitor, you can use color in your paintings, and you can use your colorful paintings in applications such as WordPad, Word for Windows, and Aldus PageMaker. If you are lucky enough to have a color printer, you can print your painting in color.

Paint has 48 colors in its palette, including black and white. You can customize the Paint palette and add up to 16 custom colors.

Defining Hue, Saturation, Luminosity, and Dithering

In order to create custom colors, you should be familiar with a few color terms. Although you can create colors by just pointing and clicking without any knowledge of these terms, they will come in handy if you ever need to create a specific color.

Term	Meaning
Hue	Amount of red/green/blue components in the color.
Saturation	Purity of the color; lower saturation colors have more gray.
Luminosity	How bright or dull the color is.
Dithering	Dot pattern of colors that can be displayed to approximate colors that cannot be displayed. In the Custom Color selector, these are the blended colors.

III

Working with Applications

Defining Custom Colors

To create a custom color, follow these steps:

1. Choose Options, Edit Colors. The Edit Colors dialog box appears.

2. Click Define Custom Colors. The Edit Colors dialog box expands to display the following items (see fig. 13.11):

   ■ Color matrix box

   ■ Color/Solid box

   ■ Luminosity bar

   ■ Color matrix cursor

Fig. 13.11

Customize your colors in the Edit Colors dialog box.

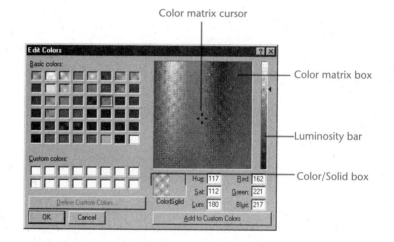

3. Click the approximate color you want in the color matrix box. The color matrix cursor moves to the spot where you clicked, and the color you selected appears in the Color/Solid box.

   You can also drag the mouse pointer around in the color matrix box while holding down the mouse button; the color matrix cursor appears when you release the mouse button. This step selects the color's hue and saturation.

   Next, drag the arrowhead up or down along the side of the luminosity bar to adjust the luminosity of the color.

   To specify a particular color whose numbers you know, click the box you want to adjust (Hue, Sat, Lum, Red, Green, or Blue), and type new numbers.

Continue adjusting until the color looks correct in the Color/Solid box.

If you want a solid color (rather than blended), double-click the solid (right) side of the Color/Solid box when the color displayed there is correct.

4. Click the Add to Custom Colors button to add this color to the custom palette.

5. Return to step 3 if you want to add more colors to the custom palette, or click OK to close the Edit Colors dialog box.

The colors you customize don't change the current painting, but they make different colors available on the palette. Your custom palette remains in effect when you start a new Paint painting. Unless you save the custom palette, however, the colors are gone when you close the Paint application. If you save a custom palette, you can retrieve it into any Paint file.

To save a custom palette, choose Options, Save Colors, type a name, and click OK. Paint assigns the extension PAL, but you can specify a different extension if you want.

To retrieve a custom palette, choose Options, Get Colors. Select a palette file or type its name; then choose Open.

Setting Up the Page

Page setup choices affect your printed paintings. Margins, for example, deter-mine where your painting is positioned on the page. You can choose either portrait or landscape paper orientation, select the size and location of the paper, and select a new printer. To set up your page for printing, choose File, Page Setup, make your selections, and click OK.

◀ See "Configur-ing Your Printers," p. 187

Saving Paint Files

When you save a Paint file, Paint assigns the extension BMP to the file name and saves the file in Windows bitmap format.

◀ See "Using Menus and Dialog Boxes," p. 92

To save a Paint file, follow these steps:

1. Choose File, Save As.

2. Type a name in the File Name text box and select from the Directories box the directory where you want to save the file.

III

Working with Applications

◄ See "Opening, Saving, and Closing Documents," p. 109

3. Click the Save as <u>T</u>ype box to select one of the following file formats:

Format	File Extension Assigned
Monochrome Bitmap	BMP
16 Color Bitmap	BMP
256 Color Bitmap	BMP
24-bit Bitmap	BMP

4. Choose <u>S</u>ave or press Enter.

To resave your file later without changing its name, choose <u>F</u>ile, <u>S</u>ave.

Troubleshooting

Many graphics files seem to use PCX format, but Paint won't save this format.

Paint saves only with the BMP format. You can open PCX files but if you want to make any changes and resave the file, you will have to save it as a BMP file.

Working with Other Applications

The paintings you create in Paint make wonderful illustrations that you can use with many other applications. If the other application does not support object linking and embedding, you can include a Paint painting by copying the painting and pasting it. You also can link or embed a painting in an application that supports object linking and embedding. You can edit linked and embedded paintings from within the other application.

► See "Using the Clipboard to Exchange Data," p. 424

To copy a Paint painting into another application, follow these steps:

1. Select the painting, or portion of the painting, that you want to copy to another application.

2. Choose <u>E</u>dit, <u>C</u>opy (Ctrl+C).

3. Start the other application, open the document into which you want to copy the painting, and position the insertion point where you want the painting to appear.

4. Choose <u>E</u>dit, <u>P</u>aste (Ctrl+V).

Embedding a Paint Object

Besides being a stand-alone painting application, Paint is also an *OLE server* application. OLE stands for *object linking and embedding.* A server is an application that can create objects that can be embedded in or linked to documents created by another application. Paint can create objects that can be embedded in or linked to documents created by applications such as WordPad and Word for Windows. (See Chapter 14, "Simple Ways of Sharing Data between Applications," for more information.)

Embedding a painting is useful when you need to have a painting within another application's document and you want to be able to edit the painting from within the other document. You can use two different methods to embed a Paint painting in a document created by an application that supports OLE. You can either copy the painting and paste it into the client application's document using the Paste or Paste Special command, or you can use a command in the client program to insert the object.

To create a new embedded painting in WordPad, follow these steps:

1. Start WordPad. (WordPad is the word processor that comes with Windows. See Chapter 12, "Using WordPad to Create Documents," for more information.)

2. Type text at the top of the document so that you can see how the embedded painting will appear in relation to existing text. Move the insertion point to a new line after the text.

3. Choose Insert, New Object.

4. Select the Create New option, select Bitmap Image from the Object Type list, and then choose OK. The menus and tools change to reflect the server application, Paint, that is being used to create the object.

5. Draw a new painting within the dashed boundaries. Use the Paint menus and tools as though you were in Paint.

6. Return to the WordPad document by clicking outside the painting and in the text of the document.

III

Working with Applications

You—or anyone receiving this WordPad document—can edit this embedded painting if you have a copy of Paint on your computer. Just double-click on the painting in the document and the Paint menu and tools will appear.

Linking a Paint Object

Linking is most often used when you have many documents that use the same painting—for example, a proposal, an engineering specification, and a marketing sheet that all contain the same Paint painting. If you link the painting to all the documents, changing the original painting's file will automatically update all the word processing documents that depend on it. Because each document contains only a description of where the painting is located on disk, the documents do not increase significantly in size. (For more information on linking, see Chapter 15, "Building Compound Documents with OLE.")

Caution

When you send via electronic mail a client document that contains links, make sure you also send the original files to which the client document is linked.

Some client applications use a command such as Paste Link or Paste Special to paste and link a painting that has been copied. Other applications use an option from within an Insert Object command to create a link to a saved Paint file.

To link a WordPad document to a Paint painting, follow these steps:

1. In Paint, create and save the file you want to link to other documents.

2. Open the WordPad application and create a document.

3. Choose Insert, New Object.

4. Select the Create from File option. This will change the contents of the Insert Object dialog box.

5. Click Browse, and find and select the file containing the painting you want to link.

6. Click OK.

7. Click the Link check box.

8. Click OK.

As with an embedded object, you can edit a linked object from within the client document. The technique for starting the server application is the same as for embedding: double-click on the linked picture, or select the picture and choose an editing command. The application starts, and you edit and save the picture.

Previewing, Mailing, and Printing Paint Files

Paint provides a preview screen where you can see your painting as it will appear in print. You can send your painting via e-mail. And Paint gives you great flexibility in printing paintings.

Previewing Your Paintings

When a painting seems complete, you can check its appearance on the page. To preview a painting, follow these steps:

1. Choose File, Print Preview. The preview screen appears (see fig. 13.12).

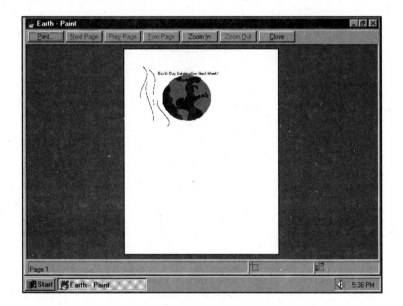

Fig. 13.12
You can examine your painting at the Print Preview screen.

2. Click the buttons to display the view you want.

3. Click Close to return to the painting, or click Print to display the Print dialog box.

You can print all or part of a painting, in draft or final quality, scaled smaller or larger. Before you print, be sure that you have the correct printer selected and set up.

Mailing a Painting

▶ See "Printing from Applications," p. 773

You can transmit a picture directly via e-mail or fax. To send a picture, display the picture you want to send and choose File, Send.

Printing a Painting

Before you print, be sure that you have the correct printer selected and set up. To select and set up a printer and print your document, follow these steps:

1. Choose File, Print. The Print dialog box appears (see fig. 13.13).

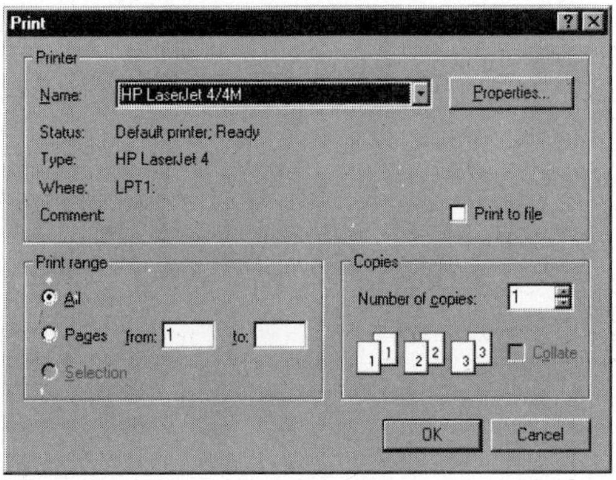

Fig. 13.13
The Print dialog box.

2. Select a printer from the Name list.

   Once a printer is selected, it remains selected for all documents—you won't have to select a printer again unless you want to change to a different printer.

3. Click the Properties button to make additional choices such as paper type and graphics quality. Click OK.

4. Select the Print Range All to print all the pages; select Print Range Selection to print only the selected text, or select the Pages, From, and To text boxes and type a range of pages to print.

5. Type the number of copies you want to print in the Number of Copies box.

6. Select the Collate check box to collate multiple copies of the document (this option is available if your printer supports collating).

7. Click OK.

To learn more about setting up your printer, refer to Chapter 6, "Controlling Printers."

Inserting Symbols with Character Map

The Character Map accessory gives you access to symbol fonts and ANSI characters. *ANSI characters* are the regular character set that you see on the keyboard and more than a hundred other characters, including a copyright symbol, a registered trademark symbol, and many foreign-language characters. One symbol font, Symbol, is included with most Windows applications. Other symbol fonts may be built into the printer. When you set up and indicate the model of the printer, font cartridges, and so on, the printer tells Windows what symbol fonts are available. (Printer fonts appear in Character Map only when they include a matching screen font.)

◄ See "Installing and Deleting Fonts," p. 217

To start Character Map, open the Start menu, click Programs, and then click Accessories. Finally, click Character Map. You are presented with the Character Map window shown in figure 13.14.

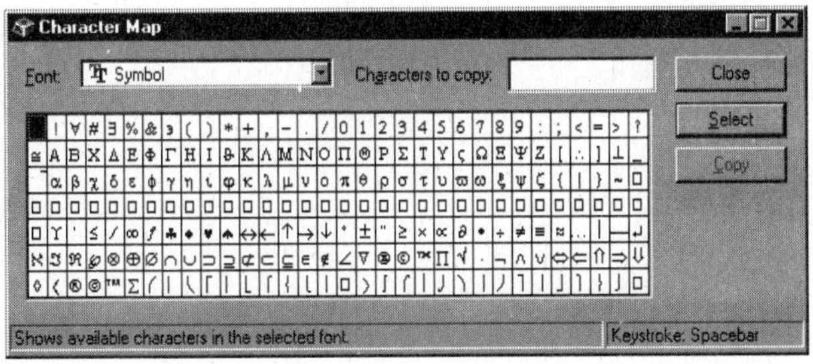

Fig. 13.14
Use Character Map to insert any of hundreds of special characters and symbols into a document.

The Character Map window includes a drop-down Font list box, from which you can select any of the available fonts on the system. After you select a font, the characters and symbols for this font appear in the Character Map table. Each set of fonts may have different symbols. Some fonts, such as Symbol and Zapf Dingbats, contain nothing but symbols and special characters.

To insert a character in a Windows application from the Character Map, follow these steps:

1. Start the Character Map accessory.

2. Select the font you want to use from the Font list.

3. View an enlarged character by clicking and holding down the mouse button on a character or by moving the selection box over a character by pressing arrow keys.

Tip
If you plan to use Character Map frequently, you may want to create a shortcut for this application so that you can start Character Map directly from the desktop.

III

Working with Applications

4. Double-click on the character you want to insert or click the Select button to place the current character in the Characters to Copy text box.

5. Repeat steps 2 through 4 to select as many characters as you want.

6. Click the Copy button to copy to the Clipboard the characters you've selected.

7. Open or switch to the application to which you want to copy the character(s).

8. Place the insertion point where you want to insert the character(s) and choose Edit, Paste (Ctrl+V).

◄ See "Creating Shortcut Icons on the Desktop to Start Programs," p. 68

If the characters don't appear as they did in Character Map, you may need to reselect the characters and change the font to the same font in which the character originally appeared in the Character Map.

Calculating with Calculator

Like a calculator you keep in a desk drawer, the Windows Calculator is small but saves you time (and mistakes) by performing all the calculations common to a standard calculator. The Windows Calculator, however, has added advantages: you can keep this calculator on-screen alongside other applications, and you can copy numbers between the Calculator and other applications.

The Standard Windows Calculator, shown in figure 13.15, works so much like a pocket calculator that you need little help getting started. The Calculator's *keypad*, the on-screen representation, contains familiar number *keys*, along with memory and simple math keys. A display window just above the keypad shows the numbers you enter and the results of calculations. If your computational needs are more advanced, you can choose a different view of the calculator, the Scientific view (see fig. 13.16).

To display the Calculator, open the Start menu and click on Programs. Then click on Accessories. Finally, click on Calculator. The Calculator opens in the same view (Standard or Scientific) as was displayed the last time the Calculator was used.

To close the Calculator, click the Close button in the title bar. If you use the Calculator frequently, however, don't close it; click the Minimize button to minimize the Calculator to a button on the taskbar.

Fig. 13.15
The Standard
Calculator.

Fig. 13.16
The Scientific
Calculator.

The Calculator has only three menus: Edit, View, and Help. The Edit menu
contains two simple commands for copying and pasting; the View menu
switches between the Standard and Scientific views; and the Help menu is the
same as in all Windows accessories.

Operating the Calculator

To use the Calculator with the mouse, just click on the appropriate numbers
and sign keys, like you press buttons on a desk calculator. Numbers appear in
the display window as you select them, and the results appear after the calculations are performed.

To enter numbers from the keyboard, use either the numbers across the top
of the keyboard, or those on the numeric keypad (you first must press the
NumLock key). To calculate, press the keys on the keyboard that match
the Calculator keys. The following table shows the Calculator keys for the
keyboard.

III

Working with Applications

Calculator Key	Function	Keyboard Key
MC	Clear memory	Ctrl+L
MR	Display memory	Ctrl+R
M+	Add to memory	Ctrl+P
MS	Store value in memory	Ctrl+M
CE	Delete displayed value	Del
Back	Delete last digit in displayed value	Backspace
+/–	Change sign	F9
/	Divide	/
*	Multiply	*
–	Subtract	–
+	Add	+
sqrt	Square root	@
%	Percent	%
1/x	Calculate reciprocal	R
C	Clear	Esc
=	Equals	= or Enter

Note

To calculate a percentage, treat the % key like an equal sign. For example, to calculate 15 percent of 80, type **80*15%**. After you press the % key, the Calculator displays the result: 12.

You can use the Calculator's memory to total the results of several calculations. The memory holds a single number, which starts as zero; you can add to, display, or clear this number, or you can store another number in memory.

Copying Numbers between the Calculator and Other Applications

When working with many numbers or complex numbers, you make fewer mistakes if you copy the Calculator results into other applications rather than retyping the result. To copy a number from the Calculator into another application, follow these steps:

1. In the Calculator display window, perform the math calculations required to display the number.

2. Choose Edit, Copy.

3. Activate the application you want to receive the calculated number.

4. Position the insertion point in the newly opened application where you want the number copied.

5. From the newly opened application, choose Edit, Paste.

You can also copy and paste a number from another application into the Calculator, perform calculations with the number, and then copy the result back into the application. A number pasted in the calculator erases the number currently shown in the display window.

To copy a number from another application into the Calculator, select the number in the application and choose Edit, Copy. Next, activate the Calculator and choose Edit, Paste.

If you paste a formula in the Calculator, you can click the equal (=) button to see the result. If you copy 5+5 from WordPad, for example, paste the calculation in the Calculator, and click the = key, the resulting number 10 appears. If you paste a function, such as @ for square root, the Calculator performs the function on the number displayed. If, for example, you copy @ from a letter in WordPad and paste it into Calculator while it is displaying the number 25, the result 5 appears.

Numbers and most operators (such as + and –) work fine when pasted in the Calculator display, but the Calculator interprets some characters as commands. The following chart lists the characters that the Calculator interprets as commands:

III

Working with Applications

Character	Interpreted As
:c	Clears memory.
:e	Lets you enter scientific notation in decimal mode; also the number E in hexadecimal mode.
:m	Stores the current value in memory.
:p	Adds the displayed value to the number in memory.
:q	Clears the current calculation.
:r	Displays the value in memory.
\	Works like the Dat button (in the Scientific calculator).

Using the Scientific Calculator

If you have ever written an equation wider than a sheet of paper, you're a good candidate for using the Scientific Calculator. The Scientific Calculator is a special view of the Calculator.

To display the Scientific Calculator, activate the Calculator and choose View, Scientific.

◄ See "Getting Help," p. 79

The Scientific Calculator works the same as the Standard Calculator, but adds many advanced functions. You can work in one of four number systems: hexadecimal, decimal, octal, or binary. You can perform statistical calculations, such as averages and statistical deviations. You can calculate sines, cosines, tangents, powers, logarithms, squares, and cubes. These specialized functions aren't described here, but are well documented in the Calculator's Help command.

Using the Taskbar Clock

◄ See "Changing the Taskbar Options," p. 126

It's convenient to have a clock always on the screen, and Windows includes one in the taskbar. If yours isn't displayed, you can turn on the clock, adjust the time, and even select a time zone. You'll be surprised at how much control you have over that little clock (see fig. 13.17).

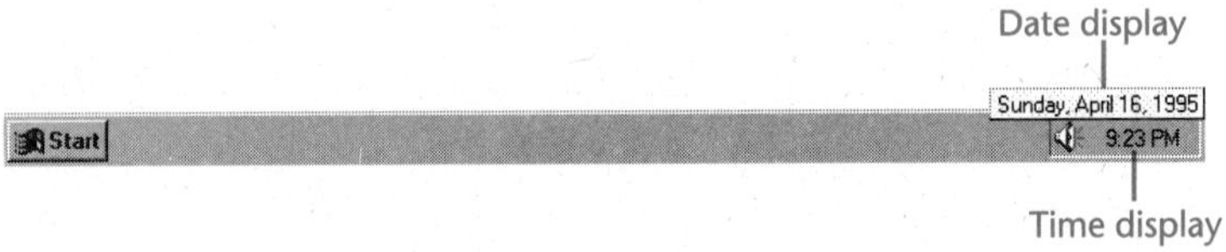

Fig. 13.17
The taskbar clock.

Date display

Sunday, April 16, 1995

Start   9:23 PM

Time display

The following table describes the taskbar clock options:

Do This...	To Do This
Point to time	Display date.
Double-click time	Display Date/Time Properties where you can set the date and time, and also select a time zone.
Right-click time, click <u>P</u>roperties	Display Taskbar Properties, where you can turn Show <u>C</u>lock on or off.

◀ See "Changing the Taskbar Options," p. 126

Note

If the taskbar Auto Hide option is enabled, the clock will only be visible when the mouse pointer is moved over the hidden taskbar.

III

Working with Applications

Chapter 14

Simple Ways of Sharing Data between Applications

by Rob Tidrow

When Windows 1.0 was introduced in 1985, Microsoft gave users the capability to use more than one software application at a time. With this capability came the need and desire to use data from one document in another document—sometimes in a document that was created by a different application. You may, for example, create a memorandum as a Microsoft Word for Windows document and then reuse all or part of that document in another Word for Windows document. You also can use the data from the Word document in a Microsoft Excel worksheet or a Lotus cc:Mail message.

You can share data from one document or application to another because Windows has *data-exchange* capabilities (also called *data sharing*). These capabilities are as simple as cutting or copying a piece of text from one program to another, and as complex as editing a piece of data in one application that you created in another application. The latter operation, known as *in-place editing*, is a component of OLE 2.0, which is discussed in Chapter 15, "Building Compound Documents with OLE." Cutting, copying, and pasting are relatively simple operations that make you more efficient in Windows.

In this chapter, you learn how to:

■ Use the Windows Clipboard and Clipboard Viewer

■ Copy text, data, and graphics between documents

- Copy text, data, and graphics between applications
- Copy text from the Clipboard to wizards and dialog boxes
- Transfer data, using file converters

Understanding Windows 95's Data-Sharing Capabilities

Windows 95 supports three types of data exchange: the Clipboard, dynamic data exchange (DDE), and object linking and embedding (OLE). Generally, all Windows applications provide some means of sharing data with another application. All applications, for example, have access to the Windows Clipboard, to which you can copy or cut data. Not all Windows applications, however, have DDE or OLE 2.0 capability.

Benefits of Sharing Data

By sharing data from one source to another, you tap into the strength of a computer in helping automate redundant tasks. How many times do you use the same word, data, or other element in a document? Do you ever write a letter and wish that you could reuse all or part of it in a different letter? Without the capability to share data, you must retype these repeated parts of your document. With the copy and paste features available in Windows 95, however, you just need to highlight the word, phrase, or element that you want to repeat; copy it to your computer's memory; and paste it in the document where you want it. In the section "Using the Windows Clipboard," you learn exactly how to copy and paste.

Take Advantage of Other Applications' Strengths

Another reason why data-sharing capabilities are popular is because they allow you to create more powerful, more informative, and more advanced documents. Many applications that adhere to Windows 95 standards let you copy an element from one type of application and use it in another application. You can, for example, create a picture from Paint and use it in a WordPad document, as shown in figure 14.1.

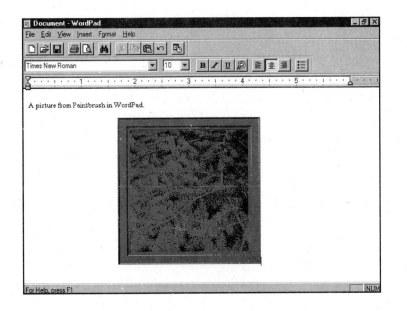

Fig. 14.1
This picture was
copied from Paint
into WordPad.

Using the Windows Clipboard

The most basic way to exchange data from one source to another is to use
the Windows 95 *Clipboard*, an area in memory that applications can access to
share data. When you use the Clipboard, you send data to the Clipboard and
then place that data in your document. This procedure is known as *copy and
paste* or *cut and paste*.

Copy means that you place a replica of the material that you selected in the
Clipboard. *Cut* means that you remove the data from your document and
place that data in the Clipboard. *Paste* is the process in which you take the
data from the Clipboard and place that data in your document.

> **Note**
>
> When you paste data from the Clipboard, you don't remove it from the Clipboard.
> You can paste the data from the Clipboard into your document as many times as you
> like. The Clipboard retains your cut or copied data until you clear the contents manu-
> ally, or until you cut or copy something else to the Clipboard.

III

Working with Applications

Cutting, Copying, and Pasting Data

Applications that let you access the Clipboard generally use standard menu commands or keyboard shortcuts. In many Windows 95 applications, you can transfer data to and from the Clipboard by choosing commands from the Edit menu (see fig. 14.2). Most Edit menus contain the Cut, Copy, and Paste commands.

Fig. 14.2
Use WordPad's Edit menu to transfer data through the Clipboard.

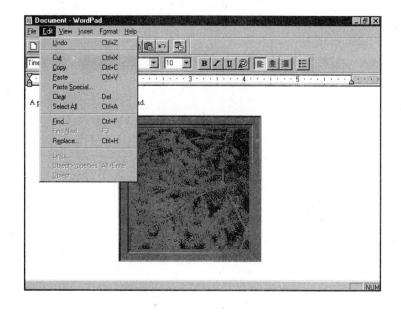

Tip
To copy information from a document to the Clipboard, use the same procedure but choose Edit, Copy instead of Edit, Cut in step 3. A copy of the data is placed in the Clipboard, but the original data remains intact.

To cut something from a WordPad document, follow these steps:

1. Start WordPad, and then open a document or start a new document and enter some text.

2. Highlight some of the text in the document, as shown in figure 14.3.

3. Choose Edit, Cut to cut the text to the Clipboard. Notice that the text disappears from your WordPad document.

Now that you have something in the Clipboard, you can paste that element into another document, such as a Paint drawing. To paste, follow these steps:

1. Open Windows Paint (it's usually in the Accessories item in the Programs folder), and open a drawing or create a new one.

2. Pull down the Edit menu. Notice that the Cut and Copy commands are grayed out (see fig. 14.4). This display tells you that you have not selected an item to be cut or copied.

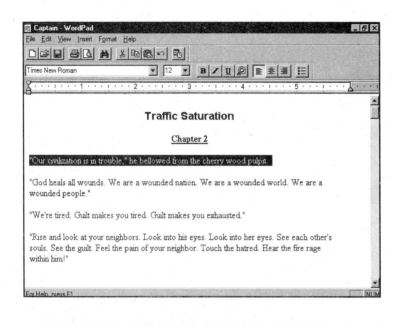

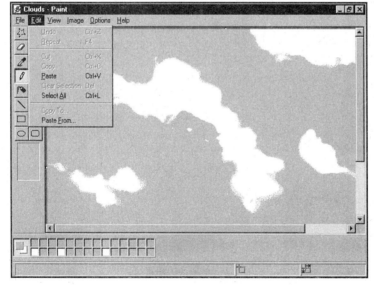

3. Choose Paste to paste the contents of the Clipboard (in this case, the text from the WordPad document) into the Paint drawing. Figure 14.5 shows what this text looks like when it's pasted into a drawing.

III

Working with Applications

Fig. 14.5

Pasting text from a WordPad document into a Paint drawing.

Another standard way to use the Clipboard is to use the buttons in an application's toolbar. Many Windows 95 applications provide toolbar buttons that let you perform routine tasks quickly and easily—for example, cutting, copying, and pasting data to and from the Clipboard. Figure 14.6 shows an example of these buttons.

Fig. 14.6

Cut, Copy, and Paste buttons provided in the WordPad toolbar.

Paste
Copy
Cut

Using Keyboard Shortcuts

Many times when you use Windows 95, you don't have access to menus or toolbars. Dialog boxes, wizards, and simple text boxes (such as ones in which you type data to open a file) don't have menus or toolbars that allow you to cut, copy, and paste data from the Clipboard. Fortunately, the Cut, Copy, and Paste commands have keyboard shortcuts.

Tip

By learning these keyboard shortcuts, you can speed data exchange within and between applications.

Windows 95 supports a common set of keyboard shortcuts that, unless the shortcut has been reassigned, you can use in any application that supports data sharing. Table 14.1 shows these shortcuts.

Table 14.1 Cut, Copy, and Paste Keyboard Shortcuts	
Action	**Windows 95 Shortcut Keys**
Cut	Ctrl+X or Shift+Delete
Copy	Ctrl+C or Ctrl+Insert
Paste	Ctrl+V or Shift+Insert

Copying Information to a Dialog Box

You can use a keyboard shortcut to help you fill in a dialog box. The dialog box shown in figure 14.7, the Letter Wizard from Windows 95, is requesting your name and address and the recipient's name and address. You can type the information or copy it from somewhere else, if the information is available. For this example, assume that you have the recipient's name and address stored in a Notepad document and that you want to copy and paste that information into the dialog box.

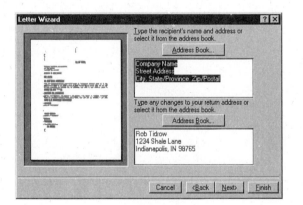

Fig. 14.7
You can cut or copy information to Windows 95 dialog boxes and wizards.

To copy information from the Notepad document to the Word Letter Wizard dialog box, follow these steps:

1. Select the information that you'll replace.

2. Switch to the open Notepad document by clicking the button in the taskbar at the bottom of the screen.

3. In the Notepad window, select the information that you want to copy, as shown in figure 14.8.

Tip
If the document isn't open, you can click the Start button in the taskbar to open programs or documents.

III

Working with Applications

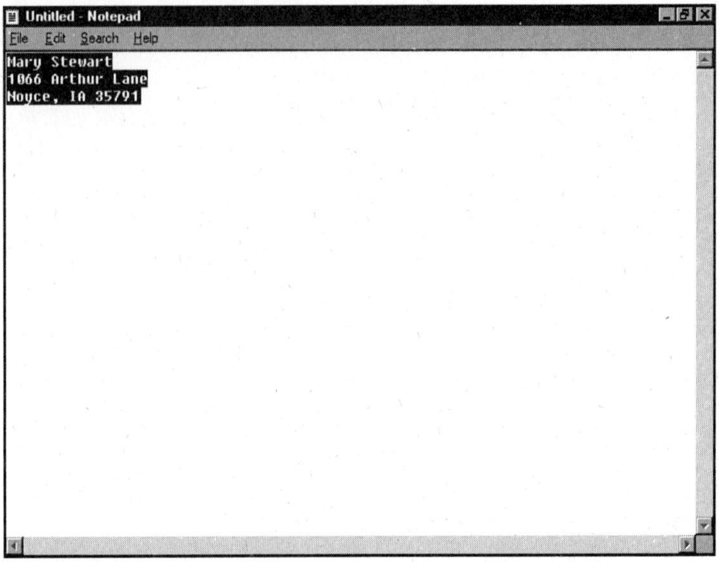

Fig. 14.8
Highlight text
in the Notepad
document to copy
to the Clipboard.

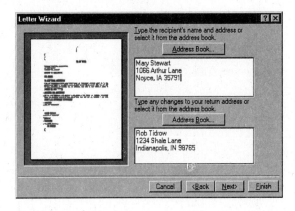

4. To copy the highlighted text, choose Edit, Copy, or press Ctrl+C.

5. Click the Word button on the taskbar to return to the Letter Wizard dialog box in Word. The old entry in the recipient's text box should still be highlighted.

6. Press Ctrl+V to copy the information from the Clipboard to the text box. Figure 14.9 shows the completed text box.

Fig. 14.9
The information
from the Clip-
board is pasted
into the text box.

> **Note**
>
> You can't use the Edit menu or any button on a toolbar while you're in a dialog box. The only way to copy from the Clipboard is to press Ctrl+V or Shift+Insert. The same holds true when you're trying to cut or copy from a dialog box. Press Ctrl+X or Shift+Delete to cut, or press Ctrl+C or Ctrl+Insert to copy highlighted text in a text box.

Capturing Screens with the Clipboard

Many Windows screen-capturing programs are available, but you also can use the Clipboard to capture the contents of the screen. When the screen image is captured, it's held in the Clipboard in bitmap format.

To capture the entire screen and paste it into a WordPad document, follow these steps:

1. Press the Print Screen key to capture the entire screen and place it in the Clipboard.

2. Open or switch to WordPad.

3. In a new or existing document, choose <u>E</u>dit, <u>P</u>aste. The screen image, in bitmap format, is pasted into the WordPad document.

Using the Clipboard Viewer

Windows 95 includes a utility called the *Clipboard Viewer*, which allows you to view and save the contents of the Clipboard. You can start the Clipboard Viewer by choosing Start, <u>P</u>rograms, Accessories, Clipboard Viewer. If you recently cut or copied an item to the Clipboard, you see it in the Clipboard Viewer (see fig. 14.10).

> **Note**
>
> The Clipboard Viewer isn't installed during the Typical installation of Windows 95. You need to specify this option during installation, using Custom setup. If Windows 95 is already installed on your computer, start the Add/Remove Programs utility in Control Panel, and install the Clipboard Viewer.

Tip
You also can capture the contents of the active window on-screen by pressing Alt+Print Screen or Shift+Print Screen, depending on your keyboard.

◄ See "Using Windows Paint," p. 378

III

◄ See "Adding and Removing Windows Components," p. 313

◄ See "Installing Windows 95 Applications in Windows 95," p. 309

Working with Applications

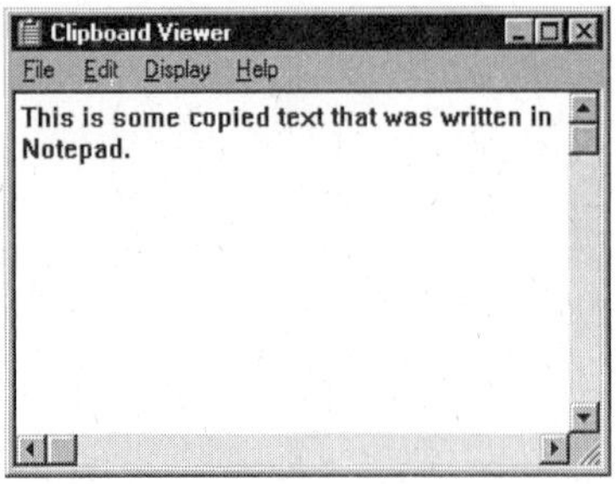

Fig. 14.10

The Clipboard
Viewer with
copied text.

Saving the Contents of the Clipboard Viewer

You can save the information that you cut or copied to the Clipboard to
reuse later. You may want to save information if you copy a large amount of
data that you can use over and over. To save information that's in the Clipboard Viewer, follow these steps:

   1. Choose File, Save As in the Clipboard Viewer. The Save As dialog box
   appears (see fig. 14.11).

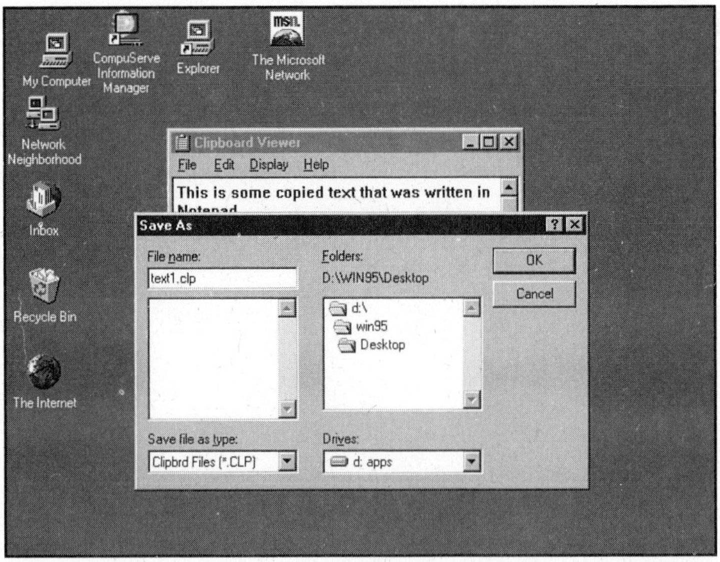

Fig. 14.11

You can save the
contents of the
Clipboard Viewer.

   2. In the File Name text box, type a file name (the Clipboard Viewer automatically uses the extension CLP).

   3. Click OK.

If you want to open a saved Clipboard file, follow these steps:

1. Choose File, Open in the Clipboard Viewer. The Open dialog box appears.

2. In the File Name list box, select the file you want to open. If necessary, select the file location in the Folders list box.

> **Note**
>
> Every once in a while, Windows displays a warning message, asking whether you want to clear the Clipboard's contents. You usually see this message when you've cut or copied a large item (such as an entire spreadsheet or large picture) to the Clipboard. If you answer yes, Windows keeps the item in the Clipboard. If you answer no, Windows erases that item from the Clipboard to free system memory and resources while you work.

3. Click OK. The Clear Clipboard message appears (see fig. 14.12).

    If you already have something in the Clipboard, this message asks whether you want to clear the contents of the Clipboard so that you can open the CLP file that you selected. (Remember that the Clipboard can hold only one cut or copied item at a time.)

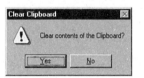

Fig. 14.12
The Clear Clipboard message asks whether you want to clear the contents of the Clipboard.

4. If you want to clear the contents and open the selected file, click Yes.

    If you don't want to clear the contents of the Clipboard, click No. You return to the Clipboard Viewer.

Viewing Text in the Clipboard Viewer

The Clipboard Viewer lets you view the Clipboard contents in different file formats. The Clipboard stores information in multiple formats so that you can transfer information between programs that use different formats.

Tip
The Display menu shows only the formats that are available for the current data that's in the Clipboard. All other formats are grayed out.

◀ See "Reviewing Types of Fonts," p. 213

On the Display menu, you have several options for viewing the contents. Following are the most common of these options:

- *Text* displays the contents in unformatted text, using the current Windows system font.

- *Rich Text Format* displays the contents in RTF (Rich Text Format). RTF retains any character formatting, such as font and font style.

- *OEM Text* displays the contents in the unformatted OEM character set. You usually use this option when you copy text from the Clipboard to DOS applications.

To view the contents in another format, follow these steps:

1. In the Clipboard Viewer, pull down the Display menu and choose a format. The Clipboard Viewer changes to reflect your choice. In figure 14.13, the content shown in figure 14.10 has changed from text to OEM text.

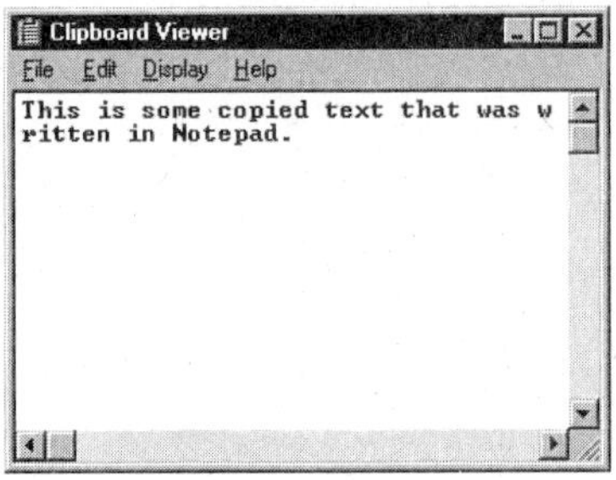

Fig. 14.13
Viewing the Clipboard contents with the OEM text option.

2. To return to the original format, choose Display, Auto.

Viewing a Picture in the Clipboard Viewer

Tip
Use the Picture option to view cut or copied formatted text before you paste it into a document.

The Display menu's Picture option lets you view a picture or formatted text that you cut or copy to the Clipboard. The formatted text shows all the characterizations you add to the text, such as color, fonts, and other formatting. To use the Picture option in the Clipboard Viewer, follow these steps:

1. Cut or copy a picture to the Clipboard, such as from Paint. If you want to view formatted text, open a document in WordPad or a similar application and cut or copy formatted text to the Clipboard.

2. Open the Clipboard Viewer.

3. Choose Display, Picture to display the item that you copied or cut to the Clipboard (see fig. 14.14).

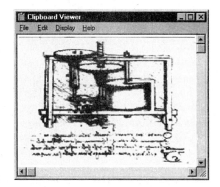

Fig. 14.14
Use the Picture option in the Clipboard Viewer to view graphics or formatted text you cut or copy to the Clipboard.

> **Note**
>
> The picture option stretches the Clipboard image to fit the current size of the Clipboard Viewer window. For a more accurate view of the image, try viewing the image in Bitmap or DIB Bitmap mode.

Using Drag-and-Drop to Copy Information between Documents

With Windows 95, you can drag and drop items to copy or move them. You learned in Chapter 2 how to use drag and drop to perform file management in the Explorer. In this section, you learn how to use drag-and-drop to copy information between documents.

Using drag-and-drop to copy between separate applications creates an embedded object. For more information on object linking and embedding (OLE), see Chapter 15, "Building Compound Documents with OLE."

> **Note**
>
> To use drag-and-drop, you must be working in an application that supports it. Most applications in the Microsoft Office suite, for example, support drag-and-drop, including Word, Excel, PowerPoint, and Access. Check the manual that comes with your application for information on using drag-and-drop.

One way to learn how to copy text by dragging and dropping it is to use WordPad. To copy information with drag-and-drop in WordPad, follow these steps:

1. Open WordPad, and then open a document or create a new document that contains some text.

◄ See "Learning about Drag-and-Drop," p. 105

III

Working with Applications

Tip
When you hold down the Ctrl key, a plus sign appears with the insertion point.

2. Select the text that you want to copy.

3. Position the mouse pointer over the selected area and drag the text.

   In some applications, you must hold down the Ctrl key and then drag the mouse pointer to copy text. If you simply drag the item, the information is moved to another spot in the document. WordPad allows you to copy text without holding down the Ctrl key first.

   The mouse pointer changes as you drag, as shown in figure 14.15.

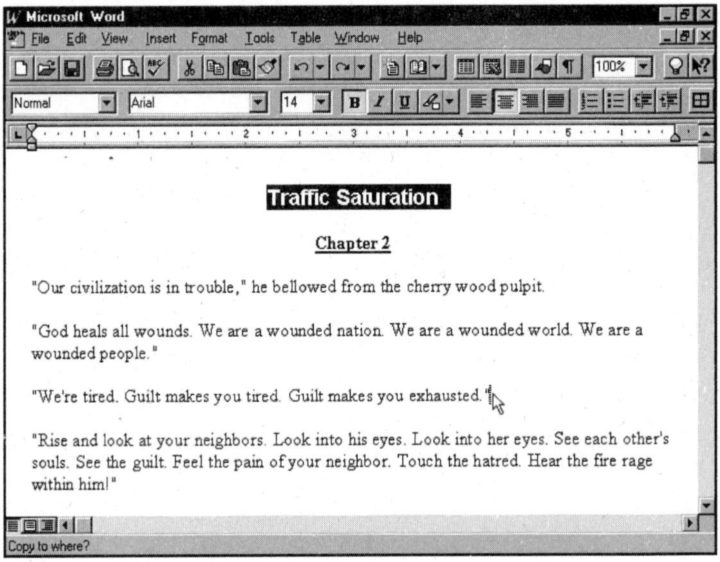

Fig. 14.15
The gray dashed line indicates where the text will be placed.

4. Drag the text to the position in the document where you want to place it. The gray vertical bar indicates the position of the new text.

5. Release the mouse button to complete the copy procedure.

Note

Some applications, such as Word for Windows, allow you to drag text between two documents. To do so, make sure that you can see both documents on-screen at the same time, and then drag the item from one document to another.

Troubleshooting

When I copy information with drag-and-drop, the original document loses its information.

You used the move feature instead. Make sure that you hold down the Ctrl key throughout the process. Release the mouse button first and then release the Ctrl key.

My copied text appears in the middle of existing text.

Don't forget to watch the gray dashed line that's part of the mouse pointer. This line shows exactly where the copied text will be inserted.

I get a black circle with a slash through it when I try to copy.

The black circle with the slash indicates that you can't drop the item in the area where the mouse is, such as the title bar or status bar. Make sure that you go all the way into the other document before you release the mouse button.

Copying and Pasting Data with DOS Applications

Although most Windows 95 users use Windows-based applications, millions of copies of DOS applications are used on Windows systems. Applications such as Lotus 1-2-3 for DOS, WordPerfect 5.1, and the MS-DOS prompt remain very popular. Windows 95 lets you copy information from a DOS application or from a DOS command prompt to a Windows application.

Windows 95 supports the following ways to transfer information from DOS applications to Windows documents:

- You can transfer text from DOS to Windows, from Windows to DOS, and between DOS applications by means of the Clipboard.

- You can transfer graphics from DOS to Windows applications by means of the Clipboard.

- You can copy text from the MS-DOS command prompt to the Clipboard.

III

Working with Applications

Using the Clipboard to Exchange Data

Some DOS applications use their own Clipboard equivalent, but none provide an area that lets you transfer text and graphics between applications. When you want to transfer text between applications, you usually have to use text converters or file-conversion utilities that transform the text into a format that the application can read. In many cases, you have to convert the text to an ASCII text file; this process strips out your formatting and special character enhancements.

When you want to share data from a DOS application to a Windows application, you use a process known as *mark, copy, and paste.* The Mark, Copy, and Paste commands are located in the control menu of a DOS window. You also can find the Mark button on the MS-DOS Prompt toolbar.

◀ See "Understanding and Configuring MS-DOS Application Properties," p. 347

To copy a list of your files at the DOS command prompt to a WordPad document, follow these steps:

1. Open the MS-DOS Prompt into a window (see fig. 14.16). You can change the way your DOS window looks by going into its properties and then changing the font or screen options.

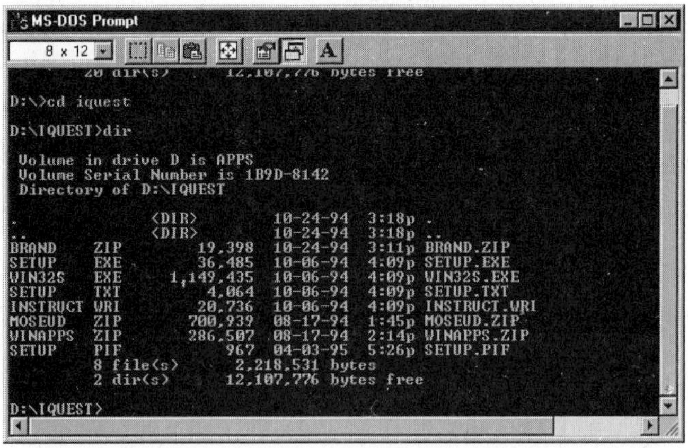

Fig. 14.16
You can copy a directory listing from the DOS window to a Windows document.

2. Type **DIR** to generate the directory listing.

3. Click the Mark toolbar button, or choose Edit, Mark from the Control menu. A blinking cursor appears at the top of the DOS window, indicating that you're in marking mode.

4. You now need to mark the area that you want to copy by drawing a box around it with your mouse pointer. To do so, place your mouse pointer where you want to start marking, hold down the left mouse button,

and then drag the box around the text that you want to copy. Your screen should look something like the one shown in figure 14.17.

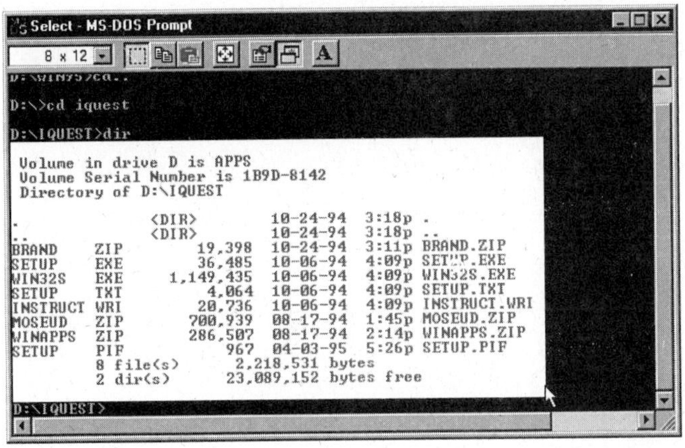

Fig. 14.17
Marking the text that you want to copy.

5. When you're satisfied with the selection, release the mouse button.

6. Click the Copy button in the toolbar; choose Edit, Copy from the Control menu; or press Enter to copy the selection to the Clipboard.

7. Switch to WordPad, and place the cursor where you want the text to be placed.

8. Click the Paste toolbar button, or choose Edit, Paste. The text from the DOS window is placed in your WordPad document (see fig. 14.18).

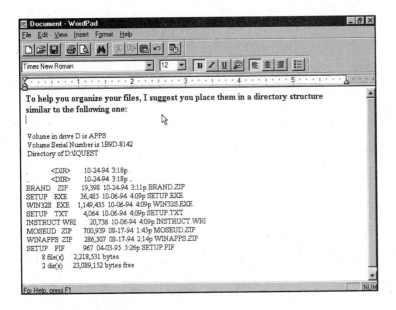

Fig. 14.18
You can place a list of your files in a WordPad document.

III

Working with Applications

Copying Data from Windows to DOS

You also can copy data from a Windows application to a DOS application by cutting or copying the data to the Clipboard and then pasting the data into the DOS application. When you do this, all the formatting that you placed in the Windows document is lost.

To copy data from Windows to DOS, follow these steps:

1. In your Windows application, such as WordPad, select the text that you want to copy.

2. Choose Edit, Copy, or Edit, Cut.

3. Switch to the DOS application, such as WordPerfect 5.2 for DOS. (Make sure that the application is in a window and not full-screen.)

4. Place the text or mouse cursor where you want to paste the text.

5. Choose Edit, Paste from the Control menu of the DOS application. The text now appears in the document.

Transferring Data by Using File Converters

Rather than cut and paste parts of a document into another document, you sometimes need to import an entire file into a different application. You may, for example, want to import a Windows Write file into WordPad. (Write was distributed with Windows 3.x.) Many software companies distribute Write files with their software to announce updates or changes in the software.

To open files that were created in other programs, many Windows applications include built-in file converters. *File converters* take the file format and transform it to a format that the application can read. During a file conversion, text enhancements, font selections, and other elements usually are preserved. Sometimes, however, these elements are converted to ASCII format.

To convert a Write file to WordPad format, follow these steps:

1. Start WordPad and choose File, Open.

2. Open the Files of <u>T</u>ype drop-down list and choose Windows Write (*.WRI).

3. Select a file with the extension WRI and open it.

   WordPad starts to convert the file. Look at the lower-left corner of the status bar, which shows the percentage of the file that WordPad has converted. When the display reaches 100%, WordPad displays the converted file.

You now can edit the file as a WordPad file.

Many other Windows applications include file converters to allow you to read and edit file formats that are created in other applications. Depending on the type of installation you perform, Word for Windows, for example, includes the following set of converters:

- Rich Text Format

- Text File

- Schedule+ Contact List

- Microsoft Excel Worksheets

- Word for DOS 3.x-5.x

- Word for DOS 6.0

- Personal Address Book

- WordStar

- WordPerfect 5.x

- WordPerfect 6.x

- Works for Windows 3.0

- Works for Windows 4.0

Tip

The type of converters you have installed for an application may depend on the installation options you choose at setup. See the application's documentation for specific converters.

Another way to convert files is to save the file in a different format during the Save As process. When you need to import a Word for Windows file into WordPerfect or Word for Macintosh, for example, you can select those formats from the Save As <u>T</u>ype drop-down list in the Save As dialog box. This list contains the types of formats in which you can save a Word for Windows document (see fig. 14.19).

III

Working with Applications

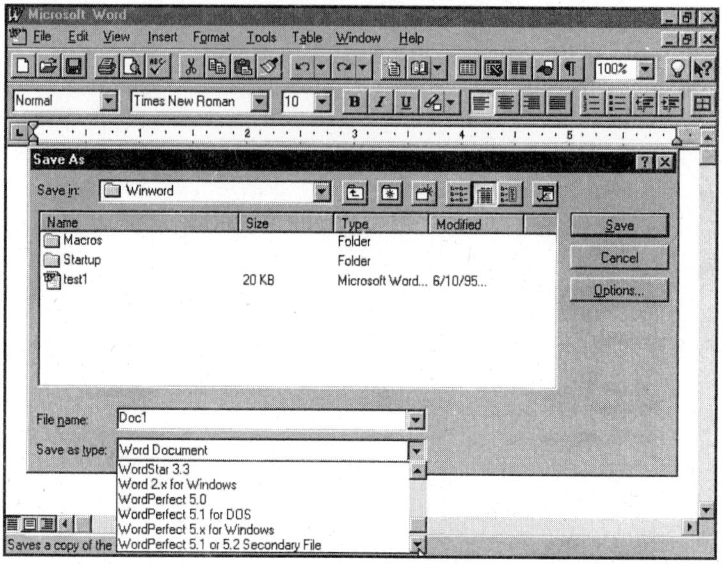

Fig. 14.19
Use the Save As
Type list options
to transfer files
to different
applications.

Understanding Dynamic Data Exchange (DDE)

A more sophisticated way to exchange data in Windows 95 is through the use of dynamic data exchange. DDE allows you to create links from one document or file to another document or file. These links can be between documents that are created in the same application (such as Word for Windows) or documents that are created in different applications (such as Word and Excel).

After you establish a link, you can update the information automatically by editing the original source of the information. This procedure lets you use data in various places but update it in only one place. To use DDE, you must set up a *link* between two applications (or two documents) that support DDE or OLE. The application that requests data is called the *client* application. The other application, called the *server* application, responds to the client application's request by supplying the requested data.

▶ See "Using
Embedding to
Link Informa-
tion," p. 440

During a DDE link, you can work in the client application and make changes in data that's linked to the server application. When you change the data in the client application, Windows 95 automatically changes the data in the server application. The advantage to exchanging data by DDE links is that data is kept up-to-date in the client and server applications.

One possible use of DDE is taking data from an Excel worksheet and placing it in a Word document. If you need to change the Excel data, you need to change it only in Excel; the data is updated in Word automatically. In figure 14.20, for example, data for the regional sales of TechTron is shown in an Excel worksheet. Figure 14.21 shows the same numbers in a Word document that can be distributed to the staff in the form of a memorandum.

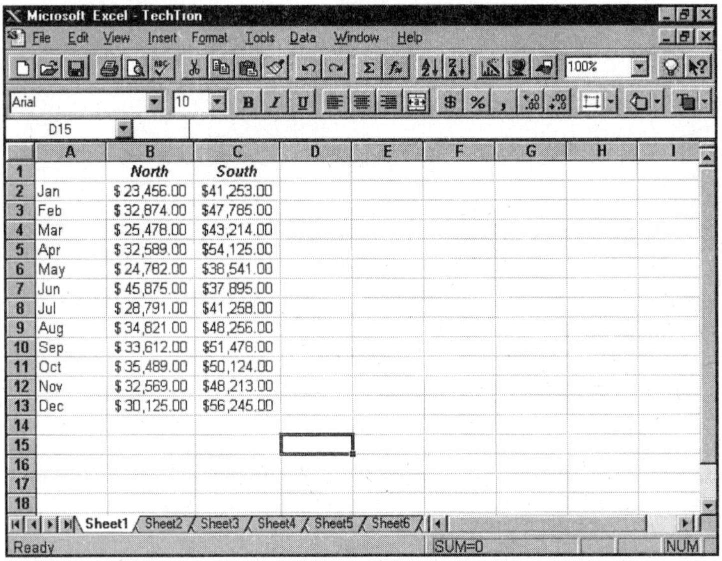

Fig. 14.20
Data from an Excel spreadsheet can be linked to a Word document.

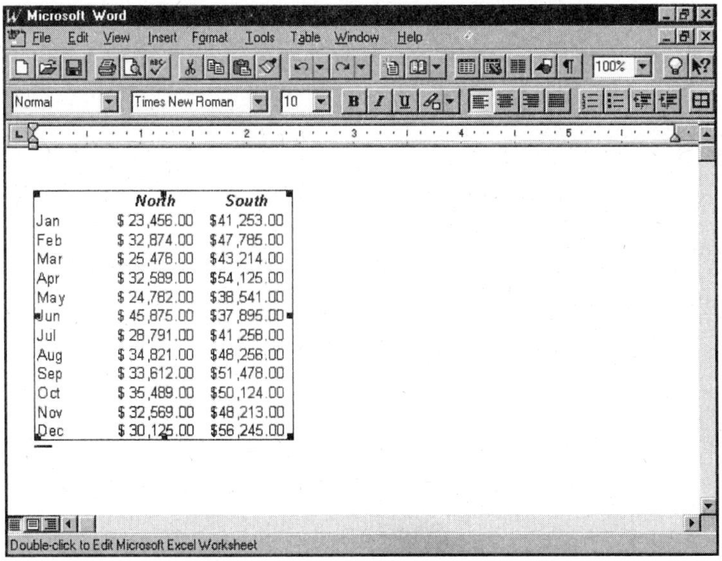

Fig. 14.21
The Word document reflects any changes that you make in the Excel document.

III

Working with Applications

Suppose that you want to put together a new memo each month to detail sales for the entire year, but you want to create the memo document one time and update the sales data in the Word document automatically. You can do this by using a DDE link. In this example, to change the worksheet data in the Word document, you need to change the data while you're working in Excel.

Windows 95 provides two ways to use DDE: interactively and through a macro language. The easiest way to use DDE is the interactive method, which is based on the Clipboard copy-and-paste method that you used earlier in this chapter but has some important differences. The macro method, which involves creating a macro in the application's macro language, isn't discussed in this book.

When you establish a DDE link between applications, you use the Edit menu's Copy and Paste Link or Paste Special commands. Suppose that you have an Excel worksheet that you want to link to a Word for Windows document. Follow these steps:

1. Open Excel and then open a worksheet. You also can create a new worksheet to link data from.

2. Highlight some data in the worksheet, as shown in figure 14.22.

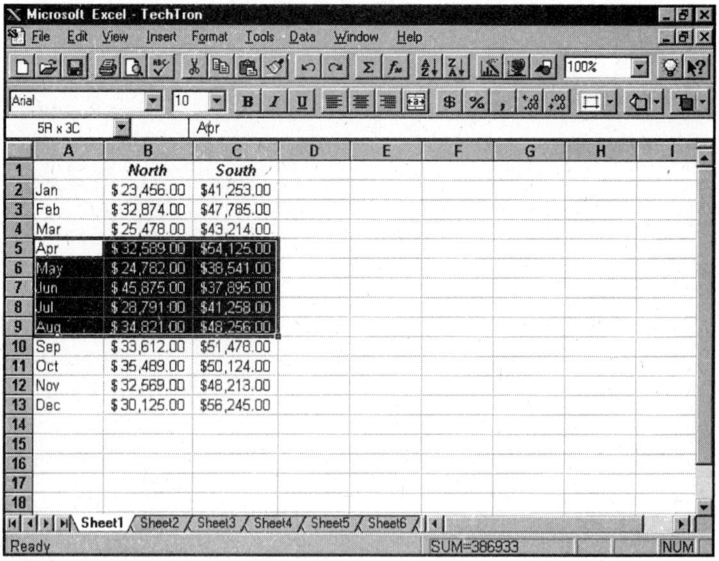

Fig. 14.22

Highlighting data in Excel to link to Word.

	A	B	C	D	E	F	G	H	I
1		North	South						
2	Jan	$23,456.00	$41,253.00						
3	Feb	$32,874.00	$47,785.00						
4	Mar	$25,478.00	$43,214.00						
5	Apr	$32,589.00	$54,125.00						
6	May	$24,782.00	$38,541.00						
7	Jun	$45,875.00	$37,895.00						
8	Jul	$28,791.00	$41,258.00						
9	Aug	$34,821.00	$48,256.00						
10	Sep	$33,612.00	$51,478.00						
11	Oct	$35,489.00	$50,124.00						
12	Nov	$32,569.00	$48,213.00						
13	Dec	$30,125.00	$56,245.00						

3. Choose <u>E</u>dit, <u>C</u>opy to copy the highlighted data to the Clipboard.

4. Open Word for Windows and then open an existing document or start a new document.

5. Choose <u>E</u>dit, Paste <u>S</u>pecial (see fig. 14.23). The Paste Special dialog box appears.

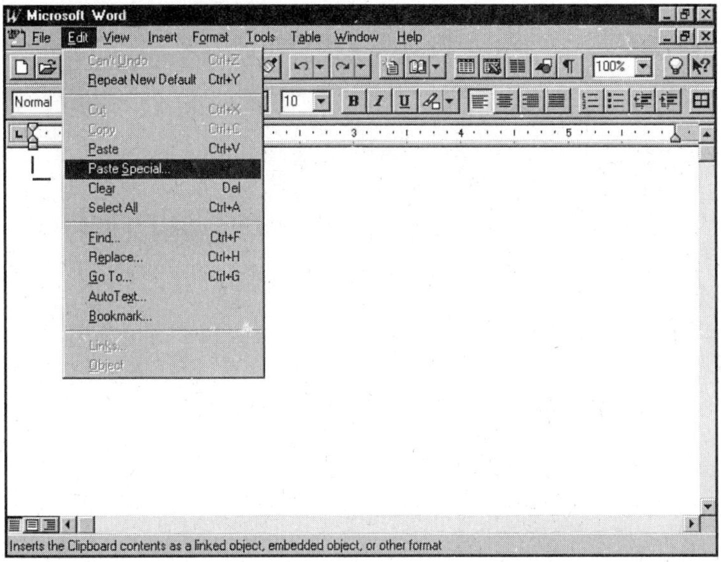

Fig. 14.23
Linking the Excel data to a Word document by using the Paste <u>S</u>pecial command.

6. In the Paste Special dialog box, click the Paste <u>L</u>ink option (see fig. 14.24). If you don't click this button, Word inserts the data from Excel as an OLE 2.0 object rather than set up a DDE link.

7. In the <u>A</u>s list box, select Microsoft Excel Worksheet Object.

8. Choose OK. The Excel data is inserted into the Word document as a picture (see fig. 14.25).

▶ See "Inserting a New Object into Your Document," p. 442

You can't change the data in Word; you can only view it. When changes are made in the data in Excel, those changes are reflected in the Word document.

III

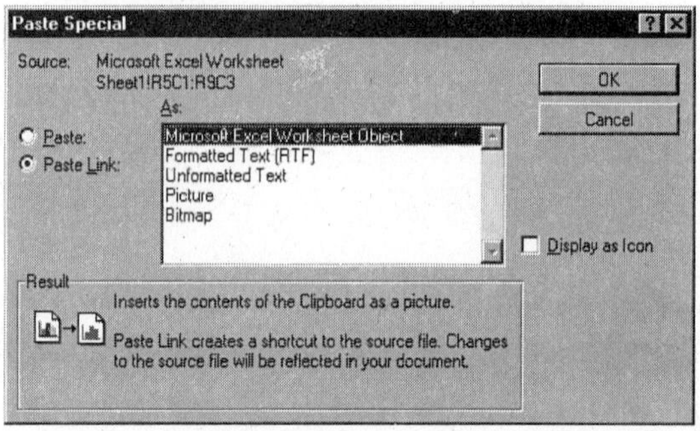

Fig. 14.24
Make sure that
you click the Paste
Link button to
establish a DDE
link.

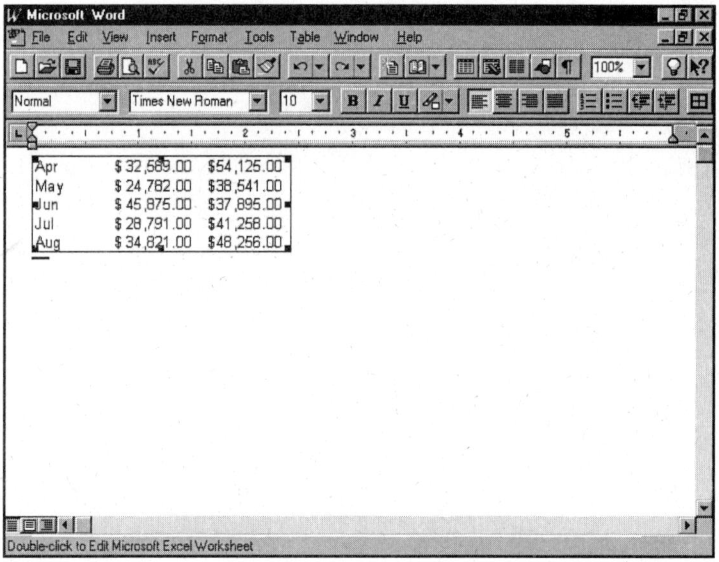

Fig. 14.25
Excel data is now
linked to the
Word document.

To see changes take place, switch back to the Excel worksheet and then follow these steps:

1. Change some of the data or formatting in the area that you linked to the Word document (see fig. 14.26).

2. Press Enter or click outside the cells that you edited. The data changes in the Word document to reflect your changes.

3. Switch to the Word document to see the updated data (see fig. 14.27).

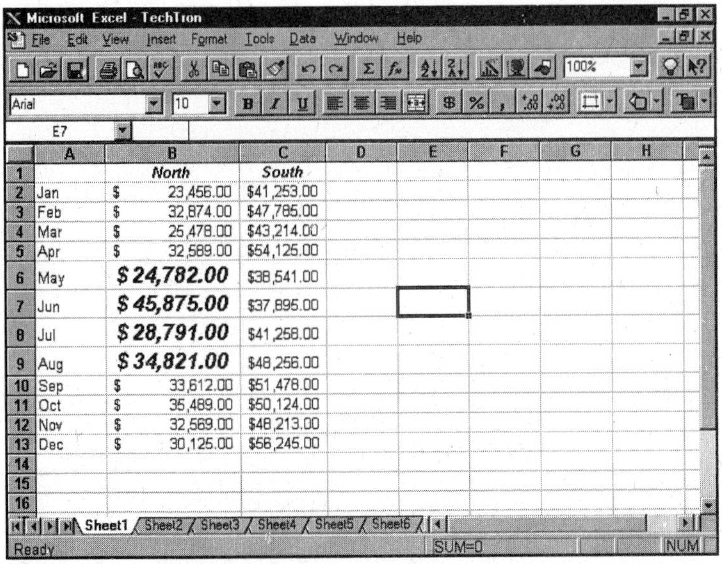

Fig. 14.26
Change some data
in the Excel
worksheet.

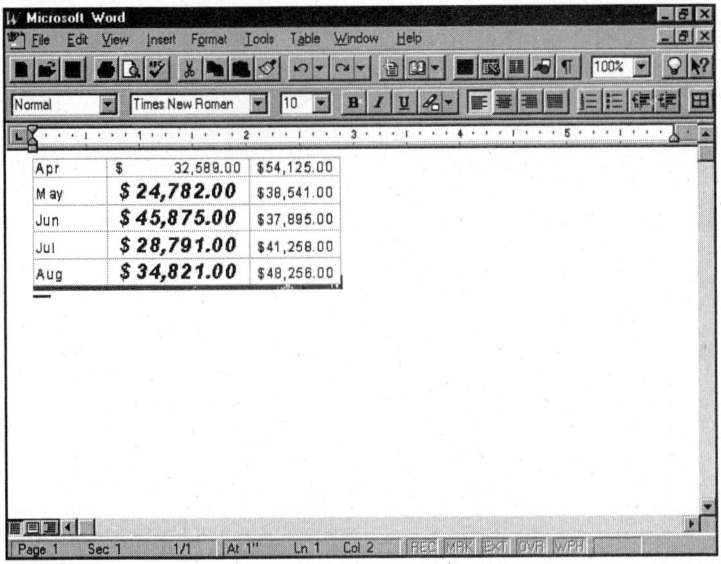

Fig. 14.27
The Word
document is
updated to reflect
your changes.

III

Working with Applications

Note

If you change the name or path of your client or server documents, you must reestablish your DDE links. You should make a habit of changing or creating file names
and directories for your documents before you create a DDE link. Otherwise, your
data won't update properly, causing you to work with old data.

Chapter 15

Building Compound Documents with OLE

by Rob Tidrow

In Chapter 14, you were introduced to two ways that you can exchange information in Windows 95. The first way was through the Clipboard and the Cut, Copy, and Paste commands. The other way was linking documents by using DDE (dynamic data exchange). Both methods are helpful when you create documents, drawings, spreadsheets, and other Windows files.

As you learned in the preceding chapter, the primary reasons to exchange and share data are to increase efficiency and to keep your information as current as possible. Keeping everyone informed and up-to-date is a difficult task, especially when you have several types of applications that can create and manipulate the information. By using Windows 95's capabilities to exchange information, you streamline the task of providing information to a diverse audience.

Expanding on the topic of data exchange and information sharing, this chapter introduces you to compound documents and object linking and embedding (OLE). *Compound documents* are documents you create by using multiple types of data. *Object linking and embedding* is a technology invented by Microsoft that allows you to build compound documents.

In this chapter, you learn to

- Look at information in a new way
- Understand compound documents and objects
- Embed information within documents

- Edit OLE objects in a document

- Understand OLE automation

Gaining a New View of Information

If you've been around the computer industry for a year or so, you've probably encountered a few obscure terms. Terms such as *compound document*, *objects*, *document-centricity*, and *component reuse* probably confuse you, or at least leave you scratching your head a little. For the most part, these terms and phrases are used to describe the way computer users interact with information.

As the personal computer industry matures and more powerful operating systems (such as Windows 95) are developed, users gain the ability to create documents that include almost any type of data, from almost any source. Today, for instance, your children can use sound and video clips from documentaries in their school book reports. You can include charts and graphs from your company spreadsheets in your monthly reports. An architect can include examples of floor plans in a proposal without redrawing a single line.

In the future, you'll be able to access any data on the Internet or online service, link it to your local document, and have it update automatically as the data source updates. You'll no longer be hampered by the boundaries and limitations that your applications and operating system have forced you to work under for years. You don't, for instance, *not* eat if your refrigerator stays empty for days. You find ways to eat. You go to the grocery, you order takeout, or you ask your neighbor for a free meal. The refrigerator doesn't dictate that you eat or how you eat. Why, then, should a word processor or spreadsheet application dictate the way in which you gather and disseminate information?

Introduction to Compound Documents

This section gets you familiar with the concept of compound documents and some of the terms associated with them. When you think about the elements that you place within a document—a sound clip, a picture, a spreadsheet—think about them as objects. An *object* is simply a piece of data that has a characteristic (such as sound) and a behavior (it plays a sound when you click it).

Objects are the basic building blocks of Microsoft's programming interface called object linking and embedding, or OLE (pronounced "oh-lay"). OLE allows you to build *compound documents*, which are documents that you create in one application but with objects from several different applications.

One technical definition of a compound document is that it's a data file maintained by a container application and that it contains one or more embedded objects. If you break this all down, it means that you can, for example, use Word for Windows as your container application and have a Visio drawing be your embedded object. You might be asking yourself, "What's all the fuss about? The Clipboard and DDE did that in Chapter 14."

The major difference between OLE (specifically OLE version 2.0) and simple data exchange (via the Clipboard) or DDE is that OLE lets you edit your Visio drawing (your embedded object) while still in Word for Windows. You can't do that with a simple Clipboard cut-and-paste operation or with a DDE link. With a DDE link, you have to return to the original application (in this case, Visio) to edit or modify the drawing. When you want to edit an OLE object in the compound document (in this case, a Word document), you just double-click the object, and elements common to the Visio interface appear on the Word for Windows interface. Figure 15.1 shows an example of this.

Tip
To edit an object in a compound document, the application that created the object must be installed on your computer.

You're still in Word...

...but these are the Visio menus and tools

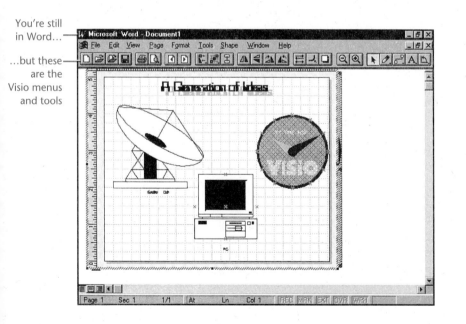

Fig. 15.1
While in Word for Windows, you can edit a Visio drawing using OLE 2.0 capabilities.

III

Working with Applications

The obvious benefit of having the capability to edit an embedded object within a compound document is that you don't have to return to the source application every time you want to change the object. Many times you just need to change the spelling of a word, the position of a graphical element, or one or two entries of data after you place an element in your document. By using OLE 2.0, you double-click the object, wait a few seconds (or minutes, depending on your system) while your application changes, and then make the necessary changes to the object. On the other hand, when you link data using DDE, you must open the application that created the data, open the file that contains the data, change the data, and then update the DDE link.

OLE Technology

Entire books have been written on the topic of OLE technology and the way in which it's implemented in a particular application. Microsoft designed and released OLE 1.0 with the introduction of Windows 3.1 in 1992. In OLE 1.0, users could embed items in a document and then activate the original application by double-clicking the object. When the original application started, the embedded item appeared in the application ready for you to edit it. After editing it, you updated the object in the compound document by using menu commands. You might recall this type of action if you used Microsoft Draw in Word 2 for Windows.

Note

Many applications still support only OLE 1.0 compatibility and haven't upgraded to OLE 2.0. Keep this in mind when you make software upgrades or decide to buy new programs—particularly if you want the capabilities of OLE 2.0 instead of OLE 1.0.

OLE 2.0, released in the last quarter of 1993, coincided with the release of a new suite of Microsoft Office applications, including Excel 5 for Windows, Word 6 for Windows, and Access 2.0. Each application includes OLE 2.0 capabilities. After these applications came others from third-party vendors, including Shapeware's Visio, CorelDRAW!, and Autodesk's AutoCAD for Windows. The benefit to end users is that OLE 2.0 is becoming a standard feature in many applications, increasing the opportunities for creating compound documents.

Some of the advantages of OLE include the following:

■ *OLE objects can be updated dynamically.* Like DDE links, OLE objects can be updated dynamically when the source data is edited or changed.

- *OLE enables applications to specialize.* Rather than have one giant application that tries to be everything for everybody, OLE allows applications to do what they do best. A drawing package, for instance, can focus on drawing; spreadsheets can focus on sorting and analyzing data; word processors can focus on creating documents; and so on.

- *OLE lets users get tasks done.* When users use embedded objects, they can focus on getting their task done rather than on the application necessary to get the job completed.

As you become more familiar with OLE and use it in your everyday work, you'll find that it becomes transparent. In fact, many users think OLE is a feature of all applications and are puzzled when they can't perform a task in an application that doesn't support OLE integration when they have done the same task in an OLE-compliant application. They become frustrated, for instance, when they can't drag a piece of text from their word processor to their favorite desktop publishing application. Or they can't share their contact manager information with their database application.

OLE Terminology

Similar to DDE links, OLE uses terms for each part of the embedding and linking stages. Two terms that you need to understand are *client* and *server*. The *client application* uses the services of another application through OLE. The *server application* provides OLE services to a client application.

For example, when you embed a Visio drawing in a Word document, Visio is the OLE server and Word is the OLE client. You can think of this relationship in the same way you think of a relationship with your attorney. The attorney is the *server* because she provides a service to you (legal help). You're the *client* because you're requesting services from the attorney (better known as the server). The services you obtain from the attorney can then be thought of as *objects*. You can use these objects, but if you need to update them or expand them (gain more knowledge of incorporating your business, for instance), you must go back and request help from your attorney. This is the same way you can update your embedded objects by using OLE. The client requests services from the server to help update the object.

Other OLE terms that you need to understand include in-place editing, drag-and-drop, container object, and OLE automation. These terms are defined in the following list:

- *In-place editing.* Refers to the capability to modify an embedded object within the client application without leaving the client application.

III

Working with Applications

- *Drag-and-drop*. Refers to the capability to grab an object, move it across the screen, and place it into a client document. An example of dragging and dropping an object is selecting an Excel chart in Excel, dragging it to Microsoft Word, and dropping it in a document.

- *Container object*. An object that contains another object or several objects. In the preceding example, the Word document is the container object that holds the Excel object.

- *OLE automation*. Refers to the capability of a server application to make available (this is known as *expose*) its own objects for use in another application's macro language. This term is used a great deal among advanced users and software developers. One example of this is Microsoft's Visual Basic for Applications (VBA) programming language. VBA Excel version, for example, can use objects in Microsoft Project's VBA environment, enabling developers to create powerful custom applications.

Using Embedding to Link Information

If you're confused by linking (DDE) and embedding (OLE), keep in mind one major difference between the two—where the information is stored. Linked (DDE) information is stored in the source document. The destination contains only a code that supplies the name of the source application, document, and the portion of the document. Embedded (OLE) information is actually stored in the destination document, and the code associated with OLE points to a source application rather than a file.

In some cases, you can't use the source application by itself; you have to use your destination application to start the application. These applications are called applets and include WordArt, ClipArt, Microsoft Graph, and others. You generally launch the source application by choosing Insert, Object.

Embedding Information in Your Documents

When you embed an object, the information resides in the destination document, but the source application's tools are available for use in editing. You can use any of the following methods to embed information in a document:

◀ See "Understanding Dynamic Data Exchange (DDE)," p. 428

- Copy the information to the Clipboard; choose Edit, Paste Special; and select an object format. (This method was discussed in Chapter 14 when you linked data from one document to another, but you selected the Paste Link To option from the Paste Special dialog box in that chapter.)

■ Arrange two windows side by side, and use drag-and-drop to copy infor-mation between the applications.

■ Choose Insert, Object and open an existing file.

■ Choose Insert, Object and create a new object. The following section describes this method.

◀ See "Using Drag-and-Drop to Copy Information between Documents," p. 421

Inserting a File into a Document

You can insert a file into documents by choosing Insert, File, which allows you to insert an entire file as an object. When you use Paste Special to link a file (as you did in Chapter 14), only the text you select before using the Edit, Copy command is part of the target file. If you later go back and insert text before or after the source-document selection, the target document doesn't include the entire text. Choosing Insert, File alleviates this problem.

Tip
The file that you insert can be from the same applica-tion or a different application.

To insert a file into a document, follow these steps:

1. Move to the position in the target document where you want to insert the file.

2. Do one of the following, depending on the application you use:

■ In WordPad, choose Insert, Object. Click the Create From File option. The Insert Object dialog box appears (see fig. 15.2).

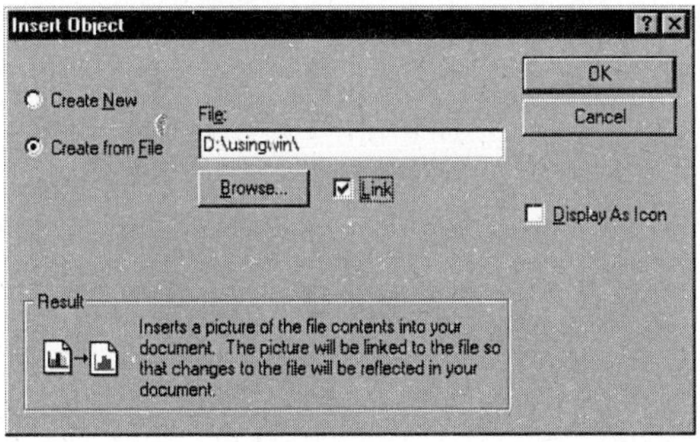

Fig. 15.2
Enter the file name or use the Browse button to indicate the file you want to embed in a WordPad document.

III

Working with Applications

■ In Word for Windows, choose Insert, File. The Insert File dialog box appears (see fig. 15.3).

- In Microsoft Excel, choose Insert, Object. The Object dialog box appears. Click the Create From File tab and choose the application and file.

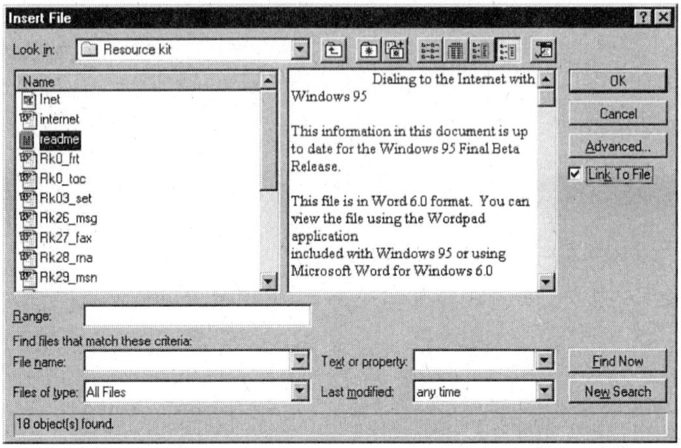

Fig. 15.3

Use the Word for Windows Insert File command to embed a file in a Word document.

3. Identify the file you want to insert, including the drive and directory, if necessary.

4. Select the Link or Link To File option.

5. Click OK.

To see that the file you inserted is a linked object, click anywhere in the document to show a gray highlight or to show the object's field codes.

> **Note**
>
> If you want to insert several word processing documents into a single larger document, give your documents a consistent appearance by using the same formats for each one. You also can use templates and styles to help ensure consistency among documents.

Inserting a New Object into Your Document

If you want to use the features of another application in your compound documents, you can choose Insert, Object and select an application from the provided list. As pointed out at the beginning of this chapter, many applications now support this feature of OLE 2.0, including the standard Microsoft Office applications, the Windows applets, and other Windows applications.

Applets are small applications that can't be run by themselves. When you buy a Windows application, one or more applets may be available.

As examples of the types of applets that support OLE as a server application or client application, the following list of applets come with Microsoft Office. When you install Microsoft Office on your system, these applets are installed in a centralized location, usually in a folder called MSAPPS, which allows many Office applications to access them easily. The WordPad application, which comes with Windows 95, can embed files that have been created in the following list.

Applet	Use
Microsoft ClipArt Gallery	Inserts clip-art pictures
Microsoft Data Map	Inserts a map showing different levels associated with data
Microsoft Equation	Creates mathematical expressions
Microsoft Graph	Inserts charts from data in a Word table
Microsoft Organization Chart	Creates organization charts
Microsoft Word Picture	Inserts a picture and the tools associated with the Word drawing toolbar
Microsoft WordArt	Creates logos and other special text effects

To use the tools from another application or applet within your document to create a new object, follow these steps:

1. Position the insertion point in the destination document.

2. Choose Insert, Object. The Insert Object dialog box appears (see fig. 15.4).

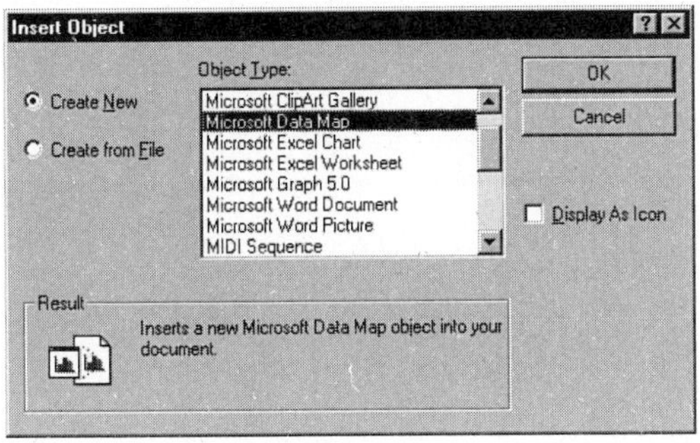

Fig. 15.4
The Insert Object dialog box lists applets as well as Windows applications.

III

Working with Applications

Tip

The title bar identifies the application you are viewing. Applications that support OLE 2.0 display the name of the container application. Applications that support OLE 1.0 display the name of the source application.

3. Select the Create New radio button, and then select an application or applet from the Object Type list.

4. If you want to see only an icon for the object, select the Display as Icon check box.

5. When you finish with the Insert Object dialog box, choose OK.

After you complete these steps, one of two things occurs. You might enter a separate window for the application or the applet (see fig. 15.5). Or you'll remain in your client document window, but the menu bar and toolbar change to reflect the source application (see fig. 15.6).

Create the object by using the application's toolbar and menus. When you finish creating the object, you can exit the object in one of two ways:

- If you launched a separate window for the application or applet, choose File, Exit.

- If you stayed in your destination document, click outside the object.

Fig. 15.5

When you choose Microsoft Graph 5.0 Chart, a separate window opens. After you finish with the chart program, click anyplace on the Word document window to return to the Word document.

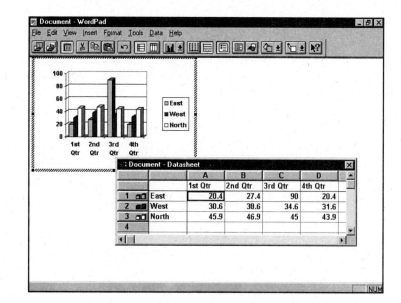

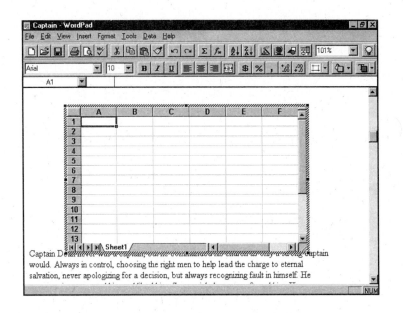

Fig. 15.6

When you choose Microsoft Excel Worksheet, you get in-place editing. The menu bar and toolbar change to Microsoft Excel, enabling you to use Excel features such as the AutoSum button.

Editing an Embedded Object

Regardless of which method you use to embed information into your document, you can edit the embedded object with the tools of the source application. To edit the object, follow these steps:

1. Click the object. Handles appear around the object, and the status bar tells you to double-click the object (see fig. 15.7).

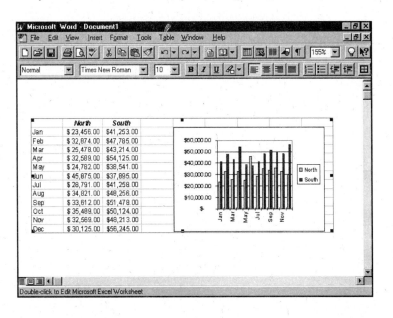

Fig. 15.7

The status bar displays instructions on how to get to the source-application tools.

III

Working with Applications

2. Double-click the object. Depending on the source and destination applications, a separate window for the program appears, or the current window's toolbar and menu bar change to those of the source application.

3. Edit the object, using the application's toolbar and menus.

4. When you finish editing the object, exit the object. If you launched a separate window for the application or applet, choose File, Exit. If you stayed in your destination document, click outside the object.

Creating an Example Compound Document

Much of what you read in this chapter may be brand new information for you. The best way to learn how to use OLE is to actually use it a few times. This section uses Microsoft Excel and some common Windows 95 applications, such as Paint and Sound Recorder, to show you how to build a compound document. If you don't have Excel, you can use another OLE 2.0-compliant application to simulate this exercise.

Embedding a Paint Object in WordPad

To start your document, open WordPad. WordPad will be the container application where you'll embed server objects. In English, this means you'll use WordPad as your main program and embed a Paint bitmap, an Excel chart, and a sound file into your WordPad document.

1. In WordPad, create some text, such as **Let's embed a Paint object first:**.

2. Switch to Paint and open SANDSTONE.BMP, which is provided with Windows 95.

3. Click the Select tool on the Paint tool box. Mark an area on the drawing that you want to embed in your WordPad document. Choose Edit, Copy.

4. Switch to WordPad and place the cursor where you want to insert the drawing object. Choose Edit, Paste Special. The Paste Special dialog box appears (see fig. 15.8).

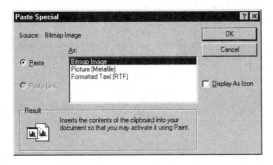

Fig. 15.8
You can imbed
objects using the
Paste Special
dialog box.

5. In the Paste Special dialog box, make sure that the Paste Link check box isn't marked. You don't want to link this object to your document. Also, select Bitmap Image in the As list box. Click OK.

6. After a few seconds, your WordPad document displays an embedded Paint object. How do you know it's embedded? Click the object, and a thin border surrounds it. This is a frame that WordPad puts around the object. Double-click the object, however, and the entire WordPad interface changes to look like Paint (see fig. 15.9).

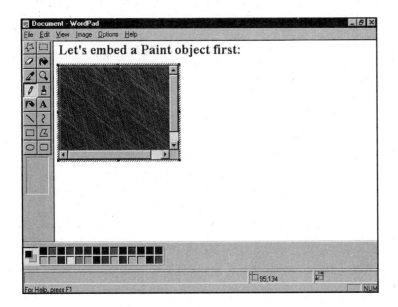

Fig. 15.9
Double-clicking
the Paint object
changes the
WordPad interface
to show Paint tools
and menus.

III

Working with Applications

Embedding an Excel Object by Dragging and Dropping

Another way to embed an object into your WordPad compound document is by dragging and dropping it from a server application. To drag a chart from Excel into WordPad, use these steps:

1. Open Excel and create a chart. You don't have to load it down with a lot of data, but do a simple one, as shown in figure 15.10.

Fig. 15.10
You can drag this chart into your WordPad document.

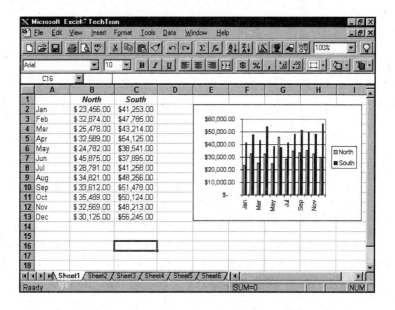

◀ See "Switching between Document Windows," p. 115

2. Arrange your desktop so that you can see WordPad and Excel at the same time, as shown in figure 15.11.

3. Select and drag the chart into the WordPad window. Place the gray box with a plus sign in it at the spot where you want the chart embedded. If you want it in a special place in the document, you should prepare the document for the object before you start the drag-and-drop process.

4. Release the mouse button. The Excel chart now appears in the WordPad document as an embedded object.

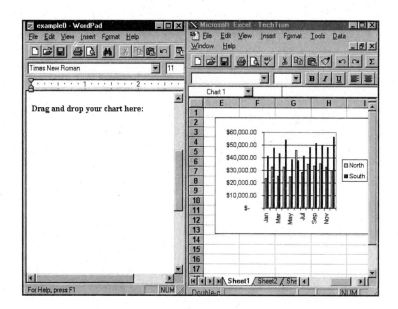

Fig. 15.11
To drag and drop, you should arrange your desktop to see both applications.

Embedding a Sound Clip in WordPad

To add a little flavor to your WordPad compound document, include a sound clip that your readers can click. You need to have a sound card and microphone to create and hear these sounds, but you still can embed the sound clips even if you don't have a sound card installed. To embed a sound clip in your document, follow these steps:

1. In WordPad, choose Insert, Object.

2. In the Insert Object dialog box, select Wave Sound from the Object Type list.

> **Note**
>
> If you have a specific sound clip that you want to embed, click the Create from File option and select the file you want to embed. If you don't click this option, the default setting is to create a new sound clip.

3. Click the Display As Icon check box to embed an icon of the sound clip in your WordPad document. When you use an icon, you reduce the system resources necessary to store the object.

4. Click OK. An icon of the sound object appears in the WordPad document (see fig. 15.12).

III

Working with Applications

5. Double-click the icon to start the Sound Object in Document applet (see fig. 15.13). This applet allows you to record a new sound clip in your document. After you create a message, you can play it back by double-clicking the sound object in your WordPad document.

Fig. 15.12
The sound object appears as an icon in your document.

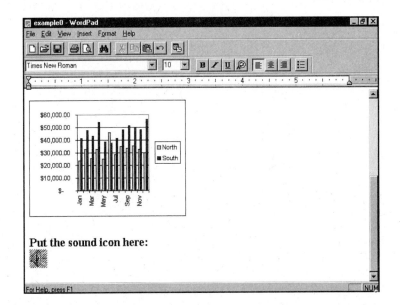

Fig. 15.13
By double-clicking the sound object icon, you activate the sound recorder applet to create a new wave file.

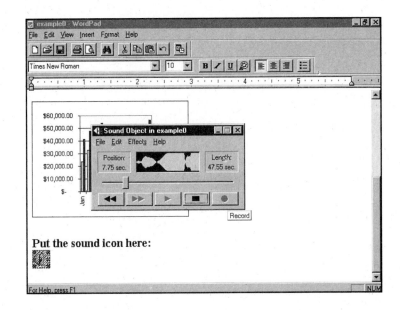

Editing an Embedded Object in Your Compound Document

If your data changes, if your taste in art differs now from what it did when you embedded the graphic object, or if you want to add something to your sound clip, you can edit each object without leaving WordPad. This section shows you how to edit the Excel chart that you embedded earlier, in the section "Embedding an Excel Object by Dragging and Dropping."

To edit the chart, follow these steps:

1. Double-click the Excel chart in your WordPad compound document. The WordPad interface automatically changes to the standard Excel interface (see fig. 15.14).

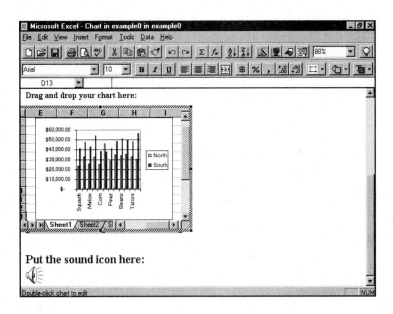

Fig. 15.14
With OLE 2.0, your container application takes on the appearance of the source application.

2. Make changes to the chart by using the toolbars and menu options. When you finish, click outside the chart. This returns the WordPad interface to its original state (see fig. 15.15).

Fig. 15.15
WordPad's
interface returns
to its original
state, but the Excel
chart has changed.

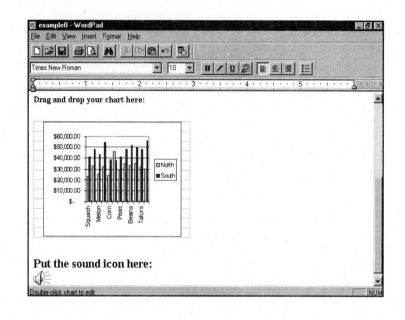

Troubleshooting

When I double-click a linked or embedded object, a `Cannot edit` *error message appears.*

This means that the source file can't be opened. Make sure that the application needed to edit the file is on your machine. Also make sure that you have enough system memory to run both the container and source applications. Keep in mind that compound documents demand more memory than simple documents.

The margins are 0 (zero) in all my embedded Microsoft Word objects.

Word sets the margins at 0 (zero) inches in a document object to eliminate excessive white space around the object. To change the margins, double-click the Word document object to open it for editing. Choose File, Page Setup; click the Margins tab; then enter new margin settings.

When I double-click an embedded Microsoft Excel object, Microsoft Excel doesn't open.

You probably have the Ignore Other Applications check box selected, which causes Microsoft Excel to ignore all requests from other applications. In Excel, choose Tools, Options and then click the General tab. Clear the Ignore Other Applications check box.

OLE Automation for Interapplication Programming

As mentioned earlier in the chapter, OLE automation allows developers to use objects from different applications. An Excel program, for instance, can create and edit Microsoft Project objects. The following is a list of some of the applications that you can use to start OLE automation:

- Visual Basic

- Access Basic

- Visual Basic for Application, Excel version

OLE automation is used so that programmers can control and reference objects without worrying about complex and problematic interapplication details during the development cycle. Sophisticated business solutions can be created by using the capabilities of multiple applications with OLE automation. With more and more applications using OLE 2.0 and exposing objects to programmers, businesses can mix and match the applications on their users' desktops and (it's hoped) diversify the vendors who supply the applications. This makes for a much richer computing environment, giving the user more to choose from.

If just one vendor is providing one application to the end user, the end user must devise ways to modify her work to get the desired results. More than likely, these users spend a great deal of time creating workarounds or end up not getting the task done, lowering productivity. With OLE automation, many customized applications can be created to help businesses get done what they need to get done.

Understanding OLE Automation Functions

If you're a developer or power user interested in OLE automation basics, this section briefly describes some of the functions available. By understanding three primary functions in OLE automation, you can begin developing applications that rely on exposed objects or control objects in other applications.

> **Note**
>
> For information on OLE automation, many Que books are available that teach you the fundamentals and expert techniques. A few of these include *Special Edition Using Visual Basic for Applications* and *Special Edition Using Excel for Windows 95*.

III

Working with Applications

The Set function is used to set a variable in the application in which you're programming to reference an object in a different OLE 2.0 application. This reference is commonly referred to as *pointing*. If, for example, you're in Microsoft Project and want to reference the active worksheet in Excel, you would use the following syntax:

```
Set ExampleSheet = MSExcel.ActiveSheet
```

When you reference the properties and methods of the ExampleSheet object in Project, you affect the worksheet in Excel.

The CreateObject function creates the specified object and then returns an object that's linked to the new object. After you get the returned object, you use the Set function to link it to an object variable. To use the CreateObject function, use the syntax CreateObject ("*ApplicationName.ObjectType*"). The following is an example of using the CreateObject function:

```
Set NewObject = CreateObject("Excel.Sheet")
```

In this example, you automatically start Excel, create an object, and create an object variable that can reference the created object. You then use the new object throughout your subroutine.

The last of the primary three OLE automation functions is GetObject. This function is similar to the CreateObject function, except it accesses its source object from a file. The syntax for GetObject is GetObject("*completePathname*"). To reference an object that's on your C:\ drive in the OLE folder, for example, use the following syntax:

```
Set ExampleObject = GetObject("C:\OLE\SAMPLE.OBJ")
```

Creating a Sample OLE Automation Subroutine

This brief introduction to OLE automation isn't intended to teach you how to write OLE automation applications. The intention is to introduce you to what OLE and OLE automation can do if you decide to create a custom application to take full advantage of Windows 95's built-in support of OLE 2.0.

The short sample code, denoted as listing 15.1, creates a Word for Windows object within Excel and then embeds a Word document in an Excel worksheet with the phrase "Sample OLE Automation," as shown in figure 15.16. To create this code, create a new Excel macro and copy this code into the macro window. Try to follow along by reading the lines that start with an apostrophe ('). These *comment lines* are included to *document* (explain) the code. For a subroutine this simple, you can see that OLE automation follows the same basic procedures that you perform when you manually embed objects. On the other hand, more sophisticated OLE automation is very complicated and involves hundreds or thousands of code lines to complete.

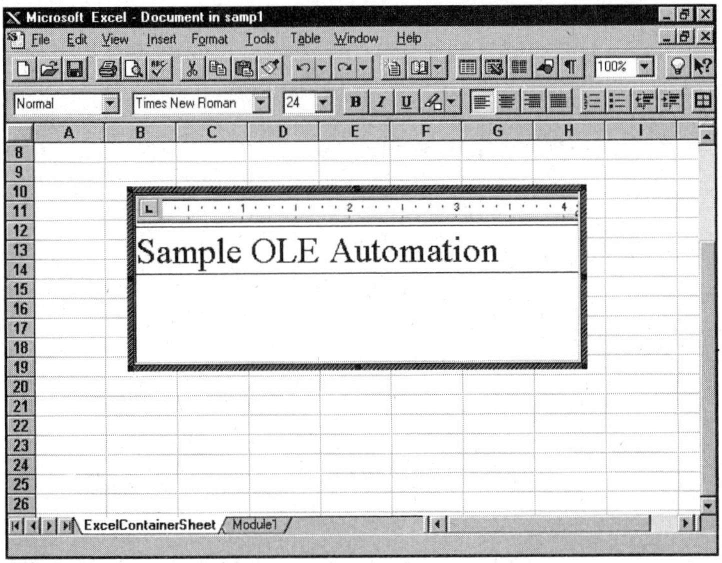

Fig. 15.16
This is an example of OLE automation controlling a Word object from within Excel.

Listing 15.1   <OLE Automation Example>

```
'
' OleAutomationExample Macro
' Macro recorded 6/13/95 by Rob Tidrow
'
'
Sub OLEAutomationExample()
    ' Use DIM to assign two variables as Object data type
    Dim WordObject As Object
    Dim WordBasicObject As Object

    'Displays the Excel worksheet that contains the Word object
    Worksheets("ExcelContainerSheet").Activate

    'Create and assign the Word object to the WordObject variable
    Set WordObject = ActiveSheet.OLEObjects.Add("Word.Document.6")
    Set WordBasicObject = WordObject.Object.Application.WordBasic

    'This line activates the Word object
    WordObject.Activate

    'This line applies a border to the outside of the text
    WordBasicObject.BorderOutside
```

(continues)

Listing 15.1 Continued

```
    'This line sets the typeface
    WordBasicObject.Font Arial$

    'This line sets the font size
    WordBasicObject.FontSize 24

    'This line places the Word text into Excel
    WordBasicObject.Insert "Sample OLE Automation"
End Sub
```

Part IV

Working with Disks and Files

Chapter 16

Working with Disks and Disk Drives

by Ron Person with Jerry Cox

Before you learn about organizing files on a computer, which is covered in detail in the next chapter, you need to learn how to work with and maintain your floppy disks and hard disks. For example, before you put data on a floppy disk, you usually have to format it to get it ready to receive data. If you want, you can also name your drives to make them easier to identify. Floppy disks and hard disks, not being perfect, are susceptible to damage—which can be very trying if you are dealing with irreplaceable data. Windows 95 comes with a tool to help you check for and repair some kinds of damage.

Everyone likes to get more performance out of their computer. You can monitor the performance of your system using the System Monitor. You can improve the performance of your hard disks using Disk Defragmenter. You can enable your system to act as though it has more memory (RAM) than is actually installed by using virtual memory. You may want to periodically refer back to this chapter when it's time to do maintenance work on your floppy disks and hard disks.

In this chapter, you learn to

- Format your floppy and hard disks
- Name your disks
- Monitor your system's performance
- Increase the effective size of your disks with DriveSpace

- Defragment your hard disk to improve performance

- Use ScanDisk to check for disk damage

- Use virtual memory

Understanding What Your Disk Drive Does

The computer does all calculations and work in electronic *memory*. (Electronic memory is known as *RAM*, or Random Access Memory.) RAM is where Windows and your programs work. The data you work on also resides in RAM. If the computer loses electrical power, the data, program, and Windows are lost from memory. Because electronic memory is limited in size and disappears when electrical power is removed, the computer needs a way to store large amounts of data and applications for long periods of time.

You use *magnetic storage* to store applications and data for long periods of time or when the computer is turned off. Magnetic-storage media include *floppy disks* and *hard disks*. Floppy disks are removable and don't contain much space. Hard disks are internal to the computer and have much larger amounts of space.

> **Note**
>
> There are larger floppies on the market but they are not standard equipment from any of the manufacturers yet. An example is the new 20M and 100M floppies for the Iomega Zip Drives.

▶ See "Understanding Files and Folders," p. 498

The hard disk you store your data and programs on does not have to reside in the computer at your desk. If you are connected to a network, you can access information stored on the hard disk in the *file server*, the computer that serves the *clients* on the network. When you start an application or open a data file, the computer places a *copy* of the information stored in magnetic storage (on floppy disks or a hard disk) into electronic memory (RAM). If power is lost, the magnetic copy still is available.

▶ See "Using the Explorer with Shared Resources on a Network," p. 544

You save the work you do in your programs in magnetic *files*, which are stored on a floppy disk or hard disk. Over time, you may have hundreds or even thousands of files. Searching for a specific file among the thousands of files can be very time-consuming.

Large computers and networks have multiple hard disks, each disk with its own drive letter. Figure 16.1 shows two hard disk drives (see the icons for drives C and D), a floppy disk drive (see the icon for drive A), and a CD-ROM drive (drive E). Each disk acts as a separate filing cabinet and can have its own unique folder organization.

> **Note**
>
> Some drives may have more than one letter depending on the controller versus drive size. If the drive is larger than the controller or BIOS can read, it can be partitioned as two drives. It is still only one piece of hardware, but software sees it as two drives. It also is possible for a drive to have more than one letter if it is compressed. In this case, the software doing the compression addresses the drive with one letter, and all other software accesses it using another drive letter, which is controlled by the compression software.

Drive icons —

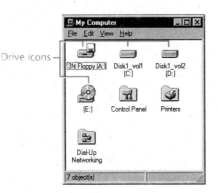

Fig. 16.1
The My Computer window displays all the resources on your computer, including all the floppy disk drives and hard drives.

Formatting Disks

You usually cannot use new disks until you format them (but some disks come already formatted). *Formatting* prepares disks for use on a computer. Formatting is similar to preparing a blank book for use by writing in page numbers and creating a blank table of contents. If a disk contains data, formatting it completely erases all existing data. Part of the process of formatting is checking for bad areas on the disk's magnetic surface. All bad areas found are identified so that data is not recorded in these areas.

Formatting a Floppy Disk

To format a floppy disk, follow these steps:

1. Insert the floppy disk to be formatted in the disk drive.

Tip
If you attempt to open an unformatted floppy disk in My Computer or Windows Explorer, you will be asked if you want to format the disk. The Format dialog box immediately displays.

2. Open the My Computer window by double-clicking its icon.

3. Select the floppy disk drive containing the floppy disk to be formatted.

4. Choose File, Format (or right-click the drive icon and select Format from the shortcut menu). The Format dialog box appears (see fig. 16.2).

> **Note**
>
> If you are working in the Windows Explorer, there is no File, Format command; instead, right-click a floppy disk drive icon in the left pane of the Explorer and select Format from the shortcut menu.

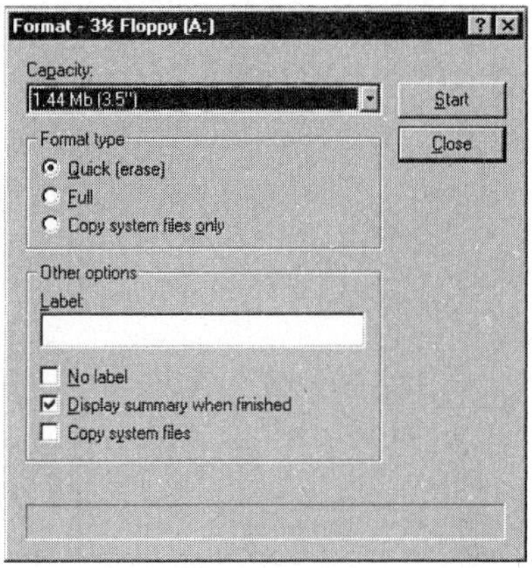

Fig. 16.2
Set up a formatting operation in the Format dialog box.

5. Select the size of the floppy disk from the Capacity drop-down list.

6. Select the type of format you want from the Format Type options:

Option	Function
Quick (Erase)	Formats the disk without scanning it for bad sectors first. Speeds up formatting, but you should be sure that the disk is undamaged. You can use the Quick format option only on disks that have already been formatted.
Full	Checks for bad sectors on the disk before formatting and marks them so that these areas are not used.
Copy System Files Only	Adds the system files to the disk without formatting it so that the disk can be used to start the computer.

7. If you want to assign a label to the disk, type the label in the Label text box. Otherwise, select the No Label option.

8. Select the Display Summary When Finished option if you want to see a screen of information about the disk after it is formatted (see fig. 16.3).

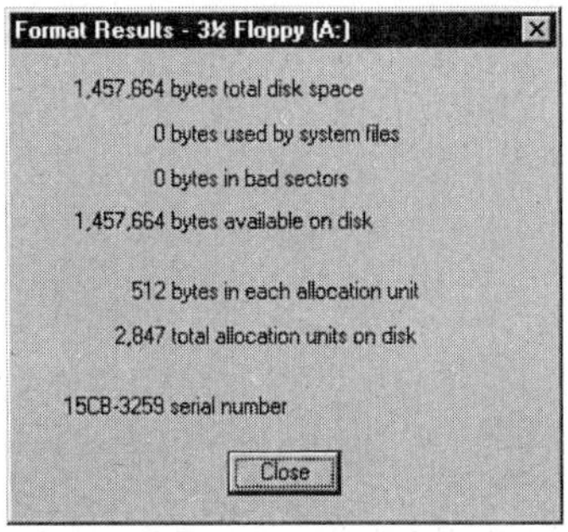

Fig. 16.3
You can get information about a formatted disk in the Format Results message box.

The Format Results message box tells you how much total disk space there is, how many bytes are used by system files and bad sectors, and how many bytes are available.

9. If you want to use the disk to start the computer, select the Copy System Files option. Do not use this option unless you need to, because system files use storage space on the disk that can otherwise be used for data.

10. Choose Start. The progress of the formatting operation is displayed at the bottom of the Format dialog box.

11. To format another disk, insert a new disk and repeat steps 5 through 10.

12. When you are finished formatting disks, choose Close.

Caution

When you format a disk, you remove all the information from the disk. You should check a disk for important files before formatting.

Format an entire box of disks at one time and put a paper label on each disk when it is formatted. This system lets you know that open boxes contain formatted disks; paper labels confirm that the disks are formatted.

Troubleshooting

Windows will not format a disk drive. A dialog says there are files open but all applications and documents on the drive are closed.

Windows 95 prevents you from formatting a disk that has a file open or a disk that is open in My Computer or the Windows Explorer. Close any documents or applications that are open on that disk and close any My Computer or Windows Explorer windows open into the disk.

Caution

Drives that have been compressed with DriveSpace or another compression software must be formatted from DriveSpace or the appropriate compression software.

Formatting Your Hard Disk

Before you can use a new hard drive you need to format it. You also may want to format a hard drive that has been used and is cluttered with data or other operating systems. Formatting does more than just erase old data, it magnetically scrubs the disk so that the files do not exist.

If you have purchased a preassembled computer that contains a hard disk and the computer starts and runs Windows or DOS, then you do not need to format the hard disk. If, however, you install additional hard disks in your computer, you may need to format them before you can use them.

Note

You should format a disk that contains confidential or secret information before giving the computer to someone who should not have access to that data. The erase or delete commands only remove a file's name and location from a disk's table of files. The data still exists on the disk until it is overwritten by another file. Formatting erases the name and location table and magnetically erases the actual data.

Using FDISK to Partition a New Hard Drive

If you are installing a new hard disk as your primary drive, place the Windows 95 Startup disk in the A: drive and turn on your computer. Windows sees the new drive and asks if you want to allocate all of the unallocated space on your drive. Answer "yes" and it will run FDISK behind the scenes and restart your computer. After the restart, it formats the new partition automatically.

Your other alternative is to boot to DOS Mode by pressing F5 during startup and running FDISK from the DOS prompt. When you type FDISK at the DOS prompt it puts a menu on the screen. Be sure to check to see that the drive that you want to partition is the drive that is selected. Option 5 on the menu allows you to select a different drive. After you have confirmed that you have the correct drive selected, choose option 1 from the menu. This option creates a DOS partition on your drive and asks if you want to use the entire drive for your DOS partition. The most common answer is yes. Once the DOS partition is created, your computer will restart and be ready for the formatting of the drive.

As you can see by the two choices of partitioning a hard drive, Windows 95 has made this step much easier.

Formatting an Uncompressed Hard Drive from MS-DOS

To format an uncompressed drive from the MS-DOS prompt, type "Format d:". Where d: is the drive letter of the drive that you want to format.

▶ See "Compressing a Drive," p. 471

Formatting an Uncompressed Hard Drive from Windows

Before you format an uncompressed hard drive make sure you have backed up or copied any file that may be needed again. Once the formatting process begins you will be unable to retrieve previous data from the drive.

To format a hard drive, follow these steps:

1. Close all documents and applications that are on the drive you want to format. Close any windows from My Computer that look at that drive. Collapse all folders in Windows Explorer for the hard drive you want to format.

2. Open My Computer and select the icon for the drive you want to format. Choose File, Format.

   or

   Open Windows Explorer, and right-click on the hard drive icon you want to format. Choose Format.

   The Format dialog box displays as shown in figure 16.4.

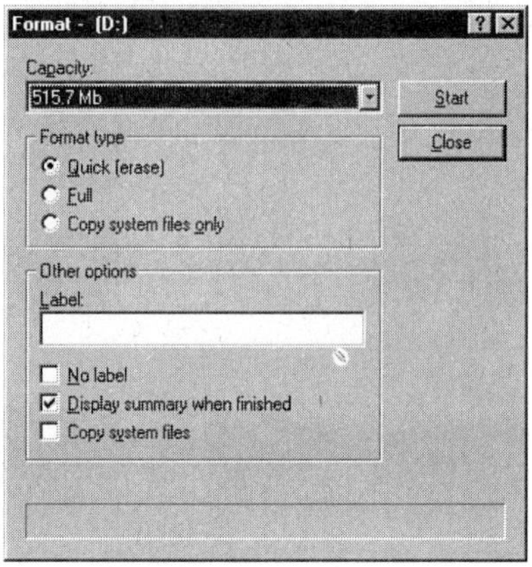

Fig. 16.4

You can use the Format dialog box to do a full format, erase files, and copy system files onto a disk.

3. Select the option you want for formatting your disk:

Option	Function
Capacity	Click the drop-down list arrow to select a different capacity for the drive.

Format Type

Option	Function
Quick (Erase)	Erases all the files, but does not use ScanDisk to check for bad areas of the disk. The disk must be formatted to use this command. If you think your disk may have bad areas or has shown erratic behavior, be sure to run ScanDisk after the Quick format.
Full	Prepares a disk for use. All files are completely removed. Disks are checked for bad sectors, but hard disks are not. If this is a new hard disk or a disk that has shown erratic behavior, be sure to run ScanDisk after the Full format.
Copy System Files Only	Does not format the disk but it does copy system files to the disk so the floppy or hard disk can be used to start the computer.

Other Options

Option	Function
Label	Creates a magnetic label on the disk. This label appears in the title bar of My Computer and Windows Explorer.
No Label	Disables the label so the disk will not have a label.
Display Summary When Finished	Displays a report when formatting is complete. The report shows the space available on the disk, the room taken by system files, and the number of bad sectors.
Copy System Files	Copies system files onto the disk after formatting. Select this check box if you need to use this floppy or hard disk to start the computer.

4. Choose Start. A dialog box displays telling you that all files on the disk will be destroyed. Are you sure you want to format this drive? Choose OK to format or Cancel to stop.

5. If you choose OK, you will see the Format dialog box showing you the progression of the file format as shown in figure 16.5.

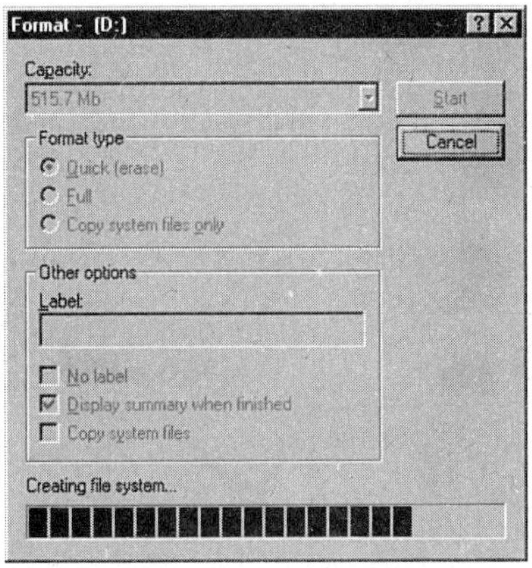

Fig. 16.5
A progression bar at the bottom of the dialog box shows you the progress of disk formatting.

6. When formatting is complete the Format Results dialog box displays the properties of the formatted drive as shown in figure 16.6.

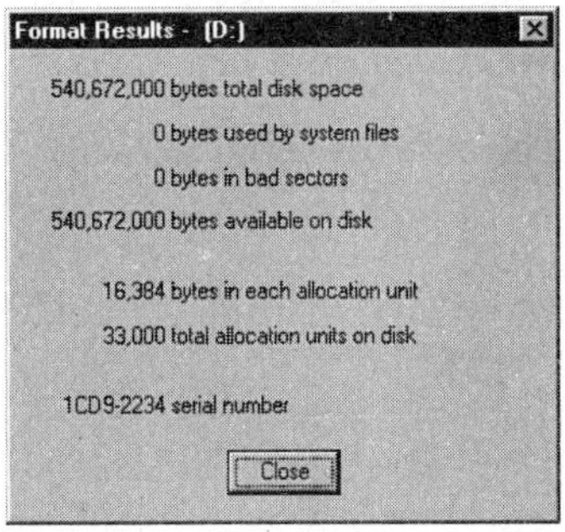

Fig. 16.6
The Format Results dialog box displays a report on disk statistics when formatting is complete.

Note

If you use the Full format option on a hard disk drive, you are reminded to use ScanDisk.

7. Choose Close to close the Format Results dialog box; then choose Close to close the Format dialog box.

IV

Disks and Files

◀ See "Using
FDISK to Parti-
tion a New
Hard Drive,"
p. 464

▶ See "Using
ScanDisk to
Check for Disk
Damage,"
p. 489

If My Computer or Windows Explorer does not display the icon for the hard
drive you want to format, then you may need to recheck the drive connections to the drive adapter or partition the hard drive using the FDISK command. You also need to check setup to be sure the proper drive type is
selected.

Caution

You cannot format the hard disk containing Windows while Windows is running. If
you need to format the hard disk containing Windows, you will need either a disk
copy of MS-DOS with the FORMAT command or a set of the Windows 95 upgrade
disks which contains a disk for formatting hard disks.

The system files, FDISK, and Format are created on the Startup disk that Windows 95
asks if you want to create it during the install. It is *highly* recommended that you
create the Startup disk.

Naming Your Drive with a Volume Label

Although you may be accustomed to putting a paper label on disks, both
hard disks and floppy disks can have magnetically recorded labels, known as
volume labels. Volume labels can help you identify disks. You can read the
volume label for a disk by looking at the disk's properties.

In the preceding section, you learned how to create a volume label when you
format a disk. If you want to create or change a volume label on a previously
formatted disk, follow these steps:

1. Open the Explorer or the My Computer window.

2. Select the drive having the volume name you want to change.

Tip
You can view the
name of a disk by
right-clicking the
disk icon in the
My Computer or
Explorer window
and selecting the
Properties com-
mand.

3. Choose File, Properties. Alternatively, right-click the drive and choose
Properties from the shortcut menu. The Properties sheet appears, as
shown in figure 16.7.

4. Type the name you want to give the disk in the Label text box and
choose OK.

If there is already a name in the box, select it first and then type a new
name. The Properties sheet also gives you information on the total size
of the disk (in bytes), how much space is used, and the amount of remaining space.

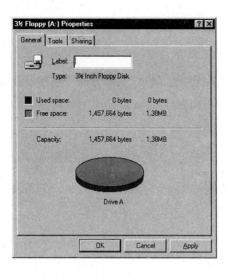

Fig. 16.7
Enter a volume label for a disk in the Properties sheet.

Compressing a Disk

If you are like many computer users, you may find yourself bumping up against the limits of the storage space on your computer as you install new programs and generate more and more data files. You've probably also discovered that new releases of Windows programs seem to take up more and more room on your hard disk. One solution is to install a new hard disk in your computer. But if your finances are limited, or you are working with a laptop in which it is not possible to add another hard disk, you have another option. Windows 95 comes with a program called DriveSpace that enables you to squeeze more storage space from your existing hard drive. DriveSpace is a software solution to your hardware problem. DriveSpace works by compressing the files on your hard disk so that they take up less room. When you need to use a file, DriveSpace automatically decompresses it. The compression and decompression of files happens transparently—you are not even aware that it is happening. You will notice very little delay in file access when you use DriveSpace.

DriveSpace is an optional program that can be installed when you install Windows 95, or you can install it at a later time. To see if you have DriveSpace available, open the Start menu and choose Programs, Accessories, System Tools. If DriveSpace is not listed in the System Tools menu, you will need to install it. For information on how to install DriveSpace after you have installed Windows, see Appendix A, "Installing and Uninstalling Windows 95."

> **Note**
>
> The DriveSpace programs work with disks compressed with DoubleSpace. DoubleSpace was included with MS-DOS 6.0 and 6.2. DriveSpace was initially released in MS-DOS 6.22.

When you run DriveSpace, it creates a compressed drive on your existing hard disk. The compressed drive is actually a file, not a physical hard drive, called a *compressed volume file* (CVF). The CVF is stored on a physical, uncompressed drive, called the *host drive*. The compressed drive is assigned a drive letter, just like a physical drive, and can be accessed like any other drive. From the user's point of view, the only difference after running DriveSpace is that the original drive has a lot more free space and there is a new drive, the host drive.

The file that DriveSpace creates on your hard drive is a hidden, read only, system file; thus, it is not acted upon by most normal DOS commands.

You can run DriveSpace in one of two ways. Typically, you use DriveSpace to compress your entire existing drive to free up more storage space. If you have a C drive, for example, you can run DriveSpace to compress your C drive, which then becomes a compressed volume file on the host drive H. You can also use DriveSpace to compress a specified amount of the free space on your hard drive to create a new, empty compressed drive. The rest of the hard drive is not compressed. If, for example, you have 80M of free space on your C drive, you can use DriveSpace to compress 25M of the free space to create a new drive D with roughly 50M of free space. You then have 55M free on drive C and 50M on drive D for an effective 105M of free space.

DriveSpace only allows the maximum compressed drive size to be 512M or less. If you have a drive of 420M, for example, you could compress the first 256M to 512M compressed and the remaining 163M to 326M compressed. These numbers are based on 100 percent compression.

▶ See "Changing the Estimated Compression Ratio for Your Compressed Drive," p. 480

As a rule of thumb, DriveSpace will add 50 to 100 percent more capacity to your disk. The amount of actual compression depends upon the types of files stored on the disk. Some files, like text files or certain graphics files, compress significantly, while other files, like an application's EXE file, may barely change.

Troubleshooting

Large files will not copy onto the compressed drive.

The available free space displayed for compressed drives is only an estimate. It is based on the average compression for all files on your disk. If the file you are attempting to save does not compress as much as the average, then it may not fit in the available space.

Compressing a Drive

The DriveSpace that comes with the initial release of Windows 95 does not compress drives larger than 256/512M. If your drive is larger than 256/512M you need to purchase the Microsoft Plus! Pak from Microsoft. This package adds extensions to Windows 95. It will enable you to compress drives up to 2 gigabytes. For information or to order Microsoft Plus! Pak, contact Microsoft at 800-426-9400.

To compress a drive using DriveSpace, follow these steps:

1. Open the Start menu and choose Programs, Accessories, System Tools, and then choose DriveSpace. The DriveSpace window appears, as shown in figure 16.8.

   A drive that has already been compressed will display the phrase "Compressed drive" next to it and will have an associated host drive in the list.

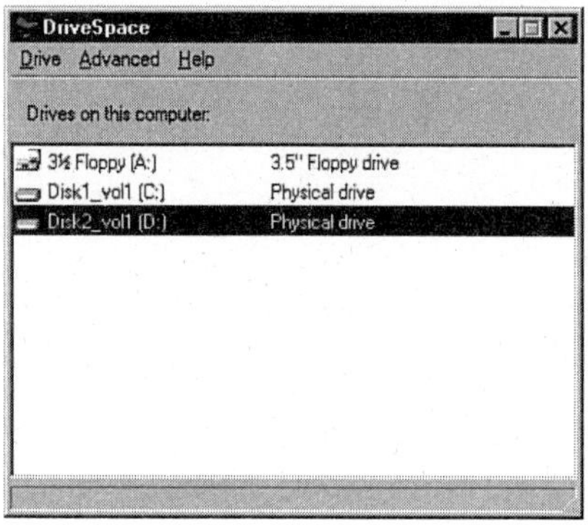

Tip
DriveSpace automatically runs ScanDisk before compressing a drive.

Fig. 16.8
Use DriveSpace to create more free space on your hard drive.

> **Note**
>
> DriveSpace is optional in installation. If it isn't in the System Tools menu, you need to use Add/Remove Programs, Windows Setup to add it.

2. Select the drive you want to compress from the Drives on This Computer list.

▶ See "Returning a Drive to Normal Compression," p. 475

> **Caution**
>
> Although you can compress a floppy disk using DriveSpace, you can use compressed floppy disks only in computers that have either DriveSpace for Windows or DoubleSpace for DOS or Windows installed. To use a compressed floppy disk in Windows 95, choose Advance, Options. Select the Automatically Mount Compressed Removable Media option and choose OK.

3. Choose Drive, Compress. The Compress a Drive dialog box appears (see fig. 16.9).

Fig. 16.9
The Compress a Drive dialog box displays information on the size of the selected disk and how much space there will be after running DriveSpace.

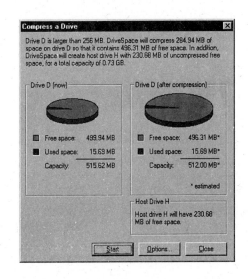

4. Choose Options to change the compression options if you want. The Compression Options dialog box displays (see fig. 16.10).

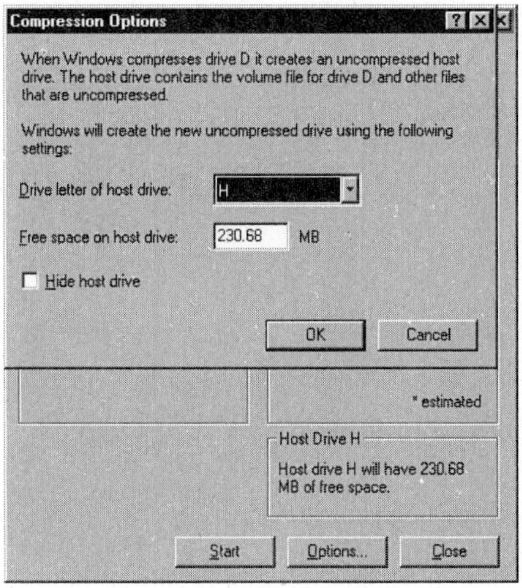

Fig. 16.10
Change the options used for compressing a drive in the Compression Options dialog box.

IV

Disks and Files

You can change the following three options:

- To change the drive letter assigned to the host drive, click the down arrow next to the Drive Letter of Host Drive drop-down list and select a new drive letter. You may have to select a new drive letter if you plan on using the default drive letter for another purpose (for example, for a new hard disk).

- To change the amount of free space reserved on the host drive, type a new value in the Free Space on Host Drive text box. Windows will calculate the smallest acceptable size for the Host drive and will not allow you to enter a number that is too small.

- If you don't want the host drive to appear in the Windows Explorer, My Computer, or various dialog boxes such as the Open and Save As dialog boxes, select the Hide Host Drive option. You may want to do this if you are creating a system for novices who may accidentally delete important files from the Host drive.

When you finish making changes, choose OK.

5. Choose Start. A confirmation dialog box appears (see fig. 16.11). (This dialog box does not appear if there are no files on the disk.)

6. If you haven't backed up your files, choose the Back Up Files button to open Backup. See Chapter 18, "Backing Up and Protecting Your Data," for detailed information on how to back up files.

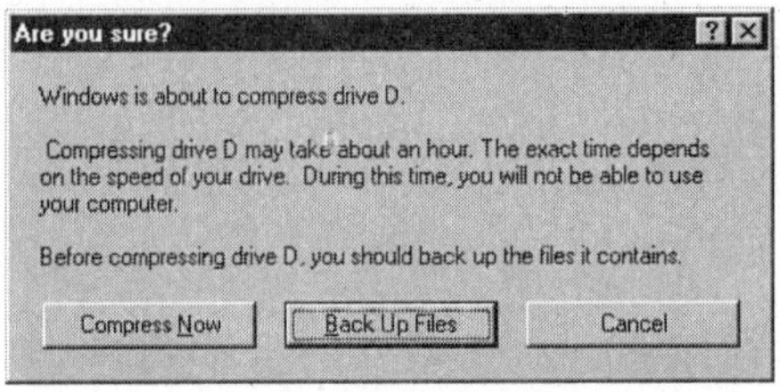

Fig. 16.11

Back up your files before you run DriveSpace by choosing the Back Up Files button.

> **Are you sure?** [?] [X]
>
> Windows is about to compress drive D.
>
> Compressing drive D may take about an hour. The exact time depends on the speed of your drive. During this time, you will not be able to use your computer.
>
> Before compressing drive D, you should back up the files it contains.
>
> [Compress **N**ow] [**B**ack Up Files] [Cancel]

7. Choose Compress Now to start the compression operation. The progress of the compression operation is displayed in the Compress a Drive message box (see fig. 16.12). Choose Close after examining the results.

   The DriveSpace program will check your hard disk for errors and defragment it as part of the compression operation.

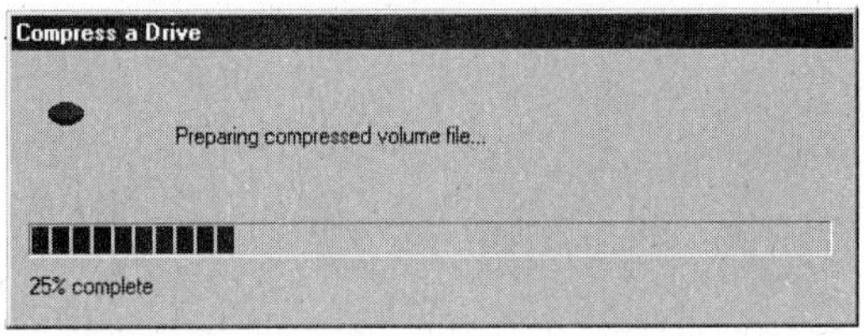

Fig. 16.12

You can monitor the progress of a drive compression operation in the Compress a Drive message box.

> **Compress a Drive**
>
> ⬭ Preparing compressed volume file...
>
> ▮▮▮▮▮▮▮▮▮▮
> 25% complete

8. When the compression operation is completed, the Compress a Drive dialog box informs you that the drive has been compressed and displays how much free space is now on the compressed drive (see fig. 16.13).

Fig. 16.13

The results of a drive compression operation are displayed in the Compress a Drive dialog box.

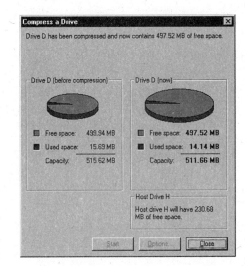

> **Compress a Drive** [X]
>
> Drive D has been compressed and now contains 497.52 MB of free space.
>
> Drive D (before compression)
> ◻ Free space: 499.94 MB
> ◼ Used space: 15.69 MB
> Capacity: 515.62 MB
>
> Drive D (now)
> ◻ Free space: 497.52 MB
> ◼ Used space: 14.14 MB
> Capacity: 511.66 MB
>
> Host Drive H
> Host drive H will have 230.68 MB of free space.
>
> [Start] [Options...] [Close]

9. A Restart Computer dialog box will display asking you if you want to restart your computer. Choose Yes to restart, No to continue working.

Do not set up new software, change system settings, or run MS-DOS programs until you restart your computer.

> **Note**
>
> Drives compressed with the MS-DOS 6.0 or 6.2 version of DoubleSpace or with the MS-DOS 6.22 version of DriveSpace for MS-DOS are compatible with DriveSpace. You can have drives compressed by both DoubleSpace and DriveSpace on the same computer using Windows 95.

Returning a Drive to Normal Compression

DriveSpace also enables you to decompress a drive. Before you decompress a drive, make sure that there will be enough space on the drive to hold all the files on the drive after it is decompressed.

When you choose to decompress a drive and there is not enough room, you get an error dialog that tells you how much data you have, how much free space is needed, and how much data needs to be deleted or moved off of which drive.

To decompress a drive, follow these steps:

1. Open the Start menu and choose Programs, Accessories, System Tools, and then choose DriveSpace. The DriveSpace window appears.

2. Select the drive you want to decompress from the Drives on This Computer list.

3. Choose Drive, Uncompress.

4. Choose Start. A confirmation dialog box appears. (This dialog box does not appear if there are no files on the disk.)

5. If you haven't backed up your files, choose the Back Up Files button to open Backup. See Chapter 18, "Backing Up and Protecting Your Data," for detailed information on how to back up your files.

6. Choose Uncompress Now to start the uncompression operation. The progress of the uncompression operation is displayed at the bottom of the Uncompress a Drive dialog box.

7. When the message box informing you that the drive has been uncompressed appears, choose OK.

Setting Up Your Floppy or Hard Disk to Read Compressed Files

When you are working with compressed removable storage media (such as floppy disks), you must mount the compressed drive if it wasn't present when the computer was started. Mounting a drive links a drive letter with a compressed volume file (CVF) and enables your computer to access the files on the compressed volume files.

To mount a compressed drive, follow these steps:

1. Open the DriveSpace window and select the drive you want to mount in the Drives on This Computer list.

   For example, if you want to read a floppy disk in drive A and the floppy disk has DriveSpace or DoubleSpace compression, then you would select the A drive.

2. Open the Advanced menu and choose Mount.

3. Select the compressed volume file you want to mount.

   Once you mount a drive, it shows up in the Drives on This Computer list as a compressed drive.

You can select an option so that newly compressed devices are automatically mounted. Choose Advanced, Settings. Select the Automatically Mount New Compressed Devices option and choose OK. Windows now automatically mounts new compressed devices so that you don't have to mount the compressed device each time you insert it in the computer.

To unmount a compressed drive, follow these steps:

1. Open the DriveSpace window and select the compressed drive you want to unmount from the Drives on this Computer list.

2. Choose Advanced, Unmount.

3. When the message box appears informing you that the operation is complete, choose OK.

Compressing Part of a Disk

You don't have to compress your entire hard disk; you can compress some or all of the free space on your hard disk to create a new compressed drive. To create a new compressed drive from part of a hard disk, follow these steps:

1. Open the DriveSpace window and select the drive with the free space you want to use to create a new compressed drive. You cannot select a compressed drive.

2. Choose <u>A</u>dvanced, <u>C</u>reate Empty. The Create New Compressed Drive dialog box appears, as shown in figure 16.14.

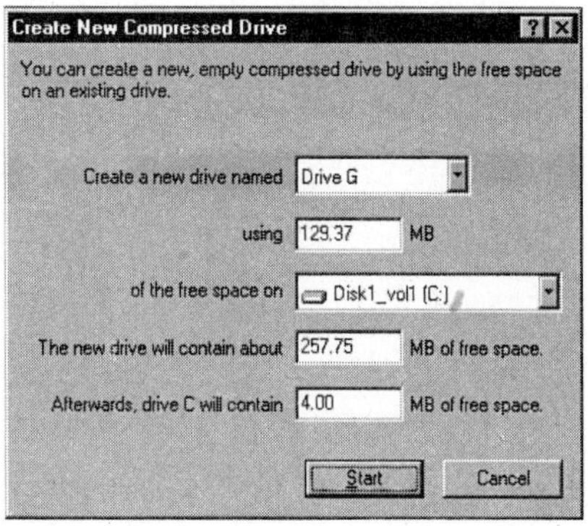

Fig. 16.14
Create a new compressed drive using the free space on your hard disk.

3. Accept the default name for the new drive or select an alternative name from the Create a New Drive Named drop-down list.

4. Enter the amount of free space (in megabytes) you want to use to create the new drive in the Using text box. If you enter a value here, the amount displayed in The New Drive Will Contain about...MB of Free Space text box changes to reflect how much free space will be created in the new drive.

5. Select the drive that has the free space you want to use to create the new drive from the Of the Free Space on drop-down list.

6. If you know how much free space you want the new drive to have, enter that figure in The New Drive Will Contain about...MB of Free Space text box. If you enter a value here, the amount displayed in the Using text box is automatically adjusted to show how much free space on the selected drive will be used for the new drive.

   The amount of free space that will be left on the uncompressed drive is displayed in the Afterwards, Drive *letter* Will Contain...MB of Free Space text box.

7. Choose <u>S</u>tart.

8. When the message box appears informing you that the operation is complete, choose OK.

Deleting a Compressed Drive

◀ See "Returning a Drive to Normal Compression," p. 475

Deleting a compressed drive is something you want to think seriously about before doing. Deleting a compressed drive removes all the data from the compressed drive, returning the drive to a blank decompressed state. One reason for deleting a compressed drive is so that you can remove the physical drive from your computer and have it accessible by any MS-DOS computer. If you only want to return the compressed data to its decompressed form and retain the data on the drive, then use the decompress feature.

When you delete a compressed drive, Windows 95 deletes the compressed volume file (CVF) that contains all the compressed data and application files. (The contents of the CVF file are what looks like a compressed disk drive.) The CVF has the name DRVSPACE.000 and is located on the host drive. (The file name extension is different for every file that DriveSpace creates. The first starts at 000, the second at 001, and so forth.) You shouldn't manually delete the DRVSPACE.000 file. Deleting the compressed drive is better.

In addition to deleting the CVF file, deleting a compressed drive also removes from the DRVSPACE.INI file the line ACTIVATE DRIVE= for the drive represented by the CVF. If you have only one compressed drive on your hard disk, then you will also be asked whether you want to delete the DriveSpace driver, DRVSPACE.BIN. You can delete this driver if you do not have other compressed drives on this drive.

Caution

When you delete a compressed drive, you lose all the information stored on that drive, so be sure that you have backed up or moved any files you need on this drive before deleting it.

Troubleshooting

An overzealous novice removed the system attribute from the DRVSPACE.000 file and deleted it. Is there a way to recover the data that was on the compressed drive?

If the user has not saved files to that disk after deleting DRVSPACE.000 the drive may be able to be recovered. Use the Recycle Bin to restore the deleted DRVSPACE.000 file; then exit Windows and restart.

To delete a compressed drive, follow these steps:

1. Open the DriveSpace window and select the compressed drive you want to delete from the Drives on This Computer list.

2. Choose Advanced, Delete.

3. When the confirmation message box appears, choose Yes.

4. A message box appears asking if you want to delete the DriveSpace driver. Choose Yes if this is the only compressed drive on your computer and you will not be using compressed floppy disks. Choose No if you have other compressed drives or if you will be using compressed floppy disks.

5. When the message box appears informing you that the operation is complete, choose OK.

6. You will be prompted to restart Windows 95 or continue. (If you are using floppy disks, you won't be prompted to restart Windows.) Switch to any open applications and save the documents, then choose Yes. If you choose No, you will not be able to change system settings, install applications, or use MS-DOS until you restart. (If you are able to, the system may not be stable.)

◀ See "Setting Up Your Floppy or Hard Disk to Read Compressed Files," p. 476

If you are in doubt about whether to delete the driver for DriveSpace, remember that it is much easier to reinstall than it is to deinstall the driver. You can remove it now and add it back at any time using the procedure to mount a compressed drive.

Adjusting the Size of the Free Space on a Compressed Drive

You can adjust the distribution of free space between a compressed drive and its host. When you increase the free space on the compressed drive, you decrease the free space on the host drive and vice versa. To adjust the free space on the compressed and host drives, follow these steps:

1. Open the DriveSpace window and select either the compressed drive or its host from the Drives on This Computer list.

2. Choose Drive, Adjust Free Space; the Adjust Free Space dialog box appears (see fig. 16.15).

3. Drag the slider to change the distribution of free space between the compressed and host drives. The pie charts will reflect the amount of free space and used space.

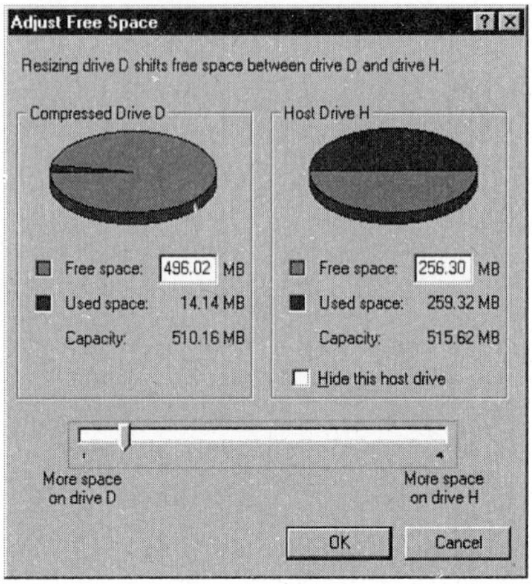

Fig. 16.15

Adjust the distribution of free space between a compressed drive and its host in the Adjust Free Space dialog box.

4. Choose OK.

   A message box shows you the amount of free space on the compressed and host drives when the operation is complete.

5. A Restart Computer dialog box displays asking you if you want to restart your computer. (This dialog box does not appear if you are doing this with floppy disks.) Choose Yes to restart, No to continue working.

   Do not set up new software, change system settings, or run MS-DOS programs until you restart your computer.

Troubleshooting

There seems to be enough space on the hard disk to store some very large video and sound files, but even after resizing the compressed drive there still isn't enough space.

Some files, such as application, video, and music files, may not compress very much. The estimated free space on a compressed drive however, is calculated from the average amount of compression for all files on the drive. As a consequence, files that look like they may fit, may not.

Changing the Estimated Compression Ratio for Your Compressed Drive

DriveSpace contains a command that enables you to change the estimated compression ratio. This does not change how tightly data is compressed on your hard drive. It is just an estimate used by Windows 95 to calculate how much free space remains on your hard drive. The remaining free space as calculated by the estimated compression ratio is then used in Windows 95 dialog boxes to give you an estimate of how much drive space remains. Changing the compression ratio to a larger number would not compress files tighter, but it would give you a very misleading idea of how much free space remains.

You may want to change the estimated compression ratio in order to see a more accurate calculation of the free space available on your compressed drive. There is a reason that you may be able to calculate this number more accurately than Windows 95. Windows 95 calculates the estimated compression ratio from an average of the actual file size and the compressed file size for all files on the drive. Everytime a file is saved or erased, Windows 95 recalculates the estimated compression ratio and then uses that number to calculate the estimated free space remaining.

The problem with accepting the estimated compression ratio is that Windows 95 has no idea what types of files you will be storing on the hard disk. Since you are familiar with the types of files you store, you may be able to estimate a better compression ratio. This in turn will give you a better idea of the amount of free space available.

To understand the problem, you must know that different files compress by different amounts. Files such as text files and some graphics files contain a lot of repetitive information that can be tightly compressed into a small space. Other files, such as an application's EXE files or a video's JPEG or MPEG files, have little room for compression and may not change significantly in size.

If you have just installed a lot of application files on a compressed drive with few data files, then Windows 95 will calculate a low compression ratio. Conversely, if your compressed drive has few application or multimedia files, then the estimated compression ratio will be higher. As long as you continue saving and removing the same type of files, Windows 95 will report a fairly accurate estimated free space. But if you change the type of files you save, the estimated free space will be wrong because the new files compress to a different amount.

If you will not be adding more application or multimedia files to your compressed drive, but you will be adding a lot more data files, then you may want to increase the estimated compression ratio to get a more accurate reading of free space. Conversely, a drive that has stored word processing files may have much less space available than it appears to have when you begin storing sound, video, and application files on it.

Tip

In general, do not change the compression ratio to more than a two to one, 2:1, ratio.

IV

Disks and Files

Caution

What you see is not necessarily what you get when dealing with compression ratios. Some files, such as EXE application files or JPEG and MPEG video files compress very little. This means that even though the estimated free space may be 15M, it's doubtful that 12M of JPEG, MPEG, or EXE files would fit because they do not compress as tightly as other files have.

To adjust the compression ratio, follow these steps:

1. Open the DriveSpace window and select the compressed drive whose compression ratio you want to adjust from the Drives on This Computer list.

2. Choose Advanced, Change Ratio; the Compression Ratio dialog box appears (see fig. 16.16).

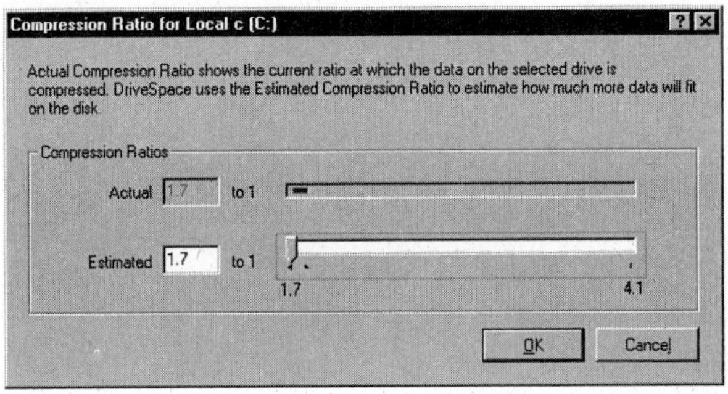

Fig. 16.16

Adjust the compression ratio of a compressed drive in the Compression Ratio dialog box.

3. Drag the Estimated Compression Ratio slider to adjust the compression ratio.

4. Click OK to begin the change. When the message box appears informing you that the operation is complete, choose OK.

Viewing the Properties of a Compressed Drive

You can view the properties of a compressed drive or its host using the Drive Properties command. You can find out the name of the compressed volume file and what drive it is stored on, the amount of free and used space on the drive, and the compression ratio if it is a compressed drive.

To view the properties of a drive, follow these steps:

1. Open the DriveSpace window and select the drive whose properties you want to view from the Drives on This Computer list.

2. Choose Drive, Properties. The Compression Properties sheet appears, as shown in figure 16.17.

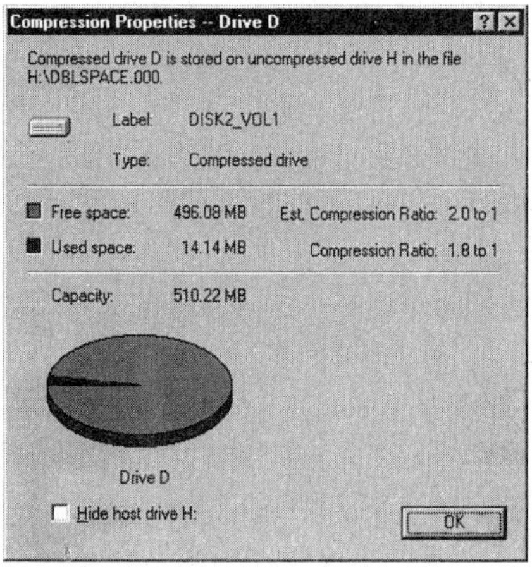

Fig. 16.17
View the properties of a compressed drive or its host in the Compression Properties sheet.

3. You can select the Hide Host Drive option to hide the display of this drive when the drive contents display in the Explorer or My Computer window and in some dialog boxes such as Open and Save As. If you select this option, a message box informs you that you will not be able to use the data or free space on the drive. Choose Yes to confirm that you want to hide the drive.

   You can use the DriveSpace Properties sheet to unhide the host drive if you change your mind at a later time.

4. Choose OK.

Monitoring Your System

Windows 95 comes with an application called System Monitor that enables you to monitor the resources on your computer. You can see if you have the System Monitor installed by opening the Start menu, clicking Programs, Accessories, System Tools, and checking for the System Monitor item. If you do not see it on the menu or if it does not start, then you need to rerun Windows 95 and reinstall the System Monitor. Appendix A describes how to install and reinstall Windows 95.

You can see information about the 32-bit file system, network clients and servers, and the virtual memory manager, among other things. Most of this information is highly technical in nature and useful only to advanced users. You can display the information in either bar or line charts or as numeric values. To open the System Monitor, open the Start menu; choose Programs, Accessories, System Tools, and then System Monitor. The System Monitor window appears, as shown in figure 16.18.

Fig. 16.18

Use the System Monitor to monitor the resources on your computer.

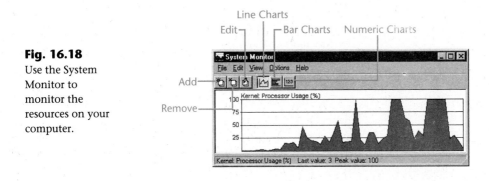

To monitor an item in System Monitor, follow these steps:

1. Select the item you want to monitor by choosing Edit, Add Item; alternatively, click the Add tool. The Add Item dialog box appears (see fig. 16.19).

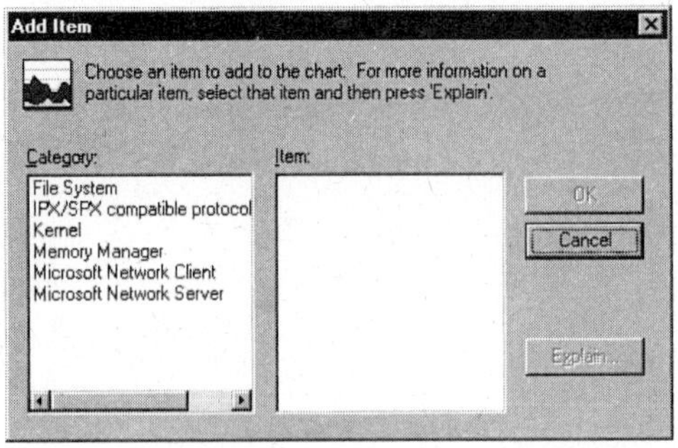

Fig. 16.19

Select the items you want to monitor in the Add Item dialog box.

You can obtain information on what an item is by selecting the item and clicking Explain. When you select an item in the right hand box the explain button becomes an option.

IV

2. Choose OK.

3. Repeat steps 1 and 2 to add additional items to the window.

To remove an item from the window, follow these steps:

1. Choose Edit, Remove Item; alternatively, click the Remove tool.

2. Select the item you want to remove and choose OK.

You can edit an item that is being monitored, changing its display color and the scaling used in its chart. To edit an item, follow these steps:

1. Choose Edit, Edit Item, or click the Edit tool, to display the Edit Item dialog box.

2. Select the item you want to edit and choose OK. The Chart Options dialog box appears, as shown in figure 16.20.

Fig. 16.20
Change the display of an item being monitored in the Chart Options dialog box.

3. Choose Change to change the color of the item.

4. Select Automatic to let System Monitor set the maximum value on the y-axis.

   or

   Select Fixed and type a value in the Value text box to set your own maximum value for the y-axis.

5. Choose OK.

You can display the items being monitored as either a line or bar chart or as a numeric value. To change the display, open the View menu and choose Line Charts, Bar Charts, or Numeric Charts; alternatively, click the appropriate tool on the toolbar.

Tip

Pressing Esc also will hide the title bar if pressed when the title bar is visible.

If you want the System Monitor window to stay on top of other windows, even when you are working in another program, open the View menu and choose Always on Top. This is handy if you want to monitor some resource as you work in a program. You can shrink the window so that it doesn't take up too much room. Choose the View, Always on Top command again when you don't want the System Monitor window to stay on top of other windows. You can also hide the title bar so that all the System Monitor window is devoted to displaying the chart: choose the View, Hide Title Bar command. To redisplay the title bar, double-click the chart or press Esc.

You can adjust the frequency at which the chart is updated by choosing the Options, Chart command and moving the slider to change the update interval. If you are on a network, choose File, Connect to connect to a different computer.

> **Note**
>
> You can quickly find out how much free disk space there is on a hard disk or floppy disk. Select the disk you want to check in either the Explorer or My Computer and choose the File, Properties command (alternatively, right-click the desired disk and choose Properties from the shortcut menu). The amount of free space on the disk is displayed in the Properties dialog box.

Improving Performance with Disk Defragmenter

Tip

To optimize the performance of your hard disk, use Disk Defragmenter on a regular basis to defragment your hard disk.

Information written to a hard disk is not necessarily stored in a *contiguous* (adjacent) block. Rather, fragments of information are more likely spread across the disk wherever the system can find room. The more you use the hard disk, the more fragmented the disk becomes. Obviously, the drive takes more time to hunt for information located in several places than it takes to fetch the same information from a single location. Because of this extra time, disk fragmentation can slow the computer's operation considerably.

The Windows Disk Defragmenter can significantly improve file access time by restructuring files into contiguous blocks and moving free space to the end of the disk.

To defragment a disk, follow these steps:

1. Open the Start menu and choose Programs, Accessories, System Tools, and then choose Disk Defragmenter. The Select Drive dialog box appears (see fig. 16.21).

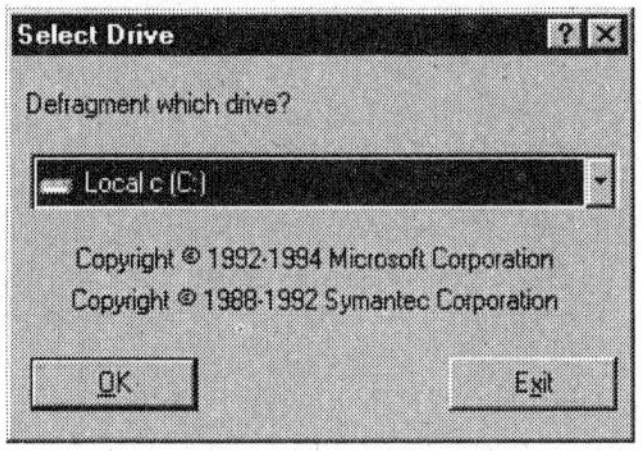

Fig. 16.21
Select the drive you want to defragment in the Select Drive dialog box.

2. Select the drive you want to defragment from the Defragment Which Drive drop-down list and choose OK.

   The Disk Defragmenter dialog box appears, as shown in figure 16.22. The percent fragmentation of the selected drive is displayed in the dialog box. You are also informed whether defragmentation will improve performance.

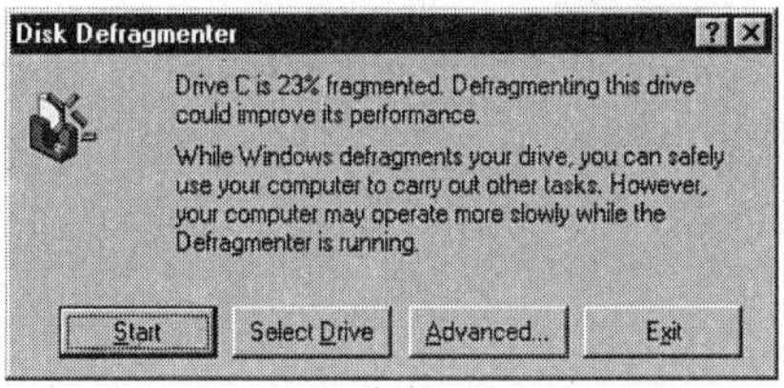

Fig. 16.22
The Disk Defragmenter dialog box tells you how fragmented your drive is and whether defragmenting it will improve its performance.

3. To change the Disk Defragmenter options, choose Advanced. The Advanced Options dialog box appears (see fig. 16.23). Use this dialog box to change the following options:

Option	Function
Full Defragmentation (Both Files and Free Space)	Defragments all the files on the selected disk.
Defragment Files Only	Defragments only the files on your hard disk, without consolidating the free space.
Consolidate Free Space Only	Only consolidates the free space on the selected disk without defragmenting the files.
Check Drive for Errors	Checks the files and folders on the drive for errors before defragmenting.

(continues)

Option	Function
This Time Only. Next Time, Use the Defaults Again	Uses the selected options for this defragment operation only.
Save These Options Use Them Every Time	Saves the selected options and uses them each time you run Disk Defragmenter unless you change them again.

Select the desired options and choose OK. You return to the Disk Defragmenter dialog box.

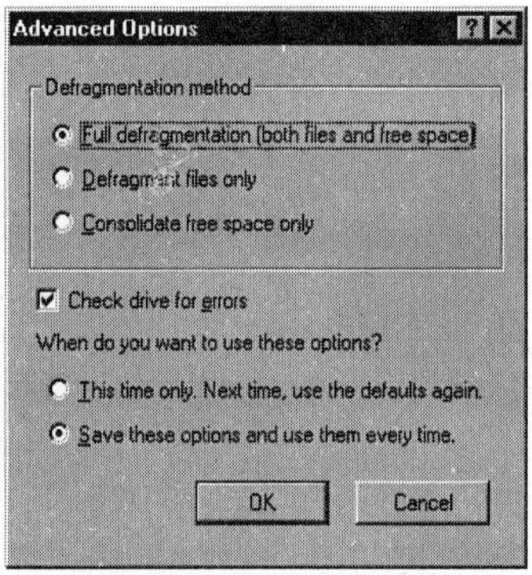

Fig. 16.23
Change the way Disk Defragmenter works in the Advanced Options dialog box.

4. Choose **S**tart. The progress of the defragmentation operation is displayed in the Defragmenting dialog box (see fig. 16.24).

5. When the defragmentation operation is complete, choose **E**xit to close the Disk Defragmenter, or choose **S**elect Drive to defragment another drive.

Defragmenting a hard disk can take a long time. Although you can continue working on your computer during the defragmentation operation, you will notice a significant slowdown in your computer's operation. For this reason, it is advisable to run the Disk Defragmenter during a time when you do not need to use the computer, for example, after you leave work for the day.

You can pause the defragmentation operation if you need to use your computer before defragmentation is completed and you don't want performance slowed down. Choose **P**ause from the Defragmenting dialog box to pause Disk Defragmenter. To resume defragmentation, choose Resume. You can also cancel the defragmentation operation by choosing **S**top. Choose Show

Details to open a window that displays the details of the defragmentation operation. To close the window, choose Hide Details.

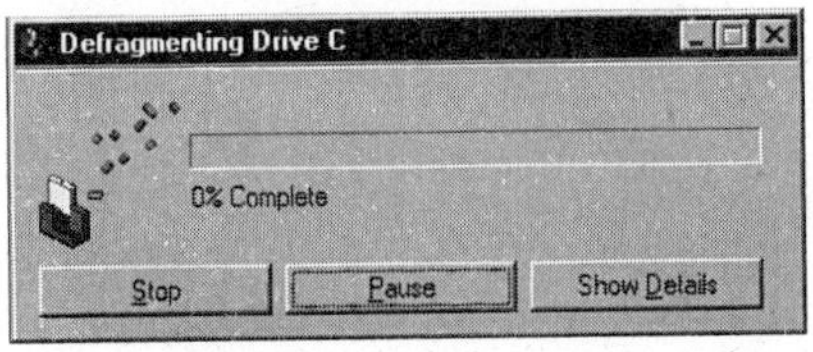

Fig. 16.24
Monitor the progress of the defragmentation operation in the Defragmenting dialog box.

Using ScanDisk to Check for Disk Damage

In an ideal world, you would never have to worry about errors occurring on your hard disk or floppy disks. This not being the case, Windows 95 comes with a program called ScanDisk you can use to check for, diagnose, and repair damage on a hard disk or floppy disk. Part of your routine hard disk maintenance, along with defragmenting your hard disk as described in the previous section, should be to periodically run ScanDisk to keep your hard disk in good repair.

In its standard test, ScanDisk checks the files and folders on a disk for logical *errors*; if you ask it to, ScanDisk also automatically corrects any errors it finds. ScanDisk checks for *cross-linked* files, which occur when two or more files have data stored in the same *cluster* (a storage unit on a disk). The data in the cluster is likely to be correct for only one of the files, and may not be correct for any of them. ScanDisk also checks for *lost file fragments*, which are pieces of data that have become disassociated with their files. Although file fragments may contain useful data, they usually can't be recovered and just take up disk space. You can tell ScanDisk to delete lost file fragments or save them in a file.

You also have the option of having ScanDisk check files for invalid file names and invalid dates and times. When a file has an invalid file name, you may not be able to open it. Invalid dates and times can cause problems when you use a backup program that uses dates and times to determine how current a file is.

You can run a more thorough test in which ScanDisk checks for both logical errors in files and folders and also scans the surface of the disk to check for physical *errors*. Physical errors are areas on your disk that are actually damaged and shouldn't be used for storing data. If ScanDisk finds bad sectors on your hard disk, any data in them can be moved to new sectors, and the bad sectors are marked so that data is not stored in them in the future.

To check a disk for errors, follow these steps:

1. Open the Start menu and choose Programs, Accessories, System Tools, and then choose ScanDisk. The ScanDisk window appears, as shown in figure 16.25.

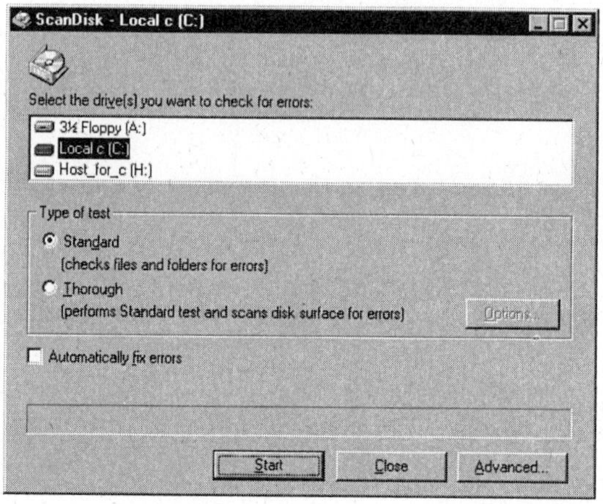

Fig. 16.25

Use ScanDisk to check your hard disk for logical and physical errors and repair any damage.

2. Select the drive you want to check in the Select the Drive(s) You Want To Check for Errors box.

3. To check only for logical errors in the files and folders on the selected disk, make sure that the Standard option is selected.

   To check for logical errors and to scan the disk for physical errors, select the Thorough option.

4. Click the Advanced button to change the settings used for checking files and folders for logical errors. The ScanDisk Advanced Options dialog box appears (see fig. 16.26). Use this dialog box to change the options in table 16.1.

Table 16.1 ScanDisk Advanced Options	
Option	**Function**
Display Summary Options	
Always	A summary with information about your disk and any errors found and corrected is displayed whenever you run ScanDisk.
Never	A summary is never displayed when you run ScanDisk.

Option	Function
Display Summary Options	
Only If Errors Found	A summary is displayed only if errors are detected.
Log File Options	
Replace Log	Saves the details of a ScanDisk session in a log file named SCANDISK.LOG in the top-level folder on drive C. Replaces any existing file with the same name.
Append to Log	Saves the details of a ScanDisk session, appending the information to the end of SCANDISK.LOG.
No Log	The results of the ScanDisk operation are not saved to a log file.
Cross-Linked Files Options	
Delete	Deletes cross-linked files when such files are found.
Make Copies	A copy is made of each cross-linked cluster for each of the cross-linked files.
Ignore	Cross-linked files are not corrected in any way. Using a cross-linked file may lead to further file damage and may cause the program using it to crash.
Lost File Fragments Options	
Free	Deletes lost file fragments, freeing up the space they use.
Convert to Files	Lost file fragments are converted to files, which you can view to see whether they contain data you need. Files are given names beginning with FILE (for example, FILE0001) and are stored in the top-level folder of the disk.
Check Files For Options	
Invalid File Names	Files are checked for invalid file names. Files with invalid file names sometimes cannot be opened.
Invalid Dates and Times	Files are checked for invalid dates and times, which can result in incorrect sorting and can also cause problems with backup programs.
Check Host Drive First	If the drive you are checking has been compressed using DoubleSpace or DriveSpace, ScanDisk checks the host drive for the compressed drive first. Errors on the host drive often cause errors on the compressed drive, so it is best to check it first.

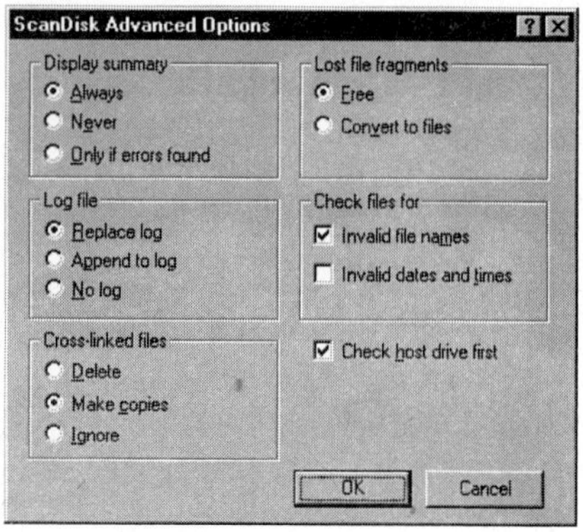

Fig. 16.26

You can change the settings ScanDisk uses to check files and folders for logical errors in the ScanDisk Advanced Options dialog box.

5. If you selected the Thorough option, choose Options to change the settings used to scan the disk for physical errors. The Surface Scan Options dialog box appears (see fig. 16.27). Use this dialog box to change the following options:

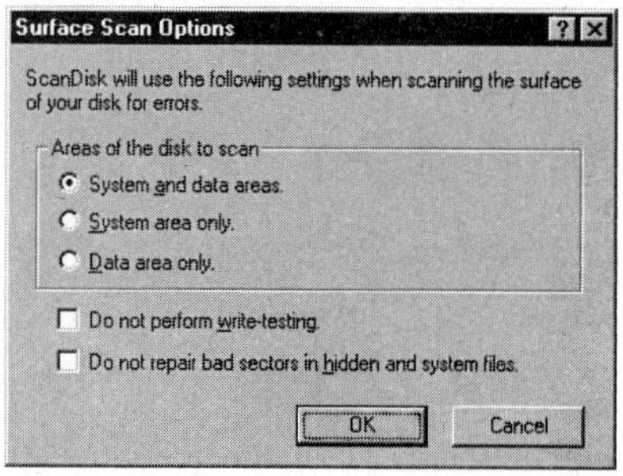

Fig. 16.27

You can change the settings ScanDisk uses to scan the disk for physical errors.

Option	Function
System and Data Areas	Scans the entire disk for physical damage.
System Area Only	Scans only the system area of the disk for physical damage. This is the disk area that contains files used to start the computer and hold the operating system.
Data Area Only	Scans only the data area of the disk for physical damage. The data area contains application and data programs. Use this if Windows behaves erratically even if you have reinstalled it.

Option	Function
Do Not Perform Write-Testing	If this option is not selected (the default), ScanDisk reads and writes every sector to verify both read and write functions. If this option is selected, ScanDisk does not write-verify the sectors.
Do Not Repair Bad Sectors in Hidden and System Files	ScanDisk will not move data from bad sectors in hidden and system files. Some programs look for hidden system files at specific locations and will not work if data in these files is moved.

6. Select the Automatically Fix Errors option if you want ScanDisk to auto-matically fix any errors it finds without first reporting the errors.

   If you don't select this option, ScanDisk informs you when it finds an error, and you can determine how ScanDisk fixes it.

7. Choose Start to begin the test. The progress of the test is displayed at the bottom of the ScanDisk dialog box. You can halt the test by choosing the Cancel button. If you told ScanDisk to scan your disk for physical errors, the test can take several minutes. When the test is complete, a summary report like the one in figure 16.28 may appear, depending on the options you selected in the ScanDisk Advanced Options dialog box. Click Close to close the Results dialog box.

8. Click Close to exit ScanDisk.

Fig. 16.28
The results of a ScanDisk opera-tion can be displayed in the ScanDisk Results dialog box.

◀ See "Improving
Performance
with Disk
Defragmenter,"
p. 486

Troubleshooting

Whenever a file is retrieved, the hard disk light seems to come on a lot. It even sounds like the hard disk is chattering. The more we use the computer the worse this problem gets. ScanDisk didn't show any problems with the disk.

The problem is probably not with the physical quality of your hard drive's magnetic surface, which is what ScanDisk checks. The problem is more likely that files on the hard disk are fragmented. Fragmented disks have pieces of files scattered all over the disk. Rather than being able to read a file at one location in one quick continuous movement, the read-head on the drive must skitter around on the disk searching for all the pieces that belong to a file. Once fragmenting is bad it gets worse, which is why your computer seems to be slowing down the more you use it. Windows comes with a defragmenting utility that will reorganize your files on the disk so they are contiguous and can be read quickly.

Improving Memory Use with Virtual Memory

Your computer has a certain amount of physical memory (RAM) installed. Typically, computers running Windows have at least 4M of RAM, and often 8M or more. The more memory you have, the more programs you can run at the same time and the faster your system operates. However, with Windows 95, you can use a special area of the hard disk as an extension of RAM, called *virtual memory*, to increase the amount of memory available to programs. Using virtual memory, you may be able to run more programs at the same time than is normally possible using only the RAM on the system.

When RAM is tight, Windows begins to move *pages* of code and data from RAM to the hard disk to make more room in RAM. Windows uses a *least-recently-used* technique to move pages of memory to the disk, selecting first the pages of code and data not recently accessed by a program. If a program requires a piece of data no longer in physical memory, Windows retrieves the information from disk, paging other information from memory to disk to make room. To programs running in Windows, no difference exists between RAM in the system and virtual memory on the disk.

When you install Windows 95, it automatically determines how much hard disk space to use for virtual memory, depending on the amount of free disk space. Windows 95 also automatically resizes virtual memory as needed. In most cases, you should let Windows determine the settings used for virtual memory on your computer. Unless you know what you are doing, changing the settings manually can adversely affect the performance of your computer. If you do want to specify your own virtual memory settings, follow these steps:

1. Open the Start menu and choose Settings, Control Panel.

2. Double-click the System icon to display the System Properties sheet; select the Performance tab.

3. Click the Virtual Memory tab to display the Virtual Memory dialog box shown in figure 16.29.

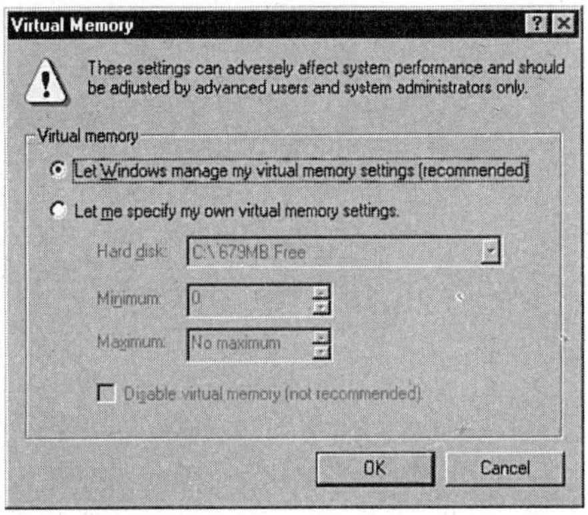

Fig. 16.29
You can let Windows manage your virtual memory settings or specify your own in the Virtual Memory dialog box. Microsoft recommends you let Windows manage virtual memory settings.

4. Select the Let Me Specify My Own Virtual Memory Settings option.

5. If you want to use a different hard disk for virtual memory than is already specified, select a new disk from the Hard Disk drop-down list. The amount of free space on the hard disk is displayed next to the drive letter.

6. Specify the minimum amount (in megabytes) of hard disk space you want Windows to use for virtual memory in the Minimum text box.

7. Specify the maximum amount of memory (in megabytes) you want Windows to use for virtual memory in the Maximum text box.

8. Choose OK.

The Virtual Memory dialog box contains a Disable Virtual Memory (Not Recommended) check box at the bottom. This turns off all use of virtual memory and is not recommended.❖

Chapter 17

Managing Your Files with Explorer

by Ron Person

The information you work with on your computer is stored in files. The programs you use to do your work and the documents you create with these programs are files. For this reason, it is essential that you learn how to work with and manage files. You need to know how to name and save files, as well as how to organize the files on your computer so that you can locate them when you need them. The Windows Explorer is a program that comes with Windows that has all the tools you need for managing your files.

The first part of this chapter explains how Windows organizes files. The remainder of the chapter shows you how to use the Windows Explorer to work with and manage the files on your computer. You also learn how to carry out many file-management tasks using My Computer.

In this chapter, you learn how to

- ■ Use files and folders to store data

- ■ Use the Explorer to view files and folders

- ■ Manage your files and folders

- ■ Protect documents

- ■ Synchronize files by using Briefcase

- ■ Register file types

- ■ Use the Explorer on a network

- ■ Use My Computer to manage files

◀ See "Formatting Disks," p. 461

> **Note**
>
> Before you can store information on a floppy disk, you must format the disk. To learn how to format a floppy disk, see Chapter 16, "Working with Disks and Disk Drives." Chapter 16 also describes how to create a system disk you can use to start your computer.

Understanding Files and Folders

Windows uses the file folder metaphor for organizing the files on your computer. You store the files you create with your programs, as well as the program files themselves, in folders. You store information in folders in the same way you store the paper files in folders in your office. And, just as you can create a filing system in your office to make it easy to locate your files whenever you need them, you can create a filing system on your computer to help you keep track of your files. This system consists of named folders in which you store your files, arranged in a way that makes sense to you.

You may, for example, want to create a folder for each of your clients. In each of your client folders you store any files associated with that client. This is an easy way to quickly locate all the information for a particular client, whether the information is recorded in a word processing document or in a spreadsheet file.

If you're a project manager, you can create a folder for each project in your department and then store any files related to a particular project in its folder. Or perhaps you think in terms of the tasks you perform—for example, completing budgets, writing reports, and sending out memos. In this case, you can create a folder for each type of task you deal with and store your files in the appropriate folders.

Tip

If you installed Windows 95 over Windows 3.1, File Manager is still available. You can continue to use File Manager or use the more powerful Explorer.

There is no limit to how creative you can be in setting up your filing system. With the skills you learn in this chapter, over time you can easily change your system and develop new ways of working. Creating new folders and moving files and folders is easy in Windows.

If you are familiar with the MS-DOS system for organizing files, a folder is analogous to a directory, and a folder within a folder is analogous to a subdirectory of a directory. If you like to think hierarchically, you can continue to visualize the organization of your files in exactly the same way as you did with DOS and earlier versions of Windows. The only difference is that instead of directories and subdirectories, you have folders and folders within folders. And, as you see in the next section, you can view the hierarchical arrangement of your folders by using the Explorer.

Many people don't like to think hierarchically, and they find the directory/ subdirectory metaphor confusing. If you're one of these people, simply imagine that your files are stored in folders, and that you can have folders within folders. This capability to have folders within folders enables you to refine your filing system, categorizing your files in a way that makes it easy for you to locate a file even if you haven't used it for a long time.

Using the Windows Explorer to View Files and Folders

Windows 95 comes with a new tool, the *Windows Explorer,* that you can use to see how the files and folders on your computer are organized. With the Explorer, you can view the hierarchical arrangement of the folders on your computer and can look into each folder to see what files are stored there. You can also use the Windows Explorer to reorganize and manage your files and folders. You can create new folders; move and copy files from one folder to another, to a floppy disk, or to another computer (if you are on a network); rename and delete files and folders; and perform other file-management tasks.

To open the Windows Explorer, follow these steps:

1. Open the Start menu and choose <u>P</u>rograms.

2. Choose Windows Explorer to open the Windows Explorer (see fig.17.1).

> **Note**
>
> Once you've opened the Windows Explorer, you can minimize it rather than close it. After minimizing the Explorer, you can reopen it instantly by clicking on its button in the taskbar.

Tip
The Explorer is a tool you will use frequently for working with your files and folders, so you may want to add it to the Start menu. "Customizing the Start Menu" in Chapter 5 shows how to add programs to the Start menu.

Tip
To quickly start Windows Explorer, right-click on Start, and then choose <u>E</u>xplore.

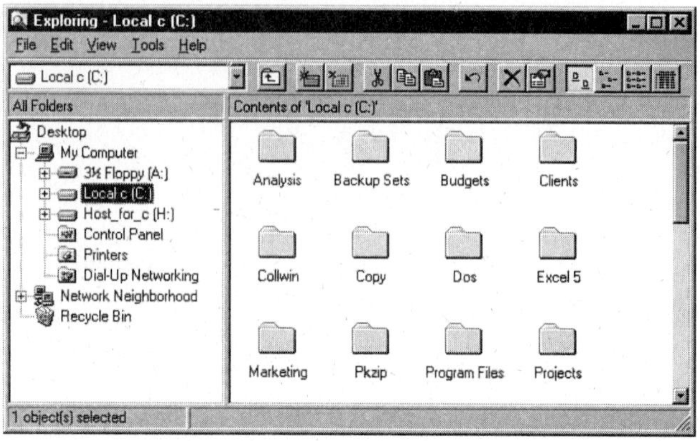

Fig. 17.1

Use the Windows Explorer to view the files and folders on your computer. This view shows the Windows Explorer with large icons and a toolbar.

Viewing Your Computer's Resources

◀ See "Managing Print Jobs," p. 173

◀ See "Managing Fonts in Windows 95," p. 223

One of the first tasks you will use the Windows Explorer for is to view the organization of the folders and files on your computer. The Explorer window is divided into two panes (refer to fig. 17.1). The left pane displays a hierarchical view of the organization of the folders on your computer. At the top of the hierarchy is the Desktop icon. This represents all the hard disks and resources available to your computer. Just beneath Desktop is My Computer, represented by an icon of a computer. Under My Computer are listed all the resources on your computer. These resources include floppy drives (represented by a floppy drive icon) and local hard drives (represented by a hard drive icon). Two special folders—the Control Panel and Printers folders—are used for managing the printers on your computer and for customizing your computer's settings. (You may also have other special folders listed here, depending on what optional components—such as dial-up networking—you have installed.)

▶ See "Deleting Files and Folders," p. 518

Two other folders that are branches off the Desktop icon are *Network Neighborhood* and the *Recycle Bin*. Network Neighborhood appears on your desktop if you are connected to a network. Open this folder to browse the computers in your workgroup or on your entire network. The Recycle Bin is where files are temporarily held when you delete them from a folder. By holding deleted files, you have the opportunity to recover them if you accidentally delete a file or change your mind.

Tip

If the toolbar is not displayed, choose View, Toolbar to display it.

Depending on the resources on your computer, you may see other folders displayed underneath My Computer. If you have a CD-ROM drive installed on your computer, for example, you will see its icon under My Computer. You may also see an icon for the *Briefcase* folder. The Briefcase is a special folder used for working on the same files at two locations and keeping them synchronized. See "Synchronizing Files" later in this chapter for more information on using the Briefcase.

Just beneath the menu bar is the toolbar. You can use the drop-down list at the left end of the toolbar to open the main folders in the Desktop and My Computer folders. This drop-down list shows all the drives on your computer, including network drives. If you scroll through the list, you'll also find your Control Panel, Briefcase (if installed), printers, Network Neighborhood, and Recycle Bin at the bottom of the list. This list also displays the folder hierarchy of the currently open folder, as shown in figure 17.2. You can, for example, quickly select the Recycle Bin folder without having to scroll to the bottom of the list in the left pane of the Explorer. To select from the list, click the down arrow next to the text box and click the folder you want to open.

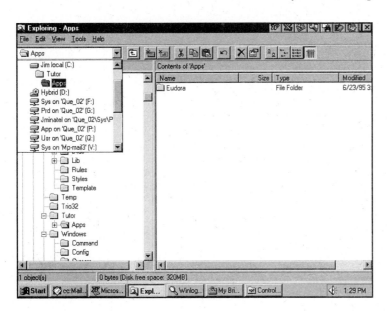

Fig. 17.2

The folders in the hierarchy above the current folder (Apps) are shown in addition to the list of drives and other main resources. The rest of the folder hierarchy is collapsed for quick access.

Browsing the Contents of a Folder

The right pane of the Explorer window displays the contents of whatever folder is selected in the left pane. If you select the Local C: drive under My Computer, for example, you see a list of all the resources on your computer, including the floppy and hard drives (see fig. 17.3). To display the contents of your hard disk, click its icon in the left pane. To see the contents of a folder, select the folder on the left and its contents are listed on the right. You can select a folder by clicking it with the mouse or by using the up and down arrow keys on the keyboard.

You can expand and collapse the hierarchical view to display more or less detail. If a plus sign (+) appears next to an icon in the left pane of the Explorer, additional folders are within this folder. To display these folders, click

Tip

You can jump to a specific folder without wading through the Explorer hierarchy by selecting Tools, Go To. Enter the path of the folder to go to and then click OK.

the plus sign (or double-click the folder). All the folders within this folder are displayed. Some of these folders, in turn, may have folders within them, which you can view using the same procedure. To hide the folders within a folder, click the minus sign (–) next to the folder (or double-click the folder). By collapsing and expanding the display of folders, you can view as much or as little detail as you want. Figure 17.3 shows an expanded view of the Local C: drive folder, which is collapsed in figure 17.1. Notice that some of the folders on the C drive have plus signs next to them, indicating that they contain additional folders.

Fig. 17.3
An expanded view of the Local C: drive in the My Computer folder, showing its folders. A plus sign indicates additional folders within a folder.

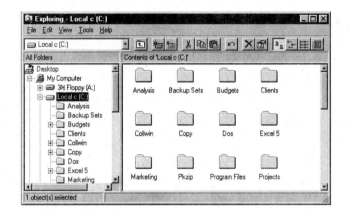

Understanding the File Icons in Windows

Windows uses various icons to represent folders and different types of files. In figure 17.4, folders within the Windows folder are represented with a folder icon. You can quickly display the contents of a folder within a folder by double-clicking its icon in the right pane of the Explorer. The easiest way to redisplay the original folder is to click the Up One Level button on the toolbar. (If the toolbar isn't displayed, choose View, Toolbar.) The Up One Level button is a picture of a folder with an up arrow in it. You also can redisplay the contents of the original folder by clicking its icon in the left pane of the window.

> **Note**
>
> Icons that have a small curved arrow in the lower left corner are shortcut icons. They are pointers to the actual file and folders that may be located in another folder.

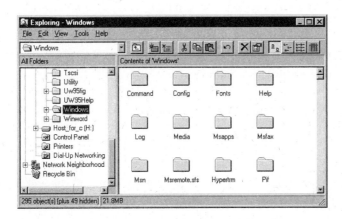

Fig. 17.4
Folder icons in the right pane of the Explorer represent folders within the folder selected in the left pane.

In addition to folders, many types of files can appear in the list of contents. Each type is represented by its own icon. Calendar files, for example, are represented by a calendar icon, and help files have their own special icon, as shown in figure 17.5. These icons are helpful for visually associating a file with its program. You can, for example, readily distinguish a file created in the Calendar program from a file created in Paint (see fig. 17.5).

Tip
You can open a file in its program by double-clicking the file's icon in the Explorer.

Calendar file

Paint file

Help file

Calendar program

Fig. 17.5
Different icons are used to represent different file types.

You may need to update the display of files and folders in the right pane of the Explorer. If you are viewing the contents of a floppy disk, for example, and you switch disks, you won't see the contents of the new disk unless you *refresh* the window. To refresh the window, click the icon for the folder you want to refresh—in this case, the icon for the floppy drive—in the left pane of the Explorer. You also can refresh by choosing <u>V</u>iew, <u>R</u>efresh or by pressing the F5 key.

Tip
Unlike in the Windows 3.1 File Manager, you don't need to refresh the Explorer to see changes to the disk contents that were made from the DOS prompt.

Customizing the Windows Explorer

Windows offers many options for changing how the Explorer window looks. You can change how folders and files are listed; hide or display the toolbar and status bar; sort the folder and file icons by name, type, size, or date; hide the display of certain types of files; and make other changes to the Explorer window. Any changes you make remain in effect until you make new changes, even if you close and reopen the Explorer. By customizing the Explorer window, you can make it look and feel the way you want, making it easier for you to view and manage the files on your computer.

> **Note**
>
> If you're used to opening multiple windows in the File Manager, note that you can't do that in the Explorer. You don't need to open multiple windows in the Explorer because you can drag from any file or folder in the right pane into any drive or folder in the left pane. You can display drives or folders in the left pane by clicking on their + sign without disturbing the contents of the right pane. If you ever need to have multiple windows in the Explorer, just open additional copies of the Explorer. You can then copy or move files between them.

> **Note**
>
> If you are wondering where the options for Backup and Drivespace from the Windows for Workgroups 3.11 File Manager are, these are both gone from Explorer. You can still access these features, however, as discussed in chapters 16 and 18. Also gone is the ability to customize the tools on the toolbar.

Changing the Width of Panes

You can use the mouse to change the size of the left and right panes of the Explorer. You can, for example, make the left pane wider if it isn't wide enough to show all the hierarchical levels (folders within folders within folders). To change the width of the two panes of the Explorer window, move the mouse pointer over the bar dividing the two panes (the mouse pointer changes to a double-headed arrow), hold down the left mouse button, and drag the bar left or right to adjust the size of the two panes to your liking. However, you can't hide one pane or the other completely as you could in the Windows 3.1 File Manager.

Changing the Status Bar

The status bar at the bottom of the Explorer window provides information on the item you select. If you select a folder, for example, you see information on the number of items in the folder and the total amount of disk space used by the folder. If you don't use it, you can hide the status bar to make more room for displaying files and folders. To hide the status bar, choose View, Status Bar. Choosing this command again displays the status bar.

Customizing the Toolbar

The tools on the toolbar are shortcuts for commands you otherwise access with menu commands. These tools are discussed in the appropriate sections in this chapter. If you don't use the toolbar, you can hide it by choosing View, Toolbar. To display the toolbar, choose the command again.

Changing How Folders and Files Are Displayed

When you first start using the Windows Explorer, you will notice that folders and files are represented by large icons in the right pane of the window, as in figures 17.4 and 17.5. You also can display files and folders as small icons, as a list, or with file details.

To change the way folders and files are displayed, follow these steps:

1. Open the View menu.

2. Choose one of the following commands:

Command	Result
Large Icons	Large icons
Small Icons	Small icons arranged in multiple columns
List	Small icons in a single list
Details	Size, type, and date modified

The currently selected option appears in the View menu with a dot beside it. Figure 17.6 shows files displayed using small icons.

Fig. 17.6
You can view
more files and
folders in the
Explorer when
you use small
icons.

Large Icons

Exploring - Windows
File Edit View Tools Help
Windows
All Folders	Contents of 'Windows'

Details

List

Small
Icons

295 object(s) (plus 49 hidden) 21.8MB

If the toolbar is displayed, you can also click one of the four tools at the right end of the toolbar to change how items are displayed. From left to right these are Large Icons, Small Icons, List, and Details.

When you select the <u>D</u>etails option, information on the size, type, and date the folder or file was last modified appears in columns next to the item in the list, as shown in figure 17.7. You can change the width of these columns by moving the mouse pointer over the line that divides the buttons at the top of each column (the mouse pointer changes to a double-headed arrow), holding down the left mouse button, and dragging the line to change the width.

Fig. 17.7
To see information
on the folders and
files in the Ex-
plorer window,
choose the Details
view. Resize col-
umns by dragging
the line between
header titles.

Exploring - C:\Program Files\Accessories
File Edit View Tools Help
Accessories
All Folders	Contents of 'C:\Program Files\Accessories'

Name	Size	Type	Modified
HyperTerminal		File Folder	4/12/95 4:14 PM
Log		File Folder	4/28/95 12:03 PM
Quick Back...		File Folder	5/10/95 3:52 PM
Accounting ...	9KB	File Set f...	6/9/95 1:59 PM
backup.cfg	24KB	CFG File	4/27/95 12:00 PM
Backup.exe	799KB	Application	4/27/95 12:00 PM
Downloads...	9KB	File Set f...	6/9/95 1:59 PM
Full System ...	9KB	File Set f...	6/9/95 2:24 PM
Mspaint.exe	299KB	Application	4/27/95 12:00 PM
mswd6_32...	159KB	WPC File	4/27/95 12:00 PM
Partial.Set	12KB	File Set f...	6/9/95 1:25 PM
Wordpad.exe	179KB	Application	4/27/95 12:00 PM
write32.wpc	61KB	WPC File	4/27/95 12:00 PM

13 object(s)   1.51MB [Disk free space: 717MB]

Arranging File and Folder Icons

If you select either the Large Icons or Small Icons option for displaying your files and folders, you can choose to let Windows automatically arrange the icons, or you can move the icons around to locate them wherever you want. To arrange the icons automatically, choose <u>V</u>iew, Arrange <u>I</u>cons. If a check mark appears next to the <u>A</u>uto Arrange command in the submenu, the command is already selected. If not, select <u>A</u>uto Arrange. The icons are now automatically arranged in a grid. If you want to arrange icons at any location in the right screen, deselect <u>A</u>uto Arrange. Some people prefer to have their files and folders arranged in an order of priority, frequency of use, or some other creative arrangement. Figure 17.8 shows PowerPoint files arranged in a circular pattern.

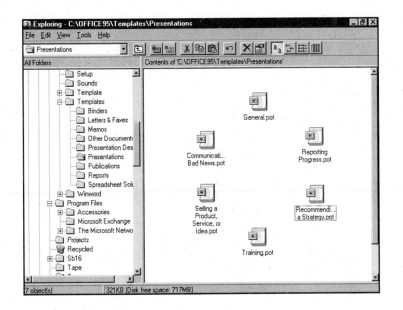

Fig. 17.8
When Auto Arrange is off, you can arrange icons in any way you want.

Tip
To automatically adjust column widths in the Detail view of the Windows Explorer to show the full content width, double-click the line between the column heads.

If the Auto Arrange command is not enabled, you can quickly arrange your icons in a grid by choosing <u>V</u>iew, Lin<u>e</u> Up Icons.

Sorting Files and Folders

You can sort the files and folders in the right pane of the Explorer by name, type, size, and date. To sort the items in the Explorer display, follow these steps:

1. Choose <u>V</u>iew, Arrange <u>I</u>cons.

2. Select one of the four options from the submenu.

Command	Result
by <u>N</u>ame	Sort folders and then files by their name
by <u>T</u>ype	Sort folders and then files by the type column (this may not be the same as file extension)
by <u>S</u>ize	Sort folders and then files by their size
by <u>D</u>ate	Sort folders and then files by their date

If you selected the Details option for displaying your folders and files, you can quickly sort the list of items by name, size, type, and date modified by clicking the button at the top of the column you want to sort by. Click Size, for example, to sort the list of items by size.

Changing Other View Options

You can change several other options in the Options dialog box. To change these options, follow these steps:

1. Choose <u>V</u>iew, <u>O</u>ptions to display the Options dialog box (see fig. 17.9).

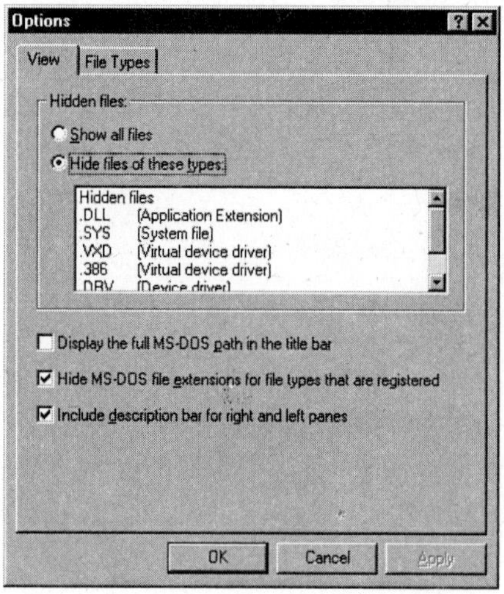

Fig. 17.9
You can change several options on the View page of the Options dialog box.

2. Select <u>S</u>how All Files to list all file types in the Explorer window.

   or

   Select Hide Files of These <u>T</u>ypes to hide the display of several types of system files.

Hiding these files, which you normally don't have to deal with, shortens the list of items displayed for some folders, and also prevents you and other users from accidentally deleting or moving crucial system files.

3. Select the Display the Full MS-DOS Path in the Title Bar option if you want to see the full DOS path for the folder selected in the left pane.

4. Select the Hide MS-DOS File Extensions for File Types that Are Registered option if you don't want the extensions for files associated with a particular program to be displayed.

   In Windows, a file's icon indicates what program it is associated with, if any. A file created in Calendar, for example, which has the MS-DOS file extension of CAL, is depicted with a Calendar icon. For this reason, you can determine a file's association by its icon and no longer need to see the file's extension. You have the option, therefore, of not displaying the extension in the list of files.

5. Select the Include Description Bar for Right and Left Panes option to display a descriptive bar at the top of the right and left panes of the Explorer window. The Description Bar appears above the panes and shows you such information as the drive letter and path name for the current view.

6. Click OK when you have finished making the selections you want.

Tip

To keep the list of file names in the Explorer manageable and easy to read, limit file names to about 75 characters.

Working with Long File Names

File and folder names help you organize and remember the contents of files and folders. Windows gives you the capability to type file and folder names up to 255 characters long and include spaces. This makes understanding file and folder names much easier than in older versions of Windows or DOS.

Another improvement is that you can now retype a file or folder name without having to display a dialog box—you just click on a name and edit or retype it.

Both of these improvements do not restrict your ability to use Windows files with older Windows or DOS systems that do not use long file names. The file names are compatible.

Tip

If you're using a keyboard, you can rename a file or folder by selecting it and then either choosing <u>F</u>ile, Re<u>n</u>ame, or pressing F2.

Renaming Files and Folders

As part of your efforts to keep the files and folders on your computer organized, you may want to rename a file or folder. This is easy to do in the Windows Explorer.

To rename a file or folder, follow these steps:

1. Click the file or folder to select it.

2. Click the name (not the icon) for the file or folder.

   Notice that a box surrounds the name and a blinking insertion point appears.

   > **Caution**
   >
   > If you accidentally double-click the file name, the program for that file opens and loads the file. To return to naming the file, close the program and click once on the file name.

3. Type the new name and press Enter.

 If you change your mind while typing a new name, just press Esc to return to the original name. If you have already pressed Enter and the file has been renamed, click the Undo button in the toolbar, choose <u>E</u>dit, <u>U</u>ndo, or press Ctrl+Z.

> **Caution**
>
> If you change the three-letter DOS file extension for a name, you will see a Rename alert box with this message: If you change a file name extension, the file may become unusable. Are you sure you want to change it? This box warns you that by changing the extension you will not be able to double-click the file and open its program. You can still open the file from within the application by choosing <u>F</u>ile, <u>O</u>pen.

Using Long File Names with Older Windows and DOS Systems

Folders and files with long names can be used on older Windows and DOS systems. The *FAT (File Allocation Table)*, an area on the disk that stores file information, has been especially modified to store both old-style 8.3 file names as well as long file names.

Windows 3.1 used an 8.3 file name convention, where eight characters were used for the first part of a file name, a period was inserted to separate the parts of the file name, and then three letters were used for a file's extension. The file extension usually indicated the type of data in the file and the application that created the file.

Caution

Beware of using MS-DOS based or previous Windows versions of file management software or file utilities with files that have long file names. The software or utilities will probably not correctly recognize long file names and will destroy the long file names. The data in the files may remain usable, however.

In Windows 95, you can have file and folder names up to 255 characters long, and the names can include spaces. This long file name is stored in an extended location in the FAT of the disk. This extended location does not hamper the normal 8.3 name also stored in the FAT.

Caution

Long file names cannot use the following characters:

/ \ : * ? " < > |

When you use a long file name, Windows automatically creates a file name fitting the 8.3 convention. This 8.3 file name is saved in its normal location in the FAT so that older Windows and DOS systems can still use the 8.3 file name.

You can see the MS-DOS file name that will be used for a file by right-clicking on the file name and choosing Properties. Figure 17.10 shows the Properties sheet for that file. The long file name is shown at the top of the box; the MS-DOS name appears near the middle.

Some of the rules involved in converting long file names to 8.3 file names are as follows:

- Blank spaces are deleted before truncating long file names.

- File names where the first characters fit in eight characters or less are left unchanged.

■ File names involving multiple periods, such as Proposal.Hodgkins.DOC, will use the file name to the left of the first period and the extension to the right of the last period.

■ File names longer than eight characters but having a first word that is eight characters long and is followed by a space use the first word as the file name.

■ File names that are created by truncating long file names end with ~#, where # is a number.

■ No truncated file name will duplicate a file name existing in the same directory. ~# will be placed as the seventh and eighth characters and the # will be a number used to differentiate files with the same names.

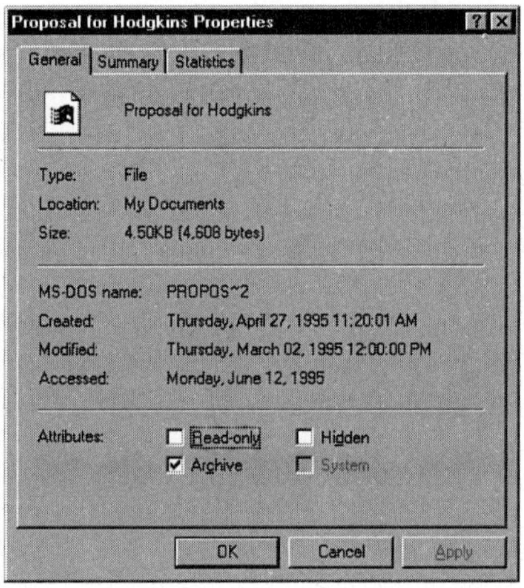

Fig. 17.10
Find out about a file by right-clicking its name and then choosing Properties.

If you often exchange files with someone who uses an older version of DOS or Windows, try to use 8-character file names and the naming conventions you adopted with Windows 3.1 within your long file names. For example, advbgt- Advertising Budget.xls will be easier to identify when it is shortened to an 8.3 file name (advbgt~1.xls) than Advertising Budget.xls (advert~1.xls).

> **Note**

If you use a DOS command from the command prompt, such as `dir` to list a directory containing files with long names, you see the normal file information as well as the long file names. The long file name is displayed in the far right column when using the DOS `dir` command.

Managing Your Files and Folders

You can do much more with the Windows Explorer than display files and folders. The Explorer is an essential tool for managing the files and folders on your computer. You can use the Explorer to create new folders, move folders from one location to another, copy and move files from one folder to another, and even move files from one disk drive to another. You can also use the Explorer to delete and rename files and folders. The Windows Explorer can become your office assistant, helping you keep your files in good order so that you can use your computer more efficiently.

Selecting Files and Folders

Before you learn how to manage files and folders, you need to learn how to select them. Selecting a single file or folder is easy. You simply click on the file or folder with the mouse or use the up- and down-arrow keys on the keyboard. The selected file is highlighted.

You can also select multiple files and folders. This is extremely useful when you want to move or copy more than one file or folder at once. You can, for example, select several files in a list at once, and then copy them to a floppy disk to back them up.

To select more than one file with the mouse, click the first file; hold down the Ctrl key and click on each additional file you want to select. To deselect a file, continue holding down the Ctrl key and click a second time on the file. To quickly select a group of contiguous files, select the first file in the group, hold down the Shift key, and select the last file in the group. All the files between the first and last file will also be selected. Another way to select a group of contiguous files is to drag a box around the group of files with the mouse.

If your files are arranged free form, you may find it convenient to select groups of files by dragging a rectangle around them using the mouse. Figure 17.11 shows how you can click and drag a rectangle around multiple icons. All the icons within the rectangle will be selected. Once they are selected, you can deselect or select additional files by holding down Ctrl and clicking on icons.

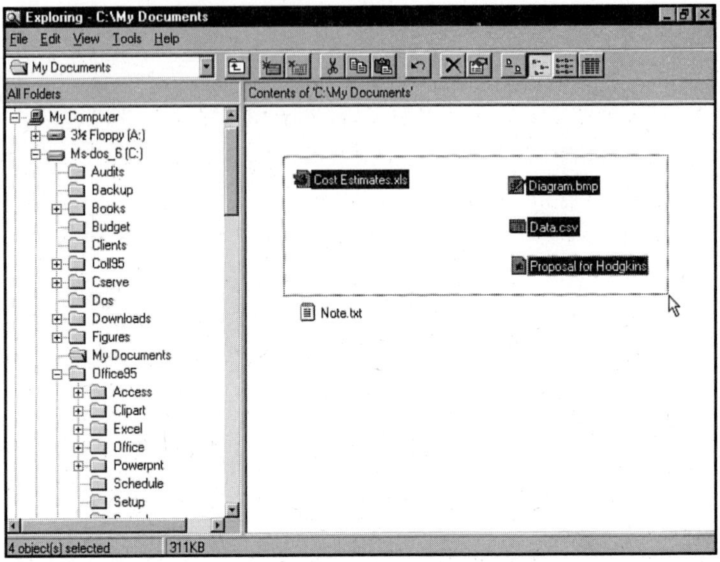

Fig. 17.11

Drag a rectangle around the group of file icons you want to select.

You can also select multiple files with the keyboard. To select multiple adjacent files, press Tab to move to the right pane and then press the down-arrow key to move to the first file. Then hold down the Shift key while pressing the down-arrow key to move to the last file you want to select. To select nonadjacent files, select the first file, hold down the Ctrl key, use the arrow keys to move to the next file to be selected, and press the space bar. While you continue to hold down the Ctrl key, move to each file you want to select and press the space bar. To deselect a file and retain the other selections, hold down the Ctrl key, use the arrow key to move to the file, and press the space bar.

To select all the files and folders displayed in the right pane, choose Edit, Select All (or press Ctrl+A). If you want to select all but a few of the files and folders in the right pane, select the files and folders you don't want to select; then choose Edit, Invert Selection.

To cancel the selections you have made, simply select another file or folder by using either the mouse or the keyboard.

Creating New Folders

You can create as many folders as you want to organize the files on your computer. As you produce more and more files with the programs on your computer, you will probably want to develop a filing system that helps you keep track of those files, just as you do with the paper files in your office. The more files you create, the more you may need to categorize those files to make them easy to locate.

Folders are the key to organizing your files. For example, you may start off with a file where you keep all your business letters. Over time, this folder will fill up with so many files that it becomes difficult to locate a file. At that point, it makes sense to subcategorize those files in some way—for example, by client or by company—and to create a folder for each of those categories. You can use the Windows Explorer to create these new folders. In the next section, "Moving and Copying Files and Folders," you learn how to move files from one folder to another.

To create a new folder, follow these steps:

1. Select the folder in the left pane of the Windows Explorer in which you want to create a new folder.

2. Choose File, New, Folder.

    A new folder appears in the right pane of the Explorer, ready for you to type in a name.

3. Type a name for the folder and press Enter.

Folders can use long names just like files. Folder names can be up to 255 characters long and can include spaces. They can't use these characters:

    \ ? : " < > |

Moving and Copying Files and Folders

As essential task when managing the files on your computer is moving and copying files and folders. If you create new folders to break the files in an existing folder into subcategories, you need to move each file from the original folder into its new folder. You may also want to move entire folders from one folder to another. Or you may want to copy files from your hard disk onto a floppy disk to back them up or transfer them to another computer. By using the Explorer and the mouse, you can quickly move and copy files and folders without ever touching the keyboard.

You can use two approaches for moving and copying files and folders. You can either use the Cut or Copy commands or use the mouse to drag-and-drop the files.

To move or copy files by using the menu, follow these steps:

1. Select the files or folders you want to move in the right pane of the Windows Explorer.

2. To move the items, choose <u>E</u>dit, Cu<u>t</u>; click the right mouse button on the selected items to display the shortcut menu and click Cu<u>t</u>; click the Cut button on the toolbar; or press Ctrl+X.

   or

   To copy the items, choose <u>E</u>dit, <u>C</u>opy; click the right mouse button on the selected items to display the shortcut menu and click <u>C</u>opy; click the Copy button on the toolbar; or press Ctrl+C.

3. In the left pane of the Explorer, select with the right mouse button the folder that will contain the moved or copied items and choose <u>P</u>aste; click the Paste button on the toolbar; or press Ctrl+V.

   You may have to scroll the folders in the left pane to make the new folder visible.

To move or copy files using the drag-and-drop method, follow these steps:

Tip

Drag selected items to the destination folder with the right mouse button. When the shortcut menu appears, click Move Here to move items or Copy Here to copy items to the new location.

1. Select the files or folders you want to move in the right pane of the Windows Explorer.

2. If the folder to which you want to move the selected items is not visible in the left pane of the Explorer, use the scroll bar to scroll it into view. If you need to display a subfolder, click on the + sign next to the folder containing the subfolder.

3. To move the selected items, drag the selected items to the new folder in the left pane of the Explorer.

   or

   To copy the selected items, hold down the Ctrl key and drag the selected items to the new folder in the left pane of the Explorer.

   A plus sign (+) appears beneath the mouse pointer when you hold down the Ctrl key, indicating that you are copying the files.

   Make sure that the correct folder is highlighted before you release the mouse button.

◀ See "Creating Shortcut Icons on the Desktop to Start Programs," p. 68

If you attempt to drag-and-drop a program file to a new folder, Windows creates a shortcut for that program in the new location. This is to prevent you from inadvertently moving a program file from its original folder. When you attempt to drag a program file, an arrow appears beneath the mouse pointer, indicating that you are about to create a shortcut for that program.

Note

If you routinely copy or move files to particular folders or a disk drive, you can create a shortcut for the folder or drive on your desktop. Then you can quickly drag-and-drop files onto the shortcut icon rather than have to scroll to the folder or drive in the Explorer. To create a shortcut for a folder (or drive), select the folder (or drive) in the Explorer, drag it with the right mouse button onto your desktop, and release the mouse button. Choose the Create Shortcut(s) Here command. You can now drag-and-drop files onto this shortcut icon to copy or move files to this folder (or drive).

Copying Disks

At times, you may want to make an exact copy of an entire floppy disk. This is easy to do in either the Explorer or My Computer.

You can copy from one floppy disk to another using the same drive, but both disks must have the same storage capacity. The disk you copy onto will be erased in the process.

To copy a disk, follow these steps:

1. Insert the floppy disk you want to copy.

2. Right-click on the disk in My Computer or in the left pane of the Explorer window.

3. Choose Copy Disk from the shortcut menu. This opens the Copy Disk dialog box shown in figure 17.12.

Tip
To quickly move selected items to a floppy disk, click the selected items with the right mouse button. Click Send To and then click the disk drive to which you want to send the selected files from the submenu.

Tip
The right mouse button has become invaluable in Windows 95. Try right-clicking on different parts of your screen to learn about tasks you can complete using the shortcut menus.

Fig. 17.12
The Copy Disk dialog box shows the selected drives for the copy operation.

If you have only one drive of this size, that drive will be highlighted for both the Copy From and Copy To areas of the dialog. If you have another drive of this same size, it will be listed as well, and you can select it to copy from drive to drive.

4. Choose Start.

5. If you are using the same drive for the master and the copy, you will be prompted to switch floppy disks when necessary.

6. When the disk is duplicated, you can copy another disk by choosing <u>S</u>tart, or choose <u>C</u>lose if you are done.

Copying disks is much faster in Windows 95 than in prior versions of Windows because of the addition of a high-speed floppy driver. If you frequently copy disks, you will notice the speed improvement.

Deleting Files and Folders

Inevitably, the time will come when you will want to delete a file or folder. This may be because you no longer need the file, or maybe you've created several new folders to subcategorize the files in an existing folder, and you want to delete the original folder after you move the files to their new locations. Deleting files and folders is an essential part of keeping your computer from getting cluttered with excessive and unnecessary files and folders.

Tip
If you realize right away that you have accidentally deleted a file or folder, choose <u>E</u>dit, <u>U</u>ndo Delete to restore the files. Press F5 to refresh the file listing and see the restored file or folder.

You must delete files and folders with care so that you don't accidentally delete a file that you still need. Fortunately, Windows now has a folder called the Recycle Bin, where deleted files are temporarily stored until you empty it. You can restore files from the Recycle Bin if you change your mind or accidentally delete a file.

Caution

Files deleted from a floppy disk are not sent to the Recycle Bin. Once you delete them, they cannot be restored.

To delete a file or folder, follow these steps:

1. Select the file or folder you want to delete.

   You can select multiple files or folders by using the techniques described in "Selecting Files and Folders" earlier in this chapter.

2. Click the selection with the right mouse button and click <u>D</u>elete.

   or

   Choose <u>F</u>ile, <u>D</u>elete (or press the Delete key or click the Delete button on the toolbar).

3. Click <u>Y</u>es when the Confirm File Delete dialog box appears (see fig. 17.13). Or click <u>N</u>o if you want to cancel the file deletion.

   If you are deleting multiple files, Explorer displays the Confirm Multiple File Delete dialog box.

Fig. 17.13
The Confirm File
Delete dialog box
gives you a chance
to check your
decision before
deleting a file.

IV

Disks and Files

Caution

If you delete a folder, you also delete all the files and folders contained in that folder. The Confirm Folder Delete dialog box reminds you of this. Be aware of what you are doing before you delete a folder.

You also should be careful not to accidentally delete a program file. If you attempt to delete a program file, the Confirm File Delete message box warns you that you are about to delete a program. Click No if you don't mean to delete the program, but other selected files will be deleted.

Note

To archive files to a floppy disk before you delete them, select the files, click the selected files with the right mouse button, and click Send To. Click the correct floppy drive to copy the files to the floppy disk. Now click the selected files with the right mouse button and click Delete.

▶ See "Backing Up Files," p. 559

Note

You can delete files and folders by dragging them onto the Recycle Bin icon on the desktop and dropping them.

When deleting some files, you may see a message warning you that the file is a system, hidden, or read-only file. System files are files needed by Windows 95 to operate correctly and should not be deleted. Hidden and read-only files may be needed for certain programs to work correctly, or they may just be files that you have protected with these attributes to prevent accidental deletion. Before deleting any of these file types, you should be certain that your system does not need them to operate correctly.

▶ See "Viewing and Changing the Properties of a File or Folder," p. 529

Restoring Deleted Files

Deleted files are moved to a folder called the Recycle Bin. You can open this folder just as you do any other folder and select a file and restore it to its original location. You can also move or copy files from the Recycle Bin to a new location, in the same way you learned how to move and copy files from other folders. The Recycle Bin provides you with the comfort of knowing that you have a second chance if you inadvertently delete a file or folder.

To restore a deleted file or folder, follow these steps:

1. Double-click the Recycle Bin icon on the desktop to open the Recycle Bin window, as shown in figure 17.14.

Fig. 17.14

Select files to restore in the Recycle Bin.

2. Select the file or files you want to restore.

   You can use the techniques described in the "Selecting Files and Folders" section to select multiple files.

3. Click the selected files with the right mouse button and click Restore, or choose File, Restore.

   The files are restored in the folders from which they were deleted. If the folder that a file was originally in has been deleted, the folder also is restored.

◀ See "Moving and Copying Files and Folders," p. 515

You can also restore a file to a different folder than the one it was deleted from. The easiest way to do this is to use the Explorer. Open the Recycle Bin folder in the Explorer, select the files you want to restore, and use one of the techniques discussed earlier in this chapter.

Emptying the Recycle Bin

Periodically, you may want to empty the Recycle Bin to free up space for more files. To empty the Recycle Bin, follow one of these procedures:

- If the Recycle Bin is already open, choose File, Empty Recycle Bin.

- Click the Recycle Bin icon on the desktop with the right mouse button and click Empty Recycle Bin.

Be aware of the fact that once you have emptied the Recycle Bin, you can no longer recover the deleted files and folders that were stored there.

You can also delete selected files from the Recycle Bin. To delete selected files from the Recycle Bin, follow these steps:

1. Open the Recycle Bin and select the files you want to delete.

2. Click the selected files with the right mouse button and click Delete.

3. Choose Yes to confirm the deletion.

Caution

The Recycle Bin can be a lifesaver if you accidentally delete a critical file. But don't forget to delete confidential files from the Recycle Bin so that others can't retrieve them.

Changing the Properties of the Recycle Bin

The Recycle Bin has a couple of properties that you can change. You can change the amount of disk space used for the Recycle Bin, and you can choose to have files permanently purged when deleted rather than be stored in the Recycle Bin.

To change the size of the Recycle Bin, follow these steps:

1. Right-click the Recycle Bin icon on the desktop or in the Explorer and click Properties.

   The Recycle Bin Properties sheet appears, as shown in figure 17.15.

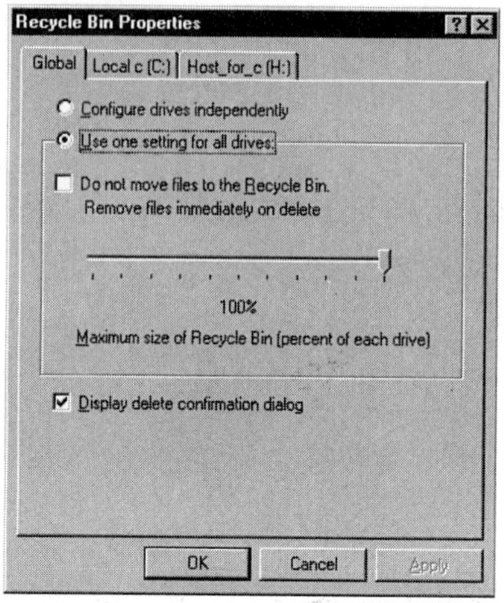

Fig. 17.15

Change the size of the Recycle Bin on the Recycle Bin Properties sheet.

2. Select the Configure Drives Independently option if you want to change the Recycle Bin size separately for each drive.

   or

   Select the Use One Setting for All Drives option if you want to use the same size Recycle Bin for all drives.

3. Drag the slider to change the maximum size of the Recycle Bin, as a percentage of the total disk size.

4. Click OK.

If you don't want to use up disk space storing deleted files, you can tell Windows to purge all files when they are deleted instead of storing them in the Recycle Bin. To purge all files when deleted, follow these steps:

1. Right-click the Recycle Bin icon on the desktop or in the Explorer and click Properties.

2. Select the Purge Files Immediately on Delete option.

3. Click OK.

When you select this option and delete a file, the Confirm File Delete dialog box warns you that the file will not be moved to the Recycle Bin.

> **Note**
>
> You can turn off the confirmation message for the Recycle Bin by deselecting the Display Delete Confirmation Dialog check box on the Recycle Bin Properties sheet.

Finding Files

Despite your best efforts to carefully organize your files, there inevitably comes a time when you can't locate a file you want to use. Windows comes with a tool to help you out when this happens. If you are familiar with the Search command from the Windows 3.1 File Manager, you should be impressed by the new features added for finding files in Windows 95.

The Find tool enables you to look for a specific file or group of related files by name and location. When searching by name, it's no longer necessary to use "wild cards" to specify your search, although you can still use them to fine-tune a search. In addition to this improvement, you can search by date modified, file type, and size. The most powerful new feature allows you to search by the text contained in the file or files. If you ever need to look for a file and can remember a key word or phrase in it but don't know the name of the file, this will be a real time-saver.

To find a file or group of related files, follow these steps:

1. Open the Start menu, choose Find, and then choose Files or Folders.

   or

   In the Explorer, choose Tools, Find, Files or Folders.

   The Find dialog box appears (see fig. 17.16).

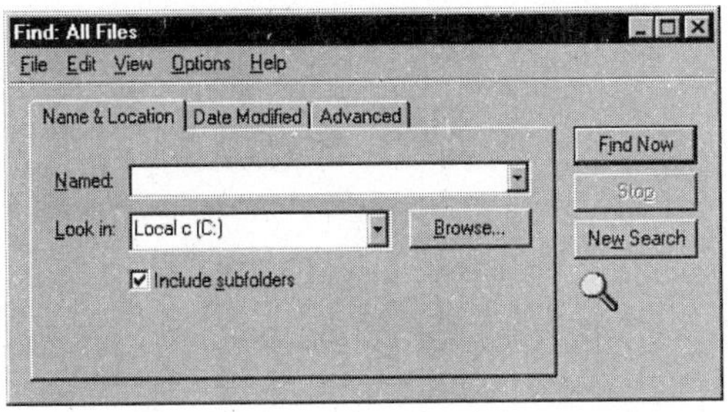

Fig. 17.16
Specify information about files you are searching for in the Find dialog box.

2. If you know the name of the file, type it in the Named text box. If you don't know the complete name of the file, just type whatever portion of file name you do know. Windows 95 will find all files that have these characters anywhere in the name.

   You can also use wild cards to look for all files of a particular type. (You could also use the Type criteria discussed in step 6 to limit files by type.) The following are some examples of how to use wild cards to look for groups of related files:

Entry	What It Finds
*.xls	Files with XLS extension (Excel worksheet files)
d*.xls	Excel worksheet files with file names beginning with the letter d
report??.txt	TXT files beginning with file names starting with *report*, followed by two more characters

   To reuse the same search criteria as one used previously, click the arrow at the right end of the Named text box and select the name search criteria you want to use from the list.

Tip
To search an entire drive, select the drive letter from the drop-down list and select Include Subfolders.

3. Specify where Find should look for the file in the Look In text box. You can type a path name in the text box, select from the entries in the drop-down list, or click the Browse button to select the location to which you want to restrict the search.

   Select the Include Subfolders option if you want to include the subfolders of whatever folders you selected in the search.

4. To limit the search to files created or modified within a specific time period, click the Date Modified tab (see fig. 17.17).

   You can restrict the search to files created or modified between two specified dates, or you can search for files created or modified during a specified number of months or days prior to the current date.

5. Click the Advanced tab to refine your search even more (see fig. 17.18).

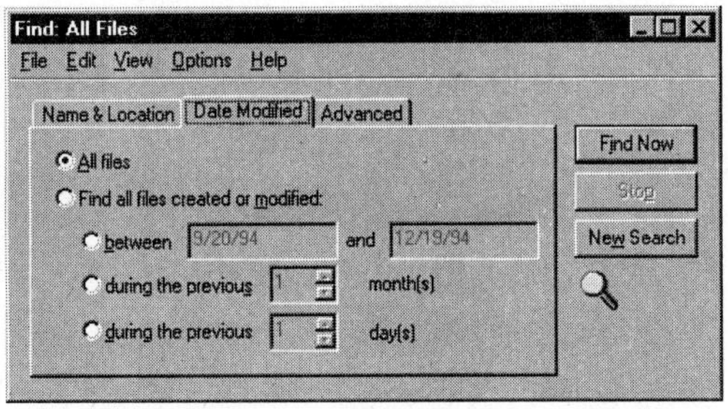

Fig. 17.17
You can narrow your search to a specified time period by using options on the Date Modified page.

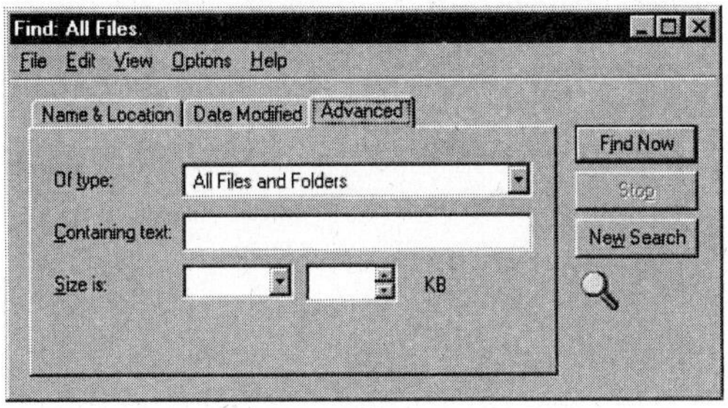

Fig. 17.18
Restrict your file search to files containing specific text or files of a specific size on the Advanced page of the Find dialog box.

6. Select a file type from the Of Type drop-down list to restrict the search to a specific file type. The types listed here are the registered file types discussed in "Registering Files to Automatically Open an Application" later in this chapter. These include document types created by application programs, as well as various types of files needed by Windows such as icons, control panels, and fonts.

7. Enter a text string in the Containing Text text box to search for files containing a specific string of text. If you enter several words separated by spaces, Windows treats the entry as a phrase and finds only documents containing those words in that order.

8. Specify the size of the file in the Size Is box. You can specify that the file be exactly a particular file size, or at least or at most a specified size. Select from the drop-down list the option to use, and then specify a size in the Size Is box.

9. When you have finished setting up your search parameters, click the Find Now button.

The Find dialog box expands at the bottom to show the results of the search (see fig. 17.19). If your search parameters were very specific, the search may take a few moments, especially if you told Find to look for files with a specific text string. All files matching the search specifications are listed, along with their location, size, and file type.

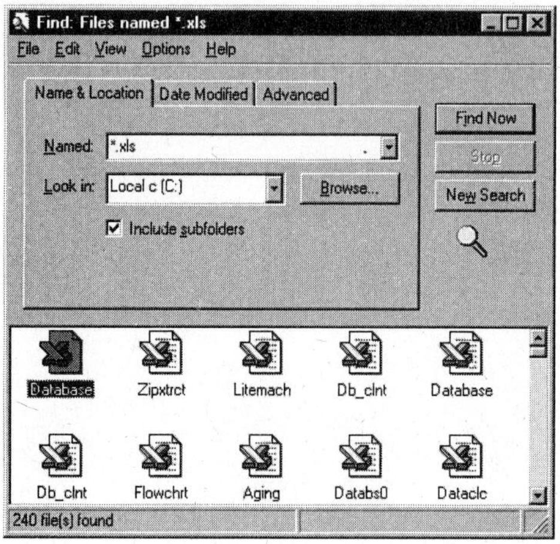

Fig. 17.19
The results of a search are listed at the bottom of the Find dialog box.

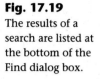

At this point, you can perform all the same operations on any of the found files that you can on a file in the Explorer. To work with a file in the Find dialog box, select the file and choose the File menu, or click on the file with the right mouse button to open the shortcut menu. You can open, print, preview, move, copy, delete, rename, or view the properties of the file. You can also drag-and-drop the file to any folder in the Explorer. This is handy if the file you located is in the wrong folder, and you want to quickly move it to the correct folder. The Edit menu contains commands for cutting and copying files.

You can save the search criteria as well as the results in an icon on your desktop. You also can save just the search criteria without saving the results. If you want to save the results with the search criteria, choose Options, Save Results so that Save Results is selected and shows a check mark. To save the criteria (and the results, if you specified that) choose File, Save Search. The saved criteria (and the results, if you specified them) will appear on your desktop as a document icon. You can label the icon by changing its name.

To open the Find dialog box using the saved criteria and result, double-click on the icon. The Find dialog box will show the criteria and results as they were when saved. To redo the search, click Find Now.

The <u>V</u>iew menu has the same commands as the Explorer for selecting how you want the files to be displayed in the results pane and for sorting the list of files. See "Changing How Folders and Files Are Displayed" earlier in this chapter to learn how to change the display in the results pane.

The <u>O</u>ptions menu has two commands for fine-tuning your search. Choose the <u>C</u>ase Sensitive command if you want Find to distinguish between upper- and lowercase characters in any text you specified in the <u>C</u>ontaining Text text box.

If you want to set up a new search, click Ne<u>w</u> Search to clear the criteria for the current search. Now you can enter the criteria for the new search.

Previewing a Document with Quick View

As you manage the files on your computer, you may want to look at the contents of a file before you make decisions about moving, copying, deleting, and backing up the file. It can be very tedious and time-consuming to open each file in the program that created the file. Windows has a tool called *Quick View* for previewing many types of files without having to open the original program. You can access Quick View from the Explorer or from any folder window.

To preview a file using Quick View, follow these steps:

1. Select the file you want to preview.

2. Choose <u>F</u>ile, <u>Q</u>uick View. The <u>Q</u>uick View item does not appear on the menu if the file type you select does not have a viewer installed.

    or

    Click the selected file with the right mouse button and click <u>Q</u>uick View.

    The Quick View window opens, displaying the contents of the file, as shown in figure 17.20.

You can scroll through the document using the scroll bars or keyboard. If you decide you want to open the file, choose <u>F</u>ile, <u>O</u>pen File for Editing (or click the Open File for Editing button at the left end of the toolbar).

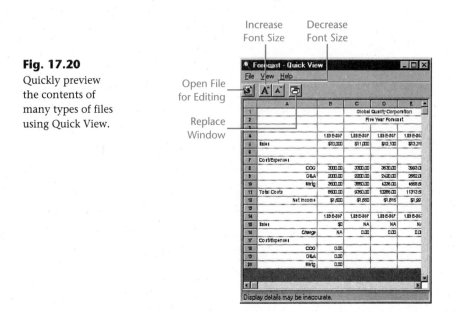

Fig. 17.20

Quickly preview the contents of many types of files using Quick View.

Tip

If you want to compare the contents of two files, you should have a new window opened for each file.

You can choose to have a new Quick View window open each time you select a file to preview, or you can view each new file in the same window. By default, Quick View opens a new window for each file. If this default has been changed, or you need to change it back, choose View and look at the menu. If a check mark appears next to Replace Window in Quick View, choose that option to deselect it and have a new window opened for each file. If you want the contents of the current Quick View window to be replaced when you select a new file for previewing, choose View, Replace Window to select this option. You can use the Replace Window button on the toolbar to activate and deactivate this option.

When you first open Quick View, you see a portion of the page of your document. To view whole pages, choose View, Page View. A check mark appears next to the command when it is activated. When you are in page view, you can click the arrows in the upper-right corner of the page to scroll through the document. To return to viewing portions of a page, choose the command again.

When you are in page view, you can rotate the display to preview the file in landscape orientation by choosing View, Landscape. Choose the command again to return to portrait orientation.

You can also change the font and font size used in the display by choosing View, Font and selecting a new font or size. To quickly increase or decrease the font size, click the Increase Font Size or Decrease Font Size tools on the toolbar. When you change the font and font size, it affects only the display in Quick View and does not alter the original file. It's handy to be able to increase the font size if you can't easily read the contents of the file, especially when you are in Page view.

To exit Quick View, choose File, Exit or double-click the Quick View icon at the left end of the title bar.

Viewing and Changing the Properties of a File or Folder

In Windows, it is easy to check the properties of a selected file or folder. You can find out the type of a file; the location and size of the selected item; the MS-DOS name; and when the file or folder was created, last modified, and last accessed. Each file and folder on a disk also has a set of *attributes,* or descriptive characteristics. Attributes describe whether the file has been backed up, is a Windows system file, is hidden from normal viewing, or can be read but not written over. With the Windows Explorer, you can display these attributes and change them.

To display the properties of a particular file or folder, follow these steps:

1. In the Explorer (or any folder), select the file or folder whose properties you want to check.

2. Right-click and choose Properties, or choose File, Properties. Windows opens a Properties sheet (see fig. 17.21).

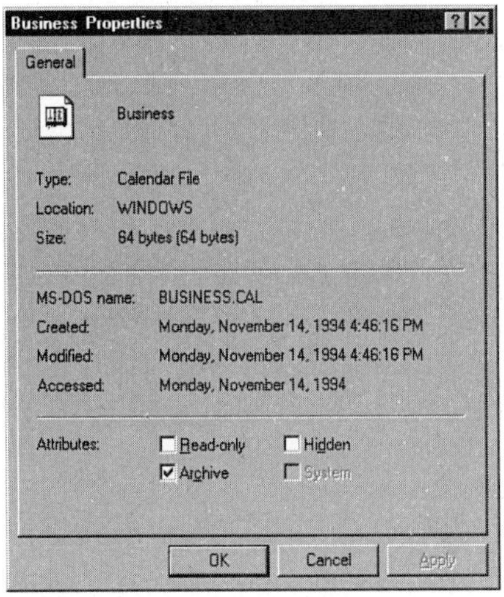

Fig. 17.21
You can check the properties of a file or folder on its Properties sheet.

3. View the file or folder's properties.

4. If you want, change the attributes for the file or folder, as described in the following table:

Attribute	Description
<u>R</u>ead Only	Sets the R or Read-Only attribute, which prevents a file or folder from being changed or erased. Set this attribute for a file or folder when you want to prevent someone from accidentally changing a master template or erasing a file that is critical to system operation.

Caution

Read-only files can still be deleted from within Explorer. You will see one additional warning dialog box prompting you if you attempt to delete a read-only file. So, setting this attribute does not entirely protect it from deletion.

Attribute	Description
Ar<u>c</u>hive	Sets the A or Archive attribute. Marks with an A any file that has changed since being backed up using certain backup programs, including Backup, which comes with Windows. If no A appears, the file has not changed since you backed it up.
Hi<u>d</u>den	Sets the H or Hidden attribute, which prevents files from displaying in the Explorer and My Computer.
<u>S</u>ystem	Sets the S or System attribute, which prevents files from displaying. System files are files that your computer requires to operate. Deleting a system file could prevent your computer from working. Folders cannot have the System attribute set.

5. Click OK.

Note

If you want to reduce the odds of accidentally changing or erasing a file, set the attributes to Read Only and Hidden or System. These attributes prevent the file from being accidentally changed and hide the file from standard display. However, hidden files can still be displayed depending on the View options you choose in Explorer, and Read Only and System files require only one additional confirmation to delete. So be careful when confirming the messages prompting you to delete files.

IV

Note

Assigning the Hidden or System attribute to hide files is a good way to prevent tampering or accidental erasure. As an experienced Windows user, however, you may need to see these files to change, erase, or copy them. To display files with the Hidden or System attribute, choose View, Options. Click the View tab and select the Show All Files option. Now hidden and system files are displayed in the list of files. You can carry out these steps in either the Explorer or My Computer window.

Opening a Document from the Explorer

Although you may usually open your documents from within the program that created the document, you can open documents directly from the Explorer. In fact, if you like to think in terms of opening documents instead of opening programs and then opening documents, you can use the Explorer as your primary interface with your computer, doing all your viewing, opening, and printing of files from the Explorer.

To open a document from the Explorer, the file type for that document must be registered with a program. Registering a file type with a program tells Windows what application to use to open and print the document. TXT files, for example, are registered with Windows Notepad, so Windows uses Notepad to open any TXT files. Windows automatically registers certain file types. Microsoft Word for Windows files, for example, are automatically registered with Word.

▶ See "Registering Files to Automatically Open an Application," p. 539

To open a document in the Explorer, follow these steps:

1. Open the folder containing the file you want to open.

2. Select the file you want to open.

3. Double-click the file or press Enter.

   or

   Right-click the file and choose Open.

The Explorer starts the program for the file and opens the file.

If Windows does not recognize the file type of the file you double-click, it displays the Open With dialog box shown in figure 17.22. This dialog enables you to tell Windows which application should be used to open the file.

Choose the program you want to open the file from the Choose the program list. If you want the program to always be used to open a file of this type, make sure that the Always Use This Program to Open This File check box is selected.

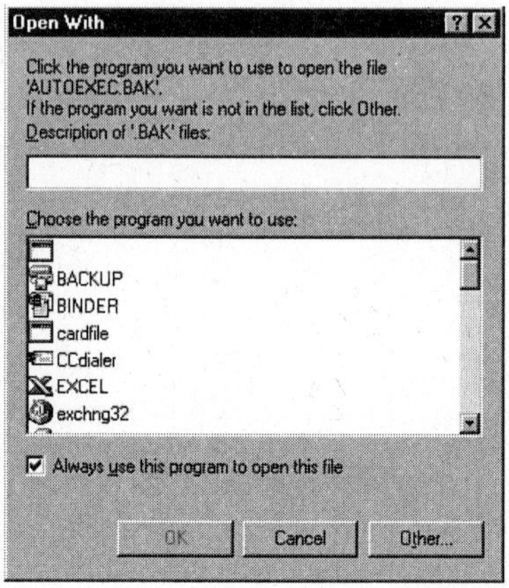

Fig. 17.22
Double-clicking a file that is not recognized produces the Open With dialog box, so you can tell Windows which program to use to open the file.

Printing Files

◀ See "Printing from the Desktop," p. 179

You can send files directly to the printer from the Explorer. For example, many software programs come with last-minute corrections and additional information stored in a text file. The information usually is not in the printed manual. These text files, which usually have the MS-DOS extension TXT, contain information such as helpful tips, corrections to the manual, and hardware configuration settings not covered in the manual. It is often helpful to print these files.

When you print with the Explorer, you send the file to the default printer. To change the default printer, use Control Panel.

To print a file with the Explorer, the file must be registered with a program. TXT files, for example, are registered with Windows Notepad.

To print a file using the Explorer, follow these steps:

1. Open the folder that contains the file or files you want to print.

2. Select the file or files you want to print.

3. Choose File, Print.

   or

   If you have created a shortcut for your printer on your desktop, drag-and-drop the selected file or files onto the Printer icon on the desktop.

Synchronizing Files

With the proliferation of home computers, laptop computers, and networks, you may often find yourself working on the same file on different computers. The inherent difficulty in working with the same file at more than one location is keeping the files synchronized—that is, making sure that the latest version of the file is at both locations. This used to be a daunting and dangerous task. It is not too difficult to accidentally copy the older version of a file on top of the newer version, rather than the other way around. A new feature in Windows, *Briefcase*, makes the task of synchronizing files in different locations much easier.

◀ See "Maintaining Laptop and Desktop Files with Briefcase," p. 292

Briefcase is really a folder with some special extra features. When you want to work on files at a different location—for example, on your laptop while you are away from your office—you first copy the files from your desktop computer into Briefcase. You then transfer Briefcase to your laptop and work on the files in Briefcase. When you return to the office, you transfer Briefcase back to your desktop and issue a command that automatically updates any files on your desktop that were modified while they were in Briefcase. The files on your desktop are then synchronized with the files in Briefcase.

The Briefcase procedure works whether you transfer Briefcase using a floppy disk, keep Briefcase on one of two computers that are physically connected, or use Briefcase to synchronize files across a network.

Creating the Briefcase

If you don't already have a Briefcase folder on your desktop, you need to create one. Unless you chose the Portable option when you were setting up Windows or specified the installation of Briefcase in a custom installation, you will not see the My Briefcase icon on your desktop. To create a Briefcase, follow these steps:

1. Open the Start menu; then choose Settings and Control Panel.

2. Double-click the Add/Remove Programs icon.

3. Click the Windows Setup tab.

4. Select Accessories in the Components list and then click Details.

5. Select Briefcase in the Components list and then click OK.

> **Note**
>
> Briefcase will be listed in these options only if it is not installed. Unlike the other accessories, which are listed here regardless of whether they are currently installed, Briefcase disappears from the list once you install it. If you delete your Briefcase, it will not appear in the list and you won't be able to reinstall it without rerunning the Windows setup.

6. Click OK again and insert the Windows disk specified in the Insert Disk message box that appears. Click OK again.

7. Click OK to close the dialog box.

Synchronizing Files with a Laptop or Another Computer on the Network

You can use Briefcase to keep files synchronized between a laptop and a desktop computer. This is useful because you may update files on the laptop while it is disconnected from the desktop. On reconnecting the two computers, you can ask Windows to synchronize the files between the two computers—comparing and updating files between the two computers. The most up-to-date file replaces the unchanged file. If files on both computers have been changed, you will be asked to choose which file should replace the other.

> **Caution**
>
> Be sure that the times and dates are correctly set on any computer that you use synchronization on. Incorrect dates or times could cause the wrong file to be overwritten.

Tip
The recommended approach is to put Briefcase on the computer you use less often.

Keeping synchronized files between your laptop and desktop computers is most convenient if they can be physically connected by a cable or network. Physically linking two computers is a much faster way to transfer files than by using a floppy disk. Using Briefcase helps you keep synchronized the files you are using on both computers. You can work on either the file on the original computer or the file in Briefcase, and use the Update command to keep the files synchronized.

You may have two computers on which you need to keep synchronized files, but you don't have the computers connected. You can still keep files synchronized by putting Briefcase on a floppy disk and using the disk to move the

Briefcase between computers. You can use this method to synchronize files between your work computer and your home computer or between your desktop and laptop computers. Although it's not as fast as synchronizing files between two connected computers, it works well if you are not working with a large number of files and don't have the means to physically connect the computers.

To synchronize files on two computers that are connected by cable or network or that use a floppy disk to transfer the Briefcase, follow these steps:

1. Copy the files and folders you want to use on both computers into Briefcase.

   The simplest way to copy the files to Briefcase is to drag-and-drop them on the My Briefcase icon on the desktop.

   ◄ See "Moving and Copying Files and Folders," p. 515

   > **Note**
   >
   > The first time you copy a file to My Briefcase or open My Briefcase, Windows 95 displays a Welcome to the Windows Briefcase Wizard. There's nothing you need to do in this Wizard except read the explanation and click Finish.

2. Move Briefcase to the computer on which you will be working with the Briefcase files. If your computer is not connected to the other computer, move the Briefcase to a floppy disk.

   Once you move the Briefcase, it will not be located on the original desktop. It can be at only one place at a time.

   The idea is to move, not copy, Briefcase onto the other computer, so that it exists in only one location. An easy way to move Briefcase is to select the My Briefcase icon with the mouse, drag it to the new location with the right mouse button, and choose Move Here from the shortcut menu that appears.

   Tip

   The fastest way to move the Briefcase is to right-click the My Briefcase icon, click Send To, and then click the floppy drive you want to move Briefcase to.

   ◄ See "Sharing Local Resources via Parallel or Serial Connection," p. 278

3. If you are using a floppy disk, transfer the floppy disk to the other computer you want to work on.

4. Open and edit the files in Briefcase, as you normally would.

   If Briefcase is on a floppy disk and the other computer you are working on has Windows installed on it, you can transfer the files to the hard disk on that computer to speed up editing. Drag the files to the hard disk; after you edit them, drag the files back to Briefcase.

   ► See "Understanding File Sharing," p. 643

If you are working on computers that are physically connected, open and edit the files from Briefcase. You can work on the files on your portable or laptop even when it is not connected to the desktop.

> **Caution**
>
> If the other computer you are working on does not have Windows, you shouldn't transfer your files to the hard disk. Open and edit them in the Briefcase on the floppy disk. Otherwise, you will defeat the purpose of using Briefcase for keeping the files synchronized.

5. Once you are finished editing the files and you need to synchronize the files between the two computers, reconnect the computers if a cable or network connects them.

   If Briefcase was on a floppy disk, you can open Briefcase from the floppy or move Briefcase back to the desktop of the original computer. Then open Briefcase.

   Double-click the My Briefcase icon to open it (see fig. 17.23).

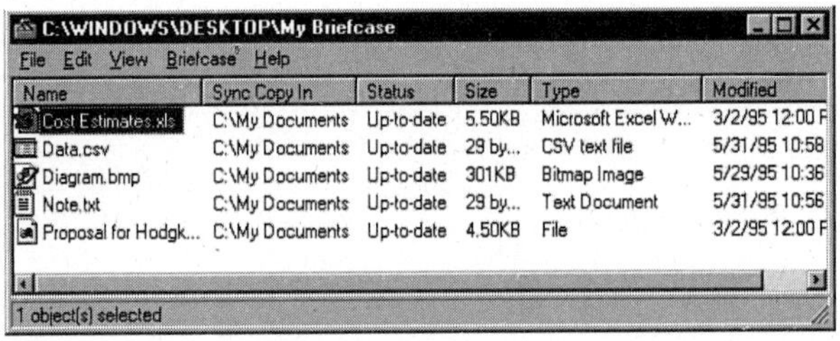

Fig. 17.23
Use Briefcase to keep files in different locations synchronized.

> **Note**
>
> By default, My Briefcase displays files in the Details view. This view is much like the Details view in Explorer with two additional columns. The Sync Copy In column lists the location of the original file. The Status column indicates whether the file is up-to-date, or whether it's older or newer than the original. Like the other columns in the Detail view of a folder, you can sort the list by clicking on the column headings.

6. Choose <u>B</u>riefcase, Update <u>A</u>ll.

or

Select only those files you want to update and choose <u>B</u>riefcase, <u>U</u>pdate Selection.

The Update My Briefcase dialog box appears, as shown in figure 17.24.

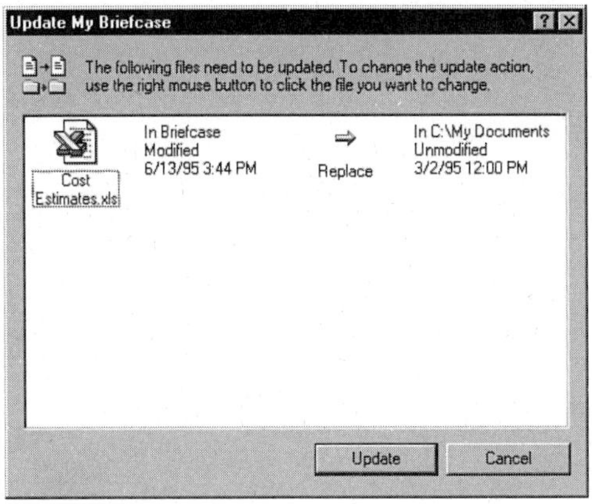

Fig. 17.24

All files that need to be updated are listed in the Update My Briefcase dialog box.

7. Check the proposed update action for each file as it is synchronized with its corresponding file on the other computer.

The default update action is to replace the older version of the file with the newer version. If you want to change the update action for a file, right-click the file name and change the action using the pop-up menu that appears (see fig. 17.25).

8. Click the Update button to update the files. (The computers must be connected for you to update the files.)

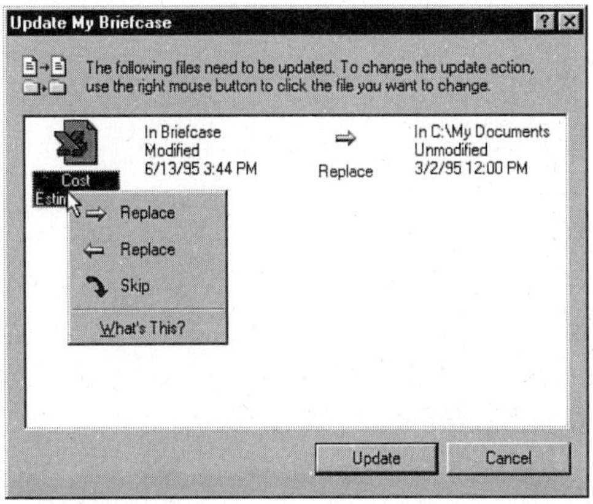

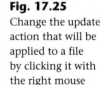

Fig. 17.25

Change the update action that will be applied to a file by clicking it with the right mouse button and then selecting the desired action.

IV

Disks and Files

Checking the Status of Briefcase Files

You can check the update status of the files in the Briefcase at any time. To check the status of a file or folder in Briefcase, open My Briefcase by double-clicking on it. Examine the Status column in the window.

If you have the Briefcase files displayed in a view other than Details, you will not see this Status column. To check the status, you can choose View, Details to switch to Details view. Or you can select the file to check and choose File, Properties; then click the Update Status tab (see fig. 17.26). The middle portion of the Update Status page shows the status of the file in the Briefcase on the left and that of the original file on the right. If the files are the same, Up to Date is indicated in the center. If the files are not the same, Replace is shown in the center along with an arrow. The arrow points to the file that is out-of-date and should be replaced.

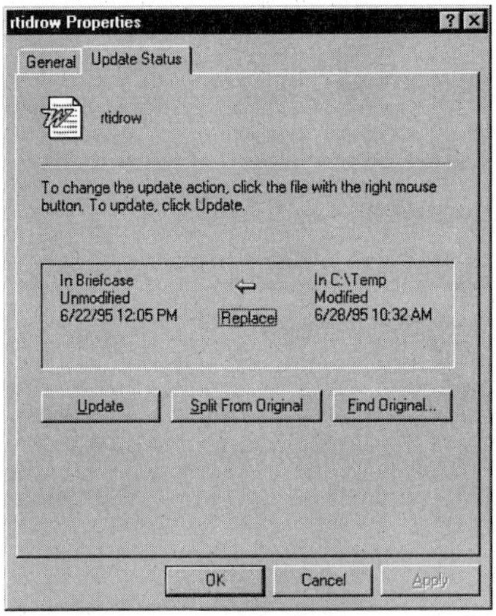

Fig. 17.26

In this figure, the copy of RTIDROW in C:\TEMP is newer than the Briefcase copy, so Windows indicates that the copy in the Briefcase should be replaced.

From within this Properties sheet, you can update the file (as described in the preceding section) by choosing Update. You also can prevent a file from being updated (which is discussed in the next section) by choosing Split from Original.

You can choose Find Original to open the folder with the original file, without having to work your way through the hierarchy of folders in Explorer or My Computer.

> **Troubleshooting**
>
> *I modified the original of a file in My Briefcase, but the status still shows* Up to Date.
>
> If you have Briefcase or the folder with the original open, the status may not be updated immediately. Choose View, Refresh both in My Briefcase and in the folder containing the original file. This ensures that the status indicates any recent changes.

Preventing a File from Synchronizing

You may want to break the connection between a file in Briefcase and its original file, so that when you issue the Update command, the two copies of the file are not synchronized. You may want to do this to preserve the original file or if the portable file is now a file that has changed into a document unrelated to the original.

To split a file from its original, follow these steps:

1. Open Briefcase and select the file you want to split.

2. Choose Briefcase, Split From Original.

    Notice that the file is now referred to as an orphan in the Status field of the Briefcase window.

You can also split a file by clicking the Split from Original button on the Update Status page of the Properties sheet.

Registering Files to Automatically Open an Application

When you register a file type with Windows, you tell Windows that the file type has a certain MS-DOS extension and that a particular program should be used to open the file. The most useful reason for registering a file type is that you can then double-click any file of that type, and the file will be opened using the program you have instructed Windows to use.

Registering a New File Type

Registering a file type is analogous to associating a file in Windows 3.1, although you can now tell Windows even more about the file type; for example, you can now tell Windows which program to use to print a type of file.

To register a new file type, follow these steps:

1. In the Explorer, choose View, Options.

2. Click the File Types tab to display the dialog box shown in figure 17.27.

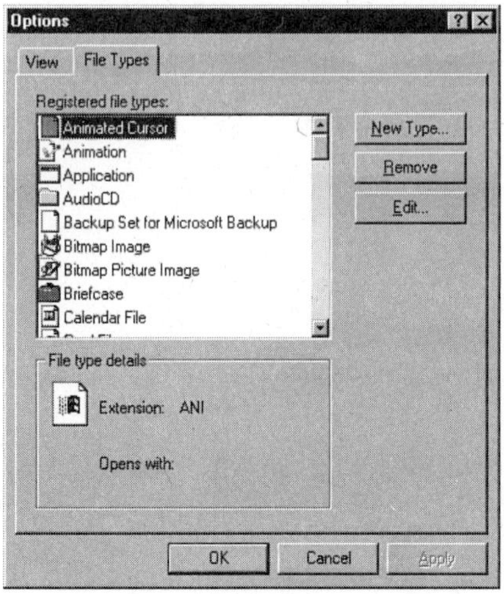

Fig. 17.27

Register and modify file types on the File Types page of the Options dialog box.

3. Choose New Type. The Add New File Type dialog box appears (see fig. 17.28).

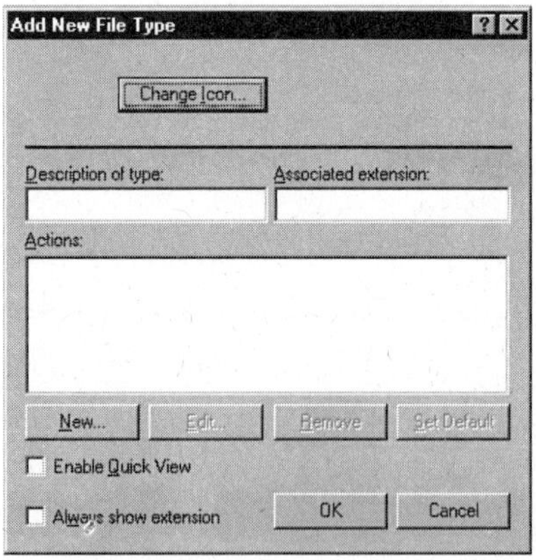

Fig. 17.28

Enter the information for a new file type in the Add New File Type dialog box.

4. Enter a description of the file type in the Description of Type text box.

   This description appears in the Registered File Types list on the File Types page of the Options dialog box. For example, if you want to be able to double-click on mainframe text files that use commas to separate data and have that file load into Excel, you might use a description similar to Comma Separated Values (CSV).

5. Enter the file extension to be associated with this file type in the Associated Extension text box. This is the three-letter file extension associated with DOS-based files. For example, a comma-separated values file uses the extension CSV.

6. Choose New to add a new action to the file type in the New Action dialog box.

   The action is actually a custom command that appears on the shortcut menu when you right-click on the file.

7. Type an action—for example, **Open CSV in Excel**—in the Actions text box.

   What you type will appear as an item on the shortcut menu for this file type. You can type anything, but commands usually start with a verb. If you want the command to have an accelerator key, precede that letter with an ampersand (&).

8. Select the application to be used to perform the action in the Application Used to Perform Action text box.

   In the example used so far, you would enter the path and directory to the EXCEL.EXE file—for example, **C:\OFFICE95\EXCEL\Excel.exe**. You can also use Browse to find and select the application to use.

   The New Action dialog box with information filled in is shown in figure 17.29.

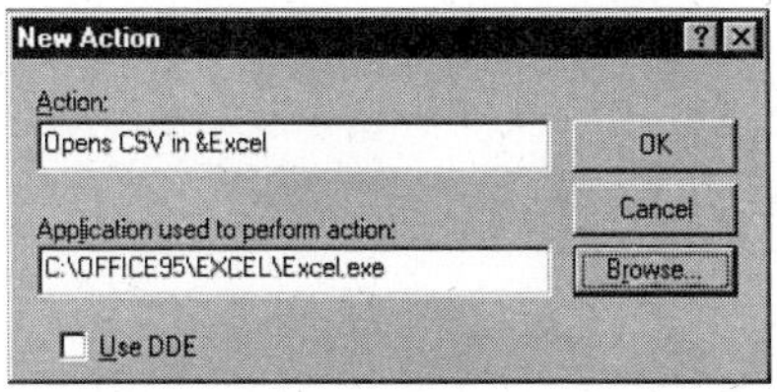

Fig. 17.29
Designate a shortcut menu action and the program used to perform that action in the New Action dialog box.

9. While the New Action dialog box is still displayed, select the Use DDE check box if the program uses DDE (dynamic data exchange).

If you select the Use DDE check box, the dialog box expands (see fig. 17.30), displaying the DDE statements used to communicate with the DDE application. If you know how to write DDE statements, you can customize the action performed with the associated application.

Fig. 17.30
You can enter your own DDE statements to customize the action associated with a registered file type.

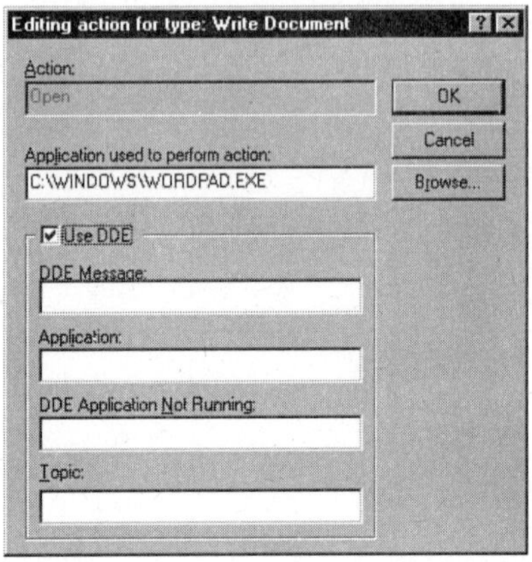

10. Click OK.

11. If you have more than one action listed in the Actions text box, select the one you want to be the default action and choose the Set Default button.

    The default action is the one that is performed when you double-click a file of this type in the Explorer or My Computer.

◀ See "Previewing a Document with Quick View," p. 527

12. Select the Enable Quick View box if the file type supports Quick View. Quick View allows you to view a file without opening it.

13. Select Always Show Extension if you want the MS-DOS file extension for this file type to always be displayed in the Explorer and My Computer windows, even when you have selected the Hide MS-DOS File Extensions option on the View page of the Options dialog box.

14. Choose Close twice.

Editing an Existing File Type

At times, you may want to change existing file-type options. For example, say you wanted to change the action that opens BMP files in Paint so that they would open in a different image editor. You would edit the BMP open action to include the path and file names for that image editor instead of Paint. You also can change the description, icon, and other aspects.

To edit an existing file type, follow these steps:

1. In the Explorer, choose <u>V</u>iew, <u>O</u>ptions.

2. Click the File Types tab to display the File Types page of the Options dialog box (refer to fig. 17.27).

3. Select the file type you want to edit in the Registered File <u>T</u>ypes list.

4. Click the <u>E</u>dit button.

5. Edit the characteristics for the file type using the same procedures outlined earlier for creating a new file type.

    To edit an action, you must first select that action from the list. Actions for a file type depend on parameters or arguments understood by that file type. Some applications may be able to accept macro names as actions, others accept "switches," and still others accept arguments leftover from DOS commands. Check the technical reference manual for the application you are starting to learn more about the actions.

6. Click OK.

7. Repeat steps 3 through 6 for any other file types you want to edit.

8. Click Close.

Removing a File Type

If you no longer want a document to start a specific application, you will want to change or remove its file type description.

To remove a file type, follow these steps:

1. In the Explorer, choose <u>V</u>iew, <u>O</u>ptions.

2. Click the File Types tab to display the File Types page of the Options dialog box (refer to fig. 17.27).

3. Select the file type you want to remove in the Registered File <u>T</u>ypes list.

4. Click <u>R</u>emove.

5. Click OK.

Changing the Icon for a File Type or Other Object

You can also change the icon used to designate a file type, drive, folder, and other objects on your computer. To change the icon used for a particular file type or object, follow these steps:

1. In the Explorer, choose View, Options.

2. Click the File Types tab to display the File Types page of the Options dialog box (refer to fig. 17.27).

3. Select the file type or other object whose icon you want to change in the Registered File Types list.

4. Choose the Edit button.

5. Click the Change Icon button to display the Change Icon dialog box shown in figure 17.31.

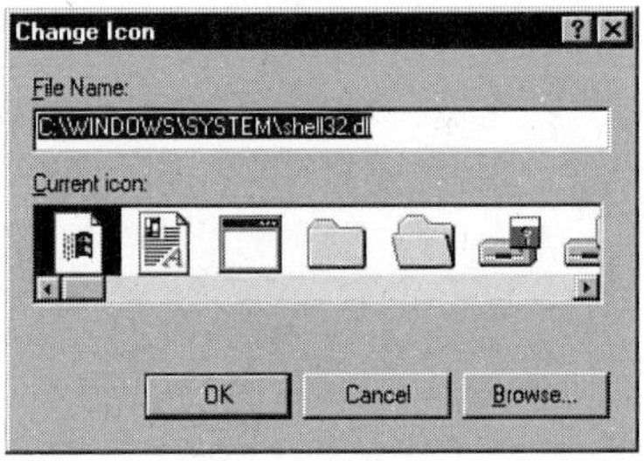

Fig. 17.31
Use the Change Icon dialog box to select a new icon for a file type or other type of object.

6. Select a new icon from the Current Icon scrolling list.

The name of the file containing the icons currently shown is listed in the File Name text box. You can use the Browse button to search for a new file containing different icons. All Windows programs come with their own icons, and you can also obtain collections of icons on computer bulletin boards and from other sources. Programs are even available that allow you to create your own icons.

7. Click OK three times.

Using the Explorer with Shared Resources on a Network

▶ See "Setting Up File Sharing," p. 643

▶ See "Sharing Your Resources," p. 688

If you are using Windows on a network, you can share resources with other users in your workgroup and use resources that other users have designated as shared. You can open the files in any folder that has been designated as shared by another user, and you can share any of your folders so that the files in that folder can be used by other users. You can use the Explorer to designate resources on your computer as shared and to browse the shared resources in your workgroup or on your entire network.

Browsing Shared Folders

You can open any folder that has been designated as shared by any user on your network. (To learn how to share a folder, see the next section, "Sharing Resources on Your Computer.") You browse a shared folder using the Explorer in the same way you browse a folder on your computer.

▶ See "Understanding File Sharing," p. 643

To browse a shared folder, follow these steps:

1. Under Network Neighborhood in the left pane of the Explorer, find the computer on Your network where the folder you want to browse is located.

   If a plus sign appears next to the name of the computer, click the plus sign to display the shared resources on that computer (see fig. 17.32).

   Shared resources can include folders, entire drives, CD-ROM drives, and printers, as you can see in figure 17.32.

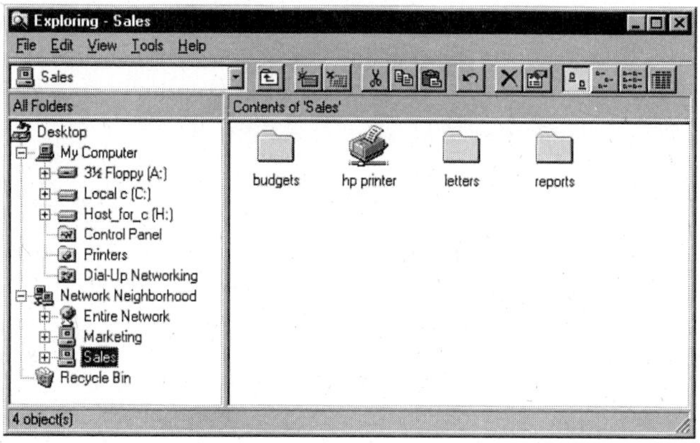

Fig. 17.32
View the shared resources on another user's computer in the Explorer.

2. Select the shared folder to display its contents in the right pane of the Explorer, as shown in figure 17.33.

3. To open a shared file from the Explorer, double-click the file name in the right pane.

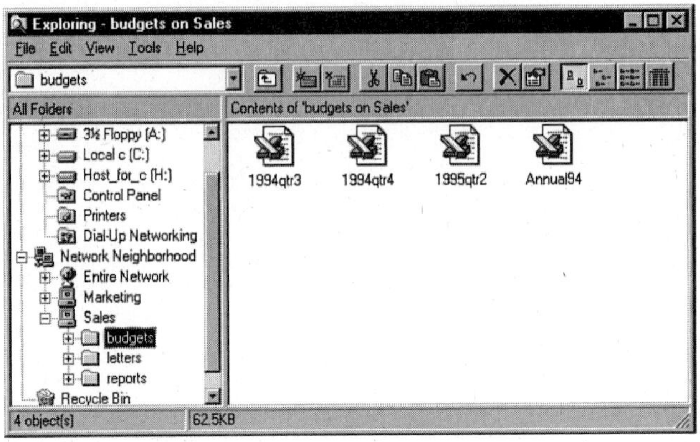

Fig. 17.33

View the contents of a shared folder by selecting it in the Explorer.

Sharing Resources on Your Computer

▶ See "Setting Up File Sharing," p. 643

▶ See "Sharing Your Re- sources," p. 688

You can designate any folder on your computer as shared. When you share a folder, you can assign a *share name* and *password* to that folder. You can also specify what type of access users have to the shared folder. Once you have shared a folder, other users have access to the files in that folder. The com- puters that have the folders you want to share must be on and logged in to the network.

To share a folder, follow these steps:

1. In the Explorer, select the folder you want to share.

2. Right-click the folder, and then click Sharing to display the Sharing page on the Properties sheet.

3. Select the Shared As option, as shown in figure 17.34.

4. You can accept the default share name for the folder or type a new name in the Share Name text box.

5. Enter a comment in the Comment text box, if you want.

   The comment appears in the Details view of your computer when other users select it in the Explorer or Network Neighborhood. Comments can help users locate shared information.

6. Select one of the Access Type options to specify the access for the shared resource.

   You can grant users two levels of access to a shared folder. If you want users to be able only to read files and run programs in a folder, select the Read-Only option. If you want users to be able to read, modify, rename, move, delete, or create files and run your programs, select the Full option. If you want the level of access to depend on which password the user enters, select the Depends on Password option.

If you want to limit access to the files in the shared folder to certain users, assign a password to the folder and give the password to only those users. If you select the Depends on Password option, you need to enter two passwords—one for users who have read-only access to your files and one for users with full access. If you want all users to have access to your files, don't assign a password.

7. Click OK.

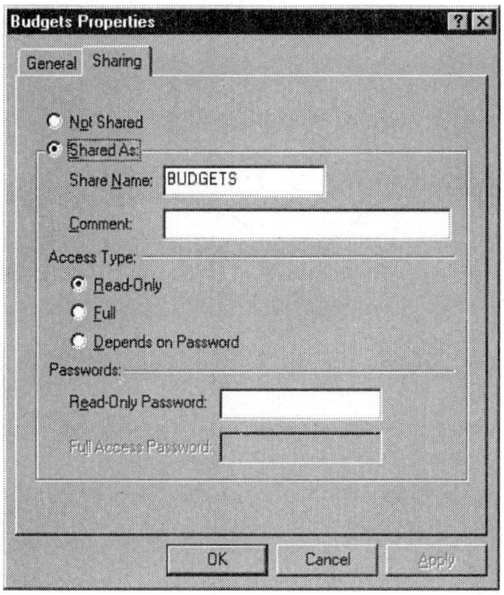

Fig. 17.34
Designate a folder as shared on the Sharing page of the Properties sheet.

You can share an entire disk drive by selecting the drive and following the preceding steps.

You can quickly tell if you have designated a folder as shared by looking for a hand beneath its folder icon in the Explorer or Network Neighborhood, as shown in figure 17.35.

To change the properties of a shared folder, click the folder with the right mouse button and change the share name, comment, access privileges, or password for the shared folder.

Fig. 17.35
Shared folders are
indicated by a
hand beneath
their folder icons
in the Explorer.

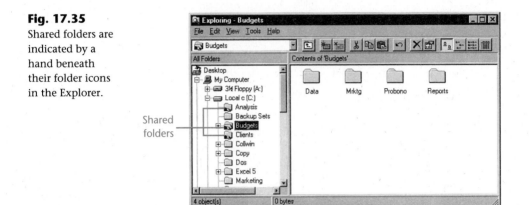

Shared folders

> **Caution**
>
> If the Sharing tab is not visible when you open the Properties sheet, you must enable file and printer sharing services.

Stop Sharing a Folder

To stop sharing a folder, follow these steps:

1. Select the folder you want to stop sharing.

2. Right-click on the folder and then click Sharing.

3. Select the Not Shared option and click OK.

Mapping a Network Drive

In earlier versions of Windows, you had to connect to a shared directory to be able to view and use its files. When you connected to a shared directory, Windows created a *network drive* for that directory and assigned a letter to that drive. To view the files in the shared directory, you selected the drive in File Manager. Windows 95 has greatly simplified working with networks by listing all shared resources in the Explorer and Network Neighborhood. You no longer have to map a drive to the shared folder. However, if you prefer to map a drive to a shared resource on another computer, you can still do it. The mapped drive appears under My Computer just like any other drive.

To map a drive to a shared directory, follow these steps:

1. Select the shared folder you want to map in the Explorer or Network Neighborhood.

2. Right-click the folder, and then click Map Network Drive. The Map Network Drive dialog box appears, as shown in figure 17.36.

Fig. 17.36
You can map a shared directory to a drive letter in the Map Network Drive dialog box.

3. By default, Windows assigns the next available drive letter on your computer to the folder you select to map. To assign a different letter, click the drop-down arrow and select a letter from the list.

4. If you want to automatically reconnect to this shared folder at log on, select the Reconnect at Startup option.

5. Click OK.

To remove the mapping for a shared directory, click the Disconnect Network Drive button in the Explorer or Network Neighborhood, select the network drive you want to disconnect, and click OK. Or select the drive in the left pane of the Explorer, click the right mouse button, and then click Disconnect.

Finding a Computer on Your Network

If you know its name, you can quickly find a computer on your network by using the Find Computer command. To find a computer on your network, follow these steps:

1. Open the Start menu; then choose Find, Computer.

   or

   In the Explorer, choose Tools, Find, Computer.

2. Enter the name of the computer you want to find in the Named text box of the Find: Computer dialog box, as shown in figure 17.37.

3. Click the Find Now button.

   The dialog box expands, listing the location of the specified computer if it is found on the network, as shown in figure 17.38.

▶ See "Finding a Computer on the Network," p. 614

▶ See "Identifying Your Workgroup Computer," p. 635

Fig. 17.37
Find a computer
on your network
by using the Find
Computer
command.

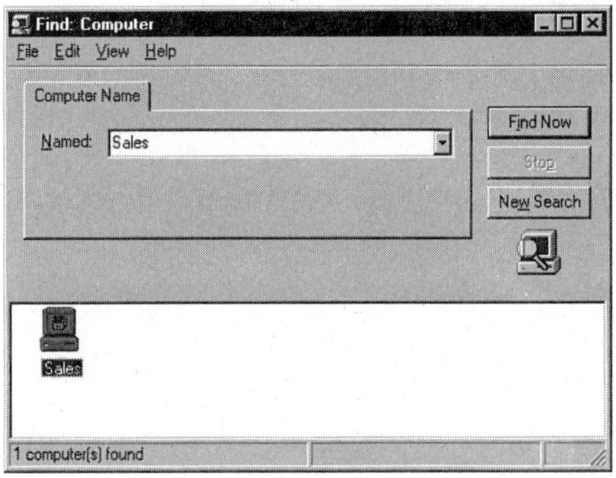

Fig. 17.38
The location
of the found
computer is listed
at the bottom of
the Find: Com-
puter dialog box.

4. To open a browse window displaying the shared files and folders on the found computer, double-click on the name of the computer at the bottom of the dialog box, or right-click on the name and click Open.

Using Network Neighborhood to View Network Resources

When you install Windows and are connected to a network, you see an icon for Network Neighborhood on your desktop. You can open Network Neighborhood and use it to work with the shared resources on your network by using the same techniques described in the preceding section. When you first open Network Neighborhood by double-clicking its icon on the desktop, the Network Neighborhood window appears, as shown in figure 17.39.

To view the shared resources on a particular computer on your network, double-click the icon for the computer to open a new window. You can continue this process to open shared folders and view the contents. Many options discussed in the sections on using the Explorer earlier in this chapter are also available in Network Neighborhood. You can, for example, change the way files are displayed; add or remove the toolbar; and move, copy, and delete files.

Fig. 17.39
The Network
Neighborhood
window displays
all the resources
on your network.

Note

If you have file sharing enabled for your computer, it will appear in Network Neighborhood. However, you can't access your own computer from within the Network Neighborhood. Use Explorer or My Computer to access your computer.

By default, each time you open a folder, a new window appears. This can result in a desktop full of windows and lots of confusion. If you prefer to have a single window open for browsing files, with the contents of that window changing as you open new folders, choose View, Options; and then click the Folder tab, select the Browse Folders by Using a Single Window option, and click OK.

Whether you use the Explorer or Network Neighborhood to work with the files on your network depends on your style of working. Try them both and see which works best for you.

Using My Computer to Manage Files

This chapter has focused on using the Windows Explorer to view and manage your files and folders. For seasoned users of earlier versions of Windows who are used to using File Manager to manage their files, the transition to using the Explorer should be smooth. And these users will appreciate the added power of the Explorer. The many shortcuts available using the right mouse button and Quick View are powerful features that make file management much quicker and easier with the Explorer.

New users of Windows may prefer to use My Computer to work with their files. My Computer is a folder containing folders for all the resources on your computer. When you first open My Computer, by double-clicking its icon on the desktop, the My Computer window displays an icon representing each of the resources on your computer, as shown in figure 17.40.

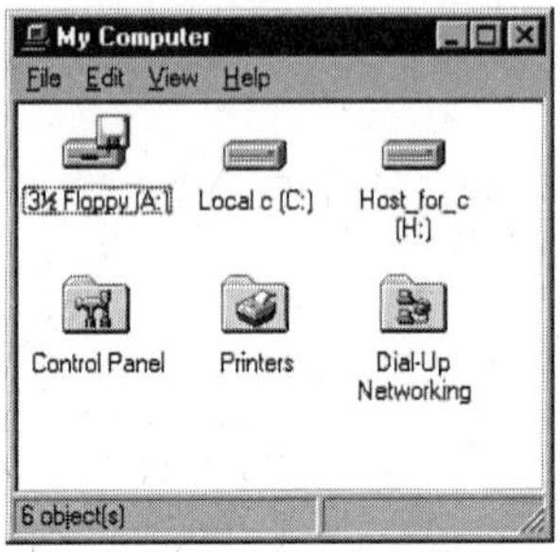

Fig. 17.40

The My Computer window is another way to view the files and folders on your computer.

To look at the contents of a resource, double-click its folder. To view the folders on your hard drive, for example, double-click the hard disk icon. A new window opens, displaying the folders on your hard drive (see fig. 17.41). You can continue browsing through the folders on your computer by double-clicking any folder whose contents you want to view.

Fig. 17.41

You can browse through the folders in My Computer by double-clicking the folders whose contents you want to see.

As you open up new windows in My Computer to view the contents of the different folders, you won't really have a sense of the organization of the folders the way you do in the Explorer. In the Explorer, you always have a map of the organization of your folders in the left pane. With My Computer, it is more difficult to visualize the hierarchical structure of your folders. If you don't think hierarchically, this may be a relief, as you may prefer to simply think of folders inside other folders that you open up one by one. You can move back through a series of opened folders by clicking the Up One Level button in the toolbar. This is a handy way to retrace your steps.

If you find it annoying to end up with layer upon layer of folder windows as you open the folders on your computer, you can choose to have the contents of a newly opened folder replace the current contents of the My Computer window, rather than open a new window. Choose View, Options and select the Browse Folders by Using a Single Window option. Now when you open a new folder, the folder's contents replace the contents of the current window. You can still use the Up One Level button to move back through a series of folders that you opened.

You can perform virtually all the file management tasks in My Computer that you learned to carry out in the Explorer. To manage your files in My Computer, use the same techniques described throughout this chapter. You can use either the menus or the mouse to open, move, copy, rename, delete, and preview your files. You can drag-and-drop files from one folder window to another. And all the shortcuts accessible with the right mouse button in the Explorer can also be used in My Computer. The display options described for customizing the Explorer work exactly the same way in My Computer as well.

As you work with Windows, you can decide whether you prefer to use the Explorer or My Computer to manage your files. You may find a combination of the two approaches works best for you. Because the commands are identical in both, you can move back and forth between the two with ease. Whichever approach you take, you will undoubtedly come to appreciate how easy it is to manage your files in Windows.❖

Chapter 18

Backing Up and Protecting Your Data

by Ron Person

Managing your files means more than just your daily work of creating, naming, and deleting files. If you consider your work valuable, part of your file management routine should be to back up your data by creating a duplicate copy.

The backup program that comes with Windows enables you to create backups onto a removable storage device such as floppy disks, a tape, or a removable hard disk. Windows also includes a virus protection program that can prevent viruses from entering your system and can remove them should they get onto the hard disk. In this chapter, you learn how to

- Copy one or more files from your hard disk to another disk (usually a floppy disk, a tape drive, or another computer on your network).

- Restore your backed-up files to any location you choose (including their original locations).

- Compare files on your backup disks with the original files to ensure their validity.

Backing Up Your Files

As you know, there is more information stored on your hard drive than you can possibly fit on a single floppy disk. The Windows Backup program automatically overcomes this problem by creating a duplicate image of your hard disk's data on a magnetic tape or by spreading an image across multiple floppy disks—as many as necessary to back up your data. During the backup operation, each disk in the set is filled to capacity before the next disk is requested. The collection of all these duplicate files and folders is referred to as the *backup set*.

As hard disks grow in capacity, it becomes more and more laborious to use floppy disks to back up your data. A much more convenient method is to use a tape backup system. You can fit much more data on a magnetic tape and may be able to back up your entire hard drive with one tape. With tape backups, you also avoid the inconvenience of having to sit at your computer swapping floppy disks. In fact, you can initiate the backup when you leave for lunch; when you return, it will be done.

> **Caution**
>
> You put the entire concept of having secure data at risk if your backups are not kept in a safe location, physically separate from the original data. For a small company, the physical location for the backup set can be a safe deposit box or the president's house. For a large company, there are services that pick up tapes and store them in disaster-proof vaults. I personally know of two instances in which the backups were lost along with the original system. In one case, a thief stole the backup floppy disks that sat next to the computer. In the other case, the fire that destroyed the legal firm's computers also destroyed their backups, which were in a closet in an adjacent room.

> **Note**
>
> Backup does not install as part of a typical or minimum installation. If Backup is not installed and you want it, refer to Chapter 10, "Installing, Running, and Uninstalling Windows Applications," on how to add programs. On the Windows Setup page of the Add/Remove Programs Properties sheet, look for Backup in the Disk Tools items in the Components list.

◄ See "Adding Windows' Component Applications," p. 312

Tip
Create a Full System Backup occasionally. It has all the configuration and registry files necessary to rebuild your system from a disaster.

To start the backup program, open the Start menu and click Programs, then Accessories, then System Tools, and finally Backup. When you first start Backup, you may see a Welcome to Microsoft Backup dialog box that describes the process of making backups. You can select the Don't Show This Again check box if you do not want to see this dialog box again. You also may see a message box that says Backup has created a full system backup file set for you. This means that until you specify otherwise, Backup marks all files and folders to be part of the backup. It is a very good idea to do a Full System Backup at least once a week or once a month, depending on the value of your data and how often program configurations change.

Once you are past these initial dialog boxes, the Backup dialog box appears, as shown in figure 18.1.

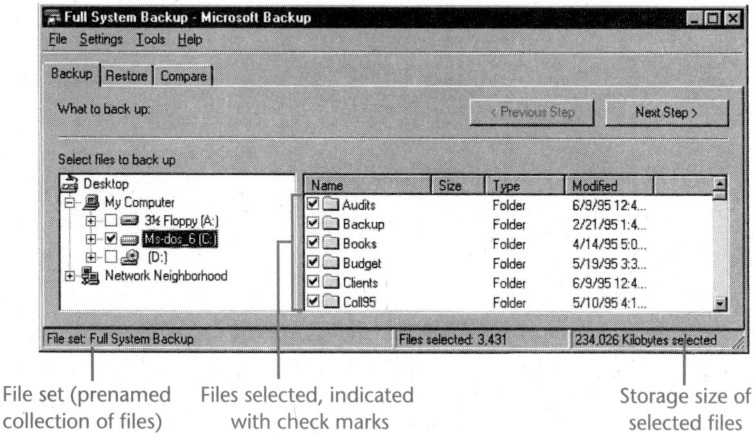

IV

Fig. 18.1
Windows Backup creates duplicate copies of files and folders, compares backups to original files, and restores duplicate files and folders.

Disks and Files

File set (prenamed collection of files) | Files selected, indicated with check marks | Storage size of selected files

The three basic functions of Backup are divided into tabs in the Backup dialog box:

- *Backup*. Copies one or more files and folders from your hard disk.

- *Compare*. Compares the files in a backup set to make sure that they match the source files on the hard disk.

- *Restore*. Copies one or more files from your backup set to the hard disk or to another floppy disk.

In addition to these major functions, several other operations can be accessed from the pull-down menus:

- The File menu enables you to load and save setup files that define settings to be used when backing up and restoring files. The File menu also enables you to print a list of files contained in a backup set.

- The Settings, File Filtering command enables you to filter the folders or file types you want to include in a backup set (this command is discussed in detail later in this chapter). Using the Settings, Options command, you can set various options for each of the major functions, as well as options that affect the program generally.

- The Tools menu contains commands for working with tapes.

An Overview of How to Back Up Your Hard Disk

The Backup program makes it very easy to create backup sets of your data. No longer should you be put off from doing the important chore of backing up. Backup makes it easy to name different sets of backup files so that you don't have to select the files and folders each time. When you aren't using your computer (at lunch time, when you return phone messages, or when you leave work), you can start a backup.

Here is the general procedure for creating a backup:

1. Have enough formatted floppy disks or tapes to store the backup.

2. Start Windows Backup.

3. Select the name of a backup set you previously created. Alternatively, manually select the drives, files, and folders you want to back up.

4. Select the Next Step button, then select the destination to which you want to back up. This could be to a tape, a floppy disk drive, or to another hard disk.

5. Start the backup.

When Backup is finished, you should store the backup media in a safe location physically separate from the computers.

Tip

For an extensive list of tape drives compatible with Backup, choose Help, select the Contents tab, then select the Using Tapes for Backup item.

Windows Backup supports the following tape drives and backup devices:

- Hard disks

- Network drives

- Floppy disks

- QIC 40, 80, 3010, and 3020 tape drives connected to a primary floppy disk controller

- QIC 40, 80, and 3010 tape drives, manufactured by Colorado Memory Systems and connected to a parallel port

Backup supports compression using the industry standard QIC-113 format. It can read tapes from other backup programs that use the same format with or without compression. Full backups can be restored to a hard disk of another type.

Preparing a Backup Schedule

When you back up important or large amounts of data, it's important to have a backup schedule and a rotation plan for the backup tapes.

Basically, the backup schedule for most businesses should consist of a full system backup followed by partial or differential backups spread over time. Should your computer ever completely fail, you can rebuild your system using the full backup (which restores Windows, the system Registry, all applications, and their data files as they existed on a specific date). You can then use the partial or differential backups (which store only changed files) to bring the restored system back to its current status. Do a full system backup once a week and a differential backup daily.

Never use one set of tapes for all your backups. If you have only one set of tapes, composed of a full backup and partials, creating another backup means that you overwrite one of the previous backups. Should the tape or computer fail during backup, you might be left with no backups capable of restoring your system.

Some companies create a full system backup every day. At the end of the week, the tapes are taken to an off-site vault and a new set of tapes are started. Multiple sets of backup tapes are used and rotated between the on-site and off-site storage locations.

Tip

Creating a full backup is important to preserving your entire system. Full backups take care of merging Registry settings and the file replacements necessary when restoring a Windows system.

Backing Up Files

Running a backup operation consists of selecting the files you want to back up, specifying the destination for the backup files, and starting the backup. The files that you select for backup will be stored in a single backup file with the extension QIC. To perform a backup, follow these steps:

1. Open the Start menu, click Programs, Accessories, System Tools, and then Backup.

2. Select the drive containing the files you want to back up. To select the drive, click the check box for the drive in the left pane of the Backup window.

   In figure 18.1, local drive C is selected. The files and folders on the drive are displayed in the right pane. You can expand and collapse the hierarchical display in the left pane by clicking the plus (+) and minus (–) signs next to the folders.

3. Select the files and folders you want to back up. If you want to back up using a file set you have previously named, choose File, Open File Set and select the file set you want to back up.

Tip

Whenever you frequently work with the same files and settings, save them as a file set.

▶ See "Saving File Sets," p. 563

You can select all the files in a folder by clicking the check box next to the folder's name in the left pane of the Backup dialog box.

To view the files and folders inside a folder, in the left pane, open the folder containing the folders or files you want to view. Then in the left pane, click the name of the folder whose contents you want to see; its contents are displayed in the right pane. You can then select individual files or folders inside that folder.

To select the entire drive, click the box next to the drive in the left pane.

If you select a folder with many files, a File Selection dialog box momentarily appears, notifying you that file selection is in progress; the box displays the number of files and their total size as the selection progresses.

The total number of files currently selected and their cumulative size appears in the status bar at the bottom of the window.

4. When you have finished selecting the files and folders you want to back up, click the Next Step button.

5. Select the destination for the backup files (see fig. 18.2).

If you select a tape drive, the volume name for that tape appears in the Selected Device or Location box. If you select a disk drive, this box shows the drive letter or path, such as A:\.

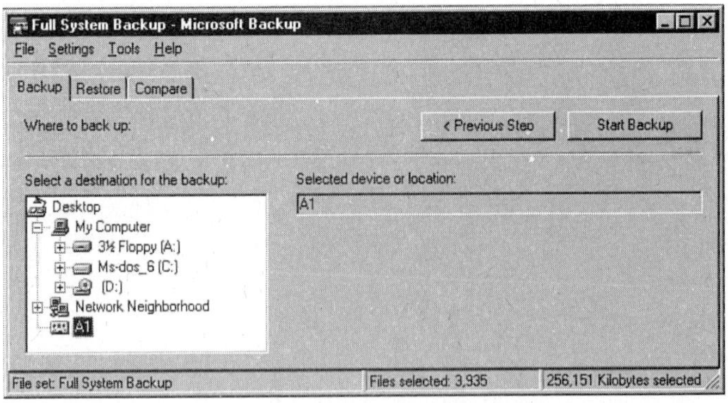

Fig. 18.2
Select the destination for the files you want to back up.

6. Save the file settings for this backup set if you will be doing this backup frequently (see "Saving File Sets," later in this chapter, for more information on saving backup sets).

7. Click the Start Backup button.

8. Type a name for the backup set in the Backup Set Label dialog box that appears (see fig. 18.3). This will be the name of the file containing all the files you have selected for backup.

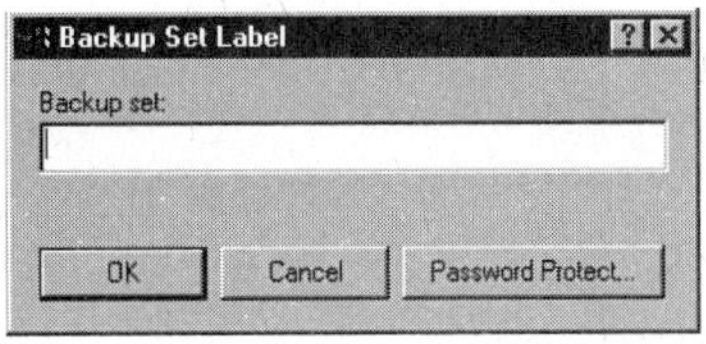

Fig. 18.3
Name the backup set in the Backup Set Label dialog box.

If you want to prevent unauthorized people from restoring the backup and stealing your data, click the Password Protect button in the Backup Set Label dialog box and enter a password.

The name you enter for the backup set is used by you and the computer to identify the data if you ever need to restore or compare it. You can use meaningful names that include spaces, symbols, and numbers. You may want to use a name such as *Accounting, full backup 5/10/95*.

Caution

Do not forget the password you assign to your backup set. Without it, there is no way to use your backup.

When you have specified a backup label and an optional password, choose OK. The Backup message box appears (see fig. 18.4), showing you the progress of the backup operation. You can cancel the operation by choosing the Cancel button.

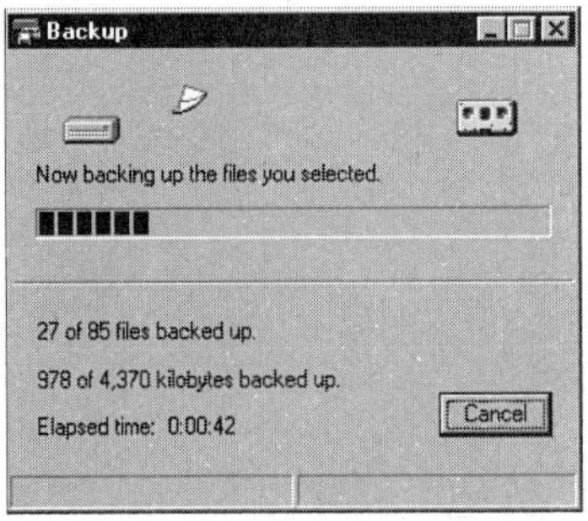

Fig. 18.4
You can monitor the progress of a backup operation in the Backup message box.

Disks and Files

IV

If you are backing up to floppy disks, a message box prompts you when you need to insert the next disk, if necessary.

9. When the message box appears informing you that the backup operation is complete, click OK; click OK again to return to the Backup dialog box.

Using Backup to Create an Archive

The Backup program is a handy way to archive files. Suppose that you want to make room on your hard disk by deleting some files you are not currently using but want to use at a later date. Use Backup to archive the files to floppy disks or a tape; then delete the files from the hard disk. If you need the files later, use the restore function to put them back on your hard disk.

Using Backup to Copy Files to Another Computer

▶ See "Restoring Files," p. 566

Another use for Backup is for transferring folders and files to another computer. The benefit of using Backup for this task is that it takes care of spreading the files across multiple floppy disks when necessary, and it preserves the arrangement of folders, so that you can duplicate your folder organization on another computer. If you purchase a laptop, for example, you can use Backup to transfer the information on your desktop computer to the laptop, including the arrangement of your folders.

Changing Backup Settings and Options

You can change several settings and options that affect your backup operations. To change the settings and options for the backup operation, follow these steps:

1. Open the Settings menu and choose Options.

2. Click the Backup tab to display the dialog box shown in figure 18.5.

3. Change or select from the following options and then choose OK:

Option	Function
Quit Backup After Operation Is Finished	Closes Backup when the backup operation is completed.
Full: Backup of All Selected Files	Backs up all selected files, regardless of whether file has changed since the last backup.
Differential: Backup of Selected Files that Have Changed Since the Last Full Backup	Backs up only selected files that have changed since the last full backup.

Option	Function
Verify Backup Data by Automatically Comparing Files After Backup Is Finished	Compares each file that is backed up with the original file to verify accurate backup.
Use Data Compression	Compresses files as they are backed up to allow more files to be backed up on a tape or floppy disk.
Format when Needed on Tape Backups	Automatically formats an unused tape before backup operation. This only works on tapes that have not already been formatted.
Always Erase on Tape Backups	Erases the tape on backup. When this option is not selected, backups are added to the tape if there is room.
Always Erase on Floppy Disk Backups	Automatically erases floppy disks before they are used in a floppy disk backup operation. When this option is not selected, backups are added to the floppy disk if there is room.

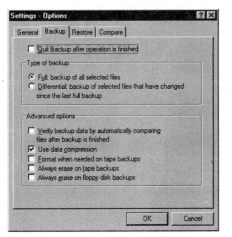

Fig. 18.5
Use the Backup tab in the Settings—Options dialog box to change the settings and options that affect the way backup operations work.

Saving File Sets

If you back up the same set of files regularly, you can save the settings for that file set. Saving backup settings saves you the trouble of reselecting the files and destination each time you want to back up the files.

To save a file set, follow these steps:

1. Open the Backup program. On the Backup page select the files you want to back up, as described earlier in this chapter. Click the Next Step button.

IV

Disks and Files

2. Select the destination for the backup files from the Select a Destination list.

3. Choose File, Save As. The Save As dialog box appears (see fig. 18.6).

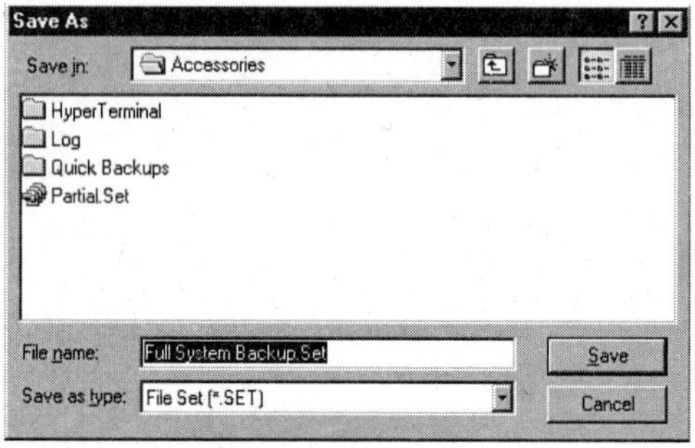

Fig. 18.6

Name your file set with a recognizable name for what it contains and when it was created.

4. Type a name for the backup set in the File Name text box.

5. Choose the Save button.

6. Choose the Start Backup button if you want to continue the backup operation and create a backup using the file set you just specified.

If you make changes to an existing file set, choose the File, Save command to save the file set with the same name without opening the Save As dialog box.

To open a file set for use in a backup operation, follow these steps:

1. Open the Backup program, and then click on the Backup tab. Choose File, Open File Set to display the Open dialog box shown in figure 18.7.

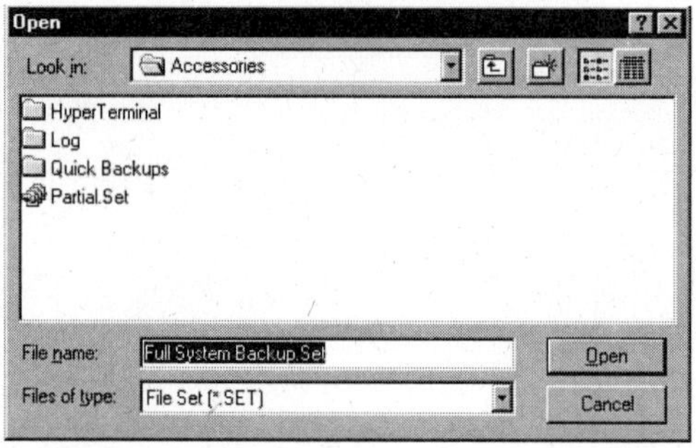

Fig. 18.7

Open a file set to use in a backup or restore operation from the Open dialog box.

2. If you cannot see the file set you want to open, open the folder that contains the file set.

3. Select the file set and choose Open.

The file set is opened, and the files named in this file set are selected in the Backup dialog box.

Filtering Folders and File Types Included in Backup Operations

Backup's file-filtering commands enable you to filter out specific folders and types of files so that they are not included in the backup set. These commands can save you a lot of time when you are creating a file set to be backed up.

You may not want to include all the files on your hard disk in a backup operation. In some cases, you may want to back up all but a few folders; it is easier to specify the folders you *don't* want to include in the backup set than to select all the folders you do want to include. You may not want to include program files in your daily backups because you can always reinstall your programs if your system crashes. You can dramatically reduce the number of disks you use in a backup if you limit the file set to data files only.

To exclude files of a specific type or date from a backup, follow these steps:

1. Choose Settings, File Filtering. The File Filtering—File Types dialog box appears, as shown in figure 18.8.

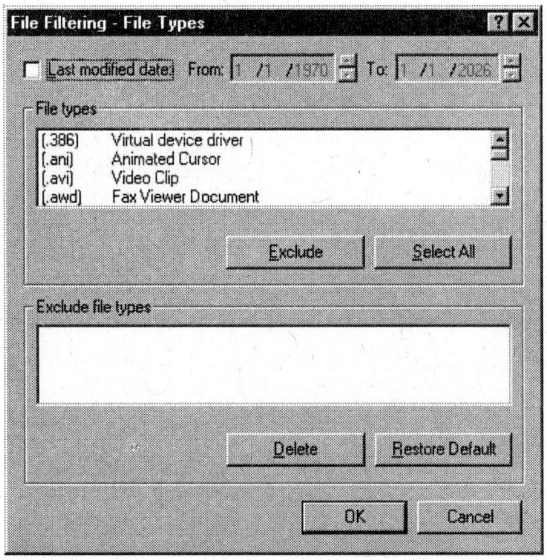

Fig. 18.8
You can exclude files of a specific type or files with specific dates.

2. To exclude files modified between two dates, select the Last Modified Date check box. Enter From and To dates that *exclude* the files you do not want copied. Click the insertion point in the date segment you want to change and then click the up or down spinner arrow to change the date.

Tip
If you want to
exclude all but
a few of the
file types in
the File Types
list, click Select
All, and then
click the types
of files you
don't want to
exclude.

For example, if you want to exclude files before November 30, 1995, enter a From date of 1/1/1970 and a To date of 11/30/95.

3. To exclude specific file types from the backup operation, select the types of files you want to exclude from the File Types list and click Exclude. Continue to select file types and click the Exclude button until all the file types you want to exclude appear in the Exclude File Types list at the bottom of the dialog box.

   To select all of the file types in the list, click Select All.

4. To delete a file type from the list in the Exclude File Types box, select the file type and click Delete.

5. To clear the Exclude File Types box, click Restore Default.

6. When you finish making your selections, choose OK.

Restoring Files

If you're lucky, you may never have to use Backup's restore function. When you do need it, however, it's as easy to use as the backup function. You can restore all the files from a backup set or select specific files or folders to restore. You can also choose where you want to restore the files.

To restore files, follow these steps:

1. Open the Backup program and click the Restore tab (see fig. 18.9).

Fig. 18.9
In the Restore tab
of the Backup
dialog box, select
the files you want
to restore.

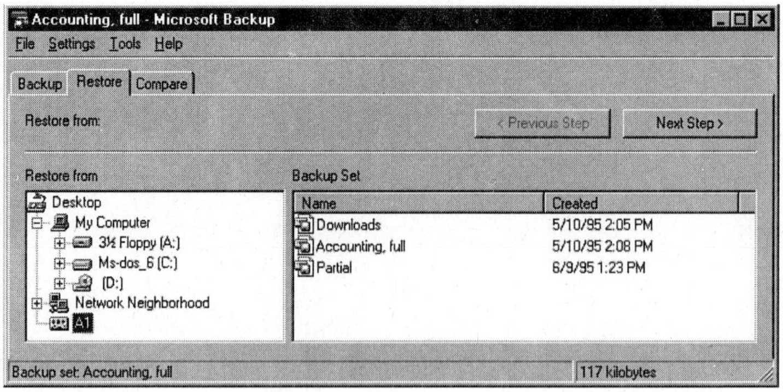

2. Select the drive containing the backup files from the left panel of the window. In figure 18.9, the tape drive has been selected as the backup source.

3. Select the backup set containing the files you want to restore from the right pane. If you have more than one backup file on a floppy disk or tape, select the one containing the files you want to restore. A single backup file, with the extension QIC, contains the files you backed up.

4. Click the Next Step button.

5. Select the folders or files you want to restore as shown in figure 18.10.

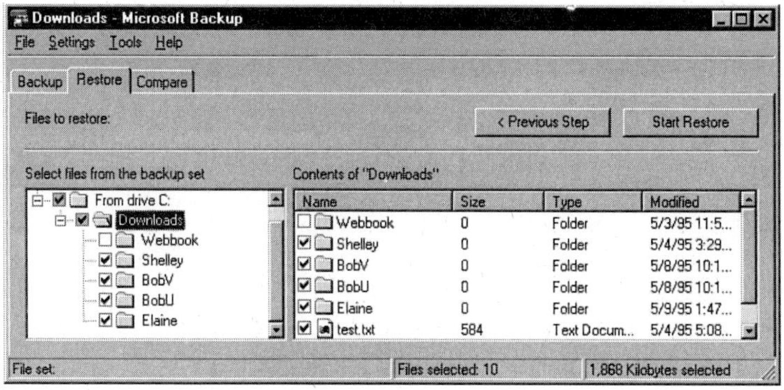

Fig. 18.10
You can select all or part of a backup set when you restore.

6. Click the Start Restore button. The Restore message box appears, showing you the progress of the restore operation (see fig. 18.11).

    By default, the files are restored to their original location. You can choose to restore the files to another location by changing one of the restore options, as described below.

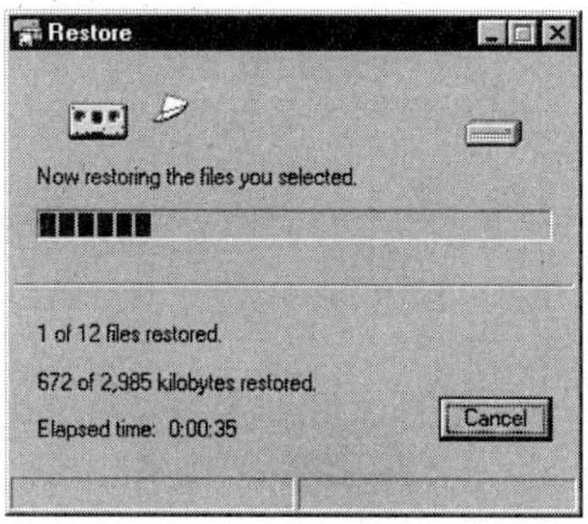

Fig. 18.11
The Restore message box tells you how the restore operation is progressing.

7. When the Operation Complete message box appears, choose OK.

Restoring Files to Other Locations

You can restore files to a location other than their original location (the location from which they were initially backed up). To restore files to an alternate location, follow these steps:

1. Choose Settings, Options.

2. Click the Restore tab.

3. Select the Alternate Location option and choose OK.

4. Perform steps 1 through 6 of the restore procedure described in the preceding section (stop just before you have to click the Start Restore button).

5. Click the Start Restore button. The Browse for Folder dialog box appears (see fig. 18.12).

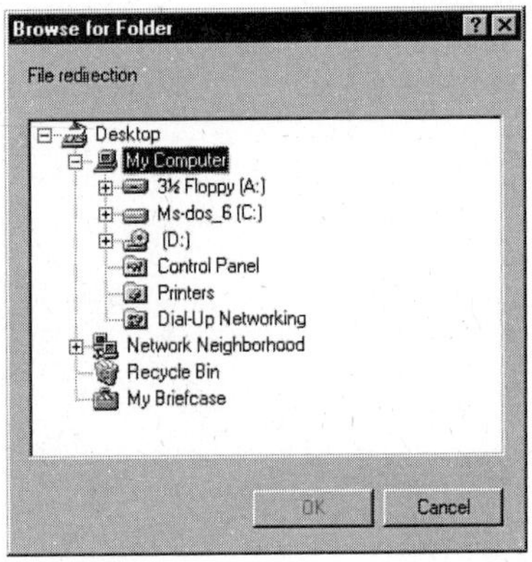

Fig. 18.12
Select the location to which you want to restore files from the File Redirection box.

6. Select the location to which you want to restore the files and choose OK.

7. When the Operation Complete message box appears, choose OK.

Changing Restore Settings and Options

You can change several settings and options that affect your restore operations. To change the settings and options for the restore function, follow these steps:

1. Choose Settings, Options.

2. Click the Restore tab to display the dialog box shown in figure 18.13.

Fig. 18.13
Use the Restore tab in the Settings–Options dialog box to change the settings and options that affect the way restore operations work.

IV

Disks and Files

3. Change or select from the following options and then choose OK:

Option	Function
Quit Backup after Operation Is Complete	Closes Backup when the restore operation is completed.
Original Locations	Restores files to their original locations.
Alternate Location	Restores files to an alternate location. (See "Restoring Files to Other Locations," earlier in this chapter.)
Alternate Location, Single Directory	Restores files to a single directory at an alternate location. Doesn't duplicate original folder structure.
Verify Restored Data by Automatically Comparing Files after the Restore Has Finished	Compares each file to file on disk or t⌐,⌐⌐ after it is restored to check for accuracy of restore.
Never Overwrite Files	Files that are already on the destination location are not overwritten during a restore operation.
Overwrite Older Files Only	Only files that are older than the files in the backup set are overwritten during a restore operation.
Overwrite Files	All files are overwritten during a restore operation. Use the Prompt Before Overwriting Files check box to specify whether you want to be prompted before a file is overwritten.

Verifying Backup Files

The first time you use a series of disks or a tape for a backup, or any time you want to be absolutely sure of your backup, you should do a comparison. When you compare backups to the original files, you verify that the backup copies are both readable and accurate. To perform a compare, follow these steps:

1. Open the Backup program and click the Compare tab.

2. From the left pane, select the device containing the backup files you want to compare (see fig. 18.14).

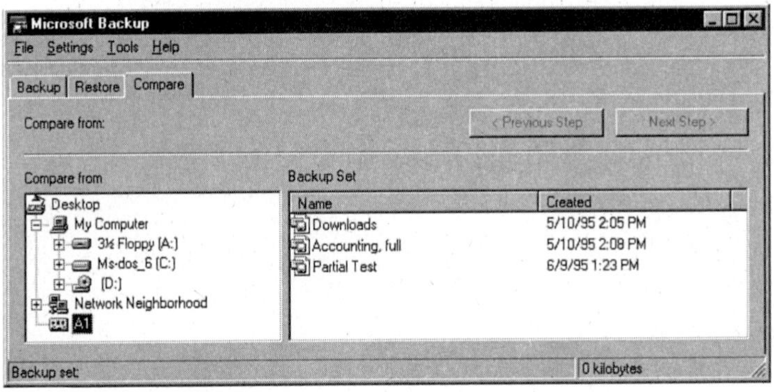

Fig. 18.14

Use the Compare function to verify the accuracy of your backup operations.

3. From the right pane, select the backup set containing the files you want to compare.

4. Click the Next Step button.

5. Select the files or folders you want to compare to the original files.

6. Click the Start Compare button. The Compare message box informs you of the progress of the compare operation.

7. Choose OK when the Operation Complete message box appears; choose OK again to return to the Backup dialog box.

Changing Compare Settings and Options

You can change several settings and options that affect your compare operations. To change the settings and options for the compare function, follow these steps:

1. Choose Settings, Options.

2. Click the Compare tab to display the dialog box shown in figure 18.15.

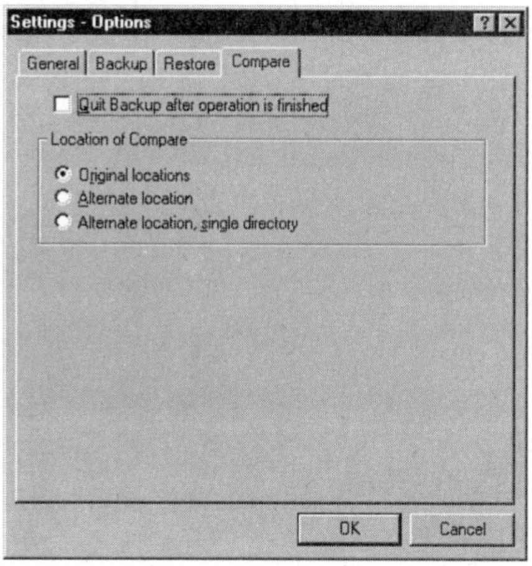

Fig. 18.15
Use the Compare tab in the Settings—Options dialog box to change the settings and options that affect the way compare operations work.

3. Change or select from the following options and then choose OK:

Option	Function
Quit Backup after Operation Is Finished	Closes Backup when the compare operation is completed.
Original Locations	Compare files to files at their original locations.
Alternate Location	Compares files to files at an alternate location.
Alternate Location, Single Directory	Compare files to files in a single directory at an alternate location. Doesn't look for duplicates of the original folder structure.

Changing the General Settings in Backup

You can change two options in Backup that affect the backup, restore, and compare functions. To change these options, choose Settings, Options. Select the General tab to display the dialog box shown in figure 18.16.

■ Select the Turn on Audible Prompts option if you want to hear beeps from your computer's speaker during backup, compare, and restore operations.

■ Select the Overwrite Old Status Log Files option to replace the old status log with the new one generated by the current backup. The status log records errors and completions of file backups.

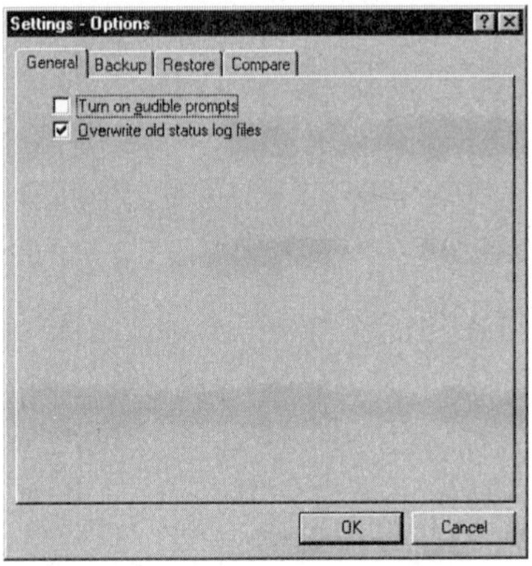

Fig. 18.16
Use the General tab in the Settings—Options dialog box to change the settings and options that affect the way Backup's operations work.

Backing Up with a Simple Drag-and-Drop

Tip
Experienced Windows users may want to set up other users' computers with drag-and-drop backup so they can easily protect their data.

Once you understand the importance of backing up files and see how easy it is to do, you will back up frequently. There is an easy way to back up your files if you have created file sets (as described earlier in this chapter). You can drag a file set and drop it onto the Backup icon or you can double-click a file set name. Either of these actions immediately starts the backup. With the appropriate settings, the entire backup operation can go on in the background and you can continue to use the computer for other tasks.

To prepare Backup for drag-and-drop operation, follow these steps:

1. Choose Settings, Drag and Drop to display the Drag and Drop dialog box shown in figure 18.17.

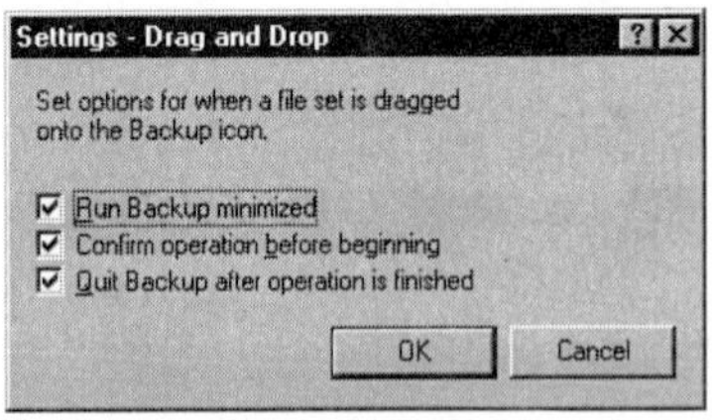

Fig. 18.17
Change the Backup settings to make drag-and-drop backup operate in the background while you work.

2. Change or select from the following options and then choose OK:

Option	Function
Run Backup Minimized	After dragging a file set onto the Backup icon, the Backup window minimizes.

Option	Function
Confirm Operation <u>B</u>efore Beginning	Displays a message showing which files will be backed up. Asks you to confirm that you want the files backed up.
<u>Q</u>uit Backup after Operation Is Finished	Quits Backup after the file set is backed up.

If Backup is operating in the background, you do not see it as a window on-screen. If you need to stop a backup that is in the background, display the taskbar and click the Backup button. A dialog box displays the current backup status and gives you the opportunity to Cancel the backup.

> **Note**
>
> If you have multiple file sets, but you don't want them all as Shortcuts on your desktop, you can still start them quickly to do a backup. In the Windows Explorer or My Computer window, double-click the name of the file set you want to back up. You are prompted whether you want to make a backup; the backup runs with the settings specified for that file set.

Before you can create backups with a drag-and-drop procedure, you must display the Backup program icon. You can open the Program Files/Accessories folder in a window in the Windows Explorer or My Computer. A more convenient method is to create a shortcut to BACKUP.EXE and display it on your desktop.

If you also want a quick way to find and display the SET files that specify your file sets, create a shortcut to the directory containing the SET files. You can do this by using the Find command (available on the Start menu) to find all files that end with SET. Create a new folder and drag the SET files into the new folder. Now create a shortcut to this folder and put that shortcut on the desktop (see fig. 18.18). (Creating shortcuts is described in Chapter 3, "Getting Started with Windows 95.")

◀ See "Starting Programs from a Shortcut Icon on the Desktop," p. 68

> **Note**
>
> Normally, the file sets are stored in the Program Files\Accessories folder. If you are unsure where your backup file sets are stored on your hard disk, open the Start menu and choose Find. Search for all files ending with .SET by entering ***.SET** in the <u>N</u>amed box.

Fig. 18.18
Once drag-and-drop is enabled, backing up is as easy as dropping a file-set icon onto the Backup shortcut.

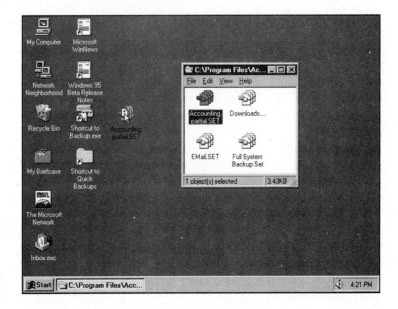

To back up a file set, you only need to double-click the shortcut to the folder containing the file sets. This opens the folder containing the file sets as a Window on your desktop. Figure 18.18 shows such an open folder. Now drag the file set you want to back up onto the shortcut to BACKUP.EXE and drop it. You are prompted whether you want to continue with the backup operation. Respond by clicking Yes or No.

Formatting and Erasing Tapes

If you use tapes to do your backups, Backup includes two tools for working with tapes. When you purchase a new tape, you must format the tape before you can use it, just as you format a floppy disk. The Format Tape command formats a tape for you. If you want to erase the contents on a tape before you use it for a new backup operation, you can use the Erase Tape command.

To format a tape, follow these steps:

1. Insert the tape in the tape drive.

2. Open the Backup program and choose Tools, Format Tape. If the Format Tape command is grayed out, choose the Redetect Tape command, which enables Backup to detect the tape.

3. When the Format Tape dialog box appears (see fig. 18.19), type a name for the tape and choose OK. You use this name to identify the tape relative to other tapes you use.

Formatting begins. The progress of the formatting operation is displayed in the Format Tape dialog box.

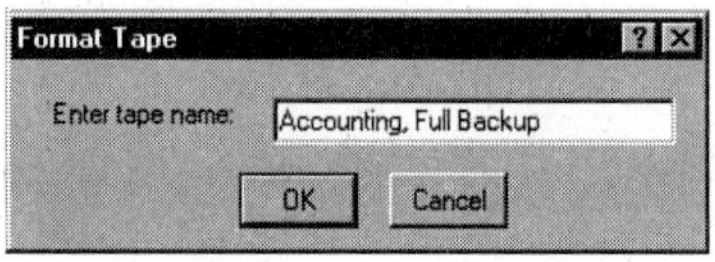

Fig. 18.19
Enter a name for
the tape you are
formatting in the
Format Tape dialog
box.

4. When the message box appears telling you the operation is complete, choose OK; choose OK again to return to the Backup dialog box.

To erase a tape, follow these steps:

1. Insert the tape in the tape drive.

2. Open the Backup dialog box and choose Tools, Erase Tape. If the Erase Tape command is grayed out, choose the Redetect Tape command, which enables Backup to detect the tape.

3. Choose Yes when the confirmation message box appears. The progress of the erase operation is displayed in the Erase dialog box.

4. When the message box appears telling you the operation is complete, choose OK; choose OK again to return to the Backup dialog box.

Protecting Your Files from Viruses

You need to take measures for protecting your computer against viruses, a scourge of the modern day computer world. In addition to backing up your system regularly, you should obtain an anti-virus program and make a habit of using it on a regular basis to protect your files against infection, especially if you frequently introduce files onto your hard disk from outside sources.

Understanding How Viruses Hurt Your Computer

A *computer virus* is a program designed to do damage to either your computer or your computer's data. Viruses make copies of themselves and spread from one computer to another, just as they do in people. Just as fitness, good food, and medicine can protect you from sickness, you can use an anti-virus program to protect your computer from a virus.

The best method of protection is prevention. There are only two ways in which viruses can be transmitted between computers:

■ Loading and running infected software

■ Booting up with an infected floppy disk

If you don't do either of these things, your system won't acquire a virus. But because such an insulated approach to computers is virtually impossible, you should consider using an anti-virus program. Used correctly, a good anti-virus program can protect you against the vast majority of known viruses before they damage your computer.❖

Part V

Networking with Windows 95

Chapter 19

Understanding
Networks

by Michael Marchuk

This chapter is dedicated to discussing the basics of networking. Although many people might use computers on a network at work, the concepts behind the system are still unfamiliar. By reviewing the ideas presented in this chapter, you can understand how your computers share information on a basic level. Understanding these basic networking concepts will enable you to participate with other users in your workgroup to design and maintain the best possible network for your situation.

Specifically, this chapter addresses

- The importance of networking in today's businesses

- The basic concepts that make your network run

- The four building blocks of the Windows networking architecture

- Sharing network resources

The Value of Networks in Business Computing

Networking computers together to share information is not a new phenomenon. In fact, universities and the government have been doing it for several decades. Even some large corporations have been involved with networking their computer resources for 20 or more years. But some companies, both large and small, are still relatively new to networking.

Computing without Networks

With the introduction of the PC in the early 1980s, many companies began to realize the benefits of computers within their own businesses. For the first time, computing power was available to companies that didn't have the personnel to staff mainframe operations. Spreadsheet and word processing software became the software of choice in the workplace.

However, as companies bought more computers for their staff, the complications of sharing the information became more difficult. Sharing a data file with someone else in the office meant making a copy of the current file and putting it on a disk. Even this method of file sharing was sufficient when there were few computers. But spreadsheet files began to get larger than one disk could hold and disk-swapping became cumbersome in larger companies. Additionally, since printers were still relatively expensive, they were often either wheeled around on carts, or set up at one computer which was designated as the "print station" for a department.

Businesses needed a way to share information quickly without the need for disks and to share printers without the need for a printer station. In time, the problems and solutions encountered by businesses became common to the PC market.

Business Networking Evolves

The networks of computers that evolved allowed businesses to spend more time working on their data than moving hardware or disks between offices. Networks with central servers could offer hundreds of megabytes of storage that could be shared with others in the office. Expensive printers could be centrally managed by the network server that provided faster printing.

Information sharing within this environment has continued to progress to the point where spreadsheets between departments or divisions can be merged to provide a better picture of their company's health. For example, daily store receipts can be analyzed at the end of each day to provide an up-to-date picture of sales projections, inventory amounts can be managed for many locations using centralized warehouses for distributing products, and customers can be informed about new products and services using fax-back or recorded message systems run by computers.

Inter-Business Networking

Networking continues to expand its importance within the business environment. With Electronic Data Interchange (EDI), businesses can maintain acceptable inventory levels by ordering raw materials from suppliers electronically. Also, many banks are beginning to offer businesses account management software to handle banking transactions through their computer networks.

Another network that is quickly becoming the most important business tool is the world-wide network known as the Internet. Businesses on the Internet can transfer data files with branch offices world-wide as easily as they could exchange data with someone in the local office. Additionally, office workers who once were required to be at an office can now be spread across the globe to handle customer requests for account information.

Future Business Networking

As businesses continue to grow, their physical office space becomes more expensive. Adding workers to handle the workload of increased sales often means moving to larger facilities. But some businesses are beginning to experiment with new networking concepts that will help them maintain a competitive advantage.

Telecommuting

Office workers that handle functions, such as data entry, customer support, accounting, or other tasks, can often do the same work from home as they can from the office. These workers don't physically commute to their offices, rather they use the phone lines to connect into the company's network. These workers are called *telecommuters*. The network saves the business expensive office space as well as providing the worker with the comfort of a home setting in which to work. The jury is still out on this subject, but initial indications show that some workers are more productive at home than at the office.

Video Conferencing

Businesses also are looking into the realm of *video conferencing*, which allows meetings to occur between many people in different parts of the world. Cameras and microphones at each user's workstation transmit their images to the other participants which in turn are seen on the user's workstation. These types of meetings could save businesses a considerable amount of time and travel expenses.

Online Shopping

Shopping from home via catalogs, mail-order, and cable television is a multibillion dollar business. Some companies are beginning to see computer networks as an extension of this market. By promoting and selling through a world-wide network, such as the Internet, companies can lower their costs of

V

Networking

doing business while providing the customers with the goods and services they want. This type of networking opportunity is still in its infancy, but a considerable amount of work is being done to make shopping through your computer more convenient.

Approaches to Networks

A network is a way of connecting individual computers so they can share resources. These resources include items such as disk drives, files (databases), printers, and communications equipment. In addition, the network enables greater interaction and communication between the members of the network by using electronic mail, databases, and other data sharing.

The computers connected to a network are called *nodes*. If the nodes are in close proximity (typically within a building) to each other, the network is called a *local area network*, or *LAN*. If the nodes are more widely dispersed (across the state, nation, or world), the network is called a *wide area network*, or *WAN*. If you are using Windows 95, you typically are connected to a LAN, which is the focus of this chapter.

LAN networking uses two general approaches, both of which Windows 95 supports. These approaches are client/server and peer-to-peer networks.

Client/Server Networks

Client/server networks use a dedicated computer (the server) that centrally handles all file and print services for many users. A network may have many servers to handle file and print sharing for specific groups of users or to handle database services for the network.

The clients on the network are *workstations* that connect to the server. Client workstations are typically computers at a worker's desk that they use for spreadsheet or word-processing tasks. Network clients can print to the server's printer or save files to the server's hard drive. Figure 19.1 shows an example of a client/server network.

While clients in a client/server network may be powerful machines used for heavy-duty spreadsheet calculations, they also can be low-powered PC's that are only used for word-processing tasks. Servers, on the other hand, are typically powerful machines that are optimized for providing the fastest response to network clients and the most protection for the network's data. Additionally, since servers must be able to handle the requests of many clients simultaneously and secure the network data from unauthorized users, the server has to run an advanced operating system that is dedicated for this purpose. Some of the client/server operating systems that Windows 95 can connect to include:

- Novell NetWare

- Windows NT Server

- IBM OS/2 LAN Server

- Banyan Vines

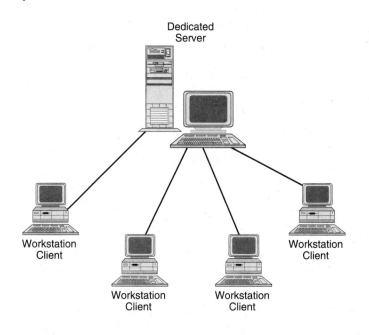

Dedicated
Server

Workstation
Client

Workstation
Client

Workstation
Client

Workstation
Client

Fig. 19.1
Clients access a dedicated server in a client/server network.

V

Networking

Peer-to-Peer Networks

Peer-to-peer networks do not use a central server to store files or to host printers. In a peer-to-peer network, the workstations share hard drives and printers, acting as part-time servers (see fig. 19.2). In addition to providing computing services to the user at a workstation, the computer must service file and print requests from other computers on the network. Of course, if a workstation is not sharing a printer or any hard drive space, then the workstation acts only as a client to another workstation that provides file and print services on the network. Windows 95 has built-in peer-to-peer networking capabilities.

> **Caution**
>
> While peer-to-peer networks offer great flexibility because any workstation can share printers or hard drive space, low-powered workstations can easily become over-loaded with tasks related to both sharing resources and performing work tasks for the local user. If you plan on sharing your printer or hard drive with others on the net-work, expect to see some performance degradation with your local tasks when others are printing or sharing files on your system. If your computer is sluggish all of the time while sharing resources, you may need to consider moving the shared resources to another workstation with a more powerful CPU, dedicating a workstation as a server, or purchasing a client/server network that can handle the load.

Fig. 19.2

Peer-to-peer networks enable workstations to be both clients and servers on the network.

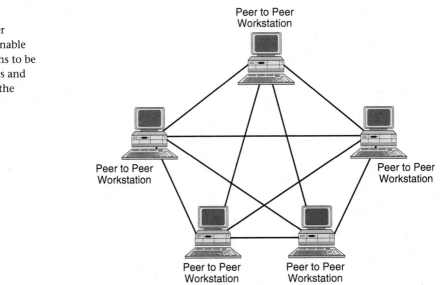

Although the peer-to-peer networking functions are built into Windows, you may need to connect to one of several other peer-to-peer networks. Other peer-to-peer networks supported by Windows 95 include:

■ NetWare Lite

■ Artisoft LANtastic

The Different Layers of a Network

In the world of networking, the concept of *one size fits all* does not apply. Each network can be tailored to fit the needs of the company using different technologies to assemble the right network. This section focuses on the various types of networks and the advantages and disadvantages of each.

You can think of networking as many different layers of software that interact with the hardware connecting computers together. The Open Systems Interconnect (OSI) networking model breaks networking into seven layers to illustrate this concept. This discussion is going to present the five layers that most users have the highest need to understand. To begin, try to conceptualize two basic layers on which the communication of the network takes place. These two layers are the *physical layer* and the *logical layer,* as shown in figure 19.3.

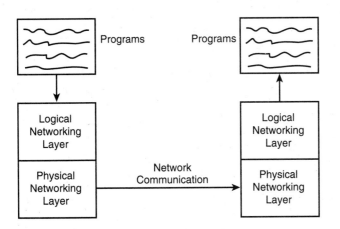

Fig. 19.3
Two networking layers—the physical layer and logical layer— interact to perform the communications between other computers.

Physical Layer

Think of the physical layer as the wire connecting your workstation to others on the network. The physical layer is the tangible piece of the networking system; this layer includes the network interface cards, cabling, connections, and any additional hardware such as concentrators and repeaters.

The logical layer is the layer that interprets the electrical voltage signals and translates them into binary data (0's and 1's) that can be passed to the next layer and interpreted by the computer.

Network Layer

The network layer is responsible for identifying the computers on the network. Each computer on the network uses the addressing mechanism that is run through the network layer to send data to the appropriate workstation.

Transport Layer

The transport layer is responsible for making sure that all of the data sent from one computer is received properly. The transport layer also makes sure that the data that may have been received out-of-order is reassembled into the right order.

Application Layer

The application layer is the software you run on your workstation. When you access a network drive letter or print to a network printer, your program is using the application layer to send the data over the network.

LAN Topologies

Many different methods are used for arranging the computers in a network and connecting them to each other. These various arrangements are called *topologies*. Each topology has certain advantages that make it more desirable in particular situations. By understanding these advantages, you can make sure your network is tailored appropriately.

Bus Networks

In a bus network, all the computers on the network are connected to the main wire of the network (see fig. 19.4). Like a highway with on/off ramps, the bus network funnels all traffic along the main wire that acts as a backbone for the network.

Fig. 19.4
Each computer on a bus network has equal access to the wire for sending data.

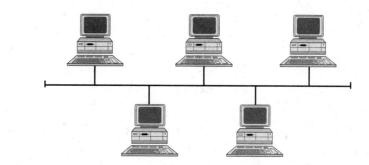

Computers connected in a bus network all have equal access to the wire at any point in time. To govern the use of the wire, the logical layer must wait until the wire is free before sending data to another computer on the network. Again, like a highway ramp, the logical layer manages the merging function to prevent collisions.

Bus networks have the advantage of incremental addition. As the network grows, additional workstations can be added to the network one at a time. The disadvantage for bus networks is the dependence on the backbone for all of the traffic. If the network is cut at any point, either by accident or by adding another network node, the entire network is out of service. The bus style network, though, is usually the least expensive to implement since it only requires the cable itself to connect each of the nodes.

An example of a bus network is Ethernet, which is discussed in the "Logical Networks" section later in this chapter.

Star Networks

Star networks connect computers through a central hub (see fig. 19.5). The central hub distributes the signals to all the connecting cables.

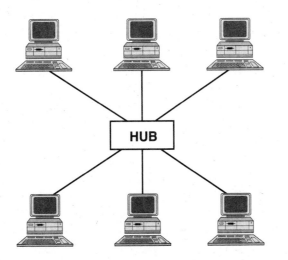

Fig. 19.5

Each node on a star network is linked to the rest of the network through a central hub.

A main advantage of using the star configuration is that each cable connecting the computer with the hub is protected from all the other cables. If one cable connection is broken or the wire is cut, only one of the computers on the network is affected. The other computers can continue to communicate with each other through the central hub. For overall reliability, this type of configuration is best.

V

Networking

The drawback of using a star network configuration affects only very small networks. The central hub equipment can be expensive, up to several thousand dollars depending on the brand of hub and number of connections you purchase. However, some manufacturers have been developing workgroup hubs with four to eight connections that sell for under $200.

Ring Networks

Ring networks connect computers using an In port and an Out port for data. Each computer sends information to the next computer down the wire. Data flows from one computer's Out port to the next computer's In port (see fig. 19.6).

Fig. 19.6
A ring network circulates data between computers on the network.

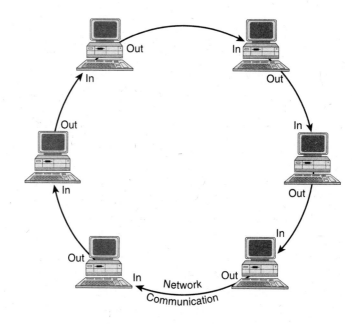

Most manufacturers do not set up true rings like the one shown in figure 19.6. This setup would make wiring very difficult. Instead, a special central hub is used to complete the ring yet maintain a star network cabling layout. Figure 19.7 shows how this special hub, called a Media Access Unit (MAU), works.

Star-Bus Networks

Like the hybrid star-ring network shown in figure 19.7, the star-bus network makes use of a central hub called a concentrator to connect the nodes of the network. All traffic that is sent by any node on the network is then sent to every other node through the concentrator.

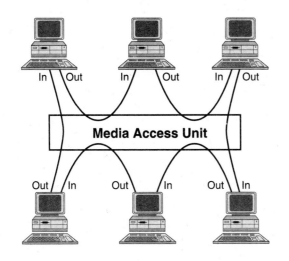

Fig. 19.7
A central Media
Access Unit
combines the
advantages of a
star network and
a ring network.

This type of network is popular in larger installations and in installations where the physical wiring in a bus network configuration is either undesirable or impractical.

Connecting Network Devices

Once you have decided on a network topology for your network, if you are just adding a Windows workstation to your current network, you need to choose networking equipment to meet your needs. This section covers some of the topics you need to know when connecting network devices.

Network Adapter Cards

Network adapter cards function as the link between the wiring of your network and your workstation. These adapter cards give you connection points to which your network cables connect. The adapter card contains a small amount of memory that is used to buffer some of the incoming network data while your computer is processing it. Some newer network cards even have their own processor that assists in handling network traffic.

Windows 95 probably supports any PC network adapter currently available from any vendor, or any network adapter that has been available for the last five years or more (see table 19.1). Because of the vast range of legacy PC hardware, this statement may have some exceptions, but there are few network adapters that Windows 95 does not support either directly or by using the existing 16-bit drivers for pre-existing hardware. For example, if you are using an adapter to connect to a NetWare network, the same adapter likely

V

Networking

works with Windows 95. The specific network topology ultimately determines the type of adapter you must use, but taken as a whole, Windows 95 makes connecting a PC to a NetWare network easier than it has ever been.

Remember these main things when choosing a new network adapter:

- Choose a product that has been designed for Windows 95

- Choose a Plug and Play adapter or modem if available

- Choose the fastest technology available

Table 19.1 lists all of the network cards that are supported by Windows 95 as the product ships out of the box. Any card on this list will work with Windows 95 without any additional drivers. Other cards will work as well, if the manufacturer provides a Windows 95 driver with the card. This list includes all of the model names of cards supported. Some cards have many different submodels supported as well for different interfaces (ISA, VLB, PCI, MCI, PC Card, etc.). In that case, the list includes the main model name to avoid cluttering the table. If you are shopping for cards, keep this list handy (make a photocopy to take to the store with you) to help ensure you get a supported card.

> **Note**
>
> The PCMCIA (Personal Computer Memory Card International Association) designation is now referred to as PC Card.

> **Note**
>
> Windows 95 also supports connecting to networks via a modem rather than a network card. Windows 95 probably supports any Hayes-compatible modem that is currently available or has been available for many years. In the case of dial-up networking, the server you are connecting to might have some requirements that constrain your choice of modem. These requirements can be related to the minimum and maximum speed of the modem connection and also the connection protocol and login methods. Consult the network administrator to confirm specifics that you need to know. Keep in mind that a modem connection is much slower than a network card.

Table 19.1   Network Adapter Cards Supported by Windows 95

Vendor	Models
3COM	Etherlink 16, Etherlink II and IITP, Etherlink III (16 different models of this card are supported), Etherlink Plus, Etherlink/MC, Fast Etherlink 10/100MB TokenLink, TokenLink III (3 models)
ACCTON	EN1660, EN 2216
Allied Telesyn	AT1510
Alta Research	PCMCIA Adapter
AMD	AM2100/AM1500t, PCNET Family (PCI, ISA, ISA+ and VL-Bus)
ArcNet	ARCNET
Artisoft	AE-1, AE-2, AE-3
AST	Token Ring Credit Card Adapter
Boca Research	BOCALANcard, PCMCIA 10BASE-T
Cabletron	E2000, E2100, E2200, E3000, E3100, T2015 4/16 Mbps
Cogent	Cogent Emaster + EM960
Compaq	NetFlex, NetFlex-2 (4 models supported), Elite Ethernet, 16E, Contura Integrated
D-Link	DE220 ISA, DE650 PCMCIA
DCA	IRMATrac (5 models)
DEC	DE100, DE101, DE102, DE200, DE201,DE202, DE210, DE211, DE212, DE425, DE434, DE435, DE500, DEPCA, EE101, Ethernet, Etherworks 3, TokeRing Auto 16/4, 433 WS, Ethernet DECchip 21040, Ethernet DECchip 21041, Fast Ethernet DECchip 21140
Dell	LATITUDE XP
Eagle Technology	NE200T
Everex	SpeedLink
EXOS	Exos 105
Farallon	EtherWave
Fujitsu	MBH10302

V

Networking

(continues)

Table 19.1   Continued

Vendor	Models
HP	Ethertwist, J2573A, J2577A, 16 TL Plus, 16 TP, 16 TP Plus, 8 TL, 8 TP
IBM	Auto 16/4 ISA Token Ring Adaptor, Ethernet Credit Card Adapter, Ethernet Credit Card Adapter II, Token Ring, Token Ring II, Token Ring Credit Card Adapter, Token Ring Credit Card Adapter II
Intel	82595-based, EtherExpress 16, EtherExpress 16TP, EtherExpress 32, EtherExpress PRO/10, EtherExpress PRO/100, TokenExpress
Kingston	Etherx Ethernet PCMCIA Adapter, Token Ring PCMCIA Adapter
Linksys	Combo PCMCIA, Ether 16, EtherFast, EtherPCI
Madge	Smart 16 (13 different models supported)
Microdyne	IRMAtrac (3 models), Novell 4000 PCMCIA Adapter, PCI Ethernet, NE2500, NE2500T
Mitron	LX2100+, PCI Ethernet
National Datacomm	NDC Credit Card Adapter
National Semiconductor	AT/LANTIC EtherNODE, Ethernode 16, NE2000 Plus Informer, NE4100 Infomover
NCR	StarCard, Token Ring 16/4 Mbps, Token Ring 4 Mbps, WaveLAN,
Novell/Anthem	NE/2, NE1000, NE1500T, NE2000, NE2100, NE3200, NE3200T
Olicom	Olicom Token Ring, Olicom Token Ring Server
Ositech	Trumpcard
Piiceon	Piiceon PCMCIA
Proteon	ProNET Token Ring (12 models supported)
Pure Data	PDI508+, PDI516+, PDI9025-32, PDuC9025, Token Ring Credit Card Adapter
Racal	ES3210, NI5210, NI6510
REALTEK	RTL8019
Silicom	Ethernet PCMCIA, Ethernet Pocket

Vendor	Models
SMC	SMC 3000, PC100, PC110, PC120, PC130, PC200, PC210, PC220, PC250, PC260, PC270, PC600W, PC650W, PS110, PS210, ARCNETPC, EtherCard, EtherCard Plus, EtherCard Plus Elite, EtherCard Elite Ultra, EtherElite Ultra, StarCard Plus, TokenCard Plus, TokenCard Elite, ELITE CARD, SMC 9000, Ether EZ, Tiger Card, EtherPower, EtherPower 2
Socket Communications	EA Credit Card Ethernet Adapter
SVEC	FD0421, FD0455
Sys Konnect	Sk-Net
TDK	TDK PCMCIA LAN
Thomas-Conrad	TC5041 PCMCIA, All Arcnet types, TC4035, TC4045, TC4046, TC6042, TC6045, TC6142, TC6145, TC6242, TC6245, TC Card PCMCIA, TC5048, TCTX048 100Base-TX, Token Ring TC4046, Token Ring TC4145Toshiba, Noteworthy PCMCIA, NWETH01 PCMCIA
Tulip	NCC-16
Ungermann-Bass	NIC, NIU, pcNIU
Xircom	CE-10, CE-10/A, CE2, CreditCard Token Ring Adapter, Pocket Ethernet I, Pocket Ethernet II, Pocket Ethernet III, Ethernet+Modem
Zenith	NE2000, Z-Note

V

Networking

> **Note**
>
> If you are buying a network PC Card to use with a laptop for networking, get a card with connectors for both twisted-pair and coaxial cabling. Then you can travel with the laptop and connect to networks with different cabling.

Cabling

The second major physical component of networks is the cabling connecting the nodes. The term *cabling* usually indicates a physical wire of some sort. As networking technology has advanced, other wireless means of connecting nodes have been developed. Therefore, the broader term *media* also applies to cabling. *Bound media* refers to traditional physical cabling, and *unbound media* refers to various wireless forms of connections. This book uses the more generic term *cabling* when referring to both bound and unbound media.

> **Note**
>
> Use a wireless network only in situations where you cannot run a wire or where a long-range connection is too costly via a wired alternative. Wires provide the best security and throughput for almost every application.

Coaxial Cable

The primary reason to use coaxial cable in the bus layout is cost. In most cases, running coaxial cable between your computers is much less expensive than using any of the other types of networks to be discussed. Of course, situations will arise in which coaxial cable will not work. For example, coaxial cabling is quite thick compared to twisted-pair cable. If you have to run cable for several computers through a small hole in a wall or floor, it my be easier to run twisted-pair cable than coaxial cable.

Another aspect of cost savings is very apparent for small networks. You can use coaxial cable to connect several computers in close proximity without the need for costly repeaters, hubs, or MAUs. As you see in the next section, twisted-pair cabling requires additional hardware when connecting more than two devices.

Another advantage that coaxial cable has over some of the other network types is that it is relatively good at shielding the networking signals in the cable from outside electrical "noise," such as the sound fluorescent lights generate.

A disadvantage of coaxial cable is that it is harder to work with and more difficult to install in the walls.

> **Caution**
>
> Because the bus networking architecture requires that computers be connected together sequentially, you are limited on the configurations you can create with coaxial. Also, bus networking relies heavily on all the connections working properly. If a cable has a bad connector, the entire network can stop working. Then finding the bad connector with coaxial cable becomes very difficult because everything might look normal from the outside. It can take hours to find and replace a bad connector, during which time the entire network may be out of service.

Twisted-pair wire has several pairs of wires that are braided within a plastic sheath. By twisting the wires around each other, the electrical signals carried on each individual wire are protected from interference from the other wires in the sheath.

The following list shows several wire types that can be easily confused when installing twisted-pair wiring. We will discuss each one briefly to expose its uses for networking.

> Category 3 Twisted Pair
>
> Category 5 Twisted Pair
>
> ATT phone wire
>
> Silver Satin wire

The Category 3 and Category 5 wires are the most common when dealing with twisted-pair networking installations. The Category 3 wire is less expensive than the Category 5 wire due to the less-advanced signaling properties of the Category 3 wire. Category 3 wire is typically used for Ethernet installations that run at 10M. Category 5 wire has much better signaling properties and can be used for high-speed networking up to 100M.

POTS (Plain-Old Telephone Set) phone wire, which looks similar to twisted-pair wiring, is only good for phones and modems. This wire does not have the same advanced data properties as the Category 3 and 5 wires.

Silver Satin wire was used quite extensively for proprietary printer sharing systems before networking was readily available. This wire should not be used for network installations since it too has poor signaling properties.

Fiber Optic Networks

A *fiber optic* network uses light, rather than electrical pulses, to carry the network signal. The fiber optic cable is a thin glass filament that connects to optical equipment on either end.

The main advantage of using fiber optic cabling involves signal strength. Not only is the fiber optic cable immune to electrical interference, which makes it great for factories or other electrical signal jungles, but fiber optic cable can also transmit a signal for two kilometers. A 10BaseT network can transmit for a maximum of 300 feet with a hub in the middle. The capability to transmit a signal over long distances makes fiber optic cable a good choice for underground cabling run between buildings.

Because of the signal characteristics of the fiber optic cabling, network speeds can increase from the 10M (10,000,000 bits per second) to over 1G (1,000,000,000 bits per second). Although personal computer networks are running 100M using FDDI, the capability of the cabling to run much faster can pay for itself over the years as networking technologies continue to increase network speeds.

The disadvantage of using fiber optic cabling is cost. Both the optical equipment that decodes the light signals and the fiber optic cable itself are expensive. For example, a FDDI network adapter may run around $1,000 while the hub to which it connects runs $500 per connection. However, if the conditions require long cable runs through electrically hostile environments, or when potential ground differences exist between buildings, then fiber optic cable may be the only way to go.

Light-Wave Connections

The light-wave transceivers use either infrared light beams to communicate in close proximity to other computers or lasers to communicate between buildings in relatively close proximity. Light-wave connections work well in many conditions but are very susceptible to interference. Because light waves cannot penetrate walls or ceilings, this type of interface is best-suited for communicating between a laptop and a desktop unit or between two computers that are fairly close together. Also, the speed of these units is typically much slower than other network speeds.

Tip

Use light-wave network bridges when distances are short and the view between the two points is unobstructed. Lasers are easily interrupted if any object passes between the two network bridges.

Laser connections can be made between buildings where the cost of running a cable between them may be prohibitive. These units have the capability to transmit a few hundred feet at network speeds, which makes them a good bridge between buildings. Lasers, like the infrared units, are also susceptible to interference and weather conditions.

Radio-Wave Connections

The second camp of wireless networks involves using radio waves. These units have the capability of transmitting between a few hundred feet and several miles. Typically, as the distance increases, the speed of the connections decreases. A big advantage that radio waves have over light waves is their ability to penetrate walls and ceilings.

A network can choose to use internal radio-wave transceivers for two purposes: either the network cannot be wired conventionally or the network includes laptop computers that require mobility.

The other major use for radio-wave networking is to span larger distances between buildings on a network. Whereas the laser-based network bridge requires an unobstructed view with a range of a couple hundred feet, you can use the radio-wave network bridge over several miles with trees in between. The speed is somewhat less than the laser, and radio waves are also susceptible to interference, but the alternative of leasing a network connection from the phone company is much more expensive.

A good application for a radio-wave based network would be a distribution center where fork trucks need computers to identify what location the driver should go to.

> **Note**
>
> Radio-wave network bridges can be affected by weather or nearby sources of radio transmissions. Check your local area for cellular towers or other radio towers before installing radio-wave network bridges.

Direct Cable Networking

Windows 95 supports a direct-cable network between two computers. This is typically used for a laptop to desktop computer connection; however, it also can be used for two desktops.

The cabling that connects the two computers can be either a serial cable with a null-modem adapter that allows the two computers to connect or a special parallel-port cable that connects directly to each computer. The parallel-port cable (also known as a LapLink cable from the software company that created it) is faster than the serial cable, but the parallel-port cable is not as easy to obtain.

These cables are convenient ways to connect two computers, but the distance between the computers is limited to around 50 feet for a parallel-port cable and around 1,000 feet for a serial cable.

Additional Hardware for Connecting Networks

The hubs and MAUs that were mentioned in several of the sections covered earlier are an integral part of all star networks. Many companies use star networks or hybrid-star networks.

Many smaller companies cannot afford to purchase elaborate network hubs for their networks. In these cases, the companies will be purchasing the low-end of the market in terms of price (and probably quality, too). When you are looking for an inexpensive hub, make sure it supports your network type. If you are running a Token-Ring network, you will be looking for a MAU to connect your computers. You cannot use a 10BaseT hub for this type of network, even though the hardware will most likely be much less expensive. Also, when you do purchase a hub, make sure that the number of connections will be able to support your network for a few years. If you fill up your hub when you install it, you will not be able to add any more network nodes unless you buy another hub.

V

Networking

For mid-sized or larger networks, hubs that offer expandability offer the greatest flexibility. Some hubs have stackable units that allow you to add incrementally to the network. Others are chassis-type systems that allow you to plug in add-in cards to grow the network. Which one is right for you depends on your individual needs. In either case, remember that your entire network will be running through these hubs. If they break, the whole network will be down. Buy quality equipment from a reputable vendor or suffer the consequences

Network Layer Protocols

To communicate on the network, your computer must be speaking the protocol of a particular network. The protocols that run on the network allow the computers to exchange information and maintain the integrity of the data transmissions.

Major network operating systems use particular protocols to communicate with their servers. The following list shows the protocol and the network operating system that uses it. Windows 95 supports all of these protocols:

- IPX/SPX—Novell NetWare, Windows NT Server

- NetBIOS—Windows NT Server, OS/2 LAN Server

- TCP/IP—UNIX, Windows NT Server

Logical Networks

The discussion thus far has concentrated on the physical layer of the network. This section covers the logical layer of the network, which determines how the computers communicate with each other over the physical media.

Ethernet

Ethernet is one of the most popular networks because the network adapters, network hubs, and cabling are relatively inexpensive. Also, the 10M network speed in considered acceptable for most networks. If you are considering building a new network, Ethernet is a good choice.

Ethernet uses the bus or star network types to communicate with other computers on the network. Ethernet 10Base2 and 10Base5 use a coaxial cable in a bus network while 10BaseT uses a twisted-pair wire in a star network. Ethernet uses a Carrier-Sense Media-Access Carrier-Detect (CSMA/CD) to determine when the computer can send data. When a computer wants to send data, it must listen on the wire to ensure that no other computer is sending data. If another computer is sending data, your workstation must wait until the line becomes clear before sending.

Token-Ring

Token-Ring was developed by IBM and until recently, you didn't have many alternatives from which to choose. The Token-Ring network tends to be more expensive than the Ethernet network. The adapters are two to three times as expensive as the Ethernet network adapters, and the hubs are also at least twice as expensive. However, for that additional cost, your network can run at 16M. This additional speed is also complemented by the way computers access the wire.

Unlike Ethernet, which requires the computer to listen for a clear line, Token-Ring computers take turns in sending data. A token is passed between computers in a round-robin fashion. When a workstation has the token, it can send data for a certain amount of time. Then that workstation passes the token to the next computer down the line. Token-Ring networks are set up as a ring network to provide this token-passing capability and to increase the throughput of the network.

Unless your network requires Token-Ring for communications to other network nodes or to mainframes, or you will have very heavy traffic loads on a particular network segment, you may want to stick with Ethernet for general purposes to keep the costs down.

FDDI

To get the most speed from the network, some companies are using FDDI, which stands for Fiber Distributed Data Interchange. As the name suggests, this network type requires fiber optic cabling to work, but the throughput is 100M. You might not need to use fiber-optic cabling or FDDI on your network, but now you have a high-speed networking option if you need it.

ATM

This ATM doesn't stand for Automated Teller Machine, but rather Asynchronous Transfer Mode. This networking option is destined to become the high-speed networking option of choice. The ATM network speeds start at 25M and go up to 155M. Future ATM networks may be as fast as 2G. But all this speed comes with a high price tag. Also, because the technology is still evolving, early equipment still has some glitches to work out, such as inoperability between vendors. Look for ATM to be the future network standard for high-speed needs.

V

Networking

Windows 95 Enhancements for Networking

One of the biggest issues with networking prior to Windows 95 was the problem of setting up a workstation to connect to the network. Typically, a workstation would need to have the network software loaded manually, the adapter card configured manually, configuration files edited manually, and start up batch files created manually.

With Windows 95, the process of installing the network has become much easier. The following list describes some of the networking enhancements of Windows 95.

- Automatic installation of networking components when upgrading to Windows 95 from a previous network

- Automatic detection of the network adapter card

- Built-in Novell NetWare support

- Built-in Peer-to-Peer networking

- Multiple network configurations to connect to different network servers simultaneously

- No conventional memory used for network software

- Enhanced network software is twice as fast as older implementations

- Single login for multiple networks

- Graphical setup and configuration for network software

- Automatic reconnection to servers upon login or after a server was down

- Built-in networking support in the Explorer and the Network Neighborhood

The Four Building Blocks of Windows 95 Networking

Now that you have learned the basic building blocks of the networking architecture, you can apply them to Windows 95. Under Windows, networking functions rely on these four building blocks:

- Adapter

- Protocol

- Client

- Services

Figure 19.8 shows how these layers fit together in Windows.

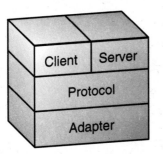

Fig. 19.8
The four building blocks provide the necessary functions for networking in Windows.

The following sections explore how these building blocks work to provide networking services.

Adapter

The adapter is the lowest level of the networking architecture. The adapter provides the interface between the physical wire that connects the computers and the internal networking of Windows. Windows provides a software layer for each network adapter that enables the network adapter card to fit into the structure of the Windows networking environment. Network adapter cards can be Ethernet, Token-Ring, Arcnet, FDDI, or ATM.

Protocol

The protocol is the basic language that computers use to communicate on a network. The protocol defines how computers can find other computers and what rules they use to transfer data. The most popular protocols are IPX/SPX, TCP/IP, and NetBIOS. Windows has built-in support for all of these network protocols.

Client

The network client enables computers to communicate with a specific network operating system. Each network server type from Novell, Microsoft, Banyan, and others requires a client to be loaded to communicate with the

V

Networking

server from each of these vendors. Network clients provide the capability to share network drives and printers on the network server.

Services

Services enable your computer to share your hard drive or printer with others on the network. Services also enable central network administrators to manage the software and hardware in your computer. Each service you load enables you to provide value to the network in which you participate.

Fitting Your Workgroup Network into Company Network

Many companies have large mainframe computers that process the volume of core business data. Additionally, these companies might have central network servers that provide large amounts of data storage and high-speed network printers. Unfortunately, even with all of these resources, companies need to provide more personalized services to smaller departments and groups of users.

Tip

Check with your network's system administrator before you set up a peer-to-peer network on the company's network. Often, traffic loads from unknown sources cause system administrators undue troubleshooting time (and stress).

These smaller networks, called *workgroups*, can install their own networking solution that meets their needs. Some of these networks, however, do not fit into the company's network very well because the department did not know how to plan for the connections to the local workgroup server and the connection to the company's main servers.

Windows 95 enables this type of multiple connectivity to occur without the same obstacles that once stood in the way. Your Windows 95 network can use its four building blocks to make connections to almost any type of network in addition to the local workgroup network. Also, your workgroup can load special networking services that enable central computer departments to manage your workgroups as part of the overall company's network.

Finding the Right Networking Solution

As you can see from the earlier sections of this chapter, you have many possible options for networking in Windows 95. No one solution is best for everyone. This section looks at a few benchmark situations and provides some recommendations for each.

Connecting to an Existing Network

This choice is the easiest to make. If you need to connect to an existing network, you should use the same network client, protocol, and cabling as the rest of the network. Ask the system administrator what is right for you in this case.

Networking Two Computers

This situation is common for many home and small business network users. You might have two computers in your home office that you want to network so you can share a printer, transfer files easily from one to the other, or share a CD-ROM drive or other device.

The best solution is to use Windows 95 built-in peer-to-peer network with coaxial cable. The peer-to-peer network with Windows 95 is powerful and enables you to share any drive or device connected to either computer. Because peer-to-peer networking is included with Windows 95, you have no additional software expenses. You can buy two network cards, cabling, and connectors you need for less than $100.

If you need a lower cost solution, you can substitute a serial (null-modem) cable connection for the coaxial cable. However, this solution is much slower. If you plan to use the network frequently, the coaxial cable and network cards will pay for themselves in saved time.

For the protocol, you should use the NetBEUI. This option is the default option when installing Windows 95 peer-to-peer networking.

Networking 3 to 20 Computers

This network is common in small businesses or in workgroups in larger businesses. The type of network you choose here depends on how you plan to use it. If your primary use is enabling users to access data on each other's computers, a Windows 95 peer-to-peer network using Ethernet adapters with coaxial cabling is the best bet (as described in the previous section) up to around eight workstations. This solution also is the most economical. However, depending on your office layout it may be impractical to install coaxial cable for this configuration.

V

Networking

Tip

If you are setting up a small network in a larger company, you should consider compatibility with other networks in the company— even if you don't have immediate plans to connect to these other networks.

If you are planning on having more than eight workstations, invest in a hub and use a star topology. This will allow you more wiring flexibility and will avoid the coaxial cable problems discussed earlier in the chapter.

If you want to use a common printer, share data on a CD-ROM, or store files in a central location, you probably want to consider a client/server network such as Novell. With this many users, a peer-to-peer network might result in unacceptably slow performance if many of the users will be accessing the same computer to print or share a drive when someone else is using it locally. A dedicated server might be the best solution, especially if you have plans for expanding the network in the future. For Novell networks, use the IPX/SPX protocol. For Windows peer-to-peer, use NetBEUI.

The choice of cabling here depends on your plans for the future. If you think your network needs will never grow beyond 30 closely located computers, coaxial is the most economical choice. If you are looking for expandability for the future, go with twisted-pair.

Tip

To add Internet connectivity along with other networking capabilities, add the TCP/IP protocol to the other protocol you use.

Networking More Than 30 Computers

If your networking needs are this large, you should consider only a Novell or other client/server network using twisted-pair cabling. IPX/SPX is the protocol of choice.

Tip

If you haven't bought your network card yet, a Plug and Play card is a good choice. Even if your computer is not Plug and Play compatible, you might buy a computer that is; then you will have a network card ready to use with it.

Installing Network Components in Windows 95

This section examines the basics of installing network components in Windows 95. Regardless of what type of network you install, many of the procedures here are similar or even identical.

Installing a Network Card

The installation of a network card is the same for every type of network. The configuration of the card can depend on your choice of cabling.

If your network card was already installed when you installed Windows 95, the card was probably properly identified and configured by the Windows installation.

Using Plug and Play Configuration

Plug and Play is probably demonstrated no better than in identifying a network adapter. When you have a Plug and Play BIOS and install a Plug and Play adapter, Windows 95 dynamically sets up the adapter with a minimum of user intervention. When Windows 95 starts, it enumerates the hardware resources and sets up each Plug and Play device so no conflict will occur.

Installation of a Plug and Play network adapter results in a similar sequence of events as the preceding dynamic detection. Windows either locates any drivers it needs for the adapter or prompts you for a driver disk if it cannot find a driver specific to the adapter. After Windows installs the correct driver for your Plug and Play adapter, you still need to install the correct protocol driver for your LAN.

Using the Add New Hardware Wizard

Windows 95 has built-in support for hundreds of network cards, most of which are listed in the table 19.1 earlier in this chapter. If your card is on that list, you can use the Add New Hardware Wizard to configure it. After installing your network adapter cards, follow these steps:

1. Open the Start menu and choose Settings, Control Panel.

2. Double-click the Add New Hardware icon.

3. Choose Next in the Add New Hardware dialog box to continue.

4. Choose No when prompted to let Windows detect your hardware. Choose Next.

5. Select Network Adapter and then choose Next to proceed to the Network Adapter choices.

6. Select the card manufacturer in the list on the left side of the dialog box, and then choose the card model on the right side (see fig. 19.9). Click OK.

   If your Windows 95 driver for this card is not included with Windows 95 but came on a disk from the manufacturer, choose Have Disk and provide the drive letter or path for the driver.

V

Networking

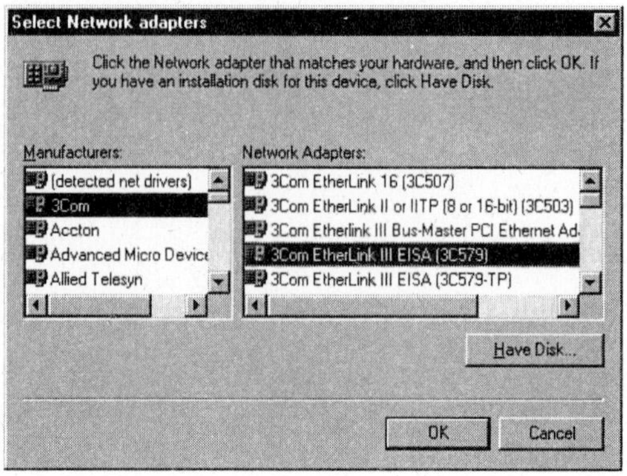

Fig. 19.9

Choose the Manufacturer and the Model of your network adapter board you are installing.

7. Windows displays the hardware settings for this card that will work with your computer (see fig. 19.10).

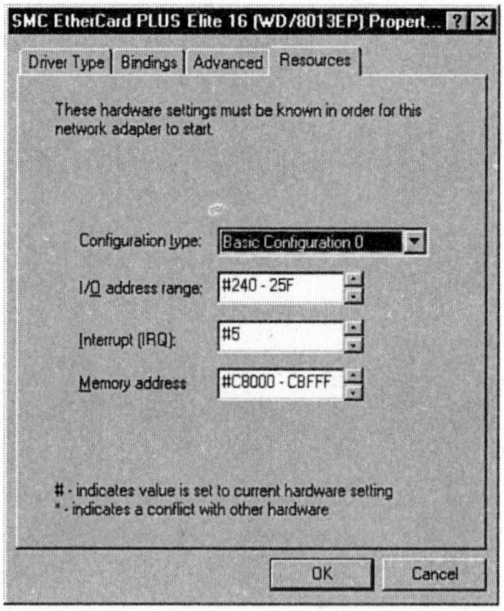

Fig. 19.10

You should review and write down the settings for your installed network adapter to save for future reference.

◄ See "Dealing with Legacy Hardware," p. 247

8. Configure the card to use these settings. Follow the card manufacturer's user manual to change any settings.

9. Click Next.

10. Insert your Windows 95 installation disks or CD-ROM as prompted.

11. Click Finish.

12. When prompted to restart the computer, select Continue.

Troubleshooting

I let Windows 95 detect my network card and it installed the NE2000 Compatible driver. This is isn't the type of card I have and my network connection doesn't work.

Many cards are compatible with the NE2000, which is a popular card. If Windows 95 cannot correctly determine what type of card you have and the card is NE2000 compatible, it will install this driver. Unfortunately, some of these cards are "less compatible" and may not function correctly with this driver. To fix the problem, delete the driver and repeat the installation process. This time, choose the proper card yourself from the list instead of having Windows choose for you. If the card isn't on the list, contact the manufacturer to see if a driver is available.

Installing a Real Mode Driver

Some older network adapters will not have Windows 95 drivers available. In this case, you need to load the Real-Mode drivers for the network card. You probably already have these drivers installed on your machine since they are older cards, so leave your current installation as it is.

You may want to consider replacing your network adapter if Windows 95 does not support it. While this is a strong statement, you must realize that the performance of your computer will be hindered if you are using an old network adapter.

Most new adapter cards from major vendors support Windows 95. But, as always, check before you purchase a network adapter card to see that Windows 95 supports it.

Adding and Changing Network Clients, Protocols, and Services

Now that you have learned about the four major types of network components Windows 95 uses, you need to know how to add, remove, and manage the different components. This information is presented in the following three sections.

▶ See "Setting Up a Windows 95 Peer-to-Peer Network," p. 617

Adding Network Components

To add a network component, follow these steps:

1. Open the Start menu and choose Settings, Control Panel.

2. Double-click the Network icon to display the Network dialog box (see fig. 19.11).

▶ See "Connecting Windows 95 to a Novell Network," p. 673

V

Networking

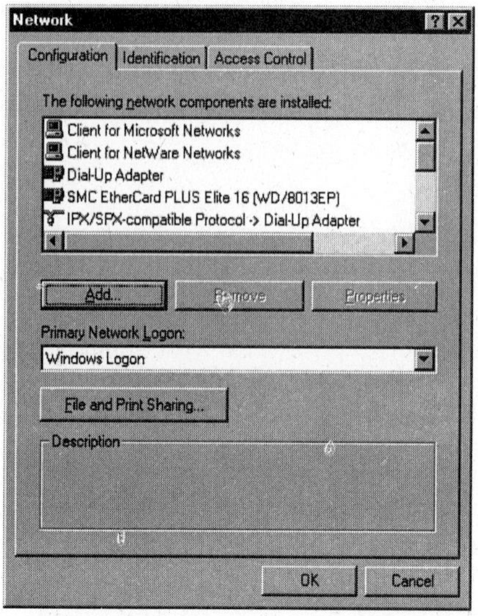

Fig. 19.11
Network settings
are configured on
the Network dialog
box.

3. Click Add, and the Select Network Component Type dialog box appears, as shown in figure 19.12.

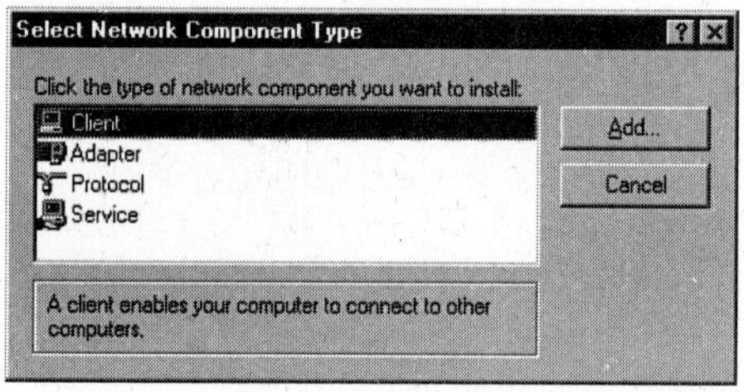

Fig. 19.12
You can add one
of four types of
networking
components to
your Windows
installation.

4. From the four types of components available, highlight the type you want to add and click Add. A dialog box appears where you can specify exactly what you want to add. Figure 19.13 shows the dialog box you see if you choose to add a network client.

   Regardless of the type of network component you are installing, the dialog box looks essentially the same. The left side lists the various vendors of the component, and the right side lists models supported for that vendor.

5. To add a component, choose a vendor and a model, and click OK.

   If your Windows 95 driver for this component is not included with Windows 95 but came on a disk from the manufacturer, choose Have Disk and provide the drive letter or path for the driver.

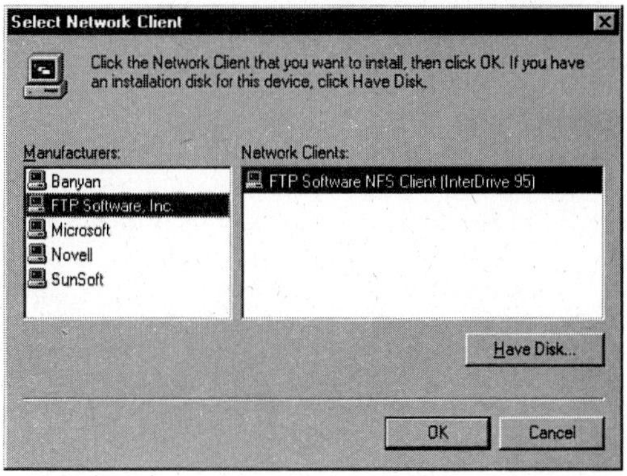

Fig. 19.13
Choose the Client
option to add a
network client to
Windows.

After you have selected a vendor and model for the component and
clicked OK, Windows 95 displays the component in the Network
dialog box.

When you close the Network dialog box, you might see a message indicating
that you need to restart Windows 95. Depending on the components you
add, restarting is necessary to reinitialize all components to work together
properly. Until you restart the system, you cannot take advantage of the network component changes you have made.

▶ See "Selecting a
Primary Cli-
ent," p. 612

> **Note**
>
> In addition to using Windows 95 to connect to multiple networks simultaneously,
> you can use this capability to connect to different networks at different times without
> making any changes to your system settings. For instance, if your office runs a Novell
> network and you have a Windows 95 network connecting the computers in your
> home office, you can have both the Microsoft and Novell clients installed. Windows
> 95 detects which network is running and presents the proper login dialog box. In
> previous versions of Windows and DOS, connecting to different networks required
> having multiple boot configurations or changing your startup settings for each
> network.

Removing Network Components

As your hardware and network environment changes over time, you might
want to delete older networking components you no longer need. Doing so
can free up memory and speed up the responsiveness of Windows 95.

Tip
Removing unnec-
essary network
drivers will let
Windows focus on
providing CPU
and memory
resources for net-
work components
that you are still
using. If you won't
need a compo-
nent, remove it.

V

Networking

To delete a network component, follow these steps:

1. Open the Start menu and choose <u>S</u>ettings, <u>C</u>ontrol Panel.

2. Double-click Network.

3. In the Network dialog box, click the Configuration tab.

4. At the top of the dialog box, highlight the network component you want to remove.

5. Click Remove. The component is removed from the network component list.

6. Repeat steps 4 and 5 until you have removed all the components you want removed. When you are finished, click OK.

   Windows 95 is then reconfigured to reflect your new selection of components.

Changing Component Properties

You already know that objects in Windows 95 have properties that determine how they or how the operating system treats them. Network components, as objects, are no different—they also possess properties you can control.

> **Note**
>
> In most instances, you will not need to change the properties of a network component—99 percent of the time Windows 95 sets up components to work properly. Change properties only if you keep track of the previous settings and if you have a firm understanding of what the change will accomplish.

To change the properties of a network component, follow these steps:

1. Open the Start menu and choose <u>S</u>ettings, <u>C</u>ontrol Panel.

2. Double-click Network.

3. In the Network dialog box, click the Configuration tab.

4. At the top of the dialog box, highlight the network component whose properties you want to change.

5. Click the <u>P</u>roperties button. The Properties sheet for the selected network component appears.

The types of properties available depend on the type of component you are configuring. You can see the following Properties sheet pages:

■ *Advanced*. Appears for network adapter, protocol, and resource components. Use this page to set the unique advanced settings for the card memory and configuration settings for the protocol, or general options for the resource.

■ *Bindings*. Appears for network adapter and protocol components. Bindings define relationships between network components. The settings on this page control which components use this particular adapter card or protocol.

■ *Driver Type*. Appears for network adapter components. Use this page to set the access mode used by the driver.

■ *General*. Appears for network client and some resource components. Use this page to set miscellaneous properties for the component.

■ *NetBIOS*. Appears for IPX/SPX protocol components. This page enables you to control whether NetBIOS applications can be executed through the protocol.

■ *Protocol*. Appears for some resource components. In a multi-protocol network environment, use this page to set the protocol that the resource should use.

■ *Resources*. Appears for network adapter components. Use this page to set hardware configuration information (such as IRQ and I/O address) for the card.

These pages are the common properties pages; other pages specific to individual network components also may be available. Typically, the use of these pages is very technical and depends on the implementation of your network. Chapters 20 and 22 look at some of the properties in more detail as they apply to Windows 95 networks and Novell networks. If you need more information on properties, refer to the system documentation for your network or contact your network administrator.

After you are finished making changes to the properties, click OK to return to the Network dialog box. You can then make changes in the properties of other network components, if you want. When you are done, close the Network dialog box. Windows 95 then attempts to reconfigure your network system according to your changes. You might receive a message to close Windows and reboot the system so your changes can be implemented with a fresh system.

V

Networking

Selecting a Primary Client

You already know that Windows 95 enables you to have multiple network clients installed in your system. Information is sent over the network one client at a time. Windows 95 enables you to specify which client you want as your primary network client (the client receiving information first).

To select a primary network client, follow these steps:

1. Open the Start menu and choose Settings, Control Panel.

2. Double-click Network.

3. In the Network dialog box, click the Configuration tab.

4. Make sure the network client you want to use is installed. If it is, the client appears in the component list at the top of the dialog box.

5. In the Primary Network Logon list at the bottom of the dialog box, select the name of the network client you want as the primary client.

6. Click OK.

Networking Components of the Windows 95 Interface

Tip
Using the Network Neighborhood is very similar to using My Computer. Both use icons to show the various resources available to you.

Windows 95 is built for networking. In addition to the Network Neighborhood that allows you to browse the servers on your network, you also can access network servers and printers through Explorer. This section describes the components that let you access your network resources easily.

Using Network Neighborhood

If you access a network from Windows 95 or if you manage your network with Windows 95, you should see an icon on your desktop labeled Network Neighborhood. Double-click that icon and you can see how easy it is to travel around your network.

◄ See "Using My Computer to Manage Files," p. 551

The Network Neighborhood depicts the network in a format just like a folder on your own computer (see fig. 19.14). Each device or computer attached is displayed as a computer icon, and depending on the access each computer or device yields, you can access data or explore further with a simple point and click. For example, if want to access a laser printer attached to a computer on the network, you simply double-click the computer icon to reveal the available resources for that computer and then choose the printer you want.

Fig. 19.14
The Network Neighborhood lets you browse your network for servers and printers available to you.

Moving around the Network

Navigating the network is easy from the Network Neighborhood window. Double-click an icon to connect to a computer. When you do, a window shows you the available resources (including shared folders and printers) on that computer. If you find that you consistently use a specific network resource, you can create a shortcut to that resource and place it on your desktop or in any of your folders.

◀ See "Creating Shortcut Icons on the Desktop to Start Programs," p. 68

The Network Neighborhood window displays a toolbar you can use to navigate the network, map network drives, and modify the way network resources appear in the window. If this toolbar is not visible, choose View, Toolbar. On the left side of the toolbar is a drop-down list box. This list box is an aid for navigating and determining your location relative to other network resources.

If you select a different resource from this list, such as your local hard drive, notice how the Network Neighborhood window changes to display that information.

Accessing the Entire Network

The network you can access is simply your local network. However, you can also view and access separate networks that are interconnected with yours. Double-click the Entire Network icon in the Network Neighborhood window. After a moment of searching, Windows 95 displays all the networks it can find. From this window, you can select any listed network and navigate as if it were your own local network.

Tip
As you move farther down the directory structure of your network resources, you can return to the previous directory by clicking the Up One Level icon on the toolbar.

V

Networking

Accessing the Network from Explorer

The Explorer also can be used to browse your network resources. Within Explorer's list of All Folders, (see fig. 19.15) you will notice a section titled Network Neighborhood. Clicking this icon will bring up a list of servers in the same way the Network Neighborhood does.

Fig. 19.15
Network Neighborhood browsing also is available through Explorer.

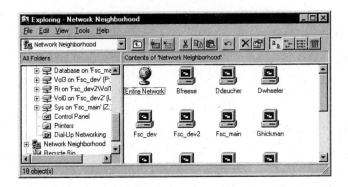

To map a drive letter to a servers folder through Explorer, follow these steps:

◀ See "Using the Explorer with Shared Resources on a Network," p. 544

1. Select the server you want to connect to.

2. Right-click on the shared folder that you want to map to a network drive letter.

3. Select Map Drive Letter from the pop-up menu.

4. Select a drive letter and click OK. If you want to permanently map the drive letter so that it is available the next time you login, mark the Reconnect at Logon check box.

Finding a Computer on the Network

If you have a large network, finding a computer using the Network Neighborhood or Explorer can be difficult. So Windows 95 has a built-in feature for finding computers quickly without scrolling through long lists.

Tip
You can enter any portion of the server name and Windows will find computers that match your selection. This is helpful if you don't know the whole name.

To find a computer, follow these steps:

1. Open the Start menu and choose Find, Computer.

2. The Find Computer dialog box appears. Enter the name of the computer you're searching for in the Named box (see fig. 19.16).

3. Choose Find Now.

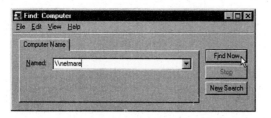

Fig. 19.16
Finding a server
on a large network
is easy using the
Find Computer
function in
Explorer.

When the computer is located, the dialog box shows the result of the search
(see fig. 19.17).

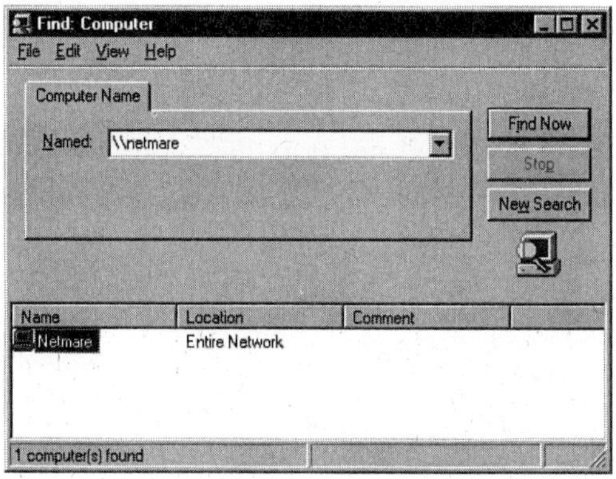

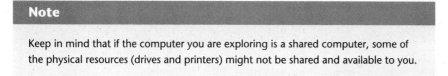

Fig. 19.17
The Find Com-
puter dialog box
shows it has
located the
Netmare server.

This Find Computer dialog box works the same way whether you're looking
for a native Windows 95, Windows NT, or NetWare server. The same function, locating a certain computer, uses the same familiar tool.

After you have located the computer you want to explore, use the File, Explore command or double-click the server name to display the contents of
the server.

> **Note**
>
> Keep in mind that if the computer you are exploring is a shared computer, some of
> the physical resources (drives and printers) might not be shared and available to you.

V

Networking

Chapter 20

Setting Up a Windows 95 Peer-to-Peer Network

by Glenn Fincher with Sue Plumley

Windows 95 peer-to-peer networking brings all the resources of the network to your desktop. You can share any of your PC's resources with other PCs on the network. You also can easily use the printer down the hall or the CD on your associate's new high-speed desktop. You accomplish all this through Windows 95's built-in peer-to-peer networking.

The network can be as simple as two PCs set up with Windows 95's Direct Cable Connection or a typical business-network connection where your PC is one of many on a local area network (LAN), wide area network (WAN), or even a city, or metropolitan, area network (MAN). Peer-to-peer networking with Windows 95 can even enable your machine to access the vast shared resources on the Internet. In peer-to-peer networking, each computer can act as both server and client.

In this chapter, you learn about

- System requirements and recommendations

- Installing and configuring your network adapter

- Installing the network drivers and protocol

- Identifying your computer for the network

- Establishing workgroup security

- Setting up and sharing your printer

Windows 95 Peer-to-Peer Networking Features

Windows provides many peer-to-peer networking capabilities, including resource sharing, communication, and compatibility with other networks, including Windows NT, the Microsoft Network, the Internet, and so on. This section explores what you can do with your workstation as part of a peer-to-peer network.

Resource Sharing

Tip
You can set automatic backup if you're using a Novell NetWare or Windows NT server.

▶ See "Using Network Tape Drives," p. 714

▶ See "Sharing an Entire Drive," p. 643

▶ See "Using Your CD-ROM Drive," p. 970

The primary networking feature that you use with a Windows 95 peer-to-peer network is resource sharing. Even though each user may need a different type of computer, all users need access to corporate data and resources. In Windows 95, resource sharing enables you to make any of the following computer devices available to the rest of the network:

- *Hard drives.* Sharing hard drives means you can access the other computers on the network and they can access your computer. Each user specifies which folders, files, printers, and so on, to make available; you don't have to share everything on your hard drive. Additionally, hard drive sharing allows for files to be backed up and restored from a central location, saving time, energy, and storage space.

- *CD-ROMs.* CD-ROM drives, although becoming more prevalent in newer computers, might still be in short supply on your network. You can share CD-ROMs over the network with others in your workgroup; you use CDs to install programs, supply files for copying, view multimedia clips, plus much more. Using CDs saves time in that installation and file access is much faster than with a tape or floppy disks. Sharing a CD-ROM drive saves a workgroup money because you need not purchase a CD-ROM drive for each workstation on the network. Also, by sharing CD-ROMs, you can share information with users who, because they lack CD-ROM drives, may never before have been able to view data distributed on CD-ROM.

Tip
Accounting programs and databases are the most commonly shared programs on peer-to-peer networks.

- *Applications.* Many applications are licensed to run on a network, thus saving installation time and space on individual workstations, and guaranteeing every user has the same version of the application. Additionally, upgrades are faster and easier since you're only upgrading one program instead of many.

> **Caution**
>
> Check your licensing agreements to see if your applications allow network sharing. If your software does not mention network usage and you install it to a network, you could run into problems when running the software. You could even lose valuable data or damage the program; this is especially true for specialized programs, such as those written specifically for churches, real estate offices, clinics, and so on. If there's any question about whether an application is suitable for a network, *always* call the manufacturer before installing.

■ *Files*. In addition to sharing applications between workstations, you also can share files. The files are stored in folders on each workstation's hard disk. You can choose to share specific folders and you can limit the access of any folder you choose to share. Only certain files, such as a database file, may be used at the same time.

▶ See "Under-standing File Sharing," p. 643

■ *Printers*. Although printers are less expensive than they once were, it rarely makes sense to have one for each workstation. By installing one or two shared printers for a workgroup—such as a laser for general output and a color inkjet for special presentations—you can save money and enable all users to print when they need to. Windows makes it easy for you to share your printer with one or more in your network; you also can easily stop sharing the printer, if you need to.

▶ See "Sharing Printers," p. 650

Communicating from the Network

Windows 95 offers several methods of communicating between workstations set up in a peer-to-peer network; you can use one of the built-in applications, such as Microsoft Exchange or MS-Mail; or you can use a third-party e-mail application, such as Lotus Notes. Using the computer to communicate with your co-workers is often more efficient than running over to their office or calling them on the phone. Using e-mail over the network, you can send not only messages or memos, but files as well, thus saving the time you would take to copy the file to a disk and walk it over to the other person's office.

V

Networking

▶ See "Creating and Sending Mail Messages," p. 738

▶ See "Introducing Hyper-Terminal," p. 861

▶ See "Connecting to The Microsoft Network," p. 1110

▶ See "Overview of Exchange Features," p. 724

In addition to communicating within the network, Windows offers ways you can communicate outside of the network to remote computers. First, you can use the Fax application to send and receive faxes to other computers; you can even send faxes from within certain programs, such as MS Word. Second, you can use HyperTerminal to connect to bulletin boards, to send or receive files, and to otherwise connect to a remote computer. Third, you can use the Microsoft Network to exchange messages with people around the world and to obtain information about various technical, financial, and entertainment subjects. Use the MS Network to connect to the Internet, as well. Fourth, you can use the Phone Dialer to dial phone numbers from your computer over your modem.

> **Note**
>
> If the Inbox icon is not on your desktop, then Microsoft Exchange is not installed. You must install both Microsoft Exchange and Microsoft Fax to send and receive fax messages. To install these two programs, open the Control Panel and open the Add/Remove Programs dialog box. In the Windows Setup tab, select the Components you want to install; The Microsoft Exchange component includes both the Exchange and Fax applications.

Windows 95 Compatibility with Other Microsoft Networks

▶ See "Exploring the Windows 95 Resource Kit," p. 1133

If other computers in your office are on networks that run the Windows NT Server, Microsoft LAN Manager 2.x, or Windows for Workgroups networking, Windows 95 peer-to-peer networking is compatible with them. This chapter focuses primarily on the Windows 95 peer-to-peer network by itself. Although the chapter discusses some issues that you might encounter when working with other Microsoft networks, you should refer to the Networking section of the Windows 95 Resource Kit for detailed discussions of using Windows 95 with those networks. Note that Microsoft's other networks work seamlessly with Windows 95 peer-to-peer networking.

System Requirements and Recommendations

The basic system requirements for running Windows are detailed in the *Getting Started with Windows 95* manual that you receive with your copy of Windows 95. There are some additional items you will need for networking and some optional items you may want to add.

To be connected to a network, you must have the following:

- Network adapter card installed to your computer

- Software for the adapter card containing both configuration and driver (if your card is not included in the Windows 95 list, you'll need this software on a manufacturer's disk to install to Windows)

- Cabling (compatible with network topology)

You also may want to include the following hardware when connecting to a network:

◄ See "Connecting Network Devices," p. 589

- Modem (for use with HyperTerminal, Microsoft Exchange, or other e-mail applications)

- Parallel or serial cable (for use when gaining access to a computer on a network when your computer is not connected to the network, such as with a portable computer)

Tip

If you're using 10BaseT (twisted pair) for your network, you'll need a hub; if you're using 10Base2 or Thin Ethernet (coaxial cable), you need no hub.

> **Note**
>
> If you use a parallel cable, it must be a bi-directional cable, also known as a laplink or interlink cable.

Before purchasing additional hardware to set up your peer-to-peer network, make a plan for how you will use the network. If you're sure the network you need is a peer-to-peer network as opposed to a client-server, then you must plan for and purchase the resources you want to share. Consider sharing such items as modems, CD-ROMs, printers, plotters, large disks, optical drives, and, above all, information as you plan for both the present and the future.

If, for example, one workstation will contain most of the software applications to be shared, or a specific application such as accounting software, then supply that workstation with a faster processor, more hard disk space, and more RAM so it can run faster and better provide for the needs of the other workstations. You may also want to include a CD-ROM drive on this more powerful computer for quick and easy installation of programs.

◄ See "Approaches to Networks," p. 582

◄ See "Finding the Right Networking Solution" p. 602

Additionally, if you plan to share a CD-ROM drive, the drive should be the fastest you can afford (4x or 6x) with a quality interface, or controller, card. A slower drive may not be able to serve everyone who needs it and could create a bottleneck on the network.

V

Networking

Similarly, if several users use the network for printing, you may need a higher speed printer than an individual user would use. You may also consider connecting two printers instead of one, or adding a plotter or color printer, as well.

Consider, too, how effectively the resources can be shared among the number of users on the network. If you have only five users, for example, one printer is probably enough; however, if your network has ten users, you may need two or more printers to keep a flood of documents from being released on one printer all at once.

Modems for Dial-Up Networking

Tip

Use dial-up networking for connecting a notebook computer to your network.

This section presents some general guidelines to keep in mind as you start to set up a dial-up network with a modem. In short, get the fastest modem that you can afford. The newest standard, V.34, enables your computer to communicate at 28.8K baud. Because V.34 modems are relatively inexpensive, they are becoming widely available. Even a 14.4K baud modem (the V.32 standard) provides a robust connection for most peer-to-peer resources.

Tip

Dial up the server computer from your home computer to connect to the network and get some extra work done in the evenings and on weekends.

With a modem, a notebook or other computer becomes a *client* by dialing in to another Windows 95 PC. The Windows 95 PC, attached to the network through conventional means, becomes the *server*. The modem connection physically connects the client to the network of the server, or *host,* computer and becomes another computer on the network, enabling connection to and use of any resources for which access has been given. Both the client and server computers must be connected to modems.

Troubleshooting
I can't connect to a remote computer.
Open the Modems Properties sheet by double-clicking the Modems icon in the Control Panel. In the General page, choose the Properties button. Also, in the General page, check to be sure the Maximum speed is the highest that can be used by both your modem and the remote computer's modem. Deselect the Only Connect at This Speed option and choose OK. Choose Close to close the Modem Properties sheet and try the call again.
If you still cannot connect to the remote computer, open the Modems Properties sheet again and choose the Properties button. Choose the Connection page and check the information in Data Bits, Parity, and Stop Bits is correct. If you are not sure about the information, contact your system's administrator or check the modem's documentation. Choose OK and Close and try again.

Network Adapters for Connecting to a LAN

When you install Windows 95, it probably will recognize the network adapter already installed on your computer. Microsoft provides drivers for most manufacturers' hardware. The Network Adapter Wizard takes you step by step through the configuration of your adapter, whether it conforms to the Ethernet, Token Ring, or even the ISDN standard. Adding your network's protocols is equally easy. If Windows does not recognize your adapter, you must use the manufacturer's disk to install the configuration files and driver for your adapter card.

◀ See "Connecting Network Devices," p. 589

◀ See "Network Layer Protocols," p. 598

▶ See "Installing and Configuring the Network Adapter Cards," p. 624

> **Note**
>
> If you are purchasing a network adapter for the first time or replacing an older adapter, try to select a Plug and Play compatible adapter. Windows 95 can set itself up dynamically for a Plug and Play adapter. Probably more importantly, however, pick a card that is both fast (32-bit) and reliable by evaluating the vendor's reputation, longevity, and technical support services.

If you have a laptop computer with a PC Card (formerly called the PCMCIA) network adapter, Windows 95 can load or unload the network drivers for the card dynamically when you are connected to the network. This important new feature enables you to have separate "connected" and "unconnected" configurations, with Windows 95 maintaining the connection properties.

◀ See "Installing Plug and Play Hardware," p. 246

Finally, if you have a stand-alone PC but periodically must connect it to another PC to avoid doing the "floppy shuffle" (copying to a disk and then walking it to or from another office), you can do so by using the Direct Cable Connection, which is actually another form of peer-to-peer networking. Using either a null-modem cable or a special parallel cable, you can connect to and use the shared resources on another PC as if those resources were actually part of your own PC.

Tip

Even if you don't see an immediate need for the Direct Cable Connection, the cables are relatively inexpensive and come in handy if you eventually buy a laptop or another PC.

> **Troubleshooting**
>
> *My PC Card was installed but it isn't working. What can I do?*
>
> In the Control Panel, open System Properties by double-clicking the System icon. Select the Device Manager page. Locate the Network adapters in the list and click the plus sign beside it; your network adapter should appear below the heading.
>
> If the device is not listed, locate the PCMCIA Socket in the hardware list and select it. Choose Properties. In the Properties sheet, choose the Global Settings page.
>
> (continues)

V

Networking

(continued)

In the Card Services Shared Memory area, deselect the Automatic Selection option. You can change the memory in the Start and End boxes; check the adapter card documentation for correct settings. Choose OK to close the dialog box, and then choose OK again. Restart the computer.

If the adapter has a red X through it, it's probably disabled. To enable the adapter, double-click the device and the Device Properties sheet appears. In the General page, Device usage area, make sure the current configuration is checked and choose OK.

If the adapter has a red circle and an exclamation point through it, double-click the device and read the Device Status area of the Properties sheet to see what type of problem exists. You can open the Device Manager (from the System icon in the Control Panel) and try disabling the device, identifying a free resource and assigning the device to that resource, or rearranging resources used by other devices to free up those resources needed by the device.

◀ See "Connecting Network Devices," p. 589

◀ See "Installing Network Components in Windows 95," p. 604

Tip
You also can connect to the WDL through Compu-Serve in the Microsoft Software Library; type **go msl**.

Installing and Configuring the Network Adapter Cards

If you already have a network adapter installed in your computer when you install Windows 95, the Install program probably will automatically detect the adapter and install the appropriate driver. If you add a network adapter after installing Windows 95, the Add New Hardware Wizard takes you step by step through the process of installing the hardware.

If Windows 95 does not contain the driver you need to configure the adapter card and you do not have a manufacturer's disk, check the Windows 95 CD Drivers folder for additional drivers added when Windows shipped. If you still cannot find the driver, and you have a modem, you can connect to the Microsoft Network and perhaps find the driver you need in the Windows Driver Library (WDL) in the Windows 95 section. The WDL contains a list of compatible hardware and many device drivers for printers, display, multimedia, network, and other adapters; drivers are updated as they become available.

Installing the Microsoft Network Client

Install the Client software so you can use the shared resources on the network. If you install networking support while installing Windows 95, the Install program installs Client for Microsoft Networks and the appropriate drivers (unless you choose not to install them). If you want to install the network after installing Windows 95, you must install the client as follows:

1. Open the Start menu and choose Settings, Control Panel.

2. Double-click the Network icon in the Control Panel. The Network dialog box appears (see fig. 20.1).

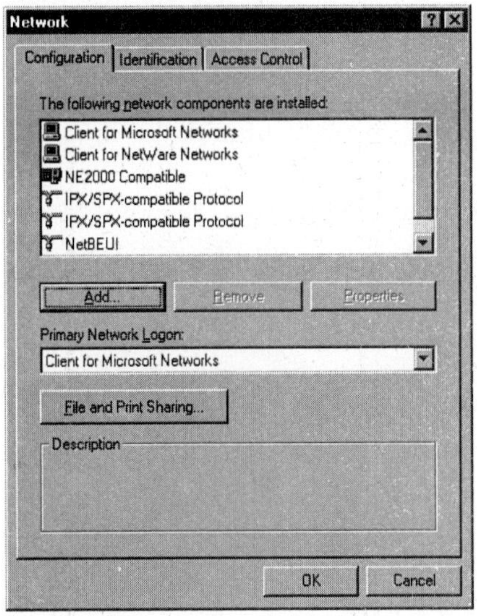

Fig. 20.1
Use the Network dialog box to install the Client software.

V

Networking

3. In the Configuration tab, choose Add. The Select Network Component Type dialog box appears (see fig. 20.2).

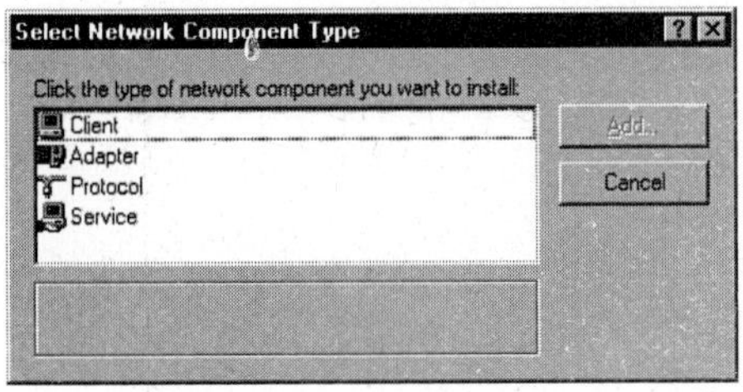

Fig. 20.2
Select the component you want to install from the list.

4. In the Component list, select Client and then choose <u>A</u>dd. The Select Network Client dialog box appears (see fig. 20.3).

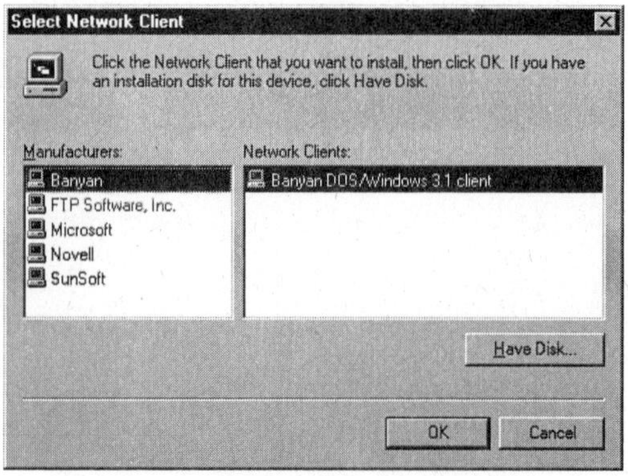

Fig. 20.3
Choose the network client you want to install in the Select Network Client dialog box.

5. In <u>M</u>anufacturers, select Microsoft and then select Client for Microsoft Networks from the Network Clients list on the right (see fig. 20.4).

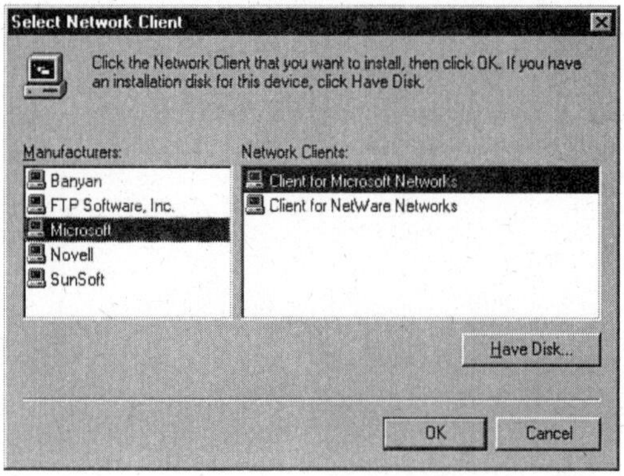

Fig. 20.4
Choose the Client for Microsoft Networks to set up a Windows 95 peer-to-peer network.

6. Click OK to install the Client. Windows may ask what type of network adapter you are using. Select the adapter from the list or, if you don't know the type of adapter you're using, choose OK and Windows will use the adapter it detected.

> **Note**
>
> If you still need to install a protocol or service, you might want to proceed to one of the following sections and take care of that installation before choosing OK in step 7.

7. When installation is complete, Windows returns to the Network dialog box. Choose OK to close the dialog box. Windows displays a System Changes message prompting you to restart the computer. Choose Yes.

After you restart the computer, Microsoft networking support is added.

You also can change the settings for the network client by opening the Network Properties sheet and selecting the client you want to modify in the Configuration page, Components list. Choose the Properties button and change any of the settings in the Properties sheet. Choose OK to close the sheet and OK again to close the Network Properties sheet.

◄ See "The Four Building Blocks of Windows 95 Networking," p. 600

Installing the Network Protocol

The Protocol is the language, or set of rules, the computer uses to communicate with other computers over the network. Protocols govern format, timing, sequencing, and error control. All of the computers on the network must use the same protocol to communicate with each other.

◄ See "Network Layer Protocols," p. 598

V

Networking

After correctly installing the network adapter, you must install the correct protocol for the network. To do so, follow these steps:

1. Open the Start menu, and choose Settings, Control Panel.

2. Double-click the Network icon in the Control Panel. The Network dialog box appears.

3. In the Configuration page, choose Add without choosing a component from the list. The Select Network Component Type dialog box appears.

4. In the Component list, select Protocol and then choose Add. The Select Network Protocol dialog box appears.

5. Select Microsoft from the Manufacturers list, as shown in figure 20.5. A list of Network Protocols appears in the list on the right.

6. Select a protocol from the Network Protocols list and click OK. (The next several sections explain the best protocol choices for Windows 95 peer-to-peer networking.)

Tip
If you want to connect to the Internet, select TCP/IP from the Network Protocols list.

> **Note**
>
> If you have a protocol that is not listed but is written for Windows 95, you can choose Have Disk in the Select Network Protocol dialog box and follow the instructions on-screen to install the protocol.

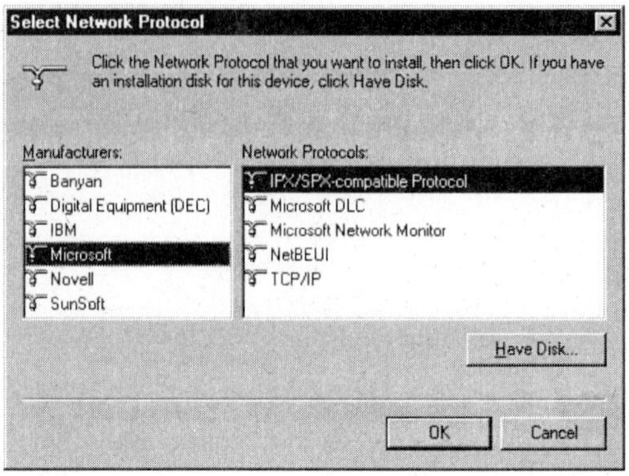

Fig. 20.5
Microsoft supports
the most common
network protocols.

Microsoft provides drivers for the most common protocols:

■ NetBEUI, the protocol for LanMan networks, Windows for Workgroups, and Window NT

■ IPX/SPX, the protocol for Novell networks

■ TCP/IP, the protocol for UNIX networks and the language of the Internet

Microsoft provides 32-bit, protected-mode drivers for each of these protocols, offering high performance with no conventional memory footprint (drivers are not installed in memory below 640K). These drivers are all also Plug and Play compliant, enabling Windows 95 to load and unload the drivers dynamically as needed.

Using NetBEUI Protocol Drivers

IBM introduced NetBEUI (NetBIOS extended user interface) in 1985. The protocol was primarily designed for small LANs of around 20–200 workstations. Since the mid-1980s, Microsoft has supported the NetBEUI protocol in its networking products. The protocol is well suited for its task because of its powerful flow control, tuning parameters, and robust error detection. The NetBEUI protocol is compatible with Windows for Workgroups peer networks as well as Windows NT Server and LanMan networks. Windows 95 includes both real and protected mode support for NetBEUI. One potential problem with NetBEUI is that it is not *routable*—that is, to cross a router to another LAN, you must also install TCP/IP or IPX/SPX protocols.

You can add, or install, NetBEUI to the list of components in the Network dialog box. See the section "Installing the Network Protocol" earlier in this chapter for information. The default properties for the NetBEUI protocol work fine in most cases; but if you need to change any of the properties, you can. See "Modifying Protocol Properties," later in this chapter.

If you are setting up only a small, localized LAN that doesn't have to cross a router or communicate with mainframes, you need not install any protocol other than NetBEUI; however, Windows automatically installs the IPX/SPX compatible protocol in addition to the NetBEUI. IPX/SPX protocol is used with Novell networks. You can use the IPX/SPX protocol to run programs that normally require NetBEUI and to cross a router to another network.

Using IPX Drivers

Microsoft supplies with Windows 95 both a real and protected mode implementation of the Novell NetWare IPX/SPX (Internetwork Packet Exchange/ Sequential Packet Exchange) protocol. The Windows 95 IPX/SPX protected mode protocol (NDIS 3.1-compliant) supports any Novell NetWare-compatible network client. The protocol supports Windows Sockets, NetBIOS, and ECB programming interfaces, and offers a packet-burst mode to improve network performance. With automatic detection of frame type, network addressing, and other configuration settings, Microsoft's IPX protocol is easy to install. Using the IPX/SPX protocol enables you to connect to servers and workstations on NetWare or Windows NT Server 3.5 networks, as well as mixed networks. Also, IPX/SPX is routable for connectivity across all network bridges and routers configured for IPX/SPX routing. With IPX/SPX installed, your computer can share peer resources across the *enterprise*, or to networks that connect to virtually all parts of an organization.

> **Note**
>
> Since IPX/SPX is also applicable to Novell client-server networks, see Chapter 22, "Connecting Windows 95 to a Novell Network," for more information.

▶ See "Windows 95 Support for NetWare," p. 674

Using TCP/IP Drivers

The Internet uses the TCP/IP (Transmission Control Protocol/Internet Protocol) protocol to enable all computers on the Internet to communicate seamlessly. TCP/IP is actually made up of a hundred protocols; two of the most important are TCP, a transport protocol, and IP, which operates on the session layer. The TCP/IP protocol is from the Department of Defense for use over large internetworks, such as the Internet, and uses Unix and other large computer operating systems to connect government, scientific, and academic internetworks.

V

Networking

◀ See "Network
Layer Proto-
cols," p. 598

Microsoft's TCP/IP is implemented as a 32-bit protected-mode driver with
built-in support for the Point-to-Point Protocol (PPP) used for Dial-Up Networking. TCP/IP enables you to connect across heterogeneous networks of
different operating systems and hardware platforms. The following are some
of the additional features that make the Microsoft TCP/IP protocol powerful:

- Automatic TCP/IP configuration with Windows NT Dynamic Host
  Configuration Protocol (DHCP) servers

- Automatic IP-address-to-NetBIOS computer-name resolution with
  Windows NT's Windows Internet Naming Service (WINS) servers

- Support for the Windows Sockets 1.1 interface, which many client-
  server applications and public-domain Internet tools use

- Supports an interface between NetBIOS and TCP/IP

- Supports for many commonly used utilities, such as Telnet, ping,
  and FTP, which the protocol installs

Chapter 29, "Getting Connected to the Internet," explains in detail how to
install and configure TCP/IP. You'll particularly want to note the section
"Connecting to the Internet via a LAN."

You can connect to the Internet by using a terminal that's connected to an
Internet host. Since the terminal is not a computer itself, you use the terminal to access a computer that is on the Internet. If you don't have a terminal
to connect to an Internet host, then you can connect to the Internet over the
phone lines by use of a modem.

Tip

In using PPP to
access the Internet,
remember that
unless you have a
dedicated phone
line, your com-
puter is not always
connected to the
Internet; you must
arrange for the
connecting com-
puter to save mail
messages for you
while you are not
online.

If you choose to use a dial-up connection over the phone line to the Internet,
you need a modem. A modem converts computer signals to telephone signals
and back again. The computer signal is "digital" and the telephone signal is
"analog." The device that converts from digital to analog is called a *modulator*;
the device that converts the signal from analog to digital is called a *demodulator*. A modem is a modulator-demodulator. To use a dial-up connection over
the phone line, both computers must have a modem.

When you use your computer and modem to dial-up the Internet, your computer emulates a terminal. You first arrange for some other Internet host to
act as your connection point; then you install PPP (Point-to-Point Protocol)
programs to your computer. After the connection is made between the two
computers, PPP gives your computer TCP/IP capabilities, allowing your computer to be an Internet host with its own official electronic address.

Since your computer is attached to a peer-to-peer network, the Internet becomes available to all computers on the network.

Modifying Protocol Properties

Although the default protocol settings should be sufficient in most cases,
Windows enables you to modify protocol properties to suit specific needs, if
necessary. Each protocol presents various settings you might change, but the
Bindings options are common to all protocols.

Binding is the process of assigning and removing protocols to and from the
network adapter. Each network adapter needs at least one protocol bound to
the driver, else the driver cannot communicate across the network.

To set binding properties, open the Network dialog box by double-clicking
the Network icon in the Control Panel. In the Configuration tab, select the
protocol you want to modify from the list of components and choose the
Properties button. The protocol Properties sheet appears, as shown in
figure 20.6.

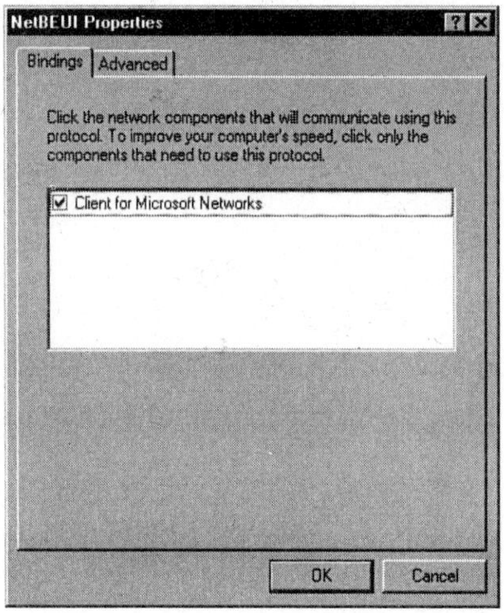

V

Networking

NetBEUI Properties

Bindings | Advanced

Click the network components that will communicate using this
protocol. To improve your computer's speed, click only the
components that need to use this protocol.

☑ Client for Microsoft Networks

OK   Cancel

Fig. 20.6
Modify the
protocol's settings
in the protocol's
Properties sheet.

Choose the Bindings page, and in the list select the components that will
communicate using that particular protocol. In the Advanced page, you can
select any settings you want to change by choosing the setting in the Property list and then entering or choosing the Value. Choose OK when you are
finished.

NetBEUI

The Propertites sheet for NetBEUI offers two pages:

■ The Bindings page reveals the service to which the protocol is bound.

■ The Advanced page enables you to adjust the maximum number of simultaneous connections and the number of network control blocks (NCBs). The default settings are Maximum connections: 10 connections and 12 NCBs.

IPX/SPX

The protocol Properties sheet for IPX/SPX offers three pages:

■ The Bindings page reveals the components that use this protocol to communicate.

■ The Advanced page enables you to change or adjust several settings.

■ The NetBIOS page lets you enable or disable NetBIOS over IPX/SPX.

TCP/IP

Figure 20.7 shows the TCP/IP Properties sheet. The TCP/IP Properties sheet contains six tabs:

■ The Bindings page lets you select the components that will use this protocol.

■ The Advanced page lets you set properties.

■ The DNS Configuration page lets you enable or disable DNS (Domain Name System), a TCP/IP service that translates domain names to and from IP addresses.

■ The Gateway page enables you to add and remove gateways, or links to other systems.

■ The WINS Configuration page lets you disable or enable WINS (Windows Internet Naming Service) resolution for use with a WINS Server. WINS enables you to use programs that require NetBIOS protocol.

■ The IP Address page enables you to assign an IP address to the computer from either a Dynamic Host Configuration Protocol (DHCP) server or a PPP dial-up router.

When you're finished setting changes to the properties for a protocol, choose OK to close the Properties sheet. Choose OK again to close the Network dialog box.

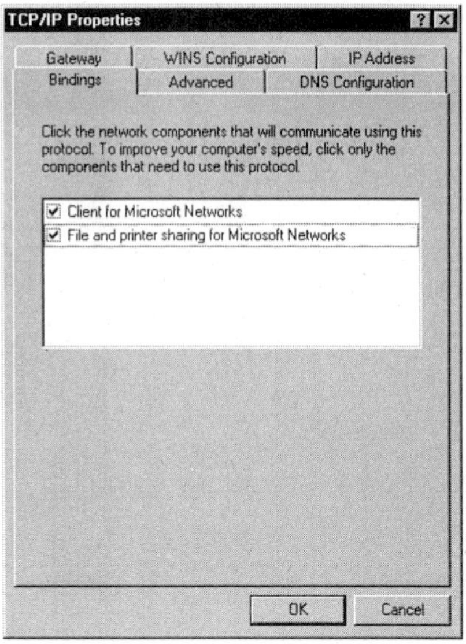

Fig. 20.7
Set the TCP/IP properties for bindings, DNS configuration, gateways, and so on.

Sharing Files and Printers

Many files on your computer are applicable only to you and your work, as are many of the files on other computers in your network. However, some of your files may be useful to your co-workers just as some of their files may be useful to you.

Peer-to-peer networks also enable printer-sharing, but if the printer is connected to your computer, you govern whether to share that printer with others on your network.

When working on a peer-to-peer network, you can choose to share or stop sharing the files and printer on each computer.

To set file and print sharing, follow these steps:

1. Open the Start menu and choose Settings, Control Panel.

2. Double-click the Network icon in the Control Panel. The Network dialog box appears.

3. In the Configuration page, select Client for Microsoft Networks from the list of installed network components.

4. Choose the File and Print Sharing button. The File and Print Sharing dialog box appears as shown in figure 20.8.

Tip
You also can control who can access your files with a password or with a list of specific users. See "Controlling Access to Shared Files and Printers" later in this chapter.

V

Networking

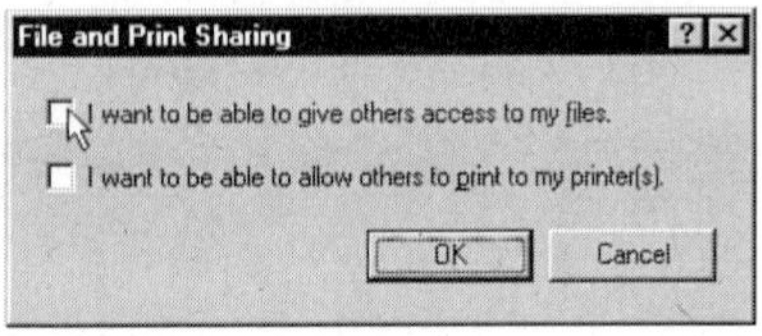

Fig. 20.8
Choose whether to share files and/or your printer with others on the network.

Caution

You cannot have Microsoft and NetWare file-and-print sharing installed at the same time. If you try to do this, you get an error message. If you use both Microsoft and NetWare networks, you have to decide which you want to use for file sharing.

Tip
You can share a specific folder by changing its sharing properties in the Explorer.

5. If you want to give other users on the network access to your files, select the option I Want to Be Able to Give Others Access to My Files. If you want to enable other users to use your printer, select the option I Want to Be Able to Allow Others to Print to My Printer(s). A check in the box means the option is on; no check mark signifies the option is turned off.

6. Choose OK to close the dialog box and Windows returns to the Network dialog box.

7. Choose OK to close the Network dialog box; alternatively, you can modify any of the other settings in the dialog box.

◀ See "Using the Explorer with Shared Resources on a Network," p. 544

This procedure doesn't set up any of your devices (drives, printers, and so on) for sharing. To share your devices, you select each individually and set up the security options for them to determine which users can access the devices. Chapter 21, "Sharing Windows 95 Peer-to-Peer Resources," describes how to set up sharing for specific devices.

Controlling Access to Shared Files and Printers

▶ See "Securing Your Network Resources," p. 640

After choosing to share your files and printer with others on your network, you can choose who, in particular, will have access to your files. You can choose to specify people or groups who will have access to each shared resource, or you can provide a password for each shared resource and only those with the password will have access.

To set access control, open the Network dialog box and choose the Access Control tab, as shown in figure 20.9. Select either Share-Level Access Control to set a password or Under-Level Access Control to provide a list of people. If you choose share-level, you can assign a password to each shared file or printer.

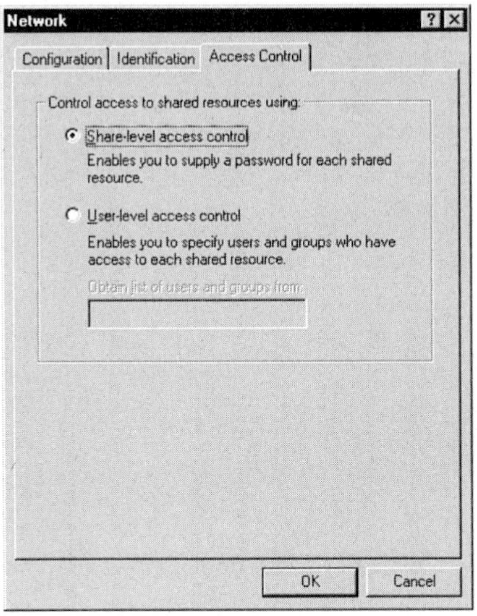

Fig. 20.9
Control the access to shared resources on your computer.

Identifying Your Workgroup Computer

If you did not give your computer and workgroup a name when you first installed Windows, you can name it at any time, or change the names, using the Network dialog box.

You name your computer to identify it to the other people on the network. When naming your computer, you can use up to fifteen characters, with no blank spaces.

The workgroup name identifies the group of computers you are most likely to communicate with—those computers on your network containing most of the resources you'll want to share. You can enter an existing workgroup name in the Workgroup text box or you can enter a new name. The name can contain up to fifteen characters.

> **Caution**
>
> To avoid confusion and erroneous workgroup names on your network, check with your network administrator before creating a new workgroup name.

To identify your computer on the network, follow these steps:

1. Open the Start menu and choose Settings, Control Panel.

2. Double-click the Network icon in the Control Panel. The Network dialog box appears. Click the Identification tab (see fig. 20.10).

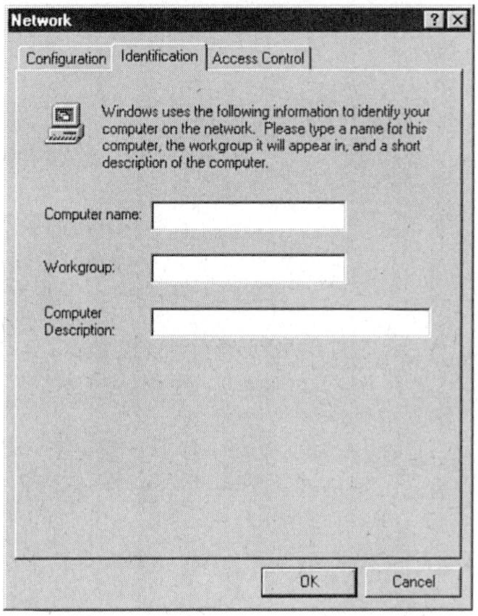

Fig. 20.10
The Identification tab enables you to identify your computer to the rest of the network.

3. In the Computer Name text box, type the name of your computer. The name of your computer must be a unique name on the network but it can be any name, such as Fred, Director, BookEditor12, and so on.

4. In the Workgroup text box, type the name of your computer's workgroup.

Tip
Use the Computer Description to enter your name or department, or perhaps resources connected to your computer.

5. An optional description of your computer appears in the Computer Description text box. You can enter a different description of your machine, if you want. The text that you enter here is used to identify your machine when users browse the network.

6. Click OK to close the Network dialog box.

Identifying the Primary Network Logon

To get onto a network, you usually use a logon, or a password, that initializes your security rights, thus enabling you to access the network and its resources. When you log on, Windows prompts you for a password and perhaps other information, such as a server name.

You can specify the logon option you use most often when logging onto the network or you can choose an option to use when you're not logging onto the network, such as when you're using a portable computer away from the office.

You select the primary logon option in the Network dialog box. Choose the Configuration tab, click the Primary Network Logon down arrow and a list of available network connections appears. Choose the logon option you use most of the time:

■ *Client for Microsoft Networks.* Use this option when logging onto the Windows peer-to-peer network.

■ *Client for NetWare Networks.* Use this option when logging onto a Novell network.

■ *Windows Logon.* Use this option if you don't want to view error messages when you're not logging on to the network.

Logging On to the Network

After you successfully install all the components for Windows 95 networking, the next time that you restart Windows, the Enter Network Password dialog box prompts you to log on to the network. To log in, enter the correct user name and password.

You can set options for the network logon in the Client for Microsoft Networks Properties sheet (see fig. 20.11). To display the sheet, open the Network dialog box and choose the Configuration tab. In the components list, choose the client you want to set logon options for. Choose the Properties button to display the Client for Microsoft Networks Properties sheet.

Following are the options you can choose in the General page of the Client for Microsoft Networks Properties sheet:

■ *Logon validation.* Select the Log On to Windows NT Domain option and enter the domain's name in the Windows NT domain text box to connect to the Windows NT domain when you log on to Windows.

■ *Network logon options.* Choose Quick Logon to make your previous network connections available but not connected until you use the drive. Choose Logon and Restore Network Connections to restore all network connections when you start windows.

V

Tip

Use the Passwords Control Panel (as discussed in the section "Restricting Access to Your Computer" in Chapter 4) to add or change the passwords and users that Windows recognizes.

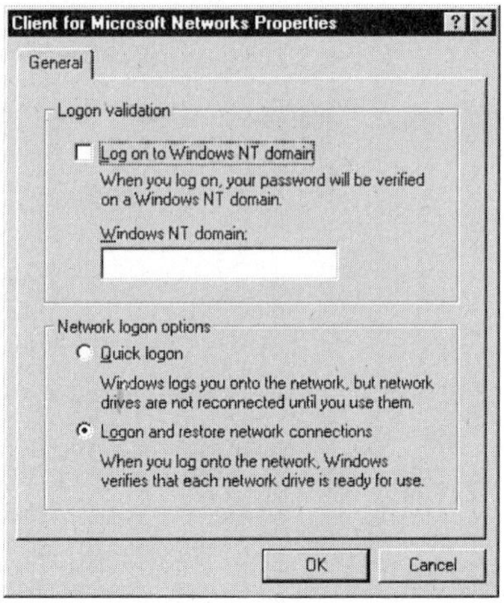

Fig. 20.11
Set logon proper-
ties for Windows
NT or Windows 95
peer-to-peer
networks.

To log off the network, choose the Start button and the Shut Down command. In the Shut Down Windows dialog box, choose Close All Programs
and Log On as a Different User? and then choose Yes. When Windows starts
again, the Enter Network Password dialog box appears. Choose Cancel and
Windows restarts without logging you onto the network.

> **Note**
>
> To change your Network and/or Windows passwords, open the Passwords icon from
> the Control Panel. In the Change Passwords tab, choose either Change Windows
> Password or Change Other Passwords.

▶ See "Network
Security,"
p. 820

> **Note**
>
> If you also have installed the Novell network client and chose it as the primary net-
> work logon, you'll see that dialog box first, then the Microsoft client logon. Chapter
> 23, "Using Novell Network Resources in Windows 95," discusses the Novell logon.
> If you have installed the Novell client but not the primary logon, you first see the
> Microsoft logon dialog box, then the Novell logon dialog box.

◀ See "Network-
ing Compo-
nents of the
Windows 95
Interface,"
p. 612

After connecting your computer to the network, you can browse any of the
available resources.❖

Chapter 21

Sharing Windows 95 Peer-to-Peer Resources

by Glenn Fincher with Sue Plumley

As discussed in Chapter 20, "Setting Up a Windows 95 Peer-to-Peer Network," peer-to-peer resource sharing with Windows 95 is much simpler than it has been in previous versions of Windows including Windows NT. This chapter discusses specific steps to sharing certain resources and covers other issues relating to sharing resources.

In this chapter, you can learn about these topics:

- Securing network resources

- File, directory, and drive sharing

- Drive usage policies

- Sharing printers

- Fax modem sharing

- Remote access to your network

- Peer-to-peer network management

Connecting to a Windows 95 peer-to-peer network offers a huge advantage over maintaining a stand-alone computer—resources. Using a network enables your computer to share resources—such as printers, plotters, optical disks, modems, applications, files, and so on—with other computers on the network. In addition, you can share in the resources of the other computers.

Securing Your Network Resources

If your PC is connected to another computer over a LAN, or dial-up network, you probably have given security more than a passing thought. Perhaps you've asked yourself these questions:

- Can others on the network gain unauthorized access to my data files?

- Should others be given *any* access to my data?

- If I do share a resource, can I revoke that access at a later time?

- Can an administrator or other person monitor my computer's resources without my knowledge?

Windows 95 Peer-to-Peer Security Principles

Although security is one of the key features of Windows 95, it is also the main reason that system administrators often do not like peer-to-peer networks. Control of resources resides with each user rather than with a centrally administered server. In other words, if a resource becomes essential for a workgroup, such as a specific directory on a single machine, then that machine becomes a server with expectations that the service or resource will always be available. The administration of these resources becomes a harder task as more power trickles down to the desktop. However, Windows 95 has tools to help track and administer this dilemma.

When you share a resource, you choose to control access to the share in two ways. You can use a password for the resource, called *share-level access control*. Or you can define users with access to the resource, called *user-level access control*. Additionally, you can choose whether to share your files and printer. At any time, you have the control to share or stop sharing your own resources. Of course, everyone else on the network also has those same rights.

> **Note**
>
> User-level access depends on *pass-through validation*—a Windows NT or Novell server authenticates the user from its database of accounts. Windows 95 does not maintain a general user list of its own for this authentication. Windows 95 does maintain the list of users' rights.

◀ See "Controlling Access to Shared Files and Printers," p. 634

◀ See "Sharing Files and Printers," p. 633

As to the questions you may have about the security of shared resources, no one can gain access to data unless you allow it by careful use of Windows 95's built-in access controls. You or the system administrator decide what resources or data, if any, is shareable, and you can revoke the access by simply un-sharing the resource or data at a later time. As long as you assign passwords for share-level access or rely on trusted users from a server with user-level access, only users who *should* have access to the resource can actually access it.

Some points to remember for security:

■ If you set up temporary access for a short time, remember to remove the access after the allotted time.

■ Always assign passwords for share-level access to a resource; never share a resource with a blank password.

■ Consider the cost in performance to a computer set up as a print or fax server. With constant use of these resources, this computer's performance may be affected.

■ After a resource is shared and regularly used, the resource might become so necessary that it can be used for little else.

User IDs and Passwords

In Windows 95, each user's unique identification information is stored in separate password USERNAME.PWL files. Each user on the network has a separate PWL file. These password files contain all password information for the respective user, including passwords for these items:

■ Resources protected by share-level security

■ Password-protected applications specifically written to the Master Password API

■ Windows NT computers not in a domain, or the Windows NT logon password if it isn't the Primary Network Logon

■ NetWare servers

These PWL files are stored in the Windows directory with each resource having a separate password. The passwords are encrypted in the PWL file, and the encrypted password is sent intact over the network. For any password scheme to work, the passwords must be protected by the user.

◀ See "Identifying the Primary Network Logon," p. 636

An administrator also can enforce certain password policies by implementing system policies using the Policy Editor in the Windows 95 Resource Kit. System policies override local Registry settings, so using system policies allows you to do these things:

▶ See "Network Security," p. 820

- Restrict a user from changing hardware settings using Control Panel

- Customize parts of the Desktop like the Network Neighborhood or the Programs folder

▶ See "What Utilities are Included in the Resource Kit," p. 1138

- Maintain centrally located network settings, such as network client customizations or the capability to install file and printer services

- Set policies for a group of users

Virus Protection on Your Network

◀ See "Protecting Your Files from Viruses," p. 575

An argument against allowing peer-to-peer networking is that the increased connectivity gives an easier path for the spread of computer virus infections. A *computer virus* is a program designed to propagate itself throughout the host computer. This propagation can be as simple as attaching its executable code to the beginning or end of an existing file, or as complex as mutating from one form to another to avoid detection and thereby quietly doing its damage.

Well-known viruses like the Michelangelo virus have gotten a lot of press because of their perennial nature. Michelangelo activates on March 6, at which time it formats the system hard disk by overwriting it with random characters from system memory. While it waits for March 6, Michelangelo dutifully copies itself to all disks accessed on the host computer. Then if another computer is booted using the newly infected disk, Michelangelo infects the next computer.

In cases where a documented virus case is discovered, multiple computers and floppy disks are also infected. Virus infections are a real problem, so steps must be taken to prevent their spread.

Regular use of one or more of the popular anti-virus packages decreases the chances of a virus hiding on your computer, and also prevents your own inadvertent propagating of a virus. MSDOS 5.*x* and up shipped with the Microsoft anti-virus MASV.EXE, but Windows 95 does not include an anti-virus product. Several products on the market can both detect and eliminate most virus infections. Because of the relative ease with which a new virus can be created, and the recent spread of so-called *polymorphic* viruses, it is wise to use more than one anti-virus product.

Note

Anti-virus software written for MSDOS or Windows 3.x may not work correctly on Windows 95. Consult your vendor for updated versions of the software.

Understanding File Sharing

Among the many resources you can share in a peer-to-peer Windows 95 network, information is the most crucial. Whether several people on the network share the accounting duties or two people exchange a spreadsheet, you'll be surprised at the amount of information that travels the network during a common workday.

Windows 95 allows workstations on the network to enable drive and directory sharing to help the users complete their work efficiently and effectively. In addition to sharing drives and directories, a user can choose to limit access to certain resources or to stop sharing at any time. This section describes how to share drives and directories and how to access shared drives and directories.

Tip

Drives you can share include the hard drive, floppy drives, CD-ROM drives, and tape drives.

Setting Up File Sharing

When attached to the peer-to-peer Windows 95 network, you can choose to share entire drives or specific folders (directories) on your computer. However, before you choose files or directories to share, you must enable file sharing by choosing that option in the Configuration tab of the Network dialog box.

◀ See "Installing Network Components in Windows 95," p. 604

> **Note**
>
> When choosing to share files or directories with other computers on your network, remember that you also can grant access to those who may share those files or directories.

◀ See "Sharing Files and Printers," p. 633

Sharing an Entire Drive

You can share your entire hard drive with other computers on the network. Additionally, you can choose to share floppy drives, CD drives, optical drives, and so on. When you choose to share a drive with the other computers on the network, those other users can access the files and directories on your computer.

◀ See "Controlling Access to Shared Files and Printers," p. 634

To share an entire drive with the network, follow these steps:

1. Open the My Computer window and select the drive you want to share.

2. Choose <u>F</u>ile, S<u>h</u>aring. The drive's Properties sheet appears with the Sharing page displayed.

3. To share the drive with the others on the network, choose the <u>S</u>hared As option. The options in the Shared As area are now ready to view and choose from, as shown in figure 21.1.

V

Networking

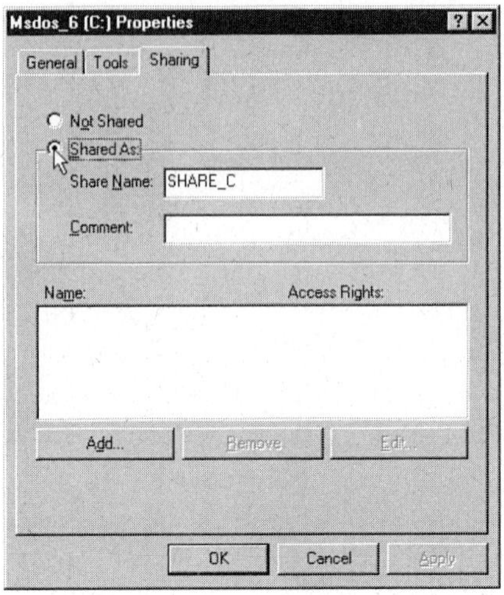

Fig. 21.1

After choosing to share the selected drive, you can choose access types, passwords, and so on in the Sharing page.

4. In the Shared As area, choose the appropriate options as described in table 21.1.

Table 21.1 Sharing Options	
Option	**Description**
Shared As	
Share Name	Enter a new name for the shared drive if you do not want to use the suggested name. This name is the name others will use when accessing the shared drive on your computer.
Comment	Add a comment, if you want, about the shared drive that others can see in Detail view. You can add a comment that will help others locate data on the drive, if you want.
Access Type	
Read-Only	Others can only view the drive and data, even copy files, but they cannot modify or remove data in any way.
Full	Others can change, add, or remove files.
Depends on Password	Enables different people different access, depending on the password they use.

Option	Description
Passwords	
Read-Only Password	Enter a password in this text box that enables those who know the password read-only access to your drive. A confirmation box appears in which you must type the password a second time to confirm.
Full Access Password	Enter a password in this text box that enables those who know the password full access to the drive. A confirmation box appears in which you must type the password a second time to confirm.

Caution

When you grant someone full access to your disk, they can delete files and folders or move items around if they want. Make sure you give full access only to people you trust.

5. Choose Apply and then OK to close the sheet.

Note

You can turn off sharing at any time by selecting the drive and then choosing File, Sharing, Not Shared, and then choose OK.

Note

If you want to share a *resource* but not make the name of the resource available by browsing, simply use the dollar sign ($) as the last character of the share name. For example, the share name SHARE$ is accessible as you define it, but it will not show up in a list of available resources when someone is browsing the network. You can name that shared device in a batch file, for example, so a user can access it without really seeing it as being available.

Tip
Windows adds a hand icon (palm up) in front of the shared drive icon in icon view to indicate it is shared.

V

Networking

Sharing a Directory

Just as you can share a drive, you also can share one or more directories on a drive. You might want to share a document, an application, or another directory with others on your network. Once again, you can limit the access for any directory you share.

To share a directory, open My Computer and locate the directory you want to share. Select the directory; choose File, Sharing. In the Sharing tab, choose the Shared As option and choose any options in the Shared As area as described in table 21.1. A small open hand icon appears in front of the folder's icon to indicate it is shared.

> **Note**
>
> When you share a directory or folder, you share *all* files in that directory. You can, however, make any file in that directory read-only or hidden to keep the file safe. To limit access to a file, open My Computer and then the folder containing the file. Select the file and choose File, Properties. In the General tab of the Properties sheet, choose Read-only or Hidden in the Attributes area. Choose OK to close the sheet.

Troubleshooting

Why can't I use any resources from another computer?

If you cannot see the resources, that computer might not have any resources available. If you can see the resources but cannot access them, you might not have permission to access those resources. Contact the system administrator.

I can't find a computer on the network. What should I do?

Choose Start, Find, Computer. The Find Computer dialog box appears. Enter the computer's name in the Named text box and choose Find Now. Windows should find the computer for you.

If you still cannot find the computer, it might be disconnected from the network. Contact the system administrator.

I tried to access a floppy disk on another computer to which I previously had access, and I received a message saying \computername\drive is not accessible. The device is not ready. *What can I do?*

That error message appears when the drive you're accessing is empty; for example, there is no disk in the floppy drive or CD-ROM drive. Contact the system administrator or send an e-mail to the computer you're trying to connect to and let them know you need the resource.

Some of the files I share are missing.

If you've given full access to someone else on the network, they can delete files from your disk. When someone deletes files from your disk, those files go to their Recycle Bin; you might check with everyone on the network who you've given full access to see if your files are still in their Recycle Bin.

Working with Shared Files

When you assign read-only and full passwords to shared drives and directories, the user must know the password to access those files. Without a read-only password, for example, the user cannot make changes to the file.

The Network Neighborhood window has two workstations: Asst. Director and Director. To open a computer on the network, double-click the icon of that computer; a window appears listing all available resources and/or directories or folders. Finally, to open a directory, double-click that directory. If the directory has read-only or full access, the directory's window opens and displays the contents. If, however, the directory allows only password access, the Enter Network Password dialog box appears (see fig. 21.2). Enter the password and choose OK to open the file. If you choose the Save This Password in Your Password List option, that password saves so you don't have to retype it the next time you open that folder.

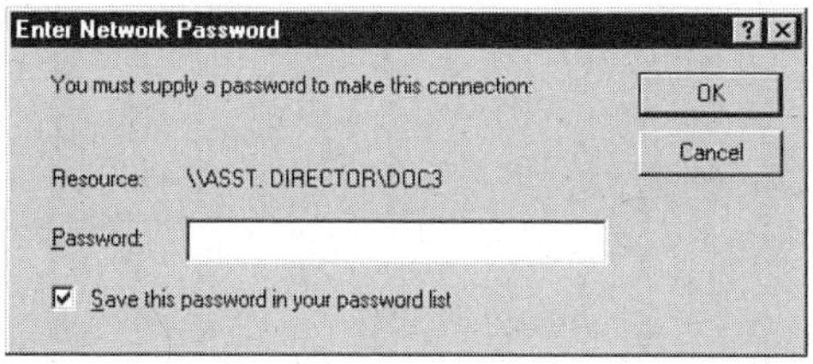

V

Networking

Fig. 21.2
You cannot open password-protected folders without entering the correct password.

Figure 21.3 shows the resulting message box from choosing File, Save while in a read-only shared file in WordPad. You can, however, choose File, Save As and save the document under another name. When saving the file, you can place it on your own drive, on another computer's drive, and in any folder to which you have access.

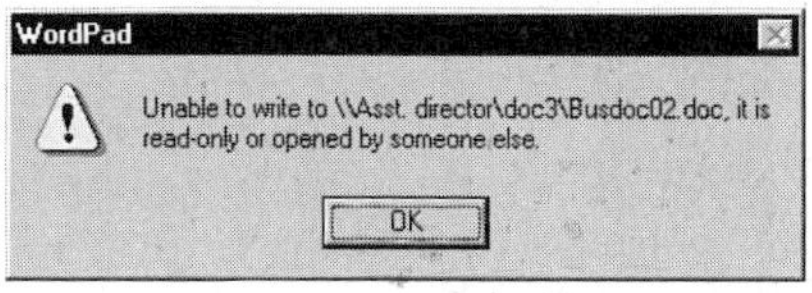

Fig. 21.3
Read-only password protection keeps you from saving changes to someone else's file.

Mapping Drives

Windows enables you to use drive mapping in peer-to-peer networking. *Drive mapping* is a method of assigning a drive letter to represent a path that includes the volume, directory, and any subdirectories leading to a directory or resource. The drive mapping you create follows the path for you, thereby saving you time; instead of opening folder after folder, you can use the drive map to quickly go to the directory or resource. Mapping is especially handy when you're constantly using a file or resource on another workstation.

To map a drive, follow these steps:

1. Open the window in which you want to place the mapped drive.

2. Choose View, Toolbar to display the Toolbar if it is not already showing.

3. Click the Map Network Drive icon on the toolbar (see fig. 21.4).

Fig. 21.4
Click the Map Network Drive icon to create a drive mapping shortcut.

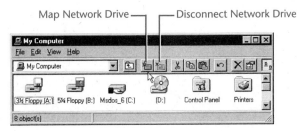

4. The Map Network Drive dialog box appears, as shown in figure 21.5. Click the Path down arrow. If you have recently connected to the drive, the path appears in the list box. If the path is not in the list box, enter the path in the following format: //*computername*/*foldername*.

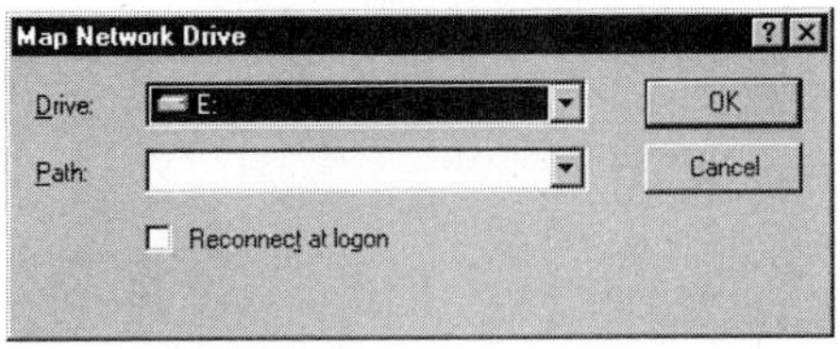

Fig. 21.5
Enter the Path of the resource or directory you want to map.

Tip
To make the mapping permanent, choose the Reconnect at Logon option.

5. Choose OK to complete the path. Figure 21.6 shows the resulting mapping icon in the My Computer window.

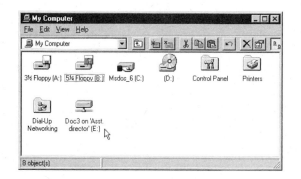

Fig. 21.6
Double-click the
mapped drive icon
to quickly open
the folder.

Note

To break the connection to the mapped drive, select the icon and click the Disconnect Net Drive icon. The Disconnect Network Drive dialog box appears; choose OK to remove the connection and the icon.

V

Networking

Understanding Drive Usage Policies

When working in a peer-to-peer environment, the workstations with the most used resources can easily become burdened and bottlenecks will often form. You must consider some simple resource usage policies to guarantee the most efficient use of those resources.

For example, the computer that contains the accounting or database program that all workstations use is a good candidate for hard drive management. To prevent a bottleneck of activity centered around the workstation containing the application, you might designate that the data files for that application be stored on another computer. Traffic then will be divided between two computers instead of concentrated on just one.

As another example, consider a network that uses MS Office daily. To guarantee the most efficient use of the applications, consider installing Office on each machine instead of sharing the application from one workstation. The applications will run faster, the user's time will not be wasted waiting for access to specific programs, and network traffic will be cut considerably.

Additionally, you might want to assign different workstations for the storage of the shared files used in the Office applications. One workstation can store shared Word files and another can store shared Excel files. Use a different workstation to store PowerPoint files, and so on. In this manner, traffic is disseminated for more efficient use of the network.

> **Note**
>
> Make sure each workstation is assigned only what is necessary for that user to do the work. For example, if a user needs to access only specific folders on the Director's drive, those are the only folders that should be available to that user. Limiting access not only ensures security, but also saves the user time searching for needed files and folders.

An additional shared resource you might want to keep an eye on is the CD-ROM drive. Windows enables each workstation to access a CD in the shared drive and run applications or copy files from that CD. Because workstations might need to access the drive at the same time, traffic can become congested. To alleviate the problem, you could limit specific workstation access to the drive. If all workstations need to use the CD-ROM drive, consider scheduling times for its use; something as simple as having workstations one through eight use the drive in the mornings and the rest using it in the afternoons.

As you become more familiar with how the Windows peer-to-peer network operates, you'll find ways to make sharing resources efficient and effective.

> **Note**
>
> A tool you might overlook when thinking about disk usage is the Recycle Bin. Not emptying the Recycle Bin leaves you with less space than you thought you had. If you use your drive in a networked environment, this extra lost space may be valuable.

◀ See "Changing the Properties of the Recycle Bin," p. 521

Sharing Printers

▶ See "Understanding Network Printing," p. 772

▶ See "Managing Print Files and Sharing," p. 784

You can designate a printer attached to your machine as a shared printer. Anyone on the network with access can then print to your printer from their workstation. With a shared printer, users can print from applications or use the drag-and-drop printing method. Users also can cancel, view the print queue, and pause printing.

When sharing your printer with others on the network, you can choose to limit access by assigning a password. Then, only those with the password can use your printer. Additionally, you can stop sharing your printer at any time.

Setting Up Printer Sharing and Security

For others to use your printer, you must designate it as a shared resource. When you choose to share the printer, you also can assign a password to limit access to the printer. Before you can share your printer, you must enable file and printer sharing from the Network dialog box.

◀ See "Sharing Files and Printers," p. 633

To designate a printer for sharing, follow these steps:

1. Choose Start, Settings, and then Printers.

2. In the Printers window, select the printer you want to share and choose File, Sharing. The printer's Properties sheet appears.

3. Choose the Shared As option to activate the shared area of the sheet (see fig. 21.7).

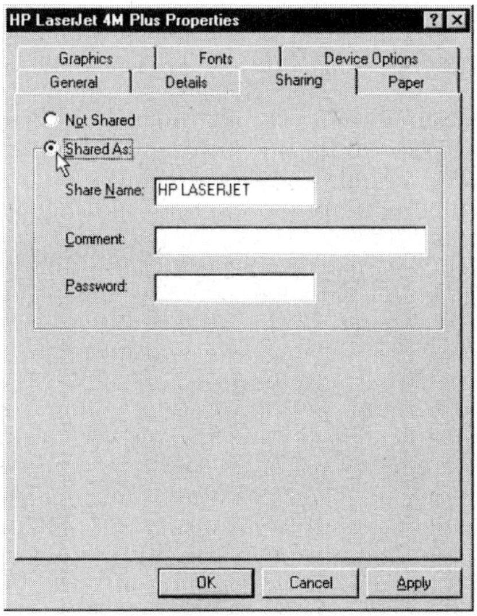

Fig. 21.7
When choosing to share a printer, you can assign a password to limit user access.

V

Networking

4. Accept the default name or type a new name in the Share Name text box.

5. If you want, describe the printer in more detail in the Comment text box.

6. Optionally, give the resource a Password.

7. To implement the changes you have made to the sheet, click the Apply button.

8. Choose OK to close the Properties sheet; the printer icon now displays the shared icon.

Connecting to a Shared Printer

Before you can attach to a shared printer, you must install the network printer to your list of printers. Windows includes a printer wizard to help you install the network printer. After installing it, you can use the printer to print from your applications as you would any printer that's attached to your computer.

To install a shared printer, follow these steps:

1. Open the Network Neighborhood and double-click the computer to which the printer is attached. The computer's window opens and the printer icon appears.

2. Select the printer icon and choose File, Install.

   You also can open the Printers folder and double-click the Add Printer icon.

3. The first Add Printer Wizard dialog box appears. Choose Yes if you plan to print from MS-DOS-based programs to this printer. Otherwise, accept the default selection, No, by choosing the Next button.

4. The second Add Printer Wizard dialog box appears, as shown in figure 21.8. Choose the Network Printer option and choose Next.

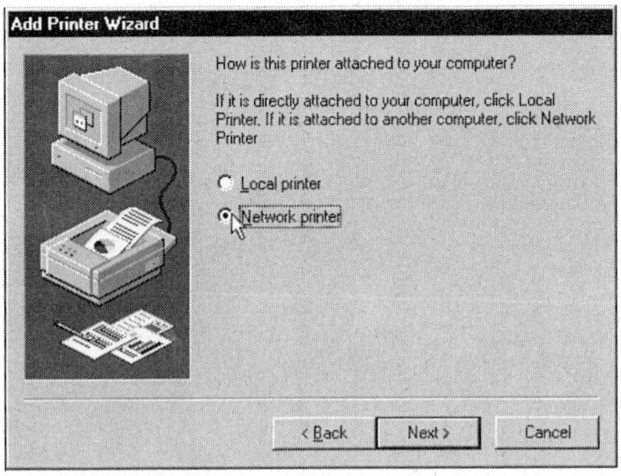

Fig. 21.8
The wizard dialog box specifies Local Printer as a default; use this option only if the printer is physically attached to your computer.

5. The next Add Printer Wizard dialog box appears (see fig. 21.9). In the Network Path or Queue Name text box, enter the path to the printer.

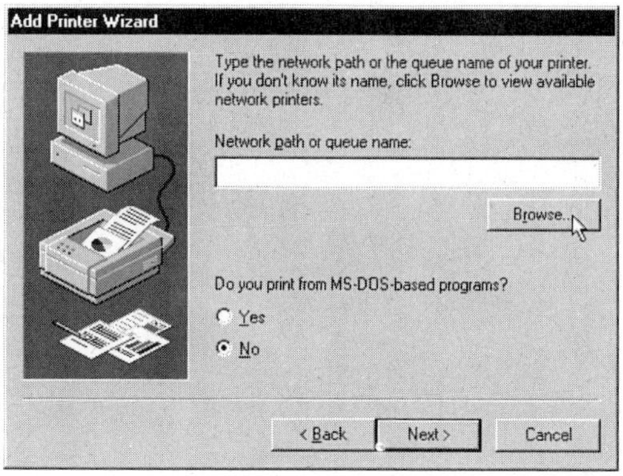

Fig. 21.9
Enter the path
to the printer or
choose the Browse
button to find the
correct path.

If you don't know the path, choose the Browse button. The Browse for
Printer dialog box opens (see fig. 21.10). Double-click the remote computer and then select the printer. Choose OK to return to the wizard
dialog box. The path appears in the Network Path text box.

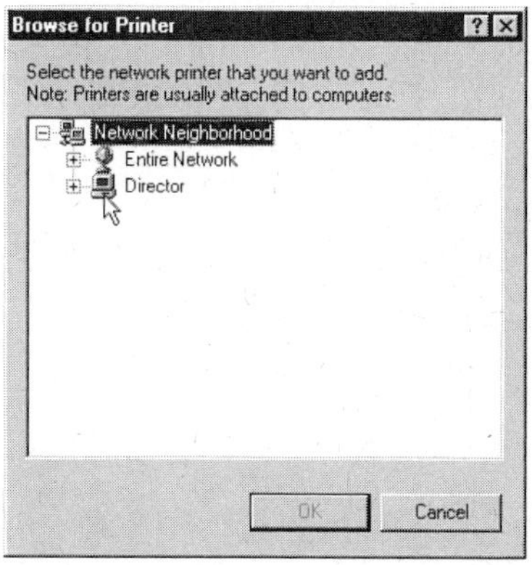

Fig. 21.10
You can select
the printer in this
dialog box and the
path will automati-
cally appear in the
Network Path text
box.

6. Choose Next. The next wizard box enables you to enter a printer name
   other than the default, if you want. Choose Next.

7. The final wizard dialog box enables you to print a text page. Choose Yes
   to print a test page; choose No if you don't want to print a test page.
   Choose Finish to install the printer.

Windows adds the network printer to your list of printers. Use the printer as
you would any printer attached to your computer.

Applying Printer Sharing Policies

When you share a printer in a peer-to-peer network, all jobs sent to the printer are entered into the print queue, where they wait for the printer to become available. Jobs are normally serviced in first-come-first-serve order, although most printers allow users to prioritize print jobs so they can be moved up in line.

While some of the resource users might print jobs with one or two pages of text, there are also those who print 90-page jobs with heavy graphic use. Those large jobs are the ones that can cause frustration for everyone else on the network who needs to print.

The solution? There are a couple of common sense ideas you can apply to the situation. First, you should make available two printers to the network, if at all possible. To justify the expense of two printers, choose one printer (such as a laser) as the workhorse—the most commonly used printer. Choose a second printer (such as a color inkjet or laser) to use for special presentations or reports. Because most color printers also can print black ink, use the second printer for general printing when the first printer is overloaded.

The second idea for controlling printer use is to set forth some common courtesy guidelines for those attached to the network. Anyone having especially large or complex print jobs should contact all concerned and perhaps even schedule a time to print the job. If everyone on the network understands they must cooperate in using all shared resources, almost any problem can be solved.

▶ See "Under-
standing Net-
work Printing,"
p. 772

▶ See "Managing
Print Files and
Sharing,"
p. 784

Troubleshooting

It's taking a long time for my document to print. Can I speed it up?

In the Printers window, double-click the printer icon to see the printer's window. Locate your job and see where you are in line. If there are a lot of jobs in the queue ahead of you, you'll have to wait for the other jobs to print.

If your job is the one printing and progress seems to be slow, graphics added to the document might be causing the problem. You can cancel the print job and then select the printer icon in the Printers window and choose File, Properties. Choose the Graphics tab and choose a lower resolution. Choose OK and try printing the document again.

Sharing a Fax Modem

Windows 95 enables users to easily share a fax modem with other users in the workgroup. Every user can take advantage of the service and send faxes and even editable files using the shared fax modem. Windows 95 makes this capability as easy as printing a file or sending an e-mail message.

Microsoft Fax is compatible with Group 3 faxes worldwide, yet it also offers secure fax transmission as well as binary file transfer to another Microsoft Fax recipient. Microsoft Fax uses MAPI (Mail Application Programming Interface) so you can easily send a fax using an application's File, Send command or File, Print command. The fax printer driver is accessible from any application's Print command, enabling fax in all users' applications. This power makes a shared fax a great addition to a workgroup. This section discusses the features of Microsoft Fax specifically when used as a shared fax server.

Understanding Fax Modem Sharing Policies

For the most part, a peer-to-peer network makes use of each computer's resource while each computer's user continues to work on the computer. When you find the shared resources are so heavily used that one computer becomes overloaded, it is time to consider changing one computer into a server.

Consider these primary issues when determining whether to set up a Windows 95 computer as a fax server:

◀ See "Approaches to Networks," p. 582

- Is the computer on which the fax modem is installed going to be used only as a fax server, or will it also be used as a workstation?

- Which users will need the fax service?

- Is this computer going to host the only fax that the company uses?

- Is this computer also going to serve as a print server?

If the fax server computer is also going to be used as a workstation, you may need to increase the amount of memory installed on the computer. Microsoft makes these recommendations:

- Standalone fax server minimum configuration:

  80486 computer with 8M of memory

V

Networking

■ Dual purpose fax server and workstation minimum configuration:

80486 computer with 12M of memory

If you want to share a fax modem, you must install Microsoft Exchange on each workstation that needs to use the fax service. All faxes are sent to the users through Microsoft Exchange. The Microsoft Exchange InBox of the fax server receives all the incoming faxes for those using the service. The faxes are not automatically routed; this operation is done manually by the administrator of the fax server.

If this fax is the only one the company uses, the fax volume needs to be monitored to assure that the needs of the company are being met. Microsoft states that the preceding recommended configuration typically supports a workgroup of 25 users.

If the computer is also a print server—a common configuration since users can print their faxes from the same computer—additional monitoring may be necessary to assure that the workstation is handling the additional load.

Setting Up Fax Modem Sharing

After you have made the decision to set up a fax server, you take these steps:

▶ See "Installing a Plug and Play Modem," p. 833

1. Install the modem.

2. Install the Exchange client on the server computer.

3. Install Microsoft Fax on the server.

4. Establish the fax share.

You use similar steps to set up each workstation:

1. Install the Exchange client.

2. Install Microsoft Fax.

3. Connect to the shared fax.

Before configuring the fax modem for sharing, you need to install it on the sharing computer. If the fax modem is not yet set up, see Chapter 27, "Installing and Configuring Your Modem." You also need to have Exchange and Microsoft Fax installed on the server. Both of these topics are explained in Chapter 24, "Using Microsoft Exchange." After that, you are ready to configure Exchange to enable sharing:

1. Open the Start menu and choose Settings, Control Panel.

2. Double-click the Mail and Fax icon. The MS Exchange Settings Properties sheet opens as shown in figure 21.11.

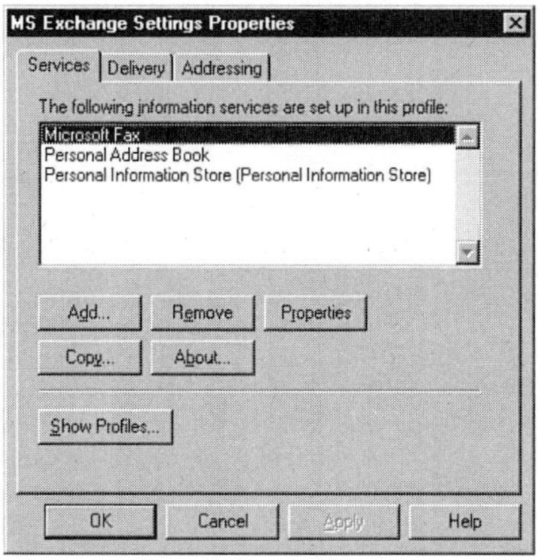

Fig. 21.11
The MS Exchange
Settings Properties
sheet shows the
Microsoft Fax
selection.

V

3. Select Microsoft Fax and click Properties. The Microsoft Fax Properties
   sheet appears (see fig. 21.12).

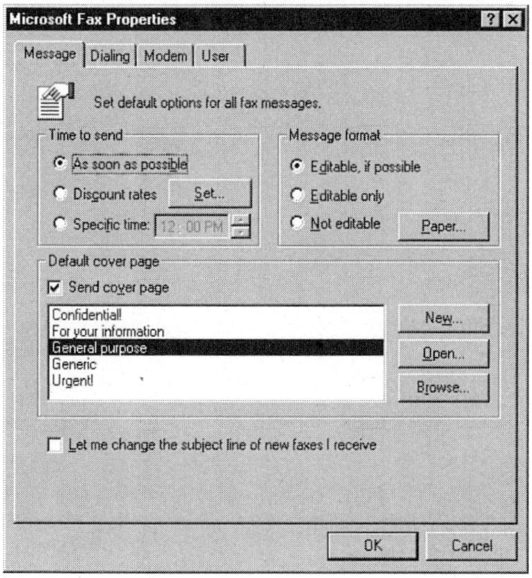

Fig. 21.12
The Message tab
appears in the
Microsoft Fax
Properties sheet.

Networking

4. Choose the Modem tab and select the option Let Other People on the
   Network Use My Modem To Send Faxes, as shown in figure 21.13.

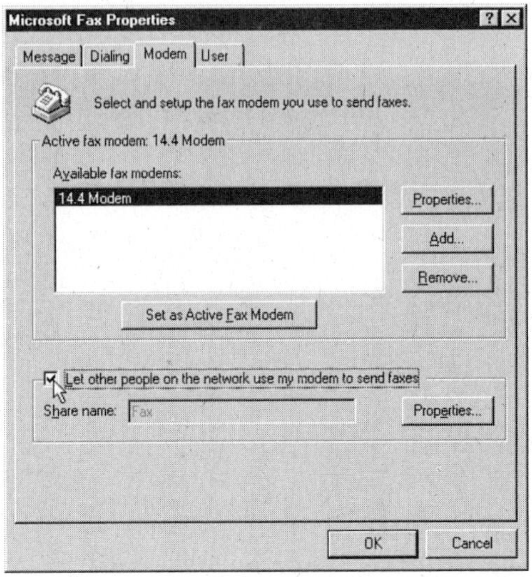

Fig. 21.13
Choose to share
the modem in the
Modem tab of the
Microsoft Fax
Properties sheet.

5. Choose the Properties button on the Modem page. The NetFax dialog box appears (see fig. 21.14).

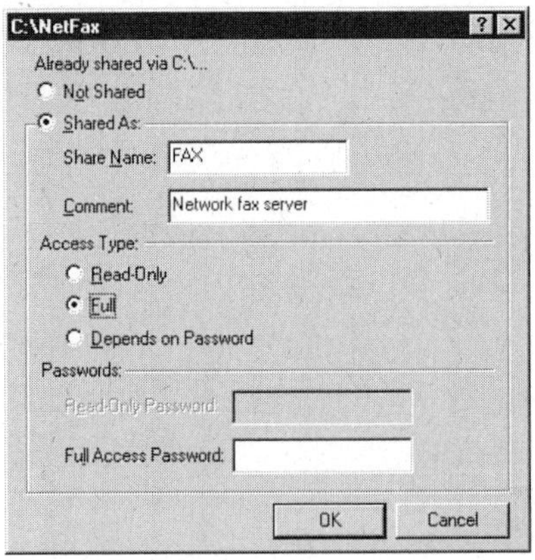

Fig. 21.14
Use the NetFax
dialog box to
assign a share
name, comment,
and to limit access
to the fax modem.

6. Enter the Share Name, a Comment if you want, and set the Access Type for the fax modem.

7. Enter a password. The Confirmation of Password dialog box appears; enter the password again and choose OK.

8. Click OK in each dialog box to complete the configuration.

Configuring Workstations to Use a Shared Fax Modem

You are now ready to install and configure each workstation to connect to and use the server. Installation is simply a repeat of the steps from Chapter 24 to install Microsoft Exchange and Microsoft Fax software, then you configure Microsoft Fax to use the shared fax modem instead of looking for a local modem. This section doesn't repeat the software installation but just steps through locating and connecting to the shared fax server:

▶ See "Installing and Configuring Microsoft Exchange," p. 727

1. Open the Start menu, choose Settings, Control Panel.

2. Double-click the Mail and Fax icon. The MS Exchange Settings Properties sheet opens (refer to fig. 21.11).

3. Select Microsoft Fax and click Properties. The Microsoft Fax Properties sheet appears (refer to fig. 21.12).

4. Click the Modem tab and choose Add. The Add a Fax Modem dialog box appears.

5. Click Network Fax Server, as shown in figure 21.15.

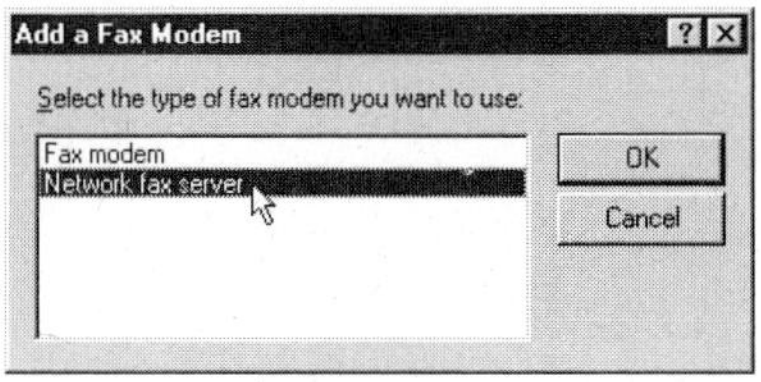

Fig. 21.15
Choose a Network Fax Server to connect to the fax modem on another computer.

6. Choose OK and the Connect To Network Fax Server dialog box appears (see fig. 21.16).

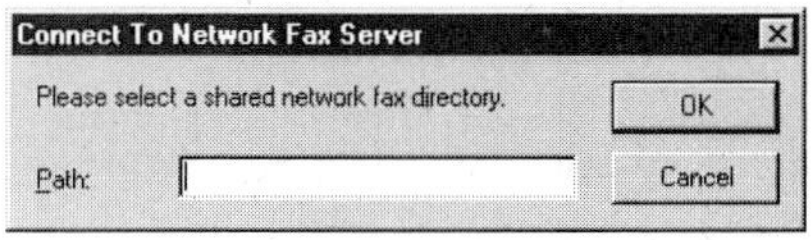

Fig. 21.16
Enter the path to the fax server.

Type the UNC share name for the fax server (for example, \\SERVER\NETFAX).

7. Click OK to close each dialog box.

You're now ready to use Windows 95's Microsoft Fax.

V

Networking

Using a Shared Fax Modem

You can easily use a shared fax modem from Microsoft Exchange through Microsoft Fax, or from an application such as WordPad or Word.

To use Microsoft Exchange to send a fax, double-click the Inbox to start the application. Compose the fax as you normally would.

▶ See "Faxing a Quick Message or a File," p. 743

To send a fax from an application, compose the fax and then choose File, Send. The Choose Profile dialog box appears. Use the default profile or choose a new one, then choose OK. The New Message dialog box appears. Complete the message as you would in Microsoft Exchange. You can, alternatively, choose File, Print to send a fax. In the Print dialog box choose Microsoft Fax as the name of the printer and choose OK.

▶ See "Working with User Profiles in Exchange," p. 763

To use Microsoft Fax, open the Start menu and select Programs. Choose Accessories, Fax, and Compose New Fax to create a fax to send.

> **Note**
>
> If someone tries to access the fax modem while it is in use, the fax messages are placed in a queue, similar to when jobs are placed in a print queue.

> **Note**
>
> If you send or receive faxes on the network using a shared fax modem, you may want to take advantage of Microsoft Fax's security features to ensure privacy of your fax transmissions. This topic is discussed in Chapter 24, "Using Microsoft Exchange."

Gaining Remote Access to Your Network

▶ See "Connecting to the Internet with a LAN," p. 899

Remote access with Windows 95 is easier and more robust than in any previous version of Windows. If you are connecting to an Internet service provider, using remote mail from home, or simply connecting to another Windows 95 workstation, Windows 95 Remote Network Access (RNA) and Dial-Up Networking can make the connection for you and enable you to use all the resources on the network as if you were physically connected to the LAN rather than remotely connected through a modem.

◀ See "System Requirements and Recommendations," p. 620

Remote access is accomplished with new 32-bit networking components and a dial-up adapter, so you can take advantage of all the interfaces of Windows remote networking. Because remote networking is built-in at the core of Windows 95, programs that require networking invoke the Dial-Up Networking component when they run to automate the connection. A good example is the Internet Explorer that is part of the Plus! Pack for Windows 95. When you attempt to connect to a resource that requires a network connection, the Internet Explorer automatically opens the Dial-Up Networking dialog box to attempt a connection to the network.

As indicated in Chapter 20, "Setting Up a Windows 95 Peer-to-Peer Network," Remote Network Access with Windows 95 requires only the addition of a modem, installation of Dial-Up Networking components, and the phone number for the remote connection. This connection can be an Internet service account, a Windows 95 or Windows NT server, a NetWare Connect server, or Shiva's LanRover and NetModem remote-node servers. This section discusses connecting to a Windows 95 server and to a Windows NT server.

Preparing Your Computer

With Dial-Up Networking, you can connect to a network and access shared information, even if your computer is not a part of the network. You can use a home computer, notebook, or other computer to dial up a server on the network.

1. In the Configuration tab of the Network dialog box, select Client for Microsoft Networks from the Network Components list, as shown in figure 21.17.

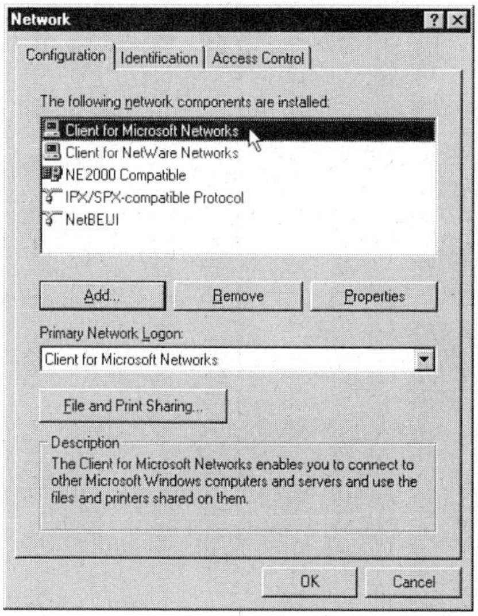

◀ See "Modems for Dial-Up Networking," p. 622

Tip
Connecting to an Internet service provider is covered in Chapter 29, "Getting Connected to the Internet."

◀ See "Installing the Microsoft Network Client," p. 625

◀ See "Identifying Your Workgroup Computer," p. 635

V

Networking

Fig. 21.17
You must first select the client before identifying the host and workgroup.

2. Click the Identification tab of the Network dialog box (see fig. 21.18).

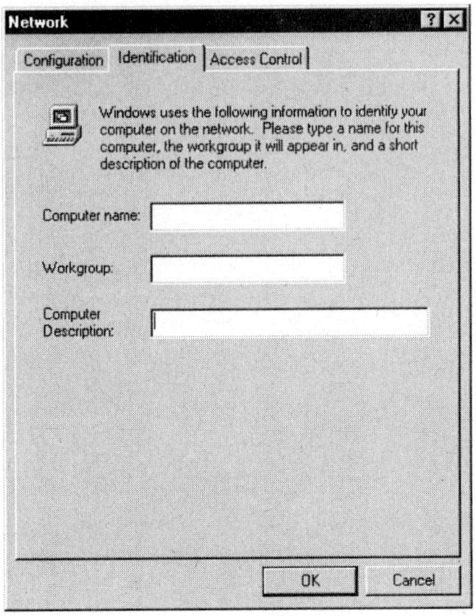

Fig. 21.18

Identify the host
and workgroup in
the Identification
tab.

3. Enter the name of the remote, or host, computer in the Computer Name text box. Enter the Workgroup name; Workgroup refers to a Windows NT, Windows 95, or Windows for Workgroup workgroup, the logical grouping of peer machines in a Windows network.

4. Click the Access Control tab. The Access Control tab appears as shown in figure 21.19.

5. For peer-to-peer networking, choose Share-Level Access Control. A LAN user can choose either option, depending on whether pass-through account validation is needed or desired.

6. Click OK.

7. Window 95 states that you must restart your computer before the new settings will take effect and asks if you want to restart the computer. Choose Yes to restart with the new settings.

Congratulations, you have made it through the hardest part of installation and configuration of your dial-up connection. Now you can proceed to configuring a dial-up connection.

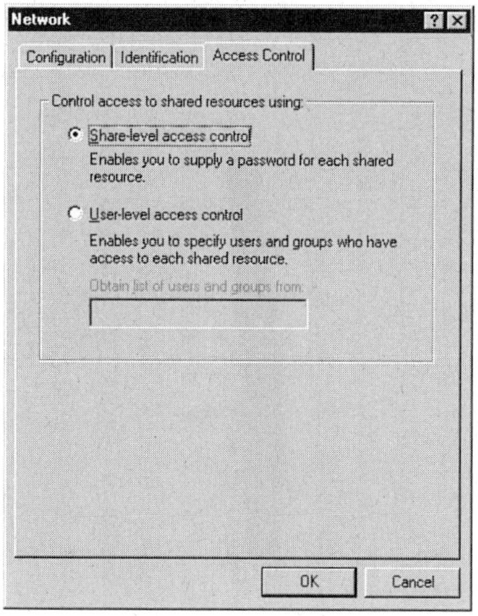

Fig. 21.19
Choose the access
control you want
for shared
resources.

Making the Connection

Windows provides a Dial-Up Connection wizard that makes it easy to create connections for Dial-Up Networking. After the wizard leads you through the process, you're ready to make your call. To run the wizard, follow these steps:

1. Open the Start menu and choose Programs, Select Accessories, and then Dial-Up Networking. The Dial-Up Networking window appears.

2. Double-click Make New Connection. The first box of the Make New Connection wizard appears (see fig. 21.20).

> **Note**
>
> After you have added at least one new connection, opening the Start menu and choosing Programs, Accessories, and then Dial-Up Networking has a different result. Once a connection exists, choosing this as in step 1 opens the Dial-Up Networking Folder instead of the Wizard.

3. Enter the name to identify the computer to which you will attach; for example, use the resource's name such as Laser Printer on Director's.

4. Select your modem.

   Choose the Configure button if you need to set any specific options. The modem's Properties sheet will appear, containing such information as port, speaker volume, baud rate, data bits, parity, and so on. Choose OK to return to the wizard.

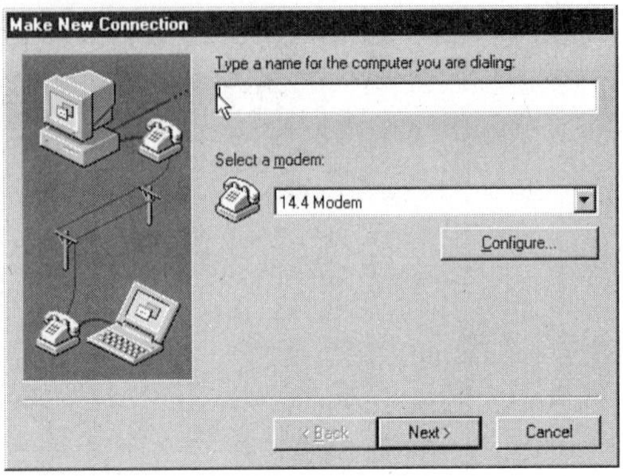

Fig. 21.20
Enter a name for
the computer to
which you are
making the
connection.

5. Choose Next. The second wizard dialog box appears (see fig. 21.21).

6. Enter the Telephone Number to the modem of the remote (host) computer and your Country Code.

7. Click Next. The next wizard dialog box appears, telling you the connection was successfully created.

8. Click Finish. The new connection is added to the Dial-Up Networking window.

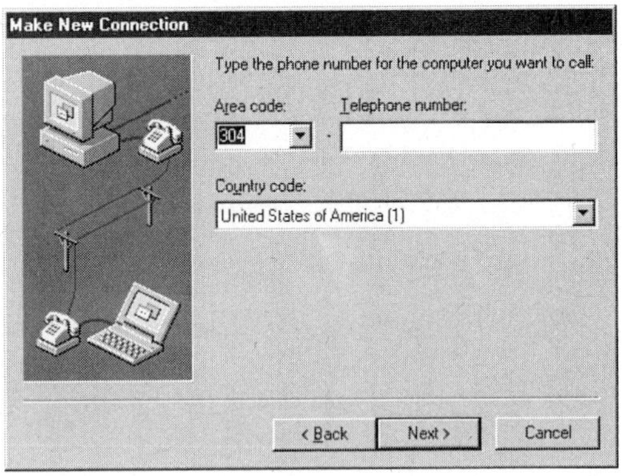

Fig. 21.21
Enter the tele-
phone number
and choose a
country, if other
than the United
States.

Modifying a Connection

You can change a phone number, modem configuration, and even the server type for a Dial-Up connection. First, you must open the Dial-Up Networking window and select the connection you want to modify. Then follow these steps:

1. Right-click the Dial-Up Connection icon you want to modify.

2. Select the Properties command. The connection's properties sheet appears, as shown in figure 21.22.

3. To reconfigure the modem, choose the Configure button. The Modem Properties sheet appears and offers options such as port, speaker volume, speed, parity, and so on.

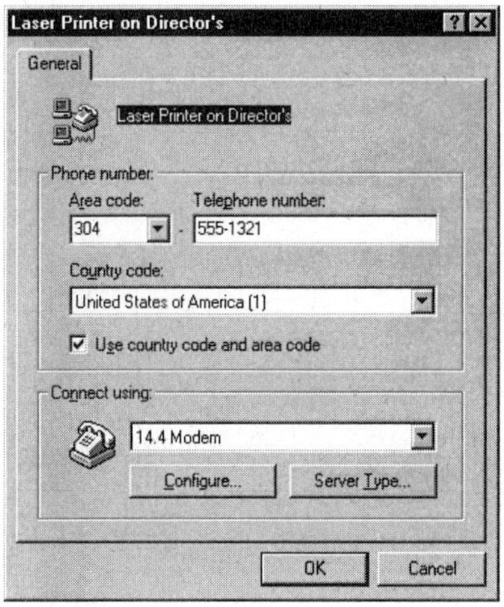

Fig. 21.22
Use the connection's properties sheet to change phone numbers, modem connections, and so on.

V

Networking

4. To set the server, choose the Server Type button. The Server Types dialog box appears (see fig. 21.23).

5. In the Type of Dial-Up Server drop-down list, choose the type of server to which you want to connect from the following:

   PPP; Windows 95, Windows NT 3.5, Internet. Choose to connect to a Windows 95 peer-to-peer network, a Windows NT 3.5 network, or to the Internet.

Windows for Workgroups and Windows NT 3.1. Choose to connect to either of these versions of Windows.

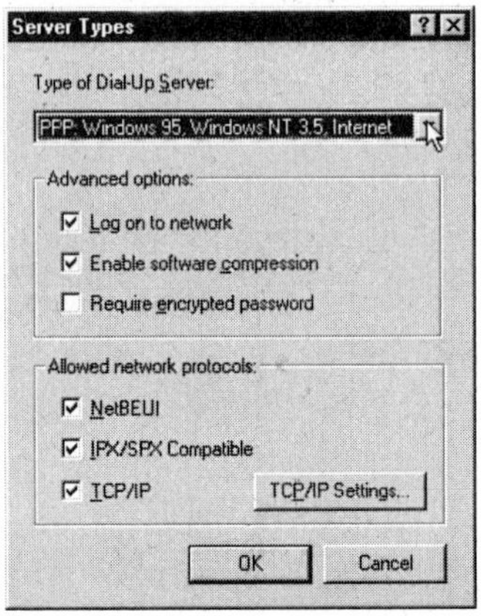

Fig. 21.23

Choose the type of server you want to connect to, such as a Windows NT or Windows 95 server.

6. In the Advanced options area, choose from the following options:

Log On to Network. Dial-Up Networking logs onto the network using the name and password you use to log into Windows.

Enable Software Compression. Specifies whether data is compressed before it is sent. Speeds up the transfer but both computers must be using compatible compression.

Require Encrypted Password. Specifies that only encrypted passwords can be sent to or accepted by your computer.

7. In the Allowed Network Protocols area, choose NetBEUI to connect to the peer-to-peer network.

8. Choose OK to close the dialog box. Choose OK again to close the connection's properties dialog box.

Connecting the Dial-Up Network

You can add more connections to your Dial-Up Networking window at any time. When you're ready to connect to the network, open the Dial-Up Networking window, turn on your modem, and follow these steps:

1. Double-click the connection icon in the Dial-Up Networking window. The Connect To dialog box appears (see fig. 21.24).

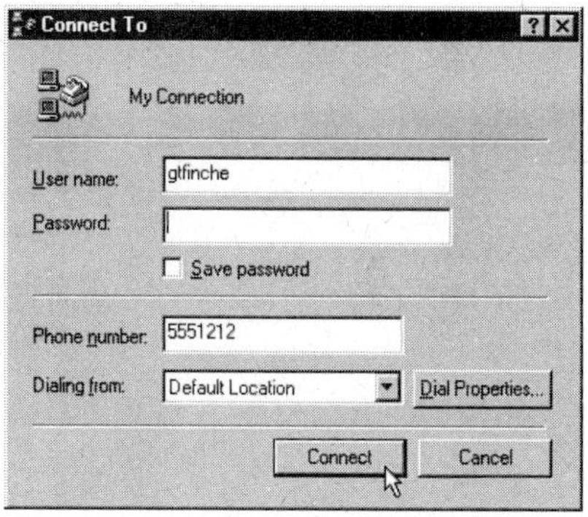

Fig. 21.24
Make any last
minute changes in
the Connect To
dialog box.

2. Enter the Password. You can choose Dial Properties if you have any last minute changes to make to the information.

3. Choose the Connect button. The Connecting To dialog box shows your progress. When the connection is made, Dial-Up verifies your user name and password with the remote computer.

4. When your login is complete, Windows 95 shows the connection status dialog box that monitors the connection. You're connected to the remote network and can access any resources to which you have been given access.

Troubleshooting

The remote computer hangs up on me unexpectedly. What makes it do that?

There might be noise over the phone lines that's interrupting the connection. You could try calling again and hope for a better connection.

If you're still having problems, ask the administrator whether the computer you're trying to connect to is up and running.

Alternatively, you might have gone too long without typing anything. Try again. Also, ask your administrator if there is a time limit on how long you can remain connected to the network. Perhaps the administrator can increase the time.

Managing a Peer-to-Peer Network

With all the useful peer-to-peer features in Windows 95, you may think the network must be a nightmare to administer. But Microsoft has assembled a set of tools to assist in managing this usually unmanageable network topology. The tools range from the fairly simple but powerful Net Watcher to the robust agents that enable remote monitoring in an automated fashion.

► See "What Utilities are Included in the Resource Kit," p. 1138

The tools that ship as part of Windows 95 are Net Watcher, System Policy Editor, Registry Editor, and Backup Agents; these tools do not install by default. The System Policy Editor, for example, is an Accessory System tool you can install through Windows Setup, if you did not install it at the same time you installed Windows. Other utilities can be found in the Windows 95 Resource Kit.

Net Watcher

Net Watcher enables you to monitor and manage network connections, as well as create, add, and delete shared resources. To use this powerful tool, you need to configure each workstation to allow remote administration.

To enable remote administration, follow these steps:

1. Double-click the Passwords icon in the Control Panel. The Passwords Properties sheet appears.

2. Click the Remote Administration tab, as shown in figure 21.25.

3. Select Enable Remote Administration of the Server.

4. Enter a Password and then enter it again in the Confirm Password text box. Choose OK.

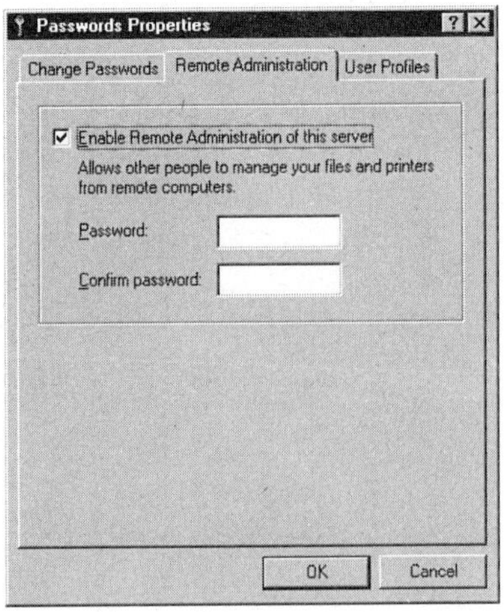

Fig. 21.25
Enable remote administration and enter a password to limit access.

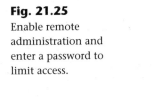

After you have configured the workstations to allow remote configuration, run Net Watcher on the administrator's workstation. To run Net Watcher, click the Start button and then choose Programs, Accessories, System Tools, and then Net Watcher. The Net Watcher window appears as shown in figure 21.26.

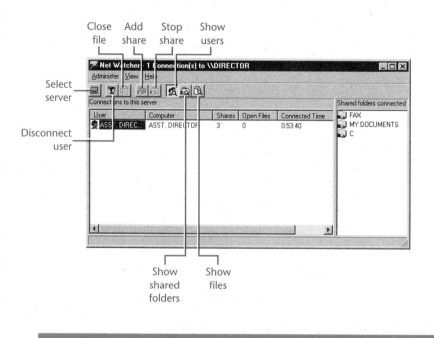

Fig. 21.26
You can view the computers on the network and the folders shared with them.

V

Networking

> **Note**
>
> To install Net Watcher, use the Add/Remove Programs icon in the Control Panel. In the Windows Setup tab, Net Watcher is listed as an Accessory.

This accessory enables a remote administrator to actively monitor and manage shared drives and folders, printers, or even the fax server. Using the icons in the Net Watcher, you can show users, shared folders, and files currently being shared. Additionally, when you show the shared folders, Net Watcher lists access type and comments, as shown in figure 21.27.

◀ See "Adding Windows' Component Applications," p. 312

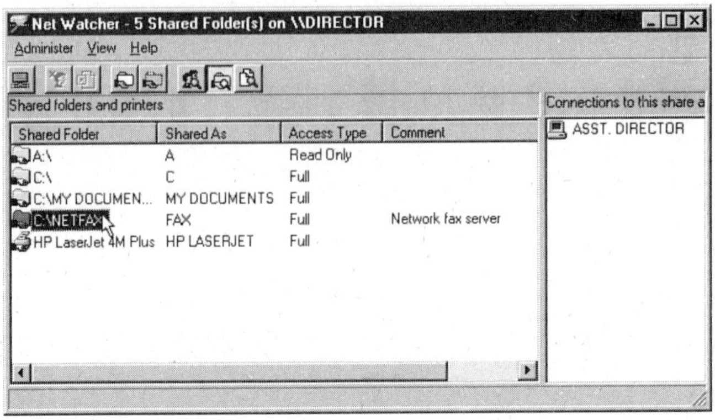

Fig. 21.27
Select a shared
folder and view
the computer
connection to that
folder on the right
side of the Net
Watcher window.

Net Watcher - 5 Shared Folder(s) on \\DIRECTOR

Administer   View   Help

Shared folders and printers

Shared Folder	Shared As	Access Type	Comment
A:\	A	Read Only	
C:\	C	Full	
C:\MY DOCUMEN...	MY DOCUMENTS	Full	
C:\NETFAX	FAX	Full	Network fax server
HP LaserJet 4M Plus	HP LASERJET	Full	

Connections to this share a

ASST. DIRECTOR

Tip
You can use the
Administer menu
to add shared
folders or to stop
sharing a folder;
you can even
change the shar-
ing properties of
any selected
folder.

System Monitor

The next tool in the administrator's arsenal is the System Monitor, which
gives a graphical picture of network traffic, file system performance, and
other settings. Though System Monitor ships with Windows 95, remote
monitoring requires the Microsoft Remote Registry service from the Resource
Kit. Once this service is installed, you can monitor running processes,
memory usage, network traffic, and so on. Figure 21.28 shows the System
Monitor on a local machine.

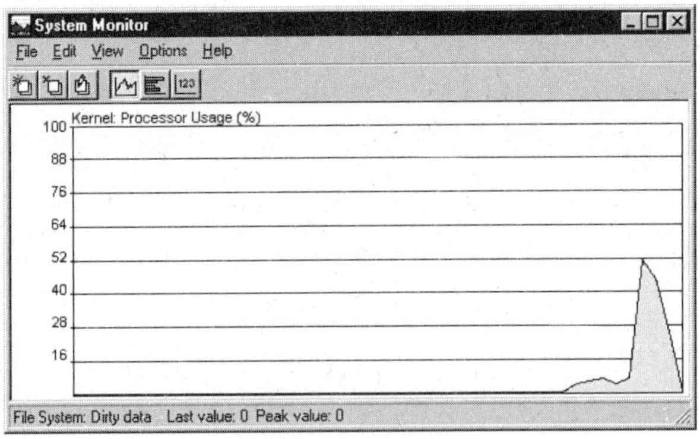

Fig. 21.28
System Monitor
dialog box
showing processor
usage.

System Monitor

File   Edit   View   Options   Help

Kernel: Processor Usage (%)

```
100
 88
 76
 64
 52
 40
 28
 16
```

File System: Dirty data   Last value: 0 Peak value: 0

▶ See "What
  Utilities are
  Included in the
  Resource Kit,"
  p. 1138

Note the graphical element showing the current processor usage. This
parameter could be useful in determining whether a specific workstation is
being overworked.

Install the System Monitor using the Add/Remove Programs icon in the Control Panel. The System Monitor is located in the Accessories component. After
installation, open the System Monitor by choosing Accessories, System Tools.

> **Note**
>
> Using both System Monitor and Registry Editor for remote administration requires Microsoft Remote Registry service from the Resource Kit. You also need to configure the workstations for User-Level access control.

Registry Editor

Registry Editor is another powerful but also dangerous tool. With the Registry Editor you can fine-tune Windows 95 performance by adjusting or adding settings to key system information. Because Windows 95 has placed WIN.INI and SYSTEM.INI file settings in the Registry, you can remotely edit these parameters. Often, Microsoft issues "knowledge base" articles with previously undocumented settings in the Registry to fix or work around problems with Windows. But remember, if you edit the Registry directly with Registry Editor, you can cause a running workstation to cease running. The Resource Kit is a required tool when working in the Registry.

Figure 21.29 shows a view of the Registry running on a local workstation. It shows the HKEY_CURRENT_USER\ControlPanel\desktop setting for full-window drag operation; DragFullWindows is set to "1," which enables this option. If a user has problems with that setting, you can remotely edit the setting to change the operation.

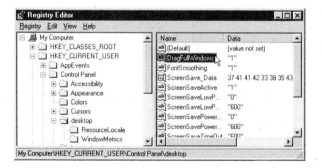

Fig. 21.29
The Registry Editor window.

Network Backups

You can use Windows Backup to back up files from one computer on the network to another. Back up the files to a hard disk or tape drive and then restore the files if the originals are damaged or lost. Start the backup by choosing Start, Programs, Accessories, System Tools, and then Backup.

> **Tip**
> You also can choose the Backup program from the Accessories, System Tools menu to restore backed-up files.

V

Networking

If Windows Backup is not installed, you can install Backup by opening the Add/Remove Program Icon and choosing the Windows Setup. The Backup is listed in the Disk Tools.

System Policy Editor

◀ See "Adding Windows' Component Applications," p. 312

The System Policy Editor is another tool from the Resource Kit. As with the tools previously described, the Policy Editor requires the Microsoft Remote Registry service from the Resource Kit. With this tool, an administrator can manage the desktop of a remote workstation by installing system-wide policies that override the local workstation's default parameters. With System Policy Editor, an administrator can force the use of alpha-numeric passwords for resources, as illustrated in figure 21.30.

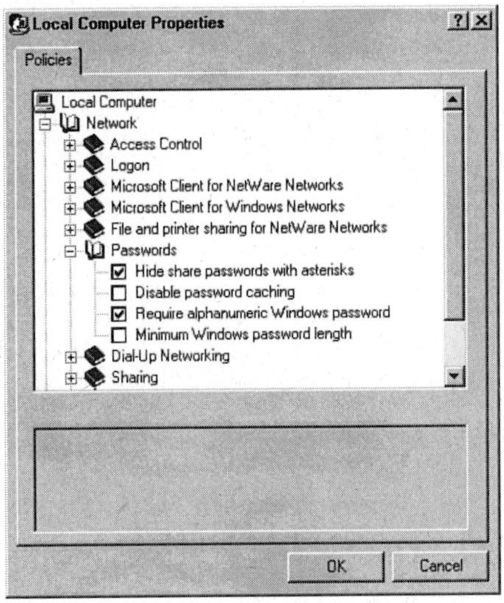
Local Computer Properties
Policies
Local Computer
Network
Access Control
Logon
Microsoft Client for NetWare Networks
Microsoft Client for Windows Networks
File and printer sharing for NetWare Networks
Passwords
Hide share passwords with asterisks
Disable password caching
Require alphanumeric Windows password
Minimum Windows password length
Dial-Up Networking
Sharing
OK
Cancel

Fig. 21.30
The System Policy Editor dialog box shows your password options.

▶ See "Who Needs the Windows 95 Resource Kit?" p. 1134

Using the tools described in this section, a system administrator can manage even the unruliest of peer-to-peer resources on the network. Microsoft rounds out the toolkit with two additional remote agents: Microsoft Network Monitor and an SNMP (Simple Network Management Protocol) agent. Both agents enable further monitoring and control using industry-standard, industrial-strength tools such as Microsoft Systems Management Server, Intel® LANDesk™, and HP® Open View for Windows.❖

Chapter 22

Connecting Windows 95 to a Novell Network

by Glenn Fincher with Sue Plumley

This chapter continues the discussion of Windows 95 networking by talking specifically about Windows 95 and Novell NetWare compatibility. If your primary network is currently Novell NetWare, Windows 95 seamlessly integrates with your current network. In most cases, you can accomplish this installation without any additional work besides simply installing Windows 95. If you are running NetWare client software during installation, Windows 95 correctly detects and installs the Microsoft Client for NetWare Networks. With this feature alone, Windows 95 makes installation on an existing NetWare network a breeze.

However, Microsoft has many other reasons for calling Windows 95 "the well-connected client." After reading this chapter, and especially after using Windows 95 with NetWare, you'll undoubtedly agree that Microsoft has really done its homework in designing this piece of the Windows 95 phenomenon.

In this chapter, you learn about the following issues regarding Windows 95 and Novell NetWare:

- System requirements

- Windows support features for NetWare

- Automatic installation of NetWare

- Manually installing a network card

- Manually installing the NetWare client

- Testing and troubleshooting your NetWare installation

System Requirements

As discussed earlier in Chapter 20, "Setting Up a Windows 95 Peer-to-Peer Network," the requirements for networking with Windows 95 are simple. With the addition of either a network adapter for a local area network (LAN) connection or a modem and Microsoft's Dial-Up Networking "adapter," you can connect your computer to virtually any network topology. Because Windows 95 has integrated support for NetWare networks, the only actual requirements to connect Windows 95 to a NetWare network are the following:

■ An existing NetWare network

■ A PC network adapter for a LAN connection, or a Hayes-compatible modem attached to your computer (the NetWare server must also have a modem attached and modem server software) for a Dial-Up Networking connection

■ A method of attaching to the network, such as cabling, infrared interfaces, laser, and so on

Windows 95 Support for NetWare

◀ See "Remote Access to Your Network," p. 660

◀ See "Connecting Network Devices," p. 589

This section looks at some of the specifics of NetWare connectivity as provided in Windows 95, such as built-in drivers and protocols, 32-bit virtual device driver components, and the capability to run the NetWare command-line utilities.

Microsoft provides such excellent support for Novell NetWare because of NetWare's popularity and dominance of the networking market. The opportunity to sell and implement Windows 95 greatly increases if it's easy to use with NetWare—and it is.

Built-In Network Drivers and Protocols

Windows 95 supports simultaneous communication with multiple networks by including clients, protocols, and services that are easy and quick to install. These network components are available for the following networks:

◀ See "Windows 95 Peer-to-Peer Networking Features," p. 618

■ *Microsoft Network.* A peer-to-peer network composed of other workstations using Windows 95 with Windows used as the networking software.

■ *Novell NetWare 3.x and 4.x.* Client/server software.

The Novell NetWare connectivity components included in Windows 95 are a client, a protocol, and a service. These components enable Windows 95 to connect to any NetWare resource. For example, with Windows 95 you can log in to a NetWare server, use print queues, map NetWare volumes, and share files and printer resources with other NetWare users.

- *Client for NetWare Networks.* The Microsoft Client for NetWare Networks has the built-in connectivity required to connect to any NetWare resources, including NetWare 2.15 and above, NetWare 3.x, and NetWare 4.x. This client also facilitates running all the standard NetWare command-line tools, as Chapter 23, "Using Novell Network Resources in Windows 95," discusses in greater detail. (Netware 4.x commands that require NDS aren't supported.) With the Microsoft Client for NetWare Networks installed, a Windows 95 computer can access NetWare resources, including applications, files, and printers.

- *IPX/SPX-compatible protocol.* Windows supplies a NetWare-compatible protocol—IPX/SPX (Internetwork Packet Exchange/Sequenced Packet Exchange)—that you can install to communicate with a NetWare server.

- *File and printer sharing for NetWare Networks.* Windows also provides file and printer sharing, which enables you to share your files and printers with other computers on the network. When you enable file and printer sharing, you can then choose specific directories and printers to share, limit access to the shared resources, and turn sharing off when you don't want to share.

Note

Windows also provides two versions of the Novell NetWare workstation shell that you can install instead of the Client for NetWare Networks.

Figure 22.1 shows the Network dialog box with the installed client, protocol, and service for use with Netware.

Note

Since Windows 95 makes the three protocols—IPX/SPX, TCP/IP, and NetBEUI—available to you, it's a good idea to install all three as network components if you will be connecting to different networks. IPX/SPX and TCP/IP are routable protocols, meaning they can use other resources across the enterprise. NetBEUI is limited to a single network, such as the Microsoft Network, and is extremely popular; additionally, some vendors have established an interface between NetBEUI and TCP/IP.

Fig. 22.1
The Network
dialog box
displays the
installed features
to use with your
network.

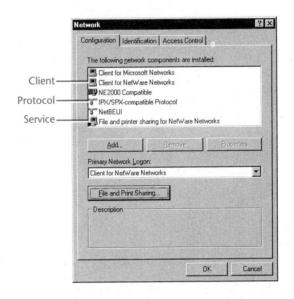

Windows supplies the client, protocol, and service you need to attach to a
NetWare server. The installed components include the Client for Microsoft
Networks and its primary protocol (NetBEUI). The components necessary for
using Windows with NetWare include the Client for NetWare Networks, IPX/
SPX-Compatible Protocol, and File and Printer Sharing for NetWare Networks. Naturally the adapter, in this case the NE 2000 Compatible, is necessary to attach to either network.

The 32-Bit Virtual Device Driver Components

The major breakthrough of Windows 95 is the use of the 32-bit virtual device
driver. The advantage is that the 32-bit driver is a protected-mode driver, as
opposed to real mode. Basically, when running in real mode, only one application or process can be run at a time. Although processors running in real
mode operate at a fast clock rate, they are not multitasking. Also, real mode
requires 32-bit requests to be translated into 16-bit requests, which slows
down the process.

Windows' 32-bit driver runs in protected mode, thus allowing more than one
application or process to run at a time. Protected mode allocates memory to
the various processes running at one time to allow for multitasking.

> **Note**
>
> An additional benefit derived from using protected-mode components is the in-
> creased speed that they inherently achieve. Without the constant overhead of real-
> mode to protected-mode transitions, the network drivers' performance increases
> impressively from 50 to 200 percent.

Before Windows 95, communication between a DOS client (operating in real mode) and the Windows client (operating in protected mode) was slow and sometimes caused problems.

Another example of a real-mode versus protected-mode problem occurs when a NetWare server shuts down for some reason. With previous versions of Windows, the real-mode client would often lock up in such situations, and thus caused Windows to lock up. If a lockup didn't occur and the server came back up, the connection was still broken. To restore the connection, you had to exit Windows and then reboot—or at least log out and then log back in. With protected-mode components, the system can handle the error gracefully and actually reconnect the resource automatically, with no lockup or rebooting necessary.

No Conventional Memory Footprint

Another important advantage of the Windows 95 components for NetWare is that their use does not result in conventional memory footprint, meaning these components do not load into the first 640K, thus leaving that memory free for other drivers, programs, and so on. Because all the components were developed to run in protected mode, none of them install in CONFIG.SYS or AUTOEXEC.BAT file. Windows 95 replaces or makes obsolete many of the traditional DOS settings from these files, so in most cases the network components may be the only ones remaining.

Full Interoperability with Novell NetWare 3.x and 4.x Clients and Servers

Windows 95 is particularly the "well-connected client" in regard to interoperability with any Novell NetWare server running NetWare 2.15 and above, including bindery-based NetWare 3.x servers and NetWare 4.x servers that use bindery emulation. Additionally, one advantage of Windows 95 that wasn't possible with Windows for Workgroups is the capability to run all the NetWare command-line utilities, such as LOGIN.EXE, SETPASS.EXE, and SLIST.EXE, to perform network tasks.

▶ See "Using Windows 95 and Novell Utilities," p. 701

> ### Note
>
> Windows 95 does not, as yet, support Novell's Directory Services (native to version 4.1) if you log in through Windows—only the bindery-based and bindery emulation. The bindery database contains definitions for entities such as users, groups, and workgroups. See the section, "Logging in to the Server," later in this chapter for more information about NDS.

V

Networking

Automatic Installation of Windows 95 NetWare Support

When you install Windows 95 on your PC, the Setup program tries to detect any existing networking components. If you have Plug and Play hardware, this detection proceeds with little or no user intervention. However, even with "legacy" network hardware, the detection program is smart enough to install a working configuration during installation. You might have specific reasons to change things after installation, but such reasons are unlikely to include a completely nonworking configuration.

Windows 95 Setup over Existing NetWare Software

◀ See "Installing Plug and Play Hardware," p. 246

During installation, the Windows 95 Setup program determines whether your computer has NetWare networking components installed. To do so, Setup searches for the following clues:

- An active NetWare connection that uses ODI (Open Data-Link Interface), a standard interface for transport protocols

- A monolithic IPX/SPX driver

- Either NETX or VLM to access NetWare services (executable programs located at a workstation that enable communication with the NetWare server)

- A call to NETSTART.BAT in the AUTOEXEC.BAT file

- At least version 3.26 of NET*.COM or NET*.EXE

When the Windows 95 Setup program detects any of these conditions, it also locates any irreplaceable real-mode terminate-and-stay-running (TSR) programs that may be running. If you are running any TSRs like DOSNP.COM, 3270 emulation software, or TCP/IP software such as Telnet, Windows 95 Setup does not replace them. After detection, Setup installs protected-mode networking components based on Microsoft Client for NetWare Networks unless Setup also discovers incompatible components or the user indicates that the existing network connectivity is to remain unchanged.

Table 22.1 lists some of the conditions that prevent Windows 95 from installing either the Microsoft protected-mode protocol or Microsoft Client for NetWare Networks.

Table 22.1   How Setup Responds after Detecting NetWare-Related Components

Detected Condition	Setup's Response
VLM.EXE with NetWare 4.x using NetWare Directory Services (NDS)	Leaves existing components unchanged
TSRs that require ODI	Installs Microsoft Client for NetWare over ODI
Incompatible TSRs	Installs only the "new" IPX/SPX or leaves existing components unchanged

To complete the configuration, the Windows Setup program makes several adjustments to the existing startup files such as AUTOEXEC.BAT and SYSTEM.INI. Setup comments out unnecessary lines in the SYSTEM.INI file as well as existing lines in AUTOEXEC.BAT that are no longer required when using Microsoft Client for NetWare. Setup also adds to the AUTOEXEC.BAT file lines that invoke the required protected-mode components. The program might move TSRs to the WINSTART.BAT file so that they are executed only when entering Windows 95. Setup also moves settings from NET.CFG to the Registry.

Table 22.2 lists Windows 95's NetWare components.

Table 22.2   Windows 95's NetWare Network Components

Component	Function
NETWARE.DRV	Emulation of the WinNet driver that some applications require
NWLINK.VXD	IPX/SPX-compatible protocol
NWLSPROC.EXE	32-bit login script processor
NWLSCON.EXE	32-bit console
NWNET32.DLL	Common NetWare networking functions for the 32-bit network provider and print provider
NWNP32.DLL	32-bit network provider
NWPP32.DLL	32-bit print provider
NWREDIR.VXD	32-bit file system driver (redirector) to support the NetWare Core Protocol (NCP) file-sharing protocol
NWSERVER.VXD	File and print services

V

Networking

Plug and Play Configuration

With Plug and Play, connecting to NetWare networks couldn't be simpler. If you have Plug and Play-compatible hardware, Windows 95 configures and assigns all the resources dynamically. You then no longer need to worry about network board settings, such as Interrupt Level (IRQ), input/output (I/O) ports, or DMA (Direct Memory Access) channel. Windows 95 therefore resolves problems that sometimes may have taken hours to iron out.

◀ See "Installing Plug and Play Hardware," p. 246

A Plug and Play adapter enables dynamic configuration of network protocols with the capability to load or unload the driver based on detection of resources. Therefore, when you are on the road, your laptop can use Dial-Up Networking; then, when you return to your office, you can install your network adapter or attach to your docking station. In either case, Windows 95 can automatically sense the change and silently reconnect you to the network. This scheme also works in reverse; if you remove your laptop's Ethernet adapter (PC Card, formerly referred to as the PCMCIA card), Windows 95 senses the change and gracefully unloads the network drivers, enabling you to continue working. This capability is another benefit of Windows 95's 32-bit driver architecture.

Windows can easily detect a non-Plug and Play or "legacy" adapter in an otherwise Plug and Play system. The system can correctly detect a vast array of existing hardware types. Windows 95 determines the Plug and Play devices, then offers to detect the legacy adapter, and even suggests the correct settings to choose to ensure that no conflicts exist.

Manually Installing the Network Card

Tip

Access the Add New Hardware Wizard by double-clicking the Add New Hardware icon in the Control Panel; follow the directions on-screen.

◀ See "Installing Network Components in Windows 95," p. 604

If you add a network adapter after installing Windows 95, the Add New Hardware Wizard takes you step-by-step through the process of installing the hardware. Using the Add New Hardware Wizard, you can let Windows find the newly installed hardware and configure it for you or you can configure the hardware yourself.

If you let Windows detect your card, it automatically determines the settings for the card and then installs the correct driver. If you choose, you can select the card from a list provided by Windows. First, choose the manufacturer of the card; second, choose the model. If Windows does not include configuration and driver files for that particular model, you can choose to use the manufacturer's disk to install those files. When you complete the wizard's step-by-step process, the adapter card is successfully installed.

Manually Installing the NetWare Client

Windows 95 enables you to install one of three clients for use with NetWare: one supplied by Microsoft or either of two supplied by Novell. The client you choose depends on your NetWare configuration. Following are a few examples:

- Your site uses NetWare NCP Packet Signature

- Your site uses NetWare IP (Internet Protocol)

- Your site uses 3270 emulators that require a DOS TSR

- Your site uses custom VLM components

- Your site uses NetWare Directory Services (NDS)

In each of the preceding instances, you should not use Microsoft Client for NetWare Networks.

However, if none of the previous examples are true for your network, you can safely and confidently use Microsoft's Client for NetWare Networks. Microsoft's Client for NetWare Networks uses the IPX/SPX-compatible protocol, which works very well with Novell NetWare. Additionally, the Microsoft Client includes file and printer sharing for NetWare networks service, which means you can share your files and resources with other computers on the network.

Of the two clients supplied by Novell, NETX and VLM, you choose the client that best fits the version of the server. NETX works with NetWare versions up to 3.11 and with a 3.12 and 4 server that's configured for 802.3 protocol. VLM requires NetWare DOS Requester software to be installed to complete installation.

Table 22.3 lists the Novell files required for using the Novell-supplied clients with Windows 95.

V

Networking

Table 22.3 Required Novell-Supplied Drivers	
File Name	**Description**
NETWARE.DRV	A Windows-compatible network driver that provides network-redirector functionality from 16-bit applications. Different versions are available for NETX or VLM usage.
NETWARE.HLP	Associated Help file.

(continues)

Tip
Before installing
the Novell-
supplied client to
your workstation,
copy the required
files to a disk from
the Novell server
and keep the disk
handy along with
your NetWare
disks.

Table 22.3 Continued	
File Name	**Description**
NWPOPUP.EXE	NetWare messaging utility.
VNETWARE.386	A virtual device driver that provides virtualization services in Windows 95 and in Virtual Machines (VMs).
VIPX.386	Virtual device driver.
NW16.DLL	32-bit to 16-bit interactive link. Required only for use with VLM.

When you install Windows 95 for use with NetWare, Setup looks for these files in the existing Windows directory. If it cannot find these files, Setup requests a location for them. You'll also need the NetWare disks supplied by Novell for setting up the workstation.

Manually Installing the Microsoft Client for NetWare

If you are installing the support for NetWare networks after previously installing Windows 95, you must install the client. The Microsoft Client for NetWare works extremely well with both Windows and the NetWare network. The client provides fast access to the network resources, easy access to your login scripts, and is quite intuitive when it comes to using the network resources.

To install the Microsoft Client for NetWare Networks, follow these steps:

1. Open the Start menu and choose Settings, Control Panel.

2. Double-click the Network icon in the Control Panel.

3. Click the Configuration tab and choose Add. The Select Network Component Type dialog box appears (see fig. 22.2).

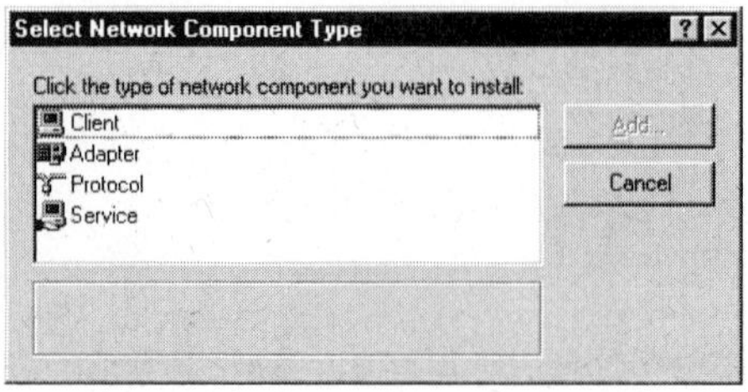

Fig. 22.2
Choose the component type you want to install and then choose Add.

4. Select Client and then choose Add. The Select Network Client dialog box appears (see fig. 22.3).

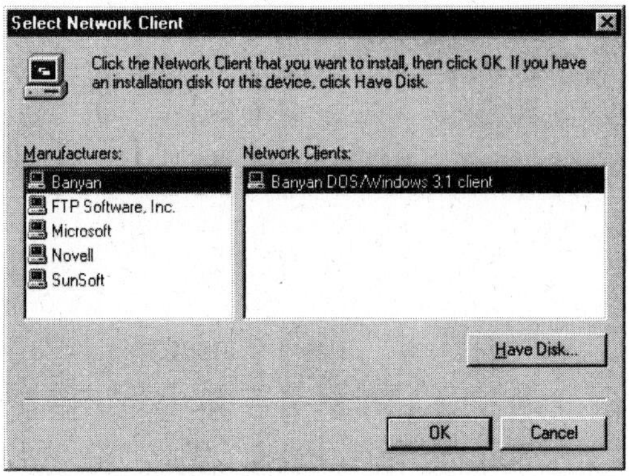

Fig. 22.3
Select a manufac-
turer and then
select a network
client.

5. Choose Microsoft from the list of manufacturers on the left and then
   Client for NetWare Networks from the list on the right.

6. Choose OK. Windows returns to the Network dialog box.

If you still need to install a protocol or service, proceed to the following sections on installation and take care of that before choosing OK. When you do
choose OK in the Network dialog box, you will be prompted to restart the
computer so the changes can take effect.

After you restart the computer, the NetWare Client is added.

Configuring the NetWare Client

Before you can use the client, you must configure it for your network. To do
so, follow these steps:

1. In the Network dialog box, select Client for NetWare Networks and
   choose Properties. The Client for NetWare Networks Properties sheet
   appears, as shown in figure 22.4.

2. In the Preferred Server list box, select the server's name or enter it in the
   text box.

3. In the First Network Drive list box, select the first available drive letter
   for drive mappings.

4. Select the Enable Logon Script Processing check box.

5. Choose OK to complete the setup for the client; however, leave the
   Network dialog box open if you want to set protocol or other options.

Tip
Running your
logon script auto-
matically sets
options for your
system when you
log on to the
network.

V

Networking

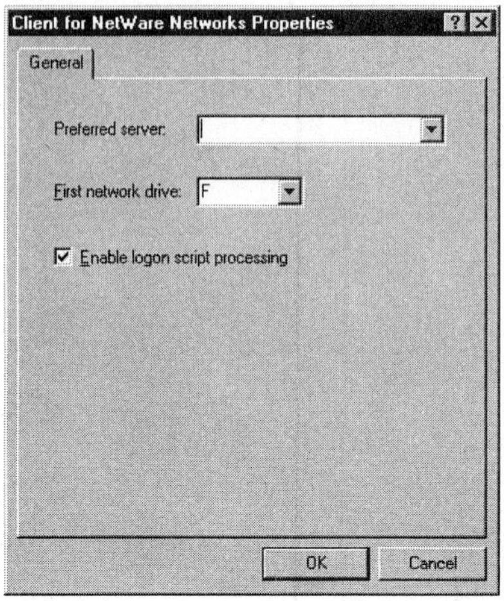

Fig. 22.4
Specify the
preferred server
and the first
network drive on
the Client for
NetWare Networks
Properties sheet.

After you set these properties, the next time that you log in, Windows 95 automatically logs in to the NetWare server, runs the login script, and makes any connections, including any drive mappings that the script defines.

Troubleshooting

I enabled logon script processing, but the mapped drives available in DOS were not available to me in Windows. What did I do wrong?

You did nothing wrong; the login script did not run, perhaps because of real-mode TSRs included in the login script. Contact your system administrator, who can move the TSRs to either the AUTOEXEC.BAT (which executes before Windows 95 starts) or WINSTART.BAT (which executes when Windows 95 initializes).

Installing the Network Protocol

Your next step is to install the NetWare protocol, IPX/SPX-compatible protocol, using the Configuration page of the Network dialog box. To install the protocol, follow these steps:

1. Open the Network dialog box by double-clicking the Network icon in the Control Panel.

2. Click the Configuration tab and choose Add. The Select Network Component Type dialog box appears (refer to fig. 22.2).

3. Select Protocol in the components list and then choose Add. The Select Network Protocol dialog box appears.

4. In Manufacturers, choose Microsoft. A list of available protocols appears on the right side of the dialog box (see fig. 22.5).

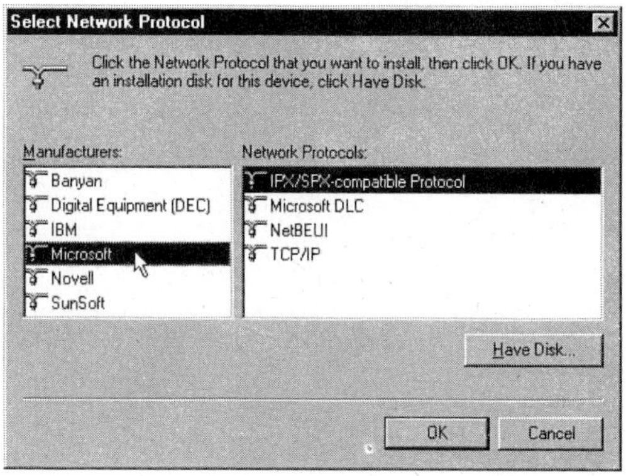

Fig. 22.5
Choose Microsoft as the manufacturer and then select the IPX/SPX-compatible protocol.

5. In Network Protocols, choose IPX/SPX-Compatible Protocol. Windows closes the dialog box and adds the protocol to the list of installed components in the Network dialog box.

6. Leave the Network dialog box open so you can set the primary network logon and install file-sharing support.

Setting the Logon

You must set the logon for NetWare to show which network you will be using. Choose the logon on the Configuration page of the Network dialog box. In the list of components, choose Client for NetWare Networks. In the Primary Network Logon list, choose Client for NetWare Networks.

> **Note**
>
> Windows uses the term "logon" and Novell uses "login," although both terms refer to the same process.

Installing File-Sharing and Printer-Sharing Support

Windows 95 enables you to install file and printer sharing services for NetWare networks. The functional equivalent of Windows 95's file and printer service for Microsoft networks, this service provides peer-to-peer networking connectivity to other NetWare clients using Windows 95.

To use Windows 95's built-in file and printer sharing with Novell NetWare, you must be using Microsoft Client for NetWare Networks. To install file-sharing and printer-sharing support, follow these steps:

1. In the Network dialog box, click the Configuration tab.

◄ See "Understanding File Sharing," p. 643

2. Choose File and Print Sharing. The File and Print Sharing dialog box appears (see fig. 22.6).

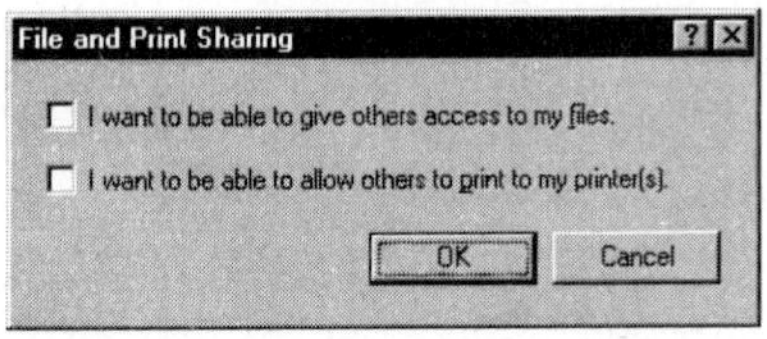

Fig. 22.6

Choose to share your files, printer, or both, with others on the network.

3. You can choose one or both options:

Choose I Want To Be Able to Give Others Access to My Files if you want to share your files.

Choose I Want to Be Able To Allow Others To Print to My Printer(s) if you want to share your printer(s) with those on the network.

4. Choose OK to close the dialog box and return to the Network dialog box.

Note

You cannot use file and printer services for both Microsoft and NetWare networks simultaneously. Windows notifies you to remove one service if you try to install the other while one is listed in the component's box. To remove a component, select it and choose Remove.

Setting Access Control

When sharing the files on your local hard drive, and/or your local printer, in a NetWare environment, Windows sets access to your files to user-level access control.

When other computers browse the network, the Windows 95 computer seems as though it has a split personality. To other Windows 95 computers running Client for NetWare Networks, the resources behave like any other Windows resources. To Windows 95 computers running NETX or VLM, shared printers look like NetWare print queues, and shared directories appear to be NetWare volumes. Shared resources, such as a CD-ROM or a printer, are immediately available to any user on the NetWare network with access to the shared resource.

To set access control, follow these steps:

1. In the Network dialog box, click the Access Control tab.

2. Choose the <u>U</u>ser-Level Access Control option if it is not already selected (see fig. 22.7).

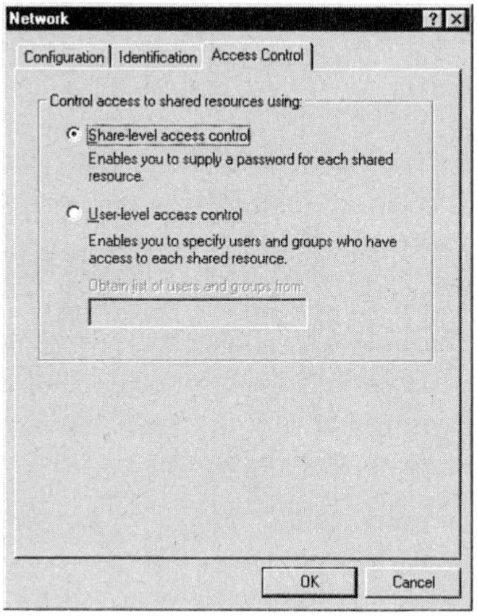

Fig. 22.7

User-level access enables others on the network to use your shared resources.

3. In the Obtain <u>L</u>ist of Users and Groups From text box, enter the name of the NetWare server.

Completing Installation

When you've completed installing the client, protocol, and service and you've set access control in the Network dialog box, you're ready to complete the installation.

> **Note**
>
> As far as the Identification page of the Network dialog box goes, you do not need to identify your computer or workgroup for NetWare. NetWare identifies your computer by a unique identification number on your network adapter card.

To complete the installation, follow these steps:

1. Choose OK in the Network dialog box.

2. The System Settings Change dialog box appears (see fig. 22.8).

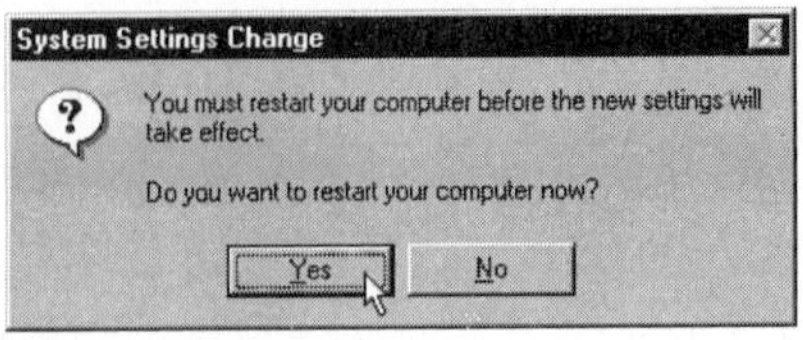

Fig. 22.8
You can choose to reboot the computer later if you do not want to stop work at this time.

System Settings Change dialog box

You must restart your computer before the new settings will take effect.

Do you want to restart your computer now?

[Yes] [No]

3. Choose Yes to reboot the computer.

4. When Windows starts again, the Enter Network Password dialog box appears with your name in the User Name text box, the server's name in the Login Server's text box, and a Password text box in which you enter a password assigned to you by your system or network administrator. Enter your password and choose OK.

5. The Welcome to Windows dialog box appears. Enter your password and choose OK. The Login Script window, if you chose to enable it, flashes by, and then the Windows desktop appears as it normally would.

To view the server's resources, double-click Network Neighborhood.

You also can access the server resources made available to you by your login script in the My Computer window. Figure 22.9 shows the My Computer window with four drives mapped to the NetWare server by the login script.

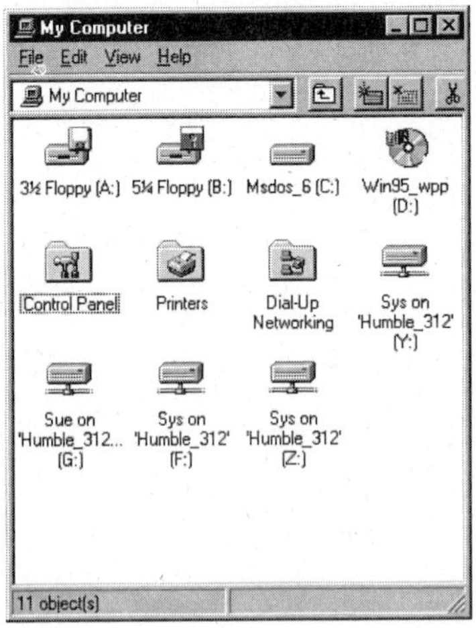

Fig. 22.9
Access mapped drives through the Control Panel after connecting to the network.

My Computer window showing drives: 3½ Floppy (A:), 5¼ Floppy (B:), Msdos_6 (C:), Win95_wpp (D:), Control Panel, Printers, Dial-Up Networking, Sys on 'Humble_312' (Y:), Sue on 'Humble_312...' (G:), Sys on 'Humble_312' (F:), Sys on 'Humble_312' (Z:). 11 object(s)

Sharing Your Resources

▶ See "Using Windows 95 and Novell Utilties," p. 701

If you choose to share your files and printer with other users on the network, you must specify the shared resources and indicate who on the network may gain access to your resources. Basically, designating a directory, printer, CD-ROM drive, or any other resource as a shared resource follows the same steps.

To share a resource, follow these steps:

1. Open the window containing the resource to be shared (My Computer to share a drive, Printers to share a printer, and so on).

2. Select the folder or item you want to share and choose <u>F</u>ile, <u>S</u>haring. The Properties sheet appears.

3. Click the Sharing tab, and then choose <u>S</u>hared As to activate the Shared As area of the page, as shown in figure 22.10.

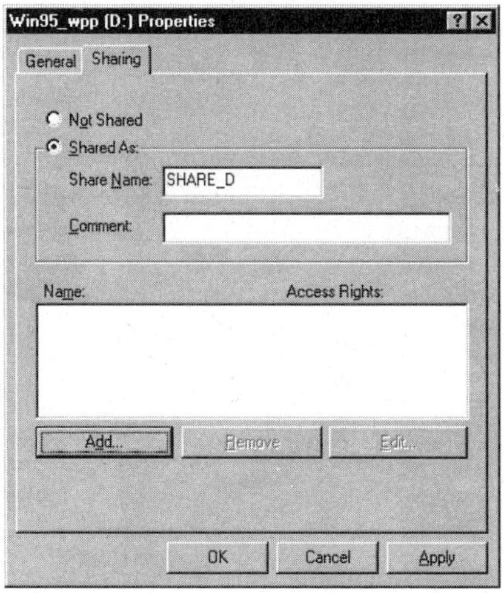

▶ See "Managing Print Files and Sharing," p. 784

▶ See "Creating Network Resources Wisely," p. 796

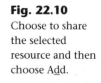

Fig. 22.10
Choose to share the selected resource and then choose A<u>d</u>d.

V

Networking

4. Choose A<u>d</u>d. The Add Users dialog box appears (see fig. 22.11).

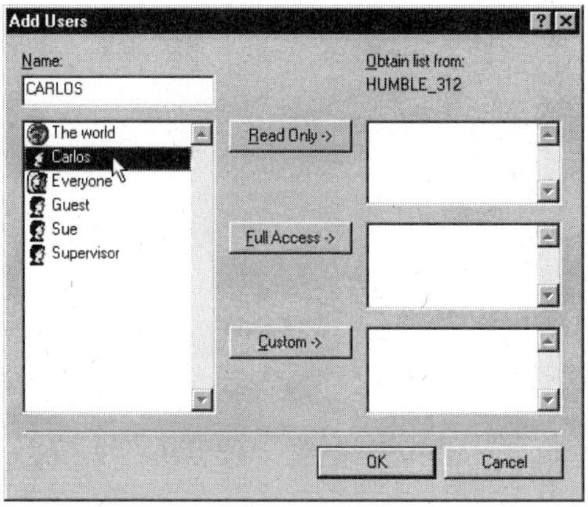

Fig. 22.11
The Add Users dialog box enables you to define a user's access.

5. In <u>N</u>ame, enter a name of the user or choose the name from the list. You can choose from the following options:

- *Read Only*. Selected user can open, read, and copy files but cannot modify the files in any way.

- *Full Access*. Selected user has full access to your drive, including modification and deletion capability.

- *Custom*. Enables you to specify specific rights to the selected user. If you choose <u>C</u>ustom, the Change Access Rights dialog box appears when you select OK. In this dialog box, you can define whether the user can read, write to, create, list, or delete files or change file attributes or access rights.

6. Choose OK to close the Add Users dialog box. Choose OK again to close the Properties sheet.

Troubleshooting

When I installed the Client for NetWare Networks and chose OK to close the Network dialog box, a message appeared stating I needed to change the Access Control. What do I do?

If you previously installed the Client for Microsoft Networks, your access control was share level; when you install the Client for NetWare Networks, you must change access to the user level and enter the name of the server. Click the Access Control tab of the Network dialog box and choose <u>U</u>ser-Level Access Control. Enter the server name in the text box and choose OK. You'll have to reboot the computer to change the system settings.

I tried to specify the client for file and print sharing in the Network dialog box as NetWare, but it doesn't appear in the installed components list.

You can only specify one client at a time for file and printer sharing. If you've already specified the Client for Microsoft Networks as available for file sharing, remove it from the components list and then choose the Client for NetWare Networks.

I'm using a notebook computer away from the office and every time I start the computer, I have to verify my network logon and then I get an error message. Is there any way I can skip this when I'm not connected to the network?

Yes. Open the Network dialog box and click the Configuration tab. In the Primary Network <u>L</u>ogon list, choose Windows Logon. You will no longer see the error messages; however, don't forget to change the logon back to NetWare when you're ready to connect to the network again.

Manually Installing the Novell Client for NetWare-NETX

You can, as an alternative to the Microsoft NetWare client, install a Novell client supplied with Windows but suited specifically for version 3.11 and below and version 4.0 and above.

The two choices for the NetWare clients in Windows are:

> Novell NetWare (Workstation Shell 3.x [NETX])

> Novell NetWare (Workstation Shell 4.0 and above [VLM])

The NETX choice applies to the workstation shell up to version 3.11; additionally, you can use this choice for version 3.12 and 4.0 *if* the server is configured for 802.3 protocol.

> **Note**
>
> When you install either Novell-supplied client, Windows automatically installs the IPX ODI protocol needed to communicate with the server. Additionally, you should make sure the access control (Network dialog box, Access Control page) is set to Share-Level Access Control instead of User-Level Access Control.

Installing the NETX Client

To install Novell's NETX client, follow these steps:

1. In the Network dialog box, click the Configuration tab.

2. Choose Add. The Select Network Component Type dialog box appears.

3. Select Client in the component list and choose Add. The Select Network Client dialog box appears.

4. In Manufacturers, choose Novell. The list of Network Clients changes.

5. In Network Clients, choose Novell NetWare (Workstation Shell 3.X[NETX]).

6. Choose OK. Windows installs the client as well as the Novel IPX ODI Protocol.

> **Note**
>
> Before choosing OK in the Network dialog box, make sure that control access is set to Share-Level Access Control on the Access Control page.

Tip
Electronic sources for updated client software are always available from Novell's CompuServe forum, World Wide Web page **http://www. novell.com/,** or FTP server at **ftp.novell.com**.

V

Networking

7. Choose OK to close the Network dialog box. Windows prompts for several Novell NetWare disks, as well as the Windows 95 CD-ROM. Follow the directions on-screen. The following list is of files you will need to complete the installation:

> IPXODI.COM
>
> NETX.EXE
>
> LSL.COM
>
> NWPOPUP.EXE
>
> NETWARE.DRV
>
> VIPX.386
>
> NETWARE.HLP
>
> VNETWARE.386
>
> A network adapter driver such as NE2000.COM

Windows completes the installation. You must restart the computer to attach to the network.

Manually Installing the Novell Client for NetWare-VLM

If your network is using VLMs, you must run at least version 4.0 of NETX.VLM on the workstations and have at least version 1.02 of the VLM client-support files from NetWare.

The VLM choice for NetWare client refers to the workstation shell 4.0 and above. If you choose the VLM option, however, you must also install Novell's NetWare DOS Requester software; Windows cannot complete the installation of the VLM client without the requester.

To install the Novell-supplied VLM client for NetWare, follow these steps:

1. Close all programs in Windows and then open the Start menu and choose Sh<u>u</u>t Down. The Shut Down dialog box appears.

2. Select the Restart the Computer in <u>M</u>S-DOS Mode option and choose <u>Y</u>es.

3. Install the Novell-supplied NetWare 4 client (NetWare Client for DOS and MS Windows disks). See your system administrator if you need help.

4. Before starting Windows, edit the AUTOEXEC.BAT by adding **REM** before the following statement:

   ```
   @CALL C:\NWCLIENT\STARTNET.BAT
   ```

5. Save the file and restart your computer.

6. In Windows, open the Network dialog box and click the Configuration tab.

7. Choose <u>A</u>dd. The Select Network Component Type dialog box appears.

8. Select Client and then choose <u>A</u>dd. The Select Network Client dialog box appears.

9. In the list of <u>M</u>anufacturers, choose Novell.

10. In the list of Network Clients, choose Novell NetWare (Workstation Shell 4.0 and above [VLM]).

11. Choose OK. Windows installs the client and may prompt you to insert the Windows 95 CD-ROM or specific NetWare disks. Insert the disks and follow the directions on-screen.

> **Note**
>
> Windows also installs the Novell IPX ODI protocol when you install the client.

12. Choose OK to close the Network dialog box and Windows prompts for you to restart the computer. Choose <u>Y</u>es.

13. When Windows starts, it will prompt for a Network password. Enter the password and choose OK. Windows starts with your workstation logged on to the server. To view the server and its resources, open Network Neighborhood.

Troubleshooting

I have installed the Novell client 4 and I get a message saying the VLM is not loaded or disabled just as Windows starts and I'm not connected to the network. What can I do?

This is a NetWare message stating Windows is not loading the VLM. Edit the AUTOEXEC.BAT to change the following lines from

```
C:\WINDOWS\LSL.COM
```

(continues)

(continued)

```
C:\WINDOWS\NE2000.COM

C:\WINDOWS\ODIHLP.EXE

C:\WINDOWS\IPXODI.COM
```

to

```
C:\NWCLIENT\LSL.COM

C:\NWCLIENT\NE2000.COM

C:\NWCLIENT\ODIHLP.EXE

C:\NWCLIENT\IPXODI.COM
```

and add the following line:

```
C:\NWCLIENT\VLM.EXE
```

I'm using NetWare 4 but I can't access Network Directory Services. Does Windows support NDS?

Yes. However, to make Network Directory Services (NDS) work with Windows 95, the login must be in the AUTOEXEC.BAT, as discussed in the next section.

Logging In to a NetWare Server

When you restart Windows, Windows attaches to the network and displays a login dialog box for the network and one for Windows. Login is quick and easy. Also, listed in the following section is an alternate method of logging in so that your login scripts run; login scripts contain drive mapping, search drives, and other Login commands.

You also can log out of the network and reattach with very little effort. These procedures are the same whether you're using the client for Microsoft NetWare or either of the two Novell clients.

Logging In to the Network

Windows prompts you to log in to the network when you first start Windows. You are also prompted to log in to Windows. To log in, follow these steps:

1. Turn your computer on to start Windows.

2. The Enter Network Password dialog box appears with your name in the User Name text box, the server's name in the Login Server's text box,

and a _P_assword text box in which you enter a password assigned to you by your system or network administrator. Enter your password and choose OK.

3. The Welcome to Windows dialog box appears. Enter your password and choose OK.

   After logging in to the network, you can view the network server in Network Neighborhood.

The capability to run NetWare login scripts is an important topic for many Novell users. When using Microsoft Client for NetWare, you can set the login scripts to run automatically; however, you cannot run login scripts in the same manner when using the Novell-supplied client.

When using the Novell-supplied client, you can only run the login script if you edit your AUTOEXEC.BAT file to include the LOGIN.EXE. When you add the LOGIN.EXE to your AUTOEXEC.BAT, you're prompted to log in before Windows starts and so your login script runs. Make sure you also add the first network drive letter (usually F:) before the LOGIN.EXE line in the AUTOEXEC.BAT so the login command can be found.

If you don't want to execute the login script, you can log in to the network from Windows. If the login script consists of only drive mapping, log in to Windows and then map the drives in the My Computer window. However, if it consists of search paths and other login script commands, add the command to your AUTOEXEC.BAT. See your system administrator for help.

> **Tip**
>
> If you want to use NDS with NetWare 4.0 and above, you must add the LOGIN.EXE to your AUTOEXEC.BAT.

Logging Out of the Network

Logging out of the network means you will no longer have access to the Network resources; your workstation will be a stand-alone computer.

To log out of the network, follow these steps:

1. Open Network Neighborhood and select the network server. Right-click the mouse to display the pop-up menu (see fig. 22.12).

2. Choose _L_og Out. A confirmation dialog box appears. Choose _Y_es to log out or _N_o to cancel the procedure.

3. The Logging Out message box appears, as shown in figure 22.13. Choose OK.

Fig. 22.12
You can quickly log out from the quick menu.

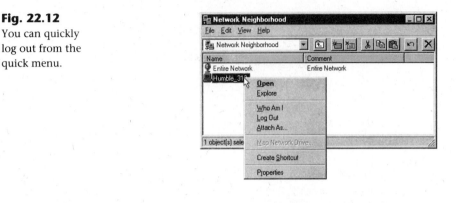

Fig. 22.13
This message informs you that you've logged out from the server.

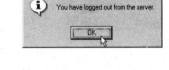

Attaching to the Network

When you log in to the network, more than one server may appear in the Network Neighborhood. You can attach to any server, as long as you have a password, using the Attach To command.

To attach to a server, follow these steps:

▶ See "Connecting to Other Servers," p. 713

1. Select the network server in the Network Neighborhood dialog box and right-click the icon.

2. Choose File, Attach As. The Enter Network Password dialog box appears (see fig. 22.14).

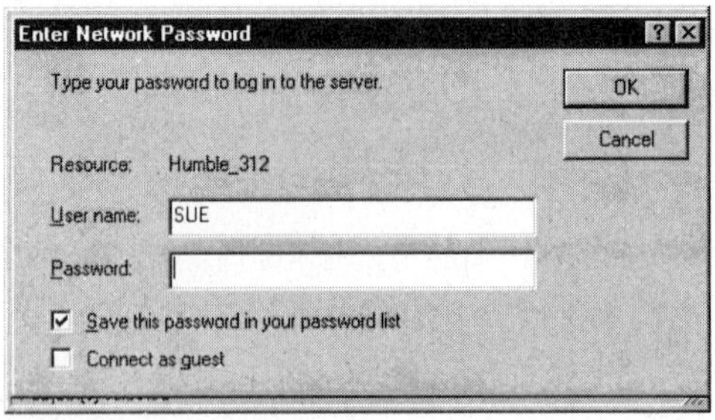

Fig. 22.14
Enter your password to log on to the network.

3. Enter your password and choose OK. Windows attaches you to the network.

Troubleshooting

My search paths before installing Windows are not available to me now.

That problem is occurring because the login script did not run. This problem does not occur when you use Microsoft Client for NetWare or when using the Novell NetWare clients with a login in the AUTOEXEC.BAT.

When I try to access commands or applications from the network, I get a message saying `Cannot find the file... Make sure the path and filename are correct...` *What have I done wrong?*

You may have accessed and modified the search paths without knowing it. When the login script sets search paths, it represents them with drive letters starting at the end of the alphabet: Z, Y, X, and so on. If you are using either the Microsoft Client for NetWare or you added the `LOGIN.EXE` line to your AUTOEXEC.BAT, those search path drives were added to your My Computer window with other mapped drives.

If you opened one of the search drives and moved around in it, you could have altered the search path. When you tried to access the command or application, the search path was wrong so the network couldn't find the file for which you were looking. To alleviate the problem, restart the computer; the login script will run again and set the search paths straight.

From now on, leave the search path drives Z, Y, X, and so on alone and use only those drives represented by letters from the front of the alphabet.

> **Tip**
> When you log in using LOGIN.EXE with the Windows Run command, the scripts run.

Testing and Troubleshooting Your NetWare Installation

Although Microsoft has expended extraordinary effort to ensure that you can run and install Windows 95 networking without any problems, every installation differs and sometimes a problem may occur. This section presents a few testing and troubleshooting tips for fixing several problems that you might encounter.

Testing your setup is a simple task in Windows 95. To ensure that everything is working, try performing the following actions:

- Start Windows 95 successfully

- Log in to the network

- Access the drives and note whether they are mapped correctly

▶ See "Solving Common Network Printing Problems," p. 788

▶ See "Troubleshooting and Network Management Tools," p. 827

V

Networking

- Access the printer resources

- Run your Windows applications

- Use all resources from within your Windows applications

- Run your DOS applications

- Use all resources from within your DOS applications

- Access the other tools and resources

- Log off the server, and then access the mapped drives, and so on

Make note of which of the above actions failed and refer to the troubleshooting sections in this and other chapters throughout this book for information on possible problems.

Logon Problems

While processing its startup files, Windows 95 displays the Windows 95 logo screen. To see the output of startup processing, you can press the Esc key, which causes the logo screen to disappear and leaves you with a familiar MS-DOS text screen until Windows 95 actually starts. As the screens flash by, keep an eye out for login and other NetWare information. If you're not logging on to the network, the screen would reveal that.

If you're not logging on to the network, check with the system administrator to make sure the server is on and operating properly. Check the cabling to your computer to see that it is properly attached. Try restarting the computer again.

If you get the message that the Server name is not valid or the server is not available, check with the system administrator to see if you have access to that server and that the server is working properly. If you're using Microsoft Client for NetWare Networks, check to see that you have the correct server listed in the client's Properties sheet. (From the Network dialog box, select the client and choose Properties.)

If the login script didn't run and your search drives are not mapped, make sure that if you're using the Microsoft Client for NetWare that you checked the Enable Logon Script Processing option on the client's Properties sheet (Network dialog box). If you're using a Novell-supplied client, you must enter the LOGIN.EXE line in the AUTOEXEC.BAT before the login scripts will run.

If the problem persists, check all of the settings in the Network dialog box to make sure you haven't neglected or accidentally changed something.

If you still cannot log in to the network after Windows 95 starts, try the following technique. Turn on your computer. You first see the standard BIOS banner; then, when you see the text string Starting Windows 95. . ., press Shift+F5. This starts the computer in safe mode, in which you get a command prompt. Windows 95 provides a real-mode network client in this configuration to assist you in determining problems.

◀ See "Starting and Quitting Windows," p. 50

At the command prompt, enter **NET START** to load this real-mode client. If you can log in with this driver loaded, you might simply have a problem with the NetWare client settings that you specify in the Network dialog box. If you can log in using this real-mode driver, also verify that you can access mapped drives and other expected resources.

> **Note**
>
> Sometimes Windows 95 cannot locate your NetWare server. This typical problem is easy to fix. Check that the frame type in the Advanced Properties sheet for the IPX/SPX-compatible protocol is set for your server. If necessary, change this setting to your server's frame type.

Following are a few more common problems with NetWare networks:

- If you forgot your password, contact the system administrator and ask her to issue you a new password.

- The network denies access to servers. Run SETPASS to synchronize your passwords.

- The network constantly asks you to enter NetWare passwords. Set Windows and NetWare passwords to be the same.

▶ See "Using Windows 95 and Novell Utilties," p. 701

- Can't connect to a server. Ask the system administrator to verify that you have access rights.❖

V

Networking

Chapter 23

Using Novell Network Resources in Windows 95

by Glenn Fincher with Sue Plumley

You can add a Windows 95 computer to an existing NetWare network by using Microsoft's enhanced NetWare connectivity tools. These tools are the first and best choices in almost every situation to ensure complete compatibility and integration with the very different architectures that Microsoft and NetWare represent. Additionally, Windows 95 has included many utilities and features you can use to communicate and connect to the NetWare network. This chapter discusses those Windows 95 utilities as well as several NetWare utilities and commands you can use from within Windows.

In this chapter, you learn about the following:

- User Maintenance and Novell Utilities

- Drive mapping and changing passwords

- Connecting to other servers

- Using network tape drives

Using Windows 95 and Novell Utilities

Windows' support for Novell's NetWare makes performing general maintenance tasks, as well as requesting information from the server, quick and easy. You can perform many NetWare functions through Windows, such as mapping drives, listing your server connection, managing network print jobs, and so on, without ever using a command line.

Windows enables you to use many of NetWare's commands and utilities directly within Windows. You can check the status of network volumes, change your password, and use several administrative utilities from the MS-DOS prompt or the Run dialog box.

Mapping Drives

Windows provides an easy method of mapping drives from within the Network Neighborhood so you can avoid using Netware's MAP command. When you map a drive, you assign a drive letter to a network resource, such as a drive or folder. Mapping drives makes access to network resources faster and easier than opening several layers of windows to find the resource on the server or network.

Tip
You can make mapping permanent so you don't have to set the mapping each time you login to the server.

◄ See "Logging in to a NetWare Server," p. 694

Additionally, if you're running a login script, mapping drives provides the search and drive maps created by the system administrator. If you choose to not run the login script, you can map the drives yourself within Windows.

You also can choose to connect the map as a root of the drive, which not only helps keep path statements from getting too long but makes your maps a bit more permanent. For example, you can map to a document directory using the path F:\CARLOS\NOTEBOOK\WPDOCS.

Now suppose you go into the F:\CARLOS\NOTEBOOK directory and access another folder, say the REPORTS directory. The next time you want to use the original mapping, to the WPDOCS directory, the map has changed to the F:\CARLOS\NOTEBOOK\REPORTS directory.

Connect the map as a root of the drive to alleviate this problem. In this example, connect F:\CARLOS\NOTEBOOK\WPDOCS as J. Whenever you want to access the WPDOCS folder, you simply type in **J**. Not only is the path shorter and easier to enter, the path remains the same even if you access different folders within the NOTEBOOK directory.

Note

If you have used Windows for Workgroups, mapping a drive in Network Neighborhood should seem familiar because it is similar to mapping a drive from File Manager.

The basic procedure for mapping a network drive is as follows:

1. Open the Network Neighborhood and select the shared folder you want to map to.

2. Choose File, Map Network Drive. The Map Network Drive dialog box appears, as shown in figure 23.1.

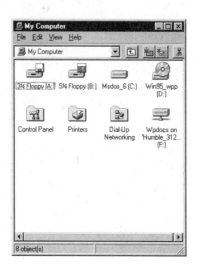

Fig. 23.1
Windows displays the path you've mapped out by selecting each folder.

3. By default, Windows assigns the next available drive letter on your computer to the folder that you select to map. To assign a different letter, select it from the Drive drop-down list.

4. To reconnect to this drive or directory automatically, select the Reconnect at Logon check box. Choosing this option makes the mapping permanent.

5. If you want, choose Connect as Root of the Drive.

6. Choose OK to close the dialog box. View drive mappings in the My Computer window (see fig. 23.2).

Fig. 23.2
Click on the mapped drive icon to open the folder you want without wading through six, eight, or ten other folders.

Tip

If the toolbar is not showing in the Network Neighborhood window, choose View, Toolbar.

> **Note**
>
> Windows supplies the Map Network Drive icon on the toolbar of the Network Neighborhood. However, mapping in this dialog box does not work with NetWare, but it does work with Microsoft peer-to-peer networking.

To disconnect a mapped drive, open My Computer and select the mapped drive. Right-click the mouse while pointing to the selected drive and choose Disconnect. The drive icon disappears from the window and the drive is disconnected.

If you want a list of the drives and mappings on your system, you might find the NetWare MAP command the best way to do so even though you can view mapped drives in the My Computer window. Enter **MAP** at the DOS prompt or in the Run dialog box, and you should see a screen similar to figure 23.3.

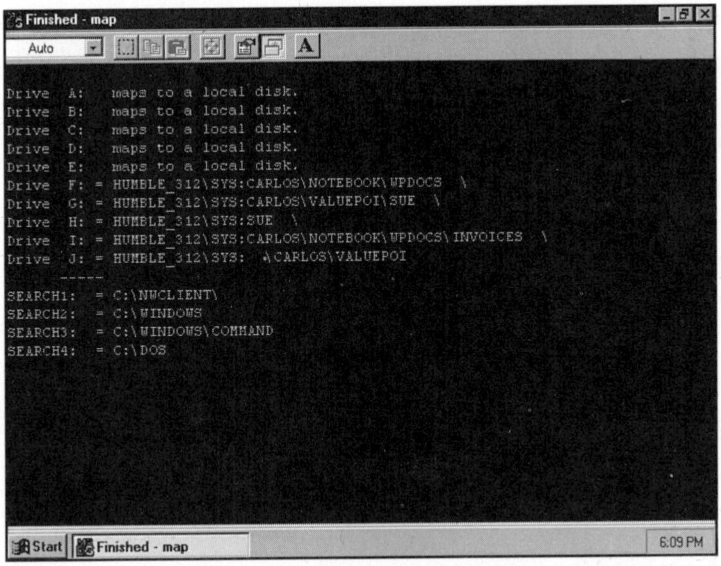

Fig. 23.3

The MAP command lists all the drive letters and the actual resources to which they are connected.

The drive mapping displayed in the figure shows drives F through J are mapped drives you've created in Windows. These drives make it easier for you to access your work on the server. The search section of the drive mapping shows the search paths that the server follows when you try to access a file or folder. The search drives were added by the login script that ran when Windows first logged in to the server.

Troubleshooting

I connected a path as a root of the drive but now I cannot move up one level in the path. What am I doing wrong?

You're not doing anything wrong; the problem is with connecting as a root of the drive. You cannot move up a level within the path. If, for example, you want to move up one level from F:\CARLOS\NOTEBOOK\WPDOCS to F:\CARLOS\NOTEBOOK, you have to create a new mapping or enter the entire path. When connecting as a root of the drive, your only choice is the entire path.

*I typed **MAP** in the Run dialog box, but I got a message that said* Cannot find the file 'run'.... *What do I do now?*

If you ran the login scripts and the search paths are established, then you can just type **MAP** in the Run dialog box; otherwise, type the path to the MAP command, beginning with the server, public folder, and then the command. A sample path might be \\HUMBLE_312\SYS\PUBLIC\MAP. HUMBLE_312 is the server and SYS is usually the name given to the first drive volume on the server. PUBLIC is the directory normally used to store NetWare commands.

Changing Your NetWare Password

The best way you can change your NetWare password, short of asking the system administrator, is to use the SETPASS command. SETPASS enables you to create or change a password on one or more file servers. You must be attached to the server before you can set the password on it.

To use SETPASS, follow these steps:

1. Open the Start menu and choose Run. The Run dialog box appears.

2. In the Open text box, enter the path and the SETPASS command. An example of the path might be \\HUMBLE_312\SYS\PUBLIC\SETPASS.

3. Choose OK. Windows opens the MS-DOS prompt with the prompt asking for a new password, as shown in figure 23.4.

> **Note**
>
> As a security measure, some versions of NetWare will prompt you for your old password before asking you to enter a new password.

4. Enter the new password and press Enter.

Tip

If you don't want to go through two lonin dialog boxes when Windows starts, change your Windows password to match your Netware password using theh Passwords Control Panel.

V

Networking

Tip

If you're attached to more than one server with the *same* password, SETPASS enables you to synchronize passwords (setting all passwords at one time to the same word).

Tip

If you're unsure of the path, choose the Browse button and look for the PUBLIC folder; then find the command.

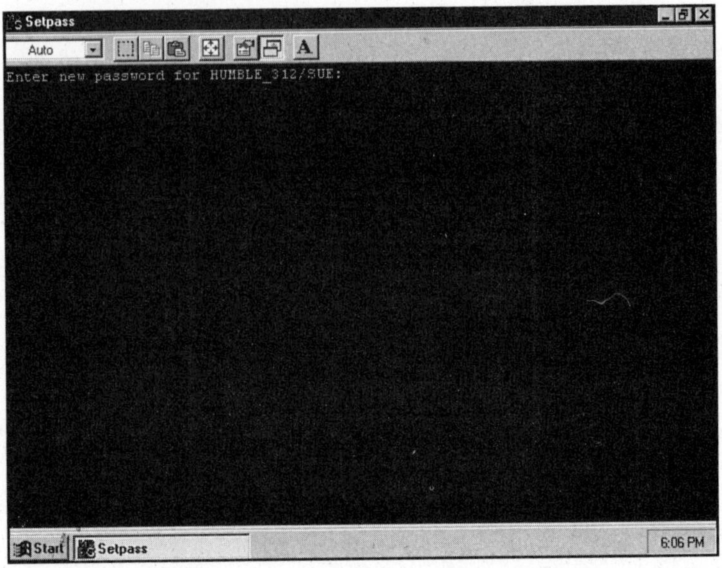

Fig. 23.4
Set a new
password using
the SETPASS
command.

```
Setpass                                              _ □ ×
Auto    ▼  [ ] 🗈 🗎  ⊠  🗃 🖨  A
Enter new password for HUMBLE_312/SUE:




















Start  Setpass                              6:06 PM
```

Tip
You also can find
the NetWare
server version
information
by running
NVER.EXE in a
DOS window.

Tip
You also can
display the
Properties
sheet by right-
clicking the server
icon and choosing
the Properties
command.

5. Reenter the new password to confirm and press Enter. SETPASS notifies you the password has been changed.

> **Note**
>
> If the new passwords entered in steps 4 and 5 are not identical or if you are prompted for your old password and do not enter it correctly, the password will not be changed.

6. Click the Close button to close the MS-DOS prompt.

Checking the NetWare Version

You can check the version of the NetWare server from within Windows. You'll need to know the NetWare version if a specific application you use is version-specific or version-sensitive.

To find the version of the NetWare used on the server, follow these steps:

1. Open Network Neighborhood and select the server.

2. Choose File, Properties. The Properties sheet appears, as shown in figure 23.5.

3. Once you have the version information, choose OK to close the Properties sheet.

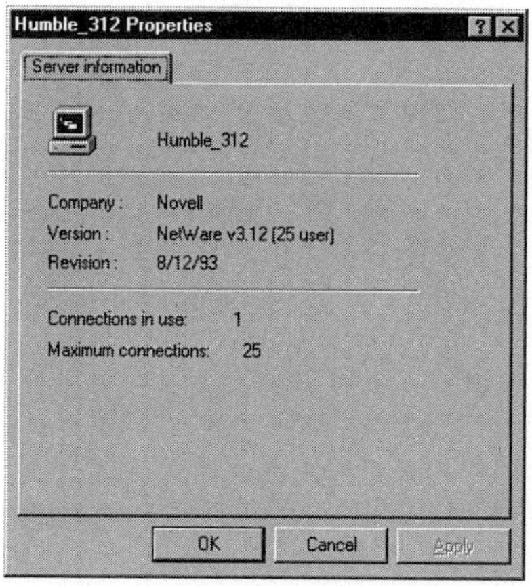

Fig. 23.5
The Properties
sheet lists
NetWare server
version
information.

Checking the Status of Network Volumes

A *volume* is a physical portion of the hard disk that stores information on the file server. You can check the space on a volume as well as find out other information about different volumes on the server, using two NetWare utilities: CHKVOL and VOLINFO.

> **Note**
>
> Usually the SYS is the first volume on a server and VOL1 is the second, VOL2 the third, and so on. Although these are the names Novell suggests, they are not always the names used.

To check on the status of the current volume, follow these steps:

1. Open the Start menu and choose Programs, MS-DOS Prompt.

2. At the MS-DOS prompt, change the directory to the primary server drive (usually F:).

3. Type **CHKVOL** and then press Enter. The results appear, as shown in figure 23.6.

> **Note**
>
> You may need to enter a path to the CHKVOL.EXE command; an example path might be \\HUMBLE_312\SYS\PUBLIC\CHKVOL.EXE.

V

Networking

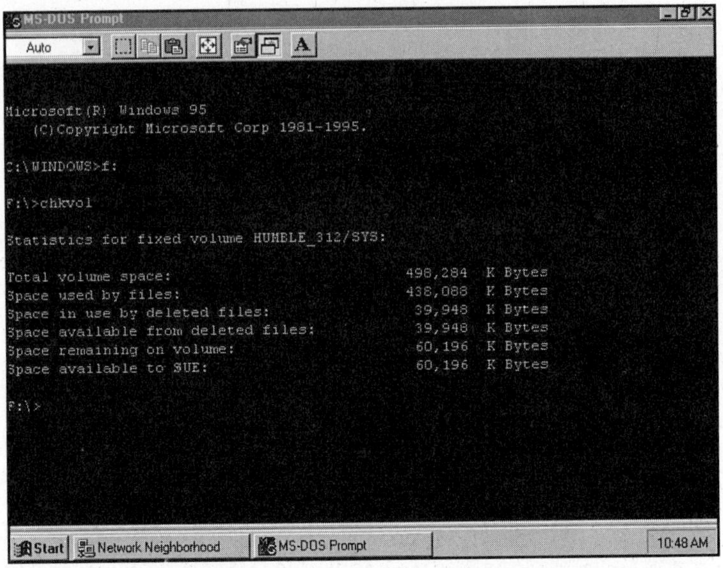

Fig. 23.6
Run CHKVOL
at the MS-DOS
prompt or from
the Run dialog
box.

```
MS-DOS Prompt                                              _ 8 X
Auto          [icons]  A

Microsoft(R) Windows 95
    (C)Copyright Microsoft Corp 1981-1995.

C:\WINDOWS>f:

F:\>chkvol

Statistics for fixed volume HUMBLE_312/SYS:

Total volume space:                498,284  K Bytes
Space used by files:               438,088  K Bytes
Space in use by deleted files:      39,948  K Bytes
Space available from deleted files: 39,948  K Bytes
Space remaining on volume:          60,196  K Bytes
Space available to SUE:             60,196  K Bytes

F:\>
```
```
Start   Network Neighborhood   MS-DOS Prompt              10:48 AM
```

4. Close the DOS window when you finish looking at the CHKVOL statistics.

The CHKVOL statistics list the total amount of space on the volume, the space used by files, the space in use by deleted files and the space available from deleted files, space remaining on the volume, and the space available to you.

Another NetWare information tool that you can use is VOLINFO.EXE, which quickly checks the status of drive usage. To use VOLINFO, follow these steps:

1. Open the MS-DOS Prompt and change to the primary server drive.

2. At the prompt, type **VOLINFO** and press Enter. The Volume Information utility appears (see fig. 23.7).

3. After viewing the volume information, press the Esc key. The Exit VolInfo dialog box appears.

4. Choose Yes and then press Enter.

5. At the MS-DOS prompt, type **exit** and press Enter, or click the Close button in the title bar, to return to the Windows desktop.

VOLINFO reports the name of the volume you are viewing and refers to the storage capacity of that volume in kilobytes, unless the server has more than one gigabyte of storage space, in which case VOLINFO reports space in megabytes.

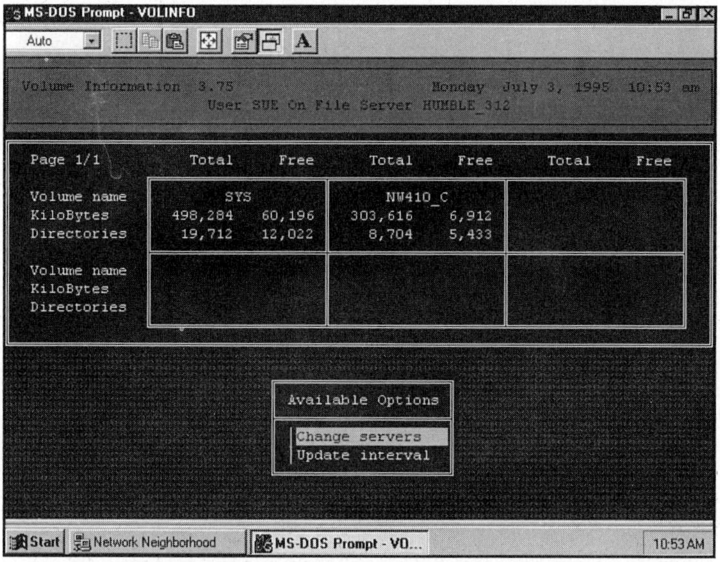

Fig. 23.7
Use Volume
Information to
view various
volumes and their
resources.

Listing Your Server Connections

Windows 95 provides a WhoAmI feature that is a graphical user interface
(GUI) approach to NetWare's WHOAMI utility. This simplified version of the
command shows only the most basic results: your user name and connection
number. To see this information, right-click on a server in the Network
Neighborhood and choose <u>W</u>ho Am I. The results are similar to figure 23.8.

Fig. 23.8
The WhoAmI
feature shows your
user name, the
server to which
you're connected,
and the connec-
tion number.

The NetWare command-line version is much more useful. For instance, if you
enter **WHOAMI** at the DOS prompt, you get the same user, server, and connection information. Additionally, WHOAMI lists the NetWare version and
allotted user number, date, and time, as shown in figure 23.9.

If you're connected to more than one server, the WHOAMI command also
lists those servers and your name on each, the software version on each, your
login date and time for each server, and your rights and security equivalen-
cies on each server.

You can enhance the command-line version's output with several parameters. Enter the command as **WHOAMI [servername] [option]**. The most
useful parameters are the following:

Parameter	Description
/s	*Security* lists the security equivalencies on each server you specify.
/g	*Groups* lists your membership in groups on each server specified.
/w	*Workgroup* lists workgroup manager information.
/r	*Rights* lists your rights on each server to which you're attached.
/a	*All* lists all the available information, including your group memberships, your security equivalencies, your rights, object supervisor, workgroup manager, and general system information.

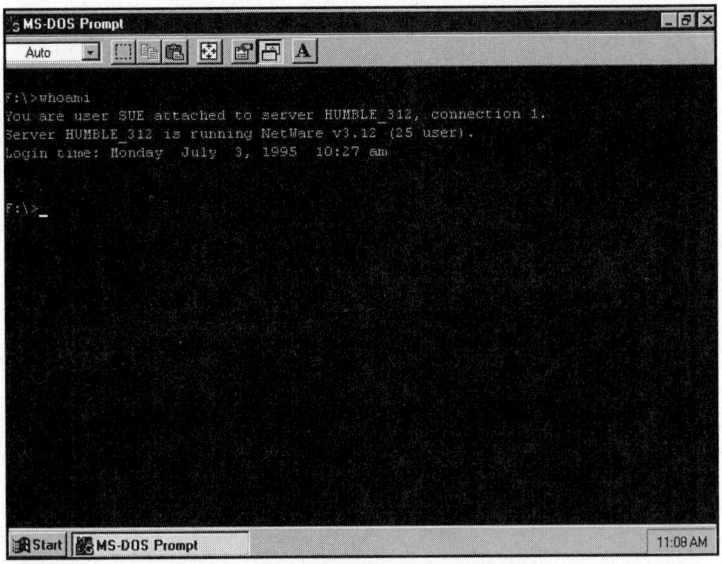

Fig. 23.9
Typical output
from NetWare's
WHOAMI utility.

Managing NetWare Printers

► See "Understanding Network Printing,"
p. 772

► See "Solving Common Network Printing Problems,"
p. 788

If you are comfortable with using NetWare and have done much work printing to a NetWare printer, you have probably seen or used NetWare's PCONSOLE utility for controlling print jobs. Windows 95 improves on PCONSOLE by adding to the printer's control applet in Windows 95 almost all these printer control functions for NetWare printers. Every common task for which you are likely to use PCONSOLE—such as checking the status of a print job and rearranging jobs in the queue (if you have sufficient user rights)—can be done from Windows.

> **Note**
>
> Even though Windows shows nine printer ports you can capture, Novell limits you to capturing on three: LPT1, LPT2, and LPT3. With Novell NetWare, Windows also tells you LPT4 and up are out of range.

PCONSOLE runs just as before, so if you are already familiar with it and want to continue using it, or if you want to access some advanced feature not available in Windows, you can still do so. However, if you only want to see how many print jobs are in front of you in the queue or to delete a print job that you sent accidentally, you can perform all these basic tasks in Windows, as described in Chapter 25, "Working with Network Printers."

Using Administrative Utilities

Most other NetWare utilities that you previously ran from a DOS prompt should now work in Windows 95 as well as from the DOS prompt. You might even find that some network utilities that were difficult to run in DOS 6.X due to memory constraints are easier to run in Windows 95 because more conventional memory is now available.

Table 23.1 lists some common Novell utilities that run in Windows 95. Many other unlisted utilities run as well.

Table 23.1   Some Novell DOS Utilities that You Can Run under Windows 95 Command Prompts

Novell DOS Utility	Function
FCONSOLE	Monitors the file server and lets you perform such functions as broadcast console messages, down the file server, check file server status, and so on
RCONSOLE	Gives you access to the file server console from a workstation (NetWare versions 3.11, 3.12, 4.02, and 4.1)
FILER	Determines file creation date, last access date, size, owner, and so on
SALVAGE	Undeletes files from a NetWare volume
SESSION	Maps network drives with a menu
CAPTURE	Assigns network printers to local LPT ports
SLIST	Displays all NetWare servers on the network (through version 3.x)
SYSCON	Controls accounting, file servers, group, and user information (through version 3.x)

> **Caution**
>
> Deleted files and folders from a network drive do not go to the Windows Recycle Bin; they are deleted permanently. There is no Undo, so be careful. If you do mistakenly delete an item you want, try the SALVAGE command as quickly after deleting the item as possible. When you delete files, the space it occupied remains on the server until the server needs space and is recoverable until that time. Your system administrator may have set NetWare to wait a minimum amount of time before reusing deleted space. You should check with your administrator about this option.

Some utilities cannot run under Windows 95 when you use the Windows Client for NetWare Networks rather than the Novell VLM network drivers. You use these commands in NetWare 4.x networks that employ the NetWare Directory Services (NDS) to manage a multiserver domain. Table 23.2 lists these utilities, which operate under Windows 95 only when the Novell VLM network drivers are used.

Table 23.2   Novell Utilities that Work Only with Novell VLM Network Drivers

Novell Utility	Function
NWADMIN	Administers the NDS directory tree under Windows
CX	Changes contexts within the NDS directory tree
NETADMIN	Administers the NDS directory tree under DOS

◄ See "Using the Explorer with Shared Resources on a Network," p. 544

In addition to the utilities listed in table 23.2 that do not work with the Windows Client for NetWare Networks, the NWUSER Windows 3.x utility is not supported under any configuration in Windows 95. This should not pose a problem because the Explorer application provides all the functionality of the NWUSER utility.

NWPOPUP, a utility that administrators use to broadcast messages across the network, does not work in Windows 95; however, you can install WinPopup to work in its place. WinPopup is a Windows utility in which you can send and receive messages on the NetWare network. Find the WinPopup utility on the migration Planning Kit CD that ships with Windows 95; look in the Admin95 folder, Apptools.

You can add WinPopup to your Startup group (Start menu, <u>S</u>ettings, <u>T</u>askbar, Start Menu Programs tab) so WinPopup automatically starts when you start Windows, so you'll always know when a network message is broadcast.

Tip

In WinPopup, choose <u>M</u>essages, <u>O</u>ptions and select Pop up Dialog on Message Receipt to be notified immediately of messages from the network.

Troubleshooting

I tried to enter a NetWare command in the Run dialog box but I got the message `Cannot find the file....` *What did I do wrong?*

You may need to specify a path to the server and the folder in which the command or utility resides. If that still doesn't work, close the Run dialog box and use the MS-DOS prompt instead. In the DOS window, change the drives to the primary network drive (usually F:) and then enter the command and the path. Some NetWare commands just do not work from the Run dialog box.

I've forgotten where I placed a file on the server. Is there a NetWare command I can use to find the file?

The easiest way to find a file or a folder in Windows is to use the Windows Find feature. You can use it for network drives as well as for your own drive. Choose Start, <u>F</u>ind, and then <u>F</u>iles or Folders. In the Find Files dialog box, choose the <u>B</u>rowse button. In the Browse for Folder dialog box, double-click the Network Neighborhood. Double-click the server and then choose OK. Enter the file or folder name in the <u>N</u>amed text box and choose Fi<u>n</u>d Now. Windows searches the server drive for your file or folder.

Connecting to Other Servers

Connecting to and using the resources on servers within the local network is easy, but how do you connect to servers other than your usual "preferred server"? You accomplish this connection just as you would expect: by using all the standard tools previously discussed.

◀ See "Logging in to a NetWare Server," p. 694

To connect to other servers, follow these steps:

1. Open the Network Neighborhood; all attached servers appear in the list.

2. Select the server name and then choose <u>F</u>ile, <u>A</u>ttach As, or right-click on the server name and choose <u>A</u>ttach As. The Enter Network Password dialog box appears.

V

Networking

3. Enter your user name and password. Additionally, you can choose from the following options:

- Save this Password in Your Password List. Choose this option to save your password in a list so the next time you make this connection, you do not have to retype the password.

- Connect as Guest. Log on as a guest if you do not have access to that server. Logging on as a guest gives you only limited access to the server.

4. Click on OK to establish the connection. Note that your user name and password may vary from server to server.

◀ See "An Easier but More Powerful Interface," p. 22

If you have logins on multiple servers, this method is probably the easiest. Of course, if you frequently need to connect your computer to the same server, you might create a shortcut on the desktop for this connection.

Using Network Tape Drives

Windows includes a Backup program you can use to back up your files to a network tape drive. Windows 95 works only with 1992 or later versions of certain tape drives (find the list in Backup Help). You might also call the tape drive manufacturer for information about backup software you can use with Windows 95.

Several drives are not compatible with Windows 95, including Archive drives, Irwin AccuTrak tapes and Irwin drives, Mountain drives, QIC Wide tapes, QIC 3020 drives, SCSI tape drives, Summit drives, and Travan drives.

◀ See "Backing Up Your Files," p. 555

In addition, Windows 95 includes an automatic backup feature, a backup agent that efficiently and regularly backs up your system, using industry-standard technology from Arcada (Backup Exec) and Cheyenne (ARCserve). These agents require network connections to a server.

> **Note**
>
> These backup agents require the appropriate software running on the NetWare server. Windows 95 does not include the Arcada or Cheyenne backup software. Additionally, Arcada and Cheyenne are not Novell's native TSA backup agents.

Microsoft considers these agents a service. To install the service to Windows 95, follow these steps:

1. Open the Network dialog box from the Control Panel.

2. On the Configuration page, choose <u>A</u>dd. The Select Network Component Type dialog box appears.

3. Select Service and choose <u>A</u>dd. The Select Network Service dialog box
   appears (see fig. 23.10).

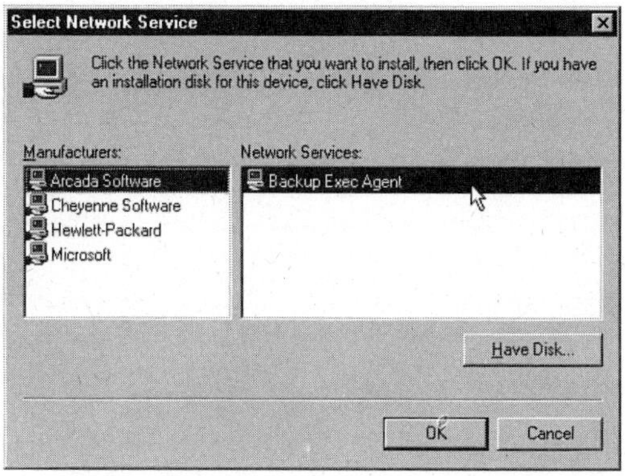

Fig. 23.10
Choose the service
from the Select
Network Service
dialog box.

4. In <u>M</u>anufacturers, choose Arcada Software and in Network Services,
   Backup Exec Agent becomes selected.

   Alternatively, choose Cheyenne Software in the <u>M</u>anufacturers list and
   choose ARCserve Agent.

5. Choose OK to select the service. Windows may prompt you to insert
   the Windows 95 CD. Follow directions on-screen.

6. Windows returns to the Network dialog box. Choose OK to close the
   dialog box. Windows may copy more files from the Windows 95 CD.

7. Windows prompts you to restart your computer. Choose <u>Y</u>es.

The following sections take you step by step through a typical setup of both
of these services. Remember, without one of these backup servers, you cannot
use the backup agents.

> **Note**
>
> If your NetWare server uses different backup software, you probably can still use it if
> you can run it from a DOS command line. Although Windows 95 might not support
> the software directly, you should still be able to run the software from DOS just as
> you could with previous releases of Windows.

V

Networking

Backing Up with Arcada

The Arcada Backup Exec agent as delivered with Windows 95 requires Arcada Backup Exec for NetWare, Enterprise Edition or Single Server Edition, version 5.01. If your NetWare server is running either of these Arcada products, you can use the Arcada backup agent to archive important data regularly from your workstation.

Setting Properties

After installing the Arcada service from the Select Network Service dialog box, follow these steps to set up the service:

1. In the Network dialog box, click the Configuration tab.

2. In the components list, double-click on Backup Exec Agent. The Backup Exec Agent Properties sheet appears, as shown in figure 23.11.

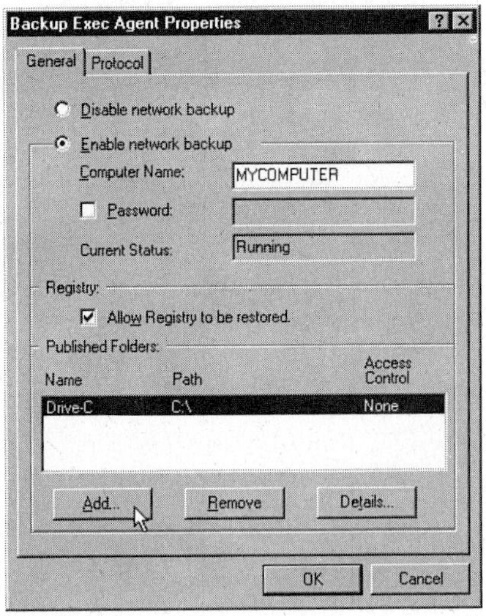

Fig. 23.11
Configure the Backup Exec Agent in the Backup Exec Agent Properties sheet.

3. Click the General tab and choose to Enable Network Backup. The NetWare server software now considers the Windows 95 computer to be a backup source.

4. Enter the name of your computer (as the network knows it) and your password.

Note

Select the Allo<u>w</u> Registry to Be Restored check box if you want to enable the software to restore the Registry. If you select the Allo<u>w</u> Registry to Be Restored check box, the software overwrites any changes that you made since your last backup.

---

5. In the Published Folders area, Drive C indicates your entire drive. If you do not want to backup the entire drive, choose <u>R</u>emove.

   To add specific folders, choose <u>A</u>dd; the Select Folder To Publish dialog box appears (see fig. 23.12). Choose the folders you want to add to the backup and choose OK. The selected folders are added to the Published Folders list on the Backup Exec Agent Properties sheet.

   Tip
   You also can choose to backup floppy and CD-ROM drives in the Select Folder To Publish dialog box.

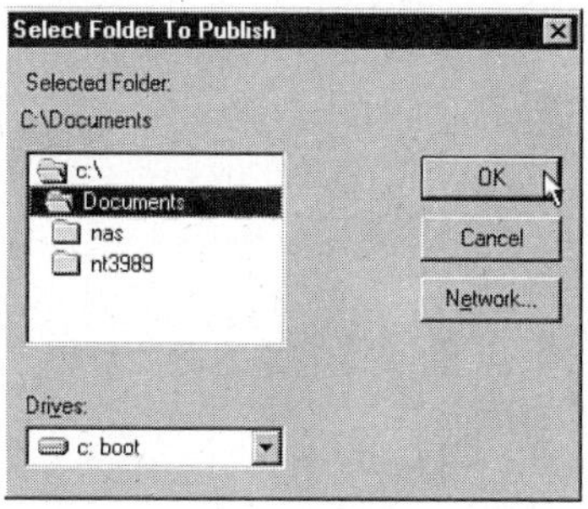

Fig. 23.12
Add drives and/or folders to the Published Folders list (backup list).

6. In the Published Folders area of the Backup Exec Agent Properties sheet, select a folder or drive and choose De<u>t</u>ails. In the Folder Details dialog box, you can browse the folder's contents and set access limits (see fig. 23.13).

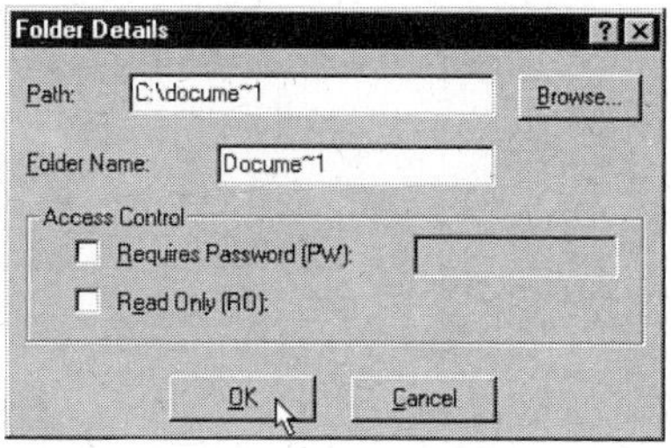

Fig. 23.13
In the Folder Details dialog box, you can assign the required access control.

V

Networking

7. Choose OK to close the Folder Details dialog box. The dialog box closes and the access control limits appear in the Published Folders area of the Backup Exec Agent Properties sheet (see fig. 23.14).

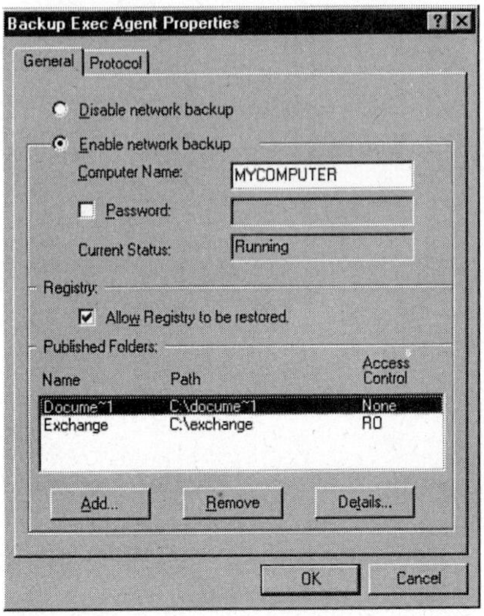

Fig. 23.14
The Published
Folders area of the
Backup Exec Agent
Properties sheet
indicates the
access control that
you have set.

8. Click OK to close the Backup Exec Agent Properties sheet.

> **Note**
>
> When you first install your software, the Properties sheet's Current Status indicates Not Running. After you install and configure the agent, this status changes to Running.

Setting Protocol

You must set the protocol of the agent to match that of the server. To set the protocol for the Backup Exec Agent, follow these steps:

1. On the Backup Exec Agent Properties sheet, click the Protocol tab (see fig. 23.15).

2. Choose the SPX/IPX protocol for the backup agent.

3. Choose OK to close the sheet.

4. Choose OK in the Network dialog box.

5. When Windows prompts you to restart the computer, choose Yes.

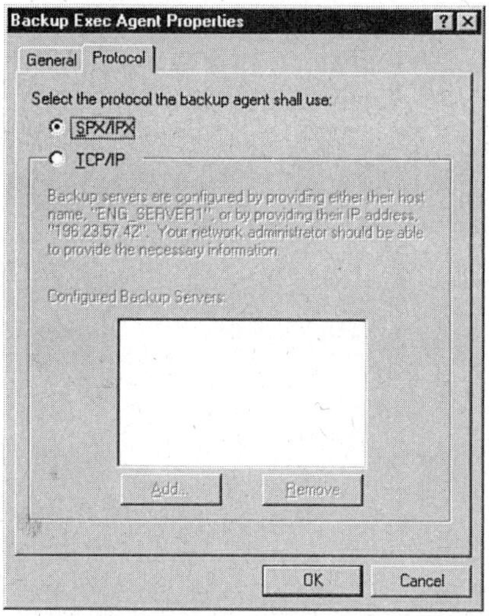

Fig. 23.15
The Protocol page
of the Backup Exec
Agent Properties
sheet.

Note

To use the Arcada Backup Agent, you might have to check whether the system administrator has the latest versions of the Arcada network loadable modules (NLMs) that have been updated for Windows 95. The necessary updated files are NRLTLI.NLM, TNRLAPT3.NLM, TNRLAPT4.NLM, TNRLTCP.NLM, and TNRLSPX.NLM. To get these files, you can contact Arcada directly or call Arcada's BBS at (407) 262-8123.

Backing Up with Cheyenne

If your server is running the Cheyenne backup software, and you've installed the ARCserve backup agent, you can set properties for the agent by following these steps:

1. In the Network dialog box, double-click on ARCserve Agent. The ARCserve Agent Properties sheet appears.

2. Click the General tab and choose Enable Network Backup. The Enable Network Backup area becomes available, as shown in figure 23.16.

3. Specify the settings to configure the Cheyenne software, as follows:

   ■ *Password*. Enter your password.

   ■ *Confirm Password*. Enter your password again.

V

Networking

- *Do Not Restore Registry*. Select this option if you do not want your system's registry settings restored when your system is restored.

- *Display Status Information*. Displays information during the backup.

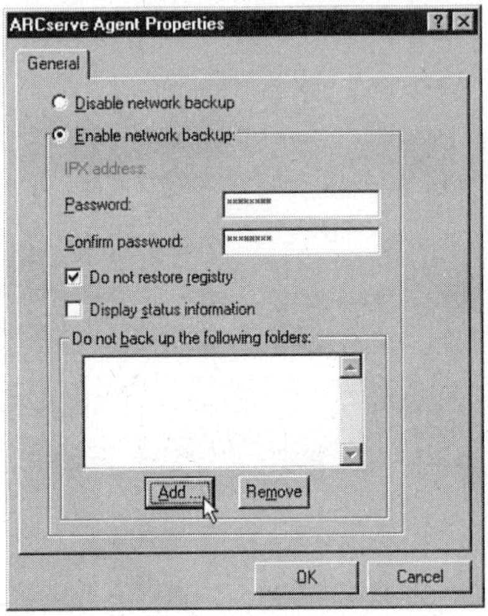

Fig. 23.16
Enable network backup on the ARCserve Agent Properties sheet.

4. Choose Add to enter folders in the Do Not Back Up the Following Folders list. The Add dialog box appears (see fig. 23.17).

In the Do Not Back Up the Following Folders list, enter only those folders you *do not* want to back up. By default, all folders will be backed up.

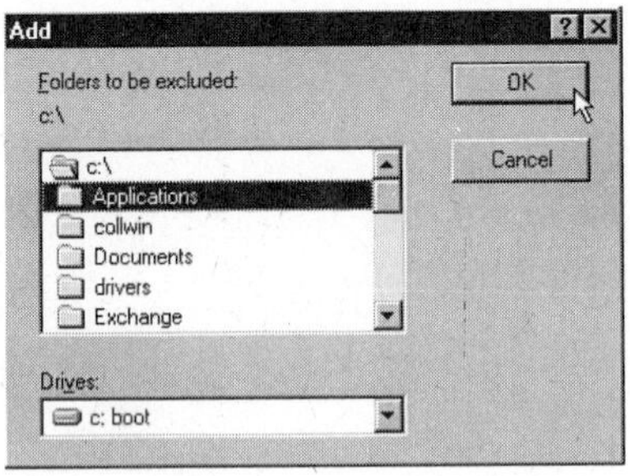

Fig. 23.17
Select the folder you *do not* want to back up in the Add dialog box for Cheyenne ARCserve agent.

Note

If you mistakenly added a folder you do want to back up, select the folder and choose Remove.

5. Choose OK in the Add dialog box to return to the ARCserve Agent Properties sheet. The folders you do not want to back up appear in the Do Not Back Up the Following Folders list box, as shown in figure 23.18.

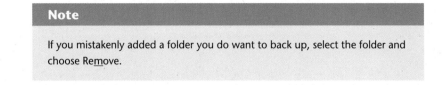

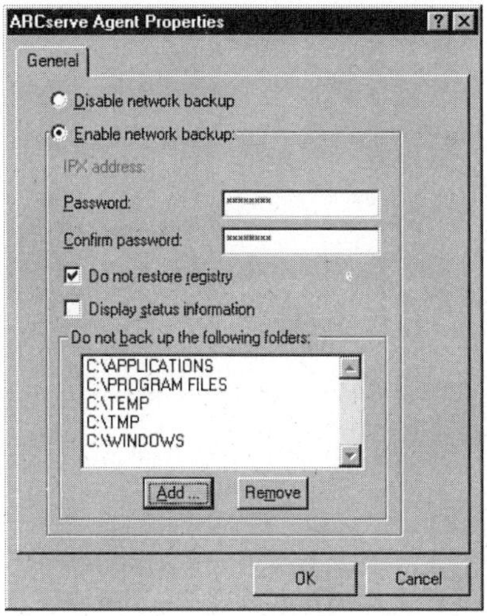

Fig. 23.18
The folders listed in the dialog box are those the agent will *not* back up.

6. Click OK to close the Properties sheet.
7. Choose OK in the Network dialog box.
8. When Windows prompts you to restart the computer, choose Yes.

Note

Cheyenne has updated the network loadable modules (NLMs) specifically for Windows 95. These updated files are APROCESS.NLM, ARCOPY.NLM, and WSTAPE.NLM. To obtain these files, contact Cheyenne directly at (800) 243-9832.

As you have seen in this chapter, Windows 95 and NetWare servers can coexist, and in fact, Windows 95 makes it easier to use NetWare server resources than previous releases of Windows. Microsoft has made Windows 95 truly a "well-connected client."❖

Chapter 24

Using Microsoft Exchange

by Gordon Meltzer with Peter Kent

Microsoft Exchange is a central communications client that organizes the electronic mail and faxes that you receive in one convenient location. Exchange operates not only as your universal in-box, but also as a tool that can compose, store, organize, and send messages via e-mail and fax.

In its basic configuration, Exchange coordinates communication among members of your Local Area Network (LAN) workgroup and handles communications via the Microsoft Network, yet still finds time to send and receive faxes in several formats. In more advanced configurations, Exchange handles communications with other message services, like CompuServe and Internet mail.

In this chapter, you learn to do the following:

- Install Microsoft Exchange
- Configure your Exchange user profile
- Create a Personal Address Book
- Choose and install messaging services
- Create and send messages
- Work with received messages
- Use Exchange remotely from a laptop or other location

Overview of Exchange Features

So that you know how to set up Exchange during the installation process, you should have some detailed information about what Exchange can do. Knowing about Exchange's abilities will help you to make the right installation and setup choices.

You call on Microsoft Exchange when you want to compose a fax. You visit Exchange again when you want to send a message to a workgroup colleague down the hall or to everyone on your workgroup network. When those folks on your workgroup reply to you, your Exchange Inbox is where their missives will land. Faxes sent to your fax card head for the Exchange Inbox, too.

Your messages don't have to be just plain text, either. Because Exchange supports Rich Text Format, messages can be delivered in any font on your system, at any size, in any color. The first time you see a mail message that has been passed around your workgroup and each member has contributed his or her thoughts in a different color, you'll begin to appreciate the power of Exchange.

More important than Rich Text is the ability to work with Object Linking and Embedding (OLE). Your messages can contain OLE documents created in applications that are OLE servers, like Microsoft Word for Windows, Microsoft Excel, or any of the many OLE server applications.

Finally, you can use Exchange to communicate via Microsoft Network, the online service available through Windows 95.

So far, we've looked at Exchange from the point of view of a member of a local area network workgroup. But even if you're on a stand-alone system, Exchange will have value to you, as long as you have a modem and a phone line. In this type of configuration, you can communicate via fax, and your e-mail can reach into the membership of Microsoft Network, and beyond, right out onto the Internet!

Clients and Servers

In the introduction, we said that Exchange was a central communications client. The word *client* is so important in Exchange, and in Windows 95 generally, that we need to explain it and its comrade term, *server*.

For the purposes of programs like Exchange, a server is a program, running on a network, that holds information accessible by users on the network.

These users employ programs called clients to get at the server-based information.

If the server is a mail or fax server, it provides a place to store mail and fax messages for all the clients (users) on the network. This is the kind of server to which the Exchange client connects.

> **Note**
>
> Clients don't have to be permanently connected to the network to get information from or send information to the server. The network connection can be dial-up, the way you access CompuServe.

Inbox

Discussions of Microsoft Exchange have commonly referred to Exchange as the "universal inbox." In fact, one way to start the Exchange program is to double-click the Inbox icon on your Windows desktop. The inbox function is a very important part of Exchange, as this section explains.

You'll be using Exchange to communicate, and a good part of communication is finding out what others have to say. You may receive messages by fax or e-mail. In Windows 95, these received messages are directed to Microsoft Exchange where they can be conveniently read. In this way, Exchange functions as an inbox. We call Exchange a *universal inbox* because all messages, both fax and e-mail, no matter where they come from, go to your Exchange inbox.

In Windows 3.1, incoming messages went to the inboxes of various applications. Faxes would go to WinFax or another fax program, depending on what you had installed. E-mail would go to cc:Mail, Microsoft Mail, or whatever program you were using for e-mail. CompuServe Mail, likewise, would go to the inbox in whatever program you used to access CompuServe.

Windows 95's designers have reasoned that collecting all these messages in one place would be more convenient. That is why the inbox function of Exchange is so important.

Microsoft Workgroup E-Mail

If you're connected to a local area network (LAN), Exchange is the program you'll use to send and receive e-mail with your workgroup colleagues. Windows 95 contains a Microsoft Mail Postoffice so you can set up an e-mail system on your workgroup network.

▶ See "Installing the Workgroup Postoffice," p. 769

V

Networking

Once you have your Postoffice running, Exchange collects all e-mail addressed to you. You then can read, reply to, and forward them, all while using the Exchange program. Other accessory programs, installed on your network, will let Exchange send and receive e-mail over networks wider than your workgroup LAN.

Microsoft Fax

Exchange, working hand in hand with Microsoft Fax, provides a convenient place to compose your fax, attach or embed documents to be included with your fax, and address your fax. Exchange gives you several ways to create faxes. You can use the Compose New Fax Wizard to send a simple typed message or an attached file. (Yes, you can transfer computer files using fax, as you'll find out later.) You can use the same New Message window that you use to compose e-mail, or you can create your fax in another application and send or print it to the fax system. Your faxes can include text, pictures, OLE objects, and files. This richness of function is one of the key features of Microsoft Exchange.

Microsoft Network

The Microsoft Network (MSN) is an online service, similar in concept to CompuServe and America Online. One service Microsoft Network provides to its members is e-mail.

Microsoft Exchange provides a way to dial into MSN and quickly retrieve any e-mail waiting for you. You also can use Exchange to send e-mail to an MSN member.

Rich Text Format

Exchange supports Rich Text Format (RTF). This means you can create messages using any font on your system. You also can change the text's size and use different colors. These text-formatting capabilities let you personalize your messages, and they can be quite useful when messages are routed to various people for comment. Individuals can use different colors and various typefaces and type sizes, which helps set off each set of comments.

OLE Support

OLE allows you to put part of one document into another. This capability has been used by every major Windows applications publisher. You can highlight a section of a document, copy it into Windows Clipboard, and paste-link or paste-embed it into another program. The original program might be a spreadsheet, and the target program might be a word processor. It doesn't matter, as long as the source program is an OLE server, and the target pro-gram is an OLE client. Most major programs are both.

> **Note**
>
> The data you copy and paste-link or paste-embed is called an *OLE object*. Often in Windows 95, OLE objects have an associated icon. You can drag the icon into other programs or drop it on the Windows desktop. In other cases, the OLE object simply appears in its original format, such as rows from a spreadsheet.

Exchange extends your powers to work with OLE objects by allowing you to drop them into its universal message form (message window). From the form, you can mail or fax objects as part of your message.

Most modern Windows applications are OLE enabled. Although we men-tioned Microsoft Word and Excel objects previously, any OLE object can be embedded in an Exchange message and sent with that message.

> **Note**
>
> Chapter 15, "Building Compound Documents with OLE," explains how to get the most out of OLE.

Installing and Configuring Microsoft Exchange

You can install Microsoft Exchange during your initial Windows 95 installa-tion or afterward. After the first few steps, however, the process is the same. The following sections explain how to install and configure Exchange for your needs.

> **Note**
>
> Microsoft Exchange requires a minimum of 6M of memory in your system to run. For good performance, plan on having at least 8M. Exchange also takes 10M of space on your hard drive for required swap files. The Exchange basic program files take 3.7M of disk space. Due to Exchange's ability to work with all sorts of different data, you should allow a few M for your incoming messages, too. It's easy to end up with 5M or more of faxes and e-mail.

V

Networking

Installing Exchange during Windows Setup

During Windows setup, the Windows 95 Setup Wizard displays the Get Connected dialog box, shown in figure 24.1. In this dialog box, you can choose to install The Microsoft Network online service, Microsoft Mail for use on workgroup networks (LANs), and the Microsoft Fax service.

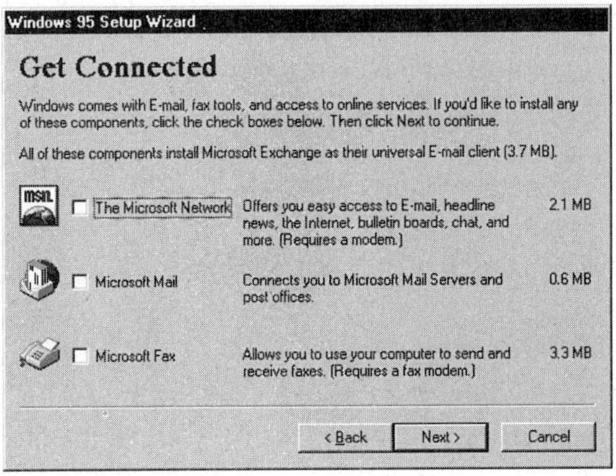

Fig. 24.1

The Get Connected dialog box is the first step to installing Exchange.

![Windows 95 Setup Wizard Get Connected dialog box]

You can install any or all of these three connectivity components. (You can always add them later, too.) MSN, Microsoft Mail, and Microsoft Fax all require Microsoft Exchange to work, so when you choose any of them, Microsoft Exchange is installed for you.

> **Note**
>
> For more information on installing and setting up Windows 95, see Appendix A, "Installing and Uninstalling Windows 95."

It's also possible to install Exchange without installing any of these items; for instance, if you want to use Exchange for Internet e-mail. To do so, you must choose a Custom installation—you'll then be able to select Exchange from a list of optional components.

Adding Exchange after Windows Is Installed

If you did not install any of the connectivity components during your Windows 95 installation, you can add Exchange later.

On your Windows desktop, you will see an icon called Inbox. If you right-click the Inbox icon and then choose Properties, Windows confirms that Exchange is not installed (see fig. 24.2).

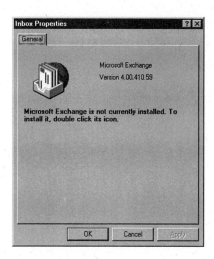

Fig. 24.2
Windows confirms
that Exchange is
not yet installed.

Follow this procedure to install Microsoft Exchange:

1. Double-click the Inbox icon on your desktop. You'll see a Get Connected dialog box similar to the one shown in figure 24.1 (though it's now called the Inbox Setup Wizard).

> **Note**
>
> If you've installed an Exchange service and now want to install one or more other services, you won't be able to use this procedure; this procedure only works when no Exchange services have been installed. To install Microsoft Fax or Microsoft Network, open the Start menu and choose Settings, Control Panel; then double-click on the Add/Remove Programs icon, click on the Windows Setup tab, and select the item from the list of components. To install Microsoft Mail or Internet Mail, right-click on the Inbox icon, choose Add, and select the service you want to install.

2. Choose one or more of the three information services you are offered. The services are The Microsoft Network, Microsoft Mail, and Microsoft Fax. (To make this example most useful, we'll cover what happens when you choose all three).

3. After selecting the information services you want, choose OK.

4. The Inbox Setup Wizard asks you to insert your Windows 95 CD-ROM or floppy disk. Insert the CD-ROM or disk and choose OK. Windows then installs the needed files.

5. The Inbox Setup Wizard now asks whether you've used Exchange before. Since you're setting up Exchange for the first time, choose <u>N</u>o. Then choose Next. Windows displays the dialog box shown in figure 24.3.

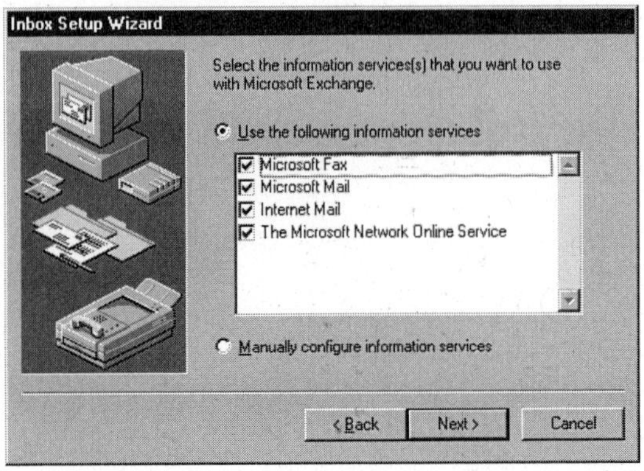

Fig. 24.3

The Inbox Setup Wizard offers you a choice of services.

Inbox Setup Wizard

Select the information services(s) that you want to use with Microsoft Exchange.

⦿ <u>U</u>se the following information services

☑ Microsoft Fax
☑ Microsoft Mail
☑ Internet Mail
☑ The Microsoft Network Online Service

○ <u>M</u>anually configure information services

[< <u>B</u>ack] [Next >] [Cancel]

6. The services you just selected in step 2 are already checked, along with Internet Mail. If you plan to use Exchange for receiving e-mail from an Internet service provider (other than Microsoft Network), leave this check box checked. Otherwise—if you are not going to use Internet e-mail—*clear* the check box.

> **Note**
>
> Microsoft Network has a level of service that provides full Internet access, and it also allows *all* users, at all levels, to send and receive e-mail across the Internet. However, the Internet Mail service referred to by the Inbox Setup Wizard is intended for use with other Internet service providers, not with the Microsoft Network.

7. Choose Next.

The basic setup of Exchange is done, but the Inbox Setup Wizard continues, setting up each of the services you have selected. In the next sections, we work with the Wizard to configure the individual communications services we just chose to use with Exchange.

Troubleshooting
I followed this procedure but couldn't get Exchange to install correctly.
The Inbox Setup Wizard may run into problems—it may even "crash" while setting up your information. For instance, you may get a message telling you that the Wizard was unable to complete something and telling you to click on the Finish button to end the procedure. If this happens to you, double-click on the Inbox icon and the Wizard should start again.

Configuring Microsoft Fax

If you chose to install Microsoft Fax, you see the dialog box shown in figure 24.4. (If you didn't choose to install Microsoft Fax, you can skip this section.) The Wizard asks you to enter information about your telephone number: your area code, the number (if any) that you dial to get an outside line, and whether you are using pulse or tone dialing. Enter all this information, and then choose OK.

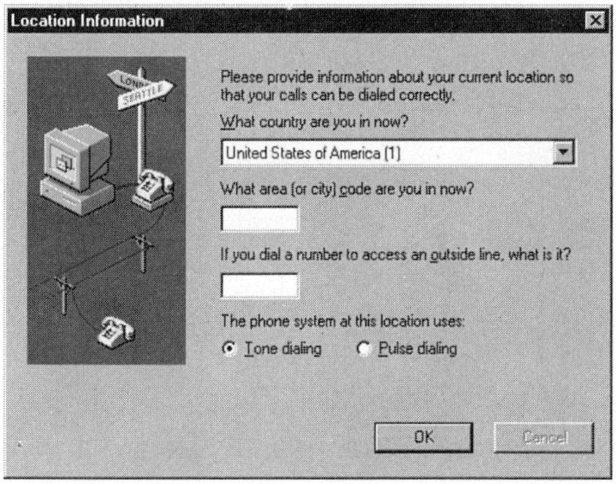

Fig. 24.4
The Wizard's Location Information dialog box.

V

Networking

You are then asked whether you want to use a ems modem or a network-fax service (you can choose only the latter if you have installed network software; if you haven't, the Wizard ignores your selection and assumes that you want to use a modem). Select the appropriate option button and choose Next.

The Wizard now asks for information about the modem or network-fax service. If you have already installed a modem, you see something like the dialog box in figure 24.5. (If you haven't yet installed a modem, the Install New Modem Wizard starts.)

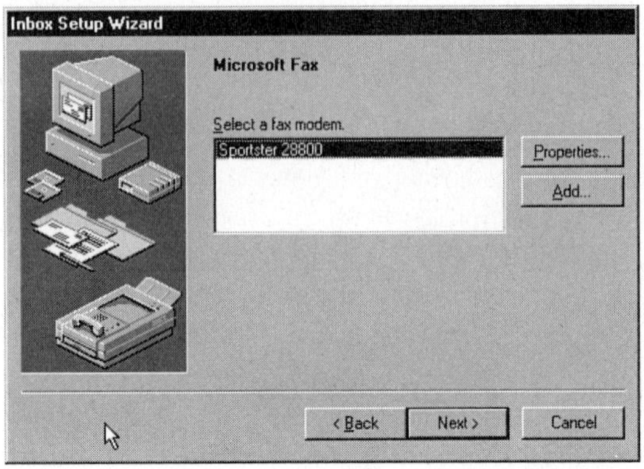

Fig. 24.5
The Microsoft Fax dialog box lets you specify the kind of device you want to use for sending and receiving faxes.

▶ See "Installing and Configuring Your Modem," p. 831

Select which modem you want to use for your fax messages—in the illustration there is only one choice. You can add another fax modem—or a Network Fax Server—by clicking on the Add button. Or modify the selected fax modem's properties by choosing Properties. When you've selected the fax modem (or added a Network Fax Server), choose Next.

Tip

If you use the modem line to receive phone calls as well as faxes, tell Microsoft Fax not to answer each incoming call. This way, voice calls can be answered by a person, not the modem.

If you select a modem rather than a Network Fax Server, the Wizard asks you whether you want Microsoft Fax to answer each incoming call on the phone line the modem is connected to. Choose Yes or No. (If you choose Yes, you may also want to change the Answer After n Rings value—you'll probably want the smallest value, 2 rings. Then choose Next.

Next, the Inbox Setup Wizard asks you for some personal information. This information will be used on any fax cover sheets you send along with your outgoing faxes, so people will know who sent them and how to fax back to you.

Enter your name and other information as requested in the dialog box shown in figure 24.6—you must enter the fax number (the number of the line to which the fax machine is connected) or you will be unable to continue. Then choose Next.

That's all their is to installing the Fax service. If you selected another service, the Wizard now asks for information about that service. If not, skip to "Completing Your Microsoft Exchange Installation," later in this chapter.

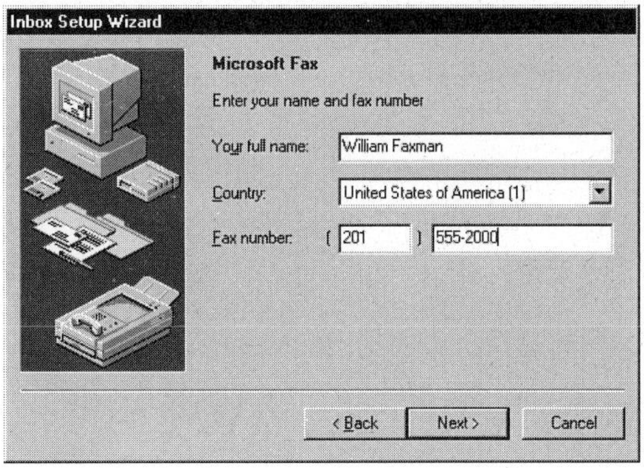

Fig. 24.6
Enter the personal information you want included on your faxes in this dialog box.

Configuring Microsoft Mail

If you chose to install Microsoft Mail, you see the dialog box shown in figure 24.7 now. (If you did not choose to install Microsoft Mail, you can skip this section.)

Fig. 24.7
You need to specify a Postoffice location to use Microsoft Mail.

Microsoft Mail requires that one of the computers on the workgroup LAN be set up as a Postoffice. You may have a network administrator who has already done this. If so, ask the administrator for the path to the Postoffice. Then, put the path to the Postoffice in the text box shown in fig. 24.7 (use the Browse button and search for the path if necessary), and choose Next.

> **Note**
>
> When the administrator creates a Postoffice, a folder called WGPO000 is created. For instance, if the administrator creates a folder called Mail and tells the Microsoft Workgroup Postoffice Admin Wizard to place the Postoffice there, the Wizard places the WPGO000 folder inside the Mail folder. You must specify where the WPGO000 folder is. For instance, you would enter C:\MSMAIL\WGPO0000, not C:\MSMAIL.

If you don't have an administrator to set up your Postoffice, go right now to the "Installing the Workgroup Postoffice" section later in this chapter. Then return to this section.

You are shown a list of people who've been given access to the Postoffice. Select your name from this list (if it's not on the list, ask the administrator to add it). The Inbox Setup Wizard then asks for your password. Again, ask your administrator what password he used when creating your account, and carefully type that into the text box. Then choose Next.

The Wizard has finished setting up Microsoft Mail, and you are ready to use it on your workgroup LAN.

Configuring Internet Mail

If you chose to install Internet Mail, you see the dialog box shown in figure 24.8. (If you did not choose to install Internet Mail, skip this section.) The first step is to specify your Internet access method.

> **Note**
>
> In order to use Internet Mail, you must have the TCP/IP protocol installed on your computer. If it isn't, you'll see a message reminding you to install it. To install TCP/IP open the Start menu and choose Settings, Control Panel; double-click on the Network icon and choose Add; select Protocol and choose Add; select Microsoft and TCP/IP, and then choose OK.

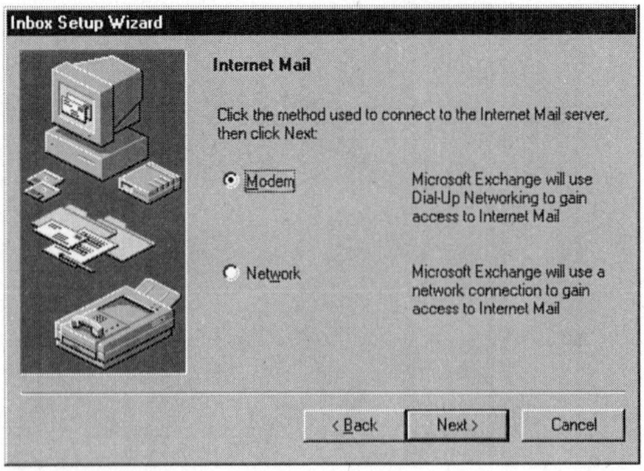

Fig. 24.8
You need to choose an access method to the Internet for Internet Mail.

▶ See "Installing and Configuring Windows 95 Dial-Up Network Adapter," p. 888

Internet Access Method

The Wizard offers Modem and Network options for Internet access. If you connect to the Internet by modem and Dial-Up Networking, follow these steps:

1. Choose <u>M</u>odem and then choose Next.

2. Now select the connection you created in Dial-Up Networking that dials your Internet Service Provider.

   If you haven't created a connection yet, choose <u>N</u>ew and create a connection. (Chapter 29, "Getting Connected to the Internet," provides detailed instructions for creating a connection.)

▶ See "Creating a Configuration for Your Access Provider," p. 892

> **Note**
>
> If you haven't yet installed the TCP/IP software, the Wizard skips this step; it doesn't ask you which service provider to use. Later you can specify a service provider by choosing <u>T</u>ools, Ser<u>v</u>ices in the Inbox, clicking on Internet Mail, choosing P<u>r</u>operties, and clicking on the Connection tab.

3. Choose Next.

If you connect to the Internet via your LAN, choose Net<u>w</u>ork and then choose Next.

Selecting Your Internet Mail Server

Now tell the Wizard about your Internet Mail server. You can tell the Wizard either the N<u>a</u>me of the server where your Internet mail is stored, or you can tell the Wizard its <u>I</u>P Address. (Figure 24.9 shows an example, with a mail-server name filled in.) Then choose Next.

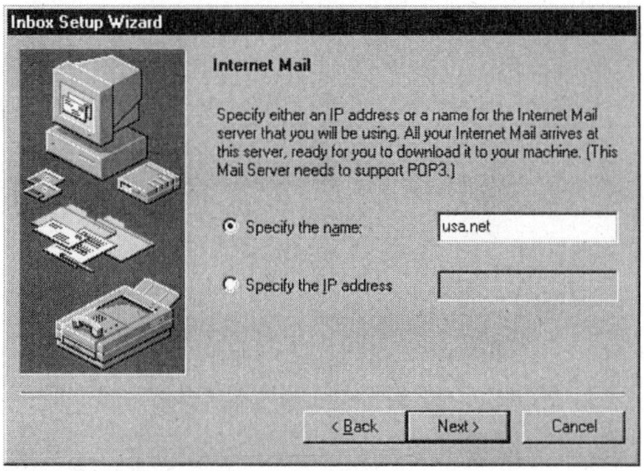

Fig. 24.9
Enter your Internet Mail server information.

Internet Mail Transfer Method

You can choose Off-line or Automatic mail transfers:

V

Networking

- Off-line lets you use Remote Preview to view only incoming mail headers. You selectively decide which messages to download to your Inbox, based on the header contents.

- Automatic instructs Exchange to connect to your Internet Mail server and retrieve all new mail to your Inbox automatically. The Automatic option also automatically sends any outbound Internet mail you've created.

Make your choice, and then choose Next.

Your Internet E-Mail Address

Next, the Wizard wants you to fill in your e-mail address in the form user@domain. Enter this in the text box called E-Mail Address. Also, put your full name in the text box called Your Full Name. When you're finished, choose Next.

Internet Mailbox Information

The Inbox Setup Wizard needs the Mailbox Name and Password you use to access your account in your Internet Mail server. Enter them in the text boxes provided and then choose Next.

Internet Mail is set up and ready to use with Exchange.

Confirming The Microsoft Network Mail System

You cannot set up MSN with the Inbox Setup Wizard. At this point, if you've chosen to install MSN, the Inbox Setup Wizard displays a dialog box confirming you have chosen to install MSN Mail to work with Exchange (see fig. 24.10).

Fig. 24.10
The Wizard confirms that you want to install The Microsoft Network online service mail.

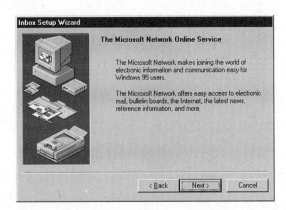

When you choose Next, the Wizard confirms that you've chosen to install MSN Mail to work with Exchange. All setup and configuration of MSN is done by the MSN Setup program—the Setup program begins when you double-click on the MSN icon on your desktop, or open the Start menu and choose Programs, The Microsoft Network. (Appendix B, Using Microsoft Network," covers MSN installation and setup.)

▶ See "Connecting to The Microsoft Network," p. 1110

Completing Your Microsoft Exchange Installation

Now you've set up the various services you selected, the Wizard finishes off the more general Exchange settings. First, it asks you which Personal Address Book it should use.

You probably haven't created a Personal Address Book (as we're assuming that you are installing Exchange for the first time), so simply choose Next.

You then see a similar dialog box, this time asking where your Personal Folder file is. This is the file that stores all your messages. Choose Next to accept the file that the Wizard is suggesting.

Next, the Wizard asks whether you want to run Exchange automatically every time you start Windows. This choice requires some thought; Exchange uses many system resources and can affect performance in low-memory configurations. If you are going to use Exchange only on a dial-up basis, such as with The Microsoft Network or an Internet service provider, choose No.

Running Exchange at Windows startup wastes system resources if you don't need to use Exchange's services constantly. If you don't expect much e-mail and will use Exchange and its communications services infrequently, select the Do Not Add Inbox to StartUp Group check box.

If your messaging needs require constant connectivity or periodic automatic logon to an online service to check for new mail, choose To Add Inbox to the StartUp Group.

To complete the installation, choose Next. The Inbox Setup Wizard displays a final dialog box confirming that Exchange is set up to work with all the communications services you selected (see fig. 24.11).

Choose Finish, and after this long setup and configuration process, you are ready to start using Microsoft Exchange. (The Exchange window opens automatically immediately after the Wizard closes.)

Tip
If you're connected to a LAN, start Exchange automatically every time you start Windows so that you won't miss any e-mail from workgroup members.

V

Networking

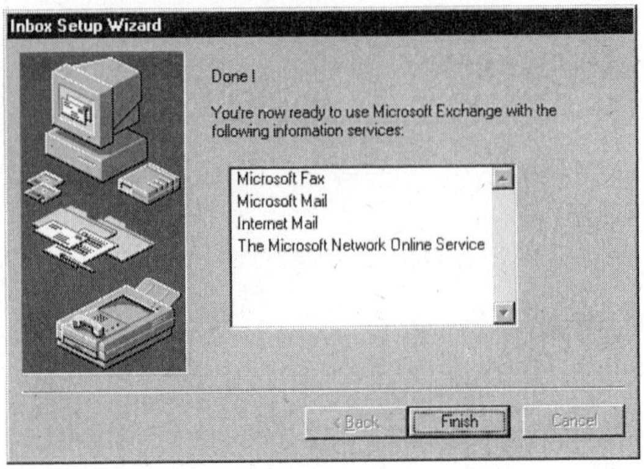

Fig. 24.11
Inbox Setup
Wizard confirms
that the setup
of services is
complete.

Creating and Sending Mail Messages

After you configure one or more information services, you can create and
send a message with the Exchange client. If Exchange were perfect, it would
have a universal composition screen in which you could compose any type of
message for any type of recipient and for any delivery method. Because of the
differences between fax recipients and electronic-mail recipients, however,
you have to decide whether to compose a mail message or a fax.

In this section, we explain how to create and send a Microsoft Mail e-mail
message to members of your workgroup LAN. Then, in the next section, we
describe how to compose and send a fax with Microsoft Fax.

Creating a Mail Message

Tip
You also can get to
the New Message
window by press-
ing Ctrl+N in the
main Exchange
window.

First we'll explain how to send an e-mail message to a member of your
workgroup LAN. You'll be working with the message form we discussed earlier in this chapter. Remember that you'll have all the power of Rich Text
Formatting and OLE at your fingertips when you create your e-mail message.

If the Exchange window is not open, start the Exchange program by double-
clicking the Inbox icon on the desktop. Then choose Compose, New Message.
If you prefer to use the toolbar, choose the New Message button. Exchange
opens the New Message window.

Figure 24.12 shows the initial blank composition window, which is
Exchange's New Message form, or window. You will see this form frequently
while you work in Exchange. Now you can work on your message.

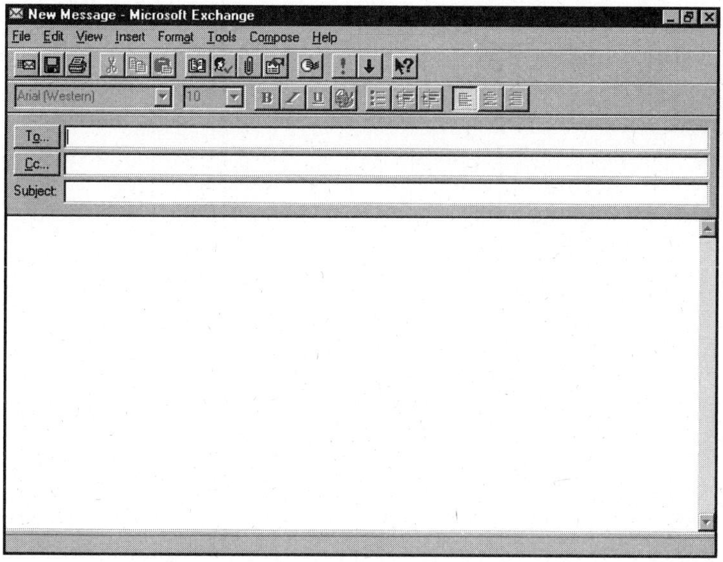

Fig. 24.12
Exchange displays
the New Message
window in which
you compose your
message.

Choosing a Recipient

When you click To in the New Message window, your Personal Address Book pops up, showing the list of recipients that you have created. Select the names of the people to whom you want to send your message; you can select names for the To box and names for the Cc box.

You may want to send a blind carbon copy, called a Bcc. The blind copy will be sent to any recipients on the Bcc list. The recipients of the original message and any Cc recipients will not know a copy has gone to the Bcc recipient. The New Message form does not show the Bcc text box by default. You can display this text box by choosing View, Bcc Box.

▶ See "Working
with Your
Address Book,"
p. 757

Entering Text

Start with the Subject box and type the subject of the message.

Pressing Tab takes you to the main message-entry space, where you can write what you have to say. Start entering text now.

Formatting Message Text

Do you see a remarkable similarity between the menus and toolbars of the New Message form and a good Windows word processor? You do, indeed. The toolbars and menus give you the option of choosing the following formatting options for your message text (the options are listed as they appear on the toolbar, from left to right):

Tip

Enter your text for the message first and format it later.

V

Networking

◀ See "Under-
standing
Fonts," p. 210

◀ See "Reviewing
Types of
Fonts," p. 213

■ Font (limited to the fonts on your system)

■ Font Size (as small or large as the TrueType font scaler can handle)

■ Bold

■ Italic

■ Underline

■ Text Color

■ Bullets

■ Indents

■ Text Alignment (left align, center, and right align)

You combine these options to create messages in Rich Text Format. Whenever you use fonts in varying sizes, colors, and alignments, or other formatting options, you are adding depth to your communications.

Entering OLE Objects in Exchange Messages

You are not limited to text messages, even Rich Text Format messages. One of Exchange's most useful capabilities is that of including objects in messages. When you use objects in your messages, you can add a lot of extra content to those messages with very little work.

You can insert the following types of Windows 95 objects into your messages:

■ Audio Recorder

■ Bitmap images

■ Media clips

■ Microsoft Word documents or pictures

■ MIDI sequences

■ Packages

■ Paint pictures

■ QuickTime movies

■ Video clips

■ Wave sounds

■ WordPad document

Tip
If the person
receiving your
message needs a
document from
you such as a text
document, spread-
sheet, or a picture,
be sure to insert it
in the document
using the tech-
niques we discuss
in this section.

Each application on your system that is an OLE server can create OLE objects that you can place in your messages, so the preceding list is not exhaustive. See Chapter 15, "Building Compound Documents with OLE," to learn how to create OLE objects.

Follow these steps to insert an OLE object in an Exchange mail message:

1. In Exchange, choose Insert, Object. The list of available object types appears (see fig. 24.13).

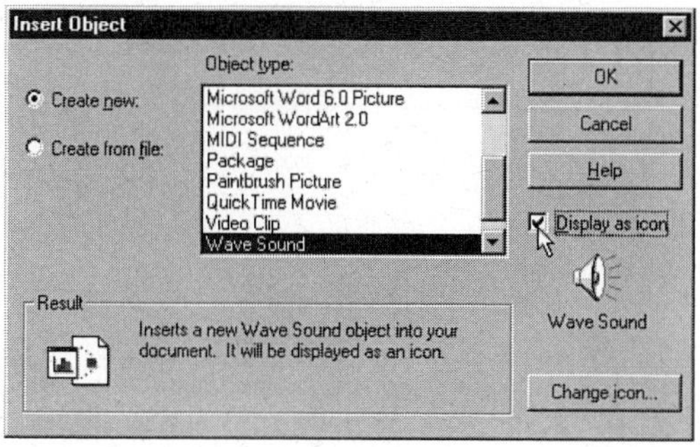

Fig. 24.13

You use the Insert Object dialog box to choose an OLE object type to insert in an Exchange message.

2. Select the type of object that you want to include in your message, and then choose OK. Select Wave Sound, for example, to insert a sound recording in the message. The application used to create the object starts. In the case of a Sound Wave object, the Sound Recorder applet starts.

> **Note**
>
> Notice that the OLE server application that opens will have a special kind of title bar. Instead of saying Sound Recorder, for instance, the title bar says Sound Object in Mail Message. The OLE server applications also have slightly different menus and options from when they run normally. The File menu in Sound Recorder, for example, has a new option: Exit & Return to Mail Message.

3. Use the application to create the object that you want to mail. In this case, record the audio that you want to send with your mail and then choose File, Exit & Return to Mail Message. The application disappears, leaving the Wave Sound icon in your message.

If you are inserting a form of data that can be displayed, and if you didn't choose the Display as Icon check box in the Insert Object dialog box, you see

Tip

If you want your OLE option to appear as an icon, select the Display as Icon option while in the Insert Object dialog box. Leave the check box cleared if you want the data—the spreadsheet rows, word processing text, picture, or whatever—displayed rather than the icon. (Some objects—sounds, for instance—can't be displayed, so their icons will display automatically.)

V

Networking

the actual data rather than the icon. You can move this data or the icon around in your message, and you can give the icon a more useful name than the default name (Wave Sound).

When recipients get a message containing an icon, they must double-click the icon. This starts the application that created the OLE object. The object is then played or displayed.

> **Note**
>
> When you insert objects in Exchange messages, rename the icon, including text such as *Click here to play*, to make the icon's intended function obvious to the receiver. Rename the icon by right-clicking it, choosing Rename, and then typing the new name in the text box over the old name. Press Enter when finished.

Embedding an object or file in an Exchange message is an example of OLE at work in Microsoft Exchange.

Rich Text Format and Object Linking and Embedding functions are illustrated in the sample Exchange message shown in figure 24.14.

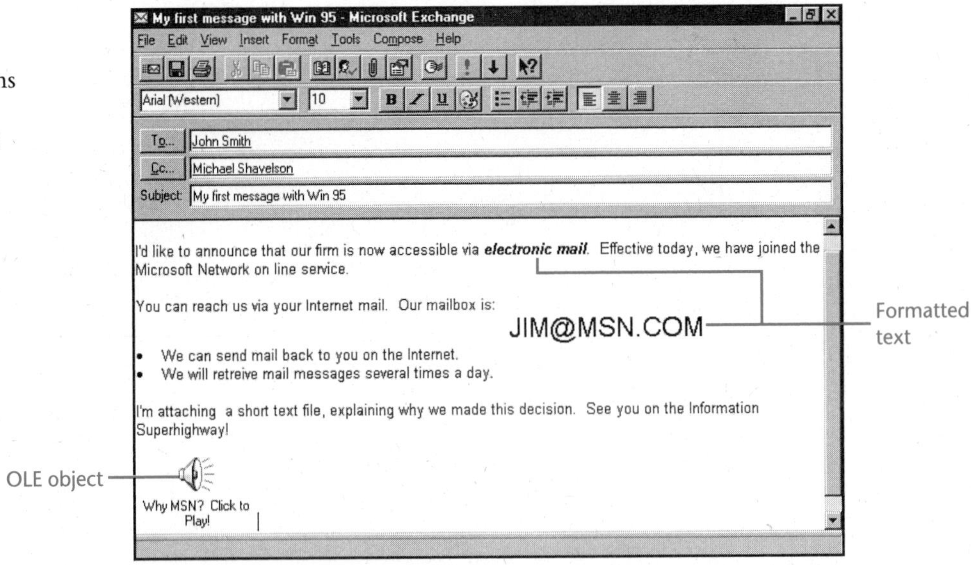

Fig. 24.14
This Exchange message contains Rich Text Formatting and an OLE object.

Finishing and Sending Your Mail Message

After you've written your message and added any formatting or OLE objects that you want, there are a few more options you may want to execute.

Choose <u>T</u>ools, <u>O</u>ptions, and then click the Send tab. This following list describes the items on the Send page:

- *Read Receipt and Delivery Receipt*. Requests that a receipt be sent back when the message has been delivered to or read by the recipient.

- *Sensitivity*. Sets sensitivity rankings to your message such as Normal, Personal, Private, and Confidential.

- *Importance Ranking*. Checks whether you want High, Normal, or Low priority for your message. You can always choose the High/Low icons to perform this task.

- *Save a Copy in 'Sent Items' Folder*. Saves a copy of the message in the Sent Items folder.

Close the Properties sheet. Now you are ready to send your message. Simply choose <u>F</u>ile, <u>S</u>end, or click the Send toolbar button.

Troubleshooting

I sent a Microsoft Mail message on my workgroup network, but the message wasn't received.

Make sure that only one Postoffice is installed for your workgroup and that the Postoffice is located in a shared folder that everyone in the workgroup can access.

Faxing a Quick Message or a File

There are several ways to send a fax. We'll begin by looking at how to send a very quick text message, or "fax" a file. This method lets you type a quick note (you won't be able to format the note) or transmit a file attached to the fax using the new BFT fax technology. If you want to do more—such as send a nicely formatted fax message, put pictures inside it, or fax from your word processor—see "Sending a More Complete Message," later in this chapter. In the main Exchange window, choose Co<u>m</u>pose, New Fa<u>x</u>. The Compose Fax Wizard appears.

▶ See "Working with Phone Dialer," p. 857

The Wizard first verifies the location from which you are sending the message, as shown in figure 24.15. If you have created other Dialing Locations and moved your portable computer to one of them, choose I'm Dialing From: and specify the new location. (Notice also that you can click on the check box at the bottom of the dialog box to tell the Wizard not to display this next time.) Then choose Next.

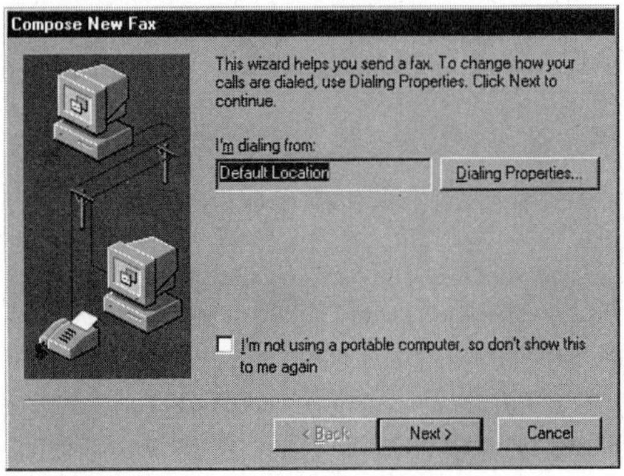

Fig. 24.15
The Compose
New Fax Wizard
confirms your
dialing location.

Addressing a Fax

▶ See "Working
with Your
Address Book,"
p. 757

The Wizard next prompts you for a recipient and offers to show you your Personal Address Book. If you want to choose a name from the Book, choose Address Book to display the Book (see fig. 24.16). Select a recipient and choose OK.

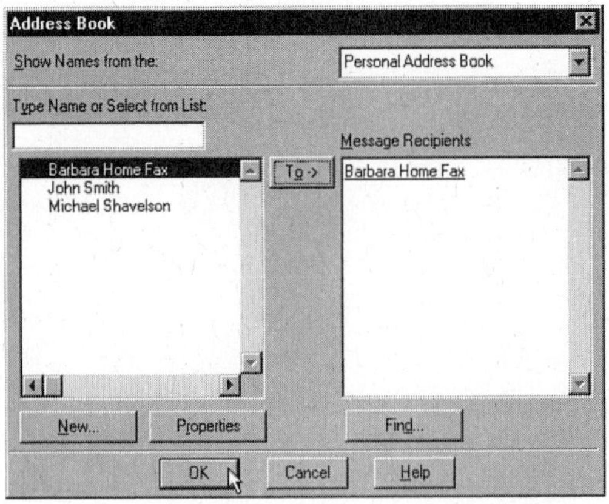

Fig. 24.16
Choose a fax
recipient from
your Personal
Address Book.

You also can just type the recipient information in the text boxes named To and Fax #, without using the Personal Address Book. Use the Add to List button if you want to send the fax to several different numbers. Select the first and choose Add to List; select the second, and choose Add to List; and so on. Choose Next when you are ready to continue.

Selecting a Cover Page

Next, the Wizard asks whether you want to send a cover page with your fax. Windows has the following built-in cover pages:

- Confidential!

- For your information

- Generic

- Urgent!

If you wish to use a cover page, select the page you want from the displayed list. Click on the No button if you don't want to send a cover page.

Options for Fax Transmission

There are a variety of fax options that you can set before you move on. Choose Options to display the Compose New Fax Wizard's Send Options dialog box (see fig. 24.17). Use these options to control when your fax is sent, the format you use to send it, the paper size, and the security applied. In this dialog box, you also can choose the Dialing Location or a cover page to send with your fax, as you did in the preceding section.

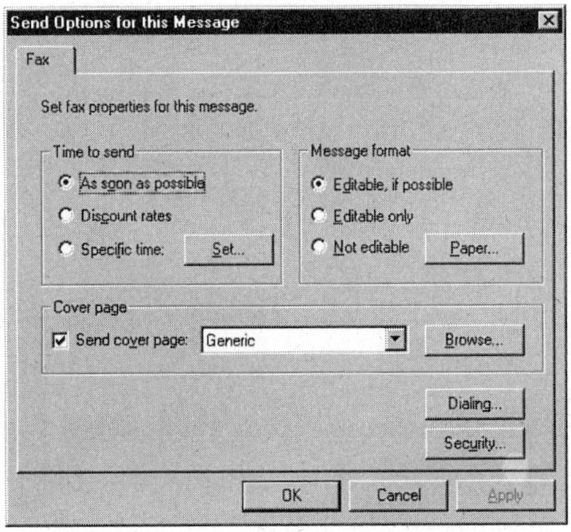

Tip

If you don't like any of the predesigned cover pages, use the Cover Page Editor to customize one of them or to create your own. See "Fax Cover Page Editor" later in this chapter.

V

Networking

Fig. 24.17
This dialog box lets you specify various fax sending options.

These seven options are available for fax transmissions:

- Message format
- Time to send
- Cover page
- Security
- Dialing
- Paper size and orientation
- Image quality

The following sections explain these options and how to use them.

Message Format

The Message Format option deals with a new technology called *editable faxes*. Editable faxes are something of a misnomer. A traditional fax is a single graphics image. Editable faxes are more like file transfers between computers, with the optional addition of a cover page. In fact, editable faxes are so much like file transfers that the technology behind them is called BFT for *Binary File Transfer.*

An editable fax can be edited by the recipient in the application that created it or in any application that can open its file type. If you send a document created in Microsoft Word for Windows (a DOC file), the recipient can open it in Word, WordPad, AmiPro, or WordPerfect, using import filters if necessary.

Sending editable faxes is very convenient because the receiver's options are increased. The recipient can view or print the fax as you sent it or edit the fax first.

You have three choices with the Message Format option:

- *Editable, If Possible.* Editable faxes can be exchanged only between computers using Microsoft Exchange and Microsoft Fax. This is the optimum way to send a fax.

  If the receiver is using a traditional fax machine, using editable format is not possible, so the fax is sent the old-fashioned way, as a graphic. If the recipient has a fax card in a computer but doesn't have Microsoft Exchange installed, the fax is delivered as a graphic. Exchange automatically determines which way to send the fax when it connects to the receiving machine.

> **Note**
>
> In the near future, other systems may implement BFT in a way that is compatible with the Microsoft system. When that happens, you will be able to exchange editable faxes with those systems, too.

■ *Editable Only*. This option works only for transfers between two Microsoft Exchange systems. If the receiving system is not a Microsoft Exchange system, the fax will not go through.

■ *Not Editable*. You use this option when you want all your faxes to be sent as a single graphic image in traditional fax format.

> **Tip**
>
> Editable faxes can be exchanged between Microsoft Exchange systems very quickly because the format used is much more compressed than the format that regular fax machines use.

Message Security

Choose the Security button to see the Security options. Security works only with editable faxes. You have two basic choices: None and Password-Protected. If you choose None, your fax can be read immediately upon receipt. Choosing Password-Protected requires the recipient to type the password that you applied to that fax transmission in order to see it.

> **Caution**
>
> If you activate password security on a fax that is sent to a non-Microsoft Exchange recipient or fax machine, your fax will not go through. Do not enable security on such faxes.

Time to Send

You can select a time to send your fax. Your choices are these:

■ As Soon as Possible

■ Discount Rates (at night and on weekends)

■ Specific Time (which you can choose)

Paper Size and Orientation, and Image Quality

Choose Paper to access the Paper Size and Orientation options. These options are usable with noneditable faxes. You can choose letter or legal paper. You also can choose Portrait (horizontal) or Landscape (vertical) page orientation.

V

Networking

You also can change the Image Quality in this dialog box. This determines the resolution at which Exchange prepares the fax. As with a laser printer, the higher the resolution, the crisper and cleaner your fax will be when printed.

Pick one of the following three Image Quality options, based on your need for a high-quality fax balanced against the additional time it takes to send the fax at a higher resolution:

- *Best Available.* This setting is recommended; it makes your fax look as good as possible on the receiving end.

- *Fine* (200 dots per inch, or dpi). Fine mode can result in incompatibilities if the receiving side doesn't support it. If it works with your recipient's hardware, it will look as good as possible.

- *Draft* (200 × 100 dpi). Draft mode looks coarser than Fine or Best Available but transmits faster.

When you've finished selecting all the options you want to use, choose Next, and the Compose New Fax Wizard moves on to let you enter the Subject of the fax and, if you wish, a note to put on the cover page.

Fax Subject and Note

When you've finished working with all the options described in the preceding sections and chosen Next, the Compose New Fax Wizard displays a dialog box where you can enter the subject of the fax and add a note to accompany your fax.

Type the subject in the Subject text box provided for you. Then, if you want to type a note to go along with your fax, type the note in the Note text box. Click in the Start Note on Cover Page check box to start your note on the cover page. If you leave the box unchecked, the note will start on a new page in your fax.

When you've finished with the subject and the note, choose Next.

Adding Files to Your Fax

◀ See "Windows Explorer for Powerful File Management," p. 27

You are able to add a file to be transmitted with your fax. After the Compose New Fax Wizard finishes with the fax subject and note (covered in the preceding section), it offers you a dialog box where you can select files to include with the fax.

If you want to include a file, choose Add File. You can use Explorer to browse and find the file you want to send with your fax.

When you've chosen the file or files to send with your fax, the Wizard shows the files you've selected in the Files to Send text box. When you've finished selecting files to add to your fax, choose Next.

Caution

The files you've chosen to send with the fax can be sent only if the fax is sent in editable format. If you use any other format, Microsoft Fax will not send the fax at all, not even the cover sheet.

For this reason, choose to add files to your fax only if you are certain that the recipient's system can support editable format, and that both your sending system and the recipient's receiving system are configured for editable faxing. (Configuring your fax in editable format was covered in "Options for Fax Transmission," earlier in this chapter.)

After you have added any files you want to send with your fax, it's ready to be sent. Choose Finish, and Microsoft Fax sends your fax.

V

Networking

Troubleshooting

I'm trying to send a fax, but it won't go through.

Do you hear the modem dial the fax? If not, make sure that you have a fax modem selected and that the settings are correct for your modem type. In Exchange, choose Tools, Services, Microsoft Fax, Properties; then click the Modem tab. You should see your fax modem displayed; if not, click Add to configure your modem.

If you can hear the modem dial the phone, but the modem disconnects just after dialing, repeat the preceding procedure. When you see your modem, select it and then click Properties. Make sure that the modem is set to allow enough time to connect after dialing (60 seconds is a good choice). This parameter often is set to one second by Windows for no apparent reason.

▶ See "Configuring Your Modem," p. 843

Sending a More Complete Message

There are a couple of other ways to send fax messages. First, you may want to use the same window you used to create an e-mail message. The only difference between creating a fax message and an e-mail message is in the way you address it. If you address the message to a Fax "address," the message will be a fax message.

▶ See "Adding Names to Your Address Book," p. 759

How do you address it to a fax address? Start by adding a fax address to your Address Book. Then use the To button in the New Message window to add this address to the To line of your message.

The advantage of sending a fax using this method is that you have all the New Message window's tools available. You can write a message, using all the text-editing capabilities. You can also attach files, and insert pictures into your fax.

The other way to fax is directly from an application. For instance, you could fax from your word processor. Many applications have a Send option on the File menu. If an application you want to use *doesn't* have such an option, you can "print" to the Microsoft Fax on FAX print driver.

Fax Cover Page Editor

The Cover Page Editor is a miniature word processor that allows you to work with graphics as well as Rich Text. Use the Fax Cover Page Editor to create your own custom-made cover pages or to modify one that is supplied with Exchange. You can do the following things with cover sheets that you create or edit:

- Insert data from the Personal Address Book into your cover page

- Paste items from the Clipboard into your cover page

- Import text or graphics (such as a logo) into your cover page

To use the Cover Page Editor, open the Start menu and choose Programs, Accessories, Fax; and then click Cover Page Editor. The Cover Page Editor program starts up.

When you first start the Cover Page Editor program, there is no cover page file loaded. From here, you can design a new cover page. If you start designing a new cover and then decide you want to start over again, choose File, New or click the New File icon on the toolbar.

To edit and customize an existing cover page, choose File, Open on the Cover Page Editor menu. Then select the cover page you want to work with.

The most useful feature of the Cover Page Editor is the ability to insert information from your Personal Address Book into your cover sheets. You do this by choosing Insert from the menu bar and then choosing from the options on that menu and successive submenus. Some of the kinds of information you can insert include:

- Recipient's or Sender's <u>N</u>ame

- Recipient's or Sender's <u>F</u>ax Number

- Recipient's or Sender's <u>C</u>ompany

Figure 24.18 shows a menu of all the different types of information you can insert from your Personal Address Book into your cover sheets.

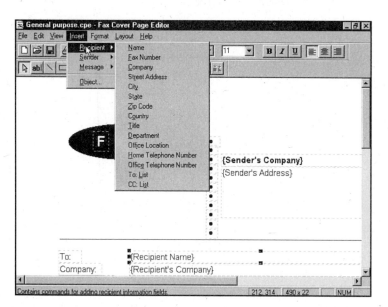

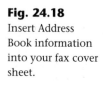

Fig. 24.18
Insert Address Book information into your fax cover sheet.

V

Networking

Viewing Received Mail and Faxes

To view and work with your received mail and faxes, you must have the Microsoft Exchange program running. This section explains how you can see your received mail and faxes and how to keep the Exchange window organized at the same time.

How Things Are Organized in Exchange

First, let's look at the kind of things we'll be organizing. Exchange contains, by default, four Personal Folders, each of which holds a different kind of message. The folder names show the function of the folders:

- *Inbox*. Where messages coming in to you are stored at first.

- *Deleted Items*. Where messages you've deleted from any of the other folders go.

- *Outbox.* Where messages you are sending are stored until you actually send them.

- *Sent Items.* Where messages you have sent are stored after they are successfully sent.

To display all four folders described above, choose View, Folders on the Exchange menu bar. You can also click the Show/Hide Folder List icon on the Exchange toolbar.

Tip

It is very useful to be able to see all four Exchange folders on your screen. If you display all four folders, you can tell what kind of message you're seeing.

When you choose to display the folder list, your Exchange window divides into two parts. On the left side of the window, you see the list of the four folders. When you highlight a folder on the left side of the Exchange window, the contents of that folder are displayed on the right side of the window. For example, if you highlight the Inbox folder, you then see the contents of your Inbox folder on the right side of the window. The contents of the Inbox folder are your received messages and faxes. If a message in the Inbox appears in **boldface**, the message is new and has not yet been read.

The types of messages that you can see in your Inbox depend on the Exchange services that you installed. If you installed Microsoft Fax, for example, you can see faxes. If you installed The Microsoft Network, you can see mail from MSN members and from the Internet. If you have Microsoft Mail installed for your workgroup network, you can see workgroup Mail messages. With Internet Mail installed, you can see mail from your own Internet mailbox. Figure 24.19 shows an Exchange Inbox with several types of messages.

Fig. 24.19

The Exchange Inbox showing received messages.

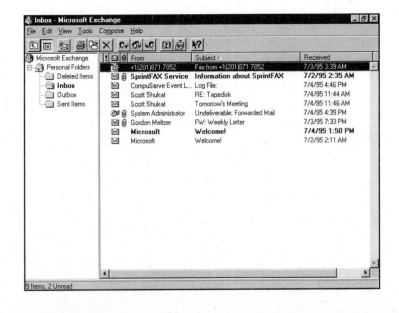

You can manipulate these messages in several ways. We examine how to manipulate and work with those received messages in the next sections.

Viewing Faxes

When you double-click on a normal, noneditable fax, the Fax Viewer opens and displays the fax. When you double-click a received editable fax, though, or a fax that has attached files, the message window opens. Inside this window, what you see depends on what you received. If you received a fax that the author created in the New Message window, you see exactly what the author saw; the text looks the same, any icons representing attached files look the same, and so on. If, however, you are receiving a fax from another application (sent using the File, Send option), you see an icon representing the fax. Double-click on this icon to open the application associated with that type of file. For instance, if you receive a DOC file, when you double-click on it the program associated with DOC opens: Word for Windows or WordPad.

> ### Note
>
> If you receive a fax that the author "printed" to the Microsoft Fax on FAX driver, it comes through as if it were a normal fax from a fax machine; double-clicking on the fax in the Inbox opens the Fax Viewer, not the Message window.

For instance, figure 24.20 shows a fax received from Notepad. Notice the Notepad icon in the message form to the left of the Notepad window. When the icon was double-clicked, Notepad opened and displayed the fax text. You can edit the text just as though you created the file on your own computer.

Troubleshooting

Someone is trying to send me a fax, but I'm not receiving it.

Make sure that your fax modem is installed. From the Exchange window, choose Tools, Services. Highlight Microsoft Fax and choose Properties. Then click the Modem tab and make sure your modem is shown in the list of Available fax modems. If it is, click the Properties tab and check to see whether the modem is set to answer automatically. If not, select the Answer After check box, and set the number of rings to wait before your fax modem answers calls.

V

Networking

Fig. 24.20
Viewing an editable fax in the application that created the fax.

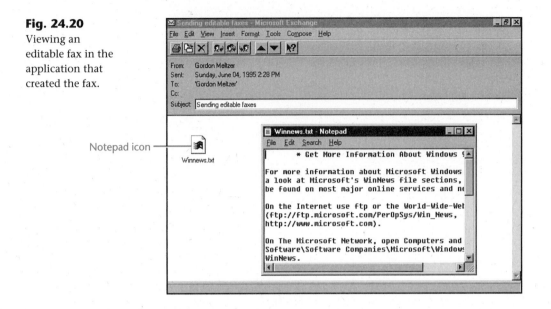

Notepad icon

Reading Mail Messages

To read a mail message, double-click the message in your Inbox. The standard message form opens, displaying the message. The Subject appears in the message form title bar. Figure 24.21 shows a received mail message.

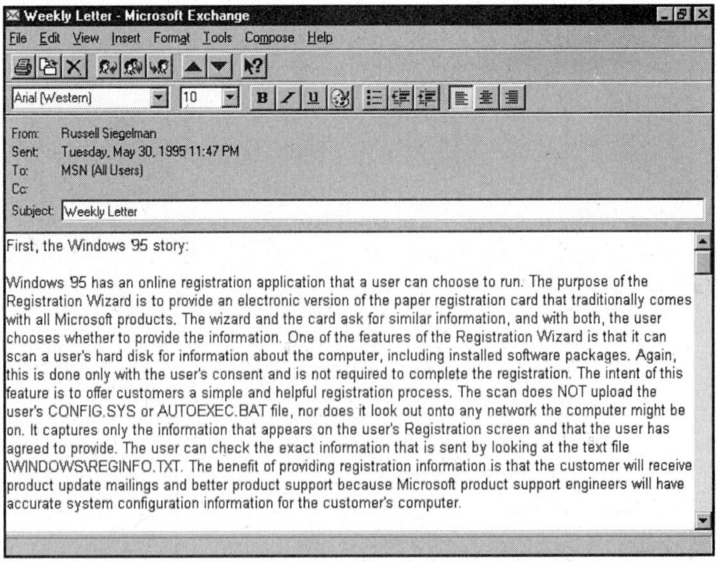

Fig. 24.21
A received mail message.

Editing, Replying to, and Forwarding Messages

The standard message form (refer to fig. 24.21) is an important place where a great deal of messaging action takes place. Notice that the form looks very much like a Windows word processor, complete with formatting toolbar. All the Rich Text tools are available, just as they are when you compose a message. In fact, the standard message form for composing a message is identical to the form for viewing, editing, replying, and forwarding mail messages.

While you're working with a received mail message, you can edit it if you want. Add text, files, or OLE objects. Then use the tools in the Compose menu to whisk your reply on its way (see fig. 24.22).

Sorting Messages

Above the messages in any of the Exchange folders are column headings. These headings indicate the following things:

- The importance of the message (according to the sender)

- The item type

- Whether files are attached to the message

- The sender's name

- The subject

- The date and time when the message was received

- The size of the message (in kilobytes)

Tip

As a shortcut to send, reply to, forward, or edit a message without displaying it first, highlight the message in your Inbox and then right-click.

V

Networking

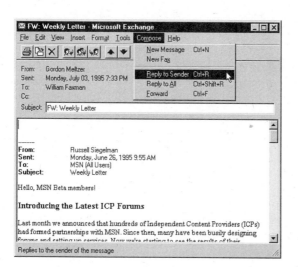

Fig. 24.22
The Compose menu has Reply and Forward options.

You can sort the messages in any of the Exchange folders in the following ways:

- Click the column heading to sort the messages in the folder by the value in that column, in ascending order.

- Right-click the column heading to change the sort from ascending to descending order.

- Choose <u>V</u>iew, <u>S</u>ort in the main Exchange window to access more elaborate sorting functions. Figure 24.23 shows these functions.

> **Note**
>
> The default From, Subject, Received, and Size columns in Exchange are only the tip of the iceberg. You can display many more columns if the column headings are relevant to your work. You'll find loads of column options, many of which are rather obscure. The options available depend on the message services you have installed, and what works for one service may not work for another.

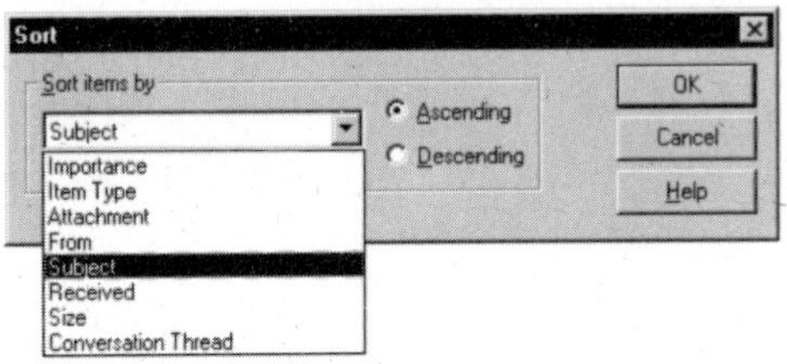

Fig. 24.23
Advanced options
you can use to sort
your messages.

Deleting Messages

When you finish working with a message in your Inbox and you want to delete it, highlight it and press the Delete key. It's removed from the Inbox, but it's not really deleted. Rather, it's transferred to the Deleted Items folder.

> **Caution**
>
> Deleting a message from the Deleted Items folder removes it completely from your system, not to the Recycle Bin.

Using the Message Finder

You can use Exchange to search through all your Exchange folders, looking for messages that match certain criteria. You can choose among many options, shown in the list below. You can find items matching

- The name of a sender you specify with the From option.

- A message you sent to a certain recipient with the Sent To option

- A message sent Directly to you or Copied (Cc) to you.

- A message with a particular subject by choosing the Subject option.

- Certain text in the message with the Message Body option.

To use Message Finder, choose Tools, Find in the main Exchange window. Then choose the search option you want to use. For example, if you're looking for messages sent to John Jones, enter **John Jones** in the Sent To text box. Exchange then displays a list of messages matching the criteria you have chosen.

Working with Your Address Book

Microsoft Exchange contains an Address Book feature. The Address Book is, logically enough, the place where you store contact information for the people with whom you correspond. The Address Book can help you keep track of how to contact your correspondents. You enter names into the Book and specify the type of communications to use (fax, Internet mail, Microsoft LAN Mail, and so forth). The Address Book makes sure that your messages are addressed properly.

◀ See "Installing and Configuring Microsoft Exchange," p. 727

The entire Address Book in Exchange is built from several different modular, building-block address books. The number of these building-block address books is determined by the communications services you installed when you set up Exchange.

Some of the services you installed come with their own building-block address book modules. For example, if you installed The Microsoft Network online service, a building-block address book for MSN was installed in your Address Book. The MSN Address Book is configured by Microsoft to contain the names and e-mail addresses of all the members of The Microsoft Network.

V

Networking

Microsoft Mail for your workgroup LAN has a building-block address book, built by the network administrator, that is part of your Exchange Address Book. In Exchange, the Microsoft Mail Address Book is called Postoffice Address List.

The final module making up your Address Book is called the Personal Address Book. In it you can store the names and addresses you use most often. You can transfer names into your Personal Address Book from the other address books. For instance, you could copy a name from the MSN address book to the Personal Address Book. Or you can add new names and addresses to your Personal Address Book.

The Address Book also has options that you can use to control how it displays the names you store.

Now, to display and work with the Address Book from the Microsoft Exchange window, choose Tools, Address Book; or press Ctrl+Shift+B.

Setting Display Preferences

How do you like to look for people's names in a list—by first names or by last names? Exchange gives you the flexibility to display names either way. By default, names are displayed with the first name followed by the last name (John Jones). If, however, you have a rather long list or know several men called John, you may find viewing the list sorted by last names to be faster.

You can use the Personal Address Book Properties settings to change the order in which first and last names are displayed. To change the order, follow these steps:

1. From the Exchange main window, choose Tools, Address Book. The Address Book opens.

2. Select Personal Address Book from the Show Names From The drop-down list. The names in your Personal Address Book display.

3. Choose Tools, Options. The Addressing dialog box appears.

4. In the When Sending Mail list, highlight Personal Address Book.

5. Click Properties. The Personal Address Book Properties sheet appears.

6. Now you can choose to show names by first name or last name. Click First Name or Last Name on the Personal Address Book page, as shown in figure 24.24.

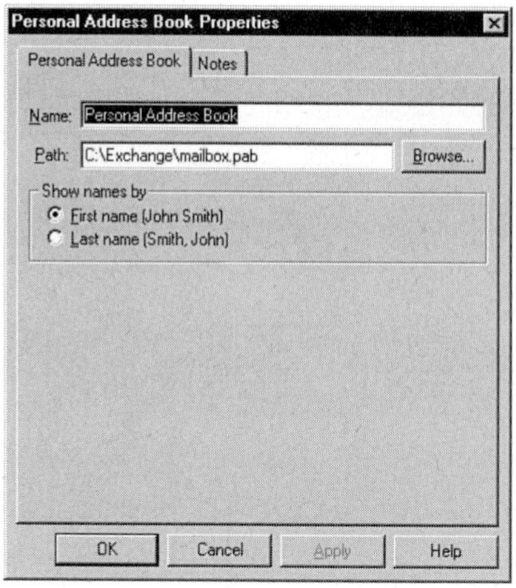

Fig. 24.24
You use this
Properties sheet
to select how to
display names in
the Personal
Address Book.

7. You also can give the Personal Address Book a more descriptive name. You might want to call it Business Contacts, for example. Type the name you want to use for the Personal Address Book in the Name text box.

8. Click the Notes tab and type, in the text box provided, any information you wish to record about your Personal Address Book.

Adding Names to Your Address Book

You want to use Exchange as the powerful communications tool it can be. Part of harnessing the power of Exchange is as simple as keeping a well-organized Address Book so that you have all the mail addresses and fax numbers you need conveniently at hand. This section focuses on the procedure for putting new names in the address book.

1. Display the Address Book by choosing Tools, Address Book. You also can click the Address Book button on the toolbar.

2. In the Show Names From The drop-down list, select Personal Address Book.

3. Choose File, New Entry. You can also choose the New Entry button on the toolbar. The New Entry dialog box appears (see fig. 24.25).

4. Select the type of address you want to add to your Personal Address Book. In this example, we're adding a Microsoft Fax entry to the Book. Then choose OK. The New Fax Properties sheet appears.

Fig. 24.25

The power of Exchange is evident in the range of address types to which you can send messages.

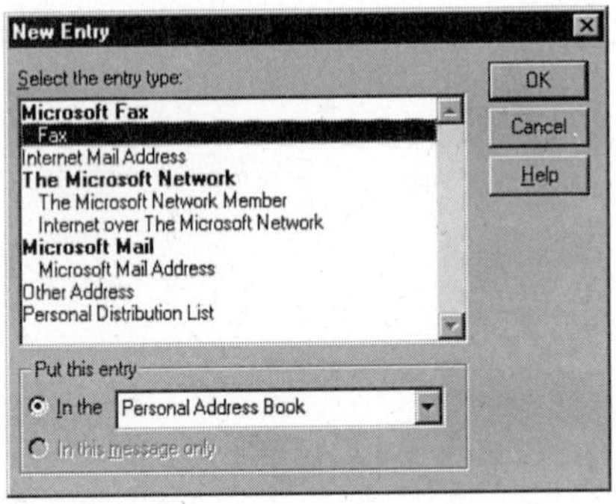

5. The Properties sheet that you see in figure 24.26 has text boxes for all the names and numbers required to reach your recipient. Type the pertinent information in each page. Then choose OK. The Properties sheet closes, and the new entry appears in your Address Book.

Fig. 24.26

The New Fax Properties sheet is typical of the Properties sheets you fill out when adding entries to your Address Book.

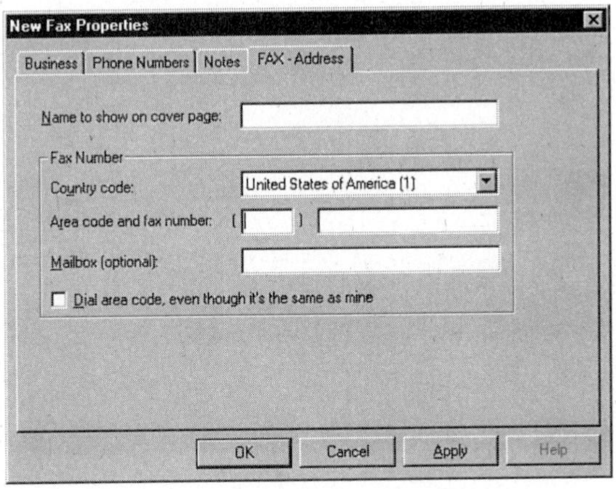

You follow the same steps as those for a Microsoft Fax entry to add different types of addresses, like Microsoft Network addresses or Internet Mail addresses.

The difference between adding the fax address we illustrated and the other possible address types is that after you select the entry type from the New Entry dialog box (step 4 above), the New Properties sheet that appears will be different.

For example, if you choose to add a Microsoft Mail address to your Address Book, the New Mail Properties sheet has a space for the recipient's mailbox, Postoffice, and Workgroup Network name, instead of a space for a fax number. Similarly, a Microsoft Network address needs an MSN Member ID, and an Internet Mail address needs a mailbox name in the form of name@domain.

Adding Groups to Your Address Book

You may want to send a message to a group of recipients. To do this conveniently, create a Personal Distribution List. Once you have a Personal Distribution List, you only have to create a message once, and you can send it to all the members of the list with one click.

Follow these steps to create your Personal Distribution List:

1. Display the Address Book by choosing <u>T</u>ools, <u>A</u>ddress Book.

2. Choose <u>F</u>ile, New <u>E</u>ntry. The New Entry dialog box appears (refer to fig. 24.25). The New Entry dialog box contains a scrolling list of address types. You can view all the types by scrolling through the list.

3. The last entry in the scrolling list is the Personal Distribution List entry type. Highlight Personal Distribution List at the bottom of the list.

4. In this example, we're putting our Personal Distribution List in our Personal Address Book. At the bottom of the New Entry dialog box is a setting which says Put This Entry <u>I</u>n The. Make sure Personal Address Book shows in the text box. If it doesn't, click the down arrow and scroll to select Personal Address Book.

5. Choose OK. The New Personal Distribution List Properties sheet appears.

6. Name your list. Type the name for your list in the Name text box. In this example, we'll name our Personal Distribution List **Staff Members on Project X**.

7. If you want to make some notes about the list, click the Notes tab and type your comments in the text box. You might use this space to document how the group members were chosen. You can enter anything that's useful in this text box.

8. Click the Distribution List tab.

V

Networking

9. Build the Distribution List now. You do this by adding members to the list. Choose Add/Remove <u>M</u>embers. A dialog box appears, titled Edit Members of (name of your Distribution List).

10. Perhaps one of the people you want to add to the Personal Distribution List is already in another of your building-block address books. If so, choose the proper address book by selecting it from the scrolling list, which is shown in <u>S</u>how Names From The. When you choose an address book in <u>S</u>how Names From The, all the address entries in that address book become visible. In this example, we'll choose to <u>S</u>how Names from The Microsoft Network. Next, we'll add some addresses from The Microsoft Network online service to our Personal Distribution List.

> **Note**
>
> You can only use The Microsoft Network address book while online. If you select this address book while offline, the Connect dialog box appears so you can log on.

11. Select The Microsoft Network members you want to add to your Personal Distribution List. The best way to do this is to highlight the names, one at a time (hold the Ctrl key and click on each one that you want to add), and then choose <u>M</u>embers. The names you've highlighted become members of your Personal Distribution List (see fig. 24.27).

To add other names from existing address books, select <u>S</u>how Names From The, and select the next address book from the scrolling list. Then repeat the steps above from step 10.

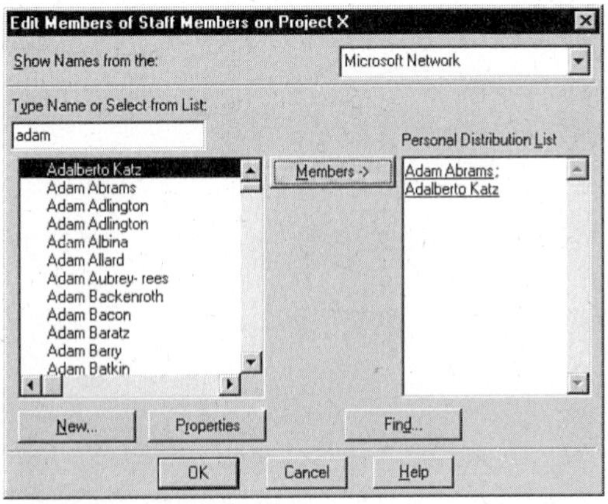

Fig. 24.27
The Edit Members dialog box has two Microsoft Network member names added to the Personal Distribution List.

You also can put people on your Personal Distribution List who are not already in any of your address books. However, you have to put that person into your Personal Address Book first.

◀ See "Adding Names to Your Address Book," p. 759

Choose New. Then follow the steps discussed earlier for adding a name to your Personal Address Book. Once you've made the addition to the book, that name is added to the Personal Distribution List automatically. When you are finished adding members to your Personal Distribution List, choose OK.

Your Personal Distribution List appears in your Personal Address Book, along with any individual addresses you have stored there. By choosing the list as a recipient in a message you create, the message is sent to all members of the Personal Distribution List.

Working with User Profiles in Exchange

When you installed Exchange, you worked with the Inbox Setup Wizard. You gave the Wizard information about yourself, and you installed one or more communications services in Exchange. You also gave the Wizard information about the communications services you chose, such as User ID and Mailbox Name.

When you finished installing Exchange, the Wizard saved all the information you gave it. The Wizard saved your information in something called a *User Profile*.

The User Profile in Exchange is where all your personal information and the information on all your communications services are stored. The name of the User Profile created by the Wizard for you is MS Exchange Settings. MS Exchange Settings becomes the default User Profile for your computer.

Tip

You can add as many User Profiles as you need by following the steps in this section.

This default profile is fine for one user. If your computer has more than one user, however, you may want to create a special User Profile for everyone who uses your machine.

Suppose that you share a computer with a coworker who works the second shift. If you don't use The Microsoft Network but your coworker does, they may want to set up their own User Profile. Then they can configure and personalize Exchange to suit their needs without disturbing the settings that you use during your shift.

V

Networking

Adding Multiple User Profiles in Exchange

To create an additional User Profile, follow these steps:

1. Open the Start menu and choose Settings, Control Panel.

2. In Control Panel, double-click the Mail and Fax icon.

3. Choose Show Profiles. You see the list of existing Exchange profiles.

4. Choose Add to create a new user profile. The Inbox Setup Wizard starts to run.

5. Select the communications services that you want to use with the new User Profile you're creating (see fig. 24.28). Then choose Next.

6. Now give a name to your new User Profile. Type the name in the Profile Name text box (see fig. 24.29). Then choose Next.

◀ See "Installing and Configuring Microsoft Exchange," p. 727

7. You then work with the Wizard to set up the communications services you chose in the step above. This works the same way as it did when you first installed Exchange.

When you've finished with the Inbox Setup Wizard, your new User Profile will be set up for use. Your screen returns to the Microsoft Exchange Profiles dialog box you saw in step 3. You see your new User Profile added to the list of profiles. Figure 24.30 shows Sheila's Exchange Settings, along with the default profile, MS Exchange Settings.

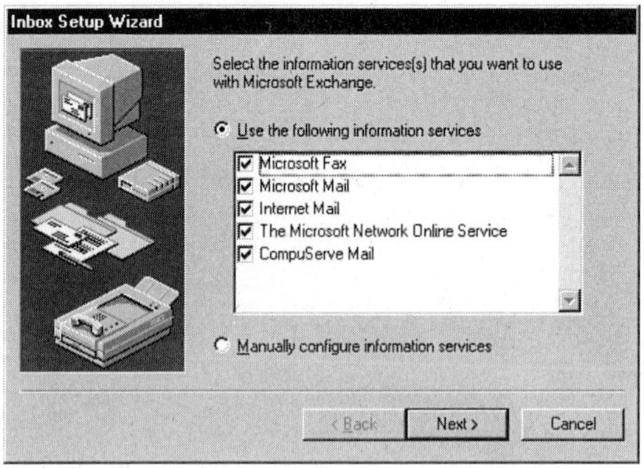

Fig. 24.28
Choose the services to use with your new User Profile

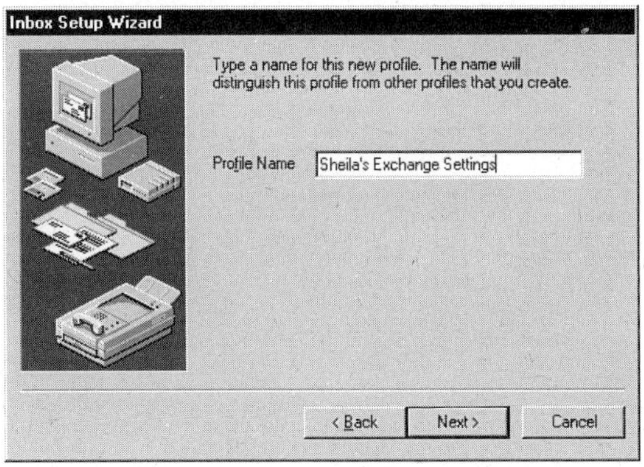

Fig. 24.29
In this example,
we called the
new User Profile
**Sheila's Ex-
change Settings**.

Fig. 24.30
Your new User
Profile has been
added to
Exchange.

V

Networking

Note

Notice that, in the Microsoft Exchange Profiles dialog box shown in figure 24.30, there is a setting called When Starting Microsoft Exchange, Use This Profile. Ignore this setting for now. We'll choose what profile to use when starting Exchange in the next series of steps.

When you have more than one User Profile installed, you'll want to choose which profile to use when you run Exchange. You'll want Exchange to ask you which profile to use each time Exchange starts. Follow these steps to set up Exchange so that it asks which User Profile to use:

1. Start Microsoft Exchange. You can do this by double-clicking the Inbox icon on your desktop.

2. Choose Tools, Options. The Options dialog box appears.

3. In the When Starting Microsoft Exchange area of the General page, check the Prompt for a Profile To Be Used box (see fig. 24.31).

4. Choose OK.

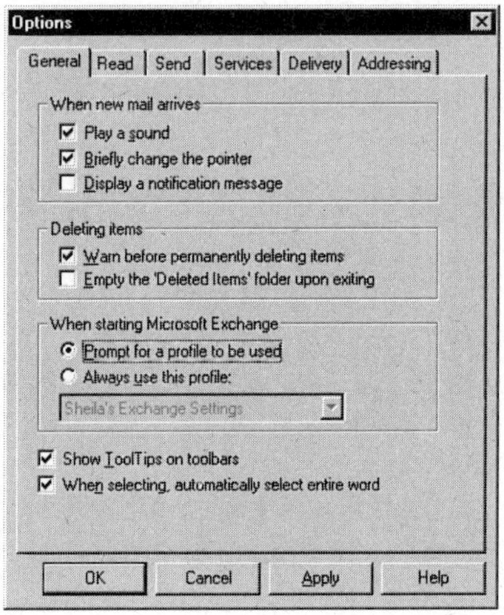

Fig. 24.31
Setting up Exchange so it prompts you for the User Profile to use when you start Exchange.

When you tell Exchange to prompt you for a User Profile, you are ensuring that each user of your computer has the opportunity to pick their own Exchange User Profile.

Troubleshooting

I want to use Microsoft Fax, The Microsoft Network, and Microsoft Mail, but I don't see any references to those services in my Exchange menus.

Install the desired services in Microsoft Exchange. In the main Exchange window, choose Tools, Services, choose Add, and select the desired service from the list. A Wizard guides you in setting up the service, if necessary.

> **Note**
>
> If you have set up your computer with a different session profile for each user—so the user has to log on when Windows starts—you can ensure that each person's profile starts automatically. Each user should log on to Windows; open Exchange; choose Tools, Options; then click on the Always Use This Profile option button and select the appropriate profile.

Enabling Mail and Message Security

Normally, when you run Exchange, your mail folders display immediately in the Exchange window. You can see and work with Inbox, Deleted Items, Outbox, and Sent Items as soon as Exchange is running. This means that anyone who starts Exchange on your computer can access all your mail, in the four folders just listed.

To make your mail secure, you must set a password for access to your mailbox so that nobody else can open your mailbox and read or work with your messages without your permission. Follow these steps to set up password security for your mail folders:

1. With Exchange running, choose Tools, Options. The Options dialog box appears.

2. Click the Services tab, highlight Personal Folders, and choose Properties.

3. When the Personal Folders Properties sheet appears, choose Change Password. The Microsoft Personal Folders dialog box opens (see fig. 24.32).

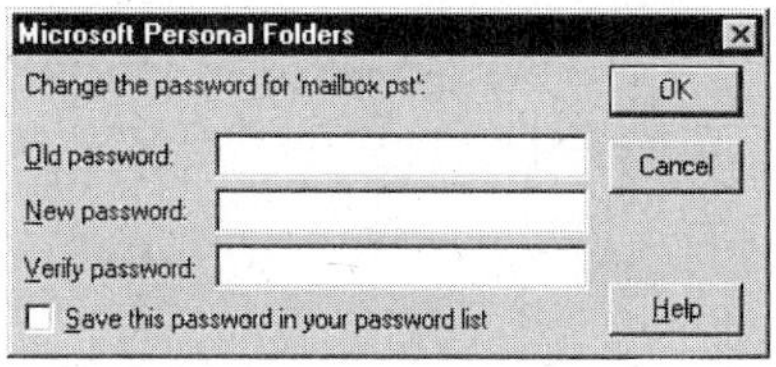

Fig. 24.32
Set a password for your mail folders for security.

4. Enter the password of your choice in the New Password text box. Then repeat the password in the Verify Password text box.

5. Choose OK.

Tip
Don't select <u>S</u>ave
This Password in
Your Password
List, unless you've
set up Windows
for different users
and each user has
to log on using a
password. If you
do, you lose pass-
word security
because Windows
enters the pass-
word for you
whenever you
start Exchange.

The next time you run Exchange, you have to enter your password to see the contents of your mail folders.

> **Caution**
>
> If you forget your mailbox password, you cannot access the contents of your mailbox again. You have to delete your Personal Folders and set up Exchange again.

You may want to get rid of your mailbox password. To do this, follow steps 1 and 2. Then in step 3, type your current password in the <u>O</u>ld Password text box. Leave <u>N</u>ew Password and <u>V</u>erify Password blank. This means that you have changed back to having no password security for your mailbox folders. Then choose OK.

Working with the Workgroup Postoffice

Microsoft Mail requires that one of the computers on the workgroup network be set up as a Postoffice. This is usually a job for the network administrator or manager. If this is your function, this section is important for you.

The Postoffice machine is the place where all mail messages are stored for the workgroup. You can choose your machine for Postoffice duties or select another.

The Postoffice must be installed somewhere on the network in a shared folder that all members of the workgroup can access. Windows 95 comes with the Postoffice and a Wizard that helps you install it.

You have to make the following decisions about your Postoffice:

- Which machine to install the Postoffice on (choose a machine that has a shared folder that everyone in the workgroup can access)

- Who will manage and maintain the Postoffice

If you are sure that there is no Postoffice installed on your Workgroup LAN yet, and if you're sure that you are the right person to set it up, the process is simple.

Installing the Workgroup Postoffice

When you are ready to install the Postoffice, follow these steps:

1. Open the Start menu and choose Settings, Control Panel.

2. Double-click the Microsoft Mail Postoffice icon.

3. Select Create a New Workgroup Postoffice, as shown in figure 24.33. Then choose Next.

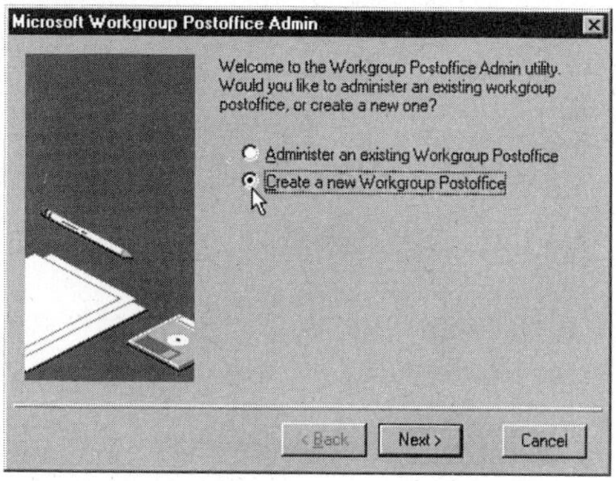

Fig. 24.33

Use the Microsoft Workgroup Postoffice Admin utility to create a new Workgroup Postoffice.

4. Type the full path to the folder you've chosen for the Postoffice in the Postoffice Location text box. Remember, this needs to be a shared folder that everyone on the Workgroup LAN can access. You'll probably want to use the Browse button to find the folder.

   ▶ See "Creating Network Resources," p. 796

5. Then choose Next. The folder you've selected for the Postoffice displays for your approval. Choose Next again.

6. The next dialog box that appears requests administration details. Type your name in the Name text box, your mailbox name in the Mailbox text box, and your mail password in the Password text box (see fig. 24.34). Choose OK.

7. You'll see a message box reminding you to allow other users access to the Postoffice—which can be done from Windows Explorer. Choose OK. You have finished creating your Postoffice.

V

Networking

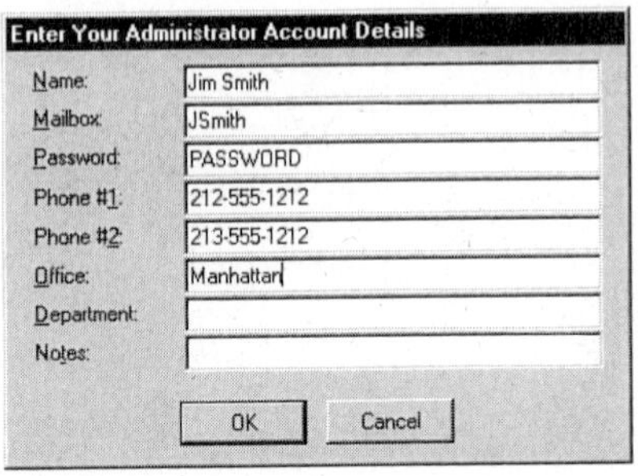

Fig. 24.34

You use this dialog box to fill out Postoffice Administrator information.

> **Note**
>
> The other text boxes shown in the figure may be filled in as you prefer, but are not required to set up the Postoffice.

> **Caution**
>
> Create only one Postoffice on your workgroup network. If you create more than one, the mail system won't work properly.

Chapter 25

Working with Network Printers

by William S. Holderby

In Chapter 6, "Controlling Printers," you learned the basics of installing and working with printers—or at least those attached directly to your computer. Of course, not all printers are connected exclusively to your PC. In many workplaces, a local area network has multiple printer connections. Although Windows 95 makes network printers appear to operate as local printers, network printing may seem more complex. Local printers usually remain attached to the same port and are under your control. Network printers can change location and are controlled by other users or a network administrator. If problems arise when you are using a network printer, troubleshooting is much easier if you understand some of the differences between local and network printing.

This chapter takes printing a step further and discusses printing issues from a network perspective. Specifically, you learn how to:

- Print to network printers
- Optimize print resources
- Manage print files
- Solve common network printing problems
- Use custom Printer Drivers and utilities

Examining Windows 95's New Network Printing Features

Windows 95 incorporates several new features and enhancements that markedly improve network printing. These new features include the following:

- *Network Point and Print* enables users to copy printer drivers automatically from network print servers to their local PC. This reduces the time it takes to set up a new printer and eliminates the need to find and copy vendor driver software. This feature also eliminates the chance of configuring the wrong printer. You can access Network Point and Print from network servers running Windows 95, Windows NT Advanced Server, Windows NT Workstation, Windows for Workgroups 3.11, or Novell NetWare.

- *Windows 95's Network Neighborhood* provides tools to configure print resources quickly on Windows 95, Windows NT, and Novell servers. You can use this feature to find, use, and manage print jobs on printers interfacing any of these devices. Formerly, the user had to memorize locations and complex network commands. Network Neighborhood virtually eliminates this need through its new network user interface.

- *Compatibility with NetWare's PSERVER* enables you to access print jobs from NetWare's print spooler.

- *Deferred printing* provides you with the ability to save printouts until you reattach your printer. Deferred printing automatically stores print jobs after you detach your PC from the network, and automatically restarts them after you reestablish the connection.

- *Printer Driver* provides command resources to remotely stop, hold, cancel, or restart print jobs located on shared printers.

Understanding Network Printing

Before delving too deeply into the nuts and bolts of network printing, you first must become familiar with the terminology you will see frequently in this discussion:

- *LAN Administrators* provide a management function to the local area network by assisting users and directing what resources are available on the network.

- *Systems policies* are software controls that are created by LAN Administrators to define what users can and cannot do on their desktops and the network. For example, you might use a system policy to restrict access to certain network programs.

- A *client* is a workstation that uses the services of any network server that can include server-based software systems, printers, and mass storage devices.

- *Print queues* contain print jobs that are not immediately printed. A queue holds the job until the printer is ready to print.

- *Windows Redirector* is the software module contained in the Windows network architecture that identifies software references to network devices and connects those devices to the workstation through the network.

- *Network resources* are software and hardware features that are available from servers and other workstations on the LAN. Resources such as shared drivers and server-based programs are available for network users.

- *Printing resources* are LAN resources that are dedicated to serving network users for the purpose of printing. These include shared printers, network printers, and print queues.

- *Print servers* service the printing needs of network clients.

Three network printer types are found on most networks:

- Printers attached to the network through a Microsoft Network compatible server.

- Printers connected to a server running a compatible network operating system other than Windows, such as Novell NetWare and Banyan VINES.

- Printers directly attached to a network through a special printer network interface card (NIC).

Printing from Applications

Printing to network printers from within applications requires the same commands and menu items that you use to print locally. Windows handles the network communications and creates a Printer Driver for each attached

V

Networking

network printer. As with local printers, you can access network printer configuration information in the Printer Properties sheet. In this sheet, you can change the network printer's properties for default or specific printing tasks.

◀ See "Options
for Your
Printer," p. 187

> ### Caution
>
> Remember that other users can change a network printer configuration. Before printing, check all important print settings for this printer on your PC, including paper orientation and resolution. Don't assume that they are already set the way that you want them. Printing mistakes on network printers take extra time to recover.

When applications create a print file, they send a print stream to the network server through the Windows 95 Network Redirector. A print file contains spooled printer data and commands that are being temporarily stored prior to printing. The Network Redirector, which is part of Windows 95 network architecture, determines whether the print stream destination is a local printer. A print stream is the data that is being sent to a printer containing both printable and unprintable characters. Unprintable characters are used to control the printer. It also uses Windows network drivers to locate the designated printer.

Drag-and-Drop Printing

◀ See "Drag-and-
Drop Printing
from the Desk-
top," p. 178

To perform drag-and-drop printing, you use the same procedure as you do for local printing. Remember, however, that drag-and-drop printing sends the print job to the system's default printer. If the selected printer is not the default printer, Windows will ask you to make it the default printer prior to printing the file. When initially connecting your PC to a network, this printer might not be available. Be sure to log in to the network and verify the printer's network connection before setting it as the default printer (unless you plan to use deferred printing with your default printer in which case anything you print is saved by Windows until the printer becomes available).

Installing a Network Printer

Network printers are usually installed in one of two ways:

■ The *Add Printer Wizard* from the Printers folder can be used for any printer connected to the network. The installation of a network printer doesn't change the printer, it simply loads an appropriate printer driver on your PC. Windows 95 uses that driver during printing.

■ *Point and Print installation* from the desktop can be used for printers attached to servers that are Microsoft Client compatible.

Using the Add Printer Wizard

Installing a network printer involves the same Add Printer Wizard as the local printer installation described in Chapter 6, "Controlling Printers." However, there are some differences.

When you configure a local printer, the location of your cable to a specific printer port determines the port's selection. The network printer, on the other hand, requires a network resource name. In the example shown in figure 25.1, an HP 1200 CPS print named HP1200CPS is located on the AlphaNT server.

◀ See "Connecting Windows 95 to a Novell Network," p. 673

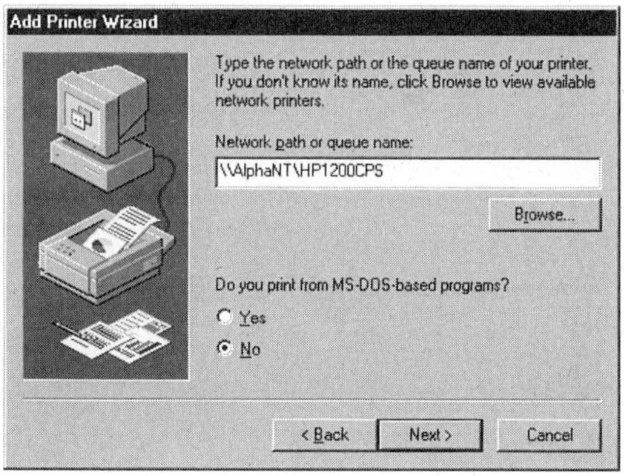

Fig. 25.1
The Add Printer Wizard requires a network address for printer installation.

If you're not sure of the correct address for the network printer, you can choose to browse the network. Browsing enables you to check which network printers are currently available. Some servers require passwords to view what network resources they have available. If you desire access to a server, but do not know the password, contact your LAN Administrator.

◀ See "Setting Up a Windows 95 Peer-to-Peer Network," p. 617

To configure a network printer, you need to know its make and model. You can get this information from your network administrator. Microsoft network servers enable you to install printer drivers quickly.

To set up a network printer with the Add Printer Wizard, follow these steps:

1. Choose Start, Settings, Printers, then double-click on the Add Printer folder.

2. From the first Add Printer Wizard screen, click the Next button. Windows 95 then displays the next Wizard screen, which asks you to decide if you are adding a Network or a Local Printer.

3. Choose the Network Printer option to connect your PC to a network printer. Choose the Next button located at the bottom of the window.

4. Next, you must identify the network path to the printer (refer to fig. 25.1). Select the Browse button to view the Network Neighborhood.

5. The Network Neighborhood displays a list of all servers and workstations connected to your network. Find the appropriate printer and select it. Then choose the Next button.

   The Wizard accesses the selected printer and determines whether its server can download an appropriate printer driver. If a driver is available, the Wizard automatically loads the driver and sets a default configuration for the printer. If a driver is not available, the Wizard asks you to specify the printer's make and model.

Tip

Use the Add Printer Wizard again if you have difficulty connecting to a printer using the Point and Print procedure.

6. Select the manufacturer and printer model by scrolling the Wizard screen lists; then click Next. The screen now offers a default name for your printer. The name should adequately describe the printer for later identification.

7. The Wizard asks whether you want this printer to be your default printer; select Yes or No. Follow this decision by selecting the Next control.

8. The final wizard screen provides the controls to print a test page on the printer you just installed. You can print the test page by selecting Yes; or select No to not print the test page. As a general rule, you should always print a test page to verify the successful completion of the Add a Printer Wizard.

9. Click Finish.

Using Point and Print

Point and Print enables a workstation user to quickly connect to and use a printer shared on another Windows 95 workstation, a Windows NT

Advanced Server, or a Novell NetWare server. When first connecting to the shared printer, Windows 95 automatically copies and installs the correct driver for the shared printer from the server.

1. Choose the Network Neighborhood icon on the Windows desktop.

2. Choose the Entire Network icon. Windows displays all of the servers attached to your network.

3. Choose the Server that supports the printer you want to attach to your workstation. If you don't know which Server that is, ask the LAN Administrator or select each server in sequence until you find the name of the appropriate printer or print queue. Windows displays the server's screen showing its shared resources.

4. Drag a network printer icon from a server's window and drop it on the desktop. You receive a diagnostic message that says You cannot move or copy this item to this location. Do you want to create a shortcut to the item instead? Answer Y̲es. Windows creates a shortcut icon and drops it on the desktop.

5. Drag a document from a local folder and drop it on the New Printer folder icon. Windows displays an information screen such as that shown in figure 25.2. If you select Y̲es, Windows automatically connects to the printer and downloads the appropriate printer driver from the network printer's server. After loading and configuring the driver, Windows 95 begins printing to the network printer.

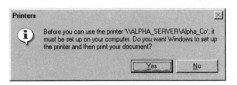

Fig. 25.2

If the printer driver is not loaded when you use Point and Print, Windows lets you install the driver on the fly.

Printing on a NetWare Network

To use a NetWare print queue, you must be logged onto a NetWare server. Windows 95 utilizes a PSERVER that can redirect print jobs from NetWare print queues to printers connected to Windows 95 workstations. In addition to the PSERVER capability, your PC must also use the Microsoft Client for NetWare Networks. Windows 95 automatically adapts to NetWare's security for printer and print queue access.

> **Note**
>
> The network administrator can control how NetWare shares printers. If the adminis-trator uses a *policy file* to disable print sharing, the network cannot access the printers. A policy file contains a set of commands that are used by your network administrator to set rules for the operation and configuration of Windows on a net-work. When entering a new network, check with your network administrator for a sharing policy before attempting to configure shared printing.

NetWare Print Servers

Windows 95 provides printer services for NetWare networks, including a 32-bit PSERVER capability. PSERVER connects NetWare queues to printers shared by Windows 95 PCs. A NetWare print queue contains all the jobs waiting (queued) for a specific printer.

To connect your workstation to a Novell NetWare print server, follow these steps:

1. Choose the Network Neighborhood icon on the desktop. Notice that all servers (Microsoft and NetWare) appear in the Network Neighborhood screen. This screen displays an icon for each network drive currently attached to your system.

2. If you want to attach your workstation to a NetWare printer, choose the appropriate server by double-clicking its icon. The server dialog box opens and displays the shared directories, files, and print queues that are attached to the selected server.

3. Select the appropriate print queue. Choose File, Print and then select the Capture Printer Port control button.

4. The Capture Printer Port dialog box contains the names of currently unattached LPT ports. Select the Reconnect at Logon check box if you want to maintain this connection and have it attached when you re-start Windows. Then click OK to attach this print queue to your PC.

   Capturing the printer port attaches the NetWare print queue to the specified port. It does not, however, attach the associated printer to the desktop.

5. To attach the printer associated with that print queue, choose File, Create Shortcut. Windows displays a message warning that you cannot

configure a shortcut printer icon in the Create Shortcut dialog box, but that you can create the icon on the desktop. Click Yes to create the icon.

6. Double-click the printer icon. Windows asks whether you want to set up a printer. Choose Yes.

7. Windows then displays the Add Printer Wizard. Follow the Wizard to finish installing an appropriate printer for the desktop.

> **Note**
>
> You must know the type of printer attached to this print queue. This procedure is different than installing a printer attached to a Microsoft print server.

After configuring the printer, you can print by using the Point and Print procedure on the desktop.

Microsoft Client for NetWare

Windows 95 Microsoft Client for NetWare Networks enables you to connect to new or existing NetWare servers to send files and interact with server-based software. With Microsoft Client for NetWare Networks, you can browse and queue your print jobs using either the Windows 95 network user interface or existing Novell NetWare utilities. The Microsoft Client for NetWare interfaces work equally well with both NetWare 3.x and 4.x servers.

To use Microsoft Client for NetWare Networks, follow these steps:

1. Choose File, Print.

2. Your application might ask you to choose a destination printer. Most applications display a list of attached printers from which you can choose. If so, choose an appropriate network printer. Then choose OK.

   The Windows Redirector accepts the print stream and sends it to the selected printer over the network. Information concerning the status of the printing process automatically returns to you.

3. To monitor the status of your print job on a network printer, open the printer's folder and double-click the appropriate icon. The printer's local Printer Driver opens a status dialog box listing all print jobs in the printer's queue.

V

Networking

Point and Print for NetWare Print Queues

You can enable a Point and Print procedure to use a NetWare-compatible client as a destination. To do so, use the Point and Print procedure discussed earlier.

To print from the desktop to a network printer, follow these steps:

1. Open the folder that contains the document you want to print.

2. Select a document. Hold down the left mouse button and drag the selected document to the network printer's icon on your desktop. The document now appears as an outline.

3. Release the outlined document icon over the printer's icon. Windows 95 interprets the file type, starts the application associated with the file, commands the application to print the document, redirects the print job to the selected printer, and shuts down the application when the print job finishes.

> ### Note
>
> Before Windows can perform the desktop printing operation, you must associate the document with an installed application. If the document is not associated with such an application, Windows displays a message box informing you that it cannot perform the printing task.

Printing on a Microsoft Network

To share files and printers on Microsoft networks, you also can set user rights remotely through the User Manager in a Windows NT Advanced Server.

To connect to a Microsoft print server, follow these steps:

1. Click the Network Neighborhood icon on the desktop. Notice that all servers (Microsoft and NetWare) appear on the Network Neighborhood window. This screen displays an icon for each network drive currently attached to your system.

2. To attach a printer through a Microsoft server, choose the appropriate Microsoft server by double-clicking that server's icon. The server dialog box, named after the appropriate server, appears and displays the shared directories, files, and printers attached to the Microsoft server.

3. Select the appropriate printer queue. Choose <u>F</u>ile, <u>P</u>rint and then select the capture printer port. The Capture Printer Port dialog box is displayed containing the name of a currently unattached LPT port.

4. In the Capture Printer Port dialog box, select the Reconnec<u>t</u> at Logon check box if you want to maintain this connection and have it attached when you restart Windows. Then click the OK button to attach this print queue to your PC.

> **Note**
>
> Capturing the printer port attaches the printer to a specified port, but does not attach the associated printer to the desktop.

5. To attach the printer associated with the selected print queue, you must choose <u>F</u>ile, Create Shortcut. Windows displays a diagnostics message warning that you cannot configure a shortcut printer icon in the Create Shortcut dialog box, although Windows creates the shortcut on the desktop. Click Yes to create the icon.

6. Double-click the printer's shortcut icon. Windows asks whether you want to set up a printer. Choose <u>Y</u>es. Windows then displays the Add Printer Wizard.

7. Follow the Wizard to finish installing an appropriate printer for the desktop. The Add Printer Wizard identifies which printer make and model you are installing and completes the printer connection quickly.

After configuring the printer, you can print by using the Point and Print procedure on the desktop.

Troubleshooting

I can see a network printer using Network Neighborhood, but I can't print to it.

Try the following:

- Check with your network administrator about your access rights to the printer.

- Verify that the printer is properly configured on your PC.

- Check with other users to determine whether they can access the printer.

- Try to print to another printer on the network to check your network connectivity.

(continues)

V

Networking

(continued)

I can't stop, cancel, or delete a print job in a network queue.

Try the following:

■ Check whether you have proper authorization from the network administrator to change the print settings. You might be authorized to change only your own print jobs, not others.

■ If the print queue is on a shared printer, reload the printer driver or reset the printer properties. The system might not recognize that this printer is attached to your PC.

The network printer doesn't tell me that it is out of paper or toner.

Have the network administrator configure Winpopup to broadcast printer-problem announcements. Winpopup is a utility that comes with Windows. This utility allows the network and network users to send "popup" messages that identify events and get the attention of other network users.

Optimizing Print Resources

Network printing involves many of the same facilities as local printing. Applications create print files that the Network Redirector streams to the destination network printer. When working with network resources, however, you must consider several other issues to ensure that you're getting the most from your system.

Network Printer Configuration and Management

The Printer Properties sheet contains information on each local and network printer attached to your PC. Each printer's properties are specific to its make, model, and hardware configuration.

◀ See "Options for Your Printer," p. 187

You can make several changes to the properties to enhance your printing. The print quality can be enhanced by specific printers, setting device options, graphics, and the procedures for handling TrueType fonts. The following general procedure explores some of these changes:

1. After attaching a network printer, open its Printer Properties sheet by right-clicking the appropriate printer. From the pull-down menu that appears, choose Properties and then click the General tab. The pages in the Properties sheet are specific to your printer and display the options

and selections that match the printer's current hardware and print driver configuration.

2. Click the Device Options tab. Notice the options that the network printer offers.

3. Change the Device Options settings to match your printer's specifications. These options include such pertinent information as printer memory size and page protection. (If you don't see these options, check with your local area network [LAN] administrator.)

4. Click the Details tab. Check the spool settings to determine whether the printer is set to print after the first or last page spools. Usually, waiting until after the last page spools yields better results. Experiment with this setting to gain a better understanding of your configuration.

5. Click the Graphics tab. Change the dithering settings to identify which setting yields the best results for both speed and printout quality.

Troubleshooting

When I print to a printer on the network, my printout quality and settings are not consistent.

Try the following:

- ■ Before printing, check with the printer's Properties sheet. Change the settings if required.

- ■ Check with the system administrator for the printer settings, features, and hardware configuration. The printer might not be capable of handling your print job.

- ■ Relate printout quality to changes in the property settings. Change your printer's properties and make test printouts to see how these changes affect the printouts.

Network Printer Drivers

Windows uses printer drivers to deliver your print files through the network to your printer. How well Windows performs this printing depends on how well the drivers perform. If you use drivers that are several revisions old, you might experience a slowdown. It is a good policy to check your printer drivers and update as revisions become available.

V

Networking

1. In the Control Panel, choose the System icon. Then click the Device Manager tab.

2. Verify that the network interface card driver is a virtual mode driver with a VxD extension. The driver will be listed including its extension. If a real-mode driver with a DRV extension is installed, then contact your LAN administrator or printer manufacturer for an updated revision.

3. Verify that the configured printer driver is a virtual mode driver. The driver should also have a VxD extension. If a real-mode driver with a DRV extension is installed, then contact your LAN administrator or printer manufacturer for an updated revision.

4. Ask your LAN administrator whether your system is configured with the latest driver version for your network printers. If the drivers are not the most current revision, request the latest update from either your LAN manager or the printer's manufacturer.

Managing Print Files and Sharing

After creating print files and sending them to a network printer, you must verify that the print jobs are finished, on hold, or need to be purged. You can check the print job status on both local and remote printers by using the Windows Printer Driver. Print job control is a complex task that involves user security rights on remote printers.

Viewing a Network Print Queue

Although you can view queue information, you cannot change any print job characteristics unless the LAN administrator has authorized you to do so. For some systems, the network administrator is the only user who can control all print jobs, while another user can control only his or her local shared-printing resources. LAN administrator policies determine which users can delete, pause, or purge documents from the queue. Usually, users can change the status of their individual print jobs, but not those of other users.

To view the queue, simply double-click on the printer's icon in the Printers folder or on the desktop. Windows displays the Printer Driver and print queue.

Shared Printing

Shared printing or *peer-to-peer sharing* provides other network workstations access to your local printer. Shared printing access is useful for transferring documents between workstations and for sharing expensive resources with other users. It is also an excellent way to maximize the use of often expensive printing hardware.

To share a printer, follow these steps:

1. Choose Start, Settings, Control Panel. In the Control Panel folder, double-click the Network icon. The Network tabs will appear. These tabs include Configuration, Identification, and Access Control.

2. On the Configuration page, select the Add button. The Select Network Component Type dialog box appears.

3. Choose Service and then click the Add button.

4. Choose Microsoft from the Manufacturers list box.

5. If your primary network logon client is Microsoft Networks, choose File and Printer Sharing for Microsoft Networks. If your primary network logon client is NetWare, choose File and Printer Sharing for NetWare Networks.

6. Choose OK to close the Select Network Service dialog box. For these changes to take effect, you must restart the computer.

Enabling Shared Printing

After configuring the network setup by following the preceding steps, you must enable the sharing feature as follows:

1. From the taskbar, choose Start, Settings, Control Panel. In the Control Panel folder, double-click the Network icon.

2. In the Network dialog box, choose the File and Print Sharing button.

3. In the File and Print Sharing dialog box, select the I Want to Be Able to Allow Others to Print to My Printer(s) check box (see fig. 25.3).

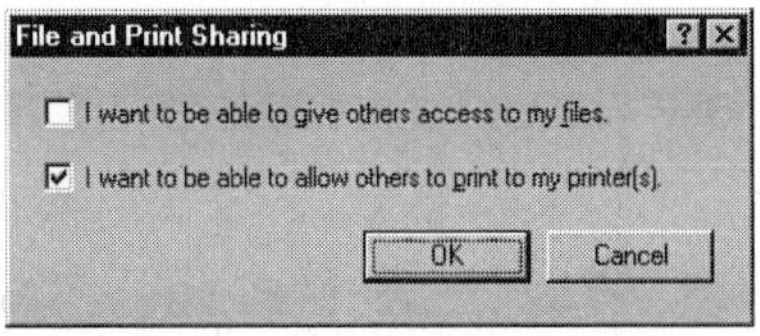

Fig. 25.3

The File and Print Sharing dialog box contains check boxes that enable you to share files and printers with other network users.

4. Choose OK to close the dialog box, and again to close the Network Control Panel. You must restart the computer for these changes to take effect.

Note

If the I Want to Be Able to Allow Others to Print to My Printer(s) check box is grayed (disabled), your system does not support print sharing.

Troubleshooting

My shared printer is unavailable to other workstations on my network.

Try the following:

■ In the Control Panel, double-click the Network icon. Choose the File and Print Sharing button. In the File and Print Sharing dialog box, verify that the I Want to Be Able to Allow Others to Print to My Printer(s) check box is selected.

■ Verify that all users are running a compatible protocol.

■ Verify that your PC shows up in the network browser on other connected PCs.

■ Verify that you can print successfully to your attached printer.

■ Use the Extended Printer Troubleshooting (EPTS) application available in your Help file.

Disabling Shared Printing

After your workstation printer is shared, you might find that too many users are creating an overload. To disable the share, follow this procedure:

1. From the taskbar, choose Start, Settings, Control Panel. In the Control Panel folder, double-click the Network icon.

2. In the Network dialog box, choose the File and Print Sharing button.

3. Deselect the I Want to Be Able to Allow Others to Print to My Printer(s) check box.

4. Choose OK to close the dialog box, and again to close the Network Control Panel.

Creating Shared-Printer Security

In Windows 95, creating shared-resource security is a multistep procedure. In order to effectively share a resource, you must be able to control who accesses that resource and, to some extent, what they do with it. If you share your printer, you can impose some level of security. Securing your printer requires several steps.

1. Choose the Passwords icon in the Control Panel folder. The Password Properties sheet appears. This Properties sheet has three tabs: Passwords, Remote Administration, and User Profiles. (The Remote Administration tab is not present if file and printer sharing are not installed.)

2. Choose the Enable Remote Administration check box on the Remote Administration page.

3. Type a user-access password in the Passwords text box.

4. In the Confirm Passwords text box, retype the password. Record the password in your system workbook or manual.

5. Select OK.

Network users can now gain access to your system by using the password that you have just created. To access your shared printer, however, users must have the appropriate password information.

Deleting Connections to a Shared Printer

When you delete a shared connection between your workstation and a workstation sharing its local printer, disabling sharing keeps your local printer from being shared by the network.

1. From the taskbar, choose Start, Settings, Printer's Folder. Windows displays a list of all printers, local or network, attached to your workstation.

2. Select the shared printer you want to delete.

3. Choose File, Delete.

4. Windows displays a dialog box warning that it will delete the selected printer. Click Yes.

5. Windows next displays a dialog box asking whether you want to delete this printer's drivers. Click Yes to delete the drivers.

V

Networking

Caution
Before you click Yes and thus delete the printer's drivers, verify that you do not have any other printers attached of the same make and model. If you delete this printer's drivers, you might also disconnect other printers.

Solving Common Network Printing Problems

Windows 95 adds some basic Help tools to aid you in solving network printing problems. These basic tools include the following:

- Windows quickly displays descriptive information in diagnostic messages that appear when Windows encounters printing problems.

- The Help facility includes an interactive Printing Problem Help tool that takes you step by step through the most common solutions to problems.

- An enhanced Help tool incorporates even more detailed steps that can solve quite difficult network printing problems.

- The System Monitor is useful in diagnosing local PC problems caused by network connections.

Diagnostics

The facilities of the Windows Help system can help you diagnose printing problems as follows:

1. Choose Help, Troubleshooting, and Print Troubleshooting from your application or Windows. Windows displays a Windows Help screen with the Print Troubleshooter dialog box.

2. Answer each question by clicking the button next to the appropriate answer. The Help screens provide suggestions for many common troubleshooting problems.

If the troubleshooting Help information is inadequate for solving your problems, Microsoft provides the Enhanced Print Troubleshooter (EPTS) on the Windows 95 CD-ROM:

1. Go to the Windows Explorer. Open the \other\misc\epts folder on the Windows 95 CD-ROM.

2. Choose the EPTS.EXE executable file. EPTS displays a Help screen that contains hypertext buttons. Next to each button is a brief statement describing a printer problem. Start by selecting the statement that best describes your problem.

3. Answer each EPTS question with the choice that best matches your problem. The EPTS helps you identify the most probable cause of your network printing problems.

Diagnosing network printing problems is more complex because the printers are not local and perhaps not readily accessible. After using EPTS, if you are still having difficulty printing to a network printer, call the local Help desk or your LAN network administrator.

Server Overload

A PC that shares a local printer with the network is a *print server*. If your PC is a print server, a percentage of your PC's resources are dedicated to the network. That percentage varies with the number of network connections to your PC. If your system slows down significantly, it might be suffering from *server overload*. This occurs when too many network users are either attached to or overusing your printer.

To test network loading, use the System Monitor to record your PC's server activities. Your Monitor charts might show large changes in network connection activity.

1. Choose Start, Programs, Accessories, System Tools, System Monitor.

2. Choose Edit, Remove to clear all Monitor chart variables.

3. Choose Edit, Add. Windows displays the Add dialog box.

4. Choose the Server Threads option from the Network Server category.

5. Choose the Bytes/sec option from the Network Server category.

6. Choose the NBs (network buffers) option from the Network Server category and then choose the OK button to complete the additions.

7. Choose Options, Chart. Set the update interval to one minute using the slide control in the Chart dialog box.

8. Choose View, Line Charts.

You have now configured the Monitor to show the level of resource loading associated with network clients. If the System Monitor displays large

V

Networking

variations in the number of threads or bytes-per-second variables, discontinue printer sharing for a test period. This test period should help you determine whether you can eliminate overload as a cause for system sluggishness.

Using Custom Print Managers and Utilities

Windows 95 provides a standard platform that other vendors use to create software drivers and applications. These custom software packages integrate a specific product with Windows. As a result, many printer vendors work with Microsoft to create new drivers. Some vendors have created printing applications that can substitute for or replace the Windows Printer Driver. Many printer vendors provide custom property configuration utilities for accessing their printers' custom features. Two of these vendors are Hewlett-Packard (HP) and Digital Equipment Corporation (DEC).

- The HP JetAdmin Utility is a substitute for the Windows Printer Driver.

- The DEC utility provides additional property screens that the Windows Printer Driver can call.

Using the HP JetAdmin Utility

You can use the HP JetAdmin Utility to install and configure networked Hewlett-Packard printers that use the HP JetDirect network interface. The HP JetAdmin Utility substitutes for the Windows standard Printer Driver. You also can use JetAdmin to interface printers connected to a NetWare LAN.

Figure 25.4 shows the JetAdmin Utility's main screen. The All Printers tab is displaying a list of printers connected to a Novell NetWare network. The network printers are of diverse makes and models. The utility can identify most of these printers. However, if incapable of identifying a printer's make, model, or network adapter card, JetAdmin displays a large, yellow question mark to designate the unknown printer.

To obtain information about the printer, double-click one of the printers shown listed. The Printer sheet shown in figure 25.5 appears. The sheet identifies the printer's make and model as well as its location, capabilities, and status.

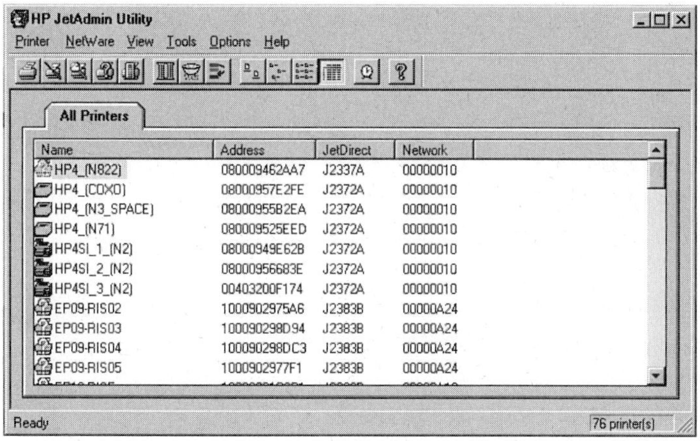

Fig. 25.4
The HP JetAdmin Utility is a vendor-supplied Printer Driver that monitors and controls HP network printers.

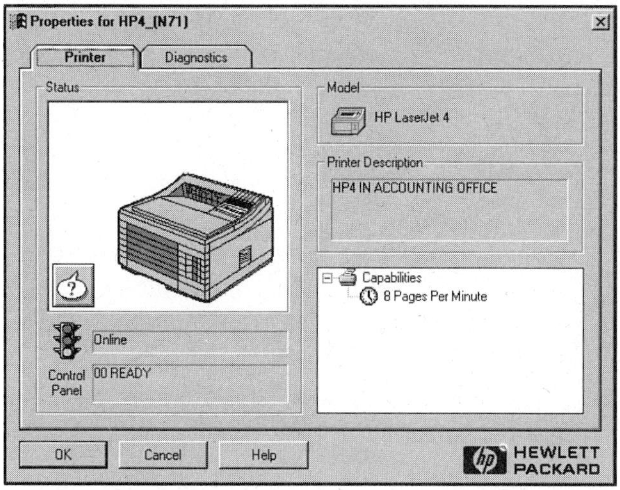

Fig. 25.5
The HP JetAdmin Utility's Printer sheet displays current information about the selected printer.

V

Networking

Notice the traffic light indicator at the screen's bottom-left corner. This indicator is useful for quickly isolating network printing problems. The following are traffic light patterns for diagnosing problem printers:

■ A red light indicates that the printer has a critical error that you must correct before printing. Such critical errors include a lack of paper or an open door interlock.

■ A yellow light signifies a noncritical error that will soon require service. For example, if the printer's toner is low, the yellow light comes on.

■ A green light indicates that the printer is online and functioning normally.

Figure 25.6 shows the Printer sheet for a problem printer. JetAdmin has identified that the printer has a problem, as the question mark in the Status section denotes. The traffic light is now red, indicating a critical error has occurred.

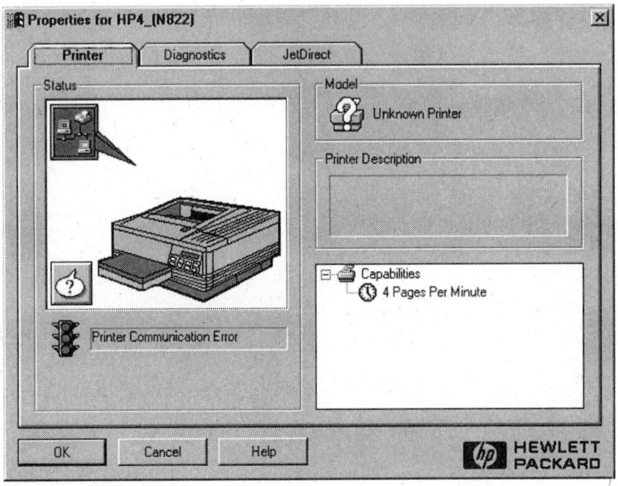

Fig. 25.6

The HP JetAdmin Utility's Printer sheet shows the status of a printer whose current configuration is unknown.

Using the DEC Printer Utility

The DEC printer utility adds features to the standard Windows 95 Printer Driver and updates printer drivers. The utility includes a detailed Help file for configuring both local and network printers. In addition, the utility creates an enhanced set of property menus and screens for configuring DEC printers.

Figure 25.7 shows the Device Options sheet, which presents in detail the current conditions associated with the network printer. This sheet also enables the user to install and quickly set special device options.

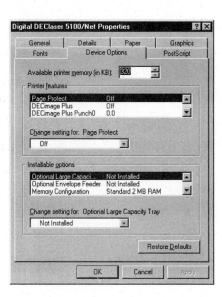

Fig. 25.7

The DEC printer utility's Device Options sheet adds unique features to the standard Windows 95 Printer Driver.

As other printer vendors change their products and software drivers, other highly customized Printer Drivers will be available for use with Windows 95. ❖

V

Networking

Chapter 26

Network Management and Security

by Gordon Meltzer

The motive for setting up a Windows 95 network is to share the resources associated with the computers on that network. *Resources* are disks (including CD-ROMs) and their files, printers, and fax modems.

A network, in which resources and information previously available only to people working on their private standalone personal computers now are available for sharing (and possible editing or deletion by the group), raises serious and complex issues. Network issues can best be understood by splitting them into two parts. This chapter examines these two parts: management and security.

In this chapter, you learn how to control the installation and configuration of your network. The chapter tries to expose weaknesses in the network design and tells you how to work around these weaknesses. The chapter provides tips for keeping your network up and running and for simplifying it without losing functionality. This chapter is a guide to help you understand the philosophy behind the Windows 95 network and make it work in your individual situation.

In this chapter, you learn about

- Creating network resources

- Monitoring network resources

- Sharing network resources

- Securing the network

- Managing the network

- Using dial-up networking

- Using Windows 95 with other networks

Creating Network Resources

The basic philosophy of peer-to-peer networks is that every file on every disk on the network is available for sharing by all members of the network. By extension, anyone can print to any printer on the network—and also delete any file, wipe out any directory, and erase any disk anywhere on the network.

That kind of peer-to-peer network, where everybody on the LAN is connected to everybody else's disks and printers, is an unmanageable network. If you draw a diagram of the connections in such a network, you'll see a crazy-quilt of connections. With more than a few machines on the LAN, you'll be unable to follow all the connections. The worst parts of thoughtlessly connecting everybody to everybody are

- *Confusion.* Time is always lost searching for data all over the LAN.

- *Data Loss.* Needed files get erased from one disk because somebody thought somebody else had a copy on another disk.

Don't be tempted to set up your Windows 95 peer network the crazy-quilt way. The problem is that after you set up your network and declare your computer's hard drive to be shared, if you take no steps to manage the network, you've opened the door to network data-loss danger and file-finding confusion. You need to bring safety and sanity to your network environment, and you need to work with the other members of your workgroup to accomplish those tasks.

Data-Storage Tips

Networks are designed to make office life easier. Peer-to-peer networks are supposed to eliminate something called the sneakernet, which is used when all computers in an office are standalone. Following are the steps involved in making a sneakernet connection:

1. You decide that you want to edit a document on which several people have been collaborating.

2. You visit each collaborator's computer, find the file in question, and record the date and time when the file was last modified. You're looking for the most recent version.

3. When you find the computer that has the most up-to-date version of the document, you find a formatted floppy disk, copy the file to the disk, and take the disk back to your computer.

4. Copy the file from the floppy disk to your hard drive.

You think you won't have to go through all that when you set up a network. All the computers will be connected, and you can copy the file to your hard disk over the wire. In fact, however, the default setup for peer-to-peer networks such as Windows 95 leaves each person's version of a collaborative file on his or her own hard disk, where other workgroup members cannot find it easily.

The solution to this problem is setting up your peer-to-peer Windows 95 network in a client/server model. The following sections show how this model enables all members of the network to get their work done but retains the flexibility that is the best feature of peer nets.

Choosing a Storage Area for Your Work

You really don't want to set up each computer on the peer network as a server; you want to make one computer on your network the server, the central storage area for data files. Data files are *work products*—the files created by the programs that you use. If you're not sure about which files are data files, remember that Microsoft Word creates files that have the DOC extension and that Excel creates worksheet files that have the XLS extension. The files with DOC and XLS extensions are the work product (data files) created by Word and Excel.

Files of this nature should be stored on only one computer in your workgroup so that everyone will know where to find them. If you don't do this, you have to search all the computers on your network for a file—not superior to sneakernet at all.

Using a Dedicated Server

You don't have to have a dedicated server in your Windows 95 network, but if you can afford to dedicate one computer on your network to storing everybody's work product, do so. Following are the benefits of storing all the workgroup's data files on one machine:

V

Networking

- The individual workstations can use smaller, slower, less expensive hard drives.

- You don't have to search for the computer that holds the files that you want.

- Complex drive mappings are eliminated.

- In a LAN where all work product is stored on one central file server, File and Printer Sharing will not need to be turned on in Control Panel, Network on most of the computers in the LAN. Memory is used more efficiently on all the machines that do not use file and printer sharing.

- Backing up everyone's work is as simple as backing up one disk because all the work is on that disk.

Setting Up a Data-File Storage Server

Once you've decided that good network management involves setting up a central server, where you and your network neighbors will store their data files, follow these steps:

1. Choose the network machine that you want to use as the data server. This machine will always be turned on.

2. Enable File and Printer Sharing on the data server. Do this by going to the machine that will be your storage server. Use Control Panel, and double-click the Network icon. Then choose File and Print Sharing and put a check in the box that says I Want To Be Able To Give Others Access to My Files.

> **Note**
>
> If the server you're working on also has a printer attached, and if you and your workgroup members want to print on that printer, also put a check in the box that says, I Want To Be Able to Allow Others To Print To My Printer(s).

3. Set up a directory structure that will make storing and finding documents easy.

> **Note**
>
> You may create one folder for each user and then create subfolders for the users' projects. You may create a folder for each client and allow the workgroup members to store their work for that client in the client's folder. Setting up folders by project is OK, too, if the projects are long-term. Ideally, the directory structure on the data server should be long-lasting and durable so that everyone in the workgroup can get used to it.

4. Map the server's network drive to each workstation, using the same drive letter (for example, Z:).

5. Set up the applications on each workstation so that the default data directory for each application is the same.

6. Have workgroup members start saving their work not to their local C drives but to the appropriate subfolder on the network drive.

Getting the Best of Peer-to-Peer and Client/Server LAN Features

Although using a central server makes our workgroup look like a big client/server network, the flexibility of a peer-to-peer network still is available. You can call on this flexibility when you want to use a resource on the network that's attached to another computer—a color printer, for example. You can designate the printer as a shared resource, no matter whose computer the printer is attached to; you can't do that in a traditional client/server network.

Drive Mappings

Following a plan like the one shown in the section "Setting Up a Data-File Storage Server" is important because, if you don't, your workgroup ends up with a drive-mapping scheme that looks like a bowl of spaghetti. You don't want everybody in the network to be connected to everybody else's machines and drives. Point everybody in the workgroup to one machine for storage of work-product data files, and you'll always be able to find what you're looking for.

Suppose that you have a 10-user workgroup. If you set up the network in full peer-to-peer fashion so that everyone is looking for files stored on other people's computers, your drive mappings look like figure 26.1.

V

Networking

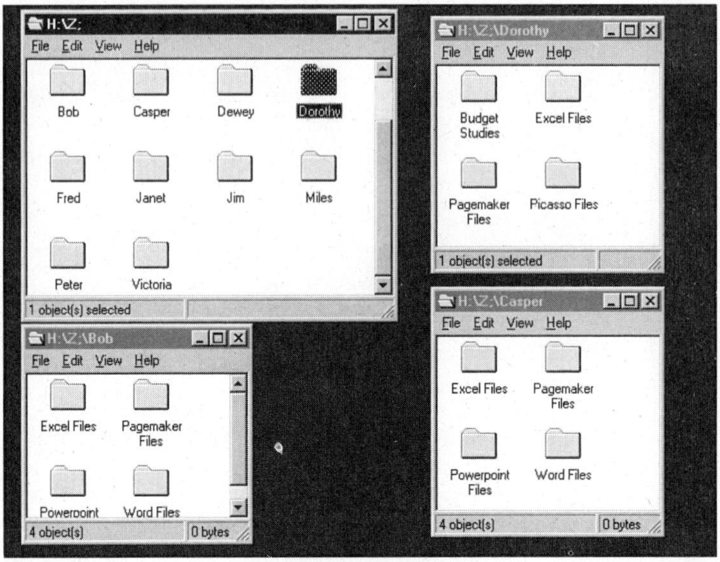

Fig. 26.1
The three smaller windows in this figure show that users have many of the same shared directories—a difficult way to find things on the network.

Since it is a 10-user version, there are 9 other mappings, or drivers, that you must contend with when searching for your data. You need to search for files on all 9 of these other drives/workstations if data files are scattered throughout the network.

Of course, you may be confused by having so many drive mappings and connections in place all the time. You may be dismayed by the drain on your system's performance caused by connecting to so many other workstations and having those workstations connect to yours. You are likely to disconnect from the other members' drives for normal work. Later, when you want to send a file to or retrieve a file from another computer, you must connect to the other computer, map that computer's drive to yours, and do your file-transfer work.

One more reason why all the computers in the workgroup should connect to one central data-storage computer is that you can keep your computer connected to that computer at all times. This persistent connection can be configured to occur automatically when you start your computer or only when you actually try to access the drive. Because you don't have to worry about drive mappings or about connecting and disconnecting network drives, you can consider the network drive to be a permanent part of your computer—the place where you store your work.

Figure 26.2 shows three windows. The parent window shows a mapped network drive called Z:. The first child window shows 10 folders on drive Z—one for each member of the workgroup. The smallest child window shows the folders in user Bob's main folder. The other users have similar folders. More or fewer folders may appear in other users' main folders, depending on the type of work that each user does and the program that he or she uses.

> **Note**
>
> A parent window is the first window displayed by a program. Child windows are subsequent windows the application displays.

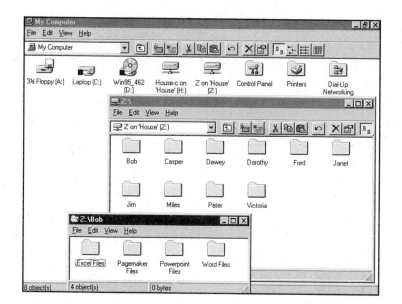

Fig. 26.2

This shows user Bob's folder structure on mapped network drive Z.

You don't have to structure the folder hierarchy on the data-server drive in any particular way. You should, however, have one data-server drive for your workgroup. All the members of the workgroup should connect to that drive permanently and store their work on that drive.

Keeping Applications and Data Separate

The preceding sections discussed only data files—the files that you generate by using your applications. But where should you store application files— your programs? The best method is to store applications locally on each user's C drive, if you have the space on your hard drive, because applications load and run noticeably faster if they run from the local hard drive.

Networks, and application-program vendors, certainly provide the capability for everyone in your workgroup to run programs from a single shared copy, located somewhere on a network file server. This method seems, at first, to be a very interesting way to operate because that huge 15M installation of your favorite word processing program won't have to go on every computer—just on a file server. But the additional network traffic generated by the continual loading of program files over the network wastes bandwidth. Since Windows programs only load part of themselves from the disk into memory at one time, there will be additional network traffic created as various parts of the program are called into memory as needed. If the application was stored on the local hard drive all this unnecessary network traffic could be eliminated.

The users may complain that the program, coming to them from a server over the network, loads and runs too slowly. Finally, if the integrity of the network is interrupted, even momentarily, while a shared copy of an application is running, chances are good that every system running that application at that time will freeze while the application is being loaded, making some users think they need to reboot their machines. This procedure, of course, means that you lose any unsaved data in all applications.

The point here of course is that your workgroup will run much more smoothly if each user has her executable program files stored on her own computer's hard drive.

Being a Good Network Neighbor

If your workgroup is to function effectively, all the members of the workgroup must be good network neighbors. You can implement this simple concept by considering what resources are available on your computer and designating those resources as shared if other members of your workgroup need access to them.

◀ See "Sharing an Entire Drive," p. 643

If yours is the only CD-ROM drive in the workgroup, for example, make it available for other members to use.

You also need to consider the continuity of shared resources. If you have the only CD-ROM drive or the only color printer and other users are connected to those resources, consider the effect on the rest of your workgroup if you turn off your computer without warning. In such a case, your resources disappear from the network and no longer are available to the other workgroup members. Don't discontinue sharing your resources without informing the rest of the workgroup. Use the WinPopup accessory program to send a message to your workgroup saying you are going to take your shared disk or printer offline. In your message, say how long it will be until you shut down. Communicating about a change in status of a shared resource you control is part of being a good network neighbor.

> **Caution**
>
> If a disk resource on your peer-to-peer network is disconnected from the network unexpectedly—if a computer that hosts a shared folder is turned off or if the folder-sharing properties are turned off—network users can lose data.

Network-Management Tools

Windows 95 includes several useful tools that help you learn about and manage your peer-to-peer network. Although *network management* is a very broad term, management tools simply allow you to see how your network is functioning and to change almost everything about the entire network from your own computer. You can use these Network Management tools to enable or disable sharing of resources, add or delete passwords, disconnect users, and so on.

When you look at network management as being a series of toggle switches, with one switch for each possible setting on each possible resource, management tools become less mysterious. The trick is knowing how to set each parameter for optimum network efficiency.

> **Note**
>
> Don't feel that you have to make every connection and map every drive just because you can. Simple is better.

Net Watcher

Net Watcher is installed in the Accessories, System Tools group, which you can find by opening the Start menu and choosing <u>P</u>rograms. This utility is useful for examining which resources on which computer are shared. Net Watcher tells you about these resources, as well as who is using the shared resources and which files are open on the shared resources.

◀ See "Understanding File Sharing," p. 643

V

Networking

◀ See "Setting Up Printer Sharing and Security," p. 651

Net Watcher is a "per-server" utility. In order to display meaningful information, Net Watcher shows information about only one server computer at a time. Net Watcher shows information about computers that are sharing their disks or printers. These computers have File and Print Sharing for Microsoft Networks enabled.

Net Watcher provides three main views of the workgroup for each server:

■ A view showing the users connected to the server called View by Connections. To see this view, start Net Watcher and choose View, Connections.

■ A view showing the shared folders on the server called View by Shared Folders. To see this view from the main Net Watcher window, choose View, Shared Folders.

■ A view showing the files that are open on the server called View by Open Files. To see this view, choose View, Open Files.

In the View by Connections, a list of users who are connected to the server appears on the left side of the screen. The right side of the screen displays the folders and printers to which the users are connected, as well as the files that the users have open. If multiple users are connected, you select one user at a time on the left side of the screen. Then you can manage how that user interacts with the network, as you'll see next.

Figure 26.3 represents the View by Connections. In this example, you are looking at a server, called HOUSE (as defined in the caption bar), to which one user, called LAPTOP, is connected.

View by Shared Folders shows detailed information about the disk folders and printers that have been declared sharable on the server. On the left side of the screen is a list of shared folders on the server, the names under which the folders are shared, the type of access available to the folder (full access or read-only), and any comment about the shared resource that was typed in the Comment box when the folder or printer was designated as sharable.

◀ See "Understanding File Sharing," p. 643

Figure 26.4 shows View by Shared Folders. In the figure, LAPTOP is connected to several shared folders and to one printer on the computer known as HOUSE.

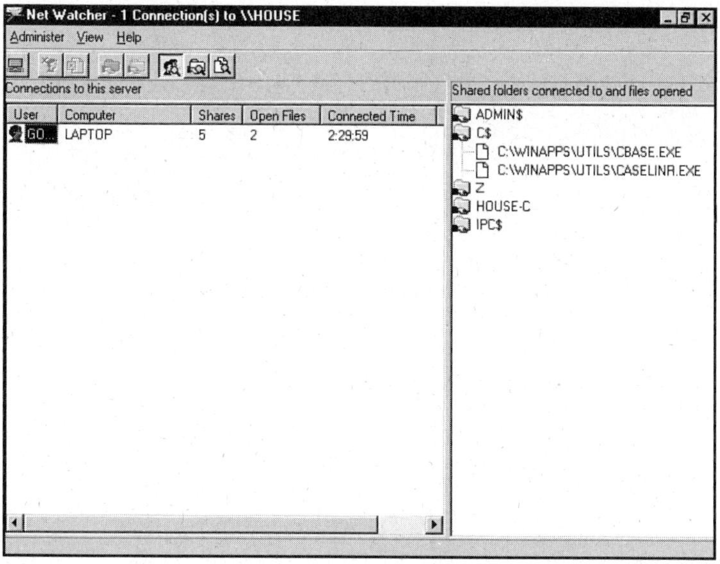

Fig. 26.3
The Net Watcher
management
program in View
by Connections
mode, showing
user Laptop
connected to
server House.

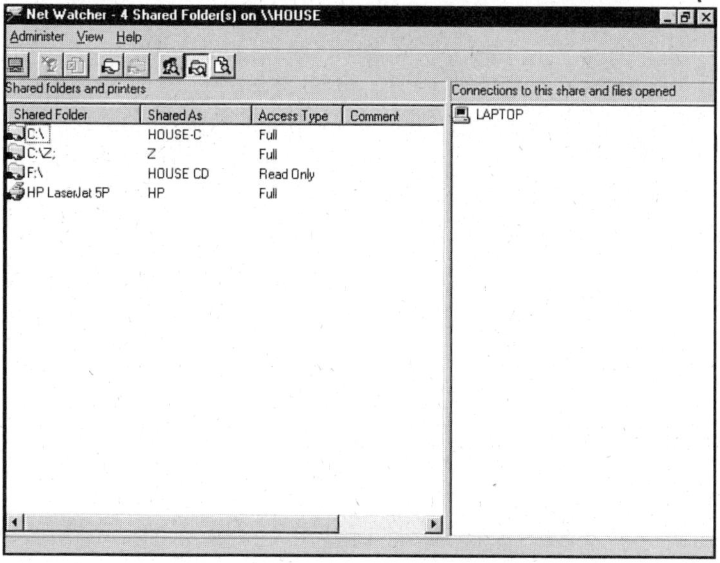

V

Networking

Fig. 26.4
The Net Watcher
management
program in View
by Shared Folders
mode, showing
four shared folders
on the server
named House.

View by Open Files is a full-screen display. In figure 26.5, Net Watcher shows
the name of two open files on the server, the share name of the server on
which the file is located, which computer is accessing the file, and whether
the file is open for reading only or for reading and writing.

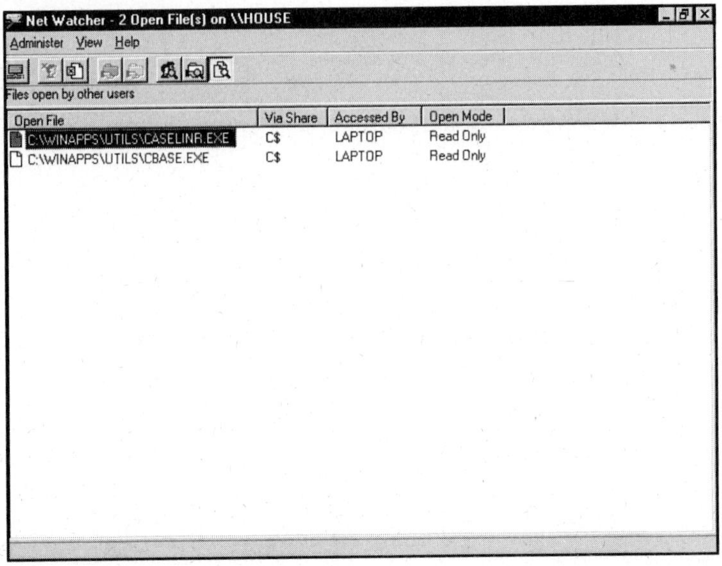

Fig. 26.5

The Net Watcher management program in View by Open Files mode, showing two open files on the server named HOUSE.

Net Watcher can do far more than simply report on network status, however; as a management tool, it can restructure the network. The following sections explain how you can use Net Watcher to accomplish these tasks:

- Disconnect a network user anywhere in the workgroup

- Close an open file anywhere in the workgroup

- Add a shared folder to any server in the workgroup

- Stop sharing folders on any server in the workgroup

- Change the properties of shared folders in the workgroup

Disconnecting a User from a Peer Server

If you want to stop a user from connecting to your computer's shared folders and printers, use Net Watcher's Show Users view. Select the user whom you want to disconnect and then choose Administer, Disconnect User.

Disconnecting a user can have serious consequences for that user; the user can lose data if he or she has unsaved data when the disconnection occurs. In fact, Net Watcher issues a warning when you issue the Disconnect User command, as shown in figure 26.6.

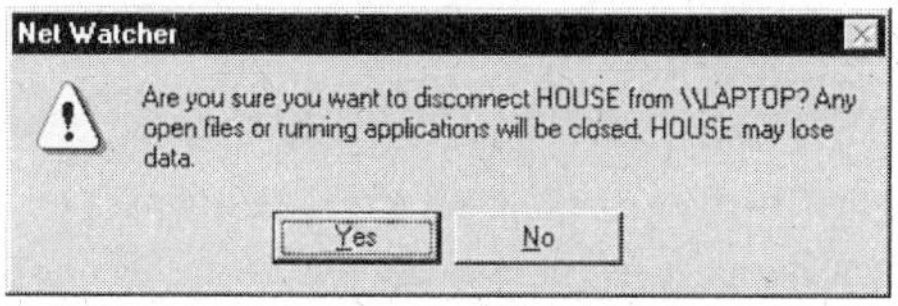

Fig. 26.6
The Net Watcher
management
program issues a
warning when you
use it to discon-
nect a server from
a connected user.

Adding a Shared Resource on a Peer Server

Adding a shared resource can be useful when you need access to a resource on another computer in your workgroup. Net Watcher can make the folder that you need sharable. Figure 26.7 shows the shared resources on the peer server called HOUSE—three shared folders and one shared printer. Anyone on a Windows 95 peer network can go and declare a share on any folder for which they have permissions on the workgroup providing the computer they are targeting is a server (has enabled File & Printer Sharing Services).

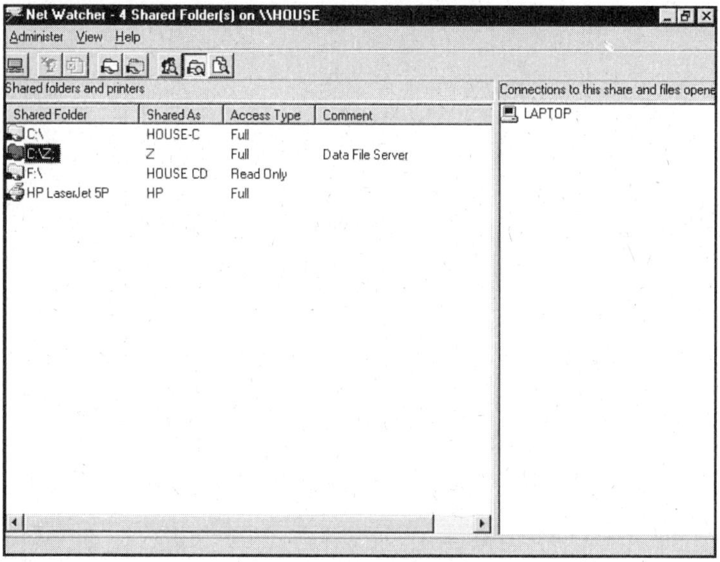

Fig. 26.7
Net Watcher in
View by Shared
Folders mode,
showing three
shared folders.

Suppose you want to access programs in the folder named SECURE on the computer named HOUSE. SECURE is not a shared folder, however, so you need to declare it to be sharable. You can do this, from any machine on the workgroup LAN, using Net Watcher. The three requirements are:

- Remote Administration is enabled on the server you are targeting (on which you want to set a resource shared).

- The folder, drive, or printer you want to share is on a server computer. A server computer has File and/or Printer Sharing enabled.

- No password has been established, controlling access to the folder or resource you want to share.

Starting from View by Shared Folders mode on peer server HOUSE, choose Administer, Add Shared Folder, or use the Add Share button on the Net Watcher toolbar. Next, you'll see the Enter Path dialog box asking for the path you wish to share. Then browse for the folder name or type it in the Path box. Figure 26.8 shows the Browse for Folder dialog box where you can find and select the path to the folder you want to share.

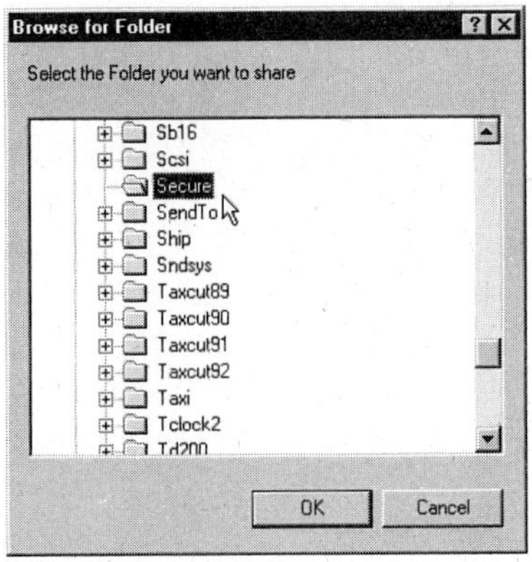

Fig. 26.8

To share a folder on your workgroup LAN using Net Watcher, browse for the folder you want to share and double-click to enter it in the Enter Path dialog box.

After you've chosen the folder you want to add, Net Watcher displays the shared folder's Properties sheet, shown in figure 26.9. In this sheet, you declare the folder to be shared and set its shared properties: Shared As, Share Name, Comment, Access Type, and Passwords.

When you choose OK on the shared folder's Properties sheet, the folder becomes a shared resource on the workgroup and is added to Net Watcher's list of shared folders (see fig. 26.10).

> **Caution**
>
> The process of adding a shared folder just described has deep implications. Any member of the Peer-to-Peer workgroup LAN can add a shared drive or folder on any server computer in the network. The owner of the computer targeted to have a drive or folder shared doesn't need to agree. In fact, the owner of the targeted computer may not even know that a drive or folder has been set as shared, until she happens to examine the drive properties with My Computer or the Windows Explorer and notices the Shared Resource icon attached to one of her drives or folders.

Notice too, that any member of the workgroup, using Net Watcher to add shared drives or folders on server computers on the LAN, can also set passwords for access to the folders he declares as shared, effectively preventing anyone but himself from accessing those drives or folders over the LAN. Again, the owner of the computer containing these shared drives or folders will not know a password has been set without examining the properties for the shared drive or folder.

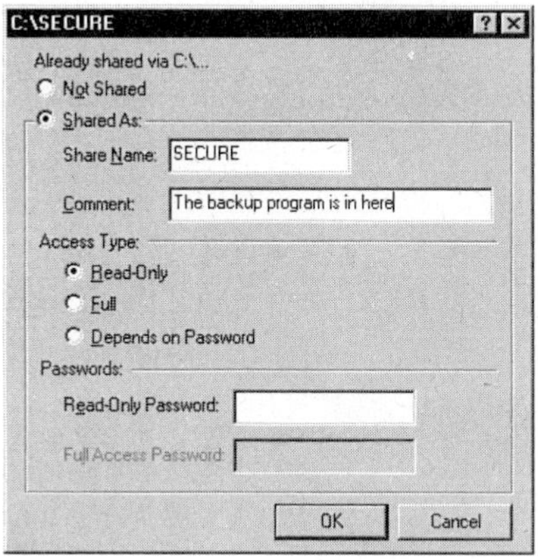

Fig. 26.9
In Net Watcher, you can edit the properties of your newly shared folder.

Troubleshooting

Files on my hard disk drive are changing. Some are being deleted, some are just being modified. I haven't done anything to them. Why is this happening?

The answer may be that another member of your workgroup LAN is causing these changes on your computer. If you have enabled File and Print Sharing in your network setup, another member of your LAN may have declared your hard drive and its folders to be shared. Then, that person can work with your files, modifying them, deleting them, or adding new files to your disk.

There are two ways to prevent having your drives and folders shared by others without your knowledge:

- Turn off File Sharing in Control Panel, Network. Then your computer is not a server, and nobody can access your drives or folders over the LAN.

- Turn off Enable Remote Administration. You do this by using Control Panel, Passwords, and then clicking the Remote Administration tab. There is only one setting on this page. In the sole check box, deselect Enable Remote Administration of this Server.

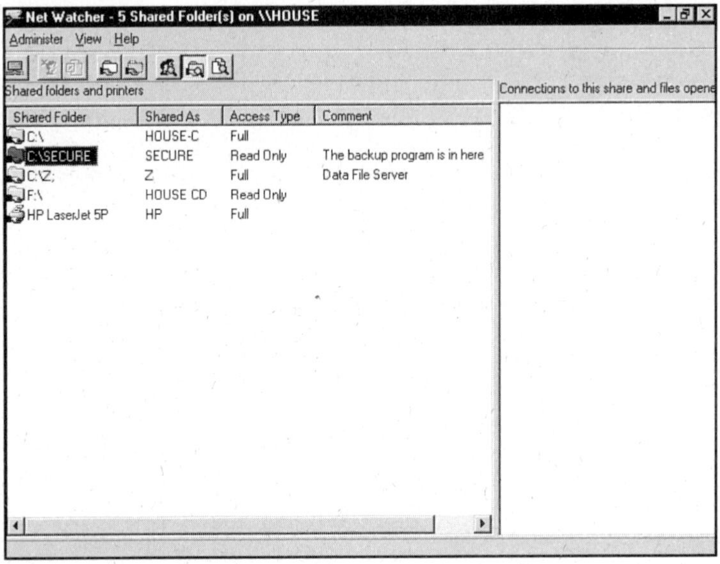

Fig. 26.10
The Net Watcher
program has
added your newly
shared folder,
C:\SECURE, to
its list of shared
folders on the peer
server HOUSE.

Stop Sharing a Folder

To stop sharing a folder, start in the View by Shared Folders view of Net
Watcher. Select the shared folder that you want to stop sharing on the network and then choose Administer, Stop Sharing Folder. You also can choose
the Stop Sharing icon on the Net Watcher toolbar. The warning message
shown in figure 26.11 appears. Click Yes to stop sharing the specified folder.

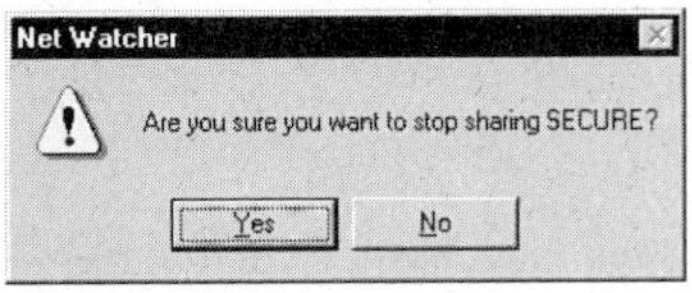

Fig. 26.11
When you use Net
Watcher to stop
sharing a folder,
this confirmation
dialog box
appears.

◀ See "Sharing a
Directory,"
p. 645

Change a Shared Folder's Properties

This option allows you to stop sharing a shared folder, but it also allows you
to change the name of the shared resource on the network, change the access
type, and set a password for access. In Net Watcher's View by Shared Folders
mode, select the folder that you want to stop sharing on the network and
then choose Administer, Shared Folder Properties.

Now, you can perform these kinds of changes on the folder you selected:

■ You can set the folder as Not Shared.

■ You can set the folder as <u>S</u>hared. If you do this, you must also enter a Share <u>N</u>ame. By default, Windows selects the folder name as the Share Name, but you can change it if you have a better description you'd like to use.

■ If you've set the folder to be <u>S</u>hared, you can set the access type to <u>R</u>ead-Only, or <u>F</u>ull, or Depends on <u>P</u>assword. You also may enter a password for access to the folder.

Figure 26.9 above shows the dialog box you work with in changing a shared folder's properties.

Stop Sharing a Printer

If you need to stop sharing a printer on the workgroup, start in View by Shared Folder mode of Net Watcher. Select the printer in the list of shared resources, and choose <u>A</u>dminister, Shared Folder <u>P</u>roperties. The printer-properties dialog box appears (see fig. 26.12), showing the name of the printer you're working with in its title bar. To stop sharing the printer, choose N<u>o</u>t Shared in the dialog box.

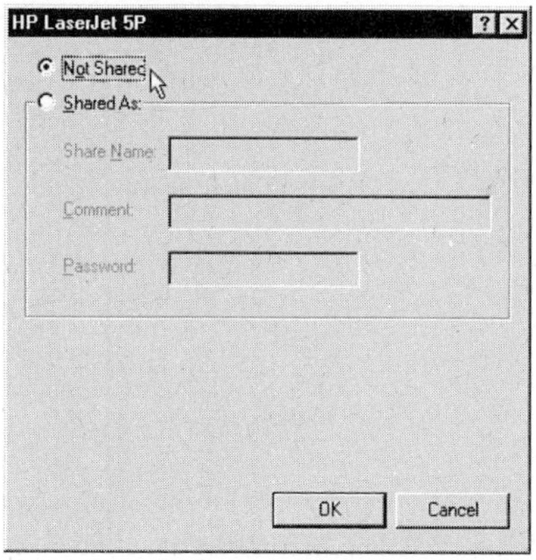

Fig. 26.12
Net Watcher uses this dialog box to allow you to stop sharing a network printer.

Then choose OK. No warning message appears before the printer is made unavailable to the workgroup.

User Profiles as a System-Management Tool

Many workgroups have users who may use more than one computer. Because Windows 95 is very customizable, a user who is sitting at what is not his or her main computer may be unable to work. Network connections may not be the same. Connections to the shared folders that the user needs may not be

◄ See "Changing Custom Settings for Each User," p. 156

available. Printer connections may not be what the user expects. Menus may be different. In general, the workstation may be so customized for the primary user that another user may be lost.

Some computers on your workgroup may have no primary user but a group of users, all of whom may have different needs or expectations. You also may have users who are true floaters—who have no primary machine but need to be able to be productive on any computer.

To deal with all these cases, Microsoft introduced User Profiles to Windows 95. With User Profiles, the following settings on any computer can be customized for any user:

- Shortcut lists and their contents

- Items in the Start menu

- Items that can be configured by Control Panel

- (For Windows 95 programs and the applications bundled with Windows 95) Menu configurations, toolbar configurations, status-bar configurations, and font and display settings

- Appearance of the desktop, including shortcuts and icons

- Fonts in use

- Screen saver, screen background, screen colors, color depth, and screen resolution

- Network settings (such as persistent connections and printer connections)

- Network Neighborhood configuration

Enabling User Profiles on the Workgroup

To use User Profiles, you must be sure the proper options are selected on the Passwords Properties sheet. Follow these steps:

1. Open the Start menu and choose Settings, Control Panel, Passwords. The Passwords Properties sheet appears.

2. Click the User Profiles tab.

3. Choose Users Can Customize Their Preferences, as shown in figure 26.13.

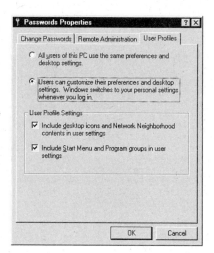

Fig. 26.13
Use the Passwords Properties sheet to enable multiple User Profiles.

V

Networking

4. To make your User Profiles more powerful, choose Include _D_esktop Icons and Include _S_tart Menu.

5. Click the Change Passwords tab.

6. Make sure that a logon password appears in this tab. You must have a password when you begin to work with User Profiles.

Working with User Profiles

When a user logs on to a Windows 95 computer that has User Profiles en-abled, the machine asks for a user name and password. The computer then creates a User Profile, using default settings.

As the user sets up network connections, desktop preferences, and all the other customizable features of the workstation, Windows 95 waits for the user to log off and shut down the machine. Then Windows saves all the settings that User Profiles can track (the settings listed in the preceding sections). Windows writes the User Profile information into the Regis-try, in the USER.DAT file, and saves the desktop and Start menu in the C:\WINDOWS\PROFILES folder, as shown in figure 26.14 . This figure shows profiles for five users on this computer; the hierarchy of subfolders is expanded for one of the users listed on the left side of the screen.

User Profiles on the Network

The preceding sections show how one machine can be customized for any number of users. This process is local use of User Profiles. An even more pow-erful type of User Profiles allows anyone to log in on any machine in the

Tip
When you finish working at a pro-file-enabled com-puter, shut down with the _C_lose All Programs and Log On as Different User option. This option prevents anyone from changing your profiled settings and preferences.

workgroup and have his or her settings restored, even if that user has never set up his or her profile at that machine before. This option requires the use of a Windows NT or NetWare server. On a Windows NT or NetWare network, you can log in from any computer on the LAN and use your customized User Profile. You can do this because your User Profile is stored on the Windows NT or NetWare file server, not on the workstation. Since the profile is stored on the Windows NT or NetWare server, it can be accessed by any workstation on the LAN.

Fig. 26.14
The Windows Explorer shows five User Profiles in the right half of the screen when five users have created Profiles.

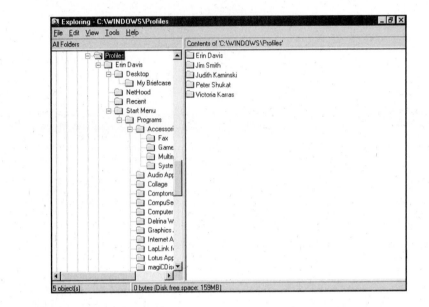

On a Windows NT server, use the User Manager tool to create a home directory for each member of the workgroup. When a user logs off his Windows 95 workstation, if User Profiles are enabled, Windows copies the profile information to the Windows NT server. When that user logs on to any other computer on the workgroup, the profile on the Windows NT server is accessed and used to set up the current workstation. (This may not work in cases when you have a shortcut to an application such as Word, and the machine you log in from does not have Word installed.)

The same system works in a NetWare environment.

> **Note**
>
> If the User Profile on the current workstation is newer than the copy on the server, the workstation copy is used, and the server is updated. The procedure also works in reverse, so that the user always has his most recent configuration available.

> **Note**
>
> If you use Microsoft Exchange on a computer that has User Profiles enabled, set Exchange to query for an Exchange profile to use at startup because User Profiles do not control Exchange profiles. (For more on Exchange, see Chapter 24, "Using Microsoft Exchange.")

System Policies and Network Management

System Policies do many of the same things as User Profiles. System Policies are not used along with User Profiles; instead, they are used in place of User Profiles. The members of a workgroup do not set System Policies, as they do their own User Profiles. In this section you will see how the System Policy Editor can change the look and feel of your Windows 95 computer. There may be Windows features that are documented in this book that are not available to you if your network administrator has disabled those features using System Policy Editor. Let's see what can happen using System Policies created by the System Policy Editor program.

> **Note**
>
> The System Policy Editor program, POLEDIT.EXE, is included on the CD-ROM version of Windows 95. It is not included on the floppy-disk version of the operating system.

The simplest way to understand System Policies is to know that these policies, which are created by a system administrator, are used to enforce predetermined User Profiles on a workgroup. The purpose of System Policies is to create a controlled workplace, in which access to certain features of Windows can be restricted or eliminated. System Policies may restrict a user from accessing Control Panel or from getting to a DOS prompt, for example. These policies also may prevent a user from connecting to or disconnecting from shared resources on the network.

Used wisely, System Policies can increase the stability of a Windows workgroup by preventing users who like to experiment from disrupting needed network connections and thereby crashing the system. Used unwisely, System Policies can prevent the natural growth of understanding that is essential if members of a workgroup are to learn how to use their computers to maximum benefit.

System Policies are set through a tool called System Policy Editor, which is the most powerful of the network-management tools included with Windows

V

Networking

95. This tool, which is designed to be used only by the network administrator, is inaccessible to users on the workgroup. The System Policy Editor should be kept in a nonshared folder on the administrator's computer.

With System Policy Editor, the administrator can set two types of policies. The first type of policy applies to individual named computers on the network. The policies created for the named computer determine the default settings that are used when a user logs on to that computer.

The second type of policy applies to individual users, determined by user name at the time of logon. If policies exist for an individual user, they are combined with the System Policies that are in effect for the computer that he or she is using.

System Policies for Individual Computers

The System Policy Editor can control the following settings on a per-computer basis:

Controlling the Network Group of Settings

- Access Control can be set to User Level. This requires the use of authentication on a Windows NT or NetWare server to access shared resources on the network.

- Logon features can display a warning at startup, saying that only authorized users should try to log on. Logon also can require validation by a Windows NT server to access Windows 95.

- Settings for Microsoft Client for NetWare can be controlled.

- Settings for Microsoft Client for Windows Networks can be controlled.

- Password settings can be modified. Use of mixed alphabetical and numeric passwords, for example, can be required, and password caching can be forced off.

- Sharing can be disabled for the computer. In this case, no resources can be declared shared, and all shared information tabs disappear from Properties sheets.

- Remote updating can be enabled.

Controlling the System Group of Settings

- The administrator can enable User Profiles.

- The network path to a shared copy of Windows Setup and Windows Tour can be specified.

■ Items to be run at startup can be specified.

System Policies for Individual Users

This area is where System Policy Editor can really show its power. Many options for individual users exist. For users, System Policy Editor works on five groups of settings.

Controlling the Control Panel Group of Settings

■ The administrator can restrict the appearance of the Network, Display, Password, Printer, and System icons in the Control Panel.

Controlling the Desktop Group of Settings

■ The wallpaper and color scheme can be controlled.

Network Settings

■ File and print sharing can be turned off for the user.

Controlling the Shell Group of Settings

■ Custom Folder Functions can be disabled.

■ Custom Programs Folders can be disallowed.

■ Custom Desktop Icons can be disallowed.

■ Start Menu Subfolders can be hidden.

■ Custom Startup Folders can be disallowed.

■ Custom Network Neighborhood can be disallowed.

■ Custom Start Menu can be disallowed.

■ The Run command can be removed from the Start menu.

■ Folders and settings can be hidden so they won't show in the taskbar.

■ The Find command can be disabled from the Start menu.

■ The display of drives in My Computer can be hidden.

■ Network Neighborhood can be hidden.

■ Hide All items on the Desktop can be hidden.

■ The Shut Down command can be disallowed.

V

Networking

■ Windows' automatic saving of settings at shutdown can be disallowed.

Controlling the System Group of Settings

■ Registry editing can be disallowed.

☑ The administrator can set up a list of allowed Windows applications and only the allowed applications can be run.

■ The MS-DOS prompt can be disabled.

■ MS-DOS mode can be disabled.

Figure 26.15 shows what the user would see if the administrator chose to restrict part of the System icon in Control Panel. The File System and Virtual Memory buttons in the System Properties sheet are missing; the Device Manager and Hardware Profiles tabs are missing, too.

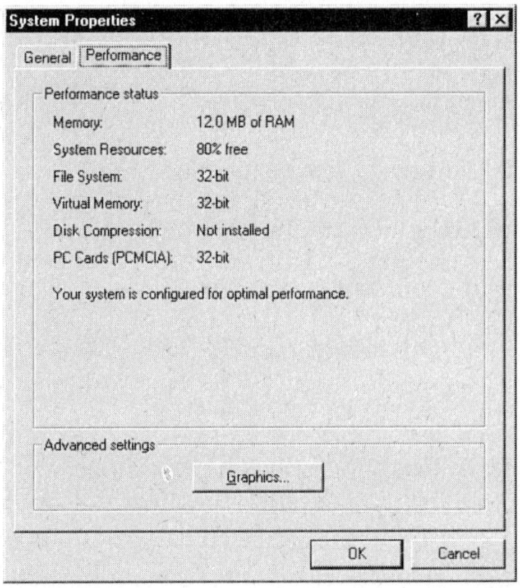

Fig. 26.15
System Policy
Editor has
removed features
from the System
Properties sheet in
Control Panel.

Figure 26.16 shows the System Properties sheet before restrictions were applied by System Policy Editor.

Caution

System Policy Editor can be unpredictable. If the administrator selects a function and then deselects it, the function may not return to the state that it was in before editing. As a result, user settings can be destroyed without warning. The workaround is to tell your administrator to leave the setting neither selected nor deselected, but dimmed. Dimmed is an option when you edit a policy file.

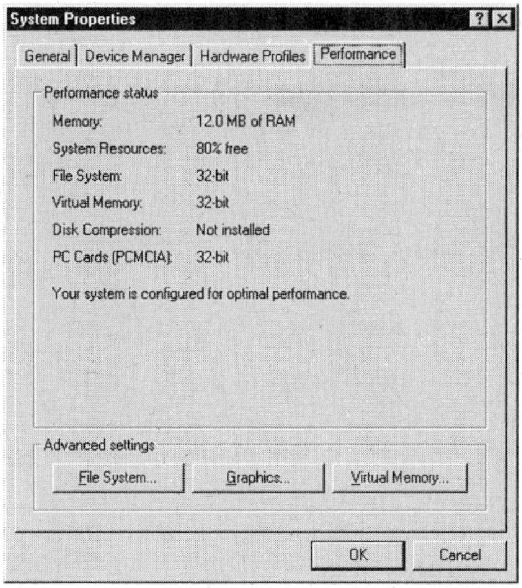

Fig. 26.16
The System Properties sheet in Control Panel looks like this before System Policy Editor removed features.

WinPopup

WinPopup is an applet that is included in the Accessories group when you install the network component of Windows 95. This tool normally is used to send short messages from one computer on the workgroup to another. WinPopup is designed so that when a message is received, the message pops up over anything else on-screen.

The real usefulness of the WinPopup program is that it automatically sends messages from a network printer when a print job finishes. WinPopup sends the message only to the computer that sent the print job for processing.

Figure 26.17 shows the simple network-management function of print-job-finished notification.

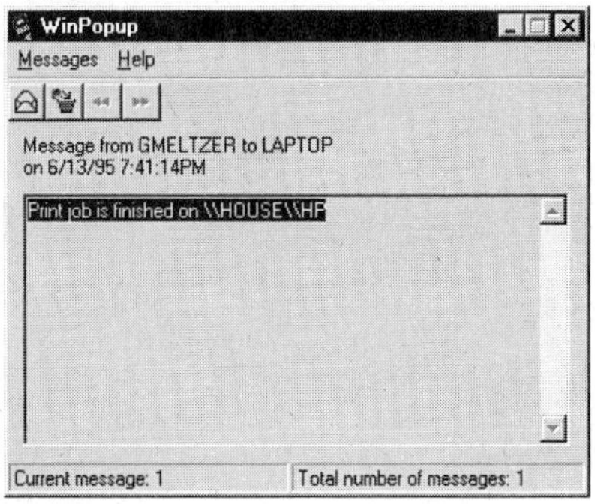

Fig. 26.17
WinPopup has sent a message to a user that her network print job is finished.

Network Security

Security on computer networks is designed to prevent unauthorized or accidental access to the information located on the disk drives on the network. Security can extend to preventing unauthorized users from using any network resource, such as a printer. Security systems also are intended to prevent unauthorized users from using computers on the network.

Windows 95 provides a wide range of network-security options. Some of the most powerful security tools, however, are not available for a workgroup network that consists of computers that run only Windows 95. These functions require that a Windows NT or Novell NetWare server be connected to the network and programmed in a special way to enable Windows 95's advanced security functions.

The following sections examine the security tools that you can use in both environments.

All-Windows 95 Workgroup Network

In an all-Windows 95 workgroup, three types of security are available:

- Logon security

- Share-level password security

- System Policies security

Next, you will learn to use each of these security methods on your workgroup LAN. Whether you use one, two, or all of these techniques, the bottom line is that using security will prevent data loss.

Logon Security

Although Windows 95 requires a logon password, you need to understand that the only things protected by this password are network resources, such as shared folders and shared printers. Windows 95 provides absolutely no password protection at the workstation level; anyone can sit down at your computer and access your local disks and attached resources.

If you need to control access to individual computers, so that only a user with the right password can start the operating system, you should consider using Windows NT, not Windows 95, on individual workstation computers. Windows NT requires a password before any user can work with the computer at all.

When Windows 95 starts, you see a screen that asks for your user ID and password. No matter what you do at this point, including clicking Cancel,

Windows continues to load and to give you access to all the drives and printers on your computer.

Now that you understand that no logon security exists for the workstation in Windows 95, consider logon security for the network.

Windows Logon Password

When Windows 95 starts for the first time, a logon dialog box asks for your user ID and password. Depending on your settings in Control Panel, Network, you will be prompted to log on to Windows 95 or the network. If your Network setting sets your Primary Network Logon as Client for Microsoft Networks, your logon screen looks like the one shown in figure 26.18.

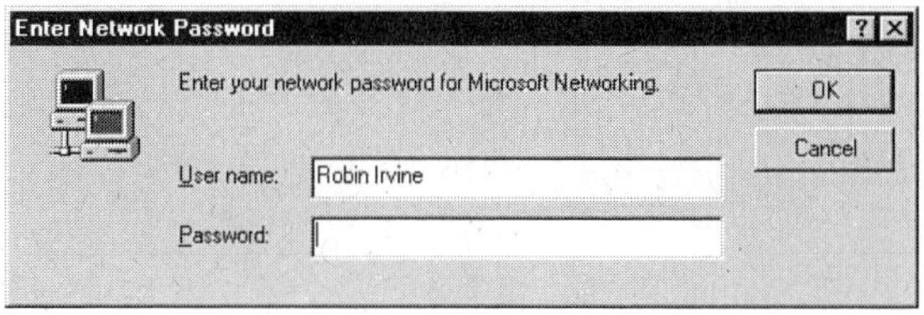

Fig. 26.18
This will be your logon screen, if your Primary Network Logon is set to be Client for Microsoft Networks.

If you set your Primary Network Logon to be Windows Logon, you see a logon prompt like the one shown in figure 26.19.

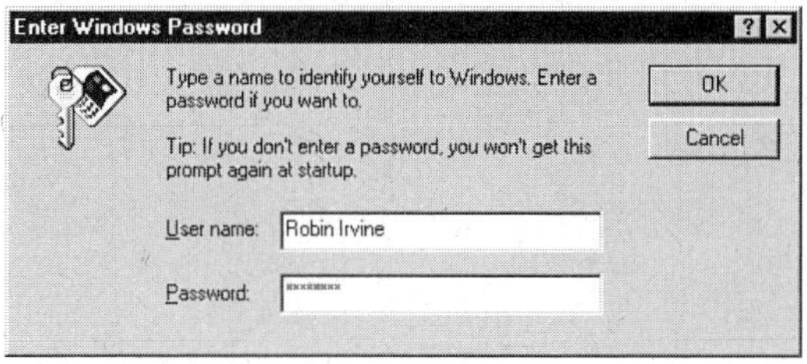

Fig. 26.19
The first time you run Windows 95 on your computer, you'll see this dialog box.

When you type the correct password for network access, you have access to all the shared resources on the network, as long as you know the password required to access them. In fact, you won't have to enter the passwords for network resources more than once; Windows stores the passwords that you enter in a cache so that they are entered for you automatically the next time you log on. Although the cache can be disabled by System Policies and by the Password List Editor program, in a normal installation, the password cache is active.

▶ See "Removing Cached Passwords," p. 824

This chapter has mentioned passwords in connection with shared resources. The following sections examine the way that passwords work.

V

Networking

Access Control in Workgroups: Share-Level-Access Control

In Chapter 20, you learned how to enable peer-to-peer resource sharing on a Windows 95 workgroup. In this section, you set some passwords for those resources so that only authorized users can find them over the network.

Figure 26.20 shows two types of shared resources.

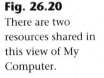

Fig. 26.20

There are two resources shared in this view of My Computer.

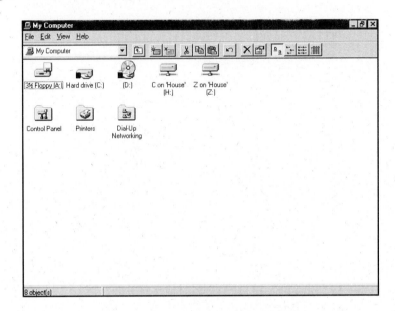

Notice that the icon for the local hard drive—drive C—is shared; the icon includes the outstretched hand that signifies sharing. The hand does not mean that the disk is completely open to any user, however. To control how you will share your drive, right-click the icon and choose Sharing from the pop-up menu.

Figure 26.21 shows the sharing properties that are enabled for the local hard drive. Two passwords are set. You want to give full read and write access to users who know the full-access password. Other users will be able only read the disk, not modify it in any way.

This type of security is called *share-level access*, and it is the only kind of access protection available to workgroups in which Windows 95 (or Windows for Workgroups 3.1x) peer server is the only type of server on the network. To see how this access control is enabled, open the Start menu and choose Settings, Control Panel, Network; click the Access Control tab, and select the Share Level access-control option. The other option is not available for peer-to-peer networks.

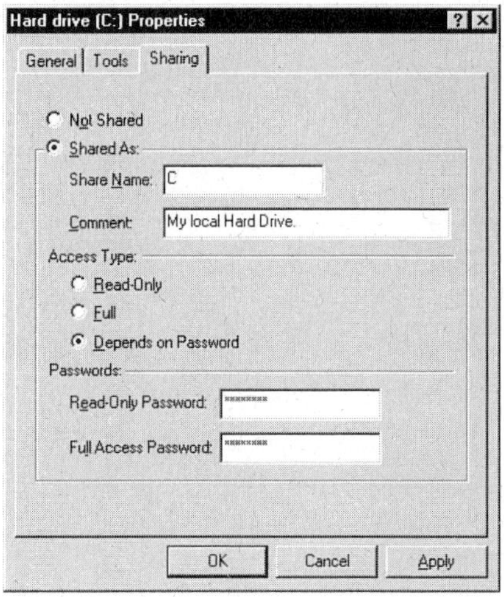

Fig. 26.21
The Hard Drive Properties sheet controls password access to the drive.

Share-Level Access and Network Neighborhood

If you enable sharing on a disk, folder, or printer on your computer, the shared resource appears in Network Neighborhood, from which users may try to connect to your resource or to map a drive letter to it.

At times, you want to share a resource but not broadcast that fact to the workgroup. A mechanism for hiding shared resources exists. To do this, add a dollar-sign character to the end of the share name. The resource still behaves in accordance with its password restrictions, but it does not appear in Network Neighborhood. Another member of the workgroup must know the exact name of the resource to connect to it.

Mapped Drives and Their Security

Figure 26.20, earlier in this chapter, showed two types of shared resources in the My Computer window. This section examines the properties of the resources whose icons look like disks attached to cables. These resources are shared drives and folders on other computers. The owners of those resources may have enabled share-level-security passwords for those resources. That security determines what you can do with the folders—whether you can write to them as well as read from them.

If the owner of a shared folder changes the password required to access that resource, your cached password no longer gives you access to the resource. You see a network drive icon with an X through the connection, like the one shown for the Z on 'House' connection in figure 26.22.

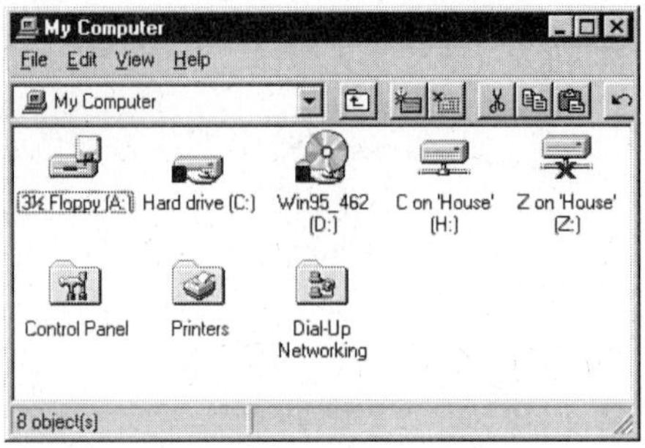

Fig. 26.22
An inaccessible
network drive is
shown with an X
through its icon.

To access the resource again, learn the new access password. Then, when you want to access the shared drive again, you will have to restart Windows.

Removing Cached Passwords

Because password caching is enabled in Windows 95 automatically, the system creates an encrypted file, in which it stores the password entries for all resources used by the computer. By default, the file name is SHARE.PWL. If User Profiles are enabled on the computer, the PWL files are not called SHARE but are created from the user names. When User Profiles are active, each user has a different PWL password-list file, such as TOM.PWL.

If you are having trouble with a cached password, use the Password List Editor program, PWLEDIT.EXE. This program does not show you the actual passwords; it shows you that a password exists and gives you the opportunity to remove the password. This procedure forces you to log in with the correct password the next time you want to connect to the resource that you edited.

> **Note**
>
> The Password List Editor program, PWLEDIT.EXE, is included on the CD-ROM version of Windows 95. It is not included on the floppy disk version of the operating system.

Figure 26.23 shows a Password List Editor screen. Password List Editor shows every password in effect on the computer on which its running. In figure 26.23, there is only one password in effect. Although the display is not very informative, the text "Rna" shown in the Resource column is a hint that the password is for dial-up networking. Rna, in Windows jargon, means Remote node access.

The only option is to remove the password.

Fig. 26.23
The Password List
Editor program
can remove
passwords from
any type of
password protected
resource on your
computer.

Using Windows 95 with a Microsoft Windows NT or Novell NetWare Server

If your network includes a Windows NT or NetWare server, your options for
workgroup security are greatly enhanced. You can use the features of those
servers to provide and enforce user-level security on the workgroup. In this
case, the Windows NT or NetWare server is acting as a security provider and
validator. This function works because those two network systems maintain
lists of authorized users and those users' network rights and access privileges.
This function does not exist in Windows 95 Peer-to-Peer networks.

Table 26.1 compares the features available in user- and share-level-access
control.

Table 26.1 Access-Control Comparison		
Feature	**User-Level**	**Share-Level**
Read Files	×	×
Write to Files	×	×
Create Files and Folders	×	
List Files	×	
Delete Files	×	
Change File Attributes	×	
Change Access Control	×	

V

Networking

You can see that user-level security gives you much finer control of shared resources because you can enable any, all, or none of the preceding sets of rights. If you enable only List Files, for example, users who connect to the folder can execute programs from the folder, but they cannot delete or change anything.

User Lists in User-Level Security

In a Windows NT environment, the administrator uses the User Manager program to set up the security permissions for each user name. Windows 95 uses these permissions to set access rights for the listed resources. A Windows NT administrator also can create groups, simplifying workgroup administration by granting the same rights to several users or perhaps an entire workgroup.

The only thing to remember is that in the case of multiple Windows NT domains, the Windows 95 computer must select one domain server to be the security and list provider.

In NetWare, the same list principles apply. Instead of using User Manager, however, NetWare relies on the Bindery feature. As a result, NetWare 4.x servers must be running Bindery emulation to act as security hosts for Windows 95 computers.

General Network-Security Guidelines

As you've seen by now, network security in a Windows 95 workgroup LAN must be configured, cooperatively, by the network neighbors who are connected to the LAN. To avoid loss of your workgroup's valuable data, accidentally or otherwise, consider the following four guiding principles:

- Although setting up a completely open, password-free network is easy, resist the temptation. Even though you may not have to enter passwords with password caching enabled, require the passwords; they will increase your options later.

- If you can make access to a shared resource read-only, do so. Use full read-write access only when you have to. This practice can prevent accidental deletion of important files and directories.

- Make sure that you and your network neighbors keep their passwords guarded—and not written in plain sight on or near the computer.

- Don't use an obvious item, such as your name, as your Windows password.

Troubleshooting and Network-Management Tools

If you're having problems accessing resources that you can see in Network Neighborhood, check to see whether you have the rights that you need to do your work. Windows provides an easy way to use Net Watcher for this purpose. In Network Neighborhood, right-click the computer that holds the resources that you need, choose Properties, and then click the Tools tab. Figure 26.24 shows the list of management tools that are available.

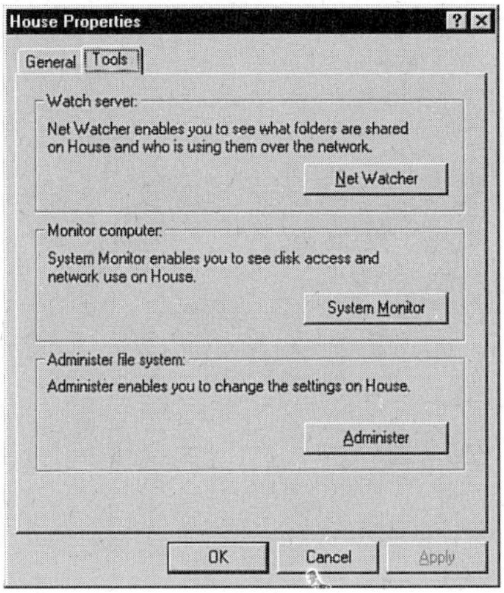

Fig. 26.24
Windows 95 provides Net Watcher, System Monitor, and Administer tools for network management.

From this point, you can select Net Watcher and use it to see whether the folder that you want to use is shared. If not, you can designate the folder as shared. If the problem is that the folder is read-only and you need full access, use Net Watcher to adjust that situation, too.

Using Dial-Up Networking

Just as you can connect to shared resources on a network using a network interface card and network wiring, you can connect to the same kind of resources using a modem and telephone wires. This type of networking is called Dial-Up Networking. Dial-Up Networking is discussed in Chapter 9, "Special Features for Notebook Users," as this feature will be of most interest to laptop and notebook PC users. However, if you want to configure dial-up networking to work on your desktop computer, all of the procedures are the same.❖

Part VI

Online Communications with Windows 95

Chapter 27

Installing and Configuring Your Modem

by Gordon Meltzer

Modems and the technology that they use—serial communications—have been a problem for Windows since Version 1.0. In Windows 95, however, Microsoft finally got it right—and then some. The operating system now incorporates a rich, reliable, full-featured communications subsystem that is capable of operating today's fastest modems. Even better, Windows 95 is an extensible system that works well with tomorrow's communications devices, such as ISDN adapters, parallel-port modems, and cable modems. These forthcoming devices work at speeds beyond even the fastest of today's modems. Windows 95 can handle all these devices, and more, at the same time.

In this chapter, you learn

- How Windows' communications system works for you

- How to install your Plug and Play modem or legacy modem

- About the Universal Standard Modem Driver and other drivers

- How to configure your modem after it's installed

- Why your modem works smarter with the new 32-bit programs

- More about TAPI

Understanding the Windows 95 Communications System

In the past, getting good performance from modems running with Windows often meant changing the part of Windows that controlled all the serial ports and, therefore, controlled the modems. Various companies supplied these *enhanced communications drivers*, which were sold with high-speed modems, by themselves, or with communications programs. (Often, you couldn't get the modem working without a special driver.) Although literally thousands of enhanced communications drivers were available, all of them took over all the modems and serial communications in Windows.

Windows 95 doesn't need these aftermarket parts to make communications fly. The sophisticated communications subsystem in Windows 95 is designed to automatically recognize, install, and configure modems if they are compatible with the Plug and Play standard.

Tip
When you hear the expression PCMCIA Card, know it is an obsolete way to refer to a PC Card, the credit card size Plug and Play devices we use as modems, network adapters, and more.

Most Plug and Play modems are located on *PC Cards* (formerly known as PCMCIA cards). These cards can support full Plug-and-Play functionality, including hot swapping.

> **Note**
>
> Hot swapping lets PC Cards be removed or inserted while the system is running. The system will load and unload any required software automatically on the fly.

◀ See "Understanding Plug and Play Architecture," p. 230

Some Plug and Play modems may be on ISA cards; these cannot benefit from hot swapping, because they are designed to be fixed inside the computer and not removed during operation.

> **Note**
>
> ISA stands for Industry Standard Architecture, and ISA cards are the familiar add-in peripheral cards that have been used in PC's since IBM set the standard.

◀ See "Using PC Card Devices," p. 266

Windows also has special capabilities for 32-bit communications programs far beyond the capabilities of its predecessor. You learn more about TAPI (Telephony Applications Programming Interface) capabilities in the section "Working Smarter with TAPI and 32-Bit Windows Programs," later in this chapter.

Even if you have a standard modem that does not support Plug and Play, a Windows Wizard can help you install and configure the modem.

Whichever type of modem you choose to install, Windows can use it to communicate more reliably and with better data throughput than ever before. The three reasons for this are:

- New 32-bit TAPI communications system for 32-bit applications

- Improved 16-bit communications driver for older 16-bit programs

- Support for the new 16550-compatible UART (Universal Asynchronous Receiver Transmitter) chips found in new modems and modern serial ports

Windows uses these features to give you more control over communications with your modem, and to make your modem do a better job for you.

Installing a Plug and Play Modem

Like other devices that support this new technology, Plug and Play modems communicate with Windows to cooperate in setting themselves up. These modems always contain the serial communications port and modulator/demodulator/dialer on the same card, so that Windows can configure them to work together at the same time.

> **Note**
>
> Internal modems consist of three main functional sections. The Serial Communications Port handles communications with your computer. The Modulator/Demodulator handles communications over the phone lines with another modem. The Dialer handles communications with the telephone network and gets your call connected.
>
> External modems don't contain the Serial Communications Port; they attach to one that is built in to your computer.
>
> Plug and Play modems add another section which identifies the modem's capabilities and resource needs to Windows 95 setup.

During Windows setup, information is exchanged between your modem and the system. This is what happens, automatically, when Windows comes to the part of setup in which your modem will be configured:

Tip

Make sure any internal ISA card modem you buy includes the modern 16550 type of UART chip. All PC Card modems already do. If you're buying a serial port card to put in an ISA slot, check to make sure you're buying one with the 16550 chip, or a compatible chip.

▶ See "Understanding Windows 95 Setup Requirements," p. 1078

VI

▶ See "How Windows 95 Setup Works," p. 1083

Online Communications

1. Windows searches through all the system's input-output (I/O) ports and finds the Plug and Play circuits on the modem.

2. The system assigns the card an identification number, which Windows stores in its information files.

3. Windows asks the modem about its speeds and specifications. The modem gives the information to Windows setup.

4. Setup then assigns a communications port number (COM1, COM2, and so on) and resources to be used by the port. These resources are an interrupt request and an I/O address. If the Plug and Play modem is on a PC Card, Windows also assigns a memory address to the modem.

Plug and Play—the Play-by-Play

If a Plug and Play modem is installed in your computer before you install Windows, the modem setup occurs automatically and transparently. This section examines what happens if you have a PC Card modem installed in PC Card slot 1 when you install Windows 95.

First, Windows configures the PC Card slots. The PC Card Wizard appears during installation. Figure 27.1 shows the wizard screen.

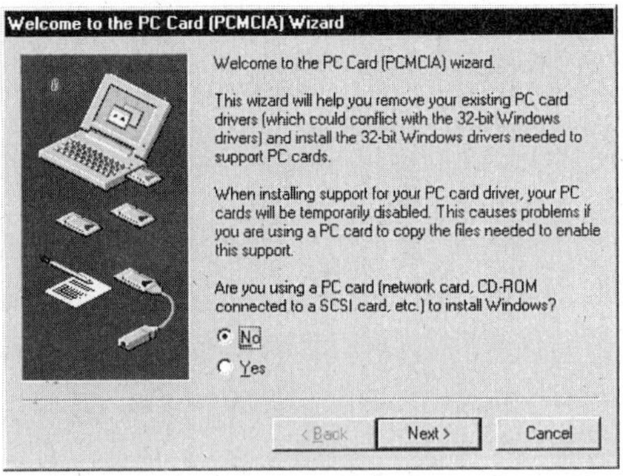

Fig. 27.1

The PC Card Wizard begins installing your PC Card modem.

Caution

Notice in figure 27.1 the wizard warns you that it is about to disable all PC Cards while it works. If you're installing Windows from a CD-ROM connected through a PC Card, setup will fail. For a workaround, use floppy disks for this portion of setup.

Next, Windows proposes removing the old DOS-based 16-bit Card and Socket Services drivers from the CONFIG.SYS, AUTOEXEC.BAT, and SYSTEM.INI files. To review the changes before proceeding, choose Yes and then click Next.

Figure 27.2 shows the real-mode 16-bit drivers in CONFIG.SYS. They are the last five lines in the file. For best results, you should permit the Wizard to remove the old drivers. Click Next to accept the changes. After the Wizard processes CONFIG.SYS, it processes the next two files in the same way.

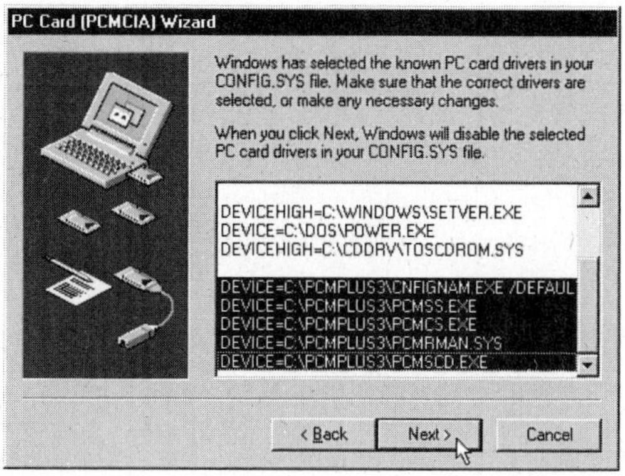

Fig. 27.2
Real mode drivers in CONFIG.SYS that will be removed by Windows 95.

Note

Technically speaking, the statements are not actually removed from the file. Instead, the wizard *comments out* (switches off) the statements by inserting a REM-Removed By PC Card Wizard statement at the beginning of each line in which the drivers are referenced.

When the wizard finishes setting up the PC Card slots, it installs the 32-bit protected mode Card and Socket Services driver software for them. These drivers control all the Plug and Play features.

After the drivers are installed, you need to restart Windows to activate the new drivers. Click Finish in the wizard dialog box, close any other applications that you may have running, and click Yes when you're ready to shut down.

VI

Online Communications

Windows loads with the 32-bit drivers enabled for the first time. Now it can "see" (and, therefore, configure) the modem in your PC Card slot. Using the new, protected-mode 32-bit Card and Socket Services, Windows can install any modem in your PC Card slot. In figure 27.3, Windows detected a new modem and installed the software drivers for it automatically.

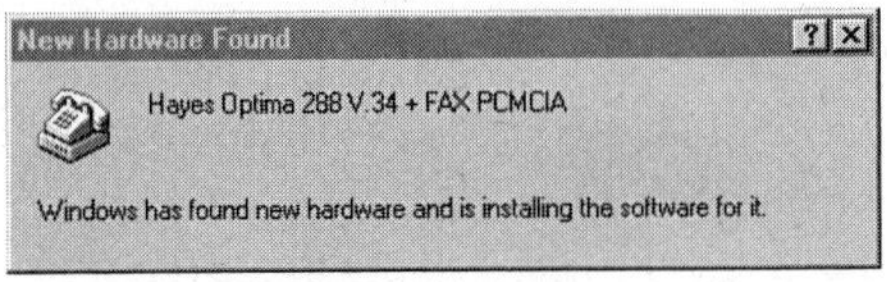

Fig. 27.3
Windows setup
finds your
modem.

Your Plug and Play modem is now installed. Next, the modem must be configured to allow all Windows advanced features to operate, which is discussed in the "Advanced Settings" section later in this chapter. The following section explains what Windows really did, via the wizard.

Plug and Play—Behind the Scenes

The Windows user interface for the installation of the Plug and Play modem is the Setup Wizard. The wizard does all the setup work, and a lot happens behind the scene.

What has actually happened during the Plug and Play modem installation is this:

1. Windows asks the modem to identify itself , the modem responds, and Windows installs the software to run the modem. Then, the wizard tells you its job is complete and your modem is installed.

2. Windows installs the Unimodem driver for any modems that support AT (Attention) commands. Most modems do. Windows then looks in its database of .INF files. If information is found on the specific modem, it installs the modem mini-driver.

> **Note**
>
> Windows will assign the IBM-compatible standard communications port names to ports and modems. The names will be assigned in order, using the standard resources:

Port Name	I/O Port Resource
Com1	3F8
Com2	2F8
Com3	3E8
Com4	2E8

Caution

If Windows finds a modem configured to a base address that is not listed in the table above, it will assign COM5 to that modem. Programs designed for Windows 3.1 or DOS may not be able to work with a modem on this port. The workaround is to change the non-standard address in Device Manager control panel.

▶ See "Using Custom Setup Mode," p. 1099

Troubleshooting

I can't get the modem to install.

First, check Device Manager to see whether the hardware Communications Port exists and is working properly. If the Port doesn't exist in Device Manager's list of Ports, follow the steps in the section "Installing a Legacy Modem" later in this chapter to install the Communications Port.

Turn your external modem off and then on again. If you are using an internal modem, shut down Windows, power down the computer, and try again.

Installing a Legacy Modem

Legacy modems don't have the hardware in them to identify themselves to Windows 95 setup—they can't tell Windows about their capabilities, or their resource requirements.

◀ See "Dealing with Legacy Hardware," p. 247

Legacy modems are not Plug and Play devices. They can, however, be either internal or external modems.

An *internal modem* is one that fits into a slot in the computer bus, and contains the serial port on the modem.

VI

Online Communications

An *external modem* does not contain the serial port. The external modem connects via cable to the serial port inside the computer.

Windows considers the serial port to be a separate device from the modem, even if you have an internal modem, in which both the modem and the serial port are on the same add-in card. Windows configures these devices separately. You should be aware of the process that Windows uses to perform the configurations.

If you're trying to install an internal modem, Windows may act differently with different modems. You may be able to install the serial port at the same time you install the modem. If Windows cannot detect and initialize the port, however, you may have to use the Add New Hardware option in the Control Panel to set up the port.

▶ See "Advanced Installation Techniques," p. 1098

In Windows 95, you can accomplish a task in several ways. You can install a legacy modem in any of the following ways:

- Use the Add New Hardware Wizard.

- Click the Modem icon, in Control Panel.

- Start a 32-bit program that uses a modem. If no modem is installed, Windows suggests you install one.

The following procedure uses the Add New Hardware Wizard to install the modem. Follow these steps:

1. Open the Start menu and choose Settings, Control Panel.

2. Double-click the Add New Hardware icon. The first Add New Hardware Wizard window appears.

3. Click Next.

4. You should allow Windows to try to find your modem by itself, so choose Yes when the wizard asks if you want Windows to detect it automatically. You'll see a progress report during the detection process.

   If Windows can, it sets up the serial port and the modem at the same time. Windows may not find the modem when it finds the port. In that case, run Add New Hardware Wizard again.

   The report from the Add New Hardware Wizard, shown in figure 27.4, shows that Windows has found a new Communications Port.

Fig. 27.4
This report from
the Add New
Hardware Wizard
shows two new
devices detected.

5. Click Finish.

6. When you are prompted, restart the computer.

After Windows restarts, look in Control Panel's Device Manager (accessed by
clicking the System icon in Control Panel). In the Ports section, you'll see a
new Communications Port, COM1, has been added, shown in figure 27.5.

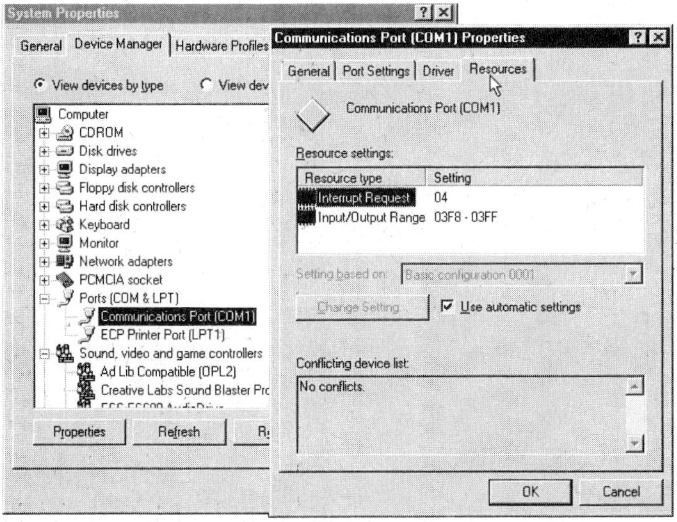

Fig. 27.5
The new Commu-
nications Port and
its resources.

VI

Online Communications

> **Note**
>
> Many times Windows will not find the port and the modem on the same pass
> through the installation process. Don't be concerned; follow the next steps.

In this common example, Windows could not detect and install the port and modem in one step. Therefore, you need to visit the Control Panel again. Now that COM1 is working properly, Windows should be able to detect and install the modem connected to that port.

 Double-click the Modems icon in the Control Panel. When the Install New Modem Wizard starts, choose Other (see fig. 27.6).

Fig. 27.6
Installing a non Plug and Play modem

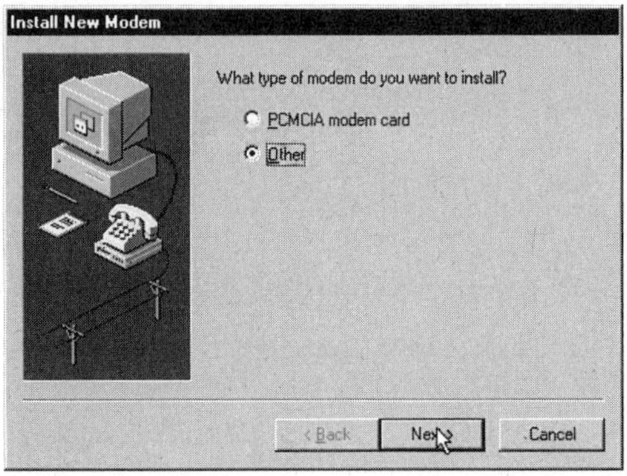

> **Install New Modem**
>
> What type of modem do you want to install?
>
> ○ PCMCIA modem card
> ● Other
>
> [< Back] [Next >] [Cancel]

In the next dialog box, the wizard asks for another chance to detect the modem. Click Next, and don't tell the wizard what modem you have; you want to see whether Windows can find out now that the port is working. Figure 27.7 shows the window that appears just before automatic modem detection.

Fig. 27.7
The Modem Installation Wizard set to auto-detect your modem.

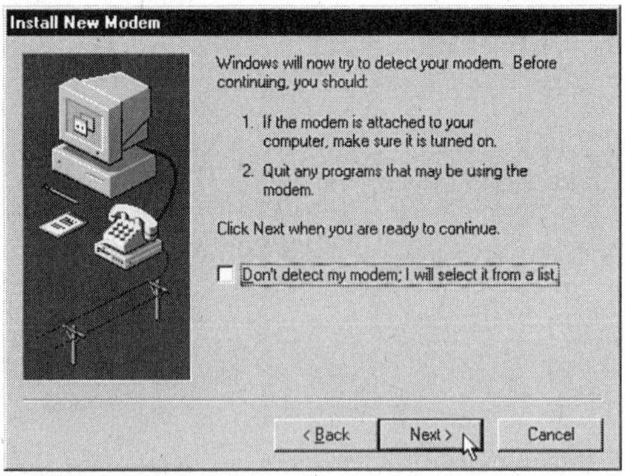

> **Install New Modem**
>
> Windows will now try to detect your modem. Before continuing, you should:
>
> 1. If the modem is attached to your computer, make sure it is turned on.
> 2. Quit any programs that may be using the modem.
>
> Click Next when you are ready to continue.
>
> ☐ Don't detect my modem; I will select it from a list.
>
> [< Back] [Next >] [Cancel]

At the end of the modem installation process, Windows reports that it found the modem attached to COM1 (see fig. 27.8). Because the reported type matches the type that is installed, you have finished the installation of the standard legacy modem. To close the dialog box, click Next.

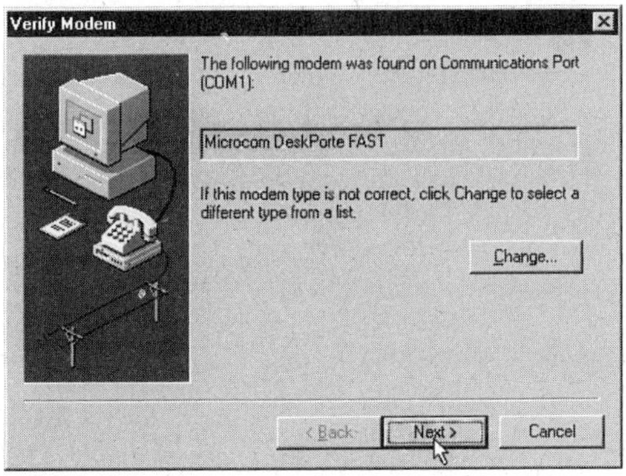

Fig. 27.8
The Modem Wizard
has detected the
new modem.

Note

Windows chooses slow port speeds by default. If you have a fast computer, change the port speeds in the Modems Properties Control Panel to the modem's maximum speed.

Troubleshooting

When I use the modem, another program—or the entire system—locks up or crashes. How do I fix it?

This problem usually results from an interrupt conflict. Two devices may be trying to use the same interrupt. If you have a serial mouse on COM1, which uses Interrupt 4, and you set up a modem on COM3, which by default also uses Interrupt 4, a conflict will exist.

Use Device Manager on the System Properties sheet (Control Panel, System) to look for a modem or mouse icon that has a yellow exclamation point. Double-click the icon and choose Resources. If a conflict is listed, Windows offers to start the Hardware Conflict Troubleshooter. This program can help you resolve interrupt conflicts by reassigning resources such as interrupts.

VI

Online Communications

Understanding the Unimodem Driver

When Windows 3.1 came on the market, one of its major advances was its capability to use installed printers with any Windows printer. Before Windows, each and every program that wanted to print had to have its own printer driver included. In Windows 3.1, if there was a Windows driver, all programs could print without drivers of their own. The problem—and the burden for programmers—was that for each printer type, a driver had to be written from scratch. Supporting the thousands of printer types on the market was difficult.

During Windows evolution, the idea of a universal driver was developed. In Windows 95, this driver is implemented beautifully.

In Windows 95, the same concept also has been extended to modems.

Most of the modems on the market use a variation of the AT command set, which Dennis Hayes developed for the original Smartmodem in 1980. The command set has evolved over the years, and each manufacturer has its own set of proprietary extensions for advanced features. Still, the most basic commands are the same for all modems that use AT commands. The fact that this lowest common denominator of commands exists for the vast majority of modems allowed Microsoft to write a universal modem driver—the Unimodem driver.

Table 27.1 shows the basic AT commands used by the Unimodem driver.

Table 27.1 Modem Commands for Unimodem Driver	
AT Command	**Function**
AT	Attention
ATZ	Reset modem
ATD	Dial modem
ATI	Identify modem
ATH	Hang up modem
ATO	Go off hook in originate mode

Once the Unimodem driver is talking to the modem, these commands provide enough functionality for the Unidriver to interrogate the modem, find its manufacturer and model number, and try to find a match in its modem database. If a match is found, the Unidriver tells Windows to install the minidriver that matches the modem. This minidriver works with the modem to enable advanced features such as data compression and error correction. These features are likely to be implemented differently by each manufacturer.

Even without a minidriver, the Unimodem driver can make a partially Hayes-compatible modem dial, connect, and disconnect. Modems that are running with only the Unidriver will be shown in Control Panel as a Standard modem.

Using Drivers Provided by Modem Manufacturers

You may encounter a modem that comes with a Windows 95 driver disk. This disk indicates that the modem has features that are not supported by the Unimodem driver and that no proper minidriver comes with Windows 95.

To install the modem with its own driver software, follow these steps:

1. Double-click the Modem icon in Control Panel.

2. Choose Add.

3. Choose Don't Detect My Modem; I will Select It From a List. Then click Next.

4. Now choose Have Disk.

5. Insert the manufacturer's driver disk into the proper disk drive when you are prompted to (or if the disk is in another drive, enter the correct drive and path), as shown in figure 27.9, and then choose OK.

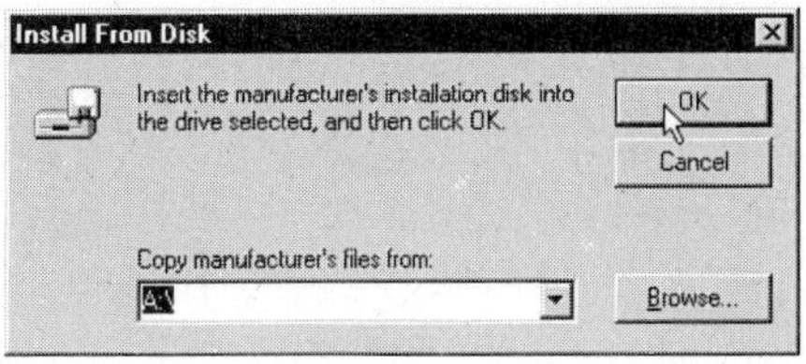

Fig. 27.9
Installing a driver provided by the modem manufacturer.

6. Choose the driver for your modem model from the list that appears (if more than one driver is on the disk), and then choose OK.

7. Choose Finish.

Your modem's drivers are installed in Windows, and the modem's special features are enabled.

Configuring Your Modem

Now that your hardware is installed, you can configure Windows to work cooperatively with it. Windows can take some information from you and supply that information to communications programs to allow them to function more effectively.

VI

Online Communications

To operate your modem with the greatest possible intelligence, Windows automatically collects the following information from you:

- Your location

- Your area code

- Access number(s) needed to get an outside line

- Type of dialing used at this location (tone or pulse)

This information, however, is not enough to make your modem operate at peak efficiency and at maximum data-transfer rates. You should tell Windows other things about your modem, including the following:

- Maximum port speed (computer to modem)

- Default data-formatting properties

- How to handle no-dial-tone situations

- How long the modem should try to connect before stopping

- When to disconnect an idle modem connection

- Your modem's error-control and compression features

- What kind of flow control to use with your modem

- How to handle low-speed connections

- How to record a log file of the modem's interaction with the system, for use in troubleshooting

- How to manually send extra AT commands to the modem during initialization

The following sections explain these items.

General Properties

Use the Modems Control Panel to select the modem that you are working with, and then choose Properties. The Modem Properties sheet, which has two pages, appears. Figure 27.10 shows the General page.

The options in this tab include the following:

- *Port.* This displays which port is in use by your modem.

- *Speaker Volume.* This slider control controls how loud you want your internal speaker.

■ *Maximum Speed.* This setting controls the speed you want your modem to work.

■ *Only Connect at this Speed.* Checking this box tells your computer to connect at only one speed.

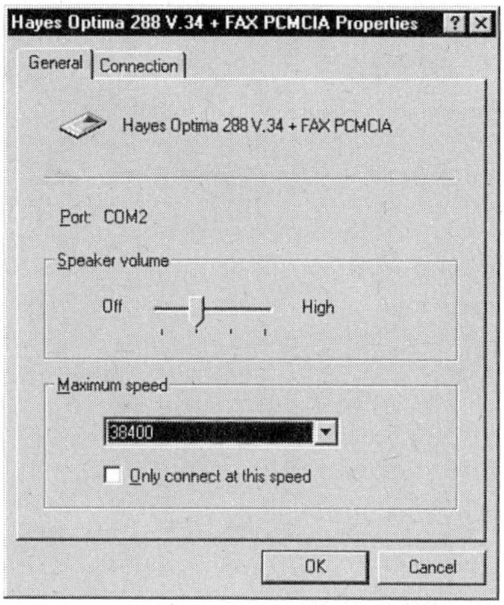

Fig. 27.10

The General page of the Modems Properties sheet displays basic information about your modem.

The General properties page contains settings that can make your modem work better, when the proper values are selected.

Port

The Port option shows the communications port to which Windows assigned the modem. If the modem is an internal Plug and Play type, in which Windows can configure the serial port, you may have a choice in setting which communications port to use with the modem. If other communications ports are used, or if the modem cannot be configured by Windows (you must use jumpers to set its port and address), you will not be able to change the communications port assigned to this modem.

Speaker Volume

The Speaker Volume control is a handy way to tell 32-bit Windows 95 communications programs how loud to set the volume of the modem's speaker.

The volume control slider works with modems that have physical speakers and with modems (such as PC Cards) that rely on the computer's speaker for their sound. If the volume control is grayed out, the modem has no speaker and no way of using the speaker in the computer. (Many ISDN Terminal Adapters will have the Speaker Volume grayed out.)

VI

Online Communicati

Note

Sixteen-bit Windows and DOS communications programs ignore the Speaker Volume setting; instead, they set modem volume themselves. These older programs set the volume themselves because when they were written, the operating system had no way to keep track of your preferences.

Maximum Speed

The Maximum Speed parameter is extremely important. This setting has nothing to do with the speed at which your modem connects to another modem; it represents the speed at which your *computer* connects to your modem.

Why is this important? Any modem that operates at 9600 bits per second (formerly referred to as the baud rate) or faster typically supports data compression. The International Telecommunications Union (ITU), the professional society that sets world-wide communications standards, has established four data-compression standards. Your modem may support one or all of these standards.

Table 27.2 shows the standards, the modem speed associated with each standard, and the port speed that you should use with your modem. These general guidelines work for almost all modems.

Table 27.2 Modem Port Speed Settings

Modem Speed	ITU Standard	Port Speed
9,600	v.32	19,200
14,400	v.32bis	57,600
19,200	v.32ter	57,600
28,800	v.34	115,200

Note

You may not be able to set the port speed as high as 115,200 on older, slower computers. These computers may not have the right type of serial-port hardware, which is based on the type 16550A chip. In such a case, use 57,600.

When two modems that are using one of the ITU standards, or one of the older, but still widely used, Microcom MNP compression standards connect, the modems examine the data that they are sending to see whether it can be compressed; if so, the modems compress the data. Sending compressed data raises the effective speed of the modem. Modem speed can approach the speed of the port if the data can be compressed greatly.

Compression works only if the port speed is fast enough to feed the data to the modem as quickly as the modem needs it. If a 14,400 v.32bis modem compresses data into half the space that the data takes up on disk, the port must feed data to the modem at least twice as fast as the 14,400 connect speed. Setting the port to 57,600 allows for the high speed data feed to the modem and also takes care of some overhead for processing.

▶ See "Advanced Settings," p. 848

Only Connect at this Speed

Check this box if you don't want your modem to adjust its speed to match the speed of the modem on the other end. Checking this box allows only high-speed connections between two modems that are each capable of high speeds.

Sometimes bad conditions on the telephone line can make two high speed modems connect at low speeds. Checking this box prevents the low speed connection from taking place. In that case, you will have to keep trying the call until the modems can connect at their full rated speed.

Connection Properties

Now open the Connection page, shown in figure 27.11.

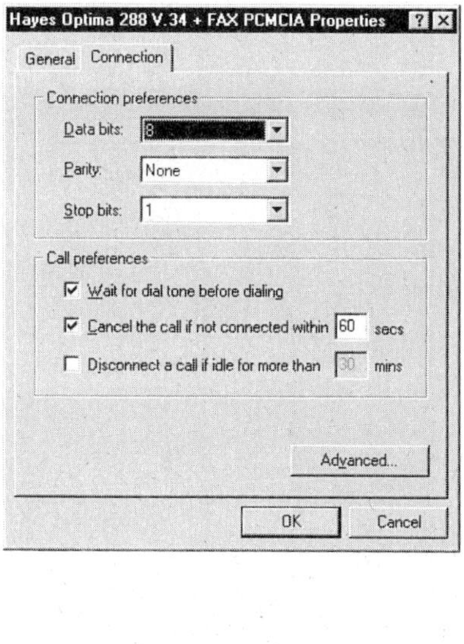

Fig. 27.11
The Connection page allows you to set your preferences.

VI

Online Communications

In this page, you can set the following options:

- *Connection Preferences.* The default settings—8 bits, no parity, and 1 stop bit—work for most online services, BBSes, remote-access and remote-control programs, data-transfer services, dial-up networking, and so on. You need to change these settings only if the resource that you are dialing requires changes.

- *Wait for Dial Tone before Dialing.* If you choose this option, you are warned if no dial tone is present when the modem tries to dial. This option allows you to check your phone line and modem cable to make sure that a dial tone is getting to the modem.

- *Cancel the Call if Not Connected Within x Secs.* If the modem that you're calling doesn't answer within 30 or 60 seconds, a problem may exist. When you choose this option, you are notified if your call didn't connect, so that you can check to see whether you have the right phone number.

- *Disconnect a Call if Idle for More Than x Secs.* You may want your communications program to hang up the phone and break the connection if the modems haven't sent any data in either direction after a specified period. This option can save you money if you use commercial online services regularly. If you get interrupted or called away from your computer, Windows disconnects from the service so that you won't continue to rack up expensive online charges.

Advanced Settings

At the bottom of the Connection page is the Advanced button. When you click this button, you see the dialog box shown in figure 27.12.

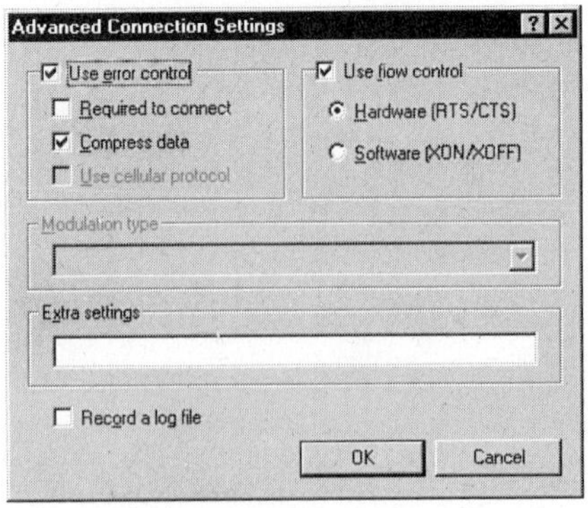

Fig. 27.12
In the Advanced
Connection
Settings dialog box
you can further
configure your
modem.

The Use Error Control, Compress Data, and Use Flow Control options in the Advanced Connection Settings dialog box work with one another and with the port-speed setting in the General page of the Modem Properties sheet. These options should be selected by default.

Your choices in Advanced Connection Settings will determine if your modem will work as fast, and as reliably, as its manufacturer intended it to.

- For modems with data speeds of 9,600 bps or faster, Windows turns on the Use Error Control option automatically.

- Windows also may turn on the Compress Data option. If it doesn't, but if your modem supports one of the compression standards, you should choose the Compress Data option.

- In the Use Flow Control section of the dialog box, you should choose Hardware on modems rated at 9,600 bps or faster. If you don't choose Hardware, the high port speed that you set in the General tab causes data errors instead of fast throughput, compression, and error correction.

These settings work well for most connections; make sure that they are enabled.

Modulation Type

The Modulation Type setting controls how Windows handles connections at 300 and 1,200 bps. If you connect with an old modem at 300 or 1,200 bps , you have to decide whether to use U.S. or European standards. Bell works with American modems, and CCITT V.21 works with modems in the rest of the world. If you want to connect to a CCITT V.21 or V.22 modem, make sure that your modem can use these standards.

> **Note**
>
> U.S. and European modems used different standards until 9,600-bps modems became popular. At that time, American manufacturers adopted the standards set by the CCITT (in English, the International Telegraph & Telephone Consultative Committee) and its successor, the ITU (International Telecommunications Union). Now modems all over the world can communicate at 9,600 bps and faster.

VI

Online Communications

Extra Settings

If you need to send the modem an AT command that Windows does not include automatically in its initialization procedure, type the command in the Extra Settings box.

Windows hides extra settings away in this obscure location because Windows architects believe the operating system should handle all details of communicating with the modem. The user should be isolated from sending raw AT commands. Because each brand of modem implements the AT command set differently, an AT command that works on one 28.8 kbps modem may not work the same on any other brand of modem.

However, if you are certain about your modem's implementation of the AT command set, Extra Settings is the place to send additional commands at modem initialization time, just before the modem dials out.

For example, if you want to turn off the speaker completely on a Hayes modem, enter ATM0 (that's a zero after the M), in the Extra Settings dialog.

Using Log Files

If you repeatedly have trouble making a connection, tell Windows to keep a record of the commands that it sends to the modem and the replies from the modem. This record can be useful in troubleshooting the problem. You can look for responses from the modem that contain the word ERROR and see what commands caused the errors. To activate this feature, choose the Record a Log File option.

> **Note**
>
> The log file is stored in the Windows directory as MODEMLOG.TXT. You can use Notepad to examine the log file.

When you are done making your choices in the Advanced Connection Settings dialog box, click OK. This returns you to the Modem Properties sheet.

Understanding Your Modem and Your Telephone System

Dialing Properties is a new concept for Windows 95. Dialing Properties gives you a way to control how your calls are dialed. You can create and choose from a list of dialing locations, each of which can be in a different area code, or different country. Windows will still dial the modem properly. Finally, the system knows how to do these things!

Dialing Properties also works with your modem to tell it whether you need to dial an access code to get an outside line. It allows you to make a calling card call with your modem. Dialing Properties can disable call waiting, so your modem calls won't be interrupted by an incoming call. And with Dialing Properties, you can tell your modem whether it can use touch-tones on your phone line, or if the modem must use rotary style pulse dialing.

To control Dialing Properties, choose Dialing Properties from the Modems Properties sheet.

The preceding sections explain how some of the properties settings for your modem control the way that the modem call is made. So far, the only actual dialing parameter that you've given the modem is whether to use tone or pulse dialing.

Many of the things that a modem needs to do to complete a call depend on where you and your computer are located. A modem that's being used at home, for example, usually dials differently than a modem that's being used in a hotel room or at the office. Knowing the phone number of the computer that you want to dial with the modem isn't enough; you also have area codes and outside-line codes to deal with. In addition, you may want to make the call a credit-card call.

These issues used to be problems. Windows 95, however, collects information from you so that communications programs deal with these issues in a seamless, elegant fashion.

Figure 27.13 shows the Dialing Properties sheet, in which you specify location information. This information tells your modem how to work wherever you go with your computer. If you are using your modem at home, where you don't need to dial a code for an outside line but do have the call-waiting feature, your settings may look like the ones in figure 27.13.

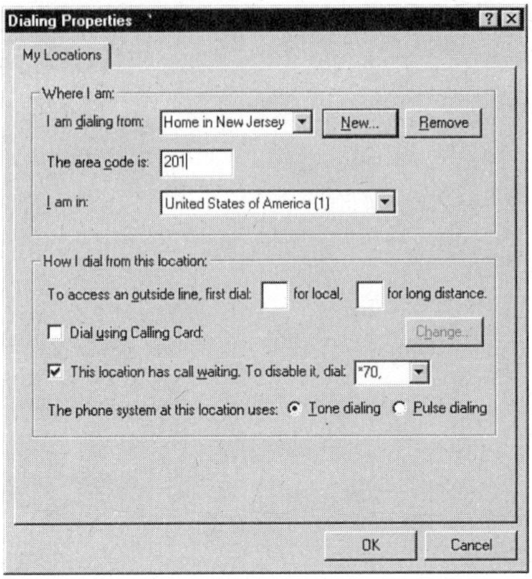

Fig. 27.13
You can set location information in the Dialing Properties sheet.

Suppose, however, that you're working in a hotel room in Washington, D.C., that you need to dial 9 to get an outside line (or 91 to get a long-distance outside line), and that you want to charge the call to a credit card.

Tip
You can create as many locations as you need.

To make a credit card call, you need to check the Dial Using Credit Card box. Your Dialing Properties settings would look like the ones in figure 27.14.

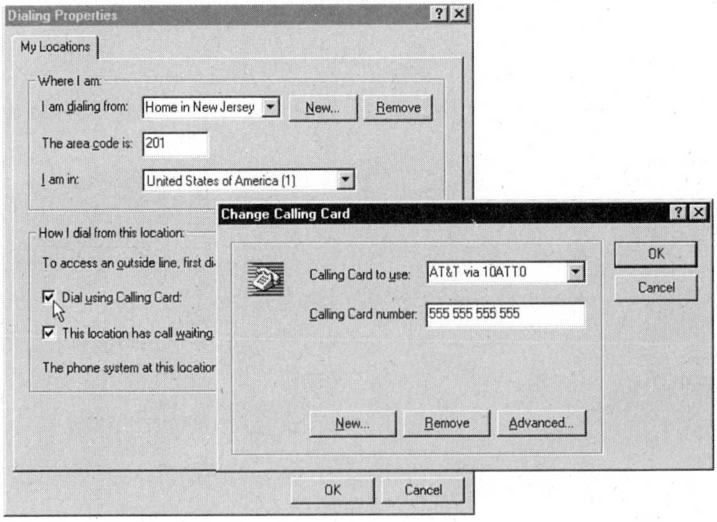

Fig. 27.14
Making a calling card call with your modem is easy.

In the Dialing Properties sheet, Windows has created your first location for you, based on information you gave setup during Windows installation. Windows has named this the Default Location.

Create additional locations by choosing Ṉew on the Dialing Properties sheet. Then, name the Location, and fill out the country and area code for the Location. You also can remove a location by choosing Ṟemove.

When you use a communications program that is TAPI-aware and Windows 95-aware, you can specify your location before dialing. Examples of programs that take advantage of Locations are Windows HyperTerminal, Windows Phone Dialer, the Microsoft Network online service, Microsoft Exchange, and any of Exchange's MAPI modules, such as CompuServe Mail and Dial-Up Networking.

To learn more about Microsoft Exchange, and MAPI modules that use modems, see Chapter 24, "Using Microsoft Exchange."

▶ See "Working Smarter with TAPI and 32-Bit Windows Programs," p. 855

Getting Your Modem to Dial

If your modem is working properly and your settings are correct, then dialing numbers through your modem should be effortless. In most cases, the program will direct-dial the modem. However, if you can't get the modem to dial, try the following procedures:

■ In the Modems Control Panel, check to see whether the modem that is displayed matches your model. If not, choose Ḁdd New Modem to install your modem. If any modems that are not in your system appear in the Control Panel, delete them.

■ In the System Control Panel, choose Device Manager. Choose Modems, select your modem, double-click to display the Properties sheet, and click the General tab. The sheet shown in figure 27.15 indicates that the device is used in the current configuration and that it's working properly.

■ Make sure that the communications port is set correctly. Click the Modem tab, shown in figure 27.16, and check the port name and port speed.

VI

Online Communications

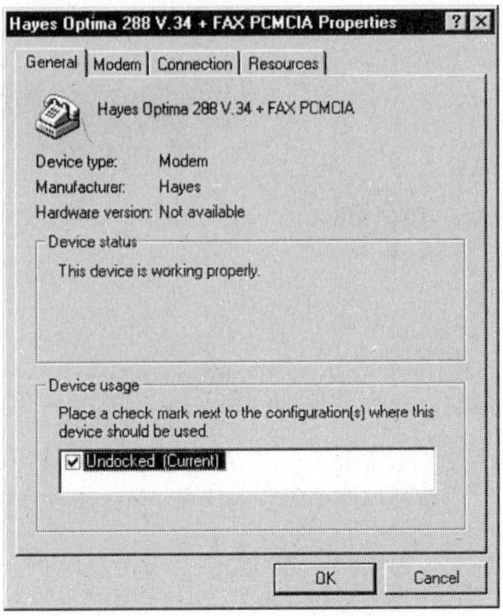

Fig. 27.15
Windows tells you
your modem is
working properly.

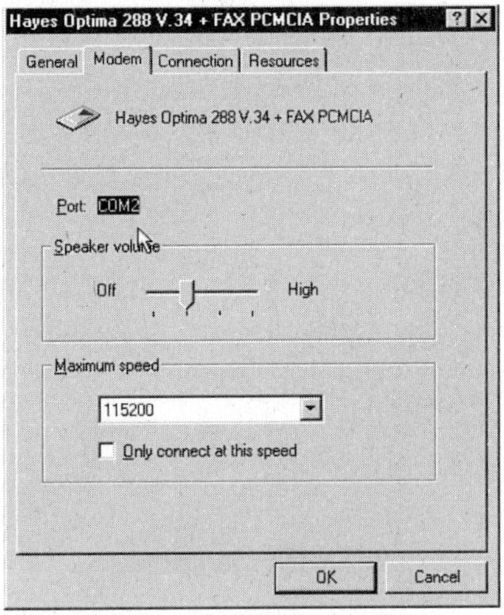

Fig. 27.16
Check the
communications
Port and Maxi-
mum Speed if your
modem is not
working properly.

■ Make sure that the port name matches the port that your application
wants to use. If the port is set to COM2, for example, make sure that
your application is trying to use the modem on COM2.

■ Try lowering the port speed. Perhaps your serial port hardware doesn't
support the selected speed. Try a range of speeds between the data
speed of your modem and the maximum speed. Use the highest setting
that works reliably.

Troubleshooting

My modem connects, but it doesn't stay connected.

If your phone line has call waiting, incoming calls may be throwing you offline. Use Dialing Properties to disable call waiting. You reach the Dialing Properties sheet by choosing <u>D</u>ialing Properties from the Modem Properties sheet.

If that doesn't work, flow control may be set incorrectly. For 9,600-bps and faster modems, make sure that flow control is set to <u>H</u>ardware.

To get to the flow control setting, use Control Panel, double-click the Modem icon, and then choose P<u>r</u>operties. Click the Connection tab, and then choose Ad<u>v</u>anced.

Also, check all cables for quality by swapping them with cables that you know to be good—serial cables for external modems as well as your regular phone cables.

My Windows 95 application keeps dialing the wrong number.

Check to see whether the Dialing Location properties are set correctly. To do this, use Control Panel and double-click the Modem icon. Then click <u>D</u>ialing Properties.

Make sure that the entry in I am <u>D</u>ialing From: matches the location you are in, and that the area code and country shown match where you are, too.

If they don't, Windows 95 programs will be dialing phone numbers incorrectly.

Working Smarter with TAPI and 32-Bit Windows Programs

Telephony Applications Programming Interface, or TAPI, is an API set that lets your modem do more for you than it ever could before Windows 95.

TAPI uses all the information that you gave Windows during the modem-configuration process to set up not only your modem, but also all the 32-bit Windows 95 communications programs. Phone dialer, HyperTerminal, Microsoft Exchange, and Dial Up Networking all share one modem because of TAPI. Communications programs that are written specifically for Windows 95 talk to TAPI, which then issues appropriate commands to the modem. The way Windows uses TAPI for all communications, instead of making each communications program learn to talk to every modem on the market, is called *device independence*. Device independence frees the program developer from having to know everything about your modem.

TAPI provides the following major benefits, which were covered earlier, in the section "Understanding Your Modem and Your Telephone System:"

- The capability to define locations to make dialing effortless

- Support for 16550A UART chips for better throughput

In addition, TAPI provides the following benefits, which are the subject of the following sections:

- Sharing of modems by applications

- Sharing fax modems over a network

Sharing a Modem under TAPI

You know the problem from Windows 3.1—your system has one modem, which is used for data and faxes, and you want to leave the modem under the control of the fax program so that the modem is ready for incoming faxes. When you try to make a data call with the modem, however, an error message appears, telling you that the port is already in use. You have to disable the fax program, use the data program, and re-enable the fax program.

Now suppose that you are using Windows 95. At 3 p.m., Microsoft Fax is waiting for an incoming fax to arrive. At the same time, the CompuServe Mail driver in Microsoft Exchange is scheduled to check CompuServe to see whether any new mail has arrived. Without missing a beat, TAPI allows the mail driver to use the modem; then TAPI hands modem control back to Microsoft Fax. The importance and convenience of this cooperation cannot be overestimated.

Troubleshooting

My Windows 95 communications programs work fine, but I can't access the modem with a DOS or old Windows communications program. How can I make my legacy communications programs work?

You ran into the TAPI gotcha. TAPI only works if all the communications programs you will be using are TAPI aware, 32-bit, Windows 95 programs. If Microsoft Fax is waiting for an incoming fax or Dial-Up Networking is waiting for an incoming call, DOS and old Windows programs cannot access the modem; this capability is reserved for TAPI-enabled Windows 95 applications.

Sharing a Fax Modem Over a Network

TAPI allows any user on a Windows 95 network to send faxes via another network user's fax modem. The user who has the fax modem enables the modem as a shared device; TAPI does the rest.

Note

Data modems cannot be shared over a network.

Working with Phone Dialer

Phone Dialer, an accessory that comes with Windows 95, is a good example of a program that is written to take advantage of the power of TAPI.

To run Phone Dialer, open the Start menu, then choose <u>P</u>rograms, Accessories, Phone Dialer. Figure 27.17 shows the main Phone Dialer dialog box.

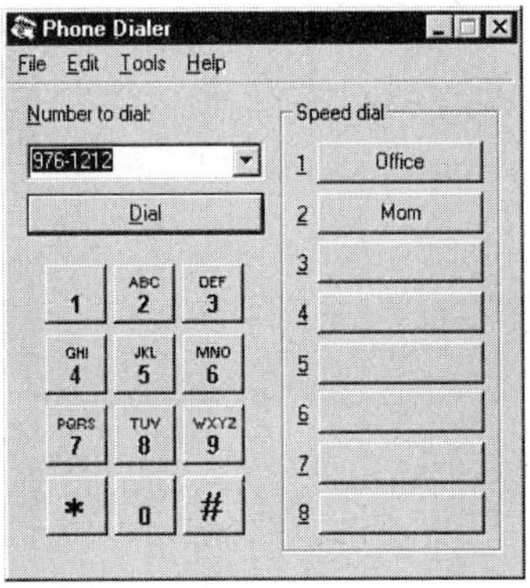

Fig. 27.17
Use Phone Dialer to make calls with your modem.

VI

Online Communications

When you tell Phone Dialer to dial the number shown in the <u>N</u>umber to Dial box, it knows how to handle the area code. Because you defined a location earlier in the section "Understanding Your Modem and Your Telephone

System," Phone Dialer knows if you're dialing a number in the same area code as your computer; in that case, it leaves off the area code and dials the call as 976-1212, as shown in figure 27.18. Phone Dialer also knows whether or not to dial 1 before the number, based on what you tell Windows about your Location.

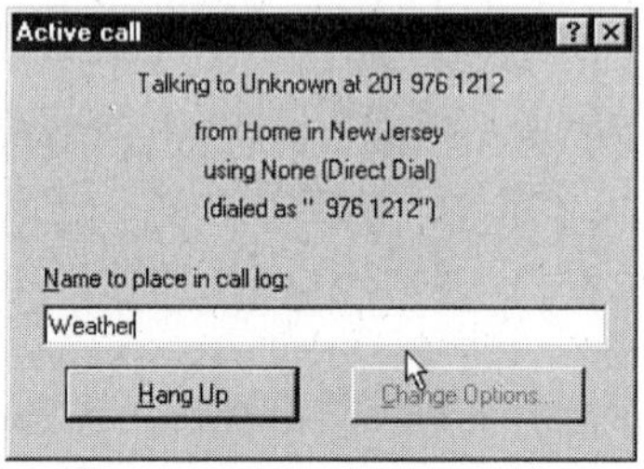

Fig. 27.18
Dialing within the same area code, Windows dials only seven digits.

All the other TAPI features work with Phone Dialer. If Microsoft Fax is waiting for a fax, for example, Phone Dialer can still dial out. When Phone Dialer finishes using the phone line, TAPI gives it back to the fax program.

> **Note**
>
> TAPI features only work with new, 32 bit communications programs that are written to support Windows 95.

If your modem is waiting for a fax under control of the TAPI program Microsoft Fax, and you need to use it to call Compuserve with your Windows 3.1 version of WinCIM, which isn't TAPI aware, you'll first have to turn off Microsoft Fax.

In the same way, if your modem is waiting for a fax under control of your legacy Windows 3.1 version of Delrina Winfax Pro, you'll have to turn Winfax off before you can use the modem with any other program.

For the TAPI features to work, all the applications in the mix must be TAPI aware, 32-bit, and written specifically to support Windows 95.

Using the Diagnostic Tool

Windows has a built-in diagnostic tool that tells you whether your modem can respond to the most basic commands. This tool is useful only to tell you that the modem is alive. Using this tool is as simple as opening the Start menu and choosing, <u>S</u>ettings, <u>C</u>ontrol Panel, Modems. When the Modem Properties dialog box appears, click the Diagnostics tab.

Select your modem and then choose <u>M</u>ore Info. Windows issues a series of interrogatory commands and notes the responses. Figure 27.19 shows sample results.

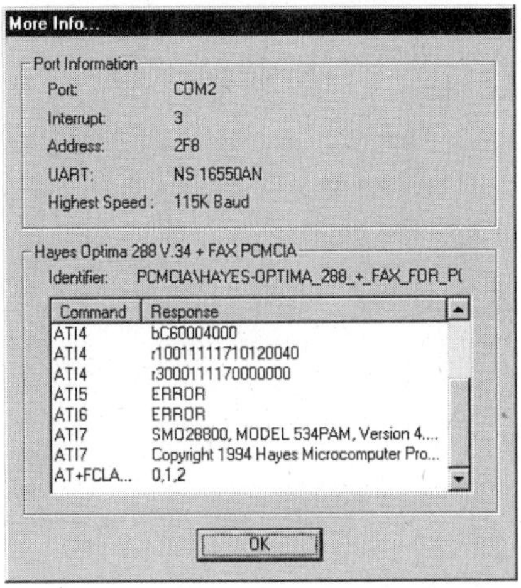

Fig. 27.19
Modem Diagnostics showing the modem responding to AT commands

Understanding File Transfer Errors

Errors occur in file transfers with DOS and old Windows programs. How do I track them down and fix them?

If you're using DOS and Windows 3.1 communications programs, you've probably upgraded from Windows 3.1 to Windows 95. There are settings in the old Windows 3.1 SYSTEM.INI file that can cause problems in your new installation of Windows 95.

To correct these problems, some manual editing of SYSTEM.INI may be necessary. You can use NOTEPAD.EXE to perform these tasks.

In the [boot] section of your SYSTEM.INI file, make sure COMM.DRV=COMM.DRV. If it doesn't, edit it so it says COMM.DRV=COMM.DRV.

This will make sure Windows 95 is using its own communications driver for older, 16-bit programs.

VI

Online Communications

In the [386Enh] section, make sure a line exists that says DEVICE=*VCD. If you don't see DEVICE=*VCD, type it on a line by itself anywhere in the [386Enh] section. Use NOTEPAD.EXE to do this.

Next, set the FIFO buffer to 512 bytes. Determine the communications port that you're using with these DOS and old Windows programs. If the port is COM2, for example, add the line COM2BUFFER=512 in the [386Enh] section of your SYSTEM.INI file. Use the same syntax for other ports. You can add COM2BUFFER=512 on a line by itself, anywhere in the [386Enh] section of SYSTEM.INI. You can use NOTEPAD.EXE to do this.❖

Chapter 28

Communicating with HyperTerminal

by Jerry Honeycutt

HyperTerminal is a Windows accessory that enables you to connect your computer to another PC or online service. HyperTerminal replaces the Windows 3.1 Terminal program. HyperTerminal is not just a clone of Terminal, however, but is a full-featured communications tool that greatly simplifies getting online. With HyperTerminal, you can connect to a friend's computer, a university, an Internet service provider, or even CompuServe.

In this chapter, you learn

- What HyperTerminal is and how it compares to the other communications tools provided with Windows

- How to use HyperTerminal for some common tasks such as creating a connection or downloading a file

- How to configure HyperTerminal and customize your connections

Introducing HyperTerminal

Before graphical interfaces to online services such as CompuServe and the Microsoft Network existed, most communications tools were character-oriented. For example, students all over the world used terminal-emulation programs to connect to their schools' computers. They typically used VT-100 terminal emulation, which made their PCs behave like any other display terminal on the system. CompuServe is another example, but instead of emulating a terminal it displays one line of text at a time. Remember the days before WinCIM?

If you can use the graphical communications tools mentioned here, why do you need a character-oriented tool such as HyperTerminal? The reason is that most bulletin boards, Internet shell accounts, and university connections are still character-oriented. Most bulletin boards do not provide a sleek, graphical interface like the Microsoft Network. HyperTerminal does the following:

- Makes the focal point of your activities the connections you create (documents), which allows you to dial or configure a connection without loading HyperTerminal first

- Automatically detects the terminal-emulation mode and communications parameters of the remote computer

- Fully integrates with TAPI and the centralized modem configuration, which provides Windows 95 applications a single interface to your modem for dialing, answering, configuration, and more

- Supports several popular terminal-emulation modes and file transfer protocols such as VT-100, VT-52, and Kermit

- Enables you to greatly customize each of your connections

What You Can Do with HyperTerminal

HyperTerminal is a communications tool with many uses. The following list describes many tasks you can do with HyperTerminal:

- Connect to another computer and exchange files

- Connect to an online service (such as CompuServe) that supports one of HyperTerminal's terminal-emulation modes

- Connect to a school's computer using VT-100

- Connect to an Internet service provider using a shell account and even access the World Wide Web using Lynx

What You Can't Do with HyperTerminal

Although HyperTerminal is a useful communications tool, it is not the only tool you will need for your communications activities. The following list describes some activities you can't do and refers you to other chapters in this book:

◀ See "Gaining Remote Access to Your Network," p. 660

- *Connect to another network.* If you need to connect your computer to another network, use Dial-Up Networking as described in Chapter 21, "Sharing Windows 95 Peer-to-Peer Resources."

■ *Connect to the Microsoft Network.* To connect to the Microsoft Network, use the graphical software provided in Windows 95, as described in Appendix B, "Using Microsoft Network."

▶ See "Connecting to The Microsoft Network," p. 1110

■ *Graphically connect to the Internet World Wide Web.* While many service providers provide Lynx, a character-oriented Web browsing tool, you'll need a graphical browsing tool to take full advantage of the Web. See Chapter 29, "Getting Connected to the Internet."

▶ See "The World Wide Web," p. 903

Using HyperTerminal

When you installed Windows, you were given the option to install Hyper-Terminal as one of your accessories. If you did not install HyperTerminal or you removed it from the Start menu, you can install it at any time by selecting Install/Remove Applications from the Control Panel. To open the HyperTerminal folder, click the Start button and choose Programs, Accessories, HyperTerminal.

◀ See "Adding and Removing Windows Components," p. 313

If you have not yet configured your modem, Windows prompts you to set it up the first time you run HyperTerminal.

Figure 28.1 shows the HyperTerminal folder. By default, each connection that you create appears in this folder as an icon.

◀ See "Configuring Your Modem," p. 843

Fig. 28.1
Double-click Hypertrm to create a new HyperTerminal connection, or double-click another icon to open an existing connection.

VI

Online Communications

Creating a New Connection

Before you can connect with HyperTerminal, you need to create a new connection. To do so, follow these steps:

1. Double-click the Hypertrm icon in the HyperTerminal folder. If HyperTerminal is already loaded, choose File, New or click the New button on the toolbar. HyperTerminal prompts you for a new connection description.

2. In the Connection Description dialog box, shown in figure 28.2, type a descriptive name for your new connection, select an icon, and click OK. HyperTerminal then displays the Phone Number dialog box.

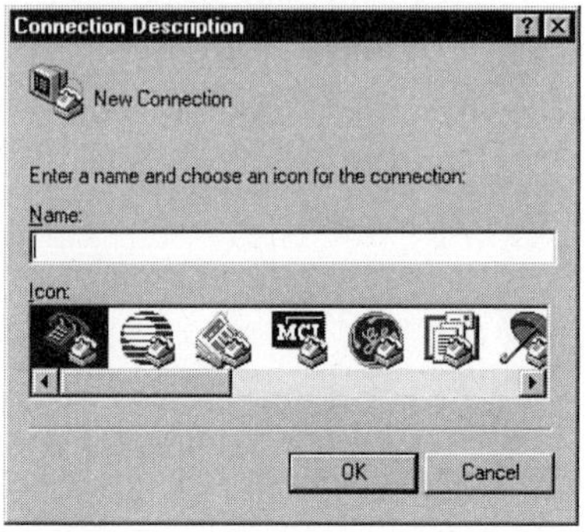

Fig. 28.2
Create a new connection and select an icon to help you easily identify it later.

3. Type the phone number for your new connection. Verify the country code, area code, and modem choice. Click OK. HyperTerminal displays the Connect dialog box, as shown in figure 28.3.

4. Select your location (usually Default Location) and click Dial if you want to establish your new connection. You can also click Dialing Properties to change the default location, outside line access, and other dialing properties.

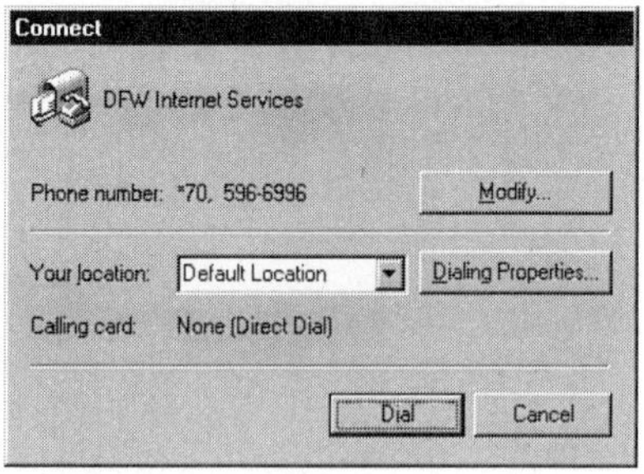

Fig. 28.3
After you have set up the connection, just click Dial to get going.

Figure 28.4 shows the entire HyperTerminal window with a session in progress. Most of HyperTerminal's features are available on the toolbar. Table 28.1 describes each toolbar button.

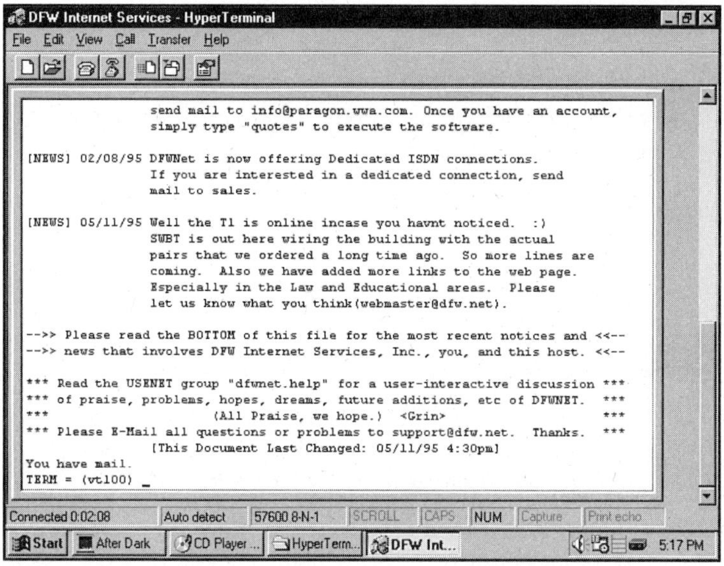

Fig. 28.4
After a connection to the remote computer is established, you interact with it just like a display terminal on the system. Click the scroll bar to review text that was previously displayed.

Table 28.1 The HyperTerminal Toolbar

Button	Name	Description
	New	Creates a new connection
	Open	Opens an existing connection
	Connect	Displays the Connect dialog box
	Disconnect	Disconnects the current connection
	Send	Sends a file to the host
	Receive	Receives a file from the host
	Properties	Displays the Properties sheet for the connection

VI

Online Communications

To save your new connection, choose File, Save As. HyperTerminal prompts you for a file name. If you want your connections to show up in the HyperTerminal folder, accept the default path. If you quit HyperTerminal without saving your new connection, HyperTerminal prompts you for a file name.

 To hang up, choose Call, Disconnect or click the Disconnect button on the toolbar.

Troubleshooting

I try to dial a connection, but I get an error that says Another program is using the selected Telephony device.

Make sure that you don't have any older Windows communications programs running in the background that might be controlling the modem. Although Windows 95 communications tools can share the modem, older Windows communications programs can't.

I connected to the service fine, but all I see on-screen is garbage—usually at the bottom of the screen.

Choose File, Properties to display the Properties sheet for your connection, click the Settings tab, and set Emulation to Auto Detect. HyperTerminal automatically determines which terminal emulation your service is using.

Using an Existing Connection

◄ See "Shortcuts Add Power," p. 29

The next time you want to use the connection you previously created, it will appear in the HyperTerminal folder. To establish this connection, double-click the icon in the folder and click Dial.

 If HyperTerminal is already running, choose File, Open or click the Open button on the toolbar.

Capturing Text from the Screen

Tip
To make access to your connection quicker, copy a shortcut to the connection onto the desktop or the Start menu.

By capturing text, you can save everything that appears in the HyperTerminal window. You may want to save the information displayed by HyperTerminal for the following reasons:

- You want to review or use it later

- The information is scrolling by so quickly that you can't read it

There are two ways to capture text from the remote computer: to a file or to the printer.

Capturing Text to a File

To capture text received from the remote computer to a file, follow these steps:

1. Choose Transfer, Capture Text from the menu.

2. Type the name for a file in which you want to put the text, or click Browse to select a file. Your screen should look similar to figure 28.5.

3. Click Start. HyperTerminal stores all text it receives from the remote computer in this file.

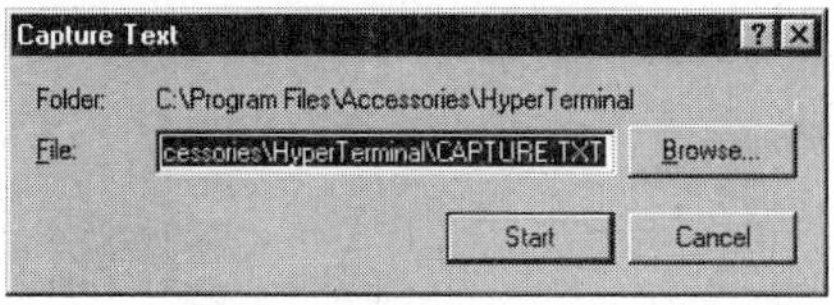

Tip
If text is scrolling by faster than you can read it, try pressing Ctrl+S to pause the screen and then press Ctrl+Q to resume.

Fig. 28.5
Type the name for a file in which to capture text.

After you start capturing text, you can stop by choosing Transfer, Capture, Stop; pause with Transfer, Capture, Pause; or resume with Transfer, Capture, Resume. Notice that these menu options are available only after you start capturing text to a file. Once you choose Stop, you will be prompted for a file name the next time you choose Capture.

Capturing Text to the Printer

Capturing text to the printer is even easier than capturing to a file. To capture to the printer, choose Transfer, Capture to Printer. All text that HyperTerminal receives will be sent to the default printer. A check mark is displayed next to Capture to Printer, indicating that the option is turned on. To turn it off, choose it again.

VI

Online Communications

Troubleshooting

I captured text to a text file, but when I view the file, I can read some of the lines, but the rest of them are garbled.

If you are using terminal emulation, such as VT-100, this condition is normal. This emulation uses escape codes, which tell HyperTerminal where to put the cursor or how to format text. Escape codes can't be displayed as normal text. However, they are still captured to the file.

Sharing Text with Other Programs

◀ See "Under-
standing
Windows 95's
Data-Sharing
Capabilities,"
p. 410

The cut-and-paste process is still one of the most useful features in Windows. With a few keystrokes or mouse clicks, you can transfer data from one program to another. HyperTerminal is no exception. To copy data from HyperTerminal using the mouse, select a block of text in the window and choose Edit, Copy or press Ctrl+C.

Pasting is simple, too. After copying data to the Clipboard from another application such as Notepad, choose Edit, Paste to Host or just press Ctrl+V.

> **Note**
>
> In applications such as Notepad, pasting text from the Clipboard puts the text in the document, which is then displayed in the window. When you paste text into HyperTerminal, it actually transmits the text to the remote computer.

Exchanging Files with the Remote Computer

You can easily exchange files with another computer using HyperTerminal. For example, you may want to download a program update from the bulletin board of your favorite software vendor. You also can download public domain software from a variety of bulletin board systems (BBSes) around the country.

> **Caution**
>
> Before running a program downloaded from a remote computer, run it through a virus scan program to make sure that it's not infected. Otherwise, severe and irreparable damage may occur to your programs and data files if you download a virus.

You also may be asked to upload a data file to a vendor's bulletin board so that the vendor can help you fix a problem. HyperTerminal can do it!

Downloading Files

Before you begin downloading a file, you must make sure that you have a connection with a host computer, as described in the previous section "Using an Existing Connection."

To download a file from a host computer, follow these steps:

1. Start the download process on the bulletin board or host computer. Bulletin boards or other host computers vary in how to start a download—follow the instructions given to you online. Make a note of the file transfer protocol you selected on the host. HyperTerminal supports several popular file transfer protocols. Table 28.2 describes each protocol.

Table 28.2	File Transfer Protocols Supported by HyperTerminal
Protocol	**Description**
Xmodem	Xmodem is an error-correcting protocol supported by virtually every communications program and online service. It is slower than the other protocols.
1K Xmodem	1K Xmodem is faster than Xmodem, transferring files in 1,024-byte blocks as opposed to the slower 128-byte blocks in regular Xmodem. Otherwise, they are similar.
Ymodem	Many bulletin board systems offer Ymodem, which is another name for 1K Xmodem.
Ymodem-G	Similar to Ymodem, Ymodem-G implements hardware error control. It is more reliable than the first three protocols. However, to use Ymodem-G, your hardware must support hardware error control.
Zmodem	Zmodem is preferred by most bulletin board users because it is the fastest protocol of those listed. Zmodem is reliable, too, because it adjusts its block sizes during the download to accommodate bad telephone lines. Zmodem has two other features that make it stand out from the rest. First, the host can initiate the download—you do nothing beyond this step. Second, you can download multiple files at one time using Zmodem. The host computer initiates a download for each file you selected.
Kermit	Kermit is extremely slow and should not be used if one of the other protocols is available. Kermit is a protocol left over from VAX computers and mainframes.

2. If you selected Zmodem as the protocol, you are done. The host computer initiates the file transfer with HyperTerminal. Otherwise, choose Transfer, Receive File from the menu or click the Receive button. The Receive File dialog box appears.

3. Type a folder name or click Browse to select a folder (see fig. 28.6). Then select a protocol to use for downloading the file. The protocol you use

should match the protocol you chose (or the system chose for you) on the host computer.

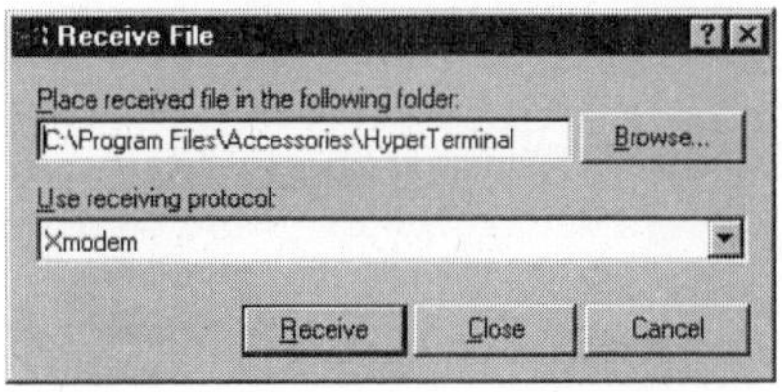

Fig. 28.6
Tell Hyper-Terminal where you want to store the file; then click Receive to begin the download.

◄ See "Opening, Saving, and Closing Documents," p. 109

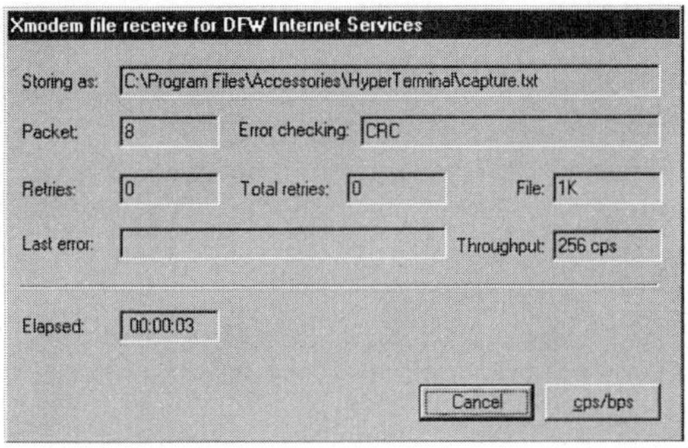

Fig. 28.7
This dialog box shows the status of your download such as the file name and time elapsed. A different dialog box is used depending on which protocol you used for the download.

4. Click Receive, type a file name, and click OK. HyperTerminal starts your download. Figure 28.7 shows the dialog box that displays the status of your download. (You may see a different dialog box depending on the protocol you chose.)

Uploading Binary Files

You can upload both binary and text files. Binary files include bitmaps, programs, and word processing documents that contain more than just readable text. For example, a program file contains code and program data that is not readable. On the other hand, text files contain characters that are easily read. This section describes how to upload a binary file. To learn how to upload text files, see "Uploading Text Files" later in this chapter.

Before you begin uploading a binary file, you must establish the connection to the host computer, as discussed in "Using an Existing Connection." To upload a binary file to a host computer, follow these steps:

1. Initiate the upload on the bulletin board or host computer by following the on-screen instructions. The host displays a message indicating that it's waiting for you to start uploading.

Note

If you are using Zmodem, you may not need to start the upload on the host computer. Zmodem can initiate the upload on the host for you. To try initiating the upload from your computer, skip step 1. However, if the host computer doesn't understand how to initiate an upload this way, you will have to start over from step 1.

2. Choose Transfer, Send File from the menu or click the Send button on the toolbar. HyperTerminal displays a dialog box similar to the one shown in figure 28.6 in the previous section "Downloading Files."

3. Type a file name or click Browse to select a file.

4. Select a protocol to use for uploading the file. The protocol you use should match the protocol you chose (or the system chose for you) on the host computer.

5. HyperTerminal starts the upload to the host computer. It displays the status of your upload in a dialog box similar to the one shown earlier in figure 28.7.

Troubleshooting

I'm trying to use Ymodem-G as the transfer protocol, but it doesn't work.

Your modem probably doesn't support hardware error control. Try using Ymodem instead.

I initiated a Ymodem upload from my computer, but the host doesn't respond.

The host computer doesn't understand how to initiate an upload this way. You will need to initiate an upload first on the host computer and then on your computer. Alternatively, you may not be at the correct prompt on the host computer.

After reviewing the preceding suggestions, I still can't download or upload a file.

Make sure that you are selecting the exact same transfer protocol the host computer is using. If you continue to have difficulty, contact the sysop (system operator) of the remote computer.

VI

Online Communications

Uploading Text Files

Before you begin uploading a text file, be sure that you're connected to a host computer, as described in the earlier section, "Using an Existing Connection." To upload a text file to a host computer, follow these steps:

1. Start the upload on the bulletin board or host computer. The host displays a message indicating that it's waiting for you to start the upload.

2. Choose <u>T</u>ransfer, Send <u>T</u>ext File from the menu. HyperTerminal prompts you for a text file name.

> **Caution**
>
> Don't try to upload a binary file using this feature. You may think that the file transferred OK, but the remote computer will receive a file with garbage in it.

3. Type a file name or click <u>B</u>rowse to select a file.

4. Click <u>O</u>pen. HyperTerminal starts uploading the text file to the host computer. Note that you do not see a dialog box showing the status of the upload.

Configuring HyperTerminal

Tip
When you change configuration items in HyperTerminal, the changes apply only to the connection you have loaded. Thus, every connection can be customized differently.

HyperTerminal is a flexible communications tool. You can customize all aspects of each of your connections and HyperTerminal automatically saves your settings. For example, you can choose which font a connection uses or which terminal-emulation mode HyperTerminal uses. The next time you use that connection, HyperTerminal uses the settings you previously set. This section shows you how to configure HyperTerminal for each of your connections.

Turning Off the Toolbar and Status Bar

You might want to turn off the toolbar or status bar for a HyperTerminal connection, especially if you do not have enough screen space to display the entire terminal area. To toggle the toolbar, choose <u>V</u>iew, <u>T</u>oolbar from the menu. A check mark beside <u>T</u>oolbar indicates that the option is turned on.

To toggle the status bar, choose <u>V</u>iew, <u>S</u>tatus Bar. Likewise, a check mark beside <u>S</u>tatus Bar indicates that it is turned on.

Changing Fonts

You can choose a specific font and style for your HyperTerminal connection. For example, if you want HyperTerminal to display a full screen in a smaller window, choose a smaller font size and resize the window.

> **Note**
>
> You can't use a small font size to display 132 columns unless you are using VT-100 terminal emulation. HyperTerminal will always resize the display area to 80 columns.

To choose a different font for this HyperTerminal connection, follow these steps:

1. Choose <u>V</u>iew, <u>F</u>ont from the menu. HyperTerminal displays the Font dialog box, which is common to most applications.

◄ See "Under-standing Fonts," p. 210

2. Set the font, style, and size. The Font dialog box shows you a preview of your choice.

3. Click OK when you are satisfied with your choice. HyperTerminal immediately resizes the display area for 80 columns, using the font you have chosen.

4. Optionally, click the right button in the display area and choose <u>S</u>nap. HyperTerminal resizes the window to fit the display area. This technique is useful if you want to use a smaller font to have a smaller HyperTerminal window.

> **Note**
>
> If the display area is larger than the HyperTerminal window, you can use the scroll bars to move the display area up, down, left, or right in the window.

Changing a Connection Setup

It is easy to change the properties for a connection after you create it. You can change the connection's icon, name, country code, area code, phone number, and modem in the connection's Properties sheet, as shown in figure 28.8.

VI

Online Communications

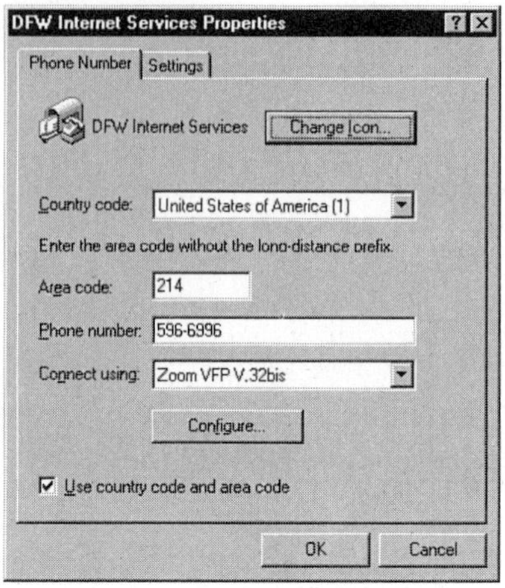

Fig. 28.8
Change the icon, name, phone number, and modem to use for this connection. Click OK to permanently save your settings.

DFW Internet Services Properties ☑ ☒

Phone Number | Settings

📶 DFW Internet Services [Change Icon...]

Country code: United States of America (1) ▼

Enter the area code without the long-distance prefix.

Area code: 214

Phone number: 596-6996

Connect using: Zoom VFP V.32bis ▼

[Configure...]

☑ Use country code and area code

[OK] [Cancel]

To change the properties of your connection, follow these steps:

1. Choose File, Properties from the menu or click the Properties button on the toolbar.

2. Click Change Icon, select another icon from the list, and change the connection name.

3. Select a country code.

Tip
To change the HyperTerminal Properties sheet without even running Hyper-Terminal, right-click the connection you want to change in the HyperTerminal folder; then choose Properties. If you do this, the Proper-ties sheet will have an additional tab, named General, with the file infor-mation.

4. Type the area code and phone number. (If you select the default location when you dial, Windows will not dial the area code if it matches your default area code.)

5. Select a modem. Windows displays the modems you currently have installed, or enables you to go directly to the port. If you go directly to the port, you can bypass the Windows 95 modem configuration, controlling the modem directly. For normal usage, select a configured modem so that you can take advantage of centralized modem configuration.

6. Click OK to save your settings.

Configuring the Connection Settings

The Settings page of the Properties sheet enables you to change the terminal properties of HyperTerminal. For example, you can change the terminal-emulation mode. Figure 28.9 shows the Settings page of this sheet. Table 28.3 describes each terminal emulation available in HyperTerminal.

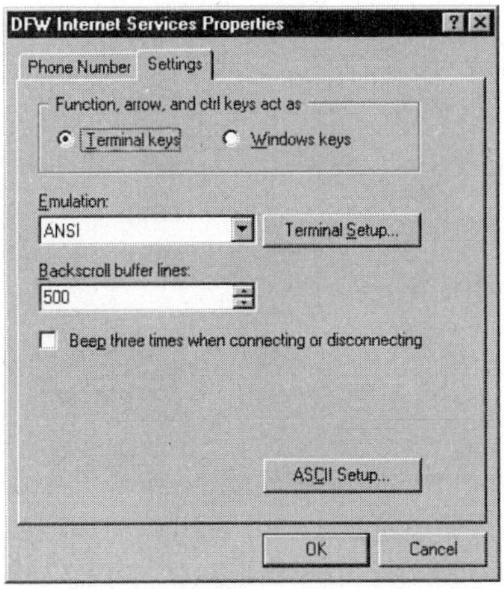

DFW Internet Services Properties

Phone Number | Settings

Function, arrow, and ctrl keys act as

⊙ Terminal keys   ○ Windows keys

Emulation:

ANSI ▾   Terminal Setup...

Backscroll buffer lines:

500

☐ Beep three times when connecting or disconnecting

ASCII Setup...

OK   Cancel

Fig. 28.9
Use the Settings page of the Properties sheet to change the terminal emulation and other useful settings.

Table 28.3	Terminal Emulation Supported by HyperTerminal
Protocol	**Description**
ANSI	A popular, generic terminal emulation supported by most Unix systems. It provides full-screen emulation.
Auto Detect	Automatically determines which terminal emulation the remote computer is using.
Minitel	An emulation primarily used in France.
TTY	Is actually absent of any terminal emulation. TTY simply displays all the characters it receives on the display.
Viewdata	An emulation primarily used in the United Kingdom.
VT-100	The workhorse of terminal emulations. Many remote systems such as Unix use it.
VT-52	A predecessor to VT 100. It provides full-screen terminal emulation on remote systems that support it.

To change the settings for this connection, follow these steps:

1. Choose File, Properties from the menu or click the Properties button on the toolbar. Alternatively, right-click a connection document in the HyperTerminal folder.

VI

Online Communications

2. On the Settings page, choose Terminal Keys or Windows Keys. Terminal Keys sends function keys F1 through F12 and arrow keys to the remote computer instead of acting on them in Windows; Windows Keys causes Windows to act on them. For example, if you choose Terminal Keys and press F1, the key would be sent to the host, and the host would respond to it. If you choose Windows Keys and press F1, Windows would display help.

3. Set Emulation to the terminal emulation you want. HyperTerminal must be using the same terminal emulation the host computer is using.

Tip

If you set Emulation to Auto Detect, HyperTerminal automatically determines what emulation the host is using and configures itself appropriately. Use this setting for normal situations.

4. Set the number of lines you want in Backscroll Buffer Lines. In the HyperTerminal main window, the current screen is displayed with a white background. If you press Page Up or use the scroll bar to scroll backwards, you see previously displayed text with a gray background. The default value for Backscroll Buffer Lines is 500 lines, which allows you to review about 20 screens and doesn't consume a large amount of memory.

5. Turn on Beep Three Times When Connecting or Disconnecting if you want to be notified when you are making or breaking a connection.

6. Optionally, Click ASCII Setup and set the options for how text files are sent and received. Figure 28.10 shows the ASCII Setup dialog box, and table 28.4 describes what each option does.

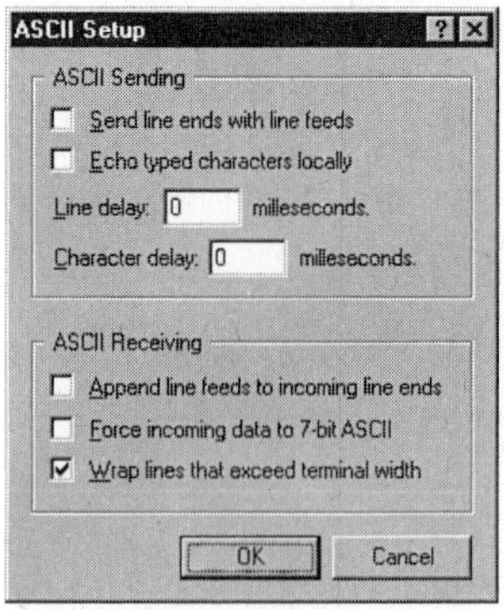

Fig. 28.10

Use the ASCII Setup dialog box to configure how ASCII files will be sent and received. For example, you can choose to send line feeds with line ends.

Table 28.4   ASCII Setup Options

Option	Description
Send Line Ends with Line Feeds	Attaches a line feed to the end of every line that HyperTerminal sends. Turn on this option if the remote computer requires it or you turned on Echo Typed Characters Locally, explained below, and pressing Enter moves you to the beginning of the current line instead of starting a new line.
Echo Typed Characters Locally	Displays each character you type on the keyboard instead of depending on the host to echo each character. Turn on this option only if you can't see the characters you type. If you see each character twice (ssuucchh aass tthhiiss), turn off this option.
Line Delay	Sets how much time to delay between lines. Increasing the amount of time between lines allows the remote computer time to get ready for the next line. Increase this setting in increments of 100 milliseconds if the remote computer frequently loses portions of each line.
Character Delay	Sets how much time to delay between characters. Increasing the amount of time between characters allows the remote computer time to get ready for the next character. Increase this setting in increments of 5 milliseconds if the remote computer randomly loses characters.
Append Line Feeds to Incoming Line Ends	Attaches a line feed to lines received. Turn on this option if the lines you receive from the host computer are displayed one on top of another.
Force Incoming Data to 7-bit ASCII	Changes 8-bit characters to 7-bit. Turn on this option if HyperTerminal displays greek or unrecognizable symbols. This option forces HyperTerminal to stick with readable characters.
Wrap Lines That Exceed Terminal Width	Turns word wrapping on or off. Turn on this option if you want lines that are longer than the terminal width to be continued on the following line.

VI

Online Communications

> **Note**
>
> If you have selected a particular terminal emulation on the Settings tab, you can
> further refine the configuration by selecting Terminal Setup. HyperTerminal displays a
> different dialog box depending on which emulation you have chosen. The following
> table shows the options available for each emulation mode:
>
> | Emulation | Options |
> | --- | --- |
> | ANSI | Cursor: Block, Underline, or Blink |
> | Minitel | Cursor: Block, Underline, or Blink |
> | TTY | Cursor: Block, Underline, or Blink
Use Destructive Backspace |
> | Viewdata | Hide Cursor
Enter Key Sends # |
> | VT-100 | Cursor: Block, Underline, or Blink
Keypad Application Mode
Cursor Keypad Mode
132-Column Mode
Character Set |
> | VT-52 | Cursor: Block, Underline, or Blink
Alternate Keypad Mode |

Configuring Your Modem for HyperTerminal

You probably configured your modem after you installed Windows. You set
options such as the port, speaker volume, and speed. In HyperTerminal, you
can override any of these options. For example, if your modem is configured
in the Control Panel to connect at 56,000 bps, you can configure your connection to connect at 2,400 bps. However, changing your connection doesn't
change your modem's configuration; it is simply overridden by the
connection.

◄ See "Installing
and Config-
uring Your
Modem,"
p. 831

Configuring your modem for a particular connection is the same as configuring it in the Control Panel.

The first two tabs, General and Connection, are the same as those displayed
for configuring the modem in Control Panel.

The Options tab is added to the HyperTerminal modem Properties sheet only when you open it from HyperTerminal. This page enables you to set additional properties for HyperTerminal. To set these options for HyperTerminal, follow these steps:

1. Choose File, Properties from the menu or click the Properties button on the toolbar. Alternatively, right-click the appropriate connection icon in the HyperTerminal Connections folder.

2. Click the Options tab. HyperTerminal displays the page shown in figure 28.11.

3. Set options as described in table 28.5 and click OK to save.

Tip

HyperTerminal automatically detects the configuration of the modem you are calling. You don't need to change the data bits, stop bits, or parity settings you might have used in the past.

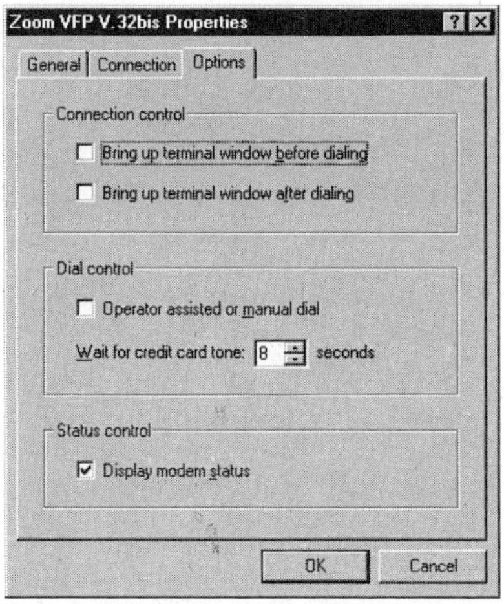

Fig. 28.11
You can refine your modem configuration on the Options page of the Modem Properties sheet by choosing to display a terminal window before and after dialing, which gives you more control over how the phone is dialed and the connection is made.

Table 28.5 Modem Options	
Option	**Description**
Bring Up Terminal Window Before Dialing	Displays a terminal window, shown in figure 28.12, before HyperTerminal starts dialing, enabling you to enter modem commands directly. (See your modem's manual for a list of commands.)
Bring Up Terminal Window After Dialing	Displays a terminal window after HyperTerminal has dialed the phone number, enabling you to enter modem commands directly.
Operator Assisted or Manual Dial	Enables you to dial the telephone number directly. HyperTerminal prompts you to dial the telephone number.

VI

Online Communications

(continues)

Table 28.5 Continued

Option	Description
<u>W</u>ait for Credit Card Tone	Allows you to specify how many seconds HyperTerminal will wait for the credit or dialing card tone.
Display Modem <u>S</u>tatus	Displays the status of the modem. Turning this option off disables the Modem icon in the taskbar.

◀ See "Under-standing Your Modem and Your Tele-phone System," p. 850

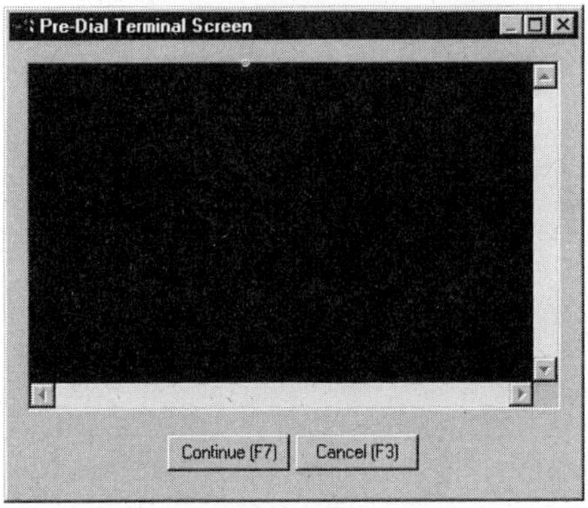

Fig. 28.12
You can use the terminal window to send commands directly to the modem before and after the phone number is dialed.

Note

HyperTerminal doesn't have a menu option or toolbar button to answer an incoming call. However, you can easily answer an incoming call if you have a Hayes-compatible modem by typing **ATA** and pressing Enter in the HyperTerminal window after the phone rings.

Chapter 29

Getting Connected to the Internet

by Francis Moss

Windows 95 provides a flexible and advanced means of connecting to the Internet, whether you are connecting from a stand-alone computer or from a network. Windows 95 has built-in support for TCP/IP dial-up access and PPP or SLIP (all Internet standards), and it supports 16-bit and 32-bit Windows Internet applications through a new Windows Sockets protocol that uses no conventional memory.

In addition, the Microsoft Internet Mail Service and the Microsoft Network provide seamless and universal connectivity.

In this chapter, you learn about the following:

- The Internet and the World Wide Web

- What TCP/IP is

- How to choose an Internet service provider

- How to connect to the Internet

- How to use other Internet applications with Windows 95

The Internet

Unless you've been living in a cave in the Himalayas, you've heard about the Internet. (There are even rumors about gurus with laptops and cellular modems who are surfing the Net!) The Internet is a "network of networks," a global linkage of millions of computers, containing vast amounts of information, much of it available to anyone with a modem and the right software... for free.

The main functions of the Internet are listed here:

- *E-mail* (electronic mail). You can send a message to anyone, anywhere in the world (as long as they have access to the Internet), almost instantaneously and for less than the cost of a regular letter, or "snailmail."

- *The World Wide Web* (the Web, or WWW). The fastest-growing part of the Internet, the Web provides access to files, documents, images, and sounds from thousands of different Web sites using a special programming language called *HyperText Markup Language*, or HTML. This language is used to create "hypertext" documents that include embedded commands.

- *UseNet newsgroups*. These are "many-to-many" discussion groups on topics ranging from science, current events, music, computers, "alternative" issues, and many others. There are currently over 10,000 newsgroups, and the list grows daily.

- *File transfer using File Transfer Protocol* (FTP). FTP is the Internet protocol for file transfer between computers linked to the Internet.

The Internet is an aggregation of high-speed networks, supported by the National Science Foundation (NSF) and almost 6,000 federal, state, and local systems, as well as university and commercial networks. It has links to networks in Canada, South America, Europe, Australia, and Asia, with more than 30,000,000 users. The Internet began with about 200 linked computers; today, there are several million linked computers all over the world. The Internet is growing so fast that no one can say how big it is today, or how large it will grow tomorrow.

The World Wide Web

The World Wide Web, also called the Web or WWW, is the fastest-growing and most exciting part of the Internet. It was developed in 1989 at CERN (which stands for *Centre Européen de Recherche Nucléaire*, but which most people call the Particle Physics Research Laboratory) at the University of Bern in Switzerland. Although the rest of the Internet is text oriented, the World Wide Web is graphics and sound oriented. Clicking a *hypertext* or *hypermedia link* (a specially encoded text or graphic image) takes you to other documents, called *Web pages*, where you can view images from the Hubble telescope, visit an art museum, watch a video clip of skiers (on a ski resort's page), or hear the haunting theme song from the Fox Network's hit show, *The X Files*—all on your computer.

Unlike other Internet file-retrieval systems, which are hierarchical in nature (you wend your way through descending layers of menus or directories to find what you're looking for), the WWW is distributed, offering links to other parts of the same document or other documents, which are not necessarily at the same Web site as the current document. With a program called a *graphical browser* (such as Microsoft's Internet Assistant or the Internet Explorer, a Web browser contained in the Microsoft Plus! Pack for Windows 95, Netscape, or NCSA's Mosaic), when you point and click a phrase on your screen that looks like this

Macmillan Publishing

you jump directly to the Web page of Macmillan Publishing USA, shown in figure 29.1.

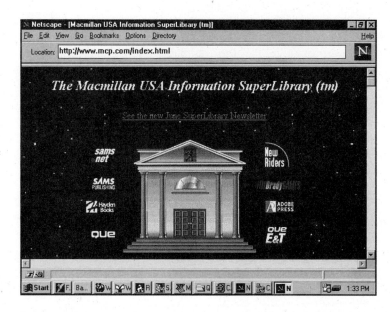

Fig. 29.1

The Macmillan Publishing Company page, as viewed from Netscape. Click elements in the graphic to move to the Web pages for those sites.

VI

Online Communications

New authoring tools, including Microsoft's Internet Assistant (to be used with Word for Windows 6.0a or later), allow anyone with an Internet account to create his or her own *World Wide Web page* (a kind of advertisement for yourself that anyone on the Web can see). You learn more about the World Wide Web later in this chapter and in Chapter 30, "Using FTP, the World Wide Web, and Other Internet Services."

TCP/IP Explained

TCP/IP stands for Transmission Control Protocol/Internet Protocol. TCP/IP is the method used by every computer on the Internet to transfer files. As the name indicates, it's actually two protocols. The earliest model was the Internet Protocol, developed in the days of ARPANET (the Advanced Research Projects NETwork, the original Internet, formed in the 1960s) to send data in packets (self-contained units of information) from one computer network to another. The weakness of IP is its inability to deal with poor transmissions. If a packet gets garbled or interrupted, the receiving IP-based machine just tosses it.

The TCP protocol makes sure that every packet is delivered to the receiving network in the same order it was sent. A kind of numbering system verifies that the packet received is identical to the one sent.

Every network and every computer on the Internet uses TCP/IP to communicate. Until recently, the TCP/IP protocol has caused some problems for DOS-based machines: a version of TCP/IP that you install on your machine may conflict with the version installed on your LAN, or with your Internet service provider's version; certain applications such as FTP or e-mail that employ TCP/IP may call different functions in their own version of the protocol than the functions the network employs. Up to now, the process of connecting to the Internet has been a good candidate for the U.S. Army's advertising slogan: "It's not just a job, it's an adventure."

Versions of Microsoft Windows after version 3.x have encouraged the development of a TCP/IP standard of sorts, called the Windows Sockets Library, or *Winsock*. All manufacturers of Windows-based Internet programs have accepted this standard, which means that, ideally (for example) any Windows mail reader you choose will work with the WINSOCK.DLL in your WINDOWS directory.

But still some problems remain. A version of Winsock bundled with one software manufacturer's Internet application may conflict with another version. Each application may install a version of Winsock in its own directory, causing conflicts with another manufacturer's version. Or an Internet provider may customize its version of Winsock, causing conflicts with Internet applications that cannot recognize the new version. Internet jockeys running Windows must periodically comb their hard drives for mismatched Winsocks.

With Windows 95, such conflicts are less of a problem. Microsoft has created two brand-new Winsocks, one for 16-bit applications and another for 32-bit applications. In addition, a Virtual Device Driver (VxD), called WSOCK.VXD, manages the TCP/IP interface. This driver resides in upper memory—your system performance isn't affected. Most Windows 3.x-based Internet applications work seamlessly with the Windows 95 Winsock. As more Internet software vendors provide Windows 95 versions, Winsock conflicts should disappear.

> **Note**
>
> CompuServe's WinCim Web browser (included with version 1.4) requires a customized Winsock that conflicts with the Windows 95 version. A work-around for this is to put the CompuServe Winsock in the CID folder.

> **Note**
>
> By default, Windows 95 installs the 16-bit WINSOCK.DLL in your Windows folder; it installs a 32-bit version, WSOCK32.DLL, in your \Windows\System folder. If you are using a 32-bit Internet application, Windows 95 knows to use the 32-bit version.

Choosing an Internet Service Provider

VI

As the Internet grows by leaps and bounds, more and more businesses, called *Internet Service Providers* (ISPs), are springing up to provide access. Typically, a local provider offers three or more computers, called *servers*, that are linked directly to the Internet. In turn, they provide a dozen or more high-speed (14.4 Kbps or 28.8 Kbps) modems connected to local telephone lines. In some cities, a new service called *Integrated Services Digital Network* (ISDN) offers modem speeds up to 128 Kbps. Unless you live in a remote part of the world, finding a service provider is not the problem it was as recently as six months ago. The problem is, what kind of service do you need?

Online Communications

Let's examine the ways to access the Internet:

- If you attend a college or university, or are employed at a business of any size, you may already have Internet access. See your supervisor, the computer science department, or an administrator. Make a case for Internet access to your home, or at least for using your organization's access during off-hours.

- Join a commercial online service, such as CompuServe, America Online, Prodigy, or Delphi. These services handle the connectivity problems for you; it's just a matter of "pointing and clicking" your way to the Net. Windows 95 can benefit you because of its improved high-speed serial port support.

- Sign on to the Microsoft Network. Although the version of MSN bundled with Windows 95 provides only limited Internet services, in response to competition from the commercial service providers, MSN is adding increased access. Offerings include: e-mail and read-only access to some UseNet newsgroups, including the following categories: rec (recreation), soc (society, social issues), sci (science), misc (miscella-neous), news (mostly Internet news), talk (online conversation), and comp (computers). Because Microsoft intends to serve young people as well as adults, their UseNet newsreader restricts access to the unmoderated alt.* newsgroups, unless you state you are over 18 years of age. However, the Microsoft Plus! Pack, a separate suite of programs released concurrently with Windows 95, offers complete Internet access through the Microsoft Network.

- Sign up with a national Internet provider, such as NETCOM, PSI Pipe-line USA, or PSI Instant InterRamp. If you live in a rural area or travel a lot, this may be your best bet. A national provider has access phone numbers in major cities and often has SprintNet or Tymnet access elsewhere.

- Sign up with a local Internet provider. This is often the most economi-cal way to get on the Net: many services cost as little as $15 to $25 per month. Every major city in the U.S. and around the world has at least one local provider. Look for advertisements in computer magazines, the newspaper, or your classified telephone directory.

What You Need to Connect to the Internet

By now, Windows 95's Hardware Wizard has installed and configured your modem, or you've done it yourself. We hope you're using at least a 14.4 Kbps modem; that's about as slow as you want to go on the Internet. Once you've chosen your Internet provider, you're ready to set up Windows 95 to surf the Net.

◄ See "Installing a Plug and Play Modem," p. 883

◄ See "Using Drivers Provided by Modem Manufacturers," p. 843

Now you have to deal with some more Net jargon: SLIP and PPP. SLIP stands for Serial-Line Internet Protocol; PPP means Point-to-Point Protocol. Both are implementations of the TCP/IP Internet protocol over telephone lines. (Unless you access the Net through a LAN and Ethernet cabling, you'll be using telephone lines and SLIP or PPP.)

There are both technical and practical differences between the two protocols: technically, SLIP is a *network-layer protocol*; PPP is a *link-level protocol*. Practically, this means that PPP is faster and more fail-safe than SLIP. Windows 95 is optimized for PPP, which is the protocol to choose if your provider offers a choice.

If you've chosen an Internet-only service, you need the following information from your Internet provider:

- The kind of connection provided: SLIP or PPP

- Your user name (You can usually choose your own, such as jsmith.)

- A password (Again, you select your own. The most secure passwords have six or more uppercase and lowercase letters and/or numbers.)

- The provider's local access phone number

- Your host and domain name

- Your Domain Name Server's IP address (Briefly, DNS is the method the Internet uses to create unique names for each of the servers on the network.)

- Authentication technique (Some ISPs require users to type in their login name and password in a *terminal window,* which is a DOS window that opens when you connect to the service. Others have automated authentication methods, called PAP or CHAP, discussed later.)

VI

Online Communications

If your service provider gives you a dedicated IP address to use every time you dial in (in other words, you always log on to the same ISP server), you may also need the following:

- *IP address for you.* This is your computer's unique address.

- *IP subnet mask.* A physical world analogy might be the apartment number following a street address as a further way of pinpointing a location.

- *Gateway IP address.* The address of your ISP's server.

Here is an example of the setup requirements for an Internet provider:

IP Address:	1.1.1.1
Subnet Mask:	255.0.0.0
Host Name:	your computer's name
Domain Name:	anynet.com
Dial:	555-0000 (your provider's phone #)
Login:	jsmith
Password:	pAssWoRd (whatever you choose)
Domain Server:	222.222.68.160

Your provider might configure your system for you. At least they will help you over the phone while you enter the information in the correct Windows 95 Dial-Up Adapter dialog boxes (except for your password, which only you and your provider will know).

Installing and Configuring Windows 95 Dial-Up Network Adapter

Now it's time to set up Windows 95 to access the Internet. Here's what to do:

1. Double-click the My Computer icon to see whether Dial-Up Networking is installed. If it is, you see a folder named Dial-Up Networking (see fig. 29.2).

2. If you have Dial-Up Networking already installed, go to the section titled, "Creating a Configuration for Your Access Provider." If you do not have a Dial-Up Networking folder, install it now. Open the Start menu, and choose Settings, Control Panel.

Fig. 29.2
A view of My Computer, showing Dial-Up Networking installed.

3. Select the Add/Remove Programs option. The Add/Remove Programs Properties sheet appears.

4. Click the Windows Setup tab.

5. Select the Communications option and click the Details button. The dialog box in figure 29.3 appears.

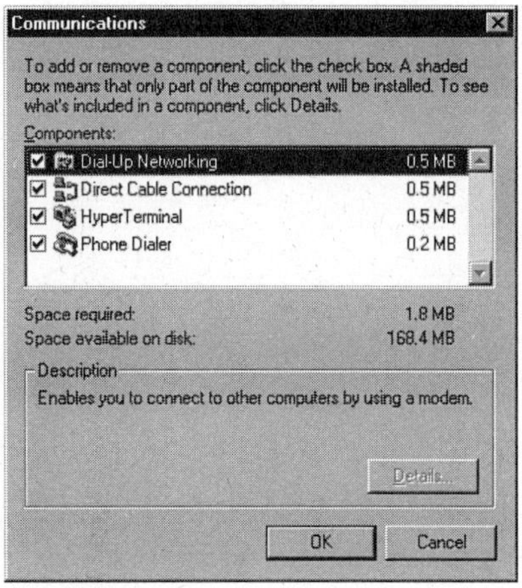

Fig. 29.3
The Communications dialog box, from which you select Dial-Up Networking to install that option.

6. Select the Dial-Up Networking option.

7. Click OK in the Communications dialog box; click OK in the Add/ Remove Programs Properties sheet to complete the installation.

Installing TCP/IP

To install and configure TCP/IP, follow these steps:

1. Open the Start menu and choose Settings, Control Panel. Double-click the Network control panel. Click the Add button, select Protocol, and

click the Add button. The Select Network Protocol dialog box appears (see fig. 29.4). Select Microsoft from the Manufacturers list, select TCP/IP from the Network Protocols list, and click OK.

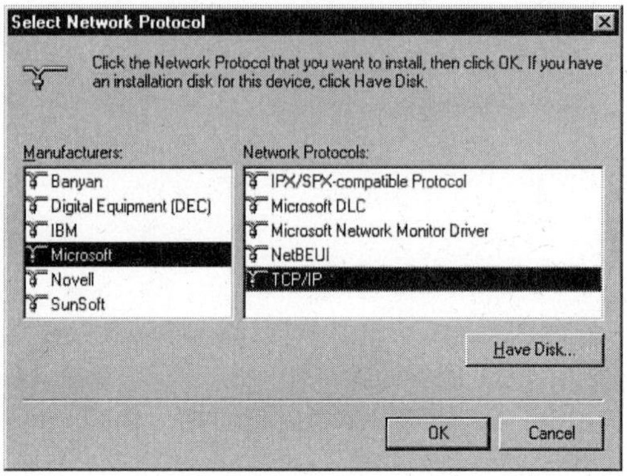

Fig. 29.4

The Select Network Protocol dialog box; select Microsoft from the Manufacturers list and TCP/IP from the Network Protocols list.

◄ See "Installing the Network Protocol," p. 627

2. Now make sure that your dial-up adapter is using (the term is, *is bound to*) the TCP/IP protocol. In the Network dialog box, click the Dial-Up Adapter to highlight it and then click Properties. Click the Bindings tab (see fig. 29.5). Make sure that a check mark is in the box next to the TCP/IP Dial-Up adapter.

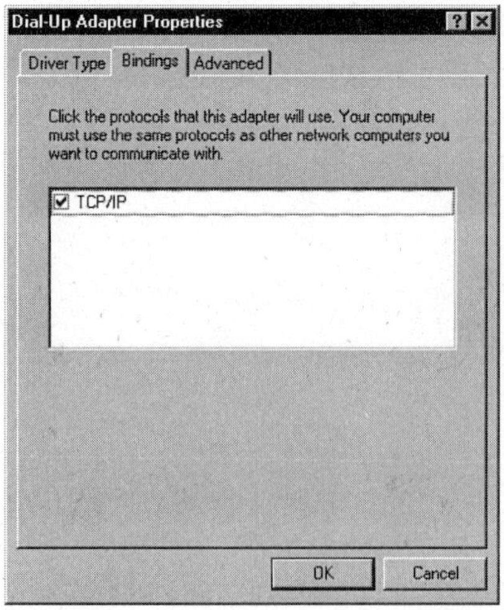

Fig. 29.5

The Bindings tab in the Dial-Up Adapter Properties sheet, showing TCP/IP bound to the adapter.

3. Set the TCP/IP properties. Open the Start menu and choose Settings, Control Panel. Double-click the Network Icon. Highlight TCP/IP -> Dial-Up Adapter in the Network box and click Properties. Select the IP Address tab and make sure that the Obtain an IP Address Automatically option is checked. This option sets your IP address to 0.0.0.0 (this will not be visible because the box will be grayed-out), which means that your Internet provider will dynamically assign you an IP address when you call in.

> **Note**
>
> If your Internet service provider assigns you a permanent IP address, enter that address manually on the IP Address tab: in the IP Address box, check the Specify an IP Address option and enter the assigned address in the IP Address field. You must also type the subnet mask address for your provider in the Subnet mask field.
>
> When you connect using PPP, the permanent IP address is used instead of the Internet service provider dynamically assigning one to you. When you connect with SLIP, the permanent IP address shows up in the Specify an IP address box to confirm your IP address for your SLIP connection.

Tip

If the address you're typing has less than three numbers before the period, use the Right Arrow key to jump to the next area between the periods in the field. If you type three numbers before the period, the cursor moves to the next area automatically.

4. In the TCP/IP Properties sheet, click the DNS Configuration tab (see fig. 29.6). Select Enable DNS; then set your Host and Domain names. Enter the Host name (this can be "User," unless you are assigned one by your network administrator).

5. Still in the DNS Configuration box, tab to the DNS Server Search Order box and enter the numeric address of the DNS server your provider said to use.

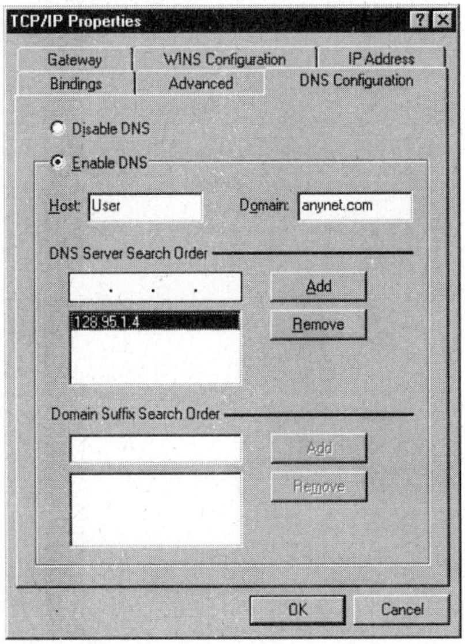

Fig. 29.6

The DNS Configuration tab of the TCP/IP Properties sheet shows the address for Microsoft.

VI

Online Communications

6. Click OK to close the Network control panel. Exit and restart Windows 95.

Creating a Configuration for Your Access Provider

In the preceding sections, you configured Windows 95 for TCP/IP connections. Now you need to tell it about the connection you'll be making to your ISP. To do this, you create and configure a new connection.

◄ See "Starting Programs and Documents from the Explorer or My Computer," p. 73

1. Open the Dial-Up Networking folder from the My Computer window. If this is the first time you've opened it, a Connection Wizard runs to help you enter all the information necessary for a dial-up connection.

2. Double-click the Make New Connection icon (see fig. 29.7). If you have not already configured Windows 95 for your modem, click Configure to do so now.

Fig. 29.7
Clicking Configure brings up the Modem Properties sheet.

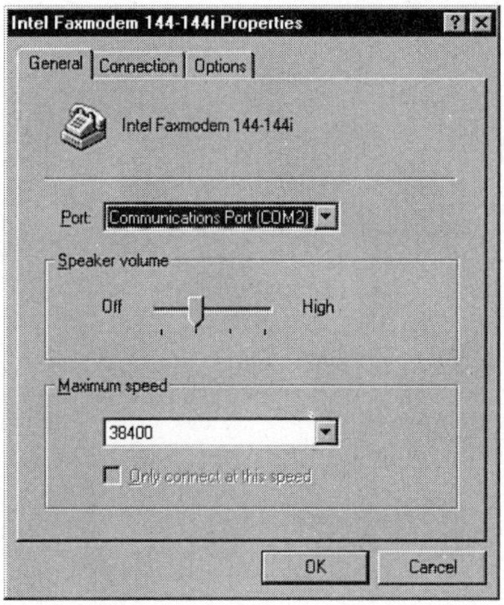

3. If you have configured your modem, continue by clicking Next; then enter the area code and telephone number for your ISP. Select your country code and area code from the drop-down menus. Click Next, and then click Finish to complete the installation. Now you have a new icon in your Dial-Up Networking Box. For easier access, drag the icon to your desktop to create a shortcut.

4. If your provider requires you to log on by means of a terminal window (it looks like a DOS window where you type in your user name and password), you must enable that function. In the Dial-Up Networking

box, right-click the connection icon you've just created and choose
Properties. In the Connect Using area of the dialog box, click Configure.
Now choose the Options tab (see fig. 29.8). In the Connection Control
section, make sure that the Bring Up Terminal Window after Dialing
box is checked. Click OK. This returns you to the first box of the Property sheet.

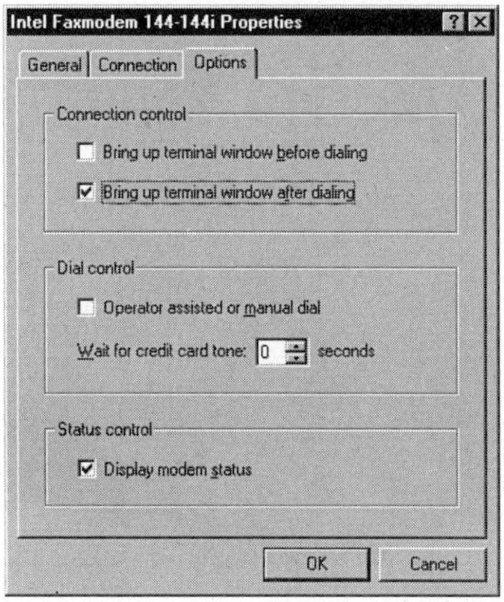

Fig. 29.8
Check the Bring
Up Terminal
Window After
Dialing option
to enable this
function.

5. In the Property sheet, click Server Type in the Connect Using section.
   This displays the dialog box in figure 29.9. From the Allowed Network
   Protocols group, check the TCP/IP option. This option provides quicker
   connect time after dialing the Internet provider. Uncheck the NetBEUI
   and IPX/SPX Compatible options because they are not relevant to connecting to the Internet.

   In the Type of Dial-Up Server section of the Property sheet, use the
   drop-down menu to select the type of connection, PPP, SLIP, or CSLIP
   (for a Compressed SLIP account). Your Internet provider can tell you
   which type of account you have. Click OK to close the dialog box for
   your Dial-Up Connection.

VI

Online Communications

Fig. 29.9

If you are using a PPP connection, your Server Types dialog box should look like this.

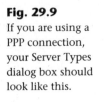

Connecting to Your Internet Provider

You are now ready to dial your Internet provider. Follow these steps:

1. To dial, double-click your New Connection icon (either on the desktop, if you've created a shortcut, or in the Dial-Up Networking folder). The Connect To dialog box should display the phone number for your Internet provider. You don't have to enter your user name and password here because you enter that information in the terminal window that appears after you've clicked Connect.

2. After the modem connects and you hear the "hiss," a terminal window appears (see fig. 29.10). Enter your user name and password, and then click Continue (F7); you should be connected within a few seconds.

Many providers are offering a more modern method of login, like PAP or CHAP. If this is true in your case, you don't have to check the Bring Up Terminal Window after Dialing option (found in the Dial-Up Networking Properties sheet under the Options tab of the Configure dialog box).

To dial your ISP, just enter your user name and password in the Connect To dialog box that appears after you double-click the Connection icon, as shown in figure 29.11.

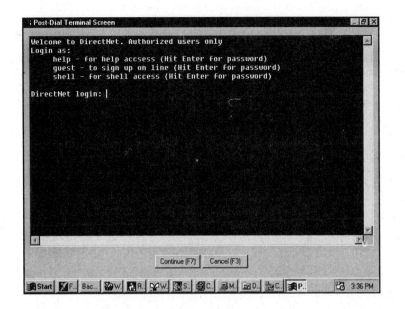

Fig. 29.10
Use the Post-Dial Terminal Screen to enter your user name and password.

Note

PAP stands for Password Authentication Protocol. *CHAP* stands for Challenge-Handshake Authentication Protocol. Both protocols allow you to log in without typing your user name and password in a terminal window.

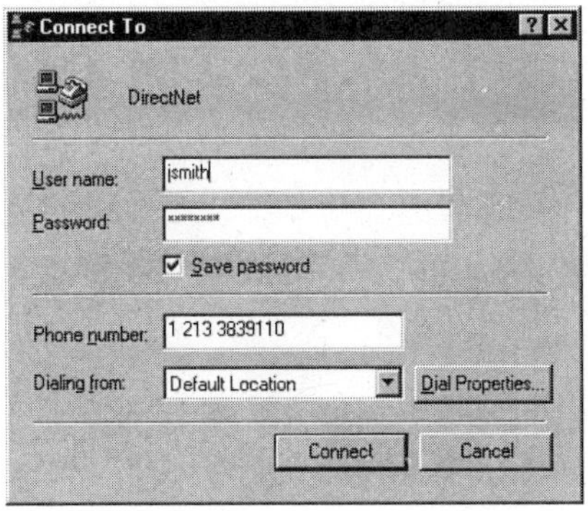

Fig. 29.11
If your provider offers CHAP or PAP, you can check Save Password in the Connect To dialog box to avoid having to retype the password each time you log in.

> **Note**
>
> Unless you configured Windows 95 to require a password at the start of each day's session, you will have to retype your password here the first time each day, or after you reboot.

If you are using a SLIP account, you will need a file called RNAPLUS.INF, available in the ADMIN/APPTOOLS/SLIP directory on the Windows 95 CD-ROM or via download from the Microsoft FTP site. Follow these steps to install it:

1. Open the Start menu and choose Settings, Control Panel. Double-click Add/Remove Programs. Select the Windows Setup tab; then click Have Disk.

2. Click Browse. Select the drive and directory where the file RNAPLUS.INF is located. When you've selected the file, click OK.

3. The Have Disk dialog box appears. Check the box (see fig. 29.12) and then click Install.

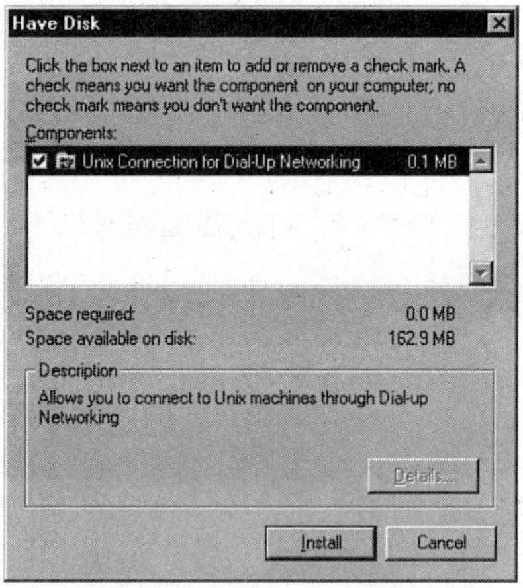

Fig. 29.12

Check the box labeled Unix Connection for Dial-Up Networking.

Now you are ready to add SLIP connectivity to your Dial-Up Networking Folder. Follow these steps to connect:

1. After you enter your user name and password in the terminal window, you should get a message from your provider telling you your IP address for this session. Most providers tell you what your IP address is with a

message like Your IP address is or SLIP session from ###.###.###.### to ###.###.###.###. The second number is usually your IP address. Write down your IP address and click the Continue button.

2. You should see a dialog box like the one in figure 29.13, asking you to confirm your IP address. Type the IP address you just wrote down and click OK. You should be connected in a few seconds. Make sure that you type the correct IP address when connecting.

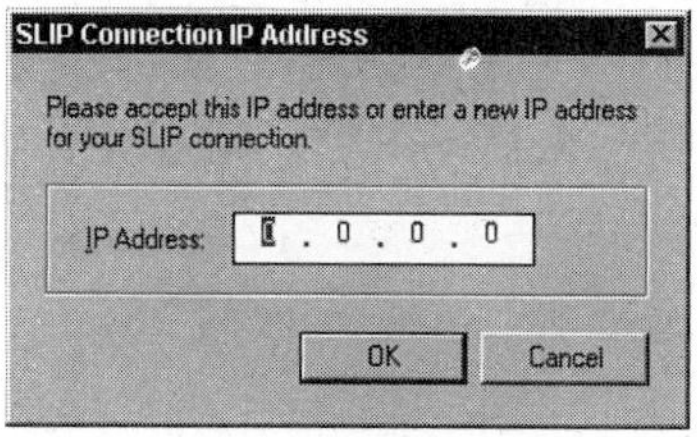

Fig. 29.13
Use this dialog box to enter your IP address. If you are not sure of it, ask your Internet provider what your address is for SLIP.

> **Note**
>
> Most Internet providers can switch your account from SLIP to PPP for no charge. PPP is faster than SLIP and offers error correction. Additionally, PPP accounts may not require you to use the terminal window to log in and do not require you to enter your IP address manually.

Troubleshooting

I've entered all the information in the Property sheet for my connection, and I've config-ured my modem correctly, but I still can't connect.

If you are having problems connecting with your service, make sure that your server type is correct. In the Dial-Up Networking folder, right-click your Connection icon; then select Properties. Click on Server Type. Make sure that the server type in the connection properties is set to PPP, not SLIP or CSLIP. Uncheck the box labeled Enable Software Compression in the Advanced Options section of the page.

If you have a SLIP account, make sure that you have changed the server type to SLIP or CSLIP (PPP is the default). Make sure that you type the correct IP address when prompted during the login process.

VI

Online Communications

Testing Your Connection

To test whether a connection is working, we'll use a program that comes with Windows 95 called PING. When executed, PING calls the remote computer you designate and sends back a response to let you know you're connected. The program's name comes from submarine sonar, which sends out a *ping* to get an echo of another hull in the water.

1. After you are connected to your ISP, open a DOS window.

2. At the DOS prompt, type **ping ftp.microsoft.com**. If the Microsoft server is busy, it may not answer right away. If so, **ping** your Internet provider's host computer by name—it may be mail, or mach1. Or **ping** 128.95.1.4, a DNS server. After a few milliseconds, the remote host replies:

   ```
   Pinging rftp.microsoft.com [198.105.232.1] with 32 bytes of data:
   Reply from 198.105.232.1: bytes=32 time=180ms TTL=18
   Reply from 198.105.232.1: bytes=32 time=185ms TTL=18
   Reply from 198.105.232.1: bytes=32 time=176ms TTL=18
   Reply from 198.105.232.1: bytes=32 time=181ms TTL=18
   ```

   This tells you that your computer is talking to the server. Unless you have ongoing problems connecting, you'll use the PING command only once.

Troubleshooting

After connecting with my SLIP account, I can ping the server, but still can't use Winsock applications to connect to a resource.

You may have to switch the server type. From My Computer, open the Dial-Up Networking folder. Right-click on your connection to open the Properties sheet. Select Server Type; then try changing the server type in the connection properties from SLIP to CSLIP or CSLIP to SLIP, depending on what it is currently set for.

I can run my Web browser, but my newsgroup reader and my mail reader won't work. What's wrong?

If you have a Winsock application that is not working properly, check to see whether that application requires a specific WINSOCK.DLL file. Some Winsock applications come with their own WINSOCK.DLL, which may not work with Windows 95. First, try renaming the application-provided WINSOCK.DLL to ensure that you're using the WINSOCK.DLL in your WINDOWS directory. If the application does not work with the Windows 95 WINSOCK.DLL, replace it with the application's WINSOCK.DLL file.

Caution

Renaming your Windows 95 WINSOCK.DLL may cause other Winsock applications not to work and is not recommended. Contact the application vendor to see whether they have an updated version that will work with the Windows 95 WINSOCK.DLL.

Troubleshooting

Everything seems to be configured properly, but I still can't connect to my ISP.

If you are having trouble connecting, open the Network icon in the control panel, select the Dial-Up Adapter, select Properties, select the Advanced tab, and set Record a Log File to Yes. This action writes a file called PPPLOG.TXT to your WINDOWS directory that contains information recorded during the connecting process. You may need this information when you talk to your provider.

I have a PPP connection and sometimes can't connect to my provider.

If you are having problems when connecting with Internet service providers offering PPP accounts, it may help if you turn off IP header compression. To do so, open Control Panel, double-click Networking, click Dial-Up Adapter to select it, and click Properties. In the Properties sheet, select the Advanced tab and uncheck the Use IP Header Compression option.

Connecting to the Internet with a LAN

If your computer is part of a Local Area Network (LAN), connecting to the Internet with Windows 95 is as easy as connecting a single user. The main difference is that instead of getting the information you need from an ISP, you will obtain it from your network administrator. Windows 95 provides seamless integration of Internet and LAN e-mail though a Microsoft API mail driver employing the Microsoft Exchange client. Mail from another computer on the LAN is treated the same as mail from out on the Internet.

Let's get started:

1. Open the Start menu and choose Settings, Control Panel. Double-click the Network icon. If you followed the previous procedures, you will now have both Dial-Up Adapter and TCP/IP installed. Select the TCP/IP protocol and click Properties.

2. Select the IP Address tab. If your LAN has a Dynamic Host Configuration Protocol (DHCP) Server, you will click the button marked Obtain an IP Address automatically.

3. If your LAN does not have a DHCP server, you will have to obtain the IP address from your network administrator. Click the button marked Specify an IP address and fill in the address. Use the arrow key to move between the fields separated by periods. You should also enter the Subnet Mask address at this time.

4. Now click the Gateway tab. This is the address of the connection point between your LAN and the Internet. Enter the address provided by your network administrator.

5. Now select the DNS Configuration tab (refer to fig. 29.6). Select Enable DNS. Obtain your Host and Domain names from your network administrator and enter them in the spaces provided. For example, your computer might be "Zeus," at IBM. The address would be zeus[Host].ibm.com[Domain] (omitting the words in the brackets). If you are part of a smaller organization, you may not have a Domain Name Server of your own, but would be given a domain name by your service provider.

6. Still in the DNS Configuration box, tab to the DNS Server Search Order box and enter the numeric address of the DNS server your network administrator gives you.

7. You are almost done. If your LAN is not using DHCP, or is running Windows NT, you may have to set up the Windows Internet Naming Service, (WINS, pronounced "WIN-S"). Click the WINS Configuration tab and follow your network administrator's instructions.

8. That's it! Click OK to close the Network control panel. Exit and restart Windows 95.

There are a few concerns for networks on the Internet with Windows 95:

◄ See "The Four Building Blocks of Windows 95 Networking," p. 600

■ *TCP/IP and System Pauses.* If you are using TCP/IP for your Internet connections and the protocol is bound to both your LAN and dial-up adapter but no DHCP server is present on the LAN, your system may pause for a few seconds every once in a while. To avoid this, unbind TCP/IP from your LAN adapter. Here's how to do it:

Open the Network folder in Control Panel. Select the Network Card (see fig. 29.14); then click on Properties. Click the Bindings tab, and then uncheck the TCP/IP option in the dialog box.

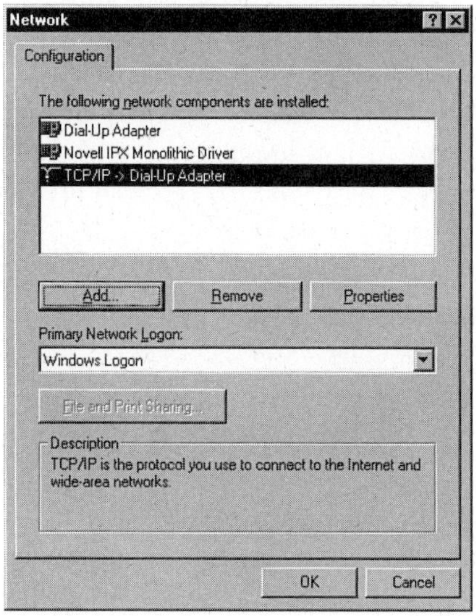

Fig. 29.14
Notice that the TCP/IP protocol is only bound to the Dial-Up Adapter, as it should be.

■ If Microsoft's TCP/IP is the only protocol you have loaded on your system, the IP address is not added during setup. If you have a DHCP server, just open the Network control panel applet and then close it; this action updates the IP address. Otherwise, open the Network control panel applet, select Properties on the TCP/IP page, and manually enter your IP address.

Software You Can Use with the Internet

After all the configuration work you went through to get onto the Internet, it may seem that getting connected was the goal. But the real power of the Internet lies not in the connection, but in what you do after you are there. Windows includes the following three Internet applications, but they are of somewhat limited usefulness; you will want to find freeware or commercial software for your Internet applications.

VI

Online Communications

- *Telnet* is a Windows-based program you use to log on to Internet sites as if your computer were a terminal connected to that computer. This version of Telnet is almost identical to the shareware version available at many sites on the Net; it is minimalist but has a good help file. For more information, see the section "Services Available on the Internet," later in this chapter.

- *FTP* is a command-line program, not for the faint of heart, used to download files from remote computers connected to the Internet. FTP is examined further in Chapter 30, "Using FTP, the World Wide Web, and other Internet Services."

With the mushrooming popularity of the Internet, more and more software packages are appearing every day. To make full use of the Internet's potential with Windows 95, you need the following kinds of applications:

- *A World Wide Web browser.* Available browsers include Microsoft's Internet Explorer, Netscape, Mosaic, or Microsoft's Internet Assistant, an add-on to Word for Windows (currently available as freeware from Microsoft's FTP site). You also need programs to view downloaded graphics and play sound files. In some cases, these applications are included with your Web browser.

- *A mail program.* Among the better known Windows programs are Eudora, by Qualcomm, available as both a shareware and a commercial program; OS Mail, from Open Systems; and Z-Mail, from Network Computing Devices, Inc.

- *An FTP program.* A very good freeware Windows-based program is WS_FTP, copyright by John A. Junod, available from your Internet provider or at many FTP sites.

- *A newsreader.* You use newsreaders with UseNet newsgroups. Trumpet News Reader is a freeware version, as is WinVN, by Mark Riordan. Also available are NewsXpress and Free Agent.

- *A file search utility.* There are millions of files on Internet servers all over the world; how do you find the one you're looking for? Three time-tested systems, each performing slightly different functions, are Gopher, Archie, and Veronica. Windows programs to access these Internet tools are available.

See Chapter 30, "Using FTP, the World Wide Web, and other Internet Services," for more information on these and other Internet applications.

Services Available on the Internet

The Internet is a combination communications tool, library, and catalog. Many think it is the most important source of information available today. More realistic Net surfers have found that, although the Internet has more *data* than anyone can ever begin to comprehend, there's not much *information* (defined as *useful* data). The Net-speak phrase that defines this situation is "a high signal to noise ratio."

The best way to decide is to find out for yourself. Windows makes getting connected fairly simple, but you'll have to get other software to do your own Net cruising. The following sections take a detailed look at some of the services on the Net.

The World Wide Web

The most exciting development on the Internet in recent months has been the explosive growth of the World Wide Web. It seems that everyone with access to the Internet has a Web page; you can find pages for groups from Microsoft (see fig. 29.15) to The Whole Internet Catalog (see fig. 29.16).

All Web pages, or World Wide Web sites, are identified by a unique address, called a *Universal Resource Locator* (URL). The Microsoft page's URL address looks like this:

http://www.microsoft.com/

The Whole Internet Catalog page's URL looks like this:

http://www.gnn.com/wic/newrescat.toc.html

All World Wide Web addresses begin the same way: http:// (which stands for *HyperText Transfer Protocol*, the "language" of the Web). With a Web browser, you can also visit FTP sites (described later in this chapter), which have addresses beginning with ftp://.

VI

Online Communications

Fig. 29.15
This is the
Microsoft Web
page.

Fig. 29.16
This is The Whole
Internet Catalog, a
Web search tool
you can use to
search for any
type of document
accessible from the
Web.

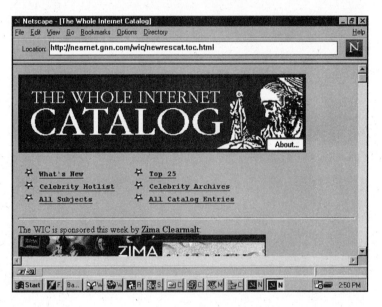

Windows 95 does not currently provide a Web browser, but excellent ones are available as freeware and shareware from NCSA Mosaic, Netscape, Quarterdeck, and many other vendors. The Microsoft Plus! Pack, a CD-ROM with many Windows 95 tools, includes a browser.

After you install your browser, you can configure it to view and download graphical images on many Web sites, listen to music and voice clips, and use hypertext links to jump to other World Wide Web sites around the world.

Time magazine has a Web page (see fig. 29.17). Begin at the Time-Warner Web page at:

http://www.pathfinder.com

The *Time* magazine site has pictures and articles from its recent issues, a database of past issue contents, and even a BBS for chatting with other *Time* aficionados. The Time-Warner page also provides links to other publications like *Sports Illustrated, People,* and *Fortune.*

Fig. 29.17

A Netscape browser view of the *Time* magazine Welcome Web page.

> **Caution**
>
> Like DOS file names, URLs have *no* spaces. Type the URL—or any Internet address you see—without spaces.

Electronic Mail

The most widely used service the Internet provides is electronic mail, or e-mail. With e-mail, you can be in almost instantaneous contact with anyone else on the Internet, no matter where they live or work.

Suppose that you've arranged to meet an associate the next morning in a distant city. It's late at night, your plans have changed, and you need to get in touch with him or her. Send an e-mail message. E-mail users check their mail every day.

How do you send an e-mail message? Just as in the physical world, where addresses include numbers, streets, cities, and states, on the Internet, everyone has a unique e-mail address that looks like this:

username@anynet.com

Businesses, Internet organizations, and services such as Listserv (a program that keeps track of mailing lists) also have addresses. Your address is composed of your user name (such as jsmith) and your provider's domain. If Jane Smith signs on to America Online for her Internet access, she may have an e-mail address like this one:

jsmith@aol.com

If Joe Smith is already using that login name on AOL, Jane has to pick another one.

The Internet also has *mailing lists*, or e-mail discussion groups, on many topics (such as writing, pets, running a small business, and so on), comprised of members who subscribe to that mailing list.

> **Note**
>
> To *subscribe* to a mailing list—in other words, to join the discussion or just read others' postings—you send an e-mail message to the *listserver* who manages that mailing list.

> **Note**
>
> To *send a message* to the members of a mailing list, once you've joined, you post a message to the mailing list itself. You respond to messages in the mailing list in the same way you answer an e-mail message from an individual.

UseNet Newsgroups

Newsgroups are another important service on the Internet. Where e-mail is a one-to-one communication, newsgroups are many-to-many discussions, organized by topics. There are over 10,000 newsgroups currently on the Internet, dealing with every imaginable—and unimaginable—topic. The wildest are the unmoderated alt.* groups (alt is an abbreviation for *alternative*), on topics from **alt.0d** (which seems to be a bunch of test messages) to **alt.zine** (a newsgroup about alternative magazines). You can read messages from a newsgroup to see whether you want to subscribe or not.

Most newsreaders identify *threads* (series of messages on the same topic) by indenting follow-up messages and by allowing the use of Re to indicate the topic of original posting (see fig. 29.18). Some newsreaders allow you to sort messages by thread so that you can follow threads that interest you and avoid those that don't.

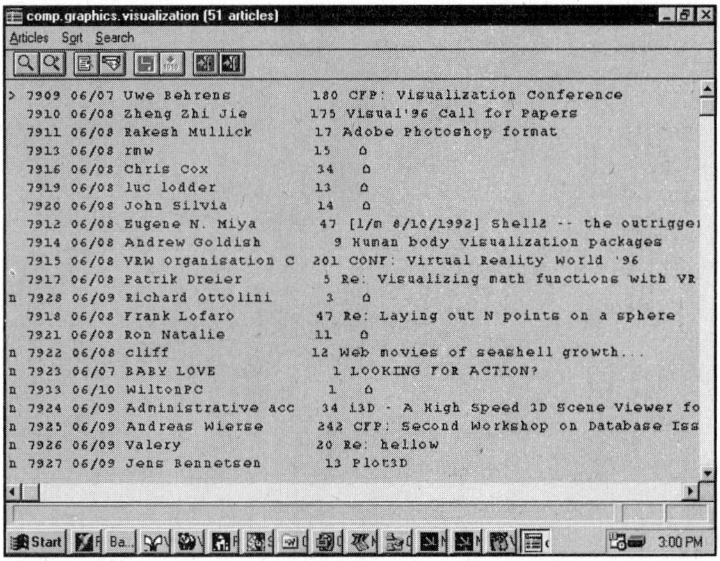

Fig. 29.18
A WinVN newsreader listing of messages in the newsgroup **comp.graphics. visualization**. Notice the indenting for threads.

When you first log on to the Internet and boot up your newsreader program, the newsreader will prompt you to download the current list of newsgroups from the news server. With more than 10,000 newsgroups this might take a few minutes, but you only have to do it once. You can refresh the list from time to time. To read the messages in a newsgroup, you then select it from the list. You can read messages from a newsgroup to see whether you want to subscribe or not. Once you have subscribed, you can just lurk (that's what Net-surfers call it when you read articles but do not post any) or you can enter into a discussion.

VI

Online Communications

FTP

File Transfer Protocol (FTP) is one of the earliest functions of the Internet. FTP enables the movement of files from one computer to another over the Internet. Computers that allow you to dial in to them and download files from them are called *FTP servers*. There are hundreds of FTP servers all over the globe, each with tens of thousands of files. How do you find what you're looking for?

Archie servers are computers that index the files available on FTP sites. Without going to each FTP site and browsing (a project that can take days and tie up Internet resources), you can go to an Archie server and find files by their names. Of course, if the file is about drug use in ancient Egypt, for example, but is named Dr3aeg91.txt, Archie has no clue about what the file contains.

Gopher

That's where Gopher comes in. *Gopher servers* are computers on the Internet that maintain lists of the files residing on their own as well as other computers. With a *Gopher client* (a menu-based Gopher program you run on your computer) you can search many places on the Internet for the files you need. Gopher also allows descriptive comments to be attached to file names. Another advantage is that many Gopher servers have World Wide Web menus: you can use a Web browser, click a file name, and begin downloading a file to your computer.

Another search tool, *Veronica,* allows the user to search menu items on Gopher servers. Veronica servers compile databases of Gopher menus and provide information about the files, in addition to the file names and their locations.

WAIS

Let's say that you're looking for as many documents as you can find about (to continue the previous topic) drug use in ancient Egypt, but you don't know the names of the files. *WAIS* (Wide Area Information Server) is the most useful search tool for this kind of search. WAIS has an index of keywords contained in all the documents on servers all over the world. Using WAIS, you can type **drugs** and **Egypt** to get information on your topic, even if the file names of the documents containing that information are obscure.

Telnet

Telnet, another Internet protocol, allows users to log in to a remote computer and treat that machine as though it were their own computer. In other words, if you want to get a file located on a machine halfway around the world, you can Telnet to a local computer, use that machine to Telnet to still another, and so on, until you reach your destination. Telnet can save you the cost of a long-distance call. All you need is the name of the local host computer. Recently, Telnet has provided a means for participants in *MUD* (Multiple User Dimension) games to play one another on-line.

Chapter 30, "Using FTP, the World Wide Web, and other Internet Services," discusses all these Internet services in detail.

Tip

Because you use it to connect to several computers, Telnet is slow and uses a lot of system resources. If you have a better way to access a remote site, use it.

Sample Fees

The following chart compares what you'll spend logging on to the Internet. Although Windows 95, aside from its modem setup and serial port configuration, plays no part in connecting to the commercial services, the service fees are included as a basis for comparison. "Anynet" is representative of many local access providers.

	AOL	Compu-Serve	Delphi	IBM-Net	NET-COM	Prodigy	Anynet
10 hrs/mo.	$24.90	$24.95	$23	$29.95	$19.95	$29.95	$25
20 hrs/mo.	$54	$24.95	$23	$29.95	$19.95	$29.95	$25
30 hrs/mo.	$83	$44.95	$41	$29.95	$19.95	$29.95	$25
60 hrs/mo.	$122	$102	$95	$89.95	$19.95	$118	$25

It's easy to see, that, for a dedicated Net surfer, a local provider is the least expensive way to go. But those interested in the additional forums and libraries of the commercial services, and who intend to be on the Internet less than 10 or 20 hours a month, may want to investigate CompuServe, Prodigy or America Online. Notice also that, as of this writing, Microsoft has not posted fees for their Internet access.❖

VI

Online Communications

Chapter 30

Using FTP, the World Wide Web, and Other Internet Services

by Francis Moss with Paul Robichaux

Windows 95 provides advanced SLIP and PPP connectivity, but once you're connected to the Internet, you're pretty much on your own. The Internet applications provided with Windows 95 are—to be generous—minimal. While the Microsoft Network provides some Internet (read-only UseNet newsgroups and e-mail), for full access you'll need an Internet service provider and other Net tools.

To fully explore the Internet, you'll need a World Wide Web browser, UseNet newsreader, and an e-mail client in addition to the software that Windows 95 provides. Fortunately, there are servers on the Internet that make these software packages—and hundreds of others—available for free.

In this chapter, you learn the following skills:

- How to use Microsoft's FTP program to connect to large archives of shareware and freeware

- How to find and download software using FTP

- How to log in to remote computers on the Internet with Telnet

- How to use Microsoft's Internet Assistant as a Web browser

- How to use e-mail and UseNet to send private messages or post and read messages that millions of other users can see

- How to explore the World Wide Web (WWW) with Microsoft's Internet Explorer (part of the Microsoft Plus! Pack for Windows 95)

- How to create your own Web pages using the HyperText Markup Language (HTML)

Microsoft is introducing the Microsoft Plus! Pack, which includes the Internet Jumpstart Kit. In the kit are a World Wide Web browser and an e-mail reader for use with the Microsoft Exchange mail client. One feature of the Web browser includes the ability to drag your favorite Internet locations to the desktop to create shortcuts.

Using FTP

The Plus! Pack tools are nice, but Plus! doesn't include all the tools you need. How can you find the software you need to start cruising the Internet now? The best way to get the software (and learn about the Internet at the same time) is to use the command-line version of FTP included with Windows 95.

Before you begin, you need an Internet connection, either through Windows 95's Dial-Up Networking or a direct LAN connection. (To find out more, see Chapter 29, "Getting Connected to the Internet.")

> **Note**
>
> This book is about Windows 95, so we can only scratch the surface of the Internet. For more coverage of the Internet and related software, check out *Special Edition Using the Internet*, Second Edition, *Special Edition Using the World Wide Web with Mosaic, Using FTP, Using Netscape, Easy World Wide Web with Netscape, Using UseNet Newsgroups, Web Publishing with Word for Windows*, or any of the other Que books about the Internet and its parts. Visit the Macmillan Publishing Web page at **http://www.mcp.com** for a complete book list.

◀ See "FTP,"
p. 908

The File Transfer Protocol, usually called FTP, is the Internet standard for file transfer. A simple, command-line version of FTP is part of Windows 95. You can use it to connect to remote FTP servers and find the files you need.

Most public archive sites allow you to log in as a special user, *anonymous*. All that means is that the FTP server allows you to enter *anonymous* as a user name instead of requiring every individual user to have a unique name and password. Whenever you log in as *anonymous*, provide your e-mail address when the FTP server asks you for a password.

To begin an FTP session, follow these steps:

1. Connect to the Internet. If your connection to the Internet is via a LAN, be sure you are properly connected to your network. If you connect by using a modem and a dial-up Internet service provider, use your Dial-up Connection to log on to your Internet Service Provider (ISP).

   ◄ See "Installing and Configuring Windows 95 Dial-Up Network Adapter," p. 888

2. When your Internet connection is active, open a DOS window and, at the C:\> prompt, type **FTP**.

3. At the ftp> prompt, type in the **open** command, followed by the name or address of the server you want to connect to (for example, **open ftp.qualcomm.com**).

4. At the login prompt, enter a user name. In most cases, this will be *anonymous*. There may be a brief message from the server along with the login prompt. If there is, read it. Some anonymous servers may ask you to log in as *guest* or some other user name. If so, follow the directions there.

5. At the password prompt, enter a password. If you logged in as *anonymous*, you should enter your e-mail address as a password. Figure 30.1 shows the results of our logon to the QUALCOMM FTP server. (QUALCOMM, Incorporated is the maker of the popular Eudora e-mail client.)

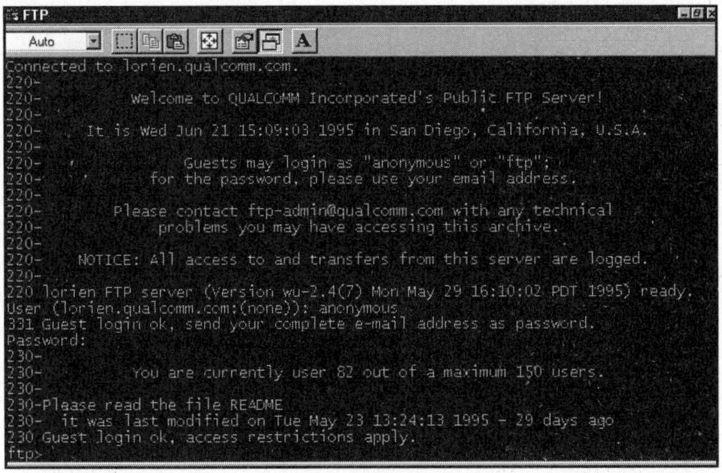

Fig. 30.1
When the QUALCOMM FTP server answers, it asks you to log in. Type **anonymous** as a user name and your e-mail address for a password.

VI

Online Communications

Tip

Every time you log
onto a remote
server, look for
"readme" or "in-
dex" files. If you
find one, down-
load it, then load it
into a word proces-
sor to search for
names and loca-
tions of files to
download.

Once you're logged in, you should see the ftp> prompt again. There may be a
message from the server, stating the server's policies or giving other information. If there is, read it. At this point, you can use the other FTP commands
discussed in the following sections to change directories and find and retrieve
files.

Navigating through Directories

Once you've connected to an FTP site, you'll most often need to change to
a particular directory to get a specific file. If you're just browsing, you may
want to poke around the directory tree. In either case, you need to be able to
move around the directory structure. Here's how to do it:

1. The dir and ls commands list the files in the current directory on the
   FTP server. dir includes more information about each file than ls does.

Tip

Some servers dis-
play messages
when you change
into particular
directories. Be sure
to read them; they
can be important.

2. The cd command works just like it does in DOS: it changes your current
   directory *on the server*. If you want to change your current directory on
   your local computer, use the lcd command.

3. At any time, you can change to a directory whose full name you know
   with the cd command. For example, cd/quest/Windows/Eudora will
   change your current directory from wherever it is to the /quest/Win-
   dows/Eudora directory.

Note

Remember that most Internet FTP servers use a forward slash (/) to indicate a directory rather than the back slash (\) used in DOS.

Figure 30.2 shows a sample session with **ftp.ksc.nasa.gov**, a public-access
server run by NASA, where you can get the WinVN newsreader.

Caution

Unlike Windows, UNIX (the operating system used by most Internet FTP servers)
distinguishes between upper- and lowercase in file and directory names. Be sure to
type directory names and file names exactly as they appear, including using the
correct capitalization.

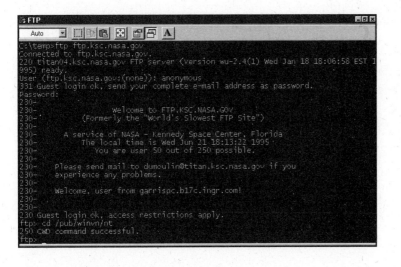

Fig. 30.2
Once you've
logged in, you
can list files and
directories and
navigate through
the server.

Getting One or More Files

Before you transfer files, you need to know that FTP allows two kinds of
transfers: ASCII and binary. On your computer, some files are human-
readable text, and others are binary data. Files on FTP servers are the same
way, and FTP provides commands for changing the transfer mode. Use them
under these circumstances:

- If you're fetching an ASCII file, you can use the ascii command before
  transferring it. The Windows 95 FTP client sets ASCII mode by default.

- If the file you're transferring isn't an ASCII file, you should use the
  binary command to tell FTP to transfer the file in binary mode. If you
  transfer a binary file, like a ZIP or EXE file, in ASCII mode, it won't be
  usable after transfer. If you transfer an ASCII file in binary mode,
  though, it doesn't do any harm.

Tip
To change modes,
type **ascii** or
binary at the ftp
prompt.

Now that you can connect to an FTP server and have browsed around until
you've found an interesting file and set the right transfer mode, you need a
way to copy that file over the Internet onto your computer.

When you copy files with FTP, the FTP client will put them in your current
local directory. If you start FTP from the C:\WINDOWS directory, that's
where your files will end up. To control where your files go:

- Before running FTP, use the DOS cd command to change to the directory where you want the downloaded files.

VI

Online Communications

■ While running FTP, use the lcd command to change FTP's current local work directory. For example, lcd c:\temp\downloads changes the current directory on your PC to that directory (assuming that directory exists on your system). Any files downloaded are then downloaded to that directory.

Tip
By default, FTP asks you to confirm each file before it transfers it when you use mget. Use the prompt command to turn off (or on) interactive prompting.

FTP provides two commands to copy files from the FTP server to your machine. Let's see how they work.

■ The get command gets a single file that you specify. For example, get wznt56.zip fetches the file named "wznt56.zip" to your local disk. You can also specify a name for the local copy; get wznt56.zip new-file.zip copies the file, then names it "new-file.zip".

■ The mget command gets all files that match the pattern you specify. For example, mget *.zip copies all files in the current server directory whose names end with ".zip" to your local machine.

Figure 30.3 puts it all together and shows a sample session with **ftp.ksc. nasa.gov**; we connect, get a directory listing with ls, and download a file in binary mode.

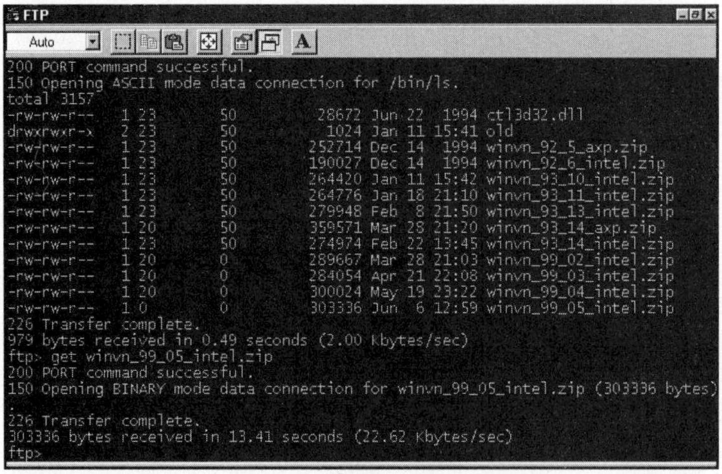

Fig. 30.3
To get files, just connect to the site, then retrieve the files you need. Don't forget to set binary mode when needed.

Leaving the FTP Site and Quitting FTP

When you're done retrieving files, you need to leave the FTP site to make it available to other users. There are several commands for doing so:

■ The disconnect command closes your connection to the FTP site, but keeps the FTP program active. You can then connect to other sites with the open command.

- The bye and quit commands close your active connection, if any, and exit the FTP program. You'll be returned to the DOS command prompt after using these commands.

Some Popular FTP Sites

Once you know how to use FTP, you can use the same methods to log in to servers all around the world. There are thousands of servers with thousands of files available. Finding what you need can be impossible if you don't know where to start. Here are the addresses of a few key FTP sites that should be of value.

- **ftp.cica.indiana.edu**

  This is the Center for Innovative Computing Applications (CICA) site. Look in the directory /pub/pc/win3 for one of the largest collections of Windows software available. There are many directories, for Windows utilities, applications, add-ins and templates for popular programs such as Word and Excel, and more.

- **ftp.ncsa.uiuc.edu**

  This is the National Center for SuperComputing Applications (NCSA) site. You will find Mosaic software for Windows here in /Web/Mosaic/Windows. Software for writing Web pages in HTML can be found in /Web/html/Windows.

- **ftp.microsoft.com**

  You guessed it, this is the home of Microsoft. Look here for software patches, press releases, technical papers, and more.

- **buckshot.usma.edu**

  This site at the US Military Academy at West Point offers the popular WS_FTP tool. WS_FTP provides a Windows GUI interface for FTP. The file you'll need is /pub/msdos/ws_ftp32.zip.

- **ftp.winzip.com**

  Many programs you get via FTP will be compressed using PKZIP. WinZip provides a slick Windows interface for using zipped files, including drag and drop and long file names. The file you need is /winzip/wznt56.exe. Even though this version is for Windows NT, it works well with Windows 95.

Tip

Type the status command to see information about whether various options are on or off. This shows if you are in ASCII or binary mode.

Tip

CICA is a busy site. There is a mirror that isn't quite as busy at **archive.orst.edu**.

VI

Online Communications

■ **ftp.mcp.com**

The Macmillan Computer Publishing site (Que is a part of MCP). Look here for software related to Que and Macmillan books.

Troubleshooting

I tried to log in anonymously but I got a message that said Anonymous User Login Denied. *Why can't I log in?*

Usually, login error messages like this one mean that the server is too busy. FTP servers limit the number of users that can log in at once so that the server doesn't get overloaded. Sometimes the sites will post a message listing the addresses of *mirror sites* (other servers that have the same files), and you can try one of those instead. Educational and business sites often have lower limits on anonymous users during the day so that their students and employees can use the sites without being slowed by anonymous users. You may have better luck logging in to these sites at night. However, more people cruise FTP sites for fun at night, so there may be more anonymous users. Take your chances and keep trying.

I connected to an FTP site, then got up from the computer for a few minutes. When I came back and typed a command, I got a message about the control connection being closed. What happened?

Most FTP sites will log you out automatically if you leave the connection open for several minutes with no activity. This frees up the connection for others to use. Just use the open command to reconnect to the site, then transfer the files you want.

Using Telnet

The Internet's Telnet protocol allows you to log in to a remote computer as though you were sitting in front of it. Windows 95 provides a Telnet client, called telnet, that you can use to connect to remote systems where you have accounts. In addition to dial-up access, many Internet service providers allow you to telnet to their hosts for direct UNIX access.

The Windows 95 Telnet client isn't flashy, but since Telnet is based on the idea of emulating a plain ASCII terminal, it doesn't need to be.

Connecting and Disconnecting to Remote Computers

The first step to connecting to remote computers with Windows 95's Telnet client is to start the client from the command prompt (its name is "telnet") or from a shortcut. Once you've done that, you can use the Connect, Remote System option to connect. Figure 30.4 shows Telnet's Connect dialog box.

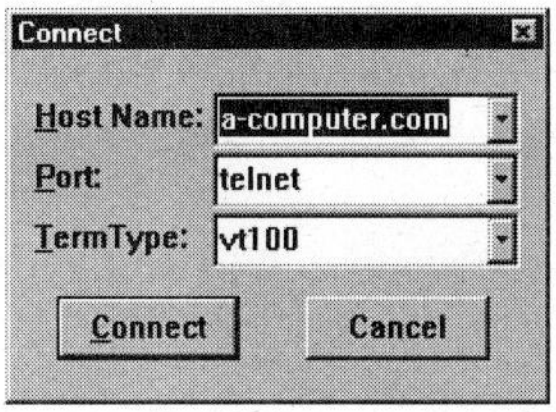

Fig. 30.4
Select a host, port, and terminal type from the Connect dialog box. Don't change the port number unless you know what you're doing.

Once you're connected, you can use all the remote computer's facilities just like you could if you had dialed into that computer via modem, or if you were sitting in front of it.

When you're done, you can choose Connect, Disconnect to close the connection; if you choose Connect, Exit, Telnet will exit. Unfortunately, you can only connect to one computer at a time.

> **Caution**
>
> If you're connected to a remote computer when you choose Connect, Exit, Telnet will exit *without* asking you to confirm.

Keeping a Log of Your Connection

Sometimes it's useful to have a permanent record of a session with a remote computer. Telnet includes a way for you to capture what appears on your screen and save it into a text file for later review.

To turn on logging, select Terminal, Start Logging. Telnet prompts you to choose a location and name for your log file. Once you start logging, your communications with the remote system goes into the log file.

To stop logging, select Terminal, Stop Logging. Telnet closes the log file.

Setting Preferences

Many users like to be able to control the cursor's appearance and behavior in a communications program. Telnet provides a preferences dialog box that allows you to adjust the cursor shape, the text font used in Telnet windows, and other aspects of the program's behavior.

To set Telnet's preferences, choose Terminal, Preferences. Set the options the way you want them, then choose OK to save your changes or Cancel to discard them. If you save changes, Telnet will remember them.

VI

Online Communications

Surfing the Web with Internet Explorer

Internet Explorer is part of Microsoft's Plus! Pack for Windows 95. Internet Explorer offers the same basic tools as other Web browsers, but it was redesigned to take advantage of the full range of Windows 95's features. It supports the full Windows 95 user interface and improves on Windows 3.1-based browsers by supporting shortcuts and long file names. Figure 30.5 shows Internet Explorer's main window and the default page that ships with the software.

Fig. 30.5

Internet Explorer's main window includes a toolbar for quick access to common functions. This is the introductory Internet Explorer start page.

Internet Explorer shares a common look and feel with Microsoft's other applications, and includes Windows 95 features like flyover help and the common file and print dialog boxes. It also has many similarities to other Web browsers; after all, it was based on Mosaic. If you're already accustomed to another browser, you'll find the Internet Explorer both comfortably familiar and excitingly different.

There *is* one difference you need to know about. Microsoft calls hypertext links shortcuts, since clicking them takes you to someplace else. To avoid confusion, I'll refer to hypertext links as "links" or "hyperlinks," and Windows 95 shortcuts as "shortcuts."

Installing the Internet Explorer

The Internet Explorer comes as part of the Plus! Pack for Windows 95. (If your computer came preloaded with Windows 95, you may already have the Plus! Pack installed; check your system documentation.) Like many other Windows 95 products, the Plus! Pack is easy to install. Here's what you should do:

▶ See "Installing Plus!," p. 1142

1. Insert the Plus! Pack disc into your CD-ROM drive.

2. Using the Windows 95 command prompt, the Explorer, or a desktop window, run D:\SETUP.EXE (assuming D is your CD-ROM drive).

3. The Plus! Pack setup installer loads and asks you to choose which modules you want to install. Choose the Internet Jumpstart option.

Navigating the Web

When you start the Internet Explorer, it displays the introductory page shown in figure 30.5 (until you customize it, that is). There are several ways to open a page. The most common way is also the simplest: just click on a hyperlink to jump to it. Hyperlinks are usually shown as underlined and colored text. The next couple let you jump to any Web document, anywhere, by bringing up the Open Internet Address dialog box (see fig. 30.6). When you type in an address, the Internet Explorer opens the Web document you've requested.

Tip
To open an HTML document from a drive on your computer, click the Open File button in the dialog box in step 2.

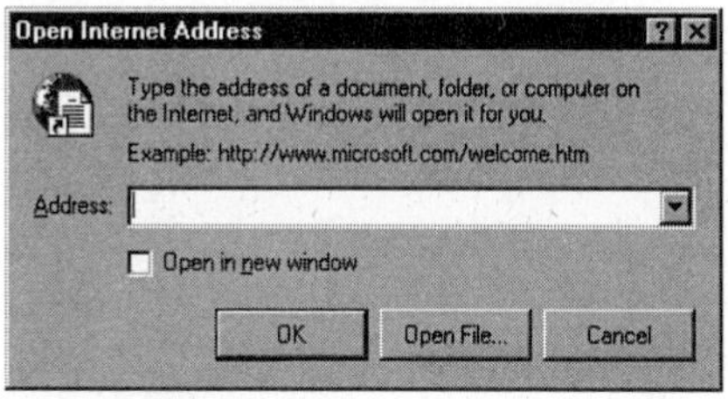

Fig. 30.6
The Open Internet Address dialog box allows you to jump directly to any site on the Internet, or to load Web pages stored on your hard disk.

To go to any page whose URL you know, use the following method:

1. Choose File, Open; or click the Open button on the toolbar.

2. Type in the address or select an address from the pull-down menu. (The pull-down menu contains pages you've previously visited.)

Tip
The Internet Explorer adds pages you've visited to the bottom of the File menu. You can also select File, More History to see a history window of pages you've visited.

3. To open a new window for the page you're opening, select the Open in New Window check box. You can easily work with multiple pages just by switching between their windows.

4. Click OK.

There are several other ways to go to Web pages. You can:

- Type an address into the Address pull-down menu just below the toolbar.

- Select a previously visited site from the Address pull-down menu.

- At any time, you can jump back to your start page (the initial page loaded when you launch the Internet Explorer) by clicking the Open Start Page icon.

- Jump directly to a Favorite site by opening the Favorites folder and then choosing a site. Click the toolbar icon or choose Favorites, Open, then select the site you want to visit.

- Use the left arrow button to go back to a page you've already visited. Once you've gone back to a page, use the right arrow button to go forward again.

Controlling Page Loading and Display

Many popular servers on the Internet are slow. Why? Because they're popular! You may find that some sites impose too long of a wait. To stop waiting for, or loading, a page, click this icon.

Once you've stopped loading a page, you might change your mind and want to reload it. You may also need to reload pages that change over time. To reload a page, click the refresh icon on the toolbar, or select View, Refresh. The Internet Explorer reloads and redisplays the page you're on.

Standard HTML lets page authors set the *relative* font sizes in a document, but you control the actual font sizes. You can enlarge or reduce the font size by using the toolbar buttons or by selecting View, Fonts, then choosing a font size from the pop-up menu.

Keeping Track of Your Favorite Sites

You've probably found that, out of the many sites you've visited on the Web, you have some favorites which you visit frequently. The Internet Explorer supplies two easy ways to keep track of your favorite sites: the Create Shortcut command and the Favorites list.

Create Shortcut creates a shortcut to the currently displayed page and puts it on your desktop. To create a shortcut, follow these steps:

1. If you're not already there, go to the page for which you want a shortcut.

2. Create the shortcut by choosing File, Create Shortcut.

3. You'll be asked to confirm that you want to create a shortcut on the desktop. Choose OK to create the shortcut.

Tip

When you create a shortcut, you can put it on your desktop, mail it to a friend, or use it anywhere else shortcuts work.

To add a page to your Favorites list, follow these steps:

1. If you're not already there, go to the page you want to add.

2. Add the page to your Favorites list by choosing Favorites, Add Favorite, or by clicking the Add to Favorites button.

3. The standard Save File dialog box appears. Choose a location for your entry, then choose OK.

Setting the Internet Explorer's Options

The Internet Explorer lets you control its behavior with the Options dialog box, displayed when you choose View, Options. We'll cover each of the tabs in the Options dialog box in more detail shortly, but feel free to experiment.

Controlling How Pages Appear

You can control settings used for displaying Web pages with the Appearances page of the Options dialog box. To open this dialog box, choose View, Options. You can change how hyperlinks are drawn, whether pictures are displayed, the text and background color for pages, and more. Figure 30.7 shows the Options dialog box when the Appearance page is selected.

VI

Online Communications

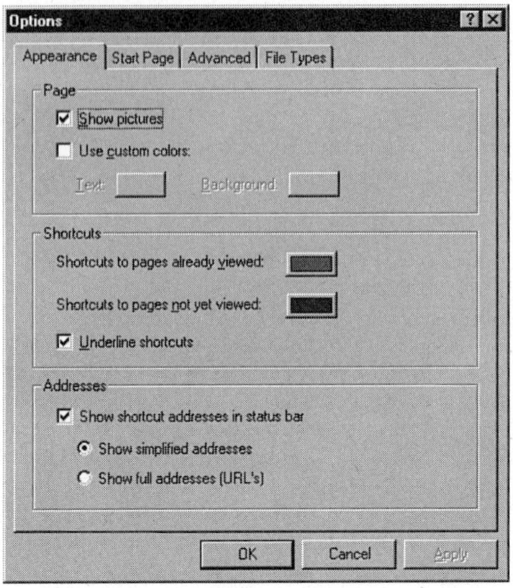

Fig. 30.7
The Appearance page gives you control over how Web pages and links appear on your screen.

Tip
These pictures are usually referred to as *inline graphics* or *inline images*.

Controlling How Graphics Are Displayed. You can ask the Internet Explorer not to download or display pictures on Web pages. This is helpful when using a modem connection, or when trying to reach a busy server. To turn image loading off or on, click the Show Pictures check box until it reflects the setting you want.

Modifying How Hyperlinks Are Displayed. The Internet Explorer lets you control how hyperlinks are displayed. Some users prefer their links underlined, while others like them to appear as plain text. You can set your preference using the Underline Shortcuts check box.

The Internet Explorer also lets you choose what colors to use when drawing links. To change those colors, choose one of these options:

- Click the Shortcuts To Pages Already Viewed button to bring up the Color Selection dialog box. Choose a color from the selected palette, or mix a custom color, then choose OK. The Internet Explorer uses that color to draw links to pages you've already visited.

- Click the Shortcuts To Pages Not Yet Viewed button to bring up the Color Selection dialog box. Choose a color from the selected palette, or mix a custom color, then choose OK. The Internet Explorer uses that color to draw links to pages you haven't yet seen.

Changing How Addresses Are Displayed. Each Web page has its own unique address, or URL. These URLs can be arbitrarily long, and many of them contain confusing query characters or computer-generated indexing markers. If you prefer, you can turn the display of page addresses off altogether, or you can make the Internet Explorer show a shortened, simpler form of the URL for each page.

To control whether the Internet Explorer shows URLs at all, use the Show Shortcut Addresses In Status Bar check box. When unchecked, the Internet Explorer won't show you the URLs. When it *is* checked, addresses appear according to the setting of the two radio buttons below it: Show Simplified Addresses and Show Full Addresses (URLs). Choose Show Simplified Addresses if you want to see a shortened, less complex form of page addresses; choose Show Full Addresses if you want to see the full URL for each link.

Changing Which Page Loads at Startup

The Start Page page of the Options dialog box allows you to specify which Web page loads when you launch the Internet Explorer. You can specify a file on your local hard disk, a shared disk (with a UNC path), or on a Web server.

Here's how to change the start page:

1. Go to the page you want to use as your starting page.

2. Open the Options dialog box (click View, Options) and click the Start Page tab.

3. Click the Use Current button to use the current page, or click Use Default to go back to the previously set start page.

Adding Helpers and New Document Types

The Internet Explorer comes preconfigured for many common file types, including Microsoft Office documents, JPEG and GIF images, WAV and AU sounds, and various other file types. However, you may need to add new file types for documents whose types Microsoft didn't anticipate, like CAD drawings, files compressed on UNIX machines, or MIDI files. You might also want to change the application launched to handle a certain file type.

Figure 30.8 shows an example of adding a file type; in this case, we've added support for PKZIP files.

Tip

To minimize waiting when first starting the Internet Explorer, use the Internet Assistant to create your own local start page on your hard drive with links to pages you use often, or to specify a page that you use often that loads quickly.

VI

Online Communications

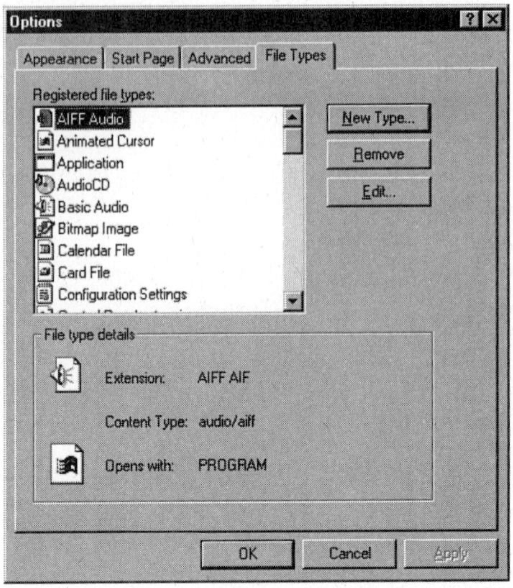

Fig. 30.8
Add new file types through the File Types page in the Options dialog box.

◄ See "Register-ing Files to Automatically Open an Appli-cation," p. 539

To register a new document type so that the Internet Explorer recognizes it, here's what to do:

1. Open the Options dialog box (click View, Options) and select the File Types tab. The File Types page appears.

2. Click the New Type button.

3. The standard Windows 95 file type dialog box appears. Fill in the fields for the file type you want to add and then choose OK.

Dragging and Dropping on the Web

Here are some ideas to get you started on dragging and dropping your way around with the Internet Explorer:

■ Drag shortcuts (created with the Create Shortcut command) from your desktop or a folder onto the Internet Explorer window to load them.

■ Drag HTML files from the My Computer window or the Explorer into the Internet Explorer window.

■ Drag images from a Web page to the My Computer window or the Explorer to copy them onto your disk, or into Exchange to mail them.

■ Drag text from a Web page into any application which accepts text, such as WordPad.

Some Popular Sites on the World Wide Web

Once you're comfortable with the Internet Explorer, you can travel to servers all around the world with a few clicks. There are more than 100,000 Web servers available, with millions of files. Finding what you need can be impossible if you don't know where to start. Here are the addresses of a few key Web sites you may find of value:

- **http://www.yahoo.com**

  Yahoo started as a project at Stanford University, but has quickly become such a popular site that it's spun off into a separate server. Yahoo offers a list of Web pages, organized into categories like law, entertainment, and business.

- **http://www.infoseek.com**

  InfoSeek offers a reliable search service that indexes Web pages, articles from computer periodicals, wire-service news articles, and several other sources. Although it's a commercial service, the rates are quite reasonable and it offers free trials.

- **http://www.einet.net**

  EINet, a company that provides electronic commerce consulting and services, operates the Galaxy as a public service. It's organized somewhat like Yahoo, but with a more varied list of topics.

Creating Your Own Pages for the World Wide Web

The World Wide Web, designed by researchers at CERN in Geneva, Switzerland, is a collection of hypertext documents served from computers throughout the world. Web documents, or *pages,* can contain pictures, text, sounds, movies, and links to other documents. Web pages can—and usually do—contain links to documents on other computers. The name "Web" came from the interlinked nature of the pages.

One of the best things about the Web is that it allows anyone with Internet access to *provide* information, not just consume it. If you have access to a Web server and information to share, the Internet lets you do so in a unique way.

VI

Online Communications

Web pages are written in the HyperText Markup Language (HTML). HTML is made up of *elements*; each element contains a *tag* defining what kind of element it is. Most elements also contain text that defines what the element represents. In figure 30.9, the sample HTML page as displayed by the Internet Explorer is shown at the top; the same page shown as HTML form is shown at the bottom.

Fig. 30.9

On-screen and HTML versions of a simple page.

Unlike traditional desktop publishing, the user—not the author—controls how the document is actually displayed. When you create HTML documents, it's important to split the content of your document from its structure and appearance on-screen. The document that looks just right in your 640 × 480 Internet Explorer window may look awful to users of other browsers.

Building Documents with HTML

HTML elements are plain ASCII text, so you can create Web pages with any simple text editor, including WordPad. This section introduces the basic elements of HTML to help familiarize you with the most common elements before we plunge into using Microsoft's Internet Assistant.

> **Note**
>
> HTML offers many features, including on-screen forms. A complete copy of the HTML specification is available from the World Wide Web Organization (W3O)'s Web server at **http://www.w3.org/hypertext/WWW/MarkUp/MarkUp.html**, and the National Center for Supercomputing Applications maintains an excellent HTML tutorial at **http://www.ncsa.uiuc.edu/General/Internet/WWW/ HTMLPrimer.html**.

How Documents Are Structured

Like those nesting Russian dolls, elements can contain other elements, and they can be deeply nested. HTML documents usually consist of one element: the HTML element, which contains head and body elements. Each of those elements can, in turn, enclose others.

The head element usually contains a title element, and it may also contain comments, author information, copyright notices, or special tags that help indexers and search engines use the contents of the document more effectively.

The body element holds the actual body and content of the document. For typical documents, most of the body element is text, with tags placed at the end of each paragraph. You can also use tags for displaying numbered or bulleted lists, horizontal rules, embedded images, and hyperlinks to other documents.

Tag Basics

All HTML tags are enclosed in angle brackets (<>). Some elements contain two matching tags, with text or hypertext in between. For example, to define a title as part of your document's <head> element, you'd put this HTML into your document:

```
<title>A Simple WWW Page</title>
```

The first tag signals the start of the title element, while the same tag, prefixed with a slash (/), tells the browser that it's reached the end of the element. Some tags don't require matching tags, like <li>, which denotes an item in a list.

The elements most often used in HTML body elements fall into three basic categories: logical styles, physical styles, and content elements.

Using Logical Styles. Logical styles tell the browser how the document is structured. The HTML system of nesting elements gives the browser some information, but authors can use the logical style elements to break text into paragraphs, lists, block quotes, and so on. Like styles in Microsoft Word, you can use the logical styles in your documents and know that they'll be properly displayed by the browser.

Table 30.1 lists some common logical styles you can use to build your document, along with examples for each one.

Table 30.1 Logical Style Elements		
Style Tag	**What It Does**	**Sample**
<p>	Ends paragraph	This is a very short paragraph.<p>
 	Inserts line break	First line Second line
<Hx>...</Hx>	Section heading	<H1>HTML Is Easy</H1>
...	Emphasis on text	Use this instead of bold text.
...	Stronger emphasis on text really gets the point across!	THIS
<code>...</code>	Displays HTML tags without acting on them	The <code><p></code> tag can be handy.

Style Tag	What It Does	Sample
<quote>...</quote>	Displays a block of quoted text	<quote>No man is an island.</quote>
<pre>...</pre>	Displays text and leaves white space intact.	<pre>E x t r a spaces are OK here.</pre>

Using Physical Styles. In ordinary printed documents, **bold**, *italic,* and underlined text all have their special uses. Web pages are the same way; you may want to distinguish the name of a book, a key word, or a foreign-language phrase from your body text. Table 30.2 shows a list of some common physical styles you can use in HTML documents, along with simple examples.

Table 30.2   Physical Style Elements

Style Tag	What It Does	Sample
...	Bold text	Bold text stands out.
<i>...</i>	Italic text	<i>Belle</i> is French for "pretty."
<u>...</u>	Underlined text	<u>Don't</u> confuse underlined text with a hyperlink!
_{...}	Subscript text	Water's chemical formula is H₂O.
^{...}	Superscript text	Writing "x²" is the same as writing "x*x."
<tt>...</tt>	Typewriter text	This tag's <tt>seldom</tt> seen.

Using Content Elements. Many Web documents just contain plain, unadorned text. Content elements enrich your documents by adding embedded graphics, lists, and links to other documents. You can quickly turn a boring, plain-text document into a rich Web page by using content elements.

One of the simplest content elements—and one of the most effective—is the <hr> tag, which inserts a horizontal rule across the page. Use it to separate different sections of material, much as you'd add a page break to a Word document to start a new section.

VI

Online Communications

<ul>...</ul> defines a bulleted or "unordered" list, and <ol>...</ol> defines a numbered or "ordered" list. Both use <li> to define list items. The list items are easy to use; if you've ever used Word or PowerPoint to build a list, you already know how to use these. Here are two quick examples:

```
<ul>
<li>First bullet
<li>Second bullet
</ul>

<ol>
<li>Item 1
<li>Item 2
</ol>
```

Many Web pages contain embedded graphics. These graphics must be in GIF or JPEG format, but they can be as large or small as you like. Embedding the images in your page is easy with the <img> tag. When a browser sees <img>, it fetches the image and displays it in the body of the document.

The simplest form of <img> lets you specify only the name of the graphics file. This instruction causes the browser to download "picture.gif" from the Web server and display it in the text:

```
<img src="picture.gif">
```

Tip

Use the alt= attribute. Users who aren't loading images can see the text tag and decide whether they want the image or not.

You can also add the alt= tag, which specifies a text string to be displayed instead of the image. Why would you want to do this? Some browsers, like Lynx, can't display images. Other browsers can display the alt tag for users who've turned off image loading to boost their connection speed. Adding alt to the above example, we end up with

```
<img src="picture.gif" alt="A pretty picture">
```

Creating Hyperlinks

Now let's talk about the key element that makes the Web different from plain static documents: hyperlinks. Each link points to an *anchor,* or destination for the link. Most anchors are implied; when you specify a page as the target of the link, it's assumed that you want that entire page to be an anchor.

You can also specify named anchors to let you quickly jump to a particular section of a document. Define anchors with <a name>...</a>. The "a" stands for "anchor," and the name attribute names the anchor. Anchors can display text labels, but they don't have to. The anchors below work identically, but the first one displays text in the browser and the other doesn't.

```
<a name="Chapter39">'s anchor</a> is the same as <a
name="Chapter39"></a> this one.
```

The basic element for hyperlinks is <a href>...</a>. The "a" still stands for "anchor," and "href" is a hypertext reference. Let's say you were setting up a Web server containing information about Windows 95. Your start page might link to a page listing new software for Windows 95, like this:

```
New <a href=Software/NewSoftware.htm>software</a> for Windows 95
```

The text in the middle of the link appears as a link on the browser's screen. Notice that the folder "Software" is part of the link. This link points to a file named "NewSoftware.htm" in the directory "Software."

Let's say you also wanted to include a link to Macmillan Publishing Company's Web page so that people visiting your page could find out about Windows 95 books. Notice that this link contains a full URL instead of the name of a local document.

```
The <a href=http://www.mcp.com>Macmillan Publishing</a> home page
has information on Macmillan's books.<p>
```

Both types of link can include anchors. If the target page contains an anchor with that name, then the browser will jump directly to that anchor and display it. For example, you could use a link like:

```
See <a href=http://www.mcp.com/Books/Win95/
UsingWin95.htm#Chapter39>Chapter 39</a>s outline for more
details.<p>
```

to specify a certain position within the link's target document.

> **Note**
>
> If you'd like a tool to check your HTML for correctness, you can use the Weblint tool. Weblint "picks the fluff" off your HTML pages and catches common errors like mismatched tags and bogus attribute names. For more details, see the Weblint page at **http://www.unipress.com/weblint/**.

VI

Online Communications

Using Microsoft's Internet Assistant

If you use Microsoft Word, you can easily create HTML files with Microsoft's Internet Assistant, a Word add-on that already knows all the rules of HTML previously discussed, and then some!

Internet Assistant gives you an HTML document template with styles representing all the major HTML elements, plus converters to let you turn a Word file into HTML with a simple mouse click.

Getting and Installing Microsoft's Internet Assistant

The Internet Assistant is available as a self-extracting executable file called WORDIA.EXE. It can be downloaded at no cost from Microsoft's FTP site at **ftp.microsoft.com** in the directory /Softlib/MSLFILES. Use Windows 95's FTP program to get this file, using the procedure described earlier in this chapter.

> **Caution**
>
> You must have Word 6.0a or later to run the Internet Assistant. If you have an earlier version of Word, you can download the 6.0a patch (WORD60A.EXE) from Microsoft's FTP server by following the instructions for getting the Internet Assistant below.

The Internet Assistant requires the English, French, or German versions of Microsoft Word 6.0a or later. It *does not* work with older versions, other languages, or Word for Windows NT. Once you've downloaded the Internet Assistant, you'll probably be in a hurry to install it and start producing HTML files. Fortunately, installation is easy; just follow these quick steps:

1. Copy WORDIA.EXE to your hard disk and then run it. This executable extracts several files into the directory.

2. Run SETUP.EXE to install the Internet Assistant into your Word directory.

Using Microsoft's Internet Assistant as a Browser

 Once you've installed the Internet Assistant, start Word for Windows. You'll discover a new button on the Formatting toolbar and a new command on the File menu.

> **Note**
>
> Before you can browse the Web with Microsoft's Internet Assistant, you need to have your connection to the Internet running. Either dial up to your service provider to log in to your network connection, or use a full-time LAN connection.

To browse the Web, choose File, Browse Web or click the Browse Web button (see fig. 30.10).

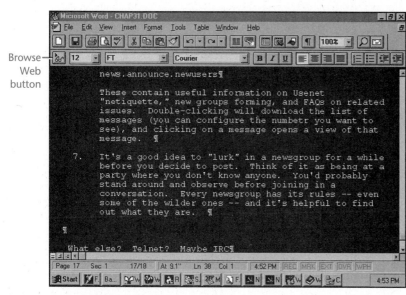

Browse Web button

Once you start the Browse Web mode, the screen changes to look like the screen shown in figure 30.11.

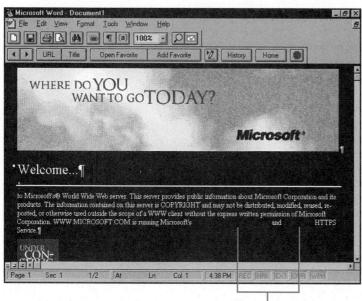

Fig. 30.11
Microsoft's
Internet Assistant
Browser, with
Microsoft's World
Wide Web page on
view.

Click hypertext links (they're in color
on-screen but barely visible here) to
jump to other Web pages.

VI

Online Communications

Creating New HTML Documents

When you use Word to create a new HTML document, select the HTML template instead of whatever you normally use. Figure 30.12 shows Word's New dialog box with the HTML template selected.

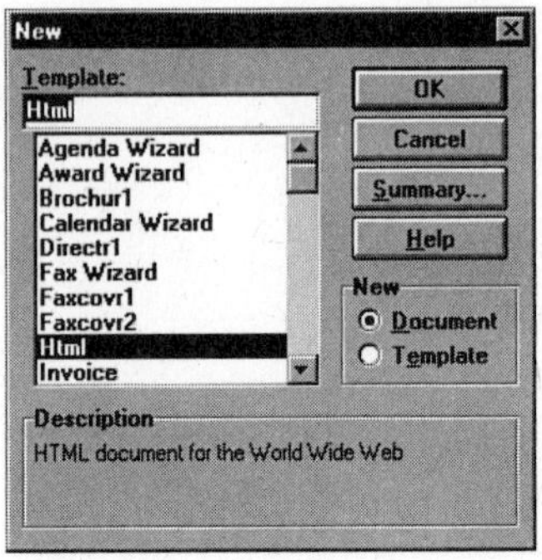

Fig. 30.12
Select the HTML template to create a new Web page with the Internet Assistant.

Tip
Use Netscape, Mosaic, or the Internet Explorer to browse the pages you create with the Internet Assistant—they're faster and use less RAM than Word.

A new document window opens, and you'll notice some new icons on the Formatting toolbar along with the familiar ones. These icons allow you to quickly format your document using HTML elements.

Formatting Your HTML Documents

You've probably noticed some new and unusual icons on the Internet Assistant Formatting toolbar. Here's how to use them to format your documents in HTML:

- The Edit and Browse Web buttons toggle Word between HTML Edit mode (the pencil) and Browse Web mode. You can also toggle with the View menu's Web Browse and HTML Edit options.

- Use the Back and Forward buttons to go backwards or forward among Web pages you've viewed. They don't do anything in normal Word mode.

- Use the Style pull-down menu (just to the right of the Forward button) to select HTML styles for your documents.

- These buttons work just like the standard Word Bold, Italic, and Underline buttons. Use them to enhance your text.

- These buttons let you create numbered and bulleted lists, just like in Word or PowerPoint.

- Use this button to insert a horizontal rule into your document.

■ Insert pictures (GIF or JPEG only) into your document with this button. You'll see a dialog box that allows you to select a picture file and enter an alternate text string for the picture. If you have BMP and PCX files that you want to use on your Web pages, convert your images with a tool like the shareware PaintShop Pro or Adobe Photoshop.

■ Use this icon to set the document's title. Clicking it brings up a dialog box that lets you specify a title to be embedded.

Building Hyperlinks

The Internet Assistant allows you to embed two kinds of links: links to external documents, and links to files and documents on your computer. This is a terrific feature, since you can quickly create links in, and between, several documents at once. Here's how to link your documents together:

Insert *bookmarks* with the Add Bookmark button. Bookmarks are HTML anchors; you can embed bookmarks in your Word documents so that you can build hyperlinks to specific pages or items. When you click this icon, the Bookmark dialog box appears, as shown in figure 30.13.

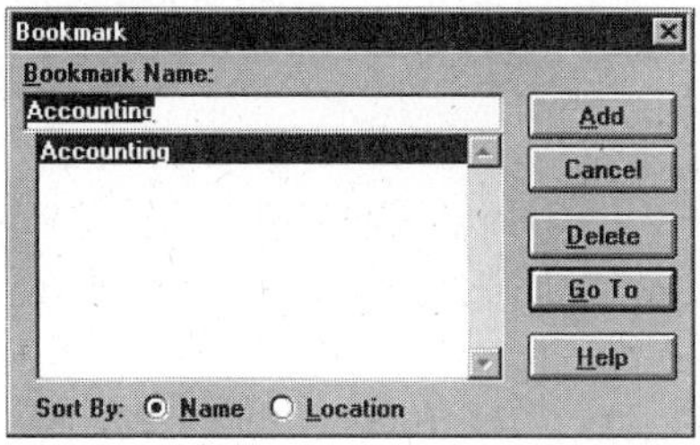

Fig. 30.13
The Add Bookmark dialog box lets you name specific locations in your document so that you can build hyperlinks to them.

Use these steps to work with bookmarks in your documents:

1. Choose Edit, Bookmark; or click the Bookmark button. The Bookmark dialog box appears.

2. To add a bookmark, type a name for the new bookmark in the Bookmark Name field and click Add.

3. To delete an existing bookmark, select it and click Delete. You'll be asked to confirm the deletion.

4. To jump to an existing bookmark, select it and click Go To.

You need to be able to embed hyperlinks in your documents, too. Fortunately, the Internet Assistant has a button for that as well. Clicking the Hyperlink button, or selecting Insert, HyperLink, brings up a dialog box with three tabbed pages: to Local Document, to URL, and to Bookmark. All of these pages have some fields in common. Figure 30.14 shows the Link to Local Document page.

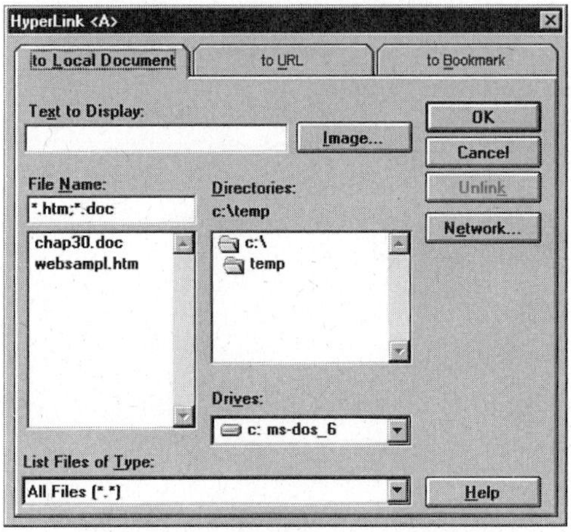

Fig. 30.14

The HyperLink dialog box gives you a quick way to build links to Web pages and Word documents on your computer or on other Web servers.

All three pages have identical upper halves, so we'll talk about the common parts first. Here's how to build hyperlinks:

1. Type the text which you want to appear in the link into the Text to Display field.

2. If you want to have an image as part of the link, click the Image button and select an image file. The Internet Assistant automatically includes it as part of your document.

3. If you're making a link to a local file using the Link to Local Document page, use the file and directory browsers, and click the Network button to find the link's target file.

4. If you're making a link to a URL somewhere on the Internet, type the URL to which you want to link into the text field, or pick a previously used URL from the list.

5. If you're linking to a bookmark you've already defined, select the bookmark to which you want to link from the list displayed.

No matter which of these steps you choose, you must click OK to accept your new link, or click Cancel to dismiss the dialog box.

Saving Your Documents

While you're creating and editing your documents, you'll need to save them to disk. You can save your documents—HTML styles and all—as regular Word documents. When you're ready to save the HTML version, see figure 30.15 for an example and follow these steps:

1. Choose File, Save As.

2. When the Save As dialog box appears, type a file name for your HTML file. You can also choose a directory to put it in from the Directories list.

3. Pull down the Save File as Type combo box and select HyperText Markup Language (HTML) as the file type. Click OK to save the file.

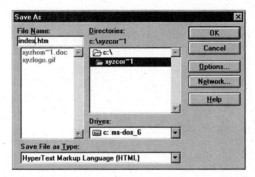

Fig. 30.15
Save your Word documents as HTML with Word's Save As dialog box.

Caution

Many Word elements don't have any equivalent in HTML. If you save a Word document as HTML and then reopen it as a Word document, those element types *will be lost*.

For a complete list of Word elements that can't be translated, use Word's Help facility to view the topic on "What Is Lost When Word Documents Are Converted to HTML."

Note

The Internet Assistant works best with relatively small pages. If you have large Word documents, consider breaking them into several smaller documents. Not only will this improve the performance of the Internet Assistant, but also Web surfers who read your pages will appreciate the reduced download time!

Translating Existing Documents to HTML

You may already have a large stock of Word documents that you want to convert into Web pages. Microsoft anticipated this and has made it easy to convert existing documents. Here's what to do:

1. Open the document you want to translate.

2. Add a title using the Title icon on the Formatting toolbar.

3. Add bookmarks as needed by choosing Edit, Bookmark, or clicking the Add Bookmark button.

4. Add links, as desired, by choosing Insert, HyperLink, or by clicking the HyperLink button.

5. Save the new document as an HTML file.

> **Note**
>
> For more detailed information on converting documents into Web pages, see Que's *Web Publishing with Word for Windows* and *10 Minute Guide to Internet Assistant*.

UseNet Newsgroups

One of the most popular services on the Internet, UseNet groups, covers topics ranging from zero-dimensional geometry ("alt.0.d"), to the "wi.*" hierarchy, consisting of groups with articles about Wisconsin.

Newsgroups are organized into a hierarchy that groups related topics with a mostly logical naming scheme. Each group name starts with a three- or four-letter prefix, followed by a group name. Here are the most common prefixes:

- *alt*. Alternative topics, everything from alien invasions to xenophobia

- *biz*. Covers business affairs, commerce, and commercial products

- *comp*. Computers and computer-related topics

- *news*. News of interest to the Internet community, like announcements of new groups

- *rec*. Recreation, hobbies, and sports

- *sci*. Scientific

- *soc.* Social issues

- *talk.* Discussions and debates

- *misc.* Everything that won't fit elsewhere

Individual regions, countries, and states have hierarchies, too, identified by their two-letter postal ID. For example, the **ca.general** group is for general discussion about Canada, and **tn.general** is for general discussion about the state of Tennessee.

Group names move from the general to the specific as you read them. For example, the **comp.infosystems.www.announce** and **comp. infosystems.www.servers.unix** groups are both about the WWW. The first has announcements about the Web, and the second is about UNIX Web server software.

In most groups, there are no rules except those enforced by the opinion of group members, but there are certain community standards for UseNet newsgroups that are generally agreed upon:

- Don't "spam." This refers to the wholesale posting of advertisements or self-aggrandizing announcements to many groups.

- Don't post sexist, racist, or demeaning messages. Doing so will usually bring down the newsgroup's wrath on the poster, whose later postings will be ignored or flamed.

- Avoid excessive cross-talk, or chatting between two posters. Keep private discussions in e-mail.

- Don't post private e-mail that you receive to a newsgroup without permission of the author.

- Keep articles short, without overly-long quoting of the message to which you're responding. In Net-speak, long, rambling postings are slammed for "wasting bandwidth."

It's a good idea to "lurk" (Net-speak for reading articles but not posting any) in a newsgroup for a while. Think of it as being at a party where you don't know anyone. You might prefer to stand around and observe before joining in a conversation.

VI

Online Communications

Getting and Installing the WinVN Newsreader

Now we'll download a freeware newsreader program called WinVN. WinVN offers an attractive interface, and it's full of useful features. Using the FTP techniques discussed earlier in this chapter, FTP to **ftp.ksc.nasa.gov** and change to the directory /pub/winvn/nt. Get the file winvn_99_05_intel.zip. If there is a file there with a later number in the file name, get it instead.

> **Note**
>
> The name of this directory may change without notice. NASA is close to releasing version 1.0 of WinVN, and they may release future versions customized for Windows 95. The files in /nt were designed for NT, but also run well in Windows 95.

After retrieving WinVN, create a folder for the files on your hard drive. Use WinZip or some other unzipping program to extract the compressed files into the folder. If you want to, set up a shortcut on the desktop or add WinVN to the Start menu.

To configure WinVN, follow these steps:

1. Start the program. WinVN detects that you don't have an INI file or news article ("newsrc") file yet and offers to create them for you by presenting the standard save dialog box for each file. Choose a location for each file, then answer Yes to the Create File confirmation dialog box.

2. WinVN presents a dialog box so you can enter communications settings, as shown in figure 30.16. (You can also bring up this dialog box by choosing Config, Configure Communications.) Enter the name of your news server, your news port, and your mail server. These are available from your ISP or system administrator. Leave the Username and Password information blank unless told otherwise by your service provider or ISP. Then click OK.

3. WinVN presents another dialog box, asking you to enter your real name, your e-mail address, the reply address that people who want to mail you should use, and an organization affiliation. Enter your real name and mail address. If your reply and e-mail address are the same, leave the reply address field blank. If you'd like, you can enter a string in the Organization field.

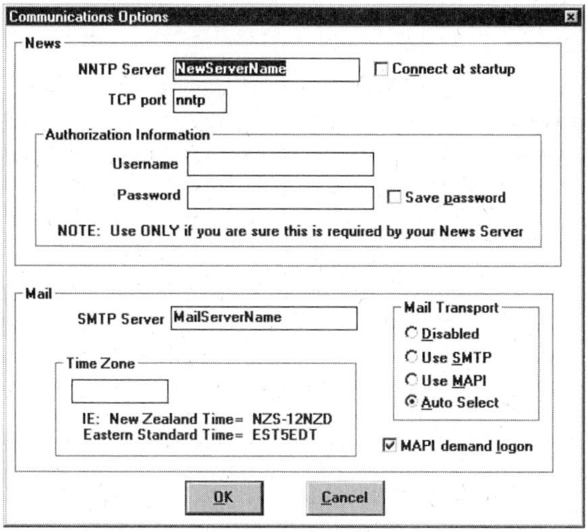

Fig. 30.16
The WinVN
Communications
Options dialog
box. You can leave
the optional
information blank
in most cases.

Reading News with WinVN

To read news, follow these steps:

1. Connect to the Internet. If your connection to the Internet is via a LAN, make sure you are properly connected to your network. If you connect by using a modem and a dial-up Internet service provider, use your Dial-up Connection to log onto your ISP.

2. If WinVN isn't already running, start it now.

3. Choose Network, Connect To Server. WinVN will connect to the news server. After you connect, WinVN asks if you want to get a list of newsgroups that your server carries.

4. Click Yes, and WinVN fetches the list. Depending on your server, there may be more than 11,000 groups, so it will take some time. You need to do it once at first, then occasionally thereafter, to refresh your list and see new groups as they're created.

5. Once WinVN has the list of groups, you'll see the New Newsgroups dialog box. This dialog box allows you to subscribe to newsgroups that interest you. Select a hierarchy from the top-left scrolling list; WinVN shows which groups under that hierarchy you're subscribed to and which you aren't.

◄ See "Installing and Configuring Windows 95 Dial-Up Network Adapter," p. 888

Tip

It's best to start with a small number and branch out once you're used to UseNet. You can always subscribe to more groups later.

VI

Online Communications

6. To subscribe to a group, double-click its name in the Unsubscribed Groups list. The group appears in the Subscribed Group list. You can subscribe to several groups while keeping the dialog box open. When you've finished subscribing, click OK to save your choices. Figure 30.17 shows the dialog box with some groups subscribed.

Fig. 30.17
Use the WinVN Subscribe dialog box to choose groups that you want to read frequently. The groups you select will be shown at the top of the WinVN groups window.

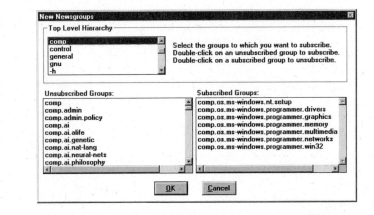

By default, WinVN subscribes you to two important UseNet newsgroups: **news.newusers.questions** and **news.announce.newusers**. These contain useful information on UseNet "netiquette," announcements of new groups, and FAQs on related issues.

WinVN's main window lists all the groups from your news server, whether you've subscribed to them or not. Subscribed groups are listed first, so you can easily find them. Double-clicking a group name downloads the list of messages in that group, as shown in figure 30.18, and displays the group's messages in a new window. Clicking a message opens another new window for that message (see fig. 30.19).

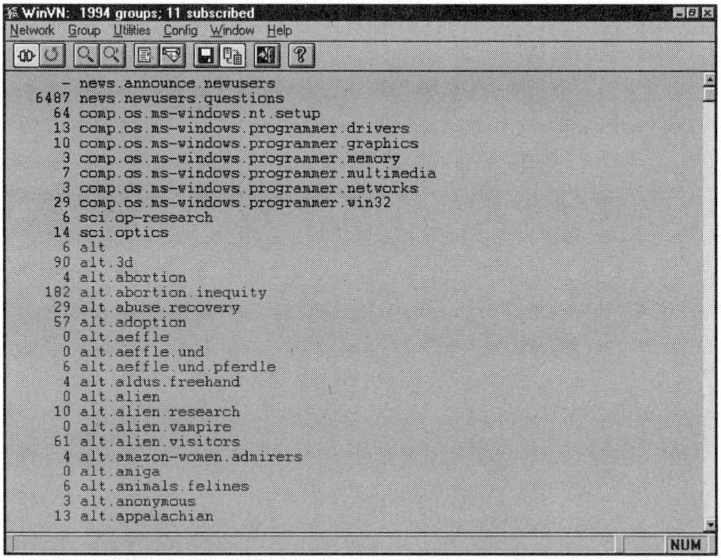

Fig. 30.18
Double-click a group to see what articles are available.

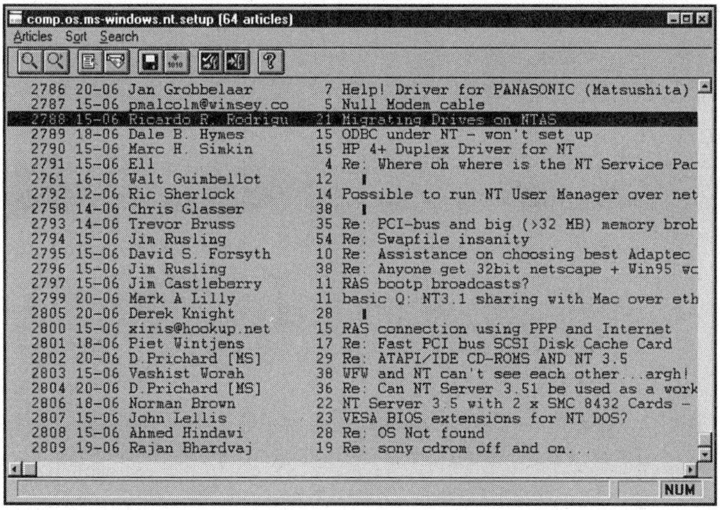

Fig. 30.19
WinVN lists each group's messages in its own window. Double-click an article line to see the article's text.

Part VII

Windows 95 Multimedia

Chapter 31

Understanding Windows 95 Multimedia

by Ian Stokell

Unless you have been secluded in a cave for the last few years, you are aware of a major evolution in the computer industry: multimedia technology. Multimedia and the move toward online services and the Internet are two of the most dominant trends in high-technology hardware, software, and telecommunications. Both topics are represented extensively in Windows 95, which includes many advanced multimedia features and the Microsoft Network.

Another major trend is the explosion in the market of home PCs. The existence of more home PCs has resulted in an increased demand for innovative non-business programs, such as multimedia reference CDs and exciting interactive games that feature sound and video. As a result, most PCs are now sold with CD-ROM drives included. In addition, the market for add-in sound boards that support advanced audio capabilities, such as MIDI, has skyrocketed. With this technology movement, it's no surprise that Windows 95 includes extensive multimedia features.

This is good for you, the end user, as it allows you to add multimedia capabilities and take advantage of multimedia features with little extra work on your part. The only thing you will need to ensure is that you either purchase a PC with multimedia hardware built-in, such as a sound board and CD-ROM drive, or add those hardware components before you begin looking toward using multimedia.

Windows 95 features a number of significant multimedia improvements over Windows 3.1, which includes Video for Windows (previously sold only as a separate product). It also includes support for a larger standard video image on-screen, which is important if you plan to view much video on your PC.

Also worth mentioning is the increased ease with which you can add various multimedia hardware components, such as a sound board or CD-ROM drive. Windows 95's Plug and Play standard allows you to add components that adhere to the standard with the minimum of problems. And Windows 95's Device Manager allows you to keep track of the many resources that are used by the multimedia components in order to minimize hardware conflicts.

Windows 95 also includes support for improved game graphics via the use of WinG, an application programming interface that allows for bitmapped graphics held in memory to appear onscreen quickly.

This chapter discusses the multimedia improvements in Windows 95, briefly touching on various multimedia options available to the Windows 95 user, and then discussing the installation of various hardware component drivers.

Specifically, you'll find coverage of the following topics:

- The effects of Multimedia on computer users
- Built-in video, audio, MIDI, and other multimedia features in Windows 95
- Microsoft's Plug and Play feature
- Using Device Manager to configure multimedia features
- Configuring multimedia properties

Multimedia Features in Windows 95

Multimedia is the point where various types of media converge. Historically, computers tended to offer users limited media choices: generally text and low-end graphics. But improved hardware performance in the industry today results in a greater range of processor-intensive products, from high-end graphics features to sound to full-motion video.

With these media choices comes the increased capability for you to interact with the program you are using. Now, many advanced CD games and products enable you to choose the route you want to travel through the program. You are no longer constrained by someone else's linear interpretation of where you should go. Now you can choose different routes each time you use the multimedia product—maybe you want to play a video or sound bite instead of just reading text on the screen or looking at a simple graphic.

Multimedia has its price. Just when you thought PCs were so cheap that anyone could have one, along comes multimedia with its increased hardware requirements. As a result, PCs equipped for multimedia are more expensive than non-multimedia-ready systems. As with all computing technology, however, prices are dropping rapidly.

Taking advantage of multimedia requires additional hardware, more RAM, and probably a larger hard disk drive to store the huge video and sound files you use. If you don't buy a multimedia-equipped PC at the outset, installing multimedia components such as a sound board and CD-ROM drive can be a study in both patience and PC knowledge. Microsoft responded to this dilemma by coming up with Plug and Play, discussed later in this chapter.

So what does Windows 95 offer the new user with regard to multimedia? The following sections provide a brief overview of various multimedia features included in Windows 95:

- Built-in video for Windows

- Larger standard video clip display

- Display Control Interface (DCI)

- MIDI and polymessage MIDI

- Support for digital joysticks

- Audio, including CD player and sound recorder

Built-In Video for Windows

Microsoft has been selling the program Microsoft Video for Windows separately since its introduction in 1992. Now the program is built into Windows 95.

With the inclusion of Video for Windows, you can distribute digital video files to other Windows 95 users using the AVI file format, without purchasing additional video-specific software.

Larger Standard Video Clip Display

Because multimedia is still in its infancy on the desktop, advances made from year to year can be significant. One example is the size of the standard video clip displayed on-screen.

The main problem with digital video is that each frame requires the transfer of a huge amount of data. As a result, the implementation and acceptance of desktop video by consumers is held captive by limited hardware and software technology. However, a number of recent hardware innovations have enabled software companies to develop advanced video applications. One such innovation is the phenomenal increase in CPU processing power and the introduction of local bus video (which increases bandwidth and therefore enables more data to be sent at the same time).

When Microsoft introduced Video for Windows in 1992, the standard video clip display was totally inadequate. The display was just 1/16 the size of a VGA screen, or 160 pixels by 120 pixels. With the inclusion of the updated Video for Windows in Windows 95 and the availability of high-end PCs at relatively low prices, video clips can appear full-screen, or 640 pixels by 480 pixels.

Display Control Interface (DCI)

▶ See "DCI Standard in Windows 95," p. 1007

Microsoft's Display Control Interface (DCI) is a display driver technology introduced in 1994 that enables Windows 95 to take advantage of a number of advanced features if they are built into display adapters. These features include *double buffering*, which speeds up block transfers; *color-space conversion*, which helps when playing back compressed digital video; *overlay*, which makes partly obstructed objects display faster; and *stretching*, which makes distorted or stretched images render faster. These features may be useful to a variety of graphics-intensive applications, such as computer-aided design, presentation preparation, and high-end desktop publishing.

MIDI

▶ See "MIDI and WAV Sound Files," p. 981

MIDI, or Musical Instrument Digital Interface, is a common protocol that enables the transfer of music-oriented digital data between electronic devices, be they keyboards or PCs. You cannot obtain sound from MIDI data without the necessary hardware, such as a MIDI-capable sound card in a PC. As such, MIDI data merely contains the instructions that enable the intended musical sound to be reproduced. For this reproduction to happen effectively, both the device that created the instructions from the original sound and the device that intends to reproduce the sound must communicate with each other using the same rules or language—which is where MIDI comes in.

One reason why this may be advantageous compared to a regular WAV file is with regard to file size. WAV files record the entire sound, and as such, can get pretty huge. MIDI files just contain the instructions to reproduce the sound, and are, therefore, much smaller.

As the number of multimedia products and games that include MIDI increases, so does the number of sound cards that are sold with those capabilities, such as a standard MIDI port for plugged-in MIDI instruments. In addition, you can use MIDI to enhance multimedia presentations, for example, where realistic sound can enhance the visual presentation appearing on-screen.

Polymessage MIDI

Windows 95's new polymessage MIDI support technology enables the transfer of multiple MIDI instructions within a single interrupt. The sound card can send and receive batch-processed multiple MIDI messages. In turn, less computing power is required, which frees up more of the CPU for other applications and processes. The CPU no longer needs to deal with each MIDI instruction separately.

This feature also enables highly efficient video playback. Any help that the PC operating system can provide is beneficial, because video playback is notoriously CPU-intensive.

Support for Digital Joysticks

Windows 95 supports the use of joysticks for use with multimedia games and CDs. After you install the joystick and select it, you must calibrate the joystick for it to work properly.

To calibrate your joystick, you need to select the joystick you are using from the Joystick Selection list on the Joystick Properties sheet. Click Custom if your joystick is not selected. Then select Calibrate and follow the instructions on-screen.

Audio

Windows 95 offers a variety of audio features for multimedia use, including the capability to play audio CDs and the customization of sound recording and playback.

▶ See "Using CD Player," p. 994

Playing audio CDs from a CD-ROM drive installed on your computer is possible using the CD Player feature. Provided you have a sound board installed, just start CD Player after you have the CD in the drive and press Start!

Windows 95 also can automatically recognize audio CDs when they are placed in the CD-ROM drive, without you doing anything. Then when you want to start the audio CD, just click on CD Player. Because CD Player operates in the background, you can listen to audio CDs while you are working in other applications on the PC.

▶ See "Using Sound Recorder," p. 998

You also can record sounds for personal use with another feature called Sound Recorder. This feature enables the recording of wave files and also their playback. Although Sound Recorder is not as sophisticated as higher-end digital recorders, it does provide a good introduction to the subject of digital recording. The resulting output is suitable for many non-professional presentations and for creating small voice files to send to other users in the form of electronic mail or embedding in documents.

Instead of just sending text e-mail, you can record a short voice message and attach it for distribution across your office network. Alternatively, for example, you can record a short voice annotation and have it run when you play a file in a presentation to a third party.

You will need a PC with enhanced sound capabilities though, such as a sound board and a microphone. Despite the prevalence of multimedia technology today, and the inclusion of multimedia capabilities in most PCs now sold in the consumer channel, you should make sure all necessary sound capabilities are included in your PC when you buy it, or you will have to add them later, which can get quite expensive.

Plug and Play

◀ See "Installing Plug and Play Hardware," p. 246

Most people who have used a PC with Windows can tell you that using the system is fine until it comes to adding a peripheral, such as multimedia components like a MIDI-capable sound card or a CD-ROM drive. Adding hardware components and getting them working often requires endless calls to technical support as you try to figure out where software drivers go and what instructions to put in startup files. Microsoft's new Plug and Play standard is the answer to this problem.

◀ See "Dealing with Legacy Hardware," p. 247

The Plug and Play standard is already supported in Windows 95. As a result, Windows 95 users who want to add a CD-ROM or sound card to their PC just need to look for one that is Plug and Play compatible. After the device is installed, Windows 95 can interact with the device with the minimum of configuration, because it already supports the necessary elements that make a PC a multimedia system (such as MIDI, digital video, and sound).

Windows 95 also includes tools that make recognizing and configuring older, non-Plug and Play devices easier, which should cut down on system conflicts. Windows 95 will automatically recognize resource conflicts for Plug and Play devices because the allocation and settings details are kept in the Registry.

> **Note**
>
> Unlike the old DOS/Windows combination, Windows 95 does not require separate AUTOEXEC.BAT and CONFIG.SYS files. The drivers required by your PC are automatically loaded, and their respective settings are automatically configured by Windows 95.

System Properties Control Panel

Windows 95 enables you to track hardware devices and the resources they are using, such as input/output (I/O) addresses and interrupt requests (IRQs), using the System Properties Registry. It is important to be able to track which multimedia hardware components are assigned which system resources so that, when adding additional peripherals, such as a SoundBlaster board, you do not assign resources that are already in use by another hardware device. Assigning resources already in use will lead to an infamous "hardware conflict," in which your PC will either crash completely or just not function properly.

With reference to multimedia components, SoundBlaster in particular has historically been difficult to configure because of the amount of resources that it uses. While this has been alleviated somewhat by Windows 95, it may be best to use SoundBlaster's own installation software to install the card in an effort to cut down on configuration problems.

Device Manager and Multimedia

Device Manager enables you to easily view the properties and resources allocated to multimedia hardware devices on your PC in a graphical way. Instead of hunting through strangely named files for such things as the IRQ settings, you can click a couple of times in Device Manager to see a familiar Windows window that lists IRQ settings and their corresponding multimedia hardware devices.

To open Device Manager, do the following:

1. Open the Start menu and choose Settings, Control Panel.

2. Double-click the System icon.

3. When the System Properties sheet appears, click the Device Manager tab.

You can view devices by type or connection. With the View Devices by Type option selected, the devices appear according to their type. For example, multimedia devices such as sound cards, full motion video, and game cards are grouped together (see fig. 31.1).

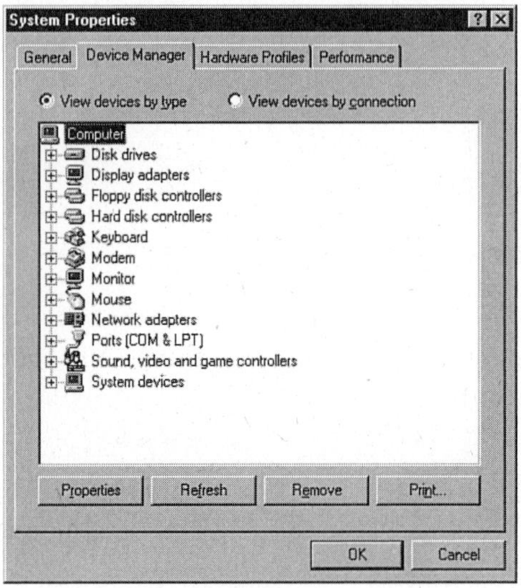

Fig. 31.1
In Device Manager you can view devices by type.

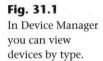

If you select the View Devices by Connection option, the connection type, such as Windows Sound System as shown in figure 31.2 on the popular Sound Blaster type sound card, appears with the corresponding device.

Fig. 31.2
In Device Manager you can view devices by what sort of connection they have, such as a Windows Sound System sound board.

Viewing Computer Properties

Device Manager enables you to view resources and settings allocated to devices attached to your PC by selecting Computer at the top of the device list in Device Manager, which appears when you select the View Devices by Type button.

You then can choose from two tabs: View Resources, which displays the resources being used by which hardware devices; and Reserve Resources, which displays the resources that are reserved system-wide. Each page offers four sets of resources: Interrupt Request (IRQ), Input/Output (I/O), Direct Memory Access (DMA), and Memory.

Interrupt Request (IRQ)

PCs are notorious for interrupt request (IRQ) conflicts when you are adding additional components. Part of the problem revolves around keeping track of which IRQ setting each peripheral or PC component has allocated to it. To make things easier, Windows 95 has the Interrupt Request (IRQ) option within the System Properties sheet's Device Manager.

To find out which IRQ setting is allocated to which component, click the Interrupt Request (IRQ) option. A list of IRQ settings appears, with the hardware using the corresponding setting next to it (see fig. 31.3).

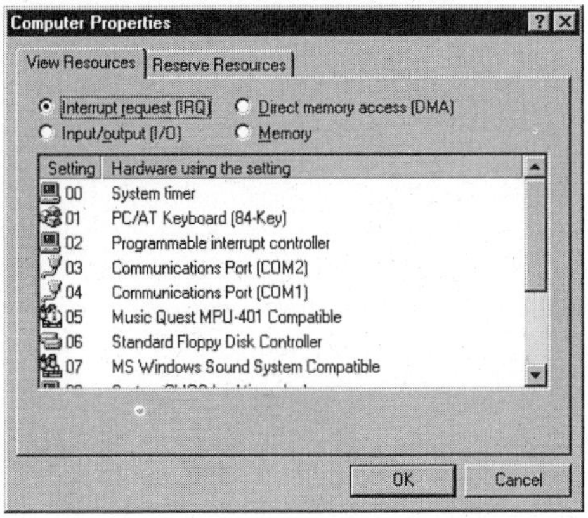

Fig. 31.3

To keep track of multimedia hardware IRQ settings, double-click Computer in Device Manager's View Devices by Type list, and you see the View Resources page.

Input/Output (I/O)

Input/output (I/O) addresses refer to locations in memory that devices use to communicate with software and/or the CPU.

To find out which I/O setting is allocated to which component, click the Input/Output (I/O) option. A list of I/O settings appears, with the hardware using the corresponding setting next to it (see fig. 31.4).

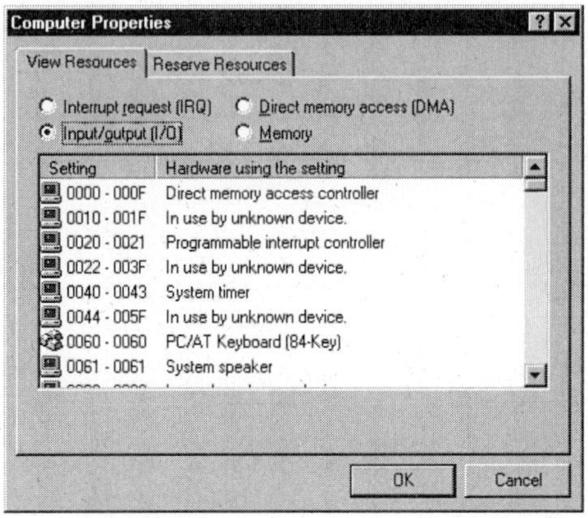

Fig. 31.4
Device Manager
enables you to
track device I/O
settings.

Direct Memory Access (DMA)

Direct memory access (DMA) is a way of improving system performance by accessing memory without using the computer's processor.

To find out which DMA setting is allocated to which component, click the Direct Memory Access (DMA) option. A list of DMA settings appears, with the hardware using the corresponding setting next to it (see fig. 31.5).

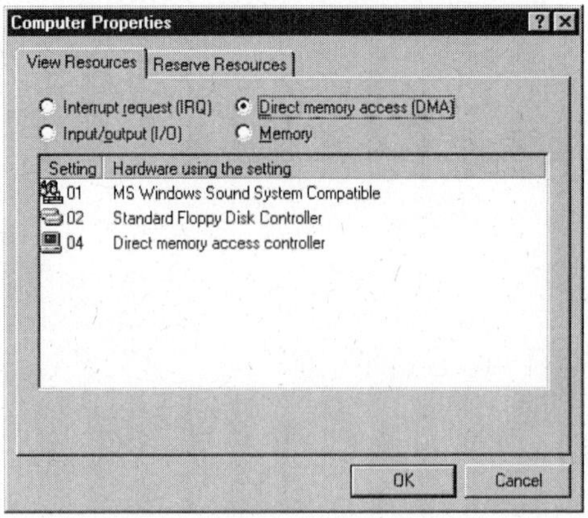

Fig. 31.5
Device Manager
enables you to
track device DMA
settings.

Memory

You can find out what memory is allocated to which component with Device Manager. Click the Memory option. A list of memory settings appears, with the hardware using the corresponding setting next to it (see fig. 31.6).

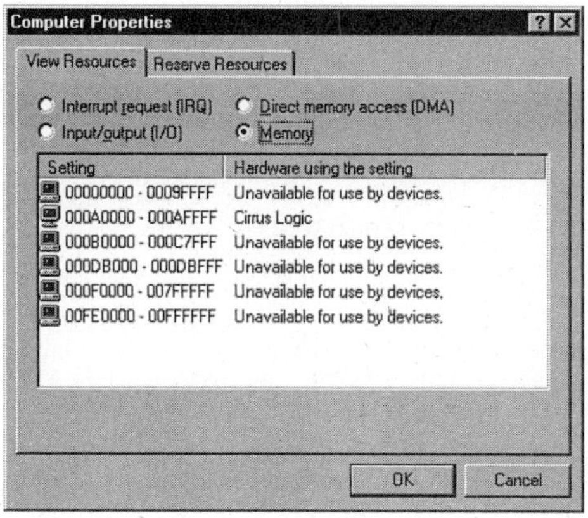

Fig. 31.6
Device Manager
enables you to
track memory
settings.

Viewing and Changing Resource Settings

You can view or change the resource setting of a device using Device Manager. From the Device Manager page of the System Properties sheet, do the following:

1. Click the plus sign along the left edge next to the hardware device type for which you want to change the settings.

2. Double-click the specific hardware device you are interested in.

3. In the dialog box that appears, click the Resources tab (see fig. 31.7).

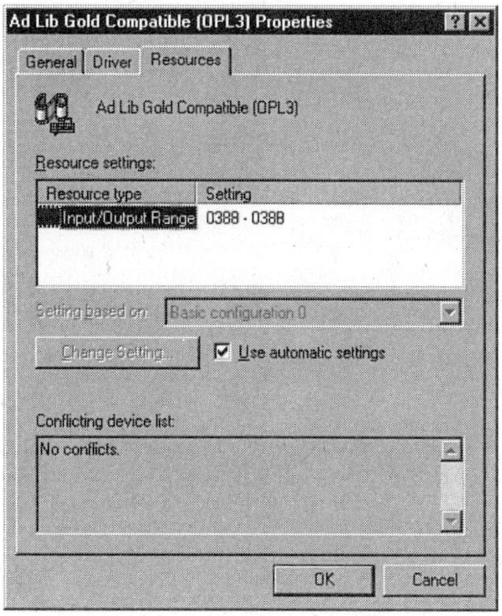

Fig. 31.7
A typical Resources page, from which you can change or view resource settings of a hardware device.

4. Click the resource you want to change. Make the change and click OK.

> **Note**
>
> Sometimes a device doesn't have a Resources tab. In such cases, the device either isn't using any resource settings, or you are not allowed to change its resources. As a result, you are not given the option to change settings.

Adding or Changing Device Drivers

Adding or changing device drivers has historically been a challenge for many people using the DOS/Windows combination. However, Windows 95 enables you to add or change device drivers using Device Manager.

As an example, try changing the driver for MS Windows Sound System Compatible. Start from the Device Manager page on the System Properties sheet, and follow these steps:

1. Click the plus sign along the left edge next to the hardware device type for which you want to change the settings, in this case Sound, Video and Game Controllers.

2. Double-click the specific hardware device you are interested in, in this case MS Windows Sound System Compatible.

3. On the sheet that appears, click the Driver tab (see fig. 31.8).

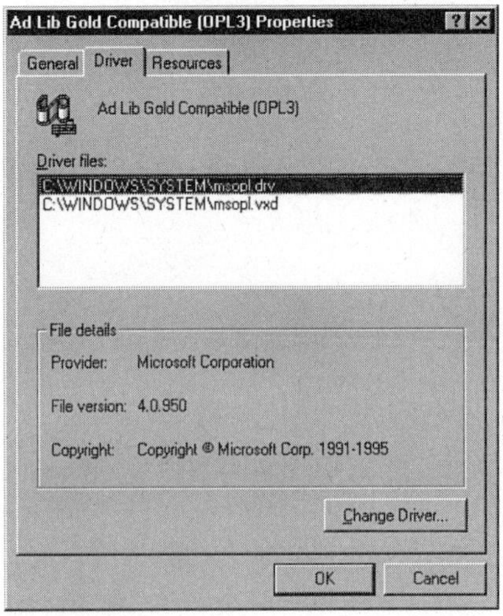

Fig. 31.8
The Driver page enables you to change drivers for a specific multimedia device.

4. Click the Change Driver button. The Select Device dialog box appears (see fig. 31.9).

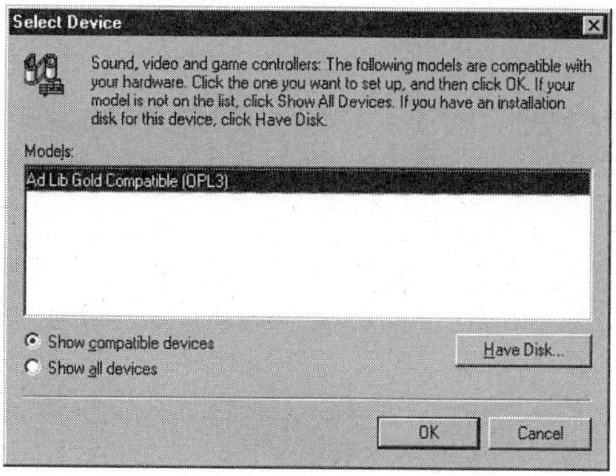

Fig. 31.9
You select the device you want to set up from the Select Device dialog box.

A list details the models compatible with your hardware. Make sure the Show Compatible Devices option is selected (if it is available). If the hardware model you want to set up is not on the list, select the Show All Devices button, if available. The list changes to show all such devices.

5. Click the device you want to set up; then click OK.

The Select Device dialog box disappears, leaving the Driver page showing the driver files and their correct directory path.

6. Select the driver you want and click OK.

7. The dialog box disappears and you find yourself back at the Device Manager list. Click Close.

If you have a separate installation disk for the device (such as a floppy disk), you need to take these extra steps:

1. From the Select Device dialog box, click Have Disk. The Install From Disk dialog box appears (see fig. 31.10).

2. Specify the directory and disk where the manufacturer's files should be copied from.

3. Click OK.

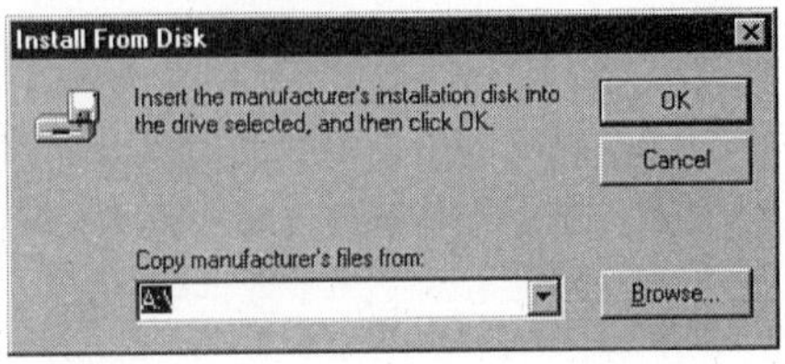

Fig. 31.10
You need to specify the drive and directory where the software drivers can be found.

Resolving Hardware Conflicts Using Device Manager

No matter how much you try to avoid it, you will probably get a hardware conflict sometime—that is, two devices trying to use the same resource at the same time. Device Manager makes resolving these conflicts easier.

If you have a conflict between two devices, open Device Manager and try one of these three things:

- Disable the device that is conflicting, which in turn frees up the device's resources.

- Assign a free resource to the device that is causing the conflict.

- Free up resources that the conflicting device needs by rearranging resources that other devices use.

> **Note**
>
> Windows 95 includes an extremely useful feature as part of Windows Help called Hardware Conflict Troubleshooter, which you can access via the Start button. Select the conflicting hardware and choose the Troubleshooting option from the Help topics index. The Troubleshooter helps you resolve conflicts on a step-by-step basis.

The Multimedia Properties Sheet

Windows 95 offers a Multimedia Properties sheet from which you can change various device properties, such as the following:

- *Audio* changes the volume level on a multimedia device.

- *Video* varies the size of the standard window in which a video clip is displayed.

- *MIDI* sets up a new MIDI instrument.

- *CD Music* adjusts the volume of an installed CD player.

- *Advanced* configures multimedia properties associated with specific attached devices.

To display the Multimedia Properties sheet, follow these steps:

1. Open the Start menu and choose Settings, Control Panel.

2. Double-click the Multimedia icon. The Multimedia Properties sheet appears.

Audio

Adjusting the volume of multimedia devices is possible using the Multimedia Properties sheet. After you display the Multimedia Properties sheet, do the following:

1. Click the Audio tab (see fig. 31.11).

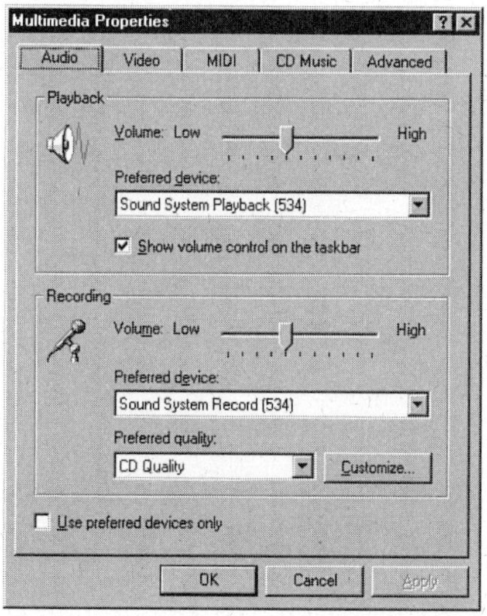

Fig. 31.11
You can adjust the volume of multimedia devices using the Audio page on the Multimedia Properties sheet.

2. Adjust the volume for Playback or Recording by dragging the respective Volume slider; drag to the right for higher, and to the left for lower.

3. Select the device you want used for playback or recording if it is not the default in the Preferred Device list.

4. Check the Show Volume Control on the taskbar if you want the volume control displayed during playback.

5. Select an option from the Preferred Quality list for the quality of the recording (for example, CD Quality).

6. If you want to customize the recording quality, click the Customize button in the Recording area. The Customize dialog box appears (see fig. 31.12).

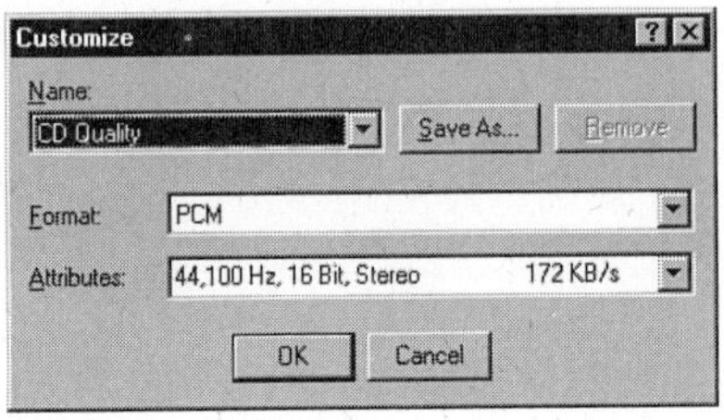

Fig. 31.12
Customize the quality of the recorded sound using the Customize option.

With this option, you can select the sound quality, format, and attributes, and then save the customized format as a special file by clicking the Save As button.

Tip
To achieve the smoothest video playback, select the Original Size option from the Window drop-down list.

Video

You can adjust the size of the standard window in which a video clip is displayed using the Multimedia Properties sheet. After the sheet appears, follow these steps:

1. Click the Video tab (see fig. 31.13).

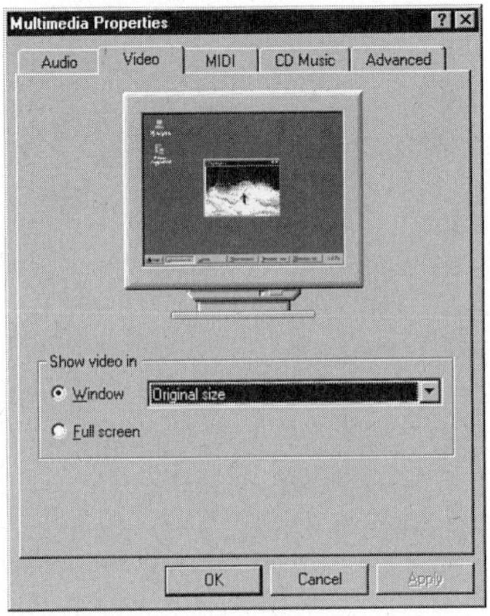

Fig. 31.13
Adjust the size of the video clip window using the Video page of the Multimedia Properties sheet.

2. Click <u>W</u>indow or <u>F</u>ull Screen in the Show Video In area to either customize the display window or use the entire screen.

3. If Window is checked, select the window size you want from the drop-down list that appears when you click the down arrow.

MIDI

You can use the MIDI page of the Multimedia Properties sheet to set up a new MIDI instrument connected to your PC.

After you display the Multimedia Properties sheet, follow these steps:

1. Connect the MIDI instrument to a MIDI port on your installed sound card.

2. Click the MIDI tab (see fig. 31.14).

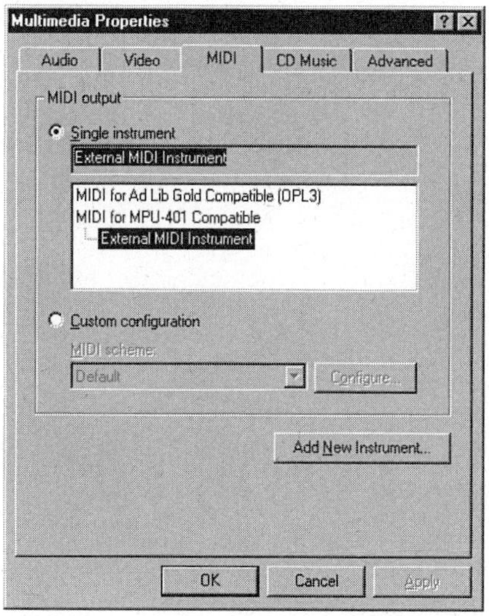

Fig. 31.14

You can set up a MIDI instrument using the MIDI page in the Multimedia Properties sheet.

3. Click the Add <u>N</u>ew Instrument button near the bottom of the page.

4. Follow the instructions on-screen to install the MIDI device, and then click the Single Instrument button.

5. The device you just installed will be displayed in the list window in the center of the MIDI page. Select the device and click OK.

Moving a MIDI Instrument to Another Sound Card

You can switch MIDI instruments between sound cards using these steps:

1. Click the Advanced tab in the Multimedia Properties sheet (see fig. 31.15).

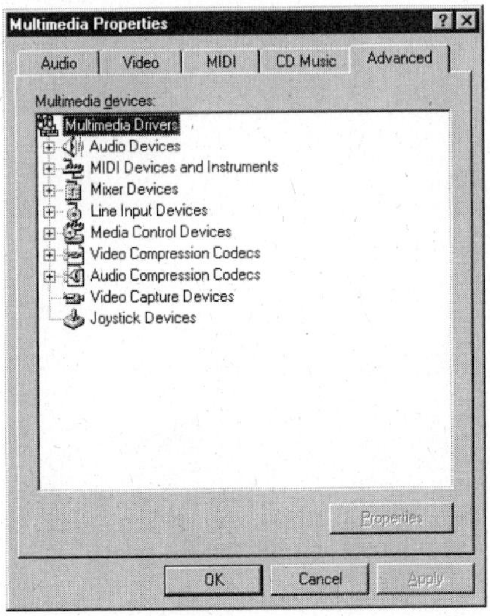

Fig. 31.15

To display multimedia properties related to different devices, click the Advanced tab.

2. Click the plus sign next to MIDI Devices and Instruments.

3. Click the plus sign next to the sound card that is connected to your MIDI instrument.

4. Select the instrument you want to move.

5. Click Properties.

6. On the resulting Properties sheet, click the Details tab (see fig. 31.16).

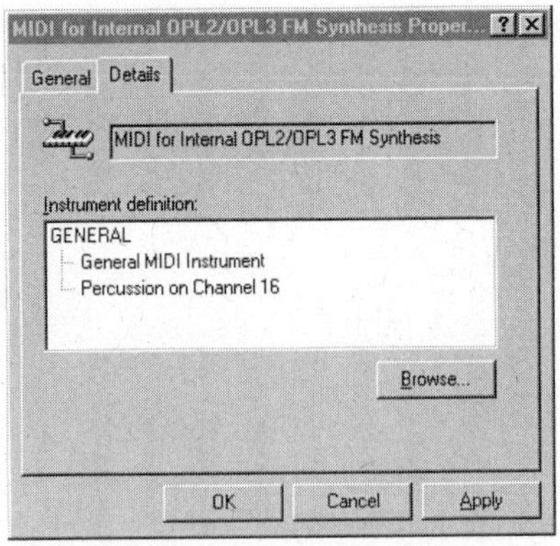

Fig. 31.16

The Details page on the MIDI Properties sheet enables you to move a MIDI instrument to a new sound card.

7. Select the sound card where you want to move the instrument from the MIDI Port list.

8. Plug the instrument into the new sound card.

CD Music

You can adjust the volume of the CD player installed on your PC using the CD Music page on the Multimedia Properties sheet.

After you display the Multimedia Properties sheet, follow these steps:

1. Click the CD Music tab (see fig. 31.17).

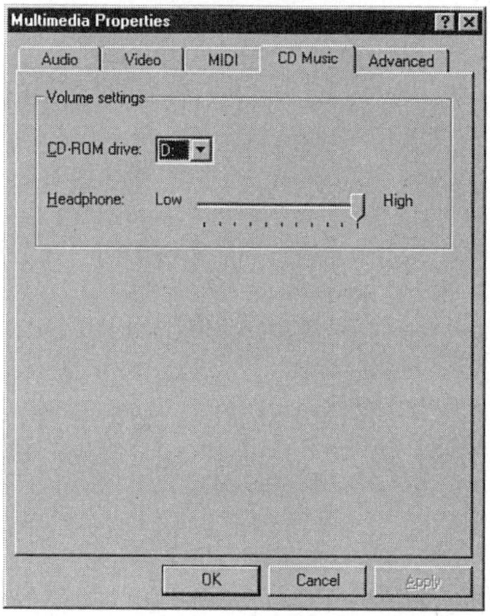

Tip

You can set volume levels for different CD drives.

Fig. 31.17

You can change the volume level for a specific CD-ROM drive using the CD Music page on the Multimedia Properties sheet.

2. To adjust the volume, just drag the slider to the right (to increase volume) or the left (to decrease volume).

3. Click OK after you have selected the correct volume level.

If you have more than one CD player installed, you can switch between CD players using the same Multimedia page:

1. Select the CD drive you want to use from the CD-ROM drive list.

2. Click OK.

Advanced

Clicking the Advanced tab of the Multimedia Properties sheet displays multimedia properties associated with different devices attached to your PC (refer to fig. 31.15).

To configure the multimedia device of your choice, follow these steps:

1. Click the plus sign next to the type of multimedia device you are interested in. A sub-list of associated devices appears.

2. Select the device you want to configure.

3. Click the Properties button at the bottom of the window.

4. Make the necessary changes on the Properties sheet and click OK. The Properties sheet is different for each type of device.❖

Chapter 32

Installing and Using a CD-ROM Drive

by Jerry Honeycutt

Do you need a CD-ROM drive in your computer? Of course you do, if you want to use any new software or games in the future. In 1995, most new computers will ship with a CD-ROM drive already installed. A trip to your local computer store reveals aisles of computers with preinstalled CD-ROM drives. In fact, only the most basic machines in current product lines are without one. The large number of CD-ROM drives in desktop computers has escalated the demand for CD-ROM software titles. And you can bet that software vendors are answering the demand.

Vendors are shipping multimedia software and games, reference material, resources, and other applications on CD-ROM. The sheer size of these titles makes the CD-ROM the only practical way for vendors to distribute them. Also, many software vendors will be shipping software on CD-ROM for economical reasons: a single CD-ROM is less expensive to ship than a handful of floppy disks, and many products include documentation on the CD-ROM instead of printed manuals. Most multimedia applications rely on sounds, videos, and images stored on a CD-ROM. For example, Microsoft Bookshelf would not be possible without CD-ROM technology. It ships only on CD-ROM and occupies over 600 megabytes. Shipping Microsoft BookShelf would require almost 500 floppy disks!

In addition to multimedia titles, many popular software packages, such as Microsoft Office, ship on CD-ROM. Installing an application as large as Office is much quicker from CD-ROM: installing Office from disks can take more than 90 minutes, whereas installing it from CD-ROM can take less than 15 minutes. As a bonus, you don't have to swap disks in and out of the drive.

The purpose of this chapter is to help you use the CD-ROM that came with your computer. This chapter also helps you install a CD-ROM drive if you don't already have one. In this chapter, you learn to

- Use your CD-ROM drive with Windows and other applications

- Run applications on the CD-ROM drive without installing them on your hard drive at all

- Install drivers for a Plug and Play CD-ROM drive

- Install drivers for an older CD-ROM drive

- Optimize your CD-ROM drive in Windows

Using Your CD-ROM Drive

◀ See "My Computer for Easy Understanding of What's in Your Computer," p. 25

With a few exceptions, using your CD-ROM drive in Windows is no different than using any other drive. Figure 32.1 shows the E drive icon in My Computer as a CD-ROM. You access it in My Computer or the Explorer just like the other drives in your computer—double-click on the icon to open its folder or right-click to display its context menu.

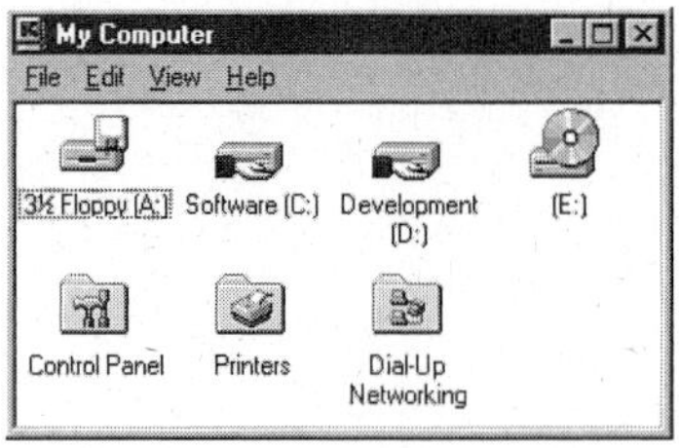

Fig. 32.1
Double-click the CD-ROM icon to open it in a folder. Right-click it and select Properties to see its size or share it.

◀ See "Dealing with Legacy Hardware," p. 247

Troubleshooting

I have a CD-ROM installed in my machine, but it doesn't show up in My Computer or the Explorer.

If you are using an external CD-ROM drive, make sure that it is turned on. At times, Windows may skip detecting your CD-ROM drive when you install Windows for the first time. In this case, use the Add New Hardware Wizard to allow Windows to automatically detect your CD-ROM as described in "Installing Legacy CD-ROM Drives" later in this chapter. If your CD-ROM drive still does not show up in My Computer, right-click My Computer and select Properties. Click the Device Manager tab, select your CD-ROM, and click Properties. A description of the problem and a possible solution is displayed in the Device Status area. If your CD-ROM does not appear in the Device Manager at all, consult the manual that came with your CD-ROM for more troubleshooting information, or call the vendor's support line.

Playing a CD-ROM Automatically

Windows automatically detects when you insert a CD-ROM into the drive. As a result, it displays the label of the CD-ROM next to the drive letter in My Computer. When you remove the CD-ROM, it clears the label.

◄ See "Adding and Removing Windows Components," p. 313

Some CD-ROMs for Windows 95 are set up to automatically run when they are inserted into the CD-ROM drive. If Windows detects an *AutoPlay* CD-ROM, it runs the appropriate program on the disc. The Windows 95 CD-ROM is a good example. After you have installed Windows 95, reinsert the CD-ROM in the drive. Almost immediately, a window opens, which gives you the opportunity to add or remove Windows components by clicking Add/Remove Software, or play a game of Hover! (see fig. 32.2).

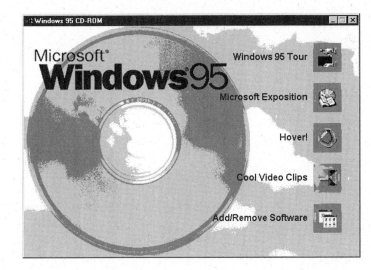

Fig. 32.2
This window opens when you insert the Windows 95 CD-ROM. You don't have to do anything!

In the future, software vendors will use AutoPlay as a significant marketing tool (or "Spin and Grin," as Microsoft calls it). However, AutoPlay is more than a marketing tool. AutoPlay simplifies installation for countless first-time users who would otherwise spend hours figuring out how to install these products. In the future, installation instructions for many programs using Spin and Grin will simply say, "Insert this CD in your drive and follow the on-screen instructions."

Tip
To disable AutoPlay, hold down the Shift key while inserting a CD-ROM in the drive.

Troubleshooting

Windows doesn't automatically recognize a CD-ROM when I insert it. I have to refresh My Computer or the Explorer to see the CD-ROM's contents.

Right-click on My Computer, select Properties, select the CD-ROM in the device list, click the Properties button, and select the Settings tab of the property sheet. Make sure the Auto Insert Notification option is checked.

Sharing Your CD-ROM Drive on a Peer-to-Peer Network

◀ See "Sharing an Entire Drive," p. 643

If other users on your peer-to-peer network don't have a CD-ROM drive, you may want to share yours. Sharing your CD-ROM drive is similar to sharing any other drive on your computer. However, there are two considerations when sharing a CD-ROM drive:

◀ See "Sharing Your Resources," p. 688

■ If a user *maps* to your shared CD-ROM drive and no disk is in it, he will receive a message that says X:\ is not available when he tries to open it.

■ You are sharing a drive, not a particular CD-ROM title. Therefore, if you share the drive with the Windows 95 CD-ROM in it, and then change the disk, you will be sharing the new disk.

Installing a Software Application from a CD-ROM Drive

Tip

With Windows 95 file sharing for Novell Networks, you can share a CD-ROM drive with other Novell clients, even though Novell is a client/server network.

Installing software from a CD-ROM drive is similar to installing from floppy disk, but it's a lot easier. You can double-click the Add/Remove Programs icon in the Control Panel or run the Setup program on the CD-ROM directly. For Windows 95 applications, you should install using the Control Panel. For legacy software (software written for older versions of Windows), either method is appropriate.

In addition to installing an application using the preceding methods, some software is AutoPlay-enabled as described earlier in this chapter. In this case, insert the CD-ROM in the drive and follow the instructions. For information on partial installations, see the section "Partial Installation" later in this chapter.

◀ See "Installing Applications in Windows 95," p. 304

Troubleshooting

When I try to install a program from a CD-ROM using the Control Panel, it complains that Windows was unable to locate the installation program.

Your CD-ROM did not have a SETUP.EXE or INSTALL.EXE file in its root directory. Click Browse to search the CD-ROM for another Setup program such as WINSTALL.EXE or try to run the program directly if there is no Setup program.

> *I successfully installed a program from a CD-ROM on my hard drive. When I run the*
> *program now, I get an error that says* File not found. *Or, if I try to use Help, the Help*
> *window pops up and displays an error that says* Help file not found.
>
> First, make sure that you have inserted the CD-ROM you used to install the program
> in the drive because the program is probably looking for program or data files on the
> CD. If you still get the error message, make sure that the CD-ROM is still assigned to
> the same drive letter it was when you installed the program. If it is not, you will need
> to reassign the drive or reinstall the program. You can change the drive letter the CD-
> ROM is assigned to by selecting the CD-ROM drive in the Device Manager, clicking
> the Properties button, and clicking the Settings tab of the property sheet. Select a
> new drive letter in the Start Drive Letter list box.

Complete Installation

Applications such as Micrografx Picture Publisher do a complete installation.
All of the files required to run the program are copied to the hard drive. This
is typical of applications that don't require a large amount of space, but are
distributed on CD-ROM for convenience. Also, some applications that by
default install only partially will give you the opportunity to do a complete
installation when performance is important.

Partial Installation

Some applications, such as Automap, shown in figure 32.3, enable you to
do a partial installation. In this case, only core components are copied to
the hard drive, whereas other files such as data or help files are left on the
CD-ROM. The advantage to this method is that you don't lose a significant
amount of hard-drive space to store the application. However, the disadvantage is that you must place the CD-ROM in the drive to run the application,
and the application will run slower than if you installed it to your hard drive.

Running Applications from the CD-ROM Drive

A very limited number of applications can be run directly from the CD-ROM
drive. Many multimedia preview discs exist that contain programs you can
run directly on the CD-ROM. However, the performance of applications that
are run directly from the CD-ROM is poorer than if you copy the files to your
hard drive because a quad-speed CD-ROM transfers data at about 600K per
second, whereas a hard drive can transfer data up to 5 megabytes per second.

◀ See "Moving
and Copying
Files and
Folders,"
p. 515

See the HoverHavoc game on your Windows 95 CD-ROM in \Funstuff\Hover for an example of an application you can run directly from the CD-ROM.

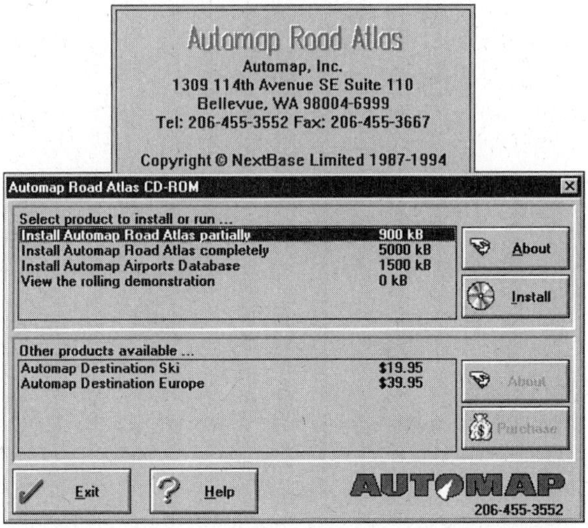

Fig. 32.3

Selecting partial installation will install only the program files, leaving the data files on the CD-ROM. Notice that a partial installation requires 900K versus 5 megabytes for a full installation.

Tip

If the CD-ROM contains a SETUP.EXE file in the root directory, you probably can't run the application from the CD-ROM.

Although programs generally can't be run directly from the CD-ROM, many other types of files can be used directly:

- *Data Files.* Data files include clip art, bitmaps, documents, and other files that you don't use often and would normally occupy a lot of space on your hard drive. You can use these files directly from the CD-ROM or copy them individually to your hard drive.

◀ See "Understanding Fonts," p. 210

- *Font.* A collection of fonts that you install via the Control Panel. Once the font is installed, you don't need the CD-ROM in the drive to use the font.

◀ See "Multimedia Features in Windows 95," p. 950

- *Multimedia.* Some CD-ROMs are packed with sounds and videos you can preview directly from the CD-ROM. For example, see the Funstuff directory on your Windows 95 CD-ROM.

▶ See "Using CD Player," p. 994

- *Audio CD.* Your favorite audio CD. Playing your favorite musical CD can pick up the pace while you are working—but it can distract you, too!

Installing Plug and Play CD-ROM Drives

In Chapter 8, "Plug and Play and Legacy Device Installation," you learned what Plug and Play is and how to install Plug and Play devices. Installing a Plug and Play CD-ROM adapter is similar to installing other Plug and Play devices. They are simpler to install than legacy CD-ROM adapters because you don't have to worry with IRQ, DMA, and I/O port settings. Driver configuration is automatic, too.

Windows will take care of the details that previously could take hours: it identifies the hardware, identifies the resource requirements, creates the configuration, programs the device, loads the 32-bit device drivers, and notifies the system of the change. It will appear in My Computer the next time you boot Windows.

Tip
Double-click on \Funstuff\Videos\ Goodtime.avi on your Windows 95 CD-ROM to see a great example video!

> **Note**
>
> For complete Plug and Play installation instructions, see Chapter 8, "Plug and Play and Legacy Device Installation."

Installing Legacy CD-ROM Drives

Installing legacy CD-ROM drives is not as easy as installing Plug and Play drives. However, Windows' Add New Hardware Wizard greatly simplifies the task. This wizard looks for clues in your computer that tell it what hardware is installed. Some clues include the following:

◄ See "Dealing with Legacy Hardware," p. 247

- ■ Signatures or strings in ROM

- ■ I/O ports at specific addresses that would indicate a specifically known hardware class

- ■ Plug and Play devices that will report their own ID

- ■ Drivers loaded in memory before you run Setup

- ■ device= lines in the CONFIG.SYS that indicate specific device drivers to the Wizard.

CD-ROM Types Supported

Windows supports three types of CD-ROM drives: SCSI, IDE, and proprietary CD-ROM drives.

- *SCSI.* Often pronounced *skuzzy*, a Small Computer System Interface adapter allows you to connect multiple pieces of hardware to a single adapter: scanners, hard drives, CD-ROM drives, and others. SCSI devices are known for their speed.

- *IDE.* An Interface Device Electronics adapter, commonly integrated into the motherboard, provides an interface for your floppy and hard disks. CD-ROM drives made for IDE adapters are less expensive than drives made for SCSI adapters.

- *Proprietary.* Some CD-ROM manufacturers, such as Sony and Mitsumi, sell drives that require a proprietary adapter. These drives require you to use an open slot for the adapter.

Note

If you haven't purchased your CD-ROM adapter or drive yet, go ahead and buy a Plug and Play adapter. Windows will still be able to take advantage of some Plug and Play features. Also, you will be using the latest technology that you can install in a Plug and Play computer later.

If you will be purchasing a sound card too, consider buying a combination sound/CD-ROM adapter card if you are running out of open slots in your computer. However, if performance is critical and you have the open slots, purchase separate sound and CD-ROM adapters.

Caution

When buying a Plug and Play adapter, be wary of packaging that says "Plug and Play *Ready*" on the box. You may be in for an expensive upgrade when you are ready to use this adapter in a Plug and Play computer. Verify that it is truly a Plug and Play device before you purchase it. See Chapter 8, "Plug and Play and Legacy Device Installation," for a discussion of the Plug and Play standard.

Installing the CD-ROM on an Existing Adapter

If you install your CD-ROM drive to an existing adapter that Windows already recognizes, you do not need to do anything else. All you have to do is complete the physical installation and connect the drive and cables as described in your manufacturer's documentation. Your CD-ROM drive will appear in your device list the next time you boot Windows.

Installing a CD-ROM and Adapter

By installing the driver for your new CD-ROM adapter before actually installing the hardware, you can let Windows suggest a configuration that does not conflict with existing devices in your computer. Therefore, make sure that you have not installed your adapter in your computer before following these steps. To install a legacy CD-ROM adapter and drive in your computer, follow these steps:

▶ See "Adding or Changing Hardware Drivers," p. 989

> **Note**
>
> If you are installing one of the popular combination sound/CD-ROM adapters, install the sound card device drivers as described in Chapter 33, "Working with Windows Sound Capabilities," before continuing installation as described in this chapter.

1. Open the Control Panel and double-click the Add New Hardware icon. The Add New Hardware Wizard opens.

2. Click Next. The wizard allows you to choose between automatically detecting new hardware and manually installing new hardware. Select No and click Next.

3. Choose your adapter from the dialog box shown in figure 32.4.

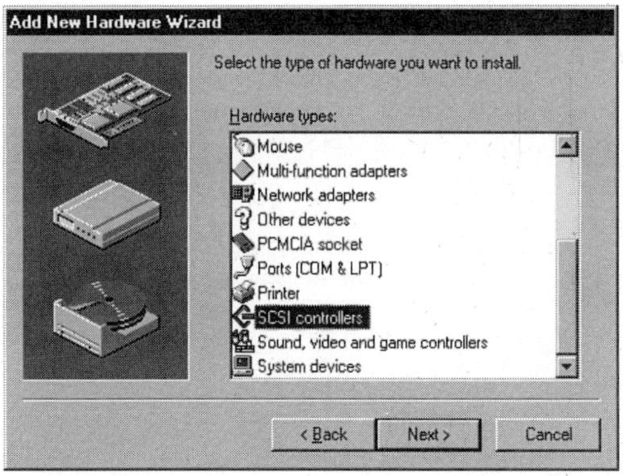

Tip
If you are absolutely sure that your CD-ROM adapter will not conflict with existing devices in your computer, go ahead and install the adapter and allow Windows to automatically detect it.

Fig. 32.4
Select either CD-ROM Controllers or SCSI Controllers from the list, depending on which type of adapter you are installing.

VII

Windows 95 Multimedia

4. Select a manufacturer from the Manufacturers list and a specific model from the Models list (see fig. 32.5). Make sure that your selection matches your adapter exactly. Click Next. The wizard displays information about the recommended settings for this device.

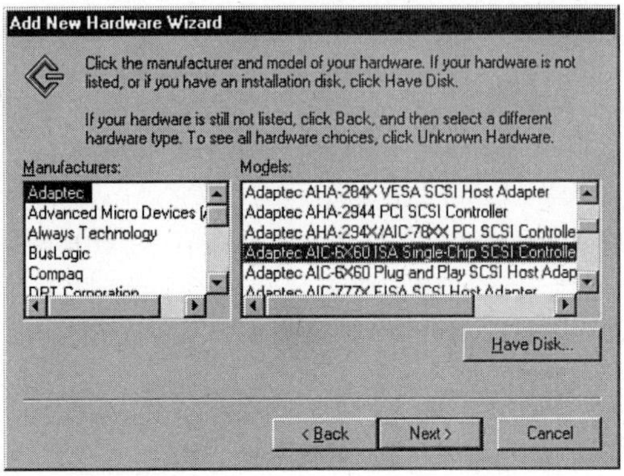

Fig. 32.5
Select a manufacturer and model. If your exact adapter doesn't appear in these lists, you'll need a disk from the manufacturer.

5. Click Print to output the recommended settings to the printer, or write them down on paper. You'll use these settings to configure your hardware before installing it in your computer.

6. Click Next; then click Finish, and Windows installs the necessary drivers on your computer.

7. After Windows has installed the drivers, shut down Windows and turn off your computer.

◄ See "Dealing with Legacy Hardware," p. 247

8. Configure and install the CD-ROM adapter and drive using the instructions provided by the manufacturer and the settings recommended by Windows. For additional information on setting an adapter's I/O address, IRQ line, and DMA address, see Chapter 8, "Plug and Play and Legacy Device Installation."

> **Note**
>
> If you are installing a separate sound card, don't forget to connect the audio output of the CD-ROM drive to the audio input of the sound card. See your manufacturer's instructions for more information.

◄ See "CD Music," p. 967

Congratulations! You have successfully installed your CD-ROM adapter and can start enjoying the benefits right away.

Troubleshooting

I successfully installed my CD-ROM (I can see the files on the CD-ROM using the Explorer), but it won't play audio CDs.

▶ See "Using CD Player," p. 994

First, check the volume by clicking on the Volume icon in the system tray. Then, run Media Player, select <u>D</u>evice, and make sure that there is a menu entry that says CD Audio. If not, install the MCI CD Audio driver as shown in Chapter 31, "Understanding Windows 95 Multimedia." Otherwise, if your CD-ROM plays but you can't hear the music, plug your speakers or headphones into the external audio jack of the CD-ROM. If you hear music using the external audio jack but not through your sound card, your CD-ROM is not properly connected to your sound card. Connect your CD-ROM to your sound card by following the manufacturer's instructions.

I tried to connect my CD-ROM to the sound card, but the cable doesn't fit both cards.

You'll need a new cable that is capable of connecting your CD-ROM drive to your sound card. If you are using commonly available hardware, contact the manufacturer, and they can provide you with a cable.

My computer dies during setup after installing my new CD-ROM adapter.

Restart your computer. Run Windows Setup again and it will ask you if you want to use Safe Recovery to continue the installation. Choose Safe Recovery and click Next. Continue using the steps described in this section. Setup will skip the portions of the hardware detection that caused the failure.

Optimizing CD-ROM Drives in Windows 95

Windows 95 incorporates a new file system specifically designed and optimized for CD-ROM drives. CDFS (CD File System) is a 32-bit, protected-mode file system that provides the following benefits:

- Replaces MSCDEX, which loads in conventional memory, with a driver that occupies no conventional memory.

- Improves performance of your applications by providing 32-bit, protected-mode caching. Your multimedia applications run more smoothly.

- Requires no configuration. CDFS is a dynamic cache.

The CD-ROM cache is separate from your disk cache because it is specifically optimized for use with a CD-ROM drive.Windows normally caches the CD-ROM to memory. However, when Windows needs more memory for your applications, it swaps the cache to the hard drive instead of discarding it altogether. The next time Windows needs that particular data, it reads it from the hard drive instead of the CD-ROM. This significantly improves performance as reading data from the hard drive is about ten times faster than reading data from the CD-ROM.

To optimize your CD-ROM, use the following steps:

1. Right-click on My Computer and select Properties.

2. Click the Performance tab of the System Properties property sheet, click File System, and select the CD-ROM tab. Figure 32.6 shows the CD-ROM tab that appears.

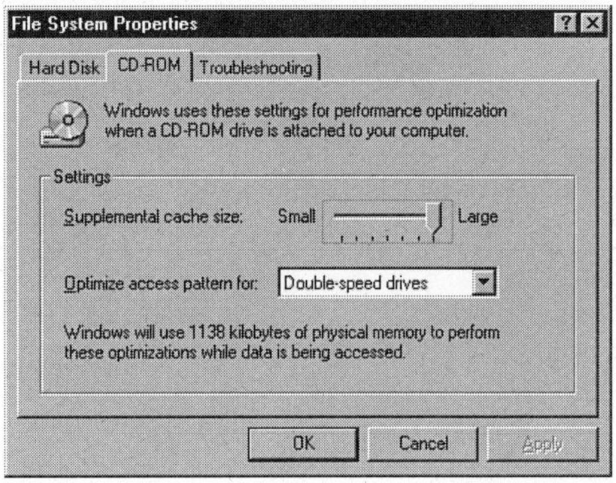

Fig. 32.6
Optimize your
CD-ROM in the
File System
Properties dialog
box.

3. Drag the Supplemental Cache Size slider to the setting indicated in table 32.1.

Table 32.1 Recommended Supplemental Cache Sizes	
Installed RAM	**Cache Size**
Up to 8M	114K
8M to 12M	626K
12M and over	1,138K

4. Select the type of CD-ROM in the Optimize Access Pattern For list, and then click OK.❖

Chapter 33

Working with Windows 95 Sound Capabilities

by Ian Stokell

The original IBM PC and resulting compatibles were not built to accommodate extensive sound features. Even today, you usually need to buy an additional audio board and speakers, often pre-installed in a new PC along with a CD-ROM drive. This type of system, advertised as "multimedia-ready," makes your PC capable of playing and recording quality sound files.

This chapter discusses sound-related topics in Windows 95:

- An overview of sound capabilities in Windows 95

- Instructions on playing sound files

- Installation of sound devices and their respective software drivers

- An overview of Windows 95 sound accessories

- Using MIDI capabilities

MIDI and WAV Sound Files

Your system has the capability to utilize two types of audio files:

- Digital audio, or WAV, files

- MIDI, or musical instrument digital interface

Windows 95 includes built-in support for both MIDI and WAV waveform audio. However, you need to install an additional sound device, such as an add-on board, before you can realize these capabilities.

WAV, or sound wave, files take up a great deal of disk storage space compared to MIDI files because WAV files record the entire sound to your hard disk. Although WAV files take up more disk space than MIDI files, the sound is generally better. MIDI doesn't save the entire sound but keeps a record of how the sound is played. The MIDI file then sends the "instructions" when you want to play the sound back and attempts to reproduce that original sound as best it can, sometimes not very successfully if you are using a less expensive 8-bit sound card. These instructions tell the card what instrument to play, the note and volume, when to play it relative to other notes, and how long it lasts.

You can use MIDI files to great effect when integrated into a computer-based presentation, for example. On the other hand, you can attach simple WAV files to electronic mail for distribution to a third party on a network.

MIDI uses either FM synthesis or wave table synthesis to reproduce the required sound. FM synthesis uses artificial sounds that are similar to the required sound, and wave table synthesis uses actual stored samples of sounds from real instruments.

With sampled sound, a small example of the instrument's sound is stored. When sound from that type of instrument needs to be reproduced, the sample is retrieved and it undergoes various changes, such as pitch variation, in order to reproduce a relatively accurate rendition.

Because a MIDI file essentially contains just the instructions on how to play a specific sound, the method of reproducing that sound depends on the quality of the sound board that will be playing it. When it comes to sound boards, what you pay for is what you get. A low-cost 8-bit board is going to give you a low-quality sound reproduction. On the other hand, if you invest in a high-end 16-bit board with extensive wave table synthesis capabilities and a good set of speakers, you are probably going to get great sound reproduction.

Note

Many new PCs are billed as "multimedia-ready" with built-in CD-ROM and sound board capabilities, but these PCs rarely contain high-end sound cards. What you often get is average quality sound, which is adequate for the average user. If you want a new PC capable of playing back recording-quality sound, buy a PC with a built-in CD-ROM drive and then add a high-end sound board of your choice.

Recording sound to your hard drive takes a great deal of disk space. Therefore, Windows 95 offers two groups of sound compression technologies, or *codecs* (coders/decoders). The first technique enables the compression of voice data, such as TrueSpeech. The second method enables you to compress high-quality musical type sound. These capabilities allow for the use of voice compression during recording, which lets the resulting sound file be compressed in real-time—that is, as it is recorded.

Another sound capability, called *polymessage MIDI support*, enables Windows 95 to handle multiple MIDI instructions at the same time. The result is that less processor resources are required, which frees up the CPU for other operations.

▶ See "Using Sound Recorder," p. 998

Sound Blaster and Windows

Creative Labs' Sound Blaster family of add-on audio boards has become something of an industry standard among multimedia PCs. If you don't have a Sound Blaster board installed, you probably have one that is Sound Blaster-compatible.

> **Caution**
>
> Boards that are advertised as Sound Blaster-compatible are not always true to their claim. The result can be distorted or inadequate sound reproduction. However, most games or CDs that fall under the multimedia label probably support Sound Blaster. Check the packaging thoroughly, and if the retail outlet is unable to verify compatibility, don't be afraid to contact the manufacturer direct.

Because of Sound Blaster's popularity, even Windows 95 comes with a compatible driver for supporting Sound Blaster programs. But if you don't want Sound Blaster, Windows 95 includes a less-popular alternative in the form of the Microsoft Windows Sound System. Windows 95's built-in audio supports capabilities required for Microsoft's own home-grown sound specifications.

Even if you use MS Windows Sound System, you are still going to need an audio board, or at least a "multimedia-ready" PC with enhanced sound capabilities and speakers, for listening to and recording CD-quality sound. The average built-in PC speakers are totally inadequate for the task.

Configuration of Sound Options

Any number of things can lead to sound features' not working properly. Many elements need to be configured properly in relation to one another.

VII

Windows 95 Multimedia

Any time one element doesn't function properly (especially with respect to the next step in the sound playing or recording process), audio problems are likely to result. This section describes how proper configuration can help you avoid sound problems.

Many times the problems are the result of hardware conflicts or wrong settings for specific components, such as IRQs or DMA channels. Hardware conflicts occur when two hardware devices want to use the same system resources. Fortunately, Windows 95 includes a very useful feature called the *Device Manager*, which keeps a centralized graphical registry of all system resources as they relate to the different PC components. As a result, you can more easily locate hardware problems in Windows 95 than you could in the previous DOS/Windows combination.

Sound problems are often the result of an error in installing a new sound device and are likely caused by wrongly assigned resources. The next section discusses the installation of a sound board using Windows 95's extremely useful Add New Hardware Wizard, which reduces the possibility of conflicts.

Troubleshooting

I get no sound at all, and when I do it is distorted.

Common settings problems, such as an IRQ conflict or a wrong DMA channel selected, can result in no sound coming out at all. A wrong DMA driver setting may also result in distorted WAV file playback.

To define the hardware settings, you need to configure groups of pins, called *jumpers*, on the audio board. Jumpers are essential to the smooth running of the audio board, and you must configure them according to available settings as defined by Windows 95 before installing the board. You can configure other necessary settings, such as IRQs and DMAs, using software after the board is installed.

◄ See "Installing Plug and Play Hardware," p. 246

Jumper configuration can vary depending on the board being installed. As a result, a thorough reading of the documentation accompanying your new board is a must.

Adding a Sound Board

The first step in configuring sound is to install a suitable audio board. Windows 95 makes adding sound and MIDI devices much easier than it was under the older DOS/Windows combination.

Windows 95 has made installation easier by implementing the Plug and Play standard and by providing an Add New Hardware Wizard. The wizard takes you through the installation of a hardware device step-by-step.

◀ See "Installing Plug and Play Hardware," p. 246

Microsoft designed its new Plug and Play standard to make it easier to add hardware components to existing PCs. Because Windows 95 supports Plug and Play, a user just has to look for a compatible component in order to en-sure that installation will be relatively easy. Windows 95 will then recognize the device being added and notify the user of the necessary resource settings that it must comply to in order to work.

> **Caution**
>
> You might want to use the sound board's own installation program instead, as the Wizard can run into problems identifying the correct interrupts for some components.

As an example of the process as it relates to sound devices, this section re-views the installation of a Sound Blaster board, in this case, the Sound Blaster 16 AWE-32.

You can access the Add New Hardware Wizard through the Control Panel feature or by choosing "sound cards, setting up" from the Help Topics Index page. This example takes you through the Control Panel option.

> **Caution**
>
> With virtually all sound boards, installation problems may occur when you try to install enhanced utilities that come with the board, after you have installed the com-ponent using Windows 95's Add New Hardware Wizard. This is because there is rarely an option that allows you to install the utilities separately from the drivers. However, this may be necessary because Windows 95 will have already installed the board without including the separate software utilities.

> **Caution**
>
> Some cards come with CD controllers already built-in. When this happens, you need to install it in Windows 95 and then configure the CD portion at the same time you install the sound card.

◀ See "Installing Legacy CD-ROM Drives," p. 975

VII

Windows 95 Multimedia

1. Open the Start menu and choose Settings, Control Panel.

2. Double-click the Add New Hardware icon. The Add New Hardware Wizard appears (see fig. 33.1).

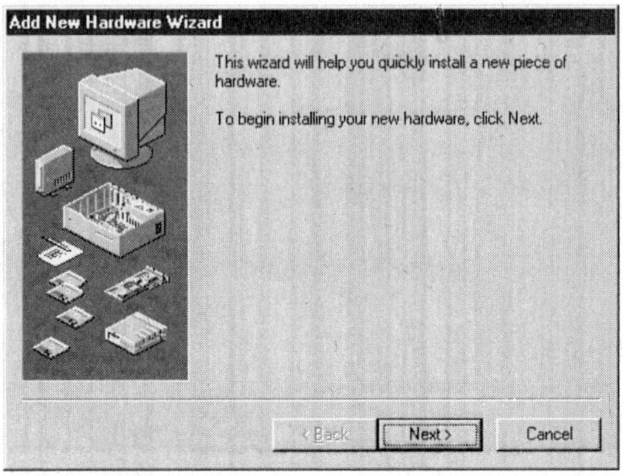

Fig. 33.1
The Add New Hardware Wizard eases the pain of adding hardware components by taking you through the installation step-by-step.

3. Click Next. The Wizard then asks you whether you want Windows 95 to search for new hardware.

4. At this point, select the No radio button as, in this case, we are only going through the steps to install sound devices (see fig. 33.2).

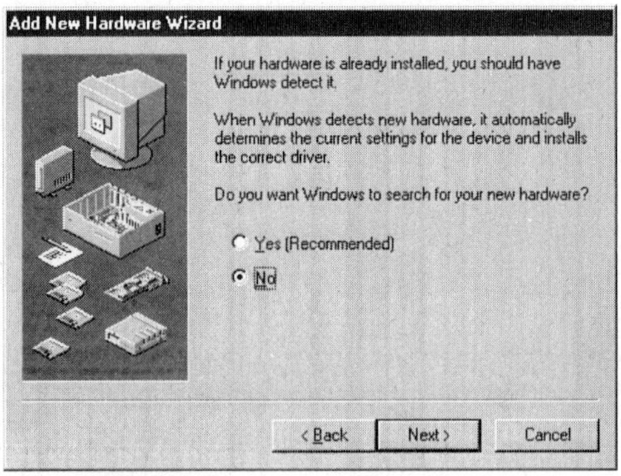

Fig. 33.2
You can choose to have Windows 95 automatically search for new hardware.

5. Click Next. The Hardware Types list appears (see fig. 33.3).

6. Select the type of hardware device you want to add from the Wizard's Hardware Type list box. In this case, select Sound, Video and Game Controllers, and then click Next >. The hardware Manufacturers and Models lists appear for the device you selected (see fig. 33.4).

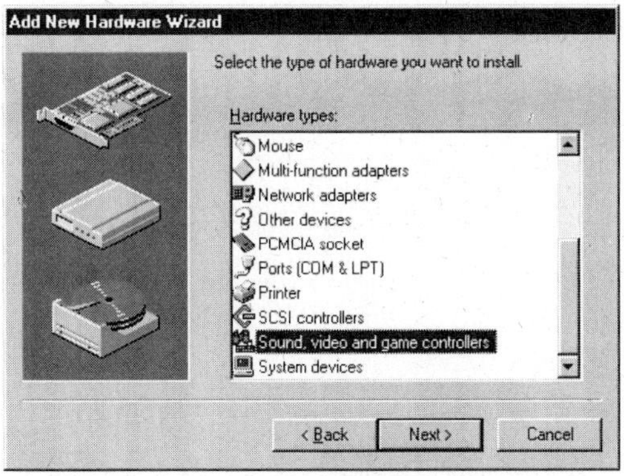

Fig. 33.3
Select the type of hardware you want to install from the Wizard's Hardware Type list.

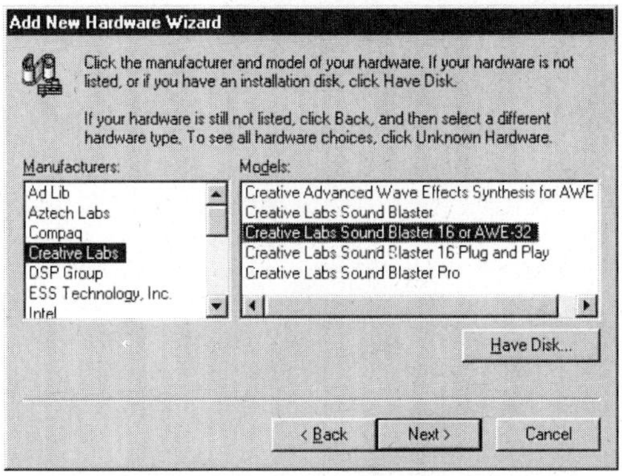

Fig. 33.4
Select the manufacturer and hardware model you want to add from these lists.

7. Click the sound board manufacturer's name in the left window. A list of products that Windows 95 is familiar with appears in the right window.

8. Select the board you want to add—in this case, Creative Labs Sound Blaster 16 or AWE-32. Click Next.

However, before moving on to the next stage, you may need to install a driver from a floppy disk. If that is the case, you need to take a couple of extra steps. Don't click Next yet, but continue with step 9. If you don't need to install a driver from a floppy disk, go to step 12.

9. From the Add New Hardware Wizard dialog box, click Have Disk. The Install From Disk dialog box appears (see fig. 33.5).

10. Specify the directory and disk where the manufacturer's files should be copied from.

11. Click OK. The Install From Disk dialog box disappears, and you are back to the Add New Hardware Wizard.

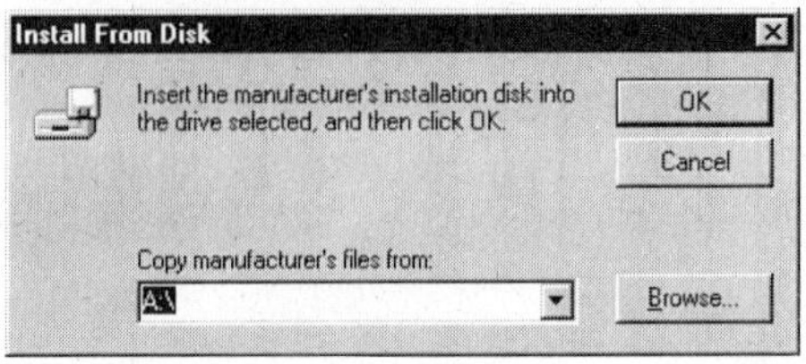

Fig. 33.5
You need to insert
the installation
disk in the
selected drive to
install a new
device driver from
a floppy disk.

> **Note**
>
> If the manufacturer's disk contains drivers for more than one sound card
> model, you will see a dialog box prompting you to select your card model
> before you return to the Add New Hardware Wizard in step 11.

12. Now you can click Next. The Wizard window changes to display the
settings it wants you to use for the new board (see fig. 33.6).

This list of settings is important; it is based on available settings as
defined in the Windows 95 Registry.

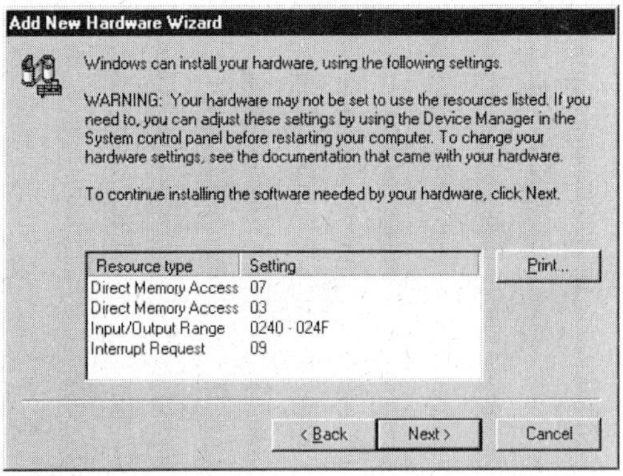

Fig. 33.6
The Add New
Hardware Wizard
gives you the
settings to use for
your new board
based on what
settings are
available.

13. Write down these settings or print them out. The new board should
have these settings before you install it.

14. Insert the floppy disks containing the drivers that the Wizard requests.

15. Shut down your PC.

16. Configure the new sound card according to the settings given during
the Wizard process. See the documentation that comes with your sound
board on how to make changes to I/O configuration settings, as well as
IRQ and DMA changes.

17. Install the sound card, using instructions that come with the card.

> **Note**
>
> You can also install the sound card prior to running the Add New Hardware Wizard; then choose the Automatically Detect Installed Hardware option in order to let Windows 95 detect new hardware, as previously described.

◀ See "Using Multiple Hardware Configurations," p. 263

Adding or Changing Hardware Drivers

Any time you add a component or peripheral to your PC, you need to make sure a software driver is also installed. The driver acts as a liaison between the computer operating system and the device, so they can communicate.

◀ See "Device Manager and Mutimedia," p. 955

With Windows 95, you can add or change hardware device drivers using Device Manager, which is the centralized registry of system properties and configurations.

As an example, these steps explain what to do to change the driver for Microsoft Windows Sound System:

1. Open the Start menu and choose Settings, Control Panel.

2. Open the System control item in the list box.

3. When the System Properties sheet appears, click the Device Manager tab (see fig. 33.7).

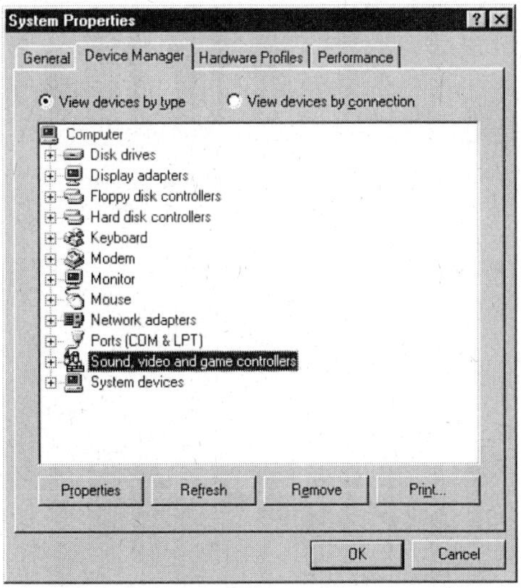

Fig. 33.7
Device Manager enables you to change driver settings.

4. Click the plus sign next to Sound, Video and Game Controllers.

5. Double-click the specific hardware device you are interested in, in this case MS Windows Sound System Compatible.

6. In the Properties sheet that appears, click the Driver tab (see fig. 33.8).

Fig. 33.8
The Driver page for MS Windows Sound System Compatible enables you to change drivers.

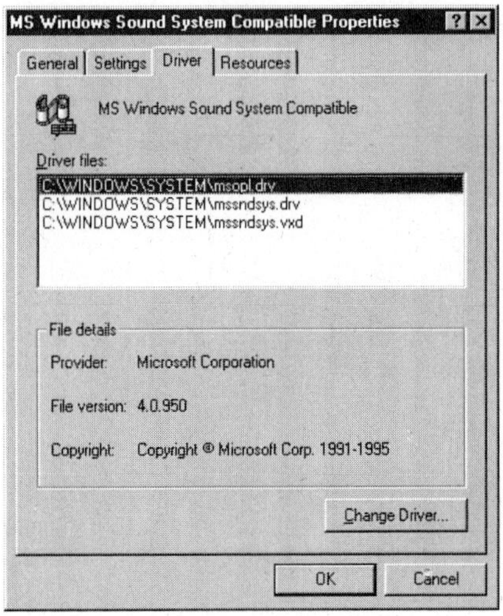

7. Click Change Driver. The Select Device dialog box appears (see fig. 33.9).

Fig. 33.9
You select the device you want to set up from the Select Device dialog box.

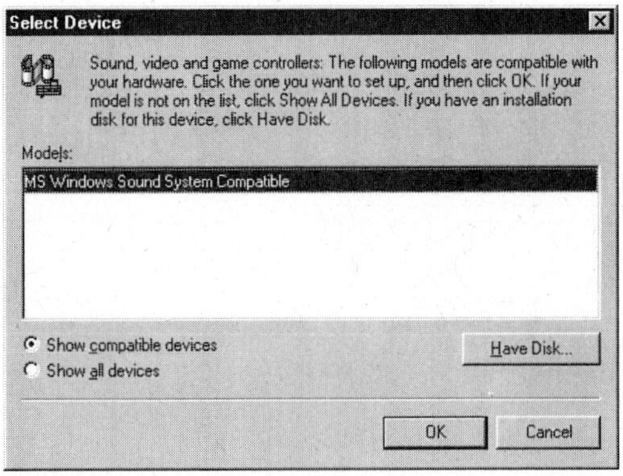

A list details the models compatible with your hardware. Make sure the Show Compatible Devices option is selected. If the hardware model you want to set up is not on the list, you should select the Show All Devices option. The list changes to show all such devices.

8. Click the device you want to set up, and then click OK.

The Select Device dialog box disappears, leaving the Driver page showing the driver files and their correct directory path.

9. Click OK to return to the Device Manager device type list.

10. Click OK to exit System Properties.

Troubleshooting

I get a hissing sound during playback of sound files.

If you hear a hissing sound during the playback of a sound file, the file may be recording in 8 bits and playing back in 16 bits. The 16-bit board doesn't realize that
the 8-bit file isn't the same high quality as a 16-bit file, so playing the file with expectations of higher sound quality emphasizes the lower detail.

Setting Up a MIDI Instrument

One of the added features of a relatively high-quality sound board is the ability to plug a MIDI instrument into a MIDI port and play sampled sound. Here
is a quick overview of setting up a MIDI instrument:

1. Plug the instrument into the sound card's MIDI port.

2. Open the Start menu and choose Settings, Control Panel.

3. Double-click the Multimedia icon.

4. In the Multimedia Properties sheet that appears, click the MIDI tab (see
fig. 33.10).

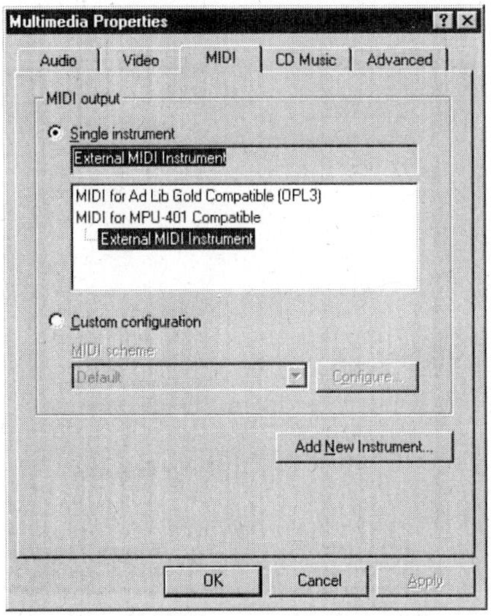

Fig. 33.10
Configure your
new MIDI
instrument using
the Multimedia
Properties sheet.

5. Click Add New Instrument.

6. Follow the instructions on-screen to install the instrument.

7. Choose Single Instrument on the MIDI page.

8. Select the instrument you just installed and click OK.

Your new MIDI instrument is now installed.

Moving a MIDI Instrument to Another Sound Board

You can move MIDI instruments between sound boards using these steps:

1. Open the Start menu and choose Settings, Control Panel.

2. Double-click the Multimedia icon.

3. On the Multimedia Properties sheet, click the Advanced tab (see fig. 33.11).

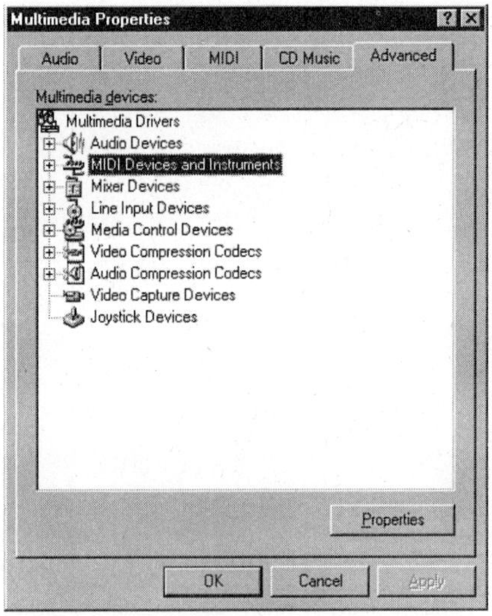

Fig. 33.11
The Advanced page in Multimedia Properties is where you specify the MIDI instrument you want to move.

4. Click the plus sign next to MIDI Devices and Instruments. A sub-list of devices appears under MIDI Devices and Instruments (see fig. 33.12).

5. From the resulting list, click the plus sign next to the sound board your MIDI instrument was connected to.

6. Click the instrument you want to move, and then click Properties.

7. Click the Detail tab.

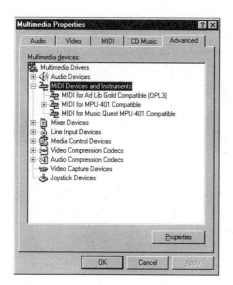

Fig. 33.12
Clicking the plus
sign next to MIDI
Devices and
Instruments brings
up a list of devices.

8. Select the name of the sound board you want to connect the instrument to from the MIDI Port list.

9. Connect your MIDI instrument into the new sound board you just specified, using the appropriate port, according to the instructions that come with your sound board.

Changing Multimedia Device Settings

You can change multimedia device settings via the Multimedia Properties sheet:

1. Open the Start menu and choose Settings, Control Panel.

2. Double-click the Multimedia icon.

3. On the Multimedia Properties sheet, click the Advanced tab (refer to fig. 33.11).

4. Click the plus sign next to the multimedia device category you are interested in.

5. Click the device you want from the resulting list.

6. Click Properties.

7. Make whatever changes you want using the different tabs, and click OK when you are done.

Windows 95 Sound Accessories

Windows 95 has some useful sound accessories related to the recording and playing of sound, either from audio CDs or specially recorded files.

CD Player enables you to play audio CDs from your CD drive while you are working in another application. CD Player offers many of the controls found in standalone audio CD players and looks and operates much the same way. In addition, CD Player enables you to edit your playlist that corresponds to the audio CD being played, playing the tracks in the order you want.

Sound Recorder is a good introduction to digital recording using a microphone that plugs into your multimedia PC. This feature enables you to make small recorded files that you can edit and mix into other sound files, although these capabilities are somewhat limited.

Using CD Player

CD Player enables you to play audio CDs in the background while you are working in another application. To access CD Player follow these steps:

1. Open the Start menu and choose _P_rograms, Accessories.

2. Choose Multimedia and then choose CD Player.

If you have used a standalone audio CD player, the controls on CD Player should be quite familiar (see fig. 33.13).

Fig. 33.13
The CD Player allows you to play audio CDs and edit play lists just like a regular high-end CD player.

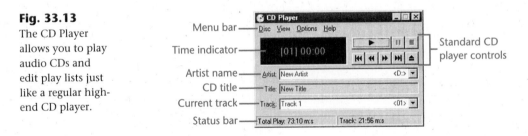

CD Player includes a number of advanced functions that you access from the menu bar, such as Random Order, Continuous Play, and the ability to edit your play list.

The main CD Player screen offers four menus: _D_isc, _V_iew, _O_ptions, and _H_elp. The _D_isc menu offers two options:

■ Edit Play _L_ist enables you to edit your personal play list (see fig. 33.14).

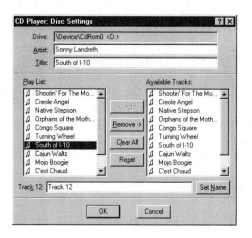

Fig. 33.14
You can customize each CD's play list by choosing the Edit Play List option from the Disc menu.

- Exit closes the CD Player window and turns off the audio CD at the same time.

The View menu offers three sets of options. The first set of options enables you to customize the general CD Player screen:

- Toolbar enables you to display or remove the toolbar. There are seven icons on the toolbar:

  - Edit Play List enables you to edit your play list.

  - Track Time Elapsed tracks the time elapsed since the start of the track.

  - Track Time Remaining lets you know how much time is remaining on the track.

  - Disc Time Remaining shows you how much time is left on the audio CD currently playing.

  - Random Track Order plays the track in random order.

  - Continuous Play starts the CD over again after the last track has played.

  - Intro Play plays the beginning 10 seconds of each track before moving to the next one.

- Disc/Track Info enables you to display or remove the CD disc and track information at the bottom of the general CD Player screen.

- Status Bar enables you to display or remove the status bar at the bottom of the window.

The second set of options on the <u>V</u>iew menu enable you to change the time displayed in the time indicator window:

- Track Time <u>E</u>lapsed shows how much time has elapsed on the current track.

- Track Time <u>R</u>emaining shows how much time is left on the current track.

- Dis<u>c</u> Time Remaining shows how much time is left on the current CD.

The third set on the <u>V</u>iew menu has a single option:

- <u>V</u>olume Control enables you to set the control levels for volume, wave, and MIDI (see fig. 33.15).

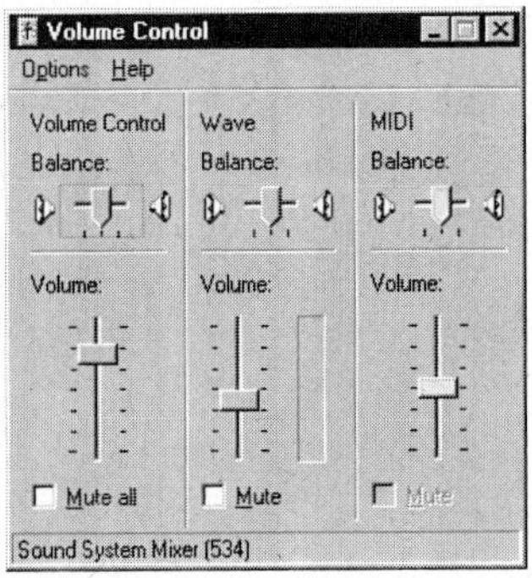

Fig. 33.15
In addition to controlling volume, you can also set WAV and MIDI file balance via the Volume Control option in the View menu.

The <u>O</u>ptions menu offers four options:

- <u>R</u>andom Order enables you to play tracks from different CDs in random order, which can be especially useful if you have more than one CD drive.

- <u>C</u>ontinuous Play enables you to repeat the track.

- <u>I</u>ntro Play plays the first ten seconds of each track.

- <u>P</u>references enables you to set preferences for the CD Player (see fig. 33.16).

The <u>H</u>elp menu offers two options:

- <u>H</u>elp Topics offers help concerning CD Player (see fig. 33.17).

- <u>A</u>bout CD Player lets you know how much memory is being used.

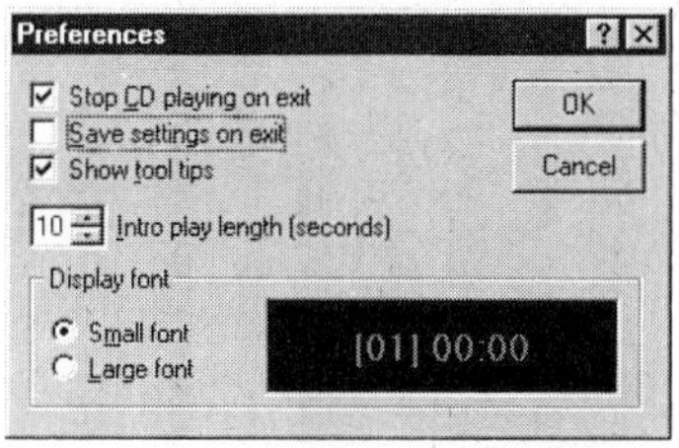

Fig. 33.16
Preferences enables you to set general preferences for CD Player, such as the length of the introduction for each track in seconds for when you choose Intro Play from the Options menu.

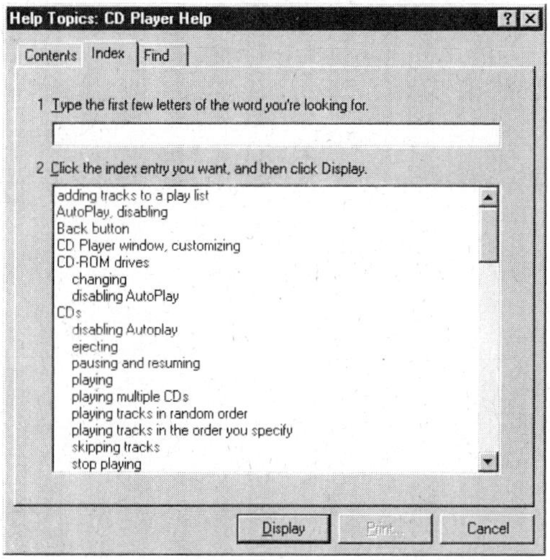

Fig. 33.17
Find help by topic with the Help Topics index option.

Editing a Play List

A play list is a list of tracks from an audio CD that you want to play. With CD Player, you can specify the tracks you want played from a CD and the order in which they should run.

You can change the play list by first choosing the Edit Play List from the Disc menu in CD Player. The CD Player: Disc Settings dialog box appears (refer to fig. 33.14).

The left window shows the desired Play List, and the right window lists all Available Tracks on the audio CD. To remove a track from the Play List, highlight it and choose Remove. To add a track to the Play List from the Available Tracks list, highlight it and click Add.

Using Sound Recorder

The Sound Recorder feature in Windows 95 provides a good introduction to the world of digital recording. Using Sound Recorder you can record small sound files to your hard drive to include in multimedia presentations or attach to documents for distribution among colleagues. You can even e-mail the file across your in-house local area network or the Internet. Sound Recorder does not have the advanced features of high-end digital recorders, but it does provide a feature suitable for most users' needs.

This section provides an overview of the basic features of Sound Recorder. To access Sound Recorder, you do much the same as you do to access CD Player:

1. Open the Start menu and choose Programs, Accessories.

2. Choose Multimedia.

3. Choose Sound Recorder to open the Sound Recorder dialog box (see fig. 33.18).

Fig. 33.18
Sound Recorder enables you to record sounds for future playback.

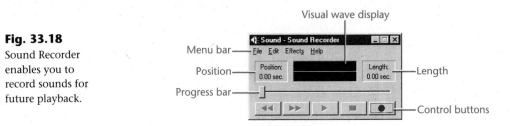

The *menu bar* lists the menus that are discussed briefly here. *Position* represents the current position in the audio file, whereas *Length* tells you the complete length of the file in seconds. The *visual wave display* offers a visual demonstration of the audio file, and the *progress bar* indicates how far along in the file you are. Finally, the *control buttons* control such operations as fast forward and rewind, like a regular tape recorder.

The File menu contains a number of familiar and self-explanatory options, in addition to two not-so-common ones. Revert enables you to undo a deleted section of a sound file, and Properties enables you to change the properties of the file and change the quality of the recording (see fig. 33.19).

> **Note**
>
> The Revert command works only if you have *not* saved the sound file you partially deleted.

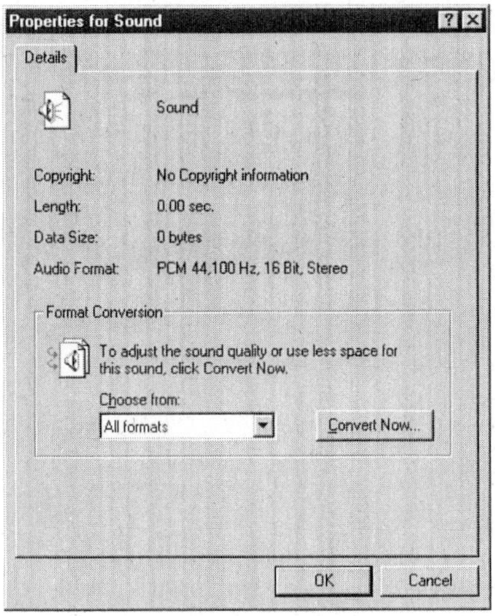

Fig. 33.19
The Properties option from the File menu enables you to change the quality of the recording, by changing the format.

The Edit menu offers a variety of options, some of which may sound familiar but actually accomplish tasks not normally associated with those commands:

- Copy copies a sound (used in conjunction with Paste).

- Paste Insert inserts a sound into a sound file.

- Paste Mix mixes two sound files together. The open file and the pasted clips are mixed and played at the same time.

- Insert File enables you to insert a file into another file at the point where you position the slider.

- Mix with File enables you to mix another file with the file playing at the point where you position the slider.

- Delete Before Current Position deletes everything before a specified point, once you have moved the slider to the point in the sound file where you want to cut.

- Delete After Current Position deletes everything after a specified point, once you have moved the slider to the point in the sound file where you want to cut.

- Audio Properties opens the Audio Properties sheet, from where you can change various properties for both recording and playback, such as volume (see fig. 33.20).

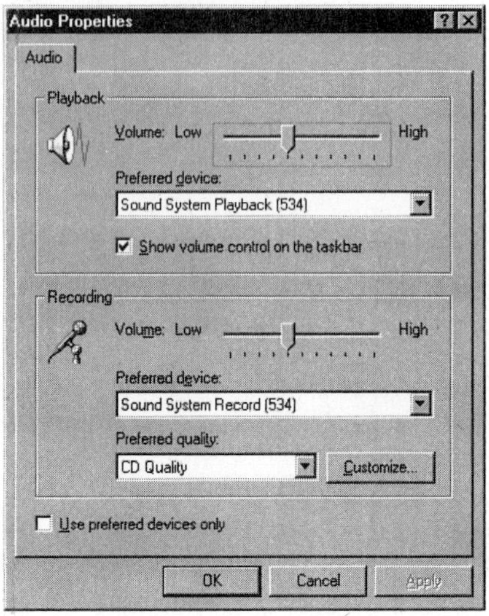

Fig. 33.20
Change recording and playback specifications, such as volume level and designated reproduction device, using the Audio Properties option.

The Effects menu offers options that allow for effects to be added to the sound file:

- Increase Volume [by 25%] increases the volume of a sound file.

- Decrease Volume decreases the volume of a sound file.

- Increase Speed [by 100%] increases the speed of a sound file.

- Decrease Speed decreases the speed of a sound file.

- Add Echo adds an echo to a sound file.

- Reverse plays a sound file in reverse.

The Help menu offers two options:

- Help Topics accesses the Sound Recorder Help section of the general Windows 95 Help Topics feature.

- About Sound Recorder lets you know who the product is licensed to, how much memory the PC contains, and how much is currently being used.

Tip
You cannot change the speed of a sound file, or add an echo to a sound file, if it is compressed.

◄ See "Compressing a Disk," p. 469

> **Troubleshooting**
>
> *When I play video and sound files together they appear out of step with each other.*
>
> If you are trying to play video that includes a soundtrack and the sound and video aren't synchronized, you again may have a computer that isn't fast enough. You can try improving performance and adding RAM, but if you have an older, slower processor and a relatively slow hard drive, you may need to think about upgrading to a new PC with fast video capabilities built in.

Common Problems with Sound

Many problems can occur when you are trying to get sound capabilities working on a PC because of the complexity of the operation between the system and the components. Windows 95's Plug and Play and easy-to-use Windows Registry help keep track of available IRQs and I/O addresses, but things can still go wrong.

One of the most problematic and intimidating steps required in installing sound devices, or any hardware for that matter, is figuring out available IRQ, DMA, and I/O settings that you can use. If you get the setting wrong and use one that is already assigned to another device, the sound component you are adding will not work properly.

Fortunately, the Windows Registry keeps track of which device is using which resources. This feature is useful because when you want to add a new hardware component you can just start the Add New Hardware Wizard, which takes you step-by-step through installing the device. During the installation process the Wizard gives you suggested free I/O, IRQ, and DMA settings that you should use for the new device, such as a sound board. You then take those settings and configure your board or hardware component to match the settings before you install it. The new device should then work because Windows 95 figured out what free settings to give you in the first place. For more information, refer to the "Adding a Sound Board" section earlier in this chapter.

Should hardware conflicts occur, Windows 95 includes the Help option from the Start menu, plus an especially useful feature: the Hardware Conflict Troubleshooter. You access the step-by-step Troubleshooter by choosing "hardware, troubleshooting conflicts" from the Help Topics Index. If you have a hardware conflict, start the troubleshooting wizard and it will take you through an investigative process that should resolve most hardware conflicts, or at least identify the conflict.❖

Chapter 34

Using Windows 95 Full-Motion Video Options

by Jerry Honeycutt

Before 1991, Windows was silent. The best Windows could muster was a beep when you missed a button. However, in mid-1991 Microsoft introduced the first multimedia extensions for Windows 3.0. These extensions enabled Windows to produce sounds and high-quality images—but not video.

In 1992, Microsoft introduced Video for Windows 1.0, which provided synchronized video and audio. But CD-ROM drives were not as prolific as they are now, sound cards didn't fill the computer store shelves, and video/audio compression technology was just starting to grow. A video was 160×120 pixels—barely 1/16 the size of a VGA monitor. While the computer industry held video as a major achievement, the consumer barely noticed. Video hadn't proven to be useful or exciting enough to stimulate demand for multimedia titles.

In 1993, vendors were delivering hardware with stepped-up performance, CD-ROM drives, sound cards, and local bus video. Now that the hardware could handle the increased demands of multimedia, the stage was set for a technological advance. Thus, Microsoft introduced Video for Windows 1.1. Software audio and video compression became a standard part of Windows multimedia. A video was a respectable 320×240 pixels, and some users realized a 50 percent improvement in video performance. This time consumers noticed. The demand for multimedia titles skyrocketed. Today, computer stores are lined with shelves full of multimedia games, reference material, and other audio/video applications.

◄ See "Using Your CD-ROM Drive," p. 970

In 1995, Microsoft introduces Windows 95, calling it an immediate multimedia upgrade. Before Windows 95, users had to install Video for Windows separately when they installed their multimedia applications. Video was not a standard part of the Windows architecture—it was more like an afterthought. However, multimedia support such as audio and video are an integral part of the Windows 95 architecture. Windows 95 performance improvements such as *CDFS* (CD File System) and *DCI* (Display Control Interface), coupled with hardware improvements such as PCI (Peripheral Component Interconnect) and local bus video, have made the limiting factor the amount of data you can put on a CD-ROM, not the throughput from a CD-ROM to a display device.

You'll see full-motion video used in many applications designed for Windows 95. For example, you'll find full-motion video used for training, reference materials, and entertainment. Products such as Intuit's Quicken present expert advice in the form of full-motion video. Also, products such as Microsoft Encarta or Automap provide videos so you can visually experience the reference material. And don't forget music videos.

The purpose of this chapter is to discuss the video technology available using Windows and how you can apply it. In this chapter, you can find information on these topics:

■ Video enhancements in Windows 95

■ The effect DCI has on increasing the performance of video in Windows

■ Video compression and decompression drivers available for Windows

■ System requirements for using full-motion video in Windows

■ Installation and configuration of Plug and Play and legacy video devices

■ Using Windows Media Player to play videos

■ Multimedia games in Windows

■ Apple's QuickTime for Windows

Video for Windows 95

Windows 95 incorporates significant enhancements for the Video for Windows architecture. Windows has made video easier to set up and more exciting with improved video performance. In short, Windows 95 has made multimedia accessible to virtually every desktop with a computer.

This section describes enhancements to full-motion video. For more information about other multimedia capabilities, see Chapter 31, "Understanding Windows 95 Multimedia," and Chapter 33, "Working with Windows 95 Sound Capabilities."

▶ See "Desktop Video Production under Windows 95," p. 1019

Easy Video Setup

The Video for Windows architecture is built into Windows. When the user installs Windows, the program automatically installs and configures the components necessary to use video, such as device drivers and video compression. Therefore, setting up and configuring video is a much less painful task than in previous versions. Users are more likely to tap into the power of video. An additional benefit of built-in support for video is that you can distribute multimedia files such as AVI to any Windows 95 user without worrying about whether they have Video for Windows installed.

Default Video Devices

Figure 34.1 shows the multimedia devices that Windows installs by default. As you can see, Windows installs device support for media control, video compression, video capture, and others. To see the list of devices installed on your computer, double-click the Multimedia icon in the Control Panel and select the Advanced tab of the property sheet.

◀ See "The Multimedia Properties Sheet," p. 962

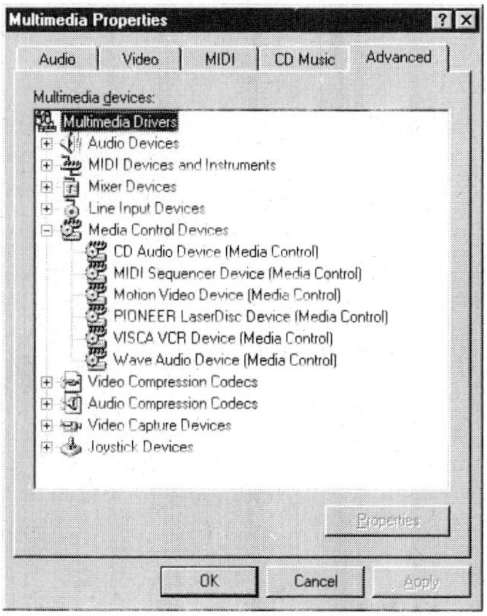

Fig. 34.1
These Multimedia devices were installed by Windows.

VII

Windows 95 Multimedia

Plug and Play Devices

◄ See "Installing Plug and Play Hardware," p. 246

Plug and Play and the Add New Hardware Wizard are new Windows 95 features that enable users to easily install new video hardware such as MPEG (Motion Pictures Experts Group) co-processors. Users can literally insert a Plug and Play video device in their computers, turn their computers on, and Windows automatically recognizes it.

As well, the Add New Hardware Wizard simplifies the task of setting up legacy devices by automatically detecting the hardware and configuring the drivers. Windows comes with drivers for most of the popular video devices available on the market today.

Improved Video Performance

A 60-second video that is 320 × 240 pixels and 15 frames per second requires over 200M of video data—3M per second! Even with video compression, the performance of the CD-ROM and video devices can be a bottleneck to a satisfying video experience because of the sheer amount of information involved. Thus, previous incarnations of Video for Windows were stressed when playing these videos. The perceived symptom was a "jerky" video as opposed to smoothly displaying frame after frame.

The performance improvements incorporated into Windows 95 make it possible to play high-quality videos in a larger window, potentially up to 640 × 480 pixels with the right hardware. Windows 95 includes these performance enhancements:

- *DCI*. The Display Control Interface greatly accelerates the rate at which video memory is updated. DCI enables video software to get closer to the hardware.

- *CDFS*. The CD File System improves throughput from the CD-ROM by providing an optimized, 32-bit, protected-mode file system. The improved performance of CD-ROM drives in Windows means you are not waiting on your system to read data from the drive. Videos look better.

- *Multitasking*. Windows' preemptive multitasking minimizes the pauses and delays during video playback. The video continues to play while other processes, such as decompressing additional video from the CD-ROM drive, are running in the background.

More Exciting Video

Very few multimedia games have been published for Windows and with good reason: performance was too slow for graphically intense games such as DOOM. Many games learned to rely on painting directly to the video device and using device-dependent features. Both traits are a no-no for well-behaved Windows applications. Thus, games were cast to the depths of DOS. In addition, the GDI and windowing environment were just too slow to support gaming software.

Windows 95 provides a significant improvement that opens the door to game developers. WinG (pronounced Win Gee) provides for virtually direct access to the display device while remaining compatible with the GDI. The compatibility with the existing GDI means that programmers can easily port applications to take advantage of WinG's speed. WinG makes it possible for graphics-intensive games such as Doom to run well in Windows.

Developing intense multimedia games for Windows is now practical with WinG. Having a place to play, you can count on vendors to provide the games. The "Gaming in Windows" section later in this chapter has more information on games for Windows 95.

DCI Standard in Windows 95

Display Control Interface (DCI) is the result of a joint effort between Microsoft and Intel to produce a display driver interface that enables fast, direct access to the video frame buffer in Windows. Also, DCI enables games and video to take advantage of special hardware support in video devices that improves the performance and quality of video. For example, a video player can take advantage of color-space conversion that enables color conversion to RGB (Red Green Blue) to occur in hardware rather than software. Although DCI enables direct access to the frame buffer, it remains compatible with the GDI.

DCI is available for the complete spectrum of display devices in Windows. DCI improves access to SVGA display devices and newer devices that include hardware support for stretching, double buffering, and so on. Some of the possible hardware-specific features are described in this list:

- *Stretching.* Stretching enables the hardware to change the size of the image instead of having the software do it. Therefore, the software sends the same number of pixels as before, but the hardware stretches the image to the requested size.

- *Color-space conversion.* Colors are stored in a video using YUV—a representation of color based on how people perceive colors. Before the image can move to the display device, it must be converted to RGB values. Hardware conversion saves a lot of time—potentially up to 30 percent—by freeing the software from this task.

■ *Double-buffering.* Double-buffering is the process of displaying the screen currently in the frame buffer while painting the next screen in memory or an additional hardware buffer. Because the new screen is quickly copied to the frame buffer, video playback and animation appear much smoother.

■ *Chroma key.* Chroma key enables two streams of video to merge. A particular color in one of the streams is allowed to be transparent before they merge. This process is similar to the "blue screens" that weather forecasters use on your local news broadcast or movies use for special effects.

■ *Asynchronous drawing.* In conjunction with double-buffering, asynchronous drawing provides for faster screen painting outside the frame buffer.

Applications using the Video for Windows architecture notice performance improvements automatically. On a 486 DX/2 66 with local bus video, DCI provides reasonable 640 × 480 video at 15 frames per second. This is full-screen video, but you will perceive it as being very jerky video playback.

On the same computer, DCI provides smooth video in a 320-×-240-pixel (quarter-screen) window at 30 frames per second. This playback is much better, but you may have a problem finding videos recorded using 30 frames per second. Figure 34.2 shows a quarter-screen video playing.

Fig. 34.2
A frame from WEEZER.AVI found in the FUNSTUFF\VIDEOS directory of your Windows 95 CD-ROM.

Note

DCI doesn't work with hardware video co-processors such as MPEG. DCI is a software-level interface. MPEG video processors don't use software to draw pixels on-screen and therefore receive little or no benefit from DCI.

Codec Implementation in Windows 95

As noted earlier, a 320-×-240-pixel video playing at 15 frames per second requires the file system to deliver 3M of uncompressed data each second. This demand is not even remotely possible with quad-speed CD-ROMs. Thus, *codecs* have evolved over the last few years to handle *c*ompression and *de*compression of video. Windows 95 comes with software support for four video codecs. Figure 34.3 shows the codecs installed in Windows 95. The four entries for Indeo are really just multiple versions of the same driver.

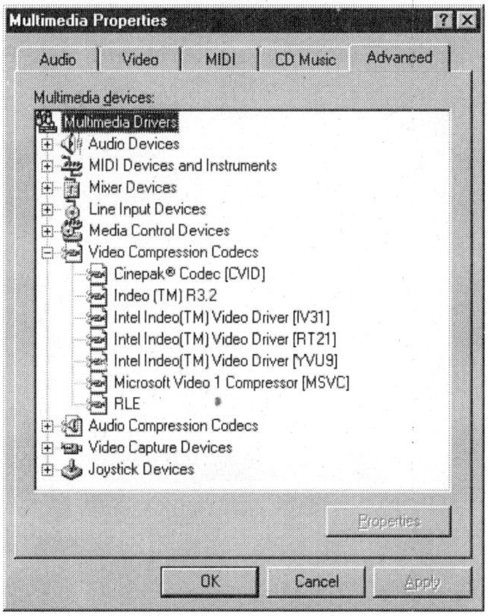

Fig. 34.3
Video codecs installed with Windows 95.

The following list describes the video codecs in Windows 95:

■ *Cinepak*. Cinepak is licensed from SuperMac. It provides good quality video playback at 15 frames per second or better and 320 × 240 pixels. Cinepak is a common codec used for both Windows and the Macintosh.

■ *Indeo*. Indeo was developed by Intel (*In*tel Vi*deo*). It provides good quality video playback at 15 frames per second or better and 320 × 240 pixels. Indeo is another common codec used for both Windows and the Macintosh.

- *Video 1*. Video is easy on the processor; it has low overhead and is a good, average quality codec. This codec was developed by Microsoft.

- *RLE.* RLE stands for *run length encoding.* RLE is not good for video because it cannot handle the rapidly changing frames. RLE is better-suited to compressing bitmaps.

> ### Note
>
> MPEG (Motion Pictures Experts Group) is a codec, not supplied by Windows, that provides high-quality 640×480 video at 30 frames per second. Approximately 75 minutes of VHS-quality video can be compressed and stored on a single CD-ROM. A full-length feature film can be distributed on two CD-ROMs.
>
> MPEG is computationally intensive. It is supported by an MPEG co-processor, usually implemented on a separate interface board. Microsoft has recently licensed a software MPEG codec that will be available for Windows 95. This software codec will play MPEG movies on computers with fast (Pentium) processors.

To see which codec a particular video uses, right-click the AVI file and click the Details tab of the property sheet. Figure 34.4 shows the property sheet for GOODTIME.AVI as found on your Windows 95 CD-ROM.

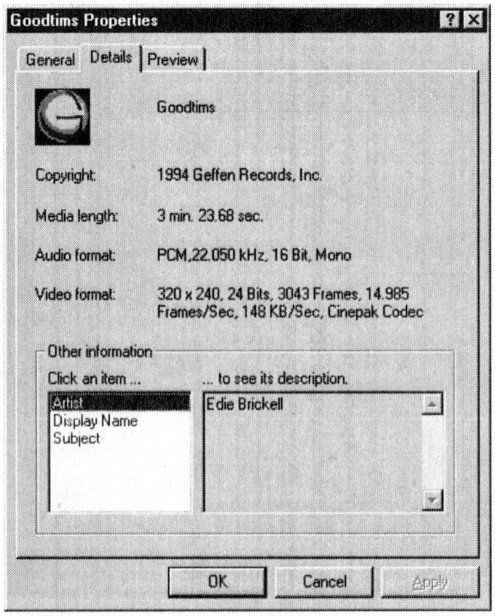

Fig. 34.4
The details of
GOODTIME.AVI
on your Windows
95 CD-ROM.

Windows System Requirements for Full-Motion Video

Playing full-motion video puts a tremendous burden on the PC. The CDFS must not fall behind or the video will appear to pause in the middle for no reason. In addition, the video data must go through computationally expensive decompression, and the bus must pump megabytes of data to the video device every second to play smoothly. If any one of the components falls down on the job, your video experience will be disappointing.

Modern CPUs are generally not the problem when identifying bottlenecks to video performance. The two primary places to point your finger are the CD-ROM and the video device. The following list shows the minimum hardware requirements for high-quality, 320-×-240-pixel video at 30 frames per second:

- Microsoft recommends a balanced system where each of the components is equally matched. What good does a local bus video device do you if you are using a single-speed CD-ROM? The fastest Pentium processor available doesn't do any good without a fast video device.

- Make sure your computer has at least a super VGA with 16-bit color (65,536 colors), preferably 24-bit true color (16.7 million colors). Eight-bit (256 colors) video just doesn't have enough colors to make a reasonable-looking image. Most new computers have display adapters, such as Cirrus Logic, which support at least 16-bit color.

- A local bus video device is essential for the multimedia experience in 1995, preferably with a DCI provider for improved performance. Local bus video devices are up to 10 times faster than some ISA devices. In addition, an adapter that provides a DCI driver offers substantial improvements by supporting color conversion and other DCI functionality.

- Make sure you purchase a CD-ROM drive with a transfer rate of at least 300K per second (double speed). This rate is required to play 320-×-240-pixel video at 15 frames per second with reasonable quality. As video quality rises, so do file sizes, so you may want to consider a triple- or quad-speed CD-ROM drive to match that local bus video device you bought.

- Use at least 16-bit audio. Before purchasing a sound card for your computer, play samples of WAV (Waveform-audio) and MIDI (Musical Instrument Digital Interface) formats on the demo units at the store. Only the ear can tell.

Installation of Full-Motion Video Device Drivers

◀ See "Installing Plug and Play Hardware," p. 246

If you are installing a Plug and Play video device, install the hardware using the manufacturer's instructions and power up your computer. Windows should literally recognize the device and install its device drivers.

To install device drivers for a legacy video device, follow these steps:

1. Power off your computer.

2. Configure the video device using the manufacturer's instructions.

3. Install the video device in your computer if it isn't already installed. Because installation instructions vary greatly, follow the manufacturer's instructions included with the drive.

4. Power on your computer. Windows may detect the new display device when it starts up. If it doesn't, open the Control Panel and double-click Add New Hardware icon. The Add New Hardware Wizard opens as shown in figure 34.5.

Fig. 34.5
The Add New Hardware Wizard simplifies driver installation.

5. Click Next and select Yes (Recommended) to allow the wizard to automatically detect your new hardware.

6. Click Next. The wizard displays a warning saying the detection process could take a long time. Be patient.

7. Click Next. The wizard displays the dialog box shown in figure 34.6 while it is detecting your new hardware.

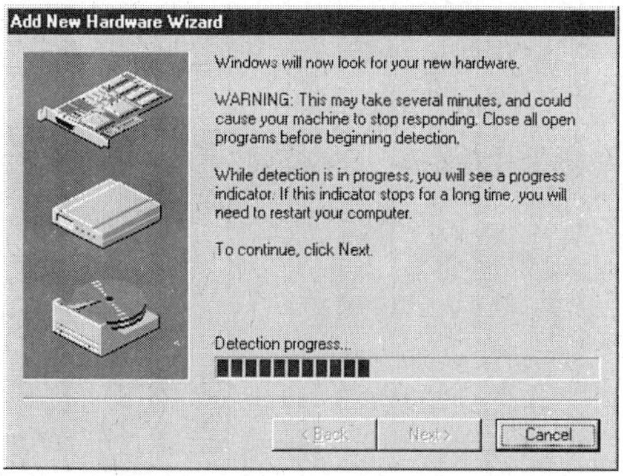

Fig. 34.6
The Add New
Hardware Wizard
is detecting the
display device.

> **Note**
>
> Following the 80/20 rule, the wizard spends 80 percent of its time in the last
> 20 percent of the progress indicator shown in the dialog box. This slow-down
> does not indicate a problem.

8. If it found your new display device, the wizard displays the dialog box
   shown in figure 34.7. Click Finish to install the drivers. If the wizard
   doesn't prompt you to reboot Windows, shut down using the Start
   button.

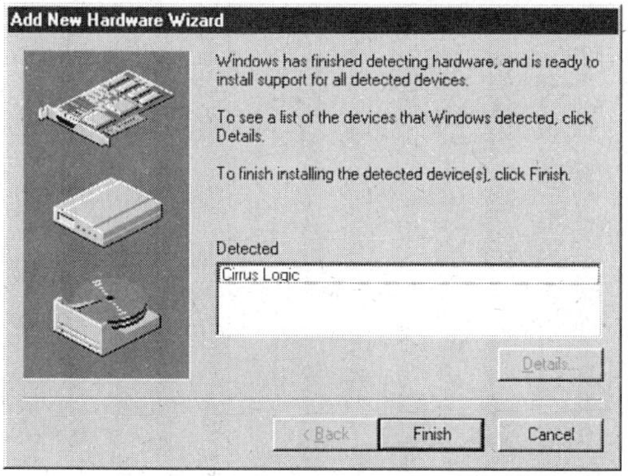

Fig. 34.7
Click Finish to
install the drivers
for your display
device.

9. If the wizard didn't find your display device, click Next. You need to
   choose your device from the dialog box shown in figure 34.8.

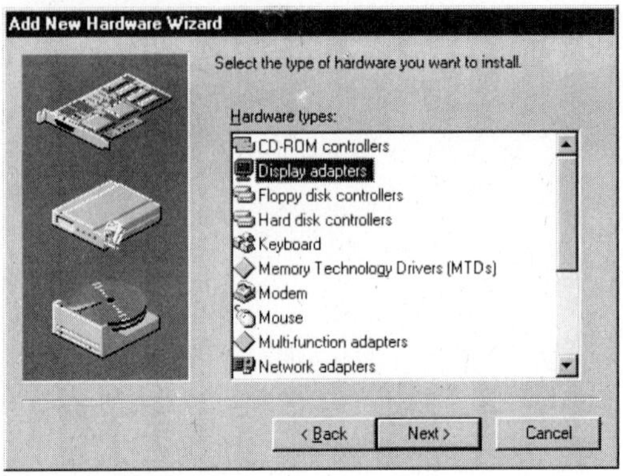

Fig. 34.8

Select your new adapter from the list.

10. Select the type of device you are installing from the list: Display Adapters. Click Next. The wizard displays the dialog box shown in figure 34.9.

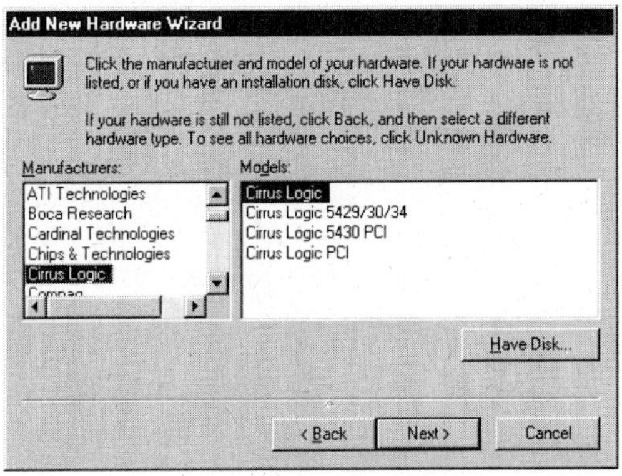

Fig. 34.9

Select an adapter from this list of manufacturers and models.

Tip

If you find that the driver doesn't work properly, contact the vendor or look on the online services for an updated driver.

11. Select a manufacturer from the Manufacturers list and a specific model from the Models list. Make sure your selection matches your display device exactly. Click Next. The wizard displays information about the driver you have chosen and the resources it uses.

12. Click Next to install your drivers. If the wizard doesn't prompt you to reboot Windows, shut down using the Start button.

Using Windows Media Player

Media Player is a Windows accessory that allows you to play multimedia files. It supports Video for Windows (AVI), sound (WAV), MIDI (MID), and CD audio. However, you'll primarily use Media Player to play videos. This section shows you how to play videos, insert portions of a video in your document, and configure Media Player.

Playing Videos in Media Player

Using Media Player to play a video is simple: double-click an AVI file in the explorer. Media Player loads the AVI file and immediately starts playing it. Alternatively, you can load Media Player first and use the following instructions to play a video.

1. Select Device, 1 Video for Windows.

2. Select an AVI file in the Open dialog box and click Open.

3. Click the play button in Media Player (see fig. 34.10).

When a video is playing, the play button changes to a pause button. You can stop the video by clicking the stop button or pause the video by clicking the pause button.

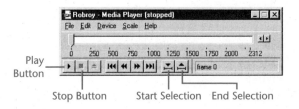

Fig. 34.10
Click the play button to play your video. The play button will change to a pause button while the video is playing.

You also can put a portion of a video in your documents. Then, you can play the video by double-clicking it. To copy a portion of a video to your document, use the following instructions.

1. Position the trackbar thumb on the starting frame of the portion you want to copy.

2. Click Start Selection.

3. Position the trackbar thumb on the last frame of the portion you want to copy.

4. Click End Selection.

5. Select Edit, Copy Object to copy that portion of the video to the Clipboard.

6. Open the document and paste the video clip by choosing Edit, Paste.

If you want to deselect a selection, select Edit, Selection from Media Player's menu, select None, and click OK.

Video Options in Video for Windows

You can change many aspects of how Media Player plays a video. For example, you can have Media Player use time or frames to display its progress by choosing Scale, Time or Scale, Frames respectively.

To choose whether Media Player plays a video full screen or in a window, choose Device, Properties. Then select Window or Full Screen in the Video Properties sheet.

Use the following instructions to set additional options for Media Player.

1. Choose Edit, Options from the Media Player menu.

2. Select Auto Rewind if you want the video clip to automatically rewind after it has finished playing.

3. Select Auto Repeat if you want the video clip to play repeatedly.

4. Select Control Bar On Playback if you want the Media Player controls to be available while a video clip is playing inside another document.

5. Select Border Around Object if you want a border around the video while it is playing.

6. Select Play In Client Document if you want the video to play in the document instead of as a separate window.

7. Select Dither Picture To VGA Colors if the color of your video looks distorted.

Gaming in Windows

All the exciting multimedia PC games, such as DOOM, have typically been targeted at DOS. The reason is performance. Multimedia games are graphically intensive. However, these games are now feasible in Windows 95.

High-quality games for Windows are sprouting up everywhere. A three-dimensional Pinball game is included in the Microsoft Plus! Pack for Windows 95 (see fig. 34.11). Other games you can purchase separately include The Incredible Machine by Sierra, Lode Runner by Sierra, and DOOM by id Software.

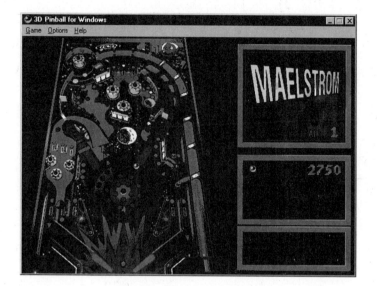

Fig. 34.11
3D Pinball for Windows (with the author getting badly beaten).

Apple's QuickTime for Windows

QuickTime is the standard codec for Apple computers. Why do you care? Because Apple has released a version of QuickTime for Windows that edges out Video 1 for performance. Also, QuickTime enables developers to include MIDI with the video and audio tracks.

Because QuickTime is available for both Windows and Apple, many game developers have used it for their video. By using a single video format for both platforms, developers can significantly reduce their multimedia development time. For example, Cyan uses QuickTime for the video in MYST.

You can expect to see a lot of games developed using QuickTime. However, QuickTime doesn't replace Windows AVI video format. For most Windows applications, AVI is still the format of choice.

Apple has made QuickTime 2.0 for Windows available for download off CompuServe. To download, GO QTIME. Select Download QuickTime 2.0 for Windows from the list and follow the instructions. It is also available on other online services, such as America Online, or directly from Apple.

QuickTime 2.0 for Windows is not a Windows 95 application. Therefore, you do not see the same type of property sheets when you right-click a QuickTime file and choose Properties as you do with AVI files.❖

Chapter 35

Desktop Video Production under Windows 95

by Roger Jennings

Desktop publishing (DTP) with Apple Macintosh computers and Windows-based PCs revolutionized the graphics arts industry in the late 1980s and early 1990s. DTP applications, such as PageMaker, QuarkXPress, and Interleaf, greatly reduced the cost of producing virtually every type of print publication.

A similar revolution is taking place today in the video postproduction industry. (Editing videotape, adding special effects, and creating animated graphics collectively are called *postproduction. Production* is the process of shooting the video with studio cameras or portable camcorders.) *Linear* postproduction systems use PCs to control multiple videotape players and recorders, and to add digital special effects, still graphics, and titles during the video editing process. *Nonlinear* editing uses PCs to digitize video and audio content; you assemble the finished production by combining digital video clips stored on large, fast fixed-disk drives. As the television industry moves toward digital video production and distribution in 1996 and beyond, nonlinear digital editing with PCs will dominate the video postproduction business.

Desktop video (DTV) has come of age with the release of Windows 95. DTV hardware and software running under Windows 95 ranges from modest 16-bit home video editing software to 32-bit nonlinear digital video editing applications used for professional video production. Virtually all of the new high-end video editing systems announced in 1995 are 32-bit applications that run only on Windows 95 or Windows NT 3.51+. These new professional-level products, ranging in cost from $5,000 to more than $20,000, are a bit pricey for most Windows 95 users.

Thus, one of the objectives of this chapter is to demonstrate the compatibility of today's low- to moderate-cost 16-bit Windows video editing applications with Windows 95. Windows 95 includes new Media Control Interface (MCI) device drivers for Sony ViSCA (Video System Control Architecture) VCRs and laserdisc players that weren't included with Windows 3.1+. Windows 95 has new features to aid the digital video capture process. This chapter covers the following topics:

- Editing home movies with Video Director 2.0

- Setting up and using Windows 95's new ViSCA and Laserdisc MCI drivers

- Using ViSCA devices for A-B roll editing with Video Magician 1.1

- Capturing digital video under Windows 95 with the Intel Smart Video Recorder Pro

- Nonlinear digital video editing with Adobe Premiere 4.0

Migrating Desktop Video Production to Windows 95

The coming transition from conventional analog to fully digital video production, postproduction, and distribution ensures DTV a major role in cable, satellite, and broadcast TV programming. Windows 95 has an important role in both analog and digital DTV postproduction for the following reasons:

- Traditional postproduction operations require a collection of dedicated video equipment, which typically costs at least $250,000. Windows-based DTV systems reduce this cost by a factor of 10 or more, finally making professional-quality video production affordable to small firms and families.

- DTV needs 32-bit applications with preemptive multitasking and multithreaded execution to provide precise timing of the heavy-duty computations and high-speed disk access required to process digital video and audio.

- Windows 95's Display Control Interface (DCI) makes full-screen, full-motion (30 frames per second) digital video a reality (with the assistance of a DCI-compliant video accelerator card).

- Plug and Play takes the mystery out of installing new DTV adapter cards.

- The new 32-bit CD-ROM file system (CDFS) and 32-bit Video for Windows codecs (*co*mpressor/*dec*ompressors) greatly improve delivery of video and audio from AVI (Audio-Video Interleaved) files on CD-ROMs.

Windows 95 is where the action's at in DTV.

Editing Your Home Videos with VideoDirector

Industry experts estimate that about 75 million North American households own one or more VCRs and that about a third of these households have a camcorder. Most owners use their camcorders infrequently, but several market research studies indicate that between 10 and 15 percent of camcorder owners include amateur video making among their hobbies and also own a home PC. Most home video enthusiasts use traditional linear editing techniques, which presently dominate the video postproduction business, because linear editing lets you use your existing video gear—usually a camcorder and a VCR. Several firms supply dedicated devices, called *edit controllers*, for consumer-level video editing that range in price from about $200 to $500 or more. The combination of a home PC and specialized video editing software is an effective alternative to a dedicated edit controller and provides many useful features that aren't available from low-end dedicated edit controllers.

The sections that follow describe the linear editing process and the use of the most popular PC-based editing software for home video postproduction, Gold Disk, Inc.'s VideoDirector 2.0.

Linear Editing, Control Protocols, and Timecode

Linear editing involves copying selected segments of the video and audio content of one or more source (camcorder) videotapes to a second tape called the *edit master*. The objective of video editing is to add only "good" video content to the edit master, rearranging the sequence of the content to fit a "story line." Linear editing often is called *analog editing* because the audio and video signals remain in the traditional analog formats (VHS, S-VHS, 8mm, and Hi8) used by today's camcorders and VCRs, as well as by broadcast TV. PC-based analog editing systems use the PC only as a control device; no video or audio content is stored on your PC's fixed disk. (You can, however, add still graphics images, such as bitmaps and titles, plus sound stored in WAV files to the video content, if you have the required PC adapter cards.) Storing all motion video and accompanying sound on videotape distinguishes linear analog editing from nonlinear digital editing, which stores digitized video and audio content on very large (multigigabyte) fixed-disk drives.

Analog editing requires the capability to control playback from the source deck and recording to the destination deck. (*Deck* is a term that includes any type of videotape player or recorder.) Virtually all camcorders and VCRs come with infrared remote control devices, and higher-priced decks also offer wired remote control. The following list describes the most common wired remote-control protocols found on consumer camcorders and VCRs:

- *Control-S* (also called *SynchroEdit*) is a simple one-way, start-stop protocol that uses the pause feature of a camcorder or VCR to control playback and recording.

- *Control-L* (also called *LANC*) is a Sony two-way protocol that also is used by several other camcorder manufacturers. Control-L duplicates all of the capabilities of an infrared remote control, including play, record, pause, rewind, and fast-forward functions.

- *Control-M* (also called *Panasonic 5-pin*) is a protocol similar to Control-L that uses a different connector and is found only on camcorders and VCRs manufactured by Panasonic (Matsushita).

Because of Sony's success in the consumer video equipment market, Control-L has become the most popular of the control protocols for advanced consumer camcorders. Control-L has another advantage—the capability to transmit Sony's RC (Rewritable Consumer) *timecode*. Timecode which identifies each frame with the time in *Hours:Minutes:Seconds:Frames* (*HH:MM:SS:FF*) format, makes analog editing much more accurate than other methods of determining tape position, such as reading a tape counter or counting seconds from the beginning of a tape. RC timecode also includes date and time-of-day information and is accurate to within about +/- one frame. Unfortunately, Sony's few high-end consumer camcorders that offer RC timecode, such as the TR-700, record but don't play back timecode data through the Control-L cable. High-end Sony VCRs, such as the EV-S7000, record and play back RC timecode.

VideoDirector 2.0's Editing Features

Gold Disk, Inc.'s VideoDirector 2.0 is a low-cost (about $100), PC-based home video editing application designed for amateur videomakers. The following are some of the highlights of this remarkably economical analog video editing product:

■ VideoDirector 2.0 includes a "Smart Cable" that plugs into a COM port of your PC; the cable splits to provide a Control-L (LANC) connector for your camcorder and an infrared remote control (called an I-R wand) for your record VCR. (Control-L is a camcorder control protocol used by high-end Sony, Canon, and a few other brands.) Gold Disk also offers a special Smart Cable capable of controlling Panasonic VHS VCRs and camcorders that use the Control-M (five-pin) protocol.

■ VideoDirector 2.0 supports the ViSCA (Video System Control Architecture) protocol described in the "Using Sony ViSCA Devices under Windows 95" section later in this chapter. You can use a Sony CVD-1000 Vdeck as the source or record VCR or use a CI-1000 Vbox to control a Sony EV-S7000 VCR. VideoDirector also reads Sony RC timecode.

■ You can add sound effects, narration, and music from digital audio (WAV) and MIDI (MID) files with your MPC2-compliant sound card. You also can mix in music from audio CDs if your CD-ROM drive has an internal analog audio connection to your sound card's CD audio input connector.

■ If you have a video overlay card, you can capture still video clips and use thumbnail-images (called *picons*) to represent the in and out points of your source video segments. Picons are small bitmapped images of the first frame of your clip.

■ With a video output card or genlock box (NTSC video encoder), you can use VideoDirector 2.0's Title Editor utility to add still images from graphics files and create titles. You record the still images or titles as source video segments, then add the segments during the editing process.

■ Gold Disk offers *Coolclips,* an extra-cost, 8mm videotape that includes video segments for calibrating the preroll times of your source VCR and record VCRs. *Coolclips* also has about 20 minutes of animated titles and effects for home movie production.

VideoDirector 2.0 is an entry-level, cuts-only editing system designed to be easy to use. VideoDirector 2.0 runs on any PC that will run Windows 95. If you have compatible video gear, you can't beat VideoDirector's performance-to-cost ratio for editing home movies or creating simple training tapes. You can learn how to use VideoDirector 2.0 and start making trial edits in three or four hours. The sections that follow briefly describe how to set up and use VideoDirector 2.0 under Windows 95.

> **Note**
>
> In 1995, Gold Disk introduced the Video Director Suite, a home video editing product with two infrared remote control wands. Video Director Suite is designed for use with VHS-C and S-VHS-C (compact cassette) camcorders that don't have Control-L or Control-M connectors but do have infrared remote control features.

Setting Up VideoDirector 2.0 and Calibrating Your Decks

After running VideoDirector's Setup application, which adds a VideoDirector 2.0 entry to the Start menu's Programs list, you shut down your PC and make the video, audio, and Control-L connections shown in figure 35.1. This figure illustrates connections for using a camcorder, such as the Sony TR-700, as the video source, and a Panasonic AG-1970P S-VHS VCR for recording.

Fig. 35.1

Making video, audio, and control connections for assemble editing with Gold Disk's VideoDirector 2.0.

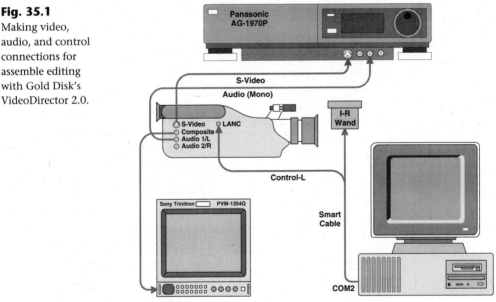

> **Note**
>
> Using as the source deck a VCR with Control-L capability, such as the Sony EV-S7000, saves wear and tear on the more delicate tape-transport mechanism of your camcorder. The EV-S7000 also reads RC timecode, which makes your editing more accurate. (The example editing process described in the following sections uses an EV-S7000 VCR as the source deck.)

> **Caution**
>
> Make sure you set the Control-L port of your camcorder or source VCR to Slave rather than Master mode. (Most camcorders default to Slave or videotape player/recorder VTR mode, but many VCRs default to Master mode.) Slave mode sets the Control-L port to receive control signals and send tape timecode data, if your VCR supports timecode. Master mode outputs control signals to camcorders and other source VCRs for editing with a built-in edit controller. If you set the source VCR set to Master mode, VideoDirector does not work.

The following steps describe the process of setting up VideoDirector 2.0 for insert editing:

1. After making your video, audio, COM port, and Control-L connections as shown in figure 35.1, position the infrared wand directly in front of your record VCR's remote control window.

2. Launch VideoDirector from the VideoDirector 2.0 entry of the Start menu.

3. In VideoDirector, choose Setup, Source Deck to open the Source Deck Setup dialog box.

4. Select LANC from the Drivers list, choose the NTSC or PAL option, and select the appropriate Options check boxes for your equipment. (The EV-S7000, used as the source deck for this example, has high-speed search, cassette eject, and timecode capability.)

5. Choose the Options button to open the LANC Options - V2.00 dialog box (see fig. 35.2).

6. Choose the Auto Configure button. VideoDirector's LANC driver then tests the control capabilities of your source deck and automatically marks the appropriate check boxes in the Transport Features frame.

7. Choose Setup, Record Deck to open the Record Deck Setup dialog box.

8. Select Infrared from the Drivers list, then choose the Options button to open the Infrared Options - V1.34 dialog box, as shown in figure 35.3. You also can select a ViSCA or Selectra (VuPort) driver if you have compatible equipment.

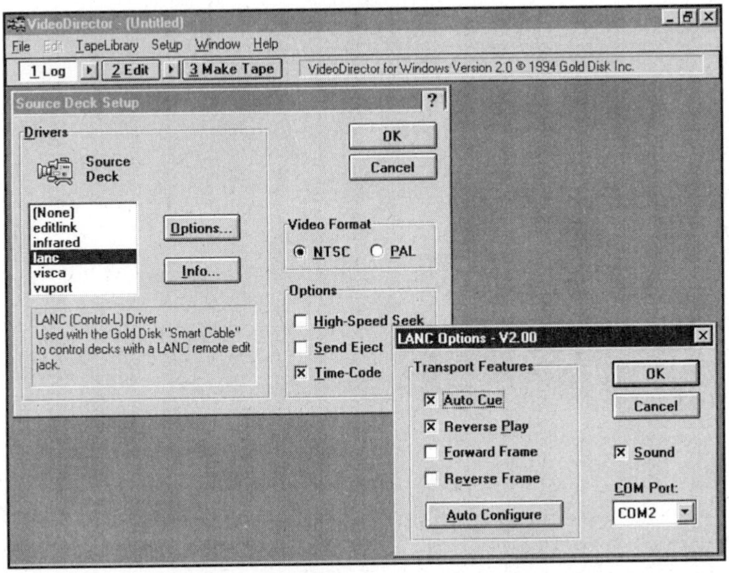

Fig. 35.2

VideoDirector 2.0's dialog boxes for setting up source deck Control-L parameters.

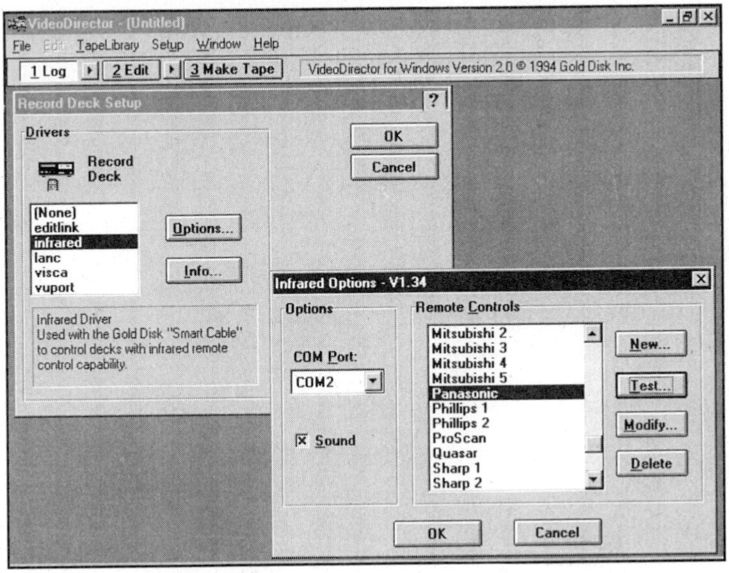

Fig. 35.3

VideoDirector 2.0's dialog boxes for setting up record deck infrared control parameters.

9. When the COM Port drop-down list appears, select the COM port to which the VideoDirector's Smart Cable is connected. Then in the Remote Controls list box, select the name of your record deck's manufacturer. (Some manufacturers use more than one remote control protocol, so you might have to experiment to find the correct selection.) Select

the Sound check box if you intend to add a sound track from your source tapes' audio content.

10. Choose the Test button to have VideoDirector check your selection, and then click OK to accept your settings and close the dialog box.

11. To achieve optimum editing accuracy, you must set record and pause delay parameters (frame-accurate decks use timecode). These settings calibrate your record deck to prevent overdubbing the end of the preceding segment or adding gaps between segments. Click the Record Delay and Pause Delay buttons of the Record Deck Setup dialog box (refer to fig. 35.3) to display the corresponding dialog boxes (see fig. 35.4). The default record delay is 45 frames and the pause delay is 0 frames. If you have a problem calibrating your decks, the Coolclips videotape calibration segments and detailed delay calibration instructions provide welcome assistance.

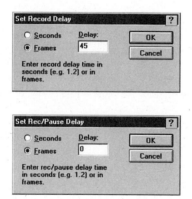

Fig. 35.4
Setting the record and pause delay parameters for the record deck.

12. If you have a video capture or video overlay card, choose Setup, Video Window to add to VideoDirector's Source Deck window a small, on-screen video display. Displaying video in a window enables you to capture picons to identify your segments.

Caution

Before using VideoDirector to log videotapes or edit, make sure that you set the record-protect tab on your source videotapes. There is a very slight chance that a computer malfunction might send a record command to your VCR or camcorder. Making sure that your source tapes are record-protected is cheap insurance against such an accident.

Note

If you have a ViSCA record deck, such as the Sony CVD-1000, or a Selectra VuPort controlling a Panasonic VCR, select the ViSCA or Selectra driver for the record deck. Using VideoDirector's Smart Cable for source deck control and ViSCA or VuPort control of the record deck requires two free COM ports and IRQs. If you're using a serial-port mouse, you probably will have to add a user-definable COM3 or COM4 port for the Smart Cable. Mouse Systems' Serial Bus Card is the simplest and least expensive way to add a COM3 or COM4 port with user-definable IRQ and I/O base address settings.

Troubleshooting

When I open VideoDirector or use the LANC Auto Configure feature, I get a message box indicating that the LANC driver isn't working.

The Control-L mode setting is the most common origin of source VCR problems. Make sure that your VCR's LANC mode is set to Slave, not Master. (Camcorders ordinarily don't offer a Control-L mode setting; most camcorders operate in Slave mode only.) With a camcorder as the source deck, make sure that the camcorder is set to VCR operating mode if the setting is available. Verify that the Control-L stereo miniplug is fully seated in its jack. You must have a tape in the source deck to use VideoDirector's Auto Configure feature.

Logging Tapes with VideoDirector 2.0

The first step in the editing process is to define the video segments that you want to use in the final edits. You use the VCR buttons of the Source Deck window, shown in figure 35.5, to position the source videotape. You can replace the standard VCR buttons with VideoDirector's Smart Buttons to provide two replay options, plus slow advance. The slider below the VCR buttons emulates the jog-shuttle control of high-end VCRs: you use the slider to position the tape to the exact in and out frames of the clip. The slider's behavior depends on your source deck's tape-positioning capabilities.

The following steps describe VideoDirector 2.0's clip-logging process:

1. Place the source tape in the source deck and click the Load Tape button of the Source Deck window to open the Select Source Tape dialog box. (The Load Tape button appears at the top of the Source Deck window prior to entering a tape name in the steps that follow.)

Tape name (Load Tape button)

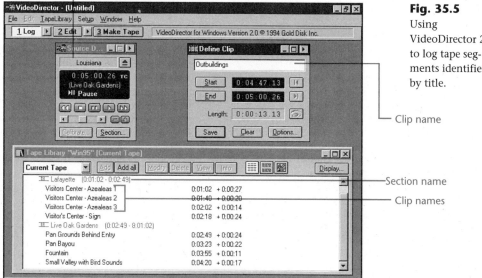

Fig. 35.5
Using
VideoDirector 2.0
to log tape seg-
ments identified
by title.

Clip name

Section name

Clip names

2. Select [NEW TAPE] in the Tapes list box to open the Create New Source Tape dialog box. Enter the name of the tape and an optional section name in the text boxes. Click the OK button of the Create New Source Tape and Select Source Tape dialog boxes to return to the Source Deck window.

3. Using the VCR buttons and the jog-shuttle slider, position the source tape to the first frame of the segment.

4. Choose the Start button of the Define Clip window to enter the in point (starting frame) in *HH:MM:SS:FF* format. The value derives from the timecode, a frame counter, or tape counter, depending on your source deck's capabilities.

5. In the Define Clip window's text box, enter a descriptive name for the clip.

6. Position the source tape to the out point (ending frame) of your clip, and then choose the End button to enter the clip's out point.

7. Choose the Save button of the Define Clip window to add the segment to the clip list in the Tape Library "Win95" [Current Tape] window (refer to fig. 35.5) and clear the entries in the Define Clip window. Video-Director then adds the segment data and picon as a new record

in its Tape Library database. The Tape Library window and database define the clip by its in point and length, rather than by the in and out points of conventional edit decision lists (EDLs).

8. Repeat steps 3 through 7 for each clip that you want to log.

VideoDirector 2.0 has an intuitive user interface and a variety of searching and editing options for the Tape Library database. The detailed 128-page *User's Guide* that accompanies VideoDirector fully describes the searching and editing options. The two-step process of defining clips enables you to proceed from the beginning to the end of the source tape. This minimizes clip search time and the wear and tear on your precious source tapes. The process also prolongs the life of your camcorder's transport mechanism.

Creating an Edit Decision List and the Edit Master Tape

After logging the tapes that you need for your production, you try a first-cut edit to determine whether your source and record decks are calibrated properly. VideoDirector's Event List is the equivalent of an edit decision list (EDL) used by professional video online-editing systems. The following steps briefly describe the process of creating an EDL and recording your video production on an edit master tape:

1. Choose the 2 Edit button at the top of VideoDirector's window to display the Tape Library window above the Event List window as shown in figure 35.6.

Fig. 35.6

Creating an edit decision list with VideoDirector 2.0.

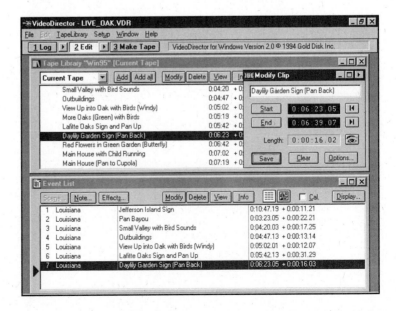

2. In the Current Tape list of the Tape Library window, select the clip to add to the Event List, drag the clip to the Event List window, and drop it in position. Alternatively, click the Add or Add All button of the Tape Library window to place selected clips at the end of the current Event List.

3. Repeat step 2 for each segment of your production. You can add clips from any tape that you log in the Tape Library. When the Event List encounters clips from another tape, VideoDirector prompts you to insert the new tape.

4. When your Event List is complete, choose File, Save to open the Save File dialog box. Assign a file name to your EDL. The default extension for VideoDirector 2.0 Event List files is VDR.

5. Insert a blank videocassette in your record deck and choose the 3 Make Tape button at the top of VideoDirector's window. The Source Deck, Record Deck, and Make Tape windows replace the Tape Library window, as shown in figure 35.7.

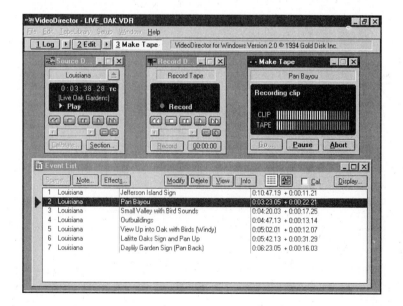

Fig. 35.7
Recording an edit master from the VideoDirector 2.0 Event List.

6. Choose the Record button in the Record Deck window to display the Make Tape dialog box and start recording a 30-second to one-minute black leader (recorded with no audio or video) on the record tape. If you use a ViSCA or VuPort device as the record deck, the Record Deck window includes VCR control for positioning the record tape.

7. As you record the leader, choose in the Make Tape dialog box the Assemble and Calibrate options that you want, then click the OK button to begin the automatic clip assemble process. The Make Tape window displays the progress of recording each clip and the edit master, as shown in figure 35.7.

Note

VideoDirector 2.0 can export edit decision lists from its Event List in the following formats: CMX 216 (CX1), 3400 (CX2), and CMX 3600 (CX3); Grass Valley Group A12V (GG1) and 41 (GG2); and EMME (EME). The equipment in professional video postproduction facilities uses these EDL formats. Thus you can use VideoDirector to define the edits (a process called *offline editing*), then take your tapes to a postproduction facility that can then produce a high-quality edit master.

Troubleshooting

The record deck doesn't go into record mode when I choose the Record button.

The most common cause of record deck control failure is improper positioning of the Smart Cable's IR wand. You should place the wand within six inches of the deck's IR remote control window and at the same level as the window. You might have to experiment to find the IR window on decks that incorporate the IR sensor in the operating display window, such as the Panasonic AG-1970P. You might also have to choose the <u>R</u>ecord button twice to place the VCR in record mode.

Adding Titles, Graphics, and Special Effects to Your VideoDirector 2.0 Productions

You can add a variety of audio, graphic, and Video Toaster special effects to your production. To do so, select an event and then choose the Event List window's Effect<u>s</u> button to display the Add Effect dialog box shown in figure 35.8. Audio effects add waveform audio, audio CD, or MIDI behind one or more segments. If you have a suitable video-output overlay encoder or a genlock card, you also can add graphic special effects, such as animation, still graphics, and titles. For Video Toaster effects, you must have a NewTek Video Toaster connected to your PC. VideoDirector 2.0 also enables you to use the Video Toaster's transition, title, and framestore capabilities.

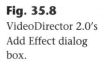

Note

NewTek, Inc.'s Video Toaster single-handedly brought about the DTV era. The original Video Toaster was an adapter card plus very advanced software (in its time) for the Commodore Amiga computer (which is no longer in production) that let videomakers create special effects, titles, and 3D animation sequences for video postproduction. The Video Toaster has the largest installed base of any linear DTV editing and special effects system. NewTek announced in mid-1995 its new Video Toaster for Windows that runs under Windows 95 and Windows NT.

Fig. 35.8
VideoDirector 2.0's
Add Effect dialog
box.

Note

To mix audio for video with sound from the source tape, plug the source camcorder or VCR's audio outputs into your sound card's line input. Connect the sound card's speaker or line output to the audio inputs of the record deck. Use Windows 95's Volume Control applet to set the levels of your Line, Wave, MIDI, and CD audio sources.

Taking Advantage of Windows 95's New MCI Drivers

Windows' Media Control Interface (MCI) is an intermediary layer that connects hardware devices (such as a sound card) and software devices (such as a video codec) to Windows applications. The purpose of the MCI layer is to make multimedia applications independent of the hardware installed on your PC. MCI defines several generic *device types*, such as *waveaudio* (waveform audio in WAV files), *digitalvideo* (video in AVI files), and *vcr* (videotape player or recorder).

◀ See "Codec Implementation in Windows 95," p. 1009

Manufacturers of adapter cards and other multimedia hardware write MCI-compliant device drivers (usually named MCI*.DRV) that specify the MCI device type and inform MCI of the device's capabilities. Figure 35.9 shows the MCI drivers that come with Windows 95, plus the Apple QuickTime for Windows and Video Blaster SE100 overlay video drivers. MCI devices are identified by the driver name preceded by the prefix [MCI] or followed by a (Media Control) suffix.

Fig. 35.9

The Advanced page of Control Panel's Multimedia Properties sheet with the Media Control Devices entry expanded.

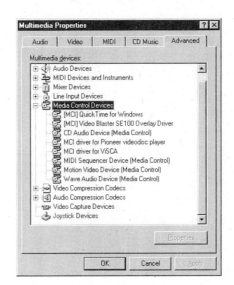

Windows 95 includes in \WIN95\SYSTEM two MCI device drivers, MCIVISCA.DRV and MCIPIONR.DRV, that Windows 3.1+ did not include. In figure 35.9, these two drivers appear as MCI driver for ViSCA and MCI driver for Pioneer videodisk player. (You can download from CompuServe's Windows Multimedia Forum, WINMM, the Windows 3.1 versions of these two drivers.) The following sections briefly describe how to set up and use these MCI drivers.

Using Sony ViSCA Devices under Windows 95

MCIVISCA.DRV is a driver for the MCI *vcr* device type that enables you to control Sony video gear that has ViSCA control connections. The following Sony products support the ViSCA control protocol:

- CVD-500 (8mm) and CVD-1000 (Hi8) Vdeck videotape player/recorders (VTRs). The term *VTR* refers to a VCR that doesn't include a built-in tuner and other features designed for off-air TV recording.

- The XV-D1000 digital video mixer and special-effects generator used for A/B roll editing, a process described in the section "Using Multi-Media Computing's Video Magician 1.1 for A/B Roll Editing" later in this chapter.

- CI-1000 Vbox, which translates ViSCA commands to Sony Control-L and Control-S protocols. You can connect a Carlson-Strand GPI-1 interface to the Control-S connector of a Vbox to generate a GPI (general-purpose interface) trigger to control video switchers, mixers, titlers, or special-effects generators. GPI is a pulse-type (on-off) signal that causes the device to execute a predetermined action or a series of actions stored in the device's memory.

> **Note**
>
> Sony's ViSCA products have gained a substantial following among amateur and professional videomakers, but you won't find the Sony products in the preceding list at consumer electronics superstores. ViSCA devices are *prosumer* (a cross between *pro*fessional and con*sumer*) video equipment. Most videomakers purchase prosumer equipment by mail order. B&H Photo-Video (New York City, 800-947-9901, 212-444-6601), for example, stocks the complete line of Sony ViSCA-compliant products.

You can connect as many as seven ViSCA devices in a daisy-chain configuration to a single serial (COM) port of your PC. You need a special cable to connect the COM port to the ViSCA IN connector of the first ViSCA device in the chain. Additional devices connect with standard ViSCA cables from ViSCA OUT to ViSCA IN connectors. Figure 35.10 shows the ViSCA connections for the video device setup used to create this chapter's examples. Each ViSCA device automatically assigns itself a device number (1 through 7) during the device initialization process. Most Windows video editing applications support the ViSCA protocol, and you can write your own Visual Basic programs to control ViSCA VCRs using the MCI custom control (MCI.VBX) or the `mciSendString()` function of Windows 95's MMSYSTEM.DLL.

Fig. 35.10

A diagram of a Sony ViSCA setup with two CVD-1000 play decks, a XV-D1000 special-effects generator, an EV-S7000 record deck, and a GPI interface.

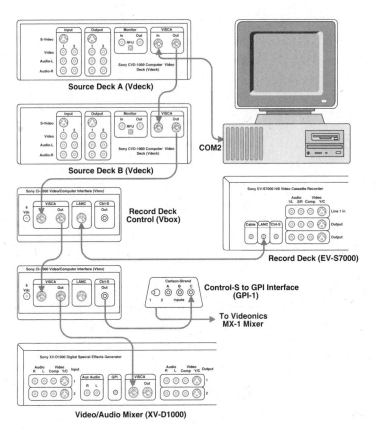

To set up the ViSCA driver, double-click the driver's entry in the Multimedia Devices list of the Advanced page of Control Panel's Multimedia Properties sheet. The Properties sheet for the ViSCA driver opens. (Alternatively, select the ViSCA driver item and choose the Properties button.) Choose the Settings button to open the MCI ViSCA Configuration dialog box. The ViSCA driver needs to know the COM port (COM1 through COM4) to which the ViSCA cable is connected and how many ViSCA devices are connected in the daisy-chain. Choose the Detect button to have the ViSCA driver automatically initialize the ViSCA chain and set the number of ViSCA devices. In figure 35.11, the Number of VCR's field indicates the detection of the five ViSCA devices shown in figure 35.10.

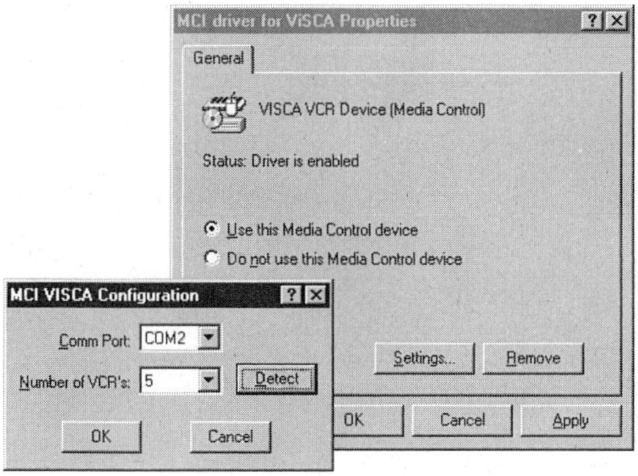

Fig. 35.11
Setting the COM port number and the number of ViSCA devices in the MCI ViSCA Configuration dialog box.

Troubleshooting

The MCI ViSCA Configuration dialog box doesn't report as many devices as in my ViSCA chain.

When you initialize the ViSCA driver, all ViSCA devices in the chain must be turned on. If any ViSCA device is unpowered, your PC terminates the daisy-chain. For example, if the Vbox for the record deck shown in figure 35.10 isn't turned on, the ViSCA driver recognizes only the two source Vdecks "upstream" of the Vbox. If all your ViSCA devices are turned on and you still don't get the correct number of devices, carefully check whether the ViSCA connectors are fully seated in the Vdeck and Vbox connectors.

Note

The version of MCIVISCA.DRV included with Windows 95 has some unfortunate characteristics. The Windows 95 ViSCA driver (developed and maintained by Sony) does not uniquely identify each device with a type, model, or number, and thus treats each device as a VCR—even if the device is a Sony XV-D1000 special-effects generator. If you have more than one ViSCA device, you need to know its device number when using most video-editing applications that support the ViSCA protocol. If you are using the ViSCA driver, opening Media Player might start all your ViSCA VTRs without warning.

Controlling Laserdisc Players

The burgeoning home theater business is breathing new life into an otherwise lackluster market for laserdisc players and videodiscs. Movies and other video content played from 12-inch videodiscs offers *much* better video and audio quality than standard VHS videocassettes offer. The videodisc is the antecedent of audio CDs and CD-ROMs, all of which technically fit in the laserdisc category. Most home theater installations include at least a rear-projection TV set, enhanced audio reproduction system, and a laserdisc player. According to market research data, most home theater enthusiasts also have home PCs. High-end laserdisc players, such as Pioneer's CLD-V2600, include a serial RS-232-C remote-control connector that enables your PC to emulate the player's infrared remote control.

> **Note**
>
> One of the most interesting uses of videodisc players is to calibrate your video equipment. Reference Recordings, Inc. (San Francisco) produces Joe Kane's *A Video Standard*, a CAV (constant angular velocity) videodisc/book combination that serves as an interactive guide to calibrating your TV set or the video and audio settings of your home theater system. Joe Kane, the founder of Imaging Science Foundation, Inc. and a columnist for several home theater periodicals, is an internationally recognized authority on projection TV systems and their calibration.

The Pioneer LaserDisc Device driver is of the MCI *videodisk* device type and has many capabilities (except recording) in common with the MCI *vcr* device. CAV videodiscs offer single-frame accuracy; you can move to any frame on a CAV disc in less than a second or so. Several firms offer recordable CAV videodisc dubbing services at about $350 for 30 minutes of high-quality video and sound. A videodisc played from a CLD-V2600 in conjunction with a digital video capture card, such as the Intel Smart Video Recorder Pro, enables you to step-capture video clips, one frame at a time, to AVI files. The advantage of step-capturing from a videodisk is that you don't need an expensive, frame-accurate VCR or a super-fast PC and fixed-disk drive to capture high-quality video images and sound tracks. Recordable videodiscs are great for archiving valuable video source material that you use repeatedly in your video productions. The laser read head doesn't touch the videodisc, eliminating the tape wear that occurs with repeated playback by VCRs.

Using Multi-Media Computing's Video Magician 1.1 for A/B Roll Editing

A/B roll editing, which enables you to use two video source (player) decks and add a variety of digital special effects during transitions from one player deck to another, is the next step above the cuts-only assemble-editing capability of

VideoDirector 2.0. Multi-Media Computing Solutions, Inc.'s (MMCS's) Video Magician is a Windows A/B roll-editing application designed exclusively for Sony ViSCA devices, as well as VCRs or camcorders with Control-L inputs. (You connect Control-L devices through the Sony Vbox's Control-L output.) Video Magician also enables you to play waveform audio files and control a CD-ROM drive (with an audio CD inserted) to add narration, sound effects, and music to your edit master tape. If you have an MCI-compatible video overlay card, such as the Orchid Videola or Creative Labs Video Blaster SE100, you can view overlay video in Video Magician's Monitor window. (Creative Labs only recently replaced the Sound Blaster FS200 overlay card with the less-expensive SE100.) When you specify the Video Monitor option, another option enables you to capture the beginning and ending frames of each clip that you define as a picon.

Figure 35.10, in the previous section "Using Sony ViSCA Devices under Windows 95," shows the ViSCA control connections that you use to test Video Magician. Figure 35.12 illustrates the video and audio connections between the two Sony CVD-1000 Vdeck source VTRs, the XV-D1000 SEG (special-effects generator), and the EV-S7000 record VCR. The configuration shown in figure 35.12 is not specific to editing with Video Magician; you can use the same setup with other ViSCA-oriented editors, such as Homrich Communication's EzV[2] editor. Video Magician includes a 25-pin serial-to-ViSCA (8-pin mini-DIN) cable, so you don't have to order the special cable for Intel-based PCs with your Vdecks or Vboxes.

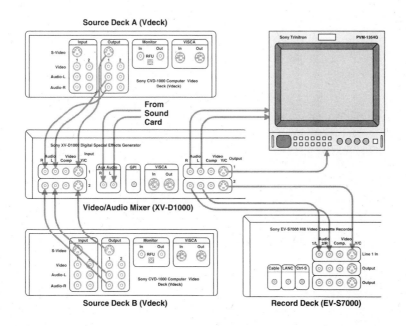

Fig. 35.12

Making video and audio connections for A/B roll editing with Sony ViSCA components.

The sections that follow describe how to set up and use Video Magician for professional-quality video A/B roll editing under Windows 95.

Setting Up Video Magician for A/B Roll Editing

MMCS makes setting up the Video Magician for a typical ViSCA A/B roll-editing suite almost automatic. You follow these steps to set the required parameters:

1. Make sure that your ViSCA cabling is properly connected and that all ViSCA devices are powered on. As was noted earlier in this chapter, any unpowered ViSCA device disables the entire ViSCA chain. The most common chain configuration is source deck A, source deck B, video mixer/special effects generator (if present), record deck, and any other auxiliary devices in the chain.

2. Run the Video Magician's Setup application. During installation, the application asks you to specify the COM port to which the ViSCA cable is connected (usually COM2). Close and relaunch Windows after Setup completes.

3. Launch Video Magician. During startup, Video Magician polls the ViSCA chain for devices and attempts to identify each device. Recognized devices are CVD-1000 or CVD-500 Vdecks, the XV-D1000 special-effects generator, or the Vbox, which is identified as a VCR. During polling, Video Magician exercises each ViSCA device. Figure 35.13 shows Video Magician's five default windows after startup.

Fig. 35.13
Video Magician's five default windows that appear on startup.

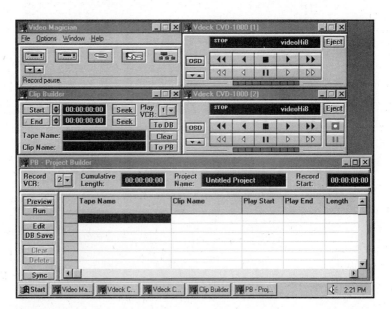

4. Click the button with the up and down arrows (below the OSD button) to expand the window of each of the two playback decks. If you're using CVD-1000 source decks, select the settings shown in figure 35.14 to start.

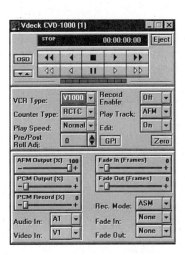

Fig. 35.14
Setting source deck parameters in one of the windows for a Sony CVD-1000 Vdeck.

5. Choose Window, VCRs, then select the submenu's number for the record VCR. The window for the record deck then opens. For the configuration shown in figure 35.10, for example, the record deck is VCR4. Figure 35.15 shows the record deck parameters for a Sony EV-S7000 VCR, which uses the Control-L protocol translated by a Vbox.

Fig. 35.15
Setting record deck parameters in the window for a Sony EV-S7000 VCR.

VII

Windows 95 Multimedia

6. If you have a Sony XV-D1000 video mixer/SEG, choose <u>W</u>indow, <u>X</u>V-D1000 to open the XV-D1000 window, which emulates the appearance of the main Control Panel of the XV-D1000. (Video Magician 1.1 does not implement the additional controls under the Digital SEG region of the window, corresponding to the lift-up panel of the XV-D1000's control unit.)

7. If you have an MCI-compatible video overlay and capture card, choose <u>O</u>ptions, Video <u>M</u>onitor. To save picons of the beginning and ending frame of each clip that you specify, choose <u>O</u>ptions, <u>T</u>humbnails.

8. Most PC users now have a sound card and a CD-ROM drive, so Video Magician enables you to add waveform audio (WAV) and audio CD material to your sound tracks. If you have these devices, choose <u>O</u>ptions, <u>C</u>ompact Disk Player, and <u>O</u>ptions, <u>D</u>igital Wave Player to open dialog boxes that let you select the track or a file to use for your soundtrack.

Like VideoDirector 2.0, Video Magician requires preroll and postroll calibration of your source and record decks to achieve maximum editing accuracy. The 120-page, spiral-bound instruction manual included with Video Magician provides step-by-step calibration instructions and includes example calibration logs for a pair of CVD-1000 Vdecks or a combination of a CVD-1000 and a Sony SLV-R5UC VCR as playback and record decks.

Editing with Video Magician 1.1

You use Video Magician's Clip Builder to define the videoclips that you want to use in the edit. The process of defining clips is similar to that described for VideoDirector 2.0 earlier in the chapter. The Clip Builder creates a succession of records in the Project Builder that comprise your production's EDL. Figure 35.16 shows how to define a segment in the Clip Builder window. (The clips defined in the Project Builder in fig. 35.16 are imported from a VideoDirector 2.0 Event List saved as a VTX file.)

You click the To PB button in the Clip Builder window to add the clip to the Project Builder. When you complete the list of clips in Project Builder, you save the project to Video Magician's database. Video Magician uses the Microsoft Access 1.1 MDB file format for the MAGICIAN.MDB database, so you can write your own Access 1.1 or Visual Basic 3.0 application to manipulate Video Magician's three database tables. Thumbnail images created with a video capture card are stored as bitmap files in a hierarchical \MAGICIAN*YEAR**MONTH**WEEK* folder structure rather than in a field of the OLE Object data type in the clips table of MAGICIAN.MDB.

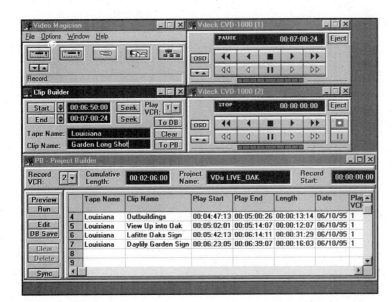

Fig. 35.16
Using Video
Magician's Clip
Builder window
to define a video
segment played
on VCR1.

Caution

Video Magician 1.1 is a Visual Basic 3.0 application that uses the Access 1.1 file
format, so you cannot save changes to the database made with Access 2.0+.
Access 2.0+ cannot save MDB files in Access 1.1 format; if you modify and save
MAGICIAN.MDB with Access 2.0+, Video Magician 1.1 can no longer read the
database.

To edit an entry in the Project Builder, you click the clip number to select the
row containing the clip data, then click the Edit button to display the Properties Editor window shown in figure 35.17. The Properties Editor includes
controls to change the value of each of the fields of the open database's clip
table. Video Magician enables you to apply a property setting to all the
records in the Project Builder; the global property feature is especially useful
when you import an edit decision list created by Homrich Communications'
EZ-V² A/B roll-editing application or VideoDirector 1.0 or 2.0.

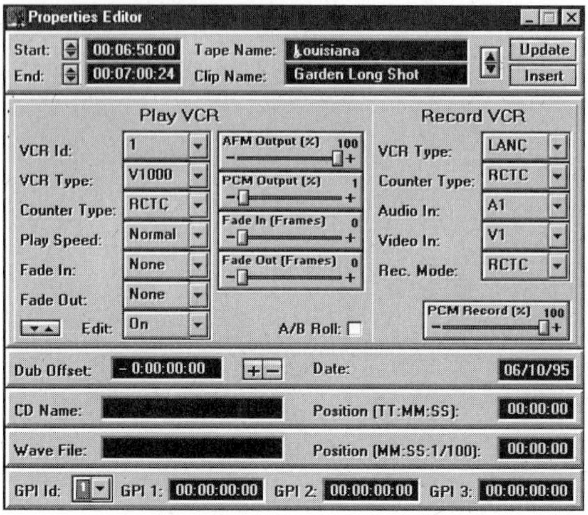

Fig. 35.17

Video Magician
1.1's Properties
Editor window
for editing clips
contained in the
Project Builder.

Unlike VideoDirector 2.0, which saves videoclip data in a database separate from the EDL, Video Magician uses a single-step EDL building process. However, you can emulate VideoDirector's two-step process with Video Magician by following these steps:

1. Create a project that consists of a sequential list of all the clips on a particular tape. (If you have VideoDirector 1.0 or 2.0, create an Event List from all the clips in the appropriate tape library, save the Event List in both VDR and VTX formats, then import the VTX file into Video Magician.)

2. Save the project, identified by the tape name or ID, to the default MAGICIAN.MDB database or to a new database with a different file name, such as *CLIENT*.MDB.

3. Repeat steps 1 and 2 for each tape required for your editing session. Make sure to identify in the Clip Builder the playback VCR ID for tapes that you plan to use for A/B roll editing. Also mark the tapes with the VCR ID.

4. After logging each of the tapes required for your editing session, open Video Magician's Database and Project Builder windows.

5. Select the project in the Database window and select Clips in the View drop-down list to display all clips in the database, as shown at the top of figure 35.18.

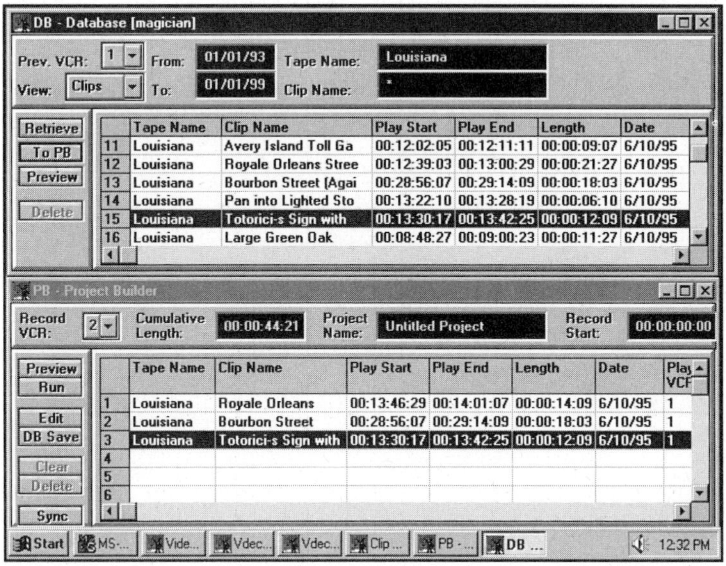

Fig. 35.18
Copying the clips for a new project from a previously saved tape log project.

6. Click the Clear button of the Project Builder window to remove all entries from the grid.

7. Select the first clip for your new project in the Database window and click the To PB button to add the clip to the Project Builder grid.

8. Repeat step 7 to add the other clips that comprise your editing project (see the bottom of fig. 35.18).

9. Use the Properties Editor to alter the properties of each clip as necessary.

10. Give your new project a name and save it in the appropriate database.

A/B Roll Editing with Video Magician 1.1

A/B roll edits involve two source decks playing simultaneously, so their EDL entries are called *roll-edit pairs*. Defining an A/B roll-edit pair with Video Magician 1.1 involves the following steps:

1. Define in the Project Builder two adjacent clips that comprise your A/B roll-edit pair. Each member of the pair must specify a different source VCR. The most common method of creating roll-edit pairs is to define a clip for the A and B elements that is slightly longer than the transition period. You get the best results when the A and B clips are the same length.

2. Define the mixer/SEG transitions for your clips and store the transitions sequentially in the mixer/SEG's memory. (Version 1.1 of Video Magician doesn't support "live" transitions with the XV-D1000; the ViSCA equivalent of a GPI signal triggers stored XV-D1000 transitions.)

3. Select the first member of the roll-edit pair. Click the Project Builder's Edit button to display the Properties Editor window, and select the A/B Roll check box. The source VCR specified in the first entry is defined as the A deck. Video Magician automatically assigns the VCR for the second clip as the B deck.

4. Set the device number for your mixer/SEG in the GPI Id drop-down list, then enter the start points of as many as three transitions in the GPI1, GPI2, and GPI3 text boxes.

5. Click the Update button to store the A/B roll-edit data in the Project Builder grid.

6. Select both members of the A/B roll-edit pair in the Project Builder grid and click the Preview button to verify that you have specified the desired transition.

7. Save the project in the database of your choice.

Creating the Edit Master

After verifying your EDL with Video Magician's Preview feature, you follow these steps to create the edit master on your record VCR:

1. If the EDL for the edit master is not in the Project Builder grid, copy the EDL from the database in which you saved the project.

2. Double-click anywhere in the Project Builder grid to remove any empty rows.

3. Insert the required tapes in the source VCRs.

4. Position the edit master tape in the record VCR.

5. Click the Project Builder window's Run button to start Video Magician's Run Engine to create the edit master. If you have as many source VCRs as tapes for the edit, the process is completely automatic; if not, the Run Engine prompts you to change tapes for the source deck specified for the clip in the EDL.

Video Magician 1.1 is a versatile assemble- and A/B roll-editing application and costs less than $400. Video Magician's imaginative use of the project and clip database and capability to import VideoDirector 1.0 and 2.0 Event List files makes the application the next logical step for videographers who upgrade from consumer-level gear to prosumer-grade ViSCA decks like the CVD-1000. Support for A/B roll editing, Control-L devices (through the Sony Vbox), and dedicated mixer/SEGs (with a Vbox and a Carlson-Strand GPI-1) makes Video Magician 1.1 an ideal editing application for videographers making the transition from dedicated edit controllers to the realm of computer-controlled linear analog editing.

Capturing Digital Video under Windows 95

Just a couple of years ago, PC-based digital video was a curiosity. Early 1/16-screen (160 × 120 pixel) "dancing postage stamps" with telephone-grade audio gave way to 1/4-screen "dancing credit cards" with high-fidelity stereo sound tracks, as Windows users migrated from 80386SX16 to 80486DX2/66 and faster PCs. Windows 95 and Pentium PCs now promise full-screen, full-motion digital video from double-speed CD-ROM drives. Even if you don't have a Pentium PC, new digital video accelerator cards such as the Diamond Viper Pro Video use video interpolation to expand 1/4-screen images to a full 640 × 480 pixels. Windows 95's 32-bit CD-ROM file system (CDFS), Display Control Interface (DCI), and 32-bit video codecs provide the power to make full-screen, full-motion video a reality on high-end home PCs.

> **Note**
>
> Software-only MPEG (Motion Picture Experts Group) decompression for White Book Video CDs is on its way to Windows 95. Microsoft announced in June 1995 a license agreement with Mediamatics, Inc. for a playback-only MPEG-1 codec that will be included "in future releases of Windows 95." Windows 95 currently supports MPEG-1 AVI files, but today you need a $200+ hardware-assisted MPEG-1 decoder card to play video CDs from your CD-ROM drive. You need a 90-MHz Pentium PC to watch 24 frames per second (fps) of full-color video and listen to 11-kHz digital audio with the Mediamatics codec. Motion pictures use 24 fps, so the frame rate is likely to be acceptable; whether 11.025-kHz digital audio will satisfy users remains to be seen.

To create digital movies, you start with a digital video capture process that converts the standard analog NTSC (PAL and SECAM in Europe) video and analog audio signals into a digital format compatible with Windows' Audio-Video Interleaved (AVI) files. A variety of digital video capture cards are available from U.S. and European suppliers, at prices starting at less than $500. The digital version of standard NTSC video that you watch on your TV set today has a data rate of about 135 Mbps (17 megabytes per second, or M/s) and today's highest-quality digital video (D-1, CCIR-601 with 4:2:2 encoding) runs at 270 Mbps (35 M/s), so compression of the video data is vital. Thus all PC digital video capture cards provide some type of built-in video compression circuitry. The sections that follow describe the PC hardware and software required to capture digital video under Windows 95.

A Brief Introduction to Digital Video Technology

Most Windows 95 users gain their introduction to digital video through 1/4-screen video clips that are included with virtually every successful CD-ROM title produced today. The image size and quality, as well as the frame rate of conventional CD-ROM video clips, is determined primarily by the maximum sustained data rate of your CD-ROM drive, which is at least 10 times slower than the data rate of today's fixed-disk drives. If you have a single-speed CD-ROM drive, you must copy most 1/4-screen video clip files to and play them from your fixed disk to view the clips without skipping frames or encountering audio breaks (stuttering). The speed of your PC also influences the playback rate because Windows 95's video codecs, such as Indeo 3.2 and Cinepak, require a substantial percentage of your PC's horsepower to decode the compressed video to the RGB data required by your PC's graphics adapter.

Capturing and playing back professional-quality digital video for nonlinear editing requires hardware assistance for both compression and decompression. The final product is a high-quality videotape rather than an AVI file on a CD-ROM. Video capture and nonlinear editing for industrial and broadcast productions involves the following basic steps:

1. Convert the analog video and audio data of selected segments of the source video tape(s) to uncompressed digital form, a process called *video decoding* or *digitizing*.

   The video-decoding process uses analog-to-digital converters (ADCs) to sample the analog video and audio signals and to create the digital data; video sampling occurs at a much faster rate than audio sampling because the video signal carries much more information (has a greater bandwidth) than the audio signal. Professional-quality ADCs sample

640 or 720 times each line of active video (480 or 486 lines for NTSC). 640 × 480 sampling is called "square pixel format," corresponding to the PC's VGA display. 720 × 486 sampling corresponds to the NTSC version of the CCIR-601 international standard for broadcast-quality digital video.

2. Compress the digital video with a compression ratio that results in a data rate your PC can handle.

   Compression must be done in real time by a very complex digital signal processing (DSP) chip, because there is no way your PC can store uncompressed video data. (It is uncommon to compress audio data; you reduce the audio data rate by reducing the sample rate.) With Motion-JPEG compression, described in the "Moving Up to Motion-JPEG Compression" section later in this chapter, a compression ratio of 4:1 or 5:1 is considered "industrial" quality that's suitable for most broadcast TV purposes.

3. Store the compressed digital video and audio clips in real time on your PC's fixed disk.

   High-quality digital video requires a sustained fixed-disk read/write data rate in the range of 3M/s to 6M/s. As a rule of thumb, it takes 1G of disk space to store n minutes of video, where n is the compression ratio. As an example, a 1G drive can hold about 5 minutes of 5:1 compressed video, which has a data rate of about 3.3M/s. These values don't include the disk space required to store the digitized sound track.

4. Edit the compressed video and audio data, adding special effects between transitions, plus titles, still graphics, sound effects, and narration.

   Depending on the type of editing system you use, the digital edit master may be an entirely new file or a combination of selected parts of original files, plus new special effects files played in sequence. (Adobe Premiere, as an example, creates a new movie file from your edited digitized clips.)

5. Decompress the video content of the file(s) in real time with the same DSP chip used to compress the data. Decompression also is called *inverse transformation* (the inverse of the compression process).

6. Decompress digital video data to the original analog video format with a digital-to-analog converter (DAC), called *video encoding*. The analog video and audio data is recorded on videotape for playback or distribution.

> **Note**
>
> The terms *video decoding* and *video encoding* commonly refer to the use of video ADCs and DACs, respectively, for uncompressed conversion. When used in conjunction with digital-only compression and decompression, encoding usually refers to compression, and decoding means decompression.

The sections that follow describe the requirements for performing the first two steps of the preceding list, decoding and compression. The "Building Digital Movies with Adobe Premiere 4.0" section later in this chapter describes the remaining four steps. Although the digital video focus of the remainder of this chapter is on CD-ROM-quality video, the techniques described are applicable to industrial- and broadcast-quality digital video productions.

Defining the Video Capture Platform

Successfully capturing and recording live digitized video and audio requires a PC with plenty of horsepower. Fortunately, the cost of Pentium PCs and fast disk drives is decreasing at such a rapid rate that today's "standard" multimedia home PC sports a 75-MHz or 90-MHz Pentium and at least a 500M fixed-disk drive. The following list provides a set of recommended specifications for a Windows 95 PC used to capture digital video:

◀ See "Understanding Plug and Play Architecture," p. 230

- *Processor, chipset, and motherboard.* A 90-MHz or faster Pentium PC is required to obtain optimum performance from low-cost video capture cards and, with a few exceptions, is essential for high-end video capture. The Intel Triton chipset provides somewhat better performance than the Neptune. The PC absolutely must have a PCI (Peripheral Component Interconnect) bus; low-end capture cards plug into ISA slots, but the future of digital video capture and processing is on the high-speed PCI bus. Plug and Play isn't critical for video capture, but almost all high-end 80486DX and Pentium motherboards produced in mid-1995 and afterward include Plug and Play in the system BIOS.

- *Cache and DRAM memory.* For video capture applications, 256K of high-speed cache RAM is adequate. Intel recommends at least 32M of DRAM, but you can get by with 16M if you use the Intel YVU9C video capture codec described in the next section. 32M of DRAM decidedly improves the performance of digital video editing applications.

- *Fixed-disk drives and controllers.* For standard video capture, fast 1G and larger SCSI-2 drives that have an average seek time of 10 milliseconds or less are normally required. However, if you're on a budget, you can get by with high-speed EIDE (Enhanced Integrated Device Electronics) drives connected to a built-in PCI-to-EIDE bridge. The Adaptec AHA-2940 currently is the "standard" PCI SCSI-2 controller card for video capture. Fast, wide SCSI-2 drives connected to an Adaptec AHA-3940W PCI multichannel SCSI controller provide as much as 20 M/s of synchronous data transfer across two drives. If you're buying a new PC, you can minimize the risk of your system's obsolescence by choosing wide SCSI. (You can connect conventional SCSI-2 devices in a wide SCSI chain with special cabling.) For heavy-duty video capture, specify audio-video (AV) drives that don't interrupt data writing with internal thermal recalibration processes.

■ *Graphics adapter card and video display unit.* A Windows DCI-compliant graphics accelerator card that provides 24-bit color at 800 × 600 pixel or greater resolution is a necessity; specify at least 2M of VRAM (special Video RAM), not DRAM. If your video capture card decimates the incoming video signal (by capturing alternate video frames) and doesn't include its own interpolated scaling circuitry, you need digital video acceleration to output digital video to tape. A 17-inch multisynchronous monitor with 0.28-mm dot pitch or smaller is the minimum specification for heavy-duty digital video editing.

■ *Audio adapter card.* Low-end video capture cards don't include audio digitizing and playback capability, so you need a sound card to handle audio-for-video chores. For reasonable sound quality and optimum Windows 95 compatibility, the Sound Blaster 16 AWE card or the recently announced Sound Blaster 32 is the low-budget choice. Professional-quality audio adapter cards, such as the Turtle Beach Tahiti, deliver full CD-quality audio and better control of audio recording levels.

Windows 95's 32-bit VFAT (virtual file allocation table) file system brings high-speed 32-bit disk access to SCSI drives and supports 32-bit file operations. (Windows 3.1+'s 32-bit disk access doesn't accommodate SCSI drives.) You can mix IDE drives connected to the built-in IDE interface with SCSI-2 drives under Windows 95 without difficulty. The optimum configuration is an IDE drive for your C (boot) drive to hold Windows 95, your applications, and SCSI-2 drives for video capture. By using an IDE drive to boot your PC, you ensure that no problem in the SCSI cabling and termination or a failed SCSI device prevents booting.

Tip

Don't use *any* type of disk data compression system for drives that store digital video data; compression slows disk writes and reads.

VII

Windows 95 Multimedia

> **Note**
>
> Some high-end digital video capture and editing systems, such as the FAST Video Machine with Digital Player/Recorder (DP/R) and Play Incorporated's Trinity system with the Preditor ™ digital video option, provide their own SCSI-2 interfaces to dedicated video disk drives. The Video Machine with DP/R (ISA) and Trinity/Preditor (PCI) both have digital audio recording and playback capability.

Capturing Digital Video for CD-ROM Titles

Tip
Make sure that you install your digital video capture and editing software *before* installing your video capture card under Windows 95.

Windows 95 includes several video codecs, the most important of which are Intel's Indeo 3.2 (IV32) and Supermatch's Cinepak (CVID). Indeo 3.2 predominates on the PC and Cinepak is the preferred codec for Apple QuickTime movies, although Indeo 3.2 is also available for the Macintosh. Both the Indeo and Cinepak codecs use *intraframe* and *interframe* compression. Intraframe compression compresses the video by removing redundancy from individual video images; interframe compression eliminates redundant data between successive compressed frames. Both of these compression methods are called *lossy* compression, because some of the detail or motion is lost during the compression process. By combining lossy intraframe and interframe compression, you can reduce the video and audio data rate for a 1/4-screen, 15-fps movie to about 240 K/s, the limit for reliable playback by double-speed CD-ROM drives. The minimum value required to achieve a semblance of full-motion video is 15 fps. Digital video producers generally consider Cinepak to be the better codec for scenes that contain fast motion, but give Indeo the nod for better overall image quality.

> **Note**
>
> CD-ROM publishers, such as Medio Multimedia, that include substantial amounts of digital video content in their titles are eagerly awaiting the Intel Indeo 4.0 video codec, which is expected to appear in late 1995. Indeo 4.0 is rumored to provide better image quality and to improve rendering of high-motion scenes, rivaling MPEG-1's compression capabilities.

Quality 1/4-screen video capture for subsequent compression with IV32 or CVID uses the Indeo Raw Video capture codec, YVU9, which requires hardware capture assistance from the original Intel Smart Video Recorder (ISVR) or the newer ISVR Pro video capture cards. YVU9 (nine bits per pixel YUV-encoded) video is compressed from the original NTSC signal, but isn't considered a lossy-compressed digital video format.

YUV is a method of determining color by specifying luminance (Y), hue (U), and saturation (V). A lossy compression codec discards video data that isn't needed to provide video of a predetermined image quality. If you use the YVU9 codec for capture, you can choose the final lossy compression codec that best suits your video material. Making this choice often requires trial and error. (If you capture in a lossy-compressed format, subsequent editing is difficult, recompression gives poor quality, and you cannot change codecs.)

The ISVR Pro, which has won several "editor's choice" awards, is the standard of comparison for digital video capture cards designed for creating videos to be distributed on CD-ROM. The ISVR Pro accepts both composite and S-video inputs and comes with Asymetrix Digital Video Producer for video capture and editing.

> **Note**
>
> Creative Labs' Video Blaster RT300 uses the same capture chipset as the ISVR Pro, but comes with its own version of IVU9. The primary advantages of the RT300 over the ISVR Pro are the slightly lower cost and the bundling of Adobe Premiere 1.1 digital video capture and editing software. For only $129, you can upgrade Premiere 1.1 to the $695 Premiere 4.0, described in the "Building Digital Movies with Adobe Premiere 4.0" section later in this chapter.

The data rate for 1/4-screen, 15-fps video capture with the YVU9 codec is about 1.2 M/s, which is within the sustained data-writing capability of Pentium 90s with high-speed SCSI-2 drives. However, most PCs in today's installed base cannot handle this data rate, which results in many dropped frames. Traditionally, Intel's response to this problem was to recommend installing 64M of RAM and then capturing to RAM rather than directly to disk. If you implement Intel's solution, however, you're limited to 60 seconds or less per clip. In Spring 1995, Intel released a "nearly lossless" version of YVU9, YVU9C, that cuts the capture data rate nearly in half. Tests of the YVU9C codec, which works with both the ISVR Pro and Video Blaster RT300 under Windows 95, show no discernible difference between most YVU9 and YVU9C images.

Tip

If you find that you're dropping frames using the YVU9C codec, try immediately repeating the capture. In most cases, you won't drop frames the second time.

> **Note**
>
> The YVU9C codec and example .AVI files captured with the ISVR Pro using the YVU9C codec are included in the YVU9C folder of the accompanying CD-ROM. The video source material for the sample file is from Reference Recording's *A Video Standard* videodisc described earlier in this chapter, and is used with the permission of the copyright holder and publisher.

95 CD

Before late 1994, almost all PC video capture cards included video capture (VidCap) and editing (VidEdit) applications from the Microsoft Video for Windows (VfW) 1.1 Developer's Kit. Today, commercial digital video editing applications, such as Adobe Premiere and Asymetrix Digital Video Producer, have built-in video capture capability based on the original VidCap design. In late 1994, Microsoft announced the termination of active support for the VfW 1.1 Developer's Kit. The "Capturing Digital Video with Premiere 4.0" section later in this chapter shows you how to use the ISVR Pro and Premiere 4.0's capture features under Windows 95.

Moving Up to Motion-JPEG Compression

The Indeo 3.2 and Cinepak codecs described in the previous section are designed primarily for creating video content for distribution on CD-ROMs. If you want to take advantage of digital editing, titling, and special-effects applications such as Adobe Premiere, and output the movie to videotape, you need a codec that can create high-quality, full-screen video images. Motion-JPEG, a variation on the Joint Photographic Experts Group's compression method for still images, is currently the preferred codec for high-end digital video capture (decoding) and playback to analog video (encoding) for recording. Motion-JPEG, which uses only intraframe lossy compression based on the discrete cosine transform (DCT), has the advantage of precise control of compression ratio and thus of image quality. Digital VTRs use 2:1 DCT compression for broadcast TV. A DCT compression of 5:1 is generally accepted as corresponding to the quality of the Betacam SP component recording format, the most widely used VTR format in the television industry.

Motion-JPEG video capture and playback cards fall into one of the following two categories:

- *Consumer/prosumer.* Relatively inexpensive ($500 to $600) Motion-JPEG adapter cards or daughterboards are limited to 16:1 or higher compression ratios and capture every other pixel of alternate video fields to create a 320 × 240 pixel image. Examples are miro Computer Products' miroVideo DC1 and FAST Multimedia's Movie Line with Motion-JPEG. Usually, the minimum compression ratio that you can achieve is limited by your PC's capture data rate, not by the card's capability. The quality of the 2:1 (line-doubled with interpolation) video output of these cards is about the same as VHS tape: about 200 horizontal lines of TV resolution. With good video gear and a fast PC and disk combination, you can achieve close to Hi8 or S-VHS quality under Windows 95. You capture the audio track with a separate sound card.

- *Industrial/broadcast.* High-end Motion-JPEG cards sample every video field to create a full 720 × 640 pixel (CCIR-601) digitized image and enable you to reduce the compression ratio to as low as 3:1, but require large, high-speed fixed-disk drives to handle the higher data rates. The practical minimum compression ratio is 5:1, but 7:1 or 8:1 is used for most digital video productions. Most suppliers of professional-quality Motion-JPEG cards provide their own 32-bit video capture and editing applications with the cards. For example, D-Vision Systems, Inc.'s OnLINE capture and editing system runs only under Windows 95 and Windows NT 3.5+. By early 1996, probably all suppliers of professional-quality Motion-JPEG capture cards will provide 32-bit versions of their bundled applications. Many high-end Motion-JPEG systems include digital audio capture and playback capabilities; a few, such as Interactive Images' Plum system, use a separate sound card.

> **Caution**
>
> The drivers for many Motion-JPEG adapter cards aren't fully compatible with Windows 95. Check Windows 95 compatibility with the manufacturer's technical service group before purchasing any Motion-JPEG card, except those designed specifically for use under Windows 95 and Windows NT 3.5+.

> **Note**
>
> The forthcoming consumer digital video cassette (DVC) recording format and professional variations on the DVC theme (Panasonic's DVCPRO format) use fixed 5:1 DCT compression. DVCPRO equipment is designed for broadcast field recording, electronic news gathering (ENG), and electronic field production (EFP).

The primary threat to the market for high-end Motion-JPEG video capture systems comes from MPEG-2, the second iteration of the MPEG compression codec. Digital MPEG-2 video compression is used for transmission of DirecTV and USSB programming (as of late 1995) to 18-inch Thomson/RCA and Sony satellite dishes connected to set-top decoder boxes. MPEG-2 is the compression standard for the forthcoming digital videodiscs (DVDs) and U.S. high-definition television broadcasting, or Advanced TV (ATV). MPEG-2 uses DCT intraframe compression, but adds sophisticated motion prediction to improve interframe compression. New, high-powered RISC (reduced instructor set computer) processors provide the capability to capture video with intraframe compression (I-frame) only, so you can edit the MPEG-2 video before applying interframe compression to reduce storage requirements. By the end of 1996 or sooner, MPEG-2 probably will be the preferred format for almost all digital video applications.

Step-Capturing with Frame-Accurate VTRs and Videodisc Players

One way to avoid the issue of high data rates altogether is to use frame-by-frame (step-frame) capture of video content. Step-frame capture requires a single-frame VTR, such as the Sony EVO-9650 Hi8 or Sanyo GVR-S955 S-VHS record deck, or a remotely controlled videodisc player, like the Pioneer CLD-V2600 described earlier in this chapter. Single-frame VTRs are used primarily for recording computer-generated animated graphics onto videotape. (You need a Sony EVBK-66 ViSCA interface board to control the EVO-9650 with most Windows digital video capture and editing applications.)

Most professional-quality videoclips for commercial CD-ROM distribution are step-frame captured. In many cases, the source video content is transferred from Betacam SP or a higher-quality component or digital video format to a recordable CAV videodisc, then step-captured with the YVU9 codec for editing and subsequent compression. Step-capturing enables you to use lower Motion-JPEG compression ratios if your fixed-disk drive has a higher sustained read than write data rate.

> **Note**
>
> You cannot step-capture the sound track of a videotape or videodisc, so the capture applications use an automatic two-step process. The applications first capture the video content (at a rate of about 1 to 2 fps) and then digitize the audio for the range of captured frames in a continuous process. The process is frame-accurate, so it maintains lip-sync.

Building Digital Movies with Adobe Premiere 4.0

Traditional video-editing suites consist of two playback VTRs, a record VTR, an edit controller, and a video switcher/special-effects generator (SEG). Computer-based A/B roll-editing systems, such as FAST Multimedia, Inc.'s Video Machine, replace the edit controller and video switcher/SEG with a PC adapter card and a Windows-based editing application. Videotape-based editing methods, whether traditional or computer-based, are referred to as *linear*, because of the need to position the source videotapes by linear movement past the playback device's read head. Linear video editing remains the prevalent methodology for industrial- and higher-quality video production, despite linear editing's dependence on highly accurate (and thus expensive) source and record VTRs, plus time-consuming tape-positioning operations. Linear editing also takes its toll on the limited-life mechanical components of VTRs because of the need for constant fast-forward and rewind operations; rebuilding VTRs with worn components is extremely expensive.

Digital video technology offers *nonlinear* editing capability, which provides nearly instantaneous random access to digitized video source material. Nonlinear editing eliminates the need for frame-accurate VTRs and minimizes wear and tear on the VTR head and drives, as well as on your valuable source videotapes. Nonlinear editing is ideal for creating short movies for distribution on CD-ROMs. You also can "print to video" to record your digital production on videotape. Even if you don't have the computer horsepower or fixed-disk space to capture Motion-JPEG video at an 8:1 or lower compression ratio, you have another option: offline editing. Capture clips at 15 fps either with Motion-JPEG with a high compression ratio or with the Indeo YVU9C codec, and then create an offline edit decision list (EDL) for later online editing. You don't need to dub your source videotapes to protect them; therefore, you don't encounter generation loss or the timecode offset problems that result from dubbing with lower-cost VCRs that don't have a separate timecode connector. Many professional video editors use offline, nonlinear editing for experimentation because random access to video segments makes trial edits quick and easy.

Adobe Premiere is an inexpensive digital video capture and nonlinear editing and special-effects application that works with most video capture cards. Premiere is available for both Intel-based PCs and Macintosh computers. The 16-bit Premiere 4.0, which works quite well under Windows 95, clearly is the leading contender in the nonlinear editing software market. Most manufacturers of digital video capture boards bundle Premiere 1.1 or Premiere 4.0 LE (Limited Edition) with their products. Premiere 4.0 is compatible with all digital video capture, video overlay, and video output/genlock cards that have drivers adhering to Microsoft's published guidelines for Video for Windows 1.1+ capture and display drivers. Premiere offers many features, including a variety of digital special effects and the capability to overlay bitmapped images and titles on live video. The following sections look briefly at the use of Premiere 4.0 under Windows 95.

Capturing Digital Video with Premiere 4.0

The demise of Microsoft's VidCap and VidEdit applications resulted in a classic video-capture problem: neither the capture card manufacturer nor the capture and editing application's publisher explains how to use the products together. Premiere's *User's Guide* refers you to the capture card documentation, and both the Intel and the Creative Labs hardware manuals suggest referring to your video-editing application's instructions. In case you lack prior VidCap experience, the following sections explain how to set up and capture digital video with the ISVR Pro and Adobe Premiere under Windows 95. Whether you use Digital Video Producer with the ISVR Pro or use Premiere 1.1/4.0 with the Video Blaster RT300, the process is similar; the menu choices and appearance of the capture window and setup dialog boxes vary, but not significantly.

Setting Up to Capture with the Intel IUV9C Codec

Before capturing video with Adobe Premiere 4.0, you must set your capture options. Follow these steps to use the Intel YVU9 or YVU9C codec to capture 320 × 240 pixel images at 15 fps:

1. Install Adobe Premiere 1.1, 4.0, or 4.0 LE under Windows 95.

2. Install the ISVR Pro in an open ISA slot of your PC, following the Intel manual's instructions.

3. Connect a source of live video to either the composite or S-video input of the ISVR Pro, then install the ISVR Pro drivers from the accompanying disk. (You need a live video input to test the video input during the diagnostics process.) Click the <u>D</u>iagnostics button to verify the choices made by the ISVR Pro's Setup program and test the functions of the card. Reboot Windows 95, open Control Panel, double-click the ISVR Pro icon, and rerun the diagnostics to double-check that the card operates properly.

4. Connect the audio output from your live video source to the line input of your sound card. (For mono recording, use the left channel.)

5. Open Windows 95's Volume Control applet and set the Line-In and Volume Control audio levels to the mid-scale position. (You might have to readjust the audio levels after making a test capture.)

6. Install the YVU9C driver from the accompanying CD-ROM if you want to take advantage of YVU9C's lower data rate. (Run Setup from the YVU9C folder of the CD-ROM and restart Windows 95.)

7. Launch Adobe Premiere. In the New Project Presets dialog box, select Presentation - 320 X 240 from the Available Presets list box. Then click OK to close the window.

8. Choose File, Capture, Movie Capture to open the Movie Capture window. If you use the default composite video input of the ISVR Pro, your live video image, updated at about 2 fps, appears in the Movie Capture window's preview area. If your video source is connected to the S-video input of the ISVR Pro, the video image is black.

9. Choose Movie Capture to display the choices for setting your video and audio capture options (see fig. 35.19). Choose the Record Video and Record Audio choices as necessary to toggle the options. The adjacent check marks indicate that Adobe Premiere will capture video and audio.

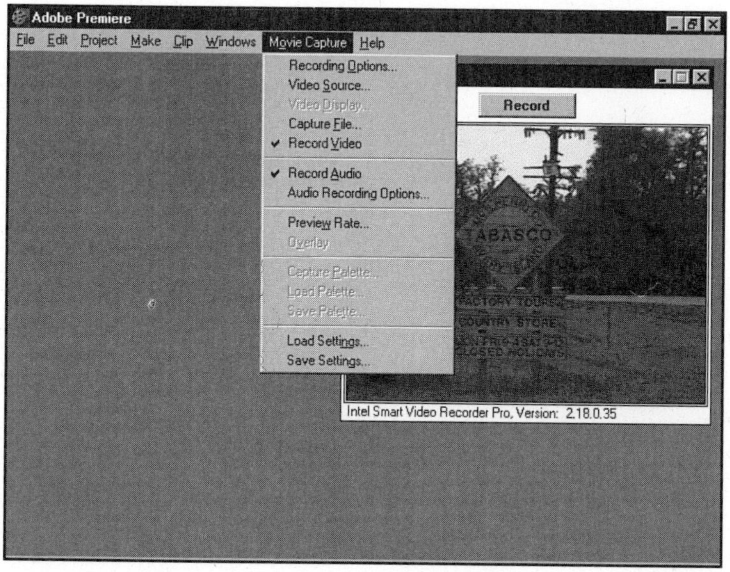

Fig. 35.19
Turning on video and audio capture in the Movie Capture menu. The adjacent check marks indicate that both video and audio capture are enabled.

10. If your live video source is connected to the S-video input, choose Movie Capture, Video Source to open the Video Source dialog box (see fig. 35.20). Select the S-Video (Y/C) option, then choose the Save button to set S-video as the default video input and close the dialog box. Your live S-video image appears in the preview area. (You can also use the Video Source dialog box to adjust the color in your video source material.)

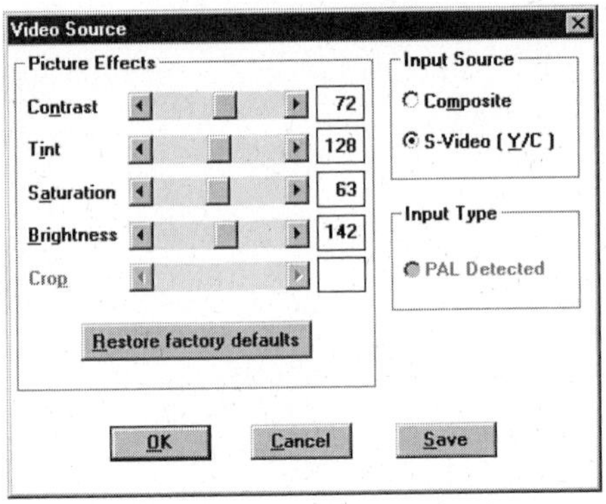

Fig. 35.20
Choosing the input
connector of the
ISVR Pro capture
card. The Video
Source dialog box
also enables you to
correct the color of
your video clips.

11. Choose Movie Capture, Recording Options to open the Recording Options dialog box. The defaults—a capture rate of 15 fps and the reporting of dropped frames—are satisfactory for initial capture tests. (If you use the YVU9 codec, select the Capture Directly to Memory check box unless you have a fast fixed-disk drive.)

12. Click the Video Format button to open the Video Format dialog box. Select the video capture codec (YVU9C if you installed the "nearly lossless" codec) from the Video Compression Method drop-down list (see fig. 35.21). Select 320 X 240 from the Size drop-down list (if necessary), choose the Save as Default button, then choose OK to close the Video Format dialog box.

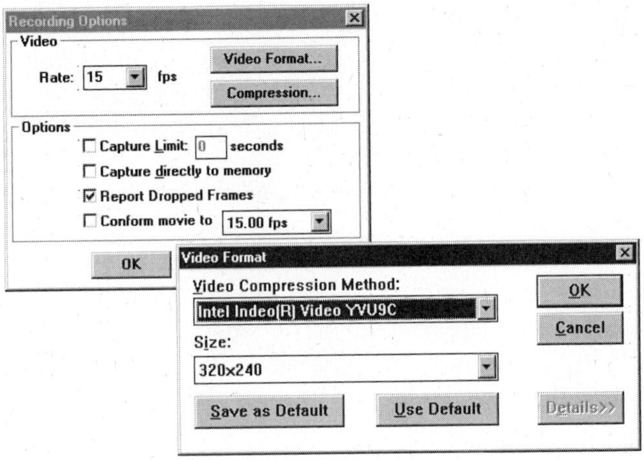

Fig. 35.21
Selecting the video
capture codec and
the image size.

13. Click the Compression button of the Recording Options dialog box to open the Video Compression dialog box. Verify that No Recompression appears in the Compressor drop-down list (see fig. 35.22). As noted earlier in this chapter, you should capture video clips that you want to edit later in YUV9 or YUV9C uncompressed format. Click OK to close the dialog box.

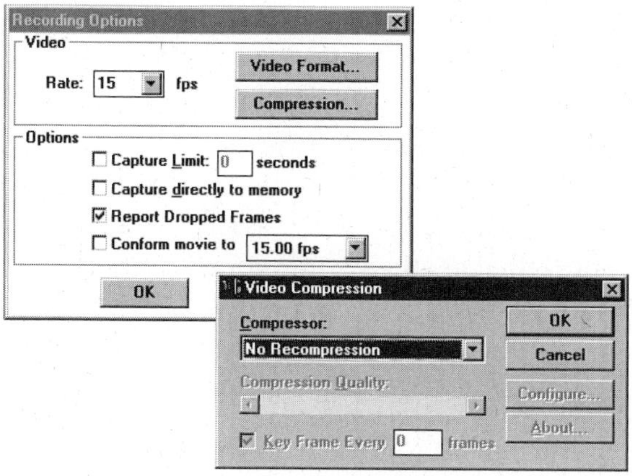

Fig. 35.22
Verifying the use of uncompressed video during the capture process.

14. Choose Movie Capture, Audio Recording Options to open the Audio Options dialog box. Select the audio capture format from the drop-down Format and Rate lists (see fig. 35.23). A format of 22-kHz, 16-bit mono is adequate for most video clips. Click OK to close the dialog box.

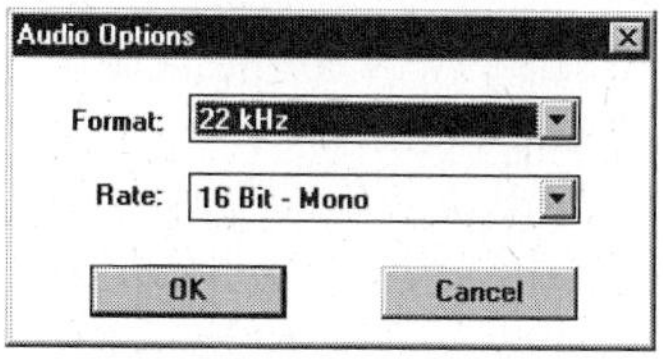

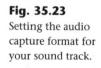

Fig. 35.23
Setting the audio capture format for your sound track.

Note

Motion-JPEG video capture and playback cards use the same capture methodology as the ISVR Pro. The primary differences are in the frame rate, which is 30 fps rather than 15 fps, and the image size settings; high-end (60 fields per second) Motion-JPEG cards capture full 640 (or 720) × 480 pixel images.

Troubleshooting

Windows 95 locks up when I run the ISVR Pro's diagnostics function so that I have to reboot.

The interrupt setting for the ISVR Pro conflicts with another card's interrupt or an interrupt used by a device built in to the motherboard. Choose another interrupt and retry the diagnostics function. (A conflict in an I/O base address results in failure to pass most diagnostic tests, but doesn't lock up Windows 95.)

Using Machine Control for Video Capture

Adobe Premiere 4.0 provides built-in support for several third-party VTR machine control systems, including Arti, VLAN, and MCI VCR (for Sony ViSCA and other MCI drivers that use the MCI *vcr* device type). If you have a VTR that supports timecode, Premiere's device control feature enables you to use timecode to set the in (start) and out (stop) points to capture a series of individual clips. Capturing a separate, trimmed clip for each segment of your movie saves disk space and makes subsequent editing easier.

To use Windows 95's new ViSCA driver with Adobe Premiere, follow these steps:

Tip
Add a couple of seconds to the beginning and end of each clip to provide for transitions, unless you plan to use cuts-only editing.

1. Choose File, Preferences, Device Control to open the Device Control Preferences dialog box.

2. Select MCI VCR from the Device drop-down list, then click the Device Options button to open the ViSCA Device Options dialog box (see fig. 35.24). Premiere polls the ViSCA connection to determine the number and type of devices in the chain. (Premiere 4.0 recognizes the Sony CVD-1000 Vdeck and Sony CI-1000 Vbox as ViSCA devices. The XV-D1000 SEG appears as a CVD-1000.)

3. If you have more than one ViSCA device in the chain, select the source video device for capture from the ViSCA Device drop-down list, and then click the OK button to close the ViSCA Device Options dialog box.

4. Click the OK button of the Device Control Preferences dialog box, and then close the Movie Capture window to return to Premiere's main window.

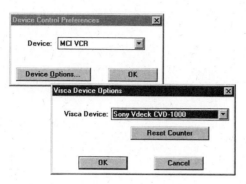

Fig. 35.24
Selecting the ViSCA device to serve as the video and audio source for capture.

Troubleshooting

The ViSCA devices don't appear in the ViSCA Device list in the order of their location in my ViSCA daisy-chain, so I can't tell which device to select for capture.

This is a known problem with the ViSCA driver included with Windows 95, not with the ViSCA device control protocol itself. (The same problem occurs under Windows 3.1+.) The simplest work-around is to connect only the source Vdeck or the Vbox controlling the source deck with the ViSCA serial cable. Click the Reset Counter button in the ViSCA Device Options dialog box to repoll the ViSCA connection so that only one device appears in the ViSCA Device list.

Like Adobe Photoshop, Premiere 4.0 is extensible through the use of Adobe and third-party *addins*. Addins are special Windows applications, stored in the \PREMIERE\ADDINS folder, that take advantage of documented "hooks" into Adobe software. When you launch Premiere, all the addins in the folder automatically are attached to Premiere. Abbate Video, Inc. (Millis, MA) publishes the Video Toolkit (VTK) addin for both the Windows and Macintosh versions of Premiere 4.0. VTK consists of a set of drivers for a remarkable variety of professional (RS-422-A), industrial (RS-232-C), and prosumer (ViSCA, LANC, and Panasonic five-pin) device control protocols. Abbate supplies the appropriate PC serial cable with the VTK for your choice of protocol. (You can order additional cables to support more than one protocol.) Figure 35.25 shows the VTK Setup dialog box for the VTK PlugIn device, displaying in the VCR Family list box just a few of the device control protocols that the VTK addin supports.

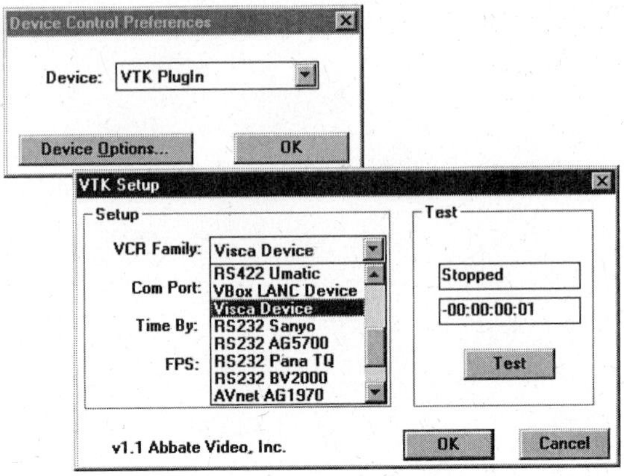

Fig. 35.25

Selecting a device
control protocol
with Abbate
Video's Video
Toolkit (VTK)
Setup dialog box.

In mid-1995, Abbate Video introduced its new AV/net video device control
network. AV/net consists of a connector that plugs into a serial port of your
PC and has an RJ-11 (modular telephone) jack at the back. Individual AV/net
devices are small, plastic boxes with RJ-11 input and output jacks and a cable
that connects to RS-422-A, RS-232-C, Control-L (LANC), Control-M
(Panasonic five-pin), and other popular device control interfaces. Abbate even
offers an AV/net device with an infrared wand for controlling consumer electronic devices, including low-end VCRs. You interconnect the AV/net boxes
with conventional modular telephone cables in a daisy-chain similar to the
ViSCA approach. AV/net components are inexpensive and support virtually
any collection of VTRs from a single serial port.

Capturing a Test Video Clip

After specifying your capture options and setting up your machine control
device, you're ready to capture live video and audio-for-video directly to disk.
The following steps describe how to record a video clip with timecode-based
machine control:

1. Open the Movie Capture window, which now has expanded to provide
   additional control objects, as shown in figure 35.26. (Compare fig.
   35.26 with the Movie Capture window shown in fig. 35.19.)

2. Click the Reel button to enter in an input box the name of the source
   videotape. Then click OK to continue.

3. Select the Auto Record check box to use machine control and timecode
   to automate the capture process.

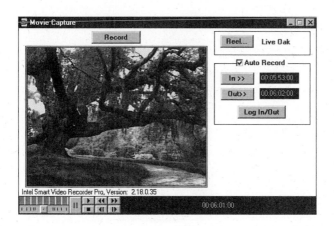

Fig. 35.26
Setting In and Out points to capture a video clip in Premiere 4.0's Auto Record mode.

4. If you know the clip's exact in and out points, you can click the In and Out buttons and then enter the timecode values in the In and Out text boxes using the format *HH:MM:SS:FF*. Otherwise, use the VCR controls at the bottom of the Movie Capture window to position the tape at the In point. Click the In button to transfer the start timecode to the text box, then position the tape to the Out point and click the Out button.

5. Click the Record button to start the Auto Record capture process to a temporary file named TEMP#.AVI, where # is a sequential integer that Premiere automatically assigns. When the capture process completes, a message box appears to indicate the number of frames, if any, dropped during capture. Click OK to close the message box and display the first frame of the clip in the Clip window, as shown in figure 35.27.

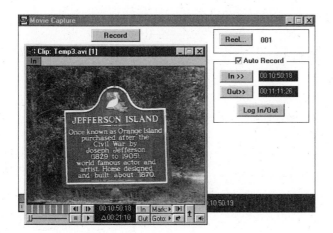

Fig. 35.27
Viewing the captured video file in Premiere's Clip window.

6. Use the VCR controls at the bottom of the Clip window to audition your clip. The sound track plays through the Speaker Out or Line Out of your sound card. Verify that the audio level is correct during playback; if not, use the Volume Control applet to alter the level as necessary.

7. Close the Clip window to open the File Save dialog box. If your clip is what you want and you didn't drop more than one percent of the frames during capture or have problems with the audio level, save your clip with a conventional DOS file name and an AVI extension. Otherwise, don't save the file but instead repeat steps 5 and 6. Recapturing the same clip usually eliminates the dropped frames.

8. Repeat steps 4 through 6 for each clip that makes up your movie.

Troubleshooting

No matter how many times I retry capturing a clip, I get a message indicating more than five percent of the frames were dropped.

Make sure that the disk volume in which your Windows swap file and in which Premiere TEMP#.AVI files are located is not compressed. The most common cause of dropped frames on uncompressed disk volumes is disk fragmentation. Use Windows 95's disk defragmenter regularly to ensure optimum disk-write performance. If defragmentation doesn't solve your dropped-frame problem and you have a network adapter card installed, temporarily remove all network drivers.

Assembling Your Videoclips on the Timeline

Nonlinear editing applications use a timeline rather than an edit decision list to specify the in and out points of each clip used in the movie. Picons identify each clip and its duration on the timeline, with longer clips represented by picons taken from beginning, intermediate, and ending frames. You can expand the timeline's time scale to make your edits more precise or contract the time scale to see an overall view of your movie. To provide A/B roll-editing capability with digital special effects at the transition between clips, Premiere provides A and B timeline tracks, separated by a transition (T) track. Premiere defines a movie by a project (PPJ) file that includes pointers (references) to each of the objects that make up the movie; the default project file is NONAME1.PPJ.

Adobe Premiere 4.0 is a full-featured application for digital video editing that offers a wide variety of editing options. A full explanation of editing with Premiere is beyond the scope of this book, so this chapter provides only a short explanation of the editing process. To assemble your clips into a movie, follow these basic steps:

1. Choose File, Import, File to open the Import File dialog box. Select one of the video clips captured for your movie, then click the OK button to add the clip to the Project window.

2. Repeat step 1 for each of the video clips that comprise your movie.

3. Drag the picon for the first video clip from the Project window to the A timeline of the Construction Window (see fig. 35.28).

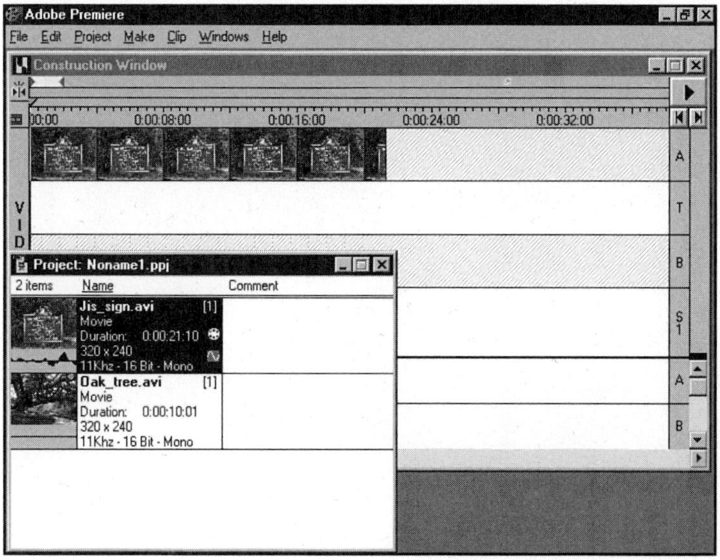

Fig. 35.28
Adding clips from the Project window to the timeline of the Construction Window.

4. Drag the picon for the second video clip from the Project window to the B timeline of the Construction Window.

5. If you want to add effects for the transition between the first and second clip, offset the in point of the second clip to the left of the out point of the first clip.

6. Repeat steps 3 through 5 for each of the clips in sequence, alternating between the A and B timelines.

7. With the focus on the Construction Window, choose Project, Preview and save your project with an appropriate DOS file name and PPJ extension. After you save the file, Premiere assembles the preview and displays your edited movie in the Preview window.

Adding Titles and Digital Special Effects

Adobe includes a title design and editing feature that takes advantage of all TrueType and Adobe Type 1 fonts installed on your PC. Figure 35.29 shows a simple title with a transparent (white) background to be superimposed on live video at the beginning of the movie. After creating the title, you save it as a file with the PTL extension and add the title file to the Project window. Drag the title to the Superimpose (S1) timeline and adjust the width of the title picon to correspond to the length of time of its appearance (see fig. 35.30).

Fig. 35.29

Creating a title with a transparent background for superimposition over live video.

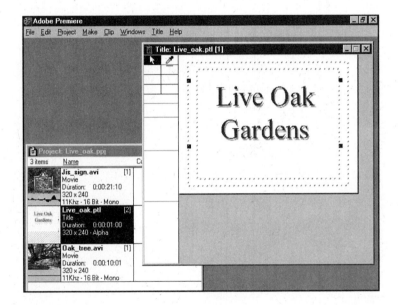

You also can add a variety of digital special effects (DSEs) for transitions between your clips that alternate on the A and B timelines of the Construction Window. You drag the icon for the effect that you want from the Transitions window to the Transitions (T) timeline, as shown in figure 35.30. You can preview the superimposed title and special effects at any time during the editing process. Premiere must compile each of the superimposed titles and special effects before creating a preview or compressing the final movie. Each time that you change any of the timeline's items, expect a substantial wait for the recompilation process to complete.

A/B cross-dissolve   A clip   Transition (special effects)

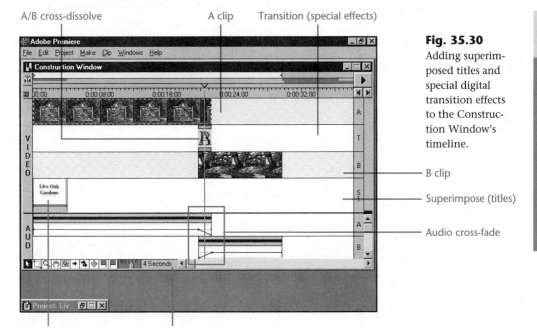

Fig. 35.30
Adding superimposed titles and special digital transition effects to the Construction Window's timeline.

B clip

Superimpose (titles)

Audio cross-fade

Superimposed title   Time-scale adjustment

Compressing Your Movie or Printing Digital Video to Tape

After you complete the nonlinear editing process, you have two options for completing your movie:

- Compression to an AVI file with a data rate suitable for distribution on CD-ROM

- Printing a full-screen image to videotape

To compress the movie for CD-ROM distribution, follow these steps:

1. Drag the right arrow of the yellow line at the top of the Construction Window to the end of your last clip or a title that defines the movie work area.

2. Select a clip in the Project window and press Ctrl+C to copy the still image to the Clipboard.

3. Choose Make, Make Movie to open the Make Movie dialog box with Premiere's default compression settings specified (see fig. 35.31). Enter the DOS file name for your compressed movie file with an AVI extension.

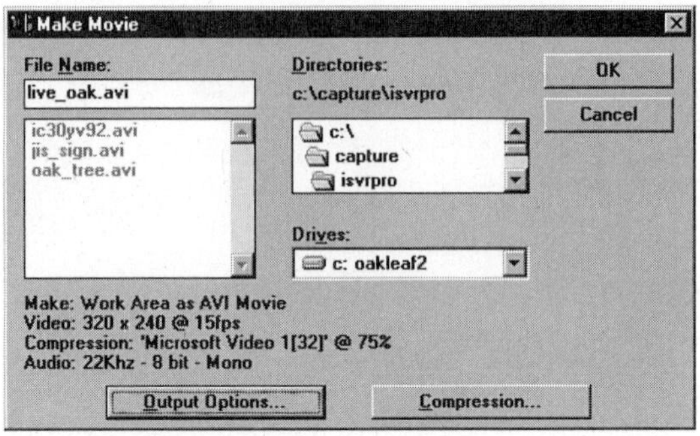

Fig. 35.31

Specifying the file name for the compressed movie.

4. Choose the Output Options button to open the Project Output Options dialog box (see fig. 35.32). In this dialog box, you define the movie's video and audio options. Accept the video options and set the audio options to the sound format that you want. Click OK to close the Project Output Options dialog box.

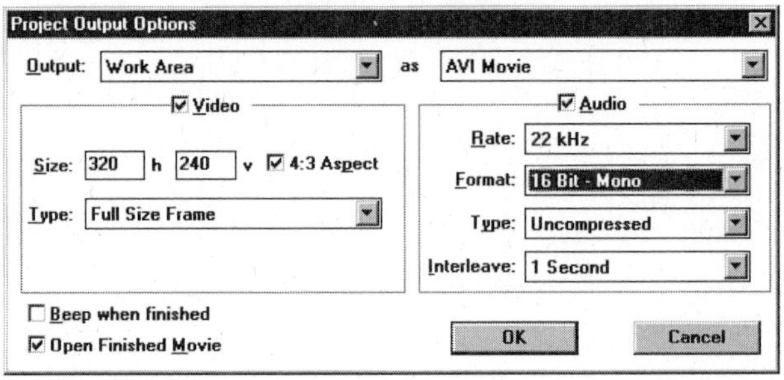

Fig. 35.32

Setting the video and audio output options.

5. Choose the Compression button in the Make Movie dialog box to open the Compression Settings dialog box (see fig. 35.33). Select the compression codec from the Method drop-down list. The video clip that you copied to the Clipboard in step 2 appears in the Sample frame; move the Quality slider to see the effect of varying quality percentages, then set the quality at the High limit.

6. Set the frame rate (usually 15 fps for CD-ROMs) and the key frame ratio. For movies with relatively low motion content, such as talking heads, a key frame every 15 frames is usually adequate. For higher motion videos, use a key frame every four to seven frames. Using fewer key frames allows a lower interframe compression ratio at a constant data rate.

7. Select the Limit Data Rate check box and enter the maximum data rate; 200K/s is a safe starting rate for double-speed CD-ROM drives. Select the

CD-ROM check box to create full 2K blocks (sectors) on the CD-ROM, a process called *data padding*.

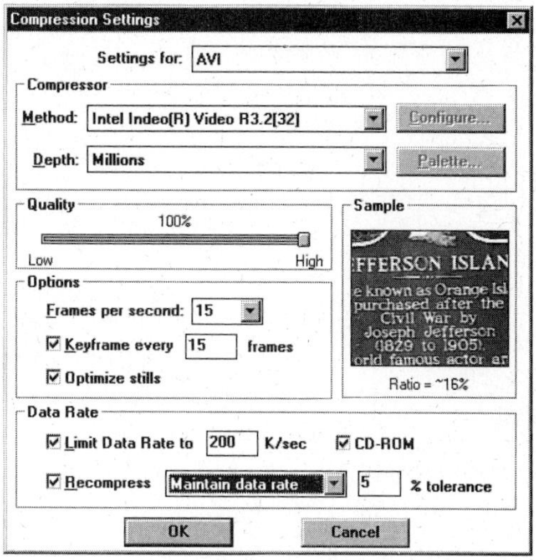

Fig. 35.33
Setting the compression options for a movie to be distributed on CD-ROM.

8. Select the Recompress check box and choose Maintain Data Rate from the drop-down list. Enter the % Tolerance value for the data rate. You can set up to 40-percent tolerance at 200 K/s, which limits the peak data rate to about 280 K/s. The rate is within the range of a double-speed CD-ROM drive's 300 K/s maximum data rate.

9. Click OK to close the Compression Settings dialog box. Click the OK button of the Make Movie dialog box to begin the compression process. Premiere estimates the time required to compress the movie, which depends primarily on the movie's length, your computer's speed, and the compression settings that you choose. A ratio of one minute of compression time for five seconds of work area is common for Pentium PCs with fast fixed-disk drives.

10. When Premiere finishes compiling your compressed movie, the resulting file opens in the Clip window automatically. Use the VCR controls to review the effect of compression on the video quality.

11. To verify that Premiere maintained the data rate and your other compression settings, open the Clip window's Control menu and choose Movie Analysis to open the Analysis dialog box. Click the Data Rate button in the Analysis dialog box to display a graph of the data rate for the entire movie (see fig. 35.34).

Fig. 35.34

A data rate graph generated by Adobe Premiere.

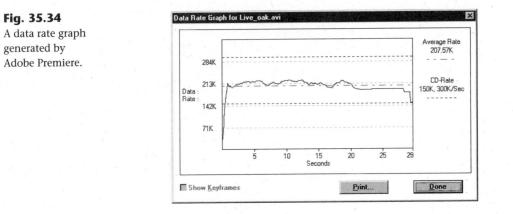

Troubleshooting

My compressed clips have "fuzzy" areas in them.

Out-of-focus image regions are called *compression artifacts*. All video compression codecs have problems dealing with image regions that contain high-frequency content (small objects in the background, such as leaves on trees). Motion also degrades images compressed at low data rates. You need very high-quality source video to create an acceptable-quality movie at CD-ROM data rates. When shooting video with a camcorder, always use a tripod and turn off both the autofocus and automatic white-balance features. If your camcorder has automatic image stabilization, turn off that feature as well.

To print a movie to videotape, you need a video output card or box (encoder) that converts the RGB (red-green-blue) signals output by your graphics adapter card to the standard NTSC (or PAL in Europe) video signal for recording. You also must connect the Speaker or Line Output of your sound card to the record deck's audio inputs. The following are the basic steps for printing a movie to videotape:

1. After final editing, compile the movie without compression (in the Compression Settings dialog box's Compressor frame, select None from the Method list).

2. With the movie in the Clip window, choose File, Export, Print to Video. The Print to Video dialog box appears.

3. Mark the Full Screen check box to expand the 1/4-screen video image to the full display area. You also can add a specified period of color bars followed by black.

4. Click the OK button and start the record deck.

Printing to video 1/4-screen images captured with the ISVR Pro or Video Blaster RT300 results in sub-VHS quality movie videotapes, but you can have a lot of fun learning the ropes of nonlinear digital video editing with a camcorder, a $400 video capture card, and Adobe Premiere 4.0. If you want to create S-VHS/Hi8 or better-quality edit master tapes, you need a high-end video capture and playback card that uses Motion-JPEG compression and, as noted earlier in this chapter, a fast PC with a large, fast fixed-disk drive.❖

Part VIII

Appendixes

Appendix A

Installing and Uninstalling Windows 95

by Dick Cravens

Everyone knows the old saying about first impressions. Setup is the first exposure you'll have to Windows 95, and it will positively affect your opinion of the newest addition to the Windows product family. Microsoft has completely rewritten Setup for Windows 95, adding significant capabilities and stability to the program. You'll be amazed at the depth of Setup's capabilities as it automatically detects and configures hardware and software that literally brought earlier versions of the program to their knees. This appendix explains the basics of installing Windows 95 for the first time. Specifically, you learn about

- Windows 95 system requirements

- Improvements in Windows 95 Setup

- How Windows 95 Setup works: four basic phases

- Using Windows 95 Setup for a typical installation

- Advanced installation techniques

- Configuring for dual-boot operation

- Removing Windows 95

Understanding Windows 95 Setup Requirements

Before you begin to install Windows 95, be sure that your system meets the minimum system requirements. To run Windows 95, you need a system that includes the following:

- A 80386 or later processor (25 MHz or faster) minimum (use at least a 486/33 for serious multitasking)

- A Microsoft- or Logitech-compatible mouse (if you have another type of mouse, be sure to have the drivers for it handy when you begin installation)

- A high-density (1.44M) 3.5-inch floppy drive or CD-ROM drive

- 4M of RAM (8M recommended, 16M preferred)

- VGA graphics video display (Super VGA recommended)

- Microsoft Windows 3.0 or later (including Windows for Workgroups) if you're installing the upgrade version of Windows 95 (the full, non-upgrade version of Windows 95 doesn't require a previous installation of Windows)

- 417K free conventional memory

- 25M to 40M of free hard drive storage space (depending upon your upgrade path and installation options) partitioned with the FAT file system

- Up to 14M of additional free hard drive storage space for the Windows 95 swap file (depending upon the amount of RAM installed on your system)

Windows 95 comes in two versions. The first is an upgrade-only product, which means you must have a previous version of MS-DOS or Windows to install Windows 95. Because Windows 3.x requires MS-DOS, most users will have both. This version is available on CD-ROM and floppy disks.

The other version is a full Windows 95 setup. This doesn't require a previous version of Windows. This is designed mostly for new computers. Most existing PCs that are capable of running Windows 95 have Windows 3.1 installed so they can use the upgrade version of 95. The upgrade version costs about half of what the full version does.

While Windows 95 will certainly install on a 386 computer with 4M of RAM, you won't be able to do a lot with it. To experience the full performance potential of the new Windows, you really need at least 8M of memory. Processor speed is certainly important, but if you have an older 386 system, you may be better off adding additional RAM, or upgrading to a faster hard drive or video system before you splurge on a 486 or Pentium. Processors are usually bottlenecked by one or more of these subsystems. Lack of RAM causes Windows to swap portions of its own code, but mostly application code, to the hard drive. Quick drive access is thus critical to Windows performance, but the fastest hard drive will appear slow if your display takes seconds to paint.

On the other hand, if you're looking at adding significant amounts of memory, plus replacing *both* your drive and video subsystems, it may pay to check out a complete new computer, with the faster CPU. Check with your hardware vendor and review your options.

Note

Windows 95 works with the major drive compression utilities on the market:

- Microsoft DriveSpace and DoubleSpace

- Stacker versions 3.x and 4.x

- Addstor SuperStor

Other compression software may work fine, but it's best to check with the vendor to confirm this prior to installation.

Also, be aware that disk compression may affect the estimate of free drive space available for installation. If you're using compression, be cautious about trusting space estimates. Compression yield depends upon many factors, including data types, so allow extra space if you're installing on a compressed drive.

Improvements in Windows Setup

Microsoft has worked hard to strengthen the Setup program for Windows 95. Among the major improvements:

- New modular architecture for greater customization and flexibility

- Vastly improved hardware detection and configuration accuracy

- Smart recovery modes for problem installations

VIII

Appendixes

- Automatic verification of installed components, with correction and replacement of corrupted files or components

- Completely graphical-based installation

- Support for automated installation

- Integrated network installation

Windows 95 is a complete operating system for your PC. As such, it is responsible for installing and integrating the disk operating system, the graphical user interface, and all network support. In addition, it provides support for an incredible number of peripheral devices including monitors, video systems, sound cards, scanners, removable drive media, and modems. While Windows 95 Setup is not perfect, you will be impressed by the simplicity and thoroughness of the new installation approach, the burdens it lifts from the average user, and the backwards-compatibility it provides for older peripheral systems and legacy applications.

Preparing for Windows 95 Setup

While Windows 95 Setup does an amazing job configuring most systems, there are some useful tips and tricks for preparing your machine for installation that will save you time and trouble. Before you begin your installation, be sure to do the following:

- Confirm your system meets the minimum Windows 95 hardware and software requirements

- Confirm the boot drive sequence for your system

- Confirm that you have a working boot floppy disk for your current operating system configuration

- Back up your critical data and system configuration files (a complete system backup is preferred)

- Confirm that your current Windows installation is in the best possible working order

- Defragment your hard drive(s)

- Know the location of all required drivers for any peripherals (including network interface cards)

- Know all user names and passwords you'll need to log in to your network

While this list may seem to suggest a lack of confidence in the Windows 95 Setup program, don't be cynical. You should follow most of these procedures for any major change in your computing system. Anything less is simply flirting with the computing demons well-known to the experienced PC user.

> **Note**
>
> While it's usually wise to make backup copies of the installation disks for a new program before you begin, you can forget about it with Windows 95. Microsoft uses a proprietary disk format for Windows 95 floppies that neither MS-DOS nor Windows 3.x can duplicate. Take care of your original disks!

The first item in this list is obvious. Less clear is the need to have a confirmed boot backup plan for your system. This comes in two parts: having a boot floppy disk and configuring your system to use it. A good boot disk is not just a bootable floppy but one that configures your system as closely as possible to the current boot session configurations you normally use via your hard drive. It's worth the time it takes to create this "boot backup." The few minutes to do this can save you hours of hair-pulling later.

A great boot disk is worthless if your system can't read it. Most systems are configured to search the drives during startup to find a bootable disk, but some are configured to look only at a specific drive, to save time at startup, or for security reasons. If in doubt about your system, *test it*. If you create a boot disk and the system won't read it from a cold start, check the system CMOS settings and correct the boot sequence (see your computer's manual regarding access to the CMOS setup). The ideal is for the system to search drive A and then continue to the next floppy (if present) before looking for startup information on drive C. While you can configure a system for a reverse of this order (C, then A), some systems will fail by looking at C and then staring off into digital space. Check yours to make sure it's set to search A first, before you learn the hard way.

While having a system backup is obvious to experienced users, the new and the brave may blithely go forth without such safety nets. Don't be computing roadkill. If you don't have a backup plan or system, get one before you invest hours of valuable time configuring your system, and before you lose hours of work due to a power failure or drive crash. This is especially true when installing a new operating system, which involves changes to the configuration of almost every component of your computer, including the storage media systems. Much effort has gone into making today's operating systems and hardware as reliable as is affordably possible, but *nothing* can prevent *all* accidents. (Do you have children, pets, or coworkers? Elbows, coffee cups, sleepy fingers?)

VIII

Appendixes

Don't expect miracles from the Setup program. If you slapped a sound card in your machine four months ago and never bothered to configure it correctly, how can you expect Windows 95 to do so? If your Windows 3.1x system is working, Windows 95 can use those previous settings to confirm your peripheral configurations. If those settings are incorrect, Windows 95 has no real choice but to try them and fail. Even if your current installation and peripherals are working perfectly, be sure to have your device driver floppy disks handy in case Windows 95 Setup needs to refer to them during installation (especially if you're setting up a dual-boot system).

Defragmenting your hard drive prior to installation insures that Windows 95 will find enough contiguous drive space to create the swap files it needs for virtual memory support. Defragmentation also makes your system run faster (especially during file copy sessions) since the drive system doesn't have to search frantically for free drive clusters.

Backing Up Your Critical Files

A complete system backup is part of the most ideal preparation for any system change. If you don't have the facility for a full backup, then consider backing up your critical operating system data as a minimum preparation. These are the recommended files:

- CONFIG.SYS and AUTOEXEC.BAT (located in the root directory of your boot drive, usually C)

- Any files listed in CONFIG.SYS and AUTOEXEC.BAT

- Any network configuration files (include any login scripts) such as CFG, INI, or DAT files in your network driver or root directory

- Your complete DOS directory

- Any initialization (INI) files for Windows applications

- Any Program Information Files (PIF) for MS-DOS applications

- Registry data files (DAT) in your Windows directory

- Password files (PWL) in your Windows directory

Tip
You can search painlessly by using the recursion function of the MS-DOS dir command (**dir c:*.ini /s** will search your entire C drive for initialization files).

While most INI and PIF files reside in the Windows directory, some applications store them in their own directory. Be sure to search all the nooks and crannies of your system. (You can save hours of reconfiguration pain if the worst should occur.)

Or you can skip the search step and copy all the desired files using the recursion switch for the xcopy command. For example, the **xcopy c:*.pif /s a:**

command copies all PIF files on drive C to your A drive in one fell swoop, complete with a directory structure if you need to re-create it later.

If you routinely use a backup utility, you may want to simply rely upon your last backup prior to installation, or make a new one for just the file types mentioned here. Consult your backup software documentation for more information on how to accomplish this.

How Windows 95 Setup Works

Before you begin to install Windows 95, it's probably a good idea to know what to expect and when to expect it. Windows 95 Setup has four basic phases:

- Detection
- Question and answer
- File copy
- Startup

Phase One: Setup Detection—Software, then Hardware

Windows 95 Setup starts by detecting what environment it was started from. If you opt to install from within a running Windows 3.1x installation, Setup skips a few steps and gets straight down to the business of analyzing your hardware. If you don't have Windows installed, or choose to start from the MS-DOS prompt, Setup first copies and executes a "mini-window" that runs the remainder of the Setup program and then moves on to hardware detection.

Setup checks your system for the following:

- Installed hardware devices
- Connected peripherals
- IRQs, I/O, and DMA addresses available
- IRQs, I/O, and DMA addresses in use

Don't be surprised if the hardware detection phase takes a few minutes. Windows 95 Setup uses a variety of techniques to perform this hardware query.

Most PCs respond well to this procedure, which results in the creation of a hardware tree in the Registry. Older PCs may represent a problem if the devices are not industry-standard for IRQs or I/O addresses; newer machines with Plug and Play technology report their configurations more quickly, fully, and accurately.

Phase Two: Providing Additional Information

Once Setup has the basic information regarding your hardware, it knows most of what it needs to install Windows on your system. However, there are still a few details to complete, and you also can exercise options regarding exactly which Windows components you want to install. Setup guides you through this process with a few clear dialog boxes. You'll look at these options in more detail when you install Windows later in this chapter.

Phase Three: Copy Chores

Unlike Windows 3.1, Windows 95 Setup asks most questions up front and lets you relax during the actual installation process. Once you tell it what you want, it completes the dreary chores by itself, asking only for disk changes (and if you are installing from a CD-ROM drive, you don't even have to worry about that!).

When all Windows 95 files are copied, Setup upgrades the existing version of MS-DOS on your boot drive with the Windows 95 operating system.

Phase Four: Home Stretch—System Startup

When it has replaced the MS-DOS operating system, Setup then restarts your system and finishes the final cleanup chores required for installation. When this is finished, you're ready to roll with Windows 95.

Using Windows 95 Setup

Now that you have an overview of the basic logic and operation of Windows 95 Setup and some tips for how to prepare your system, you can get down to the nitty-gritty of an actual installation.

This section begins by showing you two primary ways to install Windows 95:

- Installing from a working Windows 3.1x system

- Installing from an MS-DOS-only system (or Windows 3.0, Windows NT, and OS/2)

How do you know which way to install Windows 95? If at all possible, run Setup from within a working installation of Windows 3.1x or later (this includes all versions of Windows for Workgroups). Started this way, Setup can use your existing Windows installation for information on how best to configure your system.

If Windows is not on your computer, Setup installs a "mini-window" to run from. If you're running Windows NT, you need to return your system to MS-DOS (via NT's dual-boot option) before starting Windows 95 Setup. The same is true if you're running OS/2 or Windows 3.0.

If your computer system is completely new and has no operating system installed, or does not have at least Windows 3.0, be sure you have the non-upgrade version of Windows 95. Otherwise, you'll be up the creek, since the standard upgrade version requires a previous version of Windows, or at least earlier Windows disks, to operate.

The question of when to install a dual-boot system is inherently problematic. There are many variables involved, but you can boil it down to a simple question: Am I truly prepared to kiss my current Windows installation good-bye? If you're installing Windows 95 for the first time, you may want to keep your previous installation intact until you've proven Windows 95 is compatible with all of your applications and peripherals. If you do opt for the "dual-Windows" approach, be prepared for some serious impact on your disk space reserves, and be prepared to mentally juggle when you switch from version to version. No matter which approach you choose, *make a backup before you begin.*

▶ See "Setting Up a Dual-Boot System," p. 1105

VIII

Appendixes

Installing Windows 95 from Windows 3.x

You can run Windows 95 Setup from any installation of Windows 3.1 or later. If you don't have at least version 3.1, then skip to the section covering MS-DOS installations, later in this chapter.

▶ See "Installing Windows 95 from MS-DOS," p. 1097

Starting Windows 95 Setup is just like running any other Windows Setup program. If you haven't already, start your current version of Windows. Once it's running, you have a couple of choices of how to start Setup—from the Program Manager or File Manager.

Before you go further, make sure you have the installation disk set or CD-ROM in the appropriate drive. These examples assume you are using floppies in drive A. If you have a CD-ROM drive, simply substitute the appropriate drive letter for A.

Starting Setup from Program Manager

To start Setup from Program Manager, choose File, Run from the main Program Manager menu. Windows displays the Run dialog box (see fig. A.1). Type **a:\setup** and click OK to begin the installation process.

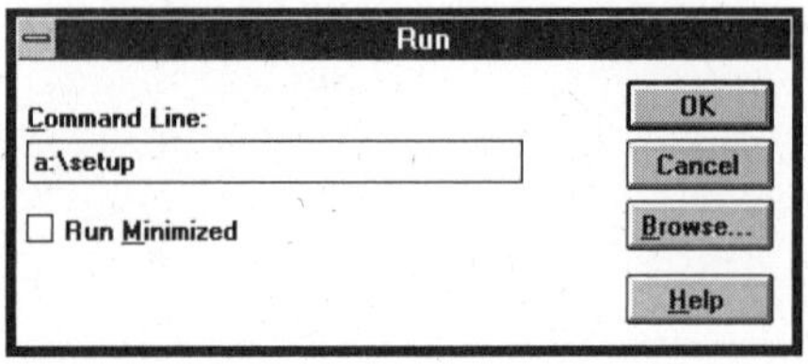

Fig. A.1
Specify the
appropriate drive
letter, followed
by **setup**.

If you're not sure what drive your Windows 95 Setup disk is in, don't despair.
You can choose Browse to find it. Windows displays the Browse dialog box to
help you (see fig. A.2).

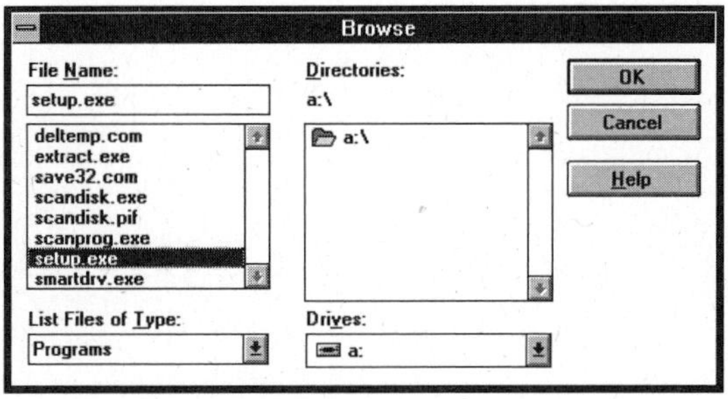

Fig. A.2
You can search for
the Setup disk
using the Browse
dialog box tools.

When you select SETUP.EXE, Windows loads and runs the Windows 95 Setup
program. After a few seconds, Setup displays the welcome screen shown in
figure A.3.

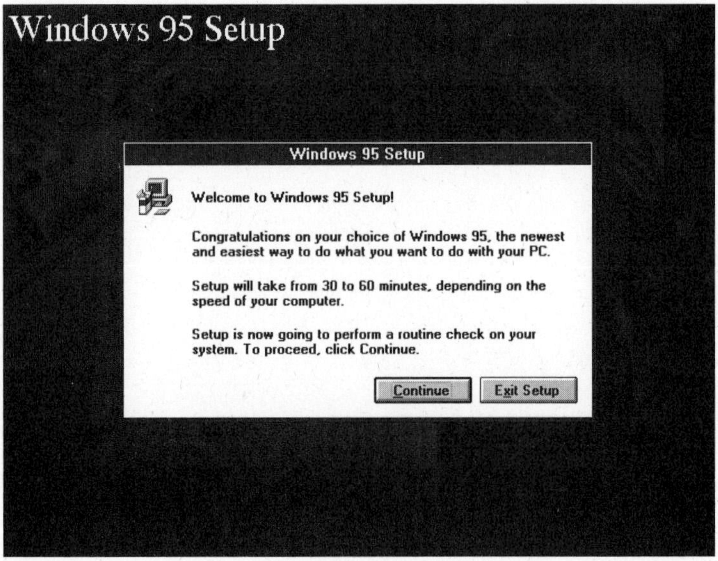

Fig. A.3
You're on your
way when you
see the big blue
screen.

Starting Setup from File Manager

Some users may be more familiar with File Manager. If you prefer to work
there instead of Program Manager, feel free. If you haven't already, start File
Manager from the Program Manager Main program group by double-clicking
the File Manager icon. When the File Manager window appears, click on the
icon for the appropriate drive where you've loaded your Windows 95 installation disk or CD-ROM. File Manager then displays the contents of the drive as
shown in figure A.4.

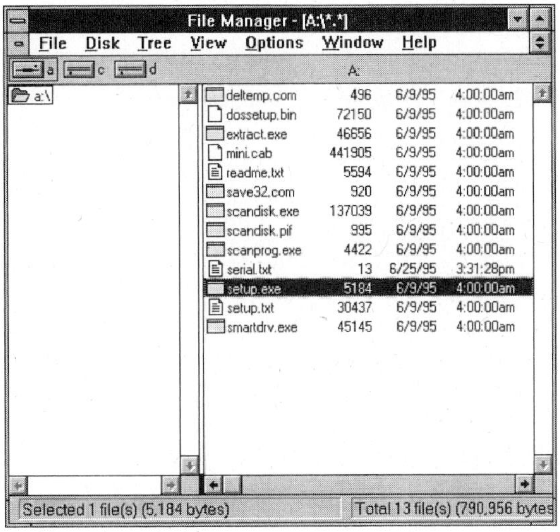

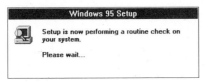

Fig. A.4
You can start
Windows 95 Setup
from File Manager.

To start Setup, double-click SETUP.EXE. Windows loads the program, and
Setup displays the welcome screen.

Getting Down to Business with Setup

To continue Windows 95 Setup, click Continue. Setup displays the message
box shown in figure A.5.

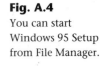

Fig. A.5
Setup keeps you
posted during its
investigations.

Setup performs a brief check of your hardware, current operating system, and
current running programs before proceeding. It then displays the End-User
License Agreement. Read it and click Yes to continue.

If you're installing from floppy disks, Setup frequently asks you for new disks via the Insert Disk dialog box (see fig. A.6). You can speed the process by having the disk ready and pressing the Enter key after you switch disks.

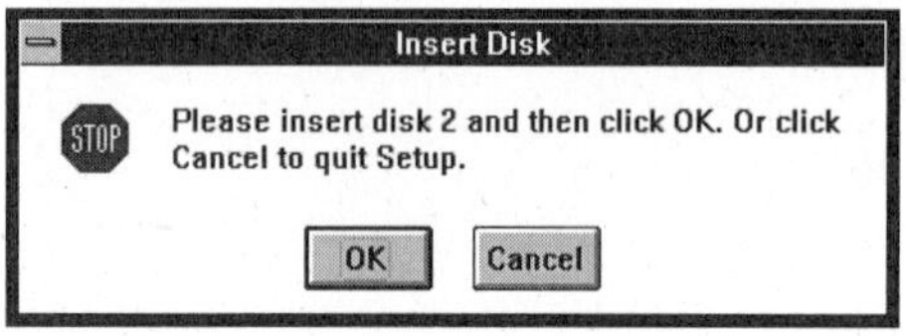

Fig. A.6
Setup asks you most of the important questions upfront, but unless you're installing from a CD-ROM, you'll still have to feed it disks.

When the Setup loader finishes creating the Setup Wizard, Windows may display the dialog box seen in figure A.7. If you have any open programs, it is strongly suggested you close them before proceeding. This is especially wise if you have any unsaved documents in other applications.

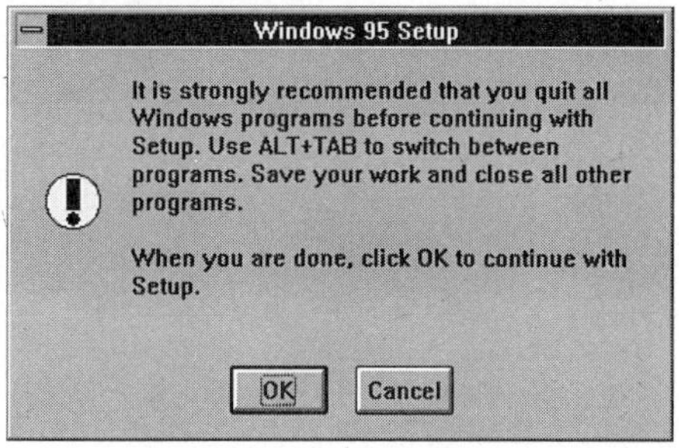

Fig. A.7
While Windows 95 Setup is well-behaved, it's always better to be safe than sorry.

Take the time to use Alt+Tab to close any other open applications or documents. (You won't be able to close Program Manager without exiting Windows.) When you finish, use Alt+Tab to return to Windows 95 Setup, and click OK to proceed. Setup then displays the main Windows 95 Setup Wizard dialog box (see fig. A.8).

Fig. A.8
We're off to see the Setup Wizard.

Setup begins the first major phase requiring user interaction by collecting information about your system and how you'll use it. Click Next to proceed. Windows displays the Choose Directory dialog box (see fig. A.9).

If you want to install Windows 95 over your current Windows installation, click Next to proceed. If you want to install to another directory, choose Other Directory and Next; then see "Setting Up a Dual-Boot System," later in this appendix.

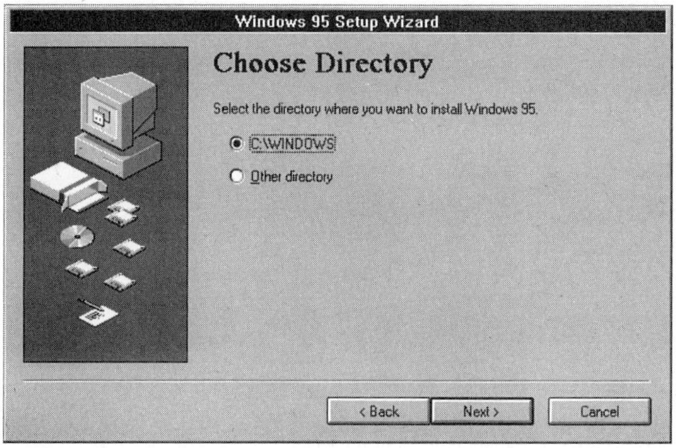

Fig. A.9
Most users will choose to install Windows 95 as an upgrade to their existing Windows 3.x installation (usually in C:\WINDOWS). Choose Next to confirm this option.

The next option is a great idea. Windows 95 setup presents the dialog box shown in figure A.10 and asks if you would like to save your Windows 3.1 and DOS system files. Saving these files takes only about 6M of disk space and it's highly recommended that you do this. Saving these files will allow you to uninstall Windows 95 (as described later in this appendix) at a later time should you ever need to revert to your Windows 3.1 setup. Notice this is *not* a full backup of your system or applications. This just saves files needed to start DOS, Windows, and Windows configuration files. Choose to save these files and then click Next to continue.

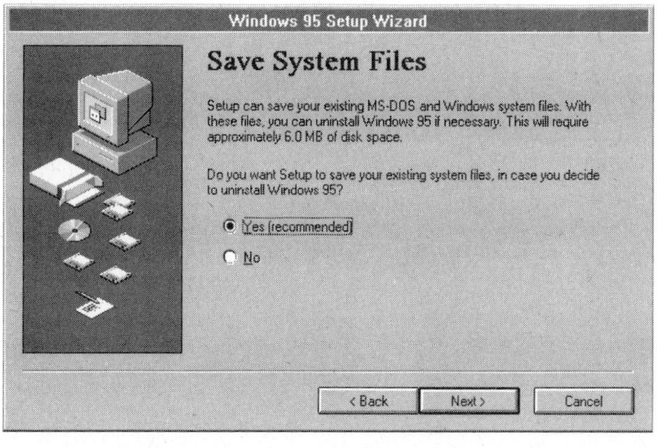

Fig A.10
Save your old Windows 3.1 and DOS system files now and save yourself some grief if you ever need to uninstall Windows 95.

Setup next checks your system for available installed components and disk space. You don't need to take any action for Setup to move to the next stage, Setup Options. As soon as Setup determines your available drive space, it asks you to confirm what type of installation you need (see fig. A.11).

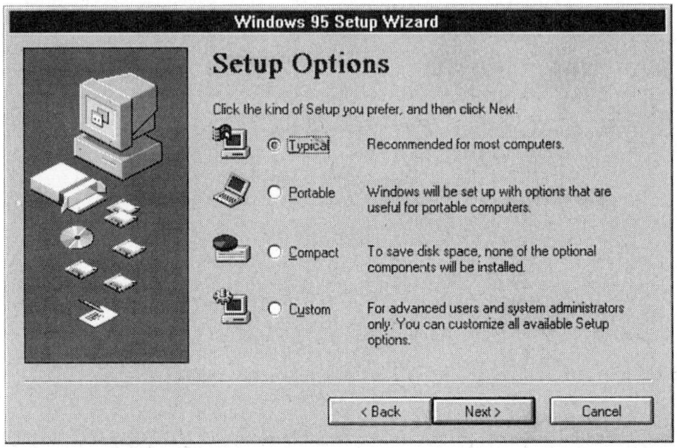

Fig. A.11

You can choose from Typical, Portable, Compact, or Custom installation profiles.

Your choice here depends upon how you use your computer and how you use Windows. The Typical installation option is truly that, fitting most installation types to a "t." With this option, you need only provide some user and computer information, and tell Setup whether you want an emergency startup disk (highly recommended).

> **Note**
>
> The Typical selection won't install all Windows accessories or games that you may expect. To confirm all components, use the Custom option described below.

The Portable setup option is best for laptop or mobile computer users. Setup installs the Windows Briefcase tools for file synchronization and transfer.

The Compact setup option is for systems where you must absolutely minimize the Windows "footprint." This option is for those with truly frugal drive budgets. Windows itself is completely installed, but all extraneous accessories are not (disk compression and maintenance tools are the only accessories installed).

▶ See "Using Custom Setup Mode," p. 1099

The Custom installation option allows the experienced user near-total control over Windows installation. If you are the master of your computing domain, this selection lets you specify network settings, device configurations, and most other variables in your Windows 95 setup. You'll find more information on the Custom option later in this appendix.

The Typical Windows 95 Setup Process

For now, let's look at a typical setup, as that is what most Windows 95 users need. To continue the installation, confirm the default selection (Typical) by clicking Next or pressing Enter. Windows displays the User Information dialog box (see fig. A.12).

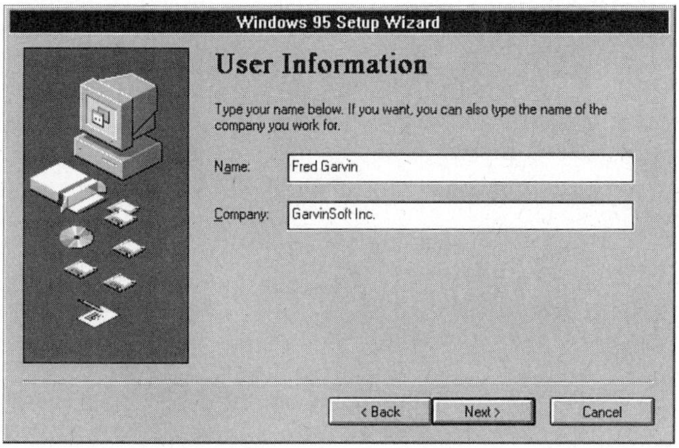

Fig. A.12
Windows Setup wants to get to know you better. Providing your name helps Windows properly identify you in later application installations and helps Windows identify your system on the Windows Network.

Fill in the appropriate information for your installation, and click Next or press Enter. The next stage in Setup is further analysis of your peripheral hardware. Setup displays the Analyzing Your Computer dialog box as shown in figure A.13.

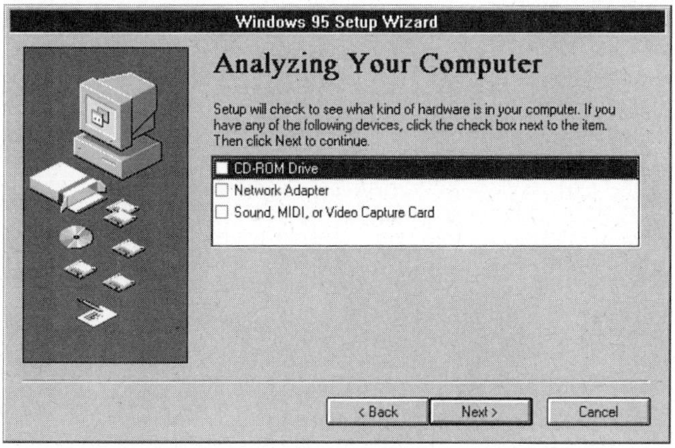

Fig. A.13
Depending upon what hardware is installed on your system, Windows will display several options in this dialog box. Confirm or deny your peripheral stance, and Setup does the rest.

Click Next or press Enter, and Setup then checks your entire system to profile your peripherals (display adapter, sound cards, and so on). When Setup finishes this investigation, Windows Components dialog box appears (see fig. A.14). Be sure to check any items you want Windows to sense, or it will skip them!

> **Note**
>
> If you don't check an item, Setup won't try to detect that class of device. If you do have a network adapter or multimedia card, and you want Setup to find it, you must check these options.

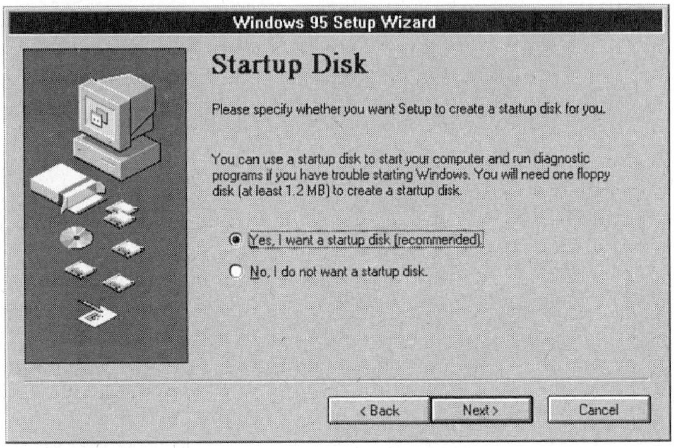

Fig. A.14
In the Typical setup mode, Setup allows you to alter the Windows component defaults.

If you're setting Windows up on a single-user, non-networked machine, odds are the default settings are just fine for you. Click Next or press Enter, and Setup displays the Startup Disk dialog box (see fig. A.15).

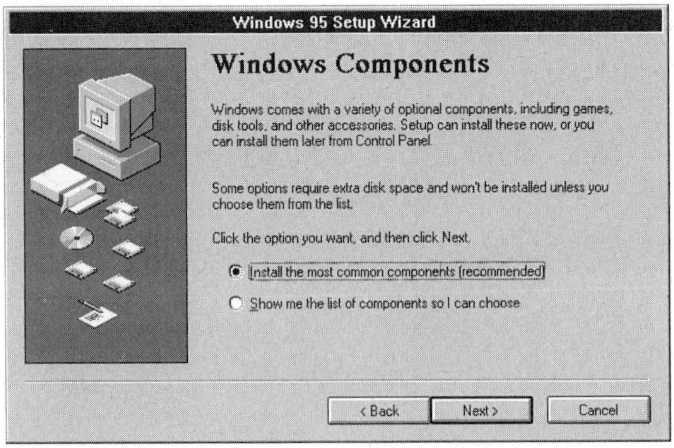

Fig. A.15
Choose wisely. Create a Startup Disk now and avoid regrets later.

Be smart and either click Next or press Enter to tell Setup to create a startup disk. Setup won't prompt you to do it immediately, so you have a few minutes to find a blank floppy disk (see, you really don't have an excuse). The Startup Disk contains all the files your computer needs to run in case the system files on your hard drive should become corrupt.

Click Next or press Enter, and Setup proceeds to the next major section of Windows 95 installation.

The Big Copy Job

Having completed its inquiries, Setup can now get down to the business at hand—moving the Windows 95 program(s) to your hard drive. Setup displays the Start Copying Files dialog box.

Simply click Next or press Enter, and Setup continues. The next displayed screen is the by now familiar Windows 95 Setup background, with a "gas gauge" at the bottom to indicate copy progress (see fig. A.16).

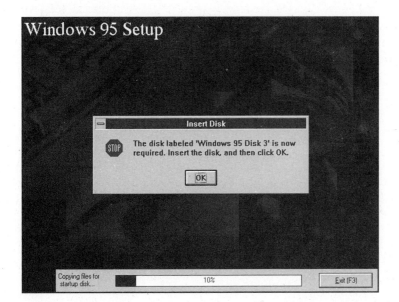

Fig. A.16
Windows 95 Setup won't be bashful about asking for the next floppy disk.

This part of installation can be either a bore or a joy, depending on how your day is going and how close your computer is to your other work. You can actually stray a little as Setup performs its work, but keep an ear or an eye open for disk requests (see fig. A.17).

Right in the middle of installation may seem like a strange time to create a boot disk, but this also is a good way to get you to do it. (You can't really back out this far in, now can you?)

When the gas gauge shows full, your Startup Disk is done, and Setup returns you to the installation.

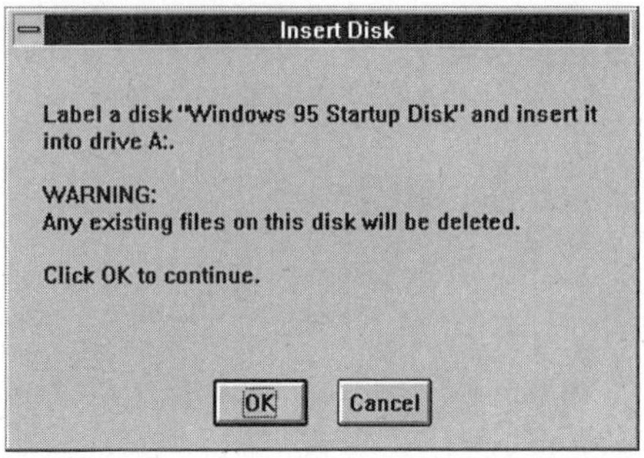

Fig. A.17

Now's the time to invest in some computing insurance by creating your Windows 95 Startup Disk. Be sure you don't need any of the data on the disk, because Windows will overwrite it.

One of the more amusing touches in Windows 95 installation is the little animations used during Setup. A tiny drum signals preparations, calling the installation troops to order (see fig. A.18).

Fig. A.18

Tiny drum rolls call the Setup cadence.

During the remainder of installation, Setup will ease your techno-ennui with informative screens alerting you to the computing delights that await. It actually pays to read these screens, especially if you are new to Windows. Even experienced Windows users can learn from these initial orientation messages (see fig. A.19).

Fig. A.19

Microsoft doesn't waste any real estate using Setup's lag times to inform you of Windows 95 features and benefits. Windows 95 has many new interface components and capabilities.

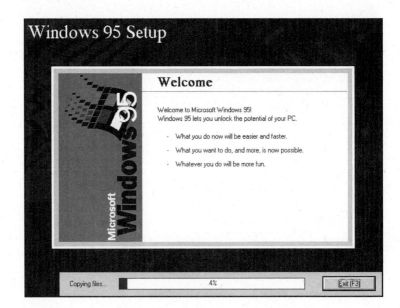

Completing the Setup Process

After Setup has copied all Windows 95 files to your hard drive, the Finishing Setup dialog box appears, as shown in figure A.20.

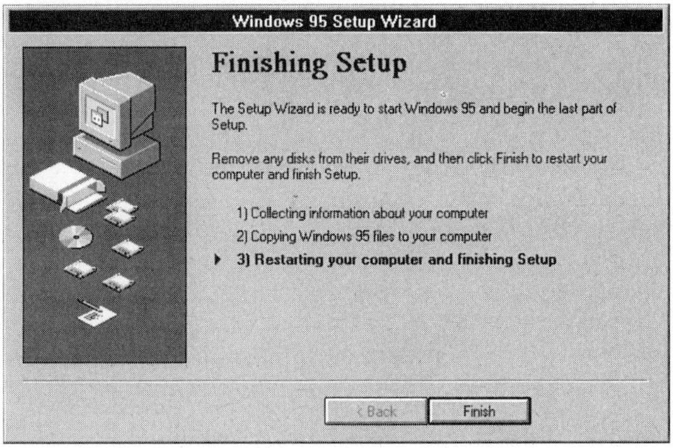

Fig. A.20

Setup needs to restart your system to complete the installation process.

Up to this point, Setup has operated as a 16-bit Windows 3.1 application. When you choose Finish and your system reboots, you'll actually be entering the world of Windows 95 computing for the first time.

Restarting Setup, Starting Windows 95

During the Copy phase of Setup, all primary Windows 95 files were created on your hard drive, and many other components of the operating system were initialized as well. When you restarted Windows 95 Setup, MS-DOS was replaced with the new Windows 95 Real Mode kernel, and your hard drive's boot sector was updated to run the new operating system.

When Setup resumes, it continues the Windows 95 installation by updating remaining configuration files and asking you a few more questions regarding your system peripherals. Most of these tasks are done by a system called the Run-Once Module, which basically fires up the appropriate system wizards to help you complete your installation.

The process begins with a quick scan of the system hardware. After this quick scan, Setup runs several short routines that can only be performed from within Windows 95 (setting up Control Panels for all appropriate devices, setting up program icons in the Start menu, initializing Windows Help, and confirming the local time zone) as shown in figure A.21.

VIII

Appendixes

Fig. A.21
Once Windows
95 is running, it
can complete
Windows 95-
specific setup
tasks.

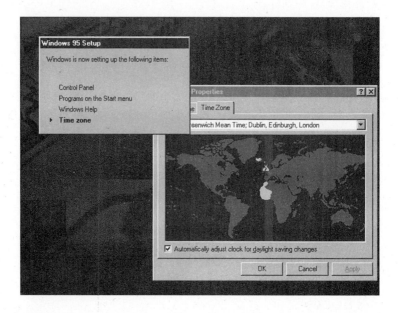

A really nice touch is the Time Zone dialog box. Simply click on the map near your part of the planet, and Windows 95 adjusts the system clock accordingly.

When the Run-Once tasks are complete, Setup is complete, and you're in the world of Windows 95 at last (see fig. A.22).

Fig. A.22
The Welcome
to Windows 95
dialog box gives
you the basic tips
for navigation and
registration.

The demonstration of a "typical" Windows 95 Setup run is complete. Next, you can learn how to install Windows 95 from MS-DOS; then you can visit some issues regarding Custom Setup and other advanced setup options.

Installing Windows 95 from MS-DOS

If you don't have an installation of Windows version 3.1 or later, or are using Windows NT or OS/2, you need to start Windows 95 Setup from the venerable MS-DOS prompt.

Starting Windows 95 Setup from MS-DOS is just like running any other MS-DOS program. If you're using a plain MS-DOS machine, you need version MS-DOS 3.2 or later. To begin, simply boot the machine just as for any other computing session. If you're using another operating system, you need to use the dual-boot feature or boot from a floppy disk to attain MS-DOS operation.

Again, it is assumed that you are using floppy disks in drive A. If you have a CD-ROM drive, simply substitute the appropriate drive letter for A in the following examples.

The first step in starting Windows 95 Setup from the MS-DOS prompt is to enter the command at the prompt. At the prompt, type **a:\setup** and press Enter.

MS-DOS then runs the Windows 95 Setup program, which starts by running the Windows 95 version of ScanDisk. The first thing you see on-screen is a message saying, `Please wait while Setup initializes. Setup is now going to perform a routine check on your system. To continue, press ENTER. To quit Setup, press ESC.` Press Enter to continue. Setup then starts ScanDisk (as shown in fig. A.23), which runs automatically to check out your drives to make sure they're sound before beginning the Windows 95 installation. Follow the prompts to deal with any drive anomalies.

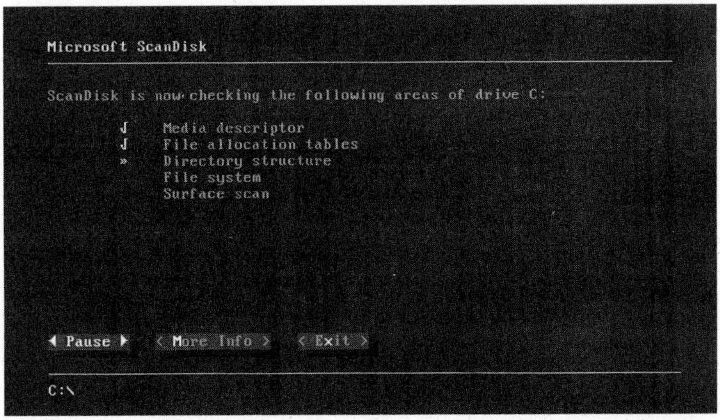

VIII

Appendixes

Fig. A.23
Setup needs to check out your disk before it begins.

When ScanDisk finishes, it automatically exits back to MS-DOS, where Setup continues.

Setup copies a small version of Windows 3.1 to your system so the graphical portions of Setup can run. Once that is complete, Setup displays the Welcome screen shown in figure A.24.

Fig. A.24
From this point on, Setup is the same whether you started from MS-DOS or the latest version of Windows.

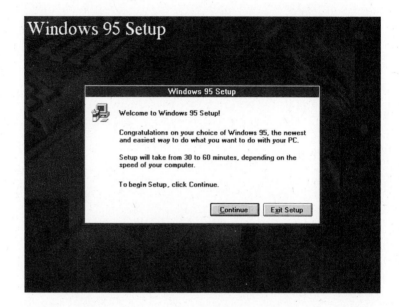

◀ See "Installing Windows 95 from Windows 3.x," p. 1085

The remaining Setup procedures are nearly identical to those listed earlier in this chapter for installing from Windows 3.1. If you're installing Windows 95 as your first version of Windows, you have to install all of your Windows applications after Windows 95 Setup is complete. If you installed from MS-DOS but didn't install over your existing Windows subdirectory, you'll have to do the same.

Advanced Installation Techniques

As simple as Windows 95 Setup can be, there are still situations that demand special considerations to meet special needs. There are as many different Windows installations as there are Windows users, and Windows 95 Setup is flexible enough to meet most needs.

In this section, you learn about

- ■ Installing with Custom options
- ■ Using Safe Recovery and Safe Detection

- Installing a dual-boot system (keeping your previous MS-DOS and Windows systems)

- Reconfiguring a single-boot system for dual-boot operation

Using Custom Setup Mode

Microsoft's Windows 95 development team has done an admirable job of establishing compatibility with a wide variety of peripheral components, but no one can perfectly predict all of the equipment variables in the churning world of the PC hardware market.

Installing Windows 95 for special setups is straightforward if you have the appropriate information ready before you begin. The Custom setup option allows you to specify application settings, network configuration options, and device configurations, and gives you more control over the installation of Windows 95 components.

VIII

> ### Caution
>
> The Custom installation mode puts a lot of power in your hands. If you don't have the specific experience in network or device configuration, you're better off leaving this to Windows 95 Setup auto-detection, or your MIS department.

Appendixes

Before you begin, know the exact name and model number of the card or device you're installing. Have any special device driver files handy (the original floppy disk is best). Find out the logical memory address defaults for the component, if applicable (see the peripheral documentation).

To use Windows 95 Setup in Custom mode, simply proceed with installation as described earlier in this chapter up to the point of selecting the Setup Options dialog box (shown in fig. A.25).

At this point, select the Custom option and click Next to proceed. Don't expect Setup to change drastically from this point on; you simply see a few more dialog boxes, where Setup asks you the appropriate questions regarding additional options. The next screen you see is the User Information dialog box. When you complete this dialog box, Setup displays the Analyzing Your Computer dialog box shown in figure A.26.

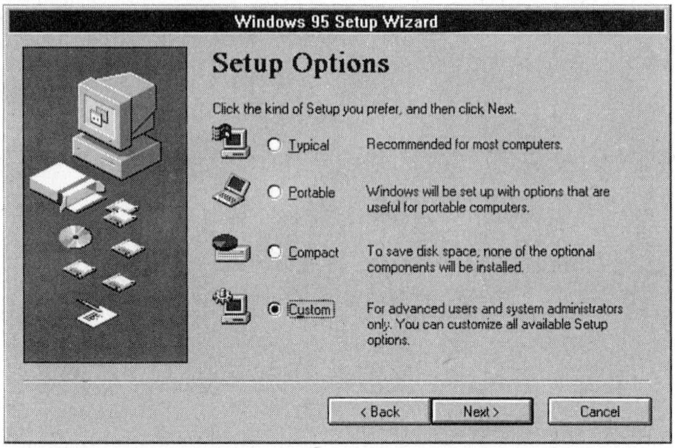

Fig. A.25

Select the Custom option to gain more control over your system configuration.

Fig. A.26

If you know you're going to need to alter your device configurations, you can select the option easily in this dialog box.

Customizing Hardware Support

If you know you have nonstandard or unsupported devices in your installation, select the No, I Want to Modify the Hardware List radio button. Then click Next to proceed. Setup displays the screen shown in figure A.27.

Here's where you need the information about your system mentioned earlier. If you *know* that you have an unusual peripheral, look for it here. Setup guides you through installing any special drivers for the device at the appropriate time.

If your device doesn't appear in the lists here, it means one of two things: either Windows 95 has native 32-bit support for the device or no support for it. If Setup didn't detect your device earlier in the installation, you need to tell it to install it now. Or, if it was detected, and the Windows installation didn't work, you can tell Windows to skip it this round. You can manually install the device later using the Add New Hardware control panel.

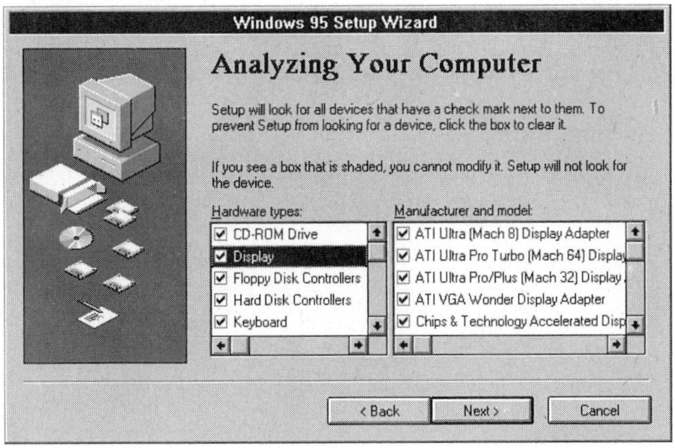

Select the device
type in the left
window and the
specific device
name in the right.
Changing the item
on the left
changes the list
on the right.

When you've selected all the device types you want configured, click Next to
proceed. After completing its analysis of your selected equipment, Setup displays the Select Components dialog box, shown in figure A.28.

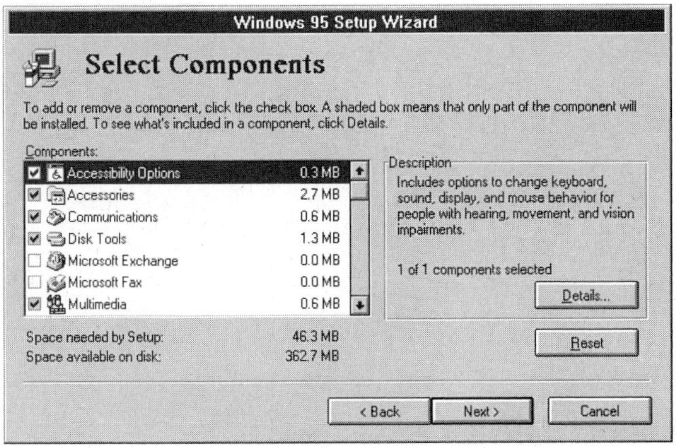

VIII

Appendixes

Fig. A.28
Select the
Windows 95
components you
want Setup to
install. Setup can
provide additional
information about
each option when
you click Details.

When you've selected all of the Windows 95 components you want installed,
click Next to proceed. The remainder of the installation depends on what
hardware and software component options you've selected. Setup attempts to
locate your devices and prompts you when it needs additional information
such as device driver files. In the next section, we look at an example of this,
specifically, the basic steps to install network support under Windows 95.

Installing Windows 95 Network Features

If you've selected network support, Setup next displays the Network Configuration dialog box shown in figure A.29.

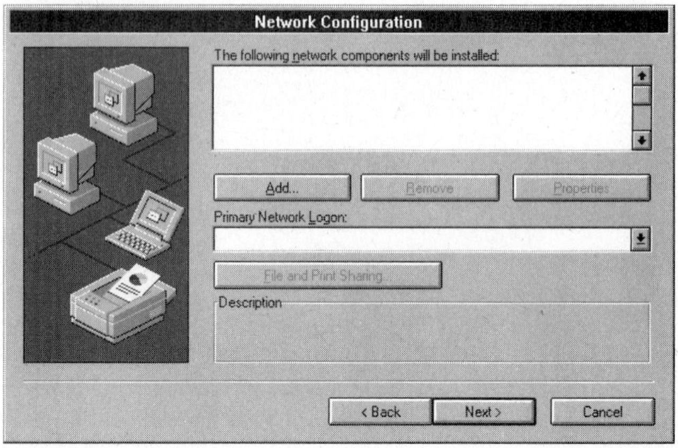

Fig. A.29
You can install network support for multiple adapters and protocols from this one Setup screen.

> **Note**
>
> See Part V, "Networking with Windows 95," for additional information on configuring network support in Windows 95.

To begin configuring your network options, click Add. Setup displays the Select Network Component Type dialog box (see fig. A.30).

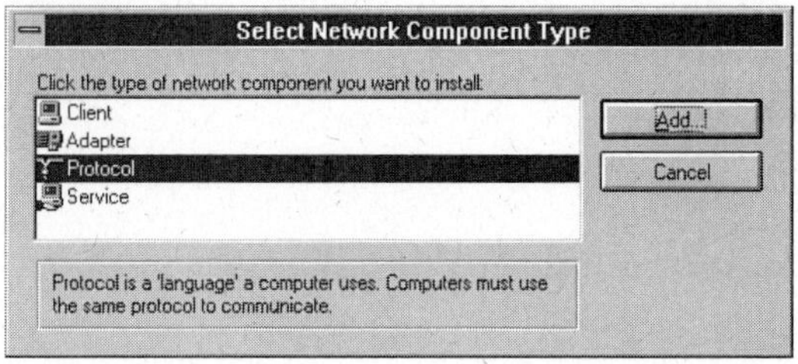

Fig. A.30
Click on the network component type you want to install.

When you select the component type you want to install, Setup displays another selection dialog box for that component classification. For example, if you select Protocol and then click Add, Setup displays the Select Network Protocol dialog box shown in figure A.31.

When you've selected the appropriate protocols network adapter, you can either click OK (to let Setup determine if Windows 95 has native drivers for these types) or click Have Disk to install your own drivers.

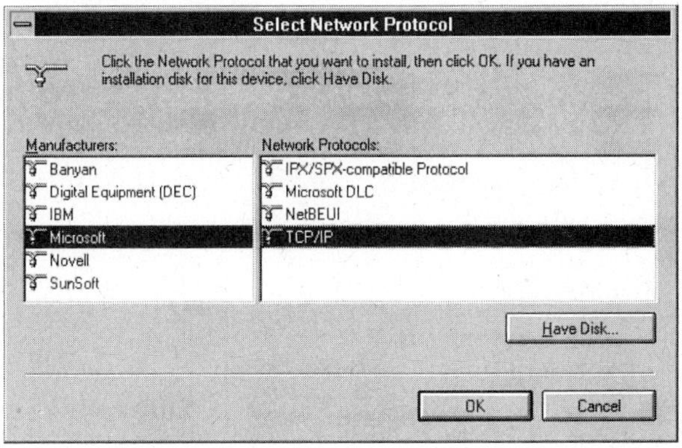

Fig. A.31
Select the protocol publisher in the left list and then the specific protocol type in the right list.

Setup may make assumptions about other network support components based upon the adapter type you select. For example, selecting the Intel EtherExpress 16 or 16TP results in Setup selecting clients and protocols for both NetWare and Microsoft network types, as shown in figure A.32.

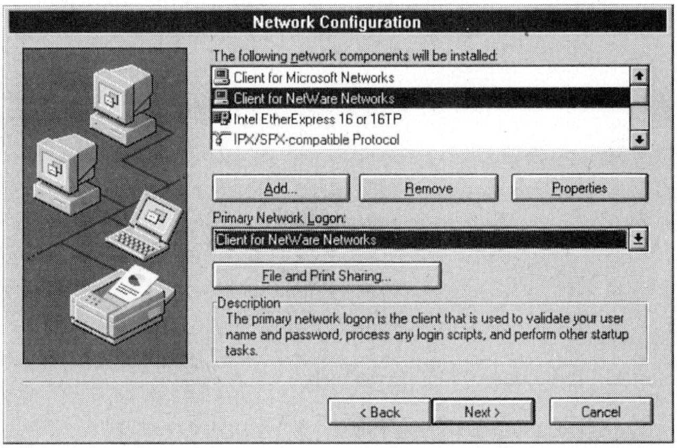

Fig. A.32
Setup may make additional choices based upon your hardware selection. You can override this by using the Remove button, but be sure you don't need the component before you proceed.

Using Safe Recovery

If Setup fails during your installation, it has the capability to recover gracefully. Setup Safe Recovery automatically skips problem configuration items to allow the installation to finish, and then allows you to go back to the problem and correct it.

Safe Recovery also can be used in repairing damaged installations. If you run Setup after a complete Windows 95 installation, it first asks whether you want to confirm or repair your installation, or whether you want to completely reinstall Windows 95 (see fig. A.33).

VIII

Appendixes

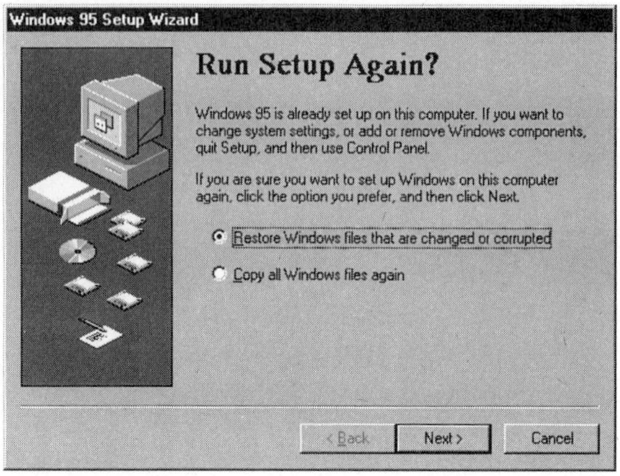

Fig. A.33
You also can use Safe Recovery after a complete installation to repair later damage.

Using Safe Detection

Windows 95 Setup looks for system components in a variety of ways. Setup can detect communication ports, display adapters, processor type, drive controllers, sound cards, and network adapters. Setup also looks for system hardware resources such as IRQs, DMA channels, and I/O addresses to avoid conflicts between devices. Setup can detect both the newer Plug and Play devices and older "legacy" peripherals.

Safe Detection works on four classes of devices:

- Sound cards

- Network adapters

- SCSI controllers

- CD-ROM controllers

One problem with such auto-detection routines is failure during the detection process itself. Plug and Play devices basically identify or announce themselves to the system, but older adapters require interactive tests to locate them and confirm operation. While most devices respond well to this, some don't. In addition, if there's any duplication of IRQ, DMA, or I/O addresses between devices, your system can lock up tighter than a drum during installation.

Windows 95 Setup can recover from such failures. Setup keeps track of the process of testing devices during installation and knows at what point a device failed. When you restart it, Setup knows not to touch that subsystem again until corrections have been applied, such as loading 16-bit device drivers, if the 32-bit native Windows 95 drivers have failed.

Setting Up a Dual-Boot System

A very popular installation option for new Windows 95 users is the *dual-boot setup*. Installing Windows 95 this way allows you to return to your previous operating system as needed or desired.

There are several ways to accomplish a dual-boot installation and several motivations for doing so. The following sections explain the techniques and options available to you under Windows 95.

Setting Up a Dual-Boot System during Installation

The simplest technique for establishing dual-boot is to simply select a new directory for Windows 95 when installing for the first time (see fig. A.34).

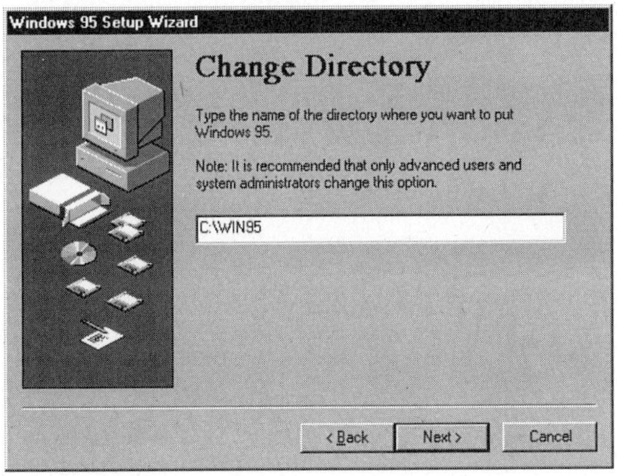

VIII

Appendixes

Fig. A.34
Specify a new directory for Windows 95, and Setup takes care of basic dual-boot details. You'll still need to configure Windows 95 for many of the applications in your previous Windows installation.

Setup preserves your current MS-DOS and Windows 3.1x settings if you follow this route, but it can't transfer settings for your current Windows applications to the new Windows 95 installation (see fig. A.35). In addition, Windows 95 will disable, redirect, or outright delete certain files from your DOS directory, so you may want to restore the complete DOS directory from the backup you made before installation.

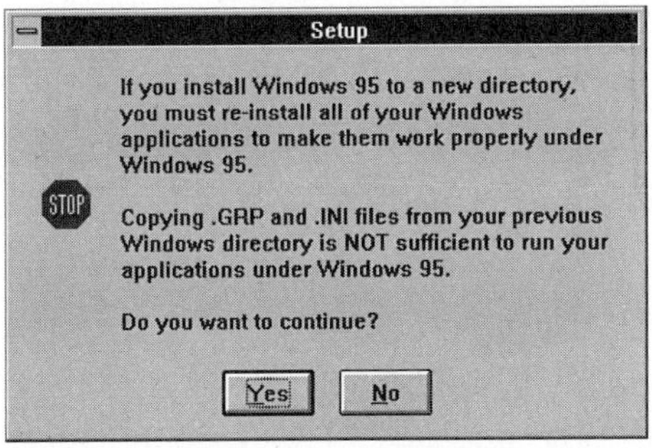

Fig. A.35
Setup warns you of the additional work dual-boot operation installation may entail.

If you're prepared to reinstall your Windows applications after Windows 95 Setup is completed, this is a clean, simple way to proceed. After you install Windows 95 this way, you can return to your previous MS-DOS installation (and from there to your previous Windows installation) with a single F4 keystroke during system startup.

Setting Up a Dual-Boot System after Installation

If you've already installed Windows 95 over your existing Windows 3.1x directory, you can easily set up your system for dual-booting back to MS-DOS. However, since your previous Windows installation was stomped, you can't return to it. In addition, you may notice that some of your favorite MS-DOS commands such as XCOPY are now dust, even when you dual-boot back to MS-DOS (Windows 95 disables some MS-DOS commands, so you'll need to restore your DOS directory from that backup you made prior to installation).

To set up your system for dual-boot to your previous version of MS-DOS, follow these steps:

1. Locate your boot floppy disk for your previous version of MS-DOS (version 5.0 or later). Make a copy of it.

2. On the copy of your boot disk, change the attributes of the IO.SYS, MSDOS.SYS, and COMMAND.COM files to allow you to rename them. (The `attrib -h -r -s filename.ext` command works for each file.)

3. Rename the IO.SYS, MSDOS.SYS, and COMMAND.COM files on your boot floppy to IO.DOS, MSDOS.DOS, and COMMAND.DOS respectively.

4. Reset the attributes of the IO.DOS, MSDOS.DOS, and COMMAND.DOS files to protect them. (Use the `attrib +r filename.ext` command for each file.)

5. Rename the AUTOEXEC.BAT and CONFIG.SYS files on your MS-DOS boot disk to AUTOEXEC.DOS and CONFIG.DOS, respectively. You may want to set these files to read-only also. (Use the `attrib +r filename.ext` command for each file.)

6. Copy IO.DOS, MSDOS.DOS, COMMAND.DOS, AUTOEXEC.DOS, and CONFIG.DOS to the boot directory of the Windows 95 drive.

You can now return to your previous MS-DOS installation with a single F4 keystroke during system startup. You also can use the F8 key during startup (when `Starting Windows 95...` appears on screen) and then select item 7,

"Previous version of MS-DOS." Bear in mind that you may need to restore certain MS-DOS files that Windows 95 has removed from your DOS directory (you can use that DOS directory backup you made prior to Windows 95 installation).

Removing Windows 95

If you decide you need to return to your previous Windows 3.1x installation, want to clean up your system before you trade or sell it, or simply don't want to use Windows 95, you can remove all traces of Windows 95. In order to use this feature to uninstall Windows 95, you had to use the (highly recommended) option to save your old Windows 3.1 and DOS system files during Windows setup.

If you were using drive compression with Windows 95, you need to uncompress your hard drive before uninstalling Windows 95. If you have more files than will fit on your uncompressed drive, you will need to delete files before proceeding.

If you have installed any programs since installing Windows 95, they probably will have to be reconfigured to work with Windows 3.1, or you may have to uninstall them from Windows 95 and reinstall them in Windows 3.1. Of course, any applications written to work with Windows 95 (like Office 95) will not run in Windows 3.1.

Once you are ready to uninstall, open the Start menu and choose Setttings, Control Panel. Double-click the Add/Remove Programs icon. Click the Install/ Uninstall tab. This shows the properties sheet shown in figure A.36.

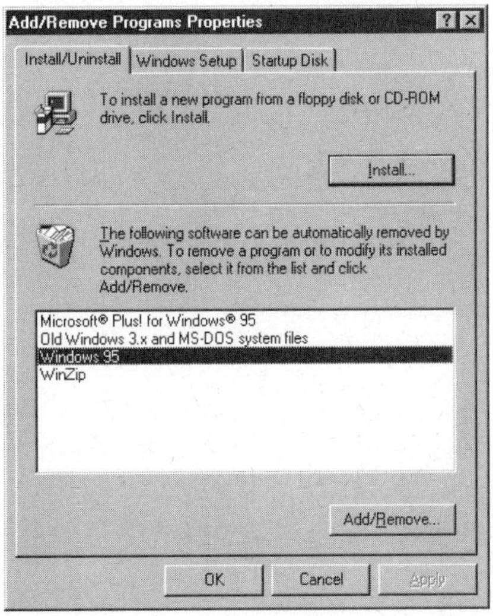

Fig. A.36
The Install/ Uninstall Programs page of the Add/ Remove Programs Properties sheet includes an option to uninstall Windows 95.

VIII

Appendixes

Select Windows 95 and then click <u>A</u>dd/Remove. This opens the warning dialog box shown in figure A.37.

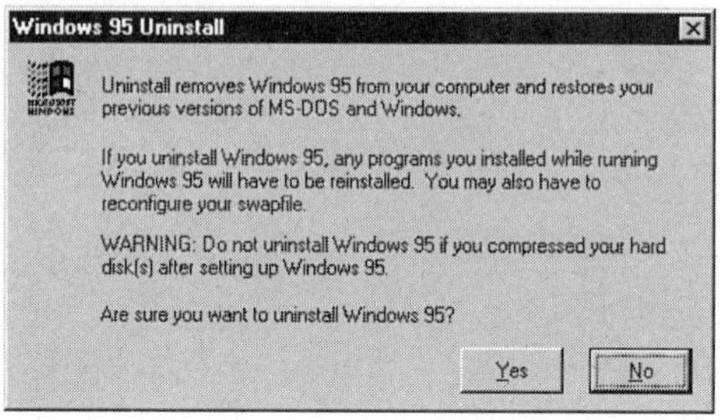

Fig. A.37

If you are sure you want to uninstall Windows 95, click <u>Y</u>es. The uninstaller will remove Windows 95 and restore your old DOS and Windows system files.

Your system should now boot straight to your previous version of MS-DOS. You may need to set up a new Windows 3.1 swap file as your old swap file (if you were using a permanent swap file) no longer exists.❖

Appendix B

Using Microsoft Network

by Jerry Honeycutt

The Microsoft Network (MSN) is an exciting addition to Windows 95. It is fully integrated into Windows and offers online access to the world by giving you access to a variety of people and resources. With MSN, you can exchange electronic mail (e-mail) with other people, exchange ideas on bulletin boards, participate in live discussions in chat rooms, access the resources of the Internet, and do even more! Why should you use this powerful accessory? Here are some important reasons:

- *Getting started is easy.* After installing Windows and MSN, you just double-click the MSN icon on your desktop and then follow the instructions.

- *Using MSN is easy.* MSN is fully integrated into Windows. You have already learned about using folders, shortcuts, drag-and-drop, and the Explorer. MSN uses these same tools to present information to you. Therefore, you can get up to speed more quickly on MSN because you already have the skills necessary to navigate.

- *Multitasking is easy.* You won't get bored in MSN! MSN takes full advantage of Windows' multitasking capabilities. If you are downloading a file from a file area, you can chat with your colleagues in a chat room and read the messages from a bulletin board at the same time.

This appendix explains how to get started using MSN and describes some interesting forum areas and services currently available.

In this appendix, you learn to:

- Create a new account and log on to MSN for the first time

- Use the variety of services available in MSN Central such as MSN Today, E-Mail, Favorite Places, Member Assistance, and Categories

- Use Internet e-mail and UseNet newsgroups in MSN

Connecting to The Microsoft Network

◀ See "Adding and Removing Windows Components," p. 313

◀ See "Understanding Windows 95 Setup Requirements," p. 1078

◀ See "Installing Windows 95 Network Features," p. 1101

As noted, getting started with MSN is easy. All you need is a modem and MSN software. If you haven't installed MSN yet, take a moment to install it now so that you can follow the examples in this chapter. To install MSN, click the Add/Remove Programs icon in Control Panel and select the Windows Setup page. Select The Microsoft Network, then click OK.

MSN automates the process of setting up your online account for the first time. MSN walks you through three major steps: updating a list of access numbers, entering information about yourself, and logging on for the first time to get a user ID and password.

Downloading Local Access Numbers

The list of MSN access phone numbers is dramatically large, covering most of the United States and large portions of the world. Microsoft updates this list periodically. MSN needs to update the list on your computer to find the best connection for you. To get started, follow these steps:

1. Double-click the MSN icon on your desktop. MSN displays a dialog box containing brief information about the services provided. Click OK to continue.

2. In the fields provided, type your area code and the first three digits of your phone number. Based on this information, MSN will find the best matching access number for you to use. Click OK to continue.

3. Click Connect to log on to MSN and update the list of access numbers.

> **Caution**
>
> The desktop icon is created as a registry key, not a file. Therefore, you can't connect to MSN if you remove the icon from your desktop.

Entering Information about Yourself

After MSN updates the list of access numbers, it asks for personal information, such as your address and payment method. This information is required for logging on to MSN. Your screen should now contain the dialog box shown in figure B.1.

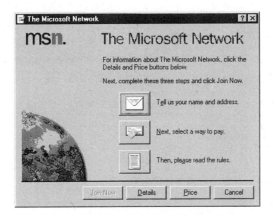

Fig. B.1
Complete each step to join MSN.

VIII

Appendixes

Before entering your personal information, take a moment to review the following:

- *Details*. Click **D**etails to see specific information about MSN.

- *Price*. Click **P**rice to see the latest fee structure for time and services on MSN. This price list is updated regularly.

To continue the sign-up process, complete the following steps:

1. Click T**e**ll Us Your Name and Address. MSN displays the dialog box shown in figure B.2. Enter the information requested in each blank field. If you do not want to accept solicitations and other special notices from MSN, click the check box labeled **Y**ou Are Entitled To... in the bottom-left corner of the dialog box. Click OK to continue, and MSN redisplays the dialog box shown in figure B.1.

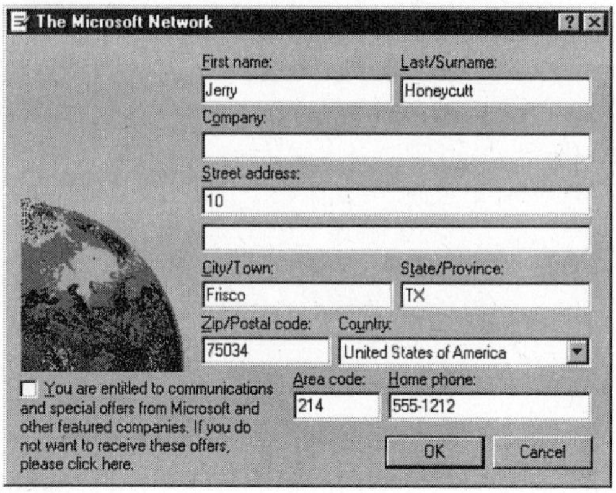

Fig. B.2

Enter information
about yourself.

2. Click Next, Select a Way to Pay. Select a payment method from the
   Choose a Payment Method list. Then enter the card number, expiration
   date, and cardholder name in the fields provided. You also may be
   asked to enter the bank's name. Click OK. MSN returns you to the dialog box shown in figure B.1.

3. Click Then, Please Read the Rules. MSN will not let you continue until
   you view the MSN membership agreement. Click I Agree if you want to
   continue, or click I Don't Agree if you want to stop. When you click I
   Agree, MSN redisplays the dialog box shown in figure B.1.

4. Click Join Now to continue the sign-up process.

Logging On for the First Time

MSN provides both primary and backup access numbers. Normally, MSN uses
the primary access number. For situations in which the primary number isn't
working, MSN uses the backup number. If you can't connect to the phone
numbers MSN chose, click Settings, Access Numbers, and then click the
Change button beside primary or backup number. Select the country, state,
and access number appropriate for your area code in the lists provided.

To log on and get your user ID and password, click Connect to log on to
MSN. MSN prompts you for a user ID and password. You will receive an error
if the user ID is already used or the password is invalid. If so, try another ID
or password.

Troubleshooting

When I dial MSN, I get a message saying that the call was canceled or the modem doesn't connect.

Your hardware may not support high-speed communications. Change your baud rate to 9,600 (or a slower rate) and try again.

I entered my new password, and MSN complained that its length was invalid even though I'm positive it was long enough.

MSN tells you that your password length is invalid if your password contains invalid characters such as spaces or other special characters. Passwords can contain only the characters A through Z, a through z, 0 through 9, "-", and ".".

◀ See "Configur-
ing Your
Modem,"
p. 843

You are now set up on MSN. To log on next time, double-click the MSN icon on your desktop, fill in your ID and password, and click Connect. If you want MSN to remember your password from session to session, click Remember My Password. Figure B.3 shows the logon screen.

VIII

Appendixes

Fig. B.3
Click Connect to log on to MSN or click Settings to change your access phone numbers, dialing properties, or modem settings.

Note

From time to time, Microsoft updates the MSN software. If so, you'll be given the opportunity to download the update when you log on to MSN. In some cases, you will not be able to continue logging on to MSN until you download the update because changes to the network may require the new software. Downloading the update is automatic. For example, you don't have to provide paths or file names because the MSN software already has this information.

Using MSN Central

You have already learned about the basic tools required to use Windows 95 folders, shortcuts, drag-and-drop, the Explorer, and many others. MSN is easy to use because it uses these same tools. For example, if you can use the Explorer to browse your hard drive, you can easily browse MSN. The following list explains how some of these tools are used in MSN:

◀ See "Managing Your Files and Folders," p. 513

■ *Folders*. These are used to present categories and forums, enabling you to move easily from area to area within MSN.

◀ See "Modifying and Deleting Shortcuts," p. 72

■ *Shortcuts*. Most documents and folders on MSN can be dragged as shortcuts to your desktop, folders, or documents. Double-clicking an MSN shortcut takes you straight to that MSN area.

◀ See "Using the Windows Explorer to View Files and Folders," p. 499

■ *The Explorer*. This tool gives you a bigger view of MSN and enables you to navigate quickly by showing the entire content of MSN in the left pane.

■ *Property sheets*. These are used to display information about an area on MSN. The information may include the type of area, who runs it, and the rating (G, PG, R, and so on).

◀ See "Viewing and Changing the Properties of a File or Folder," p. 529

■ *Exchange*. You use this tool to send and receive e-mail from other MSN members or Internet users.

◀ See "Overview of Exchange Features," p. 724

■ *Drag-and-drop*. With drag-and-drop, you can download files from a file area.

MSN Central is your home base while logged on. It is the first window you see when you log on (see fig. B.4). You can choose from a number of possible places to go:

◀ See "Moving and Copying Files and Folders," p. 515

■ *MSN TODAY*. Gives you current information about news and activities on MSN. For example, it notifies you of service changes or anticipated outages; new and exciting forums on MSN; and upcoming conferences by noted industry leaders.

■ *E-MAIL*. Starts Exchange so that you can send and receive e-mail. You can exchange e-mail with other MSN and Internet users. You can also use Exchange to search for other MSN members with interests similar to yours. See "MSN E-Mail" later in this chapter for more information about using Exchange with MSN.

- *FAVORITE PLACES.* Opens a folder containing shortcuts to your favorite places on MSN. Many of the MSN programs allow you to save a shortcut to your current location by clicking a toolbar button or selecting a menu option. You can also save a shortcut by dragging an icon from a forum's folder into the open Favorite Places folder.

- *MEMBER ASSISTANCE.* Opens the Member Assistance forum so that you can get help or find more information on MSN. This is where you'll go when you need help using MSN or want help finding a specific area on the network.

- *CATEGORIES.* Opens the Categories folder, showing all the categories of forums available on MSN. MSN has many different categories of forums such as "Computers & Software" and "Home & Family." The section "MSN Categories," later in this chapter, describes the forums available in each category. Microsoft updates these categories from time to time as forums are added or removed.

VII

Appendixes

> ### Note
>
> MSN displays MSN TODAY each time you log on. If you don't want it displayed each time you log on, choose View, Options from the menu, select the General page, and deselect Show MSN Today Title on Startup.

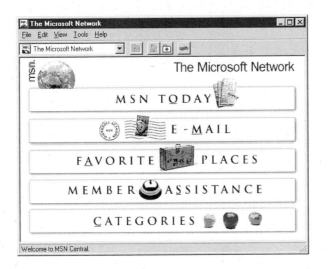

Fig. B.4
From MSN Central, you can launch into a variety of interesting areas such as MSN TODAY or CATEGORIES by clicking on its picture.

As you can see, MSN provides a wealth of tools to make your online experience a positive one. Microsoft undoubtedly will add more tools as they get feedback from users. To keep up-to-date on the latest developments, check MSN Today frequently as described in the following section.

MSN Today

MSN Today is the daily newspaper for MSN. Here, you'll find information about upcoming conferences; new and exciting forums; and service changes or anticipated outages. Figure B.5 shows MSN Today.

Fig. B.5
MSN Today keeps you informed about the latest happenings on MSN. Keep up-to-date by reading MSN Today each day.

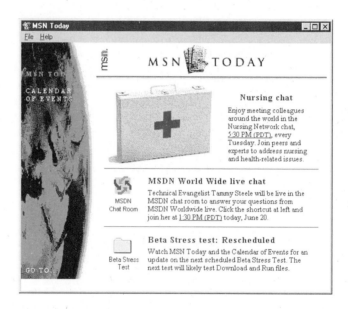

Clicking some pictures or titles in MSN Today opens a document so that you can read more information about that topic. Clicking other pictures or titles takes you to the particular area on MSN relating to that topic. For example, clicking the Nursing Chat picture in MSN Today takes you to the Nursing forum.

MSN Today also gives you a schedule for interesting events occuring during the following week. Clicking Calendar of Events shows you the public events happening each day of the following week.

MSN E-Mail

You already know how to use e-mail on MSN. In Chapter 24, "Using Microsoft Exchange," you learned how to send and receive messages, use the Address Book, use remote mail, and configure Exchange. When you installed MSN, however, it added additional features to Exchange specifically for MSN. For example, MSN added the capability to search for MSN members in the Address Book and make your personal profile available to other MSN members.

◀ See "Overview of Exchange Features," p. 724

This section describes how to use Exchange with MSN. You learn about using the Address Book, updating your personal profile, searching for other members, and setting options for using Exchange with MSN. For information about sending and receiving e-mail see Chapter 24, "Using Microsoft Exchange."

> **Note**
>
> You can share your favorite MSN shortcuts with your friends. For example, if you find an interesting BBS on Golf, you can share a shortcut to that BBS with other MSN members so that they can go to the BBS. Create the shortcut on your desktop by dragging an icon from an MSN folder to the desktop. Create and address your e-mail. Then, right-click your shortcut and choose Copy. Right-click in the body of your message and choose Paste. When the recipient opens the e-mail, she can double-click the shortcut to go directly to that item.

VIII

Appendixes

Selecting The Microsoft Network Address Book

Composing a message for MSN is the same as for any message in Exchange. However, you can choose to use MSN addresses when you use the Address Book. To see MSN addresses in the Address Book, select Microsoft Network from the Show Names From The list.

> **Note**
>
> When Exchange checks the address for an e-mail message, it automatically looks up the MSN address in the MSN Address Book. For example, if you are addressing an e-mail to "jb_smith" and type only "jb_s" in the address, Exchange completes the address for you. If more than one address matches the characters you typed, Exchange prompts you for the correct address from a list of possible choices. Clever!

Updating Your Personal Profile

Personal profiles allow other MSN members to see information about you, such as hobbies and profession. Thus, members can search their Address Books to find people with similar interests. Also, personal profiles are useful in chat rooms. If you are chatting with a person in a chat room and want to see more information about that person, such as the company for whom he works, you can right-click his name, and MSN displays his personal profile.

Providing all or part of the personal profile is optional. For example, if you don't feel comfortable broadcasting your company, leave it blank. To make sure that this information is available to other members, you need to fill in your information. To provide your personal profile, follow these steps:

1. Open Exchange by clicking E-MAIL in the MSN Central window.

2. Choose Tools, Address Book or click the Address Book button in the toolbar.

3. Select Microsoft Network from the Show Names From The list. If you are not currently logged on to MSN, Exchange starts MSN, which prompts you to log on. The Address Book displays a list of all the MSN users. This list is updated about every 24 hours.

4. Search for your name by paging down the list. Alternatively, you can start typing your name in the field provided, and MSN displays the entry that matches what you have typed.

5. Right-click your name and choose Properties. The Address Book then displays the property sheet shown in figure B.6.

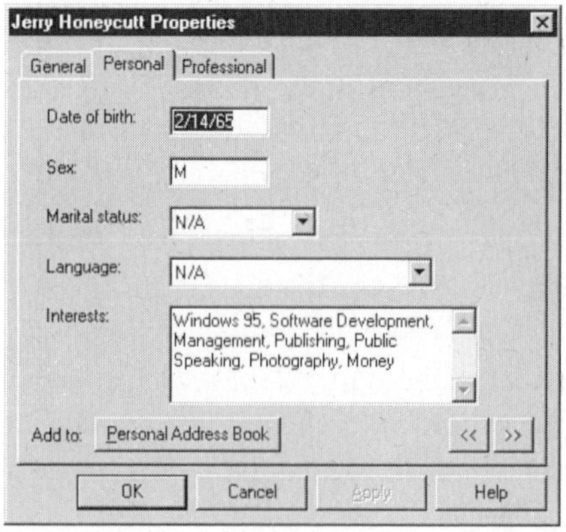

Fig. B.6

Provide useful information in the personal profile so that other users can find you! All the fields in the profile are optional, so you don't have to fill in Sex if you are uncomfortable with people knowing your gender.

6. Fill in the information in the fields provided on the General, Personal, and Professional pages of the property sheet. Click OK, and MSN will update your profile. However, the updating could take as long as 24 hours.

Finding Members in the Address Book

Finding members in the Address Book is a powerful way to find people with similar interests, professions, or even birthdays. To find members in the Address Book, follow these steps:

1. Open the MSN Address Book as described earlier. Click <u>T</u>ools, <u>F</u>ind or click the Find button in the toolbar. Exchange displays the property sheet shown in figure B.6, which you used to fill in your own profile.

2. On each page of the property sheet, fill in the information you want to match. Click OK.

3. Exchange redisplays the Address Book with the addresses that match your request. Notice that Exchange sets <u>S</u>how Names From The to Search Results.

4. Select the Microsoft Network in <u>S</u>how Names From The to return to a full list.

Troubleshooting

After starting a search in the Address Book, Exchange displays this error: `The search resulted in too many Address Book entries to display.`

Your search criteria were not narrow enough. Provide more information in the property sheet to narrow the search.

Setting Properties for The Microsoft Network in Exchange

Chapter 24, "Using Microsoft Exchange," describes setting up and configuring the various services used in Exchange such as Microsoft Fax, Personal Address Book, and Personal Information Store. When you installed MSN, it added an additional service to this list: The Microsoft Network Online Service. This service provides the capability to exchange e-mail with other MSN members.

To set options for the MSN service in Exchange, follow these steps:

1. Choose <u>T</u>ools, Ser<u>v</u>ices from the Exchange main menu.

2. Select The Microsoft Network Online Service from the list of services. Then click <u>P</u>roperties. Set the options on the Transport and Address Book pages of the property sheet. Click OK.

MSN Favorite Places

◄ See "Modifying and Deleting Shortcuts," p. 72

While you are exploring MSN, you'll come across many forums, BBSes, and other things you will want to visit again. MSN provides the Favorite Places folder, which allows you to save a shortcut to a place and then go directly to it without starting over from the Categories folder. Any document or folder you visit can be stored in Favorite Places.

Saving a Place in Favorite Places

Most of the MSN programs have the Add to Favorite Places button in the toolbar. If you want to save a shortcut to a particular icon in a folder, select the icon and click the Add to Favorite Places button. Alternatively, you can add an icon to Favorite Places by right-clicking on the icon and selecting Add to Favorite P<u>l</u>aces in the context menu.

If you want to save a shortcut to the open folder, make sure that no icon is selected in the folder and click the Add to Favorite Places button.

Going to a Place in Favorite Places

After you have saved a place in Favorite Places, you can quickly go there by double-clicking its icon. To display the Favorite Places folder, click the Go to Favorite Places button in the toolbar. Alternatively, right-click the MSN icon in the bottom-right corner of the taskbar and select Go to Favorite P<u>l</u>aces.

MSN Member Assistance

Member Assistance is the place to go if you need help or have questions about using MSN. Member Assistance is a forum that contains The MSN Member Lobby, Member Assistance Kiosk, Member Guidelines, and other documents containing news flashes about MSN. To go to Member Assistance, click the Member Assistance picture in MSN Central.

If you need help immediately, double-click The MSN Member Lobby; then double-click The MSN Member Lounge. The MSN Member Lounge is a live chat room where you can get immediate feedback to your questions, and it is always packed with interesting people from around the world.

MSN Categories

CATEGORIES, the last major section in MSN Central, represents about 95 percent of the content in MSN. Here you find forums containing BBSes to exchange messages with members, chat rooms to participate in live conversations, file libraries to download files, and more. Double-clicking CATEGORIES opens the Categories folder. This folder contains icons representing the various categories of forums on MSN. For example, under the Computers and Software category, you can expect to find forums and other information relating to computers and software. Figure B.7 shows the current categories available on MSN, and table B.1 shows the forums under each category.

Tip

The Categories folder now contains several language-independent Category subfolders, such as Categories (US), Categories (UK), and Categories (AUS).

VIII

Appendixes

Fig. B.7
You can easily find the area you're interested in by starting in the Categories folder and opening the appropriate category folder.

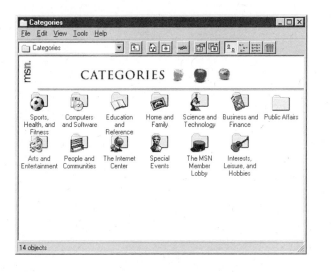

> **Note**
>
> When you first open a folder, MSN has to send information about it to your computer. This takes time, and you may perceive it as being slow. However, MSN caches (saves the information on your computer so it doesn't have to be transmitted again) the folders on your hard drive. Therefore, the next time you open the folder, it will load significantly faster.

Table B.1 Categories of Forums and Services

Category	Description
Sports, Health, and Fitness	Field and Court Sports, Health and Fitness, Indoor Sports and Recreation, Motorsports, Outdoor Sports and Recreation, Snow and Winter Sports, Sports Psychology and Medicine, Water Sports, Sports Media
Computers and Software	Computer Games, Computer Graphics, Desktop Publishing, Hardware, Multimedia and CD-ROM, Software, The BBS Industry, The MIDI Forum, *PC Magazine,* Computer Telephone
Education and Reference	Colleges and Universities, Computer Education, Educator to Educator, Fields of Study, International Students, Primary and Secondary Education, Student to Student
Home and Family	Genealogy, Home Improvement, KidSpace, Parenting in the 90s, Pets, Teen Forum, Work-At-Home Dads, Working Mothers
Science and Technology	Astronomy and Space, Biology and Life Sciences, Communications Technology, Computer Technology, Earth and Physical Sciences, Electronics, Engineering, Math, Medicine, Social Sciences, and Transportation
Business and Finance	Business Services, Jobs & Careers, News & Reference, Professions & Industries, Small Office/Home Office, UseNet Newsgroups, Wall Street
Arts and Entertainment	Art and Design, Books and Writing, Comedy and Humor, Genres, Movies, Music, Television and Radio, Theater
People and Communities	Advice and Support, Cultures, Menu Online, People to People, Religion, Women Online
The Internet Center	Internet Center BBS, Newgroups
Special Events	List changes daily. Includes special guests, shortcuts to new categories, and lists of special events happening on the network.
The MSN Member Lobby	Members Helping Members BBS, Netiquette Center, The Chat Garden
Interests, Leisure, and Hobbies	Arts and Crafts, Collecting, Games and Gaming, Hobbies and Avocations, Home Interests, Magazine, Mysteries, Outdoor Interests and Activities, Travel
Public Affairs	We the People, Armed Forces, C- SPAN, GoverNet, Inferno, Journalism World, Law Enforcement, Politics, Public Service

Double-clicking any icon in Categories opens a folder containing the forums available under that category. Forums can be nested. For example, the Software forum contains the Microsoft Forum, which is where Microsoft products are supported. Also, forums can contain any of the following six types of folders and documents:

- *Chat room.* A place where you can have a live conversation with other MSN members who see your comments immediately. Many conferences by leaders in various industries are held in chat rooms.

- *BBS.* A message area where you can exchange ideas with other like-minded people. BBSes are not live. Some are set up as file areas, which are read-only, where you can download the files attached to messages. BBSes are organized by areas of interest.

- *Media viewer title.* A file that is downloaded to your computer and viewed in the MSN Online Viewer. You view content in the right side of the viewer, and you can select different pages to view in the left side.

- *Download-and-run.* A file that is downloaded to your computer and executed. On MSN, this file is typically a Microsoft Word document. However, it can be any file type registered with Windows, such as a text file or bitmap file.

- *Kiosk.* A download-and-run document that contains additional information about the forum. Obviously, these documents are typically found in forums.

- *Forum.* A folder with a collection of related documents and subfolders. For example, a forum for cat lovers may have a BBS, chat area, and media viewer title explaining the history of cats.

Figure B.8, for example, shows the Shareware forum. This forum currently has a BBS, a chat area, a kiosk, and the Association of Shareware Professionals forum.

The path to this forum is \Categories\Computers & Software\ Software\Shareware. To get to this forum, you use the following steps:

1. Select CATEGORIES from MSN Central.

2. Double-click the Computers & Software icon representing a category.

3. Double-click the Software Forum icon.

4. Double-click the Shareware icon to go to the Shareware forum shown in figure B.8.

Tip

The Categories folder now contains several language-independent Category subfolders, such as Categories (US), Categories (UK), and Categories (AUS).

◄ See "Registering Files to Automatically Open an Application," p. 537

VIII

Appendixes

Tip

If it is not obvious what type of folder or document an icon represents, right-click on the icon and select Properties to see its type.

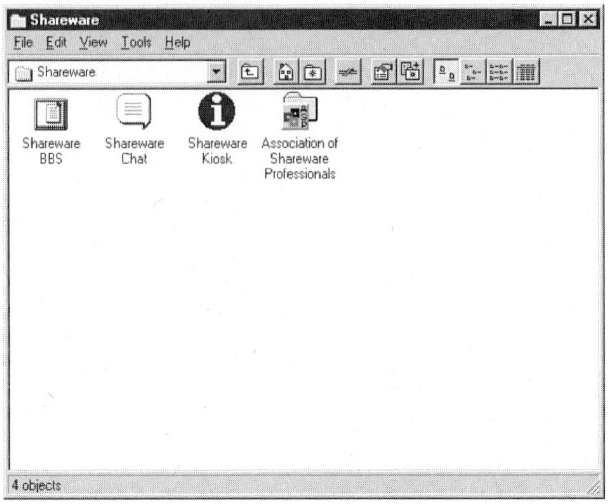

Fig. B.8

The contents of the Shareware forum. To read more information about this forum, double-click the Shareware Kiosk icon.

> **Note**
>
> You can go directly to a folder on MSN. Choose Edit, Goto, Other Location. Then type the *go word* for the folder you want. The go word is a special name given to each folder on MSN. To see a folder's go word, right-click the folder and choose Properties.

Communicating in Chat Rooms

Chat rooms are places on MSN where people gather to have live discussions. Mostly, people do chat in chat rooms. However, you'll frequently hear about conferences, debates, and other events occurring in chat rooms at predetermined times. In addition, MSN Today frequently lists upcoming events.

Tip

You can convey emotion in a chat room. For example, use the smiley *emoticon*—the emotion icon :-)—to indicate that you're grinning. See your MSN online help for more emoticons.

Chat rooms within a forum are dedicated to a particular topic. For example, a Windows 95 chat room will be used to discuss Windows 95. In reality, though, the discussion frequently wanders from the topic at hand to other mysteries of life. That is why chat rooms have *hosts*, or moderators. Hosts are provided to keep the conversation from becoming too brutal or getting off the given topic.

Figure B.9 shows a chat room, the MSN Member Lounge. This chat room is in the MSN Member Lobby forum. As indicated, there are three primary sections in this window:

- *Chat History pane.* Messages are displayed in this area immediately after they are posted. That's why they call it live!

■ *Compose pane.* You type a new message in the text box, and then press Enter or click Send. Your message is posted immediately.

■ *Member list.* You select a member name to get more information about that member. Then you can contact her or ignore her.

Notice that some members have a gavel beside their names. These members are hosts. They moderate the chat, greet people when they join the chat, and keep things civil.

Chat pane

Compose pane

Member list

Host

Fig. B.9
Chatting in the MSN Member Lounge.

VIII

Appendixes

Table B.2 shows the basic things you can do in a chat room.

Table B.2	Chat Room Tasks	
Task	**Description**	
Add the chat room to your Favorite Places folder	Choose File, Add to Favorite Places. Or click the Add to Favorite Places button in the toolbar.	
Ignore a member	Right-click a name in the member list and choose Ignore from the menu. Or select a name from the member list and click the Ignore button in the toolbar.	
Ignore many members	From the member list, select the names of the members you want to ignore. Choose View, Ignore Members from the menu. Then click Ignore Messages from Selected Members.	
	Alternatively, select the names of the members you want to ignore from the member list. Then click the Ignore icon in the toolbar.	

(continues)

Table B.2 Continued	
Task	**Description**
View member information	Right-click a name in the member list and choose Properties. Or select a name from the member list and click the Properties button in the toolbar.
Save the chat history	Choose File, Save History As. Then select or type a file name. The history can be printed with WordPad.
Receive notices when members join or leave	Choose Tools, Options from the menu. Click Join the Chat to receive messages when new members join; click Leave the Chat when members leave.

Exchanging Information in BBSs

A bulletin board is an area in an MSN forum where members exchange messages and files. The messages can be about anything, but typically they are related to the topic of the forum where the BBS is located. BBS messages are great for the following purposes:

- Exchanging ideas and opinions.

- Helping others and getting help with problems related to software, home improvements, pets, and just about any topic you can imagine.

- Reading the latest product information from your favorite vendor.

- Getting product support for hardware, software, and other products supported on the network.

- Posting files for other people to download. A file will not show up in the BBS until the forum manager, the person responsible for the forum's content, has approved it.

Tip

File areas on MSN are really just read-only BBSes. Each message in a file area has one or more file attachments. The message describes the content of the files.

Messages are grouped in a bulletin board by threads. A *thread* is a BBS conversation—a collection of messages related by subject. For example, if you post a message asking for help in a BBS and a kind person replies, both messages appear under the same subject heading as a thread.

Figure B.10 shows the Windows 95 Members To Members BBS. At this level, the BBS has only one message but contains many subfolders. You double-click a subfolder to access it. Many BBSes organize their messages into topics by creating multiple subfolders within the BBS. This approach makes it easier to find the information and the people with which you want to communicate.

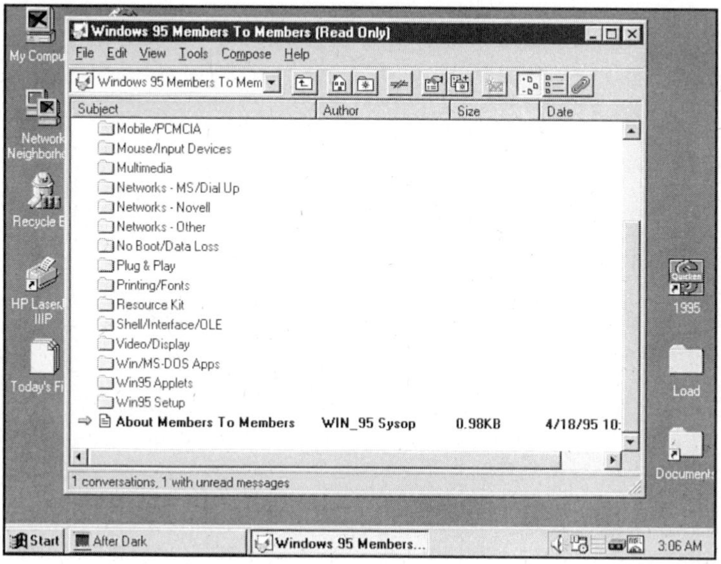

Fig. B.10
The Windows 95 Members To Members BBS.

Figure B.11 shows the General Discussion folder in the Windows 95 Members To Members BBS. As indicated in the figure, MSN provides a lot of feedback about the status of each message and thread. This feedback includes the following:

- Unread messages or threads with unread messages are indicated with the arrow pointing to the message header. When all the messages in the thread have been marked as read, the icon disappears.

- A message that is not a part of a thread or that is the last message in a thread is denoted with the Message icon next to the message header.

- A thread is indicated by the plus sign within a box next to a message header. You click the icon to expand the thread one level. You can expand additional levels of the thread by clicking the icons. The last message header in the thread will not have a plus sign beside it.

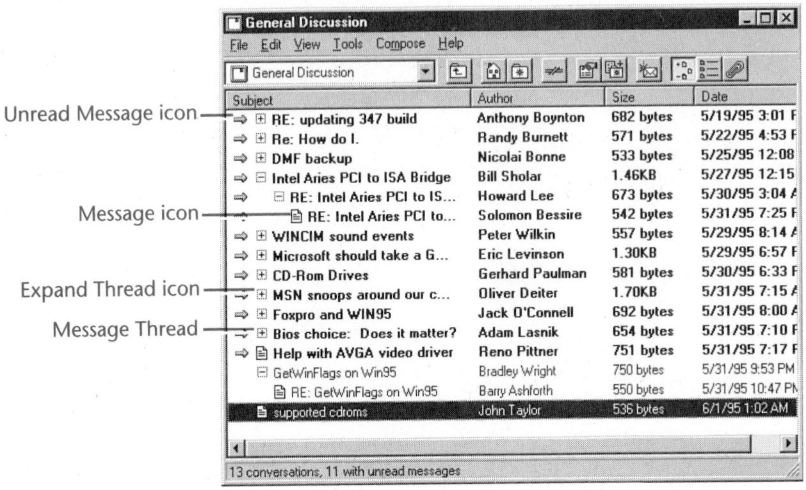

Fig. B.11
The General
Discussion
subfolder.

Unread Message icon

Message icon

Expand Thread icon

Message Thread

Table B.3 lists the basic tasks you can do in a BBS.

	Table B.3 BBS Tasks	
	Task	**Description**
	Add a BBS to your Favorite Places folder	Choose File, Add to Favorite Places. Or click the Add to Favorite Places button in the toolbar.
	Read a message	Double-click the message header.
	Compose a new message	Choose Compose, New Message from the menu or click the New Message button in the toolbar. Then type the message's subject and text. Choose File, Post Message or click the Post Message button on the toolbar.
	Reply to a message	Open the message as described earlier. Choose Compose, Reply to BBS or click the Reply to BBS button in the toolbar. Compose your message as described earlier.
	Reply via E-mail	Open the message as described earlier. Choose Compose, Reply by E-mail. Compose your message as described earlier.
	View a message's properties	Click a message and choose File, Properties. Or click a message and then click the Properties button in the toolbar.
	View attachments	Choose View, Attached Files or click the File View button in the toolbar.

Task	Description
Mark all messages as read	Choose Tools, Mark All Messages as Read.
Download an attached file	Open the message as described earlier. Double-click the attachment and click Download File. Alternatively, right-click the attachment and choose File Object, Download.
View the status of a downloading file	Choose Tools, File Transfer Status.
Send a file as	Begin composing a new message as an attachment, as described earlier. Choose Insert, File and select a file. Alternatively, click the Insert File button in the toolbar and select a file.

Note

MSN automatically decompresses or unzips files when they are downloaded. To disable this feature, choose Tools, Options from the File Transfer Status window. Then deselect Automatically Decompress Files.

Finding Folders and Files on The Microsoft Network

You've already learned how to find files on your computer. Finding folders and files on MSN is not much different. For example, you may want to find a forum about Windows 95, a chat room about golf, or any items relating to a particular company such as Symantec. To find folders and files on MSN, follow these steps:

◀ See "Finding Files," p. 523

1. Choose Tools, Find, On The Microsoft Network. MSN displays the Find dialog box shown in figure B.12.

2. In the Containing field, type the text for which you want to search. Optionally, click Description to include the description of each forum and file in the search.

VIII

Appendixes

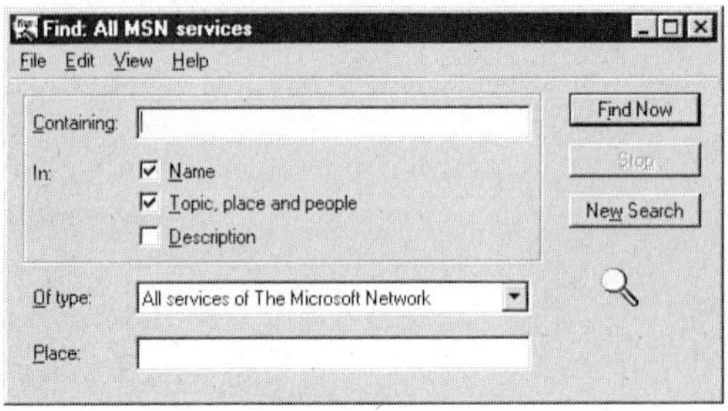

Fig. B.12
Type the text you
want to search for;
then click Find
Now.

3. Select the type of service in the Of Type list and then click Find Now.
   MSN performs the search and displays the results.

After MSN displays the search results, you can right-click a file or folder to
open it or create a shortcut to it.

> **Note**
>
> You can't search files or messages in a particular BBS.

Using the Internet through The Microsoft Network

Eventually, MSN will provide complete support for Internet e-mail,
newsgroups, and the World Wide Web. However, MSN is initially supporting
basic Internet e-mail and newsgroups. The following list describes the restrictions and plans for each Internet service:

◄ See "UseNet
Newsgroups,"
p. 940

- *E-mail.* MSN supports sending and receiving e-mail on the Internet.
  Currently, you cannot send or receive files using the Internet.

◄ See "Surfing
the Web with
Internet Ex-
plorer," p. 920

- *Newsgroups.* MSN provides support for viewing Internet newsgroups, but
  you cannot post messages to newsgroups. Microsoft intends to supply
  support for posting messages to newsgroups in the near future.

- *World Wide Web.* MSN doesn't support the Web at this time. However,
  Microsoft is working diligently on such support.

Exchanging E-Mail with Internet Users

Sending e-mail to an Internet address is no different from sending e-mail to an MSN address. Instead of typing an MSN address such as JQ_Doe, you type an Internet address such as john@msn.com. Receiving e-mail from an Internet user is just as easy. Before an Internet user can send you an e-mail message, the sender needs your Internet ID. Your Internet ID is <MSN ID>@MSN.COM, in which <MSN ID> is your MSN log-on ID.

◀ See "Electronic Mail," p. 905

Troubleshooting

I correctly addressed an e-mail message to an Internet user, but when I log on to MSN, it doesn't send the message.

Exchange determines which services will be used for Internet addresses by the order of the services in the Recipient Addresses are Processed in the Following Order list on the Delivery page of Exchange's Option menu. To use MSN to deliver e-mail to Internet users, choose Tools, Options from the Exchange menu. Then click the Delivery page and move The Microsoft Network Online Service to the top of the list.

Using Newsgroups

Internet newsgroups are identical to MSN BBSes. However, the content is not managed by MSN. You can find the Internet newsgroup BBSes at \Categories\The Internet Center\Newsgroups. Additionally, some newsgroups can be found in various forums where the newsgroup complements the forum.

Caution

The content of Internet newsgroups is not managed by MSN. Therefore, you may find some of the postings in newsgroups to be adult-oriented or particularly offensive. It is your responsibility to monitor your children's access to the Internet newsgroups, because MSN makes no provision for locking out offensive messages.

VIII

Appendixes

Appendix C

Exploring the Windows 95 Resource Kit

by R. Michael O'Mara

Microsoft split the user documentation for Windows 95 into two parts. The first part contains the User's Guide, help files, tutorial, and so on. This part is aimed at the average Windows 95 user and covers the Windows 95 user interface and features.

The Windows 95 Resource Kit comprises the *rest* of the Windows 95 user documentation. This kit provides more depth and detail about topics that (in Microsoft's estimation) the average user isn't likely to need. You can find information about customized setup and installation, network configuration, and the like. The Windows 95 Resource Kit is a manual, help files, and supplementary utilities aimed at network administrators and others who must support other Windows 95 users.

In this appendix, you learn

- Who needs the Windows 95 Resource Kit?

- How do you get the Resource Kit?

- How is the Resource Kit organized?

- What utilities are included in the Resource Kit?

It's important to understand that the Windows 95 Resource Kit is *not* a programmer's reference or software development kit—that's another area entirely. The Windows 95 Resource Kit is still part of the user-level documentation; it's just aimed at a higher-level user than the rest of the Windows 95 documentation.

Who Needs the Windows 95 Resource Kit?

Are you responsible for installing, configuring, or supporting multiple copies of Windows 95—especially on a network? If so, you need to get a copy of the Windows 95 Resource Kit.

Obviously, MIS managers, network administrators, help desk staff, and other corporate technical support personnel can benefit from the Windows 95 Resource Kit. Consultants and people serving in computer and network support roles in smaller businesses also will need the information in the Windows 95 Resource Kit.

Individual Windows 95 users are much less likely to need the Windows 95 Resource Kit. A high-end user attempting to employ Windows 95's connectivity features without assistance from a corporate network administrator may occasionally use the Windows 95 Resource Kit. However, average networked Windows 95 users are probably better off asking their network administrator for help than trying to look up answers on their own.

How Do You Get the Windows 95 Resource Kit?

The Windows 95 Resource Kit is a technical reference manual that contains information. As such, the manual is mainly text. In addition to the text-based information, the Windows 95 Resource Kit includes a few, small software utilities designed to help system administrators monitor and configure Windows 95 on networks.

If you have the full CD-ROM version of Windows 95, you already have an electronic copy of the Windows 95 Resource Kit. The Resource Kit appears as a Windows Help file in the \ADMIN\RESKIT\HELPFILE folder. The software utilities are available on the Windows 95 CD-ROM in the various subdirectories of the \ADMIN95 directory.

> **Note**
>
> Microsoft does not include the Windows 95 Resource Kit files when distributing Windows 95 on floppy disks. Also, other suppliers who are licensed to sell Windows 95 with their computer systems may not include the Windows 95 Resource Kit files.

If you don't have a copy of the Windows 95 Resource Kit, or you want a printed and bound version, you can order it direct from Microsoft Press or purchase a copy from many bookstores and software outlets. To order, call Microsoft Press at (800) 677-7377. When you purchase a copy of the Windows 95 Resource Kit, you get the Resource Kit in book form plus a CD-ROM containing help files and utility programs.

You may be reluctant to spend money for a paper copy of something you already have on disk—especially if you don't expect to use the Windows 95 Resource Kit much. However, if you expect to refer to the Windows 95 Resource Kit frequently, you will find the paper version much easier to search and use than a series of word processor files on a CD-ROM.

How Is the Windows 95 Resource Kit Organized?

This appendix gives an overview of the contents of the Windows 95 Resource Kit and how it's organized. You can get an idea of the information in the Windows 95 Resource Kit and perhaps get a head start on finding the resources you may need.

The Windows 95 Resource Kit manual is divided into eight sections. The sections of the kit are described following, complete with a list of the chapters in each section.

Part 1: Deployment Planning Guide

The first section presents Microsoft's suggested strategy for MIS managers planning to convert their users from Windows 3.1 to Windows 95. This information is of interest primarily to corporate support staff and has limited appeal for smaller businesses with more informal procedures.

- Chapter 1, "Deployment Planning Basics"

- Chapter 2, "Deployment Strategy and Details"

Part 2: Installation

This section covers installing Windows 95 on network servers and on multiple computers. You can find information on creating custom installations and setup scripts. (Sample setup scripts are included in the Windows 95 Resource Kit files.) You also can find technical details about Windows 95 setup and operating system startup in these chapters:

- Chapter 3, "Introduction to Windows 95 Setup"

- Chapter 4, "Server-Based Setup for Windows 95"

- Chapter 5, "Custom, Automated, and Push Installations"

- Chapter 6, "Setup Technical Discussion"

Part 3: Networking

Network administrators take note—this section makes the Windows 95 Resource Kit a *must have* for you. You can find technical details about configuring peer resource sharing services, configuring network adapters and protocols, and running Windows 95 on Windows NT, Novell NetWare, and other networks.

- Chapter 7, "Introduction to Windows 95 Networking"

- Chapter 8, "Windows 95 on Microsoft Networks"

- Chapter 9, "Windows 95 on NetWare Networks"

- Chapter 10, "Windows 95 on other Networks"

- Chapter 11, "Logon, Browsing, and Resource Sharing"

- Chapter 12, "Network Technical Discussion"

Part 4: System Management

Security and administrative controls are the focus of this section of the Windows 95 Resource Kit. You can gain information you need to implement system policies, user profiles, and management tools such as backup agents. The performance tuning chapter offers instructions for using Windows 95's performance settings.

- Chapter 13, "Introduction to System Management"

- Chapter 14, "Security"

- Chapter 15, "User Profiles and System Policies"

- Chapter 16, "Remote Administration"

- Chapter 17, "Performance Tuning"

Part 5: System Configuration

The system configuration section of the Windows 95 Resource Kit is a valuable reference for anyone installing, configuring, and troubleshooting devices in Windows 95 systems. The printing and fonts chapter is particularly valuable; it addresses printing on networks (both Microsoft and Novell) and using printing management utilities including the Hewlett-Packard JetAdmin utility and DEC PrintServer software.

- Chapter 18, "Introduction to System Configuration"

- Chapter 19, "Devices"

- Chapter 20, "Disks and File Systems"

- Chapter 21, "Multimedia"

- Chapter 22, "Application Support"

- Chapter 23, "Printing and Fonts"

Part 6: Communications

VIII

In addition to details on configuring modems, the Communications section includes valuable information on Microsoft Exchange (Microsoft's new universal mailbox) and Microsoft Fax. Road warriors will appreciate the chapter on dial-up networking (also known as remote network access). But the most popular chapter may be the one on Internet access. The information in this chapter provides the keys to unlocking Windows 95's built-in Internet access capabilities.

Appendixes

- Chapter 24, "Introduction to Windows 95 Communications"

- Chapter 25, "Modems and Communications Tools"

- Chapter 26, "Electronic Mail and Microsoft Exchange"

- Chapter 27, "Microsoft Fax"

- Chapter 28, "Dial-Up Networking and Mobile Computing"

- Chapter 29, "The Microsoft Network"

- Chapter 30, "Internet Access"

Part 7: Windows 95 Reference

The chapters on the Windows 95 architecture and international features may come in handy for some readers, as will the troubleshooting guidelines. But the key chapter in this section is the one on the Registry—Windows 95's repository for system configuration, networking, and software settings. This chapter may be the only place you can find information on this critical replacement for INI files.

- Chapter 31, "Windows 95 Architecture"

- Chapter 32, "Windows 95 Network Architecture"

- Chapter 33, "Windows 95 Registry"

- Chapter 34, "International Windows 95"

- Chapter 35, "General Troubleshooting"

Part 8: Appendixes

This requisite section of appendixes contains listings of settings, options, commands, and files. Note the first appendix; it contains a command summary of the Windows 95 replacements for MS-DOS commands.

- Glossary

- Appendix A, "Command-Line Commands Summary"

- Appendix B, "Windows 95 System Files"

- Appendix C, "Windows 95 INF Files"

- Appendix D, "MSBATCH.INF Parameters"

- Appendix E, "Microsoft Systems Management Server"

- Appendix F, "Macintosh and Windows 95"

- Appendix G, "HOSTS and LMHOSTS Files for Windows 95"

- Appendix H, "Shortcuts for Windows 95"

- Appendix I, "Accessibility"

- Appendix J, "Windows 95 Resource Directory"

What Utilities Are Included in the Resource Kit?

The utility programs that come with the Windows 95 Resource Kit provide system administrators with access to some of Windows 95's more powerful network and security features. If you're a system administrator, you should add these utilities to your toolbox—whether you get them as part of the Windows 95 Resource Kit or elsewhere.

You will find all these utilities on the Windows 95 CD-ROM. If you don't have the CD-ROM, you can obtain the utilities by ordering a copy of the Windows 95 Resource Kit from Microsoft. Microsoft also may make the utilities available on The Microsoft Network and other online services.

The following is a list of the utility programs that are included with the Windows 95 Resource Kit.

■ *Net Setup.* A Server-Based Setup utility that replaces the `setup /a` command and also lets you automate many Windows 95 installations across a network with installation scripts.

■ *Password List Editor.* Enables the system administrator to view a list of resources for which Windows 95 has cached passwords.

■ *System Policy Editor.* Use to create system policies that selectively control aspects of a specific Windows 95 environment when a user logs on to the network server.

■ *Net Watcher.* Enables you to check the status of all your shared resources in Windows 95.

■ *Microsoft Remote Registry Service.* Allows administrators to change Registry entries on other computers over the network.

■ *Microsoft RPC Print Provider.* Provides the full set of APIs required for a Windows 95 client to administer printer queues on Windows NT servers.

■ *Microsoft Print Agent for NetWare Networks.* Directs print jobs from a NetWare server to a computer running Windows 95 with Client for NetWare Networks and Microsoft Print Agent for NetWare Networks.

■ *SNMP Agent.* Use to monitor remote connections to Windows 95 computers with networks using Simple Network Management Protocol (SNMP).

VIII

Appendixes

Note

There are additional utilities on the Windows 95 CD-ROM in the \ADMIN\APPTOOLS directory.

Appendix D

Using Microsoft Plus!

by Lisa A. Bucki

If you previously used Windows 3.1 and have recently upgraded to Windows 95, then you're familiar with the many enhancements Windows 95 brings to your computer. As an operating system, Windows 95 provides an ample number of tools to enable you to manage your computer's resources, as well as numerous features to make your computer easier to use. The Microsoft Plus! Companion for Windows 95 provides even more tools and features to use with Windows 95.

Microsoft Plus! provides Desktop Themes, which enable you to choose new wallpaper, mouse pointers, sounds, and more to customize your Windows 95 desktop. It provides new visual settings to improve the appearance of large fonts, desktop wallpaper, and windows you're dragging. In addition, Plus! provides the System Agent, which enables you to schedule disk maintenance activities like disk backups; and ScanDisk 3, an even better version of the ScanDisk compression technology that comes with Windows 95. Finally, Plus! includes the Internet Explorer, software you can use to connect to the Internet via a local area network, the Microsoft Network, or an account you have with an Internet service provider.

This appendix introduces you to Plus! and the capabilities it adds to your system. In this appendix, you learn to

- Install all of Plus! or just the components you want, or remove Plus! from your computer

- Set up your system to connect with the Internet through the Internet Explorer

- Select and set up a desktop theme to customize Windows' appearance, and choose whether to use other desktop enhancements such as font smoothing

- Play 3D Pinball

- Schedule system maintenance with the System Agent

- Increase the amount of data you can store on a disk with DriveSpace 3

Installing Plus!

You have to install the Microsoft Plus! companion separately, after you install Windows 95 on your system. Plus! is available in both the 3.5 inch floppy disk and CD-ROM formats. For Plus! to run effectively on your system, the system must meet the following minimum requirements:

- 80486 processor or better

- 8M or more of Random Access Memory (RAM)

- Graphics display (monitor and video adapter card) that can display 256 colors or more; a 16-bit display that can handle more colors is recommended, and enables you to use all of the available Desktop Themes

- A sound card is recommended

The Plus! Setup program enables you to install the complete Plus! package (Typical installation) or only selected components of Plus! (Custom installation). Setup also includes the Internet Setup Wizard, which helps you install the Internet Explorer and set up your Internet connection. The next few sections describe how to install Plus! with Windows 95.

Performing a Typical Setup

▶ See "Performing a Custom Setup," p. 1145

Most users will use the Typical Setup option to install all of the components for Microsoft Plus! The Typical Setup requires up to 12-16M of hard disk space. If your system is low on hard disk space, or if you don't want to install all of Plus!'s features (such as when you're using a laptop computer and don't want to use some desktop features that may require more RAM), perform a Custom Setup.

> **Note**
>
> To install Microsoft Plus! for Windows 95, you need your Windows 95 Setup CD-ROM or floppy disks. Make sure these are available, or you will not be able to complete the Plus! Setup.

To perform a Typical Setup for Plus!, start your computer and wait for the Windows 95 desktop to load. Then follow these steps to complete the installation:

1. Place the first Plus! Setup floppy disk or the Plus! CD-ROM in the appropriate drive on your system.

2. Open the Start menu and choose Run. The Run dialog box appears.

3. Choose F:\SETUP.EXE from the Open drop-down list (F: represents the letter for the drive where you inserted the Setup disk or CD-ROM).

4. Choose OK. The Microsoft Plus! for Windows 95 Setup dialog box appears.

5. Click Continue.

6. At the Name and Organization Information dialog box, enter your Name and Organization. Click OK. Click OK again to confirm the entries.

7. Enter the 10-digit CD-key number or floppy disk key number from your Plus! package in the dialog box that appears. Click OK.

8. Write down the Product ID number shown in the next dialog box and store the number with your Plus! CD or disks. Click OK to confirm the Product ID number and continue Setup.

9. Setup searches your system and displays a dialog box listing the folder Setup will create to hold the Plus! files (see fig. D.1). To install Plus! to a different disk or folder, click Change Folder. In the Change Folder dialog box, specify the drive and folder to use (by choosing them from the list or typing a path in the Path text box), and then click OK. At the dialog box asking whether Windows 95 should create the destination folder, click Yes to continue. Whether you accepted the folder recommended by Setup or specified another one, click OK to accept the Install folder.

10. The next Setup dialog box asks you to specify what kind of install to perform: Typical or Custom. Click Typical. (Skip to the next section to review the Custom setup process.)

11. Setup checks your system's video installation. If your display runs in 256 colors, Setup displays the Video Resolution Check dialog box. This

dialog box asks whether you want to install the high-color Desktop Themes, even if your monitor currently displays only 256 colors. If your display is capable of displaying more colors (operating in 16-bit color or higher) and you have ample hard disk space, click Yes. Otherwise, click No.

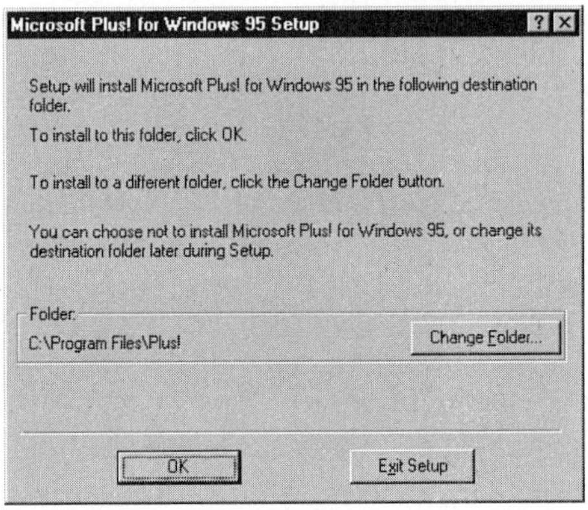

Fig. D.1

The Plus! Setup program tells you which folder the Plus! files will be installed in.

12. Setup checks your system for necessary disk space, then begins copying files to your computer (see fig. D.2). If you're installing Plus! from floppy disks, swap disks into and out of the drive when prompted. Setup displays a message that it's updating your system, then displays the Windows 95 Applet Installation dialog box, reminding you to have your Windows 95 install disks or CD-ROM available. Click OK to continue.

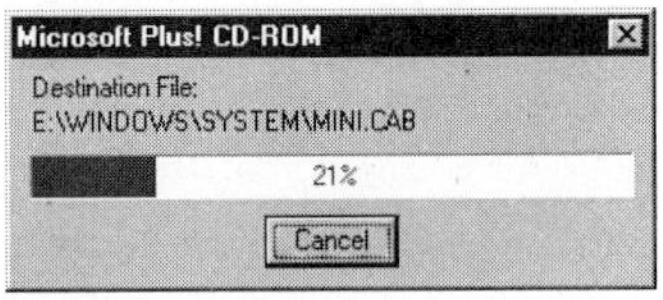

Fig. D.2

Setup shows you its progress in copying files to your hard disk.

13. Setup prompts you to insert the Windows 95 CD-ROM or a particular Setup disk. Insert it into the appropriate drive, then click OK. Windows 95 Setup tells you that it's updating the Shortcuts.

14. Setup next displays the initial dialog box for the Internet Setup Wizard (see fig. D.3). If you don't need to set up to connect with the Internet, click Cancel. If you do want to set up your Internet connection, click Next and proceed to the "Setting Up the Internet Explorer" section later in this appendix.

Fig. D.3
The Internet Setup Wizard enables you to set up Windows 95 to connect to the Internet.

15. If you clicked Cancel in step 14, the Internet Setup Wizard asks you to confirm that you want to exit the Wizard. Click Yes to do so.

16. The Set Up a Desktop Theme dialog box appears. Click OK to continue.

17. The Desktop Themes dialog box appears, allowing you to select your first Desktop Theme. Click OK to continue.

18. Microsoft Plus! Setup displays a dialog box telling you that it needs to restart Windows. To complete the setup, click the Restart Windows button. Your computer and Windows 95 restart. Notice that the Windows 95 startup screen now reads *Microsoft Windows 95 Microsoft Plus!* to indicate that you've successfully installed Microsoft Plus!

► See "Working with Desktop Themes," p. 1150

VIII

Appendixes

Performing a Custom Setup

If you want to install Microsoft Plus! but don't need to install all its features because you're short on hard disk space, you can perform a Custom Setup to pick and choose which features you really want to install. To perform a Custom Setup, use the following steps:

1. Follow steps 1 through 9 of the Typical Setup procedure described in the previous section.

2. When Setup asks whether you want to perform a Typical or Custom Setup, click Custom. The Microsoft Plus! for Windows 95-Custom dialog box appears (see fig. D.4).

3. To customize the installation for a particular component, click the component name in the Options list, then click the Change Option button.

Fig. D.4

This dialog box lets you select which components to install on your system.

Remove the check mark beside each program component you don't want to install on your system.

Space required to install the selected feature

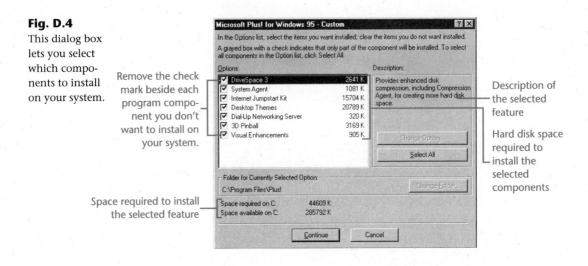

Description of the selected feature

Hard disk space required to install the selected components

4. In the dialog box that appears, click to deselect features you don't want to install in the Options list (a description of each option appears to the right of the list to help you make your selections), then click OK to return to the Custom dialog box. Repeat this step for each of the components you want to customize.

5. When you've finished specifying what components to install in the Custom dialog box, click the Continue button. After you click Continue, the Setup process progresses just like a Typical Setup.

Setting Up the Internet Explorer

The Internet Explorer software enables you to connect to the Microsoft Network or the Internet via a direct network connection or a PPP dial-up account from an Internet service provider. Microsoft Plus! provides the Internet Explorer software, plus the Internet Setup Wizard (refer to fig. D.3). You can use the Internet Setup Wizard to install the Internet Explorer while you're installing the rest of Plus!. Or, if you want to use the Wizard later, after you install Plus!, open the Start menu and choose Programs, Accessories, Internet Tools, and then Internet Setup Wizard.

> **Note**
>
> Chapters 29, 30, and Appendix B explain basic communications and Internet concepts, how to work with the Internet Explorer, and how to work with the Microsoft Network, respectively. See those chapters to learn more about the Internet. In particular, Chapter 30, "Using FTP, the World Wide Web, and other Internet Services," explains how to work with the Internet Explorer after you've installed it.

To use the Internet Setup Wizard to install the Internet Explorer, follow these steps:

1. Click Next from the Internet Setup Wizard Welcome dialog box to proceed with the setup. The How to Connect dialog box appears (see fig. D.5).

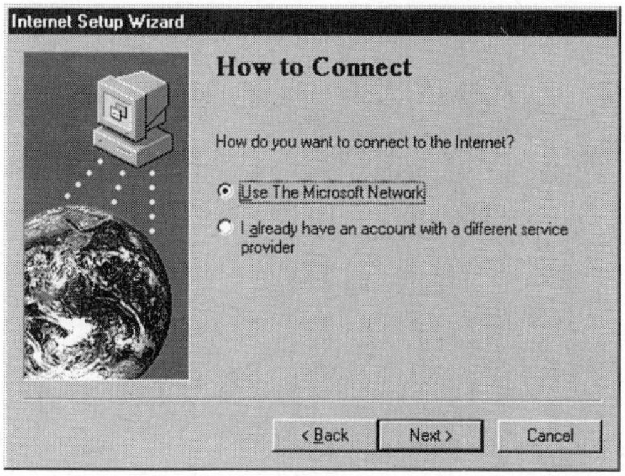

Fig. D.5
The Internet Setup Wizard asks you to specify how you will connect to the Internet—via the Microsoft Network or an existing service provider account.

> **Note**
>
> If you are connected to a LAN,Microsoft Plus! displays a dialog box prompting to see whether you want to connect to the Internet through your LAN or to connect using a modem. Choose the LAN option only if your LAN is using TCP/IP and is connected to the Internet.

2. Specify whether you want to connect via the Microsoft Network or a PPP account you have with an Internet service provider by clicking the appropriate option button. Click Next to continue.

3. The Installing Files dialog box appears, reminding you that you might need your Windows 95 setup CD-ROM or disks. Click Next to continue.

4. The Setup Wizard copies files to your hard disk. When it concludes, it displays a dialog box asking you to insert your Windows 95 Setup CD-ROM or disk into the appropriate drive. Do so, then click OK.

5. The Setup Wizard copies additional files to your system. Then, the process varies, depending on whether you chose to connect via the Microsoft Network or an Internet Service Provider. You can choose to set up a new Microsoft Network account or connect to an existing Microsoft Network or Internet account. Depending on which method you choose, the Wizard will guide you through the process. Simply

respond to each Wizard dialog box, providing information such as your Internet service provider's IP address, and your user name and password. Click Next after you provide each item of information the Wizard requests.

6. A final Setup Wizard dialog box appears, informing you that Setup is complete. Click the Finish button.

7. The Setup Wizard displays a dialog box telling you that it needs to restart Windows. To complete the setup, click Restart Windows. Your computer and Windows 95 restart.

Uninstalling When You Need To

Microsoft Plus! can take advantage of Windows 95's Add/Remove Programs feature, which enables you to automatically uninstall a program. With Plus!, you can remove the whole program or selected components from your hard disk if you no longer use them or want to replace them. To uninstall Plus!, follow these steps:

1. Open the Start menu and choose Settings, Control Panel. The Control Panel window opens.

2. Double-click the Add/Remove Programs icon. The Add/Remove Program Properties sheet appears.

Tip
You also can use this process to reinstall parts of the Plus! package, such as installing the high-color Desktop Themes after you perform the initial Plus! Setup.

3. The center of the sheet lists programs that can be added or removed from your system. Double-click Microsoft Plus! for Windows 95 in the list.

4. The Microsoft Plus! for Windows 95 Setup installation maintenance dialog box appears (see fig. D.6).

5. You can remove part of or all of the Plus! program. To uninstall all of Plus!, click the Remove All button. Or, to choose which components to remove, click the Add/Remove button to display the Maintenance Install dialog box shown in figure D.7. In the Options list, click to clear the check mark beside each Plus! component to remove from your system, then click Continue.

6. Whether you're removing all or parts of Plus!, a dialog box appears asking you to confirm the removal. Click Yes to continue the uninstall process. Setup removes the Plus! files from your system.

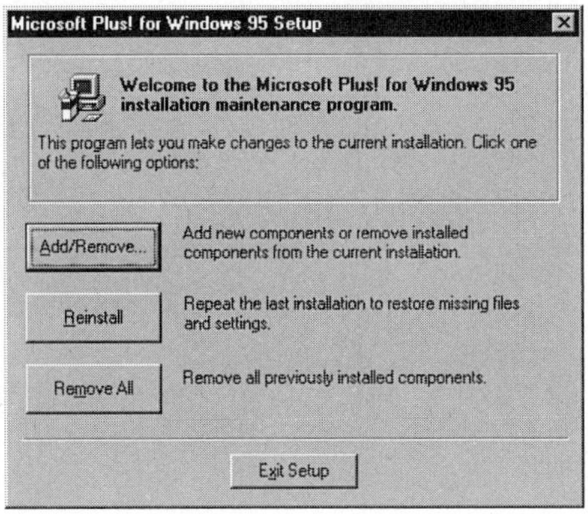

Fig. D.6
This Setup dialog
box enables you to
uninstall part of or
all of Plus!.

7. Microsoft Plus! Setup displays a dialog box telling you that it needs to restart Windows. To complete the uninstalling of Plus!, click Restart Windows. Your computer and Windows 95 restart.

Tip
Rerunning the
Setup program
from the Microsoft
Plus! CD-ROM or
floppy disks also
displays the instal-
lation mainte-
nance dialog box.

VIII

Working with Desktop Themes

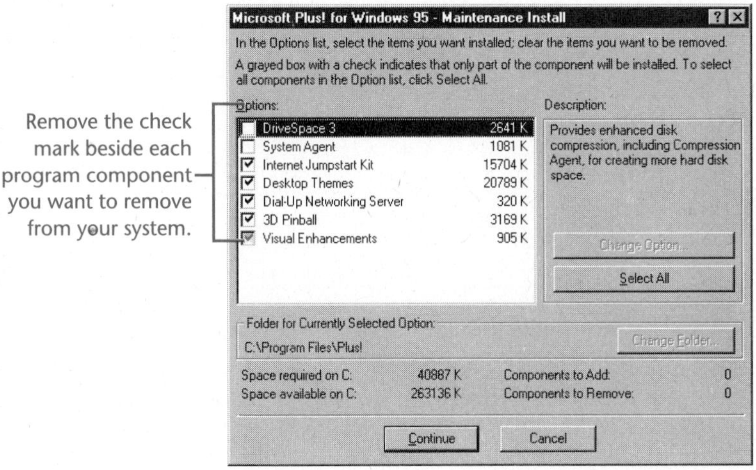

Remove the check
mark beside each
program component
you want to remove
from your system.

Appendixes

Fig. D.7
To add or remove
Plus! components,
use the Mainte-
nance Install
dialog box.

The Microsoft Plus! Desktop Themes provide you with appealing graphics and sounds to decorate your desktop and highlight system events (see fig. D.8). Each Desktop Theme offers a coordinated set of elements, so you can set the appropriate mood for your computing experience. Plus! provides Desktop

Theme combinations for computers displaying in 256 colors and for computers displaying in 16-bit or higher color. If you did not install the high-color Desktop Themes, you can rerun the Plus! Setup at any time to do so. The following are the Desktop Themes provided with Plus!:

256 Color

Dangerous Creatures (see fig. D.8)

Leonardo da Vinci

Science

The 60's USA

Sports

Windows 95

High Color

Inside Your Computer

Nature

The Golden Era

Mystery

Travel

Fig. D.8
Make every
workday a safari
by choosing the
Dangerous
Creatures Desktop
Theme.

When you choose a Desktop Theme, you can specify whether to replace Windows screen elements you specify using the Control Panel. (To learn how to change various desktop elements with the Control Panel, refer to Chapter 5, "Customizing Windows 95.") Desktop Themes provides these desktop elements; you can choose which of these you want to use for your system:

- *Screen Saver*. Displays the Theme screen saver when you leave your computer idle.

- *Sound Events*. Assigns the Theme sounds to system events such as Windows startup and exit.

- *Mouse Pointers*. Applies the Theme pointer styles for different types of pointers, such as the pointer used to select text or the one that appears while Windows is busy performing an operation.

- *Desktop Wallpaper*. Covers the desktop with the decorative background provided by the Theme.

- *Icons*. Assigns custom Theme icons to desktop objects like the My Computer object and the Recycle Bin.

- *Icon Size and Spacing*. Makes desktop icons use the icon size and spacing specified by the Theme; keep in mind that larger icons use more computer memory, so if your system is low on memory, don't use this option.

- *Colors*. Applies the Theme colors to windows and other screen elements.

- *Font Names and Styles*. Uses the Theme fonts for screen elements like window titles.

- *Font and Window Sizes*. Uses the Theme font sizes and default window sizes.

Tip

If you need a high degree of accuracy when pointing with the mouse, the <u>M</u>ouse Pointer option for several Themes might make your pointing more difficult because of the pointer shapes assigned by the Theme. If you have trouble with this, deselect the <u>M</u>ouse Pointer option for the current Theme.

VIII

Appendixes

As mentioned earlier, the Theme replaces the desktop elements you specify using the Control Panel. You should note, however, that the most recent element you select using either method (Desktop Themes or the Control Panel) becomes active. So, for example, if you apply a Desktop Theme, but aren't quite satisfied with the screen saver, you can use the Control Panel to choose another screen saver to use.

Selecting and Setting Up a Theme

Plus! Setup! creates an object icon for the Desktop Themes in the Windows 95 Control Panel, which contains other objects for controlling Windows' appearance and operation. Use the following steps to use the Desktop Themes object to select a Theme:

1. Open the Start menu and choose <u>S</u>ettings, <u>C</u>ontrol Panel.

2. In the Control Panel window, double-click the Desktop Themes icon (see fig. D.9).

Fig. D.9

Select a Desktop Theme using the Control Panel.

Double-click this icon

3. The Desktop Themes dialog box appears, as shown in figure D.10. Use this dialog box to select and set up a Theme.

Select a Theme from this drop-down list.

Click one of these buttons to preview a screen saver, sound, or other element.

Fig. D.10

Plus! provides numerous options for setting up the Desktop Theme of your choice.

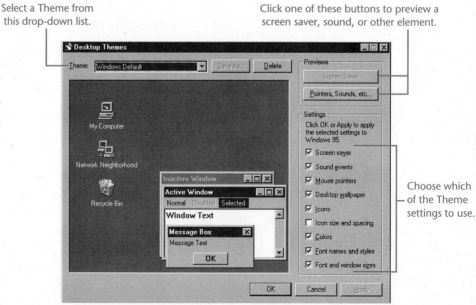

Choose which of the Theme settings to use.

Click the down arrow beside the Theme drop-down list to display the available Desktop Themes. Click the name of the Theme you want to use. A dialog box tells you that the Theme files are being imported. When that dialog box closes, the preview area of the Desktop Themes changes to display the appearance of the Theme you selected, as shown in figure D.11.

This is how the Leonardo da Vinci theme looks.

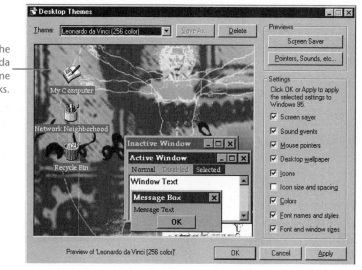

Fig. D.11
After you select a Desktop Theme, you see a preview of your Windows desktop.

4. At the right of the dialog box, choose the Settings to use for the Theme you selected. To deselect a setting, click to remove the check from the box beside it.

5. (Optional) To preview the selected Theme's screen saver, click Screen Saver in the Previews area. The screen saver appears on-screen. Move the mouse or press a key to conclude the preview.

6. (Optional) To preview several of the selected Theme's other elements, click Pointers, Sounds, etc. in the Previews area. A Preview dialog box for the Theme appears; the dialog box has three tabs for Pointers, Sounds, and Visuals. Click the tab you want to view. Each tab offers a list box with the elements for the theme. For the Pointers and Visuals tabs, simply click an element in the list to see a preview in the Preview or Picture area. For the Sounds tab, click an element in the list, then click the right arrow icon near the bottom of the dialog box to hear the sound. Click Close to conclude your preview.

7. After you have selected a theme, chosen settings, and previewed elements to your satisfaction, choose OK to close the Desktop Themes window. The selected Desktop Theme appears on your system.

Saving a Custom Theme

Any Control Panel changes you make after selecting a Theme take precedence over the Theme settings. In fact, you can make desktop setting changes in Control Panel, and then save those settings as a custom Theme. To do so, follow these steps:

Tip
To permanently delete a Desktop Theme, select it in the Theme drop-down list, then click Delete. Click Yes in the dialog box that appears to confirm the deletion.

1. Use Control Panel to change any settings you want, including the wallpaper, screen colors, sounds, and so on. See Chapter 5 to learn how to use Control Panel to customize Windows 95.

2. If the Control Panel window isn't open, open the Start menu and choose Settings, Control Panel.

3. In the Control Panel window, double-click the Desktop Themes icon.

4. Click the Save As button. The Save Theme dialog box appears (see fig. D.12).

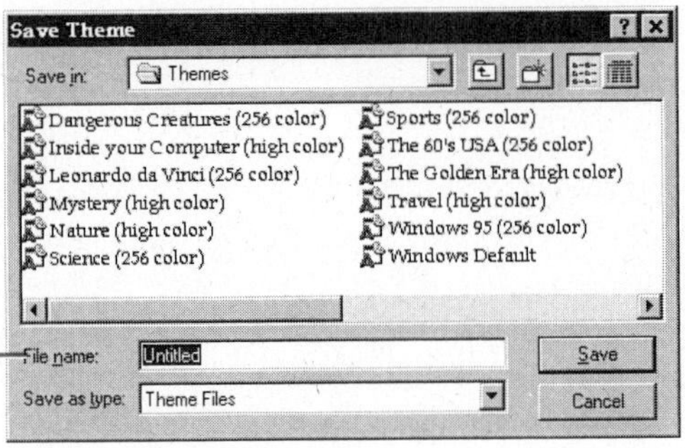

Fig. D.12
You can enter a file name in the File Name text box to save a custom Desktop Theme.

Enter the Theme
name here.

5. (Optional) Choose another folder in which to save the Theme.

6. Enter a unique name for the Theme in the File Name text box.

7. Click Save to save the Theme and return to the Desktop Themes dialog box. The newly saved Theme appears as the Theme selection.

8. Click OK to accept your new Theme and apply it to Windows 95.

Adjusting Plus! Visual Settings

Plus! adds new features to the Display settings available in the Windows 95 Control Panel. These visual settings are designed, primarily, to make your desktop more attractive. Plus! enables you to specify new icons for the My Computer, Network Neighborhood, and Recycle Bin desktop icons. You can choose to show the contents of a window (rather than just an outline) when you drag the window. Choose whether you want to smooth the appearance of large fonts on-screen. You also can choose to show icons with all possible colors or expand the wallpaper (when centered using the Background tab of the Display Properties dialog box from Control Panel) so it stretches to fill the entire screen.

> **Note**
>
> Most of the Plus! visual settings require more system resources than the normal display settings. In particular, showing window contents while dragging and using all colors in icons consumes more RAM. Consider all your computing requirements before you use up RAM by selecting any of these features. If you notice that Windows 95 runs considerably more slowly with any of these features enabled, turn off the features.

To work with the Plus! visual settings, open the Start menu and choose Settings, Control Panel. In the Control Panel window, double-click the Display icon. The Display Properties sheet appears. Click the Plus! tab to display its options, as shown in figure D.13. To assign a new Desktop icon, click the icon you want to change in the Desktop Icons area. Click Change Icon. In the Change Icon dialog box that appears, scroll to display the icon you want, then click OK to accept the change.

To enable any of the other Plus! display features, select the feature in the Visual settings area of the Plus! page. When a check appears beside the feature, that feature is selected. If you want more information about a particular feature, right-click the feature, then click What's This?. A brief description of the feature appears. Click or press Esc to clear the description. To accept your visual settings and close the Display Properties sheet, click OK. Close the Control Panel window, if you want.

VIII

Appendixes

Fig. D.13
Plus! enables you
to make additional
adjustments to the
Windows Display
Properties.

Playing 3D Pinball

Most of you already know that playing games is really the best use for your
$2,000 computer. Windows 95's smoothly integrated multimedia capabilities
promise to make your game-playing experience more satisfying than ever.
Plus! gives you an opportunity to take advantage of Windows multimedia via
the 3D Pinball game included with Plus!. 3D Pinball offers well-crafted on-
screen graphics, fun sounds and music, and a true-to-life pinball game feel—
flippers and all.

Starting 3D Pinball and Setting It Up

To start 3D Pinball, open the Start menu and choose Programs, Accessories,
Games, Space Cadet Table. After an opening screen briefly displays, the 3D
Pinball window appears.

> **Note**
>
> If there is no shortcut to the pinball game in the Start menu, use find file to search for
> the Pinball program on your hard drive. It should be in the PINBALL folder wherever
> Plus! was installed which would be \PROGRAM FILES\PLUS!\ PINBALL by default.
> The file name to run is PINBALL.EXE..

Before you begin playing, you might want to set up a few of the features in
3D Pinball. Here's a review of the key features you can control:

- To toggle between displaying 3D Pinball in a window or as a full screen without the menu bar, choose Options, Full Screen or F4.

- Choose Options, Select Players to set up a game for one to four players.

- Choose Options, Sounds or Options, Music to toggle those features on and off.

- Choose Options, Player Controls, or press F8 to display the Player Controls dialog box. Here, you can change the keys you press to play the game, such as which keys represent the flippers, the plunger, and various table bumps.

Playing and Exiting 3D Pinball

When you initially start the 3D Pinball program it appears ready to begin a new game. At any other time, you can start a new game by choosing Game, New Game or by pressing F2. When you do so, you'll see the Awaiting Deployment message in the lower-right corner of the Pinball window.

You use the keyboard to play the game, although there are menu equivalents for several operations. Following are the key commands you'll use:

- Control the plunger with the spacebar. Press the spacebar for a second, then release it to launch the ball. The length of time you depress the spacebar affects the strength of the launch. The Game, Launch Ball command performs a simple launch.

- Press the Z key for the left flipper and the / key for the right flipper. You can press F8 to display the Player Controls dialog box to change these keys.

- You can bump the table with simple keystrokes: X (left table bump), (right table bump), up arrow (bottom table bump).

- Pause or restart the game by choosing Game, Pause/Resume Game or by pressing F3.

As with other Windows applications, close 3D Pinball by clicking the Window close box. You also can choose Game, Exit.

Tip

Bumping the table too much will result in a tilt, just like on a real pinball game.

VIII

Appendixes

Managing Utilities with the System Agent

Most users tend not to perform system-maintenance operations until after a disaster strikes. Some of us simply rebel at having to perform any kind of regularly scheduled maintenance; others simply can't keep a schedule. For users in either category, Microsoft Plus! for Windows 95 provides the System Agent, a program that enables you to schedule when to run other programs, especially system-maintenance utilities like Disk Defragmenter, ScanDisk (for more about using these system utilities, see Chapter 16, "Working with Disks and Disk Drives"), and Compression Agent (see the last section in this appendix). The System Agent can run other programs, as well, and notify you when your hard disk is low on space.

By default, the System Agent is enabled after you install Plus! This means that each time you start Windows 95, the System Agent starts automatically and runs in the background, only becoming active when it needs to start a scheduled program or notify you of low disk space. Even though System Agent is active by default, it isn't fully set up. After you install System Agent, it automatically places Low Disk Space Notification, ScanDisk for Windows (Standard Test), Disk Defragmenter, and ScanDisk for Windows (Thorough Test) programs in the System Agent. You need to manually tell the System Agent which other programs to run, when to run them, and which program features to use. To schedule programs with the System Agent, use the following steps:

Tip

Schedule time-consuming programs like Disk Defragmenter for a time you won't normally use your computer. Then, leave your computer on during that time, and System Agent will handle the task for you.

1. Open the Start menu and choose Programs, Accessories, System Tools, and then click System Agent. The System Agent window opens.

2. Choose Program, Schedule a New Program. The Schedule a New Program dialog box appears (see fig. D.14).

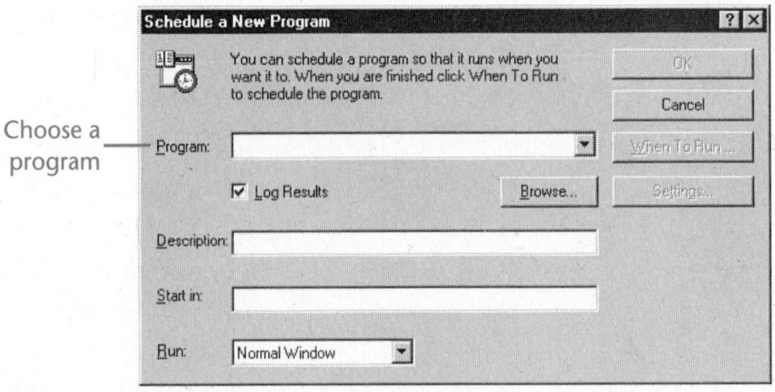

Fig. D.14

Use this dialog box to select programs for System Agent to run according to the schedule you set.

Choose a program

3. Click the drop-down list arrow to open the Program list. Choose a program from the list that appears. You can choose ScanDisk for Windows, Disk Defragmenter, Compression Agent, or Low Disk Space Notification. If you want to run a program other than one of these, click Browse, select the program to run in the Browse dialog box, and click OK. No matter what method you use, the selected program appears as the Program choice.

4. (Optional) If needed, you can edit the Description for the program and the Start In folder, which specifies the folder containing files the program needs to run.

5. (Optional) Open the Run drop-down list and specify whether you want the program to run in a Normal Window, Minimized, or Maximized.

6. To specify the schedule for the program, click the When to Run button. The Change Schedule Of... dialog box appears (see fig. D.15).

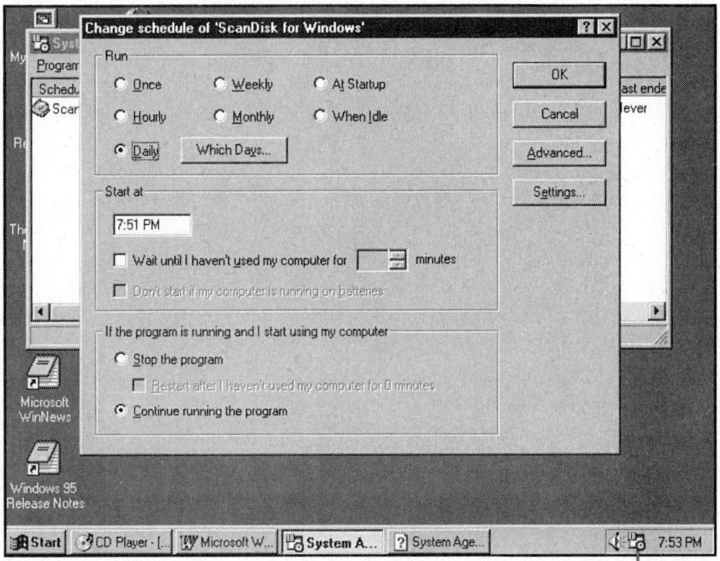

Fig. D.15
Use the Change Schedule dialog box to set up a schedule for the selected program.

This icon in the status area of the taskbar lets you know that System Agent is loaded.

7. Click a Run option, such as Weekly or Monthly. Your choice here affects the options available in the Start At area of the dialog box.

8. Specify the options you want in the Start At area. Although there might be other options, depending on your choice in step 7, you always need to enter a starting time. Also, you can specify a number of minutes to tell System Agent to wait if you're using your computer when the scheduled program runtime occurs.

9. Choose whether System Agent should Stop the Program or Continue Running the Program should you start using your computer when the scheduled program is running. Stopping the program can protect against data loss while running system utilities.

10. Click Settings to accept your changed schedule of options and to control which features the selected program uses when the System Agent runs the program. The Scheduled Settings dialog box that appears varies depending on the selected program. For example, figure D.16 shows the Scheduled Settings dialog box for the Disk Defragmenter program.

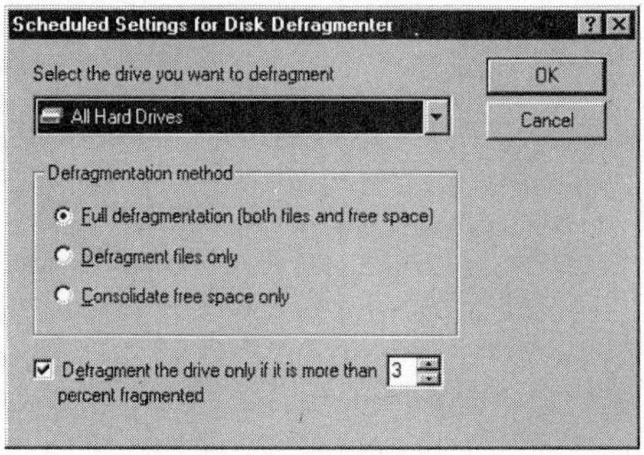

Fig. D.16
Choose which settings to use for the selected program when System Agent runs it.

11. Specify the settings you want for the selected program, then click OK to close the Scheduled Settings dialog box.

12. Click OK again to finish scheduling the program. System Agent adds the program to the list of scheduled programs. Figure D.17 shows the System Agent window with two scheduled programs.

> **Note**
>
> Keep in mind that you can schedule the same program to run at different times with different settings. For example, you can schedule a Standard ScanDisk check once a week, plus a thorough check once a month.

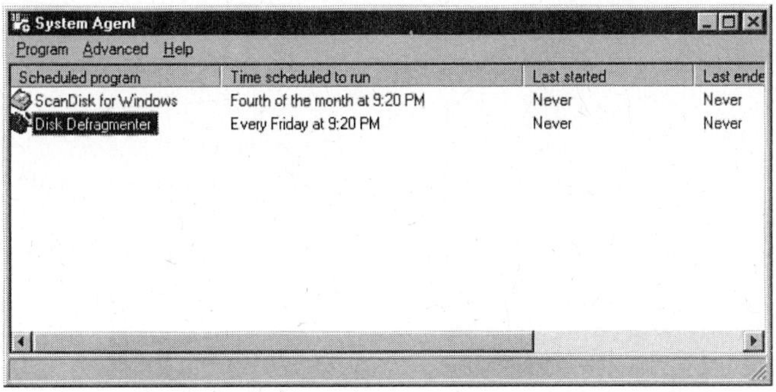

Fig. D.17
Use the System
Agent window to
view the currently
scheduled
programs.

Although you can use the Program menu choices to make changes to the
schedule and settings for one of the listed programs, it's faster to simply
right-click on the program you want to make changes for. A shortcut menu
appears, from which you can choose the following:

■ Choose Properties to change things like the program startup folder and
settings (click the Settings button in the dialog box that appears).

■ Use the Change Schedule option to adjust how often System Agent runs
the program.

■ Choose Run Now to run the program immediately, using the settings
you've specified.

■ Choose the Disable option to prevent the listed program from running
at the designated time, but leave the program on the list; choose Disable again to reinstate the program's schedule.

■ Choose Remove to delete the selected program from the System Agent
list; confirm the deletion by clicking Yes at the warning that appears.

The Advanced menu in System Agent offers two commands for controlling
System Agent itself. Toggle the Suspend System Agent option off whenever
you want to stop all your regularly scheduled programs from running; then
toggle this choice back on when you need to. The Stop Using System Agent
choice completely stops System Agent operation; after you use this option,
System Agent no longer loads when you start Windows, and you have to
select System Agent from the System Tools Shortcuts to start using it. To close
System Agent after setting it up, choose Program, Exit.

VIII

Appendixes

Working with DriveSpace 3

Windows 95 offers DriveSpace disk compression, which enables you to pack more data on your hard and floppy disks. Chapter 16, "Working with Disks and Disk Drives," introduces DriveSpace and disk compression; you won't revisit the basic concepts here. Although DriveSpace provides many benefits, it also has its limitations. That's where DriveSpace 3, offered as part of the Microsoft Plus! package, comes in.

For starters, DriveSpace 3 can handle larger disks—up to 2G—than the Windows 95 DriveSpace, which can only handle hard disks up to 512M in size. To be more efficient, DriveSpace 3 works with smaller units of data on the disk—512-byte sectors as opposed to the 32K byte cluster size regular DriveSpace works with. This ensures that DriveSpace 3 wastes less space on the disk. Finally, DriveSpace 3 offers two new, more dense compression formats—one of which is particularly suited for Pentium systems.

Keep in mind that, although compression provides you with extra disk space, it's often slower to used a compressed disk. And, the greater the compression, the slower your system is likely to perform when working with the compressed disk. Also, compressing your system's primary hard disk can take quite a bit of time, during which you won't be able to work with your system. Plan to compress this disk only when you don't have any critical work to perform.

Use the following steps to compress a disk with DriveSpace 3:

1. Open the Start menu and choose Programs, Accessories, System Tools. Click DriveSpace (after Plus! installation, the icon beside the DriveSpace will include a 3 to indicate DriveSpace 3). The DriveSpace 3 window appears (see fig. D.18).

Fig. D.18
The DriveSpace 3 window displays the available drives on your system.

Click the drive to compress.

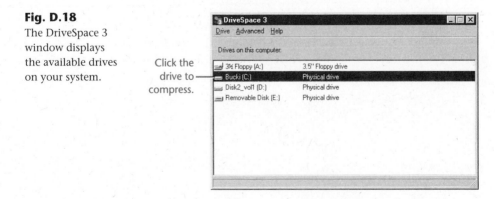

2. Click the drive that you want to compress.

> **Note**
>
> If you've previously compressed a hard disk with DoubleSpace or DriveSpace (for Win 95 or for earlier DOS versions), you can select the disk, then choose Drive, Upgrade to convert the disk to DriveSpace 3 format.

3. Choose Advanced, Settings. The Disk Compression Settings dialog box appears (see fig. D.19).

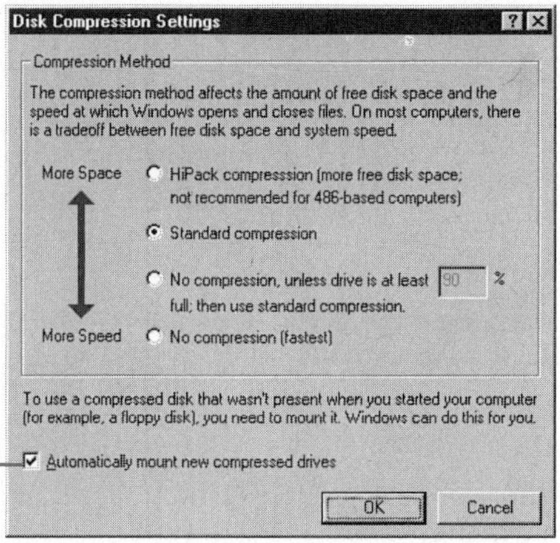

Leave this check-box enabled when compressing a floppy disk so that Windows will mount it auto-matically when-ever you insert it into your drive.

Fig. D.19
Be sure you understand the trade-offs associ-ated with the different compres-sion methods before choosing one.

VIII

Appendixes

4. Click the option button for the compression method you want to use:

No Compression

No Compression, Unless Drive Is at least X% Full...only compresses the disk after it's more full than the percentage you specify

Standard Compression compresses the disk contents by approxi-mately a 1.8:1 ratio

HiPack Compression compresses the disk contents by up to 2.3:1

> **Note**
>
> As always, the compression ratio on your hard drive will depend on the type of files being compressed.

5. Click OK to close the Compression Settings dialog box and accept the specified compression method.

6. Choose Drive, Compress. The Compress a Drive dialog box appears, informing you of the estimated results of the compression operation—that is, how much free space and used space the disk will have after compression.

7. Click Options. The Compression Options dialog box appears. Use it to specify a drive letter and free space for the Host drive where DriveSpace 3 will store compressed information about the drive. You should only need to change these first two options if your system is connected to a network that uses drive H for another purpose. If you're compressing a floppy disk you might use on another computer that doesn't have DriveSpace 3, click to select the Use DoubleSpace-Compatible Format check box; note that you do need to select this option for Windows 95 systems without DriveSpace 3 or for systems using DriveSpace from a DOS 6.X version. Click OK to accept the Compression Options you set.

8. Click the Start button in the Compress a Drive dialog box. The Are You Sure? dialog box appears, asking you to confirm the compression operation.

◀ See "Backing Up Your Files," p. 555

9. Click the Back Up Files button to make a backup copy of the files on the disk before you compress it. This is an important safety measure; skipping it isn't recommended.

10. DriveSpace 3 runs the backup utility installed to work with your system. Follow any on-screen instructions to complete the backup process.

11. When the backup is finished, click Continue to compress the disk. DriveSpace 3 compresses the disk, then redisplays the Compress a Drive dialog box to report on the compression results.

12. Click Close to complete compressing the disk.

DriveSpace 3 offers numerous other tools for mounting and unmounting compressed disks, uncompressing disks, and more. As you work more frequently with compressed disks, these features will come in handy and help you make your disks much more efficient in the amount of data they handle and the way they perform.

Managing Compression with the Compression Agent

After you compress a disk, you might want to recompress it later to ensure that the compression is optimized and that all files are compressed. Microsoft Plus! for Windows 95 offers the perfect tool to handle this task—the new Compression Agent.

To start the Compression Agent, open the Start menu and choose <u>P</u>rograms, Accessories, System Tools. Click Compression Agent. The Compression Agent window appears. Select a drive to work with in this window. Compression Agent will recompress this drive file by file, using the best method for each file. When you click the S<u>e</u>ttings button in Compression Agent, you can specify whether Compression Agent should use UltraPak compression for some or all of the files on the drive. While UltraPak reduces files to about a third of their normal size, this option isn't generally recommended for 80486 systems; this compression method can be very slow.

After you choose the settings you want in the Compression Agent, use the System Agent (as described earlier in the "Managing Utilities with the System Agent" section) to run the Compression Agent and recompress the specified disk.❖

VIII

Appendixes

Appendix E

What's on the CD

by Alex Leavens

The CD-ROM included with this book has a wide variety of software on it that can greatly enhance your productivity (and enjoyment, too) with the new Windows 95 operating system. This appendix describes many of the products on the CD-ROM, as well as how to access them.

Accessing the Software

When you insert the CD-ROM into your CD drive, Windows 95 automatically runs the installer on the CD-ROM. This installer lets you install many of the software products on the CD. You also can manually run the installer by double-clicking the CD-ROM drive icon, and then double-clicking the "Install" icon that is displayed there.

Each of the software packages lives under it's own directory entry; if you are having problems, then simply change to the appropriate directory; run the installer that is there.

What's Included

The CD comes complete with a fabulous list of software packages that will liven up your experiences with Windows 95. The following is a partial list of what packages are included:

- *Icon Safari.* This is a fabulous full-blown icon editor that lets you edit, import, and export icon images from various files (such as ICO (icon) files, and various executable and system driver files), as well as allowing you to edit cursors and small bitmaps. You can attach sounds to different windows events and buttons, which makes your cursor come alive with animation. It even includes a pop-up program launcher that lets you launch programs from anywhere within Windows. It's an even faster way to get to your programs than the taskbar!

- *WinCom Lite.* WinCom Lite gives you a full working terminal on your Windows 95 system so that you can access various information services (such as bulletin boards). You get complete control of your modem settings, your phone dialing settings, and more! WinCom Lite is a powerful terminal product, which can be upgraded to the even more powerful WinCom Pro. WinCom is provided by the folks at Delrina, who also make the popular WinFax utility.

- *WinBatch.* This is a batch file language utility. It allows you to script actions under Windows, such as a series of mouse clicks or menu entries. It can be used to automate a series of repetitive actions that could not otherwise be performed. By using WinBatch, you can create a script for actions that you perform over and over again (such as loading and printing a particular file).

- *WinEdit.* This is a programmer's editor, designed for writing code under Windows. It features many creature comforts needed by programmers, rather than just general text editing usage. If you're writing code for Windows, then this editor is a perfect example of simple power and functionality. If you've balked at paying $300 and more for some of the more expensive Windows editors, then give WinEdit a try—it might be just what you're looking for!

- *Address Manager for Windows.* This is a full-fledged miniature database for Windows, with the purpose of helping you organize your names, addresses, and phone numbers into something approaching a working system. (If you're like me, this product is a real life saver.)

- *TrueSpace2.* If you've ever wondered how they do those great realistic-looking graphics of buildings, ships, and alien scenery, here's your answer! TrueSpace2 lets you create fabulous 3D objects in a matter of minutes. You can add textures, distort images, and much, much more! You can build animations of solid-shaped objects, moving them about in space at your command. TrueSpace2 has been used to create the graphics for some of the most popular CD-ROM games on the market. Now, you too can explore the creation of futuristic worlds, alien artifacts, and anything else you can imagine. TrueSpace2 makes it easy (you'll find some wallpaper that's been created in TrueSpace in the \MEDIA\GRAPHICS subdirectory of your CD).

■ *Fauve Matisse in Grey.* If you're looking for something a little more powerful than Paint, then this is the product for you. Fauve Matisse allows you to draw with a variety of different substances, and allows you great control over things like your brush style and type of paint that you use. Even non-artists will have a ball with this one! This version of the software is the full working version! You can load and save all of your artwork to disk, as well as print and edit your documents.

■ *Mathematica.* For those of our readers who deal with higher mathematics, Mathematica is a great solution to your problems. This demo of the Mathematica software shows many of its capabilities that you'll need if you do lots of math-related work. (Even if you don't do higher math, it's still a cool demo to show your friends—they'll be impressed at how smart you are!)

■ *MapInfo.* If you want information about streets, cities, or other places that have a map, then this demo of MapInfo will show you how your computer can help. Geographic Mapping Software is an area of Windows few people know about, but more people should—you can use your computer to get directions to a specific place, find out more about how streets are organized, and map various kinds of data that you have (such as store sales data) to the positions of people within a geographic location (such as ZIP code areas).

■ *CorelDRAW!.* For many years the leading object-oriented drawing package, CorelDRAW!, just keeps getting better and better. The version included on this CD lets you use all of Corel's many drawing features. CorelDRAW! can be used for things like box art, flyers, brochures, business cards, product information sheets, and a hundred more uses (one person I know used it to create classroom materials for her fifth grade science class). See for yourself why CorelDRAW! is the leader in the marketplace.

■ *CompuServe, WinCIM 1.4.* Yes, it's true—we've included the *full version* of CompuServe's famous Windows product to access the full power of CompuServe! Not only do we include the entire product, but you'll also find a special 800 number listed in this book that will let you call for a free introductory account! (See the MCP/CompuServe ad at the back of the book.) If you're already a CompuServe member, you can have the latest version of WinCIM without having to spend all that time trying to download it.

VIII

Appendixes

- *MorphStudio SE.* If you've been fascinated by those cool looking Morphing effects seen on TV and in the movies, then MorphStudio can help you explore this new world for yourself! Not only can you view several sample "Morphs," but you also can create your own morphs!

Our Internet Section

The Internet is one of the hottest new areas of interest for many people. If you want to get on the Information Superhighway, we're here to help. Here's what we have to help you "surf the Net:"

- *MKS Internet Anywhere.* This software allows you to cruise the net in style—browsing for files, and traversing cyberspace. You'll need an Internet provider to use this software (in English, that means you have to have someone that will give you access to the Internet—this software will do the rest).

- *Netcruiser software from NETCOM.* Not only is NETCOM a leading Internet access provider, but they've got their own Windows-based software to let you browse the Internet, FTP to different sites, surf the World Wide Web, read and post to Internet newsgroups, and more!

In addition, we've gathered the best of the software from several of Que's best-selling Internet books, including

- *WS_FTP.* A GUI FTP client.

- *Microsoft Internet Assistant.* Writes Web pages in Word for Windows.

- *LView.* A graphics file editor recommended for use with Netscape and Mosaic.

- *MPEGWin.* An MPEG movie player.

- *VuePrint.* A graphics editor and utility with a great slideshow mode.

- *Eudora.* The definitive Internet e-mail software.

- *HTML Assistant for Windows.* Another program for writing Web pages.

- *HTML Writer.* Yet another program for writing Web pages.

- *HTMLed.* One more program for writing Web pages.

- *NewsXpress.* A newsreader for reading UseNet newsgroup articles.

- *Windows FTP Daemon.* Be your own FTP site with this!

- *WinCode.* A file decoder for translating encoded mail and news from the Internet into a usable form.

Other Cool Goodies

One of the big new features of Windows 95 is it's multimedia capabilities and we've got lots to help you out here! The CD holds more than 150M of graphics files, wallpaper, bitmap patterns for your desktop, sound files, digital video files, and more!

All of these files are listed in the \MEDIA subdirectory on your disk, with appropriate subdirectories of the different items listed. Since Windows 95 understands many of these formats, you can simply double-click a file that grabs your interest to either view it or hear it.

For those of you doing your own Video for Windows editing, we're including the famous VidCap and VidEdit utilities from the Microsoft Multimedia Jumpstart CD.

You'll also find a ton of Windows Shareware and Freeware utilities on this CD. These include:

- *WinZip.* The famous Windows-hosted Zip/Unzip utility. No longer do you have to shell out to DOS to unzip things! This version supports Windows 95 long file names and several popular Internet file formats, in addition to ZIP files.

- *BmpView.* A program that lets you preview bitmap files in thumbnail (miniaturized) form, and then load them into your favorite editor.

- *PolyView.* A graphics file viewer that handles a wide variety of graphic file formats, including PhotoCD, JPG, GIF, BMP, and more. It also has a slideshow feature!

We've also included the following games:

- *Gravity Well.* A cool game!

- *Insecta.* Design and build your own insects, then bring them to life!

With all that stuff, this CD is sure to make Windows 95 a more enjoyable experience for all levels of computer users. Be sure to check the CD out in detail!❖

VIII

Appendixes

Appendix F

Glossary

16-bit   In Windows, this refers to the way memory is accessed. 16-bit applications access memory in 16-bit "chunks" (2-bytes). Most pre-Windows 95 applications are 16-bit (*see 32-bit*).

32-bit   In Windows, this refers to the way memory is accessed. 32-bit application access memory in 32-bit "chunks" (4-bytes). Large portions of Window 95 and many of its new applications are 32-bit applications, and may run faster because it has become more efficient to access chunks of memory.

16550A UART   The name of the most modern chip controlling the serial port. Older chips could not support the data throughput that today's high-speed communications protocols and modems support.

A

accelerator key   A keyboard shortcut for a command. For example, Shift+Delete is an accelerator command for the Edit Cut command.

activate   To bring a window to the front and make it active.

active printer   The printer that will be used by programs.

active window   The window that is currently being used. Active windows show the "active window color" in their title bar (settable through the control panel). Other windows are inactive. To activate an inactive window, you must click somewhere in the inactive window or use the taskbar to select the window (*see taskbar*). On the taskbar, the active window looks like a pressed button; inactive windows are represented by unpressed buttons.

address book   A list of persons, phone numbers, and other information used by various Windows 95 programs, including Microsoft Fax and HyperTerminal.

Adobe Type Manager (ATM)   An Adobe program that enables you to work with Postscript fonts in Windows 95.

Advanced Program-to-Program Communications   A communications standard defined by IBM. The APPC standard is intended to allow multiple users to share the processing of programs.

airbrush   In "paint" and graphics programs, a tool that "sprays" dots in a randomized pattern around the point indicated by the user. In most programs, the output of the airbrush can be configured to modify the color, pattern, and density of the dot pattern.

alert message   A critical warning, confirmational, or informational message appearing in a dialog box.

annotate   To add notes. For example, you can add your own notes to Windows Help.

ANSI   A standard for ordering characters within a font.

anti-aliasing   A graphics technique used to hide the diagonal edges and sharp color changes ("jaggies") in a graphic or font. Because a computer screen possesses limited resolution, such changes highlight the pixels on the screen and don't look smooth. Using anti-aliasing smoothes out the changes and makes them appear more attractive.

Anti Virus   A program included with Windows 95 that helps eradicate viruses (*see virus*) from your hard drive or floppy disks.

API   *See Application Programming Interface.*

APPC   *See Advanced Program-to-Program Communications.*

applet   A small application unable to run by itself. When you purchase Windows 95 or another application, it may come with additional applets. For example, Word comes with applets for manipulating fonts (WordArt), drawing graphs (MS Graph), and creating graphics (MS Draw).

application   A computer program.

Application Programming Interface (API)   A set of interface functions available for applications.

archive bit   A single bit stored in a disk directory to indicate if a file has been changed since it was last backed up. Backup programs clear a file's archive bit when they back up the program. Modifying the program resets the bit and a backup program knows to make a backup the next time you do a backup.

ASCII characters   A subset of the ANSI character standard.

ASCII file   A file consisting of alphanumeric characters only. Although virtually every file can be converted to an ASCII file, all formatting (for example, bold, italics, underline, font size, and so on) will be lost in the ASCII file.

associate   Linking a document with the program that created it so that both can be opened with a single command. For example, double-clicking a DOC file opens Word for Windows and loads the selected document.

ATAPI   A specification for devices to attach to EIDE buses. This specification is almost identical to the EIDE specification.

AT command set   A set of commands, originally developed by Hayes, for modems. Its name originates from the fact that each command starts with "AT" (attention). Today, most modems support the AT command set, enabling Microsoft to supply the Unimodem driver with Windows 95.

ATM   Asynchronous Transfer Mode is a high-speed, but expensive, networking solution. ATM networks reach speeds of 155 Mb/s.

attribute   A property or characteristic.

attributes (FAT)   Settings for each file indicate if the file is used by an operating system, has read-only status, has its archive bit set, or is a hidden file.

auto arrange (Explorer)   In Explorer, auto arrange organizes the visible icons into a regular grid pattern.

B

background operation   A job performed by a program when another program is in the active window. For example, printing or creating a backup can be done by Windows 95 as a background operation.

Backup   A program that comes with Windows 95 and enables the user to back up the files from a hard disk to a floppy disk, tape drive, or another computer on a network.

backup set   The set of duplicate files and folders created by a backup program (*see Backup*). This set is stored on tapes, diskettes, or other storage medium that can be removed and stored safely away from your computer. *See Full System Backup.*

Basic Input/Output System (BIOS)   A program—usually residing on a ROM-based storage device in your PC—that handles instructions to and from the system bus.

batch program   A text file that instructs Window 95 to perform one or more tasks sequentially. Used for automating the loading or execution of programs. Batch files have a .BAT or .CMD extension.

Bezier   A mathematically constructed curve, such as the one used in drawing programs.

bi-directional printer port   Bi-directional Printer Communications sends print files to your printer and listens for a response. Windows quickly identifies a printer that is unable to accept a print file.

binary   A numbering system with only two values: 0 (zero) and 1 (one).

binary file   Any file containing characters other than text.

binary file transfer   A data transfer in which files aren't converted. Typically used with a modem to send programs or complex documents from computer to computer.

binary transfer protocol   When using a communications program to transmit binary files, it is very important to ensure that errors are not introduced into the data stream. Various binary transfer protocols check for matches between the data transmitted and the data received. The most common protocols are Xmodem, Ymodem, and Zmodem.

BIOS   *See Basic Input/Output System.*

bit map   A screen page in memory. Most bit maps represent some sort of viewable graphics. You can use a "paint" program to edit graphic bit maps and make modifications to them. However, although objects such as rectangles and circles may appear in a graphic bit map, these objects cannot be edited as objects. You must modify these objects one bit at a time using the paint tools in the program.

bits per second (bps)   A measurement of data transmission speed, usually over a serial data link. Roughly equivalent to baud rate. A single character requires approximately 10 bits, so a transfer rate of 9600 baud results in about 960 characters per second (cps) being transferred. This speed, however, varies depending on the make of your modem.

boot partition   The hard-disk partition that contains the Windows 95 operating system.

bound media   In networks, this refers to traditional cabling connecting the nodes of a network together, and to a server, if any. *See unbound media.*

bridge   In networks, a device that joins two separate LANs but restricts LAN frame traffic to either side of the bridge (unless forwarding is required). Bridges process LAN frames (not network packets) and are governed by IEEE standards. A bridge should not be confused with a router (*see router*), which uses an entirely different layer of protocol and information for forwarding packets (not frames).

browse   To search through or examine a directory tree of files, directories, disks, workstations, workgroups, or domains. Often done via a Browse button in a dialog box.

Bulletin Board System (BBS)   An electronic service that can be accessed via a modem. BBS typically includes collections of files, notes from other computer users, and many other services. Examples of commercial BBSs include CompuServe, Prodigy, Delphi, GEnie, and America Online (AOL). Information about Windows 95 and Windows 95 applications can be found on all these BBSs.

burst mode   A mode used in MCA and EISA computers and devices to facilitate greater flow of data through the bus. When bus mastering is employed, a bus master and its slave can establish a connection and send large blocks of data without CPU intervention. Without burst mode, each byte requires CPU attention to gain control of the bus, and send a byte of data.

bus   The interface between devices in a computer. PC's incorporate bus designs, including ISA, EISA, MCA, PCI, and VLB (VESA Local Bus).

bus mastering   A function used to off-load I/O processing to a processor on the interface card. Bus mastering is only truly effective when used with a bus design that can control bus master access to the computer bus, as is the case in EISA, MCA, and PCI computers. Bus mastering alone does not fully utilize the capabilities of this design unless implemented in conjunction with accessing the 32-bit burst mode and streaming data modes of EISA, MCA, and PCI computers.

bus network   One of various network topologies. A Bus network is one in which all of the computers on the network are connected to the main wire of the network.

C

cache RAM   A small collection of very high speed RAM. In general, modern microprocessors can process information much faster than standard dynamic RAM can even supply the information. Nevertheless, fast dynamic RAM is very expensive. Instead, a very small amount (typically 256K or 512K) of very fast "cache RAM" acts as a buffer between the CPU and the dynamic RAM. If the information needed by the CPU is in the cache, it can be processed without waiting to retrieve it from the dynamic RAM.

Calculator   A program that comes with Windows 95 and enables you to perform standard or scientific calculations.

capture text   In HyperTerminal, this refers to capturing and saving the text that appears in the terminal window to either a file or the printer. This is handy when reviewing the session at a later time.

Cardfile   A program that comes with Windows 95 and enables you to record information cards and sort through them by using their index lines.

cascade (Windows)   To arrange all the windows so that they are neatly stacked; only the title bars show behind the active window.

cascading menu   A submenu that appears (usually to the left or right of the main menu item) when a menu selection is made.

CD File System (CDFS)   An optimized, 32-bit, protected-mode file system that significantly improves the throughput of data from a CD-ROM drive.

CD-ROM Drive   A CD-ROM drive uses discs (not "disks") as the storage media. These discs look much like audio CDs but can store about 600M of data on a single disc. They can only be read by a normal CD-ROM drive (hence Read-Only Memory portion of the device's name) and take special equipment to create (write) one of them. CD-ROM drives are rated in multiples of the original (1x) drives that transfer data at the same rate as audio CD Players (150kb/sec). Today, 1x drives no longer exist, and 2x drives (300-330kb/sec) are cheap. 3x (450 kbs), 4x (600 kb/sec), and even 6x (900kb/sec) drives are available. 4x drives fulfill basic requirements needed to achieve decent performance when playing animations from a CD-ROM.

CD Player   A program packaged with Windows 95. CD player lets you play audio CDs from your CD drive in the background while you are working in another application. It offers many of the controls found in standalone audio

CD players. As a result, it looks and operates in a similar fashion. In addition, it allows you to edit your playlist that corresponds to the audio CD being played. Thus, the tracks play in the order you want.

character-based   Usually used when referring to non-Windows applications. Character-Based applications display information using the ASCII character set, or characters normally found on the keyboard. Also known as "textbased."

character formatting   In word processing, this refers to formatting that is applied to individual characters. This type of formatting includes font, effects, size, and color.

chat room   A place on Microsoft Network where you can have a live conversation with other MSN members. They see your comments immediately.

check box   A square dialog box item that takes an off or on value. Clicking in a check box adds or removes an X in the box, indicating whether the setting is on (checked) or off (unchecked).

checksum   A method for creating a calculated number, frequently used as a part of an error-detection protocol. Normally, a checksum is calculated against a copy of a file or other data, and compared to the checksum calculated for the original file/data. If the two numbers match,then it is very likely that the copy matches the original. Checksums are used in some forms of transmission protocols (for example, Xmodem) as well as part of the Antivirus program.

choose   A term used in many instructions in this book and in Windows books and manuals. Usually means opening a menu and clicking a command. Also can refer to dialog box items, such as in "Choose LPT1 from the drop-downlist."

clear   Typically refers to turning off the X in an option or check box.

clicking   Quickly pressing and releasing the mouse button.

client   As opposed to *server*, a client is a workstation that connects to another computer's resources. A client also can include the server, and doesn't necessarily have to be another workstation. Basically, a client is just another application or workstation that utilizes resources from another process.

client application   In OLE context, a program that uses an object (such as a graphic) supplied by another application (the *server* application).

VIII

Appendixes

client/server networking   As opposed to *peer to peer* networking, an arrangement in which central computers called *servers* supply data and peripherals for use by *client* computers (workstations). Typically, a server contains a large, hard disk that supplies not only data, but also programs. It even executes programs. A server might also supply printers and modems for clients to use on the network. In other words, client/server refers to an architecture for distributed processing wherein subtasks can be distributed between services, CPUs, or even networked computers for more efficient execution.

clip art   A collection of images you can use in your documents. Clip art is often distributed on CD-ROM in large collections (thousands of clip art pieces) organized into categories. Various clip art formats are sold, and the most popular are CGM, WMF, BMP, and GIF format files.

Clipboard   A temporary storage area in all versions of Windows used for storing various types of data (for example, text, graphics, sound, and video). The clipboard can hold one piece of information at a time for use in a program or to pass information between programs.

Clipboard Viewer   A Windows 95 program enabling you to store and save more than the single item that the clipboard can hold.

clock   An area at the far right edge of the taskbar that displays the time (and date if you leave the mouse pointer over the time). You can configure the taskbar to show or hide the clock.

close button   A button in the upper right corner of a Window with an "x" in it. When clicked, it closes the program running in the current window.

cluster   Segment of space on a hard drive. Each file, no matter how small in actual size, takes up at least one cluster on the hard drive. As drive sizes increase, so does the cluster size. Thus, if you have a large drive and many small files, you may waste a significant amount of space on your drive. To avoid this, physically partition the drive into multiple "logical drives" of a smaller size. These smaller, logical drives also use smaller cluster sizes, wasting less space.

coaxial cable   A type of shielded cable used in wiring networks together. Although coaxial cable sufficiently shields network signals from outside electrical noise, "coax" is stiff and difficult to work with, and more difficult to run through walls and ceilings than twisted pair cable (*see twisted pair*).

codec   A technique for compressing and decompressing files, typically sound and animation files. Common codecs include Cinepak, Indeo, Video 1, MPEG (*see MPEG*) QuickTime (*see QuickTime*), and RLE.

collapse folders   To hide additional directory (folder) levels below the selected directory (folder) levels. In Explorer, you can collapse the view of a folder to hide the folders stored within by double-clicking the folder in the left pane (tree view) of Explorer. When a folder contains no additional folders, a minus sign (-) appears next to the folder.

color pattern   A color selection made up of two other colors.

color rendering intent   Provides the best ICM settings for three of the major uses of color printing (for example, presentations, photographs, and true color screen display printing).

color scheme   A selection of colors that Windows 95 uses for screen display of applications, dialog boxes, and so forth. The color scheme is set from the Control Panel.

COM   Refers to the serial port, usually to attach a mouse and/or a modem to the computer. Most computers have two serial ports, labeled COM1 and COM2. The serial port transmits data in a single bit stream. This serial transmission of bits gives the port its name.

command   Usually an option from an application's menus. Also refers to commands typed in from a command-prompt session or from the Run dialog box from the Start Menu. In essence, it's a way of telling an application or Windows 95 to perform a major chore, such as running an application or utility program.

command button   A dialog box item that causes an action when clicked.

compare files   Compares the files in a backup set to make sure they match the source files on the hard disk.

component   A portion of Windows 95. When installing Windows 95, you have the option of installing (or not) various components. For example, you might choose to not install HyperTerminal (you might have a better terminal program). Later, you can go back and add/remove components using the original install disks or CD-ROM.

complex document   *See compound document.*

compound document   A document (created using OLE) that includes multiple types of data. For example, a Word processing document that includes a Paint picture is a compound document.

compressed volume file (CVF)   A file, created by DriveSpace (*see DriveSpace*) which is treated like another "volume" (logical disk drive)—it even has a drive letter (for example, "D:") assigned to it. When you save or retrieve files compressed by DriveSpace, they are written or read from the compressed volume file. The compressed volume file exists on a hard drive (called a "host drive"), and looks like a regular file to the FAT (*see File Allocation Table*).

connection (HyperTerminal)   In HyperTerminal, a connection sets and saves all the configuration parameters for one party you wish to contact.

connection (Network)   A communication session established between a server and a workstation.

container object   An object that contains another object or several objects. For example, a Word document might be the container object that holds the Excel object. *See compound document.*

control menu   A menu that exists in every window and enables you to modify its parameters or take global actions, such as closing or moving the window.

Control Panel   A program that comes with Windows 95 that enables you to make settings for many Windows 95 actions, such as changing network, keyboard, printer, and regional settings. Some programs (including many video card drivers) may add sections to the control panel for you to use to configure that program.

conventional memory   Memory located in the first 640K.

cover page   The page preceding a fax message. The cover page often includes such information as your name, company, telephone, and return fax number. Windows 95 includes a program (Fax Cover Page Editor) that enables you to create your own fax cover pages.

CPU   Central processing unit. Also known as a microprocessor (*see microprocessor*) or processor (*see processor*). The 80386, 80486, and Pentium are examples of CPUs built by Intel.

cross-linked file   A disk error (which can be found using ScanDisk) in which at least two files are linked to data in the same cluster.

current directory   The directory that activates if you log onto the drive at the command prompt by typing the drive letter and pressing Enter. When you switch drives, the operating system remembers the directory that was current when you switched away. It will still be the active/current directory when you switch back; it becomes the default directory. Applications will store or look for files on that drive if they're not specifically told which directory to use. This concept also works in Explorer: when you switch back to a drive, the last active directory (or *folder*) is still the active one.

current window   The windows that you are using. It appears in front of all other open windows (*see active window*).

cursor   The representation of the mouse on the screen. It may take many different shapes.

Cylinder/Head/Sector (CHS)   An addressing scheme that allows IDE drives to exceed the original 512 megabyte (1/2 gigabyte) size limit. With CHS, an IDE drive can be up to 8.4 gigabytes.

D

database   A file or group of related files that are designed to hold recurring data types as if the files were lists.

data bits   The number of bits used to transmit a piece of information. Usually 7 or 8.

DCI   The Drive Control Interface is a display driver interface which allows fast, direct access to the video frame buffer in Windows. Also, it allows games and video to take advantage of special hardware support in video devices, which improves the performance and quality of video.

DDE   *See Dynamic Data Exchange.*

DEC Printer Utility   The DEC printer utility adds features to the standard Windows 95 print window and updated printer drivers. The utility includes a very detailed help file for configuring both local and network printers. Additionally, it creates an enhanced set of property menus for configuring DEC printers.

default button   The command button in a dialog box that activates when you press the Enter key. This button is indicated by a dark border.

default printer   The printer, which is established using the Printer settings, that documents will be sent to if the user doesn't specify another printer.

deferred printing   This enables people with laptop computers to print even though their laptop is not in a docking station. Once connected in a docking station, it will automatically print. This also refers to computers whose only printer access is to a network printer, and the computer is temporarily disconnected from the network. When the network connection is reestablished, the print job starts.

density   Density is a brightness control to lighten or darken a printout to more closely reflect its screen appearance and to compensate for deficiencies in toner or paper quality.

desktop   The screen area on which the windows are displayed.

desktop pattern   A bit map decorating your desktop. You can select one of Windows 95's patterns or create one of your own.

destination document   The document into which a linked or embedded document is placed.

device driver   A program that provides the operating system with the information it needs to work with a specific device, such as a printer.

dialog box   An on-screen message box that conveys or requests information from the user.

Dial Up Networking   Dialing into a network from a remote sight using a modem.

differential backup   A differential backup backs up only those files that have changed since the time a backup was made. Normally, a backup philosophy will involve making a full system backup (which includes all files on the hard drive), and then making periodic differential backups. Windows 95 can determine which files have changed (or been created) since the last backup by the condition of the archive bit (*see archive bit*). To restore a system that has been backed up using this philosophy, first restore using the full system backup, and then successively apply the differential backups *in the same order they were made.*

Disk Defragmenter   As you use your hard drive, blocks of information for a file spread across the hard drive, wherever there is room. This "fragmentation" of the information in a file can lead to a significant slow-down in file access times because the disk's read/write head must move all over the disk, looking for the various portions of a file. Disk Defragmenter arranges the blocks of information for a file into adjacent blocks on your hard drive, which may significantly improve file access times.

dither pattern   A pattern of dots used to simulate an unavailable color or gray scale in a printout or graphic. Most frequently used when specifying a printout of a color graphic on a monochrome printer or simulating more colors in a graphic than are available in the current graphics mode.

Direct Memory Access (DMA)   A PC has eight DMA channels that are used for rapidly transferring data between memory and peripherals such as a hard disks, sound cards, tape backups, scanners, and SCSI controllers. DMA is very fast because it doesn't need the computer's microprocessor to access memory.

docking station   For a portable computer, an external device that provides additional resources such as speakers, CD-ROM, keyboard, empty card slots, and so on. A docking station is typically plugged into a portable computer using the port replicator connection.

document   A file created using an application. For example, you might create a text document using a word processing application (such as WordPad) or a picture document using a graphic application (such as Paint).

document formatting   In word processing, this refers to formatting that is applied to a whole document. Document formatting includes margins, headers and footers, and paper size.

document window   The window in which a document appears.

DOS   A term used to refer to any variation of the Disk Operating System (for example, MS-DOS and PC-DOS).

double-click   To press the mouse button twice in rapid succession while keeping the mouse pointer motionless between clicks.

double buffering   The process of displaying the screen currently in the frame buffer while painting the next screen in another portion of RAM. Then the new screen is quickly copied to the frame buffer. This makes video playback and animation appear much smoother.

download   Retrieving a file from a remote computer or BBS (*see upload*).

drag   To move an object on the screen from one place to another by clicking it with the mouse, holding the mouse button down, and pulling it to where you want it to be.

drag-and-drop   "Drag-and-drop" describes a particular action you can make with the mouse. Click an object, such as a folder, then hold down the mouse button as you drag the object to a new location. You drop the object by releasing the mouse button.

VIII

Appendixes

DriveSpace   DriveSpace is a program included with Windows 95. It enables you to compress your disks and free up more space.

DriveSpace for Windows supports drives that were compressed using DoubleSpace (which was included in MS-DOS versions 6.0 and 6.2) as well as DriveSpace for MS-DOS (which was included in MS-DOS version 6.22). You can use DriveSpace and DoubleSpace drives interchangeably. For example, you can use floppy disks that were compressed using either DoubleSpace or DriveSpace. However, such floppy disks can be used only in computers that have DriveSpace for Windows or DoubleSpace installed.

If you have drives that were compressed using either DoubleSpace or DriveSpace, you can configure them by using DriveSpace for Windows.

drop-down list   A dialog box item showing only one entry until its drop down arrow is clicked.

dual boot   The ability to reboot and enter either Windows 95 or Windows 3.1 (or whatever version of Windows you had running before installing Windows 95). This option is offered during installation and involves not installing Windows 95 over your previous Windows installation. If you choose dual boot, you will have to reinstall your Windows programs under Windows 95.

Dynamic Data Exchange (DDE)   A feature of Windows 95 that allows programs to communicate and actively pass information and commands.

E

echoing keystrokes   In a communications program, you may type information at your terminal. If the receiving system doesn't "echo" your keystroke back to your terminal, then you can't see what you type. By setting your own system to echo keystrokes, you can see what you have typed. Systems that echo your keystrokes for you are termed "full duplex"; systems that do not echo your keystrokes are termed "half duplex".

editable fax   An editable fax is, essentially, a file transfer between computers, with the addition of a cover page optionally. Once received, the "editable fax" can be edited in the application that created it—or another application capable of reading that file type. For example, if you send a document created in Microsoft Word for Windows, which is a .DOC file, the recipient can open it in Word, WordPad, AmiPro, or WordPerfect, using import filters if necessary.

ellipsis   Three dots (...). An ellipsis after a menu item or button text indicates that selecting the menu or clicking the button will display an additional dialog box or window from which you can choose options or enter data.

embedded object   Data stored in a document that originated from another application. Differing from a linked object, this type of object doesn't have its own file on the disk. However, it runs its source application for editing when you double-click it. For example, a Paint drawing embedded in a Word document.

encapsulated PostScript (EPS) file   A file format for storing PostScript-style images that allow a PostScript printer or program capable of importing such files to print a file in the highest resolution equipped by the printer.

Enhanced Integrated Electronics (EIDE)   A design that improves on the Drive limitations of the IDE design. EIDE designs can use up to four devices (split into two pairs). For each pair of devices, one of the devices is the master; the drive electronics on the master control both the master drive and (if applicable) the secondary slave unit attached. Unlike IDE, EIDE supports devices in addition to hard drives, including CD-ROM drives and tape drives. EIDE devices can be up to 8 gigabytes in size, improving on the 524 megabyte limit of IDE devices. As with IDE, this type of drive is interfaced to a computer bus with an EIDE host adapter, not a controller. However, most newer computers include an EIDE host adapter right on the motherboard.

Enhanced Meta File (EMF)   The process of converting generic Spooling print instructions to the instruction set "understood" best by a particular printer. This conversion has the capability to create faster printouts of better quality.

Enhanced Small Device Interface (ESDI)   A drive controller type that utilizes a hard drive as a slave unit. ESDI controllers generally drive only two disk drives and have an on-board processor to translate drive geometry, manage I/O requests, and provide caching.

escape codes   A set of codes that appear in a text string on a terminal (*see terminal emulation*). Although these escape codes (which provide formatting information) aren't visible in terminal emulation, they will show up as non-text characters if you capture the text to the screen or printer. In fact, some escape codes may cause the printed output to skip pages, switch into bold mode, and other undesirable effects because they may coincide with printer command codes.

VIII

Appendixes

Ethernet   One of the earliest and least expensive network types. Ethernet is capable of speeds of 10Mb/s, and employs Bus and Star network types. When attempting to transmit over an Ethernet network, the transmitting workstation must "listen" to the network line to ensure that it is clear (another workstation is not currently transmitting). If the line is not clear, the workstation must wait until the line clears.

exit   When you are finished running Windows applications and Windows, you must not turn off the computer until you correctly exit Windows. Windows stores some data in memory and does not write it to your hard disk until you choose the exit command. If you turn off the computer without correctly exiting, this data may be lost. *See shutdown.*

expanded memory   Memory that conforms to the LIM 4.0 standard for memory access. Windows 95 has the capability of converting extended memory (*see extended memory*) to expanded memory (using EMM386.EXE) for programs that require it. However, most modern programs no longer use expanded memory.

expand folders   Views the structure of folders that are stored inside other folders. In Explorer, you can expand the view of a folder that has a plus sign (+) next to it to see the folders stored within by double-clicking the folder in the left pane (tree view) of Explorer. When a folder does not contain any additional folders, a minus sign (-) appears next to the folder.

Explorer   A program that comes with Windows 95 that helps you view and manage your files.

Extended Industry Standard Architecture (EISA)   A computer bus and interface card design based on 32-bit bus mastering. EISA is an extension to ISA (Industry Standard Architecture) bus design and enables EISA and ISA interface cards to be used in a single type of bus interface slot in the computer.

extended memory   Memory that can be accessed by Windows 95 beyond the first megabyte of memory in your system.

external command   Unlike an internal command, a command that requires a separate file to run.

F

FDDI   Fiber Distributed Data Interchange is a network type that requires fiber optic cable (*see fiber optic*). Although expensive, it is immune to electrical interference and can achieve speeds of 100 Mb/s.

fiber optic   A type of cable which transmits information via light signals. Although both the cable and the decoders are expensive, such cabling is immune to electrical noise, and capable of much higher transmissions rates than electrical (coaxial or twisted pair) cables.

FIFO buffers   First in, first out buffers. In communications programs that use FIFO buffers, the first information added to the buffer is also the first information transmitted when the transmission restarts.

file allocation table (FAT)   The native DOS file system that uses a table, called the file allocation table, to store information about the sizes, locations, and properties of files stored on the disk.

file converter   File converters take the file format and transform it to a format that the application can read. During a file conversion, text enhancements, font selections, and other elements are usually preserved. Sometimes, however, these elements are converted to a similar format, and then converted to ASCII format.

file name   The name that a file system or operating system gives to a file when it's stored on disk. File names in Window 95's file system can be 256 characters long. Additionally, Windows 95 assigns a file name compatible with older DOS (8 characters with a 3 character extension) naming conventions.

file name extension   The 3 character extension that you can add to a filename—either the standard 8 characters of DOS and Windows 3.1, or the long filenames of Windows 95. The file name extension is only visible in Explorer if you enable the appropriate option. Otherwise, the extension is hidden. Nevertheless, the extension is still part of the filename, even when you can't see it—it is this extension that Windows 95 (as well as earlier Windows) uses to associate a document with the application that created it.

file set   In the Windows 95 Backup program, a collection of files to back up and the destination to back them up to. By saving a file set in Backup, you won't have to reselect the files to back up the next time.

file utility   A program that can directly manipulate the information available on the disk that defines where files are found, sized, and other attributes. It is important to NOT use file utilities that were designed for earlier version of Windows, as Windows 95 stores some file information in different places—and earlier file utilities could scramble the file information, destroying the file.

fixed space font   Fonts that have a fixed amount of space between the characters in the font.

font   A description of how to display a set of characters. The description includes the shape of the characters, spacing between characters, effects (for example, bold, italics, and underline), and the size of the characters.

folder window   A window in Explorer that displays the contents of a folder.

folder   Folders represent directories on your drives. Folders can contain files, programs, and even other folders.

foreground operation   The program in the active window.

forum   On Microsoft Network, a folder with a collection of related documents and sub-folders.

frame   A unit of data that is exchanged on a LAN. Frame formatting implements an access protocol for the purpose of enabling communications between nodes on a LAN (Ethernet, Token Ring, and so on). A frame should not be confused with a packet, which is encapsulated within a frame for transport across the LAN.

full system backup   A backup set (*see backup set*) that contains all the files on your hard drive, including Windows 95 system files, the registry, and all other files necessary to completely restore your system configuration on a new hard drive.

G

grid   A background pattern that defines regular intervals—for example, a 1/4" grid displays dots in the background every quarter inch on in a rectangular pattern. Many graphics programs make a grid available. Even when turned on, a grid won't print. When you "snap to grid," your graphic endpoints are constrained to fall on a grid point.

H

handshake   A protocol used between two devices to establish communications. For example, a portable computer and a PC Card "handshake" to set up the communications between the devices.

header information   Data sent to a printer to define aspects of the printout and prepare the printer prior to printing. PostScript documents include header information.

heap   An area of memory (also known as the "System Resources area") that Windows uses to store system information (such as menus) about running applications. If the "heap" fills up, you may get an "out of memory" error, despite the fact that you have plenty of regular memory (RAM) available. In Windows 95, you have a much less chance of getting an "out of memory" error. Although Windows 95 still uses a 64K heap to store systems information for 16-bit applications, a lot of the information that was stored in this area by older versions of Windows is now stored elsewhere. As a result, there is much less chance of your application failing due to this error.

Hearts   A card game included with Windows 95 for up to four players. The winner is the player who has the fewest points.

At the end of each round (each player has played all 13 cards), the following points are given:

1 point for each Heart you collected.

13 points for the Queen of Spades.

If one player wins all the Hearts and the Queen of Spades (called Shooting the Moon), then that player gets zero while all other players are penalized 26 points.

Help   A program that gives you information about how to run Windows 95 and its programs, including how to use the Help program.

hexadecimal   A base-16 numbering scheme with values ranging from 0 to 9, and A to F. Used in many programming languages. Not particularly relevant to users, except that memory address areas are frequently stated in hexadecimal. Hex is used whenever the actual internals of the computer are being revealed as in memory addresses and I/O ports.

hidden file   A characteristic of a file that indicates that the file is not visible in Explorer under normal circumstances. However, by selecting the View Option to view all files, hidden files will still be visible.

hierarchical   A way of displaying text or graphics in a structure. In a hierarchical structure, items closer to the top of the structure are considered "parents" of items connected to them, but which are lower down in the structure. The tree structure of Windows Explorer is an example of a hierarchical structure.

Home Page   A document on the World Wide Web dedicated to a particular subject. From a Home Page, you can use hyperlinks to jump to other Home Pages to gain more information.

host drive   The physical hard drive upon which a DriveSpace compressed volume file exists (*see compressed volume file*). You can choose to either show or hide the host drive when working with Explorer.

hot docking   For a portable computer, "hot docking" refers to the ability to insert the computer into a docking station (which may provide additional resources such as a CD-ROM, speakers, hard drive, and so on) and have the computer recognize that the new resources of the docking station are now available.

hot swapping   For a portable computer, or any other computer that uses PC cards, "hot swapping" refers to the ability to remove a PC card and/or insert a new card, and have the computer recognize the change.

HP JetAdmin   The HP JetAdmin Utility is a tool that can be used to install and configure networked Hewlett-Packard printers using the HP JetDirect network interface. The HP JetAdmin utility appears as a substitute for the Windows standard Printer window. This utility can also be used to interface printers connected to a NetWare LAN.

hub   A wiring concentrator or multiport repeater (*see repeater and wiring concentrator*). Hubs may be active or passive.

hue   The numerical representation of the colors of a color wheel. It is almost always seen with saturation and brightness.

hyperlink   A link in a document that, when activated (often by clicking it), links—or jumps to—another document or graphic.

HyperTerminal   HyperTerminal is a program included with Windows 95, which enables you to easily connect to a remote computer, a bulletin board, or an online service. It replaces Terminal from Windows version 3.1.

Hypertext Markup Language (HTML)   A hypertext language used to create the hypertext documents that make up the World Wide Web.

I

I-beam   The shape the cursor takes in the area of a window where text can be entered.

icon   A small graphic symbol used to represent a folder, program, shortcut, resource, or document.

image color matching (ICM)   Image Color Matching (ICM), a technology developed by Kodak, creates an image environment that treats color from the screen to the printed page. Microsoft licensed ICM from Kodak to be able to repeatedly and consistently reproduce color matched images from source to destination.

import   An OLE term. In Object Packager, you can import a file into a package and later embed it into a destination document.

inactive   An open window that is not currently in use. On the taskbar, the active window looks like a pressed button, inactive windows are represented by unpressed buttons.

Inbox   Inbox holds incoming and outgoing messages and Faxes that are sent or received over Microsoft Exchange.

incremental backup   *See differential backup.*

Industry Standard Architecture (ISA)   This term describes the design of the 8/16-bit AT bus (sometimes called the "classic bus") developed by IBM in the original IBM PC.

in place editing   A feature of OLE 2. With in place editing, you may edit an embedded or linked object WITHOUT that object being placed into an additional window (the way it was in OLE 1.0). Instead of creating an additional window, the tools for the object you want to edit appear in the toolbar for the container object, (*see container object*). Also, the menus for the object you want to edit replace the menus of the container object. In place editing is less disruptive; it is much simpler to ensure that the changes you make to an embedded or linked object are updated to the original complex document.

insertion point A flashing vertical line showing where text will be inserted.

Integrated Drive Electronics (IDE) A later drive design that incorporated an embedded controller on a smaller (3 1/2 inch) disk drive. IDE drives can be connected together, but the second drive must be a slave to the first, using the primary disk controller and not its own embedded controller. This type of drive is interfaced to a computer bus with an IDE host adapter, not a controller.

Integrated Services Digital Network (ISDN) A special phone line that supports modem speeds up to 64Kbps. However, these phone lines can be quite expensive to acquire. Many ISDN adapters support two-channel access.

interface The visible layer enabling a user to communicate with a computer. In DOS, the interface consisted largely of typed commands and character-based feedback. Windows 95 is an entirely graphical interface, using a mouse, menus, windows, and icons to allow the user to communicate his instructions and requirements to the computer.

internal command A command embedded in CMD.EXE, the command interpreter for Windows 95, or in COMMAND.EXE, the MS-DOS equivalent. Internal commands don't require additional support files.

Internet The Internet is a "network of networks," a global linkage of millions of computers, containing vast amounts of information, much of it available to anyone with a modem and the right software...for free. The Internet is an aggregation of high speed networks, supported by the NSF (National Science Foundation) and almost 6,000 federal, state, and local systems, as well as university and commercial networks. There are links to networks in Canada, South America, Europe, Australia, and Asia, and more than 30,000,000 users.

Internet Explorer A web browser bundled with the Windows 95 Plus kit. It takes advantage of features in Windows 95, such as shortcuts and long file names.

Internet Protocol (IP) A network protocol that provides routing services across multiple LANs and WANs that is used in the TCP/IP protocol stack. IP packet format is used to address packets of data from ultimate source and destination nodes (host) located on any LAN or WAN networked with TCP/IP protocol. IP provides routing services in conjunction with IP routers, which are incorporated into many computer systems and most version of UNIX. IP Packet format is supported in NetWare 3.11 and 4.0 operating systems, and is used throughout the Department of Defense Internet—a network of thousands of computers internetworked worldwide.

interoperability   Compatibility, or the capability for equipment to work together. Industry standards are agreed upon or used by vendors to make their equipment work with other vendor's equipment.

interrupt request line (IRQ)   A line (conductor) on the internal bus of the computer (typically on the motherboard) over which a device such as a port, disk controller, or modem can get the attention of the CPU to process some data.

interframe compression   A technique that achieves compression of a video file by eliminating redundant data between successive compressed frames

intraframe compression   A technique that compresses the video by removing redundancy from individual video images.

I/O address   Input/Output address. Many I/O devices, such as COM ports, network cards, printer ports, and modem cards, are mapped to an I/O address. This address allows the computer and operating system to locate the device, and thus send and receive data. Such I/O addresses don't tie up system memory RAM space. However, there are a limited number of I/O addresses. You can access an I/O port in one of two ways: either map it into the 64K I/O address space, or map it as a memory-mapped device in the system's RAM space.

IPX   Internetwork Packet Exchange (IPX) is a network protocol developed by Novell to address packets of data from ultimate source and destination nodes located on any LAN networked with NetWare. IPX also provides routing services in conjunction NetWare and third-party routers. An IPX packet has information fields that identify the network address, node address, and socket address of both the source and destination, and provides the same functionality of the of the OSI Network layer in the OSI model.

J

jumpers   Jumpers are small devices that complete a circuit between two pins of a multi-pin header, specifying various aspects about a card—for example, which IRQ, base memory address, or I/O port address to use. Jumpers are not normally used on a card that is compliant with Plug and Play, but were common on "legacy" (pre-Plug and Play) cards.

K

kernel   The core of an operating system, usually responsible for basic I/O and process execution.

kernel driver   A driver with direct access to hardware. A hardware driver.

keyboard buffer   Memory set aside to store keystrokes as they're entered from the keyboard. Once it's stored, the keystroke data waits for the CPU to pick up the data and respond accordingly.

keyboard equivalent   *See keyboard shortcut.*

keyboard shortcut   A combination of keystrokes that initiates a menu command without dropping the menu down, or activates a button in a dialog box without clicking the button.

kiosk   In the Microsoft Network, a download-and-run document that contains additional information about a forum. Kiosks are usually found in forums.

L

legacy   Refers to pre-Windows 95 software or hardware. Legacy cards don't support Plug and Play, and legacy software is older software (although you may have just purchased it!) typically designed for Windows 3.1 or Windows for Workgroups 3.11.

license   Refers to the agreement you are assumed to have acceded to when you purchase Windows 95. As with much other computer software, you don't own your copy of Windows 95, but instead, just license the use of it. As such, there is a long list of legalese-type things you supposedly agree to when you open the envelope containing your copy of Windows 95. These legal agreements are part of the *license*.

line by line   When using terminal emulation (*see terminal emulation*), some primitive terminals only allowed you to edit text on the single line on which you were working. Once you pressed [Enter] to move to the next line, you couldn't go back and change something on the previous line(s)—because those lines had already been sent to the host computer that the PC emulates a terminal of. In line by line editing, there is a line length limit as well, so you can't simply type an entire paragraph before pressing [Enter].

linked object   In OLE terminology, data stored in a document that originated from another application. Unlike an embedded object, this type of object has its own file on the disk. The source application is run for editing when you double-click it. For example, a Paint drawing linked to a Word document. Linking saves space over embedding when a particular object must be included in more than one other document, since the data does not have to be stored multiple times. Additionally, you can directly edit a linked file, and all the documents that the link to the file update automatically.

list box   A dialog box item that shows all available options.

local area network (LAN)   A limited-distance, multipoint physical connectivity medium consisting of network interface cards, media, and repeating devices designed to transport frames of data between host computers at high speeds with low error rates. A LAN is a subsystem that is part of network.

local printer   A printer connected directly to your computer.

local reboot   The ability of Windows 95 to close down a single misbehaving application. When you use the Alt+Ctrl+Delete key sequence, Windows 95 queries you for the application to shut down. In this way, you can close down only the application you want, without affecting other running applications.

logical block addressing (lba)   A type of addressing scheme for IDE disk drives that allows the drive to exceed the original 512 megabyte (1/2 gigabyte) IDE size limit. With logical block addressing, an IDE drive can hold up to 8.4 gigabytes.

logical drive   A drive that isn't a physical drive, as in the floppy drive A or B. Instead, a logical drive is a drive created on a subpartition of an extended partition and given an arbitrary letter such as C, D, or E.

long file name   A reference to Windows 95's ability to use file names up to 256 characters long.

lossy compression   Compression techniques that lose some of the data when compressing the file. Although lossy compression isn't acceptable for compressing application file and certain types of data files (for example, database, word processing), it is often acceptable to have a low degree of loss when compressing video or graphic files, since you likely won't notice the missing data. Also, lossy compression can gain considerably higher compression ratios than "lossless" compression. However, when using lossy compression, you don't want to decompress the file, then use the result to recompress, as the loss of data gets worse with each cycle.

VIII

Appendixes

LPT   The parallel port (used for printing). Most computers have a single parallel port (labeled LPT1), but some may have two. The parallel port transmits data one byte (8-bits) at a time. This parallel transmission of all 8 bits gives the port its name.

luminosity   When working with colors, indicates the brightness of the color.

M

macro   A sequence of keyboard strokes and mouse actions that can be recorded so that their playback can be activated by a single keystroke, keystroke combination, or mouse click. Unlike Windows 3.1 and Windows for Workgroups, Windows 95 does not come with a Macro Recorder.

Mailing List (Internet)   An e-mail discussion group focused on one or more topics. The Mailing List is made up of members who subscribe that mailing list.

map network drive   The act of associating a network drive makes the drive available in My Computer. Windows 95 uses the next available drive letter, and you can access the network drive just like any other hard drive.

maximize button   A button in the upper right corner of a Window with a square in it. When clicked, it enlarges the window to its maximum size. When the window is already at its maximum size, the maximize button switches to the restore button, which returns the window to its previous size.

media control interface (MCI)   A standard interface for all multimedia devices, devised by the MPC counsel, that allows multimedia applications to control any number of MPC-compliant devices, from sound cards to MIDI-based lighting controllers.

menu   A list of available command options.

menu bar   Located under the title bar, the menu bar displays the names of all available menu lists.

menu command   A word or phrase in a menu that, when selected, enables you to view all the commands.

Micro-Channel Architecture (MCA)   A proprietary 32-bit computer and bus architecture designed by IBM to improve bus bandwidth and facilitate bus mastering. MCA is not backward compatible with ISA and requires exclusive use of MCA devices.

microprocessor   A miniaturized processor. Previous processors were built in integrated circuit boards with many large components. Most processors today use high-tech, silicon-based technology that improves performance, reduces heat generation, and increases efficiency.

Microsoft Client for Netware Networks   Windows 95 Microsoft Client for NetWare Networks allows users to connect to new or existing NetWare servers. It permits you to browse and queue print jobs using either the Windows 95 network user interface or existing Novell NetWare utilities. The Microsoft Client for NetWare interfaces equally well with both NetWare 3.x and 4.x servers.

Microsoft Exchange   Microsoft Exchange provides a universal Inbox that you can use to send and receive electronic mail (e-mail). In addition, you can use the Inbox to organize, access, and share all types of information, including faxes and items from online services.

Microsoft Fax   Microsoft Fax is a program included with Windows 95 that enables you to send and receive faxes directly within Windows 95.

Microsoft Network (MSN)   Access to The Microsoft Network, a new online service, is a feature of Windows 95.

With The Microsoft Network, you can exchange messages with people around the world; read the latest news, sports, weather, and financial information; find answers to your technical questions; download from thousands of useful programs; and connect to the Internet.

MIDI   Musical Instrument Digital Interface. Originally a means of connecting electronic instruments (synthesizers) and letting them communicate with one another. Computers then came into the MIDI landscape and were used to control the synthesizers. Windows 95 can play MIDI files.

Minesweeper   A game of chance and skill included with Windows 95. When playing Minesweeper, you are presented with a mine field, and your objective is to locate all the mines as quickly as possible. To do this, uncover the squares on the game board that do not contain mines, and mark the squares that contain mines. The trick is determining which squares are which.

If you uncover all the squares without mines, you win; if you uncover a mine instead of marking it, you lose the game. The faster you play, the lower your score. You can use the counters at the top of the playing area to keep track of your progress.

minimize button   The button in the upper right corner of the window that has an line in it. When clicked, it reduces the window to display the taskbar only.

mission-critical application   An application program considered indispensable to the operation of a business, government, or other operation. Often, these applications are transaction-based, such as for point-of-sale, reservations, or real-time stock, security, or money trading.

modem   A device usually attached to a computer through a serial port or present as an internal card. A modem makes it possible to use ordinary phone lines to transfer computer data. In addition to a modem, a communications program is required. "Modem" is short for "modulator/demodulator"—the processes whereby a digital stream of data is converted to sound for transmission through a phone system originally designed only for sound (modulator) and the conversion of received sound signals back into digital data (demodulator).

Motion JPEG   Developed by the Joint Photographic Experts Group, motion JPEG is a compression/decompression scheme (Codec) for video files. It is a variation on JPEG, this group's codec for compressing still pictures. It uses only intraframe lossy compression (*see intraframe compression, lossy compression*), but offers a tradeoff between compression ratio and quality.

mounting a compressed drive   When you are working with removable storage media—such a diskettes—that are compressed, you must mount the compressed drive if it wasn't present when the computer was started. Mounting a drive links a drive letter with a compressed volume file (CVF). This enables your computer to access the files on the compressed volume files. Mounting a compressed drive is done using DriveSpace.

mouse pointer   The symbol that displays where your next mouse click will occur. The mouse pointer symbol changes according to the context of the window or the dialog box in which it appears.

MPEG   Created by the Motion Picture Experts Group, MPEG is a specification for compressing and decompressing (*see codec*) animation or "movie" files, which are typically very large. Although extremely efficient at reducing the size of such a file, MPEG is also very processor-intensive.

MS-DOS-based application   An application that normally runs on a DOS machine and doesn't require Windows 95. Many MS-DOS-based applications will run in Windows 95's DOS box, but some will not.

multimedia A combination of various types of media, including (but not necessarily limited to) sound, animation, and graphics. Due to the generally large size of "multimedia" files, a CD-ROM is usually necessary to store files. Of course, a sound card and speakers are also necessary.

multitasking The capability of an operating system to handle multiple processing tasks, apparently, at the same time.

multithreading A process allowing a multitasking operating system to, in essence, multitask subportions (threads) of an application smoothly. Applications must be written to take advantage of multithreading. Windows 95 supports multithreading.

My Computer An icon present on the Windows 95 desktop that enables you to view drives, folders, and files.

My Briefcase An icon present on the Windows 95 desktop. My Briefcase is the way that portable computer users can take data with them as they travel. When they return to the office, Windows examines the files in My Briefcase and updates the contents of their desktop computer.

N

NetBIOS An IBM protocol (and packet structure) that provides several networking functions. NetBIOS was developed by IBM and Sytek to supplement and work with BIOS in PC-DOS-based, peer-to-peer networks. NetBIOS protocol provides transport, session, and presentation layer function equivalent to layers 4, 5, and 6 of the OSI model. The NetBIOS software that is used to implement this protocol is the NetBIOS interface.

NetWare A trademarked brand name for the networking operating systems and other networking products developed and sold by Novell.

Netware Core Protocol (NCP) A NetWare protocol that provides transport, session, and presentation layer functions equivalent to layers 4,5, and 6 of the OSI model.

Net Watcher A tool included with the Windows 95. Net Watcher allows you to monitor and manage network connections, as well as create, add, and delete shared resources.

VIII

Appendixes

network   A group of computers connected by a communications link that enables any device to interact with any other on the network. The "network" is derived from the term "network architecture" to describe an entire system of hosts, workstations, terminals, and other devices.

Network Interface card (NIC)   Also called a network adapter, an NIC is an interface card placed in the bus of a computer (or other LAN device) to interface to a LAN. Each NIC represents a node, which is a source and destination for LAN frames, which in turn carry data between the NICs on the LAN.

Network Neighborhood   An icon which Windows 95 displays only if you are connected to a network and Windows has been installed for a network. Double-clicking the Network Neighborhood icon displays all the resources available on any network to which you are connected.

non-volatile RAM   RAM memory on a card that is not erased when power is cut off. Cards that don't use jumpers often store their resource requirements (IRQ, I/O Base address, I/O port, DMA channel, and so on) in non-volatile RAM. Non-volatile RAM is not normally used on a card that is compliant with Plug and Play but was common on "legacy" (pre-Plug and Play) cards.

non-Windows program   A program not designed to be used specifically in Windows. Most non-Windows applications or programs are character-based in nature (for example, DOS programs).

Notepad   A program that comes with Windows 95 and enables you to view and edit text files.

null modem cable   A serial cable link between computers. Standard modem software is often used to transmit information, but because there are no actual modems in the connection, very high transfer rates with good accuracy are possible. The cable must be different from a regular serial cable, however, because several of the wires in the cable must be cross connected to simulate the modem's role in acknowledging a transmission.

O

object   Any item that is or can be linked into another Windows application, such as a sound, graphics, piece of text, or portion of a spreadsheet. Must be from an application that supports Object Linking and Embedding (OLE).

object linking and embedding   *See OLE.*

OEM Fonts   OEM fonts are provided to support older installed products. The Term OEM refers to Original Equipment Manufacturers. This font family includes a character set designed to be compatible with older equipment and software applications

offline   A device that is not ready to accept input. For example, if your printer is offline, it will not accept data from the computer, and attempting to print will generate an error.

OLE   A data sharing scheme that allows dissimilar applications to create single, complex documents by cooperating in the creation of the document. The document consists of material that a single application couldn't have created on its own. In OLE, version 1, double-clicking an embedded or linked object (*see embedded object*, and *linked object*) launches the application that created the object in a separate window. In OLE version 2, double-clicking an embedded or linked object makes the menus and tools of the creating application available in the middle of the parent document. The destination document (contains the linked or embedded object) must be created by an application which is an OLE client, and the linked or embedded object must be created in an application that is an OLE server.

OLE automation   Refers to the capability of a server application to make available (this is known as expose) its own objects for use in another application's macro language.

online   Indicates that a system is working and connected. For example, if your printer is online, it is ready to accept information to turn into a printed output.

Open Data Link Interface (ODI)   A Novell specification that separates the implementation of a protocol and the implementation of the NIC hardware driver. Novell's MLID specification enables NIC drivers to interface through Link Support Layer with IPX ODI and multiple ODI-onforming packet drivers.

option button   A dialog box item that enables you to choose only one of a group of choices.

orientation   For printer paper, indicates whether the document is to be printed normally (for example, in "portrait" mode) or sideways (in "landscape" mode).

VIII

Appendixes

OSI Model   Opens Systems Interconnect 7-layer Model is a model developed by International Standards Organization to establish a standardized set of protocols for interoperability between networked computer hosts. Each layer of the model consists of specifications and/or protocols that fulfill specific functions in a networking architecture. Novell's UNA was patterned against the OSI model. The OSI model consists of specific protocols that are nonproprietary and offered in the hope of unifying networking protocols used in competing vendor's systems.

P

packet   A limited-length unit of data formed by the network, transport, presentation, or application layer (layers 3-7 of the OSI Model) in a networked computer system. Data is transported over the network, and larger amounts of data are broken into shorter units and placed into packets. Higher-layer packets are encapsulated into lower-layer packets for encapsulation into LAN frames for delivery to the ultimate host destination.

Paint   A program that comes with Windows 95 and enables you to view and edit various formats of bit maps.

palette   A collection of tools. For example, in Paint, there is a color palette that displays the 48 colors available for use in creating a graphic.

pane   Some windows, such as the window for Explorer, show two or more distinct "areas" (Explorer's window shows two such areas). These areas are referred to as "panes."

Panose   Panose refers to a Windows internal description that represents a font by assigning each font a PANOSE ID number. Windows uses several internal descriptions to categorize fonts. The PANOSE information registers a font class and determines similarity between fonts.

paragraph formatting   In a word processing program, this refers to formatting that can be applied to an entire paragraph, including alignment (left, center, right), indentation, and spacing before and after the paragraph.

parallel port   A port (usually used for printing) that transmits data 8 bits at a time. This parallel transmission of 8 bits at a time gives the port its name.

parity   An additional portion of data added to each byte of stored or transmitted data. Used to ensure that the data isn't lost or corrupted. In HyperTerminal, parity is used to ensure that the data is transmitted and received properly. Parity is also used in RAM chips to determine if RAM errors have occurred.

partial backup   *See incremental backup.*

partition   A portion of a physical hard drive that behaves as a separate disk (logical drive), even though it isn't.

path   The location of a file in the directory tree.

PC Cards   Formerly called PCMCIA cards, these are small (usually only slightly larger than a credit card) cards that plug into special slots provided in notebook computers. PC Cards can provide functionality for additional memory, modems, sound, networking, hard drives, and so on. PC Cards normally identify themselves to the computer, making configuring them quite simple.

PCMCIA   The old name for PC Cards (*see PC Cards*).

peer-to-peer   A type of networking in which no workstation has more control over the network than any other. Each station may share its resources, but no station is the sole resource sharer or file server. Typically less expensive than client/server networks, peer-to-peer networks are also more difficult to administer and less secure because there is no central repository of data.

personal information store   The Personal Information Store is Exchange's term for the file that contains the structure of folders that make up your Inbox, Out box, sent files, deleted files, and any other personal folders you may choose to create.

Phone Dialer   Phone Dialer is a program that is included with Windows 95 that enables you to place telephone calls from your computer by using a modem or another Windows telephony device. You can store a list of phone numbers you use frequently and dial the number quickly from your computer.

picon   Picons are small bitmapped images of the first frame of your video clip. They can be used to represent the in and out source of your video segments.

PIF   A file that provides Windows 95 with the information it needs to know in order to run a non-Windows program. Unlike earlier versions of Windows, there is no PIF editor in Windows 95. Instead, you set up a PIF file from the properties for the file. Access the file properties by right-clicking the file from My Computer.

Ping   A network utility that determines if TCP/IP is working properly. Simply executing the Ping command (from a DOS prompt) and specifying the IP address should produce a response (the response will depend on how the remote machine has been programmed to respond to a Ping), but virtually any response that references the remote machine's identity indicates that the Ping was successful and TCP/IP is working correctly.

Play List   In CD Player, a list of tracks from an audio CD that you want to play.

Plug and Play   An industry-wide specification supported by Windows 95 that makes it easy to install new hardware. Plug and Play enables the computer to correctly identify hardware components (including plug-in cards) and ensures that different cards don't conflict in their requirements for IRQs, I/O addresses, DMA channels, and memory addresses. In order to fully implement Plug and Play, you need an operating system that supports it (as stated, Windows 95 does), a BIOS that supports it (most computers manufactured since early 1995 do) and cards that identify themselves to the system (information from these cards stored in the Windows Registry). If you have hardware, such as modems that aren't Plug and Play (so called "legacy hardware"), then Windows 95 will prompt you for the information necessary for setup, and store such information in the Registry.

pointer   The on-screen symbol controlled by the mouse. As you move the mouse on the desk, the pointer moves on-screen. The pointer changes shape to indicate the current status and the type of functions and selections available.

polygon   A multisided shape, in which each side is a straight line.

port   A connection or socket for connecting devices to a computer (*see I/O address*).

port replicator   On portable computers, a bus connection that makes all bus lines available externally. The port replicator can be used to plug in devices which, in a desktop computer, would be handled as cards. Port replicators are also the connection used to connect a portable computer to its docking station.

Postoffice   This machine that will be the place in which all mail messages are stored for the workgroup.

Postproduction editing   The steps of adding special effects, animated overlays, and more to a "production" video.

Postscript   A special description language, invented by Adobe. This language is used to accurately describe fonts and graphics. Printers which can directly read this language and print the results are termed "postscript printers."

preemptive processing   In a multitasking operating system, multiple tasks (threads) are generally controlled by a scheduler that preempts or interrupts each process, granting processor time in the form of a time slice. This enables multiple tasks to apparently run at the same time. However, each task runs for a time slice and is then preempted by the next process, which in turn is preempted—rotating processor time among active threads. In preemptive multitasking, the operating system is empowered to override (or preempt) an application that is using too much CPU time, as opposed to cooperative multitasking, where the application is responsible for relinquishing the CPU on a regular basis.

primary partition   A portion of the hard disk that can be used by the operating system and that can't be subpartitioned like an extended partition can. Only primary partitions are bootable.

printer driver   A Windows 95 program that tells programs how to format data for a particular type of printer.

printer fonts   Fonts stored in the printer's ROM.

printer settings   A window that displays all the printers for which there are drivers present. You can select the default printer from the installed printers, as well as configure each printer using the shortcut menu and the options dialog box.

printer window   For each installed printer, you can view the printer window. The printer window displays the status of each print job in the queue, and enables you to pause, restart, and delete the print job.

processor   The controlling device in a computer that interprets and executes instructions and performs computations, and otherwise controls the major functions of the computer. This book discusses Intel 80x86-series processors, which are miniaturized single-chip "microprocessors" containing thousands to millions of transistors in a silicon-based, multilayered integrated circuit design.

program file   A program that runs an application directly (not via an association) when you click it.

program window   A window that contains a program and its documents.

property sheet   A dialog box that displays (and sometimes enables you to change) the properties of an object in Windows 95. To access a property sheet, right click the object to view the shortcut menu, and select Properties from the shortcut menu. Property sheets vary considerably between different objects.

proportional-spaced fonts   Proportional spaced fonts adjust the inter-character space based on the shape of the individual characters. An example of a proportional spaced font is Arial. The width of a character is varied based on its shape. Adjusting inter-character spacing is really a function of kerning, which is a similar but not exactly the same. For instance, the letter 'A' and the letter 'V' are typically stored in each font as a kerning pair where they will be spaced differently when appearing next to each other. Where in a mono-space font vs. a proportional font you will see a difference in the width of the letter 'i.'

protected mode   A memory addressing mode of Intel processors that allows direct "flat memory" addressing (linear addressing) rather than using the awkward "segmented" scheme required by real mode, which was pioneered on the Intel 8088 and 8086 processors. Protected mode derives its name from the fact that sections of memory owned by a particular process can be protected from rogue programs trying to access those addresses.

protocol   Rules of communication. In networks, several layers of protocols exist. Each layer of protocol only needs to physically hand-off or receive data from the immediate layer above and beneath it, whereas virtual communications occur with the corresponding layer on another host computer.

Q

QIC A formatting standard for tapes used by various tape backup devices. The amount of information that can be stored on a tape varies by the QIC number. Windows 95's Backup program supports QIC 40, 80, 3010, and 3020 formats. It also supports QIC 113 compression format.

queue   Documents lined up and waiting to be printed, or commands lined up and waiting to be serviced. Use the Printer window to view the print queue for a printer.

quick format   A quick way to format a floppy disk, quick format doesn't actually wipe the whole disk, nor does it test the media for bad sectors. It just erases the FAT.

QuickTime   Developed by Apple, QuickTime is a compression and decompression (codec) scheme for animation files. It is unique in that versions are available for both Windows and Macintosh, enabling software designers to provide their data in a format compatible for both platforms.

Quick View   A program included with Windows 95 that enables you to view files stored in 30 different file formats without needing to open the application that created the file. Quick View is available from the File menu of Explorer IF a viewer is available for the selected file type.

R

RAM   Random-Access Memory. Physical memory chips located in the computer. Typically, Windows 95 machines have 16 million bytes (16M) of RAM or more. However, Windows 95 will run on machines with 8M of RAM.

raster font   A font in which characters are stored as pixels.

read-only   Characteristic of a file indicating that the file can be read from, but not written to, by an application. Note however, that a "read-only" file can be deleted in Explorer, although you will get a warning (beyond the normal "are you sure" you normally get when you try to delete a file) if the file is read-only.

real mode   As opposed to *protected mode*, real mode is a mode in which Intel x86 processors can run. Memory addressing in real mode is nonlinear, requiring a program to stipulate a segment and memory offset address in order to access a location in memory. Originally appeared on the Intel 8086 CPU and has been the bane of PC programmers ever since. Although subsequent CPU chips supported protected-mode linear addressing, backward compatibility with the thousands of real-mode applications slows the evolution of operating systems. Note that all Intel CPUs boot in real mode and require specific software support to switch into protected mode.

Recycle Bin   An icon that appears on the Windows 95 desktop. To discard a file, you drag the file from Explorer, My Computer, or any other file handler to the Recycle Bin. This action hides the file—but doesn't actually erase it from the disk. You can "undelete" the file by dragging it from the recycle bin back to a folder. To actually delete the file, select the recycle bin menu selection to empty the recycle bin.

VIII

Appendixes

registering a program   The act of linking a document with the program that created it so that both can be opened with a single command. For example, double-clicking a DOC file opens Word for Windows and loads the selected document.

Registry   A database of configuration information central to Windows 95 operations. This file contains program settings, associations between file types and the applications that created them, as well as information about the types of OLE objects a program can create and hardware detail information.

Registry Editor   The Registry Editor ships with Windows 95. Using this tool you can fine tune Windows 95 performance by adjusting or adding settings to key system information. Since Windows 95 has placed WIN.INI and SYSTEM.INI file settings in the registry, the ability to remotely edit these parameters is an extremely powerful tool. Warning: you can totally destroy a workstation using this tool!

repeater   A device that repeats or amplifies bits of data received at one port and sends each bit to another port. A repeater is a simple bus network device that connects two cabling segments and isolates electrical problems to either side. When used in a LAN, most repeaters take a role in reconstituting the digital signal that passes through them to extend distances a signal can travel, and reduce problems that occur over lengths of cable, such as attenuation.

resize button   A button located in the lower left corner of a non-maximized window. When the mouse pointer is over this button, it turns into a two-headed arrow. You can click and drag to resize the window horizontally and vertically.

resource (card)   When installing a card, certain "resources" are needed: these often include a DMA channel, I/O Base address, and IRQ. Although these are detected and set automatically with Plug and Play compliant cards, you will have to set them using jumpers or the setup program to store the resource values in non-volatile RAM when installing a "legacy" (pre-Plug and Play) card.

restore button   A button in the upper right corner of a Window that has two squares in it. When clicked, it returns the window to its previous size. When the window is at its previous size, the restore button switches to the maximize button, which returns the window to its maximum size.

restore files   Copies one or more files from your backup set to the hard disk or to another floppy.

Rich Text Format (RTF) Rich Text Format (RTF) is compatible with several word processors and includes fonts, tabs, and character formatting.

ring network One of a variety of network topologies. Ring networks connect computers by using an In and an Out port for data. Each computer sends information to the next computer down the wire. Data flows from one computer's Out port to the next computer's In port.

ROM Read-Only Memory. A type of chip capable of permanently storing data without the aid of an electric current source to maintain it, as in RAM. The data in ROM chips is sometimes called firmware. Without special equipment, it is not possible to alter the contents of read-only memory chips, thus the name. ROMs are found in many types of computer add-in boards, as well as on motherboards. CPUs often have an internal section of ROM as well.

routable protocol A network protocol that can work with non proprietary routers. Traditional routers use the network packet header fields to identify network addresses (network numbers)/node addresses for ultimate source and destination nodes (or hosts) for packets of data. This scheme for routing packets across internetworks is used OSI, NetWare (IPX), TCP/IP, and AppleTalk network protocols.

router In a network, a device that reads network layer packet headers and receives or forwards each packet accordingly. Routers connect LANs and WANs into internetworks, but must be able to process the network packets for specific types of network protocol. Many routers process various packet types and therefore are termed multiprotocol routers.

S

safe mode A special mode for starting Windows 95 that uses simple, default settings so that you can at least get into Windows and fix a problem that makes it impossible to work with Windows otherwise. The default settings use a generic VGA monitor driver, no network settings, the standard Microsoft mouse driver, and the minimum device drivers necessary to start Windows.

safe recovery An installation option provided by Windows 95 to recover from a faulty or damaged installation of Windows 95.

saturation When working with colors, saturation indicates the purity of a color; lower values of saturation have more gray in them.

ScanDisk   A program used to check for, diagnose, and repair damage on a hard disk or disk. Part of your routine hard disk maintenance (along with defragmenting your hard disk) should include a periodic run of ScanDisk to keep your hard disk in good repair. In its standard test, ScanDisk checks the files and folders on a disk or disk for *logical* errors, and if you ask it to, automatically corrects any errors it finds. ScanDisk checks for *crosslinked* files, which occur when two or more files have data stored in the same *cluster* (a storage unit on a disk). The data in the cluster is likely to be correct for only one of the files, and may not be correct for any of them. ScanDisk also checks for *lost file fragments*, which are pieces of data that have become disassociated with their files.

screen fonts   Font files used to show type styles on the screen. These are different from the files used by Windows to print the fonts. The screen fonts must match the printer fonts in order for Windows to give an accurate screen portrayal of the final printed output.

screen resolution   The number of picture elements (or "pixels") that can be displayed on the screen. Screen resolution is a function of the monitor and graphics card. Higher resolutions display more information at a smaller size, and also may slow screen performance. Screen resolution is expressed in the number of pixels across the screen by the number of pixels down the screen. Standard VGA has a resolution of 640 by 480, although most modern monitors can display 1024 by 768, and even higher (larger monitors can usually display a higher resolution than smaller ones).

screen saver   A varying pattern or graphic that appears on the screen when the mouse and keyboard have been idle for a user-definable period of time. Originally used to prevent a static background from being "burned into" the screen phosphors, this is rarely a problem with modern monitors. Many screen savers (including those that come with Windows 95) can be used with a password—you must enter the correct password to turn off the screen saver and return to the screen. However, someone could simply reboot the machine, so a screen saver password is not very sophisticated protection.

scroll arrow   Located at either end of a scroll bar, it can be clicked to scroll up or down (vertical scroll bar) or left or right (horizontal scroll bar). Clicking the scroll arrow will move your window in that direction.

scroll bar   Scroll bars allow you to select a value within a range, such as what part of a document to see, or to what value to set the Red, Green, and Blue components of a color.

scroll box A small box located in the scroll bar that shows where the visible window is located in relation to the entire document, menu, or list. You can click and drag the scroll box to make other portions of the document, menu, or list visible.

select To specify a section of text or graphics for initiating an action. To select also can be to choose an option in a dialog box.

selection handles Small black boxes indicating that a graphic object has been selected. With some Windows applications, you can click and drag a selection handle to resize the selected object.

serial port *See COM.*

Serif Fonts Serif Fonts have projections (serifs) that extend the upper and lower strokes of the set's characters beyond their normal boundaries, for example, Courier. Sans-Serif Fonts do not have these projections, for example, Arial.

server A centrally-administered network computer, which contains resources that are shared with "client" machines on the network.

server application In OLE terminology, an application that supplies an object, (such as a drawing), to a client application, (such as a word processing program), for inclusion in a complex document.

shareware A method of distributing software, often including downloading the software from a BBS or the Microsoft Network. With shareware, you get to use the software before deciding to pay for it. By paying for the software and registering it, you usually receive a manual; perhaps the most up-to-date version (which may include additional functionality). Shareware versions of software often include intrusive reminders to register—the registered versions do not include these reminders.

shortcut A pointer to a file, document or printer in Windows 95. A shortcut is represented by an icon in Explorer, on the desktop, or as an entry in the Start menu. Selecting the program shortcut icon or menu entry runs the program to which the shortcut "points." Selecting a document shortcut runs the application that created the document (provided the document type is associated with a program). Dragging and dropping a document onto a printer shortcut prints the document. Note that a shortcut does NOT create a copy of the program or document itself.

VIII

Appendixes

shortcut keys   A keystroke or key combination that enables you to activate a command without having to enter a menu or click a button.

shortcut menu   A pop-up menu that appears when you right click an object for which a menu is appropriate. The shortcut menu displays only those options which make sense for the object you select and current conditions.

Small Computer System Interface (SCSI)   An ANSI standard bus design. SCSI host adapters are used to adapt an ISA, EISA, MCI, PCI, or VLB (VESA Local Bus) bus to a SCSI bus so that SCSI devices (such as disk drives, CD-ROMs, tape backups, and other devices) can be interfaced. A SCSI bus accommodates up to eight devices, however, the bus adapter is considered one device, thereby enabling seven usable devices to be interfaced to each SCSI adapter. SCSI devices are intelligent devices. SCSI disk drives have embedded controllers and interface to a SCSI bus adapter. A SCSI interface card is therefore a "bus adapter," not a "controller."

Small Computer System Interface-2 (SCSI-2)   An ANSI standard that improves on SCSI-1 standards for disk and other device interfaces. SCSI-2 bandwidth is 10 Mbytes/sec, whereas SCSI-1 is 5 Mbyte/sec. SCSI-2 also permits command-tag queuing, which enables up to 256 requests to be queued without waiting for the first request. Another SCSI-2 feature is the bus' capability to communicate with more than one type of device at the same time, where a single SCSI-1 host adapter only supported one type of device to communicate on the bus.

SCSI Configured Automagically (SCAM)   The specification for Plug and Play or SCSI buses. This specification makes it unnecessary to set a SCSI Id, as the configuration software negotiates and sets the id for each connected SCSI device (that is Plug and Play compliant!).

soft fonts   Depending on your printing hardware, soft fonts may be downloaded to your printer. Downloading fonts reduces the time taken by the printer to process printouts. Although downloading soft fonts is done only once (per session), benefits are realized through subsequent printing.

Solitaire   A card game included with Windows 95 for a single player. The object of solitaire is to turn all the cards in the seven face-down stacks face-up on top of each of the four aces for each of the four suites.

Soundblaster   An extremely popular family of sound boards developed and marketed by Creative Labs. Because of the popularity and large market share of this product family, most sound boards advertise themselves as

"Soundblaster compatible," meaning that drivers provided in Windows, Windows 95, and programs such as games will work with these boards. However, some board's compatibility is not perfect.

source document   In OLE, the document that contains the information you want to link into (to appear in) another document (the destination document).

spool   A temporary holding area for the data you want to print. When printing a document, it can take some time (depending on the length of the document and the speed of your printer) for the document to come off your printer. By spooling the data, you may continue using your computer while the document is printing, because the computer "feeds" the spool contents to the printer as fast as the printer can handle it. When the print job is completed, the spool file is automatically deleted.

star network   One of a variety of network topologies. Star networks connect computers through a central hub. The central hub distributes the signals to all of the cables which are connected.

Start menu   A menu located at the left end of the taskbar. Clicking the button marked "Start" opens a popup menu that makes Help, the Run command, settings, find, shutdown, a list of programs (actually, program shortcuts), and a list of recently accessed documents available for you to run with a single click. For some items (such as the Documents item), a submenu opens to the side of the main item to display the list of choices. You can configure the Start menu to specify which programs are available to run from it.

Startup Folder   A folder that contains any programs that you want Windows 95 to run whenever you startup. You can drag-and-drop program shortcuts into the StartUp Folder to add them to the list of programs to run.

static object   In OLE, where objects have a "hot link" to their original application, static objects are simply pasted into a destination document using the Clipboard. These objects are not updated if the original object is updated. This is the simple "pasting" that most Windows users use on a daily basis.

stroke font   A font that can have its size greatly altered without distorting the font.

stop bits   In a communications program, the number of bits used to indicate the "break" between pieces of information (*see data bits*). Usually 1 or 2.

submenu   A related set of options that appear when you select a menu item (*see cascading menus*).

swap file   A file that gives Windows 95 the ability to use a portion of hard drive as memory. With the use of a swap file, you can load and run more programs in Windows 95 than you actually have RAM memory for. A swap file allows Windows 95 to "swap" chunks of memory containing currently unused information to disk, making room in RAM memory for information you need to run the currently selected program. Using a swap file is slower than holding everything in RAM memory, however.

system disk   The disk containing the operating system, or at least enough of it to start the system and then look on another disk for the support files.

system fonts   System Fonts are used by Windows to draw menus, controls, and utilize specialized control text in Windows. System fonts are proportional fonts that can be sized and manipulated quickly.

System monitor   A program that enables you to monitor the resources on your computer. You can see information displayed for the 32-bit file system, network clients and servers, and the virtual memory manager, among other things. Most of this information is highly technical in nature and most useful to advanced users. You can display the information in either bar or line charts, or as a numeric value.

system policies   Policies, established by a system administrator, which override Registry settings on individual machines. By setting up policies, a system Administrator can restrict a user from changing hardware settings using Control Panel, customize parts of the Desktop like the Network Neighborhood or the Programs folder, and maintain centrally located network settings, such as network client customizations or the ability to install file & printer services. This program can also control access to a computer, enable user profiles, and maintain password control.

System Resources   *See heap.*

T

tab (dialog boxes)   In dialog boxes, there may be multiple panels of information. Each panel has an extension at the top that names the panel. This small extension is called a "tab."

TAPI   Telephony Applications Programming Interface, or TAPI, provides a method for programs to work with modems, independent of dealing directly with the modem hardware. All the information you give Windows during the modem configuration is used for TAPI to set up its interface. Communications programs that are written specifically for Windows 95 will talk to TAPI, which will then issue appropriate commands to the modem. This is called device independence.

taskbar   An area that runs across the bottom of the Windows 95 desktop. The Start button (*see Start menu*) is at the left end of the taskbar, and the clock can be displayed at the right end of the taskbar. Running applications are represented as buttons on the taskbar, the current window is shown as a depressed button, all other applications are displayed as raised buttons. Clicking the button for an inactive application activates that application and displays its window as the current window.

task list   A list of currently running applications. You can switch tasks by clicking an item in the task list. The task list is accessed by pressing Alt+Tab on the keyboard.

TCP/IP   Transmission Control Protocol/Internet Protocol is a set of networking protocols developed in the 1970s. TCP/IP includes Transport Control Protocol, which is a connection-oriented transport protocol that includes transport, session, and presentation layer protocol functions, which is equivalent to layers 4,5, and 6 of the OSI Model and Internet Protocol, and a widely used routable network protocol that corresponds to layer 3 of the OSI model. User Datagram Protocol (UDP) can be substituted in cases where connectionless datagram service is desired. TCP/IP is an entire protocol stack that includes protocols for file transfers (FTP), termination emulation services (telnet), electronic mail (SMTP), address resolution (ARP and RARP), and error control and notification (ICMP and SNMP). TCP/IP is used extensively in many computer systems because it is nonproprietary—free from royalties. Its use was mandated by Congress for use in computer systems for many government agencies and contract situations. TCP/IP is also used in the Internet, a huge government and research internetwork spanning North America and much of the world. TCP/IP is the most commonly used set of network protocols.

terminal emulation   In the "old days" of computing, a "terminal" was an input/output device that was a slave of a CPU, such as a terminal for minicomputer or mainframe. Generally, terminals, had no computing power of their own, but simply provided an interface to a remote host computer.

VIII

Appendixes

"Terminal emulation" refers to a mode (character-based) in which a PC emulates one of these terminals to communicate with a remote host—typically a BBS computer or a corporate mainframe that only "knows" how to talk to a terminal.

text-based   *See character-based.*

text box   A space in the dialog box where text or numbers can be entered so that a command can be carried out.

text file   A file containing only text characters .

thumbnail   A miniature rendition of a graphic file. A thumbnail gives a idea of what the full-size graphic looks like, and is usually used as a gateway to view the full-size graphic.

thread (program execution)   A "thread" is a chunk of a program. In a multi-threading environment such as Windows 95, multiple threads (multiple portions of a program) can execute at the same time—provided the program has been programmed to take advantage of this feature.

thread (BBS/Communications)   A set of messages pertaining to one general idea.

tile   To reduce and move windows so that they can all be seen at once.

time slice   A brief time period in which a process is given access to the processor. Each second is divided into 18.3 time slices; multiple tasks can be scheduled for processing in these slices, yet outwardly appear to be occurring simultaneously.

time-out   A time period after which a device or driver might signal the operating system and cease trying to perform its duty. If a printer is turned off, for example, when you try to print, the driver waits for a predetermined period of time, then issues an error message. In computer terminology, the driver has *timed out.*

title bar   The bar at the top of a program or document window that shows you what its title is. The control menu, maximize, minimize, restore, and taskbar buttons can be accessed in the title bar.

token ring   A network type developed by IBM. It is more expensive than Ethernet to implement, but can run at 16Mb/s. Unlike Ethernet, where the workstations must listen for a clear line before transmitting, workstations on a token ring take turns sending data—passing the "token" from station to station to indicate whose turn it is.

toolbar   A collection of buttons that typically make the more common tools for an application easily accessible. Although often grouped in a line under the menus, a toolbar can be located on the left or right side of the working area—or even be relocatable to any area of the screen the user wishes. In some applications (for example, MS Office applications such as Word), the toolbar is user-configurable—the user can display different toolbars, and add or remove tool buttons from the bar.

topology   The layout or design of cabling on a network.

TrueType fonts   A font technology developed by Microsoft in response to Adobe's success in the scaleable font business with its own Type 1 and Type 3 PostScript fonts. Used as a simple means for all Windows applications to have access to a wide selection of fonts for screen and printer output. TrueType fonts greatly simplify using fonts on a Windows computer. The same fonts can be used on Windows 3.1, Windows NT, Windows 95, and other Windows products, such as Windows for Workgroups. Consisting of two files (one for screen and one for printer), hundreds of TrueType fonts are available from a variety of manufacturers. Depending on your printer, the TrueType font manager internal to Windows, in conjunction with the printer driver, generates either bitmapped or downloadable soft fonts.

twisted pair   Cabling that consists of lightly insulated copper wire, twisted into pairs and bundled into sets of pairs. The twists enhance the wire's capability to resist "crosstalk" (bleeding of signal from one wire to the next). This cabling is used extensively in phone systems and LANs, although even moderate distances in a LAN require "repeaters" (*see repeaters*).

U

unbound media   In a network, this refers to connections that are not implemented using traditional cabling. Instead, unbound media is wireless—implemented through use of various portions of the radio wave spectrum.

Unimodem driver   A universal modem driver supplied by Microsoft as part of Windows 95. The modem driver assumes that the modem supports the Hayes AT command set (most do).

uninstalling applications   When you install an application in Windows 95, it places the necessary files in many different places on your hard drive. You can't remove all of a program by simply erasing the contents of its main subdirectory. To uninstall the application—and remove all the files it placed on your hard drive—you must run a special program that should have been included with the application. Many applications do not include the "uninstaller" program. Although, to be certified under Windows 95, the uninstaller program must be included.

Universal Naming Convention (UNC)   With UNC, you can view, copy, or run files on another machine without assigning it a drive letter on your own. It also means if you are running short of logical drive letters, you can get to servers that you use only intermittently with a simple command from the MS-DOS prompt.

unprintable area   The area, usually around the extreme edges of the paper, in which the printer is incapable of printing. For example, a laser printer cannot print in the 1/4" at the left and right edges of the paper. It is important to know the unprintable area, since graphics or text you place in this area will be cut off when printed.

Upload   The act of sending a file to a remote computer (*see download*).

V

VCACHE   Windows 95 uses a new 32-bit VCACHE which replaces the older SmartDrive that ran under DOS and previous versions of Windows. VCACHE uses more intelligent caching algorithms to improve the apparent speed of your hard drive as well as your CD-ROM and 32-bit network redirectors. Unlike SmartDrive, VCACHE dynamically allocates itself. Based on the amount of free system memory VCACHE allocates or de-allocates memory used by the cache.

vector fonts   A set of lines that connect points to form characters.

video for windows   A set of utilities and protocols for implementing full-motion video in Windows 95.

virtual machine   A "logical" computer that exists inside a PC. Multiple virtual machines can be running in a PC. Applications that run on one virtual machine are unlikely to affect the applications running on a different virtual machine. 16-bit applications (for example, Windows 3.1 applications) all run on the same virtual machine in Windows 95, thus, if one crashes, it is likely to make the rest of the 16-bit applications unusable as well. However, such an occurrence will likely NOT affect 32-bit applications that are running simultaneously.

virtual memory   The use of permanent media (for example, hard drive) to simulate additional RAM (*see swap file*). This allows large applications to run in less physical RAM than they normally would require. When RAM runs low, the operating system uses a virtual memory manager program to temporarily store data on the hard disk like it was in RAM, which makes RAM free for data manipulation. When needed, the data is read back from the disk and reloaded into RAM.

virus   A virus is a computer program written to interrupt or destroy your work. A virus may do something as innocuous as display a message, or something as destructive as reformatting your hard drive—or almost anything in between. Your computer can "catch" a virus from a floppy disk, or even from a file downloaded from a remote source, such as a BBS. Once your computer has become "infected," the virus may spread via connections on a network or floppy disks you share with others. A variety of virus-detecting software exists (including one packaged with Windows 95).

ViSCA   A protocol for daisy chaining up to seven video devices together and connecting them to a single serial port.

volume   Disk partition(s) formatted and available for use by the operating system.

volume label   The identifier for a volume (*see volume*) or disk. This is specified when formatting the volume or disk.

W

wallpaper   A backdrop for the Windows desktop, made up of a graphics file. The graphics can be either *centered*, appearing only once in the center of the desktop, or *tiled*, repeating as many times as the graphic will fit.

WAV files   Named for three-character extension .WAV (for sound wave) these files have, a WAV file is a file containing a digitized sound. Depending on the sampling rate and resolution, the sound recorded in the WAV file seems realistic (provided you have the sound card and speakers to hear it). These files can be quite large, running into the multi-megabyte range for high-quality recordings.

Web browser   A software program that enables you to view Home pages and retrieve information from the Internet.

What's This?   A new feature of Windows 95 help. In a dialog box, click the small button with a question mark (?) on it. Then, click where you want help. A small description should pop up to explain what the item is and how to use it. Click in the description popup to remove it.

Winpopup   Winpopup is an applet that is included in the Accessories group when you install the network component of Windows 95. This tool normally sends short messages from one computer on the workgroup to another (or from a shared printer to a workstation). It is designed so that when a message is received, the program will pop up over anything else on the screen and show the message.

wiring concentrator   In a network, a multiple port repeating device used in Ethernet LANs to connect multiple cable segments into one LAN. Sometimes called a "hub" (*see hub*) or "multiport repeater" (*see repeater*), this device isolates cabling problems by separating each workstation connection on an isolated cabling segment.

wizard   Microsoft's name for a step-by-step set of instructions that guide you through a particular task. For example, there are many wizards included with Windows 95 for installing new hardware, configuring the Start menu, and changing other aspects of the environment.

World Wide Web (WWW)   The fastest growing part of the Internet, the 'Web,' or WWW, is a collection of hypertext documents. It provides access to images and sounds from thousands of different Web sites, via a special programming language called **H**yper**T**ext **M**arkup **L**anguage, or **HTML**. This language is used to create "hypertext" documents, which include embedded commands.

WordPad   A program included with Windows 95 that enables you to do basic word processing and save the results in plain text format, Word 6 format, or Rich Text Format.

word wrap   In word processing, this refers to words that cannot be completed on one line automatically "wrapping" to the beginning of the next line. Most word processors use word wrap automatically—an exception is Notepad, where you must turn on word wrap.

workgroup   A collection of networked PCs grouped to facilitate work that users of the computers tend to do together. The machines are not necessarily in the same room or office.

WYSIWYG   Short for "What you see is what you get," this term refers to the ability of an application to display an accurate representation of the printed output on the screen.

X

x coordinate   The position of an item relative to the left side of the screen. Values increase as you move to the right.

Xmodem   An error-correction protocol (*see binary transfer protocol*) used by the DOS application XMODEM and many other communications programs. Xmodem using CRC (cyclical redundancy check) is a means of detecting errors in transmissions between modems or across wired serial links.

Y

y coordinate   The position of an item relative to the bottom of the screen. Values increase as you move down the screen.

Ymodem   Another form of Xmodem that allows batch transfers of files and (in Ymodem G) hardware error control.

Z

Zmodem   ZModem is a full functional streaming protocol where XModem is a send and acknowledge protocol which causes delays in the transfer equal to twice the modem lag on a connection. ZModem is the preferred way of exchanging data since it is reliable, quick, and relatively easy to implement.❖

Part IX

Indexes

Index of Common Problems

Windows Setup

If you have this problem...	You'll find help here...
Adding components also removes components	p. 315
Accessibility options aren't available	p. 150
New IDE drive is inaccessible	p. 238
Get a "resource conflict" message while installing a Plug and Play device	p. 247
Network card is not working	p. 623
Can't get the modem to work	p. 837
Modem causes Windows to crash	p. 841
Can't see your CD-ROM drive	p. 970

Windows 3.x and DOS Applications

If you have this problem...	You'll find help here...
Alt+Tab only alternates between two applications	p. 60
Can't see the taskbar when running an older Windows 3.x application	p. 64
Windows 3.x applications seem to forget your settings when you dual boot	p. 308
A DOS application won't respond	p. 330
Mouse doesn't work in DOS applications	p. 334

(continues)

IX

Indexes

Windows 3.x and DOS Applications (continued)

If you have this problem...	You'll find help here...
Windows shuts down completely when you set the Command prompt for MS-DOS mode	p. 338
DOS programs run very slowly now under Windows 95	p. 344
Can't open very many DOS sessions	p. 344
Can't double-click on a DOS data file to start a DOS program	p. 69
DOS data files don't seem to work from within Explorer	p. 75

Printing

If you have this problem...	You'll find help here...
Printer has started to print, but you can't stop it	p. 173
It takes a long time to print a document	p. 654
Can't see a network printer in Network Neighborhood	p. 781
Network printer doesn't let you know when it is out of paper	p. 782
Network printer gives you inconsistent printout quality	p. 783
Shared printer is unavailable to other workstations on the network	p. 786

Working with Documents

If you have this problem...	You'll find help here...
Need to fix a mistake in a Paint document?	p. 381
Paint gives you an error when you try to add text to the picture	p. 384
Paint won't let you resize an object you've drawn	p. 392

If you have this problem...	You'll find help here...
Can't save a PCX file in Paint	p. 396
Original document loses information when you use drag-and-drop	p. 423
Copied text doesn't go where you want it to	p. 423
Get a black circle with a line through it when you try to copy text	p. 423
Can't edit a linked or embedded object document	p. 452
Excel doesn't start when you click on an embedded spreadsheet	p. 452

Disks and Drives

If you have this problem...	You'll find help here...
Windows won't format a disk	p. 464
Large files won't copy on to a compressed drive	p. 471
Deleted the DRVSPACE.000 to save some space on a compressed drive	p. 478
Resized compressed drive still doesn't seem to have enough space	p. 480
Disk makes a lot of noise and seems kind of slow	p. 494
Modified a file in Briefcase, but it still shows as Up to Date	p. 539

Modems

Modem doesn't connect while you're dialing MSN	p. 1113
Dialing MSN tells you your password is invalid	p. 1113
E-mail isn't sent when you dial MSN	p. 1131
Modem connects but doesn't stay connected	p. 855

IX

Indexes

(continues)

Modems (continued)

If you have this problem...	You'll find help here...
Modem keeps dialing the wrong number	p. 855
Older DOS or Windows 3.x applications cannot use the modem	p. 857
Windows says another application is using the modem when you try to dial out	p. 866
Modem connects OK, but only displays garbage	p. 866
Modem captures text to a file, but the file looks like it has extra characters	p. 867
Modem can't upload or download files	p. 871
Modem won't connect as a dial-up network adapter	p. 897
Your dial-up SLIP or PPP account doesn't connect	p. 899
Your dial-up SLIP or PPP connection won't work after it has connected	p. 898

CD-ROM

If you have this problem...	You'll find help here...
Windows won't automatically recognize your CD-ROM	p. 971
Windows complains when you try to install from your CD-ROM	p. 972
CD-ROM application installed OK, but won't run	p. 973
CD-ROM won't play audio CDs	p. 979
CD-ROM won't connect to the sound card	p. 979
Windows hangs after installing CD-ROM drive	p. 979

Multimedia and Sound

If you have this problem...	You'll find help here...
Sound is distorted or doesn't play	p. 984
Sound seems to hiss during playback	p. 991
Video and sound files don't play back in sync	p. 1001
VideoDirector says your LANC driver isn't working	p. 1028
Can't record video when you press the Record button	p. 1032
MCI ViSCA doesn't show all of your devices	p. 1037
Windows locks up when you run the ISVR Pro's diagnostics	p. 1062
ViSCA doesn't show your devices in right order	p. 1063
Movies always seem to drop 5% of your frames when captured	p. 1066
Compressed movie clips have fuzzy areas	p. 1073

Networking

If you have this problem...	You'll find help here...
Can't connect to remote computer	p. 622
Can't use shared resources on another networked computer	p. 646
Can't find a computer on the network	p. 646
Remote computer on your dial-up connection hangs up on you unexpectedly	p. 667
Can't access a floppy drive on a network computer	p. 647
Some of the files you share are missing	p. 646

IX

Indexes

(continues)

Networking (continued)

If you have this problem...	You'll find help here...
Get a message about Access Control when you changed to the NetWare Client	p. 690
NetWare file-and-print sharing doesn't show up in your components box	p. 690
Network logon gives you an error on your notebook when you're not connected to the network	p. 690
The NetWare VLM client doesn't work	p. 693
Can't use NetWare Directory Services with Windows 95	p. 694
NetWare search paths aren't available	p. 697
Can't access network applications	p. 697
Can't move up a directory level when connecting to a NetWare server	p. 705
Can't use NetWare's MAP command utilities	p. 705
NetWare login scripts don't seem to be working	p. 681
Can't enter a NetWare command in the Run dialog box	p. 713
Some of the files on your hard drive are changing or being deleted without your knowledge	p. 809

Index

Symbols

IX

Indexes

IX

Indexes

IX

Indexes

IX

Indexes

IX

Indexes

IX

IX

Indexes

IX

Indexes

IX

Indexes

IX

Indexes

IX

Indexes

IX

Indexes

W

IX

Indexes

IX

Indexes

PLUG YOURSELF INTO...

The Macmillan Information SuperLibrary™

Free information and vast computer resources from the world's leading computer book publisher—online!

FIND THE BOOKS THAT ARE RIGHT FOR YOU!

A complete online catalog, plus sample chapters and tables of contents give you an in-depth look at *all* of our books, including hard-to-find titles. It's the best way to find the books you need!

- **STAY INFORMED** with the latest computer industry news through our online newsletter, press releases, and customized Information SuperLibrary Reports.

- **GET FAST ANSWERS** to your questions about MCP books and software.

- **VISIT** our online bookstore for the latest information and editions!

- **COMMUNICATE** with our expert authors through e-mail and conferences.

- **DOWNLOAD SOFTWARE** from the immense MCP library:
  - Source code and files from MCP books
  - The best shareware, freeware, and demos

- **DISCOVER HOT SPOTS** on other parts of the Internet.

- **WIN BOOKS** in ongoing contests and giveaways!

TO PLUG INTO MCP: ➔ **WORLD WIDE WEB: http://www.mcp.com**

GOPHER: gopher.mcp.com

FTP: ftp.mcp.com

Complete and Return this Card
for a *FREE* Computer Book Catalog

Thank you for purchasing this book! You have purchased a superior computer book written expressly for your needs. To continue to provide the kind of up-to-date, pertinent coverage you've come to expect from us, we need to hear from you. Please take a minute to complete and return this self-addressed, postage-paid form. In return, we'll send you a free catalog of all our computer books on topics ranging from word processing to programming and the internet.

Mrs. ☐   Ms. ☐   Dr. ☐

(first) ☐☐☐☐☐☐☐☐☐☐☐☐☐   (M.I.) ☐   (last) ☐☐☐☐☐☐☐☐☐☐☐☐☐☐☐

☐☐☐☐☐☐☐☐☐☐☐☐☐☐☐☐☐☐☐☐☐☐☐☐☐☐☐☐☐☐☐☐☐

☐☐☐☐☐☐☐☐☐☐☐☐☐☐☐☐☐☐☐☐☐☐☐☐☐☐☐☐☐☐☐☐☐

☐☐☐☐☐☐☐☐☐☐☐☐☐☐☐   State ☐☐   Zip ☐☐☐☐☐ ☐☐☐☐

☐☐ ☐☐☐☐☐☐☐☐   Fax ☐☐☐ ☐☐☐ ☐☐☐☐

y Name ☐☐☐☐☐☐☐☐☐☐☐☐☐☐☐☐☐☐☐☐☐☐☐☐☐☐☐☐☐☐

ddress ☐☐☐☐☐☐☐☐☐☐☐☐☐☐☐☐☐☐☐☐☐☐☐☐☐☐☐☐☐☐

e check at least (3) influencing factors for hasing this book.

back cover information on book .... ☐
pproach to the content .... ☐
eness of content.. ☐
reputation .... ☐
r's reputation .... ☐
ver design or layout .... ☐
table of contents of book .... ☐
book .... ☐
ffects, graphics, illustrations .... ☐
lease specify): _____ ☐

did you first learn about this book?

Macmillan Computer Publishing catalog .... ☐
nended by store personnel .... ☐
book on bookshelf at store .... ☐
nended by a friend .... ☐
advertisement in the mail .... ☐
dvertisement in: _____ ☐
ok review in: _____ ☐
lease specify): _____ ☐

many computer books have you hased in the last six months?

k only .... ☐   3 to 5 books..................... ☐
.... ☐   More than 5..................... ☐

4. Where did you purchase this book?

Bookstore .... ☐
Computer Store .... ☐
Consumer Electronics Store .... ☐
Department Store .... ☐
Office Club .... ☐
Warehouse Club .... ☐
Mail Order .... ☐
Direct from Publisher .... ☐
Internet site .... ☐
Other (Please specify): _____ ☐

5. How long have you been using a computer?

☐ Less than 6 months   ☐ 6 months to a year
☐ 1 to 3 years   ☐ More than 3 years

6. What is your level of experience with personal computers and with the subject of this book?

	With PCs	With subject of book
New	☐	☐
Casual	☐	☐
Accomplished	☐	☐
Expert	☐	☐

Source Code ISBN: 1-56529-921-3

7. Which of the following best describes your job title?

Administrative Assistant ☐
Coordinator ☐
Manager/Supervisor ☐
Director ☐
Vice President ☐
President/CEO/COO ☐
Lawyer/Doctor/Medical Professional ☐
Teacher/Educator/Trainer ☐
Engineer/Technician ☐
Consultant ☐
Not employed/Student/Retired ☐
Other (Please specify): _____ ☐

8. Which of the following best describes the area of the company your job title falls under?

Accounting ☐
Engineering ☐
Manufacturing ☐
Operations ☐
Marketing ☐
Sales ☐
Other (Please specify): _____ ☐

9. What is your age?

Under 20 ....
21-29 ....
30-39 ....
40-49 ....
50-59 ....
60-over ....

10. Are you:

Male ....
Female ....

11. Which computer publications do you read regularly? (Please list)

_____
_____
_____
_____
_____
_____
_____
_____
_____
_____

Comments: _____

Fold here and scotch-t

B. oaden You. Mind And Your Business With Que

The *Special Edition Using* series remains the most-often recommended product line for computer users who want detailed reference information. With thorough explanations, troubleshooting advice, and special "Techniques from the Pros" sections, these books are the perfect all-in-one resource.

Special Edition Using Word
for Windows 95
0-7897-0084-0
$34.99 USA
Pub Date: 8/95

Special Edition Using Excel
for Windows 95
0-7897-0112-X
$34.99 USA
Pub Date: 8/95

Special Edition Using
PowerPoint for Windows 95
0-7897-0464-1
$34.99 USA
Pub Date: 9/95

For more information on these and other Que products, visit your local book retailer or call 1-800-772-0477.

Special Edition Using Microsoft
Works for Windows 95
0-7897-0462-5
$29.99 USA
Pub Date: 10/95

Source Code ISBN:0-7897-921-3

"MagnaRAM—get up to 2, 3, even 4 times more available Windows™ Memory!"

End the frustration of low Windows Memory, without installing more RAM.

Now you can increase RAM just by adding software. Introducing MagnaRAM for Windows, the RAM compression software that expands the power of your available Windows Memory. With MagnaRAM's ultra-safe, data compression technology, you'll run more Windows programs at the same time, faster than ever before!

SAVE TIME

Boost system performance • Run multiple applications
Faster task switching • Installs in seconds

SAVE MONEY

Hundreds of $$$ less than physical RAM
No installation fees, no downtime

SAVE HASSLE

End the irritation of slow performance
Eliminate "out-of-memory" messages • Automatic configuration

MagnaRAM is quick to install and safe to use. It works, right out of the box, with all your existing software and hardware.

With MagnaRAM's Memory Monitors, you'll see dynamic, graphical statistics that show you how your system's memory and performance is improved - right before your eyes!

We're committed to providing you with a total solution that's guaranteed to work. That's why we're one of the few companies that offers toll-free, no-fee product support and a 90-day, money-back guarantee.*

Get the products, help and support you need to make Windows work hard for you—
only from Landmark Research.

LANDMARK
RESEARCH INTERNATIONAL CORPORATION

703 Grand Street, Clearwater, FL 34616
(800) 683-6696   (813) 443-1331   FAX (813) 443-6603

Before using any of the software on this disc, you need to install the software you plan to use. See Appendix E for directions on installing this software correctly. If you have problems with this disk, please contact Macmillan Technical Support at (317) 581-3833. We can be reached by e-mail at **support@mcp.com** or on CompuServe at **GO QUEBOOKS**.

Read this before Opening Software